Guide to Good Food

12th Edition

by

Velda L. Largen
Author of Family and Consumer Sciences Instructional Materials

Deborah L. Bence
Family and Consumer Sciences Author
Granville, Ohio

Annotations written by
Deborah L. Bence

Publisher
Goodheart-Willcox Company, Inc.
Tinley Park, IL
www.g-w.com

CONTENTS

Guide to Good Food

Prepare your students for the study of foods and nutrition!

Topics include

- the importance of food
- the management of food
- the preparation of food
- food and careers
- foods of the world

THE ESSENTIAL PROGRAM COMPONENTS

A complete package of support materials is available to aid you in teaching these important topics.

Student Text

Colorful design, easy-to-read typeface, and logical organization support reading comprehension and learning. (See pages IV-IX for a summary of text features.)

Teacher's Edition

The text provides a variety of teaching aids in the page margins to help you review and reinforce chapter content. Answer keys appear next to review questions.

Workbook

Includes a wide variety of activities to help students review and apply chapter concepts.

Teacher's Annotated Workbook

Includes answers to workbook activities right where you need them. Answers appear in blue.

Teacher's Resource Guide

Includes bulletin board ideas, introductory activities, suggested teaching strategies, reproducible masters, chapter tests, and much more.

Teacher's Resource CD

Gives you easy access to the content of the *Teacher's Resource Guide* and the *Teacher's Edition* of the text, both in PDF format. Also includes color lesson slides and a lesson planning feature for customizing daily lesson plans.

ExamView® Assessment Suite

Contains all the test master questions in the *Teacher's Resources* plus 25 percent more. Lets you choose specific questions, add your own, and create different versions of a test.

Teacher's Presentations for PowerPoint®

Includes colorful presentations for each chapter to reinforce key concepts and terms.

Companion Website

Motivates and engages students beyond the classroom with interactive activities and more.

INTRODUCTION

Guide to Good Food is a food and nutrition text designed to introduce your students to principles of food and nutrition, careers, and foods of the world. The components of the teaching package contain a variety of features that can help you develop an effective program tailored to your students' unique needs. The package can also aid you in achieving a number of other educational objectives with your students, as described below.

Strategies for Successful Teaching

You can make the *Guide to Good Food* subject matter exciting and relevant for your students by using a variety of teaching strategies. Many suggestions for planning classroom activities are given in the teaching supplements that accompany this text. As you plan your lessons, you might also want to keep the following points in mind.

Critical Thinking Skills

As today's students leave their classrooms behind, they will face a world of complexity and change. They are likely to work in several career areas and hold many jobs. Young people must develop a base of knowledge and be prepared to solve complex problems, make difficult decisions, and assess ethical implications. In other words, students must be able to use critical thinking skills.

Critical thinking goes beyond memorizing or recalling information. It requires individuals to apply what they know about the subject matter. It also requires students to use their common sense and experience. It may even involve controversy.

Critical thinking requires *creative thinking* to construct all the reasonable alternatives, consequences, influencing factors, and supporting arguments. Unusual ideas are valued and perspectives outside the obvious are sought.

Finally, the teaching of critical thinking does not require exotic and highly unusual classroom approaches. Complex thought processes can be incorporated in the most ordinary and basic activities, such as reading, writing, and listening, when activities are carefully planned and skillfully executed.

Debate is an excellent way to explore opposite sides of an issue. You may want to divide the class into two groups, each taking an opposing side of the issue. You can also ask students to work in smaller groups and explore opposing sides of different issues. Each group can select students from the group to present the points for their side.

Problem-Solving and Decision-Making Skills

An important aspect in the development of critical thinking skills is learning how to solve problems and make decisions. Some very important decisions lie ahead for your students, particularly those related to their future education and career choices.

Simulation games and role plays are activities that allow students to practice solving problems and making decisions under nonthreatening circumstances. In role-playing, students can examine others' feelings as well as their own. They can learn effective ways to react or cope when confronted with similar situations in real life.

Cooperative Learning

Because of the emphasis on teamwork in the workplace, the use of cooperative learning groups in your classroom will give students an opportunity to practice teamwork skills. During cooperative learning, students learn interpersonal and small-group skills that will allow them to function as part of a team. These skills include leadership, decision making, trust building, communication, and conflict management.

In cooperative learning groups, students learn to work together toward a group goal. Each member is dependent on others for the outcome. This interdependence is a basic component of any cooperative learning group. Students understand that one person cannot succeed unless everyone succeeds. The value of each group member is affirmed as learners work toward their goal.

The success of the group also depends on individual performance. Group members should be selected depending on the purpose of your grouping. As you differentiate your instruction, sometimes you may form groups based on interest. Other times, you may form diversified groups so a mix of abilities and talents are included. You might form groups with specific leveled learning tasks assigned to various groups. Within groups, individuals' roles can change so all students have opportunities to practice and develop different skills. In all situations, students can learn from working with one another.

As you monitor the effectiveness of group learning, you may need to intervene to provide task assistance or help with interpersonal or group skills. If you expect a group to carry out a particular skill on their own, you need to teach the skill to the large group first. Model the expected activity, assign various roles, and have students model the skills used in that role. Then, when you assign different tasks to groups, members will be able to move ahead on their own, utilizing the skills you taught.

Finally, you can evaluate each group's achievement of specific learning goals. Use rubrics to identify the extent to which the group reached the goal. In some scenarios, you may just give participation points to the group for completing their task. This is effective when you have differentiated the learning for the various groups and their tasks are not the same. In group settings, the learning that takes place is often in the discussion and processing of various ideas. In these cases, a summary of what students learned can be written in a journal or added to a portfolio.

Affirming Diversity

Your students will be entering a rapidly changing workplace—not only in the area of technology, but also in the diverse nature of the workforce. The majority of the new entrants into the workforce are women and people of varying ethnicities, all representing many different views and experiences. The workforce is aging, too, as the ranks of mature workers swell. Because of these trends, young workers must learn how to interact with a variety of people who are considerably unlike them.

Appreciating and understanding diversity is an ongoing process. The earlier and more frequently young people are exposed to diversity, the better able they will be to bridge cultural differences. If your students are exposed to different cultures within your classroom, the process of understanding cultural differences can begin. This is the best preparation for success in a diverse society. In addition, teachers have found the following strategies for teaching diversity helpful:

- Actively promote a spirit of openness, consideration, respect, and tolerance in the classroom.
- Use a variety of teaching styles and assessment strategies.
- Use cooperative learning activities whenever possible and make sure group roles are rotated so everyone has leadership opportunities.
- When grouping students, make sure the composition of each group is as diverse as possible with regard to gender, race, and nationality.
- Make sure one group's opinions do not dominate class discussions.
- If a student makes a sexist, racist, or other offensive comment, ask the student to rephrase the comment in a manner that will not offend other class members. Remind students that offensive statements and behavior are inappropriate.
- If a difficult classroom situation arises involving a diversity issue, ask for a time-out and have everyone write down thoughts and opinions about the incident. This allows everyone to cool down and allows you to plan a response.
- Arrange for guest speakers who represent diversity in gender, age, and ethnicity.
- Have students change seats occasionally throughout the course and introduce themselves to their new "neighbors" so they become acquainted with all their classmates.
- Several times during the course, ask students to make anonymous, written evaluations of the class. Have them report any problems that may not be obvious.

Instruction for Students with Varying Needs

In addition to having specific learning needs related to their abilities, students come to you with various backgrounds, interests, and learning styles. Differentiating instruction can help all students attain learning goals. The strategies you use to differentiate instruction in your classroom will depend on the specific learning needs of the students.

Several strategies for differentiating instruction will be included throughout the *Teacher's Edition*. They include suggestions for reteaching lessons for students who need more repetition; strategies to extend learning for students who need more application to real life; and strategies to enrich learning for students needing more challenge.

The following table provides descriptions of several types of students you may find in your classes, followed by some strategies and techniques to keep in mind as you work with these students. You will be asked to meet the needs of all your students in the same classroom setting. It is a challenge to adapt daily lessons to meet the demands of all your students.

	Learning Disabilities*	Cognitive Disabilities*	Behavioral and Emotional Disabilities*
Description	Students with learning disabilities (LD) have neurological disorders that interfere with their ability to store, process, or produce information, creating a "gap" between ability and performance. These students are generally of average or above average intelligence. Examples of learning disabilities are distractibility, spatial problems, and reading comprehension problems.	Students with cognitive disabilities (also known as intellectual disabilities) have limitations in their intellectual functioning compared with others their age. They may have difficulty remembering, associating and classifying information, reasoning, problem solving, and making judgments. They may also have difficulties with such adaptive behavior as daily living activities and developing occupational skills.	Students with these disabilities exhibit undesirable behaviors or emotions that may, over time, adversely affect educational performance. The inability to learn cannot be explained by intellectual, social, or health factors. Such students may be inattentive, withdrawn, timid, restless, defiant, impatient, unhappy, fearful, unreflective, lack initiative, have negative feelings and actions, and blame others.
Teaching Strategies	• Assist students in getting organized. • Give short oral directions. • Use drill exercises. • Give prompt cues during student performance. • Provide computers with specialized software (that checks spelling and grammar and/or recognizes speech) to students with poor writing and reading skills. • Break assignments into small segments and assign only one segment at a time. • Demonstrate skills and have students model them. • Give prompt feedback. • Use continuous assessment to mark students' daily progress. • Prepare materials at varying levels of ability. • Shorten the number of items on exercises, tests, and quizzes. • Provide more hands-on activities.	• Use concrete examples to introduce concepts. • Make learning activities consistent. • Use repetition and drills spread over time. • Provide work folders for daily assignments. • Use behavior management techniques, such as behavior modification, in the area of adaptive behavior. • Encourage students to function independently. • Give students extra time to both ask and answer questions while giving hints to answers. • Give simple directions and read them over with students. • Use objective test items and hands-on activities because students generally have poor writing skills and difficulty with sentence structure and spelling.	• Call students' names or ask them questions when you see their attention wandering. • Call on students randomly rather than in a predictable sequence. • Move around the room frequently. • Improve students' self-esteem by giving them tasks they can perform well, increasing the number of successful achievement experiences. • Decrease the length of time for each activity. • Use hands-on activities instead of using words and abstract symbols. • Decrease the size of the group so each student can actively participate. • Make verbal instructions clear, short, and to the point.

Academically Gifted	Limited English Proficiency	Physical Disabilities	
Students who are academically gifted are capable of high performance as a result of general intellectual ability, specific academic aptitude, and/or creative or productive thinking. Such students have a vast fund of general knowledge and high levels of vocabulary, memory, abstract word knowledge, and abstract reasoning.	These students have a limited proficiency in the English language. English is generally their second language. Such students may be academically quite capable, but lack the language skills needed to reason and comprehend abstract concepts.	Includes individuals who have physical, mobility, visual, speech, hearing (deaf, hard-of-hearing), or health (cystic fibrosis, epilepsy) impairments. Strategies will depend on the specific disability.	**Description**
• Provide ample opportunities for creative behavior. • Make assignments that call for original work, independent learning, critical thinking, problem solving, and experimentation. • Show appreciation for creative efforts. • Respect unusual questions, ideas, and solutions these students provide. • Encourage students to test their ideas. • Provide opportunities and give credit for self-initiated learning. • Avoid overly detailed supervision and too much reliance on prescribed curricula. • Allow time for reflection. • Resist immediate and constant evaluation. This causes students to be afraid to use their creativity. • Avoid comparisons with other students, which imply subtle pressure to conform.	• Use a slow but natural rate of speech; speak clearly; use shorter sentences; repeat concepts in several ways. • Act out questions using gestures with hands, arms, and the whole body. Use demonstrations and pantomime. Ask questions that can be answered by a physical movement, such as pointing, nodding, or manipulation of materials. • When possible, use pictures, photos, and charts. • Write key terms on the board. As they are used, point to them. • Corrections should be limited and appropriate. Do not correct grammar or usage errors in front of the class, causing embarrassment. • Give honest praise and positive feedback through your voice tones and visual articulation whenever possible. • Encourage students to use language to communicate, allowing them to use their native language to ask and answer questions when they are unable to do so in English. • Integrate students' cultural background into class discussions. • Use cooperative learning during which students have opportunities to practice expressing ideas without risking language errors in front of the entire class.	• Seat students with visual and hearing impairments near the front of the classroom. Speak clearly and say out loud what you are writing on the board. • To reduce the risk of injury in lab settings, ask students about any conditions that could affect their ability to learn or perform. • Rearrange lab equipment or the classroom and make necessary modifications to accommodate any disability. • Investigate and utilize assistive technology devices that can improve students' functional capabilities. • Discuss solutions or modifications with the student who has experience with overcoming his or her disability and may have suggestions you may not have considered. • Provide an opportunity for the student to test classroom modifications before utilizing them in class. • Ask advice from special education teachers, the school nurse, or physical therapist. • Plan barrier-free field trips that include all students.	**Teaching Strategies**

*We appreciate the assistance of Dr. Debra O. Parker, North Carolina Central University, with this section.

Using Other Resources

Much student learning in this class can be reinforced and expanded by exposing your students to a variety of viewpoints and teaching methods. Your providing guest speakers, panel presentations, field trip experiences, and access to media resources related to foods and nutrition can greatly enhance student learning.

Current magazines and journals are good sources of articles on various aspects of food and nutrition. Having copies in the classroom will encourage students to use them for research and ideas as they study foods and nutrition. Information can also be obtained from the Internet.

Publications

Current magazines and journals are good sources of information on various family and consumer sciences topics. Students can use these items in many activities related to the text.

Better Homes and Gardens
bhg.com

Consumer Reports
consumerreports.org

Instructor
scholastic.com/instructor

Journalism of Family and Consumer Sciences
aafcs.org

Scholastic Choices
scholastic.com

Time
time.com

Trade, Professional, Health, and Safety Organizations

These and other trade and professional organizations often provide helpful information on issues of industrywide, national, or international importance.

American Association of Family and Consumer Sciences (AAFCS)
aafcs.org

American Council on Consumer Interests
consumerinterests.org

American Council on Exercise (ACE)
acefitness.org

American Council on Science and Health
acsh.org

American Culinary Federation
acfchefs.org

American Diabetes Association
diabetes.org

American Dietetic Association (ADA)
eatright.org

American Egg Board
aeb.org

American Gas Association
aga.org

American Heart Association
heart.org

American Institute for Cancer Research (AICR)
aicr.org

American Meat Institute
meatami.org

American Medical Association
ama-assn.org

Architectural Woodwork Institute
awinet.org

Association for Career and Technical Education (ACTE)
acteonline.org

Association of Home Appliance Manufacturers
aham.org

Bread for the World (BFW)
bread.org

Center for Science in the Public Interest (CSPI)
cspinet.org

Children's Defense Fund
childrensdefense.org

Children's Nutrition Research Center
kidsnutrition.org

Consumers Union
consumersunion.org

Family, Career and Community Leaders of America (FCCLA)
fcclainc.org

Food Allergy and Anaphylaxis Network
foodallergy.org

FoodFit Company
foodfit.com

Food for the Hungry
fh.org

Food Marketing Institute
fmi.org

Food Research and Action Center (FRAC)
frac.org

Foodservice Educators Network
feni.org

Grocery Manufacturers Association/Food Products Association
gmabrands.com

Institute of Food Technologists
ift.org

International Association of Culinary Professionals
iacp.com

International Food Information Council (IFIC)
ific.org

Johns Hopkins Medicine Health Information
hopkinshospital.org/health_info

Kitchen Cabinet Manufacturers Association
kcma.org

Medline
http://www.proquest.com/en-US/catalogs/databases/detail/medline_ft.shtml

Multicultural Foodservice and Hospitality Alliance
mfha.net

National Cattlemen's Beef Association
beef.org

National Chicken Council
eatchicken.com

National Corn Growers Association
ncga.com

National Dairy Council
nationaldairycouncil.org

National Organization on Fetal Alcohol Syndrome
nofas.org

National Restaurant Association
restaurant.org

National WIC Association
nwica.org

Organic Trade Association
ota.com

Partnership for Food Safety Education
fightbac.org

Produce Marketing Association
pma.com

School Nutrition Association
schoolnutrition.org

Shaken Baby Alliance
shakenbaby.com

Shape Up America!
shapeup.org

Society for Foodservice Management
sfm-online.org

Students Against Destructive Decisions (SADD)
saddonline.com

Underwriters Laboratories, Inc.
ul.com

United Fresh Produce Association
unitedfresh.org

U.S. Poultry and Egg Association
poultryegg.org

Wheat Foods Council
wheatfoods.org

World Health Organization (WHO)
who.int

Company Resources

Companies often provide materials that showcase their products and compare them to similar products in the marketplace. Some companies also provide generic educational materials on topics related to their products.

Amana Appliances
amana.com

Black and Decker
blackanddecker.com

Dow Chemical USA
dow.com

Frigidaire
frigidaire.com

GE Appliances
geappliances.com

KitchenAid
kitchenaid.com

Kohler Co.
kohler.com

KraftMaid Cabinetry
kraftmaid.com

Maytag Corp.
maytag.com

Rubbermaid
rubbermaid.com

Sunbeam Products, Inc.
sunbeam.com

Whirlpool Corp.
whirlpoolcorp.com

Educational Resources

The following companies and associations provide teaching materials as one of their primary missions. Most provide videos and/or computer software, while many offer printed materials. Contact these organizations for their latest catalogs.

Cambridge Educational
http://cambridge.films.com/

Karol Media
karolmedia.com

Kidsource OnLine
kidsource.com

Learning Seed
learningseed.com

Meridian Education Corp.
meridian.films.com

Nasco
enasco.com

RMI Media Productions/ACT Inc.
actmedia.org

Sax Family & Consumer Sciences
saxfcs.com

The Health Connection
healthconnection.org

Online Teaching and Learning Tools

Bartleby
(online library)
bartleby.com

Bibliomania
(online library)
bibliomania.com

Click n Type
(free word prediction and keyboard)
lakefolks.org/cnt/

CMAP
(graphic organizer)
http://cmap.ihmc.us/

Co-Writer
(word prediction)
donjohnston.com

E-Text Reader
(talking word processor)
readingmadeez.com

Flickr
(image collection)
flickr.com

Freedom Scientific
(tools for vision impaired/learning disabled)
freedomscientific.com

Haiku
(teacher-friendly blog)
haikuls.com/

iLighter
(highlighter for Internet text)
i-lighter.com

Illuminations
(interactive math activities)
http://illuminations.nctm.org

in Pictures
(software tutorials in pictures)
http://inpics.net

Inspiration
(graphic organizer)
inspiration.com

Intellitalk
(talking word processor)
intellitools.com

Kidtools/KidSkills
(self-monitoring tools)
http://kidtools.missouri.edu/

Lesson Builder
(lesson builder)
http://lessonbuilder.cast.org

Microsoft Office Live Workspace
(document sharing)
http://workspace.officelive.com

Mindmeister
(collaborative graphing tool)
mindmeister.com

National Library of Virtual Manipulatives
(interactive math activities)
http://nlvm.usu.edu/en/nav/vlibrary.html

Natural Reader
(text-to-speech conversion)
naturalreaders.com

Project Gutenberg
(online library)
gutenberg.org

ReadPlease
(text-to-speech tool)
readplease.com

ReadPrint
(online library)
readprint.com

Read Write Think
(reading/language arts activities)
readwritethink.org

ScreenCast
(video sharing)
screencast.com

Shodor Interactive
(interactive math activities)
shodor.org/interactivat

Soothsayer
(word prediction)
ahf-net.com/sooth.htm

Survey Monkey
(survey tool)
surveymonkey.com

Talking Calculator
(talking calculator)
readingmadeez.com/products/
talkingcalculator.html

Teacher Tube
(videos for educational purposes)
teachertube.com

TIGed
(teacher-friendly blog)
takingitglobal.org/tiged/activity/

Trackstar
(activity creator)
http://trackstar.4teachers.org

Trailfire
(annotated web link creation)
trailfire.com

Web Poster Wizard
(interactive posters)
http://poster.4teacher.org

WebMath
(interactive math activities)
webmath.com

WordQ
(word prediction)
wordq.com

WordWeb
(dictionary and thesaurus)
http://wordweb.info/free/

Zoomerang
(survey tools)
http://info.zoomerang.com

Government Agencies and Programs

In addition to the federal government sources listed here, the Federal Citizen Information Center (FCIC) can help you learn about other United States Government agencies, programs, benefits, and services. Contact FCIC by phoning (800) FED-INFO or by going online at pueblo.gsa.gov.

Two popular publications available through FCIC are the *Consumer Information Catalog* and *Consumer Action Handbook*. The first lists hundreds of free and low-cost government booklets on various topics, while the latter provides contacts for assistance with consumer problems and questions. These publications can be viewed online, downloaded free of charge, or ordered for a small fee by calling (888) 878-3256 or writing to the Federal Citizen Information Center, Dept. WWW, Pueblo, CO 81009.

CDC National Center for Health Statistics
cdc.gov/nchs

Centers for Disease Control and Prevention (CDC)
cdc.gov

Consumer Product Safety Commission (CPSC)
cpsc.gov

Department of Agriculture (USDA)
usda.gov

Department of Education (ED)
ed.gov

Department of Energy (DOE)
energy.gov

Department of Health and Human Services (HHS)
hhs.gov

FDA Center for Food Safety and Applied Nutrition Information
foodsafety.gov

Federal Communications Commission (FCC)
fcc.gov

Food and Agricultural Organization of the United Nations
fao.org

Food and Drug Administration (FDA)
fda.gov

FTC Bureau of Consumer Protection
ftc.gov/bcp

Healthfinder–Your Guide to Reliable Health Information
healthfinder.gov

MyPlate Web Site
Choose**MyPlate**.gov

National Academy of Sciences
nasonline.org

National Clearinghouse for Alcohol and Drug Information
ncadi.samhsa.gov

National Health Information Center
health.gov/nhic

National Institutes of Health
nih.gov

President's Council on Physical Fitness and Sports
fitness.gov

FDA Center for Food Safety and Applied Nutrition Seafood Line
(888) 723-3366

U.S. Senate
senate.gov

USDA Agricultural Research Service
ars.usda.gov

USDA Center for Nutrition Policy and Promotion
cnpp.usda.gov

USDA Economic Research Service
ers.usda.gov

USDA Food and Nutrition Information Center of the National Agricultural Library
fnic.nal.usda.gov

USDA Food and Nutrition Services
fns.usda.gov

USDA Food Safety and Inspection Service
fsis.usda.gov

USDA Healthy Meals Resource System
healthymeals.nal.usda.gov

USDA Meat and Poultry Hotline
fsis.usda.gov/Food_Safety_Education/ USDA_Meat_&_Poultry_Hotline

USDA National Agricultural Statistics Service
nass.usda.gov

USDA World Agricultural Outlook Board
usda.gov/oce/commodity

Weight-Control Information Network (WIN)
win.niddk.nih.gov

Note: Phone numbers and Web addresses may have changed since publication. For some entries, reaching the correct website may require keying *www.* into the address.

Career-Related Organizations and Sites

The following sites provide a wide range of career-related information, including career exploration and planning tools, résumé-writing tips, job listings, workplace statistics, and career education information.

America's Career InfoNet
acinet.org

Career Builder
careerbuilder.com

CareerOneStop
careeronestop.org

Career Resource Center
careers.org

Family, Career and Community Leaders of America (FCCLA)
fccla.com

JobWeb
jobweb.com

Mapping Your Future
mappingyourfuture.org

Monster
monster.com

My Future
myfuture.com

National Research Center for Career and Technical Education
nccte.org

Occupational Outlook Handbook
stats.bls.gov/oco

O*NET Online
online.onetcenter.org

SkillsUSA
skillsusa.org

U.S. Department of Labor Employment and Training Administration
doleta.gov

Assessment Techniques

Various assessments strategies are included throughout each chapter. Some can be used to measure student progress in understanding the concepts (*formative assessment*), while others can be used to measure the extent to which they have mastered the concepts (*summative assessment*).

Formative assessment takes place often and is ongoing throughout a course. The many comprehension strategies used throughout the text can be used as formative assessment techniques. They measure students' grasp of the concepts as well as their abilities to internalize the skills and apply them to new situations. Many formative assessments can be completed as groups, because the main focus is on the learning that is taking place. Students can assess their team members and use a rubric to self-assess their own learning. The *Teacher's Resources* can be used to identify formative assessments for key knowledge, understandings, and skills being learned.

Written tests in the *Teacher's Resources* and **Exam**View® Assessment Suite have traditionally been used to evaluate performance. This method of evaluation is good to use when assessing knowledge and comprehension.

Performance Assessment

When assigning students some of the projects from the text that you plan to use as either formative or summative assessment, a rubric can be helpful for measuring student achievement. A *rubric* consists of a set of criteria that includes specific descriptors or standards that can be used to arrive at performance scores for students. A point value is given for each set of descriptors, leading to a range of possible points to be assigned, usually from 1 to 5. The criteria can also be weighted. This method of assessment reduces the guesswork involved in grading, leading to fair and consistent scoring. The standards clearly indicate to students the various levels of mastery of a task. Students are even able to assess their own achievement based on the criteria.

When using rubrics, students should see the criteria at the beginning of the assignment. Then they can focus their effort on what needs to be done to reach a certain level of performance or quality of project. They have a clear understanding of your expectations of achievement. Rubrics allow you to assess a student's performance and arrive at a performance score. Students can see what levels they have surpassed and what levels they can still strive to reach.

Portfolios

Another type of performance assessment that is frequently used by teachers today is the portfolio. A *portfolio* consists of a selection of materials that students choose to document their performance over a period of time. Therefore, it is a good tool for gathering formative assessment data. Students select their best work samples to showcase their achievement. These items might provide evidence of employability skills as well as academic skills. Some of the items students might include in portfolios are

- work samples that show mastery of specific skills, including photographs, video recordings, and assessments
- writing samples that show communication skills
- a résumé
- letters of recommendation that document specific career-related skills
- certificates of completion
- awards and recognition

The portfolio is completed at the culmination of a course to provide evidence of learning, and therefore can be used as a summative assessment tool. As students choose items to include in the final portfolio, they should include items that specifically show how they met or answered the key questions for each chapter studied. A self-assessment summary report should be included that explains what has been accomplished, what has been learned, what strengths the student has gained, and any areas that need improvement. *Portfolio Project* activities are included at the end of every chapter in the student text.

Portfolios may be presented to the class by students, but they should remain the property of students when they leave the course. They may be used for interviews with potential employers.

Portfolio assessment is only one of several evaluation methods teachers can use, but it is a powerful tool for both students and teachers. It encourages self-reflection and self-assessment of a broader nature. Traditional evaluation methods of tests, quizzes, and papers have their place in measuring the achievement of some course objectives, but other assessment tools should also be used to fairly assess the achievement of all desired outcomes.

Incorporating Career and Technical Student Organizations

Career and Technical Student Organizations (CTSOs) offer a wide variety of activities that can be adapted to almost any school and classroom situation. A brief introduction to CTSOs follows. If you would like more details, visit their websites.

Purpose

The purpose of CTSOs is to help students acquire knowledge and skills in career and technical areas as well as leadership skills and experience. These organizations achieve these goals by enlisting teacher-advisors to organize and lead local chapters in their schools. Support for teacher-advisors and their chapters is often coordinated through each state's education department. The chapters elect officers and establish a program of work. The program of work can include a variety of activities, including community service, cocurricular projects, and competition preparation. Student achievement in specified areas is recognized with certificates and/or public acknowledgement through awards ceremonies.

CTSOs Officially Recognized by the U.S. Department of Education		
Short Name	**Full Name**	**Web Site**
BPA	Business Professionals of America	www.bpa.org
DECA	An Association of Marketing Students	www.deca.org
FBLA/PBL	Future Business Leaders of America/Phi Beta Lambda	www.fbla-pbl.org
FCCLA	Family, Career and Community Leaders of America	www.fcclainc.org
FEA	Future Educators Association	www.futureeducators.org
FFA	National FFA Organization	www.ffa.org
HOSA	Health Occupations Students of America	www.hosa.org
SkillsUSA	SkillsUSA	www.skillsusa.org
TSA	Technology Student Association	www.tsaweb.org

Competitive Events

Competitive events are a main feature of most CTSOs. The CTSO develops events that enable students to showcase how well they have mastered the learning of specific content and the use of decision-making, problem-solving, and leadership skills. Each CTSO has its own list of competitive events and activities. Members develop career and leadership skills even though they may not participate in or win competitions.

The Adviser's Role

Preparing students for competitions takes much time and commitment, often beyond the traditional school day. Dedication to this process, however, does have its rewards. You see your students develop complex skills and grow in their roles as leaders and team members. Their ultimate goal is to become competent, successful members of the food and nutrition workforce.

Once you and your students commit to participating in one or more competitions, much responsibility is involved in your role as adviser. If this is a new experience for you or your school, there are some important first steps to take. They include, but are not limited to, the following:

- Obtain membership and competition requirements from organizations that sponsor the competitions, such as FCCLA.
- Meet with school administrators to gain permission to start a CTSO or gain support for an existing chapter. Contact advisory committee members to build support in the school and community.
- Identify competitions that best meet the needs of your students.

- Make sure local, state, and national membership requirements are met.
- Find out where state meetings and competitions are held and attend them.
- Find out about application or competition deadlines and plan accordingly.
- Build parent support for competitive events. Emphasize that through competition, students enhance their workplace skills and may also receive recognition awards (in some cases scholarships) if they win at state and national levels.

Advisory Committees

Many programs that receive reimbursement from state or federal governments require the formation of advisory committees. An advisory committee consists of members who are actively working in food and nutrition careers. Along with you, the instructor, the advisory committee helps determine the appropriate course of study and proper equipment/supplies to reach the educational standards and competencies of the program. The advisory committee will meet regularly to advise you on needs and trends in foods and nutrition. This regular interaction keeps the program up-to-date. It also helps provide you with job placement contacts for students involved in work-based learning programs or those who are graduating.

Incorporating the Career Clusters

In the mid 1990s, a project called Building Linkages began development, led by the Office of Vocational and Adult Education (OVAE). Building Linkages was funded in partnership by the U.S. Departments of Labor and Education. The goal of the project was to create a reliable set of standards for the integration of academics with workplace skills. Another goal was to show how higher levels of skills and knowledge lead to higher positions. Eventually the organization of the project emerged as *career clusters*, and The States' Career Clusters Initiative was launched in 2001.

There are 16 career clusters, and among these are 79 different career pathways. In each cluster, three levels of knowledge and skills exist, ranging from broad to specific. The *foundation* level applies to all levels of the careers. The *pathway* level lists the skills necessary for a career subgroup within a cluster. The *career/occupation* level is the highest level of skill and knowledge within a given cluster. All levels promote employability, academic, and technical skills.

The career clusters are discussed in Chapter 26. In addition, each chapter features an occupation related to chapter content that is associated with the following career clusters: *Agriculture, Food & Natural Resources*; *Health Science*; *Hospitality & Tourism*; and *Human Resources*. Typical job duties, education requirements, and job outlook are highlighted.

Integrating Academics

No matter what career path a student chooses, academic skills will be critical to his or her success. The following are core academic subjects in schools: English, reading, language arts, math, science, foreign languages, civics and government, economics, arts, history, and geography.

The *Guide to Good Food* program supports student growth and achievement in key academic areas. The academic areas are highlighted where they are covered in the *Link to Academic Skills* and *A Measure of Math* in the end-of-chapter section.

Reading, English, and Language Arts

The entire *Guide to Good Food* student text is designed to encourage reading and understanding. Each chapter begins with a *Learning Prep* activity to engage student interest. *Terms to Know* terms are shown in bold and highlighted in the text copy to draw attention to the reader. End-of-chapter activities in the *Link to Academic Skills* section strengthen students' skills in reading, writing, and speech. The *Teacher's Edition*, *Student Workbook*, and *Teacher's Resources* provide more activities designed to develop skills in English and language arts.

Teaching Reading Across the Curriculum

All teachers need to be teachers of reading. In all content areas, teachers need to teach students how to use reading as a tool to enhance their learning. The following strategies will help you teach reading skills that help students create meaning and understand what they read.

- Use prereading activities to help students prepare for learning. *Learning Prep* activities in each chapter of the text are designed to help students make the connection between what they already know and the new concepts to be learned. This connection is critical for students to be able to remember new information.
- Use strategies that help students comprehend what they read. Examples of comprehension strategies include having students question what they read, think about the concepts, talk about content with a partner or in small groups, summarize ideas, and organize ideas graphically. Strategies that help develop comprehension are included in the student text and *Teacher's Edition*. The questions at the end of each chapter help students clarify their comprehension of key concepts. The various strategies for reteaching and reinforcing concepts in the *Teacher's Resources* are also designed to help students think about what they have read and gain understanding.
- Use strategies that help students incorporate the new knowledge they have acquired into their own system of thinking. Such internalization is needed in order for students to remember concepts and be able to apply them to daily living. The various strategies listed under *Link to Academic Skills, Build Critical Thinking Skills, Apply Technology,* and *Teamwork in Action* are designed to help students incorporate their new knowledge. Strategies such as journaling allow students a time to connect new concepts to their personal situations. The *Learn More About...* boxed features motivate students to seek further information related to chapter content. The *Teacher's Resources* contain strategies for enriching and extending the text into real-life situations. As students extend and refine the new knowledge they have acquired, the learning takes on personal meaning.

It is important to model these three steps before, during, and after text reading. Explain to students why you are using various strategies. Continual practice of reading skills in all classes will help students develop these lifelong skills.

Math

Mathematics is a tool necessary for success in business as well as managing personal finances. To strengthen students' math skills, *A Measure of Math* activities are found at the end of chapters.

Science

Science plays an important role in the study of food and nutrition. Science activities appear in the *Link to Academic Skills* end-of-chapter section. Mentions of science occur as appropriate in the student text.

Social Studies

Social studies and psychology are especially helpful in understanding the cultural aspects of food. Appropriate activities are found at the end of each chapter under *Link to Academic Skills*. Additional activities appear in the *Teacher's Edition*, *Workbook*, and *Teacher's Resources*.

Planning Your Program

Program planning guides suggest ways to schedule the chapters of *Guide to Good Food* for different course calendars. Semester and full-year course planning guides are included on pages T22-T23. Chapters are grouped according to the suggested depth of coverage and duration of instruction time.

Correlation of National Standards with *Guide to Good Food*

By studying *Guide to Good Food*, students can learn to master the competencies that are key to the study of nutrition and wellness. Competency statements identify what learners should know and be able to do upon studying a textbook or instructional course. Such competency statements form the basis of national standards.

This teacher's guide presents national standards on nutrition and wellness from the National Association of State Administrators of Family and Consumer Sciences (NASAFACS). A chart showing the national standards correlated to the *Guide to Good Food* text appears later in this Introduction.

Marketing Your Program

Many students and their parents may have preconceived ideas about what the foods and nutrition curriculum includes. You need to identify these preconceptions and, if necessary, gently alter them to give students and their parents a more accurate idea of what your class entails.

To get your public relations campaign started, create a newsletter to inform parents about what their children will be studying in your class. You can also use the newsletter to encourage students to enroll in your class. Post the newsletter on your class website or pass it out to students. You might ask some of your former students what they feel they have gained from taking your class and add some of their ideas to the newsletter. (If you decide to use direct quotations, be sure to get permission from your students.)

Students and their parents are not likely to be the only ones who are not totally aware of the importance of food and nutrition classes. You can make people more aware through good public relations. It pays to make the student body, faculty, and community aware of your program. With good public relations, you can increase your enrollment, gain support from administrators and other teachers, and achieve recognition in the community. Following are some ways to market your program:

- *Create visibility.* This includes announcements of projects and activities at faculty meetings and in school newspapers, and articles and press releases in school and community newspapers.
- *Interact with educators in other subject matter areas.* Coordinate the teaching of chapter material with other departments in your school that might be covering related information.
- *Contribute to the education objectives of the school.* If your school follows stated educational objectives and strives to strengthen specific skills, include these overall goals in your teaching.
- *Serve as a resource center.* Make your department a resource center of materials related to foods and nutrition.
- *Generate involvement and activity in the community.* Involve students in community life through field trips, surveys, presentations from guest speakers, and interviews with businesspeople and community leaders.
- *Connect with parents.* Keep parents informed about classroom activities and invite them to participate as they are able.
- *Establish a student sales staff.* Encourage students to tell their parents and friends what they are learning.

Goodheart-Willcox Welcomes Your Comments

We welcome your comments or suggestions regarding *Guide to Good Food* and its supplements. Please send any comments you may have to the editor by visiting our website at www.g-w.com or writing to

Editorial Department
Goodheart-Willcox Publisher
18604 West Creek Drive
Tinley Park, IL 60477-6243

Program Planning Guides

Guide to Good Food program planning guides are provided for trimester, semester, and full-year courses. Chapters are grouped according to the suggested depth of coverage and duration of instruction time. Incorporate activities from the *Teacher's Edition*, *Teacher's Resources*, or *Workbook* to provide variety during extended class periods.

Semester Course, Eighteen Weeks

Week	Chapter Numbers and Names
1	**Part 1 The Importance of Food** 1 Food Affects Life 2 Nutritional Needs
2	3 Making Healthful Choices
3	4 Nutrition and Fitness Through the Life Span 5 Staying Active and Managing Weight
4	6 Safeguarding Health **Part 2 The Management of Food** 7 Kitchen and Dining Areas
5	8 Kitchen Appliances 9 Kitchen Utensils
6	10 Planning Meals 11 Shopping Decisions
7	12 Recipes and Work Plans **Part 3 The Preparation of Food** 13 Grain Foods
8	14 Vegetables 15 Fruits
9	16 Dairy Products 17 Eggs
10	18 Meat 19 Poultry
11	20 Fish and Shellfish 21 Salads, Casseroles, and Soups
12	22 Breads 23 Cakes, Cookies, Pies, and Candies
13	24 Food and Entertaining 25 Preserving Foods
14	**Part 4 Food and Careers** 26 Investigating Careers 27 Career and Job Success
15	**Part 5 Foods of the World** 28 The United States and Canada
16	29 Latin America 30 Europe
17	31 Mediterranean Countries 32 Middle East and Africa
18	33 Asia

Full-Year Course, Six Grading Periods, Six Weeks Each

First Grading Period

Part 1 The Importance of Food
1 Food Affects Life
2 Nutritional Needs
3 Making Healthful Choices
4 Nutrition and Fitness Through the Life Span
5 Staying Active and Managing Weight
6 Safeguarding Health

Second Grading Period

Part 2 The Management of Food
7 Kitchen and Dining Areas
8 Kitchen Appliances
9 Kitchen Utensils
10 Planning Meals
11 Shopping Decisions
12 Recipes and Work Plans

Third Grading Period

Part 3 The Preparation of Food
13 Grain Foods
14 Vegetables
15 Fruits
16 Dairy Products
17 Eggs

Fourth Grading Period

18 Meat
19 Poultry
20 Fish and Shellfish
21 Salads, Casseroles, and Soups
22 Breads
23 Cakes, Cookies, Pies, and Candies

Fifth Grading Period

24 Food and Entertaining
25 Preserving Foods

Part 4 Food and Careers
26 Investigating Careers
27 Career and Job Success

Sixth Grading Period

Part 5 Foods of the World
28 The United States and Canada
29 Latin America
30 Europe
31 Mediterranean Countries
32 Middle East and Africa
33 Asia

Full-Year Course, Four Grading Periods, Nine Weeks Each

First Grading Period

Part 1   The Importance of Food
1   Food Affects Life
2   Nutritional Needs
3   Making Healthful Choices
4   Nutrition and Fitness Through the Life Span
5   Staying Active and Managing Weight
6   Safeguarding Health

Part 2   The Management of Food
7   Kitchen and Dining Areas
8   Kitchen Appliances

Second Grading Period
9   Kitchen Utensils
10   Planning Meals
11   Shopping Decisions
12   Recipes and Work Plans

Part 3   The Preparation of Food
13   Grain Foods
14   Vegetables
15   Fruits
16   Dairy Products

Third Grading Period
17   Eggs
18   Meat
19   Poultry
20   Fish and Shellfish
21   Salads, Casseroles, and Soups
22   Breads
23   Cakes, Cookies, Pies, and Candies
24   Food and Entertaining
25   Preserving Foods

Fourth Grading Period

Part 4   Food and Careers
26   Investigating Careers
27   Career and Job Success

Part 5   Foods of the World
28   The United States and Canada
29   Latin America
30   Europe
31   Mediterranean Countries
32   Middle East and Africa
33   Asia

Correlation of National Standards for Nutrition and Wellness Practices Across the Life Span with *Guide to Good Food*

In planning your program, you may want to use the correlation chart below. This chart correlates the Family and Consumer Sciences Education National Standards with the content of *Guide to Good Food*. It lists the competencies for each of the content standards for Nutrition and Wellness. It also identifies the major text concepts that relate to each competency. Bold numbers indicate chapters in which concepts are found.

After studying the content of this text, students will be able to achieve the following comprehensive standard:

14.0 Demonstrate nutrition and wellness practices that enhance individual and family well-being.

Content Standard 14.1
Analyze factors that influence nutrition and wellness practices across the life span.

Competencies	Text Concepts
14.1.1 Explain physical, emotional, social, psychological, and spiritual components of individual and family wellness.	**1:** Food Meets Physical Needs, Cultural Influences on Food Choices, Social Influences on Food Choices, Psychological Influences on Food Choices **4:** Pregnancy and Lactation, Infancy and Early Childhood, The Elementary School Years, The Teen Years, Adulthood, The Later Years **5:** Energy Needs, Physical Activity and Fitness, Nutrition for Athletes, Weight Management, Eating Disorders
14.1.2 Analyze the effects of psychological, cultural, and social influences on food choices and other nutrition practices.	**1:** Making Choices About Foods, Cultural Influences on Food Choices, Social Influences on Food Choices, Psychological Influences on Food Choices **2:** The Nutrients, Carbohydrates, Fats, Proteins, Vitamins, Minerals, Water, Digestion and Absorption, Metabolism **3:** Benefits of Healthful Choices, Resources for Making Healthful Choices, Choosing Wisely When Shopping for Food, Choosing Wisely When Preparing Food, Choosing Wisely When Eating Out
14.1.3 Analyze the governmental, economic, and technological influences on food choices and practices.	**1:** The History of Food, Factors That Affect the Food Supply **2:** The Nutrients, Carbohydrates, Fats, Proteins, Vitamins, Minerals, Water, Digestion and Absorption, Metabolism **3:** Benefits of Healthful Choices, Resources for Making Healthful Choices, Choosing Wisely When Shopping for Food **4:** Food Assistance Programs **10:** Provide Good Nutrition, Use Planned Spending, Control the Use of Time and Energy **11:** Choosing Where to Shop, Deciding What to Buy, Using Food Labeling, Help with Consumer Problems **13:** Selecting and Storing Cereal Products **14:** Choosing Fresh Vegetables, Choosing Canned, Frozen, and Dried Vegetables **15:** Choosing Fresh Fruit, Choosing Canned, Frozen, and Dried Fruit **16:** Selecting and Storing Dairy Products **17:** Selecting and Storing Eggs **18:** What Is Meat?, Inspection and Grading of Meat, Selecting Meat **19:** Buying Poultry **20:** Choosing Fish and Shellfish **22:** Selecting and Storing Baked Products **25:** Commercial Food Preservation

Competencies	Text Concepts
14.1.4 Analyze the effects of global and local events and conditions on food choices and practices.	**1:** The History of Food, Making Choices About Foods, Cultural Influences on Food Choices, Social Influences on Food Choices, Factors That Affect the Food Supply
	3: Benefits of Healthful Choices, Resources for Making Healthful Choices, Choosing Wisely When Shopping for Food, Choosing Wisely When Preparing Food, Choosing Wisely When Eating Out
	4: Food Assistance Programs
	28: A Historical Overview of the United States, The Pennsylvania Dutch, Soul Food, Creole Cuisine, Geography and Climate of Canada, Canadian Culture, Canadian Cuisine
	29: Geography and Climate of Mexico, Mexican Culture, Mexican Cuisine, Geography and Climate of South America, South American Culture, South American Cuisine
	30: Geography and Climate of the British Isles, Cuisine of the British Isles, Geography and Climate of France, French Culture, French Cuisine, Geography and Climate of Germany, German Culture, German Agriculture, German Cuisine, Geography and Climate of Scandinavia, Scandinavian Culture, Scandinavian Cuisine
	31: Geography and Climate of Spain, Spanish Culture, Spanish Cuisine, Geography and Climate of Italy, Italian Culture, Italian Cuisine, Geography and Climate of Greece, Greek Culture, Greek Cuisine
	32: Geography and Climate of the Middle East, Middle Eastern Culture, Middle Eastern Cuisine, Geography and Climate of Israel, Israeli Culture, Israeli Cuisine, Climate and Geography of Africa, African Culture, African Cuisine
	33: Geography and Climate of Russia, Russian Culture, Russian Cuisine, Geography and Climate of India, Indian Culture, Indian Cuisine, Geography and Climate of China, Chinese Culture, Chinese Cuisine, Geography and Climate of Japan, Japanese Culture, Japanese Cuisine
14.1.5 Analyze legislation and regulations related to nutrition and wellness.	**1:** The History of Food, Factors That Affect the Food Supply
	3: Resources for Making Healthful Choices, Choosing Wisely When Shopping for Food
	4: Food Assistance Programs
	11: Using Food Labeling, Help with Consumer Problems

(Continued)

Content Standard 14.2	
Evaluate the nutritional needs of individuals and families in relation to health and wellness across the life span.	
Competencies	**Text Concepts**
14.2.1 Analyze the effect of nutrients on health, appearance, and peak performance.	**1:** Food Meets Physical Needs **2:** The Nutrients, Carbohydrates, Fats, Proteins, Vitamins, Minerals, Water, Digestion and Absorption, Metabolism **3:** Benefits of Healthful Choices, Resources for Making Healthful Choices, Choosing Wisely When Shopping for Food, Choosing Wisely When Preparing Food, Choosing Wisely When Eating Out **4:** Pregnancy and Lactation, Infancy and Early Childhood, The Elementary School Years, The Teen Years, Adulthood, The Later Years, Special Diets **5:** Energy Needs, Physical Activity and Fitness, Nutrition for Athletes, Weight Management, Eating Disorders **10:** Provide Good Nutrition
14.2.2 Analyze the relationship of nutrition and wellness to individual and family health throughout the life span.	**1:** Food Meets Physical Needs **2:** The Nutrients, Carbohydrates, Fats, Proteins, Vitamins, Minerals, Water, Digestion and Absorption, Metabolism **3:** Benefits of Healthful Choices, Resources for Making Healthful Choices **4:** Pregnancy and Lactation, Infancy and Early Childhood, The Elementary School Years, The Teen Years, Adulthood, The Later Years, Special Diets **5:** Energy Needs, Physical Activity and Fitness, Nutrition for Athletes, Weight Management, Eating Disorders **10:** Provide Good Nutrition
14.2.3 Analyze the effects of food and diet fads, food addictions, and eating disorders on wellness.	**1:** Social Influences on Food Choices, Psychological Influences on Food Choices **5:** Nutrition for Athletes, Weight Management, Eating Disorders
14.2.4 Analyze sources of food and nutrition information, including food labels, related to health and wellness.	**1:** Social Influences on Food Choices **3:** Resources for Making Healthful Choices, Choosing Wisely When Shopping for Food, Choosing Wisely When Eating Out **11:** Using Food Labeling
Content Standard 14.3	
Demonstrate ability to acquire, handle, and use foods to meet nutrition and wellness needs of individuals and families across the life span.	
Competencies	**Text Concepts**
14.3.1 Apply various dietary guidelines in planning to meet nutrition and wellness needs.	**3:** Resources for Making Healthful Choices, Choosing Wisely When Shopping for Food, Choosing Wisely When Preparing Food, Choosing Wisely When Eating Out **4:** Pregnancy and Lactation, Infancy and Early Childhood, The Elementary School Years, The Teen Years, Adulthood, The Later Years, Special Diets, Food Assistance Programs **5:** Energy Needs, Physical Activity and Fitness, Nutrition for Athletes, Weight Management, Eating Disorders

Competencies	Text Concepts
14.3.2 Design strategies that meet the health and nutrition requirements of individuals and families with special needs.	**4:** Pregnancy and Lactation, Infancy and Early Childhood, The Elementary School Years, The Teen Years, Adulthood, The Later Years, Special Diets, Food Assistance Programs
	5: Energy Needs, Physical Activity and Fitness, Nutrition for Athletes, Weight Management, Eating Disorders
14.3.3 Demonstrate ability to select, store, prepare, and serve nutritious and aesthetically pleasing foods.	**1:** Making Choices About Foods
	3: Benefits of Healthful Choices, Resources for Making Healthful Choices, Choosing Wisely When Shopping for Food, Choosing Wisely When Preparing Food, Choosing Wisely When Eating Out
	10: Provide Good Nutrition, Prepare Satisfying Meals
	11: Deciding What to Buy, Using Food Labeling, Help with Consumer Problems
	12: Choosing a Recipe, Preparing Simple Recipes
	13: Selecting and Storing Cereal Products, Cooking Starches, Cooking Cereal Products
	14: Choosing Fresh Vegetables, Choosing Canned, Frozen, and Dried Vegetables, Preparing Vegetables
	15: Choosing Fresh Fruit, Choosing Canned, Frozen, and Dried Fruit, Preparing Fruits
	16: Selecting and Storing Dairy Products, Cooking with Milk and Cream, Preparing Common Milk-Based Foods, Cooking with Cheese
	17: Selecting and Storing Eggs, Eggs as Ingredients, Methods of Cooking Eggs
	18: What Is Meat?, Inspection and Grading of Meat, Selecting Meat, Food Science Principles of Cooking Meat, Methods of Cooking Meat
	19: Buying Poultry, Storing Poultry, Food Science Principles of Cooking Poultry, Methods of Cooking Poultry
	20: Choosing Fish and Shellfish, Cooking Finfish, Cooking Shellfish
	21: Salads, Casseroles, Stock Soups, Herbs and Spices
	22: Selecting and Storing Baked Products, Quick Breads, Yeast Breads
	23: Cakes, Cookies, Pies, Candy
	24: Planning for Entertaining, Outdoor Entertaining
	28: The Pennsylvania Dutch, Soul Food, Creole Cuisine, Canadian Cuisine
	29: Mexican Cuisine, South American Cuisine
	30: Cuisine of the British Isles, French Cuisine, German Cuisine, Scandinavian Cuisine
	31: Spanish Cuisine, Italian Cuisine, Greek Cuisine
	32: Middle Eastern Cuisine, Israeli Cuisine, African Cuisine
	33: Russian Cuisine, Indian Cuisine, Chinese Cuisine, Japanese Cuisine

(Continued)

Content Standard 14.4

Evaluate factors that affect food safety from production through consumption.

Competencies	Text Concepts
14.4.1 Analyze conditions and practices that promote safe food handling.	**1:** Factors That Affect the Food Supply **6:** Foodborne Illnesses, Four Steps to Food Safety, Safety in the Kitchen **8:** Service and Safety **13:** Selecting and Storing Cereal Products **14:** Choosing Fresh Vegetables, Choosing Canned, Frozen, and Dried Vegetables **15:** Choosing Fresh Fruit, Choosing Canned, Frozen, and Dried Fruit **16:** Selecting and Storing Dairy Products **17:** Selecting and Storing Eggs **18:** Inspection and Grading of Meat, Selecting Meat **19:** Storing Poultry **20:** Choosing Fish and Shellfish **22:** Selecting and Storing Baked Products **24:** Outdoor Entertaining **25:** Food Spoilage, Canning Foods, Freezing Foods, Drying Foods, Commercial Food Preservation
14.4.2 Analyze safety and sanitation practices throughout the food chain.	**1:** Factors That Affect the Food Supply **3:** Resources for Making Healthful Choices **6:** Foodborne Illnesses, Four Steps to Food Safety, Safety in the Kitchen **8:** Service and Safety **13:** Selecting and Storing Cereal Products **14:** Choosing Fresh Vegetables, Choosing Canned, Frozen, and Dried Vegetables **15:** Choosing Fresh Fruit, Choosing Canned, Frozen, and Dried Fruit **16:** Selecting and Storing Dairy Products **17:** Selecting and Storing Eggs **18:** Inspection and Grading of Meat, Selecting Meat **19:** Storing Poultry **20:** Choosing Fish and Shellfish **22:** Selecting and Storing Baked Products **24:** Outdoor Entertaining **25:** Food Spoilage, Canning Foods, Freezing Foods, Drying Foods, Commercial Food Preservation

Competencies	Text Concepts
14.4.3 Analyze how changes in national and international food production and distribution systems influence the food supply.	**1:** Factors That Affect the Food Supply **4:** Food Assistance Programs **25:** Food Spoilage, Commercial Food Preservation **28:** A Historical Overview of the United States, Geography and Climate of Canada **29:** Geography and Climate of Mexico, Geography and Climate of South America **30:** Geography and Climate of the British Isles, Geography and Climate of France, Geography and Climate of Germany, German Agriculture, Geography and Climate of Scandinavia **31:** Geography and Climate of Spain, Geography and Climate of Italy, Geography and Climate of Greece **32:** Geography and Climate of the Middle East, Geography and Climate of Israel, Climate and Geography of Africa **33:** Geography and Climate of Russia, Geography and Climate of India, Geography and Climate of China, Geography and Climate of Japan
14.4.4 Analyze federal, state, and local inspection and labeling systems that protect the health of individuals and the public.	**1:** Factors That Affect the Food Supply **3:** Choosing Wisely When Shopping for Food **6:** Four Steps to Food Safety, Safety in the Kitchen **8:** Service and Safety **11:** Using Food Labeling, Help with Consumer Problems **18:** Inspection and Grading of Meat **19:** Buying Poultry **20:** Choosing Fish and Shellfish **25:** Food Spoilage, Commercial Food Preservation
14.4.5 Analyze foodborne illness factors, including causes, foods at risk, and methods of prevention commercially and by individuals and families.	**1:** Factors That Affect the Food Supply **3:** Resources for Making Healthful Choices **6:** Foodborne Illnesses, Four Steps to Food Safety **14:** Choosing Fresh Vegetables, Choosing Canned, Frozen, and Dried Vegetables **15:** Choosing Fresh Fruit, Choosing Canned, Frozen, and Dried Fruit **16:** Selecting and Storing Dairy Products **17:** Selecting and Storing Eggs **18:** Inspection and Grading of Meat, Selecting Meat **19:** Buying Poultry, Storing Poultry **20:** Choosing Fish and Shellfish **24:** Planning for Entertaining, Outdoor Entertaining **25:** Food Spoilage, Commercial Food Preservation
14.4.6 Analyze public dialogue about food safety and sanitation.	**1:** Factors That Affect the Food Supply **6:** Foodborne Illnesses, Four Steps to Food Safety, Safety in the Kitchen

(Continued)

Content Standard 14.5

Evaluate the influence of science and technology on food composition, safety, and other issues.

Competencies	Text Concepts
14.5.1 Analyze how scientific and technical advances influence the nutrient content, availability, and safety of foods.	**1:** Factors That Affect the Food Supply **3:** Choosing Wisely When Shopping for Food **6:** Four Steps to Food Safety **11:** Deciding What to Buy **25:** Food Spoilage, Commercial Food Preservation
14.5.2 Analyze how the scientific and technical advances in food processing, storage, product development, and distribution influence nutrition and wellness.	**1:** The History of Food, Making Choices About Foods, Food Meets Physical Needs, Factors That Affect the Food Supply **3:** Choosing Wisely When Shopping for Food **11:** Deciding What to Buy **25:** Food Spoilage, Commercial Food Preservation
14.5.3 Analyze the effects of technological advances on selection, preparation and home storage of food.	**1:** Factors That Affect the Food Supply **3:** Benefits of Healthful Choices, Resources for Making Healthful Choices, Choosing Wisely When Shopping for Food, Choosing Wisely When Preparing Food **8:** Major Kitchen Appliances **10:** Provide Good Nutrition **11:** Deciding What to Buy, Using Food Labeling **12:** Preparing Simple Recipes **13:** Selecting and Storing Cereal Products, Cooking Starches, Cooking Cereal Products **14:** Choosing Fresh Vegetables, Choosing Canned, Frozen, and Dried Vegetables, Preparing Vegetables **15:** Choosing Fresh Fruit, Choosing Canned, Frozen, and Dried Fruit, Preparing Fruits **16:** Selecting and Storing Dairy Products, Cooking with Milk and Cream, Preparing Common Milk-Based Foods, Cooking with Cheese **17:** Selecting and Storing Eggs, Eggs as Ingredients, Methods of Cooking Eggs **18:** Selecting Meat, Food Science Principles of Cooking Meat, Methods of Cooking Meat **19:** Buying Poultry, Storing Poultry, Food Science Principles of Cooking Poultry, Methods of Cooking Poultry **20:** Choosing Fish and Shellfish, Cooking Finfish, Cooking Shellfish **21:** Salads, Casseroles, Stock Soups, Herbs and Spices **22:** Selecting and Storing Baked Products, Quick Breads, Yeast Breads **23:** Cakes, Cookies, Pies, Candy **25:** Food Spoilage, Canning Foods, Making Jellied Products, Freezing Foods, Drying Foods, Commercial Food Preservation

Competencies	Text Concepts
14.5.4 Analyze the effects of food science and technology on meeting nutritional needs.	**1:** Factors That Affect the Food Supply
	3: Resources for Making Healthful Choices, Choosing Wisely When Shopping for Food, Choosing Wisely When Preparing Food
	4: Pregnancy and Lactation, Infancy and Early Childhood, The Elementary School Years, The Teen Years, Adulthood, The Later Years, Special Diets, Food Assistance Programs
	5: Energy Needs, Weight Management
	10: Prepare Satisfying Meals, Control the Use of Time and Energy
	11: Choosing Where to Shop, Deciding What to Buy, Using Food Labeling, Help with Consumer Problems
	13: Cooking Starches, Cooking Cereal Products
	14: Preparing Vegetables
	15: Preparing Fruits
	16: Preparing Common Milk-Based Foods, Cooking with Cheese
	17: Methods of Cooking Eggs
	18: Food Science Principles of Cooking Meat, Methods of Cooking Meat
	19: Buying Poultry, Storing Poultry, Food Science Principles of Cooking Poultry, Methods of Cooking Poultry
	20: Cooking Finfish, Cooking Shellfish
	25: Food Spoilage, Canning Foods, Making Jellied Products, Freezing Foods, Drying Foods, Commercial Food Preservation

Guide to Good Food

12th Edition

by

Velda L. Largen
Author of Family and Consumer Sciences Instructional Materials

Deborah L. Bence
Family and Consumer Sciences Author
Granville, Ohio

Publisher
Goodheart-Willcox Company, Inc.
Tinley Park, IL
www.g-w.com

Library of Congress Catalog Card Number 2011014169

ISBN 978-1-60525-600-9

3 4 5 6 7 8 9 – 12 – 17 16 15 14 13 12

The Goodheart-Willcox Company, Inc. Brand Disclaimer: Brand names, company names, and illustrations for products and services included in this text are provided for educational purposes only and do not represent or imply endorsement or recommendation by the author or the publisher.

The Goodheart-Willcox Company, Inc. Safety Notice: The reader is expressly advised to carefully read, understand, and apply all safety precautions and warnings described in this book or that might also be indicated in undertaking the activities and exercises described herein to minimize risk of personal injury or injury to others. Common sense and good judgment should also be exercised and applied to help avoid all potential hazards. The reader should always refer to the appropriate manufacturer's technical information, directions, and recommendations; then proceed with care to follow specific equipment operating instructions. The reader should understand these notices and cautions are not exhaustive.

The publisher makes no warranty or representation whatsoever, either expressed or implied, including but not limited to equipment, procedures, and applications described or referred to herein, their quality, performance, merchantability, or fitness for a particular purpose. The publisher assumes no responsibility for any changes, errors, or omissions in this book. The publisher specifically disclaims any liability whatsoever, including any direct, indirect, incidental, consequential, special, or exemplary damages resulting, in whole or in part, from the reader's use or reliance upon the information, instructions, procedures, warnings, cautions, applications, or other matter contained in this book. The publisher assumes no responsibility for the activities of the reader.

The Goodheart-Willcox Company, Inc. Internet Disclaimer: The Internet resources and listings in this Goodheart-Willcox Publisher product are provided solely as a convenience to you. These resources and listings were reviewed at the time of publication to provide you with accurate, safe, and appropriate information. Goodheart-Willcox Publisher has no control over the referenced Web sites and, due to the dynamic nature of the Internet, is not responsible or liable for the content, products, or performance of links to other Web sites or resources. Goodheart-Willcox Publisher makes no representation, either expressed or implied, regarding the content of these Web sites, and such references do not constitute an endorsement or recommendation of the information or content presented. It is your responsibility to take all protective measures to guard against inappropriate content, viruses, or other destructive elements.

Library of Congress Cataloging-in-Publication Data

Largen, Velda L.
    Guide to good food / Velda L. Largen, Deborah L. Bence. -- 12th ed.
      p. cm.
    Includes index.
    ISBN 978-1-60525-600-9
    1. Food. 2. Nutrition. 3. International cooking. I. Bence, Deborah L. II. Title.
TX354.L37   2012
641.3--dc23   2011014169

Cover image: Shutterstock

INTRODUCTION

Guide to Good Food includes information on a wide range of food and nutrition topics. This practical text focuses on the latest advice about diet and physical activity. It offers guidelines for using appliances, setting up a food budget, and buying and storing foods. It provides help for managing resources, organizing workspace, and working effectively as part of a team. Discussions on basic cooking methods will give you the background needed to prepare a variety of foods. *Guide to Good Food* also includes several chapters on foods from around the world.

The broad scope of information in this text is intended to show you food is more than just something to eat. Food provides a source of income for millions of people. It is at the heart of scientific research. It is also a part of people's cultural identity.

You will find *Guide to Good Food* easy to read and understand. An opening activity, main points, *Terms to Know*, and learning objectives will introduce you to the content of each chapter. As you read, hundreds of photos will help you picture the many foods and techniques that are discussed. Colorful boxes will address scientific, cultural, environmental, and health issues related to food. Descriptions of an array of food industry careers detail work tasks, needed skills, and training requirements to help you think about your future options for work. Numerous recipes will give you the chance to practice food preparation methods covered in the book. Review questions at the end of each chapter will help you assess your learning of what you read. A variety of activities are suggested to help you build skills needed for success at home, at work, and in the community. All these resources are intended to add to your experience as you study the interesting and vital subject of food and nutrition.

Promotes Successful Learning

Welcome to *Guide to Good Food*! Get ready to learn how food affects all aspects of your life.

Part 1 The Importance of Food

1 Food Affects Life
2 Nutritional Needs
3 Making Healthful Choices
4 Nutrition and Fitness Through the Life Span
5 Staying Active and Managing Weight
6 Safeguarding Health

Study Starters

1. Become familiar with the glossary in the back of this book. Look up the following words from Chapters 1 through 6 in the glossary: *hunger, fiber, processed food, diet, fitness,* and *contaminant.* Then look up the same words in a dictionary. Compare the dictionary definitions with the definitions given in the glossary. Discuss in class why the definitions from the two sources might differ somewhat.
2. Choose a food. Then design a poster illustrating the cultural/social significance, nutritional contributions, and food safety concerns associated with your chosen food.

FCCLA: Taking the Lead

As a Power of One project for the *A Better You* unit, set a goal for improving your nutritional status. You might begin by using the ChooseMyPlate.gov website to conduct personal nutrition assessments. After identifying nutrients for which your intakes are low, you can make food choices, find recipes, and write menus to plan a more healthful diet that will help you meet nutrient needs. After following the healthful diet for a set period, repeat the nutrition assessments and write an evaluation of how the dietary changes you have made have affected you physically and mentally.

Study Starters

Quick, easy activities introduce the food topics you will explore.

FCCLA: Taking the Lead

Food-related projects present opportunities for demonstrating leadership in Family, Career, and Community Leaders of America events.

CHAPTER 11 Shopping Decisions

Main Menu

○ Developing shopping skills can help consumers get the most value for their food dollars.
○ Food labeling is a helpful tool consumers can use to learn about the products available to them.

Learning Prep

Make a matching activity listing the *Terms to Know* in one column and randomly ordered definitions in a second column. Trade papers with a partner and complete one another's matching activities. Trade papers again and evaluate your partner's accuracy.

Objectives

After studying this chapter, you will be able to
○ evaluate store features to decide where to shop for food.
○ identify factors that affect food costs and comparison shop to decide what foods to buy.
○ use information on food product labels to make informed decisions about foods to buy.
○ list sources of consumer information.

Terms to Know

produce
comparison shopping
impulse buying
unit pricing
grade
brand name
store brand
national brand
precycling
organic food

pesticide
food additive
GRAS list
artificial sweetener
nutrition labeling
Daily Values
universal product code (UPC)
open dating

Learning Prep

Fun activities help you improve reading skills.

Main Menu

Brief statements preview what you will learn in each chapter.

Objectives

Objectives summarize the learning goals for each chapter.

Terms to Know

New terms important to understanding the chapter expand your vocabulary.

IV

Presents Concepts Simply

Special features make text concepts come alive.

Health and Wellness

Health and wellness feature boxes summarize the latest nutrition, dietary, and health facts and recommendations.

Colorful Tables

Attractive organizers summarize complex concepts.

Learn About...

Important facts on a wide variety of topics amplify text material.

Global Perspective

Learn the global viewpoint on environmental concerns and other food issues.

Food Science

Discover the scientific principles that affect the growing, storing, and preparing of food.

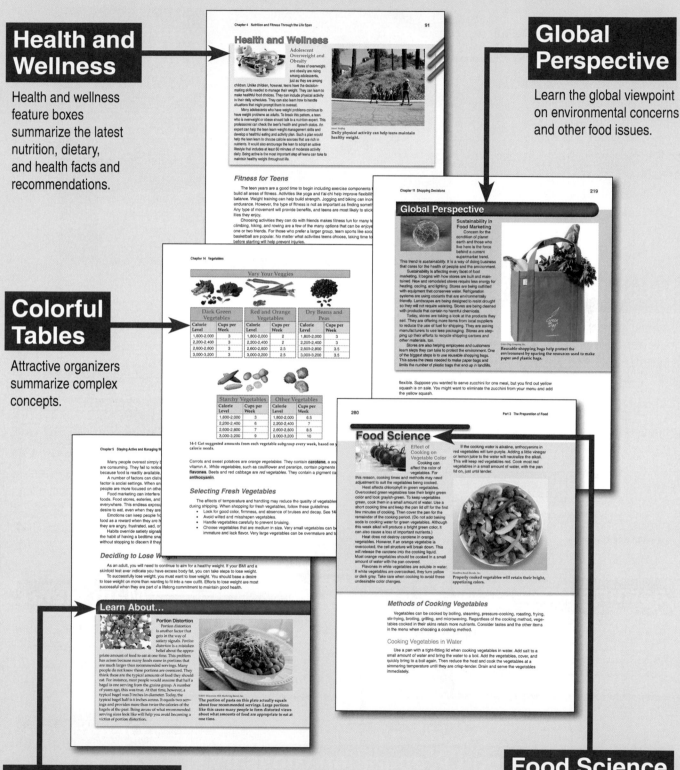

Highlights Food Preparation

Learn how to prepare nutritious, appealing meals while stretching food dollars.

The Preparation of Food

Thirteen chapters acquaint you with the basics of selecting, storing, preparing, and serving foods to preserve nutrients, flavors, textures, and colors.

Special Features

Easy-to-understand tables and charts clarify the concepts presented in the text.

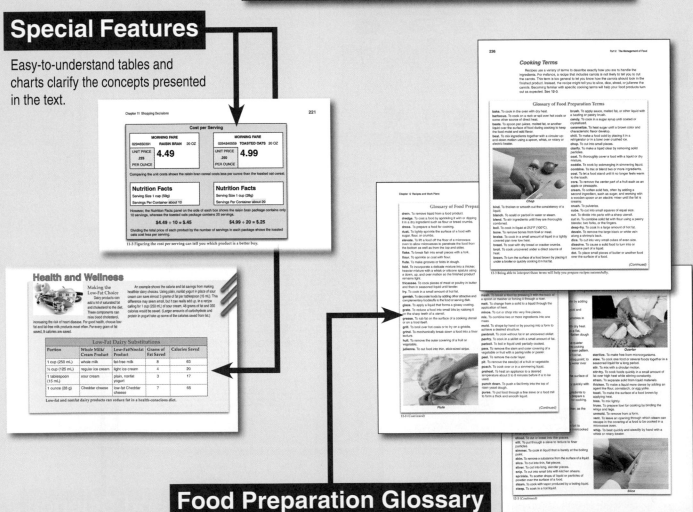

Food Preparation Glossary

A complete Glossary of Food Preparation Terms provides clear definitions for the specialized vocabulary used to describe the various preparation techniques.

Explores Food Around the World

Investigate popular foods and typical recipes served in various regions of the globe.

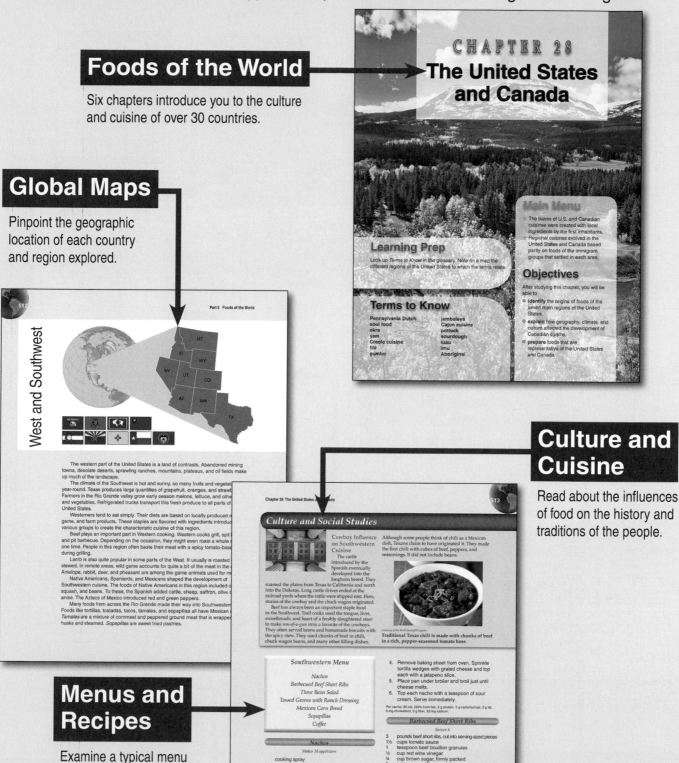

Foods of the World

Six chapters introduce you to the culture and cuisine of over 30 countries.

Global Maps

Pinpoint the geographic location of each country and region explored.

Culture and Cuisine

Read about the influences of food on the history and traditions of the people.

Menus and Recipes

Examine a typical menu of the region and prepare selected recipes.

Focuses on Your Future

Learn about food-related careers and how to prepare for your role in the workplace.

Chapters 26 and 27

Two chapters cover the basics of career planning and transitioning to the workplace. The information applies to all students, even those not planning to enter a food-related field.

Career Success

Through case studies, examine the skills and personal qualities needed to become an effective worker.

Entrepreneurship

Learn whether the option of self-employment appeals to you.

Exploring Careers

Investigate the job duties and educational requirements of various occupations in the broad and diverse food field.

16 Career Clusters

Use this helpful tool for investigating various career options in the food field and beyond.

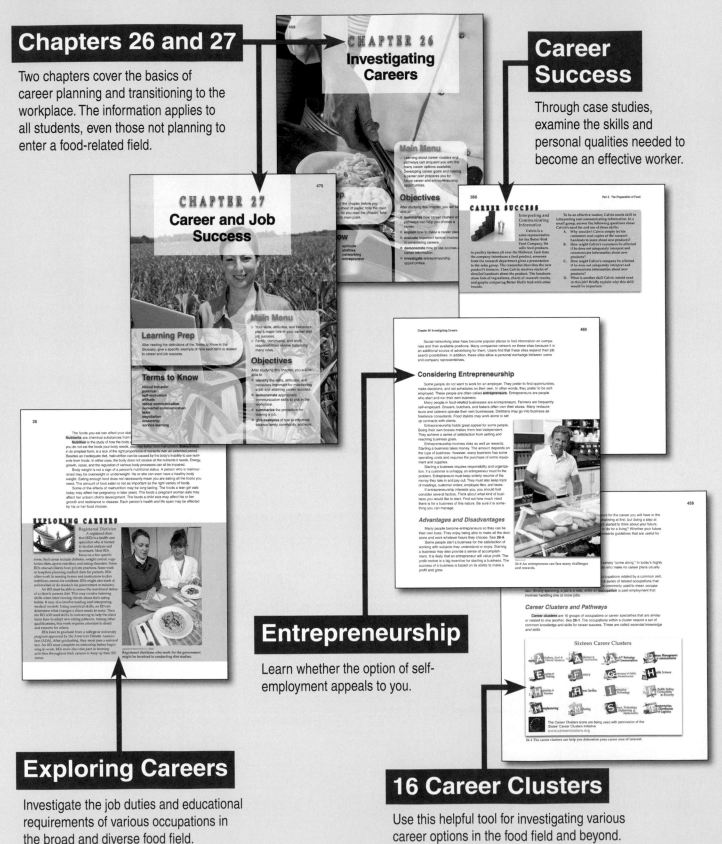

Enhances and Extends Learning

Reinforce learning by relating your knowledge to other academic areas.

Summary

A brief overview condenses the main ideas presented.

Review

Questions prompt your recall of chapter content.

Academics

Various learning activities link chapter content to academic areas such as science, social studies, and English language arts.

Critical Thinking

Use the higher-order thinking skills of analysis, synthesis, and evaluation to complete activities.

Math

Activities encourage real-life application of concepts discussed in the text.

Technology

Various technologies are used to explore chapter topics.

Companion Website

A variety of drill and practice activities help you to reinforce learning.

Service Learning

Team projects focused on food themes provide the basis for learning as you provide a valued service in your school or community.

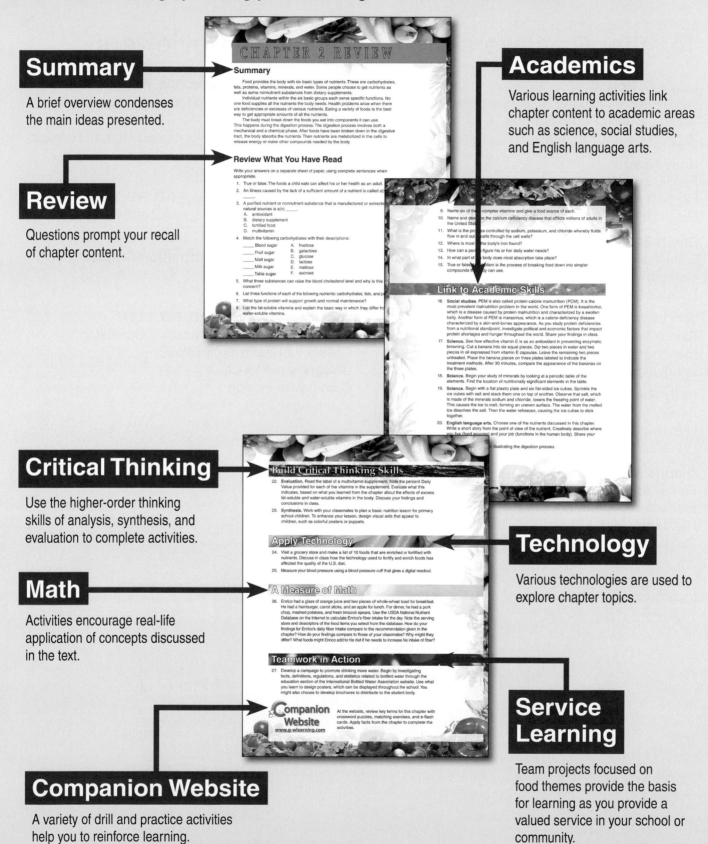

REVIEWERS

Teacher Reviewers

Linda O. Spruill
Family and Consumer Sciences Coordinator
Virginia Beach Public Schools
Virginia Beach, Virginia

Kelly Lang
Family and Consumer Sciences Instructor
Fairport High School
Fairport, New York

Sheila Mecklenburg
Family and Consumer Sciences Instructor
Lockport High School
Lockport, Illinois

Teri Lynn Fuentez
Family and Consumer Sciences Instructor
Lyman High School
Longwood, Florida

Polly Reiss-Churchill
Family and Consumer Sciences Instructor
Cleveland Heights High School
Cleveland Heights, Ohio

Dianne Meeks
Family and Consumer Sciences
Instructor/Department Chair
Highlands High School
Ft. Thomas, Kentucky

Technical Reviewers

Karen Chapman-Novakofski, RD, LD, PhD
Associate Professor and Extension Specialist,
  Nutrition
Department of Food Science and Human Nutrition
University of Illinois
Urbana-Champaign, Illinois

Barbara Ann F. Hughes, PhD, RD, LDN, FADA
Resident, B.A. Hughes & Associates
Raleigh, North Carolina

**International Food Information Council
Foundation**
Washington, DC

Jessica Schulman, PhD, RD, LDN
Adjunct Professor and Nutrition Consultant
College of Health Professions
University of Florida
Gainesville, Florida

CONTENTS IN BRIEF

CONTENTS

Exploring Careers

FCCLA: Taking the Lead

Food Science

Global Perspective

Health and Wellness

Learn About...

Career Success

Culture and Social Studies

Part 1
The Importance of Food

Study Starters

1. Become familiar with the glossary in the back of this book. Look up the following words from Chapters 1 through 6 in the glossary: *hunger*, *fiber*, *processed food*, *diet*, *fitness*, and *contaminant*. Then look up the same words in a dictionary. Compare the dictionary definitions with the definitions given in the glossary. Discuss in class why the definitions from the two sources might differ somewhat.
2. Choose a food. Then design a poster illustrating the cultural/social significance, nutritional contributions, and food safety concerns associated with your chosen food.

FCCLA: Taking the Lead

As a Power of One project for the *A Better You* unit, set a goal for improving your nutritional status. You might begin by using the Choose**MyPlate**.gov website to conduct personal nutrition assessments. After identifying nutrients for which your intakes are low, you can make food choices, find recipes, and write menus to plan a more healthful diet that will help you meet nutrient needs. After following the healthful diet for a set period, repeat the nutrition assessments and write an evaluation of how the dietary changes you have made have affected you physically and mentally.

CHAPTER 1
Food Affects Life

Learning Prep

Divide the class into two teams. Each student on one team will write the words listed under *Terms to Know* on a set of index cards. Each student on the other team will write the definitions of the terms on another set of index cards. Working with a partner from the other team, shuffle your two sets of cards together. Randomly place all the cards facedown. Take turns to see whether you or your partner can find the most matching terms and definitions.

Main Menu

⊛ Consumer food choices are impacted by a number of influences.
⊛ A range of factors affect the food supply.

Objectives

After studying this chapter, you will be able to

⊛ **explain** how the search for food led to the development of civilization.

⊛ **use** the steps of the decision-making process to make food choices.

⊛ **describe** how food relieves hunger and improves wellness.

⊛ **outline** cultural, social, and psychological influences on food choices.

⊛ **list** factors that affect the food supply.

Terms to Know

decision-making process
alternative
goal
hunger
appetite
wellness
stress
culture
custom
fasting
value
lifestyle

peer pressure
fallacy
fad
functional food
agriculture
environment
sustainability
United States Department of Agriculture (USDA)
Food and Drug Administration (FDA)
technology

Food has different meanings for different people. People who are starving see food as a means of survival. People who are proud of their culture consider traditional foods to be part of their heritage. Members of some faiths regard certain foods as religious symbols. People who are entertaining guests view food as a sign of hospitality.

Clearly, food does much more than meet a basic physical need. It meets emotional, social, and psychological needs as well.

As long as people have walked the earth, they have searched for food and the means to produce it. Efforts to improve food resources are likely to continue as long as life exists.

The History of Food

Early people probably ate food raw. At some point, they accidentally discovered cooked food tasted better and was easier to digest. By trial and error, they learned to control fire and use it to prepare food.

Eventually, these early people found they could protect themselves and secure food more easily by living in groups. They formed tribes and began to hunt for food together.

Some hunters became herders when they discovered they could capture and domesticate animals. People also discovered they could plant seeds to produce large amounts of food. This discovery led to the beginning of farming. The advances of herding and farming made the food supply much more dependable.

Enrich

Have each student research the origins of a favorite food and share his or her findings in an oral report.

Activity

Have students create and trace on a time line how the search for food led to the development of civilization.

Global Perspective

The Migration of Food

As civilizations grew and developed, people began searching for food in distant places. By the fifteenth century, Spanish, Portuguese, English, and Dutch sailors were traveling the world in search of tea and spices. These sailors discovered new lands as well as new foods. Thus the search for new food sources fostered European colonization of distant continents and the growth of powerful empires.

European explorers introduced foods they carried with them in the new lands to which they traveled. In North America, Spanish explorers introduced cane sugar and wheat. English explorers brought apples and walnuts. The explorers also carried foods from the lands they explored back to their homelands. Therefore, foods that were once native to one place are now found in many places. This type of exchange led to an increased variety of foods throughout the world.

U.S. Apple Association

Apple pie would not be a U.S. national dish if English explorers had not introduced apples to the New World.

As food became easier to obtain, not all people had to spend their time hunting and farming. Some were able to learn a craft. Others became merchants. Trading in its simplest form began, and with it came the development of civilization.

Making Choices About Foods

In the United States, many people are fortunate enough to have a variety of foods available to them. This requires them to make many choices about foods. They must decide when and where to eat. They must choose what to eat and how to prepare it. These choices require some skill in thinking and making decisions.

The Decision-Making Process

You can use a process to make decisions and solve problems about foods, activities, or any other topics. The **decision-making process** is a method for thinking about possible options and outcomes before making a choice. It involves the following series of steps:

1. Identify the problem or decision. This helps you define the specific issue you are considering so you can focus your thoughts. You may want to phrase this step as a question. A decision about food might be *What should I do for lunch?*
2. Consider your alternatives. **Alternatives** are the various options you might choose. Options for your lunch decision might include making a sandwich, reheating yesterday's leftovers, and going out for fast food.
3. Think about how your alternatives relate to your goals. **Goals** are aims you try to reach. You have goals that guide your actions in all areas of your life. You want to be sure the decisions you make are in line with those goals. Suppose you have a goal to make healthful food choices. One of your other goals is to avoid wasting food. You might also have a goal to save money. Think about how your lunch options relate to each of these goals.
4. Determine which alternatives are acceptable. Sometimes, when measuring your options against your goals, there is only one suitable choice. Other times, there will be more than one alternative that seems to fit with your goals. All three of your lunch options could meet your goal for healthful food, depending on the specific foods you select to prepare or purchase. You can safely store the leftovers for another day. Therefore, all three of your options would fit your goal to avoid wasting food if you eat everything you prepare or purchase. Both making a sandwich and reheating leftovers would go along with your goal to save money. However, buying fast food would not. Going through this step shows you that you have two acceptable alternatives.
5. Choose one alternative. If you have more than one acceptable alternative, now is the time to decide which one you will choose. Perhaps you do not feel like taking the effort to prepare a sandwich. In this case, reheating leftovers may seem like the best choice.
6. Evaluate your decision. Thinking about how happy you are with a decision can help you make decisions in the future. Perhaps after eating the leftovers, you realize you do not like eating the same food two days in a row. You determine making a sandwich would have been worth the extra effort. This evaluation will help you make a more pleasing choice the next time you are deciding what to do for lunch.

You can use the decision-making process whenever you have a problem to solve or a choice to make. It can help you with daily decisions like what to wear in the morning or how to spend your time after school, **1-1**. When making such routine choices, you may go through the process rather quickly without even realizing you are doing it. However, the process can also help you make major decisions, such as what to do after you graduate from high school. When making big decisions, you will find it worthwhile to take the time to carefully go through each step. This will help you make a satisfying choice that is in line with your goals.

Food Meets Physical Needs

Have you ever tried studying for a test when you were hungry? You may have found it hard to concentrate. This is because food is one of your most basic physical needs. The instinct to meet this need is so strong you cannot focus on other issues until this need has been addressed.

Your body needs food to provide the energy required to maintain vital functions, such as keeping your heart beating. You also need energy from food to move your muscles so you can perform tasks like walking, sitting, and climbing. Your body needs substances from food to build and repair tissues, too.

Reflect

Ask students to think of a time when they went to a restaurant or bought a food product they did not like. Ask them how this experience affected their future decisions about where to eat or what foods to buy.

For Example...

Introduce students to Maslow's Hierarchy of Human Needs. Use a visual representation to illustrate why the need for food must be met before needs at higher levels.

Rubbermaid

1-1 You can use the decision-making process to help you with everyday choices, such as how to spend your time.

Food meets two basic physical needs. First, food eases hunger. Second, it can affect your overall state of health.

Relieves Hunger

A complex system within your body senses when you need a fresh supply of the materials food provides. This system involves your digestive tract, which sends a message to your brain. Your brain receives this message and gives a signal, which you recognize as hunger. **Hunger** is the physical need for food. The hunger signal stimulates your stomach to produce hunger pangs. The hunger signal may also stimulate your **appetite**, which is a psychological desire to eat.

You can choose how you respond to the sensations of hunger and appetite. If you choose to eat, food relieves your hunger and the pangs in your stomach go away. If you choose not to eat, the pangs are likely to become more intense. You may experience other symptoms as hunger continues, such as a headache or dizziness.

Your appetite has a greater influence on your food choices than your hunger. Any food will relieve hunger, but only certain foods will satisfy your appetite. For instance, if you eat meat loaf when you have a taste for pizza, your appetite will not be satisfied.

Improves Wellness

Wellness is the state of being in overall good health. It involves mental and social health as well as physical health. Wellness is a goal most people actively try to achieve.

The three areas of wellness—physical health, mental health, and social health—all affect one another. Sensible food choices can help improve all three areas.

In terms of *physical health*, or the health of your body, food does more than relieve hunger. Food helps you grow and develop normally. It can help you avoid developing certain diseases, too. Your *mental health* is the health of your mind. One sign of good mental health and overall wellness is an ability to handle stress. **Stress** is mental tension caused by change. For instance, moving to a new community creates many changes. Some of these changes may be positive, such as living in a nicer home. Some of the changes may be negative, such as seeing less of your friends in the old neighborhood. In both cases, the changes can cause stress.

Your *social health* refers to the health of your relationships with other people. Eating healthful foods can help you feel strong and energetic. This strength and energy can give you confidence to be more outgoing as you interact with others. Food also affects the social aspect of wellness by being an important part of many social gatherings.

Health and Wellness

Managing Stress

Food can help you manage stress. When you eat the foods your body needs, you are less likely to develop certain illnesses. Illness can be a major source of stress. Therefore, preventing illness through careful food choices can help you avoid stress and improve your mental health. Eating well can also give you the strength to face stressful situations when they arise.

Cultural Influences on Food Choices

What do you choose to eat when you are hungry? Where do you usually eat? Who is with you when you eat? When do you eat? How does food make you feel?

Your answers to all these questions reflect your food habits. Each of your friends would likely answer these questions a bit differently. This is because the factors that affect food habits are a little different for everyone.

One factor that affects food habits is culture. **Culture** is the traditions and beliefs of a racial, religious, or social group. People of a certain race form a cultural group. Citizens of a given country and followers of a specific religion are also examples of cultural groups. Many people are part of more than one cultural group.

The United States is a *multicultural society*. The many cultures in this country include those of the Native Americans and the first explorers. The cultures of immigrants from Europe and Asia and slaves from Africa are also part of U.S. culture today. You might think of the United States as a cultural "tossed salad." A tossed salad is a single food item made up of a variety of vegetables. Each vegetable contributes a distinct flavor, color, and texture. In a similar way, each culture that is part of U.S. society contributes unique **customs** (typical ways of behaving) and beliefs to the nation.

National Origin

The people who colonized various lands brought with them foods from their native cultures. For instance, the French who settled in the United States introduced chowders. The Chinese introduced stir-fried dishes. When the immigrants could not obtain traditional ingredients, they had to adapt their recipes. They incorporated foods that were available locally into their diets.

In the United States, immigrants tended to settle together based on nationality. As a result, many foods are typical of particular regions of the country. For instance, foods of Mexican and Spanish origin are found in the West and Southwest. Asian influence is seen in foods of the Pacific Coast. See **1-2**.

Religion

Religion is an important cultural influence on the food habits of many people. Some religions have certain customs regarding food and how people should eat it. For instance, Hindus will not use cattle (beef) for food because they consider cattle to be sacred. Muslims can eat only with the right hand.

Through the ages, people have used food for religious offerings. They might place special foods on altars or offer prayers recognizing events symbolized by the foods. The bread and wine used in Christian churches during communion symbolize the sacrifice of Christ's body and blood. Unleavened bread is an important symbol for Jewish people during Passover, the eight-day festival that commemorates their flight from Egypt. Because the Jews had to leave their homes so quickly, they did not have time to allow their bread to rise.

Fasting, or denying oneself food, has long been a religious custom. Some Christians fast during Lent, a 40-day period leading up to Easter. Jews fast on Yom Kippur, the Day of Atonement. Muslims fast from sunrise to sunset each day of Ramadan, the ninth month of the Islamic calendar.

Some early people used food as part of their burial ceremonies. For example, the ancient Egyptians buried food with their dead. The Egyptians believed the deceased needed food for their journey into the next world. Some Shintos, Taoists, and Buddhists still offer food and coins at shrines honoring deceased relatives and friends.

Discuss
Ask students what foods are typical of the region in which they live. Ask what the national origins of these foods are.

For Example...
The foods Hindus can eat depend on social class. Muslims and Orthodox Jews cannot eat pork because they consider swine to be unclean. Jewish dietary laws state Jews cannot eat meat and dairy foods together. They also specify Jews can eat only fish with scales and fins.

Think Outside the Box
Have students investigate business etiquette in another culture. Have them give brief oral reports on their findings. Ask students how failing to be sensitive to cultural differences might have a negative impact on business transactions.

FYI
Traditionally, people have fasted as a sign of repentance or mourning. People have also used fasting to help them focus on spiritual rather than physical needs.

Enrich

Have students find recipes for any unfamiliar foods listed in 1-2 and be prepared to briefly describe the food items in class.

Enrich

Have students use the international section of this text and other resources to investigate holiday traditions in cultures other than their own. Have them share their findings in class.

Reflect

Ask each student to think about his or her favorite holiday. Have students identify what food traditions are part of their families' celebrations of these holidays.

Region	Influences on Regional Cuisine	Typical Foods
New England	English	Baked beans, clam chowder, succotash
Mid-Atlantic	Dutch, English, Germans, Italians, Swedes	Cheesecake, coleslaw, scrapple
South	African slaves, English, French, Irish, Native Americans, Scots, Spaniards	Andouille, chitterlings, jambalaya
Midwest	French, Germans, Greeks, Irish, Italians, Poles, Scandinavians, Spaniards	Apple pie, Cornish pasties, paczki
West and Southwest	Cowboys, Mexicans, Native Americans, Spaniards	Barbecued beef short ribs, sopapillas, tamales
Pacific Coast	Chinese, Japanese, Koreans, Mexicans, Polynesians	Caribou sausage, salmon steaks, sourdough bread
Hawaiian Islands	Chinese, Europeans, Japanese, Polynesians	Coconut, macadamia nuts, poi

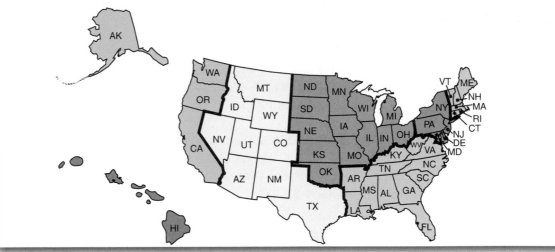

1-2 Foods typical of each region of the United States reflect the traditional ingredients and food customs of the people who settled there.

Health and Wellness

Fasting to Cleanse the Body

Some people believe fasting should be used as a health practice to periodically cleanse the body from the inside out. Health and nutrition experts do not advise depriving your body of nutrients, which is what fasting does. Your liver and digestive system work to remove waste material from your body. Your body does not require any other form of internal cleansing.

Holidays

People of all cultures have special days set aside each year for celebration. Cultural influences on food choices may be most apparent on these days. Holiday celebrations abound with food traditions. Some holiday foods have special symbolism. For instance, heart-shaped chocolates are given on Valentine's Day as a symbol of love. Other holiday foods have simply become part of the customs connected with the celebration. As an example, many people eat corn on the cob and hot dogs on Independence Day.

Social Influences on Food Choices

For many people, preparing and eating food are social activities. Food can bring people together. It brings family members together at the dinner table. It brings friends together at parties and picnics. When guests come to visit, the host usually offers them something to eat or drink. People often transact business over lunch. In each of these situations, food is part of the social interaction. Therefore, eating habits and food choices are affected by social influences.

Family

Family has a great impact on the foods people eat and how they eat them. Food choices are often a reflection of family values. **Values** are items and ideas that a person or group considers important. For instance, a family who values the environment might choose to buy foods that are locally grown and have limited packaging. Children who grow up in this family are likely to adopt these values. They will probably continue to make similar food choices as they become adults.

Many food habits are formed around family customs. As mentioned earlier, customs are typical ways of behaving. In many families it is a custom to eat dinner together. Holiday meal traditions are another example of family food customs. Adults often continue to follow the customs they learned at home as children.

Lifestyle is another way families affect food choices and eating patterns. **Lifestyle** is the way a person usually lives. Today, many families would describe their lifestyles as busy. Work, school, sports, and lessons keep family members running in different directions. This limits time family members have for tasks such as grocery shopping and preparing meals. Busy families may respond to these time constraints by having a few family members share these tasks. They may also choose more convenience food products that require less preparation time. They may opt for takeout and fast-food items as frequent food choices, too.

Busy lifestyles limit the amount of time family members have to share meals. However, most families say they want to keep family meals a priority. They realize mealtime is a great time to build relationships. Sharing a meal gives family members a chance to relax together and talk about interests and concerns.

Friends

Your friends have an effect on the foods you choose. You may feel peer pressure to eat the same foods your friends are eating. **Peer pressure** is influence that comes from people in a person's social group. For instance, suppose you are in a restaurant with friends. If they all order pizza, you are also likely to order pizza even if you would really have preferred a sandwich. See **1-3**.

Friends may also encourage you to try new foods or preparation techniques. A friend might persuade you to sample a food such as squid, which might have little appeal to you. A friend might convince someone used to eating French fries to try another vegetable instead.

Enrich
Ask students to determine ways family members assuming multiple roles can apply food management skills to help balance their busy lifestyles.

Reflect
Ask students who in their families plans menus, shops for groceries, and prepares foods.

Reflect
Ask students what foods their friends have encouraged them to try.

Time Management Tip
Have each student make a table listing favorite quick-and-easy main dishes, grain food side dishes, vegetable side dishes, salads, and desserts in separate columns. Have students post their tables in their home kitchens. Family members who help with meal management tasks can use the table to save time when planning menus or putting together last-minute meals.

Corelle®

1-3 Friends can influence food choices and eating habits.

Mass Media

Mass media, such as television, radio, magazines, and the Internet, can affect your food choices. The media acquaints you with, reminds you of, and informs you about food products and nutrition issues.

Advertising

A key way the media influence your food choices is through advertising. Manufacturers spend millions of dollars to encourage you to try new food products. They also urge you to continue buying products you have used for years.

The first level of advertising for a food product is the product package. Clearly showing the brand as well as the name of the product is an important part of the packaging. Manufacturers want you to remember what product you are buying so you can buy it again. They also want you to remember who makes the product so you will be encouraged to look for other products from the same company. Most packages show an attractive photo of the prepared food. This image is intended to appeal to your appetite. Manufacturers use package coloring to send messages about their products, too. Think about how many foods promoted as being "healthy" have a package with a green background or green lettering. Green is the color of healthy, growing plants in nature. Using this color on the package sends the message that choosing the food product will help you be healthy.

Through the media, manufacturers use a number of techniques to sell their products. The *bandwagon technique* stirs a desire to belong by saying everyone is using the product. The *humor technique* prompts you to connect products with the happy feelings you have when watching funny ads. The *nostalgia technique* urges you to buy products because of their natural qualities or old-fashioned goodness. The *transfer technique* often uses famous people to sell products. Ads encourage you to transfer qualities like fame, wealth, and beauty from the people in the ads to the products they are promoting. The *testimonial technique* triggers you to buy a product because an expert says he or she uses it.

Another common advertising practice is the use of *advertising icons*. These are characters designed to help people recognize products, **1-4**. Icons encourage people to try new products, too. For instance, suppose a box of the newest cereal bars on the market shows the smiling cow icon from your favorite yogurt. You like the yogurt, and you associate the cow with the yogurt. Therefore, seeing the cow might lead you to assume you will also like the cereal bars, so you try them.

Manufacturers know that getting you to try a product is the key to turning you into a repeat buyer. Free samples, coupons, rebates, eye-catching displays, and special offers are tools they use to prompt you to check out food products.

General Mills, Inc.

1-4 Advertising icons are the characters on product packages used to help shoppers quickly spot favorite brands.

EXPLORING CAREERS

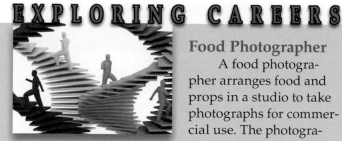

Food Photographer

A food photographer arranges food and props in a studio to take photographs for commercial use. The photographer needs to adjust the lighting and camera settings to create the effect desired by the client. Then the photographer needs to review images and choose those that best show the food product.

To fully grasp the needs of the client, a food photographer must use active listening skills. Many photographers set their own schedules. They need to be dependable and able to manage their time to plan photography sessions and meet client deadlines. Producing images that show products in unique ways requires creativity and attention to detail.

A food photographer may begin training in a technical school. One way to learn about this career could be to work as an apprentice to a skilled photographer. A photographer will probably need a few years of experience to earn a name in the field and attract clients.

Evaluating Information in the Media

Research has shown that people with a higher educational level are more likely to have a higher quality diet. However, you do not have to have a college degree to make healthful food choices.

News in the media can inform you about findings of a food's special health properties. The media can also notify you about products that are found to be unsafe. Learning this information can help you make wise food purchase decisions. However, news stories about food and nutrition are sometimes missing important points. To help you review media information critically, read or listen for answers to the following questions:

- Who conducted the research? Experts in the field of the research are likely to be most knowledgeable about how to interpret findings.
- Where were the results of the research published? A journal reviewed by professionals in the field of the research has more credibility than a popular magazine.
- How was the study set up? A valid study needs to be conducted under carefully controlled conditions. Steps must be taken to keep unplanned variables from affecting the outcomes.
- Who funded the research? You may have reason to be more skeptical if the funding party stands to gain financially from the findings.
- How many people did the researchers study? A study that involves a large group of subjects may be more relevant than one that involves a small group.
- Were the results of this study similar to the results of other studies? Findings are more significant when they match those of a number of research teams.
- How much and how often does the food or nutrient need to be consumed to experience the benefit or harmful effect? Quantities should resemble what people might normally be expected to consume. For instance, one study found eating dark chocolate could help lower blood pressure. However, the amount needed would likely cause weight gain or decreased nutrient intakes for most people.
- Do the beneficial or harmful effects of the food or nutrient build with repeated consumption? This indicates the degree to which the research findings might affect established eating habits.
- Does the food or nutrient have different effects on certain groups of people, such as children or pregnant women? This indicates how much bearing the research has for you.

Career Path

Ask students if they think they would enjoy the work of a food photographer. Why or why not?

Discuss

Ask students which advertising techniques they feel are most effective in convincing people to buy food products. Have students explain why they feel these techniques are effective.

Activity

Have each student find a recent newspaper or magazine article about a food or nutrition issue to share with the class.

Community Interaction

Ask students what food and nutrition websites they have visited that they have found to be helpful. Have students visit sites suggested by their classmates and rate them for reliability and accuracy. Have students compile their ratings and distribute them.

Learn About...

Evaluating Internet Information

A vast array of food and nutrition information is available over the Internet. When evaluating this information, look at the end of the website address. This will give you a clue about the source of the information. Websites that end in *.edu* are those of educational institutions. A government agency site ends in *.gov,* and a professional organization site ends in *.org.* These may be the most reliable resources when you are researching a topic. Website addresses that end in *.com* are sponsored by commercial groups. These sites may provide a wealth of helpful information. However, keep in mind that they exist mainly as a way to promote products.

Activity

Have students go to the library to find the names of two professional journals and two popular magazines that might report information about food and nutrition.

Enrich

Have each student visit the website of an educational institution, government agency, or professional organization that has food and nutrition information. Then have students visit websites of commercial groups related to the food industry. Ask students to compare the types of information available from the two sites.

Reflect

Ask students what food fallacies they have heard. Ask them if they have ever tried a food fad.

Online Resource

Have each student navigate the website for *Prepared Foods Magazine* to find out about a food product that was recently introduced to the market. Ask students to prepare a report.

Answers to these questions can help you evaluate the information you receive through the media. These answers distinguish a merely interesting story from one that can help you make more healthful food choices.

Food Fads and Fallacies

Incomplete or inaccurate information through the media may be behind many food fallacies and fads. A **fallacy** is a mistaken belief. Mistaken beliefs often lead to **fads**, or practices that are very popular for a short time. For instance, suppose the media reports that a component in apples helps reduce the effects of aging. Although there may be some research behind this story, the information is incomplete. Nevertheless, a fallacy spreads that eating apples will help people live longer. Suddenly it seems apples are in every new food product that hits the market, from muffins to frozen entrees. A few months later, the media issues a new story. This report states much more research is needed before any link between apples and the aging process becomes clear. However, studies show eating large amounts of apples will probably not change a person's life span. The fad comes to an end, and the popularity of apple products fades. Many food fads and fallacies are related to nutrition, weight loss, and food safety issues.

Food fads can lead to disappointment when they do not produce promised results. Some fads can even be harmful if they keep people from eating the variety of foods needed for good health.

Before jumping on the bandwagon to try a new fad, find out the facts. Take a little time to research the information on which the fad is based. The time you invest may end up saving you money and possible harm.

Food Product Trends

Whereas fads are short lived, *trends* shape the market for an extended period. Consumer demand drives trends for new products in the marketplace. In turn, what products are available influences your consumer choices. When it comes to food products, consumers demand three main qualities. They want foods that are healthful, convenient, and great tasting.

Health

A consumer concern for health has fueled a trend for functional food products. **Functional foods** are foods that provide health benefits beyond the nutrients they contain. Some of the most recent trends in this area center on products that promote *probiotics* or *prebiotics*. In simple terms, these are components found in or added to foods mainly to help improve intestinal health. Certain yogurt products were among the first foods on the market to be promoted for these benefits.

Some other functional foods are attracting attention in the market for their antioxidant values. *Antioxidants* are substances that help protect cells from damage that can result from natural body processes. They are also linked with a range of health benefits, including heart health and brain function. Antioxidants include vitamins A, C, and E and a number of compounds found widely in plant foods. Products like juices and frozen fruit bars may be advertised as natural sources of antioxidants. Antioxidants may also be added to some foods, such as cereals and drink mixes.

More consumers are using package information to help them choose foods that will meet their goals for good health, **1-5**. This is driving a trend for food companies to place brief nutrition facts on the fronts of product packages. These facts are designed to be easy to see and understand quickly. Labels also promote qualities such as reduced sodium and no *trans* fat in response to current health concerns.

Convenience

Many consumers say they enjoy cooking at home. However, they do not have a lot of time to spend on food preparation. Therefore, convenience is a key to the success of new food products. Meal kits have become a trend because they include nearly everything needed to prepare a home-cooked meal in one package. This saves the time of shopping for and measuring ingredients. Heat-and-eat breakfasts are expected to become a bigger part of this market.

The convenience trend has led to a large number of microwavable products. Some foods can be microwaved right in the package. Such products require fewer cooking utensils, saving on cleanup as well as preparation time.

Foods in single-serving packages have become popular convenience items. Many of these foods make quick snacks. Servings for one are handy for the large number of single consumers. They help with portion control, and they also allow groups to satisfy individual flavor preferences.

Great Taste

Consumers are not willing to give up taste for health or convenience. That is why food manufacturers are always introducing new and improved flavors of products. Some of these new flavors are appearing in a broader spectrum of ethnic cuisines on the market. Chinese, Mexican, and Italian foods have been sold in supermarkets for years. Today, there is a trend toward a growing number of Thai, Indian, and North African items, too.

Photo courtesy of The Sackaroos Company and Steve Rasmussen Photography— Wichita, KS

1-5 Package information can help consumers make healthful choices when shopping for foods.

Academic Connection

Invite a psychology or behavioral science teacher to give students a brief overview of research methods used in the field of psychology. Ask the teacher to discuss the basics of such techniques as naturalistic observation, interview, and survey by random sampling. Work with the teacher to help students develop a research project about psychological influences on food choices.

For Example...

Another example of the psychological influence of food is a growing trend some people call "cause cuisine." Consumers are concerned about more than the food products they buy. They are also concerned about how manufacturers treat employees, handle claims against their products, and work to protect the environment.

Another trend in the taste arena is fruit flavors. Raspberry and tropical fruits, such as mango and papaya, are among the most popular flavors for new products. These fruits are being used in everything from drinks to dressings.

A third taste trend is the growing number of gourmet chocolate products. Chocolate has always been a well-liked flavor. However, many new treats feature premium dark chocolate infused with exotic flavors like citrus and chili peppers.

Psychological Influences on Food Choices

Psychology has to do with how your thoughts and feelings affect your behavior. The way you think and feel about foods will influence what foods you choose. Many of your thoughts and feelings are based on memories of your experiences. Picture a monthly dinner at your aunt's house that always includes fried chicken. If these meals are filled with laughter and fun, fried chicken may make you think of pleasant experiences. You may choose to eat it at other times because doing so makes you feel happy. If these gatherings are filled with arguments and stress, fried chicken may bring you bad memories. You may avoid eating it because it brings you a sense of sadness.

Odors as well as events create memories that affect food choices. Odor is a key part of flavor and is more likely to trigger memories than any of the other senses. Therefore, an odor linked with a pleasant memory may lead you to choose certain foods. For instance, imagine you had a kind uncle who always used mint breath mints. The smell of mint may bring on happy memories of your uncle, and you may be drawn to mint-flavored foods. In the same way, an odor you connect with an unpleasant memory may cause you to reject some foods.

Psychology affects why you eat as well as what you eat. Food can please the senses and help meet people's need for social contact. Therefore, most people eat partly because eating is enjoyable. See **1-6**. However, some people who are underweight may stop eating because they feel sad or lonely. Some people who are overweight may eat too much because they find comfort in foods they like. Food psychologically makes up for such emotions as anger and regret in certain people.

Psychology even plays a role in food preparation. Cooking a meal that tastes good and looks attractive can give a person a psychological lift. It can also serve as a creative outlet. The cook who receives praise for a beautifully prepared dish feels a sense of pride and self-esteem.

Factors That Affect the Food Supply

Many factors affect the supply of foods from which you can choose when you go to the store. These factors include regional agriculture and the environment. The government, economics, and technology also play roles in food choices.

Agriculture and the Environment

Agriculture is the use of knowledge and skill to tend soil, grow crops, and raise livestock. Successful agriculture requires a suitable environment. **Environment** refers to interrelated factors as air, water, soil, mineral resources, plants, and animals that ultimately affect the survival of life on earth.

Hamilton Beach Brands, Inc.

1-6 People often associate happy experiences with food and food with happy experiences.

Academic Connections

Coordinate your teaching of this material with the agriculture department. You might focus on sustainability practices and how the availability of agricultural products affects consumer prices at the supermarket. An agriculture teacher might address factors that affect the prices farmers are able to get for their products on the commodities market.

Online Resource

Have students visit the USDA Agricultural Research Service website at ars.usda. gov. Have them look for information on current research to improve crop and food animal production. Ask them to share their findings in poster reports.

Discuss

Ask students what crops grow well in your region of the country.

That is why sustainability is such a key issue in the field of agriculture. **Sustainability** refers to practices that are productive and profitable while still caring for the environment. Farmers need to be able to produce the most crops and livestock possible to feed a growing number of people. They also need to protect the environment to make sure they can keep producing crops and livestock in the future. They need to reach both of these goals in a way that is not too costly so they can still make a living.

Food crops require the right air temperatures, adequate water, and fertile soil to grow. Livestock need supplies of food and water. The specific requirements vary from one type of plant or animal to another. This is why certain crops and livestock are easier to raise in some regions than in others.

In the United States, regional agriculture does not affect the availability of foods as much as it affects their costs. This is because foods are routinely shipped from one region to another. You can easily obtain foods even if they do not grow well in your local environment. However, you may have to pay more for them due to transportation costs. The environment also affects food costs when severe weather, such as a flood or drought, damages crops. The resulting shortages cause prices to rise.

In some areas of the world, the regional nature of agriculture limits food choices. In these areas, the equipment needed to preserve and ship food from one region to another may not be available. People may not be able to afford food with added transportation costs. Therefore, people's food choices are restricted to crops and livestock that are produced locally.

Global Perspective

Sustainability

Just as the environment can affect crop growth, crop growth can affect the environment. Soil that is overworked by farmers can lose its ability to support crops in the future. Watering crops can strain water reserves in areas where there is not enough rain. In addition, chemicals used in farming sometimes get into water supplies. Tainted water affects the plants and animals that live in and around it. That is why practicing sustainable agriculture is so important.

Sustainability is not just an issue for farmers. It relates to all areas of society. Companies can make sustainable choices in the way they do business. For instance, they can purchase supplies from local and regional sources. This decreases the distance supplies have to be transported. This, in turn, lessens the amount of pollution created by shipping vehicles. Manufacturers can reduce the amount of material they use to package products. This will cut down on the amount of package waste that ends up in landfills.

As a consumer, you can also make sustainable choices that help care for the planet. When choosing foods, you can buy fruits and vegetables that are grown in your region. Better yet, you can plant a garden and grow some of your own food. Stock up on fresh foods when they are in season. Then you may freeze, can, or dry them for later use. Eat a diet focused on plant foods, as more energy is required to produce meat. Limit the number of trips you make to the store or carpool to the store with a friend. Choose products that are less processed and have less packaging. All these steps will help reduce the impact you make on the environment.

Agricultural Research Service, USDA

The use of high-tech irrigation systems helps farmers make the best use of limited water resources.

FYI

The USDA also conducts nutrition research and educates the public about nutrition. Additional responsibilities of the FDA include setting standards for food composition.

Government

The government has a large impact on the food supply. Laws govern the way foods are grown, processed, packaged, and labeled. Strict guidelines keep foods safe. Government policies affect foods exported to and imported from other countries.

Two key federal agencies oversee the food supply in the United States. The **United States Department of Agriculture (USDA)** enforces standards for the quality and wholesomeness of meat, poultry, and eggs. The **Food and Drug Administration (FDA)** ensures the safety and wholesomeness of all other foods. The FDA inspects food processing plants, too. These agencies are responsible only for foods shipped across state lines. Foods sold within the state in which they are produced are controlled by state agencies.

Economics

Economics has a great effect on the food supply. A basic economic concept is the *law of supply and demand*. This means if consumers are willing to pay for a product, producers will provide it. An example of this is a food store in an ethnic neighborhood. Some people in this neighborhood will probably want to buy certain ingredients needed to make ethnic dishes. Therefore, the manager of the neighborhood store will stock these ingredients. In another neighborhood where the people are of a different ethnic group, these ingredients may not be in demand. Stores in this neighborhood are less likely to carry these items.

Consumer demand for some food products affects much more than local stores. Some foods, such as coffee, sugar, and cacao beans (used to make chocolate) are grown in faraway places. Many of the countries where these foods are grown have large populations of poor people. These people often have trouble getting enough food to feed themselves and their families. However, land that might be used to grow nourishing grains and legumes is instead used to raise crops for export. The money made from the exported crops often goes to wealthy landowners. The poor farmers who grow the crops do not earn enough to lift themselves out of poverty. In this way, food choices made by consumers in the United States can have an impact on world hunger.

Many other factors affect the problem of world hunger. People with little money cannot afford to buy quality seeds to grow hearty crops. They are not able to purchase fertilizers and pesticides that will increase the size of their harvests. They do not own modern farm equipment. Poor farmers often lack education. They may be unknowingly using farming methods that lead to shrinking crop yields. All these factors work together to limit the amount of food poor people can produce.

Activity

Encourage students to visit a food store in an ethnic neighborhood. Note what products are available that might not be carried in stores everywhere.

For Example...

Factors other than poverty that contribute to world hunger include overpopulation, natural disasters, government policies, and culture.

Global Perspective

Malnourishment
About half the world's people do not always earn enough money to buy basic foods. The number of people who cannot afford adequate food is threatening to soar due to a global food crisis. Higher fuel costs and a growing demand for food have caused food prices to rise sharply. Natural disasters and increased use of crops for biofuels and animal feed have also affected food prices.

Most people who do not have enough to eat are malnourished. However, malnutrition is caused by a lack of variety in the diet as well as a lack of food. This is because the body needs a range of nutrients, which must come from different foods. Therefore, people striving to meet the needs of the hungry must focus on food quality as well as food quantity.

Compassion International

These children receive nutritious food through an organization that is working to release them from a cycle of poverty.

Think Outside the Box

Divide students into three groups. Assign each group to investigate one of the following topics about the global food crisis: causes and effects on people in developing countries or the response of the U.S. government and relief organizations. After groups have shared their findings in oral reports, challenge the class to come up with a project to raise funds for a food crisis relief effort.

Activity

Have each student visit the website of a hunger-relief organization. Ask each student to share one fact about world hunger or hunger relief he or she learned from visiting the site.

Online Resource

Have students visit the Institute of Food Technologists website. Ask each student to investigate a topic related to improving the nutrient content, availability, or safety of the food supply. Have students summarize their findings in written reports.

A number of organizations are working to deal with world hunger. These organizations want to make an adequate supply of safe and nutritious food available to every person on earth. However, the hunger problem is widespread and complex. Many factors affect the degree to which hunger-relief organizations can meet their goals.

Technology

Technology affects every aspect of the food supply, from the farm to the table. **Technology** is the use of knowledge to develop improved methods for doing tasks. Researchers are using technology to help farmers produce more food in less space and in less time. Food manufacturers use technology to develop new products that meet consumer demands. These uses of technology affect your options when buying foods. You also use technology when you prepare many foods. For instance, your refrigerator and microwave oven help you keep foods fresh and cook them quickly. This would not be possible without technology.

Nutrient Content

Food technologists are using their expertise to affect the nutrient content of the food supply. They are developing foods that have less of some components and more of others. Food scientists are formulating processed foods to contain less sugar and fat than foods of the past. They are also working to develop crops that are more nutrient rich. Technology is being used to grow grains that are higher in protein. Fruits and vegetables are also being altered. Researchers are finding ways to increase the vitamin and mineral content of these foods.

Availability

Throughout the world, most of the land that can sustain crops is already being farmed. Researchers are studying ways to increase the amount of crops a given piece of land can produce. They are concerned with finding ways to feed the growing number of people on earth. They are also worried about placing added strain on earth's limited resources.

Food technologists are working to grow plants that can resist diseases and pests that destroy crops in the field. They are studying plants that grow larger and faster so more food can be produced in less time. Technologists are also raising plants that can grow in less suitable soil and weather conditions.

Growing healthy plants is only part of the picture when it comes to ensuring the availability of food. Large amounts of crops spoil after being harvested. Researchers are studying ways to destroy the organisms that cause this spoilage. They are also trying to develop plants that are more resistant to these organisms. All these efforts will help increase the food supply to better meet future needs.

Safety

The safety of the food supply is another issue that has drawn the interest of food technologists. Each year, millions of people get sick from something they ate. Researchers are trying to develop foods that are less likely to spread disease. They are working to improve packaging so foods will stay safer longer. They are also developing new ways to preserve foods. See **1-7**.

Agricultural Research Service, USDA

1-7 These scientists are studying ways to improve the safety and keeping quality of fresh fruits and vegetables.

Disease is not the only food safety concern for food technologists. Researchers also want to keep the food supply relatively free of harmful substances, such as some chemicals used to grow and process foods. They are coming up with faster, less costly, and more effective ways to screen foods for these substances. They are looking for ways to limit the amounts of these substances needed to produce foods, too. Through these efforts, scientists hope to create a safer food supply.

CAREER SUCCESS

Technology Tasks
      Heldia is a food technologist at Frozen Fresh, Inc. She is helping to develop and test a new line of high-fiber, low-fat frozen entrees. So far, the development process has been discouraging. All the entrees Heldia has tested have a gritty texture.
      To be an effective worker, Heldia needs skill in applying technology to specific tasks. In a team, answer the following questions about Heldia's need for and use of this skill:

   A.   What questions about the frozen entrees might Heldia try to answer using her skill in applying technology?
   B.   How will Heldia's skill in applying technology affect Frozen Fresh, Inc.?
   C.   How will Heldia's skill in applying technology affect consumers?
   D.   What is another skill Heldia would need in this job? Briefly explain why this skill would be important.

CHAPTER 1 REVIEW

Answer Key for
Review What You Have Read **questions**

1. People discovered they could plant seeds to produce large amounts of food.
2. (1) Identify the problem or decision. (2) Consider your alternatives. (3) Think about how your alternatives relate to your goals. (4) Determine which alternatives are acceptable. (5) Choose one alternative. (6) Evaluate your decision.
3. Hunger is the physical need for food. Appetite is a psychological desire to eat.
4. Careful food choices can help prevent illness, which is a source of stress. Eating well can also provide the strength to face stressful situations when they arise.
5. culture
6. true
7. (List two. Student response.)
8. (Describe two. Student response. See text page 11.)
9. true

Summary

In prehistoric times, people viewed food solely as a means of survival. Early humans spent most of their time and energy hunting and gathering food. As time passed, people learned to herd and farm. As food resources became more plentiful, people could spend more time in other pursuits. With the development of a more stable food supply, came the development of civilization.

You can use the decision-making process to make choices about the foods you eat. Sometimes you will choose foods to relieve hunger. However, your food choices can also affect your state of wellness.

Many factors influence the foods you eat and how you eat them. Cultural factors like national origin, religion, and holidays may affect your food choices. Social factors such as family, friends, mass media, and food product trends also have an impact. Even psychological factors like memories and emotions play a role in your food habits.

A number of factors affect the foods you can buy. The future of the food supply depends on the use of sustainable agriculture. The environment affects what foods can be produced in each region. Government agencies set guidelines and inspect facilities to be sure foods are safe and wholesome. The economic law of supply and demand directs managers to stock certain products in food stores. Technology influences the nutrient content, availability, and safety of the food supply.

Review What You Have Read

Write your answers on a separate sheet of paper, using complete sentences when appropriate.

1. What led early people to begin farming?
2. What are the six steps of the decision-making process?
3. What is the difference between hunger and appetite?
4. How can food help a person manage stress?
5. The traditions and beliefs of a racial, religious, or social group form the group's _____.
6. True or false. Foods of Mexican and Spanish origin are found in the West and Southwest regions of the United States.
7. Give two examples of religious customs regarding food.
8. Describe two ways family might influence a person's food choices.
9. True or false. Friends can encourage people to try new foods and preparation techniques.
10. Describe five techniques advertisers use to encourage people to buy food products.
11. What are five questions to ask when reading or listening to media reports on foods and nutrition?

(continued)

12. What three main trend-driving qualities do consumers demand in food products?

13. Which of the senses is most likely to trigger memories that influence food choices?

14. What are three ways consumers can practice sustainability to help reduce the impact they make on the environment when choosing foods?

15. What are two key federal agencies that oversee the food supply in the United States and what do they do?

16. What are two ways researchers are working to increase the availability of the food supply?

10. (Describe five:) bandwagon technique, humor technique, nostalgia technique, transfer technique, testimonial technique, use of advertising icons, free samples, coupons, rebates, eye-catching displays, special offers

Link to Academic Skills

17. **History.** Research the types of tools used by prehistoric people. Write a report describing some of these tools, noting which ones were used to hunt and prepare foods.

18. **Social studies.** As a class, prepare a survey to find out how students in your school make choices about foods. You might ask questions about what alternatives students consider for each meal. You could find out what goals they have when choosing foods and whether they are usually happy with their food choices. Divide into groups and have each group use the survey to interview a given number of students outside your class. Then compile your findings into an article for the school newspaper about using the decision-making process to make choices about foods.

19. **English language arts.** Talk with your grandparents or senior citizens in your community about food customs they followed as children. Discuss how their food customs differed from those of people today. Share what you learned in a brief oral report to the class.

20. **Government/Civics.** Debate the statement, "The government has too much control over the food supply." Conduct research to find information that will help you support your position.

11. (List five. Student response. See text page 13.)

12. health, convenience, great taste

13. smell

14. (List three:) Buy regionally grown fruits and vegetables. Plant gardens to grow some of their own food. Stock up on fresh foods when they are in season and preserve them for later use. Eat more plant-focused diets. Limit the number of trips they make to the store or carpool

Build Critical Thinking Skills

21. **Analysis.** Make a list of all the decisions you make about food in one day. Analyze each decision to determine whether you used the steps of the decision-making process to make it.

22. **Synthesis.** Analyze food customs in your community. Make a list of cultural, social, and psychological influences that affect the foods available in local restaurants and supermarkets. Compile your list with those of your classmates to create a bulletin board about food customs in your community.

23. **Evaluation.** Conduct research to evaluate the advantages and disadvantages of a technological development in the area of foods and nutrition. Based on your evaluation, decide whether you favor or oppose this development. Prepare arguments to help support your viewpoint in a class debate.

to the store with a friend. Choose products that are less processed and have less packaging.

(continued)

Apply Technology

15. The United States Department of Agriculture (USDA) enforces standards for the quality and wholesomeness of meat, poultry, and eggs. The Food and Drug Administration

24. Work with a team of students to write and videotape a commercial for a hypothetical food product. The ad should include nutritional claims about the product. Show your tape in class and ask your classmates to critique the advertising appeal and the information presented.

25. Use the Internet to find a report on a food or nutrition topic of interest. Evaluate the report using the questions listed under "Evaluating Information in the Media" in the chapter.

A Measure of Math

(FDA) ensures the safety and wholesomeness of all other foods and inspects food-processing plants.

26. Many restaurants and food manufacturers estimate the cost of the ingredients equals about 40 percent of the price of a food product. The remaining 60 percent of the product price covers such costs as labor, facilities and equipment, license fees, utility bills, transportation, and advertising. Use this information to make a poster showing the calculated food cost and "other" cost of five food products.

Teamwork in Action

16. (List two. Student response. See text page 20.)

27. As a class, plan an event in the community to raise funds for a hunger-relief organization. Put together a brochure to help educate the public about how food is a physical need. The brochure should go on to describe that having this need met is a basic right of every human being. You can distribute the brochure at the event or use it as a tool to encourage people to become involved in the event.

Companion Website
www.g-wlearning.com

At the website, review key terms for this chapter with crossword puzzles, matching exercises, and e-flash cards. Apply facts from the chapter to complete the activities.

CHAPTER 2
Nutritional Needs

Learning Prep

List each of the *Terms to Know* and its definition as you read through the chapter. Use this list to help you review material at the end of the chapter.

Terms to Know

nutrient
nutrition
malnutrition
deficiency disease
toxicity
dietary supplement
antioxidant
fortified food
carbohydrate
glucose
fiber
fat
fatty acid
hydrogenation
trans fatty acid
cholesterol
protein
amino acid
protein-energy malnutrition
  (PEM)

vitamin
fat-soluble vitamin
water-soluble vitamin
night blindness
rickets
scurvy
beriberi
pellagra
anemia
mineral
macromineral
trace element
osteoporosis
hypertension
goiter
digestion
absorption
peristalsis
saliva
metabolism

Main Menu

⊛ The body needs a number of nutrients for good health.
⊛ Eating a variety of foods is the best way to get needed nutrients.

Objectives

After studying this chapter, you will be able to

⊛ **name** the key nutrients, **describe** their functions, and **list** important sources of each.
⊛ **analyze** the effects of various nutrient deficiencies and excesses.
⊛ **explain** the processes of digestion, absorption, and metabolism.

Discuss

Other than the reasons given on this page, ask students why people might not eat the foods they need for good nutrition.

The foods you eat can affect your state of health. Food provides nutrients. **Nutrients** are chemical substances from food the body needs to live.

Nutrition is the study of how the body uses the nutrients in the foods that are eaten. If you do not eat the foods your body needs, you may suffer from malnutrition. **Malnutrition**, in its simplest form, is a lack of the right proportions of nutrients over an extended period. Besides an inadequate diet, malnutrition can be caused by the body's inability to use nutrients from foods. In either case, the body does not receive all the nutrients it needs. Energy, growth, repair, and the regulation of various body processes can all be impaired.

Body weight is not a sign of a person's nutritional status. A person who is malnourished may be overweight or underweight. He or she can even have a healthy body weight. Eating enough food does not necessarily mean you are eating all the foods you need. The amount of food eaten is not as important as the right variety of foods.

Some of the effects of malnutrition may be long lasting. The foods a teen girl eats today may affect her pregnancy in later years. The foods a pregnant woman eats may affect her unborn child's development. The foods a child eats may affect his or her growth and resistance to disease. Each person's health and life span may be affected by his or her food choices.

EXPLORING CAREERS

Registered Dietician

A registered dietitian (RD) is a health care specialist who is trained to do diet analysis and treatment. Most RDs focus on a few specific areas. Such areas include diabetes, weight control, vegetarian diets, sports nutrition, and eating disorders. Some RDs counsel clients from private practices. Some work in hospitals planning medical diets for patients. RDs often work in nursing homes and institutions to plan nutritious menus for residents. RDs might also teach at universities or do research for government or industry.

An RD must be able to assess the nutritional status of a client's current diet. This may involve listening skills when interviewing clients about their eating habits. It may also involve reading and interpreting medical records. Using analytical skills, an RD can determine what changes a client needs to make. Then the RD will need skills in instructing to help the client learn how to adopt new eating patterns. Among other qualifications, this work requires attention to detail and concern for others.

RDs have to graduate from a college or university program approved by the American Dietetic Association (ADA). After graduating, they must pass a national test. An RD must complete an internship before beginning to work. RDs must also take part in learning activities throughout their careers to keep up their RD status.

Agricultural Research Service, USDA

Registered dietitians who work for the government might be involved in conducting diet studies.

The Nutrients

Several nutrients may be described as *nonessential nutrients*. Some of these nutrients are substances the body can make. Therefore, you do not need to get them from the foods you eat. Cholesterol is an example of this type of nutrient. Other nonessential nutrients do not meet the true definition of nutrients because they are not required to sustain life. However, they are substances from foods that have an impact on health. Carotenoids in some plant foods are an example of this type of nutrient.

The main focus of this chapter will be on *essential nutrients*. These are substances the body cannot make, at least not in a quantity needed to sustain life. These nutrients must be supplied by the foods you eat.

Humans need over 50 essential nutrients for good health. Some of these nutrients supply energy for the body. All the nutrients help build and maintain cells and tissues. They also regulate bodily processes such as breathing. No single food supplies all the nutrients the body needs to function.

Nutrients can be divided into the following six groups: carbohydrates, fats, proteins, vitamins, minerals, and water. A diet that meets the body's needs contains nutrients from all six groups in the right proportions.

Failure to get enough of needed nutrients may result in a **deficiency disease**. This is an illness caused by the lack of a sufficient amount of a nutrient. Deficiency diseases are caused by the lack of different nutrients.

Some groups of people are more vulnerable to nutrient deficiencies than others. Pregnant women, infants, and children up to the age of two years are among those who are most at risk. The bodies of people in these life stages have high nutritional needs to support rapid growth. Nursing mothers are also more open to deficiencies. They need extra nutrients to aid in the production of milk.

Consuming too much of some nutrients can be just as harmful to your health as not getting enough. Getting an excess of some nutrients can result in **toxicity**, or poisoning. Symptoms of toxicity vary from one nutrient to another.

Dietary Supplements

Most health experts agree the best way to get needed nutrients is to eat a varied diet. However, some people have trouble meeting all their nutrient needs from food alone. Doctors may suggest these people take a dietary supplement to help make up for any shortages in their diets. **Dietary supplements** are purified nutrient or nonnutrient substances that are manufactured or extracted from natural sources, **2-1**.

Supplements usually come in tablet, capsule, liquid, or powder form. Some, such as vitamin C tablets, contain single nutrients. Others, like multivitamin capsules, contain a number of nutrients.

Nature Made

2-1 Many people take dietary supplements to help meet the need for nutrients that may be lacking in their diets.

Discuss

Ask students why they think some people take large doses of vitamin supplements. *(They may have the misconception that if a small vitamin intake is good for the body, a large vitamin intake will be even better.)*

Enrich

Hold a class debate on the topic "It Is Better to Get Nutrients from Foods Than from Supplements."

Meeting Special Needs

To help students with cognitive disabilities keep information about the various nutrients straight, use a consistent format in presenting the information about each nutrient. Start each class with a daily drill reviewing facts about functions, sources, deficiencies, and excesses of nutrients covered to date.

Not all dietary supplements provide nutrients. Some provide nonnutrient substances such as herbs and some antioxidants. An **antioxidant** is a substance that prevents or slows damage caused by chemical reactions involving oxygen. In the body, these chemical reactions can harm some cells. They can also break down certain materials in the body. Cell damage and substance breakdown due to oxygen exposure has been linked to such diseases as heart disease and cancer. A number of researchers believe antioxidants may lower the risk of these diseases. They think antioxidants might help improve the function of the immune system as well.

Vitamins A, C, and E and the mineral selenium all serve as antioxidants. The nonnutrient substances lutein and lycopene are antioxidants, too. Antioxidants are in a range of foods, including fruits, vegetables, nuts, and whole grains. Many health experts advise people to eat a varied diet of foods rich in antioxidants. However, scientists still have much to learn about the value of antioxidant supplements.

Supplements are considered to be neither food nor drugs. Therefore, they are not regulated by the Food and Drug Administration (FDA). No laws require manufacturers to prove their supplement products are safe. Manufacturers do not have to prove the claims they make about products are true, either. This does not mean all supplements are harmful. In fact, many products have been safely used for years. However, some products have been taken off the market because they were shown to have harmful effects. It is wise to seek the advice of a dietitian or a physician before taking any supplements. Avoid supplements that provide large doses of single nutrients.

A source of added nutrients in the diet aside from supplements is **fortified foods**. These are foods to which nutrients are added in amounts greater than what would naturally occur in the food. For instance, orange juice naturally contains very little calcium. However, calcium-fortified orange juice serves as an excellent source of this important mineral. Fortified foods give people additional options for meeting their nutrient needs through food choices.

Carbohydrates

Carbohydrates are the body's chief source of energy. Most carbohydrates come from plant foods. Three main types of carbohydrates are important in the diet—sugars, starches, and fiber.

Wheat Foods Council

2-2 The barley, wheat berries, and vegetables in this risotto are sources of complex carbohydrates.

Because of their molecular structures, sugars are sometimes called *simple carbohydrates*. The diet includes six types of sugars. At the molecular level, glucose, fructose, and galactose are made up of single sugar units. **Glucose** is the form of sugar carried in the bloodstream for energy use throughout the body. Therefore, it is sometimes called blood sugar. *Fructose*, which is also known as fruit sugar, is the sweetest of all sugars. A third sugar is *galactose*. It is found attached to glucose to form the sugar in milk.

Sucrose, lactose, and maltose are made up of pairs of sugar units. *Sucrose* is ordinary table sugar. The milk of mammals contains *lactose*, or milk sugar. Grain products contain *maltose*, or malt sugar.

Starches and fiber are often called *complex carbohydrates* because they are made from many glucose sugar units that are bonded together, **2-2**. *Starch* is the storage form of energy in plants. Because humans eat an array of plant foods, starch is the most abundant carbohydrate in the diet. When people digest plant foods, they release the energy the plants have stored as starch. The body can then use the released energy for fuel.

Fiber is a form of complex carbohydrates from plants that humans cannot digest. Therefore, it does not provide the body with energy like other carbohydrates. Fiber provides bulk in the diet and promotes normal bowel function.

Functions of Carbohydrates

The main function of carbohydrates is to furnish the body with energy. You will learn that fats and proteins can also provide the body with energy. However, carbohydrates are the only source of energy the brain can use. Also, the body can use carbohydrates as an energy source more readily than fats or proteins. Fats serve as long-lasting energy reserves. Proteins are mainly needed to build and repair body tissues—functions they cannot perform if they are being used for energy.

Functions performed by fiber are linked to the prevention of heart disease and some types of cancer. Fiber binds to a compound made from cholesterol and carries it out of the body. This helps lower blood cholesterol levels, which reduces the risk of heart disease. Fiber stimulates the action of the muscles in the digestive tract, helping speed food through the body. The bulk created by fiber may also help dilute *carcinogens* (cancer-causing agents) in food. Experts believe these functions may help reduce the risks of cancer. Therefore, experts advise men through age 50 to consume 38 grams of fiber each day. They advise women through age 50 to consume 25 grams daily. Recommended intakes drop a bit for older adults.

Sources of Carbohydrates

Many foods are rich sources of carbohydrates. Foods high in simple carbohydrates include sugars, syrups, soft drinks, jams, jellies, candies, and other sweets. Sources of starch are breads, cereals, pasta products, and rice. Some vegetables, such as corn, potatoes, and dry beans and peas, are also high in starch. Whole-grain cereal products and fresh fruits and vegetables are good sources of fiber.

Carbohydrate Deficiencies and Excesses

Foods high in carbohydrates are abundant and inexpensive. Therefore, deficiencies in the United States are usually the result of self-prescribed limitations.

A diet low in carbohydrates may cause the body to use protein as an energy source. This can interfere with the normal growth and repair of body tissues. It can also create a chemical imbalance in the body that could be dangerous if it is allowed to continue. If fiber is lacking in the diet, constipation may occur.

Food energy is measured in calories. Nutrition experts recommend that most of the calories in your diet come from complex carbohydrates, especially those high in fiber. They also recommend limiting the number of calories consumed from fat. Eating a diet high in whole-grain breads and cereals will accomplish both goals. These foods are fiber-rich sources of complex carbohydrates. By consuming more calories from these foods, you may consume fewer calories from foods high in fat.

Health and Wellness

Tooth Decay

Bacteria in the mouth act on sugar and starch to produce acid. This acid can erode teeth, causing tooth decay and gum disease. To help avoid these problems, dentists recommend limiting snacks between meals, especially sticky sweets. They also suggest brushing teeth after eating, flossing daily, and getting regular dental checkups.

Too many simple carbohydrates in the diet can be a health concern. Foods high in sugars, such as candy and soft drinks, tend to be low in other nutrients. Eating simple carbohydrates in place of other foods may deprive the body of needed nutrients. Eating too many simple carbohydrates in addition to other foods increases the risk of unhealthful weight gain.

Fats

Like carbohydrates, **fats** are important energy sources. Fats belong to a larger group of compounds called *lipids*, which include both fats and oils.

Types of Fats

All lipids contain fatty acids. **Fatty acids** are chemical chains that contain carbon, hydrogen, and oxygen atoms. Different types of fatty acids contain different amounts of hydrogen atoms. *Saturated fatty acids* are fatty acids that have as many hydrogen atoms as they can hold. *Unsaturated fatty acids* are fatty acids that have fewer hydrogen atoms than they can hold. Unsaturated fatty acids may be monounsaturated or polyunsaturated. *Monounsaturated fatty acids* are missing one hydrogen atom. *Polyunsaturated fatty acids* are missing two or more hydrogen atoms. Each type of fatty acids has different effects on the body.

Fats and oils in foods contain mixtures of the three types of fatty acids. Learning which fats and oils contain more of each type will help you make more healthful food choices. The fats in meat and dairy products are high in saturated fatty acids. Palm, palm kernel, and coconut oils are also high in saturated fatty acids. Olive, canola, and peanut oils are good sources of monounsaturated fatty acids. Safflower, corn, soybean, and some fish oils are rich in polyunsaturated fatty acids.

Most fats that are high in saturated fatty acids are solid at room temperature. Most oils that are high in unsaturated fatty acids are liquid at room temperature. A process called **hydrogenation** adds hydrogen atoms to unsaturated fatty acids in liquid oils. This turns the liquid oils into more highly saturated solid fats.

Hydrogenation creates ***trans* fatty acids**, or *trans* fats. These are fatty acids with odd molecular shapes. Most shortening and stick margarine are made from partially hydrogenated oils. Therefore, these foods, and baked goods and snack foods made with them, contain *trans* fats. *Trans* fats also occur naturally in foods such as dairy products, beef, and lamb.

Cholesterol

Cholesterol is a fatlike substance found in every cell in the body. Cholesterol serves several important functions. It is part of skin tissue. It aids in the transport of fatty acids in the body. The body also needs it to produce hormones.

Health and nutrition experts refer to two types of cholesterol. You consume *dietary cholesterol* when you eat certain foods. It occurs only in foods of animal origin, **2-3**.

Plant foods do not contain dietary cholesterol. Liver and egg yolks are especially high in dietary cholesterol.

Blood cholesterol circulates through the body in the bloodstream. Your doctor can check your blood cholesterol level. A high blood cholesterol level is a risk factor for heart disease. Doctors urge people to take steps to keep their blood cholesterol levels within a safe range. However, cholesterol in the diet has only a small effect on cholesterol in the blood.

Your body makes the cholesterol it needs. Therefore, you do not need to include cholesterol in your diet.

Photo courtesy of National Pork Board. For more information about pork, visit TheOtherWhiteMeat.com.

2-3 Foods like ham that come from animal sources provide dietary cholesterol.

Functions of Fats

Fats in the diet serve a number of important roles. They provide a source of energy. They carry certain vitamins. Fats also carry flavor substances that make food taste good. They make foods such as meats and baked goods tender, which makes these foods more appealing. Fats help you feel full after eating, too.

The body needs various fatty acids to make other important compounds, such as hormones. The body can produce some of the fatty acids it needs. These are called *nonessential fatty acids*. However, there are a few fatty acids the body cannot produce. These are called *essential fatty acids*. You must obtain these fatty acids from the foods you eat.

Fats have many other important functions in the body besides making hormones. The body stores energy in fatty tissues. In addition to serving as energy reserves, these tissues form cushions that help protect internal organs from injury. Fat under the skin forms a layer of insulation that helps maintain body temperature. Fats are also part of the membrane that surrounds every cell in the body.

Sources of Fats

Saturated fats raise blood cholesterol levels. Eggs and many dairy products and meats are significant sources of these fats. That is why health experts advise limiting eggs and choosing low-fat or fat-free dairy products and lean meats most often. Mono- and polyunsaturated fats do not raise blood cholesterol levels. Therefore, most of the fats in your diet should be mono- and polyunsaturated. Fish, nuts, and vegetable oils are rich in these types of fats. Olives and avocados are high in these fats, too.

Fat Deficiencies

Fat deficiencies are rare in the United States. However, a diet too low in fat may result in a loss of weight and energy. Also, too little fat may cause deficiencies of the fatty acids and fat-soluble vitamins carried by fats.

Discuss

Ask students why they think some manufacturers advertise plant food products, such as vegetable oil and peanut butter, as being cholesterol free when all plant foods are cholesterol free.

Discuss

Ask students why some people seem to think fats in the diet are "bad." *(They may have misinterpreted information about health problems linked with overconsumption of fat.)*

Vocabulary Builder

Feeling full after eating, a condition prolonged by fats in the diet, is called *satiation*.

Integrating Math Concepts

Moderately active 16-year-old males need 2,800 calories per day; moderately active females need 2,000 calories daily. Have students calculate the maximum number of calories moderately active 16-year-olds should have each day from fat and saturated fat. *(males: fat—980, saturated fat— 280; females: fat—700, saturated fat—200)*

Limiting Excess Fats and Cholesterol

The typical diet in the United States is high in fat. A high-fat diet can contribute to weight problems. This is because fat is a concentrated source of food energy. Fat provides more than twice as many calories per gram as carbohydrates and proteins. Therefore, a diet that is high in fat may also be high in calories. The body burns calories for the energy needed for movement and the maintenance of body processes. However, if your diet provides more fat or calories than your body needs, your body will store the excess as fat tissue.

Experts recommend no more than 35 percent of the calories in your daily diet should come from fat. No more than 10 percent of total calories should come from saturated fat. You should limit your daily cholesterol intake to 300 mg.

These recommendations are based on more than possible weight problems. Saturated fats and, to a lesser extent, dietary cholesterol can increase the blood cholesterol level. Another type of fat that raises blood cholesterol is the *trans* fat found in partially hydrogenated vegetable oils. High blood cholesterol is one of several risk factors for heart disease. High-fat diets have also been linked to increased risk of several types of cancer.

Health and Wellness

Choosing a Low-Fat Diet

Choosing a diet moderate in total fat means eating a variety of fruits, vegetables, legumes, and grain products. Opt for lean meats, skinless poultry, and fish as well as low-fat and fat-free dairy products.

For a diet low in saturated fats, limit high-fat meat and full-fat dairy products. Choose fats and oils that have less than 2 grams of saturated fat per serving. Liquid and tub margarine and olive and canola oils meet this guideline.

To reduce *trans* fat in your diet, limit foods that list partially hydrogenated oils on their ingredient lists. Such foods include many stick margarines and some cookies, chips, and crackers.

Commercially fried foods, such as French fries and doughnuts, are also usually fried in these types of oils. To keep dietary cholesterol in check, limit egg yolks and cook with vegetable oil instead of animal fat.

Agricultural Research Service, USDA

Commercially fried foods are often sources of *trans* fat and should be limited in the diet.

Proteins

Proteins are chemical compounds that are found in every body cell. They are made up of small units called **amino acids** (the building blocks of proteins). Scientists have found 20 amino acids that are important to the human body. Nine of these amino acids are called *essential amino acids*. The body cannot make some essential amino acids. It can make others, but not at a rate fast enough to meet nutritional needs. Therefore, you must get the essential amino acids from the foods you eat. The other 11 amino acids are called *nonessential amino acids*. You do not have to get these amino acids from foods because your body can make them fast enough to meet its needs.

Animal foods and soybeans have *complete proteins*. These proteins contain all nine essential amino acids. Complete proteins will support growth and normal maintenance of body tissues. Most plant foods have *incomplete proteins*. These proteins are missing one or more of the essential amino acids. Incomplete proteins will neither support growth nor provide for normal maintenance.

Activity

Explain the complementary relationship of grains, legumes, and nuts and seeds as nonmeat protein sources. Have students suggest examples of foods in each category.

Enrich

Have students investigate the essential amino acids. Then have them identify a plant source of each one.

Functions of Proteins

The body needs amino acids from proteins for growth, maintenance, and repair of tissues. Proteins aid in the formation of enzymes, some hormones, and antibodies. Proteins also provide energy. (Your diet needs to supply enough carbohydrates and fats to meet energy needs. Otherwise, your body will use proteins for energy before using them to support growth and maintenance.) Regulation of bodily processes, such as fluid balance in the cells, is also a function of proteins.

Protein needs are based mainly on age, body size, and physical state. Children need more protein per pound of body weight than adults because they are growing so rapidly. Pound for pound, adult men and women need the same amount of protein. Therefore, because men generally weigh more than women, they need more protein each day. Pregnant women need extra protein to support the growth of their developing babies. Nursing women need extra protein to produce milk.

Food Science

Complimentary Proteins

Incomplete proteins can complement one another. In other words, you can supplement a protein food lacking an amino acid with a protein food containing that amino acid. When combined, the two foods provide a higher quality protein than either would have provided alone. The two foods do not have to be eaten together. They must simply be part of a nutritious diet consumed throughout the day. The proteins in dry beans and grains generally complement each other in this way. Red beans and rice is an example of this combination.

Sources of Protein

Important sources of complete protein are lean meats, poultry, fish, milk, cheese, and eggs. Dried beans, peas, and nuts are sources of incomplete protein. Grain products and vegetables provide smaller amounts of incomplete protein.

FYI
Combining incomplete
protein sources with
complete sources can
improve protein values.
Serving cereal with
milk is an example.
The complete proteins
in the milk improve the
protein value of the
cereal. Macaroni and
cheese and tuna and
noodle casserole are
other examples.

FYI
The grains group
and vegetable group
in MyPlate supply
small amounts of
protein. A teen boy
who consumes
the recommended
amounts may meet
over half his daily
protein needs from
these groups.

Discuss
Ask students why
PEM would be
more common in
underdeveloped areas
of the world. *(Protein
sources specifically
are limited among the
poor people who live in
these areas.)*

Protein Deficiencies and Excesses

If the diet does not contain enough protein and calories, a condition called **protein-energy malnutrition (PEM)** may result. In adults, symptoms of this condition include fatigue and weight loss. In children, this condition can lead to diarrhea, infections, poor brain development, and stunted growth. PEM is common in many developing countries around the world. However, even wealthy nations have hungry people who are affected by PEM. People who fail to get enough food for reasons such as drug addictions or eating disorders may also suffer from PEM.

If the diet contains too much protein, the body converts the extra protein to fat and stores it in the fat tissue. The body cannot convert stored protein back into amino acids for use in building tissues. Eating nutritious foods at meals throughout the day will maintain your body's supply of amino acids. See **2-4**.

Vitamins

Vitamins are complex organic substances. You need them in small amounts for normal growth, maintenance, and reproduction. The body cannot produce most vitamins, at least not in large enough amounts to meet nutritional needs. The best way to get all the vitamins you need is to eat a nutritious diet.

Energy Nutrients		
Nutrient	**Functions**	**Sources**
Carbohydrates	Supply energy; Provide bulk in the form of cellulose (needed for digestion); Help the body digest fats efficiently; Spare proteins so they can be used for growth and regulation	Sugar: Honey, jam, jelly, molasses, sugar; Fiber: Fresh fruits and vegetables, whole-grain breads and cereals; Starch: Beans, breads, cereals, corn, pasta, peas, potatoes, rice
Fats	Supply energy; Carry fat-soluble vitamins; Insulate the body from shock and temperature changes; Protect vital organs; Add flavor and satisfying quality to foods; Serve as a source of essential fatty acids	Bacon, butter, cheese, chocolate, cream, dressings, egg yolks, marbling in meats, margarine, nuts, olives, salad oils
Proteins	Build and repair tissues; Help make antibodies, enzymes, hormones, and some vitamins; Regulate fluid balance in the cells and other body processes; Supply energy, when needed	Complete proteins: Eggs, fish, meat, milk and other dairy products, poultry; Incomplete proteins: Cereals, grains, legumes, lentils, peanut butter, peanuts

2-4 Carbohydrates, fats, and proteins all supply energy in the diet.

Vitamins are either fat-soluble or water-soluble. **Fat-soluble vitamins** dissolve in fats. They are carried by the fats in foods and can be stored in the fatty tissues of the body. Over time, fat-soluble vitamins can build up in the body and may reach dangerous levels. **Water-soluble vitamins** dissolve in water. The body does not store them to any great extent. Instead, excess water-soluble vitamins are carried out of the body in the urine.

Although the body does not store large amounts of water-soluble vitamins, consuming large quantities may still be harmful. You are not likely to get harmful quantities of fat- or water-soluble vitamins from the foods you eat. However, taking large doses of vitamin supplements could put you at risk of developing symptoms of toxicity.

Vitamins A, D, E, and K are the fat-soluble vitamins. Vitamin C and the B-complex vitamins are water-soluble.

Vitamin A

The body uses vitamin A to make a chemical compound the eyes need to adapt to darkness. Vitamin A promotes normal bone growth. The health of tissues such as skin and mucous membranes also depends on the presence of vitamin A.

Sources of Vitamin A

The body obtains vitamin A in two forms. The first form is the preformed vitamin. This form of vitamin A is in foods from animal sources like liver, egg yolk, and whole milk. It is also in fortified dairy products, butter, and fish oils.

The second form of vitamin A is *provitamin A carotenoids*. These are substances the body can convert into vitamin A. Provitamin A carotenoids are in plant foods. Deeper color indicates the presence of more provitamin A carotenoids. Therefore, orange and dark green fruits and vegetables normally have a higher vitamin A value than lighter colored produce.

Vitamin A Deficiencies and Excesses

If the diet contains too little vitamin A, the eyes will become sensitive to light. They may develop **night blindness**, which is a reduced ability to see in dim light. The skin will become rough, and susceptibility to disease may increase. In severe cases, stunted growth may result.

People seldom get too much vitamin A from food. However, if they take too many vitamin A supplements, fatigue, headaches, nausea, vomiting, and liver damage may eventually occur.

Vitamin D

The major function of vitamin D is to promote the growth and proper mineralization of bones and teeth. Vitamin D performs this function by helping the body use the minerals calcium and phosphorus.

Sources of Vitamin D

Vitamin D occurs naturally in a few foods. These include eggs, liver, and fatty fish. In addition, vitamin D is added to most milk as well as some cereals and margarine.

Health and Wellness

The Sunshine Vitamin

The body can make vitamin D with exposure to sunlight. Thus, some people call vitamin D the "sunshine vitamin." Sunlight helps convert a substance found in the skin to vitamin D. Advanced age, darker skin color, sunscreen, heavy clothing, and smog all decrease the production of vitamin D in the skin.

Sun exposure is linked to about 30 percent of all cancers. However, you do not have to be in the sun for long periods to manufacture vitamin D. Therefore, you should follow advice for using sunscreens, wearing protective clothes, and avoiding dangerous exposure times. Most people who drink milk and enjoy normal outdoor activities will get enough vitamin D to meet their needs.

VISIT FLORIDA

Spending time enjoying outdoor activities can help your body make the vitamin D it needs.

Shutterstock

FYI

The vitamin D deficiency disease in adults is called *osteomalacia*. It is characterized by a bent spine and bowed legs.

Vitamin D Deficiencies and Excesses

If the diet does not contain enough vitamin D, the body will not be able to use calcium and phosphorus as it should. In severe cases, children with vitamin D deficiencies can develop a disease called **rickets**. Symptoms of rickets include crooked legs and misshapen breastbones. Adults may develop other bone abnormalities.

If the diet contains too much vitamin D, the body will store the excess. Over an extended period, excesses of vitamin D may result in nausea, diarrhea, and loss of weight. In severe cases, kidneys and lungs may be damaged, and bones may become deformed.

Vitamin E

In humans, vitamin E functions mainly as an antioxidant. Some cells in the body, such as cells in the lungs, are constantly exposed to high levels of oxygen. Oxygen can destroy the membranes of these cells. When vitamin E is present, however, it combines with the oxygen before the oxygen can react with and harm the cells. Vitamin E also protects red and white blood cells, fatty acids, and vitamin A from harmful reactions with oxygen.

Sources of Vitamin E

Vitamin E is widely distributed throughout the food supply. Sources include fats and oils, whole-grain breads and cereals, liver, eggs, whole milk dairy foods, and leafy green vegetables.

Vitamin E Deficiencies and Excesses

The average diet in the United States supplies sufficient amounts of vitamin E. Therefore, deficiencies are rare. However, premature infants may have deficiencies. Babies who do not reach full term fail to receive enough vitamin E from their mothers before birth. Toxicity from excess dietary vitamin E also seems to be rare. However, people who take large doses of vitamin E supplements are at increased risk of hemorrhage.

Vitamin K

Vitamin K is known as the blood-clotting vitamin. Vitamin K performs this function by helping the liver make a substance called *prothrombin*. Prothrombin is a protein blood needs to clot. If vitamin K is not available, the liver cannot form prothrombin and blood cannot clot properly.

Sources of Vitamin K

Bacteria in the human intestinal tract can make vitamin K. Leafy green vegetables and cauliflower are good dietary sources of vitamin K. Additional sources include other vegetables, organ meats, and egg yolk.

Vitamin K Deficiencies and Excesses

Most people receive enough vitamin K from the foods they eat. Deficiencies are more likely due to a body's inability to absorb or make vitamin K. In cases where deficiency is severe, hemorrhaging can occur due to lack of blood clotting.

The amount of vitamin K consumed in a normal diet is not harmful. However, toxicity can develop through the use of vitamin K supplements. See **2-5**.

Vitamin C

Vitamin C, which is also known as ascorbic acid, performs many important functions in the body. It helps in the formation and maintenance of *collagen*, a protein that is part of connective tissue. Collagen is the cementing material that holds body cells together. Vitamin C helps make the walls of blood vessels firm, and it helps wounds heal and broken bones mend. It aids in the formation of hemoglobin (a substance in red blood cells) and helps the body fight infections. It also functions as a dietary antioxidant.

Sources of Vitamin C

Fresh fruits and vegetables are the best sources of vitamin C in the diet. Citrus fruits, strawberries, and cantaloupe are good fruit sources of vitamin C. Leafy green vegetables, green peppers, broccoli, and cabbage are good vegetable sources.

Discuss

Ask students what cooking methods would limit the loss of thiamin and other water-soluble vitamins. *(microwaving and dry heat cooking methods, such as broiling and frying)*

Discuss

Ask students why thiamin, riboflavin, and niacin deficiencies are not common in the United States. *(Most people in the U.S. eat adequate food sources of these vitamins.)*

FYI

According to the Food and Nutrition Board at the Institute of Medicine of the National Academies, no adverse effects associated with the consumption of excess thiamin or riboflavin have been reported.

Fat-Soluble Vitamins		
Nutrient	**Functions**	**Sources**
Vitamin A	Helps keep skin clear and smooth and mucus membranes healthy Helps prevent night blindness Helps promote growth	Butter; Cheddar-type cheese; dark green and orange fruits and vegetables, such as apricots, carrots, and spinach; egg yolk; fortified margarine; liver; whole and fortified milk
Vitamin D	Helps build strong bones and teeth in children Helps maintain bones in adults	Egg yolk; fish liver oils; fortified butter, margarine, and milk; liver; sardines; tuna; the sun
Vitamin E	Acts as an antioxidant that protects cell membranes of cells exposed to high concentrations of oxygen	Eggs; leafy green vegetables; liver and other variety meats; salad oils, shortening, and other fats and oils; whole-grain cereals
Vitamin K	Helps blood clot	Cauliflower, leafy green vegetables, and other vegetables; egg yolk; organ meats

2-5 The fat-soluble vitamins can be stored in the body.

Vitamin C Deficiencies and Excesses

Because vitamin C is a water-soluble vitamin, the body cannot readily store it. Therefore, you need a daily supply. People who smoke face increased oxygen damage in the body and thus need extra vitamin C for its antioxidant effects. Too little vitamin C in the diet can cause poor appetite, weakness, bruising, and soreness in the joints. A prolonged deficiency may result in a disease called **scurvy**. Symptoms of this disease include weakness, bleeding gums, tooth loss, and internal bleeding.

Vitamin C does help the body fight infection. However, scientists do not agree it will prevent or cure the common cold. Avoid taking vitamin C supplements unless directed to do so by a physician. Excess vitamin C may cause nausea, cramps, and diarrhea.

Thiamin

Thiamin, or vitamin B_1, is part of a larger group of vitamins called the *B-complex vitamins*. All the B-complex vitamins are water-soluble. Each B vitamin has distinct properties. However, they work together in the body.

Thiamin helps the body release energy from food. It forms part of the coenzymes needed for the breakdown of carbohydrates. (*Coenzymes* are chemical substances that work with enzymes to promote enzyme activity.) Thiamin helps promote normal appetite and digestion. It also helps keep the nervous system healthy and prevent irritability.

Sources of Thiamin

Nearly all foods except fats, oils, and refined sugars contain some thiamin. However, no single food is particularly high in this vitamin. Wheat germ, pork products, legumes, and whole-grain and enriched cereals are good sources of thiamin.

Thiamin Deficiencies

Too little thiamin in the diet will first cause nausea, apathy, and loss of appetite. A severe thiamin deficiency can result in a disease of the nervous system called **beriberi**. It begins with numbness in the feet and ankles followed by cramping pains in the legs. The next stage is leg stiffness. If the deficiency is prolonged, paralysis and potentially fatal heart disturbances may result.

Riboflavin

Riboflavin, or vitamin B_2, is the second member of the B-complex group. Riboflavin forms part of the coenzymes needed for the breakdown of carbohydrates. It helps cells use oxygen and helps keep skin, tongue, and lips normal. Helping to prevent scaly, greasy areas around the mouth and nose is also a function of riboflavin.

Sources of Riboflavin

Organ meats, milk and milk products, eggs, and oysters are good sources of riboflavin. Leafy green vegetables and whole-grain and enriched cereal products are good sources, too. See **2-6**.

Riboflavin Deficiencies

Too little riboflavin in the diet can cause swollen and cracked lips and skin lesions. Later symptoms include inflammation of the eyes and twilight blindness.

Niacin

Niacin forms part of two coenzymes involved in complex chemical reactions in the body. It helps keep the nervous system, mouth, skin, tongue, and digestive tract healthy. Niacin also helps the cells use other nutrients.

Sources of Niacin

The most common sources of niacin include muscle meats, poultry, peanuts, and peanut butter. The body can convert *tryptophan*, one of the essential amino acids, into niacin. Milk contains large amounts of tryptophan.

Niacin Deficiencies and Excesses

Too little niacin in the diet can cause a disease called **pellagra**. Skin lesions and digestive problems are the first symptoms. Mental disorders and death may follow if the disease goes untreated. Pellagra normally occurs only when the diet is limited to just a few foods that are not good sources of niacin.

Reflect

Ask students how often they include sources of riboflavin in their diets.

FYI

The paper and opaque plastic cartons used to package milk prevent the destruction of riboflavin by light.

Enrich

Have students research pellagra. Ask them to write reports stating where outbreaks have occurred and identifying factors that contributed to the outbreaks.

Courtesy ACH Food Companies, Inc.

2-6 Whole-grain breads are good sources of many nutrients, including riboflavin.

Excess niacin from food has not been reported to cause health problems. However, too much niacin from supplements can cause nausea, vomiting, and a red flushing of the face, chest, and arms.

Vitamin B$_6$

Vitamin B$_6$ helps nerve tissues function normally and plays a role in the regeneration of red blood cells. It takes part in the breakdown of proteins, carbohydrates, and fats. Vitamin B$_6$ also plays a role in the reaction that changes tryptophan into niacin.

Sources of Vitamin B$_6$

Vitamin B$_6$ is in many plant and animal foods. The best sources of this vitamin are muscle meats, liver, vegetables, and whole-grain cereals.

Vitamin B$_6$ Deficiencies

Vitamin B$_6$ is in so many foods that a deficiency rarely occurs naturally. In cases of prolonged fasting, however, a B$_6$ deficiency can occur. Skin lesions, soreness of the mouth, and a smooth red tongue can develop. In advanced cases, nausea, vomiting, weight loss, irritability, and convulsive seizures may result.

Folate

Folate is another B-complex vitamin. It helps the body produce normal blood cells. It plays a role in biochemical reactions in cells that convert food into energy. A form of folate called *folic acid* is especially important in the diets of pregnant women and is often given to them as a supplement. Folic acid has been shown to help prevent damage to the brains and spinal cords of unborn babies.

Sources of Folate

Folate is found in food sources, which include broccoli, asparagus, leafy green vegetables, and dry beans and peas. Liver, yogurt, strawberries, bananas, oranges, and whole-grain cereals are good sources, too, **2-7**. Folic acid is a synthetic form of folate that is added to fortified foods and dietary supplements. Folic acid is found in most enriched bread and cereal products, including flour, pasta, and rice.

Folate Deficiencies

A poor diet, impaired absorption, or an unusual need by body tissues may cause folate deficiencies. Symptoms include inflammation of the tongue and digestive disorders, such as diarrhea. Folate deficiency can also result in two types of **anemia**. This is a condition that reduces the number of red blood cells in the bloodstream. This decreases the amount of oxygen the blood can carry. Symptoms of anemia

Shutterstock

2-7 This fruit salad is a good choice for meeting folate needs. Strawberries, bananas, and oranges are all good sources.

include weakness and fatigue. People often associate anemia with a deficiency of iron. However, deficiencies of several vitamins and minerals can lead to various types of anemia.

Vitamin B₁₂

Vitamin B_{12} promotes normal growth. It also plays a role in the normal functioning of cells in the bone marrow, nervous system, and intestines.

Sources of Vitamin B₁₂

Vitamin B_{12} is in animal protein foods and brewer's yeast. Many cereals and breakfast foods are also fortified with this vitamin. A nutritious diet that includes animal foods should supply enough vitamin B_{12}. However, plant foods do not provide vitamin B_{12}. Therefore, strict vegetarians need to eat fortified foods or take a supplement to avoid a deficiency.

Vitamin B₁₂ Deficiencies

In simple cases of vitamin B_{12} deficiency, a sore tongue, weakness, loss of weight, apathy, and nervous disorders may result. In extreme cases, *pernicious anemia* can develop. This is a chronic disease typified by abnormally large red blood cells. It also disturbs the nervous system, causing depression and drowsiness. Pernicious anemia can be fatal unless treated.

Pantothenic Acid

Pantothenic acid is part of the B-complex group of vitamins. Its main function is as a part of coenzyme A. The body needs coenzyme A to use the energy nutrients. Pantothenic acid also promotes growth and helps the body make cholesterol.

Sources of Pantothenic Acid

Pantothenic acid is in all plant and animal tissues. Organ meats, yeast, egg yolk, bran, wheat germ, and dry beans are among the best sources of pantothenic acid. Milk is also a good source.

Pantothenic Acid Deficiencies

Pantothenic acid is in so many foods that deficiencies are rare. In cases where a deficiency does exist, symptoms include vomiting, sleeplessness, and fatigue.

Biotin

Of all the B-complex vitamins, biotin is one of the least well known. However, it is as essential in the diet as the other B vitamins. The body needs biotin for the breakdown of fats, carbohydrates, and proteins. It is also an essential part of several enzymes.

Sources of Biotin

Biotin is in both plant and animal foods. Kidney and liver are the richest sources of biotin. Chicken, eggs, milk, most fresh vegetables, and some fruits are also good sources.

Biotin Deficiencies

Because biotin is in most foods, deficiencies are rare. Symptoms of a biotin deficiency are scaly skin, mild depression, fatigue, muscular pain, and nausea. See **2-8**.

Enrich

Invite a dietitian to speak to your class about the importance of folate in the diet for women of childbearing age.

FYI

Some scientists believe combined deficiencies of folate, vitamin B_{12}, and vitamin C are more common than deficiencies of any one of these vitamins by itself.

Discuss

Ask students how vegetarians can avoid a vitamin B_{12} deficiency in their diets. *(Milk, cheese, and eggs provide sufficient vitamin B_{12} for lacto-ovo vegetarians. Vegans may choose brewer's yeast or supplements to meet their needs.)*

Vocabulary Builder

Have students look up the term *synergism* in a dictionary and relate it to pantothenic acid and other nutrients.

Activity

Have students make a table identifying all the B-complex vitamins.

Water-Soluble Vitamins

Nutrient	Functions	Sources
Biotin	Helps the body break down the energy nutrients Forms part of several enzymes	Chicken, eggs, fresh vegetables, kidney, liver, milk, some fruits
Folate	Helps produce normal blood cells Helps convert food into energy Helps prevent damage to the brain and spinal cord of unborn babies	Asparagus, bananas, broccoli, fortified bread and cereal products, leafy green vegetables, legumes, liver, oranges, strawberries, whole-grain cereals, yogurt
Niacin	Helps keep nervous system healthy Helps keep skin, mouth, tongue, and digestive tract healthy Helps cells use other nutrients Forms part of two coenzymes involved in complex chemical reactions in the body	Dried beans and peas, enriched and whole-grain breads and cereals, fish, meat, milk, poultry, peanut butter, peanuts
Pantothenic Acid	Forms part of a coenzyme needed to release energy from carbohydrates, fats, and proteins Promotes growth Helps the body make cholesterol	Bran, dried beans, egg yolk, milk, organ meats, wheat germ, yeast
Riboflavin	Helps cells use oxygen Helps keep skin, tongue, and lips normal Helps prevent scaly, greasy areas around the mouth and nose Forms part of the coenzymes needed for the breakdown of carbohydrates	Cheese, dark green leafy vegetables, eggs, fish, ice cream, liver and other meats, milk, poultry
Thiamin	Helps promote normal appetite and digestion Forms parts of the coenzymes needed for the breakdown of carbohydrates Helps keep nervous system healthy and prevent irritability Helps body release energy from food	Dried beans, eggs, enriched or whole-grain breads and cereals, fish, pork and other meats, poultry
Vitamin B$_6$	Helps nerve tissue function normally Plays a role in the breakdown of proteins, fats, and carbohydrates Plays a role in the reaction in which tryptophan is converted to niacin Plays a role in the regeneration of red blood cells	Liver, muscle meats, vegetables, whole-grain cereals
Vitamin B$_{12}$	Protects against pernicious anemia Plays a role in the normal functioning of cells	Cheese, eggs, fish, liver and other meats, milk
Vitamin C	Promotes healthy gums and tissues Helps wounds heal and broken bones mend Helps body fight infection Helps make cementing materials that hold body cells together	Broccoli, cantaloupe, citrus fruits, green peppers, leafy green vegetables, potatoes and sweet potatoes cooked in the skin, raw cabbage, strawberries, tomatoes

2-8 The B-complex vitamins and vitamin C are water-soluble, so you need to eat sources every day.

Minerals

Carbohydrates, fats, proteins, and water make up about 96 percent of the body weight. **Minerals** are inorganic substances that make up the other 4 percent. Minerals become part of the bones, soft tissues, and body fluids. Minerals also help regulate body processes. Scientists have found the body needs at least 21 minerals for good health. However, they do not yet completely understand the roles of some of these minerals.

The body contains larger amounts of some minerals than others. **Macrominerals** are minerals needed in the diet in amounts of 100 or more milligrams each day. Calcium, phosphorus, magnesium, sodium, potassium, and chlorine are macromin-erals. *Microminerals*, or **trace elements**, are minerals needed in amounts less than 100 milligrams per day. Iron, zinc, iodine, and fluorine are among the trace elements. They are just as important for good health as macrominerals.

Calcium

The body contains more calcium than any other mineral. Most of the calcium is in the bones and teeth. The fluids and soft tissues contain the rest. The body stores a reserve of excess calcium inside long bones.

Calcium combines with phosphorus to build and strengthen bones and teeth. Calcium helps blood clot and keeps the heart and nerves working properly. It also helps regulate the use of other minerals in the body.

Sources of Calcium

Milk and milk products like yogurt and cheese are the best food sources of calcium. Some cereals, fruit juices, and other foods are fortified with calcium. Whole fish, green vegetables, and broccoli also provide some calcium in the diet.

Calcium supplements are available. However, most experts agree food sources supply the most beneficial balance of calcium with other nutrients (like phosphorus and vitamin D).

Calcium Deficiencies

Children with severe calcium deficiencies may develop malformed bones. However, these bone disorders are most often the result of a vitamin D deficiency. This is because vitamin D affects the body's ability to use calcium.

Many teens and adults in the United States, especially females, do not get the recommended daily intake of calcium. If the diet does not supply enough calcium, the body will take the calcium it needs from the bones. This becomes an increasing problem in old age, when bone mass naturally decreases. Bones weakened further by the draw on their calcium supply become porous and brittle. This is a condition known as **osteoporosis**.

Health and Wellness

Osteoporosis

Osteoporosis afflicts millions of people in the United States. It causes many fractures of hips and other bones. Resulting complications make osteoporosis a leading cause of crippling and death. Women are most often afflicted because they have less bone mass than men. Osteoporosis is also related to hormone changes that take place in older women. Therefore, women who have gone through menopause are at the greatest risk of developing this disease.

Obtaining enough calcium (and phosphorus) can help prevent osteoporosis. This is especially important during the growth years when bones are developing and the body more readily absorbs calcium. Research has shown that being physically active throughout life can also help reduce the risk of osteoporosis. This is because performing weight-bearing activities, such as walking, helps increase bone mass.

Online Resource

Ask students to investigate information at the National Osteoporosis Foundation website on bone health or bone density.

FYI

An 8-ounce serving of milk provides about 300 mg of calcium and about 235 mg of phosphorus. A 12-ounce can of cola provides about 63 mg of phosphorus and no calcium.

Activity

Ask each student to bring in a recipe for a dish that includes a good source of magnesium.

Phosphorus

Phosphorus is second only to calcium in the amount found in the body. Phosphorus works with calcium to give strength to bones and teeth. Like calcium, the body stores a reserve of excess phosphorus in the bones.

Phosphorus helps build bones and teeth and aids the body in storing and releasing energy. It helps balance the alkalis and acids in the blood. Phosphorus also helps the body use other nutrients.

Sources of Phosphorus

Meat, poultry, fish, eggs, and milk and other dairy products are good sources of phosphorus. Many soft drinks also supply a large amount of phosphorus. However, they lack the variety of nutrients provided by other food sources. If you eat enough foods that are high in protein and calcium, you should receive enough phosphorus.

Phosphorus Deficiencies and Excesses

Most people have no trouble getting enough phosphorus in their diets. There are no known symptoms for phosphorus deficiency. On the other hand, too much phosphorus in the diet can cause problems. The ratio of calcium to phosphorus in the diet should be no lower than 1:2. However, people who drink a lot of soft drinks and not much milk may have a lower calcium to phosphorus ratio. This can cause calcium to be pulled from the bones to correct the ratio. As mentioned earlier, depleting the bones' calcium supply can lead to osteoporosis.

Magnesium

About half of the body's magnesium is in the skeleton. The other half is in the soft tissues and body fluids.

Magnesium helps cells use proteins, fats, and carbohydrates to produce energy. It helps regulate the body's temperature and keeps the nervous system working properly. Magnesium also helps muscles contract and improves the balance between alkalis and acids.

Sources of Magnesium

Whole grains and grain products are good sources of magnesium. Nuts, beans, meat, and dark green leafy vegetables also supply magnesium, **2-9.**

Magnesium Deficiencies

Healthy people who eat a nutritious diet receive enough magnesium. A deficiency, however, can occur in alcoholics. People suffering from malfunctioning kidneys, severe diarrhea, or malnutrition may also form deficiencies. Symptoms include twitching, muscle tremors, an irregular pulse, insomnia, and muscle weakness.

Sodium, Chloride, and Potassium

Like calcium and phosphorus, sodium, chloride, and potassium work as a nutrient team. Blood plasma and other fluids outside the cells contain most of the body's sodium and chloride. In addition, some sodium is in bones, and some chloride is in gastric juices. Most of the body's potassium is within the cells.

Sodium, chloride, and potassium work together to control osmosis. *Osmosis* is the process whereby fluids flow in and out of the cells through the cell walls. These minerals help maintain the acid-alkali balance in the body. They help the nervous system and muscles function properly. They also help the cells absorb nutrients.

Sources of Sodium, Chloride, and Potassium

Sodium and chloride are found naturally in many foods. Table salt provides added amounts of these minerals. However, processed foods are, by far, the largest source of sodium and chloride in the U.S. diet.

Potassium is widely found in the food supply. It is in some meats, milk products, and many types of seafood. Many vegetables, including sweet and white potatoes, tomato products, beet greens, and legumes, are good sources of potassium. Fruit sources include prune juice, bananas, peaches, and apricots.

Courtesy of the Almond Board of California

2-9 Almonds are a healthful snack. They provide an excellent source of magnesium as well as many other nutrients.

Enrich

Have students investigate the link between dietary sodium and high blood pressure. Have students share their findings in written reports.

Activity

Have students use Nutrition Facts panels on food products to identify 10 foods that provide over 500 mg of sodium per serving.

Sodium, Chloride, and Potassium Deficiencies and Excesses

Deficiencies of sodium and chloride are rare. People who sweat a lot during heavy work or exercise may lose some sodium. Cases of severe diarrhea, vomiting, and burns can cause losses, too. However, normal eating usually replaces these losses.

Unlike sodium and chloride, potassium intake is low in the diets of many people. People who do not get enough potassium may not have deficiency symptoms. However, they are not getting all the benefits of a diet rich in potassium. Potassium may help people have healthy blood pressure.

Most people consume much more sodium than they need. Normally, you excrete excess sodium through urine. In some cases, however, the body cannot get rid of the sodium, and fluids build up. The resulting swelling is called *edema*.

Research has shown there is a link between sodium and **hypertension**, or high blood pressure. The more salt people consume, the higher their blood pressure will be. Thus, people who have hypertension have a lower limit for sodium. See **2-10**.

Macrominerals		
Nutrient	Functions	Sources
Calcium	Helps build bones and teeth Helps blood clot Helps muscles and nerves work Helps regulate the use of other minerals in the body	Fish eaten with the bones; leafy green vegetables; milk, cheese, and other dairy products
Magnesium	Helps cells use energy nutrients Helps regulate body temperature Helps muscles and nerves work Improves acid-alkali balance in the body	Beans, dark green leafy vegetables, meat, nuts, whole grains
Phosphorus	Helps build strong bones and teeth Helps regulate many internal bodily activities	Protein and calcium food sources
Sodium, chloride, and potassium	Work together to control osmosis Help maintain acid-alkali balance in the body Help nervous system and muscles work Help cells absorb nutrients	Sodium: Processed foods, table salt Chloride: Table salt Potassium: Bananas, milk products, prune juice, sweet and white potatoes, tomato products

2-10 You need 100 milligrams or more of each of the macrominerals in your daily diet.

Trace Elements

The body contains very small amounts of trace elements. Experts have determined some of these minerals are vital for good health. Recommended daily intakes have been set for copper, selenium, manganese, and a number of other trace elements besides those discussed here. However, these minerals have not been shown to pose a great concern in the diets of most people in the United States.

Health and Wellness

Limiting Dietary Sodium

The best way to reduce sodium in the diet is to limit use of processed foods. Many cured meats, canned foods, frozen entrees, snack items, and condiments, such as soy sauce, are high in sodium. When you do use processed foods, be sure to read nutrition labels. The amount of sodium can vary widely in similar products. Compare labels and choose those products that are lowest in sodium. Limiting use of salt in cooking and at the table can also help you reduce sodium intake.

Iron

The human body contains about 4 g of iron. Over half of this iron is in the blood, where it combines with a protein to form hemoglobin. *Hemoglobin* is a protein pigment found in red blood cells. It takes oxygen from the lungs and carries it to cells throughout the body.

The body does not excrete iron in any quantity. The body stores iron and reuses it. When iron reserves are low, anemia can result. Loss of appetite, pale skin, and tiredness are common symptoms of anemia.

Women and infants suffer from anemia more often than other groups of people. Women lose varying amounts of iron each month during menstruation. Women who do not consume enough iron may become anemic. Infants have some iron reserves when they are born. When these reserves are depleted, however, the infant must receive iron from foods, such as iron-fortified cereal. Milk is not a good source of iron. Infants kept on a milk-only diet may develop anemia.

Liver, beef, and egg yolks are animal sources of iron. Iron is also found in such plant sources as leafy green vegetables, legumes, and enriched grains. The body absorbs iron from animal sources more easily than iron from plant sources. Eating foods rich in vitamin C with plant sources will enhance iron absorption.

Zinc

Zinc helps a number of enzymes perform their functions. It helps wounds heal and aids the functioning of the immune system. It promotes normal growth and development in children, too. Lack of zinc can stunt the growth and sexual development of children. Zinc deficiency may also result in poor wound healing and impaired taste and night vision. Large doses of zinc supplements can cause fever, nausea, and vomiting. Over time, heart disease and kidney failure can develop. Meat, poultry, seafood, legumes, and whole grains are good sources of zinc, **2-11**.

Iodine

The thyroid gland stores a third of the body's iodine. This small gland is located at the base of the neck. Iodine is an essential part of thyroxine, a hormone produced by the thyroid gland. Thyroxine regulates the rate at which the body uses energy.

If the diet does not contain enough iodine, the cells of the thyroid gland become enlarged. As the gland swells, it forms a lump at the front of the neck. This visible enlargement of the thyroid gland is called a **goiter**.

Insufficient iodine during the prenatal period and early childhood may cause severe mental retardation. Combined with a slowed growth rate, this deficiency can cause

Community Interactions

Have the class prepare a brochure directed to teenage girls about the importance of iron in the diet. It should mention health concerns associated with iron deficiency and discuss why teen girls are especially at risk. It should also include a list of food sources and a couple recipes.

Reflect

Ask students if they like liver. For those that do not, ask what other food sources of iron they prefer to eat.

Photo courtesy of National Pork Board. For more information about pork, visit TheOtherWhite Meat.com.
2-11 Meats are one of the best sources of zinc, which is needed for normal growth among other functions.

Enrich

Invite a dentist to speak to your class about the effects of fluoride on teeth.

Activity

Have each student make a set of nutrient flash cards with a card for each nutrient and its functions. Divide the class into pairs. Have students use the flash cards as they take turns quizzing their partners on functions by showing nutrients, then nutrients by showing functions.

Think Outside the Box

Invite a speaker from the American Red Cross to explain how drinking water supplies can become contaminated during a natural disaster. Ask the speaker to discuss hazards of an unsafe water supply and ways to avoid these hazards. Ask students what daily tasks require them to turn on a water tap. Ask how they could do these tasks if the taps were not working.

swollen facial features and enlarged lips and tongue. Early treatment can reverse some of these characteristics. Seafood, seaweed, and iodized salt are good sources of iodine.

Fluoride

The greatest quantities of fluoride are in the teeth and bones. The teeth need fluoride for maximum resistance to decay. Fluoride is most helpful during the development of teeth, but it serves a protective function for the life of the tooth. Studies have also shown fluoride may be effective in maintaining the health of bones.

Drinking water is the most common source of fluoride, as commonly eaten foods contain very little. Many communities add fluoride to public drinking water if it is not present naturally. However, it may not be added to bottled water. Most toothpastes also contain fluoride. See **2-12**.

Water

The body must have water to function. People can live more than a month without food. However, they can live only a few days without water.

Functions of Water

Between 50 and 75 percent of body weight is water. Water is found both inside and outside all your cells. Water aids proper digestion and cell growth and maintenance.

All chemical reactions within the body rely on water. Water also lubricates the joints and body cells and helps regulate body temperature.

Trace Elements		
Nutrient	**Functions**	**Sources**
Fluoride	Helps teeth resist decay Helps maintain bone health	Fluoridated drinking water, toothpaste
Iodine	Promotes normal functioning of the thyroid gland	Iodized table salt, saltwater fish and shellfish
Iron	Combines with protein to make hemoglobin Helps cells use oxygen	Dried beans and peas, dried fruits, egg yolk, enriched and whole-grain breads and cereals, leafy green vegetables, lean meats, liver
Zinc	Helps enzymes function Helps wounds heal Aids work of the immune system Promotes normal growth	Legumes, meat, poultry, seafood, whole grains

2-12 Trace elements are needed by the body in very small amounts. However, they are no less important than any other nutrients in your diet.

Water Intake and Excretion

The body takes the water it needs from the liquids you drink and the foods you eat. About 80 percent of water intake comes from liquids. These liquids include water, milk, broth, coffee, tea, fruit juices, and other beverages. About 20 percent of water intake comes from the food you eat. Different foods contain different amounts of water. For instance, lettuce contains more water than a slice of bread.

The body excretes most of the water it uses through the kidneys as urine. It excretes the remaining water through the skin and lungs and in the feces.

Water Requirements

Some nutrition experts suggest an easy way to figure your daily water needs. Divide your body weight in pounds by two. The result equals how many ounces of fluids you should drink each day. This means a 150-pound person should drink about 75 ounces of water and other fluids per day (150 ÷ 2 = 75).

Some people need more water. Someone who is in a coma or suffering from fever or diarrhea has increased water needs. People on high-protein diets and those living in hot climates must also increase their water intake.

Diarrhea, vomiting, excessive sweating, or the unavailability of drinking water can deplete body fluids. Thirst is the first symptom of water loss. If water is not replaced, dryness of the mouth, weakness, increased pulse rate, flushed skin, and fever can result.

For Example...

The following foods contain the indicated percentages of water: peanut butter—1, butter—16, marshmallows—17, Cheddar cheese—37, corn tortilla—45, lean ground beef—56, water-packed tuna—63, banana—74, broccoli—90, watermelon—92.

Learn About...

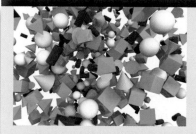

Bottled Water

Studies have not shown any health benefit of drinking bottled water over drinking tap water. However, many people like the taste and convenience of bottled water.

There are many types of bottled water. Bottled water may carry such labels as purified water, spring water, mineral water, or sparkling water. The FDA has set a precise technical definition for each of these terms that must be met by the product.

Bottled water containers are designed to be used just once. If you wish to refill a bottled water container, however, you should clean it thoroughly. Wash the container and lid inside and out with hot soapy water every day. Allow the container and lid to air dry completely between uses. Follow these same precautions when using sports bottles and other beverage containers intended for repeated use. Also make sure your hands are clean when opening a water bottle.

Once you have started drinking from a water bottle, do not leave the water sitting at room temperature for more than two hours. Taking these measures will prevent bacteria from getting into and building up in the container. This will help keep water the healthful beverage you want it to be.

Shutterstock

Bottled water provides a convenient source of one of the body's most vital nutrients.

FYI

The expansion of your stomach as you eat; the sight, smell, and taste of food; and the type of food eaten all affect the production of gastric juices. The length of time food remains in the stomach depends on the individual and the combination of foods eaten.

Discuss

Ask students what enzymes are and what the role of enzymes in digestion is. *(a type of protein produced by body cells; cause food particles to break apart into simpler substances)*

Excess water is not a problem for most healthy people. However, the kidneys cannot keep up with rapid intake of extreme amounts of fluids. This level of intake can lead to a rare but dangerous condition known as *water intoxication.*

Digestion and Absorption

Suppose you eat a hamburger for lunch. Before your body can use the nutrients in the hamburger, the hamburger must go through digestion. Then the nutrients must go through absorption. **Digestion** is the bodily process of breaking food down into simpler compounds the body can use. **Absorption** is the process of taking in nutrients and making them part of the body.

The Digestive Tract

The *digestive* or *gastrointestinal tract* is a tube about 30 feet (9 m) long. It extends from the mouth to the anus. It contains the esophagus, the stomach, the small intestine, and the large intestine. These parts of the digestive tract work together both mechanically and chemically to help the body use food.

The Digestion Process

During digestion, the body breaks down complex molecules obtained from food into simple, soluble materials. These simple materials can pass through the digestive tract into the blood and lymph systems. Vitamins and minerals undergo very little chemical change during digestion. However, fats, proteins, and carbohydrates undergo many changes.

The Mechanical Phase

The digestion process involves two phases. The mechanical phase begins in the mouth. Here, the teeth chew the food and break it down into smaller pieces.

Contractions of the muscular walls of the digestive tract carry on the mechanical action. These contractions mix food particles and break them into smaller pieces. With waves of contractions known as **peristalsis**, the muscles also push food through the digestive tract. Emotions such as sadness, depression, and fear can slow down peristalsis. Anger and aggression can speed up this process.

The Chemical Phase

Like the mechanical phase, the chemical phase of digestion begins in the mouth. As you chew, food is mixed with **saliva**. This is a mucus- and enzyme-containing liquid secreted by the mouth. It moistens food particles, helping them move down the esophagus into the stomach. Saliva also begins to break down starches.

In the stomach, *gastric juices* containing hydrochloric acid and several enzymes are secreted. These juices break down the food further. An ordinary meal usually leaves the stomach in about two to three hours. Carbohydrates leave the stomach first. Proteins are second to leave the stomach, followed by fats. This is why it is good to include some protein and a little fat at every meal. Such a meal will help you feel full longer than a meal that is made up mostly of carbohydrates, **2-13**.

A   B

A—USA Rice Federation B—Photo courtesy of National Pork Board. For more information about pork, visit TheOtherWhiteMeat.com.

2-13 This rice cereal is higher in carbohydrates and lower in fats and proteins than the Canadian bacon and egg breakfast. Therefore, you are not likely to feel full as long after eating the cereal as you would after eating the bacon and egg dish.

As digestion continues, the semiliquid food mass leaves the stomach and enters the small intestine. Here, intestinal juices, pancreatic juices, and bile act on the food. These secretions contain the enzymes needed to complete the digestion of the proteins, fats, and carbohydrates.

Digestive enzymes help break down carbohydrates, proteins, and fats into simple substances the body can absorb and use. Each type of enzyme has a specific function. An enzyme that breaks down proteins, for example, will not break down fats. Once digestion is complete, absorption can take place.

Indigestible residues, bile pigments, other wastes, and water travel from the small intestine to the large intestine. The large intestine acts as a reservoir, or storage area. Eventually, the body will excrete these materials in the feces.

The Absorption Process

The body can absorb water, ethyl alcohol, and simple sugars directly from the stomach. They pass through the stomach walls into the bloodstream. Most absorption, however, takes place in the small intestine.

Millions of hairlike fingers called *villi* line the small intestine. The villi increase the absorptive surface of the small intestine by more than 600 percent. Each villus contains a lymph vessel surrounded by a network of capillaries. Nutrients absorbed by the capillaries pass into the portal vein and travel directly to the liver.

The body absorbs nearly all carbohydrates as *monosaccharides*, or single sugar units. The body absorbs fats and other lipids in two forms: as fatty acids and glycerol and as mono- and diglycerides. (*Glycerol* is an alcohol obtained from the breakdown of fat. *Diglycerides* are compounds formed by the combination of glycerol and fatty acids.) The body absorbs nearly all proteins as amino acids.

Metabolism

Metabolism is the chemical processes that take place in the cells after the body absorbs nutrients. Enzymes cause nearly all metabolic reactions. The body uses some nutrients to replace substances used for growth. It uses some nutrients to carry out bodily processes. The body breaks down some nutrients into simpler substances to release energy. The body uses part of this energy to carry out metabolic reactions. It converts the rest into heat.

Each nutrient follows a distinct metabolic path. The body converts all carbohydrates into glucose for use as an energy source, **2-14**. If carbohydrates are not needed for immediate energy, they can be converted to *glycogen*. This is the storage form of carbohydrates in the body. Excess carbohydrates can also be stored in the body as fat tissue.

During fat metabolism, fatty acid chains are shortened. The body uses most fat for fuel.

The body can use amino acids from protein metabolism for cell maintenance or cell growth. It can also use amino acids to make enzymes, antibodies, and nonessential amino acids. The body can use amino acids as an energy source, too.

Street Surfing

2-14 Carbohydrates provide the body with glucose, which is used as an energy source to fuel physical activity.

CAREER SUCCESS

Organizing and Maintaining Files

Lupe is a dietetic technician at St. Andrew's Hospital. She consults with patients about how to modify their diets in response to specific health conditions. She has to keep detailed records on each patient for her supervisor to review and for use in follow-up visits.

To be an effective worker, Lupe needs skill in organizing and maintaining files. Put yourself in Lupe's place and answer the following questions about your need for and use of these skills:

A.   How would maintaining well-organized files help you when your patients come in for follow-up visits?

B.   How would maintaining well-organized files help your supervisor?

C.   How might your failure to organize and maintain files affect your patients?

D.   What is another skill you would need in this job? Briefly explain why this skill would be important.

CHAPTER 2 REVIEW

Summary

Food provides the body with six basic types of nutrients. These are carbohydrates, fats, proteins, vitamins, minerals, and water. Some people choose to get nutrients as well as some nonnutrient substances from dietary supplements.

Individual nutrients within the six basic groups each serve specific functions. No one food supplies all the nutrients the body needs. Health problems arise when there are deficiencies or excesses of various nutrients. Eating a variety of foods is the best way to get appropriate amounts of all the nutrients.

The body must break down the foods you eat into components it can use. This happens during the digestion process. The digestion process involves both a mechanical and a chemical phase. After foods have been broken down in the digestive tract, the body absorbs the nutrients. Then nutrients are metabolized in the cells to release energy or make other compounds needed by the body.

Review What You Have Read

Write your answers on a separate sheet of paper, using complete sentences when appropriate.

1. True or false. The foods a child eats can affect his or her health as an adult.

2. An illness caused by the lack of a sufficient amount of a nutrient is called a(n) _____.

3. A purified nutrient or nonnutrient substance that is manufactured or extracted from natural sources is a(n) _____.
   A. antioxidant
   B. dietary supplement
   C. fortified food
   D. multivitamin

4. Match the following carbohydrates with their descriptions:

   _____ Blood sugar   A. fructose
   _____ Fruit sugar   B. galactose
   _____ Malt sugar   C. glucose
   _____ Milk sugar   D. lactose
   _____ Table sugar   E. maltose
                         F. sucrose

5. What three substances can raise the blood cholesterol level and why is this a concern?

6. List three functions of each of the following nutrients: carbohydrates, fats, and proteins.

7. What type of protein will support growth and normal maintenance?

8. List the fat-soluble vitamins and explain the basic way in which they differ from water-soluble vitamins.

(continued)

Answer Key for *Review What You Have Read* questions

1. true
2. deficiency disease
3. B
4. blood sugar—C; fruit sugar—A; malt sugar—E; milk sugar—D; table sugar—F
5. Saturated fat, dietary cholesterol, and *trans* fat can raise the blood cholesterol level. High blood cholesterol is a risk factor for heart disease.
6. (List three functions of each: See text pages 28-34.)
7. complete protein
8. Vitamins A, D, E, and K are fat-soluble. They can be stored in the body whereas water-soluble vitamins cannot be stored to any great extent.

9. (List six:) thiamin, riboflavin, niacin, vitamin B$_6$, folate, vitamin B$_{12}$, pantothenic acid, biotin (Food sources are student response. See text.)

10. Osteoporosis is a condition of porous, brittle bones caused by lack of calcium in the bone tissue.

9. Name six of the B-complex vitamins and give a food source of each.

10. Name and describe the calcium deficiency disease that afflicts millions of adults in the United States.

11. What is the process controlled by sodium, potassium, and chloride whereby fluids flow in and out of cells through the cell walls?

12. Where is most of the body's iron found?

13. How can a person figure his or her daily water needs?

14. In what part of the body does most absorption take place?

15. True or false. Metabolism is the process of breaking food down into simpler compounds the body can use.

Link to Academic Skills

11. osmosis

12. in the blood

13. Divide body weight in pounds by two to figure daily fluid needs in ounces.

14. small intestine

15. false

16. **Social studies.** PEM is also called protein-calorie malnutrition (PCM). It is the most prevalent malnutrition problem in the world. One form of PEM is kwashiorkor, which is a disease caused by protein malnutrition and characterized by a swollen belly. Another form of PEM is marasmus, which is a calorie-deficiency disease characterized by a skin-and-bones appearance. As you study protein deficiencies from a nutritional standpoint, investigate political and economic factors that impact protein shortages and hunger throughout the world. Share your findings in class.

17. **Science.** See how effective vitamin E is as an antioxidant in preventing enzymatic browning. Cut a banana into six equal pieces. Dip two pieces in water and two pieces in oil expressed from vitamin E capsules. Leave the remaining two pieces untreated. Place the banana pieces on three plates labeled to indicate the treatment methods. After 30 minutes, compare the appearance of the bananas on the three plates.

18. **Science.** Begin your study of minerals by looking at a periodic table of the elements. Find the location of nutritionally significant elements in the table.

19. **Science.** Begin with a flat plastic plate and six flat-sided ice cubes. Sprinkle the ice cubes with salt and stack them one on top of another. Observe that salt, which is made of the minerals sodium and chloride, lowers the freezing point of water. This causes the ice to melt, forming an uneven surface. The water from the melted ice dissolves the salt. Then the water refreezes, causing the ice cubes to stick together.

20. **English language arts.** Choose one of the nutrients discussed in this chapter. Write a short story from the point of view of the nutrient. Creatively describe where you live (food sources) and your job (functions in the human body). Share your story in class.

21. **Science.** Make a poster illustrating the digestion process.

Build Critical Thinking Skills

22. **Evaluation.** Read the label of a multivitamin supplement. Note the percent Daily Value provided for each of the vitamins in the supplement. Evaluate what this indicates, based on what you learned from the chapter about the effects of excess fat-soluble and water-soluble vitamins in the body. Discuss your findings and conclusions in class.

23. **Synthesis.** Work with your classmates to plan a basic nutrition lesson for primary school children. To enhance your lesson, design visual aids that appeal to children, such as colorful posters or puppets.

Apply Technology

24. Visit a grocery store and make a list of 10 foods that are enriched or fortified with nutrients. Discuss in class how the technology used to fortify and enrich foods has affected the quality of the U.S. diet.

25. Measure your blood pressure using a blood pressure cuff that gives a digital readout.

A Measure of Math

26. Enrico had a glass of orange juice and two pieces of whole-wheat toast for breakfast. He had a hamburger, carrot sticks, and an apple for lunch. For dinner, he had a pork chop, mashed potatoes, and fresh broccoli spears. Use the USDA National Nutrient Database on the Internet to calculate Enrico's fiber intake for the day. Note the serving sizes and descriptors of the food items you select from the database. How do your findings for Enrico's daily fiber intake compare to the recommendation given in the chapter? How do your findings compare to those of your classmates? Why might they differ? What foods might Enrico add to his diet if he needs to increase his intake of fiber?

Teamwork in Action

27. Develop a campaign to promote drinking more water. Begin by investigating facts, definitions, regulations, and statistics related to bottled water through the education section of the International Bottled Water Association website. Use what you learn to design posters, which can be displayed throughout the school. You might also choose to develop brochures to distribute to the student body.

Companion Website
www.g-wlearning.com

At the website, review key terms for this chapter with crossword puzzles, matching exercises, and e-flash cards. Apply facts from the chapter to complete the activities.

CHAPTER 3
Making Healthful Choices

Objectives

After studying this chapter, you will be able to

⊛ **name** benefits of making healthful choices.

⊛ **explain** how to use Dietary Reference Intakes (DRIs), the Dietary Guidelines for Americans, and the MyPlate food guidance system as diet planning resources to meet daily needs.

⊛ **identify** your recommended daily intake from each food group in MyPlate.

⊛ **list** tips to use when shopping for fresh and processed foods.

⊛ **describe** suggestions for preparing healthful foods.

⊛ **apply** the Dietary Guidelines for Americans when eating out.

Learning Prep

Suggest a meaning for each word listed under Terms to Know. Then look up the terms in the glossary to see how accurate your suggested meanings are.

Terms to Know

Dietary Reference Intakes (DRIs)
Dietary Guidelines for Americans
calorie
calorie balance
nutrient dense
MyPlate
processed food

Knowing about nutrients gives you an idea of the important role food can play in health. However, you need to know a bit more to choose foods that will supply adequate amounts of nutrients. Some general guidelines can help you select a nutritious diet. You can use these guidelines when shopping for food, preparing food, and eating out.

Benefits of Healthful Choices

Choosing a diet that provides the body with needed amounts of all the nutrients can benefit people in many ways. This important choice can affect health and appearance. It can have an impact on job performance and personal life, too.

Making wise food choices can help people maintain good health and may improve their health. An adequate supply of nutrients in the diet will prevent deficiency diseases. For instance, someone who consumes the recommended amount of vitamin C will not get scurvy. Research also indicates some nutrients may lower the risk for certain chronic diseases. As an example, studies show high-fiber, low-fat diets may help protect against cancers of the colon and rectum. Nutrients also affect health in more general ways. A case in point, carbohydrates provide energy, and B vitamins help the body use carbohydrates. When people get enough of these nutrients, they will have the fuel they need to do daily tasks.

Getting enough nutrients in the diet can affect appearance as well as health. Vitamin A and the B vitamins promote smooth skin. Fluoride and calcium help form strong teeth. Protein is needed to build well-defined muscles. Nutrients also play a role in keeping hair shiny and nails healthy. Getting needed nutrients helps people look their best.

By affecting health and appearance, nutrients can affect job performance. People who are in good health will miss less work due to illness. They find it easier to stay focused on tasks and do top-quality work. They are better equipped to manage stress. Someone who looks his or her best has more confidence to accept new challenges. He or she will be more willing to approach customers to make a sale or to ask supervisors for help. See **3-1**.

In similar ways, nutrients can influence personal life. Good physical health can give people the strength and energy to manage all the tasks in their daily schedules. Their ability to concentrate will improve. They will have more positive attitudes when interacting with others.

Choosing healthful foods is not the only day-to-day decision that can help promote good health. Daily activity choices also affect the way people look and feel. Choosing to be active throughout the week can help people have more positive attitudes about themselves. They will be stronger and more flexible. They will have an easier time maintaining healthy body weight. They will reduce their risk of certain major illnesses, such as heart disease, diabetes, and some cancers. They will be less likely to become anxious and depressed.

Reflect

Ask students to think about the extent to which health issues play a role in their food choices.

FYI

Nutrients function together to do their work. Getting enough of a single nutrient will not ensure that functions associated with that nutrient are performed in the body. You need an adequate supply of all nutrients to enable each nutrient to do its job.

Agricultural Research Service, USDA

3-1 A healthful diet can give people the energy and nutrients they need to look and feel their best at work.

It is important to realize that eating wholesome foods and exercising will not guarantee good health. Habits like getting enough rest, avoiding hazards, and taking safety precautions affect each person's state of health. Heredity and environment also have an effect on physical well-being, and these factors are often beyond control. However, making healthful choices whenever possible allows people to take an active role in managing their total state of wellness.

Risks of Unhealthful Choices

Just as making healthful choices can have a number of benefits, making unhealthful choices can have a number of risks. For instance, making too many unhealthful food choices could result in a lack of some nutrients. This could lead to deficiency diseases. Choosing portions that are too large can bring about unhealthful weight gain. Choosing to spend excessive amounts of time in sedentary activities can cause a loss of muscle strength and energy.

Unhealthful choices go beyond decisions about food and activities. Lifestyle choices involving tobacco carry many health risks. Choosing to use tobacco in any form is hazardous to health. Smoking tobacco is linked with lung and heart diseases and many cancers. It can also weaken bones and damage the digestive tract. Using smokeless tobacco has been shown to cause cancers of the mouth, throat, and tongue. Choosing to be around secondhand smoke (inhaled from nearby smokers) is nearly as dangerous as smoking.

Using alcohol in excess is another lifestyle choice that has a number of health risks. These include liver disease, high blood pressure, and some cancers. Excess alcohol also causes many car accidents, suicides, and acts of violence.

Many diseases caused by unhealthful choices can lead to secondary health risks. For instance, nausea and lack of appetite are common side effects of chemotherapy drugs used to treat cancer. In response to these symptoms, patients are often unwilling or unable to eat healthful diets. This, in turn, puts them at risk for nutrition-related health problems.

Resources for Making Healthful Choices

Many reports about health issues are linked to nutrients. Supermarkets, health food stores, and pharmacies all have shelves lined with bottles of nutrient supplements. Food packages make claims about the nutrient content of products.

Having some tools can help people sort out all the nutrition information they encounter. Standards are available to help people know how much of each nutrient they should consume each day. General guidelines exist to make it easier to choose a healthful diet. A model has been developed to help plan nutritious meals. Using these resources can assist people in making healthful food choices.

Dietary Reference Intakes

People need a way to tell if they are meeting their nutrient needs. The Institute of Medicine developed a set of values to help. This set of values is called the **Dietary Reference Intakes (DRIs)**. These are estimated nutrient intake levels used for planning and evaluating the diets of healthy people. They are standards against which the

Learn About...

Types of DRI Values

Different types of DRI values are set for different nutrients. Values for some nutrients are expressed as *Recommended Dietary Allowances (RDAs)*. Values for other nutrients are expressed as *Adequate Intakes (AIs)*. The difference between these types of values has to do with the amount of research available to nutrition experts. (AIs are used when there is insufficient evidence to establish an RDA.) What is important to remember is that both types of values can be used as guides to daily nutrient intake.

One other type of DRI value is the *Tolerable Upper Intake Level (UL)*. This is the highest level of daily intake of a nutrient that is unlikely to pose risks of adverse health effects. Keep in mind that ULs are not intended to be recommended levels of intake. Health experts have found no advantage to consuming more than the RDA or AI of any nutrient. As intake increases above the UL, the risk of adverse effects increases. People can use ULs to check whether they might be consuming too much of any nutrient. See Appendix A, "Nutritional Goals for Age-Gender Groups."

Reflect

Ask students which of the steps for making changes outlined in the Dietary Guidelines they find easiest to make. Which steps are most challenging? Why?

nutritional quality of a diet can be measured. The DRIs are designed to help prevent diseases caused by lack of nutrients. They are also designed to reduce the risk of diseases linked to nutrition. Such diseases include heart disease, some types of cancer, and osteoporosis. See **3-2**.

Dietary Guidelines for Americans

A key resource for choosing a healthful diet is the **Dietary Guidelines for Americans**. These are the federal government's nutritional advice. They are intended to promote health and reduce the risk of *chronic* (long-term) diseases. They are also aimed at reducing the rate of overweight and obesity in the United States. The Guidelines urge people to use improved nutrition and physical activity to reach these goals.

This resource comes from the U.S. Department of Agriculture (USDA) and the U.S. Department of Health and Human Services (HHS). The Guidelines are based on scientific facts. They are revised every five years to reflect new findings about health and nutrition. The present recommendations urge consumers to take steps in three key areas.

DRIs for Teens		
Nutrient	**Males 14-18 years**	**Females 14-18 years**
Protein	52 g	46 g
Carbohydrate	130 g	130 g
Fiber	38 g	26 g
Vitamin A	900 µg	700 µg
Vitamin C	75 mg	65 mg
Iron	11 mg	15 mg
Calcium	1,300 mg	1,300 mg

3-2 Most healthy teens who consume these amounts of nutrients through their daily food choices are eating nutritionally adequate diets.

FYI

Activity levels for determining calorie needs can be defined as follows:

- *sedentary.* A lifestyle that includes only the light physical activity of typical day-to-day life.

- *moderately active.* A lifestyle that includes physical activity equivalent to walking 1.5 to 3 miles per day at 3 to 4 miles per hour in addition to the light physical activity of typical day-to-day life.

- Balance calories.
- Eat more of some foods.
- Eat less of some foods.

The Dietary Guidelines are for people who are two years and older. They are meant to be used by people of all ethnic backgrounds, regardless of their food preferences.

The Dietary Guidelines will have the greatest benefit when all the recommendations are followed together as part of a healthful diet. However, the Guidelines urge each person to find the steps for making changes that work best for him or her. The sooner changes are made, the sooner positive effects will be enjoyed.

Balance Calories

Balancing calories over time will help people manage their weight. In the United States, a main reason for poor health and increased disease risk is overweight. Being overweight is a risk factor for many health conditions, including heart disease and many types of cancer. Following the Dietary Guidelines will help people who have a healthy body weight avoid weight gain. It will help people who are overweight lose excess pounds and improve their weight status.

Calories are the units used to measure the energy value of foods. Body weight is partly due to how many calories people consume through foods and beverages. It is also due to how many calories they burn through movement and body functions. When calories consumed equal calories burned, a person is in **calorie balance**.

Enjoy your food, but eat less. People who consume more calories than they burn will gain weight. One step many people need to take in the area of calorie balance is to eat fewer calories. The first thing a person needs to know to take this step is his or her daily calorie needs. These needs are based on a person's age, gender, and activity level. See **3-3**.

Once people know their calorie needs, they must make sure the foods and drinks they consume meet but do not exceed those needs. An obvious way for adults to detect a problem with calorie intake is to keep track of their weight. People who are gaining weight are consuming more calories than they are burning. People can use tools like online calorie counters and cell phone apps to track their calories. This will help them enjoy healthful foods while choosing amounts that fit within their daily calorie needs.

Health and Wellness

Fat-Free and Reduced-Fat Products

Fat-free and reduced-fat products can make it easier for you to fit some foods into a healthful diet. As you consider purchasing these foods, however, be sure to read labels carefully. Some products are higher in sodium and sugars than their high-fat counterparts. Also remember that reduced-fat products are not dietary cure-alls. Just because a product is lower in fat and calories doesn't mean it is good for you.

- *active.* A lifestyle that includes physical activity equivalent to walking more than 3 miles per day at 3 to 4 miles per hour in addition to the light physical activity of typical day-to-day life.

Daily Calorie Needs			
Gender and Age Group	**Sedentary**	**Moderately Active**	**Active**
Females, 14-18 years	1,800	2,000	2,400
Males, 14-18 years	2,000-2,400*	2,400-2,800*	2,800-3,200*

*Lower calorie levels within a range are needed by younger teens; higher levels are needed by older teens.

3-3 Calorie needs are affected by body size as well as age and activity level. These calorie needs are estimates based on median body sizes for 14- to 18-year-old teens.

Health and Wellness

The Physical Activity Side of Calorie Balance

Increasing physical activity goes hand in hand with tracking calorie intake to manage weight. Being physically active does more than burn the calories consumed from foods. It also improves muscle tone and strengthens the heart and lungs. It also promotes a sense of mental well-being.

The activities chosen should call for more movement than what is needed for normal daily tasks. Moderate activities include bike riding, brisk walking, and gardening. Jogging, playing soccer, and swimming laps are more vigorous activities. They can be enjoyed instead of or in addition to activities that are less intense. Choosing some muscle-strengthening activities, such as climbing and lifting weights, is also important.

Adults should try to get at least 150 minutes of physical activity per week. Children and teens need at least 60 minutes of activity per day. Spending more time or choosing more intense activities can give added health benefits.

For many people, becoming more active means limiting screen time and other forms of inactivity. Some activity is better than no activity. People who are not already active can begin with short activity periods a few days a week. Choosing fun activities they can enjoy with others will encourage them to stay active. Then they can slowly build up the amount of activity they choose.

VISIT FLORIDA

Adults, like people in all life stages, need to be physically active to help balance calories and manage weight.

Avoid oversized portions. Another step many people need to take to balance calories is to avoid oversized portions. Unfortunately, large portions are common in many restaurants. Choosing smaller portions from appetizer or lunch menus is one way to address this concern. Splitting a meal with someone or taking part of it in a leftover container are other ways to avoid large portions when eating out.

When not eating out, be aware of the amounts of food eaten at one time. Read the Nutrition Facts panels on food labels. Check serving sizes listed on labels and compare them with the amounts of food typically eaten. Realize that eating a portion that is double the given serving size will provide twice the number of calories listed.

When dishing up foods, serve small amounts. At meals, use small plates to make modest food portions look bigger. This will keep you from putting more food on the plate than you really need or want. When eating snacks, put small portions in dishes rather than eating out of packages. This will help you avoid eating too much.

Eat More of Some Foods

While choosing foods within calorie needs, it is important to make choices that are good sources of required nutrients. This means focusing on choices that are **nutrient dense**. These are foods and beverages that provide vitamins, minerals, and other healthful substances with relatively few calories. The most nutrient-dense foods are low in solid fats. They contain little or no added sugars, solid fats, and sodium. The most nutrient-dense forms of foods also keep nutritional components that occur in them naturally. For instance, unsweetened applesauce is fairly nutrient dense. It is fat free and contains no added sugars. However, a fresh apple is even more nutrient dense than the unsweetened sauce. The whole fruit is a source of dietary fiber, some of which is lost when the fruit is made into sauce.

Many American diets are low in potassium, dietary fiber, calcium, and vitamin D. The Dietary Guidelines urge people to eat more of the foods that provide healthful sources of these nutrients. Such foods include fruits, vegetables, and dairy products.

Make half your plate fruits and vegetables. Many Americans consume less than recommended amounts of fruits and vegetables. Eating more of these foods will help people get many of the nutrients that may be low in their diets. The nutrients supplied by fruits and vegetables vary from one type to another. Choosing a variety of fruits and vegetables each day will provide a range of nutrients. Studies have shown that diets rich in fruits and vegetables are linked to lower risks of many diseases.

Most fruits and vegetables are also naturally low in fat and calories and high in fiber. Preparing and eating these foods without adding fats and sugars will allow them to remain nutrient dense. Filling up on more of these foods can help people eat fewer foods that are higher in calories. This can help people stay within their daily calorie needs.

Switch to fat-free or low-fat (1%) milk. Like fruits and vegetables, dairy products—milk, yogurt, and cheese—are low in many American diets. Increasing intake of these foods will provide needed potassium, calcium, and vitamin D. Fat-free and low-fat milk are the most nutrient-dense forms of dairy products. Flavored yogurt often has added sugars. Whole and reduced fat (2%) milk and cheese contain solid fats. Replacing higher fat products with those that are lower in fat will reduce calorie intake. People who do not wish to use cows' milk products can use fortified soy beverages instead.

Eat Less of Some Foods

For many people, choosing a nutrient-dense diet means eating less of some foods. These include foods that are high in solid fats. Fat is an essential nutrient. However, solid fats are major sources of saturated fats and *trans* fats. Animal sources of solid fats also provide dietary cholesterol. These three food components tend to raise blood cholesterol. A high blood cholesterol level is a risk factor for heart disease. In addition, too many solid fats in the diet can result in excess calories, which can lead to unhealthful weight gain.

The Dietary Guidelines recommend consuming less than 10 percent of total calories from saturated fats. Intake of *trans* fats should be kept as low as possible. Cholesterol intake should be under 300 mg per day. Reading Nutrition Facts panels on product labels will help keep fat intake within these recommended limits.

Making changes in protein food choices is one way to reduce solid fats in the diet. Replace meats that are higher in fat with lean cuts. Take the skin off poultry before preparing or eating it to greatly reduce the fat content. Include more seafood in the diet in place of some meat and poultry. Seafood is a source of oils that are low in many diets. Choose beans and peas frequently as low-fat, high-fiber meat alternates.

Compare sodium in foods like soup, bread, and frozen meals—and choose the foods with lower numbers. Foods nearly everyone needs to eat less of include those that are high in sodium. In the United States, most people consume more than the recommended amount of this nutrient. Most of the sodium in the average diet comes from salt that is added to processed foods. Read the Nutrition Facts panel to see how much sodium foods contain. Compare products and choose those that have lower amounts. Also limit the amount of salt added to foods during preparation and at the table.

Sodium is a vital nutrient. However, too much salt in the diet can cause high blood pressure. The Dietary Guidelines advise reducing sodium intake to less than 2,300 mg per day. The Guidelines urge many people to cut sodium intake to 1,500 mg per day. This lower intake level is for adults 51 and older and all African Americans. This level is also for people who have hypertension, diabetes, or chronic kidney disease. (As a reference, a teaspoon of salt has about 2,300 mg of sodium.)

Besides curbing sodium, make an effort to increase potassium intake. Potassium helps offset some of the effects sodium has on blood pressure. Foods like baked potatoes, tomato products, and yogurt are good sources of this mineral.

Drink water instead of sugary drinks. Another group of foods most people need to reduce are those high in added sugars. Food products contain two types of sugars—natural and added. *Natural sugars* are found in many nutritious foods, such as fruit and milk. *Added sugars* are ingredients that are put into foods during processing. Foods that contain a lot of added sugars often supply little more than calories. Such foods include cakes, cookies, ice cream, and candy. However, the largest source of added sugars in American diets is, by far, soda, energy drinks, and sports drinks, **3-4**. Therefore, drinking water instead of these sugary drinks would significantly reduce added sugars for many people.

Consuming too many foods and drinks with added sugars may limit intake of foods that contain needed nutrients. Excess calories from sugars can lead to weight gain. Sugars also contribute to tooth decay.

The sugars listed on a Nutrition Facts panel include natural and added sugars. Reading the ingredient list will reveal whether a food contains much added sugar. Look for such ingredients as high fructose corn syrup, sugar, honey, and molasses. If any of these ingredients appears near the beginning of the list, the food is high in added sugars.

Shutterstock

3-4 Sugary drinks like soda, energy drinks, and sports drinks are the largest source of added sugars in American diets.

For Example...
Measure out 3½ tablespoons of sugar to illustrate for students the sugar equivalent in an average 12-ounce can of cola.

FYI
According to the American Dietetics Association, the average calorie intake for adults has risen steadily over the last 50 years. Soft drink consumption has increased 5-fold in the same time period. Many soft drinks are sweetened with high fructose corn syrup (HFCS), and nearly half of the added sugars in the U.S. diet come from HFCS. However, there is currently insufficient evidence to conclude that HFCS plays a unique role in promoting increases in body fat or increased appetite.

MyPlate

To assist people in following the Dietary Guidelines, the USDA created flexible patterns for healthful eating. These patterns outline daily amounts of foods to eat from five major food groups. The recommended daily intakes are determined by a person's calorie needs. Eating the suggested amounts of foods from each group daily will provide people with required nutrients.

In 2011, the USDA released a new food guidance system called **MyPlate**, which is based on the *2010 Dietary Guidelines for Americans*. MyPlate replaced MyPyramid. The Choose**MyPlate**.gov website offers a number of interactive tools to help people make healthful eating choices consistent with the Dietary Guidelines. A key element of the MyPlate system is its simple visual message. See **3-5**. The MyPlate icon helps people visualize how the food groups fit together to build a healthy plate at mealtime. Choosing nutrient-dense forms of foods from each food group will allow people to stay within their calorie limits.

3-5 Visit Choose**MyPlate**.gov **and use the interactive tool Daily Food Plan to create and print out a personalized plan of how much food you need daily from each food group. Then use this information to help set your food and activity goals for good health.**

Discuss

Ask students what factors they think might make it difficult for some people to follow the MyPlate food guidance system. Ask what strategies they think will most assist people in adopting healthier lifestyles.

Grains Group

The grains group includes such foods as breads, cereals, rice, and pasta. These foods are excellent low-fat sources of complex carbohydrates, which supply energy. They are also good sources of B vitamins and iron. Whole grain foods are also high in fiber.

Amounts of foods in this group are counted in *ounce-equivalents*. One slice of bread; 1 cup (250 mL) dry cereal; and ½ cup (125 mL) cooked cereal, rice, or pasta each count as 1 ounce-equivalent.

MyPlate divides this group into two subgroups—whole grains and refined grains. Whole grains include whole wheat bread, oatmeal, and brown rice. Refined grains include foods like white bread, enriched pasta, and white rice. People should make at least half their daily choices from the grains group from the whole grains subgroup.

Vegetable Group

The vegetable group includes any vegetable or 100-percent vegetable juice. Vegetables may be raw or cooked; canned, frozen, or dried; and may be whole, cut up, or mashed. These foods are good sources of vitamins, minerals, and fiber.

MyPlate divides vegetables into the following five subgroups:
- *dark green vegetables*, such as broccoli, spinach, collard greens, and kale
- *red and orange vegetables*, such as carrots, sweet potatoes, and winter squash
- *beans and peas*, such as lentils, and soybean products like tofu
- *starchy vegetables*, such as white potatoes, corn, and green peas
- *other vegetables*, such as tomatoes, lettuce, green beans, and onions

People do not need to choose vegetables from each subgroup every day. However, they should be sure to include foods from all five subgroups in their diets throughout the week.

Fruit Group

The fruit group includes all forms of fruits—fresh, canned, frozen, and dried. Fruits (except avocados) are low-fat, high-fiber sources of vitamins and minerals. Pure fruit juices (not fruit drinks or punches) are part of this group, too. However, they do not provide much fiber. Therefore, choose whole or cut-up fruits most often.

Dairy Group

Foods from the dairy group—such as milk, yogurt, and cheese—are the best sources of calcium. They also provide riboflavin, phosphorus, and protein. Whole and fortified milk products also provide vitamins A and D.

A number of people avoid foods from this group for health or lifestyle reasons. Yogurt and lactose-free milk may be good alternatives for some people. Increased amounts of calcium-rich foods from other food groups can also help meet calcium needs. Such foods include fortified cereals, tofu, canned salmon with bones, and spinach.

Protein Foods Group

The protein foods group includes meat, poultry, seafood, beans and peas, eggs, processed soy products, and nuts. These foods are excellent sources of protein. They supply vitamins and minerals, including B vitamins and iron. Dry beans and peas are also rich in fiber, so choose them often as meat alternates. (Note that legumes can count toward either protein intake or toward vegetable intake, but not both.) Remember to make seafood the protein on your plate at least twice per week.

Like grain foods, protein foods are counted in ounce-equivalents. One ounce (28 g) of cooked lean meat, poultry, or seafood, and one egg can each be considered as 1 ounce-equivalent. One tablespoon (15 mL) peanut butter, ¼ cup (60 mL) cooked dry beans or tofu, and ½ ounce (14 g) nuts or seeds also each count as 1 ounce-equivalent. See **3-6**.

Oils

Oils in the diet come from cooking oil, soft margarines, and salad dressing. They are also found in such foods as fish and nuts. Oils are *not* a food group. However, they are good sources of vitamin E and essential fatty acids. Small amounts are necessary for good health.

Activity

Have each student find or make up a soup, salad, or casserole recipe that includes at least one vegetable from each subgroup. Post recipes on a bulletin board.

Discuss

Ask students how calcium intake is related to bone health at various stages of the life cycle. *(Young people need calcium to build bone tissue. Older adults need calcium to minimize bone losses associated with aging.)*

Discuss

Ask students what foods from the protein foods group would fit into a vegetarian diet. *(Dry beans and nuts fit into all vegetarian diets. Eggs fit into lacto-ovo vegetarian diets.)*

Food Group Examples

Food Group	Typical Foods
Grains group	• Whole grains: brown rice, bulgur, oatmeal, popcorn, whole grain barley and corn, whole grain cereals and crackers, whole wheat breads, wild rice • Refined grains: enriched cereals, crackers, and pasta; flour and corn tortillas; white breads; white rice
Vegetable group	• Dark green vegetables: broccoli; collard, turnip, and mustard greens; romaine; spinach • Red and orange vegetables: carrots, pumpkin, sweet potatoes, winter squash, tomatoes, red peppers, beets • Dry beans and peas: kidney, lima, and navy beans; black-eyed peas; chickpeas; lentils; tofu • Starchy vegetables: corn, green peas, white potatoes • Other vegetables: bok choy, cucumbers, eggplant, green beans, lettuce, okra, onions, pea pods, green bell peppers, summer squash
Fruit group	Apples, apricots, bananas, blueberries, cantaloupe, cherries, figs, fruit juice, grapefruit, grapes, kiwifruit, mangoes, oranges, papayas, peaches, pineapple, plums, raisins, strawberries, watermelon
Dairy group	Buttermilk, calcium-fortified soy milk, cheese, cottage cheese, fat-free milk, frozen yogurt, goat's milk, ice cream, kefir, low-fat milk, whole milk, yogurt
Protein group	Beef, dry beans and peas, chicken, eggs, fish, lamb, lentils, nuts, peanut butter, pork, rabbit, refried beans, seeds, shellfish, tofu, turkey, veal, venison

3-6 Choose a variety of foods from each MyPlate food group to get your daily recommended amounts of food

Solid Fats and Sugars

Oils are not the only foods that do not fit into the five main groups of MyPlate. Other such foods include butter, jams, jellies, syrups, candies, gravies, and many desserts and snack foods. These foods provide mostly solid fats and/or added sugars. Foods that are high in these components are often high in calories. They also tend to be low in vitamins and minerals.

Be aware that many foods in the five food groups contain solid fats and added sugars. For instance, chocolate-flavored whole milk is in the milk group. It contains about 8 grams of solid fat and almost 3 teaspoons (15 mL) of added sugars per cup. Compare this to fat-free milk, which contains 0 grams of fat and no added sugars. People must consider all sources of fats and sugars when evaluating their diets.

Most people would nearly reach their daily calorie limits if they chose just nutrient-dense foods to meet all their nutrient needs. Most healthful eating patterns can allow for only a small number of calories from solid fats and added sugars. These calories might be used to give flavor and variety to nutrient-dense foods. Examples include topping vegetables with a little butter or sprinkling some sugar on whole-grain cereal. However, foods such as cakes, cookies, and candy provide nearly all their calories from solid fats and added sugars. These foods fit only rarely into most healthful eating patterns.

Recommended Daily Intakes								
	Calorie Level							
	1,800	2,000	2,200	2,400	2,600	2,800	3,000	3,200
Grains	6 oz-eq	6 oz-eq	7 oz-eq	8 oz-eq	9 oz-eq	10 oz-eq	10 oz-eq	10 oz-eq
Vegetables	2.5 cups	2.5 cups	3 cups	3 cups	3.5 cups	3.5 cups	4 cups	4 cups
Fruits	1.5 cups	2 cups	2 cups	2 cups	2 cups	2.5 cups	2.5 cups	2.5 cups
Dairy	3 cups	3 cups	3 cups	3 cups	3 cups	3 cups	3 cups	3 cups
Protein Foods	5 oz-eq	5.5 oz-eq	6 oz-eq	6.5 oz-eq	6.5 oz-eq	7 oz-eq	7 oz-eq	7 oz-eq
Oils	5 tsp	5 tsp	6 tsp	6 tsp	7 tsp	7 tsp	9 tsp	10 tsp

3-7 MyPlate is intended to help each person choose the types and amounts of foods that are right for him or her.

Integrating Math Concepts

Have students use the information on this page to calculate the daily calorie limits from saturated fats for each of the calorie levels shown in Figure 3-7.

MyPlate is flexible. People from any ethnic background and economic level can use it. It fits any food preference, from meat lover to vegetarian. For instance, a vegetarian who enjoys Mexican food might fill a tortilla from the grains group with refried beans from the meat and beans group. This might be topped with tomatillos from the vegetable group and cheese from the milk group. Papaya from the fruit group would complete the meal. People can use their recommended amounts from each food group to form almost any combination of meals and snacks. See **3-7**.

EXPLORING CAREERS

Nutrition Epidemiologist

Nutrition epidemiologists study how nutritional factors play a role in the cause of some diseases. Through their research, they may find food intake patterns that create health risks. They may also learn about food components that help protect against certain diseases. These findings may then be used to help form public health and nutrition guidelines.

Nutrition epidemiologists may work for government agencies. They may be employed by colleges and universities to teach or carry out research. Drug companies may also hire these professionals.

Nutrition epidemiologists must be willing to take on challenges. They need patience to complete studies that may go on for years. They need leadership skills to be able to take charge of a study and work without close supervision. These professionals also need to be able to get along with fellow researchers. Nutrition epidemiologists use math skills to assess data and statistics. They need attention to detail so they do not overlook factors that could affect study outcomes. They need good communication skills for sharing the results of their studies.

Those interested in working in this area should have a strong background in math and the sciences. Their training will help them learn how to design and conduct scientific studies. Many jobs in this field require a master's degree. Some require a doctorate.

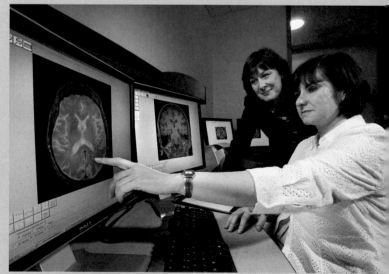

Agricultural Research Service, USDA
Nutrition epidemiologists conduct research to study the relationship between diet and disease.

Meeting Your Daily Needs

How can the DRIs, the Dietary Guidelines, and MyPlate be used to help meet daily nutritional needs? Actually, the Choose**MyPlate**.gov website includes a number of interactive tools that can help people use all these resources. To use the MyPlate *Food Tracker*, enter such personal information as age, gender, height, weight, and activity level. Then enter the types and amounts of foods eaten on a particular day. Be sure to enter all beverages, condiments, and snack foods as well as meal items.

Once all information has been entered, nutrient intakes can be calculated and compared with DRIs. This will show whether a person has consumed enough of all the needed nutrients each day. If a person is low in certain nutrients, he or she can click on those nutrients to identify food sources. Adding these sources to daily food plans will help meet nutrient needs in the future.

The *Food Tracker* also allows people to evaluate their intakes in terms of the Dietary Guidelines. They can see whether they are staying within recommended limits for fat, saturated fat, cholesterol, and sodium. The tool lets them see how their intakes compare with the suggested food group amounts from MyPlate. By using this interactive tool regularly, people can track the quality of their diets over time. The tool even includes a feature for assessing daily physical activity.

Another tool at the Choose**MyPlate**.gov website is the *Food Planner*. This tool allows people to select foods they would like to serve for meals and snacks throughout the day. It will show how each food choice helps meet daily recommended food-group amounts. It will also show the number of calories each food choice provides.

Choosing Wisely When Shopping for Food

The foods people choose at the grocery store become the foods they will later choose to eat at home. Plan nutritious menus before going to the store. Then make careful grocery purchases to ensure healthful foods are on hand. Keeping the Dietary Guidelines for Americans in mind can help people choose wisely when shopping for food.

Fresh or Processed?

When shopping for food, consider the time and energy available to prepare it. Also consider nutrition and the food budget. Many times, these factors become trade-offs. For instance, you might have to pay more for a frozen dinner in order to save preparation time. **Processed foods** are foods that have undergone some preparation procedure, such as canning, freezing, drying, cooking, or fortification. In most cases, processing adds to the cost of foods. It often decreases the nutritional value of foods. For instance, when potatoes are processed into potato chips, they lose nearly all their nutrients. In addition, their fat and sodium contents increase. There are, however, some exceptions to the processing rule. For instance, frozen and canned fruits and vegetables may be as nutritious as fresh fruits and vegetables. When whole milk is processed to remove the fat, it becomes more healthful.

Fresh foods, such as fresh meat, poultry, eggs, and produce, have not been processed. In general, the closer a food is to its fresh state, the more nutrient dense it is likely to be. However, it is important to note that some nutrients in fresh foods can be lost during storage. Fresh foods can also spoil if they are kept too long. Therefore, fresh foods should be used as soon after purchase as possible.

Shopping Tips for Fresh Foods

Evaluate whether fresh foods fit into the food budget and preparation plans. Whenever fresh foods will meet your needs, the following tips can help you buy them:

- Choose a variety of fresh vegetables. They are high in fiber, vitamins, and minerals and low in fat. They are also lower in sodium than most canned vegetables.
- Choose a variety of fresh fruits. They are higher in fiber than fruit juices and lower in sugar than many canned and frozen fruits.
- Stock up on extra fresh fruits to eat as snacks. They can take the place of other snack foods that are higher in fat, added sugars, and sodium.
- Look for lean cuts of meats, such as beef round steak, pork tenderloin, and leg of lamb.
- Choose meats with little marbling and visible fat. Choose Select grade meats when available.
- Choose light meat pieces of chicken and turkey. They are lower in fat than dark meat pieces.
- Choose fresh fish and shellfish more often to replace meat and poultry. Most varieties are low in fat, and fresh seafood is lower in sodium than canned seafood.

Shopping Tips for Processed Foods

When fresh foods will not fit into meal management plans, shoppers may decide to buy processed foods. Be aware that some processed foods are more nutrient dense than others. For instance, peaches canned in unsweetened fruit juice and peaches canned in syrup are both processed foods. However, the peaches in juice are more nutrient dense because they are lower in added sugars and calories.

Processed foods have Nutrition Facts panels on their labels. Reading and comparing package labels can help people choose more healthful options. Nutrition labeling also allows people to assess how foods fit with the Dietary Guidelines. **See 3-8**.

When reviewing nutrition labeling, always note the serving size given on the package. Be aware of how your portion compares to that serving size. Remember that eating a larger portion will provide more than the stated amounts of calories and nutrients. Likewise, eating a smaller portion will provide less than the stated amounts.

You can use the calories per serving listed on a label to help you balance calories. Keep in mind that any food providing more than 400 calories per serving is considered high in calories. Think about the calories each food provides along with those provided by other food choices throughout the day. Then decide if eating the product will fit into your total eating plan or exceed your daily energy needs.

Enrich

Have the class debate the statement "Fresh foods are more nutritious than processed foods."

Agricultural Research Service, USDA

3-8 Reading Nutrition Facts panels on food labels can help shoppers make nutritious food choices.

Activity

Give students a number of Nutrition Facts panels from food product labels. Have them look at the number of calories on each panel to determine whether the food is considered high in calories. Ask them to use the percent Daily Values to identify which foods are considered high and which are considered low in saturated fat, cholesterol, and sodium.

Integrating Math Concepts

Have students compare the two Nutrition Facts panels on the next page to determine which product is lower in (a) total fat, (b) saturated fat, (c) trans fat, (d) cholesterol, and (e) sodium. Students should also determine which product is higher in (a) fiber, (b) protein, (c) vitamin A, (d) vitamin C, (e) calcium, and (f) iron.

Enrich

Have each student make a consumer information poster about one of the shopping tips listed on this page.

Reflect

Ask students why they do or do not like fat-free and reduced fat products they have tried. Ask them to explain why previous experiences with these products would encourage or discourage their use of more of these products in the future.

Use the percent Daily Values on Nutrition Facts panels to help you choose more nutrient-dense food options. Keep in mind that the higher the percent Daily Value, the more a serving of a food product provides for a given nutrient. A percent Daily Value of 20 percent or more is considered high; 5 percent or less is considered low. Foods containing 10 to 19 percent of a nutrient would be fairly high sources of that nutrient. For food components you are trying to reduce, such as saturated fat and sodium, you will want to look for products that have lower numbers. For nutrients you want to increase, such as dietary fiber and calcium, higher numbers will help you reach your goal.

Use the ingredients list on a product to help you find the sources of food components. This can help you know whether saturated fats, *trans* fats, and sugars occur naturally or were added to a food product. For instance, beef fat and coconut oil in the ingredients list are sources of added saturated fats. If partially hydrogenated oils appear, the product contains added *trans* fat. Sugars and syrups in the ingredients list indicate added sugars.

Nutritional labeling can help you compare similar products and different brands of the same product. Suppose you are choosing between three-bean chili and cheese lasagna frozen entrees. Comparing labels can show you which product is lower in calories, fat, sodium, and sugars. Comparing labels can also tell you which product is higher in protein and listed vitamins and minerals. Perhaps you know you want chili, but you cannot decide which brand. Again, comparing labels can help you make a healthful choice. See **3-9**.

The following tips can help people choose sensibly when buying processed foods:

- Choose whole-grain bread, English muffins, rice, and pasta often for low-fat complex carbohydrates.
- Choose croissants, biscuits, and muffins less often. Many are higher in solid fats than other bread products.
- Check the labels on breakfast cereals carefully. Many are good sources of fiber. However, some are high in added sugar and sodium. Granola-type cereals also tend to supply fat.
- Select regular and quick-cooking hot cereals instead of instant products, which tend to be much higher in sodium.
- When buying canned vegetables, choose no-salt-added products, when available.
- Choose fruits canned in juice. They are lower in sugar than those canned in syrup.
- Read labels on fruit juices to be sure they are 100 percent juice. Fruit drinks and punches tend to be high in added sugar and may not contain much juice.
- Choose beans, peas, and lentils often as low-fat, high-fiber alternatives to meats.
- Buy processed meats, like luncheon meats, bacon, and hot dogs, less often. They are high in fat and sodium.
- Choose canned fish products that are packed in water. They are lower in fat than those canned in oil.
- Choose fat-free or low-fat dairy products. They are lower in fat than whole milk products.
- Choose reduced fat versions of dairy products like sour cream and cheese.
- Consider buying low-fat forms of salad dressings and mayonnaise.
- Read labels on soups, sauce mixes, and packaged entrees carefully. Many are high in sodium.
- Choose soft margarine in tubs for use as a table spread. It will be lower in saturated fat than butter and lower in *trans* fatty acids than stick margarine.

Three Bean Chili

Nutrition Facts

Serving Size 1 package
Servings Per Container 1

Amount Per Serving

Calories 280   Calories from Fat 70

	% Daily Value*
Total Fat 8g	**12%**
Saturated Fat 2.5g	**13%**
Trans Fat 1.5g	
Cholesterol 10 mg	**3%**
Sodium 690 mg	**29%**
Total Carbohydrate 43g	**14%**
Dietary Fiber 8g	**32%**
Sugars 8g	
Protein 10g	

Vitamin A 35%	•	Vitamin C 30%
Calcium 15%	•	Iron 10%

*Percent Daily Values are based on a 2,000 calorie diet. Your daily values may be higher or lower depending on your calories needs:

	Calories	2,000	2,500
Total Fat	Less than	65g	80g
Sat Fat	Less than	20g	25g
Cholesterol	Less than	300mg	300mg
Sodium	Less than	2,400mg	2,400mg
Total Carbohydrate		300g	375g
Dietary Fiber		25g	30g

Calories per gram:
Fat 9   •   Carbohydrates 4   •   Protein 4

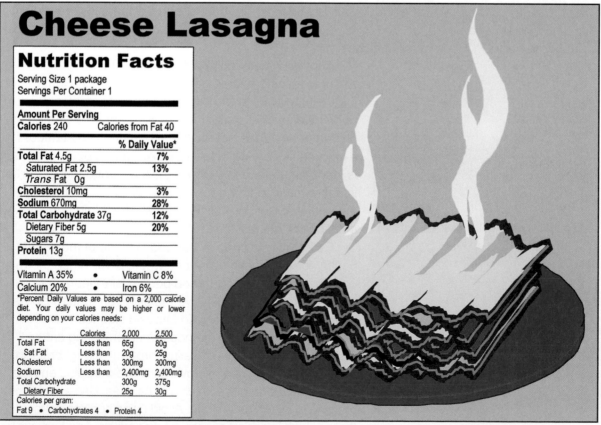

Cheese Lasagna

Nutrition Facts

Serving Size 1 package
Servings Per Container 1

Amount Per Serving

Calories 240   Calories from Fat 40

	% Daily Value*
Total Fat 4.5g	**7%**
Saturated Fat 2.5g	**13%**
Trans Fat 0g	
Cholesterol 10mg	**3%**
Sodium 670mg	**28%**
Total Carbohydrate 37g	**12%**
Dietary Fiber 5g	**20%**
Sugars 7g	
Protein 13g	

Vitamin A 35%	•	Vitamin C 8%
Calcium 20%	•	Iron 6%

*Percent Daily Values are based on a 2,000 calorie diet. Your daily values may be higher or lower depending on your calories needs:

	Calories	2,000	2,500
Total Fat	Less than	65g	80g
Sat Fat	Less than	20g	25g
Cholesterol	Less than	300mg	300mg
Sodium	Less than	2,400mg	2,400mg
Total Carbohydrate		300g	375g
Dietary Fiber		25g	30g

Calories per gram:
Fat 9   •   Carbohydrates 4   •   Protein 4

3-9 Comparing nutrition information on food labels can help people choose foods that best meet their daily nutrient needs.

Health and Wellness

Make Half Your Grains Whole

Whole grains, such as brown rice, oatmeal, barley, and whole wheat, are good sources of fiber. Getting enough fiber in the diet helps keep bowels working properly. Fiber also helps people feel full after eating, so they may be less likely to overeat.

Refined grain products do not provide all the nutrients and fiber found in whole grains. Many refined grain products, such as cakes and cookies, are also high in solid fats and added sugars.

The Dietary Guidelines recommend people get at least half their daily grain needs from whole grain sources. Look for whole grain ingredients to appear first on ingredient lists for bread and cereal products. (Be aware that *whole wheat flour* refers to a whole grain ingredient but *wheat flour* does not.) Choose a variety of grain foods to receive the most health benefits.

FYI

On average, removing separable fat from lean cuts of beef before cooking reduces calories by over 20 percent and total fat by over 50 percent.

Choosing Wisely When Preparing Food

Making wise food choices at the grocery store is a good beginning to a healthful diet. However, the way people choose to prepare these foods greatly affects their nutritional quality.

Try to prepare foods from minimally processed ingredients whenever time allows. Preparing foods from scratch gives you more control over what goes into them. You can decide how much fat to use when sautéing vegetables. You can decide when to omit salt or reduce sugar listed in a recipe. The ability to make these decisions can help you prepare foods in keeping with the Dietary Guidelines.

Start with the Main Course

Most meal managers plan meals around a main course, which generally includes a source of protein. A few pointers can help people prepare main courses that will get their meals off to a healthful start.

Try increasing the emphasis on plant-based foods. Consider preparing meatless entrees on a regular basis. Legumes, such as dry beans, peas, and lentils, are rich in protein and low in fat. You can use them to make hearty soups, stews, and casseroles to serve in place of meat dishes.

Another way to include more plant-based foods in the diet is to let side dishes become main dishes. Remember that half the plate should be fruits and vegetables. Limit portions of animal protein foods. Remember that meeting protein needs does not require a platter-sized steak or half a chicken. A serving of lean, cooked meat, poultry, or fish is just 2 to 3 ounces (56 to 84 g). A 3-ounce (84 g) portion is about the size of a deck of playing cards. To make a moderate portion look bigger, try slicing it thin and fanning it out on the plate.

Remember to choose seafood in place of meat and poultry for a couple meals each week, **3-10**. When the main course does include meat and poultry, start lean. Trim all visible fat from meat. Remove the skin from poultry. These simple steps will reduce solid fats and calories.

Use low-fat cooking methods when preparing entrees. Instead of frying, choose roasting, broiling, grilling, braising, stewing, stir-frying, and microwaving. Avoid dipping entrees in batters and breading, which add calories. Use a rack when roasting to allow fats to drain. Avoid using cooking sauces that are high in added sugars, fat, or sodium. Add herbs to

USA Rice Federation

3-10 Seafood is a source of healthful oils, and it is lower in solid fats than meat and poultry.

braising and stewing liquids to season them without salt. Use a nonstick skillet or wok to reduce the need for added fat when stir-frying. Try microwaving to save time as well as fat.

Rounding Out the Meal

After planning the main course, concentrate on other menu items. Choose sensible portions to help balance calories. Make a point of actually measuring out servings of some favorite foods. See what a serving of cereal looks like in one of your bowls. Become familiar with the appearance of a serving of rice or pasta on one of your plates. See how 6 ounces (175 mL) of juice or 8 ounces (250 mL) of milk looks in one of your glasses. Keeping these portion sizes in mind when serving food will help you avoid exceeding calorie needs.

When evaluating a menu, do not forget the items served with entrees and side dishes. Toppings and spreads used at the table can affect the nutritional value of foods. Items like sour cream, cream cheese, and jam add solid fat, sugars, and calories.

Healthful Preparation Tips

Preparation methods can be as important as food choices when it comes to healthful eating. The following tips can help reduce, replace, or omit ingredients that add solid fats, sugars, and/or sodium to foods:

- Cook and bake with liquid oils, such as corn, canola, and olive oil, instead of solid fats, like butter, lard, and shortening, whenever possible.
- Avoid adding oil or salt to cooking water when preparing pasta.
- Use only half the amount of butter or margarine suggested when preparing packaged pasta, rice, stuffing, and sauce mixes.
- Use salad dressings, mayonnaise, sour cream, and cream cheese sparingly. Try reduced fat versions, or use plain nonfat yogurt in place of these products. Season yogurt with herbs for tasty dressings and dips.
- Flavor vegetables with herbs and lemon juice instead of salt and butter.
- Omit salt from recipes calling for other ingredients that are high in sodium, such as cheese or condensed soup.
- Reduce the amount of sugar listed in recipes for baked goods. Add vanilla or spices, such as cinnamon, ginger, and cloves, to make these recipes seem sweeter.
- Dust cakes with powdered sugar instead of spreading them with frosting.
- Use fat-free or low-fat milk in place of whole milk in recipes. Use fat-free evaporated milk in place of cream, except for whipping.
- Use a gravy separator to make it easy to prepare gravies from meat drippings without the fat.
- Chill meat drippings and stocks. Then skim the fat that forms on the top before making gravies and soups.

Discuss

Ask students to name some examples of low-fat side dishes and light entrees.

Activity

Have students serve what they consider typical portions of beverages and foods such as pasta, cereal, and vegetables. Then have students measure to see what amounts these portions are.

Enrich

Challenge students to choose one of the steps for keeping foods safe—*clean, separate, cook,* or *chill*—to use as an acronym. Have them come up with a food safety tip beginning with each letter of their chosen word.

Health and Wellness

Play It Safe with Foods

The main messages in the Dietary Guidelines focus on calories and food choices. No matter how nutrient dense a food is, however, it can make you sick if it is not wholesome. Therefore, the Guidelines also touch on the topic of food safety.

Keeping foods safe involves four basic steps. Remember these steps by the words *clean, separate, cook,* and *chill.* Be sure hands, utensils, and work areas are clean before beginning to prepare foods. Separate raw foods from cooked and ready-to-eat foods while shopping for, preparing, and storing them. Cook foods thoroughly and use a food thermometer to be sure they have reached safe temperatures. Chill perishable foods in a refrigerator or freezer as soon as possible after buying or preparing them.

Reflect

Ask students which of the menus in Figure 3-11 they would say is most nutritious. Ask them to think about which menu they would be most likely to choose when eating in a fast-food restaurant and why.

Integrating Math Concepts

Ask students to identify which fast-food meal in Figure 3-11 is lowest in (a) calories, (b) total fat, (c) saturated fat, and (d) sodium; and highest in (a) fiber, and (b) calcium.

- Reduce the number of egg yolks used in recipes for baked goods. They are high in cholesterol. Use two egg whites to replace one whole egg. Stretch portions of omelets and scrambled eggs by adding extra egg whites.

Choosing Wisely When Eating Out

Cooking and eating more meals at home can help people control calorie intake. Studies show that eating out puts people at increased risk of weight gain. Planning ahead by packing healthful meals at home to eat at school or work can help people make better food choices. When people do eat out, they can follow a few tips to make choices that will fit into a healthful diet.

The more varied a menu is, the easier it is to find healthful food options when eating out. Keep this in mind when choosing a restaurant. A family restaurant is likely to give more choices than a fast-food restaurant. However, even the limited menus at many fast-food restaurants offer some health-oriented food options. Consider ordering a salad with low-fat dressing instead of French fries to accompany a sandwich. Limit calories, fat, and sodium from fast-food meals by choosing regular rather than large-sized items. See **3-11**.

In any type of restaurant, menu terms can give clues about the food. Many menu items are high in fat, sugars, and sodium. Watch out for buttered vegetables, fish broiled in butter, and pasta with butter sauce. Be aware of items served with cream sauces, gravy, or cheese. Notice items that are breaded, fried, or wrapped in pastry, too. These items are all likely to be high in fat. Keep in mind that many soups and sauces are high in sodium. Smoked, pickled, and barbecued foods are also likely to be

Fast-Food Comparison			
	Double Cheeseburger Large French Fries Chocolate Reduced-Fat Milkshake	Hamburger Regular French Fries Cola	Broiled Chicken Sandwich Side Salad Reduced-Fat Milk
Total price	$5.67	$3.38	$5.69
Calories	1203	636	560
Total Fat	51 g	22 g	26 g
Saturated Fat	23 g	9 g	7 g
Cholesterol	126 mg	46 mg	112 mg
Sodium	1291 mg	622 mg	971 mg
Carbohydrate	141 g	93 g	46 g
Fiber	6 g	3 g	3 g
Protein	48 g	15 g	36 g
Vitamin A	192 RE	46 RE	411 RE
Vitamin C	21 mg	10 mg	15 mg
Iron	5 mg	3 mg	4 mg
Calcium	539 mg	144 mg	447 mg

3-11 The calories, fat, saturated fat, and sodium in a fast-food menu can vary greatly, depending on the specific foods ordered.

high-sodium items. In addition, foods prepared by these methods have been shown to contain compounds that may cause cancer.

You can control how restaurants prepare food by requesting that items be made according to your preferences. Keep in mind what you have learned about shopping for and preparing food when ordering food in restaurants. For health-conscious menu selections, choose foods prepared with low-fat cooking methods. Ask to have foods prepared without salt or butter. Ask to have high-fat sauces and dressings served on the side. You can add just enough to flavor, rather than smother, your food. Choose whole grain rolls when they are available. Load up on fresh vegetable salads, but go easy on dressing and toppings like bacon bits and cheese. Opt for fresh fruits in place of rich pastries or heavy ice creams for dessert.

Remember, the amount of food eaten affects calorie intake as well as fat, sodium, and sugar consumption. Ask for a petite or half-sized portion. Consider ordering an appetizer instead of an entree. Split an entree with a friend. Do not feel you have to be a member of the "clean plate club." You can always ask to have a take-home bag for food you do not finish. You might even want to have half of your entree packed before you begin eating. This will keep you from accidentally eating more than you had intended. These are all ways to help keep calories in balance.

Consider having water with your meal instead of ordering a soft drink. Water is a great thirst quencher, and this choice will save you money as well as calories from added sugars.

Keep in mind that foods eaten away from home are not always eaten in restaurants. Use the guidelines given above when choosing foods from vending machines and in the school cafeteria. These guidelines also apply at the snack bar in the mall and the concession stands at ball games and festivals. See **3-12**.

Community Interactions

Have students analyze the nutritional values of food items from two local fast-food restaurants. Have them write health-conscious menu suggestions for each restaurant on one side of wallet reference cards and pass the cards out to other students.

Reflect

Ask students what types of entrees they would be most likely to split with a friend. Ask students what types of food items they would not want to split. Have students explain their responses.

Shutterstock

3-12 The principles of the Dietary Guidelines can be applied wherever food choices are made.

Eating out, like shopping for and preparing food, requires thought. Follow the Dietary Guidelines for Americans and choose the right amounts from the food groups in MyPlate. Make healthful eating a lifetime habit.

CAREER SUCCESS

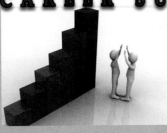

Teaching Others

Nancy is a family and consumer sciences teacher at Green Valley High School. In her foods and nutrition classes, Nancy lectures on nutrition, shows videos on food safety, and demonstrates preparation techniques. She plans labs and other experiences to help her students learn how to prepare and serve nutritious, appealing meals.

To be an effective worker, Nancy needs skill in teaching others. Imagine you are a student in Nancy's class. Answer the following questions about her need for and use of this skill:

A. What are two characteristics of Nancy's teaching techniques that would most help you learn?

B. How could Nancy's skill in teaching others have an effect on your future?

C. How might Nancy's skill in teaching others affect the number of students who sign up for her class next year?

D. What is another skill Nancy would need in this job? Briefly explain why this skill would be important.

CHAPTER 3 REVIEW

Summary

Making healthful choices has a number of benefits. Choosing a nutritious diet can protect and possibly improve health. An adequate supply of nutrients promotes healthy skin, hair, and teeth. Having a sound body and healthy appearance can, in turn, have positive effects on work and family life. Choosing to be active can lead to a strong, fit body and an optimistic outlook. On the other hand, making unhealthful choices can have a number of risks.

Several resources can help people make healthful choices. They can use Dietary Reference Intakes to evaluate the quality of their diets. Following the Dietary Guidelines for Americans will help them form good eating and activity habits. Using the MyPlate food guidance system will assist them in planning menus that meet their daily nutritional needs.

Using these resources, people can make informed choices when shopping for fresh and processed foods. They can also make wise decisions about how they prepare those foods. They can choose sensibly when eating away from home, too.

Review What You Have Read

Write your answers on a separate sheet of paper, using complete sentences when appropriate.

1. What are three factors besides food choices that can affect a person's state of health?

2. Estimated nutrient intake levels used for planning and evaluating the diets of healthy people are called _____.
   A. Adequate Intakes (AIs)
   B. Dietary Reference Intakes (DRIs)
   C. Recommended Dietary Allowances (RDAs)
   D. Tolerable Upper Intake Levels (ULs)

3. What condition describes a person who is in calorie balance?

4. Which food is more nutrient dense, a fresh pear or a pear canned in light syrup? Explain your answer.

5. What mineral helps offset some of the effects sodium has on blood pressure?

6. Name the five main food groups in MyPlate and give your recommended daily intakes from each group.

7. True or false. Foods in all five main groups of MyPlate may contain solid fats and added sugars.

8. How does processing affect the nutritional value of foods?

9. List five tips to follow when shopping for fresh foods.

10. Name five low-fat cooking methods that can be used to prepare entrees.

Answer Key for Review *What You Have Read* questions

1. (List three:) exercising, getting enough rest, avoiding hazards, taking safety precautions, heredity, environment (Students may justify other responses.)

2. B

3. A person is in calorie balance when calories consumed equal calories burned.

4. The fresh pear is more nutrient dense than a pear canned in light syrup because the canned pear contains added sugars.

5. Potassium helps offset some of the effects sodium has on blood pressure.

6. grains group, vegetable group, fruit group, dairy group, protein group (Recommended daily intakes are student response based on Figures 3-3 and 3-7.)

7. true

8. Processing often decreases the nutritional value of foods.

9. (List five. Student response.)

(continued)

10. (Name five:) roasting, broiling, grilling, braising, stewing, stir-frying, microwaving

11. Use a gravy separator or chill drippings and skim fat before making gravies.

11. How can the fat in gravies made from meat drippings be reduced?

12. Which of the following items on a restaurant menu is likely to be the best choice for a low-fat side dish?
    A. Mashed potatoes with gravy.
    B. Steamed broccoli with cheese sauce.
    C. French fries.
    D. Sliced tomatoes sprinkled with fresh herbs.

Link to Academic Skills

12. D

13. **English language arts.** Work in a small group to design a pamphlet explaining the key consumer messages of the Dietary Guidelines for Americans. The pamphlet should be geared for a teen audience. The words and design should inspire teens to adopt healthier eating habits. Vote to choose the most creative and effective pamphlet design in your class. Then make copies of the winning pamphlet and, with permission, distribute them in the school cafeteria.

14. **English language arts.** Choose which recommendation from the Dietary Guidelines for Americans you most need to improve. Set specific goals for improvement and form a plan of action for achieving those goals. Follow your plan for two weeks. Then prepare an oral report describing your progress. Share any tips you found effective for helping you change your eating and/or activity behaviors.

15. **History.** Investigate the evolution of USDA food guides, beginning with the Basic Four Food Groups. Find out when each guide was introduced and why changes were made from previous guides.

16. **Science.** Conduct a taste test to compare the flavor, texture, appearance, and nutritional value of tuna canned in oil with tuna canned in water. Investigate the functions of fats as carriers of flavor compounds.

Build Critical Thinking Skills

17. **Analysis.** Record all the foods you have eaten in one 24-hour period. Visit the Choose**MyPlate**.gov website and use the Food Tracker tool to analyze your food record. Determine whether you consumed the recommended amounts from each food group. If you did not, make a list of foods you could add to supply the missing amounts.

18. **Evaluation.** Bring in two nutrition labels from similar processed foods, such as frozen entrees or breakfast cereals. Prepare a written evaluation of the nutritional strengths and weaknesses of each product. Based on your evaluation, write a paragraph stating which product you would prefer to buy. Give reasons for your choice.

19. **Synthesis.** Work with a team of classmates to synthesize the launch of a new health-oriented menu item for a fast-food restaurant. Each team member should focus on a different aspect of the product launch: nutrition, flavor, packaging, and advertising. Put together a presentation to introduce your menu item to the rest of the class.

Apply Technology

20. Enter nutrient data about your 10 favorite grain foods, vegetables, and fruits into a table on a computer. Sort the grain foods based on fiber and iron. Sort the vegetables and fruits based on vitamins A and C. Print your tables and use them as meal planning guides to help you choose foods that are highest in these nutrients.

21. Use chapter information to write 30 nutrition tips. Use the tips as daily screen savers on your home or classroom computer.

A Measure of Math

22. Remember that foods made mostly of solid fats or sugars do not fit in any of the five main groups of MyPlate. However, foods in all groups can contain solid fats and added sugars. Use the USDA National Nutrient Database on the Internet to find the calories and nutrients provided by a 1-tablespoon serving of butter. Compare this with the calories and nutrients provided by a 1-tablespoon serving of peanut butter. Then compare a 1-tablespoon serving of jam with a 1-ounce portion of sugar-coated cereal. Discuss where each of these foods fits in MyPlate and how their nutritional values differ.

23. Prepare a food item according to a traditional recipe. Then use one of the techniques suggested in the chapter to reduce the calories, cholesterol, fat, sodium, or sugar in the food product. Use dietary charts or diet analysis software to determine the differences in nutritive values between the two products.

Teamwork in Action

24. Investigate terms used on restaurant menus that indicate the use of high-fat preparation methods. Some examples include *Stroganoff*, *Wellington*, *Cordon bleu*, *Salisbury*, and *Parmesan*. Prepare wallet cards listing these terms along with brief definitions. Laminate the cards. Make them available to the student body before a social event such as a prom to help students make healthful food choices when dining out.

Companion Website
www.g-wlearning.com

At the website, review key terms for this chapter with crossword puzzles, matching exercises, and e-flash cards. Apply facts from the chapter to complete the activities.

CHAPTER 4
Nutrition and Fitness Through the Life Span

Main Menu

⊛ Continuing to follow MyPlate will help people meet changing nutrient needs throughout the life span.
⊛ Being physically active at all stages of the life span will promote good health and fitness.

Learning Prep

Look up each of the *Terms to Know* in the glossary and use it in a sentence.

Objectives

After studying this chapter, you will be able to

⊛ **describe** health and development concerns that affect the nutritional needs of people in different stages of the life span.

⊛ **list** meal-planning tips to meet the nutritional needs of people in different stages of the life span.

⊛ **suggest** appropriate activities to help people at different stages of the life span maintain physical fitness.

⊛ **plan** a nutritious diet for yourself.

Terms to Know

diet
fitness
cardiovascular health
food allergy
food intolerance
growth spurt

vegetarian diet
therapeutic diet
medical nutrition therapy
  (MNT)
diabetes mellitus
food-drug interaction

A person's **diet** is all the food and drink he or she regularly consumes. Each stage of a person's life span is affected by his or her diet. From the prenatal period to old age, each stage is associated with nutritional needs. Poor nutrition in any stage may create health problems, shorten the life span, or both.

Discuss

Ask students how the definition of *diet* given here compares with the way they typically think of this term.

Pregnancy and Lactation

Diet during pregnancy affects both the mother and the *fetus*, or developing baby. Good nutrition is especially important during pregnancy. This is because the mother nourishes the fetus through her body. The foods the mother eats must supply the nutrient needs of the fetus. Otherwise, nutrients for the fetus may be taken from the mother's tissues. This could cause the mother to suffer deficiencies. Nutrient deficiencies can be a problem especially in the case of teen pregnancies. Teen mothers need high levels of nutrients to support their own growth. Deficiencies could negatively affect a teen mother's development as well as the development of her baby.

Enrich

Invite an obstetrician or a registered dietitian to your class to talk about prenatal nutrition.

Nutrient Needs During Pregnancy

A key nutritional need during the first *trimester* (three month period of pregnancy) is the need for folic acid. Folic acid is the synthetic form of folate found in fortified foods and dietary supplements. Folic acid helps prevent *neural tube* damage in the fetus. This is damage to the brain or spinal cord. It can occur in the early weeks of pregnancy before many women even know they are pregnant. This is why all women of childbearing age should consume 400 micrograms of synthetic folic acid per day in addition to natural food sources of folate. Once pregnancy is confirmed, a woman's doctor may advise her to increase her intake of this vitamin.

By the beginning of the second trimester, needs for almost all the essential nutrients increase. Some of the extra nutrients are needed to build the child's tissues. Others are needed to protect the mother.

Protein, calcium, and iron are especially important during pregnancy. The mother needs increased amounts of protein to support the growth of the fetus. Most women in the United States eat more than enough protein to meet this increased need.

The fetus needs calcium for well-formed bones and strong teeth. If the mother's diet does not supply enough calcium, the needs of the fetus will be taken from the mother's bone tissue. This increases the mother's risk of developing osteoporosis later in life. See **4-1**.

Iron needs are especially large during the last six months of pregnancy. This is to help the baby build up iron reserves before birth. The baby will need these reserves during the first six months of life. A pregnant woman who does not get enough iron may become anemic as her body works to meet her baby's needs.

Shutterstock

4-1 Drinking milk and eating other calcium sources during pregnancy supports the bones of both the mother and the developing baby.

Diet During Pregnancy

A pregnant woman should follow a nutritious diet made up of a variety of foods. She can visit ChooseMyPlate.gov and use the Daily Food Plan for Moms to find her recommended food group amounts. Recommended amounts are based on a woman's age, body size, and activity level before pregnancy. Calorie needs increase and recommended food group amounts change with each trimester. If the woman's diet was adequate before pregnancy, a few small additions are all she should need. These additions will meet her increased nutrient needs and help her gain weight at the correct rate. As before pregnancy, she should limit solid fats and added sugars.

Consider a woman who needs 2,000 calories a day before becoming pregnant. Her calorie needs will increase to 2,200 a day in her second trimester. To meet these needs, she needs to boost a few of her daily food group amounts. The woman should add one ounce-equivalent from the grains group and a half ounce-equivalent from the meat and beans group. She should also increase her intake from the vegetable group by ½ cup daily. The woman might have an extra slice of toast for breakfast. She could add a small tossed salad topped with a few nuts to her lunch. These small changes would be all the woman needs to get her increased food group amounts.

In the third trimester, the woman's calorie needs will go up to 2,400 calories per day. She should add one more ounce-equivalent of grain foods and another half ounce-equivalent from the protein foods group. A few whole-grain crackers for a snack and a couple extra tablespoons of black beans in her burrito for dinner would meet these needs.

Obstetricians often prescribe nutrient supplements for pregnant women. These supplements include iron along with vitamins and other minerals. Many women have low iron reserves, and supplements help them meet the increased demands of pregnancy. Pregnant women should never take supplements without consulting their doctors. Too much of some vitamins and minerals can be harmful to pregnant women and their developing babies.

A woman should ask an obstetrician how much weight to gain during pregnancy. Doctors usually suggest a gain of 25 to 35 pounds for women of healthy weight. They also advise women who are overweight not to try to lose weight during pregnancy.

Health and Wellness

Foodborne Illness and Pregnancy

Some illnesses spread through food pose greater risks during pregnancy. This includes the risk of miscarriage. Pregnant women should not eat foods linked with these illnesses. These foods include raw and undercooked meat, poultry, seafood, and egg dishes. Raw sprouts and unpasteurized milk and juice are also on the list of foods pregnant women should not eat. Advice about other foods to avoid during pregnancy changes based on new findings. Pregnant women would be wise to check the government's food safety website at foodsafety.gov to find the most current information. Carefully following safe food handling guidelines will also help prevent illness.

Fitness During Pregnancy

Fitness is the body's ability to meet physical demands. These demands include the need for *endurance*, so you can keep going when you start to get tired. This type of fitness is a sign of **cardiovascular health**, or a strong heart and blood vessels. You need *flexibility* so you can bend and reach. You need *strength* for lifting. You also need *balance* to keep you steady on your feet. Making physical activity a part of your daily life will help you improve or maintain fitness in all these areas.

Changing interests and abilities make some activities more suitable than others at each stage of the life span. The pregnancy stage is no exception. Being physically fit can help a woman have a more comfortable pregnancy and an easier delivery. However, changes in a pregnant woman's body can put her at increased risk of injury. Therefore, it is important to choose moderate rather than vigorous activities at this life stage.

Walking, swimming, and low-impact aerobics are good activities for pregnant women. Many other activities are safe as well. However, contact sports and activities that involve bouncing, twisting at the waist, or a high risk of falling are not good choices. A pregnant woman should discuss her fitness routine with her health care provider. She should listen to her body and stop activity immediately if she feels pain, dizziness, or shortness of breath.

Diet During Lactation

During *lactation* (the production of breast milk), a woman has increased energy, protein, mineral, and vitamin needs. The woman needs these extra nutrients to replace the nutrients secreted in the milk. She also needs them to cover the energy cost of producing the milk and to protect her body.

The diets of a lactating woman and a pregnant woman are similar. However, the lactating woman's needs for some nutrients are greater. Like a pregnant woman, a mother who is breastfeeding can visit Choose**MyPlate**.gov to get a food group plan. Following this plan will help her make sure she is using the right food groups to meet her extra nutrient needs.

Calorie needs may change for a nursing mother six months after her baby is born. A woman's body forms fat stores as she gains weight during pregnancy. During the first six months after delivery, some of the energy needed to produce milk comes from these fat stores. Six months after delivery, the woman is likely to have lost all the weight she gained during pregnancy. At this point, she may need a small amount of extra calories from food to supply the energy she needs to produce milk.

Lactating women need liquids to provide water in breast milk and to meet their own fluid needs. They should drink at least 2 to 3 quarts (2 to 3 L) of fluid each day. Drinking water or another beverage each time she nurses her baby will help a breastfeeding mother get the fluid she needs.

Fitness After Delivery

After having a baby, most women look forward to getting their bodies back in shape. Following a daily fitness routine is a great way to reach this goal, **4-2**. Physical activity can also help lessen feelings of depression that sometimes occur after delivery. A new mother should check with her doctor before beginning a routine. Generally, she can start moderate exercise as soon as she feels up to it.

Some of the first exercises a new mother may want to do will help her regain balance and strength she lost during pregnancy. Standing on one foot and then the other is one activity that will help improve balance. Doing modified sit-ups and pelvic tilts are among the options for building muscle strength in the back and abdomen.

Walking is a good activity for building endurance during the first weeks after having a baby. A woman can slowly increase her speed and distance as she feels able to keep up with a tougher routine. She can add more intense activities as she feels ready. However, she should avoid activities such as jogging and jumping for the first six to eight weeks after delivery. These activities put stress on joints that have been loosened by pregnancy hormones and can lead to injury.

Discuss

Ask students how the description of fitness given here applies to all stages of the life span.

Time Management Tip

Preparing nutritious snack packs in advance can help nursing moms keep up with their extra nutrient needs amid the busy schedule of caring for a new baby. Several small bags, such as carrot sticks, orange segments, and high-fiber cereal, can be packed at one time. They can be stored in a convenient location so mom can quickly grab a snack for herself whenever she nurses the baby.

Online Resource
Have students visit the National Organization on Fetal Alcohol Syndrome website at nofas.org to find out how a woman's alcohol consumption during pregnancy can affect her unborn baby.

For Example…
Nicotine, a drug found in cigarette smoke, can cause vomiting, diarrhea, and restlessness for a breast-fed baby and can decrease the mother's milk production. Maternal smoking or passive smoke may also increase the risk of sudden infant death syndrome (SIDS).

Wheat Foods Council

4-2 Walking with their babies is a great way for new mothers to make fitness part of their daily routines after delivery.

Pelvic pain, bleeding, shortness of breath, and exhaustion are all signs of trouble for a new mother. A woman who has any of these symptoms should see her doctor before continuing her fitness routine.

Health and Wellness

Avoiding Drugs During Pregnancy and Lactation

Many drugs can have harmful effects on a developing fetus or nursing baby. This is why pregnant and lactating women should not use alcohol, tobacco, and illegal drugs. Alcohol is a drug, and tobacco contains nicotine, which is a drug. During pregnancy, drugs can pass from the mother's body to the baby through the placenta. (The *placenta* is an organ that nourishes the developing child in the mother's womb.) During lactation, drugs can pass to a baby through breast milk. Pregnant and lactating women should even avoid prescription and over-the-counter medications, such as aspirin, except under a doctor's advice.

Infancy and Early Childhood

Infants and preschool children need good nutrition to grow and develop normally. A healthful diet is more important during the first year of life than at any other time in the life span.

Nutritional Needs of Infants

An infant's requirements for all nutrients are higher per unit of body weight than an adult's. Unlike adults, however, an infant has no nutrient reserves. The exception is iron. A full-term baby should have enough reserve iron to last for the first six months of life. A baby needs iron reserves because he or she consumes only breast milk or infant formula during the first few months. Breast milk is not a rich source of iron. Formula may be fortified with iron, but a baby cannot absorb it well.

Infants generally receive injections of vitamin K at birth. This meets their needs for the vitamin until bacteria in their intestinal tracts develop and begin making it. Some breast-fed infants also receive a supplemental source of vitamin D. This helps prevent *rickets*, the vitamin D deficiency disease that results in malformed bones.

Besides high nutrient needs, an infant has high energy needs to support rapid growth. Growth patterns vary, but an infant's rate of growth is fastest during the first few months of life. During the first three months, a normal, healthy infant will gain about 2 pounds (910 g) a month. The growth rate then slows to about 1 pound (454 g) a month. As growth slows, an infant's energy needs per unit of body weight decrease slightly. By the end of the first year, the infant's weight has almost tripled. His or her length is one and one-half times the birth length.

Feeding Infants

Newborns usually need to be fed seven or eight times a day. Newborns are just learning to eat, and their small stomachs cannot hold much. Feedings gradually decrease to about five a day by the time the infant is two months old. Although intake varies, most infants will drink about 1 quart (1 L) of breast milk or formula each day.

Breast Milk or Formula

Nutrition experts strongly recommend that mothers breast-feed their infants. Brain development is rapid during the first years of life. Breast milk is recognized as the best food to foster brain development. Breast milk is easy for a baby to digest. It provides nutrients in ratios that are perfectly designed for babies. It contains immune substances that help a baby resist infection. Breast milk also helps protect the baby from developing allergies.

Iron-fortified infant formulas are available for mothers who are unable or choose not to breast-feed their infants. Infant formula contains less carbohydrate and fat and more protein than breast milk. Formula also contains more of many vitamins and minerals. However, babies absorb the lower amounts of nutrients in breast milk better than the nutrients in formula. In addition, too much of some nutrients, such as protein and calcium, can place stress on a baby's immature kidneys.

Cow's milk is difficult for infants to digest and may cause intestinal bleeding. Cow's milk is not a suitable food for babies under 12 months of age. After a baby's first birthday, whole cow's milk can be introduced into his or her diet. Low-fat milk is not recommended for children under 24 months of age because they need fat for normal growth and development.

Learn About...

Bedtime Bottles

Some people believe putting cereal in a baby's bedtime bottle will help him or her sleep through the night. However, study data does not support this practice. A baby's ability to sleep through the night depends on the maturity of his or her nervous system. In addition, sleeping with a bottle that contains milk, juice, or formula can lead to tooth decay. To protect a baby's developing gums and teeth, a bedtime bottle, whether at nighttime or naptime, should contain nothing more than plain water.

©*Courtesy of California Tree Fruit Agreement*

4-3 Pureed fruits are usually the third type of solid food to be introduced into a baby's diet, after cereals and pureed vegetables.

Reflect

Ask students if they have any food allergies. Ask what happens when they eat foods to which they are allergic.

Online Resource

Have students visit the Food Allergy and Anaphylaxis Network website to investigate tips for managing allergies to common foods. Ask each student to share a tip with the class.

For Example...

Use a doll and toys to demonstrate for students how to set up a safe and stimulating "tummy time" environment for babies.

Solid Foods

The introduction of solid foods into a baby's diet should be gradual. Most infants are ready to begin eating solid foods when they are between four and six months old. The first solid food in most babies' diets is a single-grain iron-fortified cereal. Rice cereal is usually recommended because it is least likely to cause an allergic reaction. Parents may introduce single pureed vegetables and fruits into their babies' diets after cereals, **4-3**. They follow these with strained meats and poultry and then food mixtures. Parents can add chopped foods from family meals to a child's diet by his or her first birthday.

Experts advise parents not to offer juice to infants less than 6 months of age. If juice is offered to older infants, it should be 100 percent juice and be limited to 6 ounces per day.

Most pediatricians tell parents to start with a small amount of just one new food at a time. Parents should feed the baby the same food several times in a row. This will help the parents identify food allergies. A true **food allergy** involves a response of the body's immune system to a food protein. Medical tests are required to verify food allergies. Allergy symptoms may include diarrhea, vomiting, skin rashes, and runny nose. A severe allergic reaction can be life threatening and requires immediate medical attention. Foods that most commonly cause allergic reactions are milk, eggs, fish, shellfish, tree nuts, peanuts, wheat, and soybeans. Many experts recommend waiting until babies are a bit older before introducing these foods.

Infants may be sensitive to certain foods without being truly allergic to them. A **food intolerance** is a negative reaction to a food substance that does not involve the immune system. Symptoms of food intolerance may resemble allergy symptoms. Whether symptoms are due to allergy or intolerance, they should end when parents stop feeding the baby the problem food. Parents may try reintroducing the food a month or two later. Sensitivities often go away as infants mature.

Fitness During Infancy

It is never too early to begin a fitness routine. Parents should begin helping their babies exercise from the day they bring them home from the hospital. Of course babies cannot jog and do sit-ups, but they can enjoy regular "tummy time." Spending time playing on their bellies helps babies develop their muscles and motor skills. It also keeps them from getting flattened skulls caused by spending too much time on their backs.

Following a few guidelines can help make tummy time safe and enjoyable for babies. Babies should only be placed on their stomachs when they are awake. It is important to place babies on their backs for sleeping to reduce the risk of Sudden Infant Death Syndrome (SIDS). Babies should never be left alone when they are on their stomachs. Placing a folded towel or blanket under their chests will help babies lift their heads. Placing toys in front of babies and on both sides will encourage them to reach and turn from side to side.

Babies will also gain from being placed in various positions for daily tasks like feeding and diapering. Carrying babies in a choice of positions and on both sides of the body will help them build different muscles. Holding babies firmly while allowing them to put weight on their feet will strengthen leg muscles they will need for walking. Following these tips throughout the day will help parents make sure their babies develop fitness.

Nutritional Needs of Preschool Children

Growth is slower between the ages of two and six years than it is during the first year of life. However, growth is still quite rapid. The diet should supply enough calories for a weight gain that fits a child's normal rate of development.

Nutrient needs vary from child to child, depending on growth and activity. However, many young children do not get enough potassium, vitamin E, and fiber in their diets. Sweet potatoes, bananas, and dried peaches and apricots are good sources of potassium. Nuts and seeds, such as peanuts, almonds, and sunflower seeds, are rich in vitamin E. Eating plenty of fruits, vegetables, and whole grains will help children meet fiber needs. See **4-4**.

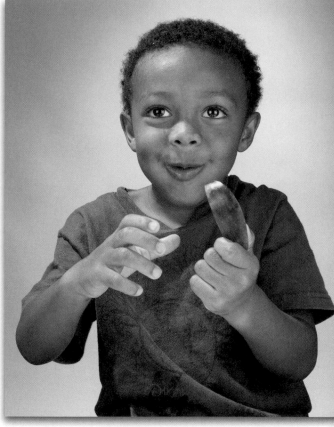

Agricultural Research Service, USDA

4-4 Fresh fruits make nutritious, high-fiber snacks for preschoolers.

Meals for Preschoolers

Preschool children can have unpredictable eating habits and are often viewed as picky eaters. Most pediatricians urge parents to be patient and continue offering healthful foods at each meal. Parents also need to set good examples by eating healthful foods themselves. Most experts agree children should not be pressured to eat. Children who do not eat at one meal will often make up for it at another. What matters most is that each day's diet includes all the needed nutrients.

When planning meals for a preschooler, follow MyPlate. Choosing finger foods will often encourage preschoolers to eat. Serve foods in a pleasant eating atmosphere. Offer younger children booster seats and smaller utensils to help them feel more comfortable.

Young children tend to like foods that are bright colored, mild flavored, soft, and lukewarm. For instance, a child may prefer orange carrots over white potatoes. He or she may enjoy a Mexican dish more if the hot peppers are left out. Soft rolls might be more appealing than crusty French bread. A bowl of soup is likely to be received better if it is just warm rather than piping hot.

Remember, young children have small stomachs and cannot eat large meals. Begin with small portions and add more as needed. Offer nutritious snacks, such as whole-grain cereal, fresh or dried fruits, and yogurt smoothies, to help meet daily needs.

Discuss

Ask students why parents should refrain from using food as a punishment or reward. *(This attitude toward food encourages children to develop inappropriate relationships with food that can lead to overeating and other problems in the future.)*

Enrich

Have the class create a coloring book preschoolers could use to learn about the foods they should eat each day. Have each student submit a simple outline of a different food item to be included in the book. Each illustration should be accompanied by a sentence explaining why that food is healthful.

Shutterstock

4-5 Caregivers need to be sure to supervise preschoolers to keep their fitness activities safe.

Fitness for Preschoolers

Just about any kind of active play can help preschoolers build fitness. The key is that the play is *active*. Children need to move and use their muscles. Running, jumping, riding a tricycle, kicking a ball, and swimming are all great activities for preschoolers. Games such as Hide and Seek and Ring Around the Rosy count as active play, too.

Knowing a few guidelines will help caregivers keep preschoolers active and safe. Limit sitting activities to 60 minutes at a time, and limit screen time to no more than 2 hours a day. Make sure young children always wear helmets when riding tricycles or bicycles. Instruct children about traffic safety and not playing too close to the street. Keep a close eye on children while they play outdoors, and always supervise children playing in a pool. Set a good example by choosing activities you can do with children, such as playing catch or going for a walk. Children who learn to enjoy being active when they are young will form fitness habits that will last a lifetime. See **4-5**.

The Elementary School Years

During the elementary school years, children grow at a fairly steady rate. Between the ages of 6 and 12, children develop many of the food habits they will follow throughout life. Parents can promote healthy attitudes about good nutrition by setting good examples. They should encourage their children to try new foods. However, parents should refrain from using food as a punishment or reward.

Nutritional Needs of School-Age Children

A 6-year-old child does not need as much food as a 12-year-old child. However, both children need the same kinds of food. The amount of food a child needs depends on his or her growth rate and physical activity. Normally, a child's appetite is a fairly reliable indication of energy needs.

School-age children should eat foods from all the food groups. They should continue to include sources of potassium, vitamin E, and fiber to be sure they are meeting daily needs. Children ages nine and over need the equivalent of a third cup of milk each day to meet increased calcium needs. Children at this age also have increased magnesium requirements. Whole grains, legumes, and nuts are all excellent sources of this mineral.

All food choices should be nutrient dense to promote growth and development. Many school-age children prefer familiar foods that are mild in flavor. As children grow older, their food tastes gradually change. They will eat larger servings and enjoy a greater variety of foods.

Community Interactions

Have the class plan an appropriate sack lunch menu for a school-age child. Have students prepare and pack the food items into paper sacks. Arrange for the lunches to be delivered to a class in a nearby elementary school. As an alternative, you might arrange a field trip for your students to deliver the lunches themselves. While your students are visiting the elementary class, have them put on a brief nutrition education program for the school-age children.

FYI

Unlike registered dietitians, pediatricians do not have the specialized nutrition training required to analyze and plan diets.

Online Resource

Have students visit the Children's Nutrition Research Center website. Ask students to view the Facts and Answers section under Consumer News and select a topic to investigate.

Planning Meals for School-Age Children

Breakfast should supply about one-fourth of the day's total nutrients for a school-age child. Children who skip breakfast do not obtain nutrients when the body needs them most—after a night without food. Studies have shown that children who eat breakfast do better in school than children who skip breakfast.

Children can eat any nutritious food for breakfast. Breakfast does not have to include traditional breakfast foods. Yogurt or a bowl of tomato soup is just as nutritious at breakfast as it is at lunch or dinner.

The basic meal patterns for a school-age child's lunch and dinner are about the same. Each meal should supply about one-third of the day's total nutritional needs. Both meals should contain foods from all the food groups.

Many school-age children have trouble eating enough at meals to meet their nutritional needs. Snacks can provide added nutrients. Most children like fresh fruit, raw vegetables, low-fat cheese and yogurt, raisins, and whole-grain crackers with peanut butter.

For Example…
Other nutritious snacks parents might provide for obese children include unsweetened whole grain cereals, such as wheat squares and toasted oat rings. Raisins and popcorn with little or no added salt and butter are healthful snacks. Snacks like fruit-flavored yogurt and graham crackers contain added sugars.

Fitness for School-Age Children

The choices of fitness activities for school-age children are almost endless. Swinging and climbing on bars and ladders at the playground will help children get their muscles moving. Playing tag or running an obstacle course in the backyard with friends gives children a chance to be active, too. School-age children enjoy swimming, jumping rope, dancing, and playing soccer. They also like using bicycles, rollerblades, and skateboards. In winter weather, sledding, ice skating, and building snow sculptures can help keep children fit. When children cannot go outdoors, they might choose interactive video games that require them to get up and move.

Caregivers of school-age children need to follow the same fitness guidelines they followed when the children were younger. Caregivers still need to limit screen time and other sitting activities. They may also need to remind children to wear helmets and other safety gear. The most important thing a caregiver can do is offer a number of activities and the encouragement to do them. This will prompt school-age children to make fitness a part of their daily lives. See **4-6**.

Health and Wellness

Childhood Overweight and Obesity

Overweight and obesity are common among children. A child is *overweight* if he or she weighs more than what is considered a healthy weight for his or her height. *Obesity* is a condition characterized by excessive deposits of body fat. Children do not have the decision-making skills to make all their own lifestyle choices. Therefore, parents have to help children manage their weight. Otherwise, children are likely to have weight problems as adults.

One of the best steps parents can take to address children's weight problems is to model healthful eating and activity habits. Parents can urge children to be more active. They can limit the time children spend watching TV and playing video games. Parents can provide healthful snacks, such as fresh fruit and vegetables. This will help children avoid high-calorie snack foods. Parents can help children learn to use hunger signals to guide eating habits. They can provide moderate portions at mealtimes and allow children to stop eating when they are full. Parents might also discourage snacking in front of the TV, when children may be too distracted to notice hunger signals. These steps will help slow children's weight gain. In time, their growth will catch up to the excess weight.

Parents should consult a registered dietitian before making major changes in a child's diet. Children need a nutritious diet to support growth. Restricting foods may result in a lack of important nutrients.

Agricultural Research Service, USDA

4-6 Using playground equipment is a fun way for school-age children to exercise their large muscles.

The Teen Years

All teens undergo a period of rapid growth called a **growth spurt**. The growth spurt varies from teen to teen. However, girls usually experience it at an earlier age than boys.

During the growth spurt, teens of both sexes need more energy. From ages 14 through 18, active teen girls need about 2,400 calories per day. Active teen boys need about 3,200 calories per day.

Many teens have busy schedules, which cause them to skip meals. Foods teens grab on the go are often low in nutrient density. Some teens limit food intake due to weight concerns. All these factors put teens, especially girls, at risk of nutrient deficiencies.

Teen diets are often low in a number of nutrients. Among these are magnesium, calcium, and potassium. Many kinds of fish and nuts are good magnesium sources. Choosing the equivalent of 3 cups daily from the milk group will help teens avoid low calcium intakes. Tomato products, baked potatoes, and cantaloupe are rich sources of potassium. Fiber and vitamin E tend to be low in teen diets, too. Eating plenty of whole grains, fruits, and vegetables will help teens meet fiber needs. Sunflower seeds, salad oils, and avocados are among the best sources of vitamin E.

Besides the nutrients mentioned above, teen girls need to be sure to get enough folate and iron in their daily diets. Orange juice, spinach, and enriched grain products provide folate. Good sources of iron include turkey dark meat and whole-grain breads.

Planning Meals for Teens

Eating a healthful breakfast will help teens have the energy they need to start the day. When needed, teens can increase portion sizes of wholesome foods at lunch and dinner to meet energy and nutrient needs.

Snacks often count for one-fourth of a teen's total daily calorie intake. Thus, nutritious snacks are especially important. Fresh fruits and vegetables, low-fat cheese and yogurt, and sandwiches make nutritious snacks. Cookies made with whole wheat flour, oatmeal, raisins, or nuts add nutrients and satisfy the desire for sweets. Reading labels will help teens make choices that are lower in sodium.

Teens should limit their intake of nondiet soft drinks, which are a major source of added sugars in the diet. Instead, teens should most often choose to drink water, fat-free milk, and juices.

Health and Wellness

Adolescent Overweight and Obesity

Rates of overweight and obesity are rising among adolescents, just as they are among children. Unlike children, however, teens have the decision-making skills needed to manage their weight. They can learn to make healthful food choices. They can include physical activity in their daily schedules. They can also learn how to handle situations that might prompt them to overeat.

Many adolescents who have weight problems continue to have weight problems as adults. To break this pattern, a teen who is overweight or obese should talk to a nutrition expert. This professional can check the teen's health and growth status. An expert can help the teen learn weight management skills and develop a healthful eating and activity plan. Such a plan would help the teen learn to choose calorie sources that are rich in nutrients. It would also encourage the teen to adopt an active lifestyle that includes at least 60 minutes of moderate activity daily. Being active is the most important step all teens can take to maintain healthy weight throughout life.

Street Surfing
Daily physical activity can help teens maintain healthy weight.

Fitness for Teens

The teen years are a good time to begin including exercise components that help build all areas of fitness. Activities like yoga and t'ai chi help improve flexibility and balance. Weight training can help build strength. Jogging and biking can increase endurance. However, the type of fitness is not as important as finding something fun. Any type of movement will provide benefits, and teens are most likely to stick with activities they enjoy.

Choosing activities they can do with friends makes fitness fun for many teens. Rock climbing, hiking, and rowing are a few of the many options that can be enjoyed with just one or two friends. For those who prefer a larger group, team sports like soccer and basketball are popular. No matter what activities teens choose, taking time to warm up before starting will help prevent injuries.

Adulthood

Energy needs begin to decrease for adults in their 20s. Adults who lead active lives require more calories than adults who lead sedentary lives. However, even active adults need to consume fewer calories than teens. During this same stage of life, nutrient needs change, with the need for several nutrients increasing.

Like teen diets, adult diets are often low in calcium, potassium, fiber, magnesium, and vitamin E. In addition, many adults need to increase their intakes of vitamin A (as

Discuss
Ask each student what his or her favorite type of fitness activity is. Ask students to identify the area of fitness targeted by each activity mentioned.

Reflect
Ask students if the adults in their homes are more or less conscious of good nutrition than the students are.

carotenoids) and vitamin C. Bright orange fruits and vegetables, such as mangoes, cantaloupe, and carrots, are rich in carotenoids. Leafy greens, like spinach and romaine lettuce, are good sources, too. Citrus fruits, along with broccoli, peppers, and tomatoes, are high in vitamin C.

Nutrient needs remain fairly constant through age 50. However, energy needs continue to gradually decrease. For adults over 50, the needs for some nutrients change again. Two nutrients that are needed in greater amounts at this age are calcium and vitamin D. Fortified dairy products are the best sources of these nutrients.

Vitamin B_{12} is also a nutrient of concern for adults over 50. Some adults in this life stage have trouble absorbing vitamin B_{12} from food sources. That is why nutrition experts advise adults in this group to meet vitamin B_{12} needs with fortified foods or supplements.

Adults over 50 need to watch their sodium intake, too. In the U.S., many people in all age groups tend to go over their daily sodium needs. Consuming too much sodium increases the risk of high blood pressure. A sodium intake that is already high becomes even more excessive for adults over 50. This is because sodium needs drop at this age. Therefore, adults in this life stage need to make a greater effort to read labels and choose foods lower in sodium.

EXPLORING CAREERS

Dietetic Technician

Dietetic technicians work in a range of settings where nutrition topics are a concern. In hospitals and weight management clinics, they might work with clients one on one. They may help assess the client's dietary needs for dealing with issues like high blood pressure and obesity. They would help teach clients about how to follow suggested eating plans and would then monitor the clients' progress. In schools and institutions, they would plan menus that meet the nutritional needs of a group of people. In food companies and restaurant chains, they might analyze recipes and test new products. In all of these settings, dietetic technicians would be likely to be working under the direction of registered dietitians.

Dietetic technicians need good speaking and listening skills. They need to be able to share information and accurately gather facts. They must give attention to details, be able to work independently, and have a concern for others.

Dietetic technicians may have two-year or four-year degrees. These workers can earn a dietetic technician, registered (DTR) credential. This gives them more credibility with employers. DTRs must pass a national exam. They must also take part in continuing education to keep up the credential.

Planning Meals for Adults

Jobs, family responsibilities, and other tasks make many demands on adults' schedules. With such busy lives, many adults do not take the time to plan nutritious meals. As a result, many adults gain unwanted weight. They may also suffer from vitamin and mineral deficiencies.

With a little planning, adults can improve their meal habits. For instance, having whole-grain breads, cereals, and fruit available can help adults eat a healthful breakfast at home. This will help them resist picking up empty-calorie foods like donuts and sweet rolls. Before going to bed, an adult can pack a sandwich and carrot sticks and put them in the refrigerator for tomorrow's lunch. The next day, the lunch will be ready to go without adding to the busy morning routine. This will make it easy to break a lunchtime habit of fast-food burgers and fries. Having some healthful foods on hand will ease dinner preparations at the end of a busy day. A jar of pasta sauce, some whole-grain pasta, and a bagged salad can quickly become a nutritious dinner.

Adults should plan their meals around MyPlate. They need to be sure to eat recommended amounts of whole grains, vegetables, and fruits. The Dietary Guidelines for Americans advise adults to maintain a calorie balance over time to get to a healthy weight and hold it. The healthiest way to cut calories is to reduce solid fats and added sugars. Choosing sorbet in place of ice cream for dessert or skim milk instead of a soft drink are examples.

Fitness for Adults

Following a daily fitness plan is another step adults can take to keep weight in a healthy range. The Dietary Guidelines for Americans advise adults to improve their health through increased physical activity. Some adults choose to join health clubs to help them stay fit. Others use a treadmill, step machine, or other piece of at-home fitness equipment. Working out with a fitness video is another option. Many adults enjoy leisure activities like golf and tennis to help them stay fit, **4-7**.

During adulthood, it becomes more important to choose a range of activities that address all types of fitness. Having a fit body can help delay or prevent some of the health issues that often occur as people age. Walking, swimming, and biking are good for endurance. Lifting weights and using resistance bands will increase strength. Exercises like leg raises that strengthen leg muscles also help improve balance. Stretching movements will build flexibility. Adults who follow a complete fitness routine will be on target for staying fit in their later years.

The Later Years

As adults age, their bodies use less energy to carry on vital processes. Therefore, calorie needs decrease for people over 70. Unlike energy needs, the needs for most nutrients do not decrease with age. Therefore, foods eaten by people in the later years must be more nutrient dense than foods eaten by younger adults.

Older adults must keep focusing on the nutrients that were concerns in the earlier adult years. They also have to boost their vitamin D intake to meet increased needs.

VISIT FLORIDA
4-7 Being physically active uses calories and helps adults avoid weight gain.

Discuss

Ask students what implications the information about osteoporosis has for their diets during the teenage years. *(Meeting calcium needs during the teen years can help prevent the development of osteoporosis later in life.)*

Online Resource

Have students visit the AARP website to research health and wellness topics of concern to older adults.

Activity

Have each student make a list of foods that must be handled carefully when being served to older adults.

Including eggs, liver, and fatty fish in the diet will provide this vitamin. Fortified cereals and dairy products are sources, too.

Remember the main role of vitamin D is to help the body use calcium to keep bones strong. A number of older people suffer from broken bones and curving of the spine due to osteoporosis. Older women are at the greatest risk of developing this disease. This is because women have less bone mass than men. Earlier in their lives, women are likely to have greater demands made on their calcium stores due to pregnancies. Hormonal changes that take place after menopause also contribute to osteoporosis.

Lack of calcium in the diet is a leading cause of osteoporosis. The need for calcium is the same for older adults as it is for adults at age 50. Older adults need to keep consuming the equivalent of 3 cups from the milk group each day. Choosing calcium-fortified foods will also help older adults meet calcium needs. High calcium intake cannot cure osteoporosis once it has developed. People must meet calcium needs all through life to prevent osteoporosis. However, meeting daily calcium needs in the later years will keep the disease from worsening.

One other nutrient that requires attention in the later years is sodium. Adults over 70 must be even more mindful of their sodium intake than they were at age 50. After age 70, daily sodium needs drop again. Processed foods provide more than three-fourths of the sodium in the average diet. Therefore, reading labels on processed foods is the best way to manage sodium intake. Limiting the use of salt in cooking and at the table will help control sodium intake, too.

Planning Meals for Older Adults

Like people in other age groups, older adults should use MyPlate to plan their meals. Whole grains, vegetables, and fruits should make up the bulk of their diets, **4-8**. Older adults also need to eat suggested amounts of fat-free or low-fat dairy foods. They must also meet their daily needs from meat, fish, beans, and other protein foods. These will help older adults maintain muscle mass and strength.

A MyPlate meal plan will provide most of the nutrients that are low in the diets of many older adults. Even with healthful diets, however, some people over age 70 need supplements to meet their needs for vitamins B_{12} and D.

Meals for older adults should consist of well-liked foods. Food likes and dislikes are hard to change. Older people who need encouragement to eat are more likely to eat favorite foods.

Taste buds decrease in number as people age. This can make some foods seem bland and unappealing. Older adults can use more herbs and spices to wake up the flavors of tasteless foods.

Tooth loss and gum disease become problems for some older adults. These problems can make certain foods more difficult to chew. Older adults may need to cut foods into smaller pieces and choose more soft-textured foods to address oral health issues.

Agricultural Research Service, USDA

4-8 Choosing nutritious foods, like fresh fruits and vegetables, is an important factor in maintaining good health during the later years in life.

Foodborne illnesses pose a greater risk to older adults than to younger adults. Therefore, taking steps to handle, cook, and store food safely is vital when preparing meals for older adults.

Fitness for Older Adults

Many adults remain quite active in their later years. However, people over 70 often begin to have problems with weak muscles and sore joints. In many cases, these discomforts cause older adults to become less active.

Sadly, some older adults do not know that staying active can help lessen many aches and pains. Keeping fit can also help reduce risks of heart disease, some cancers, and diabetes. Weight-bearing exercise can limit the normal loss of bone mass that can lead to osteoporosis. Activity can ease symptoms of depression, too. These benefits of physical activity can help older adults live on their own for many years.

Older people do not need special programs or equipment to stay fit. They can use many routine activities and household items to help them maintain the four types of fitness. Walking, climbing stairs, and gardening help build endurance. Common items like canned goods or bottled water can serve as weights to increase muscle strength. Standing on one foot and walking heel to toe will help improve balance, which is needed to prevent falls. Stretching movements, such as reaching with the arms and pointing the toes, increase flexibility. Many exercises can be done while seated. This allows even adults with limited mobility to receive the benefits of fitness. See **4-9**.

Fitness programs for older adults do not require medical supervision. However, people who are starting new routines may want to talk to a doctor first. Doctors can suggest suitable activities for people who have health concerns. Pain, dizziness, and shortness of breath may be signs of problems. Older adults who have any of these symptoms while exercising should see their doctors before continuing their fitness routines.

Special Diets

Some people choose to follow special diets. Other people follow special diets on their doctor's advice. A registered dietitian can be a resource to help make sure a special diet meets a person's nutritional needs.

Learn About...

Easing Meal Preparation

During meal preparation, older people who have limited mobility can save physical energy in many ways. They can use convenience products to save preparation steps. They can sit while preparing some foods. Older adults can store frequently used tools and basic food items on shelves within easy reach. They can install single-handled faucets, which are easy to use with one hand. They can slide heavy objects rather than lifting them. If peeling and chopping vegetables is difficult, older people can substitute precut frozen or canned vegetables for fresh. They can make some foods ahead of time to reduce preparation tasks at mealtime. When meal preparation can be made easier, older adults may be more willing to take the time to make nutritious foods.

Activity
Have students list tips older people can use to save physical energy while cooking.

VISIT FLORIDA
4-9 Walking and other daily activities can help older adults stay fit and maintain their independence.

Vegetarian Diets

A **vegetarian diet** is a diet built partly or entirely on plant foods. The types of foods included in vegetarian diets vary. For instance, *lacto-ovo vegetarians* include dairy products and eggs in their diets. *Vegans* eat no animal foods of any kind.

People choose to follow vegetarian diets for a number of reasons. These include religious beliefs, environmental concerns, and animal rights issues. Some people choose vegetarian diets for health reasons.

You might think omitting animal foods such as meat, poultry, and fish from the diet would cause a protein deficiency. However, legumes, nuts, and grains are all good sources of protein. By choosing a variety of these plant foods every day, vegetarians can easily meet their protein needs. The types of amino acids lacking in one food will be provided by another. Lacto-ovo vegetarians can also use dairy foods and eggs to increase the protein value of plant foods. Macaroni and cheese is an example of a dish that combines dairy and wheat.

A number of nutrients other than protein are concerns for vegetarians, especially vegans. Shortages of vitamins D and B_{12}, calcium, iron, and zinc are common. Some sources of these nutrients vegetarians might choose are shown in **4-10**.

Nutrient deficiencies pose greater risks for certain groups of people. Failure to meet nutrient needs can stunt the growth of infants, children, and teens. Nutrient deficiencies can affect the health of pregnant and lactating women and their babies. Vegetarians in these groups are advised to consult with a registered dietitian. The dietitian can determine whether nutrient needs are being met. He or she can also recommend nutrient supplements when needed.

Meeting Vegetarian Nutrient Concerns	
Nutrient	**Sources**
Vitamin B$_{12}$	Fortified cereals and soy milk
Vitamin D	Exposure to sunlight, fortified margarine and milk
Calcium	Fortified cereals, orange juice, and soy milk; leafy green vegetables; legumes; tofu
Iron	Leafy green vegetables, legumes, tofu, whole grains (Eat sources of vitamin C, such as citrus fruits, strawberries, tomatoes, and peppers, with iron sources to improve iron absorption.)
Zinc	Dairy products, eggs, legumes, nuts, tofu, whole grains

4-10 Vegetarians must plan their diets with care to avoid deficiencies of these vitamins and minerals.

Nutrition and Health Care

The term *therapeutic diet* has been loosely applied to any eating plan used to treat physical, mental, or emotional health. Yet a true **therapeutic diet** is an eating plan prescribed by a physician. Such eating plans may be ordered for patients in hospitals and nursing homes. Doctors often consult with dietitians when ordering therapeutic diets to make sure patients' nutritional needs are met. The foods for a therapeutic diet are prepared by workers in a diet kitchen. Patients may have little choice about the foods that are served. Therefore, counseling a patient about eating habits is not part of a therapeutic diet.

Therapeutic diets are not the only way food is used to help treat medical conditions. People with certain health problems often need **medical nutrition therapy (MNT)**. This is a health care strategy that helps people learn to use their eating habits as part of their treatment. For instance, MNT is used to treat people who have **diabetes mellitus**. This is a body's lack of or inability to use the hormone insulin to maintain normal blood glucose levels. Other health problems for which MNT is used include heart disease, cancer, allergies, and HIV/AIDS. See **4-11**.

Medical Nutrition Therapy

Medical Condition	Description	Recommended Nutrition Therapy*
Cancer	Uncontrolled cell multiplication, which interferes with normal functioning of body organs	To cope with nausea and vomiting resulting from cancer treatment and medications • Sip cool, clear liquids to prevent dehydration • Choose bland foods that are easy to digest, such as gelatin, crackers, and dry toast • Avoid strong food odors and greasy and spicy foods
Celiac disease	An intestinal disorder caused by a reaction to proteins in certain grains, which can cause symptoms including gas, diarrhea, and fatigue	Read all food labels carefully to completely avoid gluten, which may be in such ingredients as • Wheat, rye, barley, and triticale • Emulsifiers, stabilizers, and thickeners • Flour, food starch, and hydrolyzed vegetable protein
Diabetes mellitus	Lack of or inability to use the hormone insulin, which results in irregular blood glucose levels and can lead to damage of body tissues	Eat a variety of foods at regularly scheduled meals Monitor carbohydrate intake, focusing on grain-, fruit-, and milk-group sources Limit fat intake and choose adequate sources of fiber Maintain healthy body weight
Food allergy	A response of the body's immune system to a food protein, which can cause symptoms such as hives and breathing difficulties	Read all food labels carefully to completely avoid the allergy-causing food or ingredient If an allergic reaction occurs, seek immediate treatment, such as use of medication, an injection, and/or emergency room care
Gastroesophageal reflux disease (GERD)	Recurrent heartburn caused by stomach acid flowing up into the esophagus	Eat small, frequent meals and avoid overeating Drink liquids between meals rather than with meals Avoid spicy and greasy foods Avoid lying down for at least one hour after eating
Heart disease	General term for a variety of diseases affecting the heart muscle and surrounding tissue	Moderate total fat intake Limit sources of saturated fats, such as heavily marbled meats and full-fat dairy products Choose sources of monounsaturated fats more often, such as olive oil and fish
High blood cholesterol	Above average amount of cholesterol in the bloodstream, which is a risk factor for heart disease	Limit foods containing partially hydrogenated oils, such as margarine, snack foods, and commercially fried foods, to avoid sources of *trans* fats Choose sources of fiber, such as fruits, vegetables, and whole grains
HIV/AIDS	A disorder that causes the body's immune system to shut down and is often accompanied by a loss of appetite leading to wasting	When feeling well enough to eat, eat small, frequent meals and choose high-protein, high-calorie foods, such as cheese, eggs, nuts, and liquid meal replacements Limit liquids with meals to keep from feeling full Strictly follow food safety practices
Hypertension	High blood pressure, which is a risk factor for heart disease	Limit sources of sodium, such as processed foods, salty snacks, and table salt Choose sources of potassium, calcium, and magnesium Moderate fat intake and choose adequate sources of fiber
Lactose intolerance	Inability to produce the enzyme lactase, which is needed to digest the sugar in milk, results in symptoms such as gas, cramps, and bloating after consuming milk products	Choose cheese and cultured dairy products, such as yogurt Eat small amounts of dairy products with other foods Choose lactose-reduced dairy products

* This is a partial list of recommended nutrition therapies and is not intended to replace specific advice of a physician or registered dietitian.

4-11 Many patients can help control their medical conditions through diet as well as medication.

Academic Connections

Correlate information on medical diets with the health department. Focus on nutritional needs during illness and how to meet them.

MNT is provided by a registered dietitian. The dietitian begins by assessing how a client's health condition is affecting his or her body and nutritional needs. The dietitian can then recommend an eating plan that will help the client meet those special needs. The eating plan will take the client's food likes and dislikes into consideration. The dietitian will counsel the client about how to form new eating habits to make following the plan part of his or her lifestyle. This will make it easier for the client to successfully stick with the plan. The dietitian will continue to meet with the client as needed to track his or her progress in following the plan. The dietitian will also evaluate whether any changes to the plan are needed.

Health and Wellness

Nutrition During Illness

Even people who do not have ongoing health problems get sick from time to time. Knowing how minor illnesses can affect your appetite and nutrient needs can help you handle common ailments.

Drinking liquids is a recommended treatment for many everyday health problems. Warm liquids soothe a sore throat. Chilled liquids help cool a fever. Water helps flush bacteria out of your urinary tract to ease the discomfort of an infection. Liquids replace fluids lost through diarrhea and through perspiration caused by fever. They help keep sinus and nasal secretions flowing. This provides relief when you have the flu, a cold, or a sinus infection.

A number of common digestive disorders are related to food habits. Choose sources of sodium and potassium when diarrhea becomes a problem. Also avoid greasy, fried, spicy, and high-fiber foods. On the other hand, you should eat more fiber if you are trying to relieve and prevent constipation.

Nausea, vomiting, and fatigue brought on by illness can often take away your appetite. If a sore throat makes swallowing hard, you may not feel like eating either. However, your body needs nutrients to help the healing process. If you do not feel like eating, try drinking a nutritious beverage instead. Sometimes juice or a healthful smoothie made with fruit and yogurt goes down easier than solid food.

Food and Drug Interactions

Some drugs can affect the way the body uses nutrients from foods. Similarly, some foods can affect the way drugs are absorbed and used in the body. Such reactions between foods and drugs are called **food-drug interactions**.

Anytime you must take prescription or over-the-counter drugs, be sure to read labels carefully. Follow all directions about consuming foods and beverages. Unless your doctor or pharmacist tells you otherwise, take all drugs with water. Water helps most drugs dissolve quickly, and it does not hamper absorption. If you must take drugs for an extended period, you may want to consult a registered dietitian. He or she can assess how to best deal with any nutritional problems the drugs might cause.

Food Assistance Programs

Limited income makes it hard for some people to buy nourishing foods. In the United States, help is available to people at all stages of the life span through various federal food assistance programs. Most of these programs are run by the Food and Nutrition Service, which is an agency of the USDA. Nutrition education is a key part of these programs. The programs are intended to help people learn to make healthful food choices as well as giving them access to nutritious foods.

Federal food assistance funds are provided to agencies in each state. These agencies manage the programs at the state and local levels. They set standards for who is able to receive program benefits. These agencies then provide benefits to those who meet the standards.

In the earliest stages of the life span, food assistance is provided through *Women, Infants, and Children (WIC)*. This program helps women who are pregnant or who have recently had babies. It also assists infants during the first year of life and children up to the age of 5. WIC enables participants to receive foods that will meet the specific needs of people in these life stages. WIC foods include fruits, vegetables, milk, eggs, baby food, and formula.

School-age children and teens can receive food assistance through several programs. The *National School Lunch Program (NSLP)* supplies nutritious lunches for little or no cost through public and some private schools. The *School Breakfast Program (SBP)* provides breakfast for qualified children and teens. Schools that do not participate in NSLP or SBP may offer milk to children and teens through the *Special Milk Program*. During the summer months, free nutritious meals and snacks may be provided through the *Summer Food Service Program (SFSP)*. This program may operate at sites such as camps and community centers as well as schools.

Low-income households can receive help to buy food through the *Supplemental Nutrition Assistance Program (SNAP)*. (This program used to be known as the Food Stamp Program.) Participants in this program receive a plastic card that works much like a bank debit card. Each month, money is made available in the participant's SNAP account. The amount of money is based on the participant's income and household size. Participants can then use the card to make food purchases at authorized food retailers, such as most grocery, drug, and discount stores.

Older adults can receive food assistance through the *Elderly Nutrition Program*. This program is run by the Administration on Aging, which is a division of the U.S. Department of Health and Human Services (HHS). It provides funds for adults who are homebound to have nutritious meals delivered to their homes. It also provides for meals to be served in places such as senior centers, schools, and churches. These meals are called *congregate meals*, and they give older people a chance to socialize as they eat. Nutrition education and health screenings may also be offered as part of this program.

Not all food assistance is provided by the government. Many charities also offer aid to people in need. For instance, *Meals on Wheels* is a charity that delivers nutritious meals to homebound older adults. *Feeding America* is an organization that has a network of large food banks. These banks distribute food to smaller agencies that pass out food to needy people at the community level, **4-12**. Many local organizations also run food pantries, soup kitchens, and shelters that provide food. All these government and private programs share a common goal of ending hunger in the United States.

Charlie Westerman

4-12 These teen volunteers are working at a Feeding America member site to pack food boxes for distribution to hungry people in their community.

CAREER SUCCESS

Problem-Solving Skills

Carmelita is the head cook in the Hayward Heights High School cafeteria. She supervises a staff of seven workers. Each day, they prepare and serve lunch to over 1,500 students during three lunch periods. The staff gets ingredients for the lunch menus from a central warehouse. However, the weekly delivery is often short of some items.

To be an effective worker, Carmelita needs problem-solving skills. In a small group, answer the following questions about Carmelita's need for and use of these skills:

A. What is a specific problem Carmelita has to solve in her position as school cafeteria head cook?

B. How might the other cafeteria workers be affected if Carmelita lacked problem-solving skills?

C. How might the students at Hayward Heights be affected if Carmelita lacked problem-solving skills?

D. What is another skill Carmelita would need in this job? Briefly explain why this skill would be important.

CHAPTER 4 REVIEW

Summary

Good nutrition is important at all stages of the life span. During pregnancy, a woman must eat a range of foods to supply her developing baby with the nutrients it needs. For the first few months after birth, infants obtain needed nutrients from breast milk or formula. Most parents slowly begin introducing solid foods into their infants' diets when the infants are about four to six months old. Preschoolers and school-age children need help to choose foods that will meet their needs. As children become teens, they need more nutrients and calories to support their rapid growth. Adults must select foods carefully to get needed nutrients without getting too many calories. Older adults must make an even greater effort to choose nutrient-dense foods to meet nutrient needs as calorie needs continue to decrease. Throughout life, MyPlate can help people choose foods to meet their nutrient needs.

Fitness goes hand-in-hand with nutrition to help people stay in good health at all stages of the life span. Activities that help build endurance, flexibility, strength, and balance make up a complete fitness program. Activity choices may vary from one life stage to another. However, the key factor is getting some form of energetic movement on a daily basis. Being aware of signs of stress and injury will help keep activity safe.

People at any life stage may have special dietary needs. Vegetarians must choose plant foods with care to meet their nutrient needs. People with certain health problems may need to follow specific nutrition advice from a doctor or dietitian. People with limited income can choose to access a range of food assistance programs to help meet their nutritional needs.

Review What You Have Read

Write your answers on a separate sheet of paper, using complete sentences when appropriate.

1. What can happen if the calcium needs of a fetus are not provided by the foods eaten by the mother?

2. What are three types of activities that are not good choices for a fitness program during pregnancy?

3. Why should lactating mothers avoid drinking alcohol, smoking cigarettes, and taking medications?

4. True or false. Babies absorb the nutrients in breast milk better than the nutrients in formula.

5. What is the difference between a food allergy and a food intolerance?

6. What types of food choices often encourage preschoolers to eat?

7. How can school-age children who have trouble eating large meals meet their nutritional needs?

Answer Key for *Review What You Have Read* **questions**

1. If the mother's diet does not meet the calcium needs of the fetus, the needed calcium is taken from the mother's bone tissue.

2. (List three:) contact sports, activities that involve bouncing, activities that involve twisting at the waist, activities that involve a high risk of falling

3. Alcohol, nicotine, and other drugs can pass to a baby through breast milk.

4. true

5. A food allergy involves a response of the body's immune system to a food protein. A food intolerance is a negative reaction to a food substance that does not involve the immune system.

6. Finger foods, especially those that are bright colored, mild flavored, soft, and lukewarm, will often encourage preschoolers to eat.

(continued)

7. School-age children who have trouble eating large meals can meet their nutritional needs by eating nutritious snacks.

8. (List 10:) swinging, climbing on playground bars and ladders, playing tag, running an obstacle course, swimming,

jumping rope, dancing, playing soccer, bicycling, rollerblading, building snow sculptures, playing interactive video games (Students may justify other responses.)

9. A nutrition expert can check an overweight or obese teen's health and growth status. An expert can help the teen learn weight management skills and develop a healthful eating and activity plan.

10. Two nutrients that are needed in greater

amounts for adults over age 50 are calcium and vitamin D.

11. Vitamin D is needed to help the body use calcium to keep bones strong and prevent osteoporosis, which affects a number of older adults.

(continued)

8. List 10 fitness activities that are appropriate for school-age children.

9. How can a nutrition expert help a teen who is overweight or obese?

10. What two nutrients are needed in greater amounts for adults over age 50?

11. Why is vitamin D important in the diets of older adults?

12. Why is it especially important to handle, cook, and store food safely when preparing meals for older adults?

13. True or false. Lacto-ovo vegetarians include dairy products and eggs in their diets.

14. Explain what liquid should generally be used to take medications.

15. What food assistance programs are available to help school-age children and teens?

Link to Academic Skills

16. **English language arts.** Visit the government's food safety website at foodsafety.gov. Look for advice directed toward pregnant women. Use this information along with food safety guidelines to write a food safety brochure for pregnant women.

17. **Social studies.** As you study nutrient needs and fitness through the life span, identify major events, goals, and concerns of people at each life stage. Create a table summarizing this information. Discuss in class how meeting nutrient needs and staying fit can help people achieve goals and face concerns in other areas of their lives.

18. **Science.** Prepare two batches of vegetarian bean soup. Soak the beans before preparing one batch of soup. Prepare the other batch of soup without soaking the beans. Compare the two batches for taste, texture, and appearance. Investigate the reason for soaking beans before cooking.

19. **English language arts.** Choose one health condition that requires medical nutrition therapy. Find out as much as you can about that therapy and give an oral report to the class. Prepare at least one visual aid to help illustrate your report.

20. **Social studies.** Visit the Feeding America website. Investigate stories and statistics about hunger in the United States. Share a fact or anecdote with the class.

Build Critical Thinking Skills

21. **Synthesis.** Interview a group of three to five school-age children about their interests. Combine their input to come up with an activity that would encourage these children to be more physically active. For instance, their ideas might lead you to make up an active game based on a favorite cartoon character. If possible, have the children try your activity. Discuss the children's reactions in class.

22. **Evaluation.** Write a survey to assess factors that decrease the nutritional quality of teen diets. These factors include busy schedules, skipped meals, reducing diets, and low nutrient density foods. Distribute the survey to at least 10 of your classmates. Use the results to determine the key factor that should be addressed in a nutrition campaign for a teen audience.

Apply Technology

23. Research the effectiveness of new products containing antioxidant vitamins that are being developed to counter some effects of aging. Summarize your findings in a written report.

24. Investigate the features available on two blood glucose monitors used to help manage diabetes mellitus. Present your comparison in a brief oral report to the class, explaining which monitor you would recommend to a diabetic.

A Measure of Math

25. Conduct research to compare the nutrient needs of pregnancy with the nutrient needs of lactation. Identify which nutrients are needed in greater amounts during lactation.

Teamwork in Action

26. Review the text section on nutrition during illness. Read more about this topic from a website that provides medical information for consumers. Work with your classmates to summarize your findings into a chart format. Add illustrations and color to make your chart visually appealing. Be sure to site the source of your information. Also add a disclaimer reminding others that information in the chart is not intended to replace the advice of medical professionals. Then copy your chart and distribute it through the school nurse's office as a medicine cabinet reference guide.

Companion Website

www.g-wlearning.com

At the website, review key terms for this chapter with crossword puzzles, matching exercises, and e-flash cards. Apply facts from the chapter to complete the activities.

12. Handling, cooking, and storing food safely helps prevent foodborne illnesses, which pose a greater risk to older adults than to younger adults.

13. true

14. Unless otherwise directed by a doctor or pharmacist, medications should be taken with water to help the drugs dissolve quickly and avoid interfering with their absorption.

15. School-age children and teens can receive food assistance through the National School Lunch Program (NSLP), the School Breakfast Program (SBP), the Special Milk Program, and the Summer Food Service Program (SFSP).

CHAPTER 5

Staying Active and Managing Weight

Main Menu

- Making physical activity part of daily life helps manage weight and provides other health benefits.
- Managing body weight requires a lifestyle that balances the energy gained from food with the energy used through activity.

Learning Prep

Suggest definitions for each of the *Terms to Know*. Then look up the terms in the glossary to check the accuracy of your suggested definitions.

Objectives

After studying this chapter, you will be able to

- **identify** factors that affect your energy needs.
- **associate** physical activity with overall fitness.
- **examine** factors that contribute to weight problems and eating disorders.
- **explain** the philosophy behind weight management.

Terms to Know

basal metabolism
aerobic activity
dehydration
weight management
body composition
body mass index (BMI)
healthy weight
overweight

underweight
obesity
waist circumference
eating disorder
anorexia nervosa
bulimia nervosa
binge eating disorder

Weight problems and lack of physical activity have been pinpointed as major health concerns in the United States today. These concerns are also becoming more common among children and teens.

Current health issues are the basis for the Dietary Guidelines for Americans. The Guidelines urge people to maintain body weight in a healthy range. They also advise taking part in regular physical activity. These Guidelines show that eating a healthful diet requires more than choosing foods to meet your nutrient needs. It also involves choosing the right amounts of foods to meet, but not exceed, your body's need for fuel. In addition to what you eat, the Dietary Guidelines focus on how you use the food you consume. Following the Guidelines will help you avoid health problems and enjoy a greater state of wellness.

Energy Needs

What do you know about your body's energy needs? *Energy*, in one sense, is the power to do work. The human body needs energy to move. It needs energy to produce heat and carry on internal processes. During certain periods of life, the body also needs energy for growth and repair. The body produces energy by *oxidizing* (using oxygen to burn up) the foods you eat.

Basal Metabolism

Basal metabolism is the amount of energy the human body needs to stay alive and carry on vital processes. It can be measured as the amount of heat the body gives off when at physical, digestive, and emotional rest.

Basal metabolism depends on a number of factors. One factor is body size. A person who is overweight will have a higher *basal metabolic rate (BMR)* than someone of the same age who weighs less. However, two people who are the same weight and age may have different BMRs. This is because their body shapes differ. A person who is tall has more body surface area than a person who is short. Therefore, the person who is tall has a higher BMR per unit of weight.

The kinds of tissues that make up the body also affect basal metabolism. Men usually have a larger amount of lean muscle tissue than women. This causes them to require more energy per unit of body weight than women, **5-1**.

Age can affect basal metabolism. Children and adolescents have a higher basal metabolism than adults. This is because basal metabolism is greater during periods of rapid growth. After about age 20, basal metabolism gradually declines.

A person's general health can affect basal metabolism. The basal metabolism of a well-nourished person is higher than that of a malnourished person. An increase in body temperature also increases basal metabolism. For this reason, the basal metabolism of a person with a fever is higher than that of a person with a normal body temperature.

Gland secretions can affect basal metabolism. The thyroid gland affects metabolism more than any other gland. Undersecretion of the thyroid gland may lower basal metabolism. Oversecretion can raise it. Adrenaline, which the adrenal glands secrete during times of stress, also increases metabolism.

Vocabulary Builder

Have students look up the term *basal* in a dictionary. Ask them how the definition of this term relates to the concept of basal metabolism.

Enrich

Have each student make a chart or poster illustrating factors that increase basal metabolism.

Meeting Special Needs

Remind students that physical activity is just as important for people with physical disabilities as for people without disabilities. Have students use the Internet to explore the variety of exercise equipment available to meet the needs of this population group. Equipment they might find includes universal design weight machines, exercise videos, and flotation devices for aqua therapy.

VISIT FLORIDA

5-1 Men generally have a larger percentage of lean body mass than women, which causes them to have a higher basal metabolism.

Physical Activity

When you engage in any physical activity, your energy needs become greater than your basal metabolism. Different activities require different amounts of energy. For instance, it takes more energy to wash dishes than it takes to read a book. It takes still more energy to rake leaves or swim.

Several factors can influence the amount of energy a person needs to perform a physical task. The intensity with which you perform a task can affect energy needs. A person who walks briskly, for example, needs more energy than a person who walks slowly. Body size can affect energy needs. This means a 220-pound (100-kg) student requires more energy to ride a bicycle than a 120-pound (55-kg) student. The temperature of the environment also can affect energy needs. It takes more energy to wash windows when the temperature is 90°F (32°C) than when the temperature is 70°F (21°C).

Meeting Energy Needs with Food

Each food you eat has a particular energy value. Most people refer to the units used to measure the energy value of foods as *calories*.

The three nutrients that provide the body with energy are carbohydrates, fats, and proteins. Carbohydrates and proteins provide the body with 4 calories per gram. Fats provide the body with 9 calories per gram.

Because few of the foods you eat are pure carbohydrates, pure proteins, or pure fats, foods vary widely in their energy values. Foods that are high in fat and low in water have a high energy value. This means a small amount of these foods will provide a lot of energy. Some examples of high energy value foods are nuts, mayonnaise, cheese, and some meats. Foods that are high in water and fiber and low in fat have a low energy value. A serving of these foods provides only small amounts of energy. Most fresh fruits and vegetables have a low energy value. Lean meats, grain foods, and starchy vegetables have an intermediate energy value.

When the energy (calories) you obtain from food equals the energy you expend, your body weight remains the same. When the energy you obtain from food is less than the energy you expend, your body weight decreases. When the energy you obtain from food is greater than the energy you expend, your body weight increases. It takes about 3,500 calories to make up 1 pound (0.45 kg) of body weight.

Physical Activity and Fitness

Besides affecting your energy needs, physical activity can affect your health throughout life. Physical activity contributes to your overall fitness. Physical activity has other benefits, too. It speeds metabolism and helps you burn calories so you can reach or maintain a healthy weight. It tones your muscles, builds strong bones, and keeps your skin healthy. It reduces your risk of heart disease, high blood pressure, diabetes, and some forms of cancer. It helps you feel better about yourself. Physical activity can provide a fun social outlet, too.

Discuss

Ask students to give examples of high, low, and intermediate energy value foods other than those listed on the page.

Enrich

Ask each student to survey three teens in the school about which of the benefits of physical activity he or she finds most worthwhile. Have students compile their findings. Then have the class prepare a campaign using the most popular benefit to inspire their classmates to be more physically active.

Food Science

Energy Value of Foods

Food scientists measure the energy value of foods in *kilocalories*. This is the more accurate name for the units most people call calories. One kilocalorie equals the amount of heat needed to raise one kilogram of water one degree Celsius.

The total energy value of a food depends on that food's chemical composition. Placing a food sample inside a device called a *bomb calorimeter* is one way to determine the food's energy value. The food is placed in a special chamber surrounded by water and ignited. As the food burns, it releases energy as heat. The energy value of the food can then be determined by measuring the temperature change of the water.

Shutterstock

Burning a food sample in a calorimeter allows food scientists to measure the energy value of the food.

Amount of Activity

The normal movements of day-to-day living cannot give you all these health benefits. The Dietary Guidelines refer to *moderate-intensity activity*. Such activity is above the light activity of daily life. It equals the intensity of walking a mile in 15 to 20 minutes. To reduce disease risk, the Guidelines suggest adults get at least 150 minutes of moderate activity most days of the week. For additional and more extensive health benefits, the Guidelines advise adults to raise this amount to 300 minutes a week of moderate-intensity physical activity. Adults need to keep on being active as they age. Older adults who are physically active are less likely to have problems with broken bones and weak muscles.

Physical activity is not just for adults. The Dietary Guidelines recommend children and teens get 60 minutes or more of moderate activity daily. When you are moving at a moderately active level, you should still be able to talk. However, you should not have enough breath to be able to sing. Use this method to help you decide if you need to increase or decrease the pace of your activity.

Health and Wellness

Fitting Activity into Your Day

Maybe you feel like you cannot spare 60 minutes a day for physical activity. If so, look at how you currently use your time. How much time do you spend each day watching television or sitting in front of a computer? How much time do you spend talking to friends on the phone? Consider using some of this inactive time to be more active. Instead of watching television to relax, skate or take a bike ride to unwind after a busy day. Rather than looking up information on the computer, try walking to your local library to do research. Invite friends to join you for a game of tennis or basketball in place of talking to them on the phone.

What if you are already meeting the daily 60-minute activity goal? You could benefit even more by increasing your activity level. You might spend more time being moderately active. You could also try doing more vigorous activities, such as swimming and jogging.

You do not have to set aside a block of time to be physically active. If you prefer, you can accumulate your activity throughout the day. Just be sure to be active for at least 10 minutes at a time. For instance, you might ride your bicycle to and from school, pedaling 15 minutes in each direction. Before dinner, you could spend 20 minutes shooting baskets. Then in the evening, you might walk your dog for 10 minutes. By the end of the day, you would have accumulated 60 minutes of activity.

Types of Activity

Notice that physical activity does not require special classes or equipment. Everyday tasks such as gardening and climbing stairs also count as physical activity.

Remember that flexibility, strength, balance, and endurance are all part of fitness. Try to choose activities that target each of these areas. Stretching movements improve flexibility. Lifting weights or heavy objects, such as groceries, infants, and laundry baskets, can help you build strength. Exercises that strengthen your lower body will also improve your balance. **Aerobic activities**, which speed your heart rate and breathing, promote endurance. Jogging, cycling, and skating are good aerobic activities.

Make sure some of your activity choices are *weight-bearing exercises*. These are exercises done in an upright position with your weight on your feet. Such exercises strengthen the bones in your legs and hips to help prevent osteoporosis. Examples include walking, jogging, and climbing stairs.

You can use the decision-making process to help you choose which types of activity to include in your fitness plan. Think about your alternatives. Some of your options may be limited by the equipment and facilities you have available. Consider how your alternatives relate to your fitness goals. Determine which alternatives are acceptable and then choose the ones you will include in your fitness routine. Do not forget to evaluate your decision. You can always adjust your routine if you are not happy with it.

Keep community resources in mind when looking into your activity choices. Many schools, churches, and community centers offer activities such as basketball and volleyball in their gyms. Local recreation departments may set up sports leagues for people in various age groups. A lot of public parks have playground equipment for children. Some also have swimming pools and multiuse trails for walking and bicycling. These facilities provide a range of fitness options and often cost little or nothing to use. See **5-2**.

Getting Started

Including more moderate physical activity in their lifestyles should not create health concerns for most people. However, someone who is starting a new program of vigorous exercise may wish to consult with a doctor first. Consulting a doctor is especially recommended for men over 40, women over 50, and anyone with chronic health problems.

If you have been fairly inactive, you need to begin increasing your activity level slowly. Trying to do too much too soon increases the risk of injury. Setting your initial activity goals too high can also cause you to become discouraged. If you are unable to attain the goals, you are more likely to give up. Starting with a goal to jog 30 minutes every day may be too ambitious. Instead, you might begin with a goal to walk 10 minutes a day three days a week. When you reach your initial goal, you can set a new goal that is more challenging.

Making physical activity a regular part of your day is more important than the types of activities you choose. Vary your activities so you do not become bored. Choose activities that are fun and convenient for you to do. Try making physical activity a social outlet by doing it with family members and friends. If you can make physical activity part of your lifestyle, you will enjoy the benefits of fitness for a lifetime.

Agricultural Research Service, USDA

5-2 Multiuse trails in public parks are a great free fitness resource for people who enjoy walking, jogging, and bicycling.

Health and Wellness

Excessive Exercise

Getting daily physical activity is an important part of taking care of your body. However, getting too much exercise can be harmful to your health. Too much exercise can damage bones and joints. If intense exercise continues, these injuries will not have a chance to heal properly. Long-term problems could result. Too much exercise can also affect hormone balance in females, causing changes in their menstrual cycles. Excessive exercise causes the body to break down muscle tissue for energy. It can cause weakness and fatigue. It can lead to feelings of depression and low self-image. Overdoing exercise can even strain the heart.

The amount of exercise that is healthful varies from person to person. For instance, most athletes will spend more time working out than most nonathletes. However, the following signs can indicate that someone is overdoing it and may need professional help:

- Feeling guilty or anxious about failing to exercise
- Working out when sick or injured or against the advice of health professionals
- Skipping other activities in order to exercise
- Having undue concern with weight loss, appearance, or physical performance
- Combining frequent, intense exercise with unhealthful eating habits

Nutrition for Athletes

Being moderately active each day does not create special dietary needs. Most people can meet their daily nutrient needs by following MyPlate. However, intense physical activity can increase the need for some nutrients. Nutrition also plays a key role in athletic performance. Athletes should be aware of a few specific dietary concerns.

Meeting Fluid Needs

The nutrient that is most likely to affect sports performance is water. Athletes lose much water through sweat when they are training and competing. If an athlete does not replace these fluids, dehydration can set in quickly. **Dehydration** is an abnormal loss of body fluids. It can cause headache, dizziness, confusion, and a drop in overall performance. Severe dehydration can even result in death.

To prevent dehydration, athletes should begin drinking fluids before an event. They need to continue drinking ½ to 1 cup (125 to 250 mL) of fluids at 15-minute intervals throughout the event. Athletes need to drink more fluids after a competition or workout has ended.

Meeting Nutrient Needs

Athletes have some other special nutrient needs besides water. Their high level of activity increases the need for calories. Most of these calories, 55 to 60 percent, should come from complex carbohydrates. Whole-grain breads, cereals, pasta, and rice and starchy vegetables are all excellent sources of complex carbohydrates. Choosing lean meats, poultry, and fish will supply an athlete's slightly increased need for protein. Low-fat and fat-free dairy products provide needed calcium. Fresh fruits and vegetables furnish vitamins, minerals, and fiber, **5-3**.

Rubbermaid

5-3 Fruit makes a healthful snack after practice or a game, providing athletes with needed vitamins, minerals, and fiber.

Learn About...

Sports Drinks

Some athletes choose sports drinks to replace their fluid losses. Sports drinks contain carbohydrates to help athletes replace some of the fuel they are burning through activity. Many sports drinks also contain sodium to replace sodium lost through sweat. This sodium also helps increase fluid absorption. For people who engage in lengthy workouts of 90 minutes or more, sports drinks can be a good choice.

Fluid replacement is equally important for those who take part in less strenuous activities. However, plain water does a fine job of meeting their fluid needs. A normal diet can easily replace sodium and replenish carbohydrates. Although sports drinks offer no special benefits for moderately active people, the taste may encourage them to drink more. This alone makes the choice of a sports beverage worthwhile.

If this diet sounds familiar, it's not a coincidence. Like less active people, athletes can meet their nutrient needs by following MyPlate. Athletes should avoid nutrient supplements unless they are being taken on the advice of a dietitian. These costly supplements are not always what they claim to be. Tests have shown some products to be ineffective or even harmful. Adverse effects from these products have included fatigue, upset stomach, joint pain, and irregular heart beat.

Planning a Pregame Meal

Trainers once thought athletes needed protein for energy. Although athletes do need protein, they need it for growth and repair of muscle tissue—not for energy. Lean meats can easily fit into an athlete's diet at other meals. For a pregame meal, however, pasta and rice make better choices. These grain foods are packed with complex carbohydrates—an athlete's main energy source. Another reason to choose grain foods before a competitive event is that they are low in fat. Fat stays in the stomach longer than carbohydrates. Avoiding fat before a game keeps energy needed to compete from being used for digestion.

The best time to eat a pregame meal is 2½ to 3 hours before a sports event. An athlete should choose moderate portions so he or she will not feel too full during competition. The athlete should avoid unfamiliar foods, which could cause an upset stomach. He or she should also limit high-fiber foods, such as fruits, vegetables, and whole grains. Although athletes need fiber, they would not want bulk from fiber in their digestive systems while competing. This could make them feel sluggish.

Meeting Weight Goals

Achieving an optimal performance weight is a critical nutrition issue for many athletes. To compete in lower weight classes, some wrestlers use laxatives to speed food through their digestive systems. They also force themselves to vomit and avoid drinking fluids. To avoid weight gain, some gymnasts skip meals to restrict their calorie intakes. To increase body mass, some football players go on eating sprees. They consume large quantities of high-calorie, low-nutrient foods. To meet weight goals, some athletes in all sports fields have engaged in such unwise and often dangerous practices. These practices can harm health as well as sports performance.

Athletes who want to lose weight need to do so gradually and well before the start of their sports season. They should not try to lose weight while they are training and competing. They should never restrict fluids, force vomiting, or use laxatives, either.

Athletes should not skip meals or restrict calories. The body needs a steady supply of nutrients throughout the day. It needs energy to fuel activity. Teen athletes also need calories to support normal development. Failing to get enough nutrients and calories can stunt growth and make the athlete too weak to compete.

Athletes who want to gain weight need to add moderate amounts of extra calories to their diets from nutrient-rich sources. They also need to follow a steady program of muscle-building exercise. This will ensure that weight gained is due to lean body mass rather than fat.

All athletes wishing to reach weight goals should seek the advice of a registered dietitian. Many coaches lack sufficient training in sports nutrition to provide guidance about healthful weight loss, maintenance, and gain.

Discuss

Ask students what conditions affect losses of body fluids during physical activity. Ask why it is important for people to stay hydrated during physical activity. Discuss health consequences of dehydration.

Enrich

Invite an exercise physiologist to speak to your class about precompetition meals, sports drinks, and nutrient supplements for athletes.

Enrich

Have the class analyze the nutrients provided by at least three types of energy or power bars and two sports drinks marketed to athletes. Ask the class to use their findings to write a recommendation for athletes about the use of these products before, during, and after sports practices and competitions.

Discuss

Ask students why athletes should never restrict fluids. *(Insufficient fluid intake will result in dehydration, which can have serious effects on physical health.)*

EXPLORING CAREERS

Athletic Trainer

Athletic trainers work on sports teams and in other settings to help athletes avoid injuries. When injuries do occur, athletic trainers may consult with doctors to provide treatment. They then work with the athletes to help restore health and peak function to the injured areas. They also keep coaches updated on the status of injured team members.

These health professionals must have a thorough knowledge of the body. When assessing injuries, they need good listening skills. These skills will allow them to ask the right questions and accurately determine the source and extent of the damage. Their critical thinking skills help them choose the best therapies for each injury. They must be active learners so they can adopt new health information as it becomes available.

They also need skills in speaking and instructing to help athletes understand how to care for, strengthen, and protect their injured bodies.

A key personal quality for athletic trainers is a concern for others. They need leadership skills so they can take charge and offer direction in critical situations. They need to be able to work cooperatively with coaches, physicians, and athletes. They must be flexible—willing to try new therapies or adjust treatments that are not proving to be effective. These trainers also need persistence to keep treating injuries that take a long time to heal.

Athletic trainers must have at least a bachelor's degree. Most earn master's degrees. They must pass an exam to become certified athletic trainers and earn the ATC (Athletic Trainer, Certified) credential. They must meet set qualifications and have a license in the state where they practice. Athletic trainers must also take part in continuing education to keep their skills and knowledge current.

Career Path

Have students compare the job description, qualifications, and training requirements for a personal trainer and an athletic trainer.

Weight Management

Of course, athletes are not the only ones who have weight goals. The Dietary Guidelines for Americans suggest everyone should have a goal to maintain body weight in a healthy range, **5-4**.

People come in all shapes and sizes. Heredity largely determines bone size and shape. However, maintaining a healthy weight depends mostly on lifestyle. **Weight management** means using resources like food choices and physical activity to reach and/or maintain a healthy weight. Weight management is not a short-term program you follow until you lose a few pounds. It becomes part of your way of life.

Determining Healthy Weight

To maintain a healthy weight, you need to be concerned with more than just the numbers on a scale. You need to know the source of your weight.

Body weight includes the weight of bone, muscle, fat, and other tissues. People have different **body compositions**, or proportions of these types of tissues that make up their body weights. Muscle and bone tissue weigh more than fat tissue. These factors explain why two people may be the same height but have different weights. The person with greater muscle mass and heavier bones will have the

Shutterstock

5-4 Healthy weight is a weight at which your body fat and lean tissue are in an appropriate proportion. It is not a particular number on a scale.

Body Mass Index																							
Weight in Pounds																							
	90	95	100	105	110	115	120	125	130	135	140	145	150	155	160	165	170	175	180	185	190	195	200	205
4'11"	18	19	20	21	22	23	24	25	26	27	28	29	30	31	32	33	34	35	36	37	38	39	41	42
5'0"	18	19	20	21	22	23	23	24	25	26	27	28	29	30	31	32	33	34	35	336	37	38	39	40
5'1"	17	18	19	20	21	22	23	24	25	26	26	27	28	29	30	31	32	33	34	35	36	37	38	39
5'2"	17	17	18	19	20	21	22	23	24	25	26	27	28	28	29	30	31	32	33	34	35	36	37	37
5'3"	16	17	18	19	20	20	21	22	23	24	25	26	27	28	28	29	30	31	32	33	34	35	36	36
5'4"	15	16	17	18	19	20	21	22	22	23	24	25	26	27	28	28	29	30	31	32	33	34	34	35
5'5"	15	16	17	18	18	19	20	21	22	22	23	24	25	26	27	28	28	29	30	31	32	33	33	34
5'6"	15	15	16	17	18	19	19	20	21	22	23	24	24	25	26	27	28	28	29	30	31	32	32	33
5'7"	14	15	16	17	17	18	19	20	20	21	22	23	24	24	25	26	27	28	28	29	30	31	31	32
5'8"	14	14	15	16	17	18	18	19	20	21	21	22	23	24	24	25	26	27	27	28	29	30	31	31
5'9"	13	14	15	16	16	17	18	19	19	20	21	22	22	23	24	24	25	26	27	27	28	29	30	30
5'10"	13	14	14	15	16	17	17	18	19	19	20	21	22	22	23	24	24	25	26	27	27	28	29	30
5'11"	13	13	14	15	15	16	17	18	18	19	20	20	21	22	22	23	24	25	25	26	26	27	28	29
6'0"	12	13	14	14	15	16	16	17	18	18	19	20	20	21	22	22	23	24	25	25	26	26	27	28
6'1"	12	13	13	14	15	15	16	17	17	18	19	19	20	21	21	22	23	23	24	25	25	26	26	27
6'2"	12	12	13	14	14	15	15	16	17	17	18	19	19	20	21	21	22	23	23	24	24	25	26	26

Height (label along the left side of the table)

5-5 Body mass index, a calculation based on body weight and height, is used to evaluate how healthy a person's weight is.

higher weight. However, what concerns health experts most is the amount of weight attributed to fat tissue.

Vocabulary Builders

Have students compare the terms *overweight* and *obesity*.

Body Mass Index

Many health professionals assess a person's weight based on his or her **body mass index (BMI)**. This is a calculation involving a person's weight and height measurements. According to federal guidelines, **healthy weight** for adults is defined as a BMI of 18.5 to 24.9. **Overweight** is defined as a BMI of 25 to 29.9. An adult who has a BMI of 30 or more is obese. Someone with a BMI under 18.5 is considered **underweight**.

These BMI cutoffs cannot be used for children and adolescents because their bodies are still growing. Suggested BMI values for evaluating overweight in these younger age groups vary according to age. Table **5-5** can help you find your BMI. Table **5-6** can help you determine whether you are underweight or at risk of being overweight.

The use of BMI in assessing weight has limitations because it does not take body composition into account. For example, consider

Adolescent Risk for Weight Problems				
Gender	Age	BMI at Risk of Underweight	BMI at Risk of Overweight	BMI at Risk of Obesity
Female	14	15	23	27
	15	16	24	28
	16	16	24	28
	17	17	25	29
	18	17	25	30
Male	14	16	22	26
	15	16	23	26
	16	17	24	27
	17	17	24	28
	18	18	25	28

5-6 The body mass indexes that identify potential weight problems for an adolescent vary according to age and gender.

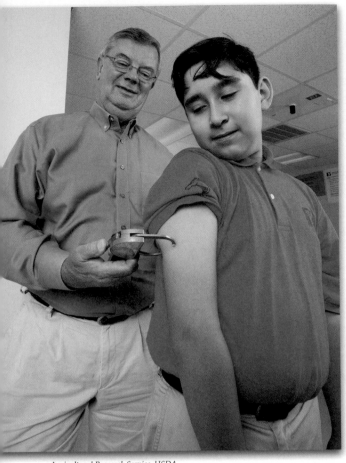

5-7 Measuring a fold of skin at the back of the upper arm indicates whether excess body weight is due to fat or muscle.

Activity

Make a photocopy of Figure 5-6 for each student. Have students use four colors of highlighters or colored pencils to shade the table into segments representing underweight, healthy weight, overweight, and obese.

Enrich

Invite a trained technician to your class to take students' skinfold measures.

a football player who has a large proportion of muscle tissue compared to fat. Because muscle weighs more than fat, the player may have a seemingly high weight. His BMI might be in the overweight range. Because his weight is due to muscle, however, it is not a health concern. Therefore, rather than being defined strictly by BMI, **obesity** is a condition characterized by excessive deposits of body fat.

One way to assess whether a high BMI is due to excess fat is to measure **waist circumference**. This is the distance around the natural waistline. For a man with a BMI of 25 or more, a waist circumference of over 40 inches indicates an increased health risk. For a woman with a BMI in this range, such a risk is indicated by a waist measurement of 35 or more inches.

Skinfold Test

A *skinfold test* can help evaluate body composition. This is a measure of a fold of skin using an instrument called a *caliper*. The back of the upper arm, below the shoulder blade, and around the abdomen are common measuring spots. About half the body's fat is located under the skin. Therefore, a skinfold test gives an indication of total body fat. See **5-7**.

An inexact variation of a skinfold test you can do yourself is the *pinch test*. Simply grasp a fold of skin at the back of your upper arm between your thumb and forefinger. A fold that measures more than an inch (2.5 cm) thick is often a sign of excess fat.

Hazards of Being Obese

Obesity is a major health issue in the United States. High blood pressure, diabetes mellitus, heart disease, some types of cancer, and other diseases are more common among people who are obese. Studies show people who are obese die at earlier ages than people who are not obese. Some insurance companies view people who are obese as "high risk" and charge them higher rates.

Too much weight puts a strain on the body's bones, muscles, and organs. A thick layer of fat interferes with the body's natural cooling system. People who are overweight use more effort to walk and breathe.

People who are obese also face social pressures. The fashion industry focuses little attention on designs for larger sizes. Television and magazines promote the image that being attractive means being thin. Some employers hesitate to hire people who are obese for certain jobs.

Factors That Contribute to Overeating

People can be overweight for several reasons. Some people inherit a tendency to be overweight. Some people are overweight because of medical problems. However, most people are overweight because they eat more calories than they need for basal metabolism and physical activity.

Many people overeat simply because they do not pay attention to how much they are consuming. They fail to notice their bodies' *satiety* (fullness) *signals*. They eat because food is readily available, not because they are hungry.

A number of factors can distract people from listening to their body signals. One factor is social settings. When snacking with friends or enjoying a family gathering, people are more focused on others than on food.

Food marketing can interfere with satiety signals. Media ads constantly promote foods. Food stores, eateries, and vending machines make food easy to get almost everywhere. This endless exposure to food and food images often spurs people's desire to eat, even when they are not truly hungry.

Emotions can keep people from noticing their satiety signals. Some people use food as a reward when they are happy. Others use food as a source of comfort when they are angry, frustrated, sad, or bored.

Habits override satiety signals for many people. For instance, some people are in the habit of having a bedtime snack. These people may reach for food in the evening without stopping to discern if they are actually hungry.

Deciding to Lose Weight

As an adult, you will need to continue to aim for a healthy weight. If your BMI and a skinfold test ever indicate you have excess body fat, you can take steps to lose weight.

To successfully lose weight, you must want to lose weight. You should base a desire to lose weight on more than wanting to fit into a new outfit. Efforts to lose weight are most successful when they are part of a lifelong commitment to maintain good health.

FYI

The following portion distortion information was gathered by the National Heart, Lung, and Blood Institute. This list shows common food portions 20 years ago compared with common portions today. Numbers in parentheses show the added calories provided by today's larger portions.

- Bagel—3 in., 6 in. (210)
- French fries—2.4 oz., 6.9 oz. (400)
- Soda, bottle—6.5 oz., 20 oz. (165)
- Muffin—1.5 oz., 4 oz. (290)
- Popcorn—5 c., 11 c. (360)

Learn About...

Portion Distortion

Portion distortion is another factor that gets in the way of satiety signals. *Portion distortion* is a mistaken belief about the appropriate amount of food to eat at one time. This problem has arisen because many foods come in portions that are much larger than recommended servings. Many people do not know these portions are oversized. They think these are the typical amounts of food they should eat. For instance, most people would assume that half a bagel is one serving from the grains group. A number of years ago, this was true. At that time, however, a typical bagel was 3 inches in diameter. Today, the typical bagel half is 6 inches across. It equals two servings and provides more than twice the calories of the bagels of the past. Being aware of what recommended serving sizes look like will help you avoid becoming a victim of portion distortion.

©2011 Wisconsin Milk Marketing Board, Inc.

The portion of pasta on this plate actually equals about four recommended servings. Large portions like this cause many people to form distorted views about what amounts of food are appropriate to eat at one time.

Reflect

Ask students what
their eating habits are.
Ask which of these
habits might contribute
to excess calories in
their diets and how
they might go about
changing these habits.

Activity

Have each student
keep a food log for one
week.

Discuss

Ask students to name
high-fat foods that can
quickly add calories to
the diet.

Once you have decided to lose weight, you might want to see a registered dietitian. A dietitian can help you design a weight management plan suited to your individual needs. The dietitian might also recommend a vitamin-mineral supplement.

Most successful weight-loss plans involve three main components: changing poor eating habits, controlling energy intake, and increasing physical activity.

Identifying Eating Habits

One of the first steps in losing weight is to keep a *food log*. This is a list of all the foods and beverages you consume. You should also note where you ate, who you were with, and how you felt when eating. Keep this list for at least a week. Studying it will help you discover some of your eating habits. For instance, you may find you often snack in front of the television. You may also learn you eat when feeling sad, frustrated, or nervous. See **5-8**.

Once you identify some of your eating habits, you can take steps to change them. If you idly snack while watching television, try keeping your hands busy with an activity instead of with food. If you eat when nervous, try taking a brisk walk when you feel full of nervous energy. If you eat when feeling lonely, call a friend when the urge to nibble strikes.

Controlling Energy Intake

Weight management involves being aware of the energy value of the foods you eat. The amount of energy the body receives from food is measured in calories. The body needs the energy obtained from the foods you eat to function. However, if you eat more calories than your body uses, you will gain weight.

The number of calories your body needs each day to maintain your present weight is called your *daily calorie need*. This need must provide enough calories to support your basal metabolism. You need additional calories to give you energy for activities.

		Food Log			
What did I eat?	How much did I eat?	When did I eat?	Where did I eat?	Who was with me?	How did I feel?
Breakfast		7:30 a.m.	kitchen	Christopher	tired
banana	1 medium				
corn flakes	1 1/2 cups				
fat-free milk	1/2 cup				
orange juice	3/4 cup				
Lunch		12:10 p.m.	cafeteria	Tanisha	excited
cheeseburger	1			Pilar	
fries	about 15				
lowfat milk	1 cup				
Snack		3:30 p.m.	living room	no one	bored
cookies	2		(watching TV)		

5-8 Keeping track of what, when, where, and with whom you eat can help you identify patterns in your eating behavior.

Your daily calorie need depends on your age, sex, body size, and level of activity. Pound for pound, children and teens need more calories than adults to support growth. Men usually need more calories than women. This is partly because men generally have a higher percentage of muscle tissue than women. Muscle tissue requires more calories to maintain than fat tissue. A large person needs more calories each day than a small person. One reason for this is a larger skin surface area allows more heat to be lost from the body. An active person needs more calories to fuel motion than an inactive person.

One of the easiest ways to determine your daily calorie need is to visit the ChooseMyPlate.gov website. The Daily Food Plan tool allows you to enter your age, sex, weight, height, and activity level. The tool will then calculate your calorie needs. (It will also recommend daily intakes from each of the food groups.)

To lose weight, you must consume fewer calories than your daily calorie need. You will want to remember 1 pound (0.45 kg) of fat equals about 3,500 calories. To lose 1 pound (0.45 kg) a week, you would need to increase the difference between your energy intake and expenditure by 3,500 calories. This is roughly 500 calories a day. You should make this adjustment through a combination of reduced calories and increased physical activity.

Losing a pound (0.45 kg) a week may not bring you to your goal weight as soon as you had hoped. However, losing weight too quickly can strain your body systems. You may deprive yourself of needed nutrients if you eat too little food. You will also be more successful in maintaining your weight goal if you lose weight slowly. Most experts recommend a steady weight loss at the rate of ½ to 1 pound (0.23 to 0.45 kg) per week. After all, you did not gain your excess weight in a week. Therefore, you should not expect to lose it in a week.

Food labels and recipes can help you keep track of the calories you eat. Packaged food products and many recipes list the number of calories per serving. Be aware of the stated serving size. Many people cannot understand why they do not lose weight when they are following a weight management plan. Often the problem is they misjudge portion sizes. When you begin following your weight-loss plan, you may find it helpful to measure portions. Soon you will become familiar with what a cup (250-mL), half-cup (125-mL), or tablespoon (15-mL) portion looks like.

You should also be aware of the amount of fat in the foods you eat. Health experts recommend that fat make up 20 to 35 percent of your total daily calories. For an active teenage boy, that would be about 70 to 123 grams of fat per day. An active teen girl should consume about 53 to 92 grams of fat daily. Food labels and recipes can help you keep track of your fat intake. A gram of fat contains more than twice as many calories as a gram of carbohydrate or protein. Therefore, calories can add up quickly when you are eating high-fat foods.

Increasing Physical Activity

Watching your food intake is only part of a weight management plan. You also need to get plenty of physical activity. As you read earlier, regular activity speeds up metabolism, promotes good muscle tone, and burns calories. See **5-9**. You can burn half of your 3,500-calorie weekly reduction goal with just 30 to 60 minutes of activity each day.

Check with your doctor to be sure there are no restrictions to the type of activity you might pursue. Then choose an activity you enjoy. You may want to participate in a sport. Perhaps you would prefer to join an aerobics class. The kind of activity is not as important as its regularity.

Along with planned activity, try to build extra movement into your daily routine. Take the stairs instead of riding the elevator. Play ball with a friend instead of watching TV.

Tips for Success

If you have a goal to lose weight, your weight management plan should meet several criteria. It should include as many of your favorite foods as possible and provide a variety of choices. It should also be nutritious and fit into your food budget.

Do not avoid all your favorite high-calorie foods when you are working to lose weight. If you feel as if you are being deprived, you may give up on your weight management plan. Simply learn to enjoy your favorites less often and in smaller portions. Go out for pizza once a week instead of twice a week. Try settling for 5 French fries instead of 10.

Avoid fad diets that focus on just a few foods or omit certain groups of foods. These plans lack variety and are not nutritionally balanced. You are likely to become bored with these diets and stop following them. If you do stick with them, you may be missing important nutrients. In addition, these diets do not help you form good eating habits. Therefore, when you go off these diets, you are likely to regain the weight you lost.

A weight-loss plan should follow MyPlate. Search the home page of Choose**MyPlate**.gov for links to *Weight Loss* or *Steps to a Healthier Weight* for health

Trek Bicycle Corporation

5-9 Following a program of regular physical activity is an important part of maintaining healthy weight and overall fitness.

Discuss

Ask students why a weight management plan should meet the criteria on this page. *(People are more likely to stick with an affordable eating plan that includes a variety of nutritious foods they enjoy.)*

Learn About...

Weight-Loss Aids

Radio, television, and magazine ads for weight-loss aids are widespread. These aids include special pieces of exercise equipment that promise to slim your waist and firm your thighs. They extend to pills promoted to make pounds melt away without any changes in your current exercise or eating patterns. They also include diet fads that claim you will lose weight if you simply eat enough of one kind of food and avoid eating another.

The age-old advice to consumers is certainly valid here: If something sounds too good to be true, it probably is. The problem with most diet aids and fad diets is they cannot live up to their claims on a long-term basis. They do not help people develop new lifestyle behaviors. Therefore, as soon as people stop using these products, they go back to their old eating and activity patterns. This causes them to regain the weight.

Another factor consumers must think about when considering weight-loss aids is cost. Prices of weight-loss aids vary, but some can be quite costly. Consumers must decide if the cost is worthwhile for products that may bring disappointment.

A few approved prescription drugs are designed to help people lose weight. Like all drugs, weight-loss medications have some side effects and cannot be used by all people. Those who take these drugs will find they still need to monitor their food intake and activity levels. With or without drugs, the only way to lose weight is to consume fewer calories than you burn.

tips and wholesome food plans that lead to weight loss. In many cases, MyPlate will recommend more physical activity. When you follow MyPlate's recommendations and reach your weight goal, maintain an active lifestyle. This will ensure you get needed nutrients while burning more calories than you eat. See **5-10**.

National Chicken Council/U.S. Poultry & Egg Association

5-10 Fresh vegetables and grilled chicken make this salad nutrient dense. It is a meal option that easily fits into a weight-loss plan based on MyPlate.

Health and Wellness

Weight Management and Social Events

Do not allow your weight management plan to cause you to miss social events. Skipping holiday meals or trips to the ice cream shop may help you resist the temptation to eat high-calorie foods. However, you may also start to resent your weight management plan and give up completely.

When a special occasion arises, feel free to attend. However, avoid going on an empty stomach so you will be less tempted to overeat. Eat a healthy snack before you go to a dinner party. At the party, eat moderate portions of the foods that are served, just as you would at any other meal. When party foods focus on appetizers, snacks, and desserts, choose just a few items to sample instead of eating everything offered.

You do not have to avoid eating in restaurants as long as you make sensible food choices. When ordering, choose fruit or vegetable juice for an appetizer. Ask to have salad dressings, gravies, and sauces served on the side. Avoid fried menu items and ask to have vegetables served unbuttered. Select fresh fruit for dessert. Put half of your food in a takeout box before you begin eating.

©2011 Wisconsin Milk Marketing Board, Inc.

Do not skip getting together with friends when you are trying to lose weight. Just remember to eat moderate portions

Reflect

Ask students if they are more likely to take stairs or an elevator when they have an option. Ask them to think about the reasons for their choices.

Discuss

Ask students to give examples of foods in each group of MyPlate that are low in fat and added sugars.

Discuss

Ask students why it is important to view weight management as a lifestyle rather than as a short-term program. *(Unless a person makes choosing nutritious foods and getting regular activity permanent lifestyle habits, he or she is likely to regain any weight that was lost.)*

When working to reduce weight, try using a smaller plate to make portions look larger. Eat slowly and chew food thoroughly to extend the length of the meal. Use herbs and spices to add variety to foods.

Avoid weighing yourself more than once a week. Your goal is a gradual weight loss. Checking your weight too often may cause you to feel discouraged.

When you are trying to lose weight, the first few pounds may come off rather quickly. (This initial loss is usually due to water loss.) However, weight loss is seldom steady. Plateaus during which you may seem to make little or no progress are normal. Do not be discouraged—be patient!

When working toward a lower weight goal, you should not skip any meal. In fact, you may want to eat extra meals. Eating six small meals each day rather than three large meals will increase your metabolic rate. It will also reduce your chances of overeating.

You are not a failure if you splurge on a pint of ice cream before bedtime. Everyone makes unwise choices now and then. Turn your mistake into a learning experience. Continuing to keep the food log you used to identify your eating habits can help you avoid repeating your mistake. Think about what might have caused you to overeat. Then try to avoid that situation in the future.

Reward yourself when you reach intermediate goals in your weight management plan. Set realistic intermediate goals that present a challenge. Choose nonfood rewards that are meaningful to you. For instance, if you meet your physical activity goal for the week, you might reward yourself with a trip to the movies. If you avoid unplanned snacking, you might reward yourself with a small purchase.

Maintaining Healthy Weight

Once you have reached your goal weight, do not give up your weight management plan. Remember, weight management is part of your lifestyle. Keeping up this lifestyle will help you enjoy food in a whole new way.

To maintain your weight, you can begin eating at, rather than below, your daily calorie need. Use MyPlate to choose food group amounts that match your activity level. Remember to select foods that are nutrient dense. Keep the Dietary Guidelines for Americans in mind to help you make healthful choices.

Keeping active is a key to maintaining healthy weight. The Dietary Guidelines advise at least 60 to 90 minutes of moderate to vigorous activity per day to help sustain weight loss.

Keep in mind that you have alternatives when it comes to food choices, eating habits, and fitness activities. Use the decision-making process to help you choose the options that best relate to your goal of maintaining a healthy weight. Do not forget to evaluate your choices. Make adjustments as needed to manage your weight throughout life.

Underweight

Body weight can be just as much of a problem for people who weigh too little as for people who weigh too much. People who are chronically underweight often suffer from more infections. They may tire easily. Some people who are underweight feel cold even when the temperature is moderate. Wearing swimsuits and other figure-revealing clothes may embarrass them.

Underweight may be due to a couple of main causes. A tendency to be underweight can be hereditary. Not eating enough food to meet the body's needs can cause a person to be underweight. Health problems may prevent the body from properly using and storing food energy to maintain healthy weight. A response to a stressful environment can also result in underweight.

Following a Weight-Gain Plan

Before trying to gain weight, a person who is underweight should see a physician. The physician will investigate if there are any medical reasons the person's body is not using the food it receives. If emotional problems are causing the weight problems, a physician may be able to recommend a therapist.

The goal of a weight-gain plan should not be a rapid weight gain. Rapid gains usually are the result of increased fat deposits. Instead, people trying to gain weight need to build up muscle tissue. To do this, they need to carefully follow a two-fold plan. First, they need to regularly take part in muscle-building activities, such as weight lifting. This will ensure that weight gain is not due just to added body fat, which would be unhealthful. Second, people who are underweight need to consume more calories than their bodies need. They should add 700 to 1,000 calories to their daily diets. This will provide enough energy to fuel the added activity plus allow for a gradual weight gain.

People who are underweight should continue to follow MyPlate. They can choose larger daily amounts from each food group. They can add modest amounts of fats and sweeteners, such as butter and sugar, to some foods. People who are underweight can boost calories by eating small meals every few hours. Nutritious snacks are a good way to add calories, too. Fats should still make up no more than 35 percent of total calories.

People who are underweight may have trouble eating large quantities of food. Therefore, they need to consume calories in more concentrated forms. They can choose nutritious, calorie-dense foods from each food group. For instance, dried fruit, cheese, and nuts are concentrated sources of calories, **5-11**. Other ways to add nutrients and calories without adding bulk include stirring nonfat dry milk into soups, casseroles, and cooked cereals. Choosing starchy vegetables, such as peas, potatoes, and corn will add more calories per serving than nonstarchy vegetables.

While eating more of some foods, a person who is trying to gain weight should limit other foods. Drinking beverages with meals and eating high-fiber foods, such as salads, will cause a person to feel full quickly.

A person who is underweight may do better to consume liquids between meals. Choosing calorie-dense beverages may be a way of increasing energy intake that is easier to swallow than eating solid foods. Some people use nutrient-loaded drinks in place of meals to lose weight. People trying to gain weight can use these drinks in addition to meals. Delicious shakes made with fruit and yogurt can be used in the same way.

©2011 Wisconsin Milk Marketing Board, Inc.

5-11 Calorie-dense snacks like cheeses, nuts, and dried fruits provide nutrients as well as concentrated energy for people who are trying to gain weight.

Vocabulary Builder

Have students compare the terms *anorexia nervosa* and *bulimia nervosa*.

Activity

Have students use online sources to identify local resources that can help people in your community with eating disorders.

Online Resource

Have students visit the National Eating Disorders Association website. Ask them to put together a sheet identifying the types of information available at this site to help family members and friends of people with eating disorders. The sheet should also include a list of links to other online resources.

Following a weight-gain plan can be just as challenging as following a weight-loss plan. With continued physical activity and careful food choices, weight will gradually increase. Once a weight goal has been reached, a person who is underweight can begin eating at his or her daily calorie need. Making good nutrition and physical activity an ongoing weight management program will help maintain healthy weight.

Eating Disorders

An **eating disorder** is abnormal eating behavior that risks physical and mental health. Eating disorders can lead to malnutrition, organ damage, or even death.

Doctors do not know what causes eating disorders. However, some type of personal stress often triggers them. The disorders become sources of more stress. They tend to progress until the victims feel unable to handle their problems.

Eating disorders most often affect young women and teenage girls. However, people of both genders and other age groups can also form eating disorders.

Common Eating Disorders

Anorexia nervosa is an eating disorder characterized by self-starvation. The term *nervosa* indicates the disorder has psychological roots. A person with anorexia has an intense fear of weight gain. He or she also has a distorted body image. This person may look like skin and bones, yet he or she may complain of being fat. An anorexic does not realize he or she has an eating disorder.

Starvation causes some body processes to slow down or stop. Blood pressure drops and respiration slows. Hormone secretions become abnormal. This causes anorexic women to stop menstruating. The body cannot absorb nutrients properly. Body temperature drops and sensitivity to cold increases. The heart cannot function correctly. In some cases, it may stop entirely, resulting in death.

Bulimia nervosa is an eating disorder that has two key characteristics. The first is repeated eating *binges*. These are episodes during which the bulimic consumes thousands of calories in a short period. The second is an inappropriate behavior to prevent weight gain. For some bulimics, this behavior takes the form of *purging*. This means trying to quickly rid the body of the food. Some bulimics purge by forcing themselves to vomit. Others take laxatives or diuretics to speed food and fluids through their bodies. Bulimics who do not purge may fast or exercise excessively to avoid weight gain. The cycle of bingeing and purging or other countering behavior is repeated at least twice a week. This pattern continues for at least three months.

Bulimics feel a lack of control over their eating behavior. This gives them a sense of guilt and shame. Unlike anorexics, however, they know their behavior is abnormal.

Frequent purging upsets the body's chemical balance. This can cause fatigue and heart abnormalities. Repeated vomiting can harm the teeth, gums, esophagus, and stomach.

Like bulimia nervosa, **binge eating disorder** involves repeated episodes of uncontrolled eating. Binge eaters consume large amounts of food. However, they do not take part in an opposing behavior to prevent weight gain. Therefore, most binge eaters are overweight.

Binge eaters often feel physical discomfort from eating large amounts of food. They may develop health problems linked to obesity, such as diabetes and high blood pressure. They may also feel shame about a lack of self-control. See **5-12**.

Treatment for Eating Disorders

Early treatment of eating disorders improves the chance of recovery with no severe health problems. These disorders require professional care. Treatment centers first on physical effects of the disorder. A person may need to be hospitalized to treat symptoms of malnutrition or other damage to the body.

Signs of Eating Disorders
Abnormal weight loss
Binge eating
Self-induced vomiting
Abuse of laxatives and/or diuretics
Excessive exercise
Absent or irregular menstrual periods in females
Depression

5-12 You should suspect a person has an eating disorder when one or more of these signs are present. Early detection leads to a better chance of recovery.

Learn About...

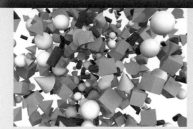

Helping Someone with an Eating Disorder

An eating disorder affects family members and friends as well as the person with the disorder. These people may feel they are somehow to blame for the disorder. They may feel helpless because they think they are unable to assist in the recovery process. Their lives may be disrupted as they seek treatment from numerous sources.

Family members and friends can help form a strong support system for someone with an eating disorder. However, they must first realize there is no value in placing blame. They must also accept that their lives are likely to be forever changed because of this illness. With this understanding, family members and friends can play key roles in the treatment of a loved one's eating disorder.

If you think you know someone who has an eating disorder, you should confront the person with your concerns. Speak to the person privately. Be honest as you express care and support. Describe the behaviors that have caused your concern. Use your knowledge of nutrition and eating disorders to counter any excuses the person may offer. Suggest that the person see a professional about these behaviors. Do not threaten or accuse the person, and avoid making promises you cannot keep. If the person seems unwilling to seek help, you should talk to a trusted adult about the situation. A parent, teacher, doctor, or counselor should be able to offer advice. Remember, the sooner someone with an eating disorder gets help, the better his or her chances of recovery are.

Shutterstock

Family members are an important part of the personal support system needed by someone recovering from an eating disorder.

Discuss

Ask students why psychological counseling is a part of the treatment for eating disorders. *(Eating disorders generally have psychological roots. If these issues are not addressed, disordered eating patterns are likely to continue.)*

Once a person's physical health has been addressed, he or she must begin psychological counseling. Counselors often urge family members to take part in therapy. Family members can learn to address issues that may have triggered the eating disorder. They can also learn to offer support as the disordered eater works to change his or her behavior. Group therapy may be used to provide peer support to people with eating disorders.

Other specialists are often part of the treatment team for someone with an eating disorder. A registered dietitian can help the person learn how to make nutritious food choices. A fitness counselor can aid in setting up a sound program of physical activity. Working as a team, health professionals can help someone with an eating disorder form a healthful relationship with food.

CAREER SUCCESS

Working with People from Diverse Backgrounds

Aja is an attendant at The New You weight management clinic. She is responsible for recording clients' weights and body measurements. She shows clients how to use the exercise equipment selected for their personalized fitness programs. She also gives clients a menu planning pamphlet prepared by a registered dietitian. Then she suggests ways clients can continue to enjoy their favorite foods while following the guidelines in the pamphlet.

To be an effective worker, Aja needs skill in working well with people from culturally diverse backgrounds. In a small group, answer the following questions about Aja's need for and use of this skill:

A. Why would Aja need to consider the cultural backgrounds of her clients?

B. How could Aja's skill in working with people from diverse cultures affect her clients' success in achieving weight management goals?

C. How would Aja's skill in working with people from diverse cultures affect business at The New You?

D. What is another skill Aja would need in this job? Briefly explain why this skill would be important.

CHAPTER 5 REVIEW

Summary

Your energy needs are based on your basal metabolism and your activity level. The energy value of the foods you eat depends on the amount of carbohydrate, fat, and protein in the food. The way the energy provided by the foods you eat compared with your energy needs affects your body weight.

The energy you use for physical activity plays a vital role in your body's state of fitness. You need to be active every day. Finding a variety of activities you enjoy will help you stay active so you can reap a lifetime of benefits.

Weight management involves balancing the energy you consume from food against the energy you expend through activity. It is a lifestyle that will help you maintain a healthy weight throughout life. Body mass index and a skinfold test can help determine whether your weight is healthy. Being overweight or obese may lead to a number of health problems. People overeat for many reasons. Deciding to lose weight and identifying eating habits are the first steps to reaching healthy weight goals. Weight management involves controlling energy intake and increasing physical activity. A number of weight-loss aids are available. However, the only sure way to lose weight is to consume fewer calories than you expend. After reaching a weight-loss goal, you need to continue to practice weight management to maintain a healthy weight. Weight management principles also apply to people who are trying to gain weight.

Eating disorders could be viewed as the opposite of weight management. They are abnormal eating behaviors that risk health. Anorexia nervosa, bulimia nervosa, and binge eating disorder are three common eating disorders. Treatment requires care of the body and mind to help disordered eaters form a healthful relationship with food.

Review What You Have Read

Write your answers on a separate sheet of paper, using complete sentences when appropriate.

1. True or false. Basal metabolism refers to the amount of energy the human body needs just to stay alive and carry on vital life processes.

2. What are three factors that can influence the amount of energy a person needs to perform a physical task?

3. How many calories are provided by a gram of each of the following: carbohydrates, proteins, fats?

4. How much physical activity do the Dietary Guidelines recommend adults get to reduce disease risk?

5. What types of physical activities help build flexibility, strength, balance, and endurance?

6. When should an athlete begin drinking fluids to prevent dehydration?

7. An athlete's main source of energy should be _____.
   A. complex carbohydrates
   B. fats
   C. protein
   D. sugar

Answer Key for *Review What You Have Read* **questions**

1. true

2. The intensity with which a task is performed, body size, and the temperature of the environment can influence the amount of energy a person needs to perform a physical task.

3. Carbohydrates and proteins each provide 4 calories per gram. Fats provide 9 calories per gram.

4. The Dietary Guidelines suggest adults get at least 150 minutes of moderate activity most days of the week. For additional and more extensive health benefits, the Guidelines advise adults to raise this amount to 300 minutes a week of moderate-intensity physical activity.

5. Stretching movements improve flexibility. Lifting weights or heavy objects can help build strength. Exercises that strengthen the lower body will also improve balance. Aerobic activities promote endurance.

(continued)

6. To prevent dehydration, an athlete should begin drinking fluids before an event.

7. A

8. Many coaches lack sufficient training in sports nutrition to provide guidance about healthful weight loss, maintenance, and gain.

9. Body mass index does not take body composition into account.

8. Why should athletes wishing to reach weight goals seek the advice of a registered dietitian?

9. Explain why the use of body mass index in assessing weight has limitations.

10. Describe three factors that can distract people from listening to their satiety signals.

11. Briefly describe a weight management plan for losing 1 pound (0.45 kg) a week.

12. Why are most weight-loss aids ineffective?

13. True or false. In a weight-gain plan, fats should make up no more than 35 percent of total calories.

14. What often triggers an eating disorder?

15. Identify three health professionals who might be part of a team for treating someone with an eating disorder.

Link to Academic Skills

10. (Describe three. Student response. See page 115 in the text.)

11. To lose 1 pound (0.45 kg) a week, you would need to increase the difference between energy intake and expenditure by roughly 500 calories a day through a combination of reduced calorie intake and increased physical activity.

12. Most weight-loss aids do not help people develop

16. **English language arts.** Visit the American Council on Exercise (ACE) website to research a specific fitness topic. Prepare a poster presentation to share your findings with the class.

17. **Social studies.** Choose a demographic group: ethnicity, age, gender, or region of the United States. Visit the Centers for Disease Control and Prevention website to research the rate of overweight and obesity in your chosen group. Prepare a graph or table showing your findings. Propose reasons for differences among people in various segments of your group.

18. **English language arts.** Write a letter to a friend expressing your concern about his or her abnormal eating behaviors. Offer support and suggest a possible course of action your friend might take.

19. **Government/Civics.** Visit the HealthyPeople.gov website. Find the goals of Healthy People 2020 that relate to physical activity and weight management. Compare how these goals differ from the goals of Healthy People 2010. In class, discuss why the federal government sets national health goals.

Build Critical Thinking Skills

new lifestyle behaviors. Therefore, as soon as people stop using these products, they go back to their old eating and activity patterns and regain lost weight.

20. **Analysis.** Plan a pregame meal that would prepare a teenage athlete for an hour of vigorous sports competition. The meal should provide 700 to 800 calories, with 60 to 70 percent of calories from carbohydrates, 10 to 20 percent from proteins, and 15 to 25 percent from fats. Use tools at the ChooseMyPlate.gov website to help you analyze your menu to be sure it meets these goals. (Remember that carbohydrates and proteins provide 4 calories per gram and fats provide 9 calories per gram.)

21. **Evaluation.** Evaluate a reducing diet suggested in a popular magazine. Give an oral report comparing the diet with the weight management principles discussed in this chapter.

(continued)

Apply Technology

22. Visit a health club and note the types of computerized monitors and performance meters that are on the exercise equipment. Report your findings in class. Discuss how you think these high-tech tools would help people using the equipment.

23. Measure your body fat using a scale with a body fat monitor. If possible, have a trained professional measure your body fat using a skinfold caliper. Compare the two measurements.

A Measure of Math

24. Bring in a Nutrition Facts panel from a food product. Use the panel information to figure the number of calories in the food product that come from proteins, carbohydrates, and fats.

25. Multiply your weight by 14 and 20 to compare your daily calorie needs for a sedentary lifestyle and an active lifestyle. Choose the figure that is most appropriate for you. Multiply this number by 0.35 to determine your daily calorie limit from fat. Then divide your fat calorie limit by 9 to calculate your daily limit for grams of fat.

Teamwork in Action

26. As a class, host an active event for the community, such as a neighborhood walk or jog, backyard volleyball tournament, or skating party. Prepare brochures about the benefits of physical activity to distribute at the event.

Companion Website
www.g-wlearning.com

At the website, review key terms for this chapter with crossword puzzles, matching exercises, and e-flash cards. Apply facts from the chapter to complete the activities.

13. true

14. Eating disorders are often triggered by some type of personal stress.

15. (Name three:) doctor, psychological counselor, registered dietitian, fitness counselor

CHAPTER 6

Safeguarding Health

Main Menu

- You can avoid getting and spreading foodborne illnesses by practicing the four steps to food safety.
- Taking precautions when working in a kitchen will help you prevent common accidents.

Learning Prep

See how many of the *Terms to Know* you can find in a biology textbook. Compare the definitions and context of the terms in the biology text with the definitions and context used here.

Objectives

After studying this chapter, you will be able to

- **discuss** causes, symptoms, and treatment of common foodborne illnesses.
- **list** the four key steps to food safety and give examples of each.
- **give** examples of how following good safety practices can help you prevent kitchen accidents.
- **apply** basic first aid measures.

Terms to Know

foodborne illness
contaminant
microorganism
bacteria
toxin
sanitation
cross-contamination
abdominal thrust

Keeping foods safe to eat and making the kitchen a safe place to work are keys to good health. Improper food handling can make you ill. Kitchen accidents can cause severe injuries. You can prevent both illness and accidents by following safety principles.

Foodborne Illnesses

A disease transmitted by food is called a **foodborne illness**. Millions of cases of foodborne illness occur in the United States each year. Many of these cases go unreported because people mistake their symptoms for the "flu." To reduce the number of cases, advice for keeping food safe is part of the Dietary Guidelines for Americans.

Food Contamination

Most foodborne illnesses are caused by contaminants. A **contaminant** is a substance that may be harmful that has accidentally gotten into food. Many contaminants are microorganisms. A **microorganism** is a living substance so small it can be seen only under a microscope. Many contaminated foods do not look or smell spoiled, but they can still cause illness.

One type of microorganism that causes many foodborne illnesses is **bacteria**. Bacteria are single-celled or noncellular microorganisms. They live almost everywhere. They are not all harmful. Some types of harmless bacteria are normally found in foods.

Harmful bacteria can get into food at any point from the farm to the table. Soil, insects, humans, and cooking tools can all transfer bacteria to foods. Improper handling can taint food that was not affected previously. For instance, leaving food at room temperature can turn it into a breeding ground for bacteria. This is why all people who produce, process, and consume food must use care to avoid contaminating it.

The Dietary Guidelines recommend avoiding foods that are often contaminated with harmful bacteria. These foods include raw and undercooked meat, poultry, fish, shellfish, and eggs. Any dishes made with these foods should be avoided, too. Unpasteurized (raw) milk and any products made from it are also on the list of foods to avoid. See **6-1**.

These foods present risks because animals raised for food often contain microorganisms that can be harmful to humans. This is true even if the animals are healthy. Thorough cooking will kill most harmful bacteria. However, when these foods are eaten in a raw or undercooked state, the bacteria can be passed on to the people who eat them.

Steer clear of unpasteurized juices. Fresh fruits and vegetables can be contaminated if they are fertilized with untreated manure or washed with tainted water. Pasteurization kills bacteria in juices made from fresh produce. However, unpasteurized juices would retain any harmful bacteria that are present. Carefully washing fresh fruits and vegetables in clean running water right before eating will help reduce risk of contamination.

Raw sprouts pose a threat, too. The conditions used to grow sprouts are also well suited for growing bacteria. Cooking sprouts will kill any bacteria they may contain.

Meeting Special Needs

Challenge students who are academically gifted in your class to attain the following higher-order objectives as they study the chapter:

- associate the causes and symptoms of common foodborne illnesses with their prevention and treatment.

- analyze how each of the four key steps to food safety can help keep foods from becoming contaminated.

- demonstrate good safety practices that can help them prevent kitchen accidents.

FYI

The Centers for Disease Control and Prevention (CDC) estimates that 48 million foodborne illness cases occur in the United States every year.

USDA

6-1 Raw poultry can contain harmful bacteria. Careful handling and proper cooking will help prevent foodborne illness.

Learn About...

Governing Food Supply Safety

Federal, state, and local governments all play key roles in helping to keep the food supply safe. Federal laws govern food plants that process foods sold across state lines. Federal regulations require some food processors to follow a quality control system called *HACCP*. This stands for Hazard Analysis and Critical Control Point. This system involves looking at food production processes to see where hazards can occur. Processors can then take steps to prevent problems and respond to problems quickly.

State laws govern food businesses like restaurants and grocery stores. Each state sets health codes based on federal food codes. State codes may include programs like HACCP.

Local governments are in charge of sending health inspectors to visit food businesses. These inspectors make sure the businesses are following state health codes. Inspectors issue warnings when they find minor code violations. When violations are severe, inspectors may close businesses until problems are addressed.

Another federal program related to the safety of the food supply is the Total Diet Study (TDS). This is a survey conducted by the U.S. Food and Drug Administration (FDA). FDA staff purchase samples of commonly eaten foods from grocery stores. They collect samples from different cities in different regions. This assures the samples reflect the food supply of the entire nation. The FDA has the food samples made into dishes that would be eaten at the table. Then they check the foods for contaminants such as pesticide residues and industrial chemicals. This allows the FDA to track the amounts of various contaminants people are likely to consume. Most contaminants are found in amounts well below levels that are thought to be unsafe.

Bacterial Illnesses

Common foodborne illnesses include *campylobacteriosis*, *listeriosis*, and *perfringens food poisoning*. All these diseases are caused by bacteria. Some other foodborne illnesses, such as, *botulism* and *staphylococcal food poisoning*, are caused by **toxins** (poisons) produced by bacteria.

The bodies of most healthy people can handle small amounts of harmful bacteria. However, when the bacterial count becomes too great, illness can occur. Foodborne illnesses pose a greater risk for some groups of people. These groups include infants, pregnant women, older adults, and people with impaired immune systems. The Dietary Guidelines suggest extra care be used when handling foods for people in these high-risk groups.

Symptoms of bacterial foodborne illnesses vary depending on the type of bacteria. However, most of these illnesses affect the digestive system. Symptoms may appear 30 minutes to 30 days after eating tainted food. The amount of time required for symptoms to develop often makes it hard to pinpoint the source of foodborne illness. The symptoms of botulism differ from those of most other foodborne illnesses. This disease affects the nervous system. The death rate for botulism is high. However, a doctor can treat botulism with an antitoxin if he or she diagnoses it in time. See **6-2**.

Bacterial Foodborne Illnesses

Illness and Organism	Food Sources	Symptoms
Botulism. Caused by toxins produced by *Clostridium botulinum*	Improperly processed home-canned low-acid foods, raw fish	Double vision, inability to swallow, speech difficulty, progressive respiratory paralysis that can lead to death Appear: 4 to 36 hours after eating
Campylobacteriosis. Caused by *Campylobacter jejuni*	Raw and undercooked beef and poultry, unpasteurized milk, and untreated water	Diarrhea, abdominal cramping, fever, bloody stools Appear: 2 to 5 days after eating Last: 7 to 10 days
Hemorrhagic colitis. Caused by *E. coli* O157:H7	Fresh fruits and vegetables, raw and undercooked ground beef and pork, raw sprouts, unpasteurized milk, unpasteurized juice	Bloody stools, vomiting, stomachache, nausea, Appear: 12 to 72 hours after eating Last: 4 to 10 days
Listeriosis. Caused by *Listeria monocytogenes*	Fresh fruits and vegetables, raw and undercooked pork and poultry, raw fish, soft cheeses, unpasteurized milk	Fever, headache, nausea, vomiting, abdominal pain, diarrhea Appear: 48 to 72 hours after eating
Perfringens food poisoning. Caused by *Clostridium perfringens*	Meat, meat products, and gravy not chilled in a timely manner after cooking	Abdominal cramping, diarrhea Appear: 8 to 22 hours after eating Last: 24 hours
Salmonellosis. Caused by multiple species of *Salmonella*	Fresh fruits and vegetables; raw and undercooked beef, pork, poultry, eggs, and fish; raw sprouts; unpasteurized milk; unpasteurized juice	Severe headache, nausea, vomiting, abdominal pain, diarrhea, fever Appear: 8 to 12 hours after eating Last: 2 to 3 days
Staphylococcal food poisoning. Caused by toxins produced by *Staphylococcus aureus*	High-protein cooked food, such as ham, egg salad, cream pies, and custard; raw and undercooked beef, pork, and poultry; unpasteurized milk	Abdominal cramping, nausea, vomiting, diarrhea Appear: 30 minutes to 8 hours after eating Last: 1 to 2 days
Yersiniosis. Caused by *Yersinia enterocolitica*	Meats, oysters, fish, unpasteurized milk	Fever, abdominal pain, diarrhea, vomiting Appear: 24 to 48 hours after eating

6-2 These are among the many foodborne illnesses that can be caused by improper handling of food.

For Example...
Other foods that have natural poisons include apricots, cherries, and peaches, which all have poisonous pits. Some types of fish also produce a natural toxin called scombroid toxin when they begin to spoil.

FYI
Toxoplasmosis is also spread through contact with infected cat stool. Cleaning the litter box daily and avoiding the handling of stray cats and kittens are precautions that will help prevent cat lovers from becoming infected.

Treating Bacterial Foodborne Illnesses

Infants, pregnant women, older adults, and those with chronic illnesses should see a doctor about symptoms of foodborne illness. If you are not in these high-risk groups, you may not need professional treatment for foodborne illness. Resting will help you regain your strength. Drinking liquids will help replace body fluids lost due to diarrhea and vomiting. If you suspect you have botulism, or if your symptoms are severe, you should call your doctor right away.

Other Foodborne Illnesses

Bacteria are not the only microorganisms that can cause foodborne illnesses. A couple of foodborne illnesses are caused by *protozoa* (tiny, one-celled animals). *Amebiasis* is caused by drinking polluted water or eating vegetables grown in polluted soil. *Giardiasis* can also be caused by drinking impure water.

Some foodborne illnesses are caused by viruses. (A *virus* is the smallest and simplest known type of microorganism.) For instance, common "stomach flu" can be spread by food handlers infected with *norovirus*. Symptoms include vomiting and diarrhea. To prevent spreading norovirus, wash hands before handling food and avoid handling food when symptoms are present.

The *hepatitis A* virus is found in some shellfish. It is highly heat-resistant. This makes disease prevention difficult because people often eat shellfish raw or just slightly cooked. Contaminated water and sewage are the major sources of this virus. The best way to avoid contamination is to buy shellfish that come only from commercial sources. If you gather fresh shellfish, be sure to stay safely away from any source of pollution.

A few foods have *natural toxins* that can cause illness. Certain varieties of mushrooms and leaves of the rhubarb plant are two such foods. Avoid picking wild mushrooms as well as fruits, roots, and berries unless you are knowledgeable about them. Some varieties can be poisonous.

Health and Wellness

Parasitic Foodborne Illnesses

Parasites are another type of microorganism that can be sources of foodborne illness. A *parasite* is a microorganism that needs another organism, called a *host*, to live. Hogs were once a common host for parasitic roundworms called *trichinae*, which cause the disease *trichinosis*. Improved standards for feeding hogs have all but eliminated this risk in pork. However, hogs and other sources of red meat are often infected with the parasite *Toxoplasma gondii*. This parasite causes the infection *toxoplasmosis*, which can damage the central nervous system. People can become infected with Toxoplasma by eating undercooked meat from animals infected with this parasite.

Another parasite that is becoming more of a concern is *anisakis*. This is a worm that causes an illness called *anisakiasis*. It is found in raw fish, which means there is some risk involved in eating raw fish dishes like sushi and sashimi. The larvae of this parasite can cause vomiting and diarrhea.

Four Steps to Food Safety

Most foodborne illnesses are spread through improper food handling. All the guidelines for keeping food safe to eat can be summed up in four basic steps—clean, separate, cook, and chill. Keep these steps in mind when you are buying, preparing, and storing food. This can help you avoid foodborne illness. See **6-3**.

Clean

One of the key steps you can take to prevent foodborne illness is to keep yourself and the kitchen clean. You need to follow good sanitation practices. **Sanitation** means maintaining clean conditions to prevent disease and promote good health. Encourage others to abide by the following sanitation guidelines when handling food:

- Wear clean clothes and a clean apron when working around food. Bacteria can accumulate on dirty clothes. Avoid loose sleeves, which can dip into foods.
- Keep long hair tied back and avoid touching hair while you work.
- Designate the kitchen as a nonsmoking area to keep ashes from falling into food.
- Cover coughs and sneezes with a disposable tissue. Wash hands immediately.
- Keep your work area clean. Wipe up spills as they happen.
- Use paper towels to wipe up juices from raw meat and poultry. Then immediately wash the area on which the juices dripped.
- Remove dirty utensils from your work area before proceeding to the next task. Bacteria grow quickly in spills and on dirty utensils.
- Wash the tops of cans before opening them. Otherwise, dust and dirt could fall into food when you open the can.

USDA

6-3 Following the four basic steps to food safety—clean, separate, cook, and chill—can help you avoid illness-causing bacteria.

Discuss

Ask students why they should use paper towels when wiping up meat and poultry juices. *(You can get rid of harmful bacteria from these juices when you dispose of the paper towels. Wiping up juices with a sponge or dishcloth would provide bacteria with a damp environment in which to breed.)*

Online Resource

Have students visit the USDA Food Safety and Inspection Service website at fsis.usda. gov to survey the variety of fact sheets available on food safety topics. Ask each student to read one of the fact sheets and give a summary of it in a brief oral report.

Reflect

Ask students which of these guidelines they routinely follow when working with food.

- Thoroughly wash cutting boards, counters, and utensils after each use. In addition, regularly sanitize counters and cutting boards with chlorine bleach solution to kill bacteria.
- Wash dishes promptly, using hot water and detergent. Wash dishes in the following order: glasses and cups, flatware, plates and bowls, pots and pans, and greasy utensils. Rinse dishes with scalding water and allow them to air dry. If you must dry dishes, be sure to use a clean dishtowel.
- Dispose of garbage properly and promptly. Frequent washing and air drying of garbage pails prevents odors and bacterial growth.
- Never store any foods under the kitchen sink. Drainpipes can leak and damage the food.
- Wash dishcloths and sponges daily. (Sponges can be washed in a dishwasher in a covered basket designed to hold small items.) Between uses, rinse dishcloths and sponges well, wring thoroughly, and allow to air dry. This discourages bacteria from breeding on damp surfaces.

Health and Wellness

Hand Washing

Washing your hands may be the most important step you can take to prevent the transmission of harmful bacteria. Wash hands for 20 seconds, rubbing briskly with soap and warm running water before starting to work with food. (Note that using a hand sanitizer will not adequately clean your hands before food preparation.) Be sure to clean under your fingernails, too. Dry hands with paper towels or use a clean hand towel.

Follow these same hand washing steps after handling raw meat, fish, poultry, or eggs before touching any other foods. Also, wash your hands after sneezing, coughing, using the toilet, or touching your face, hair, or any unsanitary object. This will prevent the transfer of bacteria.

If you have an open sore or cut on your hand, put on gloves before handling food. Open sores are a major source of staphylococcal bacteria. Wash gloved hands while working with food just as you would wash bare hands.

Separate

A second step for preventing foodborne illness is to separate cooked and ready-to-eat foods from raw foods. Following this step will avoid the risks of cross-contamination. **Cross-contamination** occurs when harmful bacteria from one food are transferred to another food. For instance, juices from a leaky package of raw chicken may contain harmful bacteria. If the juices drip on other foods in your shopping cart or refrigerator, the bacteria will be transferred to these foods. The following guidelines will help you keep foods that may be contaminated separated from other foods:

- Put raw poultry, meat, and seafood in separate plastic bags before placing them in your shopping cart.
- Store raw poultry, meat, and seafood in containers to keep them separate from other foods in the refrigerator. See **6-4**.
- Do not wash raw meat or poultry. This can spread bacteria from these foods to other foods and surfaces.

- Use one spoon for tasting and one for stirring. To taste, pour a little of the food from the stirring spoon onto the tasting spoon. Do not lick your fingers.
- Use clean utensils and containers. Never use the same utensil, cutting board, or plate for both raw and cooked meat, poultry, fish, or eggs. Utensils can transfer bacteria from raw foods to cooked foods.
- Never use a hand towel to wipe dishes. Dirty towels can transfer bacteria.
- Keep pets and insects out of the kitchen. Do not feed pets in the kitchen or wash their dishes with your dishes. Remove leftover pet food and dispose of it promptly.

- Never taste any food that looks or smells questionable. Dispose of it promptly.
- Store nonperishables in tightly sealed containers to keep them fresh and free from insects and rodents.

Cook

Raw meat, poultry, seafood, and eggs can contain harmful bacteria. Cooking these foods to a safe internal temperature is the third step to food safety. High temperatures can kill bacteria. The following guidelines will help you make sure foods are thoroughly cooked:
- Use a food thermometer to make sure the internal temperatures of foods have reached recommended safe levels. See **6-5**.
- When serving hot foods, be sure to keep them hot—above 140°F (60°C).
- Stuff raw poultry, meat, and fish just before baking. Stuffing should reach an internal temperature of at least 165°F (74°C).
- Do not partially cook foods and then set them aside or refrigerate them to complete the cooking later.
- Reheat leftovers to 165°F (74°C). When reheating sauces, soups, and gravies, make sure they come to a full boil.
- Boil low-acid, home-canned foods for 10 to 20 minutes before tasting. Dispose of any bulging, leaking, or otherwise damaged container of food.
- Use only clean, fresh, unbroken eggs for eggnog, custard, and other egg dishes. Modify recipes calling for uncooked or partially cooked eggs. Cook eggs until they are firm, not runny.
- Do not eat raw cookie dough or taste partially cooked dishes containing meat, poultry, fish, or eggs.

Chill

Chilling foods is the fourth basic step to food safety. Chilling foods promptly after buying or serving them will keep harmful bacteria from multiplying. The following tips will help you store foods correctly to keep them safe and wholesome:
- Keep cold foods cold—below 40°F (4°C).
- Bacteria multiply fastest at temperatures between 40°F and 140°F (4°C and 60°C), **6-6**. This danger zone includes room temperature. This is why you should not allow food to sit out for more than two hours.

USDA

6-4 In the refrigerator, use food storage containers to keep cooked and ready-to-eat foods separated from raw foods. Place raw meats and poultry on platters to keep them from dripping on other foods.

USDA Recommended Safe Minimum Internal Temperatures	
Beef steaks and roasts	145 °F*
Ground beef, veal, lamb, pork	160 °F
Pork steaks and roasts	145 °F*
Chicken breasts	165 °F
Whole poultry	165 °F
Fish	145 °F
Egg dishes	160 °F
*Including a 3 minute rest time after cooking.	

6-5 You can be sure foods are safe to eat when you cook them to recommended internal temperatures.

FYI

Note that color is not always an accurate indicator of doneness in meats. According to USDA research, one out of every four hamburgers turns brown in the middle before it has reached a safe internal temperature.

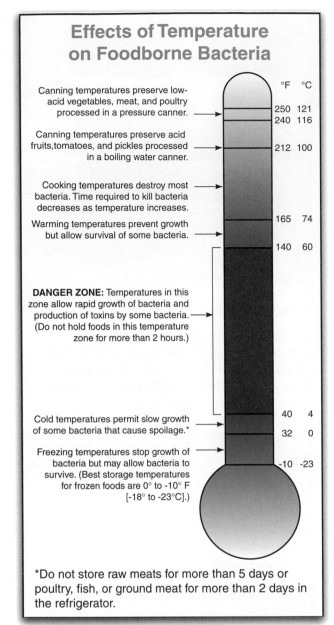

Effects of Temperature on Foodborne Bacteria

Canning temperatures preserve low-acid vegetables, meat, and poultry processed in a pressure canner. → 250 121 / 240 116

Canning temperatures preserve acid fruits, tomatoes, and pickles processed in a boiling water canner. → 212 100

Cooking temperatures destroy most bacteria. Time required to kill bacteria decreases as temperature increases. → 165 74

Warming temperatures prevent growth but allow survival of some bacteria. → 140 60

DANGER ZONE: Temperatures in this zone allow rapid growth of bacteria and production of toxins by some bacteria. (Do not hold foods in this temperature zone for more than 2 hours.)

Cold temperatures permit slow growth of some bacteria that cause spoilage.* → 40 4 / 32 0

Freezing temperatures stop growth of bacteria but may allow bacteria to survive. (Best storage temperatures for frozen foods are 0° to -10° F [-18° to -23°C].) → -10 -23

*Do not store raw meats for more than 5 days or poultry, fish, or ground meat for more than 2 days in the refrigerator.

6-6 Bacteria multiply rapidly at moderate temperatures. To prevent this, keep hot foods hot and cold foods cold.

Discuss

Ask students why they should allow custards and cream pies to cool slightly before refrigerating them. (Putting any foods in the refrigerator when they are hot can cause the temperature in the food storage compartment to climb to an unsafe level.)

- Refrigerate leftovers promptly. Eat or freeze refrigerated leftovers within three days.
- Use a refrigerator thermometer to check the temperature of your refrigerator and freezer regularly. Refrigerator temperatures should be 40°F (4°C) or just slightly below. Freezer temperatures should be 0°F (-18°C) or below. Also, check the gaskets around the doors to be sure they are tight.
- Thaw foods in the refrigerator or in the microwave oven immediately before cooking. Do not thaw at room temperature.
- Keep your refrigerator and freezer clean.
- Package refrigerated and frozen foods properly. Use moistureproof and vaporproof wraps for the freezer. For the refrigerator, cover fresh meats loosely and store leftovers in tightly covered containers. Use foods within recommended storage times.
- Read labels to identify foods that need to be refrigerated after opening, such as ketchup and salad dressings. Once opened, use these foods within about three months.
- Refrigerate custards, meringue, cream pies, and foods filled with custard mixtures when they have cooled slightly.
- Use shallow containers for refrigerator storage to help foods reach safe, cool temperatures faster. You can also hasten cooling by placing containers of food in an ice water bath.
- Remove stuffing from poultry, meat, and fish promptly after serving and refrigerate it separately. Refrigerate gravy, stuffing, and meat immediately after the meal.
- Do not refreeze foods unless they still contain ice crystals. Do not refreeze ice cream that has thawed. Use defrosted foods promptly.
- Make the supermarket your last stop on the way home. Put perishable items in your shopping cart last. Refrigerate or freeze them as soon as you get home. If you will not be going directly home after grocery shopping, take an insulated cooler to the store with you. Use it to keep perishable foods cool until you can store them properly.

Cooking for Special Occasions

Cooking for a crowd or cooking outdoor meals requires extra measures to keep food safe to eat. Before planning any big gathering, be sure your equipment can handle large amounts of food. Refrigerators must be able to chill increased quantities of warm foods without raising the temperature above 40°F (4°C). Preparing and freezing foods ahead will prevent overloading your refrigerator the day before an event. Heating appliances must be able to keep hot foods above 140°F (60°C) until serving time.

Health and Wellness

Picnic Food Safety

Picnic and barbecue foods present specific problems. You may carry these foods some distance before serving them. Use insulated containers to keep these foods at the proper temperature to prevent the growth of bacteria. Wrap raw meat, poultry, and fish carefully to keep them from leaking onto other foods. You may want to use a separate cooler for beverages. This will help you avoid repeatedly opening the cooler containing the perishable foods. Do not take perishables from the cooler until you are ready to cook or serve them.

Use sanitary procedures when preparing picnic foods. Be sure utensils are clean. Do not let hamburgers, hot dogs, or other meats sit next to the grill while the charcoal heats. Keep them in the ice chest. Do not put cooked meat on the same plate that held raw meat.

Photo courtesy of National Pork Board. For more information about pork, visit TheOtherWhiteMeat.com.

To keep barbecued meats safe, be sure to keep meat chilled until right before grilling. Also, use separate plates and utensils for raw and cooked meats.

If using buffet service, put the food in small serving dishes, which you can refill or replace as needed. Another way to keep hot foods hot and cold foods cold is to use heated serving appliances and ice.

Large amounts of food take longer to heat and chill than do small or average amounts. Divide food and place it in small, shallow containers for quicker heating and cooling.

Be sure to thoroughly cook all foods. Then serve them promptly. Refrigerate leftovers immediately after the meal.

Eating Safely When Eating Out

Most of the foodborne illness cases reported each year occur in foodservice establishments. Restaurants have strict sanitation guidelines they must follow when preparing food for the public. State health departments inspect foodservice facilities regularly to ensure that guidelines are being met. However, occasional problems still occur.

You can take several steps when eating out to protect yourself from foodborne illness. First, look at the surroundings on your way into a restaurant. The parking lot should be free from litter. The way the outside of a restaurant is maintained can give you a clue about how the inside is maintained.

When you enter the restaurant, you should see a concern for cleanliness throughout the establishment. Tables should be wiped. Walls and floors should be clean. Restrooms should be tidy.

Activity

Have students conduct food safety checks of their home kitchens.

Discuss

Why do most of the foodborne illness cases reported each year occur in foodservice establishments? *(These cases tend to affect larger numbers of people, making them easier to identify and trace to a source.)*

Reflect

Ask students how much attention they usually pay to the cleanliness of a restaurant and its employees. Ask when they have encountered foodservice establishments that did not meet acceptable sanitation standards.

Observe the employees as they wait on you. They should appear to be in good health. Their clothes should be clean. If they have long hair, they should have it tied back. When they serve you, they should not touch the eating surfaces of your tableware.

When your food is served, it should look and smell wholesome. Hot foods should be hot. Cold foods should be cold.

If you have a concern about your food, do not be afraid to speak to your server. If your server cannot answer your questions or correct the problem, ask to speak to the manager.

Most servers will wrap leftovers for you if you wish to take them home. However, be sure you are going directly home and promptly put leftovers in the refrigerator. If you cannot refrigerate food within two hours from the time it was served, discard it.

If you choose restaurants with care, you may never have a problem with foodborne illness. However, if you get ill from something you ate at a restaurant, call local health authorities. Others should be warned they may have been exposed to the infected food also.

EXPLORING CAREERS

Dishwasher

The foodservice industry offers a number of entry-level jobs for young workers. One such job is that of dishwasher. Of course, a dishwasher's main task is to wash dishes. Some dishwashing is done by hand, but most involves the use of a commercial dishwashing system. A dishwasher may also have to clean other kitchen equipment and work areas. A dishwasher may be asked to stock food and utensils in storage areas and handle minor food preparation tasks, too.

Generally, a dishwasher does not need specific education or training. Training often comes from a coworker on the job. Therefore, being able to listen to and follow directions are key skills. A dishwasher also needs to be able to read instructions and operate equipment. In time, an experienced dishwasher may need skill in training others to do the job.

A dishwasher's most important personal qualities are attention to detail and cooperation. A successful dishwasher needs to make sure all cleaning tasks are done to accepted sanitation standards. He or she needs to get along with coworkers and show a willingness to help others. A dishwasher with these traits may soon find opportunities to move into other positions in the kitchen. Such a worker is likely to have a bright future in the foodservice industry.

Shutterstock

Starting out working as a dishwasher may lead to other jobs in the foodservice industry.

Storing Food for Emergencies

No one wants to think about hurricanes, floods, tornadoes, and earthquakes. Unfortunately, such disasters can happen. When they do, people are often stranded in their homes or forced to evacuate for days. Utilities may be cut off, and stores may be closed, unreachable, or out of merchandise. That is why safely storing food and water for emergency situations is important.

The American Red Cross recommends storing at least a three-day supply of food and water for each person. Be sure to keep special needs of those such as infants and diabetics in mind. Choose nonperishable foods that do not require cooking. Many canned goods make wise choices. Foods like dried fruits and beef jerky are good choices, too. They are compact and lightweight, so they will be easy to carry if there is an evacuation. Remember to store a can opener and any other tools you might need to prepare the food. Store items in a backpack or a container with wheels and a handle for pulling. This will make it easier to transport your supplies if you have to leave your home. Replace stored food and water every six months so they will be safe and fresh when you need them.

Safety in the Kitchen

Many common kitchen items may seem harmless. However, they can be dangerous if you do not take safety precautions. For instance, people can injure themselves by bumping into open cabinet doors and drawers. Keeping all kitchen cabinets and drawers closed will prevent accidental injuries.

Hospital emergency room personnel see the results of thousands of kitchen accidents each year. Some kitchen accidents are due to ignorance. Many result from carelessness. Chemical poisonings, cuts, burns and fires, and falls are the most common of these accidents. Electric shocks, choking, and other types of injury can also occur in the kitchen. You can prevent many accidents by properly using and caring for equipment. Following good safety practices and keeping the kitchen clean will also help you avoid accidents.

Knowledge of basic first aid will help you provide treatment to someone involved in a kitchen accident. A simple first aid kit kept in the kitchen should include the items you need to treat minor injuries.

Preventing Chemical Poisonings

Children are especially susceptible to chemical poisonings. To many children, poisonous household chemicals, such as furniture polishes, cleaners, and bleach, look like food. The following guidelines will help you prevent chemical poisonings:
- Keep all household chemicals in a location where children cannot reach them.
- Keep all household chemicals in their original, clearly labeled containers. Do not put them in soda bottles or other food containers. Keep all containers tightly closed.
- Do not rely on containers with safety closures. Some children can open safety caps.
- If the phone or doorbell interrupts you while you are using a household chemical, take the product with you.

Discuss

Ask students what kinds of items they should keep in a first aid kit. *(antiseptic wipes, medicated cream, gauze, adhesive bandages)*

FYI

Some of the most dangerous household poisons for children include
- adult iron supplements
- drain openers, toilet bowl cleaners, and oven cleaners, which can cause chemical burns
- hydrocarbons in products like gasoline, motor oil, lighter fluid, and paint thinner
- windshield washer solution and antifreeze
- nail glue remover and nail primer
- alcohol in products like mouthwash, hair tonic, and food flavorings and extracts as well as alcoholic beverages

Rubbermaid

6-7 Carefully washing fresh fruits and vegetables will remove traces of agricultural chemicals that may be present.

- Pesticides and insecticides used on food can be poisonous. Wash all fresh fruits and vegetables thoroughly before use to remove any chemical residues, **6-7**. Cover all food and cooking and eating utensils before using a pesticide in the kitchen.
- Keep medication out of the kitchen and out of a child's reach. Never refer to medicine as candy. Contact a local hospital or pharmacy to find out how to properly dispose of unused medication.
- Read all warning labels, and keep a poison chart handy. This will help you know what first aid to give if someone is accidentally poisoned. It will also help you know what to tell a doctor.

Treating Poisonings

In a case of poisoning, call the nearest poison control center immediately. Have the poison container with you when you call so you can accurately describe the poison taken. If the label on the poison lists first aid instructions, follow them. Keep the victim comfortable and calm until help arrives.

Preventing Cuts

Knives, sharp appliances, and broken glass cause most kitchen cuts. The following guidelines will help you prevent cuts:
- Keep knives sharp. Dull blades can slip and cause cuts.
- Use knives properly. Move the blade away from your body as you cut. Never point a sharp object at another person.
- Do not try to catch a falling knife in midair. Let the knife fall to the floor and then carefully pick it up.
- Use a knife only for its intended purpose. Do not use it as a screwdriver or to pry open containers. To do so can cause serious injuries.
- Wash and store knives separately from other utensils.
- Never put fingers near beaters or the blades of blenders, food processors, or food waste disposers to dislodge foods or objects. Instead, disconnect the appliance and use a nonmetal utensil to remove items that are stuck. If you cannot dislodge an object, call a repair person.
- When opening a can, dispose of the lid immediately.
- Never pick up broken glass with your bare hands. Wear rubber gloves to pick up large pieces. Sweep smaller pieces into a disposable dustpan and wipe up fragments with a damp paper towel. Dispose of broken glass immediately.

Treating Cuts

To treat a cut, cover the wound with a sterile cloth or clean handkerchief. Apply firm pressure to the wound to stop bleeding. If a cut is minor, wash it with soap and water. Apply an antiseptic solution and bandage it with a sterile dressing. If a cut is severe, continue to apply pressure to the wound. Take the victim to a doctor or the hospital emergency room.

Preventing Burns and Fires

Scalding liquids, spattering grease, and hot cooking utensils cause most kitchen burns. The majority of fires are due to malfunctioning electric appliances and carelessness around hot surfaces and open flames. The following guidelines will help you prevent burns and fires:

- Use pot holders to handle hot utensils.
- Make sure pan handles do not extend over the front edge of the cooktop to prevent accidental tipping, **6-8**.
- To avoid a steam burn, open pan lids away from you so the steam will escape safely.
- Never open a pressure cooker before the pressure has gone down to zero. The pressurized steam within the cooker can rush out and cause a severe burn.
- Do not let children play near the range or cook without help. Teach them proper safety procedures.
- Turn off range and oven controls and disconnect small appliances when not in use.
- Use caution with liquids heated in a microwave oven. The water can reach temperatures over 212°F (100°C) without showing signs of boiling. Adding teabags, beverage mixes, or ice cubes to the water can cause sudden, rapid boiling to begin.
- Follow manufacturer's directions for use and care of all electric and gas appliances.
- Be sure to ground all electric appliances. Avoid using lightweight extension cords and multiple plug adapters.
- When working near the range, wear tight-fitting clothing. Roll up long sleeves.
- Do not hang towels, curtains, or other flammable materials near the range.
- If you must light a gas range manually, light the match first. Then turn on the gas to prevent an accidental explosion. If you smell gas, turn off the controls, leave the premises, and call the gas company.
- Never leave a pan of grease unattended; it could burst into flames. If grease should ignite, do not pour water on the flames as this could spread the fire.
- Use care around lit candles, canisters of cooking fuel, and other sources of open flames.
- Clean grease from exhaust hoods frequently to prevent grease fires.
- If your clothes should catch on fire, do not panic and run. Drop to the floor and roll over to smother the flames.
- Install a smoke alarm in the kitchen. Check it monthly to be sure batteries are operating.

USDA

6-8 Turning a pan's handle away from the front edge of a cooktop will help avoid accidentally spilling the hot food in the pan.

Enrich

Have each student plan an emergency escape route for his or her family to use in their home if there is a fire. Encourage students to post maps of the routes in each room in their homes. Then ask them to conduct fire drills to allow family members to practice getting out of their homes safely.

Discuss

Ask students why they should drop to the floor when there is a fire. *(Most smoke rises, so you reduce your risk of smoke inhalation if you stay low.)*

Reflect

Ask students when someone last checked the smoke detectors in their homes.

Learn About...

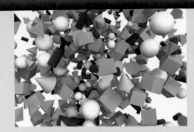

Fire Extinguishers

When buying a fire extinguisher, choose one that is ABC class rated. This type of extinguisher is a good choice for the kitchen because it is all-purpose. Also, check to be sure the extinguisher has a safety seal. This is an emblem indicating the extinguisher has met the standards of a reputable testing agency.

Store fire extinguishers in handy locations. Be sure you know how to use them. Have them checked periodically. Do not store an extinguisher over a range.

Treating Burns

When someone becomes burned, place the burned area immediately under cold running water or in a cold water bath. Do not apply ointments or grease of any kind. Do not break blisters that may form. Call a physician immediately if a burn is severe or if pain and redness persist.

Preventing Falls

Most kitchen falls result from unsteady step stools and wet or cluttered floors. The following guidelines will help you prevent falls:

- Do not stand on a chair or box to reach high places. Use a sturdy step stool or ladder.
- Wait until a freshly washed floor dries before walking across the room.
- Wipe up spills from floors immediately. Be sure no sticky or greasy residue remains.
- Do not let children leave their toys on the kitchen floor. Remove shoes, boots, sports equipment, and other objects from kitchen traffic areas.
- If you use throw rugs, find ones with nonskid backings.

Treating Falls

When someone is injured in a fall, stop bleeding if necessary. Loosen clothing around the victim's neck. If you suspect a broken bone, do not move the victim unless absolutely necessary. Make the victim as comfortable as possible. Do not give the victim anything to eat or drink. Call a physician.

Preventing Electric Shock

Faulty wiring, overloaded electrical outlets, and damaged appliances are common causes of electric shock. Electrical hazards can also be fire hazards. The following guidelines will help you prevent electric shock:

- Never stand on a wet floor or work near a wet counter when using electric appliances.
- Do not touch any electrical plugs, switches, or appliances when your hands are wet.

- Do not run electrical cords under rugs or carpeting.
- Do not use lightweight extension cords with small appliances. If possible, plug appliances directly into electrical outlets. If you must use an extension cord, choose a heavy-gauge one that is designed to carry a heavier electrical load.
- Do not overload electrical outlets by plugging several appliances into the same outlet.
- Place safety covers over unused electrical outlets to prevent children from sticking fingers or objects into them. See **6-9**.
- Unplug the toaster before trying to pry loose food that has become stuck.
- When you disconnect appliances, hold onto the plug, not the cord. Replace all cords and plugs when they become worn.
- Do not use damaged appliances.

Treating Electric Shock

If someone receives an electric shock, immediately disconnect the appliance or turn off the power causing the shock. Do not touch the victim if he or she is connected to the power source. If you do, you will receive a shock, too. Use some nonconducting material to pull the victim away from the electrical source. A rope, a long piece of dry cloth, or a wooden pole would be suitable choices. Then immediately call your local emergency number.

KidCo, Inc.

6-9 Covering electrical outlets when they are not in use will help keep children safe from electric shock.

Preventing Choking

Choking occurs when an object, such as a piece of food, becomes stuck in the throat. The trapped object blocks the airway, making it impossible for the victim to speak or breathe. Someone who is choking quickly turns blue and collapses. The choking victim can die of strangulation in four minutes if the airway is not cleared. The following guidelines will help you prevent choking:
- Chew food thoroughly before swallowing.
- Avoid talking and laughing when you have food in your mouth.
- Do not give children small, round pieces of food, such as grapes or slices of hot dogs or carrots. Cut slices in halves or quarters.

Treating Choking

The **abdominal thrust** is a procedure used to save choking victims. It involves exerting pressure on the victim's abdomen. This causes the trapped food to be expelled.

FYI

Even though a choking victim cannot speak, he or she can use the universal choking signal to alert others to the trauma. This signal is given by grasping the throat between the thumb and forefinger.

Enrich

Invite a nurse or EMT to your class to demonstrate basic first aid procedures.

Discuss

Ask students what items or situations other than those mentioned in the text create potential

Be sure a person is choking before using the abdominal thrust. Someone who can cough, breathe, or talk is not choking. If a choking victim loses consciousness, do not attempt to use the abdominal thrust. Instead, call the local emergency number for immediate medical help.

The abdominal thrust can injure a choking victim. Therefore, the victim should see a doctor as soon as possible after the rescue.

Learn About...

Performing the Abdominal Thrust

Being familiar with the abdominal thrust may help you save someone's life. For adults and children over one year of age, perform the abdominal thrust using these steps.

1. If the victim is standing, stand behind him or her. If the victim is sitting, stand behind his or her chair. Wrap your arms around the victim's waist.

2. With your thumb toward the victim, place your fist against the victim's abdomen. Your fist should be above the navel and just below the rib cage.

3. Grasping your fist with your other hand, use a quick thrust to press upward into the victim's abdomen. Repeat the thrust several times, if needed.

If no help is available, you can also perform the abdominal thrust on yourself before losing consciousness.

CAREER SUCCESS

Maintaining and Troubleshooting Technologies

Desmond is a health and safety manager at the Tempting Table food processing plant. He inspects the plant's machinery and working conditions to make sure they meet safety and health standards. When Desmond finds a piece of equipment that is not working properly, he helps get it operating safely again. Sometimes plant supervisors have to stop production while equipment is being repaired.

To be an effective worker, Desmond needs skill in maintaining and troubleshooting technologies. In a small group, answer the following questions about Desmond's need for and use of these skills:

A. How might Tempting Table be affected if their plant does not meet health and safety standards?

B. Why would Tempting Table want Desmond to identify potential hazards before problems occur?

C. How might other employees be affected if Desmond fails to identify or correct a problem?

D. What is another skill Desmond would need in this job? Briefly explain why this skill would be important.

hazards in the kitchen. *(Nearly any item can be dangerous if it is misused.)*

CHAPTER 6 REVIEW

Summary

Foodborne illnesses are very common in the United States. Although bacteria cause many of these illnesses, people are often at fault for spreading the bacteria. Bacteria can get into food at any point during production, processing, or preparation. Most symptoms of foodborne illnesses affect the digestive system and last only a few days. However, foodborne illnesses can be deadly.

Foods often become contaminated through improper handling. It is important to keep yourself and your kitchen clean when preparing food. You need to separate raw foods from cooked and ready-to-eat foods. You must cook foods thoroughly and chill them promptly after purchase or serving. You need to take special precautions when cooking for a large group or transporting food. You need to be wary when you are eating out to avoid the risk of illness. Storing supplies in a special location will ensure that you have safe food in the event of an emergency. Following these steps will help you avoid foodborne illness.

Exercising safety is another concern when you are working in the kitchen. Many kitchen injuries are the result of poisonings, cuts, burns, falls, shock, and choking. You can take steps to prevent common kitchen accidents. You should also learn how to provide proper treatment when minor injuries occur.

Review What You Have Read

Write your answers on a separate sheet of paper, using complete sentences when appropriate.

1. True or false. Raw and undercooked meat, poultry, fish, shellfish, and eggs are often contaminated with harmful bacteria.
2. For what groups of people do foodborne illnesses pose the greatest risk?
3. What are three microorganisms other than bacteria that can cause foodborne illness?
4. List eight standards for personal and kitchen cleanliness.
5. List five guidelines for keeping foods that may be contaminated separated from other foods.
6. What are the proper temperatures for serving hot and cold foods?
7. How can large amounts of food be heated or chilled quickly?
8. Where do most of the foodborne illness cases reported each year occur?
9. True or false. Older adults are especially susceptible to chemical poisonings.
10. Describe the correct way to pick up and dispose of broken glass.
11. List eight safety precautions that can prevent burns and fires.
12. List three guidelines for preventing falls.
13. What should be used to pull a shock victim away from an electrical source?
14. Briefly describe the steps for performing the abdominal thrust.

Answer Key for *Review What You Have Read* **questions**

1. true
2. Foodborne illnesses pose the greatest risk for infants, pregnant women, older adults, and people with impaired immune systems.
3. Three microorganisms other than bacteria that can cause foodborne illness are parasites, protozoa, and viruses.
4. (List eight. Student response.)
5. (List five. Student response.)
6. Keep hot foods above 140°F (60°C) and cold foods below 40°F (4°C).
7. Divide large amounts of food and place it in small, shallow containers.
8. Most of the foodborne illness cases reported each year occur in foodservice establishments.
9. false
10. Wear rubber gloves to pick up large pieces of broken glass. Sweep smaller pieces into a disposable dustpan and use damp paper towels to wipe up any remaining fragments.

(continued)

Link to Academic Skills

11. (List eight. Student response.)

12. (List three. Student response.)

13. Use a nonconducting material, such as rope, a long piece of dry cloth, or a wooden pole to pull a shock victim away from an electrical source.

14. (Student response.)

15. **English language arts.** Write a public service announcement that might be broadcast on radio or television about safe food handling. Include a jingle or slogan to help people remember a specific standard of personal or kitchen cleanliness. Record your announcement and play it for the class.

16. **English language arts.** Write a pamphlet listing simple first aid procedures for poisonings, cuts, burns, falls, and electric shock.

17. **Science.** Look at examples of parasites and protozoa under microscopes.

18. **Science.** Pour ¼ teaspoon (1 mL) of cooking oil on your hands. Try to remove the oil using just warm water. After a few seconds, put a couple drops of liquid soap on your hands to help remove the oil. Describe what difference the soap made. Note that soap is an emulsifier that surrounds the oil droplets, keeping them suspended in the water so they can be washed away.

Build Critical Thinking Skills

19. **Analysis.** Analyze how food might become contaminated during a specific aspect of food production, processing, or transportation. Make a diagram illustrating this operation and the possible points of contamination. Also note safeguards that are taken to prevent contamination at these points.

20. **Synthesis.** Work in a group of four to research one type of foodborne illness. Each group member should summarize a different one of the following aspects: cause, food sources, symptoms, or prevention. Combine your ideas to prepare a poster presentation for the rest of the class.

Apply Technology

21. Make a list of 10 antibacterial personal care and/or kitchen cleaning products that have been introduced to the market in the last five years. Investigate the active ingredient in one of these products and note the pathogens it was developed to remove. Share your findings in class.

22. Develop a segment on food safety and the correct use of food thermometers in different foods to air on your local cable access channel.

A Measure of Math

23. With proper growth conditions, bacteria can double in number every 20 minutes. If there were 100 bacterial cells on a surface initially, calculate how many bacteria would exist on the surface after 2 hours. Then calculate how many bacteria would exist on the surface after 5 hours. Discuss what these calculations show about the importance of wiping up spills as they happen and storing leftovers promptly.

Teamwork in Action

24. Divide the class into four groups. Each group should write a skit to educate young children about a different step to food safety—clean, separate, cook, or chill. Arrange to present your skits in a local elementary school. Following the skit presentations, invite questions from the elementary school audience. Be prepared with chapter information to help you address the questions.

Companion Website

www.g-wlearning.com

At the website, review key terms for this chapter with crossword puzzles, matching exercises, and e-flash cards. Apply facts from the chapter to complete the activities.

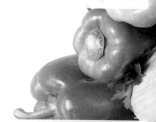

Part 2
The Management of Food

Study Starters

1. Look up the definition of *management* in a dictionary. Discuss in class how you think the concept of management would apply to meal preparation.

2. Divide a sheet of paper into two columns. In the first column, list factors you think would contribute to efficient meal preparation. In the second column, list factors you think would interfere with efficient meal preparation. Share your responses in class. Note how many of the factors cited relate to planning rather than to actual preparation.

FCCLA: Taking the Lead

Use this section of the text to help your FCCLA chapter create a *Financial Fitness* peer education project. Chapters 7, 8, and 9 describe items needed in a well-equipped kitchen. This could fit into a project for the *Financing Your Future* unit about applying financial skills when furnishing a kitchen in a first apartment. Chapter 10 includes information on planned spending. This material could serve as the basis for a budgeting education project that would relate to the *Cash Control* unit. Chapter 11 covers topics about using money wisely when shopping for food. Teaching these skills to other teens could become a project that would go along with the *Consumer Clout* unit.

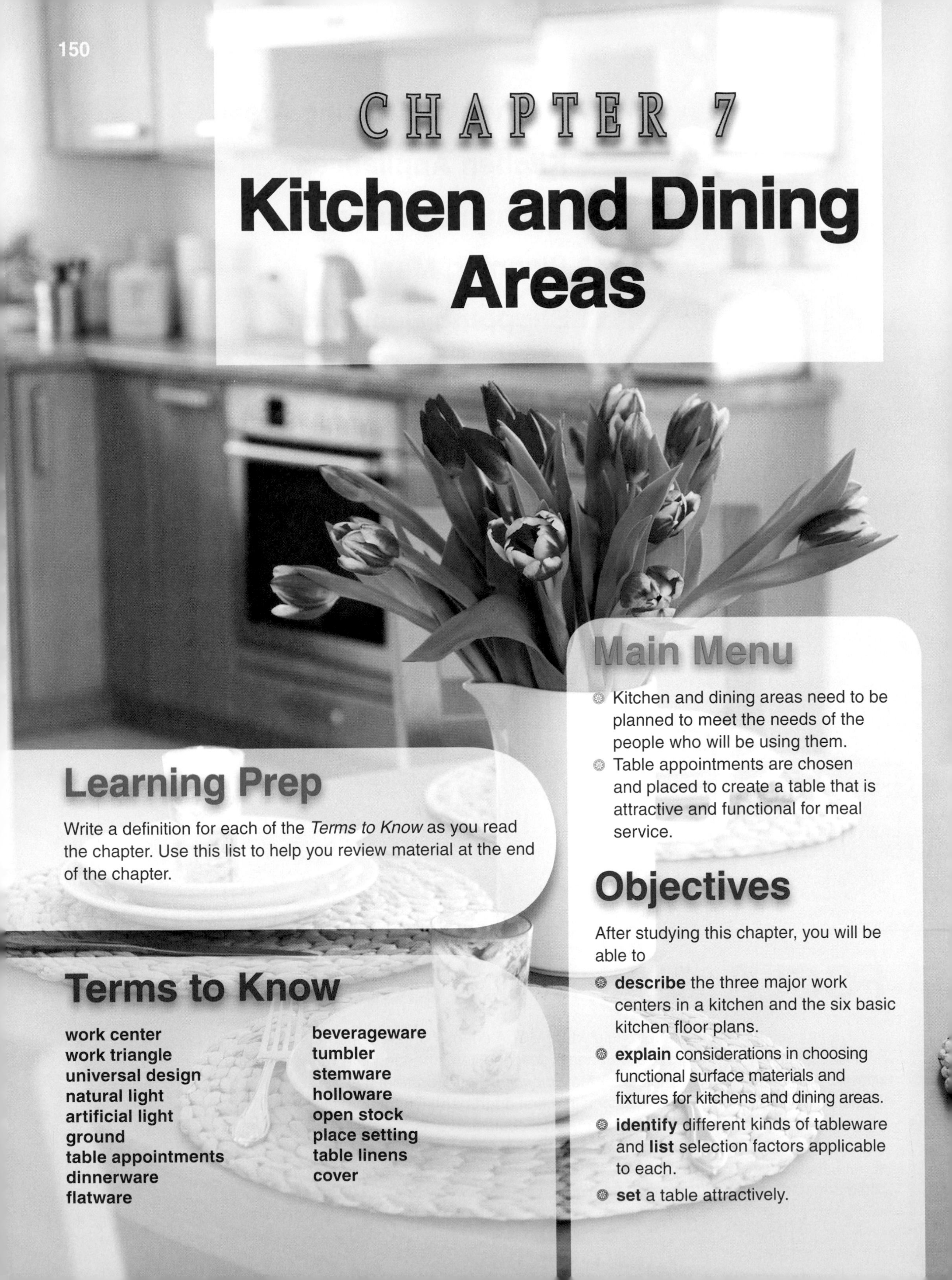

CHAPTER 7
Kitchen and Dining Areas

Learning Prep

Write a definition for each of the *Terms to Know* as you read the chapter. Use this list to help you review material at the end of the chapter.

Terms to Know

work center
work triangle
universal design
natural light
artificial light
ground
table appointments
dinnerware
flatware

beverageware
tumbler
stemware
holloware
open stock
place setting
table linens
cover

Main Menu

- Kitchen and dining areas need to be planned to meet the needs of the people who will be using them.
- Table appointments are chosen and placed to create a table that is attractive and functional for meal service.

Objectives

After studying this chapter, you will be able to

- **describe** the three major work centers in a kitchen and the six basic kitchen floor plans.
- **explain** considerations in choosing functional surface materials and fixtures for kitchens and dining areas.
- **identify** different kinds of tableware and **list** selection factors applicable to each.
- **set** a table attractively.

The kitchen and dining areas are often the busiest areas of the home. People spend a lot of time in these areas planning, preparing, and eating meals. Therefore, consider the likes, dislikes, and needs of everyone in the home when arranging these areas. Make them comfortable, convenient, and efficient places to work.

Planning the Kitchen and Dining Areas

When planning the arrangement of kitchen and dining areas, you should think about several questions. Are meals eaten in the kitchen, or is a separate dining room needed? How much storage and work space is needed in these areas? How much time will each person in the home spend in the kitchen and dining areas? What kind of atmosphere do you want these areas to have?

Major Work Centers

Most kitchens have three main **work centers**. A work center is a section in a kitchen that has been designed around a specific activity or activities. Each center focuses on one of the three basic groups of kitchen activities—food preparation and storage, cooking and serving, and cleanup.

The focal point of the *food preparation and storage center* is the refrigerator-freezer. This center requires cabinets for food storage. Cabinets also hold containers and tools used to store and serve frozen and refrigerated foods. Sometimes baked goods are mixed in this center. If so, storage space for mixing tools and workspace for mixing tasks will be needed here.

The *cooking and serving center* focuses on the range and oven. One side of the range should have at least 24 inches (60 cm) of counter space. This counter will hold the ingredients when you cook. Cabinets and drawers in this center store utensils, cookware, and serving pieces.

The *cleanup center* always contains the sink. It may also include a dishwasher and food waste disposer. Work done in this center includes dishwashing, cleaning vegetables and fruits, cleaning fresh fish, and soaking pots and pans. Plenty of counter

Learn About...

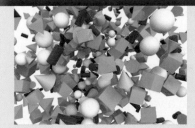

Additional Work Centers

If a kitchen is large, it may include additional work centers. A counter between the range and refrigerator can serve as a *mixing center*. It needs to be at least 36 inches (90 cm) wide. An electric mixer, a blender, mixing bowls, measuring tools, and baking utensils need storage space. Baking ingredients, such as flour and sugar, need to be stored, too.

Consider tucking a *planning center* into a corner where it can double as a communications center. Use shelves to store items such as cookbooks. A desk or countertop can hold a computer to be used for meal planning. You might keep a telephone in this area. Hang a bulletin board to post messages. Keep recipe cards, note pads, and writing utensils in a drawer.

Some kitchens have a *laundry center*. A laundry facility within the kitchen can save steps. However, be sure to locate it away from food preparation areas.

space and storage space are necessities in this work center. Keep coffeepots, teapots, dishwashing detergent, dishcloths, towels, and a wastebasket here. Canned goods and vegetables that require no refrigeration might be stored in this center. However, never store food under the sink.

Kitchen Storage Space

As mentioned, space is needed in each kitchen work center to store various items. Two points will help you evaluate how much storage space is needed and how best to use it. First, items should be stored where they will be used. Think about what tasks are likely to be done in each work center. Identify all the supplies needed to do each task. For instance, vegetables are chopped in the food preparation and storage center. This task requires knives and a cutting board. Store these items in the drawers and cupboards of that center.

The second point to think about when planning storage space is how often items will be used. Store items used most often in the most convenient places. For instance, saucepans and a double boiler both belong in the cooking and serving center. The saucepans are likely to be used almost daily. However, the double boiler may only be used occasionally. Therefore, store the double boiler in the back of a cupboard. Store the saucepans in the front of the cupboard, which is easier to reach.

Work Triangle

To make a kitchen as efficient as possible, place the focal points of the major work centers at the corners of an imaginary triangle. This triangle is called a **work triangle**.

Ideally, the work triangle follows the normal flow of food preparation. Food is removed from the refrigerator or freezer and taken to the sink for cleaning. From the sink, the food is taken to the oven or range for cooking. After cooking and eating, leftovers are returned to the refrigerator.

Spacious kitchens allow room for people to work together. However, if the work triangle is large, more energy will be used as you move from one point to another to prepare foods. The total length of the three sides of the triangle should not exceed 21 feet (6.3 m).

Kitchen Floor Plans

Work centers fit into a variety of kitchen floor plans. The shape of the kitchen depends largely on the size of the room.

The *U-shaped kitchen* represents the most desirable kitchen floor plan because of its compact work triangle. All the appliances and cabinets are arranged in a continuous line along three adjoining walls.

The *L-shaped kitchen* is popular because it easily adapts to a variety of room arrangements. Appliances and cabinets form a continuous line along two adjoining walls. In a large room, the open area beyond the work triangle might be used as an eating area.

Appliances and cabinets in a *corridor kitchen* are arranged on two nonadjoining walls. This can be an efficient floor plan if the room is not too long and is closed at one end. However, a long room can create a long work triangle that requires many steps. A room that is open at both ends allows traffic through the kitchen, which can interfere with the work triangle.

The *peninsula kitchen* is most often found in large rooms. In this kitchen, a counter extends into the room, forming a peninsula. The peninsula can serve as storage space or an eating area. It can also hold a cooktop or other built-in appliance.

The *island kitchen* is also found in large rooms. In this kitchen, a counter stands alone in the center of the room. An island and a peninsula serve similar functions. In some kitchens, the island also serves as a mixing center.

The *one-wall kitchen* is found most often in apartments. All the appliances and cabinets are along one wall. This arrangement generally does not give adequate storage or counter space. It also creates a long, narrow work triangle. Often, a folding or sliding door sets off the one-wall kitchen from other rooms. See **7-1**.

Reflect

Ask students which of the kitchen floor plans is found in their homes. Ask which floor plans they would prefer to have. Encourage students to think about the reasons for their choices.

Kitchen Floor Plans

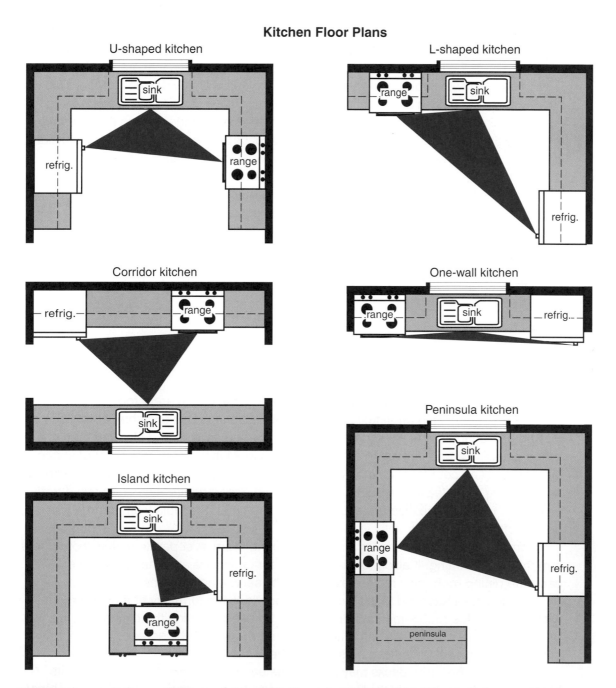

7-1 The size and shape of the work triangle depends on the kitchen floor plan.

Online Resource

Have students visit The Center for Universal Design website to investigate the principles of universal design.

Reflect

Ask students to identify the rooms in each of their homes where family members eat most of their meals.

Vocabulary Builder

A dining area attached to a living room is sometimes called a *dinette*.

Enrich

Invite a homemaker with a physical disability to speak to your class about obstacles he or she encounters in a traditionally designed kitchen. Find out what modifications the speaker has made in his or her kitchen to overcome those obstacles.

Meeting Design Needs of People with Physical Disabilities

A well-planned kitchen will help meet the special needs of people with physical disabilities. **Universal design** refers to features of rooms, furnishings, and equipment that are usable by as many people as possible. Peninsula, U-shaped, and L-shaped floor plans are examples of universal design. These floor plans provide the fewest restrictions to movement through a kitchen. A floor plan with a compact work triangle also reflects universal design. A compact work triangle prevents household members from using excess energy. This is especially important for people who have limited mobility, such as people who use walkers and crutches.

Work surfaces in a universal design kitchen need to be at a variety of levels. This allows people of all heights to work in the kitchen comfortably. Lower countertops can be reached with ease by children and people seated in wheelchairs. A narrow shelf can be installed above these counters to provide a handy place for items that are used often.

Removing lower cabinets near the sink and cooktop will provide knee space. This will allow someone sitting in a wheelchair or on a stool to move close to these work areas. A shallow sink with a rear drain also allows room for knees. Undercoating the sink and insulating the hot water pipes will protect the legs of people working in a seated position. Mounting a lever-type faucet on the side of the sink will make it easy to reach.

Contrasting trim along counters and around doorways is a universal design feature. Contrasting trim makes edges easier to see. Therefore, people will be less likely to bump into them. This feature is especially helpful for people with limited vision.

Universal design can even be used in kitchen storage spaces. Loop handles on drawers and cabinets are easier to pull open. Adjustable pantry shelves can be placed at heights that put most-used items within easy reach. Pull-out shelves reduce the need to bend and reach for items stored in the back of lower cabinets. Universal design allows all areas of the kitchen to better meet the needs of each person in the home.

Planning the Dining Area

The location of the dining area depends on the layout of the home. The number of people in the home and personal preferences affect the dining area, too.

A counter, a built-in breakfast nook, or a table can serve as a kitchen eating center. Having an eating area in the kitchen saves steps when serving and clearing meals. When planning a counter eating area, provide 18 to 24 inches (45 to 60 cm) of space per person. The counter should be at least 15 inches (38 cm) deep. If a table is serving as an eating area, leave at least 30 inches (75 cm) clearance around it. To avoid traffic problems, increase the clearance to 36 inches (90 cm) if the table is in an area where people often walk past it.

Some homes have space for a separate dining room. A separate dining room offers a more formal setting. It also provides storage for tableware and linens. However, a separate dining room may require extra steps to serve and clear meals.

A dining area attached to the living room provides the formality of a dining room without the space requirements. Screens may be used to divide the dining area from the rest of the living room. When entertaining larger groups, the screens can be taken down and additional tables can be set up in the living room.

Patios, porches, and decks may be used as eating areas when weather permits, **7-2**. Meals may also be eaten in the family room, living room, or den. In many homes, these areas are located near the kitchen. If they are not, trays and carts with wheels can help make transporting food and other items easier. Lap trays, tray tables, and card tables can be used to provide impromptu eating space.

You may want to turn to a computer for help when arranging kitchen and dining areas. A number of software programs are available to help you draw floor plans and place furniture and appliances. This will spare the effort of moving heavy items until you are sure the arrangement will meet needs. Some programs have a three-dimensional format. This feature lets you feel as though you are walking through rooms. It gives you a more realistic perspective than the overhead view provided by a standard floor plan.

Shutterstock

7-2 An outdoor eating area can provide an enjoyable dining atmosphere in warm weather.

Functional Surfaces and Fixtures

Kitchen and dining areas need to be functional. A key factor for reaching this goal is to choose surface materials and fixtures with care.

Wall and Floor Coverings

Wall coverings in kitchen and dining areas should be smooth and easy to clean. Many wall covering materials are available. Flat finish *paints* are suitable for dining rooms. Satin and semi-gloss finishes are better choices for kitchens. Other options include *ceramic* and *metal tile*, *wallpaper*, *vinyl wall coverings*, and *paneling*. Think about the cost and care requirements when choosing wall coverings. Also, find out how durable the coverings will be when exposed to heat, moisture, and grease from cooking.

Like wall coverings, kitchen and dining area floor coverings must be easy to clean. Floor coverings should also provide walking comfort and be durable. You can choose from several materials. *Solid wood*, *engineered wood*, and *plastic laminate* all offer the appearance of wood. *Vinyl sheets* or *tiles*, *ceramic tile*, and *linoleum* come in a wide range of colors and designs. *Stain-resistant carpeting* especially designed for use in the kitchen is also available. The costs of floor covering materials as well as their installation costs vary widely. Resistance to stains, scratches, dents and other signs of wear varies, too. Be sure to do your research before making a choice.

Countertops and Cabinets

In the kitchen, countertops provide workspace. In dining areas, counter space is used for serving food and holding dishes that have been cleared from the table. Common countertop materials include *natural stone*, such as granite and marble; *engineered stone*; *laminate*; *solid surface*; and *ceramic tile*. *Wood* counter surfaces are also an option. Use care to protect counter surfaces from damage due to heat, scratches, and moisture.

FYI

Illumination is measured in foot-candles. Lighting experts recommend 10 to 20 foot-candles of illumination for comfortable dining and 50 to 100 foot-candles

Cabinets are needed in kitchen and dining areas to store food, appliances, cleaning supplies, cooking utensils, dinnerware, and table decorations. Kitchen cabinets need to be easy to clean.

Cabinets may support countertops or be mounted on walls or suspended from ceilings above countertops and appliances. Tall, freestanding cabinets and special storage features, such as pull-out shelves, are also common in kitchens. *Wood*, *wood veneer*, and *plastic laminates* are popular cabinet materials.

Lighting and Ventilation

In the kitchen, good lighting is needed to prevent eyestrain and accidents while preparing food. In the dining room, there must be enough light to allow diners to see what they are eating.

Lighting can be classified as natural or artificial. **Natural light** comes from the sun. The amount of natural light available during daylight hours depends on the size and placement of windows, doors, and skylights. If there is not enough natural light to perform kitchen and dining tasks, artificial light should be added.

Artificial light most often comes from electrical fixtures. Ceiling fixtures are often hung over dining tables. They may also provide general lighting in kitchens. Extra light fixtures are often installed over ranges and under cabinets to provide *task lighting* in the kitchen, **7-3**.

Ventilation is needed in the kitchen to remove steam, heat, and cooking odors. Proper ventilation also helps maintain a comfortable dining atmosphere. If there is not enough natural ventilation, exhaust hood, wall, and ceiling fans will help circulate air.

GE Appliances

7-3 Task lighting over a cooktop reduces eyestrain and increases safety while cooking.

of illumination for food preparation tasks.

Activity

Have each student make a list of everything in his or her home kitchen that requires electricity. Ask students to share their lists in class.

Think Outside the Box

Have the class put together a list of suggestions in addition to using compact fluorescent lightbulbs that would help conserve energy in kitchen and dining areas.

Electrical Wiring

Another factor that affects the function of kitchen and dining areas is electrical wiring. Kitchens need a large supply of electricity to safely run appliances. In dining areas, electricity is needed mainly for lighting. Power is also needed to operate items such as coffeemakers and warming trays.

When wiring is inadequate, circuits often become overloaded. Be aware of the warning signs of overloaded circuits. Circuit breakers may trip or fuses may blow frequently. Motor-driven appliances, such as mixers, may slow down during operation. Lights may dim when an appliance is being used. Appliances that heat, such as electric skillets, may take a long time to become hot. If any of these signals occurs, call a qualified electrician to check the wiring.

For safety, appliances should be grounded. To **ground** an appliance means to connect it electrically with the earth. If a grounded appliance has a damaged wire, the electric current will flow to the earth instead of through your body. Thus you will not receive a severe or fatal shock.

Table Appointments

Table appointments are all the items needed at the table to serve and eat a meal. They include dinnerware, flatware, beverageware, holloware, linens, and centerpieces.

Dinnerware

Dinnerware includes plates, cups, saucers, and bowls. The material used to make dinnerware helps determine its durability and cost.

China is the most expensive type of dinnerware, but it is elegant and durable. *Stoneware* is heavier and more casual than china, but it is less expensive. Like stoneware, *earthenware* is moderately priced. However, it is less durable than stoneware. *Pottery* is the least expensive type of ceramic dinnerware. It is thick and heavy, and it tends to chip and break easily. *Glass-ceramic* is strong and durable. *Plastic* is lightweight, break resistant, and colorful, although it may stain and scratch over time. It is most suitable for very casual meals.

Flatware

Flatware, often called "silverware," includes knives, forks, and spoons. It also includes serving utensils (such as serving spoons) and specialty utensils (such as seafood forks). As with dinnerware, the material helps determine appearance and cost.

Sterling silver and *silver plate* flatware require polishing to remove tarnish caused by exposure to air and certain foods. *Stainless steel* does not tarnish, but like silver, it can be affected by eggs, vinegar, salt, tea, and coffee. To prevent staining, avoid prolonged contact with these foods and carefully rinse flatware as soon as possible.

When selecting flatware, consider the general shape of each piece, its weight, and the way it feels in your hand. A well-designed piece should feel sturdy and well balanced. Look at the finish. All edges should be smooth. Silver plate should be evenly plated.

Beverageware

Beverageware, which is often called glassware, are drinking glasses of many shapes and sizes used for a variety of purposes, **7-4**. Beverageware can be made of lead glass, lime glass, or plastic. The two basic shapes of beverageware are tumblers and stemware. **Tumblers** do not have stems. Juice and cooler are common tumbler sizes. **Stemware** has three parts—a bowl, a stem, and a foot. Water goblets, wine glasses, and champagne glasses are popular stemware pieces.

When choosing beverageware, examine the edges to be sure they are smooth and free from nicks. Glasses should feel comfortable to hold and be well balanced so they will not tip over when filled or empty. Look to see that the joints between the different parts of stemware are invisible.

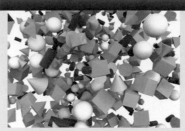

Learn About...

Grounding Appliances

The National Electrical Code requires all new homes to have Ground Fault Circuit Interrupters (GFCI) as part of the kitchen wiring system. If the outlets in a home have three holes, an equipment grounding wire has been installed. Many appliances have three-pronged plugs that fit into the three holes, thereby grounding the appliances.

If the outlets in a home have just two holes, two-pronged adapters will be needed for grounded appliances. An adapter has a small wire called a *pigtail* attached to it. Attaching the pigtail to the screw on the electrical outlet plate grounds the appliance.

Reflect

Ask students when they have eaten meals at tables that had especially attractive settings. Ask how the table setting affected the dining atmosphere.

Discuss

Ask students if they would prefer to buy sterling silver, silver-plated, or stainless steel flatware. Have them explain their choices.

Reflect

Ask students what types of beverages they usually serve with meals. Ask what beverageware pieces seem most appropriate for serving these beverages.

Vocabulary Builder

Lead glass is used to make higher-quality glassware that is more expensive. *Lime glass* is lighter and more brittle than lead glass.

Hamilton Beach Brands, Inc.

7-4 Different shapes of glasses are ideal for serving various fruit blends.

Choose pieces that are multipurpose. For instance, you can use some stemware for serving shrimp cocktails, fruit cups, and ice cream sundaes as well as beverages. Consider plastic beverageware for casual dining and when serving young children.

Holloware

Holloware includes bowls and tureens, which are used to serve food, and pitchers and pots, which are used to serve liquids. Holloware may be made of metal, glass, wood, or ceramic. Some holloware pieces have heating elements.

Holloware tends to be expensive, fragile, and difficult to store. You may purchase holloware pieces to match your dinnerware. However, unmatched holloware that complements other table appointments is less expensive and more popular.

Purchasing Tableware

Dinnerware, flatware, beverageware, and holloware are all referred to as *tableware*. All four types of tableware are available in many patterns and at a variety of prices. When purchasing tableware, you will want to consider your lifestyle and budget. If you enjoy formal entertaining and can afford the expense, you might select china, sterling silver, and lead glass. If you prefer more casual, less expensive tableware, you might choose stoneware, stainless steel, and lime glass for your table.

You can purchase tableware in several ways. You can buy some tableware as **open stock**. This means you can purchase each piece individually. Dinnerware and flatware are often sold in place settings. A **place setting** includes all the pieces used by one person. For instance, a place setting of dinnerware usually includes a dinner plate, salad plate, sauce dish or bread and butter plate, cup, and saucer. A place setting of flatware usually includes a knife, dinner fork, salad fork, teaspoon, and soupspoon. You can also buy some tableware by the set. A box of four water glasses and a set of dinnerware for eight are examples of sets.

Caring for Tableware

Proper handling and storage will extend the life of your tableware. Rinse tableware as soon as possible after use. Dried food particles are difficult to remove. You can put most tableware in the dishwasher, but you should check the manufacturer's recommendations.

Store tableware carefully. Handle dinnerware and beverageware with care to prevent chipped, cracked, and broken pieces. Place flatware neatly in a drawer to avoid scratching and bending it.

Table Linens

The term **table linens** includes both table coverings and napkins. *Tablecloths* protect the surface of the table and provide a background for your table setting. Place mats and table runners are also popular table coverings. *Place mats* come in several shapes and can be used for all but the most formal occasions. *Table runners* are narrower and slightly longer than the table. They are often used with tablecloths or place mats. *Napkins* can match the other table linens or provide a contrast. See **7-5**.

The amount of care table linens need depends on the materials used in their construction. Paper tablecloths, place mats, and napkins can simply be thrown away when a meal is finished. Vinyl-coated tablecloths and place mats can be wiped clean with a damp cloth. Most fabric cloths can be machine washed and dried. Linen cloths and napkins must be laundered carefully and then ironed while still damp. Before purchasing table linens, you should consider durability, ease of laundering, colorfastness, and shrinkage.

Centerpieces

You can buy or make centerpieces to add interest to the dining table. Floral arrangements are popular centerpieces. However, avoid using potted plants. Soil and food do not mix.

If your centerpiece includes candles, light them and be sure they burn above or below eye level. If open flames are a safety concern, consider using battery-operated flameless candles to add warmth and elegance to your centerpiece. Avoid using candles on the table during the day.

Regardless of the materials used to make your centerpiece, it should be in proportion to the size of the table. Make sure guests will be able to see over the centerpiece while they are seated.

Shutterstock

7-5 Table linens can add to the beauty and elegance of a formal table setting.

EXPLORING CAREERS

Interior Designer

Interior designers plan the use of space in buildings. They work with clients to select and arrange surface materials, appliances, furniture, and accessories to meet the clients' needs. Some designers specialize in planning space in homes. Others work on commercial buildings. Some designers also focus on certain types of design, such as color design or kitchen design.

Designers must have good listening skills as they find out from clients how the space will be used. They must learn about a client's likes and dislikes in terms of styles and colors, too. Designers must be able to manage money as they help clients set budgets for their projects. Then the designers must be able to stay within those budgets as they present ideas for clients to consider. Interior designers need to know how to read and understand blueprints. They need math skills as they take measurements and plan how to fit furniture and equipment in available space. Interior designers need attention to detail and cooperation skills as they work with architects and builders to get projects completed. They need to be able to manage time to meet project deadlines. Problem-solving skills are also important, as few projects go from start to finish without running into some snags.

Most interior designers have a four-year bachelor's degree. A few years of working with an experienced designer will help a new professional build needed skills. This type of background will help designers acquire status and attract future clients.

Setting the Table

You should set a table for convenience as well as beauty. There is no "right" way to set a table. The occasion, style of service, size of the table, and menu will help you determine how to set the table.

Begin setting the table with the table linens. A tablecloth should extend evenly on each side of the table. You may lay place mats flush with the edge of the table or 1 to 1½ inches (2.5 to 4 cm) from the table edge. Place runners down the center, along both sides, or around the perimeter of the table.

Handle all tableware without touching the eating surfaces. Start by placing the dinner plate in the center of each cover, 1 inch (2.5 cm) from the edge of the table. A **cover** is the table space that holds all the tableware needed by one person. If using a salad plate, place it to the left of the dinner plate above the napkin. If using a bread and butter plate, place it just above the salad plate, between the salad plate and the dinner plate. Each guest should be able to tell which appointments are his or hers. See **7-6**.

Place flatware in the order in which it will be used, working from the outside toward the plate. Forks go to the left of the plate. Therefore, if you are serving salad before the main course, place the salad fork to the left of the dinner fork. Place the napkin to the left of the forks or on the dinner plate.

Knives and spoons go to the right of the plate. This means a soupspoon goes to the right of the teaspoon if you are serving soup before the entree. You can place dessertspoons or forks above the dinner plate. When placing flatware, turn knives so the blades are toward the plates. Place forks and spoons with tines and bowls turned upward. The bottom of each piece of flatware should be in line with the bottom of the dinner plate.

Place the water glass just above the tip of the knife. Place other glasses below and to the right of the water glass. If you are serving a hot beverage, place a cup and saucer to the right of the knife and spoon.

Place salt to the right of pepper when placing shakers on the table. Place rolls, butter, and other foods that will be self-served to the right or left of the host's cover. Place serving utensils needed for foods to the right of serving dishes.

Corelle®

7-6 A properly set table provides each diner with the tableware pieces he or she will need for the meal being served.

CAREER SUCCESS

Learning New Information

Angelo is a cabinet and trim installer for Kitchen Works. Kitchen Works carries all the latest cabinet materials. They specialize in custom work to suit unusual kitchen designs. Angelo goes to customers' homes to measure where cabinets will go. Then he measures and cuts the materials and attaches the cabinets and trim using hand tools and power tools.

To be a successful employee, Angelo needs to know how to learn. Put yourself in Angelo's place and answer the following questions about your need for and use of this skill:

A. What new information might you need to learn to continue to perform your job well?

B. How might the customers of Kitchen Works be affected if you were unable to learn and apply new knowledge and skills?

C. How might Kitchen Works be affected if you were unable to learn and apply new knowledge and skills?

D. What is another skill you would need in this job? Briefly explain why this skill would be important.

CHAPTER 7 REVIEW

Summary

Kitchen and dining areas are heavily used spaces in the home. With careful planning, their design will meet the needs of all household members. Three major kitchen work centers focus on the tasks of preparing and storing food, cooking and serving, and cleanup. If space allows, a home may include additional work centers for such tasks as mixing, eating, planning, and doing laundry. Space is needed to store supplies required for the tasks done in each of these work centers. An imaginary line connects the three major work centers to form a work triangle. This triangle takes on different dimensions in different kitchen floor plans. Peninsula, U-shaped, and L-shaped plans reflect universal design, making the kitchen usable by as many people as possible.

Choose surface materials and fixtures that will be functional in kitchen and dining areas. Think about cost, durability, and care when selecting wall coverings, floor coverings, countertops, and cabinets. Plan ample lighting, ventilation, and electrical wiring to safely meet needs.

You will want to select dinnerware, flatware, beverageware, and holloware to suit your lifestyle and budget. Use table linens to provide a backdrop for other table appointments. Choose a centerpiece to add appeal to the dining table. The materials used to make table appointments affect their cost, durability, and care. A few basic guidelines can help you use table appointments to set an attractive table.

Review What You Have Read

Write your answers on a separate sheet of paper, using complete sentences when appropriate.

1. List two items that would be stored in each of the three major kitchen work centers.
2. What is the most desirable kitchen floor plan?
3. True or false. Work surfaces in a universal design kitchen all need to be at a level that can be easily reached from a seated position.
4. What qualities do floor coverings used in kitchen and dining areas require?
5. Name the two classifications of lighting and give sources of each.
6. What are three warning signs of an overloaded electrical circuit?
7. What type of tableware are plates, cups, and saucers and what factor helps determine their cost and durability?
8. What are the two basic shapes of beverageware? Give examples of each.
9. Describe the three ways tableware may be purchased.
10. List three types of table linens.
11. Give five guidelines for placing flatware when setting a table.
12. Make a drawing that shows how you would set the table for a family meal in which the salad is eaten before the main dish and water is the only beverage.

(continued)

Answer Key to *Review What You Have Read* questions

1. (List two items that would be stored in each of the following major kitchen work centers: food preparation and storage center, cooking and serving center, and cleanup center. Student response.)
2. The U-shaped kitchen is the most desirable floor plan.
3. false
4. Floor coverings must be easy to clean. They must also provide walking comfort and be durable.
5. Lighting can be classified as natural or artificial. Natural light comes from the sun. Artificial light most often comes from electrical fixtures.
6. (List three:) Circuit breakers may trip or fuses may blow frequently. Motor-driven appliances may slow down during operation. Lights may dim when an appliance is being used. Appliances that heat may take a long time to become hot.

Link to Academic Skills

7. Plates, cups, and saucers are dinnerware, and the material used to make them helps determine their cost and durability.

8. Tumblers and stemware are the two basic shapes of beverageware. (Examples are student response.)

9. Open stock pieces may be purchased individually. Place settings include all the pieces used by one person. Items sold by the set include a number

13. **History.** Visit a restored historic home or living history museum to see a kitchen from a previous century. Note what types of appliances and storage spaces the kitchen contained and how the work centers were arranged. Write a paragraph describing what you consider to be the biggest difference between the kitchen you visited and your kitchen at home.

14. **Government/Civics.** Investigate the National Electrical Code. Prepare a brief oral report on the history, function, or features of the Code.

15. **Science.** Clean tarnished sterling silver or silver plate flatware by lining the bottom of a sink with aluminum foil. Place tarnished flatware in the sink, making sure each piece touches the foil. Fill the sink with a solution of 1 cup of sodium carbonate washing soda per gallon of hot water. Use enough solution to completely cover the flatware. Observe how quickly the appearance of the flatware improves. Note that tarnish is silver sulfide, formed by a reaction between silver and sulfur in the air. An electrochemical reaction between silver and aluminum causes the tarnish to be transferred from the flatware to the foil.

16. **English language arts.** Find a picture of a table setting in a magazine or catalog. Attach the picture to your written critique of the table setting based on the guidelines given in this chapter.

Build Critical Thinking Skills

of the same piece or a number of place settings packaged together.

10. (List three:) tablecloths, place mats, table runners, napkins

17. **Analysis.** Pretend to make a cake in your foods lab, following the directions on a packaged mix. While you are doing this, have a partner count the number of times you walk along each side of the work triangle. When you have finished, analyze your motions. Then brainstorm with your partner to come up with ideas for reducing the distance you walked. Share your suggestions with the rest of the class.

18. **Synthesis.** Work with a partner to design a test to compare the effectiveness of various recommended cleaning products on the countertop material in your foods lab. With permission from your teacher, conduct the test. Compare a traditional cleaning product, a "green" cleaning product, and a homemade cleaning product. Present your findings in class, noting which cleaning product you preferred. Also, give your overall evaluation of the countertop material based on how easy it was to clean.

Apply Technology

19. Use a computer and the table function in word processing software to make gridlines. Then open the gridline file in a drawing program to draw the floor plan of your home kitchen according to accurate measurements.

20. Investigate two options for replacing traditional incandescent lightbulbs. Compare all three types of bulbs in terms of cost, performance, and energy efficiency.

(continued)

A Measure of Math

21. Go to a home improvement store that sells flooring and carpeting. Choose kitchen carpeting and a vinyl sheet design that appeal to you. Figure the cost of covering a 10- by 14-foot (3.0- by 4.3-meter) kitchen floor with each of these products. Compare the cost of installation as well as materials.

22. The part of a tablecloth that hangs over the edge of a table is called the drop. The drop should be 6 to 8 inches (15 to 20 cm) on all sides of a table for a casual table setting. The drop should be 8 to 10 inches (20 to 25 cm) for a formal table setting. Measure a table in the foods lab and figure what size tablecloth would be needed for casual and formal table settings.

Teamwork in Action

23. Host a table setting workshop for your community. Have class members demonstrate how to set tables to correspond to planned menus brought by those attending the workshop. Students might also demonstrate napkin folding techniques and ideas for creating simple, attractive centerpieces.

Companion Website

www.g-wlearning.com

At the website, review key terms for this chapter with crossword puzzles, matching exercises, and e-flash cards. Apply facts from the chapter to complete the activities.

11. (List five:) Place flatware in the order in which it will be used, working from the outside toward the plate. Place forks to the left of the plate. Place knives to the right of the plate. Place spoons to the right of the plate. Place dessertspoons or forks above the dinner plate. Place the bottom of each

piece of flatware in line with the bottom of the dinner plate. Turn all knife blades toward the plate. Place forks with tines turned upward. Place spoons with bowls turned upward.

12. (See page 160.)

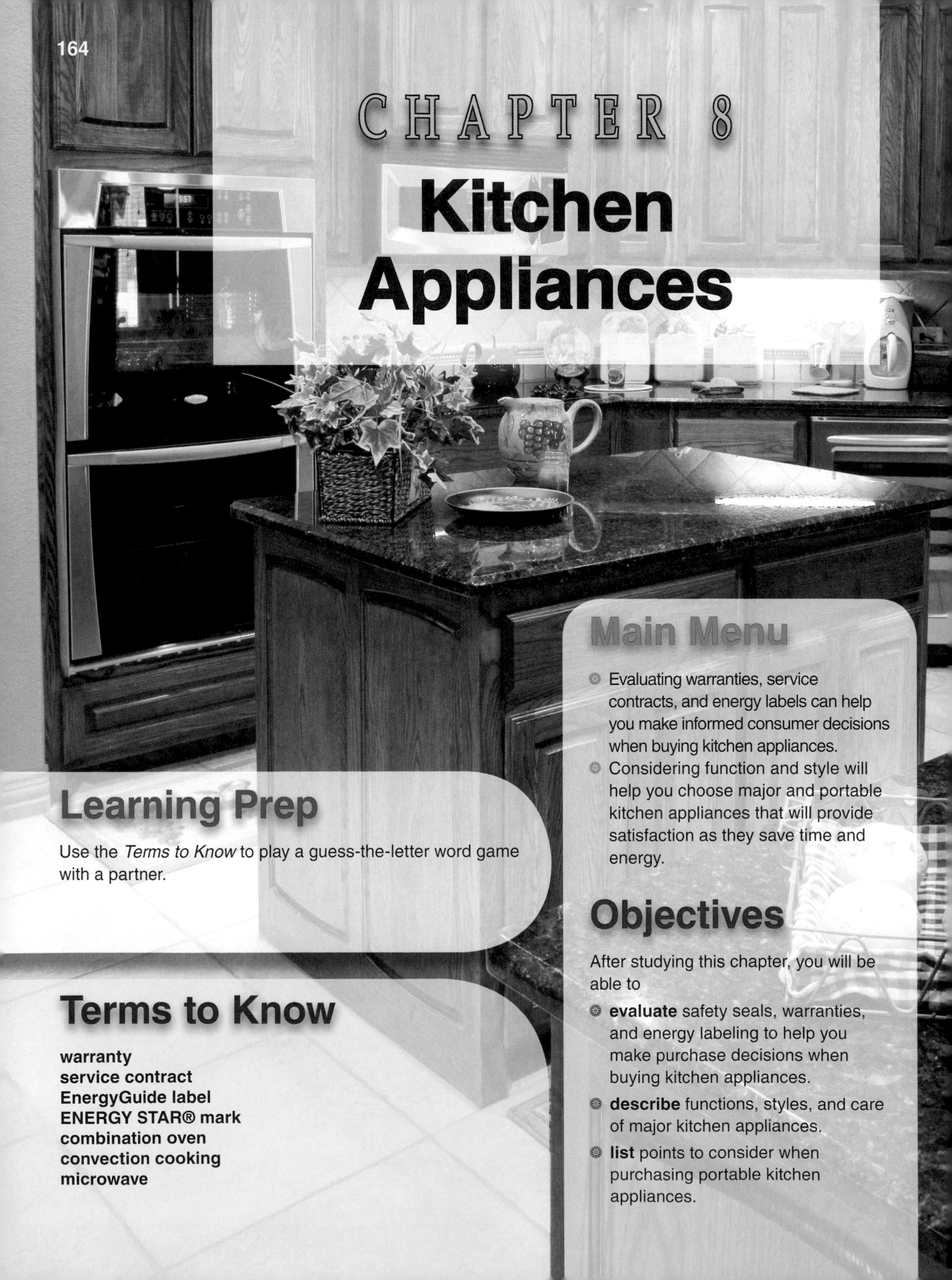

CHAPTER 8

Kitchen Appliances

Learning Prep

Use the *Terms to Know* to play a guess-the-letter word game with a partner.

Terms to Know

warranty
service contract
EnergyGuide label
ENERGY STAR® mark
combination oven
convection cooking
microwave

Main Menu

⊚ Evaluating warranties, service contracts, and energy labels can help you make informed consumer decisions when buying kitchen appliances.
⊚ Considering function and style will help you choose major and portable kitchen appliances that will provide satisfaction as they save time and energy.

Objectives

After studying this chapter, you will be able to

⊚ **evaluate** safety seals, warranties, and energy labeling to help you make purchase decisions when buying kitchen appliances.
⊚ **describe** functions, styles, and care of major kitchen appliances.
⊚ **list** points to consider when purchasing portable kitchen appliances.

Today's appliances make food preparation and cleanup easier. Major appliances are available in a range of styles and offer a wide variety of features. Portable appliances perform a multitude of kitchen tasks. Keep in mind that kitchen appliances are an investment. You can spend a lot of money for appliances. You will probably be using the appliances you choose for many years. Therefore, you will want to plan your appliance purchases carefully.

Service and Safety

Information is available when you buy an appliance to help you know what you can expect from your purchase. Using this information can help you buy safe, efficient products. Warranties, energy labeling, and safety seals can help you get your money's worth when you shop for appliances.

Warranties

A **warranty** is a seller's promise that a product will be free of defects and will perform as specified. A warranty can be full or limited. A *full warranty* states the issuer will repair or replace a faulty product free of charge. The warrantor may also opt to give you a refund for the product. A *limited warranty* states conditions under which the issuer will service, repair, or replace an appliance. For instance, you may have to pay labor costs, or you might have to take the appliance back to the warrantor.

Carefully check the warranty and be sure you understand the terms before you buy an appliance. Both limited and full warranties must state how and where you can fulfill them. Review the warranty to see if it covers the entire item or just parts. Find out if it includes labor costs. Note how long the warranty is in effect. If you have any questions, call or write to the manufacturer.

Service Contracts

A **service contract** is like an insurance policy for major appliances that you can buy from an appliance dealer. Service contracts cover the cost of needed repairs for a period after the warranty has expired. However, if your appliance does not need repairs, you receive no service for the money you spent on the contract.

If you are thinking about buying a service contract, be sure you know what you are getting. Read the terms of the contract carefully. Find out if it covers both parts and labor. Ask if the coverage will be good if you sell the appliance or move out of the service area. Check to see if there is a limit to the amount of service you may receive. Be sure you understand all the terms fully before you buy the contract.

Energy Labeling

The amount of energy appliances require can vary widely from model to model. Consumers must pay for the gas and electricity their appliances use. Energy also has an environmental cost because natural resources are used to produce it. Therefore, it is important to look into how much energy appliances will use when making buying decisions.

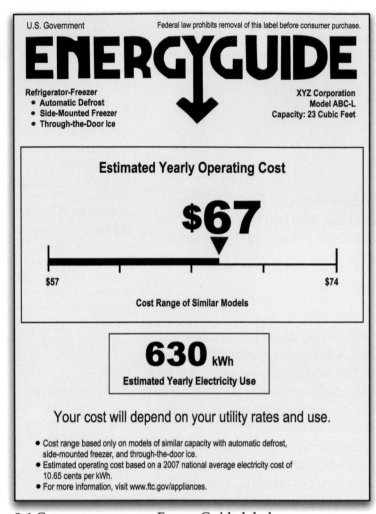

U.S. Government   Federal law prohibits removal of this label before consumer purchase.

ENERGYGUIDE

Refrigerator-Freezer
- Automatic Defrost
- Side-Mounted Freezer
- Through-the-Door Ice

XYZ Corporation
Model ABC-L
Capacity: 23 Cubic Feet

Estimated Yearly Operating Cost

$67

▼

|————————————————————————————————————|
$57 $74

Cost Range of Similar Models

630 kWh
Estimated Yearly Electricity Use

Your cost will depend on your utility rates and use.

- Cost range based only on models of similar capacity with automatic defrost, side-mounted freezer, and through-the-door ice.
- Estimated operating cost based on a 2007 national average electricity cost of 10.65 cents per kWh.
- For more information, visit www.ftc.gov/appliances.

8-1 Consumers can use EnergyGuide labels to compare the energy efficiency of various models of an appliance.

To help consumers, the Federal Trade Commission (FTC) requires **EnergyGuide labels** on many major appliances, **8-1**. These yellow tags show an estimate of yearly energy use for major appliances. This estimate is shown in kilowatt-hours. An estimate of the yearly operating cost is also given for the model on which the label appears. This cost is based on national average energy costs.

EnergyGuide labels are required on refrigerators, freezers, and dishwashers as well as a number of nonkitchen appliances. You can use these labels when you shop. Compare EnergyGuide labels on appliances of the same size. This will tell you which model is the most energy efficient and least costly to operate.

A second type of label you can use to find appliances that are energy efficient is the **ENERGY STAR® mark**. The U.S. Environmental Protection Agency (EPA) started the program in 1992. Today over 60 different kinds of products can earn the ENERGY STAR, as well as new homes and commercial buildings. Products that earn the ENERGY STAR include refrigerators and dishwashers. Unlike EnergyGuide labeling, the ENERGY STAR mark is not required. Products that earn the ENERGY STAR must meet strict guidelines set by the EPA. These appliances perform as well as similar appliances, but they use less energy. Therefore, they are better for the environment. They also save consumers money. See **8-2**.

Learn About...

Safety Seals

Most appliance manufacturers hire independent agencies to test their appliances for safety. These agencies ensure that appliances meet standards of the industry. One such agency that has been testing appliances for years is Underwriters Laboratories (UL). Appliances that pass safety tests carry a safety seal. This seal indicates the appliance has the testing agency's certification of safety.

When shopping for appliances, look for those made by well-known manufacturers. Buy appliances from reputable dealers. Look for safety seals on the appliances.

These steps are your best defense against appliances that fail to meet safety standards.

Electrical appliances carrying the Underwriters Laboratories (UL) mark have been carefully tested for safety.

Major Kitchen Appliances

Every part of kitchen activity involves major appliances. You use them to cook and store food and to clean up after preparing food. Today's appliances have many convenience features that reduce the time and effort needed to do these tasks.

When shopping for an appliance, consider how you will use it. You should also think about your space limitations and your budget.

Look for appliances with universal design styles and features. Such appliances will allow all household members to work in the kitchen with ease. For instance, you might choose a side-by-side refrigerator. This style gives wheelchair users and children access to both refrigerated and frozen foods. A built-in oven can be installed in the wall at a level that is easy to reach while seated. Front- or side-mounted appliance controls are a good choice for some households. These controls can assist people who have trouble seeing or reaching rear-mounted controls. An oven with a window and an interior light can help people who have limited vision. Audible signals on appliances can aid those who have trouble seeing. Indicator lights assist users who have difficulty hearing.

Size is an important factor to consider when buying an appliance. The size of appliance you need depends partly on the number of people in the household. For instance, a family of eight will probably need a larger range than a single person. Measure the appliance to find out if it will fit in the area where you want to put it. There must be adequate space for servicing and ventilation. Also measure the doors in your home. They must be wide enough to move the appliance into the room where you plan to install it.

Major appliances require a large financial investment. You must plan their purchase just like any other major household purchase. However, do not buy strictly on the basis of price. Service is also an important consideration. A bargain appliance may not seem to be such a good buy if no one in your area will service it.

Read the use and care manuals that come with your major appliances. Using the information in the manuals will help you get the best service from your kitchen equipment.

Trends and Technology in Major Kitchen Appliances

Each year, manufacturers bring out new appliance models in the hopes of boosting sales. They tap into the latest technology to build more efficient appliances that perform a wider range of functions. They design equipment that is easier to use and clean. For instance, the latest ranges do not just bake and broil foods. They offer faster, more even cooking than older models. They have larger interiors and flexible baking rack arrangements. They may have grilling and dehydrating functions. They have smooth surfaces for easy wiping and steam enhanced cleaning options, too.

U.S. Environmental Protection Agency

8-2 The ENERGY STAR® Certification Mark on appliances is a sign of energy efficiency.

Reflect

Ask students what styles and features they would choose if they were buying complete sets of major kitchen appliances. Ask students to think about the reasons for their choices.

Reflect

Ask students what types of convenience features on major kitchen appliances are important to them.

Reflect

Ask students what type of store they would be most likely to shop in when looking for kitchen appliances. Ask them why they would choose the types of stores they specified.

Consumers in smaller homes want compact models to conserve space without giving up style or function. Some other consumers are looking for appliances with extra capacity, such as dishwashers with three racks. Today's appliances come in a range of sizes to meet the needs of every household.

High-tech electronic touch pads are commonly used to create smooth control panels that are easy to wipe clean. Electronics also allow consumers to program appliances to do specific tasks. Some appliances have graphic display screens and/or voice modules. These features can show how a selected cycle is progressing. They can provide use and care information. They can also point out when something is not working right.

Today's consumers want appliances that reflect the latest trends in kitchen design. Smooth, stainless steel surfaces and gourmet features give appliances a professional look. Some consumers want their appliances to have an integrated look. They can use customized trim kits to make appliances mesh with the style of kitchen cabinets.

Global Perspective

Energy-Efficient Appliances

An important trend in major kitchen appliances is the continuing effort to make products more energy efficient. The latest models do more tasks with less energy than appliances of the past. Cooktops have quick-heating elements. Refrigerators have better insulation and door seals. Dishwashers are built to use less water. Some appliances are being designed to automatically wait until off-peak hours to perform tasks. This helps avoid draining public power supplies.

Consumers can also do their part for the environment when using appliances. Using the oven to bake more than one food at a time makes the best use of heat energy. Not opening the refrigerator door longer or more often than needed helps limit electricity use. Running full loads in the dishwasher and choosing the no-heat drying option save energy, too. As an added plus, conserving resources cuts utility costs.

GE Appliances

This induction cooktop is energy efficient because heat quickly goes straight to the cookware and the food without heating the cooking surface.

Cooking Appliances

Before buying cooking appliances, analyze your food preparation needs. You will need a cooktop for surface cooking and an oven for baking. These can be purchased as separate built-in units or as a single range.

Fuel

Whether you choose built-ins or a range, you will need to decide if you wish to use gas or electric fuel. Consider fuel costs, cooking needs, safety issues, appliance performance, and personal preferences when making your choice. Many times, you may decide based on the type of fuel hookups in your home.

Electric cooking appliances require a 240-volt electrical circuit. Electric current flows through coils of wire called heating elements. The current produces heat. Coils can be visible or hidden under a smooth, glass-ceramic top. Some smoothtop electric ranges feature *radiant* or *halogen* elements. These elements heat much faster than traditional electric coils.

Gas cooking appliances require both a gas line and a 120-volt electrical circuit. The ignition system and accessories, such as timers, clocks, and lights, require electricity. Gas appliances can use liquid propane (LP) or natural gas.

Dual-fuel ranges and cooktops cook with both gas and electricity. Dual-fuel ranges pair gas surface cooking with electric ovens. Modular cooktops allow consumers to place gas burners and electric elements side by side.

Cooking Appliance Styles

A built-in oven may be mounted into a wall or specially designed cabinet. A built-in cooktop is installed in a countertop. It may be placed along a wall or in an island or peninsula. These separated cooking units offer great flexibility in kitchen design.

Ranges come in three basic styles. *Freestanding ranges* have finished sides. You can place them at the end of a counter or in a cutout between cabinets. Freestanding ranges have backguards that extend above the counter surface, making them taller than other range styles. *Slide-in ranges* sit on the floor. *Drop-in ranges* are shorter and sit on a cabinet base. Both slide-in and drop-in ranges fit snugly between two cabinets. They have a more built-in look with surfaces that are nearly flush with countertops.

Ranges and built-ins may have single or double ovens. Some ovens are **combination ovens**, which can do two types of cooking. Many combination ovens offer a choice of conventional or convection cooking. **Convection cooking** uses a stream of heated air to bake and roast foods. This saves energy, reduces cooking time, and promotes more even cooking than conventional cooking. In models with double ovens, one oven may be a conventional oven while the other is a convection or microwave oven. See **8-3**.

Using and Caring for Cooking Appliances

Always practice good safety habits when using cooking appliances. Place pans on surface units before turning on the units. This will prevent accidents and also save energy. Be careful not to drop heavy objects on the cooktop. Most appliances have finishes that can crack or chip if struck. Wipe up spills immediately with a damp cloth. Do not use cold water when the cooktop is hot. Some appliance surfaces can crack from severe temperature changes.

Wash the surface of appliances regularly. Wash removable parts in warm, soapy water. Then rinse and dry them carefully. Clean the oven regularly. Also, wipe up spills when they occur to keep the oven neat between cleanings.

Enrich

Have students survey five homemakers about whether they prefer gas or electric cooking appliances. Students should ask the homemakers to note the reasons for the choices given. Ask students to share their findings in class.

FYI

Gas ranges are generally less costly to operate than electric ranges. However, the initial purchase price of an electric range tends to be lower than the price of a comparable gas range. Also, gas fuel lines are not available in all areas of the country.

Reflect

Ask students which cooking appliance styles they would prefer and why.

Reflect

Ask students to identify the tasks for which they would most often use a microwave oven.

Time Management Tip

Even when you are using a cooktop or conventional oven to perform the main cooking function for a dish, use the microwave oven to help save time with preliminary preparation tasks. For instance, a microwave oven can help save time and limit dirty dishes when melting butter, softening cream cheese, thawing foods, and toasting nuts.

KitchenAid

8-3 A built-in double oven may offer the speed and efficiency of convection cooking in one or both ovens.

Microwave Ovens

Microwave ovens vary widely in price, size, and features. When buying a microwave oven, consider what best fits your needs. Will the microwave oven be used for full cooking procedures, or will it mainly be used to defrost and reheat prepared foods? Are several levels of power needed, or will a simple model with one power level meet your needs?

Microwave ovens can defrost, cook, or reheat food in a fraction of the time required by conventional ovens. Microwave cooking can also save up to 75 percent of the energy used by conventional ovens.

Microwave cooking is done by high-frequency energy waves called **microwaves**. The oven walls, floor, and door liner are made of metal. The metal confines the microwaves and reflects the energy toward the food. This allows the microwaves to penetrate the food from the top and all sides. The energy from the microwaves causes the molecules of the food to vibrate. The friction of the vibrating molecules creates heat, which cooks the food.

Microwave Oven Styles

Two main styles of microwave ovens are available. *Countertop microwave ovens* can be placed nearly anywhere, **8-4**. With a manufacturer's kit, you can install some models under cabinets or in a wall. A *combination microwave and hood* has a light and exhaust vent on the bottom of it. This type hangs over a range or cooktop in place of a standard hood. Both styles are available as combination microwave/convection ovens. This type of oven allows you to cook with microwaves only, convection heat only, or both methods at the same time.

GE Appliances

8-4 Countertop microwave ovens are the most popular style and offer the greatest choice of features.

Using and Caring for Microwave Ovens

Do not plug a microwave oven into an extension cord. Plug it into a 120-volt grounded electrical outlet. You may want the microwave oven to be the only appliance on the electrical circuit. Sharing the circuit with another appliance can reduce the amount of electrical power to the microwave oven. This can affect the cooking time and may harm the oven itself.

Take care not to turn on a microwave oven when it is empty. This could damage the interior.

The door seal on a microwave prevents radiation leakage. Do not let anything become caught between the sealing surfaces. Immediately clean up any food spills to keep the seal intact. If the door or hinges should become damaged, do not use the oven until you have it repaired.

To clean the interior and exterior of the oven, use a damp cloth and mild detergent. Never use an oven cleaner or abrasive cleansers.

Refrigerators

A refrigerator's main job is to keep foods cold and retard food spoilage. Refrigerator space is measured in cubic feet (cubic meters). Fresh food storage compartments should provide about 3.5 cubic feet (0.11 cubic meters) of space for each adult in a household. Freezers should provide about 1.5 cubic feet (0.04 cubic meters) of space per person. If you shop less than once a week, you may need additional storage space.

Refrigerator Styles

The three most common refrigerator styles are based on the placement of the freezer. *Top-mount refrigerators* have the freezer above the refrigerator. They are the most common and energy efficient style. *Side-by-side refrigerators* have the freezer beside the refrigerator. They provide more freezer space, but the narrow compartments may make it hard to store large food items. *Bottom-mount refrigerators* have the freezer below the refrigerator. This style places refrigerated foods at a height that is easier to reach, but fewer models are available. Some bottom-mount refrigerators have double French-style doors.

Most refrigerator models are *frost free*. This means frost does not accumulate in the freezer. You can save on purchase and operating costs by buying a *manual-defrost* model. To avoid wasting energy, you should defrost the freezer on these models when frost reaches a thickness of ¼ inch (0.6 cm).

Using and Caring for Refrigerators

For food safety and energy efficiency, keep the fresh food compartment at 37°F to 40°F (3°C to 4°C). Keep the freezer at 0°F to 5°F (−18°C to −15°C). Keep foods covered to hold in moisture and prevent unpleasant odors in the refrigerator. Try to take out all the items you need from the refrigerator at one time. Each time you open the refrigerator door, warm air enters. The refrigerator then has to use more energy to lower the temperature again.

8-5 Keeping shelves, drawers, and all interior surfaces of a refrigerator clean will help keep chilled foods safe.

Water use by a dishwasher varies from about 6 to 19 gallons (24 to 76 L) per load, depending on the model and cycle. The average use of 9 gallons per load is less than many people use when washing dishes by hand.

To ensure food safety, keep both the inside and the outside of the refrigerator clean. Refrigerator parts and accessories also need regular cleaning. Wash ice cube trays, door gaskets, crisper drawers, and shelves with warm, soapy water. Rinse and dry carefully. See **8-5**.

Dishwashers

Dishwashers have a number of advantages. They can save time and personal energy. Dishes washed in a dishwasher are more sanitary. This is because the water is hotter and the detergent is stronger than the water and detergent used in hand washing. In addition, air drying is more sanitary than drying with a dish towel. Dishwashers offer a choice of wash cycles. Cycles differ in the number and length of washes and rinses, amount of detergent used, and water temperature.

Dishwasher Styles

Two basic types of dishwashers are available. *Built-in* models are the most popular type. They fit between two cabinets and load from the front. Built-in dishwashers are permanently connected to a drainpipe, hot water line, and electric circuit.

Portable dishwashers are designed to be rolled to a sink for use. A portable dishwasher connects to the sink faucet with a hose and drains into the sink. You can convert some portable models to built-ins.

Using and Caring for Dishwashers

If you will not be running the wash cycle right away, you should scrape dishes carefully before loading the dishwasher. If food hardens on dishes, it will be harder for the dishwasher to remove. Food left on dishes will also create odors in the dishwasher.

When loading the dishwasher, place dishes so they face the water source and avoid crowding them. Point knives, forks, and spoons down into the flatware basket. Angle pieces with recessed bottoms so water will run off.

To use a dishwasher most efficiently, run it only when there is a full load. Use an automatic dishwasher detergent. If the water in your area is high in some minerals, spots may form on glassware. Using a rinse agent will help reduce spotting. See **8-6**.

To maintain water temperature and pressure needed for proper cleaning, you should not use the washing machine while using the dishwasher. You should also avoid watering the lawn and taking a bath or shower.

Periodically empty the drain screen of any food particles that have collected. Occasionally wipe the outside of the machine with a soapy cloth, then rinse and dry.

8-6 Running full dishwasher loads will help save water and energy costs.

EXPLORING CAREERS

Appliance Sales Manager

Appliance sales managers are in charge of making sure appliances sell. Managers may be responsible for one store or a chain of stores. They must know the needs and desires of consumers in their geographic areas. This will help them stock the types of appliances that are most likely to sell. They may set sales quotas, hold trainings, and conduct job evaluations for salespeople who sell directly to customers. They may help set prices and discount rates, too.

Successful sales managers must show an ability to set and achieve goals. They must be leaders who can handle stress and are not afraid to take control and tackle challenges. Sales managers need to understand why people react the way they do. This will help them know how customers will react to various sales techniques. Good speaking skills are necessary so they can communicate appliance information in employee trainings. They need to be persuasive so they can encourage salespeople to try new ways of approaching customers. Sales managers also need critical thinking skills so they can correct customer issues that reflect problems with sales or service policies.

Most appliance sales managers have four-year bachelor's degrees. These degrees are likely to be in a business field, such as marketing. Many managers begin working as salespeople. Then, after a few years, they use their product knowledge and sales experience to move into management positions.

Other Major Appliances

Some people choose to buy other major appliances to help in the kitchen. A few examples include *warming drawers*, which are useful for holding prepared foods at serving temperatures for a few hours. *Food waste disposers* use sharp blades to grind food scraps into tiny particles, which wash down the drain. *Trash compactors* compress food and nonfood waste to about one-fourth its initial size.

Before purchasing any of these appliances, consider your needs and the styles and features available. Be sure the appliances will fit in your kitchen without taking away needed storage space. Look at your budget and be sure the benefits you receive from the appliances will be worth their costs.

Portable Kitchen Appliances

Major appliances are needed for basic kitchen functions. However, they cannot do many of the individual preparation tasks meal managers must perform. For these tasks, meal managers often rely on the time and energy savings provided by portable appliances. These small appliances can do many tasks faster and better than you could do them by hand.

Trends and Technology in Portable Kitchen Appliances

Modern portable appliances are designed with smooth, sleek shapes in trim sizes. Most appliances are available with white, black, or metal finishes. They are neutral enough to blend with any kitchen decor. However, many portable appliances also come in a range of popular colors to reflect the latest kitchen decorating trends.

FYI

Water spotting and cloudy filming on glassware in a dishwasher are often caused by hard water. Besides a rinse agent, filming can be avoided by using fresh, dry, high-phosphorous detergent; hot water (at least 140°F); and hot drying.

Discuss

Ask students what other means homemakers can use to dispose of garbage if they do not have food waste disposers. *(composting)*

Career Path

Have students investigate a job description, qualifications, and training requirements for the career of appliance salesperson. Have them compare this with the information provided about an appliance sales manager.

Hamilton Beach Brands, Inc.

8-7 A suite of portable appliances that are designed to go together give a kitchen a unified look.

Appliance suites are another trend. Some consumers choose each appliance by the brand that offers the most desired features. Other consumers want their appliances to have a unified look. For these consumers, manufacturers offer collections of appliances that go together. See **8-7**.

A number of needs have set the pace for technology in all of today's portable kitchen appliances. Consumers require appliances that perform quickly and safely. Sensors that turn off appliances when not in use are one safety feature found on many of today's portables. Appliances should be easy to clean. Many appliances have dishwasher-safe parts to address this need. Modern appliances should not take up much space. Cordless and under-the-cabinet appliances are conveniently sized to help consumers maximize limited space in the kitchen.

Consumers want portable appliances that simplify their work in the kitchen. However, today's appliances are used far beyond the kitchen. Coffeemakers, for instance, may be found anywhere from the office to the garage. A few models are available that will even plug into the power outlet in a car.

Purchase Considerations for Portable Appliances

When purchasing small appliances, select those that give the most satisfaction for the money spent. Consider what the appliance does, its limitations, and its special features. Then decide what to buy.

The following are some questions to consider:

- Is the appliance made by a reputable manufacturer and sold by a reputable dealer?
- Does the appliance come with a warranty?
- Who provides servicing when the appliance needs repairs?
- Will the appliance be used frequently?
- Does another appliance you already have do the same job?
- Is there adequate, convenient storage space for the appliance?
- Does the appliance have adequate power to perform its intended tasks?
- Does the appliance have a convenient size and shape?
- Is the appliance sturdy and well balanced? (Motor-driven appliances should not tip or "walk" during use.)
- Are parts easy to assemble for operation and easy to disassemble for cleaning?
- Does the appliance have quality construction features?
- Does the appliance have built-in safety features?
- Does the appliance have a safety seal to guarantee that it meets electrical safety standards?

Toasters and Toaster Ovens

Toasters are one of the most common kitchen appliances. You can choose between two- and four-slice models, depending on the number of people who will be using it. Look for a model with extra wide openings if you like to toast bagels and thick slices of bread. See **8-8**.

Toaster ovens bake and broil small food items in addition to toasting bread. These appliances are handy for small apartments and other small quarters. They use less energy and create less heat in the kitchen than full-sized ovens.

Electric Mixers

Electric mixers are popular among home bakers for blending ingredients, beating egg whites, and whipping cream. These appliances are available in stand and hand-held styles. Unlike hand mixers, *stand mixers* leave your hands free. They are also better for heavy-duty mixing jobs. You can remove some stand mixer heads from the stand and use them as hand mixers. The motor on a stand mixer should be strong enough to beat stiff mixtures without overheating. The mixer should provide even, constant mixing at every speed. The beaters should be easy to insert and remove. They should cover the full bowl diameter for thorough mixing of small or large amounts of food.

Hand mixers are smaller, lighter, and less expensive than stand mixers. However, they are not as versatile. You must hold them during the entire mixing operation. They should have stable heel rests or other means of support for standing on the counter when not in use.

Blenders

You might use a blender to blend milk shakes, puree soup, or crush cookies for a crumb crust. Unlike mixers, blenders do not incorporate air into foods.

A blender should have a removable container, molded of heat-resistant glass or plastic. The container should have a wide opening, a handle, a pouring spout, and measurement markings on the side. Also look for a self-sealing vinyl cover that resists odors and stains. A removable center cap makes it easy to add ingredients.

Food Processors

The food processor performs many time-consuming jobs quickly and easily. It blends, purees, grates, chops, and slices. It is especially helpful when you have larger amounts to prepare.

When buying a food processor, look for one that meets your needs for features. A safety interlock switch ensures that you have locked the cover in place before starting the processor. A dishwasher-safe container and cutting disks or blades will ease cleanup. You may want a food pusher that adapts to processing small or slender foods. Also make sure the control panel is easy to operate.

KitchenAid

8-8 Wide openings in a toaster are designed to accommodate thick-sliced breads and bagels.

Reflect

Ask students if they would prefer a toaster-oven over a toaster. Ask them why or why not.

Discuss

Ask students to identify the advantages and disadvantages of a stand mixer as compared with a hand mixer. *(Stand mixers are better for heavy-duty mixing jobs and they leave your hands free. However, they are more costly and less portable than hand mixers.)*

Discuss

Ask students why a blender would not be satisfactory for whipping cream and beating egg whites. *(because it does not incorporate air into foods)*

Hamilton Beach Brands, Inc.

8-9 Coffeemakers brew fresh, aromatic coffee and keep it steaming hot and ready to enjoy.

Coffeemakers

Coffeemakers have thermostatic controls that brew coffee without boiling it and then keep it at drinking temperature. The two types of automatic coffeemakers are the percolator and the drip coffeemaker. In an *electric percolator*, hot water is repeatedly pumped over a perforated basket holding ground coffee. In an *automatic drip coffeemaker*, hot water slowly drips down through ground coffee into a pot below. Special types of coffeemakers are available for brewing espresso and cappuccino. See **8-9**.

Electric Can Openers

An electric can opener quickly and easily cuts lids off metal cans. A magnet holds the lid for easy removal. Some models adjust to accommodate cans of different heights. Most have removable cutting assemblies for easy cleaning. Many can openers also sharpen knives.

Electric Skillets

A thermostat controls the temperature throughout the entire cooking process in an electric skillet. The electric skillet can take the place of the oven in some instances, thus saving energy. You can use it to fry, roast, panbroil, stew, or simmer foods. You can also use it to bake casserole dishes, quick breads, cakes, custards, and desserts.

An electric skillet should have a high dome cover to provide maximum capacity and versatility. The cover should have a vent. Also look for a clearly visible heat indicator light and a cooking surface that suits your needs. Aluminum is least expensive, stainless steel is durable, and a nonstick coating provides easy cleaning.

Slow Cookers

Slow cookers are versatile, timesaving appliances. Most models have at least two heat settings for cooking. You can use them to prepare pasta sauces, roasts, and a range of one-dish meals, such as soups and stews. You can combine ingredients in a slow cooker in the morning. At the end of the day, you will have a meal that is ready to eat without much additional preparation time. Look for a model with a removable cooking vessel that has a nonstick surface for easy cleaning. Some cooking vessels and lids are dishwasher safe.

Bread Machines

Bread machines mix and knead bread dough. They allow the dough to rise, and then they bake the bread. A manual setting allows you to use a bread machine to prepare dough for pizza, rolls, and other yeast products. You must then shape these products by hand and bake them in a conventional oven.

When shopping for a bread machine, consider the loaf size you want. Different machines produce different sizes, and some machines produce more than one size loaf.

Other Portable Kitchen Appliances

In addition to the small appliances discussed, there are many others available on the market. These include pasta makers, cappuccino makers, electric tea kettles, and iced tea makers. Electric woks, knives, coffee grinders, ice cream makers, waffle bakers, and grills are also among the variety of portable appliances offered.

Many portable appliances are versatile, performing several functions. Others do just one task. These single-function appliances are often fad items that appear on the market one year and disappear the next. Others meet real consumer needs and become lasting options for appliance buyers. See **8-10**.

When choosing a more specialized appliance, consider storage space. Think about how often the appliance will be used. Also check to see if you have another appliance that will perform the same task. As with all appliances, make selections based on need, available features, quality construction, and ease of use and care.

Hamilton Beach Brands, Inc.

8-10 A rice cooker may seem like a single-function appliance, but it can actually be used to prepare a wide range of foods.

General Use and Care for Portable Appliances

Before using any portable appliance, be sure to read the manufacturer's use and care booklet. The booklet will give directions for proper use that will help your appliance last for years. It will also include safety guidelines to help avoid mishaps in the kitchen.

The manufacturer's booklet will tell you how to clean the appliance. You should clean most portable appliances after each use. Allow hot appliances to cool. Always unplug portable appliances before cleaning. Wash most removable parts in warm, soapy water. Some parts may be safely cleaned in a dishwasher. Most appliance motor bases and heating elements should not be immersed in water. Wipe them clean with a damp cloth.

CAREER SUCCESS

Using Positive Personal Qualities

Gary works on the assembly line at the Cook Craft appliance factory. He uses hand tools to mount control knobs on ranges.

Gary has seen many of his coworkers quickly tire of doing this routine task day after day. Some workers quit; others pay little attention to their work and are eventually fired for failing to meet quality standards.

To be a successful employee and avoid the fate of his coworkers, Gary needs positive personal qualities. Put yourself in Gary's place and answer the following questions about your need for and use of these traits:

A. What positive personal qualities would you find useful as an appliance line assembler?

B. How will having each of these personal qualities help you deal with the routine nature of your work?

C. How could you use your personal qualities to have a positive influence on your coworkers?

D. What is a skill you would need in this job? Briefly explain why this skill would be important.

CHAPTER 8 REVIEW

Summary

You can do nearly every kitchen task more easily with the help of appliances. Use available information to help you make wise consumer choices. Safety seals on appliances assure you the appliances have been tested to work safely. Warranties state what you can expect from a manufacturer if an appliance does not perform as intended. EnergyGuide labels and ENERGY STAR marks help you choose appliances that are energy efficient.

Major kitchen appliances handle the basic tasks of cooking, storage, and cleanup. Cooking appliances include ranges, built-in ovens and cooktops, and microwave ovens. Refrigerators store perishable foods; dishwashers ease cleanup.

All major appliances come in several sizes and styles. Different models offer different features. Major appliances are expensive. You must weigh your options carefully to choose the appliances that best meet your needs. Following manufacturers' recommendations for use and care will help appliances work properly and last for a long time.

There are many portable appliances available to help do food preparation tasks. These include toasters, mixers, blenders, food processors, coffeemakers, can openers, electric skillets, slow cookers, and bread machines. When choosing portable appliances, choose those that are convenient to use and store. Look for well-built models that provide the desired features.

Review What You Have Read

Write your answers on a separate sheet of paper, using complete sentences when appropriate.

1. Give two suggestions for buying appliances that have met safety standards.

2. Explain the difference between a full warranty and a limited warranty.

3. Give three examples of universal design features in major appliances that will allow all household members to work in the kitchen with ease.

4. What types of fuel hookups are required to run electric and gas ranges?

5. How much energy can cooking foods in a microwave oven save compared with cooking foods in a conventional oven?

6. Name the three most common styles of refrigerators.

7. Give three use and care guidelines for dishwashers.

8. List five questions to consider when purchasing portable appliances.

9. Which type of mixer is best for heavy-duty mixing jobs?

10. What features make a food processor easier to clean?

11. What are five cooking methods that can be done using an electric skillet?

12. What are three factors consumers should consider when thinking about buying a specialized portable appliance?

Link to Academic Skills

13. **English language arts.** Investigate appliance testing at Underwriters Laboratories or another testing agency. Find out what kinds of tests appliances must pass in order to meet safety standards. Write a brief report of your findings.

14. **English language arts.** Visit an appliance or department store. Compare the prices and features of several models of the major or portable appliance of your choice. Ask about the warranties that come with each model. Find out if service contracts are available. Check safety features and energy ratings. Use your findings to give an oral report in class.

15. **Social studies.** Review four television commercials, sales flyers, and/or magazine ads promoting kitchen appliances. Note the marketing strategies used by appliance manufacturers and retailers to attract business. Use your review for input in a class discussion.

16. **Science.** Investigate how other forms of energy are converted to electrical energy. Also research how electricity flows through household wiring and how circuits are completed when appliances are turned on. Draw a diagram to illustrate one of your findings.

17. **History.** Find out when and how iceboxes were used to keep foods fresh. Compare this appliance with a modern refrigerator. Write a paragraph describing why you would or would not like to have an icebox in your home today.

18. **Science.** Place a portion of perishable food on each of two identical plates and leave them at room temperature for 24 hours. Dispose of the food and sanitize the surfaces on which the plates were sitting. Then wash one of the plates by hand and the other plate in a dishwasher. Use cellophane tape to transfer bacteria from the surface of each cleaned plate to an identified section of a petri dish filled with agar. Leave a third section of the petri dish untouched as a control. Incubate the petri dish at 99°F (37°C) for two days. Examine the bacterial colonies on the petri dish. Discuss what this reveals about washing dishes by hand as compared to using a dishwasher.

4. Electric cooking appliances require a 240-volt electrical circuit. Gas cooking appliances require a gas line and a 120-volt electrical circuit.

5. Microwave cooking can save up to 75 percent of the energy used by conventional ovens.

6. The three most common styles of refrigerators are top-mount, side-by-side, and bottom-mount.

7. (List three. Student response. See page 172 in the text.)

8. (List five. Student response. See page 174 in the text.)

9. stand mixer

10. A dishwasher-safe container and cutting disks or blades will make a food processor easier to clean.

Build Critical Thinking Skills

19. **Analysis.** Bake equal portions of a casserole, such as macaroni and cheese, in a conventional oven and a microwave oven. Compare the cooking times and the quality of the dishes. If possible, also compare the results using a convection oven. Based on your analysis, state which appliance you would prefer to use when preparing this type of casserole. Give reasons for your choice.

20. **Evaluation.** Look through a catalog or an Internet site that offers a variety of portable appliances. Evaluate the functions of each appliance. Make a three-column table on a sheet of paper. In the first column, list all the types of portable appliances that are available. Place a check in the second column beside appliances that perform a variety of functions. Place a check in the third column beside appliances that perform a function another appliance can do. Use your list as the basis for a discussion of how portable appliances meet consumer needs.

11. (List five:) fry, roast, panbroil, stew, simmer, bake

12. When thinking about buying a specialized portable appliance, consumers should consider storage space, how often they will use the appliance, and whether they have another appliance that will perform the same task.

Apply Technology

21. Use a kitchen appliance with programmable settings, a graphic display, and/or a voice module. Then evaluate whether these high-tech features would truly save a meal manager time and effort.

22. Visit the EnergyStar.gov website to find information about ENERGY STAR qualified dishwasher models. Use the **Find a Model** tool to search for models of the same size from three manufacturers. Use a computer and spreadsheet software to enter this information into a table. Then sort the table to find the model(s) that (A) used the fewest kilowatt hours of electricity per year, (B) used the fewest gallons of water per cycle, and (C) had the highest percentage of performance exceeding minimum federal standards. Compare your findings with those of classmates who searched for models from other manufacturers.

A Measure of Math

23. Investigate what the monthly payment and contract term would be for a rent-to-own kitchen appliance. Compute the total cost of the appliance. Compare this figure to the retail price of the appliance.

24. The fresh food storage compartment of a refrigerator should provide about 3.5 cubic feet (0.11 cubic meter) of space for each teen or adult household member. The freezer compartment should provide about 1.5 cubic feet (0.04 cubic meter) of space per teen or adult. Use these guidelines to calculate how many cubic feet of refrigerator and freezer space are needed to store food in your home.

Teamwork in Action

25. Choose a major or portable kitchen appliance. Investigate at least one energy-saving tip for using your chosen appliance. Compile your tip with those of your classmates into a brochure. Add color and artwork to give the brochure visual appeal. Make the brochures available at your local library just prior to Earth Day.

Companion Website
www.g-wlearning.com

At the website, review key terms for this chapter with crossword puzzles, matching exercises, and e-flash cards. Apply facts from the chapter to complete the activities.

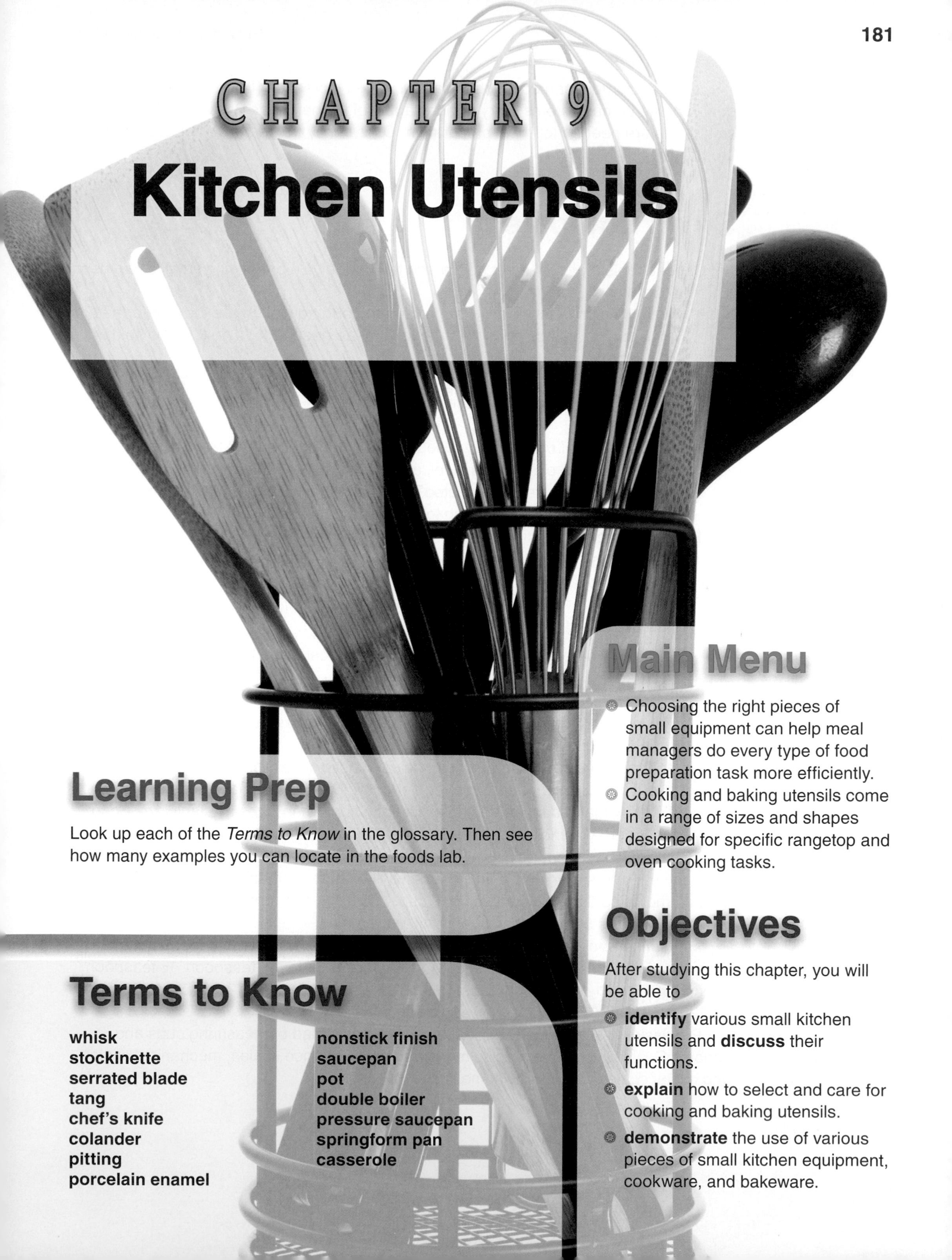

CHAPTER 9
Kitchen Utensils

Main Menu

- Choosing the right pieces of small equipment can help meal managers do every type of food preparation task more efficiently.
- Cooking and baking utensils come in a range of sizes and shapes designed for specific rangetop and oven cooking tasks.

Learning Prep

Look up each of the *Terms to Know* in the glossary. Then see how many examples you can locate in the foods lab.

Objectives

After studying this chapter, you will be able to

- **identify** various small kitchen utensils and **discuss** their functions.
- **explain** how to select and care for cooking and baking utensils.
- **demonstrate** the use of various pieces of small kitchen equipment, cookware, and bakeware.

Terms to Know

whisk
stockinette
serrated blade
tang
chef's knife
colander
pitting
porcelain enamel

nonstick finish
saucepan
pot
double boiler
pressure saucepan
springform pan
casserole

Meeting Special Needs

Challenge academically gifted students in your class to attain the following higher-order objectives as they study the chapter:

- analyze the functions of various small kitchen utensils.

- demonstrate how to select and care for cooking and baking utensils.

- evaluate the effectiveness of various pieces of small kitchen equipment, cookware, and bakeware while using them to prepare a food product.

Enrich

Invite a chef or professional cook to speak to your class about which utensils he or she uses in the workplace.

Discuss

Ask students to describe the differences between liquid and dry measures. Ask them why it matters which type of measure they use to measure ingredients. *(liquid— transparent to see ingredients poured to the desired level; dry—no extra space at the top so ingredients can be leveled off; to assure accurate measurement, which can affect the outcome of food products)*

Small equipment can do much to save time and increase efficiency. Housewares departments in many stores carry a wide variety of kitchen gadgets. Many of these small tools are needed for meal preparation. Others may not really be needed, but they are helpful.

Small Equipment

Choose tools that best meet needs and the budget. Before buying small equipment, ask the following questions.

- What kinds of kitchen tasks are performed and how often are they performed? A specialized piece of equipment may not be needed for a task that is seldom performed.
- How is the equipment designed and how does it work? Avoid complicated equipment that is hard to assemble. Choose well-designed tools that are easy to operate.
- What quality of materials are used to make the equipment? For example, many tools are made of stainless steel, a rustproof and durable material.
- How are the handles constructed? The handles should fit the hand comfortably. They should be sturdy enough to withstand frequent use.

To receive the most satisfaction from small equipment, select tools wisely. Follow manufacturers' directions for their use and care. Also, store small equipment in a convenient location.

Small kitchen utensils can make many food preparation tasks easier. Utensils can be grouped according to the types of tasks they perform.

Measuring Tools

Measuring tools are essential for baking. Failing to measure ingredients accurately can result in poor quality food products.

Liquid measures are made of glass or clear plastic. Use them to measure liquid ingredients, such as milk, water, and vegetable oil. They should have handles, pouring lips, and clearly marked measurements. The most common sizes available are 1 cup, 2 cup, and 4 cup. (Metric liquid measures are 250 mL, 500 mL, and 1 L.)

Dry measures are made of metal or plastic. Use them to measure dry ingredients, such as flour and sugar, and solid ingredients like shortening and peanut butter. They are commonly sold in sets containing ¼-cup, ⅓-cup, ½-cup, and 1-cup sizes. (Metric dry measures are 50 mL, 125 mL, and 250 mL.)

Measuring spoons are also made of metal or plastic. Use them to measure small amounts of liquid and dry ingredients. A typical set includes ¼-teaspoon, ½-teaspoon, 1-teaspoon, and 1-tablespoon sizes. (Metric measures are 1 mL, 2 mL, 5 mL, 15 mL, and 25 mL.) See **9-1**.

Professional kitchens often use *kitchen scales* instead of measuring cups and spoons. Scales give more precise measurements. Balance scales, mechanical scales, and digital scales are sold for home kitchens, too.

Mixing Tools

Virtually every recipe requires ingredients to be mixed together. Spoons can be used for many mixing tasks. *Wooden spoons* are available in many sizes and shapes for stirring and mixing. They will not scratch pan surfaces, and their handles remain cool. Use *slotted spoons* to remove pieces of food from a liquid. Use *heavy metal spoons* to stir thick mixtures.

Use a *rotary beater* to beat, blend, and incorporate air into foods. When the crank is manually turned, the beaters rotate. Beating speed depends on how fast the crank is turned.

Use a **whisk**, a mixing tool made of loops of wire attached to a handle, to incorporate air into foods. Use it for eggs, soufflés, and meringues. When preparing sauces, use a whisk to prevent lumps from forming. Most chefs prefer a whisk to a rotary beater. See **9-2**.

Goodheart-Willcox

9-1 Using the proper tools to accurately measure ingredients helps ensure the outcome of a recipe.

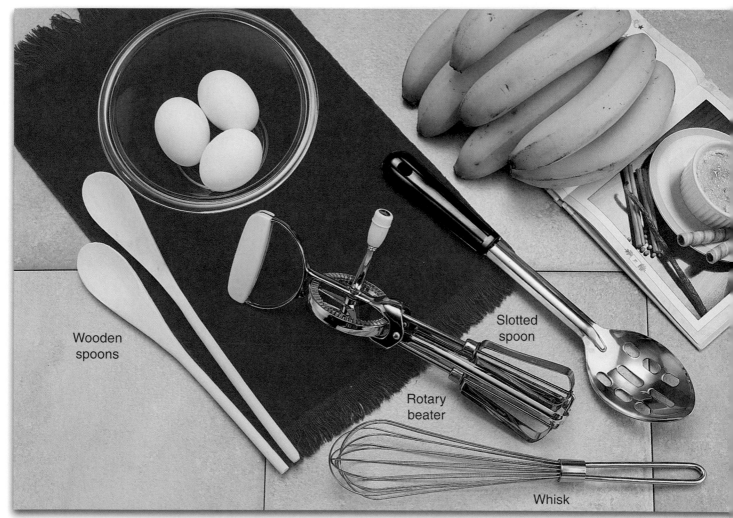

Goodheart-Willcox

9-2 Choose the best tool for each mixing task—stirring, blending, beating, or incorporating air.

Baking Tools

A number of tools are used just for preparing baked goods. One such tool is a *sifter*. Use a sifter to blend dry ingredients and remove lumps from powdered sugar.

A *pastry blender* is made of several thin, curved pieces of metal attached to a handle. Use it to blend shortening with flour when making pastry. It can also be used to blend butter and cheese mixtures.

Use *pastry brushes* to brush butter or sauces on foods. They can also be used to remove crumbs from a cake before frosting it and to baste foods in the oven. For basting, the pastry brush must be heat-resistant.

Use a rolling pin, pastry cloth, and stockinette when rolling dough or pastry. Place dough on the *pastry cloth* and roll it with the *rolling pin*. The cloth keeps the dough from sticking to the counter while it is being kneaded or rolled. The **stockinette** covers the rolling pin and prevents the dough from sticking to the rolling pin.

Spatulas can be made of plastic or metal. They come in various widths and lengths. All spatulas should be somewhat flexible. Use *bent-edged spatulas* to remove cookies from a baking tray. They can also be used to turn meats, fish, pancakes, eggs, and omelets. Use *straight-edged spatulas* to spread cake icings and meringues and to level ingredients in dry measures. Use *flexible spatulas* to scrape bowls and saucepans and to fold one ingredient into another. See **9-3**.

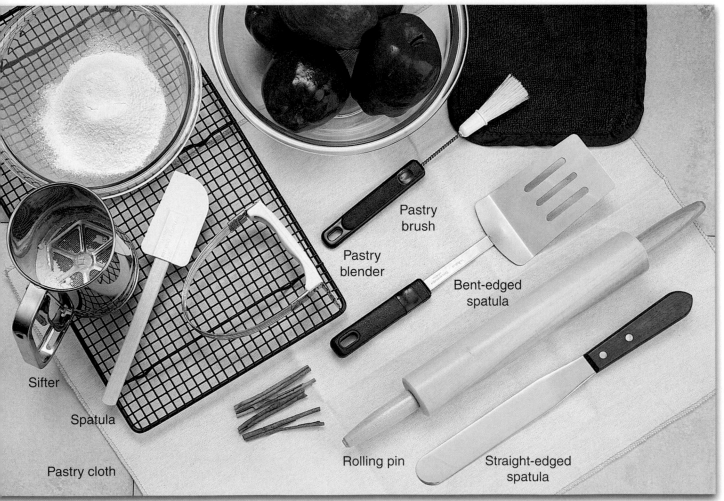

Goodheart-Willcox

9-3 Using the correct tools can affect the quality of baked products.

Thermometers

Being able to accurately measure the temperature of a food product can improve cooking success. It can also help reduce the risk of foodborne illness. Many foods contain harmful bacteria that can be killed by thorough cooking. Use a thermometer when cooking protein foods, such as meat, poultry, fish, egg dishes, and casseroles. Be sure these foods have reached recommended internal temperatures.

Several types of thermometers are available. *Oven-safe thermometers* are designed to be placed in a food while it is cooking. *Instant-read thermometers* are inserted into a food at the end of cooking time. This type of thermometer will provide an accurate reading in a matter of seconds.

Special thermometers are available for candy making and deep frying. *Candy thermometers* clip to the side of a pan. They are marked with the temperatures needed for different kinds of candies. *Deep-fat thermometers* also clip to the side of a pan. They register oil temperatures for deep frying foods like doughnuts and French fries.

For Example...

Demonstrate how to calibrate a thermometer that is found to be inaccurate. Give students an opportunity to practice calibrating thermometers.

Learn About...

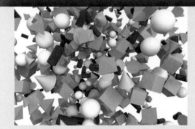

Appliance Thermometers

Two other types of thermometers are important pieces of kitchen equipment. Use a *refrigerator-freezer thermometer* to keep track of the temperatures at which foods are stored. The refrigerator should not be more than 40°F (4°C). Keep the freezer at no more than 0°F (–18°C). An *oven thermometer* can help make sure an oven heats to the temperature for which it is set. An oven that overheats can cause foods to burn, whereas an oven that underheats can lengthen cooking times.

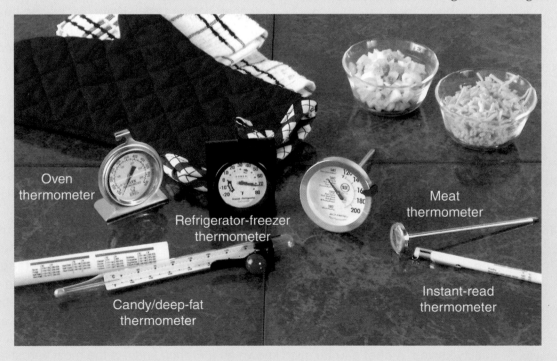

Oven thermometer

Refrigerator-freezer thermometer

Meat thermometer

Candy/deep-fat thermometer

Instant-read thermometer

Jack Klasey

Appliance thermometers, like other types of thermometers, help assure safe, quality food products.

Cutting Tools

Preparing ingredients often involves a variety of cutting tasks. Use *kitchen shears* to snip herbs and trim vegetables. They can also be used to cut meat, dough, cookies, and pizza. *Poultry shears* are heavier and sharper than ordinary kitchen shears. Use them to cut through fowl and fish bones. Use kitchen shears for food preparation tasks only.

Use a *peeler* to remove the outer surface of fruits and vegetables. A peeler removes only a thin layer, so nutrients lying near the surface are preserved. Peelers can also be used to make decorative carrot, chocolate, and cheese curls for garnishes.

A *shredder-grater* is a four-sided metal tool used to shred and grate foods such as cheese and cabbage. Openings of different sizes make it possible to grate and shred food into small or large pieces.

Cutting boards can be made of a variety of materials and are usually rectangular in shape. They are sometimes built into a cabinet or counter. Use a cutting board when cutting and chopping foods to protect tables and countertops. See **9-4**.

Goodheart-Willcox

9-4 A number of cutting tools are available so food can be cut into pieces of just the right size and shape for any recipe.

Knives

Different types of knives are used for different kitchen cutting tasks. Knife blades can be smooth or serrated. A **serrated blade** has a sawtooth edge. Some serrated knives are called *slicers*. They are especially helpful for slicing tender foods that are firm on the outside, such as tomatoes and crusty breads.

Knife blades are made of carbon steel, stainless steel, or ceramic. Carbon steel is easy to sharpen because it is soft. However, it will stain and rust easily unless the knife is washed and dried soon after each use. Stainless steel is durable and will not rust, but stainless is so hard that sharpening is difficult. (Some manufacturers, however, produce a type of stainless steel that is soft enough to sharpen easily.) Ceramic blades are very hard and will hold a sharp edge for a long time. They are excellent for slicing. However, ceramic blades are not flexible and can chip or break with misuse.

Knife handles can be made of wood, plastic, or bone. High-quality knives usually have hardwood handles. A knife handle should fit the hand comfortably. It should also be properly balanced and constructed for maximum safety. For safety, the **tang** (prong of the blade that attaches to the handle) should extend at least one-third of the way into the handle. At least two rivets should join the blade and handle. Three rivets should join larger knives. Never soak a knife, as soaking can cause the handle to loosen.

Some of the most popular kitchen knives are chef's, paring, bread, boning, and utility knives. A **chef's knife**, also known as a *French knife*, is the most versatile of all kitchen knives. It has a long, smooth blade for chopping, dicing, and mincing fresh fruits, vegetables, and herbs. A *paring knife* is the smallest knife used in the kitchen. It has a smooth blade for peeling and trimming fruits and vegetables. A *bread knife* has a long, serrated blade for cutting bread without flattening the air cells. A *boning knife* has a thin, smooth blade to easily cut and remove bones from raw meat and poultry. A *utility knife* is a good all-around knife. It can be used to trim fat from meat and cut tender vegetables, cheese, and cold cuts. See **9-5**.

Other Preparation Tools

Tongs usually are made of metal. They are helpful for turning meats and fried foods. They might also be used for handling such foods as corn on the cob, hard-cooked eggs, and baked potatoes.

Kitchen forks are made of heavy-duty metal. Use them when transferring heavy meats and poultry. A kitchen fork can also be used to turn heavy foods.

Ladles are round cups attached to long handles. They come in different sizes for different purposes. Use a ladle for dipping and pouring. A ladle might be used to serve punches, soups, sauces, gravies, and salad dressings.

Chef's Knife

Paring Knife

Bread Knife

Boning Knife

Utility Knife

Chicago Cutlery®

9-5 Choose different knives for different cutting needs.

Strainer

Colander

Ladle

Tongs

Kitchen fork

Baster

Goodheart-Willcox

9-6 Small utensils are designed to perform a variety of food preparation tasks.

A *baster* is a long tube attached to a flexible bulb. A baster uses suction to collect juices from meat and poultry for basting (covering foods with liquid). It can also be used to skim fat from soups and gravies.

Colanders are perforated bowls used to drain fruits, vegetables, and pasta. A colander should have heat-proof handles.

Strainers are available in several sizes. Use them to separate liquid and solid foods. See **9-6**.

Can openers remove the tops of cans. Some have round blades that puncture the tops of cans and cut the lids off. Other can openers decrimp the tops of cans where they are attached to the sides, leaving no sharp edges. Most can openers have handles that can be squeezed. Then a key is turned, which causes the can to rotate through the mechanism of the opener.

Cooking and Baking Utensils

Cooking and baking utensils can be purchased separately or in sets. Before buying cooking and baking utensils, think about needs and the features each utensil offers. All cooking and baking utensils should last a long time and maintain their appearance with normal care.

Consider the following features when buying cooking and baking utensils:

- Utensils should be sturdy and well balanced to prevent tipping. All edges should be smooth. Pan bottoms should be flat for good heat conduction. Beware of crevices where food particles can collect.
- Handles should be heat-resistant, sturdy, and securely attached.
- Lids should be well constructed and should fit tightly. Handles on lids should be heat-resistant and easy to grasp with a pot holder.
- Utensils should be light enough to handle comfortably and safely. They should be heavy enough to be durable and to withstand warping.
- Utensils should be able to stack or hang from a rack for storage.

Cookware and Bakeware Materials

Cooking and baking utensils are made from a number of materials. Metal, glass, ceramic, silicone, and plastics are the most popular of these materials.

Metal Materials

Several metals are used for conventional cookware and bakeware. *Cast iron* is a cookware material that distributes and holds heat well. Its porous surface holds oils that help prevent sticking. Iron is heavy, however. It can also rust, retain food flavors, and lose its nonstick qualities unless it is cared for properly.

Aluminum is a lightweight, corrosion-resistant cookware and bakeware material. It conducts heat rapidly and is reasonably priced. It comes in several thicknesses. Cast aluminum is used for heavier utensils, such as skillets. Sheet aluminum is used for lighter utensils, such as cookie sheets. Aluminum is susceptible to scratches, dents, and detergent damage. Food and minerals can cause **pitting** (marking with tiny indentations). Hard water, eggs, and alkalis, such as baking soda, can cause darkening.

Copper is a good heat conductor. However, pure copper utensils cannot be used for cooking. When heated, copper reacts with food and forms poisonous compounds. Copper cooking utensils must be lined with another material to make them safe for cooking. Copper must be cleaned with a special cleaner to keep it from discoloring.

Stainless steel is an alloy of steel, nickel, and chromium. It resists stains, does not discolor, and is strong and durable. However, it does not distribute heat evenly, so hot spots can occur. Stainless steel may darken if overheated. It is relatively expensive.

Some stainless steel pieces have a copper or aluminum bottom to improve heat distribution. Other pieces may have a core of copper, carbon steel, or other heat-conducting metal. These materials help conduct heat across the pan bottom and up the sides. A heat-conducting core prevents scorching, conserves fuel, and allows low temperature cooking. See **9-7**.

FYI

Lemon juice or vinegar can be used to remove discoloration from aluminum caused by alkalis.

Revere®

9-7 Stainless steel is not a good heat conductor and can allow hot spots that cause scorching (left). A copper or aluminum bottom or core on a stainless steel pan promotes even heating (right).

Glass and Ceramic Materials

Glass and ceramic materials are used for a range of cookware and bakeware pieces. These materials are attractive. However, they must be handled with care to avoid cracking, chipping, and breaking.

Transparent *glass* utensils allow the food to be seen while it is cooking. Glass does not react with the flavors or colors of food. However, glass is a poor heat conductor.

Glass-ceramic is strong and durable. It can withstand a wide range of temperatures. This property allows glass-ceramic utensils to be taken from the freezer and put directly in the oven. This material has the drawbacks of developing hot spots and heating unevenly.

Porcelain enamel is a glasslike material. It is fused to a base metal at very high temperatures. The outer surfaces of metal cookware and bakeware are often coated with porcelain enamel. This makes the utensils colorful and easy to clean.

Ceramic materials are made from nonmetallic minerals that are fired at very high temperatures. Ceramic materials include earthenware and terra-cotta. These materials are not suitable for rangetop cooking. However, they can retain heat well. This makes them good choices for many bakeware pieces.

Reflect

Ask students which cookware and bakeware pieces they would rather have made from metal materials and which they would rather have made from glass and ceramic materials. Ask them the reasons for their answers.

EXPLORING CAREERS

Housewares Demonstrator

A housewares demonstrator shows people how to use and care for kitchen utensils, highlighting the special features of each product. Demonstrators may work for housewares makers. They show their products to retail business owners to urge them to offer the products for sale in their stores. Demonstrators may also work for retailers. They may need to travel to various stores and set up their display areas before demonstrating utensils to store customers. They may pass out product brochures and samples and offer discounts to help boost sales.

Housewares demonstrators need to have good speaking skills as they discuss their products. They need to feel comfortable working in front of people. They need good listening skills to answer questions. Reading skills will help them understand product literature so they will be informed about the items they are demonstrating. They need attention to detail to keep their work area tidy and keep track of sales records. They must be flexible so they can adjust their demonstrations to best meet the needs of their customers.

A housewares demonstrator needs only a high school diploma. However, a few months of on-the-job training may be required. This will allow the demonstrator to become fully familiar with all the products and techniques he or she will be using. Experience speaking in front of others may also be helpful for someone in this type of work.

Career Path

Ask students what aspects of a housewares demonstrator's work they would find most challenging.

FYI

Silicone bakeware may not require greasing, and baked goods usually slip out with a gentle twist of the pan. Silicone pans should be placed on a metal tray before filling to keep them from buckling when you handle them.

FYI

Remind students to use pot holders when removing food containers from a microwave oven. Because microwaves pass through microwavable cookware, students may think the cookware itself does not become hot. However, heat transferred from the food can warm cookware.

Silicone and Plastic Materials

Silicone has a rubbery texture and comes in an array of bright colors. Many bakers like its nonstick properties for bakeware items like cake, loaf, and muffin pans. *Plastic materials* are popular for microwave cookware. Both types of materials can be placed in the freezer and dishwasher. However, both will melt when exposed to the direct heat of a broiler or rangetop. Using nonmetal utensils will protect silicone and plastic pieces from damage.

Nonstick Finishes

Nonstick finishes prevent foods from sticking to utensils. The coating may be applied to both the inside and outside of cookware and bakeware for easier cooking and cleanup. The effectiveness of a nonstick finish depends on the type of finish and how it is applied. Use cooking and cleaning tools designed for nonstick cookware to avoid scratching.

Microwavable Materials

The main requirement for a microwave cookware material is that microwaves must be able to pass through it. Otherwise, the microwaves will not be able to reach the food. Microwaves can pass through materials such as ceramic, plastics, glass, wood, and paper. These materials can all be used for cooking in a microwave oven.

Metal cookware reflects microwaves and keeps them from cooking food in a microwave oven. However, some microwave dishes have special metal surfaces to brown foods. Before using these or any metal items in a microwave oven, check the oven use and care guide.

Not all containers made from microwavable materials are microwave safe. For instance, cookware made from microwavable material should not be used if it has bands of metal trim. The trim can cause arcing. Disposable plastic containers from margarine and whipped toppings are not recommended for microwave cooking. They are made of soft plastics that may melt when they come in contact with hot food. This can cause chemicals from the plastics to get into the food. Containers that absorb liquid, such as wooden bowls, should not be used when microwaving liquids. The moisture absorbed by such a container will attract microwave energy away from the food.

Cooking Utensils

Saucepans and pots are used for cooking foods in water or other liquids over direct surface heat, **9-8**. **Saucepans** generally have one handle. **Pots** have two handles. Sizes range from a 1 pint (0.5 L) saucepan to a 12 quart (12 L) stockpot. For maximum cooking efficiency, the bottoms of pots and pans should be about the same diameter as the surface unit. Handles should be heat-resistant and comfortable to hold. Some pots and pans can be purchased with matching lids.

A **double boiler** is a small pan that fits into a larger pan. Food is put into the smaller pan. Then a small amount of water is put in the larger pan. As the water simmers, the heat produced by the steam gently cooks the food.

Pressure saucepans cook foods more quickly than conventional saucepans. This is because as pressure increases, temperature increases. Choose a pressure saucepan that carries a safety seal. Be sure to read manufacturer's directions carefully before using a pressure saucepan.

Skillets are available in a variety of sizes with and without lids. Skillets have wide bottoms and low sides. They are generally heavier than saucepans. Use skillets for panbroiling foods or for cooking foods in a small amount of fat.

Griddles and omelet pans are variations of skillets. A *griddle* is a skillet without sides. It often is coated with a nonstick finish. Use it for grilling sandwiches and making foods like French toast and pancakes. An *omelet* or a *crepe* pan is an uncovered skillet with a narrow bottom and sloping sides. Use it to make omelets and delicate French pancakes.

Baking Utensils

When selecting baking utensils, it is important to consider whether the utensil's surface is shiny or dull. The outer surface of a pan affects the amount of heat the pan absorbs. A shiny or bright surface reflects part of the heat away from the food. A dull or dark surface absorbs heat. Products baked in bright, shiny pans will have softer, lighter crusts. Products baked in dull, dark pans will have darker and crisper crusts.

Insulated bakeware is made from two sheets of metal. An air space between the two sheets creates a layer of insulation. This layer helps protect baked goods from overbrowning.

Cookie sheets are often made of aluminum. They are flat sheets of metal with a low rim on one or more sides for strength. Use them for baking cookies, toasting bread, and supporting small utensils, such as custard cups.

Revere®

9-8 Cookware comes in a variety of sizes and shapes for preparing all types of foods on top of the range.

Discuss

Ask students to identify foods that are prepared in saucepans and pots. *(soups, stews, pasta, vegetables)*

For Example...

A pressure saucepan can cook corn on the cob in 5 minutes, a two-pound chicken in 10 minutes, and vegetable soup in 20 minutes.

Reflect

Ask students whether they prefer baked goods with soft, light crusts or dark, crisp crusts. Ask what type of surface their bakeware should have to produce the type of crusts they desire.

Cake, angel food, springform, jelly roll, pizza, muffin, and loaf pans are usually made of aluminum. Cake and loaf pans are also available in glass, ceramic, and silicone materials. Many bakeware pieces are available in several sizes.

Cake pans can be round, square, or oblong. Angel food, sponge, and chiffon cakes can be made in an *angel food cake pan*. It is a deep, round pan, narrower at the bottom than at the top. It has a tube in the center, and the bottom may be removable. A **springform pan** is also round and has a removable bottom. Its sides hook together with a latch or spring. Use springform pans for making cheesecakes, tortes, and other desserts that are delicate and difficult to remove from the pan. A *jelly roll pan* is a large, shallow oblong pan. Use it to make sheet cakes and to bake the sponge cake for cake rolls. *Pizza pans* are large and round. They may have a narrow rim around the edge. *Muffin pans* are oblong pans with round depressions. Use them for baking muffins and cupcakes. *Loaf pans* are deep, narrow, oblong pans. These are used most often for breads and loaf cakes.

Pie plates are round with sloping sides. They are generally made of glass or aluminum. Use them when making dessert and main dish pies.

Casseroles are baking dishes with high sides. They can be made of glass, glass-ceramic, or earthenware. Some casseroles are designed for freezer-to-oven use. *Soufflé* dishes are a variation of a casserole. They have high, steep sides. See **9-9**.

Roasting pans can be oval or oblong. They are larger and heavier than pots, pans, and skillets. Most have high, dome lids, and many have racks or trivets.

Learn About...

Cookware Shapes for Microwaving

The shape of cookware can affect how evenly foods cook in a microwave oven. Round-shaped containers allow microwaves to hit food evenly. Microwaves can overlap in the corners of square cookware pieces. This causes food in the corners to overcook.

Ring-shaped pans give great results when microwaving cakes, meat loaves, and other foods. This shape accounts for the fact that foods tend to cook slower in the center of a microwave oven. The circular arrangement allows foods to cook more evenly. Ring shapes also allow microwaves to hit foods from the center as well as the top, bottom, and sides. This increased microwave penetration speeds cooking time.

Cookware pieces should correspond to the amount and kind of food being microwaved. Choose single-serving pieces when cooking small amounts of food. Use a rack with a slotted or raised surface when cooking meats so fats and juices can drain. Select deeper containers when cooking foods like milk that may boil over.

Use and Care of Cooking and Baking Utensils

To maintain cooking and baking utensils, proper use and care are essential. Some materials only tolerate certain temperatures. Some utensils must be conditioned before being used. Some utensils require the use of special cleaning compounds. Always read the use and care information that accompanies cooking and baking utensils. Follow manufacturer's directions for use and cleaning.

Round cake pan

Square casserole

Muffin pan

Oblong baking
dish

Pie plate

Cookie sheet

Pyrex®

9-9 Each piece of bakeware is designed for preparing specific kinds of food items in an oven.

CAREER SUCCESS

Using Creative Thinking

Regina is a housewares designer for Top Chop Company. She develops ideas for kitchen utensils.

Lately, Regina has been working on a line of utensils for people with limited ability to use their hands.

To be a successful employee, Regina needs skills in thinking creatively. In a small group, answer the following questions about Regina's need for and use of these skills:

A.   What is one of the questions about utensil design Regina must creatively answer as she plans the new product line?

B.   How will Regina's ability to think creatively affect consumers with manual limitations?

C.   How will Regina's ability to think creatively affect the Top Chop Company?

D.   What is another skill Regina would need in this job? Briefly explain why this skill would be important.

CHAPTER 9 REVIEW

Summary

Small kitchen equipment includes measuring, mixing, baking, and cutting tools as well as thermometers and other preparation tools. When selecting these items, think about the types of tasks performed. Also consider the quality and cost of the tools.

Cookware refers to items used on top of the range. Bakeware includes items used in the oven. Cookware and bakeware are commonly made from metal, glass, ceramic, silicone, and plastic materials. In addition to the material, the shape and size of microwave cookware can affect its performance. When buying cookware and bakeware, look for pieces that are well made and that are easy to handle and store. Follow manufacturers' use and care directions.

Review What You Have Read

Write your answers on a separate sheet of paper, using complete sentences when appropriate.

1. What types of ingredients are measured with measuring spoons?
2. True or false. Most chefs prefer a rotary beater to a whisk.
3. Which type of spatula would be used to level ingredients in dry measures?
   A. Bent-edged spatula.
   B. Silicone spatula.
   C. Straight-edged spatula.
   D. None of the above.
4. What type of thermometer is inserted into a food at the end of cooking time?
5. List four uses for kitchen shears.
6. What is the smallest knife used in the kitchen?
   A. Boning knife.
   B. Bread knife.
   C. Chef's knife.
   D. Paring knife.
7. A perforated bowl used to drain fruits, vegetables, and pasta is a _____.
8. List three features to consider when buying cooking and baking utensils.
9. What are the five most common types of materials used to make cooking and baking utensils?
10. True or false. Pure copper cannot be used for cooking because it reacts with food and forms poisonous compounds.
11. For which types of cooking are silicone and plastic materials not suited?

(continued)

12. Which of the following cookware materials reflects microwaves and keeps food from cooking in a microwave oven?
    A. Ceramic.
    B. Metal.
    C. Paper.
    D. Plastic.

13. What is the difference between a saucepan and a pot?

14. What baking utensil is used to make sheet cakes?

15. True or false. Round containers cook foods more evenly than square containers in a microwave oven.

14. A jelly roll pan is used to make sheet cakes.

15. true

Link to Academic Skills

16. **Social studies.** Investigate how kitchen utensils are developed and promoted in a competitive market. Identify features and characteristics manufacturers use to encourage consumers to choose their products over similar products from other manufacturers.

17. **History.** Research a kitchen utensil used in the seventeenth or eighteenth century. Prepare an oral report for the class on how the utensil was used. Be sure to explain what tool or tools would be used today to perform the functions of the antique utensil. Bring in a sketch or photograph of the utensil to use as a visual aid.

18. **English language arts.** Make a display of small kitchen tools for a showcase in your school. Write a paragraph describing each tool and explaining its use in the kitchen.

19. **Science.** Look up how to perform the boiling water test and the ice bath test for checking the accuracy of thermometers. Test the accuracy of several types of kitchen thermometers using both of these testing methods.

20. **Science.** Investigate heat transfer and the conductivity of different materials used for cookware and bakeware. Incorporate what you learn into a class discussion on the advantages and disadvantages of various materials for cookware and bakeware applications.

21. **Science.** Do a simple test to compare the performance of various microwavable materials. Choose three pieces of cookware with similar dimensions, each made from a different microwavable material. For instance, you might choose 2-quart (2-L) casseroles made from glass, ceramic, and stoneware. (For fire safety reasons, remember not to use any metal cookware in a microwave oven.) Test each piece of cookware individually by filling it with two cups of water. Measure and record the temperature of the water. Then place the cookware in the microwave oven and turn the oven on high power for one minute. Remove the cookware from the oven and measure and record the temperature of the water again. Repeat this test with the other two pieces of cookware. On an observation sheet, record the cookware materials, the results of the tests, and your conclusions about each material.

Build Critical Thinking Skills

22. **Analysis.** Make a poster chart to help you analyze different materials used for cooking and baking utensils. List the characteristics, uses, care requirements, advantages, and disadvantages of each material.

23. **Evaluation.** Using homemade or refrigerated chocolate chip cookie dough, drop six rounded tablespoons of the dough two inches apart on a cookie sheet with a shiny finish. Drop six more rounded tablespoons of the dough two inches apart on a cookie sheet with a dull finish. Bake the two sets of cookies according to recipe or package directions. Evaluate the two sets in terms of taste, texture, and appearance. Explain any differences.

Apply Technology

24. Compare the speed and accuracy of a digital food thermometer and a dial food thermometer.

25. Examine the various materials developed for use as nonstick finishes on cookware and bakeware in the last 20 years. How have these materials been rated for performance in consumer literature?

A Measure of Math

26. Make a list of cooking and baking utensils a single person would need in his or her first apartment. Then visit the cooking and baking utensil section of a department store. Figure how much it would cost to equip this hypothetical kitchen.

Teamwork in Action

27. Investigate safe cooking temperatures for various types of food products. Compile this information in a table. Include the table in a food safety brochure you prepare for consumers. Along with information about cooking foods safely, the brochure should illustrate and describe the various types of food thermometers available. Make the brochures available at your local library or community center.

Companion Website
www.g-wlearning.com

At the website, review key terms for this chapter with crossword puzzles, matching exercises, and e-flash cards. Apply facts from the chapter to complete the activities.

CHAPTER 10
Planning Meals

Main Menu

- Meal managers must meet goals for nutrition, spending, taste appeal, and time control when planning and preparing meals.
- Meal managers have resources available to help them reach their goals.

Learning Prep

In a class discussion, suggest how you think each of the chapter vocabulary terms relates to the topic of planning meals.

Objectives

After studying this chapter, you will be able to

- **plan** nutritious menus using meal patterns based on MyPlate.
- **prepare** a food budget.
- **plan** menus with an appealing variety of flavors, colors, textures, shapes, sizes, and temperatures.
- **describe** resources a meal manager can use as alternatives to time and energy.

Terms to Know

meal manager
menu
course
convenience food
budget
income
fixed expense
flexible expense

taste buds
conservation
finished food
semiprepared food
work simplification
prepreparation

A **meal manager** is someone who uses resources to reach goals related to preparing and serving food. A meal manager's resources include people, money, time, energy, knowledge, skills, and technology. Food and equipment are resources, too. Meal managers must make many decisions based on these resources. They must decide how much time and money they are willing to spend planning and preparing meals. This will affect their decisions about what foods to serve and how to prepare them.

A meal manager will use available resources to reach the following four goals:

- Provide good nutrition to meet the needs of each person eating the meal.
- Use planned spending to make meals fit into a food budget.
- Prepare satisfying meals that look and taste appealing.
- Control the use of time and energy involved in meal preparation. See **10-1**.

The meal manager is responsible for seeing these goals are reached. However, he or she may not be the only one working to reach them. Using people as a resource, the meal manager may assign various preparation, serving, and cleanup tasks to others.

Household members need to help the meal manager with planning meals as well as preparing them. The meal manager needs input to know each person's food preferences when choosing menu items. The meal manager also needs to be aware of each person's schedule to know who will be eating each meal served. He or she may need to make other plans to meet the needs of household members who will be away at mealtime. Communicating and working together under the guidance of the meal manager will help all household members make sure mealtime goals are met.

Photo courtesy of McCormick & Co., Inc.

10-1 A meal manager must use available resources to plan nutritious, affordable meals that look and taste appealing.

Provide Good Nutrition

People tend to eat foods they like. However, foods people like may not always be the foods they need to stay healthy. For good health, the foods people eat must supply their bodies with the right amounts of proteins, carbohydrates, fats, vitamins, minerals, and water. Everyone needs the same nutrients, but not in the same amounts. For instance, pregnant women need more of some nutrients than other adults. Active people need more of some nutrients than inactive people.

Meal Patterns

Some people might eat a few pieces of pizza and call it "lunch." Others might consume a plate of spaghetti and call it "dinner." Perhaps you realize a meal should be composed of more than just pizza or spaghetti. However, you might not know what else to serve with these food items to make the meals complete.

Meal managers can use a meal pattern to plan meals that provide a variety of foods. A *meal pattern* is an outline of the basic foods normally served at a meal. A meal pattern based on MyPlate can provide all the nutrients needed each day.

A MyPlate meal pattern can be set up for any calorie level. Simply divide the recommended daily amounts of food for each food group by the number of meals needed. This will indicate about how much food from each group is needed at each meal.

This basic pattern works equally well for planning breakfast, lunch, and dinner. The meal manager can use snacks to fill in added food group amounts needed by various individuals. He or she can also add servings to one meal to make up for a shortage in another meal. For instance, some people may want to skip the vegetable group at breakfast. An extra vegetable serving for lunch, dinner, or snack can easily accommodate this preference.

In a household, the meal manager must make sure each person eats the recommended amounts from each food group throughout the day. In general, breakfast supplies one-fourth of the day's total nutritional needs. Lunch and dinner each supply one-third. Snacks supply the remaining needs. See **10-2**.

Reflect
Ask students what foods they would add under each food group in Figure 10-2 for each meal.

Breakfast

Eating breakfast helps prevent a midmorning slump. A good breakfast should be rich in complex carbohydrates for energy. Enriched or whole grain toast and cereals are popular carbohydrate choices for breakfast. The morning meal is a good time to work some fruit

MyPlate Meal Pattern				
Meal	**Grains Group** (2-3 oz eq per meal*)	**Vegetable Group** (1-1 ½ cups per meal*)	**Fruit Group** (½-1 cup per meal*)	**Dairy Group** (1 cup per meal)	**Protein Foods Group** (2-2½ oz eq per meal*)
Breakfast	Buckwheat pancakes Grits Muesli Oatmeal Toasted oat cereal Whole-wheat bagels	Hash browns Onions, peppers, broccoli, mushrooms in omelets Tomato juice	Grapefruit Melon Orange and prune juices Papayas, mangoes Strawberries	Low-fat cheese in omelets Hot chocolate	Canadian bacon Eggs Ham
Lunch	Tortillas Whole-grain sandwich bread Whole-wheat pasta in soups and salads	Beans in soup Lettuce and tomato on sandwiches Spinach salad Vegetables in soups	Applesauce Bananas Cherries Fruit salad Grapes Plums	Low-fat cheese on sandwiches Cottage cheese	Ham, chicken, tuna, and egg salad Lean luncheon meats Peanut butter Refried beans
Dinner	Biscuits, cornbread, dumplings Brown rice, pasta Bulgar, kasha, couscous Whole-grain rolls	Baked beans, lentils Corn, green beans, winter squash Stir-fried vegetables Sweet potatoes Green salad	Baked apples Cranberry sauce Grilled pineapple Poached pears Spiced peaches	Cheese in casseroles Fat-free milk Pudding	Beef, lamb, pork, veal Chicken, turkey Fish, shellfish Tofu
Snacks	Matzos Popcorn Rye crackers	Carrot and celery sticks Cauliflower	Dried figs, dates, and apricots Raisins	Fat-free yogurt Kefir	Hard-cooked eggs Nuts Sunflower seeds

*Smaller amounts within a range are needed by people at lower calorie levels; larger amounts are needed by people at higher calorie levels

10-2 Using a meal pattern based on MyPlate can help meal managers plan to provide good nutrition.

Discuss

Ask students why they think so many people skip breakfast if it is supposed to be the most important meal of the day. *(They are in a hurry. Food does not appeal to them in the morning. They do not realize how important it is.)*

Reflect

Ask students if they prefer to carry a packed lunch or buy lunch in the cafeteria. Have them consider the reasons behind their responses.

Reflect

Ask students how often they eat dinner with other family members.

Reflect

Ask students how their families feel about trying new and unusual foods.

Discuss

Ask students what menu combinations come to mind when they think of the following main dishes: roast beef, hamburgers, chili.

Discuss

Ask students why a meal manger should initially consult with a registered dietitian when planning meals for a family member with special needs. *(Most meal mangers lack the expertise to plan a varied, balanced diet that will meet the health goals of a family member requiring medical nutrition therapy.)*

into a diet. Try topping cereal or pancakes with fruit instead of sugar or syrup. Breakfast should provide a small amount of fat to help the meal stay with a person throughout the morning. To help get the needed daily servings from the milk group, include a low-fat or fat-free choice for breakfast. Foods from the meat and beans group are optional at breakfast. Remember, only 5 to 7 ounce-equivalents from this group are needed each day.

Lunch

Many meal managers make good use of leftovers at lunchtime. Leftovers can be used to prepare nutritious salads, casseroles, and sandwiches. For instance, suppose there is some leftover lean roast beef. People who carry their lunches to work or school could take hearty roast beef sandwiches. Those who eat their lunches at home could add strips of roast beef to a chef's salad.

In cold weather, hot foods are popular for lunch. Those who must take their lunches can carry soups, stews, and casseroles in wide-mouthed vacuum containers. In warmer weather, the same containers can be used to carry cold fruit or main dish salads.

Dinner

Dinner is the one meal of the day many people can eat leisurely and share with family members. Dinner is often a heavier meal than lunch.

The meal manager can add variety to dinners in many ways. Occasionally serving a new dish is an easy way to add interest to meals. The meal manager can also try serving common foods in new ways. For instance, instead of serving chicken, broccoli, and rice separately, combine the chicken and broccoli. Toss in some red pepper strips and soy sauce. Serve this medley over the rice as a tasty stir-fry.

In hot weather, appetites often become sluggish. Replace a filling, hot entree with a cool, refreshing main dish salad. Hot whole grain rolls and a fresh fruit cup would complete the meal.

Varying preparation methods is another way to add variety to meals. For instance, suppose mashed potatoes are always served. Try roasted potatoes with a dash of herbs for a change of pace.

Snacks

With planning, the meal manager can make sure snacks satisfy nutritional needs as well as hunger. Fresh fruits and vegetables, low-fat cheese and yogurt, whole grain crackers, and nuts are good snacks. They supplement foods eaten at meals by adding nutrients to the diet.

Planning a Meal

A written menu can be a useful tool in helping a meal manager reach the goal of providing good nutrition. A **menu** is a list of the foods to be served at a meal. Daily menus can help meal managers assess whether they are serving foods from all the groups in MyPlate.

Some menus are planned with several courses. A **course** is a part of a meal made up of all the foods served at one time. At an elaborate dinner, appetizer, soup, salad, main course, and dessert may each be served as separate courses. At an informal supper, the salad and main dish may be served together. An appetizer, soup, and dessert may be omitted from the menu.

Generally, the best menus center on one food. In the MyPlate meal pattern, grain foods are often the largest portions on the plate. However, plain grain foods have mild flavors that can be seasoned to blend with almost any other food. Therefore, meal managers usually center their menus on a protein food instead. Foods from the meat and beans group often call certain menu combinations to mind. For instance, roast turkey calls to mind stuffing and yams. Baked ham may make some people think of scalloped potatoes and green beans. See **10-3**.

When planning a meal, meal managers may find it easiest to make menu selections in the following order:

1. Choose the main dish of the main course. Keep in mind that the main dish does not have to be from the meat and beans group. Try planning a meal around a vegetable main dish, such as vegetable soup. This can be a great way to help people get recommended amounts of vegetables.

2. Select the grain foods that will accompany the main dish, such as pasta, rice, or barley. Make sure at least half of the choices are from whole grain sources. Bread or rolls may be served along with or in place of other grain foods. Just make sure the total amount of grain foods served does not exceed daily recommended amounts.

3. Select one or two vegetable side dishes that will complement the main dish. (Vegetables and grain foods may also be part of the main dish rather than side dishes. Casseroles and hearty soups often include vegetables and grains in this way.)

4. Choose the salad. Be sure to go easy on the dressing.

5. Keeping calories in mind, select the dessert and/or first course. Remember to make nutrient-dense choices for these courses, too. Desserts and appetizers are often good places to work a serving from the fruit group into the menu.

6. Plan a beverage to go with the meal. Fat-free milk is often a good beverage choice. Serving milk is an easy way to include a food from the milk group in the menu.

Later sections in this chapter will give other points to keep in mind as individual menu items are chosen. Following these guidelines can help meal managers serve meals that are appealing as well as nutritious.

National Chicken Council/U.S. Poultry & Egg Association

10-3 You might want to plan your meal around a protein food, but be sure to fill the majority of your plate with grains and vegetables.

Time Management Tip

Use the steps on this page to plan menus for an entire week. Then plan a grocery shopping list based on these menus. This will help make sure the shopping list includes all the ingredients needed to prepare the week's meals. You will save time by avoiding return visits to the grocery store.

Health and Wellness

Planning for Special Nutritional Needs

Some people have health problems that affect their food needs. For instance, someone with heart disease may be advised to eat a diet low in sodium, cholesterol, and saturated fat. When planning meals, a meal manager must consider such special needs.

Initially, the meal manager and the person with unique needs should work with a registered dietitian. The dietitian can offer guidance in meal planning. He or she can also assess whether nutrient needs are being met.

A meal manager could plan separate meals for someone with unique needs. In most cases, however, other household members can adapt their eating habits to follow the special diet. For example, anyone could follow a low-fat, high-carbohydrate diet prescribed to someone with diabetes mellitus. Adapting eating habits has two key advantages. First, it keeps the person with special needs from feeling isolated. He or she will not feel deprived of foods others are enjoying. Second, it saves the meal manager the time and effort of planning and preparing two sets of meals. Special diets often have a third advantage of being more healthful than a typical diet.

Use Planned Spending

The second goal of meal management is planned spending. Nearly everyone finds a need to establish a spending plan for food. Families in the United States spend, on the average, a little less than 10 percent of their disposable incomes for food. Meal managers must consider a variety of information when determining the amount of money they can spend for food.

Factors Affecting Food Needs

The activity, size, sex, and age of each person affect a household's food needs. It costs more to feed some people than it does to feed others because people's nutrient needs differ. It costs more to feed an athlete, for example, than it does to feed an office worker. It costs more to feed a person who weighs 250 pounds (112 kg) than a person who weighs 110 pounds (49 kg). After the age of 12, it costs more to feed boys than it does to feed girls. It also costs more to feed a teenager than it does to feed a senior citizen.

Health problems also influence food needs. Someone who is allergic to wheat or milk, for example, might need special foods. These special foods are often expensive.

Factors Affecting Food Purchases

You might think all households with similar food needs would spend about the same amount of money for food. However, this is not always true. Similar quantities of nutrients can be acquired at very different costs, depending on the foods purchased.

Think of two baskets of food. One basket contains a beef rib roast, fresh asparagus, fresh oranges, bakery bread, and a frozen cake. The other basket contains ground beef, canned green beans, frozen orange juice concentrate, store brand bread, and a cake mix. Both baskets provide similar nutrients. However, the second basket will cost quite a bit less. See **10-4**.

Photos Courtesy of The Beef Checkoff www.BeefItsWhatsForDinner.com

A   B

10-4 Ground beef and T-bone steak both provide protein along with vitamins and minerals. However, you will spend quite a bit more money on the steak.

The following factors determine the amount of money a meal manager spends for food:

- income
- meal manager's ability to choose foods that are within the food budget
- meal manager's shopping skills and knowledge of the marketplace
- amount of time the meal manager has to plan and prepare meals
- food preferences of household members
- personal values

Income is a major factor in determining the amount of money a household spends for food. Generally, as income increases, a meal manager spends more money for food. As income increases, the use of dairy products, better cuts of meat, and bakery goods tends to increase. Meanwhile, the use of less expensive staple foods, such as beans and rice, tends to decrease.

Knowing how to choose the tastiest, most nutritious foods for the money spent is an important meal management skill. A meal manager needs to know how similar products differ in quality and nutrition. He or she needs to know when buying a brand name is important. He or she should be able to identify products that contain hidden service costs. A meal manager also needs to know how to compare prices on a per serving basis. Recognizing seasonal food values and choosing quality meats and produce are other meal management skills.

The meal manager's available time and energy affect the food budget. If these resources are limited, the meal manager will have to spend more money on convenience foods. **Convenience foods** are foods that have had some amount of service added to them. For instance, a meal manager who has ample time and energy could buy ingredients to make homemade lasagna. However, a meal manager who has little time and energy might purchase frozen lasagna instead. The frozen entree costs more, but it cooks quickly and requires no preparation.

Food likes and dislikes affect spending on food purchases. People who eat steaks and fresh produce will spend more than those who eat casseroles and canned goods.

Value systems affect spending. Some people view food as merely a basic need. They would rather spend their money on other goals. Others value meals as a source of entertainment. These people are likely to spend more money for food.

Preparing a Food Budget

Most people have a set amount of money that must cover many expenses. To keep from overspending in one area, such as food, they establish a budget. A **budget** is a plan for managing income and expenses, **10-5**. The meal manager has a responsibility to stay within the budget. The following steps will help you prepare a budget:

1. On a piece of paper, record your average monthly income. **Income** is money received. You will probably receive most income as wages earned by working. Income also includes money you receive as tips, gifts, and interest on bank accounts. Unless you can count on receiving a set amount from these sources, however, do not include them in your budget. Also, be sure to list only your take-home pay. Money deducted from your paycheck for taxes and other payments is not available for you to use for household expenses.

2. List your monthly fixed expenses and the cost of each. A **fixed expense** is a regularly recurring cost in a set amount. Fixed expenses include rent or mortgage payments, car payments, insurance premiums, and installment loan payments. You should also list savings as a fixed expense. Otherwise, you might end up spending money you intended to save.

Reflect

Ask students how they think the taste of convenience foods generally compares with the taste of homemade foods.

Reflect

Ask students if they have ever used a budget to plan their personal spending and savings.

Online Resource

Have students visit the U.S. Environmental Protection Agency website. Ask each student to find a tip for saving resources in the kitchen. Then have students try their tips at home and report back to class. Were family members willing to implement the tips? Why or why not?

Monthly Budget	
Income	$2080
Fixed expenses	
Rent	$625
Car payment	300
Insurance premium	110
Savings	100
Flexible expenses	
Food	240
Nonfood items	60
Clothing	95
Utility bills	180
Gasoline/oil	150
Entertainment	120
Gifts and contributions	100
Total expenses	$2080

Discuss

Ask students how they can accurately estimate flexible expenses. *(Track each category of flexible expenses for a couple months to figure an average amount to use as an estimate.)*

Career Path

Ask students which of a kitchen manager's work tasks they would find most challenging.

10-5 Figuring your monthly budget will help you decide how much you can afford to spend for various items, including food.

3. List your flexible expenses and their estimated monthly costs. **Flexible expenses** are regularly recurring costs that vary in amount. Flexible expenses include food, clothing, utility bills, transportation, and entertainment.

4. Figure the total of your fixed and estimated flexible expenses. Compare this amount with your income. If your income equals your expenses, you will be able to provide for your needs and meet your financial obligations. If your income is greater than your expenses, you can put the extra money toward future goals. If your expenses are greater than your income, however, you will need to make some adjustments.

Reducing Food Expenses

A budget shortage can be handled in two ways: increasing income and decreasing expenses. Working overtime or getting another job would provide you with extra income. Looking at your current spending patterns will help you see how you can reduce expenses.

Although you cannot do much to change your fixed expenses, you can adjust your flexible expenses, including food. Save your grocery store receipts for a few weeks to see what kinds of foods you are buying.

You already know the cost of food has little bearing on its nutritional value. Each group of MyPlate includes both expensive and inexpensive foods. Protein foods are the most costly, but prices of foods in this group vary widely. T-bone steak, for example, costs more than ground beef. Both, however, provide similar nutrients. Milk, eggs, and

EXPLORING CAREERS

Kitchen Manager

Kitchen managers are in charge of everything that goes on in foodservice kitchens. They must keep track of food ingredients and order more as needed to have enough supplies on hand. They hire, train, schedule, and evaluate staff. They oversee the preparation of food items and may also do some of the preparation tasks. Kitchen managers are responsible for making sure their kitchens meet standards of safety and sanitation, too.

Kitchen managers need excellent leadership skills for guiding staff. However, they also need teamwork skills to work alongside their employees. They must be good time managers and pay attention to details to avoid overlooking one of their many duties. They need good speaking skills for instructing staff and good listening skills for handling customer complaints. A busy kitchen can be a hectic place. Therefore, kitchen managers need to be able to deal with stress, adapt to sudden changes, and calmly solve problems.

Kitchen managers may not be required to have more than a high school diploma. However, they will surely benefit from culinary school training. Work experience in a restaurant, including the dining room as well as a range of kitchen stations, is essential.

---

cheese also are protein foods. Dried milk costs less than fluid fresh milk. Medium eggs usually cost less than large eggs. Domestic cheeses cost less than imported cheeses. Dried legumes are an inexpensive source of protein that can help stretch food dollars.

The fruit and vegetable groups are the next most costly food groups. However, foods in these groups vary widely in price, too. Before you buy, compare prices of fresh produce with frozen and canned products. Fresh fruits and vegetables are usually economical when they are in season. During off-seasons, however, canned and frozen products usually are cheaper. Grocers often price small pieces of fresh produce lower than larger pieces. Store brand canned and frozen fruits and vegetables cost less than national brands.

The skillful meal manager also knows margarine usually costs less than butter. Unsweetened ready-to-eat breakfast cereals usually cost less than presweetened cereals, **10-6**. Cereals you cook yourself cost even less. Store brand bread usually costs less than brand name bread or bakery bread. Large packages usually are better buys than small packages. However, wise shoppers compare prices on a per serving basis before buying one size over another.

Convenience products and snack foods are often costly. You may be able to save money by preparing more foods from scratch and buying fewer snack foods. Using coupons and taking advantage of store specials will also help you cut costs.

Remember the grocery store is not the only place you buy food. Restaurants, concession stands, and vending machines also take a portion of your food dollar. You will need to evaluate these purchases in relation to your overall budget.

After identifying ways you can reduce food costs, determine a realistic figure for your monthly food budget. If you do your shopping weekly, divide this amount by four. Then keep careful track of your food purchases for a few

FYI

Remember that price is not the only factor affected by the form of food. Canning and freezing can also affect the nutritional value of fruits and vegetables.

Agricultural Research Service, USDA

10-6 Breakfast cereals that are presweetened or have added ingredients tend to cost more than plain cereals.

weeks to see whether you are overspending. Sometimes your records may show you have spent more than your weekly budget. For instance, stocking up on sale items one week may cause you to spend more than your estimated amount. However, this may enable you to spend less money the following week.

Food is only one of the flexible expenses in your budget. You can take similar steps to reduce other spending areas, such as clothing, transportation, and entertainment.

Prepare Satisfying Meals

The third goal of meal management is to prepare satisfying meals. Everyone eating the food should find the meal appealing. This goal can be one of the most difficult to accomplish.

Food Preferences

Studies have shown people like some groups of foods better than others. People find vegetables, salads, and soups least appealing. They like breads, meats, and desserts best. Studies also show wide ranges of preferences within a liked class of foods. In the meat class, for instance, respondents listed grilled steak, fried chicken, and roast turkey among their favorites. The least-liked foods in the same group were lamb, liver, fish, and creamed and combination dishes.

The foods you prefer to eat usually are familiar foods that taste good to you. Many factors affect your food preferences, including sight, smell, and touch. As a result, the color, size, shape, flavor, texture, and temperature of foods help determine how well you like them.

Color

The way food looks can stimulate or squelch a person's appetite before the food is even tasted. Colorful foods appeal to the eyes and whet the appetite. Therefore, try to avoid too many pale foods when planning a menu. Instead, choose foods that provide a variety of colors. However, avoid colors that would clash. For instance, bright red tomatoes would not be pleasing with the purple color of red cabbage.

Garnishes can add color and eye appeal to a meal. A sprinkling of nutmeg on custard or paprika on potatoes adds a touch of color. Meal managers can use lemon wedges, green pepper strips, and parsley sprigs to add color to a plate. Peach halves, orange twists, and cucumber slices are also simple garnishes.

Size and Shape

The size and shape of food items affect how appetizing they look. Avoid serving several foods made up of small pieces. For instance, spears of broccoli would be a better choice than peas to accompany a chicken and rice casserole. When choosing a salad to serve with the casserole, a lettuce wedge would be more appealing than coleslaw. Choose foods with various shapes and sizes when planning meals.

Learn About...

Food Presentation

Presentation refers to the way food looks when it is brought to the table and presented to a diner. Along with colors, the arrangement of foods on a plate affects their presentation. Some restaurant chefs put much emphasis on the presentation of foods. They carefully fan out meat slices to make a moderate portion look bigger. They artistically sprinkle snipped herbs or grated cheese over pasta. They skillfully drizzle dessert sauces to write words or draw pictures.

If you are preparing a fancy meal, you may want to try some of these creative techniques. For everyday meals, however, two simple guidelines will help you present food attractively. First, avoid heaping foods on top of one another. Place foods side by side and spread them slightly to fill most of the space on the plate.

Second, be careful not to smear or splash food on the edge of the plate. If you happen to drip, use a paper towel to wipe the edge of the plate before serving it.

The American Lamb Board
Presenting food with color and artistry creates eye appeal.

Flavor

Flavor is a mixture of taste, aroma, and texture. Information about the taste of food is conveyed to the brain by nerves at the base of the taste buds. **Taste buds** are flavor sensors covering the surface of the tongue. The four basic tastes recognized by human taste buds are sweet, sour, salty, and bitter.

Some foods have one distinct flavor. Sugar, for example, is sweet. Other foods have a blend of flavors. Sweet and sour pork has the sweetness of sugar. It also has the sourness of vinegar and the saltiness of pork.

Aroma is closely associated with flavor. When you like a food, it will taste even better to you if it has a good smell. For example, if you like coffee, the smell of coffee brewing will stimulate your appetite and taste buds.

Flavor should be an important consideration when planning meals. Some flavors seem to go together. Turkey and cranberry sauce, peanut butter and jelly, and apples and cinnamon are popular flavor combinations. Other flavors seem to fight one another. For instance, you should not serve rutabagas and Brussels sprouts together. Their strong flavors do not complement each other.

When planning meals, do not repeat similar flavors. For instance, avoid serving tomatoes on a salad that will accompany pasta with tomato sauce. Menus should not include all spicy foods or all mild foods. Plan to serve foods with different flavors.

FYI

A number of researchers believe human taste buds recognize a fifth taste called *umami*. This taste is often described as *savory*.

Reflect

Ask students what other flavors they think go well together. Ask what other flavors they think are unappealing together.

Texture

Texture is the feel of food in the mouth. Familiar food textures are hard, chewy, soft, crisp, smooth, sticky, dry, gritty, and tough. A meal made up of foods that are all soft or all crisp lacks interest. A meal made up of a variety of textures is much more appealing.

Serve foods in combinations that have texture contrasts. Crisp cookies and soft, smooth pudding is one example. Tossing toasted, slivered almonds into a pan of green beans adds a pleasing difference in texture.

When planning meals, work for a balance between soft and solid foods. Be sure to consider chewy versus crunchy, dry versus moist, and smooth versus crisp. Avoid serving two or more chopped, creamed, or mashed dishes together.

Temperature

The temperature of foods can also affect appetite appeal. A cold salad, for example, provides a pleasing temperature contrast to a piping hot entree. Icy cold sherbet cools the sensation created by steaming chili.

Hot foods should be hot and cold foods should be cold. Imagine a steaming bowl of soup and the same soup barely warm. Picture a cold, crisp tossed salad next to a room temperature salad bowl filled with wilted greens. Foods served lukewarm do not usually stimulate the senses of taste and sight. See **10-7**.

10-7 The most appealing meals include foods with a variety of colors, sizes, shapes, flavors, textures, and temperatures.

Control the Use of Time and Energy

Meal managers use time and energy to plan menus, buy and store food, and prepare and serve meals. They also need time and energy to care for the kitchen and dining area. **Conservation** refers to the planned use of a resource to avoid waste. Meal managers want to conserve all their resources. However, busy schedules may make time and energy seem more valuable than some other resources. That is why some meal managers view controlling the use of time and energy as the most important meal management goal.

Two main factors help determine the amount of time meal managers need to plan and prepare meals. These are the number of people eating and food preferences. A meal manager will spend more time preparing meals for a large group than for a few people. A meal that provides enough leftovers to feed a small group two meals would feed a large group only once. Preparing complex dishes and five-course dinners requires more time than making simple recipes and one-dish meals.

Alternatives to the Use of Time and Energy

A meal manager can use several alternatives to time and energy. These include people, money, knowledge, skills, technology, and time itself. All these resources are limited. Each meal manager has to balance how he or she uses them to best meet his or her goals.

Meal managers can use *people* as a resource to help save time and energy. Each household member can play a role in helping with grocery shopping and various preparation tasks. Even young children can take on such responsibilities as setting and clearing the table. This gives the meal manager more time to focus on planning and organizing. However, the meal manager can help each person learn how to do assigned jobs as efficiently as possible. This will allow everyone to make the best use of available time and energy.

When *money* is available, the meal manager could use it to hire help or pay for time-saving appliances. However, a more common way to use money in place of time is to buy ready-made foods. These foods may come from restaurant takeout menus or grocery store deli counters.

Though short on time, some meal managers wish to be more involved in food preparation than takeout allows. *Meal prep kitchens* provide an option for these meal managers. These businesses supply prepared ingredients, which meal managers can use to quickly assemble provided recipes. Food items are then ready to take home and cook or freeze for future use. This saves the meal manager the time and energy required to shop, get ingredients ready, and clean up the kitchen.

Some busy meal managers meet their goal to control the use of time by spending money to eat out. With a little thought, eating out can meet the other three meal management goals, too. Meal managers can help others choose items from the menu that meet the goal of good nutrition. They can limit the frequency of dining out to meet the goal of planned spending. They can choose restaurants with varied menus to meet the goal of satisfying meals.

Meal managers' *knowledge* and *skills* can be alternatives for time and energy. Meal managers may gain some knowledge by studying and asking questions. However, much knowledge and most skills come from experience. Through practice, meal managers find shortcuts and develop speed. For instance, learning the best time, place, and method for buying groceries can save time on a shopping trip. Learning how to correctly clear a table can save energy at the end of a meal. See **10-8**.

Reflect

Ask students how often their families eat out as an alternative to spending time and energy to prepare meals at home.

For Example…

Modern kitchen appliances that speed food preparation tasks are another example of how technology can be an alternative to time and energy.

Chicago Cutlery®

10-8 As meal managers perform routine kitchen tasks, they develop skill and gain speed, which will save them time and energy in the future.

Technology can be an alternative to time and energy in the kitchen. A computer can be used to help plan menus. Recipe websites and software programs often suggest preplanned menus. These menus can be used as is or adapted to reflect personal preferences. Shopping lists can be printed that go with the menus. Saving menus for favorite meals will reduce planning time in the future.

A meal manager can use *time* itself to save time. Using time to organize the kitchen for efficiency can save time later when preparing meals. Using time to plan menus can save time later by making shopping more efficient. Make the most of the time spent cooking by preparing double recipes. Leftovers can be turned into a different dish to serve on another day or frozen for later use.

Using Convenience Foods

Most meal managers use convenience foods to reduce or eliminate food preparation and cooking time at home. Some ready-made foods are so commonly used, people do not think of preparing meals without them.

You can group convenience foods according to the amount of service they contain. **Finished foods** are convenience foods that are ready for eating either immediately or after simply heating or thawing. Packaged cookies, canned spaghetti, and frozen fruits are examples of finished foods. **Semiprepared foods** are convenience foods that still need to have some service performed. Cake mixes are semiprepared foods. The meal manager beats in eggs and liquid, pours the batter into pans, and bakes it for a specified time.

Some meal managers do not care for the taste of packaged products. Others do not want to miss having the chance to cook creatively. These meal managers may still enjoy the time savings of convenience products to do *speed-scratch cooking*. This type of cooking might involve adding a few seasonings to a convenience product like prepared pasta sauce to give it a special touch. Speed-scratch cooking also uses convenience products as the basis of recipes. For instance, a meal manager might use a cake mix as the starting point for a batch of homemade cookies.

The cost of convenience depends on the amount of service a product contains. Generally, the more built-in service a product contains, the higher the product's price will be. A product that contains more service reduces the amount of time the meal manager spends measuring, mixing, and cooking. Most convenience foods cost more than their homemade counterparts. However, there are some exceptions. Frozen orange juice concentrate and some commercial cake mixes cost less than their homemade counterparts.

Convenience foods have both advantages and disadvantages. Before buying a convenience product, ask the following questions:

- How does the convenience food help meet daily nutrient needs?
- Does buying convenience foods fit into the food budget? (Is the time saved worth the extra cost?)
- How does the cost of the convenience product compare with the cost of the homemade product?
- How costly are any additional ingredients that must be added? (Some convenience mixes require the addition of foods like meat, eggs, or sour cream.)
- How much must be bought? (The cost of a convenience product may seem reasonable if one or two people are being fed. However, it may seem costly if three or more people are being fed.)

- How do the appearance and flavor of the convenience product compare with those of its homemade counterpart? See **10-9**.

Work Simplification

Work simplification is the performance of tasks in the simplest way possible to conserve time and energy. Work simplification techniques can help meal managers reach their goal for controlling the use of time. The meal manager can simplify tasks by minimizing hand and body motions. He or she can organize workspace and tools. Changing the product or the method used to prepare the product can also simplify some tasks.

Hand and body motions can be minimized in many ways. Performing a task repeatedly can eventually result in reduced preparation time. This is because the person performing the task develops a skill. A professional cook who chops celery every day soon learns an efficient method for chopping celery.

Another way to minimize motions is to rinse and soak dishes. This simplifies the task of washing dishes.

Saving steps in the kitchen is a method of work simplification, too. Try not to walk back and forth across the kitchen while preparing a meal. Instead, get all the equipment ready first. Then go to the cabinets and then to the refrigerator to get the needed ingredients.

An organized kitchen simplifies work. Store tools in the area where they are used most often. For instance, pots and pans can be stored in a cabinet close to the range. Many experienced meal managers buy duplicates of inexpensive tools like spatulas, wooden spoons, and measuring utensils. They store these tools in different parts of the kitchen where the tools will be easy to reach. By using the correct tool for each task, the meal manager can also simplify work. Measuring flour in a dry measure is much more efficient than measuring it in a liquid measure.

Simplify work by changing the food product or the method used to prepare it. For instance, if the meal plan calls for biscuits, but time is short, opt for store-bought bread instead. Making dropped biscuits instead of rolled biscuits would be another way to save time.

Prepreparation is another work simplification technique. **Prepreparation** is any step done in advance to save time when getting a meal ready. Chopping onions and shredding cheese might be prepreparation tasks. After completing these steps, the onions and cheese can be placed in bags in the freezer. When preparing a recipe calling for these ingredients, the needed portion can be quickly measured from the freezer bag. Trimming chicken, peeling oranges, and cooking rice may be other prepreparation tasks that could be done.

Convenience Foods	
Advantages	**Disadvantages**
Time and energy are saved because the meal manager does not have to measure, mix, peel, and slice. The inexperienced cook can prepare meals confidently. The meal manager who does not like to cook can prepare nutritious meals without spending hours in the kitchen.	Many mass-produced foods do not taste as good as home-prepared foods. Frequent use of convenience foods is expensive. Many convenience foods are high in fat and sodium.

10-9 Before buying a convenience food, a meal manager should consider both the advantages and disadvantages.

Discuss

Ask students how an organized kitchen can save cleanup time as well as preparation time. *(Having a specific place for storing each item in the kitchen speeds tasks like emptying the dishwasher.)*

Activity

Give students a list of food products and ask them to suggest comparable alternatives that would be faster and easier to prepare.

Activity

Have each student make a list of all the food items on one shelf of a food storage area in his or her home. Ask students to place a check beside each item on their lists that is packaged in recyclable material.

Global Perspective

Conserving Resources in the Kitchen

Human energy is not the only type of energy that meal managers need to conserve in the kitchen. They also need to conserve fuel energy, such as gas and electricity. Steps that can be taken to conserve energy include using the oven to cook more than one food at a time. Cover pans on the range to keep in heat. Avoid unnecessarily opening the oven door and letting out heat while using the appliance. Likewise, avoid opening refrigerator and freezer doors, which lets in heat.

Water is another resource that should be conserved in the kitchen. Avoid letting the water run while washing dishes. Run the dishwasher only when it is full.

Resources can also be conserved in the kitchen by **recycling**. This means processing a material so it can be used again. Many communities collect empty metal cans, plastic bottles, and glass containers for recycling. The metal, plastic, and glass can be made into new products. Collection facilities often take cardboard from cereal, cracker, and convenience mix boxes, too. Recycling these items keeps them from taking up space in public garbage landfills. It also lessens the need for raw materials to make new products. A meal manager can easily take these steps to help care for the environment while meeting meal planning goals.

Shutterstock

Recycling containers instead of throwing them away is a simple step meal managers can take to conserve resources.

CAREER SUCCESS

Using Budgeting

Emilio owns a catering business. People hire him and his staff to prepare food and bring it to their homes or rented banquet halls. Many people also ask Emilio to stay and serve the food to their party guests. Many of Emilio's clients order fancy foods, such as shrimp cocktail and exotic fruits. They want the foods to be expertly seasoned and beautifully garnished. They often insist on ordering more than enough food to feed the expected number of guests. All these factors add to the catering bill. However, most of the clients have limited finances.

To be an effective worker, Emilio needs skill in budgeting money. Put yourself in Emilio's place and answer the following questions about your need for and use of this skill:

A. What are four expenses you must consider when deciding how much to charge your clients?

B. How might your clients react if you exceed their financial limits?

C. What would happen if you underestimate your expenses when billing clients?

D. What is another skill you would need in this job? Briefly explain why this skill would be important.

CHAPTER 10 REVIEW

Summary

Meal managers have four main goals in planning meals. The first goal is to provide good nutrition for everyone eating the meal. Meal managers can use a meal pattern based on MyPlate as a resource to help meet this goal.

The second goal is to use planned spending. A meal manager must consider factors that affect food needs and food purchases when preparing a budget. He or she can use consumer skills to reduce food expenses and stay within the established budget.

The third goal of meal management is to prepare satisfying meals. Meal managers must be mindful of diners' food preferences to achieve this goal. They must also consider flavors, colors, textures, shapes, sizes, and temperatures of foods. This will help them plan menus that are varied and appealing.

The fourth meal management goal is to control the use of time and energy. Meal managers can use a number of resources as alternatives to time and energy. They can use convenience foods and work simplification techniques to reduce the time they spend planning and preparing meals. Meal managers can use appliances efficiently and recycle to conserve fuel energy and other resources in the kitchen.

Review What You Have Read

Write your answers on a separate sheet of paper, using complete sentences when appropriate.

1. Name six resources a meal manager can use to reach goals related to preparing and serving food.

2. What portion of a day's total nutrient intake do breakfast, lunch, dinner, and snacks generally supply?

3. What is usually the first step in planning a menu?

4. True or false. All households with similar food needs spend about the same amount of money for food.

5. List four factors that help determine the amount of money a meal manager spends for food.

6. Describe the steps you would take to estimate the amount of money you could spend for food each week.

7. Which of the following statements about food costs is not true?
   A. Dried milk costs less than fluid fresh milk.
   B. During off-seasons, canned fruits and vegetables cost less than fresh.
   C. Store brands cost less than national brands.
   D. Presweetened cereals cost less than unsweetened cereals.

8. List the six elements that affect the sensory appeal of a meal. Give examples of foods that show contrast for each element.

Answer Key to *Review What You Have Read* **questions**

1. (List six:) people, money, time, energy, knowledge, skills, technology, food, equipment

2. Breakfast generally supplies one-fourth of the day's total needs. Lunch and dinner each supply one-third, and snacks supply the remaining needs.

3. The first step in planning a menu is usually to choose the main dish of the main course.

4. false

5. (List four:) income, meal manager's ability to choose foods that are within the food budget, meal manager's shopping skills and knowledge of the marketplace, amount of time the meal manager has to plan and prepare meals, food preferences of household members, personal values

6. (Student response.)

7. D

8. flavor, color, texture, shape, size, temperature (Examples are student response.)

9. (Student response. See page 209 in the text.)

(continued)

10. finished foods
11. Minimize hand and body motions. Organize workspace and tools. Change the food product or the method used to prepare it.

9. Explain how eating out can help meal managers meet all four meal management goals.

10. Convenience foods that are ready for eating either immediately or after simply heating or thawing are called _____.

11. Describe three ways a meal manager can simplify tasks.

12. Give two suggestions for conserving fuel energy and one suggestion for conserving water in the kitchen.

Link to Academic Skills

12. (List two for fuel energy; one for water. Student response.)

13. **Government/Civics.** Compare government budgeting with personal budgeting. What are the sources of income and expenses in each type of budget? What factors affect how much money is allocated to the various categories in each type of budget?

14. **English language arts.** Find and read an online article about ways to stretch food dollars. Give a poster presentation about one or more of the money-saving tips described in the article you read.

15. **Science.** Work with a partner to conduct this experiment. *Partner A* will keep the identity of the samples and serve the samples. *Partner B* will taste and evaluate the samples. *Partner A* should choose three flavors of clear sparkling water. Remove the label from each bottle and tag the bottles **1**, **2**, and **3**. Record the flavor that corresponds to each number. Make sure *Partner B* does not see the flavors. For each of three tastings, pour a small amount from each bottle into each of three glasses. Change the order of the glasses for each tasting. For the first tasting, do not add anything to the samples. For the second tasting, add a drop of an unexpected food color to each glass. For instance, you might color grape yellow or lemon red. For the third tasting, add a drop of an expected food color to each glass. Ask *Partner B* to taste each of the samples and identify the flavor. *Partner A* should record *Partner B's* responses. What does this experiment tell you about the impact of color on flavor perception?

16. **English language arts.** Visit the school cafeteria or a nearby foodservice operation and observe employees involved in food preparation. What work simplification techniques do you see employees using? How could employees make better use of work simplification techniques? Share your findings in a brief oral report to the class.

Build Critical Thinking Skills

17. **Evaluation.** Keep track of all the meals you eat for one week. Evaluate the meals according to MyPlate. If each day's meals were not nutritionally balanced, suggest where you could have added or subtracted menu items to provide the recommended daily amounts.

18. **Analysis.** Write menus for meals for one week. Attach the menus to a report analyzing how they meet the four goals of meal management.

Apply Technology

19. Use a computer and a recipe website or software to plan meals for one week.

20. Use a computer and a spreadsheet program along with the steps outlined in the chapter to prepare a monthly budget. Then use the budget to analyze your food spending.

A Measure of Math

21. Compare the costs of 10 foods with built-in convenience with their less convenient counterparts. Examples might include shredded cheese and bulk cheese, instant rice and long grain rice, and ready-made juice and frozen concentrate.

Teamwork in Action

22. In the United States, over 7 percent of the population has diabetes. Conduct library and/or online research to investigate the special nutrient needs of someone with this disease. If possible, you might also consult with a registered dietitian. Then write menus that would meet the special nutritional needs you have studied. Create a display for a school or community health fair showing how these menus compare to menus that would meet the nutritional needs of the general population. Make copies of your menus available to people visiting the fair.

Companion Website
www.g-wlearning.com

At the website, review key terms for this chapter with crossword puzzles, matching exercises, and e-flash cards. Apply facts from the chapter to complete the activities.

CHAPTER 11

Shopping Decisions

Main Menu

- Developing shopping skills can help consumers get the most value for their food dollars.
- Food labeling is a helpful tool consumers can use to learn about the products available to them.

Learning Prep

Make a matching activity listing the *Terms to Know* in one column and randomly ordered definitions in a second column. Trade papers with a partner and complete one another's matching activities. Trade papers again and evaluate your partner's accuracy.

Objectives

After studying this chapter, you will be able to

- **evaluate** store features to decide where to shop for food.
- **identify** factors that affect food costs and comparison shop to decide what foods to buy.
- **use** information on food product labels to make informed decisions about foods to buy.
- **list** sources of consumer information.

Terms to Know

produce
comparison shopping
impulse buying
unit pricing
grade
brand name
store brand
national brand
precycling
organic food

pesticide
food additive
GRAS list
artificial sweetener
nutrition labeling
Daily Values
universal product code
 (UPC)
open dating

To be a smart consumer at the grocery store, you need to know how to read labels and compare prices. You need to be able to choose foods that will give you the most nutrition for your money. You also need to understand basic marketing techniques.

Making wise decisions about where to shop and what to buy takes knowledge and practice. As you develop consumer skills, you will be able to plan appealing, nutritious meals while staying within your budget.

Choosing Where to Shop

Consumers can choose between many kinds of food stores. Some large stores stock thousands of items. Other stores are small and stock just a few specialty items. Some stores sell only food, whereas others also sell drugs, cosmetics, toys, and clothing.

Types of Stores

Being familiar with the different types of stores will help you know what to expect when you shop. You may find one store that meets all your needs, or you may shop in several stores.

Supermarkets carry both food and nonfood items. Many have special food sections, such as delis and bakeries. Some offer services, such as home delivery, check cashing, and credit. Some supermarkets have in-store pharmacy and banking services, too. See **11-1**.

Discount supermarkets sell only a limited number of products, brands, and sizes. They focus on items that offer consumers noticeable savings over other types of food stores. In order to enjoy these savings, customers may find discount supermarkets to be small with plain decor. These stores may not carry fresh meat or **produce** (fresh fruits and vegetables). Shoppers may have to bag their own groceries, too.

Wholesale clubs sell a limited selection of foods in bulk quantities. You may be able to buy some items by the case or in restaurant-sized containers. Although you may find reduced prices, be sure you can use the large amounts you buy. Also be aware these stores may not accept coupons, and they often have membership fees.

Most *convenience stores* sell gasoline and are open long hours. They are smaller than supermarkets and usually offer only a limited choice of convenience foods. They charge higher prices, which consumers are willing to pay because shopping there is handy.

Specialty stores carry one specific type of product. Dairies, bakeries, butcher shops, and ethnic markets are specialty stores. *Delicatessens* are also a type of specialty store. They sell ready-to-eat foods like cold meats, salads, and rolls. Foods sold in specialty stores are generally high in quality, but they are often high in price, too.

Photograph provided courtesy of the California Strawberry Commission. ©2010 California Strawberry Commission. All rights reserved.

11-1 Supermarkets that offer extra services, such as banking and floral centers, enable customers to complete a number of errands while doing their grocery shopping.

Outlet stores offer reduced prices on products from individual food manufacturers. Some items in an outlet store may not meet the manufacturer's standards for retail sale. However, the foods are nutritious.

Food co-ops are owned and operated by groups of consumers. They keep prices low by buying foods in bulk, leaving off profits, and requiring volunteer labor of their members. Most co-ops have limited hours and are open only to their members.

During the growing season, growers often bring their fruits and vegetables to sell at *farmers' markets*. Individual growers may operate *roadside stands* near their farms. Fresh-picked produce is available at both types of markets. Prices are generally lower because food is sold directly from the farm to the consumer. However, to make wise purchases, recognize signs of quality and know retail prices.

Learn About...

Internet Grocery Stores

Internet grocery stores offer service in many areas. They allow consumers to shop from a computer through the store's website. Consumers simply choose the brands, sizes, and quantities of products desired from menus on the screen. They can choose to read nutrition, ingredient, and other label information. When they are done shopping, they electronically send the order and arrange for delivery. Professional shoppers fill the order and deliver it to consumers.

Products from Internet grocers tend to cost a bit more than they do from supermarkets. Consumers also pay a delivery fee. However, many people feel avoiding traffic, crowded stores, and heavy shopping bags is worth the cost.

Store Features

You may shop at a certain food store because it is the only store near you. If you can choose among several stores, however, considering each store's features may help you decide where to shop. You might want to ask yourself the following questions:

*   What services does the store offer?
*   Is the store neat and clean? Are the shelves and cases well stocked?
*   Are the store's hours convenient?
*   Are the employees courteous and helpful?
*   Does the store stock a variety of foods, brands, and sizes?
*   Are the prices for both advertised and nonadvertised items comparable to those of other area stores?
*   Are the dairy and meat cases cold and clean?
*   Is the produce fresh? Is it well chilled? Is the variety good?

Deciding What to Buy

You can make most of your decisions about what to buy by writing weekly menus before you go shopping. Try to plan meals around advertised specials. For example, if ham is a good buy, plan to serve it in several ways during the week. Keep your menus

Global Perspective

Sustainability in Food Marketing

Concern for the condition of planet earth and those who live here is the force behind a current supermarket trend.

This trend is *sustainability*. It is a way of doing business that cares for the health of people and the environment.

Sustainability is affecting every facet of food marketing. It begins with how stores are built and maintained. New and remodeled stores require less energy for heating, cooling, and lighting. Stores are being outfitted with equipment that conserves water. Refrigeration systems are using coolants that are environmentally friendly. Landscapes are being designed to resist drought so they will not require watering. Stores are being cleaned with products that contain no harmful chemicals.

Today, stores are taking a look at the products they sell. They are offering more items from local suppliers to reduce the use of fuel for shipping. They are asking manufacturers to use less packaging. Stores are stepping up their efforts to recycle shipping cartons and other materials, too.

Stores are also helping employees and customers learn steps they can take to protect the environment. One of the biggest steps is to use reusable shopping bags. This saves the trees needed to make paper bags and limits the number of plastic bags that end up in landfills.

Green Bag Company, Inc.

Reusable shopping bags help protect the environment by sparing the resources used to make paper and plastic bags.

flexible. Suppose you wanted to serve zucchini for one meal, but you find out yellow squash is on sale. You might want to eliminate the zucchini from your menu and add the yellow squash.

Using a Shopping List

A shopping list can help you save time, avoid extra trips for forgotten items, and stick to your food budget. Keep a list handy in your kitchen so you can jot down items when you find you need them. Before going to the store, check the recipes you plan to prepare during the week. Be sure you have all needed ingredients on hand. Check for staples such as flour, sugar, and milk. Add any needed items to your list. Also add advertised specials if you need them and if they really are bargains.

Organize your list according to categories, such as produce, dairy, meat, and frozen foods. Place the categories in the same order as the store aisles.

Carry your shopping list with you and stick to it. You will be less tempted to buy groceries you do not need.

Enrich

Have each student make a map showing the layout of the aisles at a local grocery store. Have them note which products are stocked in each aisle. Then have students use their maps to organize shopping lists.

Using Unit Pricing

You can get the best buys if you learn to comparison shop and avoid impulse buying. **Comparison shopping** involves evaluating different brands, sizes, and forms of a product before making a purchase decision. **Impulse buying**, on the other hand, is making an unplanned purchase without much thought.

Many, but not all, grocery stores use unit pricing to help customers comparison shop. **Unit pricing** is a listing of a product's cost per standard unit, weight, or measure. Examples are the cost per dozen, pound (.45 kg), or quart (L). Unit prices generally appear with selling prices on shelf tags underneath products.

With unit pricing, you can compare different brands and package sizes. Unit pricing can also help you compare the cost of different forms of a product quickly and easily. This would tell you whether fruits and vegetables are a better buy in fresh, canned, or frozen form. You could find out if tuna in a can is more or less economical than tuna in a pouch. See **11-2**.

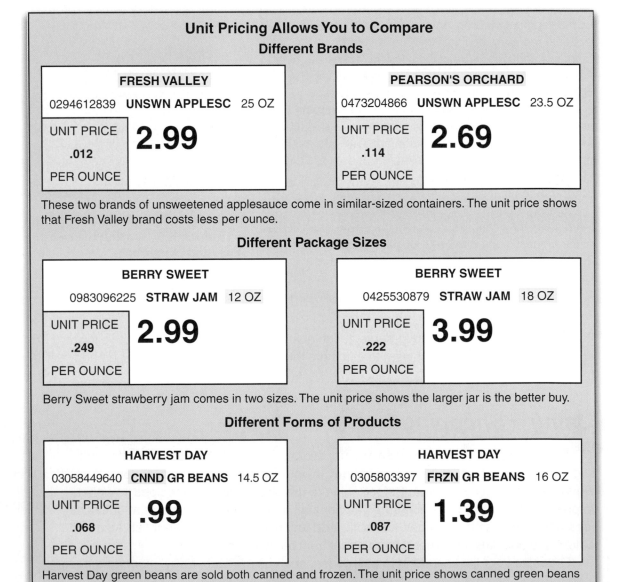

Unit Pricing Allows You to Compare
Different Brands

FRESH VALLEY	
0294612839 **UNSWN APPLESC** 25 OZ	
UNIT PRICE .012 PER OUNCE	**2.99**

PEARSON'S ORCHARD	
0473204866 **UNSWN APPLESC** 23.5 OZ	
UNIT PRICE .114 PER OUNCE	**2.69**

These two brands of unsweetened applesauce come in similar-sized containers. The unit price shows that Fresh Valley brand costs less per ounce.

Different Package Sizes

BERRY SWEET	
0983096225 **STRAW JAM** 12 OZ	
UNIT PRICE .249 PER OUNCE	**2.99**

BERRY SWEET	
0425530879 **STRAW JAM** 18 OZ	
UNIT PRICE .222 PER OUNCE	**3.99**

Berry Sweet strawberry jam comes in two sizes. The unit price shows the larger jar is the better buy.

Different Forms of Products

HARVEST DAY	
03058449640 **CNND GR BEANS** 14.5 OZ	
UNIT PRICE .068 PER OUNCE	**.99**

HARVEST DAY	
0305803397 **FRZN GR BEANS** 16 OZ	
UNIT PRICE .087 PER OUNCE	**1.39**

Harvest Day green beans are sold both canned and frozen. The unit price shows canned green beans are a better value.

11-2 Unit pricing helps consumers comparison shop.

Cost per Serving

MORNING FARE	
0294850391 **RAISIN BRAN** 20 OZ	
UNIT PRICE .225 PER OUNCE	**4.49**

MORNING FARE	
0294840559 **TOASTED OATS** 20 OZ	
UNIT PRICE .250 PER OUNCE	**4.99**

Comparing the unit costs shows the raisin bran cereal costs less per ounce than the toasted oat cereal.

Nutrition Facts

Serving Size 1 cup (59g)

Servings Per Container about 10

Nutrition Facts

Serving Size 1 cup (28g)

Servings Per Container about 20

However, the Nutrition Facts panel on the side of each box shows the raisin bran package contains only 10 servings, whereas the toasted oats package contains 20 servings.

$$\$4.49 \div 10 = \$.45 \qquad \$4.99 \div 20 = \$.25$$

Dividing the total price of each product by the number of servings in each package shows the toasted oats cost less per serving.

11-3 Figuring the cost per serving can tell you which product is a better buy.

Academic Connections

Work with the math department to prepare students to figure unit prices. Ask the math teachers to review figuring percentages along with using basic multiplication and division to solve application problems.

Online Resource

Have students visit the Savings Lifestyle website and explore strategies to save at the grocery store. Ask each student to share a tip in class.

As a smart consumer, you need to be aware that a heavier food might not provide as many servings per container as a lighter food. In this case, the unit cost will not tell you which product is a better buy. Instead, you need to find the cost per serving. Do this by dividing the total product price by the number of serving in each package. You can find the number of servings in a food container by looking at the Nutrition Facts panel on the package. See **11-3**.

Factors That Affect Costs

Several factors affect the costs of the foods you buy. These factors include food grades, product brands, and packaging. Understanding these factors can help you be a smart consumer.

Learn About...

Coupons and Unit Pricing

Consider the impact of coupons on unit cost. Small packages often have a higher unit cost than large packages of the same product. When using a coupon, however, the small package often becomes the better buy. For instance, suppose a 10-ounce (284 g) box of cereal costs $2.49 and a 20-ounce (568 g) box costs $4.39. The small box would have a unit cost of $.25 per ounce (28 g). The large box would have a unit cost of $.22 per ounce (28 g). With a $.75 coupon, the small box would cost $1.74; the large box would cost $3.64. With the coupon, the unit cost of the small box would be $.17; the unit cost of the large box would be $.18.

Grades

Many food products are given a **grade**, which is an indication of quality. Foods with higher grades usually cost more than those with lower grades. Grades are based on factors that affect the appeal of a food rather than its wholesomeness. For instance, a lower-grade peach may not have a uniform shape or a characteristic color. However, it is nutritious and safe to eat. In many cases, only products with the highest grades are sold in fresh form. Lower-grade products are often used as ingredients in processed foods.

Brands

The cost of a product is affected by its **brand name**. This is the name a manufacturer puts on products so people will know that company makes the products. A **store brand**, also called a *house brand*, is a brand sold only by a store or chain of stores. A **national brand** is a brand that is advertised and sold throughout the country. Manufacturers of national brands often package some of their products with store brand labels. However, because the store brands are not promoted with big advertising budgets, they often cost less than national brands.

Packaging

Another factor that affects the cost of food products is the amount and type of packaging material. Packaging affects the environment as well as product costs. As a smart consumer, make a habit of precycling when deciding what to buy. **Precycling** is thinking about how packaging materials can be reused or recycled before buying a product. For instance, you might plan to use a resealable plastic container to store leftovers. You might choose a product in a glass jar instead of a plastic container because you can recycle the glass. You might avoid buying a single-serving product because of the excessive packaging.

Organic Foods

As you decide what to buy, you may think about choosing some **organic foods**. These are foods produced without the use of synthetic fertilizers, pesticides, or growth stimulants. Genetic engineering methods and ionizing radiation are also banned in the production of organic products.

The United States Department of Agriculture (USDA) has set standards for organic foods. Organic plant foods must be grown on land that has been free of chemical pesticides for at least three years. (**Pesticides** are agents used to kill insects, weeds, and fungi that attack crops.) Organic standards also limit the types of fertilizers farmers can use to help plants grow. Organic meats and poultry must come from animals raised without the use of antibiotics or hormones to promote growth. Drugs may be used only to treat sick animals.

Along with fresh organic foods, you can buy processed foods that have organic ingredients. Look for the exact percentage of organic ingredients in a product to be stated on the label.

Organic foods often cost quite a bit more than nonorganic products. Many consumers are willing to pay higher prices for organic foods. These consumers often say they are concerned about the effects standard farming methods may have on foods or the environment. See **11-4**.

Food Additives

Another factor that may affect consumer decisions about what to buy in the supermarket is **food additives**. These are substances that are added to food for a specific purpose. Although about 2,800 additives are in use today, they all fill one of the following four basic purposes:

- add nutrients
- preserve quality
- aid processing or preparation
- enhance flavors or colors

The Food and Drug Administration (FDA) firmly controls the kinds and amounts of additives companies can use in foods. (The Food Safety and Inspection Service [FSIS] of the USDA shares this duty for additives used in meat, poultry, and egg products.) Before the government passed strict food additive laws, about 600 additives were in use. The FDA placed these additives on the "Generally Recognized as Safe" or **GRAS list**. The FDA has retested the additives on this list to make sure they are safe according to today's standards. Food manufacturers can use any additive on the GRAS list without permission.

When a company wants to use a new food additive, it must first receive FDA approval. Before the FDA grants approval, it needs to know the chemical makeup of the additive. The FDA also wants to know the additive's intended purpose and the amount that will be added to food products. The company must submit results of any testing it has done on the additive, too. The FDA carefully reviews all this information. Only after the additive is found to be safe and effective is approval given for its use. The FDA continues to review additive safety based on new findings to decide if approved uses need to be changed.

One type of food additive used to enhance food flavors is sugar substitutes called **artificial sweeteners**. These are products that sweeten foods without providing the calories of sugar. Artificial sweeteners include aspartame, acesulfame K, sucralose, and saccharin. These products are used in many sugar-free foods and beverages. They are also sold for home use.

Shopping Tips

Following a few guidelines will help you get the most value for your money when shopping for food. One way to cut costs is to use coupons for items you need. Coupons are available in newspapers and magazines. Many can also be downloaded from websites and printed from your computer. Most coupons have expiration dates. Some require you to buy more than one item. Be sure you have met all the qualifications before you try to redeem coupons. Also, avoid buying a product you do not need just because you have a coupon for it.

Promotions and sales can help you save money on featured products. However, decide whether a promoted product is your best buy. For instance, stores sell some items in multiples, such as three boxes of macaroni and cheese for five dollars. In a

Whole Foods Market

11-4 The USDA organic seal on a food product assures consumers the product meets national standards for organic foods.

Discuss

Ask students why a store would advertise food products that are not on sale. *(to remind consumers they need the products)*

Reflect

Ask students when the meal managers in their homes do most of the shopping.

case such as this, determine what you would pay for one box. This will help you decide if the multiple price is a good value.

Smart consumers know how to save money without sacrificing nutrition, quality, or taste when shopping for food. The following tips can help you be a smart consumer, too.

- Sign up for a frequent shopper card at stores you visit regularly. Present the card when you check out to receive special savings and earn rewards available only to card holders.
- Read labels to be sure you know what you are buying, **11-5**.
- Compare brands and then select the brand that best meets your needs.
- Compare prices on a cost-per-serving basis.
- Buy foods that are in season when possible. Foods that are in season are generally low in price and high in quality.
- Take advantage of specials advertised in sale flyers or online, but be sure advertised prices are sale prices. Some stores feature regular prices in their advertisements.
- Compare the costs of different forms of the same food, such as canned, fresh, and frozen.
- Prepare foods from scratch if you have the time. Most convenience foods cost more than homemade ones.
- Use nonfat dry milk and margarine in cooking instead of fluid milk and butter to stretch dairy dollars.
- Avoid higher costs for cubed and sliced meats and cheeses. Buy large pieces and cut them at home.
- Plan meals that focus more on plant foods, such as dried legumes, which cost less than meat.
- Resist the temptation to make impulse purchases encouraged by store displays.

Shutterstock

11-5 Reading labels can help consumers make sure they are choosing products that will meet their needs.

- Do not take a grocery cart if you plan to buy just one or two items. You will be less tempted to buy items you do not need if you have to carry them through the store.
- Shop when stores are least crowded—usually this is in the late evening on weekdays.
- Shop for groceries just after you have eaten. You are less likely to buy unneeded items when you are not hungry.
- Do grocery shopping by yourself. Shopping with another person makes some people more likely to buy foods they do not need.

EXPLORING CAREERS

Grocery Stock Clerk

A grocery stock clerk's main duty is to refill empty shelf space with products. Stock clerks may set up displays, rearrange shelves, and update product prices as directed by a manager. They may help unpack shipments, checking items against invoices to be sure orders have been filled correctly. They may also scan customer purchases at checkout, bag merchandise, and help customers take items to their cars.

To be successful in this job, store clerks need good listening skills so they can follow directions. They must be polite and use speaking skills when answering customer questions. Grocery clerks need to show self-control if they are faced with difficult customers. They must be dependable, doing assigned tasks without close supervision. They also must be able to cooperate with other store employees and accept criticism from managers.

Grocery store clerk is an entry-level position. Many stores hire teens with little or no experience while they are still in high school. On-the-job training is often provided by more experienced coworkers. Workers who start as clerks may have opportunities to advance. With time and training, they might be able to move into positions as department or store managers.

Using Food Labeling

Food labels provide a wealth of information that can be helpful to consumers. Federal law requires the following items on food labels:
- the common name and form of the food
- the volume or weight of the contents, including any liquid in which foods are packed
- the name and address of the manufacturer, packer, or distributor
- a list of ingredients, in descending order according to weight. For instance, suppose a label lists "chicken, noodles, and carrots." The product would need to contain, by weight, more chicken than noodles and more noodles than carrots. Any ingredients that have protein from milk, eggs, fish, shellfish, tree nuts, peanuts, wheat, or soybeans must also be clearly listed. This helps people who are allergic to these foods avoid products that could trouble them.

Nutrition Labeling

The FDA requires **nutrition labeling** on almost all food packages. This is a break-down of how a food product fits in an average diet. You can identify this labeling by the heading "Nutrition Facts."

FYI

Information about nutrients such as thiamin and monounsaturated fat is optional on a Nutrition Facts panel. However, foods about which manufacturers make nutritional claims and foods with added nutrients must include additional information on the label.

The first items under the heading are the *serving size* and *servings per container*. Serving sizes are stated in both familiar units and metric measures. They are the same for similar foods to help consumers compare products. Remember to compare the listed serving size with what you typically eat. Your portion size is what determines the amounts of calories and nutrients you consume.

Calories per serving and calories from fat are listed next. Remember that foods providing more than 400 calories per serving are considered high in calories. Checking these numbers can help you avoid eating more calories than you need each day. This can also help you limit fat to no more than 35 percent of your total calories.

Nutrients found in each serving of a food product also appear on the nutrition label. The list must include the amounts of total fat, saturated fat, *trans* fat, cholesterol, and sodium. It is important to limit these nutrients in your diet. Dietary fiber, vitamin A, vitamin C, calcium, and iron are also required. Be sure you consume enough of these nutrients. Total carbohydrate, sugars, and protein are listed, too. You can see how these components compare in the foods you choose. Besides these required nutrients, manufacturers may opt to list amounts of other nutrients, such as B vitamins and zinc.

A *footnote* appears at the bottom of larger nutrition labels. It shows Daily Values for 2,000- and 2,500-calorie diets. **Daily Values** are recommended nutrient intake levels that are used on food labels. The footnote is the same on all labels that include it. It reminds you to eat less than the listed amounts of fat, saturated fat, cholesterol, and sodium each day. It also reminds you to eat at least the listed amount of fiber.

Percent Daily Values based on a 2,000-calorie diet are given for each of the nutrients listed on the label. You may need more or less than 2,000 calories per day. Therefore, your percent Daily Values may be higher or lower than those shown. See **11-6**.

Health and Nutrient Content Claims

Manufacturers often want to let consumers know what food products will do for their bodies as well as their hunger. To do this, companies may petition the FDA for approval to place health claims on product labels. A *health claim* is a statement that links a food or food component to a health condition. Food products must meet certain requirements to carry these claims. The claims cannot be misleading. They must contain specified phrasing. The FDA classifies different types of claims according to the strength of the scientific evidence on which they are based. An example of one type of health claim is a statement about the relationship between dietary fat and cancer.

Nutrient content claims are another tool companies may use to make consumers aware of the ways food products can affect health. Like health claims, nutrient content

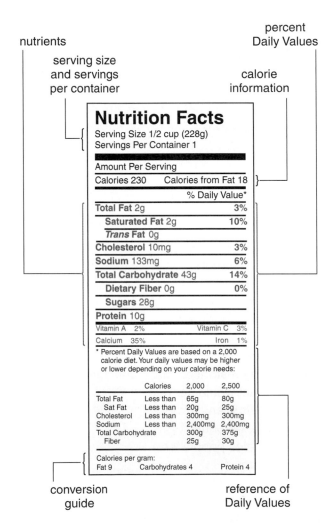

nutrients

serving size and servings per container

percent Daily Values

calorie information

Nutrition Facts

Serving Size 1/2 cup (228g)
Servings Per Container 1

Amount Per Serving

Calories 230   Calories from Fat 18

	% Daily Value*
Total Fat 2g	3%
Saturated Fat 2g	10%
Trans Fat 0g	
Cholesterol 10mg	3%
Sodium 133mg	6%
Total Carbohydrate 43g	14%
Dietary Fiber 0g	0%
Sugars 28g	
Protein 10g	

Vitamin A	2%	Vitamin C	3%
Calcium	35%	Iron	1%

* Percent Daily Values are based on a 2,000 calorie diet. Your daily values may be higher or lower depending on your calorie needs:

		Calories	2,000	2,500
Total Fat	Less than		65g	80g
Sat Fat	Less than		20g	25g
Cholesterol	Less than		300mg	300mg
Sodium	Less than		2,400mg	2,400mg
Total Carbohydrate			300g	375g
Fiber			25g	30g

Calories per gram:
Fat 9   Carbohydrates 4   Protein 4

conversion guide

reference of Daily Values

11-6 Some food products may carry a simpler version of the Nutrition Facts panel. However, all nutrition labels provide consumers with valuable information.

claims are regulated by the FDA. These claims may describe the level of a nutrient in a food. For instance, a bottle of fruit juice might have the claim "high in vitamin C." Nutrient content claims may also compare the level of a nutrient in a food with the level in another food. As an example, light mayonnaise may be labeled with the claim "30 percent less fat than regular mayonnaise." The FDA specifies terms that may be used in these claims, such as *free*, *low*, and *reduced*. FDA regulations spell out the nutrients with which each term can be used. The FDA also identifies acceptable synonyms and specific definitions for each term. Manufacturers must follow FDA guidelines so the claims will be meaningful to consumers.

Health and nutrient content claims can help consumers learn about products and make choices when shopping for food. However, keeping all the definitions straight would be too confusing. Just remember the simple guideline that 20 percent or more is high and 5 percent or less is low. Then you can apply this guideline to the information on the Nutrition Facts panel to help you reduce intakes of nutrients you want to limit. You can also use it to help you increase intakes of nutrients you want to consume in greater amounts.

Universal Product Code

Another item found on food labels is the **universal product code**, or **UPC**. This is a series of lines, bars, and numbers that appears on packages of food and nonfood items. This code is used by a computer scanner to identify a product, its manufacturer, and its size and form. Grocery checkers pass the UPC on items over a laser beam scanner. As the items pass over the scanner, the store's computer reads the codes. The correct prices are then rung up on the cash register at the checkout counter. The register prints a description of the items and their prices on the customer's receipt.

Open Dating

Dates are printed on many food product labels. Federal law does not require dates on most food products (Baby food and formula are exceptions.). However, certain states have laws ordering dates on some foods.

Some dates on food products are printed in codes, which are used mostly by manufacturers. However, **open dating** uses calendar dates on perishable and semiperishable foods to help retailers know how long to display products. Open dating also helps consumers to choose products that will maintain quality the longest and know which product to use first.

Manufacturers use a few types of dates. A *sell-by date* is the last day a store should sell a product. You should not purchase foods that are past this date. However, sell-by dates allow for some storage time in your refrigerator. Foods are still safe to eat for a few days after the date. Milk, ice cream, and cold cuts often have sell-by dates stamped on their containers or packages.

A *use-by date* is the last day a consumer should use or eat a food. On meat products, you may see the phrase "use or freeze by." A product that is kept safely frozen can be stored well beyond the date on the package.

A *best-by date* is a date suggested by the manufacturer for peak quality. You may or may not be able to notice a drop in quality if you buy and use products after this date. See **11-7**.

Rubbermaid

11-7 Herb and spice containers often have best-by dates to help consumers use seasonings before they lose their peak flavor.

Keep in mind that dates on food packages are not safety dates. It is not always necessary to throw away a food just because the date on the package has passed. Also remember that proper storage and handling affect food safety. Food that has not been stored correctly may not be safe to eat even if it is within the date on the package. If a product has a use-by date on it, follow that date. Otherwise, follow reliable food storage guidelines, such as those found for foods throughout this text.

Help with Consumer Problems

From time to time, you may have problems with food products or the businesses that sell them. Many sources of consumer help exist. The source that will best be able to assist you will depend on your particular problem.

Food stores can help you with a quality problem caused by the way they handled a food product. For instance, you might discover a loaf of bread you just purchased is moldy. If you return the bread, most store managers will refund your money or give you a new loaf.

Product manufacturers can help you with a food quality problem that is due to a processing error. Suppose when you open a package of rice mix, you find the seasoning packet is missing. Look on the package for a toll-free telephone number, website, or address you can use to contact the manufacturer. Keep the package handy so you can refer to it for specific product information the manufacturer might need. Be polite as you make a brief complaint and reasonable request for what action you would like the manufacturer to take. For instance, you might ask for a coupon for a free package of rice mix.

The *Food Safety and Inspection Service (FSIS)* can help you with a food safety problem involving meat, poultry, or egg products. The FSIS is the branch of the USDA that handles product *recalls*, or removal of products from the market. If you found metal shavings in a can of beef stew, the FSIS might contact the manufacturer to recall the product.

The *FDA* is the agency that handles food safety complaints linked to products that do not contain meat or poultry. If you found a piece of glass in a box of cereal, the FDA would handle the investigation. Be prepared to provide detailed product information when you call or complete an online form.

City, county, or *state health departments* address safety problems you might have with food from restaurants. They inspect facilities, issue warnings and fines, and close businesses when needed.

Better Business Bureaus (BBBs) can help you when you have a problem with the way a food store or restaurant conducts business. BBBs promote honest advertising and selling practices. Imagine the prices at a food store checkout regularly ring up higher than the shelf tags. If the store manager does not give you a satisfactory response, a BBB can contact the store on your behalf. The BBB can also offer to resolve your complaint by other means, if necessary.

These sources of help do more than handle consumer complaints. They can answer questions and provide a variety of consumer information. Some also do testing, grading, and inspecting to ensure the quality and safety of the food supply. See **11-8**.

Wegmans Food Markets, Inc.

11-8 Store managers are usually happy to help consumers who have questions or problems.

CAREER SUCCESS

Effective Speaking

Carine is a retail food demonstrator at Johnsen's Supermarket. She tells store customers about food products and answers their questions as she offers them samples she has prepared. The store manager expects Carine to help boost sales of the products she demonstrates.

To be a successful employee, Carine needs basic speaking skills. Put yourself in Carine's place and answer the following questions about your need for and use of these skills:

A. What are three specific speaking skills that will help you communicate with your customers?

B. How might store customers respond if you do not have adequate speaking skills?

C. How might the store manager respond if you do not have adequate speaking skills?

D. What is another skill you would need in this job? Briefly explain why this skill would be important.

CHAPTER 11 REVIEW

Summary

Smart consumers must shop carefully to get the most for their food dollars. They can choose from many types of stores. Evaluating store features can help them decide where to shop. Using a shopping list and comparing costs can help consumers know what to buy. Unit pricing makes it easy to compare costs of different brands, forms, and sizes of products. Consumers must evaluate grades, brands, and packaging to choose products that best meet their needs. Thinking about organic foods and food additives will help consumers make purchase decisions, too.

Food labeling provides consumers with information about the food products they buy. Nutrition labeling helps them get the most nutritional value for the money they spend. Health and nutrient content claims increase awareness of ways foods can affect well-being. The UPC speeds checkout. Open dating helps consumers choose products that will maintain quality the longest and know which product to use first.

Various resources can help consumers who have problems with food products. These resources can also provide information and other consumer services.

Review What You Have Read

Write your answers on a separate sheet of paper, using complete sentences when appropriate.

1. At what type of food store might consumers have to bag their own groceries?

2. What are five store features consumers might consider when deciding where to shop?

3. Explain how a shopping list can help a meal manager.

4. Consumers can easily compare the cost of different brands, sizes, and forms of the same or similar products with _____.

5. Why do store brand products often cost less than national brands?

6. Why are some consumers willing to pay higher prices for organic foods?

7. What are four basic purposes of food additives?

8. A 15-ounce can of green beans usually costs $.99. This week, a large supermarket chain is advertising 2 cans for $1.79. Is this a bargain? Explain why or why not.

9. List eight tips to help consumers save money when shopping for food.

10. True or false. The net weight shown on canned foods includes the liquids in which the foods are canned.

11. Why might food products provide people with different percent Daily Values than those listed on labels?

12. Describe how the UPC works at the checkout stand in a grocery store.

(continued)

13. The last day a product should be sold is called the _____.
   A. best-by date
   B. open date
   C. sell-by date
   D. use-by date

14. Name four sources of help with consumer problems.

Link to Academic Skills

15. **Geography.** Divide the class into seven groups. Each group will research a different geographic region of the United States: New England, Mid-Atlantic, South, Midwest, West and Southwest, Pacific Coast, or Hawaiian Islands. Each group will examine the types of food stores in two metropolitan areas and two rural areas in their region. Share and compare findings in class. Can you draw any conclusions about the popularity of various types of food stores in different regions? Are there differences in the types of stores that commonly operate in metropolitan versus rural areas?

16. **English language arts.** Visit the Food Marketing Institute website to investigate the sustainability initiative in the wholesale and retail food industry. Read a news release or industry report on the topic and summarize it for the class.

17. **English language arts.** Read an article about a food product from an issue of *Consumer Reports* magazine. Then write a summary of what was learned from the article.

18. **Government/Civics.** Mount the entire label from a can of food in the center of a sheet of paper. Identify any food additives in the ingredient list. Label each of the points of information federal law requires on food packages. Also label each part of the Nutrition Facts panel and any health and nutrient content claims that appear. Discuss in class why the government might be concerned about food product labeling.

19. **English language arts.** Write a letter to an appropriate source about a consumer problem with a food product. Be sure to use correct grammar, spelling, organization, and style.

Build Critical Thinking Skills

20. **Evaluation.** Visit several supermarkets of comparable size. Using the criteria for choosing a food store given in the chapter, evaluate each store. Write a report summarizing your findings and identifying the store at which you would most like to shop. Explain the reasons for your choice.

21. **Synthesis.** Use information about the layout of the food aisles in the store where you shop to create a master shopping form. Prepare for a trip to the store by listing needed items in the appropriate sections of the shopping form. Use the form to do your shopping. Share with the class how using the form affected the efficiency of your shopping process.

8. Yes, this is a bargain. Two cans of green beans purchased at the regular price would cost $1.98. The sale price saves the consumer $.19.

9. (List eight. Student response.)

10. true

11. Percent Daily Values listed on food labels are based on a 2,000-calorie diet. People who have higher or lower calorie needs will have higher or lower percent Daily Values, respectively.

12. As grocery checkers pass the UPC on items over a laser beam scanner, the store's computer reads the codes. The correct prices are then rung up on the cash register, which prints a description of the items and their prices on the customer's receipt.

13. C

14. (Name four:) food stores; product manufacturers; Food Safety and Inspection Service (FSIS); FDA; city, county, or state health departments; Better Business Bureaus (BBBs)

Apply Technology

22. Research the types of information stores record when shoppers scan frequent shopper cards. Find out how stores analyze and use this data. Make a list of ways the gathering of this information benefits consumers and food stores.

23. Investigate the lab procedures used to determine the nutritional values of food products itemized on Nutrition Facts panels.

A Measure of Math

24. Go to a local supermarket and record the prices of five types of fresh fruits and five types of fresh vegetables. Then visit a farmers' market and record the prices for the same fruits and vegetables. Calculate the percentage price difference for each item. Which location has the best prices overall?

25. Do a price comparison study of the cost of different forms of a food product. For example, compare the cost per serving of a chocolate cake made from scratch, a chocolate cake made from a mix, a frozen chocolate cake, and a bakery chocolate cake. (All of these cakes should be two-layer, 8-inch (20-cm) cakes with chocolate frosting.)

26. Look at the Nutrition Facts panels on three food products. Figure the percent Daily Values of listed nutrients for people needing 2,800 calories per day and for people needing 1,600 calories per day.

Teamwork in Action

27. As a class, prepare a reference card of useful websites for researching various types of consumer problems. Include factors to consider when selecting a website to make sure the information provided is reliable and accurate. Distribute the cards to students in other classes as well as to family members, faculty, and friends.

Companion Website

www.g-wlearning.com

At the website, review key terms for this chapter with crossword puzzles, matching exercises, and e-flash cards. Apply facts from the chapter to complete the activities.

CHAPTER 12
Recipes and Work Plans

Main Menu

- Learning some basic food preparation skills will make it easy to follow simple recipes.
- Being effective in the kitchen requires planning the use of time and working cooperatively with others.

Learning Prep

Use the *Terms to Know* to make a crossword puzzle. Use the definitions as clues.

Objectives

After studying this chapter, you will be able to

- **identify** abbreviations and define cooking terms used in recipes.
- **measure** liquid and dry ingredients and fats for use in recipes.
- **change** the yield of a recipe.
- **plan** time-work schedules.
- **follow** a recipe to prepare a sandwich, snack, or beverage.

Terms to Know

recipe	time-work schedule
yield	dovetail
cooking time	blend
watt	caffeine
standing time	decaffeinated
dehydration	tea
arcing	

You do not have to have cooking skills to satisfy hunger. You can eat convenience foods that require little or no preparation. However, you can add unlimited variety and interest to meals when you know how to prepare foods from scratch.

Before you can begin working in the kitchen, you need to have some basic knowledge and food preparation skills. In this chapter, you will learn how to read a recipe and measure ingredients. You will also learn how to plan your use of time in the kitchen.

Choosing a Recipe

A **recipe** is a set of instructions for preparing a specific food, **12-1**. Cookbooks are popular sources of recipes. Magazines, newspapers, appliance manuals, and recipe software can all be good places to find recipes, too. The meal manager can use these resources to help plan and prepare daily meals.

You can also explore numerous recipe websites on the Internet. Many sites allow you to search for recipes using factors such as type of dish, cuisine, and preparation method. You can easily adjust the number of servings and make a printout of any recipe. Many sites also allow you to prepare food budgets, shopping lists, and nutritional analyses. You can often save favorite recipes in a personal online recipe file, too.

Good recipes are written in a clear, concise manner. A recipe should list ingredients in the order in which you will be combining them. Amounts should be easy to measure. Directions for mixing and/or handling procedures must be complete. Baking or cooking times and temperatures and pan sizes need to be accurate. The recipe should state the **yield**, which is the average amount or number of servings a recipe makes. Many recipes also include a nutritional analysis to help you evaluate how the food will fit into a healthful diet.

A recipe is your work plan for the food you are going to prepare. Read through the recipe before you begin to prepare it. This will allow you to be sure you understand the directions and have all the needed ingredients. If you are out of a needed ingredient, you may be able to make a substitution. See **12-2**.

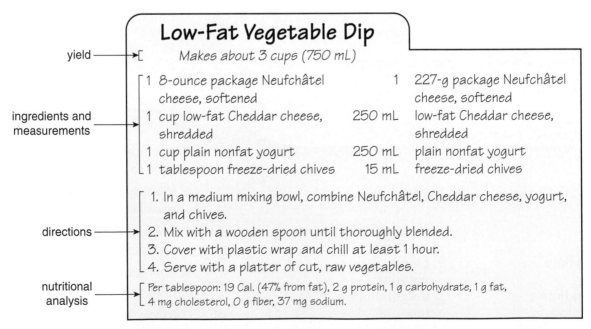

yield ⟶

Low-Fat Vegetable Dip
Makes about 3 cups (750 mL)

ingredients and measurements ⟶

1	8-ounce package Neufchâtel cheese, softened	1	227-g package Neufchâtel cheese, softened
1	cup low-fat Cheddar cheese, shredded	250 mL	low-fat Cheddar cheese, shredded
1	cup plain nonfat yogurt	250 mL	plain nonfat yogurt
1	tablespoon freeze-dried chives	15 mL	freeze-dried chives

directions ⟶

1. In a medium mixing bowl, combine Neufchâtel, Cheddar cheese, yogurt, and chives.
2. Mix with a wooden spoon until thoroughly blended.
3. Cover with plastic wrap and chill at least 1 hour.
4. Serve with a platter of cut, raw vegetables.

nutritional analysis ⟶

Per tablespoon: 19 Cal. (47% from fat), 2 g protein, 1 g carbohydrate, 1 g fat, 4 mg cholesterol, 0 g fiber, 37 mg sodium.

12-1 A well-written recipe should include all the information needed to prepare a particular food.

Substituting One Ingredient for Another

If you do not have	You may use
2 egg yolks	1 whole egg, for baking or thickening
1 cup (250 mL) fluid whole milk	½ cup (125 mL) evaporated milk plus ½ cup (125 mL) water
1 cup (250 mL) fluid fat-free milk	1 cup (250 mL) reconstituted nonfat dry milk
1 cup (250 mL) heavy cream	¾ cup (175 mL) milk plus ⅓ cup (75 mL) butter
1 cup (250 mL) sour milk or buttermilk	1 tablespoon (15 mL) vinegar or lemon juice plus milk to make 1 cup (250 mL) (Allow this mixture to stand several minutes before using.)
1 cup (250 mL) butter	1 cup (250 mL) margarine
1 ounce (28 g) unsweetened chocolate	3 tablespoons (45 mL) unsweetened cocoa powder plus 1 tablespoon (15 mL) butter or margarine
1 cup (250 mL) corn syrup	1¼ cups (300 mL) sugar plus ¼ cup (50 mL) liquid used in recipe
1 tablespoon (15 mL) cornstarch	2 tablespoons (30 mL) flour
1 cup (250 mL) cake flour	⅞ cup (220 mL) all-purpose flour

12-2 You can sometimes make substitutions for ingredients you do not have on hand.

Activity
Ask each student to find 10 of the terms in Figure 12-3 in recipes. Ask students to share their recipes in class. Note which terms are used most often.

As you read through a recipe, remember the four basic steps for keeping foods safe to eat—clean, separate, cook, and chill. Avoid recipes that include unsafe practices, such as marinating meat at room temperature. When you are ready to begin, reread the recipe one step at a time. Follow the directions carefully as you prepare the product.

Learn About...

Recipe Abbreviations

The amounts of ingredients listed in recipes are often given as abbreviations. You need to be able to interpret these abbreviations. This will help you make sure you include ingredients in the right proportions.

Abbreviations Used in Recipes

Conventional	
tsp. or t.	teaspoon
tbsp. or T.	tablespoon
c. or C.	cup
pt.	pint
qt.	quart
gal.	gallon
oz.	ounce
lb. or #	pound
doz.	dozen
pkg.	package
Metric	
mL	milliliter
L	liter
g	gram
kg	kilogram

Recipes often include these abbreviations.

Activity

Have students divide the terms listed in Figure 12-3 into categories, such as cutting techniques, moist-heat cooking methods, and cooling methods.

Cooking Terms

Recipes use a variety of terms to describe exactly how you are to handle the ingredients. For instance, a recipe that includes carrots is not likely to tell you to cut the carrots. This term is too general to let you know how the carrots should look in the finished product. Instead, the recipe might tell you to slice, dice, shred, or julienne the carrots. Becoming familiar with specific cooking terms will help your food products turn out as expected. See **12-3**.

Glossary of Food Preparation Terms

bake. To cook in the oven with dry heat.

barbecue. To cook on a rack or spit over hot coals or some other source of direct heat.

baste. To spoon pan juices, melted fat, or another liquid over the surface of food during cooking to keep the food moist and add flavor.

beat. To mix ingredients together with a circular up-and-down motion using a spoon, whisk, or rotary or electric beater.

Chop

bind. To thicken or smooth out the consistency of a liquid.

blanch. To scald or parboil in water or steam.

blend. To stir ingredients until they are thoroughly combined.

boil. To cook in liquid at 212°F (100°C).

bone. To remove bones from fowl or meat.

braise. To cook in a small amount of liquid in a tightly covered pan over low heat.

bread. To coat with dry bread or cracker crumbs.

broil. To cook uncovered under a direct source of heat.

brown. To turn the surface of a food brown by placing it under a broiler or quickly cooking it in hot fat.

brush. To apply sauce, melted fat, or other liquid with a basting or pastry brush.

candy. To cook in a sugar syrup until coated or crystallized.

caramelize. To heat sugar until a brown color and characteristic flavor develop.

chill. To make a food cold by placing it in a refrigerator or in a bowl over crushed ice.

chop. To cut into small pieces.

clarify. To make a liquid clear by removing solid particles.

coat. To thoroughly cover a food with a liquid or dry mixture.

coddle. To cook by submerging in simmering liquid.

combine. To mix or blend two or more ingredients.

cool. To let a food stand until it no longer feels warm to the touch.

core. To remove the center part of a fruit such as an apple or pineapple.

cream. To soften solid fats, often by adding a second ingredient, such as sugar, and working with a wooden spoon or an electric mixer until the fat is creamy.

crush. To pulverize.

cube. To cut into small squares of equal size.

cut. To divide into parts with a sharp utensil.

cut in. To combine solid fat with flour using a pastry blender, two forks, or the fingers.

deep-fry. To cook in a large amount of hot fat.

devein. To remove the large black or white vein along a shrimp's back.

dice. To cut into very small cubes of even size.

dissolve. To cause a solid food to turn into or become part of a liquid.

dot. To place small pieces of butter or another food over the surface of a food.

(Continued)

12-3 Being able to interpret these terms will help you prepare recipes successfully.

Glossary of Food Preparation Terms *(Continued)*

drain. To remove liquid from a food product.

dredge. To coat a food by sprinkling it with or dipping it in a dry ingredient such as flour or bread crumbs.

dress. To prepare a food for cooking.

dust. To lightly sprinkle the surface of a food with sugar, flour, or crumbs.

elevate. To lift a food off the floor of a microwave oven to allow microwaves to penetrate the food from the bottom as well as from the top and sides.

flake. To break fish into small pieces with a fork.

flour. To sprinkle or coat with flour.

flute. To make grooves or folds in dough.

fold. To incorporate a delicate mixture into a thicker, heavier mixture with a whisk or silicone spatula using a down, up, and over motion so the finished product remains light.

fricassee. To cook pieces of meat or poultry in butter and then in seasoned liquid until tender.

fry. To cook in a small amount of hot fat.

garnish. To decorate foods by adding other attractive and complementary foodstuffs to the food or serving dish.

glaze. To apply a liquid that forms a glossy coating.

grate. To reduce a food into small bits by rubbing it on the sharp teeth of a utensil.

grease. To rub fat on the surface of a cooking utensil or on a food itself.

grill. To broil over hot coals or to fry on a griddle.

grind. To mechanically break down a food into a finer texture.

hull. To remove the outer covering of a fruit or vegetable.

julienne. To cut food into thin, stick-sized strips.

Mince

knead. To work dough by pressing it with the heels of the hands, folding it, turning it, and repeating each motion until the dough is smooth and elastic.

marinate. To soak meat in a solution containing an acid, such as vinegar or tomato juice, that helps tenderize the connective tissue.

mash. To break a food by pressing it with the back of a spoon or masher or forcing it through a ricer.

melt. To change from a solid to a liquid through the application of heat.

mince. To cut or chop into very fine pieces.

mix. To combine two or more ingredients into one mass.

mold. To shape by hand or by pouring into a form to achieve a desired structure.

panbroil. To cook without fat in an uncovered skillet.

panfry. To cook in a skillet with a small amount of fat.

parboil. To boil in liquid until partially cooked.

pare. To remove the stem and outer covering of a vegetable or fruit with a paring knife or peeler.

peel. To remove the outer layer.

pit. To remove the seed(s) of a fruit or vegetable.

poach. To cook over or in a simmering liquid.

preheat. To heat an appliance to a desired temperature about 5 to 8 minutes before it is to be used.

punch down. To push a fist firmly into the top of risen yeast dough.

puree. To put food through a fine sieve or a food mill to form a thick and smooth liquid.

Flute

(Continued)

Glossary of Food Preparation Terms (*Continued*)

quarter. To cut into four equal pieces.

reconstitute. To return to a previous state by adding water.

reduce. To decrease the quantity of a liquid and intensify the flavor by boiling.

refresh. To quickly plunge blanched vegetables in cold water to stop the cooking process.

roast. To cook uncovered in the oven with dry heat.

roll. To shape into a round mass; to wrap a flat, flexible piece of food around on itself; to flatten dough to an even thickness with a rolling pin.

rotate. To turn food in a microwave oven one-quarter to one-half turn at one or more intervals in the cooking period to allow microwaves to hit it in a more even pattern.

sauté. To cook food in a small amount of hot fat.

scald. To heat liquid to just below the boiling point; to dip food into boiling water or pour boiling water over the food.

scallop. To cover with sauce and bake.

score. To make small, shallow cuts on the surface of a food.

sear. To brown the surface of a food very quickly with high heat.

season. To add herbs, spices, or other ingredients to a food to increase the flavor of the food; to prepare a cooking utensil, such as a cast iron skillet, for cooking.

section. To separate into parts.

separate. To remove one part from another, as the yolk from the white of an egg.

shape. To form.

shell. To remove from an outer covering.

shield. To use small pieces of aluminum foil to cover areas of a food that might become overcooked in an oven.

shred. To cut or break into thin pieces.

sift. To put through a sieve to reduce to finer particles.

simmer. To cook in liquid that is barely at the boiling point.

skim. To remove a substance from the surface of a liquid.

slice. To cut into thin, flat pieces.

sliver. To cut into long, slender pieces.

snip. To cut into small bits with kitchen shears.

sprinkle. To scatter drops of liquid or particles of powder over the surface of a food.

steam. To cook with vapor produced by a boiling liquid.

steep. To soak in a hot liquid.

Quarter

sterilize. To make free from microorganisms.

stew. To cook one food or several foods together in a seasoned liquid for a long period.

stir. To mix with a circular motion.

stir-fry. To cook foods quickly in a small amount of fat over high heat while stirring constantly.

strain. To separate solid from liquid materials.

thicken. To make a liquid more dense by adding an agent like flour, cornstarch, or egg yolks.

toast. To make the surface of a food brown by applying heat.

toss. To mix lightly.

truss. To prepare fowl for cooking by binding the wings and legs.

unmold. To remove from a form.

vent. To leave an opening through which steam can escape in the covering of a food to be cooked in a microwave oven.

whip. To beat quickly and steadily by hand with a whisk or rotary beater.

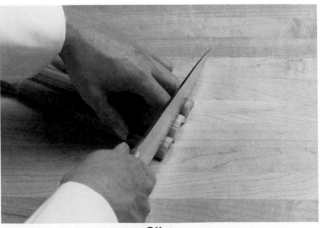

Slice

Using Microwave Recipes

Many people use their microwave ovens mainly for defrosting, reheating, and making popcorn. However, you can also cook foods in a microwave oven if you have a little specific knowledge.

Microwave cooking times vary, depending on the power of the microwave oven being used. **Cooking time** in a microwave recipe refers to the total amount of time food is exposed to microwave energy. Microwave cooking power is measured in units of power called **watts**. Most oven models produce a maximum of 600 to 1,100 watts. More watts mean faster cooking. For best results, you should always start with the shortest microwave cooking time stated in a recipe. Then check to see if more time is needed.

Many microwave recipes specify **standing time**. This is the time during which foods finish cooking by internal heat after being removed from a microwave oven. For instance, a recipe for baked potatoes may specify four minutes of cooking time and five minutes of standing time. Failure to allow for standing time can result in foods being overcooked. This can cause **dehydration**, or drying out. Wrapping foods in aluminum foil will help hold in heat during standing time.

Covering Foods

Many microwave recipes state that you should cover foods during cooking. Covering distributes heat more evenly and helps foods retain moisture so they will not dry out. The steam held in by the cover can help speed cooking time and tenderize foods. Covers are also useful for preventing spatters inside the microwave oven.

Several materials can be used to cover foods in a microwave oven. Tight fitting casserole lids and microwave cooking bags are excellent for foods that require steam for cooking. Waxed paper works well as a loose covering. Covering foods with paper towels will help absorb spatters. (Choose paper towels designed for microwave use, as they are free of materials not approved for food contact.)

Covering food with plastic wrap will help retain moisture. (Plastic wraps designed for the microwave oven work best because they will not melt during cooking.) Recipes often recommend *venting* the plastic wrap. This means turning back a corner of the wrap to form a vent so steam can escape and prevent a buildup of pressure.

Not all foods require a cover in the microwave oven. You may leave some foods uncovered to allow excess moisture to evaporate. You may need to cover other foods for only part of the cooking time. For best results, follow the directions in your recipe.

Evenness of Cooking

Microwaves are not always distributed evenly throughout the microwave oven cavity. This can cause foods to cook unevenly. Stirring foods partway through cooking will redistribute the heat and promote more even cooking. Many microwave recipes also recommend rotating food at one or more intervals in the cooking period. (Turntables included in many microwave ovens rotate food automatically during the entire cooking cycle.)

Foods tend to cook more slowly in the center of a container in a microwave oven. Therefore, recipes often suggest arranging individual foods, such as potatoes, in a circular pattern. They recommend placing large or dense foods, such as meats, around the edge of a dish. Arrange unevenly shaped foods, like chicken legs, with the thicker parts toward the outside of the container.

For Example...
Show students a topographical map of the United States and point out areas of the country where high-altitude cooking guidelines would need to be followed.

Some recipes recommend *shielding* areas of unevenly shaped foods that might overcook with small pieces of aluminum foil. Be sure to check manufacturer's directions before using any type of metal in a microwave oven. The foil will reflect the microwaves so the covered areas will not continue to cook. However, microwaves will penetrate the uncovered areas, allowing them to finish cooking.

Use care to keep foil or any metal material away from microwave oven walls. When metal meets oven walls, **arcing**, or sparking, can occur. Intense arcing can cause oven failure. The presence of narrow bands of metal, such as wire twist ties and metal-trimmed china, can also cause arcing.

Browning Techniques

Many foods cook so quickly in a microwave oven they do not have time to brown. Browning does not affect the quality and flavor of food. However, browning does affect appearance, which in turn affects appetite appeal.

Some microwave ovens have browning or crisping units, which provide excellent browning. If your microwave does not have such a unit, you can use gravies, sauces, or toppings to cover a lack of browning.

Food Science

High-Altitude Cooking

Atmospheric pressure decreases at high altitudes. At an altitude of 3,000 feet (914 m), this decrease begins to affect the outcome of food products. As the altitude increases, so does the effect on food. If you are cooking at high altitudes, you may need to make some adjustments to your recipes.

Water boils at a lower temperature at high altitudes. Therefore, most foods cooked in liquid will require more cooking time. Liquids also evaporate faster at high altitudes. You may need to add extra liquid when preparing some foods. You may need to reduce the temperature of deep fat to keep foods from overbrowning before they are thoroughly cooked.

Breads and cakes tend to rise more during baking at high altitudes. To account for this, an increase oven temperature may be needed. This will help set the batter before air cells formed by leavening gases have a chance to expand too much. A decrease baking time may be needed to keep foods from overcooking at the higher oven temperatures. Reducing the amount of leavening agents used in recipes will help compensate for excess

rising. Using larger baking pans will also keep baked goods from overflowing the pans as they rise.

For best results when cooking at high altitudes, choose recipes designed for high-altitude cooking. Many commercial mixes include high-altitude directions on the package.

©2011 Wisconsin Milk Marketing Board, Inc.

Increasing oven temperature by 25°F (4°C) will keep breads and cakes from rising too much when baking at high altitudes.

Measuring Ingredients

When preparing foods, you will need to measure different types of ingredients in different ways. Knowing how to measure ingredients correctly will help food products turn out right.

Measuring Dry Ingredients

Dry ingredients include sugar, flour, baking soda, salt, and spices. Measure these ingredients in dry measuring cups. Spoon the ingredient into the correct measuring cup until it is overfilled. Do not shake or tap the measuring cup. Hold it over the ingredient container or a sheet of waxed paper. Then use a straight-edged spatula to level off any excess. The ingredient should be even with the top edge of the measuring cup.

Flour is thoroughly sifted during the milling process and does not need to be sifted before measuring. Just stir it lightly and measure it like other dry ingredients. However, you should not skip the sifting step when a recipe tells you to sift flour with other dry ingredients. In this case, sifting helps combine the ingredients.

Measure brown sugar a bit differently from other dry ingredients. Press it firmly into a dry measure with the back of a spoon. This is called *packing*. Overfill the measuring cup and then level it with a straight-edged spatula. The brown sugar should hold the shape of the measuring cup when you dump it out.

Use measuring spoons when measuring less than ¼ cup (50 mL) of dry ingredients. Dip the correct measuring spoon into the ingredient container and level off any excess.

You may need to use combinations of dry measures to measure the amounts of ingredients you need. For instance, you would fill a ⅓-cup measure twice to measure ⅔ cup. You would fill a ¼-teaspoon measure and a ½-teaspoon measure to measure ¾ teaspoon.

Measuring Liquid Ingredients

Liquid ingredients include milk, water, oil, juices, food colorings, and extracts. Measure these ingredients in liquid measuring cups or measuring spoons. The handles and spouts on liquid measuring cups make pouring easy. The extra room at the top of the cup will help you avoid spilling.

Set the liquid measure on a flat surface. Then bend down so the desired marking on the measuring cup is at eye level. Slowly pour the ingredient into the measuring cup until it reaches the mark for the desired amount. See **12-4**.

Use measuring spoons when measuring less than ¼ cup (50 mL) of liquid ingredients. Carefully pour the ingredient into the correct spoon until it is filled to the edge.

Measuring Fats

Butter, margarine, shortening, and peanut butter are fats used in recipes. Stick butter and margarine have markings on their wrappers to help you measure needed amounts. Each stick equals 8 tablespoons or ½ cup (125 mL). Use a sharp knife to cut through the wrapper at the marking for the desired number of tablespoons.

You can measure shortening and peanut butter in dry measuring cups. Use a flexible spatula to press these ingredients into the measuring cup, making sure you eliminate any air pockets. Overfill the measuring cup, then level it with a straight-edged spatula.

Courtesy ACH Food Companies, Inc.
A

Courtesy ACH Food Companies, Inc.
B

12-4 Level off a dry measuring cup so the ingredient is even with the top edge. Fill a liquid measuring cup to the appropriate mark at eye level.

You can also use the *water displacement method* to measure solid fats. Fill a 2-cup (500 mL) liquid measuring cup with 1 cup (250 mL) of cold water. Then carefully spoon in the solid fat until the water level rises by the amount you need. For instance, suppose you need ½ cup (125 mL) of shortening. You would spoon the shortening into the measuring cup until the water level reached 1½ cups (375 mL). Make sure the fat is not clinging to the side of the measuring cup. Drain off the water before using the fat.

Learn About...

Measuring by Weight

Some recipes list amounts of ingredients by weight rather than volume. To measure these ingredients, you need a kitchen scale. Place the empty container you will use to hold the ingredients on the scale. Follow the manufacturer's directions to set the scale back to zero. (This keeps you from including the weight of the container with the weight of your ingredients.) Then spoon each ingredient into the container until the amount needed registers on the scale.

Rubbermaid
A kitchen scale allows you to precisely measure ingredients by weight.

Changing Yield

Some recipes will make more or less of a food product than you want. For instance, a recipe might make four dozen chocolate chip cookies. When making them for a large group, you may want twice that many. A recipe for a chicken and rice casserole might make eight servings. When preparing dinner for four, you might want only half that amount. Knowing *measuring equivalents* will help you adjust the yield of a recipe. See **12-5**.

Conventional units of measure used in recipes are teaspoons, tablespoons, and cups. Changing the yield of a conventional recipe can be tricky. You may have to convert from one unit to another. For instance, 3 teaspoons is the equivalent of 1 tablespoon. Suppose you are doubling a recipe that calls for 1½ teaspoons of baking soda. Two times 1½ teaspoons equals 3 teaspoons, or 1 tablespoon. Likewise, ¼ cup equals 4 tablespoons. Suppose you are halving a recipe that calls for ¼ cup sugar. You can easily figure half of 4 tablespoons is 2 tablespoons. Figure the adjusted amounts of each ingredient before you begin cooking. Write the adjusted amounts on your recipe so you will remember them as you work. See **12-6**.

The main metric unit of measure used in recipes is the milliliter. Changing the yield of a metric recipe is easy. You do not have to convert from one unit to another.

Common Equivalent Measures		
Conventional Measure	**Conventional Equivalent**	**Approximate Metric Equivalent***
¼ teaspoon	—	1 milliliter
½ teaspoon	—	2 milliliters
1 teaspoon	—	5 milliliters
3 teaspoons	1 tablespoon	15 milliliters
2 tablespoons	⅛ cup	30 milliliters
4 tablespoons	¼ cup	50 milliliters
5 ⅓ tablespoons	⅓ cup	75 milliliters
8 tablespoons	½ cup	125 milliliters
10⅔ tablespoons	⅔ cup	150 milliliters
12 tablespoons	¾ cup	175 milliliters
16 tablespoons	1 cup, ½ pint	250 milliliters
2 cups	1 pint	500 milliliters
4 cups	1 quart	1 liter

*Based on measures seen on standard metric equipment.

12-5 Knowing equivalent measures can help you change recipe yield and convert between conventional and metric measures.

Using a Time-Work Schedule

When serving a meal, you would not want the vegetable to finish cooking 20 minutes after you serve the main course. As a meal manager, you are responsible for making sure all the food is ready at the same time. You can accomplish this goal by using a **time-work schedule**. This is a written plan that lists times for doing specific tasks to prepare a meal or food product.

A time-work schedule should be specific enough to identify the order and timing of all the critical preparation steps. On the other hand, it should be flexible enough to allow you to make adjustments. If you underestimate your speed or need to substitute an ingredient, you may need this flexibility.

Preliminary Planning

Before writing your time-work schedule, you need to think about the tasks involved in preparing a meal. As you gather recipes for each menu item, think about the cooking methods required. Choosing two or more items that can be prepared by the same method can help you save time and energy. For instance, you can use the heat of the oven to roast chicken and carrots at the same time.

In addition to recipes, you will need paper and a pencil to write your schedule. (Using a pencil makes it easier to revise the plan, if needed.) You may also want a calculator to figure the total time required to prepare each food.

Reflect

Ask students when they have needed to increase or decrease the yield of a recipe.

Reflect

Ask students if they have ever prepared or been served a meal for which all the food items were not ready at the same time. How did this affect the dining atmosphere?

Time Management Tip

Try to do your menu planning a week at a time. As you plan your menus, check your refrigerator and pantry for ingredients and add anything you need to your shopping list. Do your shopping in advance. These steps will make it easier to stick to your time-work schedule.

Changing Yield

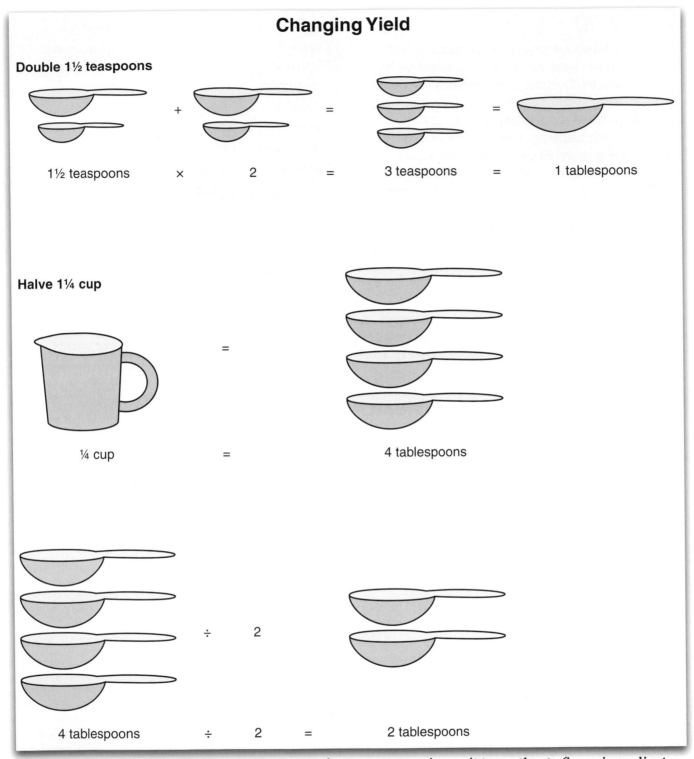

Double 1½ teaspoons

1½ teaspoons   ×   2   =   3 teaspoons   =   1 tablespoons

Halve 1¼ cup

¼ cup   =   4 tablespoons

4 tablespoons   ÷   2   =   2 tablespoons

12-6 You may need to convert from one measuring unit to another to figure ingredient amounts when changing the yield of a recipe.

Enrich

Ask each student to interview a meal manager about the extent to which he or she uses a time-work schedule when planning and preparing a meal.

The following steps outline how to do some initial planning. The example shows completed plans for the meal in **12-7**.

1. On a piece of paper, set up a *food preparation time chart*, as shown in **12-8**. List the menu items in the first column. Add table setting to this list because time needs to be reserved for this task.

2. Use the recipes to identify preparation tasks that will need to be done as you make each menu item. Remember these tasks may appear in the ingredient list as well as in the recipe directions. For instance, a recipe might call for ½ cup chopped onions or 2 strips fried bacon. List estimates in the chart for the time required to prepare, cook, and serve each food. (Some recipes give estimated preparation and cooking times, which will help you with this step.)

3. Add the total time required to prepare each item and list these totals in the chart.

4. In the last column, rank menu items in order of total time. The item ranked number 1 should be the food requiring the most time. This step will help you decide which menu items to prepare first.

Making a Schedule

Use the completed food preparation time chart to help plan the actual time-work schedule. The first decision to make when writing a time-work schedule is what time you want to begin eating the meal. Think about your daily activities and the activities of other diners when making this decision. Allow enough time to prepare the meal so you will not feel rushed. Allow other diners enough time to come to the meal leisurely. You may want to plan the serving time at least 15 minutes after a guest's intended arrival time. This will allow a time cushion for any unexpected delays.

Once you have decided when to begin eating the meal, the following steps will help you write the time-work schedule:

1. Set up a chart like the one in **12-9**. Write the time you plan to begin eating at the bottom of the time column.

2. Look at the *serving time* column of the food preparation time chart. Work backward from the eating time to determine when to begin serving.

12-7 You can prepare and serve this nutritious breakfast in just 15 minutes.

Academic Connections

Coordinate your study of scheduling in the kitchen with a discussion of the importance of long- and short-range business planning given by teachers in the business department. Have students compare and contrast a time-work schedule for preparing a meal with short- and long-range planning used in operating a business.

Food Preparation Time Chart					
Menu Item	**Preparation Time**	**Cooking Time**	**Serving Time**	**Total Time**	**Rank**
Strawberry breakfast sandwich	7 minutes	2 minutes	2 minutes	11 minutes	1
Milk	—	—	1 minute	1 minute	3
Table setting	3 minutes	—	—	3 minutes	2

12-8 Charts showing preparation, cooking, and serving times for each menu item can help meal managers plan their work.

Discuss

Ask students to identify some other examples of dovetailing meal preparation tasks.

Discuss

Ask students what kinds of problems can arise when several people are preparing food together in a kitchen. Ask how these problems can be avoided.

Time-Work Schedule	
Time	**Tasks**
7:45	Set table. Split and toast English muffins.
7:50	Wash strawberries and lemon. Hull and slice strawberries.
7:55	Grate lemon zest. Combine low-fat cream cheese, honey, and lemon zest in food processor. Process until well mixed.
7:57	Spread cheese mixture on toasted English muffin halves. Top with sliced strawberries. Pour milk.
8:00	Eat.

12-9 A time-work schedule lists actual times for doing specific food preparation tasks.

3. Look at the *cooking time* column of the food preparation time chart. Identify the time at which you should begin cooking each item.
4. Use recipes to help list all the preparation tasks needed to be done. Refer to the *preparation time* column of the food preparation time chart. It will help you decide how much time to allow for these tasks.

To keep the schedule flexible, avoid listing specific times for every task. Instead, group tasks in 5- or 10-minute blocks of time. Plan to do related tasks together. For instance, you can wash the lemon at the same time you are washing the strawberries.

Remember to dovetail your meal preparation tasks as you plan the schedule. **Dovetail** means to overlap tasks to use time more efficiently. You can often dovetail during cooking time. For example, while the English muffins are toasting, you can set the table.

Another point to keep in mind is you do not have to prepare food items ranked number 1 first. Sometimes it is helpful to get simple tasks, such as setting the table, out of the way. You may also want to prepare foods that do not need to be served hot ahead of time. This will prevent hot foods from cooling while you prepare other menu items.

Even a complete schedule is no guarantee that plans will go smoothly from start to finish. Sometimes one dish might cook in more or less time than you estimated. In these cases, you might have to keep some foods warm while you finish preparing the other foods.

As you become more skilled in the kitchen, you will be able to use less detailed schedules. Until that time, however, a schedule that is both detailed and flexible will be helpful.

Cooperation in the Kitchen

You will not always work alone in the kitchen. At home, family members may help you prepare meals. At school, you will work with classmates to prepare food products. If you work in a professional kitchen, you will have coworkers attending to a variety of tasks. The kitchen can become a chaotic place when several people are in it at the same time. To work effectively, each person will have to do his or her part as a member of a team.

Teams work best when one person takes a leadership role. In the kitchen, this person may be called a *meal manager*, *head chef*, or simply a *group leader*. No matter what this person is called, he or she will be in charge of assigning meal preparation tasks. The time-work schedule should indicate who will do each task listed. Be sure to rotate tasks from one time to the next to give everyone a range of kitchen experience.

When you are filling the leader role, consider your time frame and each person's skills before making assignments. For instance, if you are in a hurry, you may not want someone with little baking experience to make biscuits. If you have the time, however, you might want this person to help you with the biscuits. This will give him or her more baking practice. Helping team members develop their skills is another part of your role as leader.

When you are a team member, show responsibility. This means doing your assigned tasks quickly, correctly, and without needing anyone to prompt you. Accept direction from your leader and cooperate with the other members of the team. When everyone works well together, the group will be making the best use of time, space, and skills in the kitchen. See **12-10**.

Preparing Simple Recipes

Put your basic food preparation knowledge to work by making a simple recipe. While you are developing cooking skills, choose recipes with just a few ingredients and a short list of directions. As you gain experience, you can move on to recipes that require more advanced preparation techniques.

Sandwiches

Many sandwich recipes are simple to prepare. Sandwiches are a common choice for packed lunches because they travel well and can be eaten without utensils. Sandwiches are also popular party and picnic foods because they are convenient to serve to a group.

Sandwich Ingredients

All sandwiches are made with some type of bread and a filling. Any kind of bread or rolls can be used to make sandwiches. Pita bread, tortillas, bagels, and other ethnic breads and rolls add still more variety. The bread or roll chosen should be fresh and either whole grain or enriched.

Sandwich fillings are often protein foods. Leftover meats and poultry are good choices. Cheese, hard-cooked eggs, peanut butter, and canned fish also make good fillings.

Lettuce, tomatoes, onions, and other vegetables complement some sandwiches. Bacon, pitted olives, and pickles complement others. First choose the filling; then choose the extras.

Shutterstock

12-10 Learning to cooperate when sharing kitchen space and equipment with others is an important food preparation skill.

FYI

In 1765, the sandwich was invented by John Montagu, the fourth Earl of Sandwich, who gave the food its name. The Earl used to order roast beef between pieces of toast for a snack while he was at the gaming tables. This allowed him to keep one hand free to play while he ate.

Reflect

Ask students to name some of their favorite types of sandwiches. When do they like to eat them?

FYI

Snacks can fit into the food groups of MyPlate. Three cups of popcorn counts as 1 ounce-equivalent in the grains group. Two rye crispbreads, five whole-wheat crackers, and seven snack crackers also each count as 1 ounce-equivalent. In the protein foods group, 12 almonds, 24 pistachios, and 7 walnut halves each count as 1 ounce-equivalent.

Preparing Sandwiches

The following guidelines will help you prepare nutritious, attractive, and flavorful sandwiches:

- Use a variety of breads and fillings.
- Cut sandwiches into halves or quarters to make them easier to eat. For party sandwiches that are extra interesting and attractive, cut bread into shapes, such as circles, diamonds, and hearts.
- Garnish sandwiches attractively. Garnishes can improve the appearance and food value of a sandwich.
- Keep sandwiches refrigerated until serving time. Bacteria grow quickly above 40°F (4°C). Therefore, pack sandwiches in a cooler when transporting them. Use ice, frozen gel packs, or chilled drinks to keep perishable ingredients safe. Wrap sandwiches well to prevent staling. Pack lettuce, pickles, tomatoes, and other relishes separately to keep sandwiches from getting soggy.
- Make hot sandwiches just before serving. Serve them hot, not lukewarm.
- Use freshly toasted bread for sandwiches served on toast.

Snacks

Like sandwiches, many snack foods are easy to make. Some require no cooking. Others can be quickly heated in a microwave oven. Even if you are just learning your way around the kitchen, you can make simple snacks with ease.

Foods for Snacks

People choose a wide range of foods for snacks. Some snacks are hearty, such as sandwiches and leftover pizza. Other snacks are light, such as fruit and popcorn. With a little imagination, you can make a variety of snacks out of ingredients you probably have available.

With a bit of planning, you can have snacks on hand that are nutritious and simple to prepare. Stock up on foods like yogurt, whole-grain crackers, and cheese slices to grab in a hurry. Store a bag of cut up fresh vegetables in the crisper of the refrigerator. Make a healthful snack mix out of raisins, nuts, and ready-to-eat cereal. Your snack food choices can help meet your daily serving needs from the five main food groups. When nutritious snack foods are convenient, you will be less likely to choose foods that provide empty calories. See **12-11**.

Beverages

People drink beverages with meals and throughout the day. Beverages can quench thirst and help meet the body's need for water. Some beverages also provide other nutrients. For instance, milk is a good source of calcium, and many fruit and vegetable juices are high in vitamin C.

©2011 Wisconsin Milk Marketing Board, Inc.

12-11 Fresh fruit and a yogurt dip make a healthful snack that is easy to prepare.

Many beverages require no preparation. Those beverages that have recipes are usually simple enough for even the most inexperienced cooks to prepare.

Cold Drinks

Milk, bottled water, carbonated beverages, fruit and vegetable juices, lemonade, punch, smoothies, and milk shakes are popular cold drinks. Be aware that nondiet soft drinks are the number one source of added sugars in the U.S. diet. Many fruit drinks and punches also supply little more than sugar. Follow the Dietary Guidelines for Americans by balancing these beverages with more nutritious beverage choices, such as milk and juices. Also, be sure to choose pure water often.

Many drinks are ready to enjoy, right from the refrigerator. Make sure to serve drinks icy cold. Have plenty of ice on hand to keep drinks chilled.

Smoothies and milk shakes are thick, frosty treats. Ingredients can vary, but smoothies are often made with yogurt and fruit; milk shakes contain milk and ice cream. When preparing these beverages, have all ingredients as cold as possible. Using frozen fruit in a smoothie will help make the drink extra thick and cold. Combine all ingredients in a blender. Adding the liquid ingredients first will help the solid ingredients become thoroughly blended. Blend for about 20 to 30 seconds until the mixture is smooth. Pour it into tall glasses and serve with straws.

Enrich

Have each student survey three other students in the school to find out their favorite cold drinks. Compile findings into a bar graph.

Enrich

Have students research where coffee is grown and how it is processed. Share findings in an oral report.

FYI

Coffee is the most recognized smell in the world. The second most identifiable smell is peanut butter.

Learn About...

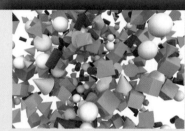

Preparing Beverages for a Party

When preparing cold drinks for a party, you can freeze fruit juices in ice cube trays. These ice cubes will not dilute drinks. You can also use fruit juices to make ice rings to float in punch bowls. Ice rings take longer to melt than ice cubes, so they keep punches cold longer. For outdoor events, pack canned beverages and drink boxes in coolers. Use insulated picnic jugs to hold large amounts of cold beverages.

When preparing sparkling punch for a party, make the punch base ahead of time and chill it well. Chill the soda for the punch separately. Make the base by mixing all ingredients except the soda. Just before the party, pour the punch base over an ice ring in a punch bowl. Add the soda at the last minute to keep the punch from getting "flat."

Coffee

Coffee is a popular beverage at breakfast and with desserts. However, many people drink coffee all day long.

Coffee is made from the beans of the coffee plant. The beans are dried, roasted, and packaged for shipment. The flavor of coffee beans depends on the variety and growing conditions. It also depends on the degree of roasting, which may be described as mild to dark.

You can buy a single variety of coffee beans. You can also buy coffee **blends**, which are mixtures of several varieties of coffee beans. Coffees that have added flavorings, such as hazelnut or French vanilla, are available, too.

You can choose ground or whole bean coffee. If you choose whole bean coffee, you can have it ground at the store. For freshness, however, you might prefer to grind it yourself just before brewing. You can choose the coarseness of the grind to suit your preparation method. Coffee stales quickly when exposed to moisture and air. Buy only enough coffee to last a week or two. To help maintain freshness, store both ground and whole bean coffee in opaque, airtight containers at room temperature.

You can purchase coffee in instant form. Instant coffee products are dry, powdered, water-soluble solids made by removing the moisture from very strong, brewed coffee. Some brands are freeze-dried. Prepare instant coffee by adding freshly boiled water to the coffee granules according to the manufacturer's directions.

Caffeine is a naturally occurring compound in coffee and some other plant products that acts as a stimulant. **Decaffeinated** coffee (and tea) is made by removing most of the caffeine. Decaffeinated coffee is available ground, whole bean, and in instant form.

Preparing Coffee

When you brew ground coffee, be sure to start with a clean pot. Thoroughly wash the inside of the coffeepot with hot, soapy water and rinse it well after each use. Oily film that collects on the inside of a coffeepot can cause coffee to be bitter.

Measuring can mean the difference between pleasing coffee and dreadful coffee. Measure fresh, cold water for the desired amount of coffee, 6 ounces (175 mL) per serving. Then measure 1 tablespoon (15 mL) ground coffee per serving for a regular strength brew. Measure 2 tablespoons (30 mL) ground coffee per serving if you prefer strong coffee. See **12-12**.

Serve coffee as soon as possible after brewing it. Heating coffee too long can cause it to become bitter. This is because bitter substances present in coffee become more soluble at high temperatures. Correctly prepared coffee is clear and flavorful. It is piping hot and has a pleasing aroma.

In addition to plain coffee, people enjoy a number of popular coffee drinks. These drinks are made with a base of plain coffee or a strong type of coffee called *espresso*. A special type of coffeemaker is available for brewing espresso at home.

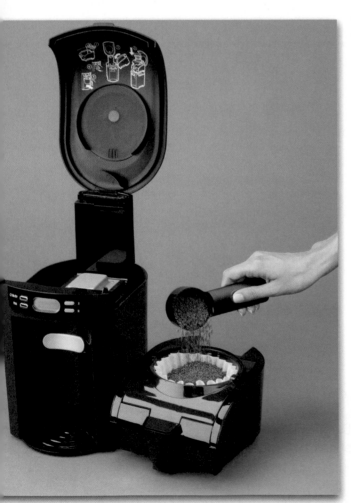

Hamilton Beach Brands, Inc.

12-12 Carefully measuring water and ground coffee will allow you to produce a flavorful brew.

Tea

Hot tea may be served in place of or in addition to coffee at brunches, dinners, and other occasions. Iced tea is popular at picnics and other warm-weather get-togethers.

Tea is the leaves of a small tropical evergreen used to make a beverage. Teas vary according to the age of the tea leaves and the way they are processed. *Black teas* are made from tea leaves that are fermented and dried. When brewed, black teas are amber in color and have a rich aroma and flavor. *Green teas* are made from tea leaves

EXPLORING CAREERS

Barista

Baristas do all the tasks involved with waiting on customers in a coffeehouse. They weigh, grind, and pack coffee. They prepare and serve coffee beverages and other menu items. Baristas order and stock supplies. They also clean work areas and equipment.

Successful baristas are friendly, helpful, and have good listening skills for accurately taking customer orders. They use speaking skills to describe menu items to customers. Baristas use math skills to make change and balance cash drawers. They need to be able to work as members of a team as they relay orders to other employees for preparation. Baristas must keep up with a fast-paced work environment when there is a rush of customers. They must see what needs to be done and take the initiative to do it.

Barista is an entry-level job. However, many coffeehouses prefer to hire people with high school diplomas. A background in foodservice is helpful but not required. Baristas will learn how to perform most tasks from coworkers and training manuals. In time, baristas may move into jobs as coffeehouse supervisors or managers. Their skills will also help them find work in other areas of the hospitality industry.

---

that are not fermented. When brewed, green teas are a greenish-yellow color. *Oolong teas* are made from partially fermented tea leaves. The color and flavor of brewed oolong teas fall between those of black and green teas. *White teas* are made from tea leaves that are gathered before they have fully opened. They are not fermented and produce a brew with a pale color and delicate flavor. All four varieties of tea are available decaffeinated.

Other Forms of Tea

Tea is available in instant form. Instant teas may be sweetened and flavored. They can be dissolved in cold or freshly boiled water.

Tea can be flavored. Spices like cinnamon, herbs like mint, and floral fragrances like jasmine are popular flavorings.

Herbal teas are made from a variety of plants. They come in many interesting flavors and they do not contain caffeine. Fennel seeds, chamomile flowers, ginger root, and blackberry leaves are just a few of the ingredients commonly found in herbal teas.

Some people have allergic reactions to some of the plants used in herbal teas. When purchasing herbal teas, choose commercial brands. Avoid herbal mixtures that claim to have special health or medicinal properties.

Preparing Tea

You can purchase tea in filter paper teabags or in loose form. To prepare either form of tea, begin by rinsing a clean teapot or cup with boiling water to preheat it. Place a teabag or loose tea in the preheated pot or cup. (Place loose tea directly in the bottom of the pot or cup, in a cheesecloth bag, or in a tea ball. A *tea ball* is a perforated ball made of silver or stainless steel.) Then pour freshly boiled water over the tea. Allow the tea to steep two to six minutes, until it reaches the desired strength. Remove the tea leaves from the pot before serving. If the tea leaves stay in contact with the water too long, the tea can become bitter. Serve cream, sugar, and lemon with tea.

Prepare iced tea by first making strong hot tea. If desired, dissolve honey or sugar in the tea. Then pour the tea over ice and stir until chilled. Making the hot tea stronger than you usually drink it will keep the ice from diluting the iced tea too much.

Career Path

Ask students if they have visited coffeehouses and seen baristas at work. Discuss any information this description provides that students did not previously know about this career.

For Example...

The tea served in Chinese restaurants is generally oolong tea.

Activity

Have students visit a grocery store and make a list of all the different varieties of tea that are available.

FYI

India, Ceylon, China, Indonesia, and Japan are the major tea-producing countries.

Reflect

Ask students when they are most likely to drink chocolate and cocoa beverages.

Chocolate and Cocoa Beverages

Hot chocolate is made from unsweetened chocolate. Cocoa is made from cocoa powder. Both of these beverages contain milk. This means you must use low temperatures to prevent scorching.

Do not allow hot chocolate or cocoa to boil after adding milk. Beating these beverages with a rotary beater until foamy will keep the milk from forming a scum layer. If desired, you may flavor either beverage with vanilla extract and top with marshmallows or whipped cream.

CAREER SUCCESS

Designing and Improving Systems

Suda is a time-study engineer. Food product manufacturers hire her to study the way their assembly line workers perform tasks. The manufacturers want Suda to help them find ways to increase production. Suda analyzes the placement of equipment and supplies. She also looks at the physical motions involved in doing each job. Then she improves the system or designs a new system that will eliminate wasted and nonproductive motions.

To be an effective worker, Suda needs skills in designing and improving systems. In a small group, answer the following questions about Suda's need for and use of these skills:

A. How will Suda's skills in designing and improving systems affect the manufacturers who hire her?

B. How will Suda's skills in designing and improving systems affect assembly line workers?

C. Why might manufacturers hire Suda to analyze their production systems instead of doing it themselves?

D. What is another skill Suda would need in this job? Briefly explain why this skill would be important.

CHAPTER 12 REVIEW

Summary

To prepare meals, it is necessary to know how to choose and follow recipes. You need to know abbreviations and cooking terms used in recipes. Learning a few special techniques will help you when using microwave recipes. You should also know the correct ways to measure dry and liquid ingredients and fats. Being familiar with measuring equivalents will help you easily adjust the yield of a recipe.

As a meal manager, you will need to know how to make a time-work schedule. This will help you plan the use of time in the kitchen. When working with others, you need to know what is expected of leaders and team members so everyone can work cooperatively.

You can put basic cooking skills to use when preparing simple recipes. Sandwiches, snacks, and beverages are good foods for beginning cooks to make.

Review What You Have Read

Write your answers on a separate sheet of paper, using complete sentences when appropriate.

1. What are the components of a well-written recipe?
2. Give the unit of measure for which each of the following abbreviations stands:
   A. c.
   B. oz.
   C. t.
   D. tbsp.
3. Complete each of the following statements.
   A. To stir ingredients until they are thoroughly combined is to _____.
   B. To cut into very small cubes of even size is to _____.
   C. To rub fat on the surface of a cooking utensil or on a food itself is to _____.
   D. To heat an appliance to a desired temperature about 5 to 8 minutes before it is to be used is to _____.
4. How can dehydration occur during microwave cooking?
5. Why should plastic wrap used to cover food in a microwave oven be vented?
6. What happens to the boiling point of water at high altitudes?
7. True or false. Dry ingredients should be spooned into a dry measuring cup until the cup is filled just to the edge.
8. Double and halve each of the following amounts:
   A. 2 tablespoons
   B. 1 ½ teaspoons
   C. ¾ cup
   D. 1 ⅔ cups
9. Explain why time-work schedules for preparing meals need to be flexible.

(continued)

Answer Key for *Review What You Have Read* questions

1. The recipe is written in a clear, concise manner. Ingredients are listed in the order in which they will be used. Amounts are easily measured. Directions are complete. Accurate baking or cooking time is given. Baking or cooking temperature is given. Pan size is given. Number of average servings is given.
2. A. cup
   B. ounce
   C. teaspoon
   D. tablespoon
3. A. blend
   B. dice
   C. grease
   D. preheat
4. Failure to allow for standing time during microwave cooking can result in foods being overcooked, which can cause dehydration.
5. Pressure from steam can build up inside containers that are tightly covered with plastic wrap.
6. The boiling point of water drops at high altitudes.

7. false
8. A. ¼ cup, 1 tablespoon
   B. 1 tablespoon, ¾ teaspoon
   C. 1 ½ cups, ⅜ cup (¼ cup plus 2 spoons)
   D. 3 ⅓ cups, ⅚ cup (½ cup plus ⅓ cup)
9. The time estimates for preparing menu items could be off target.

10. What is the first decision that needs to be made when writing a time-work schedule?

11. What two things does a leader in the kitchen need to consider before assigning meal preparation tasks to members of the work team?

12. Give two guidelines for preparing sandwiches.

13. How can you prevent cold drinks from being diluted by ice cubes?

14. Why should coffee be served as soon as possible after brewing?

15. Teas made from partially fermented tea leaves are called _____.
    A. black teas
    B. green teas
    C. herbal teas
    D. oolong teas

Link to Academic Skills

10. The first decision that needs to be made when writing a time-work schedule is what time you want to begin eating the meal.

11. A kitchen leader needs to consider his or her time frame and each person's skills before assigning meal preparation tasks to members of the work team.

12. (List two. Student response. See page 248.)

16. **Science.** Have two lab groups each prepare a different recipe calling for one of the ingredients listed in the first column of Table 12-2. Have two other lab groups each prepare one of the recipes using the appropriate ingredient substitution listed in the second column of the table. All students should sample all four food products, comparing the taste, texture, and appearance of the two versions of each recipe. Note any differences you can attribute to the ingredient substitutions.

17. **Geography.** On a photocopy of a map of the United States, color in the areas where high-altitude cooking principles would apply.

18. **Science.** This activity illustrates some of the characteristics of carbonated beverages. Drop a tablespoon of raisins into a clear plastic cup filled with a clear carbonated soft drink and note what happens. Note that a soft drink is a gas-in-liquid solution in which carbon dioxide gas is dispersed in water. The gas forms bubbles that attach to the raisins and raise them to the surface of the beverage. When the bubbles break, the raisins drop back to the bottom of the cup and the cycle is repeated.

19. **Social studies.** In a small group, research some aspect of the traditional Japanese tea ceremony. Give a group oral report to the class.

Build Critical Thinking Skills

13. Freeze fruit juices in ice cube trays to make ice cubes that will not dilute drinks.

14. Heating coffee too long can cause it to become bitter.

15. D

20. **Analysis.** Select two types of cookbooks from your school or local library. Analyze the strengths and weaknesses of each cookbook. Write a critique stating which one you prefer and why.

21. **Synthesis.** Work with your lab group to brainstorm food ideas for a breakfast or luncheon. Choose from among the suggestions to plan a specific menu. Collect recipes for the foods you have selected. Create a food preparation time chart. Plan a time-work schedule for the members of your lab group. What factors did you consider when creating your schedule?

22. **Evaluation.** Prepare several coffee blends. Evaluate the color, aroma, and flavor of each blend. Identify the blend you prefer and explain why you prefer it.

Apply Technology

23. Use a computer and a spreadsheet program to develop a spreadsheet with a formula that will calculate measurements when doubling and halving recipes.

24. Use a computer and the table function in word processing software to create a time-work schedule.

A Measure of Math

25. Each 1,000 feet increase in elevation decreases atmospheric pressure by about ½ pound and the boiling point of water by 1.9°F. At sea level, pressure is 14.7 pounds per square inch and the boiling point is 212°F. Figure the approximate atmospheric pressure and the boiling point of water at 2,000; 5,000; 7,500; and 10,000 feet.

26. Find a sandwich recipe with a yield of 8 servings or fewer. Copy the recipe and calculate how much of each ingredient would be needed to serve 40 party guests.

Teamwork in Action

27. Make a recipe yield adjustment guide by creating a four-column table of common equivalent measures. In the first column, list conventional measures. In the second column, list conventional equivalents. In the third column, list half of equivalent amounts. In the fourth column, list double equivalent amounts. See Table 12-5 to help you get started with the first two columns. Make copies of your finished guide on colored card stock. Laminate the guides. Glue magnetic strips on the backs of the guides to make them easy to hang on a refrigerator. Distribute the guides to visitors at a school open house.

Companion Website
www.g-wlearning.com

At the website, review key terms for this chapter with crossword puzzles, matching exercises, and e-flash cards. Apply facts from the chapter to complete the activities.

Part 3
The Preparation of Food

Study Starters

1. Discuss with the class what qualities you consider characteristic of well-prepared food.
2. Read the titles of Chapters 13 through 25. Make a list of topics you would anticipate covering in this part of the text. Write a couple opinion paragraphs describing how you think information on these topics would be useful to you.

FCCLA: Taking the Lead

Use information learned about various food products in this section of the textbook to help you develop a prototype formula for a Food Innovations STAR Event. Check the FCCLA national website to find this year's food product scenario for competition.

CHAPTER 13
Grain Foods

Learning Prep

See how many of the *Terms to Know* you can find on the package of a cereal, bread, or pasta product. Share your findings in class.

Main Menu

- Grains are made into a wide variety of nutritious economical food products.
- Principles of starch cookery must be followed when preparing grain foods to obtain desired characteristics.

Terms to Know

cereal
kernel
bran
endosperm
germ
whole grain
refined
pasta
enriched
starch
gelatinization
syneresis

Objectives

After studying this chapter, you will be able to

- **list** a variety of cereal products.
- **describe** how heat and liquids affect starches.
- **prepare** cooked breakfast cereals, rice, and pasta.

Cereals are major staple foods for people throughout the world. This is because they are easy to grow and store. They are also low in cost and have high energy value.

Career Path

Ask students which of the qualities needed by grain inspectors they possess and which qualities they would need to work to develop.

Types of Cereal Products

Cereals are starchy grains that are suitable to use as food. Corn, wheat, rice, oats, barley, and rye are the cereals most often used as food in the United States. They are used to make a wide variety of products, including breakfast foods, flours, meals, breads, pasta products, and starches.

Grain Structure

Grains differ in size and shape, but they all have kernels with similar structures. A **kernel** is a whole seed of a cereal. It has three parts: the bran, the endosperm, and the germ.

The **bran** is the outer protective covering of the kernel. It is a good source of vitamins and fiber (cellulose).

The **endosperm** makes up the largest part of the kernel. It contains most of the starch and the protein of the kernel, but few minerals and little fiber. It holds the food supply the plant uses to grow.

The **germ** is the reproductive part of the plant. It is rich in vitamins, minerals, protein, and fat. It makes up the smallest part of the kernel. See **13-1**.

Whole grain cereal products contain all three parts of the kernel. **Refined** products have had the bran and germ, along with the nutrients they provide, removed during processing.

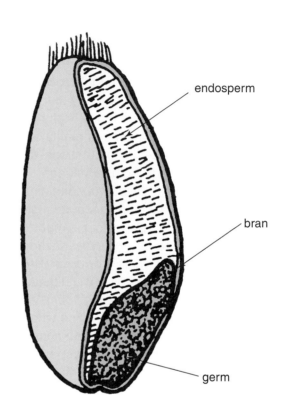

endosperm

bran

germ

13-1 Each part of a kernel of grain contains different nutrients.

Breakfast Foods

Corn, rice, wheat, and oats are made into popular breakfast foods. Breakfast foods can be made from whole grain, enriched refined grain, or a combination of both.

EXPLORING CAREERS

Grain Inspector

Grain inspectors collect and assess samples of grains, especially grains that are being exported. They check to see how the samples measure up to specific standards. They test for diseases, infestations, and chemical residues. Then they may issue quality grades based on their evaluations. Inspectors prepare written reports of their findings. They may also guide grain producers to take corrective measures when needed.

To be successful, grain inspectors should know how to ask the right questions and listen to the answers. They must be able to work independently. They need to be good time managers as they schedule inspection visits at various locations. Grain inspectors also need good analytical skills when looking at test results and making grade assessments.

A grain inspector needs a two-year degree in agriculture. Past farming knowledge and experience is also a plus.

They can be presweetened or unsweetened. Some have added ingredients, such as raisins or nuts.

Cereals may be ready-to-eat, or they may require some amount of cooking. *Ready-to-eat cereals* may be puffed, shredded, flaked, granulated, rolled, or formed into shapes. You can pour them into a bowl and eat them without any preparation.

Cereals that require cooking are available in cracked, crushed, granular, and flaked forms. They require the addition of liquid and heat. *Quick-cooking* or *instant cereals* are partially cooked and require little time to prepare. *Raw* or *old-fashioned cereals* require longer cooking times. Oatmeal and oat bran are examples of these types of cereals.

Flour

Any grain can be made into flour. However, most consumers use wheat flours for baking because the gluten in wheat flours is superior. (*Gluten* is an elastic protein substance that provides the structure in baked goods.)

You can buy many kinds of wheat flour. Both *bleached* and *unbleached all-purpose flour* are made from milled, sifted blends of different varieties of wheat. All-purpose flour is made up primarily of the endosperm. Bleached flour is whiter than unbleached, but there is no nutritional difference between the two. People use both types for general cooking and baking.

Bread flour contains more protein than all-purpose flour. It is often used in bread machines because it gives the bread more structure.

Cake flour is made from a class of wheat called soft wheat. People use it for making cakes and other baked products with delicate textures.

Instant or *quick-mixing flour* is all-purpose flour that has been specially treated to blend easily with liquids. People use it to make gravies and sauces.

Self-rising flour is all-purpose flour with added leavening agents and salt. You must adjust your recipe when using this type of flour.

Whole wheat flour is made by milling the entire wheat kernel so it contains the bran, germ, and endosperm. Whole wheat flour gives baked products a nutlike flavor and coarser texture than does all-purpose flour.

Potato flour is made from cooked potatoes that have been dried and ground. People on wheat-free diets often use potato flour.

Buckwheat flour is made from ground buckwheat grain. It is gluten free and has a nutlike flavor.

Rye and *pumpernickel flours* are made from ground rye. Both are popular for making breads. Pumpernickel flour is whole grain and produces a darker, coarser loaf. Rye flour may have some or all of the bran and germ removed and produces a lighter loaf.

Soy flour is made from ground soybeans. It has a strong flavor and must be combined with wheat flour for use in baked products.

Rice flour is made by milling white rice. It is a white, starchy flour that is popular in Asia and the Far East.

Corn flour is a gluten-free flour made from ground yellow corn. *Masa harina* is made from a different variety of corn that has been specially treated. It is an ingredient in tortillas and other Mexican dishes, **13-2**.

Photo courtesy of National Pork Board. For more information about pork, visit TheOtherWhiteMeat.com.

13-2 Masa harina is used to make corn tortillas.

Rice

Rice (also called *white rice*) is the white, starchy endosperm of the rice kernel. *Brown rice* has had the hull removed but contains the bran and germ as well as the endosperm.

Rice can be classified according to grain length or method of processing. *Long grain rice* is dry and fluffy when cooked. Many people use it as a side dish. *Short grain rice* is small and sticky when cooked. People often use it in puddings, croquettes, and rice rings.

Parboiled or *converted rice* has been steeped (soaked) in warm water, drained, steamed, and dried. Parboiling improves the nutritive value and keeping quality of milled rice.

Precooked or *instant rice* has been cooked, rinsed, and dried by a special process before packaging. You can prepare it in a matter of minutes.

Wild rice is not really rice. It is the seed of a grass that grows in the marshes of Minnesota and Canada. It has an appealing, nutlike flavor and is rather expensive.

Pasta

Pasta is a dough that may or may not be dried. Macaroni, noodles, and spaghetti are all pastas. Pasta dough is made from *semolina*, which is produced from durum wheat. *Durum wheat* is specially grown for pasta making. It gives pasta products a nutty flavor and firm shape. Noodles are made by adding egg to the pasta dough.

Pasta comes in many shapes and sizes. Commercially, pasta is made by machine. Some people, however, enjoy making homemade pasta either by hand or with a pasta-making appliance.

Other Grain Products

Cereals are used to make a variety of other products. *Cornmeal* is made from ground white or yellow corn. It is often enriched.

Hominy, a popular food in the South, is corn minus the hull and germ. When broken into pieces, it is called *hominy grits*.

Cornstarch is the refined starch obtained from the endosperm of corn. People use it as a thickening agent in cooking.

Pearl barley is the whole barley grain minus the hull. It is high in minerals, and people often use it in soups.

Bulgur wheat is whole wheat that has been cooked, dried, partly debranned, and cracked. It is a popular Middle Eastern side dish.

Wheat germ is the germ portion of the wheat kernel separated during milling. Wheat germ is high in vitamins and minerals. You can add it to foods for flavor and nutrition.

Farina is a wheat product made by grinding and sifting wheat that has had the bran and most of the germ removed. People use farina as a thickener and as a cooked breakfast cereal. Cream of Wheat® is a popular brand of farina.

Couscous is granules of precooked, dried semolina, which is the same wheat product used to make pasta. Couscous cooks quickly, so it is a convenient choice for meal managers on a tight schedule. You can use it as a side dish or as a base to top with stews or stir-fried dishes. See **13-3**.

Reflect

Ask students what kinds of rice dishes their families enjoy.

Enrich

Have students compare the nutritive values of spaghetti and egg noodles.

Enrich

Other flour and grain products include amaranth, millet, quinoa, teff, and triticale. Have students investigate the economic significance and use of one of these products, and summarize their findings in written or oral reports.

Quinoa has been grown and eaten in South America for hundreds of years. It is actually the seed of the Goosefoot plant rather than a true grain. However, it has cooking and flavor characteristics that are similar to grain. It is growing in popularity as a grain food in the United States.

Selecting and Storing Cereal Products

Cereal products are nutritious, economical, and versatile enough to serve at any meal. You can store them for extended periods without refrigeration. Therefore, you will want to keep a variety of cereal products on hand at all times.

Nutritional Value of Cereal Products

©2011 Wisconsin Milk Marketing Board, Inc.

13-3 Couscous can be used in place of rice or pasta as a nutritious side dish.

Cereal products are in the grains group of MyPlate. Most teens should eat 6 to 10 ounce-equivalents of grain foods each day. One cup (250 mL) ready-to-eat cereal and ½ cup (125 mL) cooked cereal, rice, or pasta each count as 1 ounce-equivalent.

Whole grains provide protein, complex carbohydrates, fiber, B vitamins, iron, magnesium, and selenium. Federal law requires many refined products, including white flour, white rice, pasta, and cereals, to be enriched. **Enriched** products have added nutrients to replace those lost due to processing. Enriched cereals contain added thiamin, niacin, riboflavin, folic acid, and iron.

Fat, sodium, and sugar are added to many breakfast cereals and rice and pasta mixes. Use the Nutrition Facts panel to help you choose products that are lower in these components. The Nutrition Facts panel can also help you choose products that are higher in fiber.

Health and Wellness

Choosing Whole Grains

Choosing a variety of cereal products will give you the greatest nutritional value. At least half of your grain food choices should list a whole grain first on the ingredient list. Look for the word *whole* beside any type of grain listed. Brown rice, graham flour, oatmeal, and wild rice are also whole grain ingredients. Be aware that products labeled *multi-grain, stone-ground, 100% wheat,* and *cracked wheat* may not be whole grain foods. The ingredient list can also help you avoid added sugars in the grain products you choose.

Cost of Cereal Products

Cereal products are generally inexpensive, but costs vary according to the type of item. Convenience products and products with added ingredients tend to cost more.

Breakfast foods can be costly or economical. Ready-to-eat cereals are more expensive than those that require cooking. Presweetened cereals and cereals with added ingredients cost more than plain cereals. Small boxes often cost more per unit of weight than large boxes. Single serving boxes cost the most per serving.

All-purpose flour is generally the least expensive type of flour. Specialty flours, such as cake flour and instant flour, are usually higher in price.

Most pasta products, regardless of shape or size, are low in cost. Fresh-made, gourmet pastas are more expensive. Packaged pasta dishes with special sauces and seasonings also cost more.

Long grain and short grain rice are the lowest priced rice products. The convenience of converted or instant rice adds to the cost. Wild rice and seasoned rice mixes also carry higher prices.

Storing Cereal Products

Store flours, breakfast foods, pasta products, and rice in tightly covered containers in a cool, dry place. Grain products stored uncovered will attract dust and insects. Some may also pick up moisture, which will cause them to lose their characteristic texture. Breakfast foods will keep well for two to three months. Brown and wild rice will keep for six months. White rice and pasta will keep for a year. See **13-4**.

Rubbermaid

13-4 Storing cereal products in airtight containers will keep them fresh and wholesome.

Cooking Starches

Starch is a complex carbohydrate stored in plants. Cereal grains contain plant cells that are the sources of starch granules. Wheat flour, cornstarch, and tapioca are starches commonly used in cooking.

Uses of Starch

Cooks use starches primarily as thickening agents. Mixtures thickened with cornstarch or tapioca are translucent, whereas mixtures thickened with flour are opaque. Therefore, cooks use flour to thicken gravies and unsweetened sauces. They use cornstarch and tapioca to thicken puddings and sweet sauces. They also use cornstarch and tapioca to thicken unsweetened sauces in which they want a translucent appearance.

Food Science Principles of Cooking Starches

Starches differ in chemical structure and composition. Thus, different starches behave differently. Some starch mixtures form gels; others do not. Some starches form firm gels; others form weak gels. Some cooked starch mixtures are clear; some are semiclear; others are opaque.

Granular starch is completely *insoluble* (unable to dissolve) in cold water. The granules need heat to become *soluble* (able to dissolve). Both dry and moist heat affect starch.

Dry heat causes starch to become slightly soluble and to lose some of its thickening power. This is why gravy made from browned flour is thinner than gravy made from unbrowned flour. Dry heat also causes color and flavor changes. The effect of dry heat

Discuss

Ask students what advantages there would be to buying unsweetened cereals and adding their own sweetener to taste. *(money savings and increased control over the amount of added sugars in the diet)*

Reflect

Ask students which convenience cereal products they think are worth the extra cost.

Activity

Have students find recipes for two food products—one thickened with flour and one thickened with cornstarch or tapioca.

FYI

At high altitudes, special care is needed for cornstarch-thickened mixtures to reach maximum gelatinization.

FYI

Suggest that students use the name *Matt* as a mnemonic device to help them remember the four factors that must be controlled when cooking starch mixtures—*mixing method, agitation, time,* and *temperature.*

on starch causes the dark crust of baked goods, toast, and some ready-to-eat breakfast cereals.

Mixing starch granules with water and heating them causes them to become soluble. They absorb water and swell. As starch granules swell, the starch mixture thickens. As heating continues, the starch mixture becomes thicker until it reaches a maximum thickness. This process is called **gelatinization**. It is basic to cooking all starches.

During cooling, bonds form between the starch molecules. Because of this bonding, most starch mixtures form gels. The spaces of the gel network hold water. If you cut the gel, or if it stands too long, water may leak out. This is called **syneresis**. You may have seen this leakage in a lemon pie filling.

Cooking Cereal Products

The relative low cost and high energy value of cereals make them an important part of the diet. Cereals are popular as breakfast foods. However, you can serve a variety of cereal products at meals throughout the day.

Food Science

Factors Affecting Starch-Thickened Mixtures

The temperature, time, agitation, and mixing method used when cooking with starch can all affect the outcome of the mixture. These factors must be controlled during cooking.

The *temperature* used to cook starch mixtures must be warm enough to make the starch molecules swell uniformly (the same amount). It should not be so hot that it causes uneven swelling or lumping. When lumping occurs, the molecules in the middle of the lump do not swell. They stay small and dry. Cooking starch mixtures in a double boiler or in a heavy pan over moderate heat will help prevent lumping.

The *time* needed for gelatinization to be completed depends on the kind of starch and the cooking temperature. Once gelatinization occurs, cook the starch mixture for a short time longer to thoroughly cook the starch. This will prevent a raw starch flavor in the finished product.

The amount of *agitation* a starch mixture receives can affect its texture. Gentle stirring during cooking will help keep the starch mixture smooth. If you stir the mixture too rapidly or for too long a time, the starch granules may rupture (break down). As a result, the cooked starch mixture will be thinner.

A recipe will usually tell you which *mixing method* to use when adding starch to a hot liquid. If you add starch directly to a hot liquid, the starch granules usually will lump. To prevent lumping, you must separate the starch granules from one another before you add them to the hot liquid. You can separate starch granules by using one of three techniques:

- coating with fat
- combining with sugar
- mixing with a cold liquid to form a paste

©2011 Wisconsin Milk Marketing Board, Inc.

Cornstarch was mixed with cold half-and-half to separate the starch granules before being added as a thickening agent in this soup.

Principles of Cooking Cereal Products

Cereal products contain large amounts of starch. Therefore, the principles used in cooking starches also apply to cooking cereal products. Cooking improves both palatability and digestibility of cereal products.

When cooking cereal products, you must use enough water to permit the starch granules to swell. The amount of water needed will vary depending on the product. You can find correct proportions of cereal products to water along with cooking times on cereal, rice, and pasta packages.

Food Science

Starch in Cereals

During cooking, the starch granules in cereal products absorb water and swell, causing the products to increase in volume. This swelling causes rice and dried pasta products to soften. It causes cereals to become thicker until they reach a point of maximum thickness (gelatinization).

Preparing Cooked Breakfast Cereals

To prepare cooked cereal, bring the recommended amount of water to a boil. The size of the cereal particles and whether the bran layer is present determine the amount of cooking water needed. Whole-grain cereals will cook more quickly if you first soak them to soften the bran. (If you do not soften the bran, it can block the passage of water into the center of the kernel and delay swelling.) If you soak a whole-grain cereal, you should cook it in the soaking liquid, adding more water, if needed.

All the cereal particles must have equal contact with the water and heat so the starch granules can swell uniformly. To prevent lumping, slowly add dry cereal to the boiling water. Wetting the cereal with cold water before adding it to the boiling water will also prevent lumping.

Gently stir the cereal with a fork when you are adding it to the boiling water. This preliminary stirring helps separate the cereal particles and prevent lumping. Stirring throughout the remaining cooking time should be gentle and minimal. Too much stirring will break up the cereal particles, and the cooked product will be gummy.

Cook the cereal until it thickens and absorbs all the water. Low to moderate heat is best, as temperatures that are too hot can cause lumping and scorching. Like starch mixtures, cereals should be cooked for a short time after gelatinization is complete to prevent a raw starch flavor.

Cooking time will vary depending on the type of cereal and cooking method. Cereals that are finely granulated or precooked will cook faster than cracked or whole-grain cereals. Cereal cooked over direct heat will take less time to cook than cereal prepared in a double boiler.

Cooked cereals should be free of lumps. (Flaked cereals should contain separate and distinct flakes.) Cooked cereals should be thick, but they should flow when poured into a serving bowl.

Preparing Rice

When cooking rice, the goal is to obtain tender kernels that hold their shape. Properly cooked rice is tender and fluffy. The rice kernels should not stick together and form a gummy mass.

For Example…

As a rule, fine, granular cereals, such as farina, require about five times their volume of water. Coarse, cracked cereals, such as cracked wheat, require about four times their volume of water. Flaked cereals, such as oatmeal, require about two times their volume of water.

Reflect

Ask students what their favorite cooked cereals are. Ask how they like to eat cooked cereals.

Reflect

Ask students how lumps or a gummy texture would affect the appeal of cooked breakfast cereal.

Rice may be cooked over direct heat, in a double boiler, or in the oven. The proportion of water to rice varies somewhat. As a rule, white rice requires about twice its volume of water. Milk, bouillon, or another liquid can be substituted for all or part of the cooking water. The rice should absorb all the liquid used in cooking.

The same preparation methods can be used for brown rice that you use for white rice. However, brown rice will take about twice as long to cook unless it is soaked first. Soaking softens the outer bran layer so the rice will absorb the cooking liquid more quickly. You may also want to soak wild rice before cooking. Follow package directions for soaking and cooking brown and wild rices.

Precooked or instant rice cooks in a very short time. Add the rice to boiling water. Remove the pan from the heat and cover it tightly. When the rice has absorbed all the liquid, it is ready to serve. See **13-5**.

Preparing Pasta Products

To cook macaroni, spaghetti, and other kinds of pasta, bring water to a boil. Use 2 quarts (2 L) of water for each 8 ounces (225 g) of pasta. Pasta requires more water than other cereal products so it can move freely as it cooks. Add the pasta gradually to the boiling water. The water should not stop boiling. If it does, the pasta may stick together as it cooks. As the starch granules swell, the pasta will double in size. Simmer the pasta just until tender and drain. Do not rinse pasta products after draining. Water-soluble nutrients can be lost by rinsing. Properly cooked pasta is tender, but it holds its shape.

Hamilton Beach Brands, Inc.

13-5 All types of rice should be tender and fluffy when they are properly cooked.

Microwaving Cereal Products

Cereals, rice, and pasta do not microwave much faster than they cook conventionally. However, these foods are less likely to stick and burn when prepared in a microwave oven. You can also prepare and serve them in the same dish, which saves time on cleanup.

When microwaving cereal products, be sure to use containers that are large enough to prevent boilovers. Cover these foods for microwave cooking.

You can serve pasta immediately after microwaving. Allow rice and cereal to stand a few minutes before serving. Cereals, rice, and pasta can be reheated in a microwave oven without stirring or adding water.

You may wish to use quick-cooking rather than conventional cereal products when making casseroles in a microwave oven. If using conventional products, precook them a bit less than if you were going to serve them immediately.

Activity

Have students compare prices of plain rice, quick-cooking rice, and various rice mixes.

CAREER SUCCESS

Using Negotiation

Tom is a miller at the Olde Towne Granary. The granary grinds several varieties of corn and wheat brought in by local farmers. Tom supervises and coordinates the activities of workers who run the cleaning and grinding machines. Whenever the workers have a scheduling problem or a safety concern, Tom has to handle it.

To be an effective worker, Tom needs skill in negotiating. In a small group, answer the following questions about Tom's need for and use of this skill:

A. Why can't the workers handle scheduling problems and safety concerns themselves?

B. How might the workers respond if Tom lacks skill in negotiating?

C. How might Olde Towne Granary be affected if Tom lacks skill in negotiating?

D. What is another skill Tom would need in this job? Briefly explain why this skill would be important.

CHAPTER 13 REVIEW

Answer Key to *Review What You Have Read* **questions**

1. The bran is the outer protective covering of the kernel and is a good source of vitamins and fiber. The endosperm makes up the largest part of the kernel and contains most of the starch and protein. The germ is the smallest part of the kernel and is rich in vitamins, minerals, protein, and fat.

2. Whole-grain cereals contain all three parts of the kernel. Refined cereals have had the bran and germ removed during processing.

3. (List three:) rice, pastas, cornmeal, hominy, cornstarch, pearl barley, bulgur wheat, wheat germ, farina

4. true

5. D

6. (List two:) convenience, added ingredients, package size

7. gelatinization

8. Starch granules may be separated to prevent lumping by coating them with fat, combining them with sugar, or mixing them with a cold liquid to form a paste.

(continued)

Summary

Corn, wheat, rye, oats, rice, and barley are important crops throughout the world. These grains are made into a variety of staple food products, including breakfast foods, flours, and pasta. These products are generally nutritious, inexpensive, and easy to store.

Starches obtained from cereals are used chiefly as thickening agents in gravies, puddings, and sauces. When mixed with liquid and heated, starches absorb water and swell, causing the mixture to thicken. As they cool, most starch mixtures form gels. Temperature, time, agitation, and mixing method used affect the cooking of starch mixtures.

Cooked breakfast cereals, rice, and pasta all contain large amounts of starch. Therefore, you need to keep the principles of cooking starches in mind when preparing these foods. During cooking, cereal products absorb water and increase in volume. The amount of water needed to make the starch granules in cereal products swell varies depending on the product. Cooked breakfast cereals require moderate temperatures and gentle stirring. The water for pasta should boil constantly throughout cooking. Properly cooked cereal products are tender, but they hold their shape and have no raw starch flavor. Microwaving cereal products does not save time, but it may reduce cleanup tasks.

Review What You Have Read

Write your answers on a separate sheet of paper, using complete sentences when appropriate.

1. Describe the appearance and nutrients of the three parts of a kernel of grain.
2. How do whole grain cereals differ from refined cereals?
3. List three products, other than breakfast food and flour, that come from grain.
4. True or false. Wild rice is not really rice.
5. Pasta is made from _____.
   A. all-purpose flour
   B. cake flour
   C. self-rising flour
   D. semolina
6. What are two factors that affect the cost of cereal products?
7. The swelling and thickening of starch granules when heated in water is called _____.
8. Describe three ways to separate starch granules to prevent lumping.
9. True or false. Rice should absorb all of its cooking liquid.
10. How can the cooking time of whole-grain cereals be shortened?

11. True or false. Cereals should be stirred vigorously throughout the entire cooking time.

12. How can a raw starch flavor be prevented when cooking cereals?

13. How can pasta be kept from sticking together during cooking?

14. True or false. Cereal products can be microwaved in about one-fourth the time needed for conventional cooking.

Link to Academic Skills

15. **Social studies.** Research the types of grains people in different parts of the world use as staple foods. (Use the international foods chapters in this textbook as one of your sources of information.) Summarize your findings in a two-page report.

16. **Geography.** After conducting research, make a poster illustrating which states produce the most corn, wheat, and rice. Identify the climatic conditions and geographical features in those states that make them favorable for grain production.

17. **Social studies.** Investigate factors that affect wheat prices and the operation of the grain exchange and the futures market. Share your findings in a class discussion.

18. **Science.** Explore the chemical structures of starches and the properties of starches that cause them to gelatinize. Draw a molecular diagram to illustrate your findings.

Build Critical Thinking Skills

19. **Evaluation.** Prepare two white sauces. To prepare the first sauce, make a paste with the fat and flour. Add the milk slowly, stirring constantly, and cook the sauce until thickened. To prepare the second sauce, warm the milk with the fat. Add the flour all at once. Cook until thickened, stirring constantly. Evaluate the two sauces. Which would you rather serve? Why?

20. **Analysis.** Prepare two recipes of cherry sauce. Thicken one with cornstarch. Thicken the other with flour. Analyze the differences in appearance, texture, and flavor between the two sauces. Which one would you rather serve? Why?

21. **Evaluation.** Prepare old-fashioned oatmeal, quick-cooking oatmeal, and instant oatmeal. Taste each type of oatmeal. Assess how the flavor, texture, and appearance of each product affects your preference.

Apply Technology

22. Research how modified atmosphere packaging (MAP) is used to preserve fresh pasta products.

23. Work in a small group to investigate the processes and rationale biotechnologists use to develop new varieties of grains. Share your findings with the rest of the class through a poster presentation.

9. true

10. The cooking time of whole-grain cereals can be shortened by soaking the cereal before cooking to soften the bran.

11. false

12. When cooking cereals, a raw starch flavor can be prevented by continuing to cook them for a short time after gelatinization is complete.

13. During cooking, pasta can be kept from sticking together by making sure the water does not stop boiling while gradually adding the pasta.

14. false

A Measure of Math

24. Choose one of the following types of cereal products: breakfast foods, flours, pastas, or rice products. Visit a grocery store and make a list of as many products as you can find in the group you chose. Don't forget to list canned and frozen products as well as dried products. Make a price graph of all the products you listed.

25. Oatmeal requires twice its volume of water for cooking. The volume of the cooked cereal equals the combined volume of the dry cereal and the water. For example, 1 cup of oatmeal would require 2 cups of water for cooking. This would produce 3 cups of cooked cereal. Figure how much oatmeal and how much water would be needed to make four ½-cup servings of cooked oatmeal.

Teamwork in Action

26. As a class, prepare a survey form to use in interviewing young children about their favorite breakfast cereals and the television commercials used to advertise those cereals. Individually, use the completed survey form to interview three young children. Compile your findings with those of your classmates and summarize them in a report for parents. Make the reports available at open houses or parent-teacher meetings in an elementary school.

Companion Website

www.g-wlearning.com

At the website, review key terms for this chapter with crossword puzzles, matching exercises, and e-flash cards. Apply facts from the chapter to complete the activities.

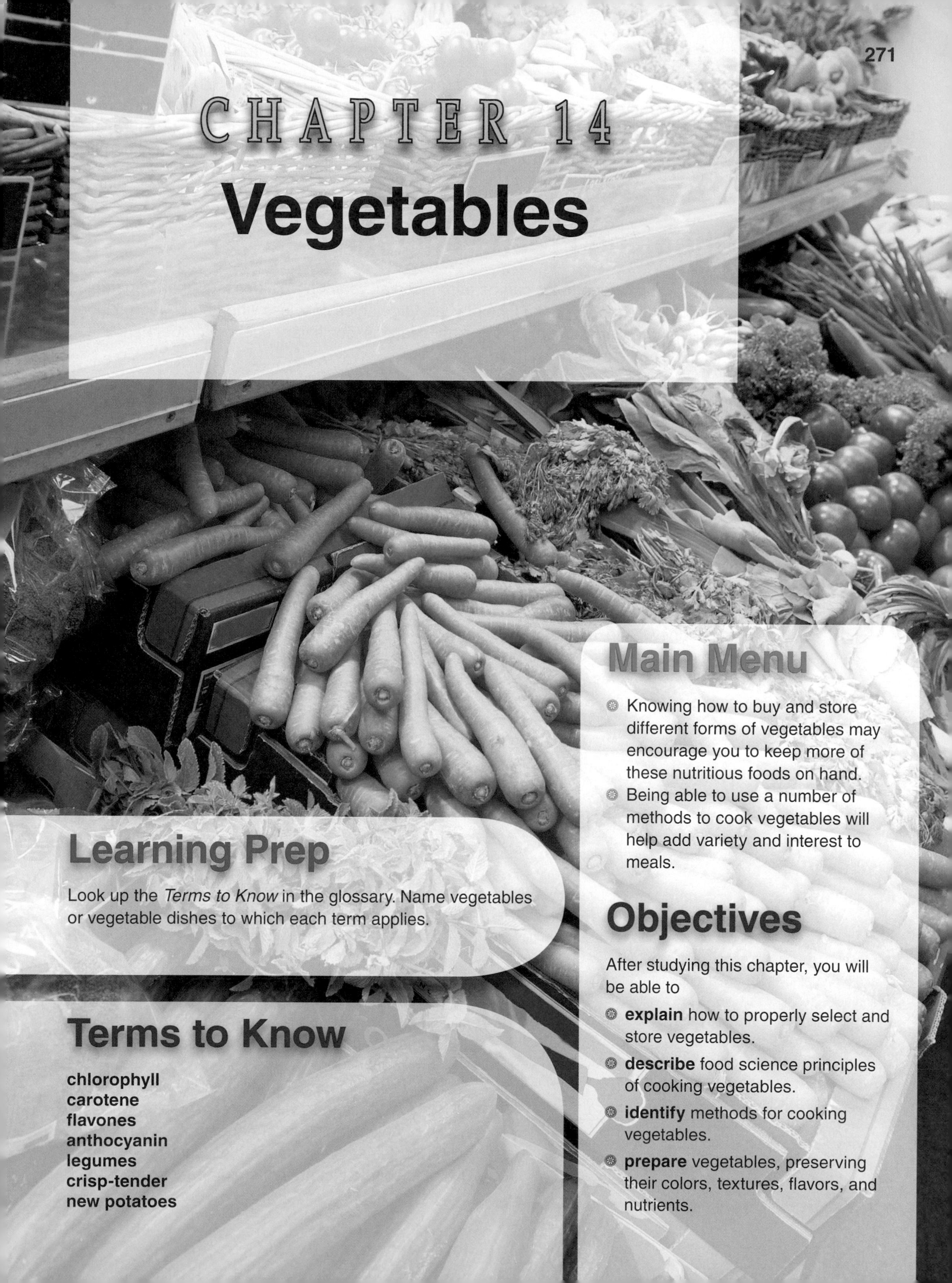

CHAPTER 14
Vegetables

Main Menu

- Knowing how to buy and store different forms of vegetables may encourage you to keep more of these nutritious foods on hand.
- Being able to use a number of methods to cook vegetables will help add variety and interest to meals.

Learning Prep

Look up the *Terms to Know* in the glossary. Name vegetables or vegetable dishes to which each term applies.

Objectives

After studying this chapter, you will be able to

- **explain** how to properly select and store vegetables.
- **describe** food science principles of cooking vegetables.
- **identify** methods for cooking vegetables.
- **prepare** vegetables, preserving their colors, textures, flavors, and nutrients.

Terms to Know

chlorophyll
carotene
flavones
anthocyanin
legumes
crisp-tender
new potatoes

Activity

Have students write breakfast, lunch, dinner, and snack menus that include vegetables.

Enrich

Ask each student to select one vegetable and investigate its nutritional value. Have students make bar graphs illustrating the levels of the various nutrients their chosen vegetables contain. Have students make posters advertising the nutritional value of chosen vegetables.

Most vegetables are fairly low in cost and calories. Vegetables are versatile enough to use in any menu. They can be served raw or cooked to add color, flavor, texture, and nutrients to meals. They are also good choices for between-meal snacks. They can be purchased fresh, canned, frozen, and dried.

Choosing Fresh Vegetables

Many fresh vegetables can be purchased all year long. The cost of fresh vegetables depends a great deal on the time of year. Vegetables cost less when purchased during their peak growing season. During other seasons, costs vary due to storage, handling, and shipping charges.

Vegetables and MyPlate

MyPlate suggests teens eat 2½ to 4 cups (625 to 1,000 mL) per day from the vegetable group. The amount you need depends on your sex and activity level. Cut vegetables and vegetable juice count cup for cup. Two cups (500 mL) of leafy vegetables count as 1 cup (250 mL) from this group.

MyPlate sorts vegetables into five subgroups based on the nutrients they provide. *Dark green vegetables* include broccoli, dark green leafy lettuce, spinach, and greens like collards and kale. All types of winter squash, carrots, pumpkin, and sweet potatoes are *red and orange vegetables. Dry beans and peas* include lentils; split peas; and kidney, pinto, and black beans. Soybean products like tofu are also part of this subgroup. Corn, green lima beans, green peas, and white potatoes are common *starchy vegetables.* The *other vegetables* subgroup includes onions, celery, cucumbers, and green beans. See **14-1.**

Health and Wellness

Vegetable Variety

Including a variety of vegetables in your diet is important because different vegetables provide different nutrients. Vegetables are low in fat and calories and rich in fiber. They are good sources of folate and vitamins A, C, and E. Vegetables like sweet and white potatoes, tomato products, and beet greens will help boost your potassium intake, too. That is why a healthful diet includes plenty of vegetables. Such a diet may reduce your risk for stroke, heart disease, and diabetes. Eating vegetables may also reduce your risk for some forms of cancer.

You do not need to eat vegetables from all five MyPlate subgroups each day to get the nutritional value of vegetables. However, try to get the suggested amount from each subgroup weekly. For most people, this means eating more legumes and dark green and red and orange vegetables. This may also mean cutting back on your intake of starchy vegetables.

Vegetable Classifications

Nutrient content is not the only characteristic used to group vegetables. Vegetables are also grouped according to the part of the plant from which they come. Garlic and onions are *bulbs.* Artichokes, broccoli, and cauliflower are flowers. Tomatoes, cucumbers, eggplant, okra, peppers, pumpkins, and squash are *fruits.* Asparagus and celery are *stems.* Brussels sprouts, cabbage, lettuce, and spinach are *leaves.* Peas, corn, and beans are *seeds.* White potatoes and Jerusalem artichokes are *tubers.* Beets, carrots, parsnips, radishes, rutabagas, sweet potatoes, and turnips are *roots.*

Color is another factor used to classify vegetables. Vegetables can be green, orange, white, or red. A vegetable's color depends on the pigments it contains. *Green vegetables*, such as broccoli and spinach, contain the pigment **chlorophyll**.

Vary Your Veggies

Dark Green Vegetables	
Calorie Level	Cups per Week
1,800-2,000	3
2,200-2,400	3
2,600-2,800	3
3,000-3,200	3

Red and Orange Vegetables	
Calorie Level	Cups per Week
1,800-2,000	2
2,200-2,400	2
2,600-2,800	2.5
3,000-3,200	2.5

Dry Beans and Peas	
Calorie Level	Cups per Week
1,800-2,000	3
2,200-2,400	3
2,600-2,800	3.5
3,000-3,200	3.5

Starchy Vegetables	
Calorie Level	Cups per Week
1,800-2,000	3
2,200-2,400	6
2,600-2,800	7
3,000-3,200	9

Other Vegetables	
Calorie Level	Cups per Week
1,800-2,000	6.5
2,200-2,400	7
2,600-2,800	8.5
3,000-3,200	10

14-1 Get suggested amounts from each vegetable subgroup every week, based on your calorie needs.

Activity
Have each student make a five-column table. Students should head each column with one of the vegetable subgroups in MyPlate. Tell students to list all the vegetables they have tried in the appropriate columns. At the bottom of each column, ask students to write the name of a vegetable from that subgroup they would like to try.

Carrots and sweet potatoes are *orange vegetables*. They contain **carotene**, a source of vitamin A. *White vegetables*, such as cauliflower and parsnips, contain pigments called **flavones**. Beets and red cabbage are *red vegetables*. They contain a pigment called **anthocyanin**.

Selecting Fresh Vegetables

The effects of temperature and handling may reduce the quality of vegetables during shipping. When shopping for fresh vegetables, follow these guidelines
- Look for good color, firmness, and absence of bruises and decay. See **14-2**.
- Avoid wilted and misshapen vegetables.
- Handle vegetables carefully to prevent bruising.
- Choose vegetables that are medium in size. Very small vegetables can be immature and lack flavor. Very large vegetables can be overmature and tough.

- Buy only what will be used within a short time. Fresh vegetables lose quality and nutrients through prolonged storage.
- Vegetables that are in season usually are high in quality and low in price.
- Keep fresh vegetables away from raw meat, poultry, and seafood in the shopping cart.
- Buy ready-to-eat vegetables and salads if they fit in the budget. These handy items may prompt you to eat more vegetables.

How to Buy Fresh Vegetables		
Parts of Plant and Vegetable Examples	**Choose**	**Avoid**
Bulbs		
Onions	Hard, smooth, and firm with small necks; papery outer covering	Wet or soft necks, woody or sprouting areas
Green onions	Fresh, green tops; well-formed, white bulbs	Yellow, wilted, or decayed tops
Flowers		
Broccoli	Firm, compact clusters of small flower buds; deep green color	Thick, tough stems; open buds; wilted, soft condition; yellow color
Cauliflower	Creamy white to white heads; compact, clean, solid florets	Discolored spots, wilting
Fruits		
Bell peppers	Bright color, glossy sheen, firm walls, heavy for size	Thin, wilted, cut or punctured walls; decayed spots
Cucumbers	Well-shaped, rounded bodies; bright green color; firm	Signs of wilting, large diameter, yellowing
Summer squash	Tender, well-developed, firm body, glossy skin	Dull appearance; hard, tough skin
Tomatoes	Well-formed, smooth, free from blemishes, bright red color	Soft spots, moldy areas, growth cracks, bruises
Leaves		
Cabbage	Firm heads, heavy for size; bright red or green color; fresh; no blemishes	Wilted, decayed, yellow outer leaves; worm holes
Lettuce	Crisp leaves for iceberg and romaine, soft texture for leaf lettuce	Very hard heads, poor color, brown or soft spots, irregular heads
Roots		
Carrots	Bright color; well-rounded, smooth, firm roots	Flabby, decaying roots; patches of green
Radishes	Plump, round, and firm; medium size; bright red color	Large or flabby radishes, decaying tops
Sweet potatoes	Deep orange color; firm, solid roots	Pale color, blemishes

(Continued)

14-2 Choose vegetables that are brightly colored, firm, and free from blemishes.

How to Buy Fresh Vegetables (Continued)

Parts of Plant and Vegetable Examples	Choose	Avoid
Seeds		
Corn	Plump, not overly mature kernels; fresh, green husks	Yellow, wilted, or dried husks; very small, very large, or dark kernels
Green beans	Bright color, tender beans, crisp pods	Thick, tough, or wilted pods, serious blemishes
Stems		
Asparagus	Rich, green color; tender stalks; compact tips; rounded spears	Open, moldy, or decayed tips; ribbed spears; excessive sand
Celery	Bright color; smooth, rigid stalks; fresh leaves	Discoloration; flabby or pithy stalks; wilting
Tubers		
Potatoes	Firm, well-shaped, free from blemishes and sunburn	Large cuts, bruises, or green spots; signs of sprouting or shriveling

14-2 *Continued.*

FYI

Vegetables are used as more than food products. Corn, for example, has more than 1,000 uses. Modified starches from corn are used in a variety of food and nonfood products. These include biscuits, mayonnaise, chewing gum, bologna, dog food, cardboard, aspirin, batteries, and glue.

Career Path

Of the different types of work agricultural engineers might do, ask students which they find most interesting and why.

EXPLORING CAREERS

Agricultural Engineer

Agricultural engineers help solve a wide range of problems related to producing food and other farm products. They might address environmental issues such as irrigation and erosion control. Some work to design and test farm machinery. Others look for ways to increase crop yields. They may also analyze how to better process, pack, and ship farm products.

To be successful, agricultural engineers must have math and science skills. They use reading skills to learn new information. They need critical thinking skills to approach problems from more than one direction to design solutions that fit each situation. They must be willing to take on challenges and adapt to changes. They also need to be able to take charge, work with little supervision, and pay attention to details.

Most agricultural engineers work with companies that sell products and services to farmers. For instance, they may work for companies that make animal feeds, pesticides, or grain silos.

Agricultural engineers need at least a four-year degree. They take a range of classes. This helps them learn to apply information from a variety of areas to

the field of agriculture. Experience working with farm equipment and systems will also help prepare people attracted to this career.

Agricultural Research Service, USDA

This agricultural engineer is measuring the water in soil to help find ways to grow successful crops in times of drought.

Storing Fresh Vegetables

Use all vegetables as soon as possible for best flavor, appearance, and nutritive value. However, most vegetables can be kept fresh in the refrigerator for at least a few days. Place most vegetables in the crisper or in plastic bags or containers. Store sweet corn in the husks. Allow tomatoes to fully ripen at room temperature before storing in the refrigerator uncovered. Wrap leafy green vegetables in a damp towel and place them in a perforated plastic bag before refrigerating.

Store onions in open containers at room temperature or slightly cooler. Air should circulate freely around them.

Store potatoes, hard-rind squash, eggplant, rutabagas, and sweet potatoes in a cool, dark, dry place. Use potatoes stored at room temperature within a week, as they will sprout and shrivel if kept longer. Potatoes that are exposed to light will turn green and develop a bitter flavor. Cut away green portions before using potatoes.

Choosing Canned, Frozen, and Dried Vegetables

Most people prefer fresh vegetables for salads and relish trays. For use in recipes or as hot side dishes, however, canned, frozen, and dried vegetables often work just as well.

Canned Vegetables

Canned vegetables can be whole, sliced, or in pieces. Most are canned in water. A few, like Harvard beets, are canned in sauces.

Most canned vegetables are packed in cans. A few are available in jars. Choose a container size to meet your needs.

Buying and Storing Canned Vegetables

Canned vegetables usually cost less than either frozen or fresh produce. Cost per serving depends on brand, can size, quality, and packing liquid. Choose house brands to save money. Choose cans that are free from dents, bulges, and leaks. Choose the quality that meets your needs and intended use. Store all cans in a cool, dry place. After opening, store unused portions in the refrigerator.

Frozen Vegetables

Frozen vegetables retain the appearance and flavor of fresh vegetables better than canned and dried vegetables. However, freezing may alter their texture somewhat. They are available in paper cartons and plastic bags. Some vegetables are frozen in combinations or in sauces.

Buying and Storing Frozen Vegetables

Frozen vegetables usually cost less than fresh. Green beans are one example. During winter months, frozen green beans are less expensive than fresh green beans. (During the summer months when green beans are in season, fresh beans may cost less than frozen.) Prices will vary according to brand, packaging, size of container, and added ingredients such as butter and sauces.

Choose packages that are clean and solidly frozen. A heavy layer of ice on the package may indicate the food has been thawed and refrozen. Store packages in the coldest part of the freezer.

Dried Vegetables

A few vegetables are dried. Dried **legumes**—peas, beans, and lentils—are the most commonly purchased dried vegetables.

Legumes are high in protein. They are also excellent sources of fiber. They are used as meat substitutes in many dishes. Many people use dried navy beans, lima beans, split peas, and lentils in soups. They use pinto and red beans in chili and many Mexican foods. Black-eyed peas are a popular side dish in the South. Garbanzo beans and kidney beans are tasty in salads. Soybeans are often used in combination with other foods.

Buying and Storing Dried Vegetables

Choose legumes that are uniform in size, free of visible defects, and brightly colored. Store them in covered containers in a cool, dry place, **14-3**.

Community Interaction

Find a vegetarian entree recipe featuring legumes. Use the USDA National Nutrient Database to calculate the total protein per serving. Identify each ingredient that supplies at least 1 gram of protein per serving. Also calculate the cost per serving. Prepare, sample, and evaluate the recipe. In class, choose the top 10 recipes based on nutrition, economy, and taste. Compile the recipes and information in a flyer on the use of legumes as meat substitutes. Ask permission to distribute your flyers at a local supermarket.

Rubbermaid

14-3 Dried vegetables kept in tightly covered containers can be safely stored for up to a year.

Preparing Vegetables

Vegetables come in a spectrum of colors and a range of flavors. These characteristics, combined with various cooking methods, allow vegetables to be used in countless ways to add interest to meals.

Preparing Raw Vegetables

Many vegetables can be eaten raw. You may have eaten raw celery and carrot sticks, pepper strips, and broccoli florets on relish trays. You may have enjoyed raw salad greens, cucumbers, tomatoes, and cabbage in salads. Raw vegetables are attractive to serve because they are colorful, and their crunchiness adds texture to meals and snacks.

To prepare clean raw vegetables for eating or cooking, trim any bruised areas, wilted leaves, and thick stems. When peeling vegetables, use a vegetable scraper or floating edge peeler rather than a paring knife. This will help protect as many nutrients as possible.

Cut raw vegetables into pieces that are easy to handle. Sticks, wedges, slices, rings, and florets are good choices. Raw vegetables also make colorful garnishes. Carrot curls, celery fans, and radish roses add nutrients and eye appeal to many dishes.

Raw vegetables taste best when served cold. Place a relish tray on a bed of ice or arrange vegetables in a bowl lined with ice. Store washed and thoroughly drained vegetables in covered containers in the refrigerator.

Health and Wellness

Washing Vegetables

If you have seen a vegetable garden, you know the edible part of most vegetables grows in or near soil. Soil can carry harmful bacteria. Therefore, whether you are preparing fresh vegetables to eat raw or cooked, the first step is to wash them. Careful washing removes dirt, bacteria, and pesticide residues. You should even wash vegetables with rinds and peels that you are going to discard, such as winter squash and onions.

Wash vegetables in cool running water. Use a vegetable brush to remove stubborn dirt from crevices. Do not allow vegetables to soak as you wash them, as this can cause a loss of water-soluble nutrients. After washing, gently dry vegetables with a clean cloth or paper towel. Removing surface moisture helps prevent the growth of bacteria.

Rubbermaid

Wash and trim fresh vegetables before eating or cooking them.

Food Science Principles of Cooking Vegetables

When vegetables are cooked, several changes take place. The cellulose (fiber) in vegetables softens to make chewing easier. Starch absorbs water, swells, and becomes easier to digest. Flavors and colors undergo changes, and some of the nutrients may be lost.

Properly cooked vegetables are colorful and flavorful. They also have a **crisp-tender** texture. This means they are tender, but still slightly firm. They can be pierced with a fork but not too easily.

Overcooked or incorrectly cooked vegetables may suffer undesirable changes in color, texture, and flavor. They also may lose many of their nutrients. The amount of cooking liquid and the cooking time greatly affect nutrient retention and degree of doneness.

Amount of Cooking Liquid

Some nutrients in vegetables, including minerals, vitamin C, and the B vitamins, are water-soluble. They will dissolve in cooking liquid. Vegetables cooked with no added water or in a small amount of water retain more of these water-soluble nutrients.

Cooking Time

Cooking vegetables too long causes several undesirable changes to take place. Heat-sensitive nutrients, such as thiamin, are lost. Unpleasant flavor, texture, and color changes also occur. Vegetables cooked for a short time retain more heat-sensitive nutrients, flavor, texture, and color.

In most cases, vegetables should be cooked for a short time in a small amount of water. Serve them when they are crisp-tender.

Effect of Cooking on Vegetable Flavor

Vegetables can have mild, strong, or very strong flavors. Cooking can affect these flavors. Therefore, consider flavors as well as colors when deciding how to prepare a vegetable.

Mildly flavored vegetables include green vegetables, such as peas, green beans, and spinach. Yellow vegetables, such as corn; red vegetables, such as beets; and white vegetables, such as parsnips, also have mild flavors. Cook most mildly flavored vegetables for a short time in a small amount of water with the pan covered.

Strongly flavored vegetables, such as cabbage, broccoli, Brussels sprouts, yellow turnips, and rutabagas, are exceptions to general cooking rules. Cover these vegetables with water. Cook them in an uncovered pan for a short time. Following these guidelines will allow some of the strong flavor substances to escape into the water and air.

Very strongly flavored vegetables, such as onions and leeks, should also be covered with water. Cook them in an uncovered pan for a longer time. As they cook, these vegetables will release strong flavor substances and develop a milder flavor.

Reflect

Ask students if they have ever eaten vegetables that were overcooked, causing them to be mushy and have off colors. Ask how students felt about eating those vegetables and whether they think they would prefer vegetables cooked to the crisp-tender stage.

Strengthening Family Ties

Have each student write seven dinner menus featuring different vegetable recipes. Have students make copies of their recipes to try at home. Ask students to encourage their family meal managers to use the menus and recipes to help family members increase the variety of vegetables in their diets. Invite students to share family members' responses to the vegetable dishes.

Food Science

Effect of Cooking on Vegetable Color

Cooking can affect the color of vegetables. For this reason, cooking times and methods may need adjustment to suit the vegetables being cooked.

Heat affects chlorophyll in green vegetables. Overcooked green vegetables lose their bright green color and look grayish-green. To keep vegetables green, cook them in a small amount of water. Use a short cooking time and keep the pan lid off for the first few minutes of cooking. Then cover the pan for the remainder of the cooking period. (Do not add baking soda to cooking water for green vegetables. Although this weak alkali will produce a bright green color, it can also cause a loss of important nutrients.)

Heat does not destroy carotene in orange vegetables. However, if an orange vegetable is overcooked, the cell structure will break down. This will release the carotene into the cooking liquid. Most orange vegetables should be cooked in a small amount of water with the pan covered.

Flavones in white vegetables are soluble in water. If white vegetables are overcooked, they turn yellow or dark gray. Take care when cooking to avoid these undesirable color changes.

If the cooking water is alkaline, anthocyanins in red vegetables will turn purple. Adding a little vinegar or lemon juice to the water will neutralize the alkali. This will keep red vegetables red. Cook most red vegetables in a small amount of water, with the pan lid on, just until tender.

Hamilton Beach Brands, Inc.

Properly cooked vegetables will retain their bright, appetizing colors.

Methods of Cooking Vegetables

Vegetables can be cooked by boiling, steaming, pressure-cooking, roasting, frying, stir-frying, broiling, grilling, and microwaving. Regardless of the cooking method, vegetables cooked in their skins retain more nutrients. Consider tastes and the other items in the menu when choosing a cooking method.

Cooking Vegetables in Water

Use a pan with a tight-fitting lid when cooking vegetables in water. Add salt to a small amount of water and bring the water to a boil. Add the vegetables, cover, and quickly bring to a boil again. Then reduce the heat and cook the vegetables at a simmering temperature until they are crisp-tender. Drain and serve the vegetables immediately.

Steaming Vegetables

Young, tender vegetables that cook quickly can be steamed. To steam vegetables, place them in a steaming basket over simmering water. Tightly cover the pan and steam the vegetables until they are tender. Shredded cabbage, broccoli, diced root vegetables, celery, sweet corn, and French-style (thinly sliced) green beans can be successfully steamed.

Pressure-Cooking Vegetables

To pressure-cook vegetables, follow the directions that accompany the pressure cooker. The pressure in a pressure cooker produces high temperatures, so foods cook quickly. Time vegetables carefully to prevent overcooking.

Roasting Vegetables

Vegetables can be roasted peeled or in their skins. Roasting is usually done in an open pan. However, peeled vegetables can be wrapped in foil before placing them in an oven. Peeled vegetables can also be placed in a covered casserole with a small amount of liquid before roasting. Potatoes, tomatoes, and onions are popular vegetables for roasting. Roasting takes longer than other cooking methods.

Frying Vegetables

Vegetables can be dipped in batter and deep-fried. They can be sautéed in a small amount of fat. Stir-frying works well with vegetables that have a high moisture content.

To stir-fry vegetables, shred them or cut them into small pieces. Place the vegetables in a heavy pan or wok. Use a small amount of oil to help prevent sticking. Place the pan over medium-high heat and stir the vegetables constantly, just until tender.

Broiling Vegetables

Tomato halves and eggplant slices are often broiled. To broil vegetables, brush the cut surfaces with oil or melted fat. Place the vegetables under the broiling unit and broil until tender. Because vegetables cook quickly under the broiler, they must be watched carefully.

Grilling Vegetables

Grilling times vary for vegetables. Dense vegetables, like potatoes, take longer to grill than less dense vegetables, like mushrooms and peppers. Whole vegetables also take longer to grill than cut pieces. Place vegetables that cook more quickly directly over the heat source on a grill. Grill slower cooking vegetables with indirect heat. Placing vegetables in a grill basket makes it easy to turn them during grilling for more even cooking. Be sure to watch them carefully to avoid charring.

Microwaving Vegetables

Vegetables cooked in a microwave oven retain their shapes, colors, flavors, and nutrients. This is due to the short cooking time and the use of little or no cooking liquid.

Use high power to cook vegetables in a microwave oven. Remember to allow standing time for vegetables to finish cooking. Stir vegetable dishes during the cooking period to redistribute heat. Rearrange whole vegetables during the cooking period to ensure even cooking. Vegetables that have tight skins can explode when cooked in a microwave oven. To prevent this, pierce their skins in several places before microwaving.

Frozen vegetables can be prepared in a microwave oven as easily as fresh vegetables. Slit pouches of vegetables to allow steam to escape. Place vegetables that do not come in pouches in a microwavable casserole for cooking.

Potatoes

Although potatoes are a vegetable, they are treated somewhat differently from other vegetables. The cooking method followed to prepare potatoes depends on the type of potato being used. See **14-4**.

Potatoes are classified on the basis of appearance and use. Common varieties are long or round with white skins or round with red skins. They can be all-purpose potatoes, baking potatoes, or new potatoes. (**New potatoes** are not a variety. They are potatoes that are sent to market immediately after harvesting.)

New potatoes and round red varieties are best for boiling, oven-browning, frying, and making potato salad. This is because these varieties hold their shape when cooked. Baking or russet potatoes are best for baking and mashing. Their mealy texture allows them to break apart easily. All-purpose potatoes can be used for both baking and boiling.

Shutterstock

14-4 A bowl of mashed potatoes makes an appealing side dish.

Preparing Potatoes

Four popular potato preparations are boiling, mashing, frying, and baking. To prepare boiled potatoes, wash, peel, and halve them. Cover the potatoes with lightly salted water and simmer until tender. (Potatoes can also be cooked in one inch (2.5 cm) of simmering salted water. Check them during cooking to be sure the water has not boiled away. Add more water, if needed.) Drain potatoes and season as desired.

Prepare potatoes for mashing the same as boiled potatoes. Then add butter, milk, and salt and beat the potatoes with an electric mixer or mash them by hand.

French fries, hash browns, and home fries are just a few of the fried potato dishes people enjoy. Some fried potato dishes are made with raw potatoes, and others are made with boiled potatoes. French fries are made by deep-frying raw potato strips. Hash browns are made from shredded or diced cooked potatoes. To prepare home fries, place sliced cooked potatoes in a heavy nonstick skillet with a small amount of melted fat. Season the potatoes with salt and pepper. Cook over low heat until the slices brown on the bottom. Then turn the potatoes to brown the other side.

To prepare baked potatoes, scrub potatoes under cool running water. Pierce potatoes in several places with a fork. This prevents steam from building up inside the skin, which could cause the potato to explode. Bake potatoes in a 400°F (205°C) oven until they are tender, about 40 to 60 minutes. (Baking time and temperature can be adjusted so potatoes can bake with other foods.) A potato can also be baked in a microwave oven in about five minutes.

Preparing Canned, Frozen, and Dried Vegetables

Canned vegetables have already been cooked. Many vegetables suffer changes in color and texture during canning. Therefore, they will look and taste better if they are heated no more than necessary before serving.

To prepare canned vegetables, place the vegetables and the liquid from the can in a saucepan. Cook over low heat until the vegetables are heated through. Add seasonings to taste.

Prepare frozen vegetables according to package instructions. Frozen vegetables have already been blanched (preheated in boiling water or steam for a short time). Blanching reduces the cooking time needed to about half that needed for fresh vegetables.

Before cooking, rinse and sort dried legumes. Remove any debris that may have been packaged with the vegetables. Dried beans must be soaked before cooking so they will absorb water and cook more evenly. To soak beans, place them in a large pot with plenty of water. Bring the water to a boil for two to three minutes. Cover the pot and remove it from the heat. Allow beans to soak for at least one hour. Discard the soaking water and use fresh water for cooking. This will help reduce the gas-causing properties of beans. Dried lentils and peas need no soaking. Reconstitute other dried vegetables according to package directions.

Serving Vegetables

Vegetables can be served in many creative and delicious ways. Some people prefer their vegetables served simply, seasoned with herbs or a sprinkling of salt. Others enjoy vegetables topped with a few toasted nuts or a bit of shredded cheese. With just a little extra effort, variety can be added to a vegetable with a low-fat sauce.

Health and Wellness

Using Vegetable Cooking Liquid

After vegetables have cooked, do not throw away the cooking liquid. It contains many valuable nutrients. A small amount of the cooking liquid can be served with the vegetables in a separate dish. If the liquid is not needed right away, freeze it in small amounts. (Ice cube trays work well.) Later, the frozen liquid can be added to sauces, soups, and gravies.

Light glazes of brown sugar or honey are also popular. See **14-5**.

Yogurt and cottage cheese are tasty, low-fat alternatives to sour cream for fresh vegetable dips and baked potato toppings. Garnish boiled potatoes with fresh chopped parsley or chives. Give ordinary mashed potatoes a new twist by combining them with roasted garlic. Try swirling them with mashed sweet potatoes. Brown small whole potatoes around a roast. Serving vegetables in these different ways adds variety to meals.

©2011 Wisconsin Milk Marketing Board, Inc.

14-5 Melted cheese makes a delicious, attractive topping for baked tomatoes.

CAREER SUCCESS

Using Writing Skills

Yoshi is a botanist who works for The Green Thumb, a seed catalog company familiar to many home gardeners. Yoshi is working to develop a strain of green beans that has a longer growing season and better keeping quality. He needs to keep detailed records of his procedures and observations. When Yoshi successfully develops the new strain, The Green Thumb will duplicate his work. They will offer seeds for the beans in their catalog.

To be a successful employee, Yoshi needs basic writing skills. Put yourself in Yoshi's place and answer the following questions about your need for and use of these skills:

A. How would having basic writing skills help you when you get to work each day?

B. How would your company's ability to duplicate your results be affected if you do not have adequate writing skills?

C. How would your writing skills affect home gardeners?

D. What is another skill you would need in this job? Briefly explain why this skill would be important.

CHAPTER 14 REVIEW

Summary

Vegetables are low in fat and calories, high in fiber, and rich in vitamins and minerals. Eat suggested amounts from each subgroup weekly to meet nutrient needs. When buying fresh vegetables, choose items that are in their peak growing season to get the best buy. Select medium-sized pieces that have good color and are free from bruises and decay. Store most vegetables in the refrigerator.

Canned, frozen, and dried vegetables can be a good buy when fresh vegetables are not in season. Choose packages that are intact. Store frozen vegetables in the freezer. Keep canned and dried vegetables in a cool, dry place.

To prepare fresh vegetables, begin by washing and trimming them. Cooking affects the pigments in green, yellow, white, and red vegetables. Cook most vegetables for a short time in a small amount of liquid. This will help preserve flavors, textures, colors, and nutrients.

Aside from cooking in liquid, vegetables can be steamed, pressure-cooked, roasted, fried, broiled, grilled, and microwaved. The method chosen will depend on taste preferences. Canned and frozen vegetables cook more quickly than fresh vegetables. Dried vegetables often require soaking before cooking.

Review What You Have Read

Write your answers on a separate sheet of paper, using complete sentences when appropriate.

1. List the five vegetable subgroups in MyPlate. Give an example of a vegetable from each subgroup.

2. The pigments in white vegetables are called _____.
   A. anthocyanins
   B. carotenes
   C. chlorophylls
   D. flavones

3. List three guidelines to follow when shopping for fresh vegetables.

4. What form of vegetables best retains the flavor and appearance of fresh vegetables?

5. What vegetables are most commonly purchased in dried form?

6. Why is it important to wash fresh vegetables? How should they be washed?

7. List three changes that take place in vegetables when they are cooked.

8. List the three flavor categories of vegetables and give cooking guidelines for each.

9. List four methods for cooking vegetables. Describe two.

10. What type of potato is the best choice when making mashed potatoes?

11. True or false. Canned vegetables have already been cooked.

12. How can vegetable cooking liquid be used?

Answer Key to *Review What You Have Read* **questions**

1. The five vegetable subgroups in MyPlate are dark green vegetables, red and orange vegetables, dry beans and peas, starchy vegetables, and other vegetables. (Examples are student response.)

2. D

3. (List three. Student response. See pages 273-275 in the text.)

4. Frozen vegetables best retain the flavor and appearance of fresh vegetables.

5. Legumes are the vegetables most commonly purchased in dried form.

6. It is important to wash fresh vegetables to remove dirt, bacteria, and pesticide residues. Wash vegetables in cool running water. Use a vegetable brush to remove stubborn dirt from crevices. Do not allow vegetables to soak. Gently dry vegetables with a clean cloth or paper towel.

(continued)

Link to Academic Skills

7. (List three:) Cellulose softens. Starch absorbs water and swells. Flavors change. Colors change. Some nutrients may be lost.

8. Mildly flavored vegetables should be cooked for a short time in a small amount of water with the pan covered. Strongly flavored vegetables should be covered with water and cooked in an uncovered pan for a short time. Very strongly flavored vegetables should be covered with water and cooked in an uncovered pan for a longer time.

13. **Government/Civics.** Visit the Fruits & Veggies—More Matters website at FruitsandVeggiesMatter.gov. Explore the site to find out why the federal government cares about the fruit and vegetable consumption of its citizens. Learn about local fruit and vegetable activities planned by the Nutrition Coordinator in your state. Discuss what you learned in class.

14. **Geography.** Working in a small group, choose a type of natural disaster or weather condition that can affect crop harvests. Investigate which regions of the United States are most affected by your chosen condition. Identify the vegetable crops that are grown in those regions. Also research how your chosen condition can affect soil quality as well as the quality, cost, and supply of various forms of vegetables. Present your findings in an oral report to the class, using a map as a visual aid.

15. **English language arts.** Research the principles behind composting and techniques and procedures for maintaining a compost pile. Find out how vegetable scraps can be used as compost. Summarize your findings in a two-page persuasive report encouraging the reader to compost at home.

16. **Science.** Cook red cabbage in water made alkaline with baking soda and in water made acidic with vinegar. Compare color.

17. **Geography.** Choose an international cuisine. Find out what vegetables are popular in this cuisine and research common preparation methods. Find and prepare a recipe for a vegetable dish from this cuisine. Share your evaluation of the dish in class.

Build Critical Thinking Skills

9. (List four:) cooking in water, steaming, pressure-cooking, roasting, frying, broiling, grilling, microwaving (Descriptions are student response.)

10. A mealy or all-purpose potato variety is the best choice when making mashed potatoes.

11. true

12. Vegetable cooking liquid can be served with the vegetables or added to gravies, soups, or sauces.

18. **Evaluation.** Evaluate the flavor, color, and texture of equal amounts of green beans prepared in each of the following ways:
    A. in a small amount of water for a short time with the pan covered
    B. in a small amount of water for a short time with the pan uncovered for the first few minutes of cooking
    C. in a large amount of water for a long time with the pan covered
    D. in a small amount of water for a short time with baking soda added and the pan covered

19. **Analysis.** Prepare two portions of small, whole onions. Use a small amount of water and a covered pan for one portion. Use a large amount of water and an uncovered pan for the other portion. Compare flavor and aroma. Based on your analysis, which cooking method would you recommend? Write an opinion paragraph to explain your reasons.

Apply Technology

20. Investigate the technology used to produce ethanol from corn as an alternative to gasoline. How is use of this technology affecting corn production, prices, and exports in the United States? Share your findings in class in a brief oral report.

21. Use the Internet to find three vegetable recipes. Compile your recipes with those of your classmates. Then use a computer to organize all the recipes according to each of these factors: type of vegetable (sorted alphabetically), cooking method, meal (breakfast, lunch, dinner, or snack), and type of dish (entree, side dish, salad, or other).

A Measure of Math

22. Choose five types of vegetables. Visit a supermarket to find the price of each type of vegetable in fresh, canned, frozen, and dried forms. Calculate the cost per serving of each type and form of vegetable. Illustrate your findings with a bar graph.

Teamwork in Action

23. Investigate tips for getting children to eat more vegetables. Find recipes for simple vegetable snacks that would appeal to young children. Write rhymes or nursery songs and/or create a puppet show to encourage young children to eat vegetables. Arrange for your class to teach your rhymes and songs and/or present your puppet show to a group of preschool or kindergarten students. Prepare and serve some of the vegetable snack recipes you found. Give each child a handout to take home to parents. Handouts should include the words to the rhymes and songs you taught as well as the tips and snack recipes you found. Be sure to site the sources of your tips and recipes.

Companion Website
www.g-wlearning.com

At the website, review key terms for this chapter with crossword puzzles, matching exercises, and e-flash cards. Apply facts from the chapter to complete the activities.

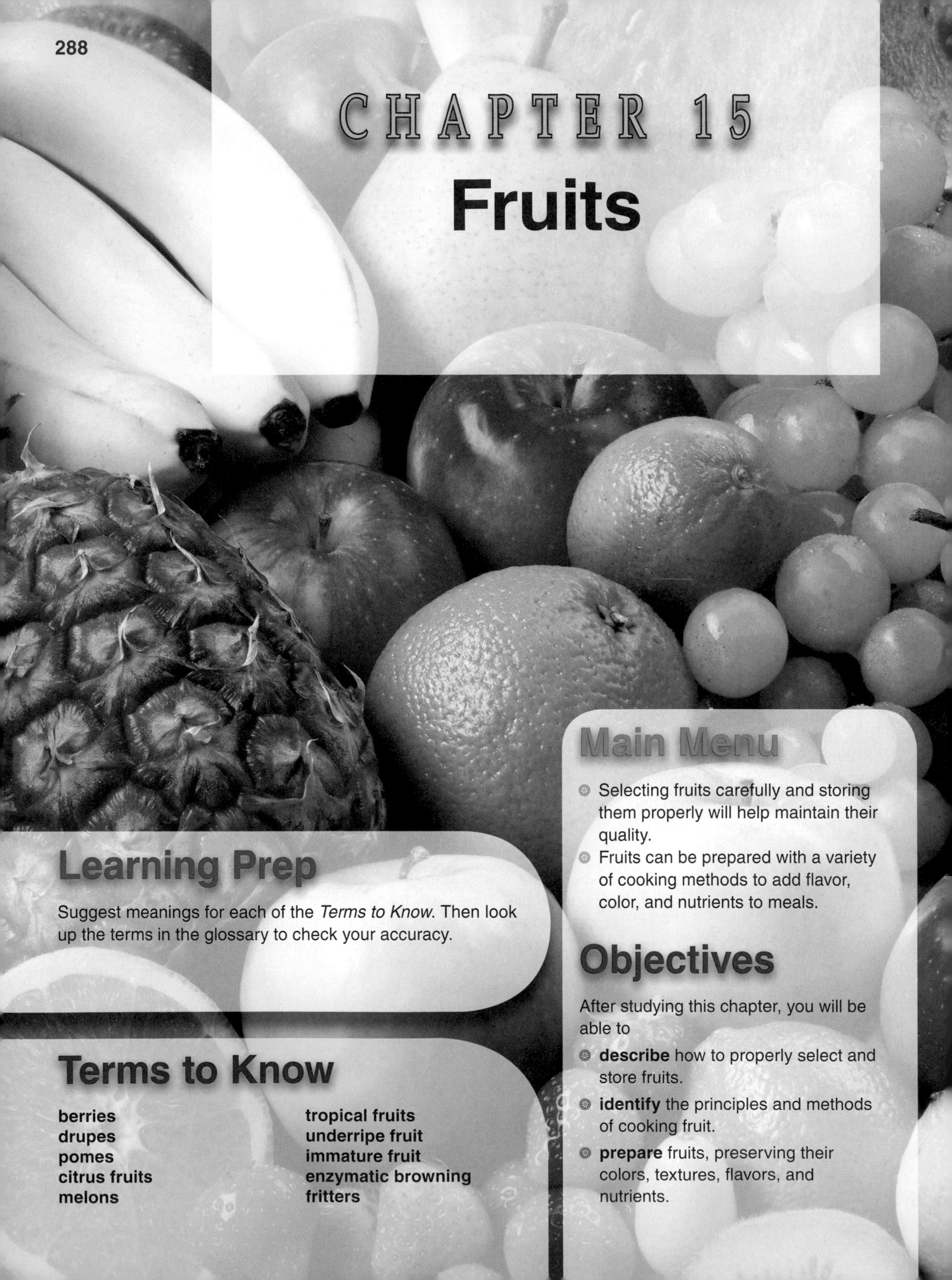

CHAPTER 15
Fruits

Learning Prep

Suggest meanings for each of the *Terms to Know*. Then look up the terms in the glossary to check your accuracy.

Terms to Know

berries
drupes
pomes
citrus fruits
melons

tropical fruits
underripe fruit
immature fruit
enzymatic browning
fritters

Main Menu

⊛ Selecting fruits carefully and storing them properly will help maintain their quality.
⊛ Fruits can be prepared with a variety of cooking methods to add flavor, color, and nutrients to meals.

Objectives

After studying this chapter, you will be able to

⊛ **describe** how to properly select and store fruits.
⊛ **identify** the principles and methods of cooking fruit.
⊛ **prepare** fruits, preserving their colors, textures, flavors, and nutrients.

Fresh, canned, frozen, and dried fruits add flavor, color, and texture contrasts to meals. They are generally nutritious and low in calories, so they are good choices for desserts and snacks.

Fruits can be eaten raw or cooked. For example, an apple can be packed in a school lunch and eaten plain. It could also be used to make applesauce or a pie. Fresh blueberries could be tossed into a fruit cup. They could be sprinkled on breakfast cereal or baked into a cobbler, too.

Choosing Fresh Fruit

Many varieties of fresh fruit are available year-round. Others are available for only a short time. Knowing how to recognize high-quality fresh fruit will help you make smart choices.

Fruit Classifications

Fruits can be divided into groups according to physical characteristics, **15-1. Berries** are small, juicy fruits with thin skins. Blackberries, cranberries, blueberries, red and black raspberries, gooseberries, and strawberries all belong to the berry family. Grapes and currants are also berries. Except for cranberries, all berries are highly perishable.

California Strawberry Commission. All rights reserved. Photograph provided courtesy of the California Strawberry Commission. ©2010

berries

©Courtesy of California Tree Fruit Agreement

drupes

U.S. Apple Association

pomes

Florida Department of Citrus

citrus fruits

National Watermelon Promotion Board

melons

Brooks Tropicals

tropical fruits

15-1 Each class of fruit has distinct qualities.

Vocabulary Builder

Ask students to use the dictionary to check for proper pronunciation of the terms *drupes* and *pomes*, as well as other unfamiliar terms introduced on this page.

For Example…

Other tropical fruits include coconut, carambola, (also called star fruit), passion fruit, atemoya, and lychee.

Vocabulary Builder

Review the meaning of the term *provitamin A carotenoids*.

Reflect

Ask students to name their favorite types of fresh fruit.

Drupes have an outer skin covering a soft, fleshy fruit. The fruit surrounds a single, hard seed, which is called a *stone* or *pit*. Cherries, apricots, nectarines, peaches, and plums are all drupes.

Pomes have a central, seed-containing core surrounded by a thick layer of flesh. Apples and pears are pomes.

Citrus fruits have a thick outer rind. A thin membrane separates the flesh into segments. Oranges, tangerines, tangelos, grapefruits, kumquats, lemons, and limes are citrus fruits.

Melons are large, juicy fruits produced by plants in the gourd family. They usually have thick rinds and many seeds. This group of fruits includes cantaloupe, casaba, honeydew, Crenshaw, Persian, and watermelon.

Tropical fruits are grown in warm climates and are considered to be somewhat exotic. Many species of tropical fruits are available throughout the world. Those most commonly available in the United States are avocados, bananas, figs, dates, guavas, mangoes, papayas, persimmons, pineapples, pomegranates, and kiwifruit.

Fruit and MyPlate

According to MyPlate, teens should eat 1½ to 2½ cups (375 to 625 mL) from the fruit group each day, depending on calorie needs. Most forms of fruit and fruit juice count cup for cup. For dried fruit, ½ cup (125 mL) counts as 1 cup (250 mL) from this food group.

Selecting Fresh Fruit

Fresh fruits are usually least expensive during their peak growing season. They are also at their best quality during this time. Peak season is a good time to buy large quantities of fruit and preserve it for future use.

Ripeness is a guide in judging the quality of fresh fruits. Ripe fruits are those that have reached top eating quality. Test fruit for ripeness by pressing it gently to see if it gives slightly. **Underripe fruits** are fruits that are full-sized but have not yet reached peak eating quality. Some fruits, such as pears and bananas, can be purchased when they are underripe because they will ripen within a few days at room temperature.

Color and fragrance are guides to ripeness. Most fruits lose their green color as they ripen. For instance, peaches turn from green to deep yellow. Pineapples and melons have a characteristic fragrance when ripe.

Maturity is another factor that will help judge the quality of fresh fruits. Do not confuse underripe fruits with immature fruits. **Immature fruits** have not reached full size. They are small and have poor color, flavor, and texture. They will not improve in quality when left at room temperature.

When buying fresh fruit, use the following guidelines:

- Buy just what can be used in a short time.

Health and Wellness

Focus on Fruits

Most fruits are high in vitamins and low in fat. (Avocados are a high-fat exception.) Citrus fruits, cantaloupe, and strawberries are excellent sources of vitamin C. Cantaloupe, apricots, and other orange fruits are good sources of vitamin A because they contain large amounts of provitamin A carotenoids. Bananas and dried fruits supply potassium. Fruits are also rich in antioxidants, and whole fruits provide needed fiber in the diet.

An overall healthful diet that includes plenty of fruits may help prevent some major health problems. These problems include heart disease, type 2 diabetes, and some types of cancer.

- Look for signs of freshness and ripeness.
- Avoid bruised, soft, damaged, or immature fruits.
- Consider needs. For instance, use smaller, blemished apples for stewing and pies. Use fancy apples for fruit trays and other dishes in which appearance is important.

Storing Fresh Fruit

Handle all fruits gently to prevent bruising. Let underripe fruits ripen at room temperature and refrigerate ripe fruits. Store strong-smelling fruits in plastic bags or airtight containers. Store other fruits uncovered in a crisper.

Use berries, melons, grapes, and fruits with pits as soon as possible. Apples, pears, and citrus fruits can be stored longer, but they too will lose quality after prolonged storage. Bananas can be refrigerated for a short time after they have ripened at room temperature. The cold temperature may darken banana skins, but the flavor and texture of the fruit will be unharmed.

Choosing Canned, Frozen, and Dried Fruit

Fruit can be purchased canned, frozen, and dried as well as fresh. Fruits are picked at their peak of quality and then preserved so they can be enjoyed all year long. See **15-2**.

Canned Fruit

Canned fruits are packed in cans or jars. Canned fruits can be whole, halved, sliced, or in pieces. They come packed in juices or in light or heavy syrup. Fruit juices are lower in calories and higher in nutrients than syrups used as packing liquids.

Buying and Storing Canned Fruits

Canned fruits are usually less expensive than frozen or fresh fruits. Costs vary depending on brand, can size, quality, and packing liquid. To receive the greatest economy, choose house brands.

When buying canned fruits, choose cans that are free from dents, bulges, and leaks. Choose jars that are free from cracks and chips. Store all cans and jars in a cool, dry place. Cover the fruit after opening and store it in the refrigerator.

Frozen Fruit

Frozen fruits are available sweetened and unsweetened; whole and in pieces. Most frozen fruits come in plastic bags or plastic-coated paper cartons.

Frozen fruits resemble fresh fruits in color and flavor. They may, however, lose some texture qualities during freezing.

U.S. Apple Association

15-2 Fruits come in a variety of forms and can be used in many ways.

Reflect

Ask students when they would choose canned, frozen, or dried fruit instead of fresh fruit.

Career Path

Ask students how a plant scientist would use math and science skills in his or her work.

Buying and Storing Frozen Fruits

The most common frozen fruits are not available in fresh form year-round. When fresh fruits are out of season, frozen fruits are often less expensive than fresh. However, prices of frozen fruits vary according to brand, packaging, size of container, and added ingredients, such as spices and sweeteners. Be sure to compare prices, especially if the fruit is in its peak growing season.

When buying frozen fruits, choose packages that are clean, undamaged, and frozen solid. Store in the coldest part of the freezer. After thawing, store the unused portion in a tightly covered container in the refrigerator. Use as soon as possible. Never refreeze.

Dried Fruits

Raisins, dried plums (also known as prunes), and apricots are the most common dried fruits. Dried apples, peaches, pears, figs, pineapple, bananas, mango, and papayas are also available.

Dried fruits usually come in boxes or plastic bags. Sometimes they are loose, so they can be purchased in any quantity. Size generally determines the price of dried apples, apricots, and plums. Larger fruits cost more than smaller fruits.

Buying and Storing Dried Fruits

Choose dried fruits that are fairly soft and pliable. Store unopened packages and boxes in a cool, dark, dry place. After opening, store unused portions in tightly covered containers. Some package labels recommend storing opened dried fruits in the refrigerator for best keeping quality.

EXPLORING CAREERS

Plant Scientist

Plant scientists study plants and factors that affect their growth. They may develop new varieties of plants that can resist pests, disease, or drought. They may work to improve the nutritional value of plant foods. They may help farmers increase crop harvests while making the best use of soil and water resources. Some plant scientists try to find new uses for plant products.

To be successful, plant scientists need strong math and science skills. They use critical thinking skills to analyze and solve problems. They must be active learners so they can understand and apply new information. Being able to communicate effectively, through both speech and writing, is important, too. Plant scientists must pay attention to details. They need to be able to work independently as well as with members of a research team. They also need to be willing to stick with a project even when it takes many attempts to achieve a desired outcome.

Taking a variety of math, science, and computer classes can help prepare someone to enter this field. Plant scientists need a bachelor's degree to work as research assistants. However, scientists who wish to direct research projects must have a master's or doctoral degree.

Agricultural Research Service, USDA

Plant scientists may help research how crops respond to various growing conditions.

Preparing Fruits

Fruits can be served in a variety of ways to add interest to meals and snacks. They can be used raw or cooked, fresh or preserved. Carefully following preparation techniques will help maintain the appealing flavors, colors, textures, and shapes of fruits.

Preparing Raw Fruits

Raw fruits are delicious when eaten out-of-hand. They can also be combined with other foods in appetizers, salads, and desserts.

To prepare raw fruits for eating, wash them carefully under clean running water. Then dry them with a clean towel. Fruits, such as oranges and melons, should even be washed before peeling or removing rinds. Washing removes dirt and microorganisms. Never let fruits soak, as this may cause them to lose flavor and some of their water-soluble nutrients.

Serve raw fruits whole or sliced. Some fruits, such as bananas and peaches, darken when exposed to the air. This is called **enzymatic browning**. Dipping these fruits in lemon, orange, grapefruit, or pineapple juice will prevent enzymatic browning and make them look more appealing.

Use a sharp, thin-bladed knife when peeling raw fruit. Peel as thinly as possible to preserve nutrients found just under the skin.

Principles of Cooking Fruit

Some fruits, like rhubarb, are cooked to make them more palatable and easier to digest. Other fruits, like pears, are cooked to give variety to a menu. Cooking allows overripe fruits that are past prime eating quality to be used. For instance, apples that are becoming overripe can be used to make applesauce. Overripe bananas are great in banana bread or muffins.

Overcooked fruits become mushy. They lose their colors, nutrients, natural flavors, and shapes. Correctly cooked fruits can retain these characteristics.

Sometimes it is necessary for a fruit to retain its shape; other times it is not. For instance, if apple slices are being poached for a garnish, the slices should retain their shape. If applesauce is being prepared, however, the apples should lose their shape and form a smooth pulp.

Methods of Cooking Fruit

Fruits can be prepared by cooking them in liquid. They can also be baked, broiled, fried, or microwaved.

Food Science

Effects of Cooking on Fruit

During cooking, several changes take place within fruit. Cellulose softens and makes fruit easier to digest. Colors change. Heat-sensitive and water-soluble nutrients may be lost. Flavors become less acidic and mellower.

Fruits that undergo enzymatic browning will keep their colors if cooked with a small amount of lemon or orange juice. Water-soluble nutrients will be retained if fruit is cooked in a small amount of water just until tender. Natural flavors will be preserved if fruit is not overcooked. Fruits will hold their shapes if they are cooked in sugar syrup instead of plain water.

FYI

Not all apple varieties are equally suited for all uses. For instance, Fuji, Red Delicious, and Winesap apples are best used only for eating and salads. Rome apples are great for baking and making sauce, but they are not very appealing for eating fresh. Braeburn, Golden Delicious, and Granny Smith apples are suitable for all uses.

Discuss

Ask students why fruits covered with a tight skin need to be pierced before microwaving. *(to keep steam pressure from building up inside the fruits, which could cause them to explode)*

Cooking Fruit in Liquid

When cooking fruits in liquid, water or sugar syrup can be used. Fruits cooked in sugar syrup will retain their shape. Those cooked in water will not. The intended use of the fruit will determine the cooking method.

When cooking fruits in syrup, use a two-to-one ratio of water to sugar. (Too much sugar will cause the fruit to harden.) Use a low temperature and cook the fruit just until it is tender and translucent. Serve cooked fruit warm or chilled.

When fruits are cooked in water, use as little water as possible. Cook the fruit over low heat until tender, then add sugar as the recipe directs. When sugar is added at the end of cooking, it will thin a fruit sauce. Thus, the amount of cooking water used must be small so the sauce will not be too thin. For a smoother sauce, force the cooked fruit through a sieve or run it through a food mill. Serve cooked fruit sauces warm or chilled.

Baking Fruit

Apples, pears, and bananas can be baked. Baked fruits should be tender, but they should keep their shape. If fruit is baked in its skin, the skin will hold in the steam that forms during baking. This steam cooks the interior of the fruit. If the fruit is skinned before baking, a covered casserole dish will serve the same purpose as the skin. Bake fruits in a small amount of liquid just until they are tender. See **15-3**.

Broiling Fruit

Bananas, grapefruit halves, and pineapple slices often are broiled. Sprinkle these fruits with brown sugar or drizzle them with honey before broiling. Fruits broil quickly, so watch them carefully to prevent overcooking.

Frying Fruit

Some fruits can be fried in a small amount of fat in a skillet. This is called *sautéing*. Fruits can also be dipped into a batter and deep-fried. These deep-fried fruits are called **fritters**. All fried fruits should be tender, but they should retain their shape.

©2011 Wisconsin Milk Marketing Board, Inc.

15-3 A warm baked pear makes a tempting, healthful dessert.

Microwaving Fruit

Fruits cooked in a microwave oven maintain their flavors and nutrients because they cook quickly using little or no water. When microwaving several pieces of fruit, choose pieces of similar size to ensure even cooking. Pierce fruits covered with a tight skin if they are being microwaved whole.

When microwaving fruit, the type of fruit, its size, and its ripeness will affect cooking time. Fruits with a higher moisture content, such as strawberries, will cook more quickly than dense fruits, like rhubarb. Berries and other small pieces of fruit will cook more quickly than larger pieces like apples. Ripe fruit requires less cooking time than firmer, underripe fruit.

Preparing Preserved Fruits

Canned fruits may be served right from the can. They may be drained or served in the syrup or juice in which they were packed. Canned fruits can be used like fresh or frozen fruits. Unless a recipe says otherwise, drain canned fruits well before using them in baked products.

Use frozen fruits in the same ways fresh and canned fruits are used. Completely thawing frozen fruits causes them to become soft and mushy. Therefore, serve frozen fruits with a few ice crystals remaining in them.

Dried fruits can be used for cooking or baking or eaten right from the package. Before cooking, soak dried fruits in hot water for about an hour. Soaking helps restore the moisture removed during the drying process. Cooking softens the fruit tissues. Because dried fruits vary in moisture content, follow package directions. See **15-4**.

Cherry Marketing Institute

15-4 Dried tart cherries add a tangy sweetness and a moist, chewy texture to this snack mix.

CAREER SUCCESS

Using Math Skills

Margery is a produce broker for citrus growers in Texas. She sells large shipments of oranges and grapefruit to fruit wholesalers throughout the country. Margery is authorized to offer various discounts depending on how much a wholesaler buys. Her computer figures exact discounts when it prints invoices. However, Margery's customers frequently ask her to give them quick estimates of costs when they call to place orders.

To be a successful employee, Margery needs basic math skills. Put yourself in Margery's place and answer the following questions about your need for and use of these skills:

A. What are three specific math skills you would use as a produce broker? Give an example of how you would use each skill.

B. How might wholesalers react if your estimates are too high?

C. How might wholesalers react if your estimates are significantly lower than the amounts shown on their invoices?

D. What is another skill you would need in this job? Briefly explain why this skill would be important.

CHAPTER 15 REVIEW

Summary

Fruits can be grouped into six basic classifications. No matter what their classification is, fruits are high in nutrition. Choose fresh fruits that are mature, ripe, and high in quality. Fresh fruits should be stored promptly in the refrigerator.

When fresh fruits are not available, choose canned, frozen, and dried fruits. Look for undented cans and solidly frozen packages. Store canned and dried fruits in a cool, dry place. Store frozen fruits in the freezer.

Wash fresh fruits and cut them as desired for serving raw. If necessary, treat cut fruits to prevent enzymatic browning.

Cooking affects the textures, colors, flavors, and nutrients of fruits. Fruit can be cooked in liquid. It can also be baked, broiled, fried, or microwaved.

Serve canned fruits right from the can or drain them to use in recipes. Serve frozen fruits with a few ice crystals on them. Eat dried fruits straight from the package or soak them and cook them.

Review What You Have Read

Write your answers on a separate sheet of paper, using complete sentences when appropriate.

1. List the six fruit families and give one example of each.

2. The citrus fruits are one of the best dietary sources of _____.
    A. vitamin A
    B. the B vitamins
    C. vitamin C
    D. calcium

3. Explain the difference between underripe and immature fruit.

4. When are fresh fruits usually least expensive?

5. Give three guidelines for buying fresh fruit.

6. In what types of liquids are canned fruits packed?

7. What should consumers look for when buying frozen fruits?

8. How should unused portions of dried fruits be stored?

9. Some fruits darken when they are exposed to air. This is called _____.

10. Describe three changes that take place in fruit during cooking.

11. True or false. Fruits will retain their shape if they are cooked in syrup instead of water.

12. Fruits that are dipped in batter and deep-fried are called _____.

13. List three factors that will affect the microwave cooking time of fruit.

14. What is the general guideline for using canned fruits in baked products?

Link to Academic Skills

15. **Geography.** Identify climatic conditions that make various fruit crops economically important in different regions of the United States. In a class discussion, be prepared to tell which state is the leading producer of a specific type of fruit.

16. **English language arts.** Visit the produce section of a grocery store. Note the different varieties of the same fruit in terms of shape, size, and color. Use visual aids to give a presentation of your findings to the class.

17. **Science.** Slice a banana. Place half the slices on a plate and set aside. Dip the remaining slices in lemon juice, place on a plate, and set aside. Compare slices 30 minutes later.

18. **Science.** Observe what happens immediately when you drop a peeled orange and an unpeeled orange into a container of water. Investigate to explain what you observed.

9. enzymatic browning

10. (Describe three:) Cellulose softens and makes fruit easier to digest. Colors change. Heat-sensitive and water-soluble nutrients may be lost. Flavors become less acidic and more mellow.

11. true

Build Critical Thinking Skills

19. **Synthesis.** Sample and compare one type of fruit in all its available forms. For instance, compare fresh peaches with canned peaches, frozen peaches, and dried peaches. Synthesize your findings into a chart describing the differences in flavors, textures, and colors and suggesting ways to serve each form.

20. **Analysis.** Slice an apple into rings. Cook half the slices in sugar syrup and the other half in plain water until tender. Analyze the differences in appearance, texture, and flavor of the two sets of apple rings.

12. fritters

13. (List three:) type of fruit, size, ripeness, moisture content

14. Unless a recipe tells you otherwise, drain canned fruits before using them in baked products.

Apply Technology

21. Choose a specific fruit. Then use the Internet to research where and how your selected fruit is grown and harvested. Make printouts from any websites that provide worthwhile information.

22. Use a computer and the table function of word processing software to make a table listing 10 popular fruits. Columns of the table should identify how many calories and how many micrograms of vitamin A, milligrams of vitamin C, and grams of dietary fiber a serving of each fruit provides. Sort the table in ascending order according to the number of calories per serving and make a printout. Then resort the table in descending order according to the amounts of each of the nutrients and make printouts.

A Measure of Math

23. Choose five types of fresh fruit and record the price per pound of each. Using a precision scale from the science department, weigh each piece of fruit. Remove and weigh the inedible portions, such as peels, cores, and pits. Record both sets of weights. Calculate the percentage of inedible waste in each type of fruit. Then figure the cost per pound of the edible portions.

Teamwork in Action

24. Survey four students from other classes to identify their five favorite fruits. Compile your results with those of your classmates. Make posters illustrating the 10 most popular fruits among students in your school. Conduct research to find out which of these are good or excellent sources of fiber, folate, potassium, vitamin A, and vitamin C. The Daily Values for these nutrients for a 2,000-calorie diet are as follows:
    - fiber — 25 grams
    - folate — 400 micrograms
    - potassium — 3,500 milligrams
    - vitamin A — 5,000 International Units (IU)
    - vitamin C — 60 milligrams

   Remember that good sources are those that contain 10 to 19 percent of the Daily Value per serving. Excellent sources contain 20 percent or more of the Daily Value per serving. Display your posters in the school cafeteria to encourage your schoolmates to make fruit part of their daily diet.

Companion Website

www.g-wlearning.com

At the website, review key terms for this chapter with crossword puzzles, matching exercises, and e-flash cards. Apply facts from the chapter to complete the activities.

CHAPTER 16
Dairy Products

Learning Prep

Look at each of the *Terms to Know*. Which of these terms have you seen on dairy product packages or in recipes calling for dairy products?

Terms to Know

pasteurization
ultra-high temperature
  (UHT) processing
homogenization
milkfat
milk solids
coagulate
curd
whey
unripened cheese

ripened cheese
process cheese
scum
curdling
scorching
white sauce
roux
slurry
bisque
chowder

Main Menu

- Dairy products include a range of foods made from milk, all of which require careful storage to prevent spoilage.
- Care must be taken when cooking with dairy products to ensure desirable results.

Objectives

After studying this chapter, you will be able to

- **list** factors affecting the selection of dairy products.
- **describe** guidelines for preventing adverse reactions when cooking with dairy products.
- **prepare** a variety of dishes using milk, cream, cheese, and other dairy products.

The dairy group of MyPlate consists of foods made from milk that retain their calcium content. Such dairy products include yogurt, cheese, and milk-based desserts. Besides calcium, foods in this group contain high-quality protein, potassium, riboflavin, and vitamins A and D.

Foods like cream cheese, cream, and butter are made from milk and are discussed in this chapter. However, they contain little or no calcium. Therefore, they are not considered part of the dairy group.

All people ages 9 and older need 3 cups (750 mL) from the dairy group each day. Children ages 2 and 3 need 2 cups (500 mL) daily, and ages 4 through 8 need 2½ cups (625 mL). While all dairy products provide calcium, they do not all provide it in the same amounts. When counting foods from the dairy group, count milk and yogurt cup for cup. Cottage cheese and ice cream provide about half as much calcium as equal portions of milk or yogurt. Therefore, count each cup of these foods as half a cup from the dairy group. Also, count 1½ ounces (42 g) of natural cheese or 2 ounces (56 g) of process cheese as 1 cup (250 mL) from the dairy group.

Selecting and Storing Dairy Products

Choose dairy products to use fresh or as ingredients in cooking and baking. Pudding, pizza, and scalloped potatoes are just a few well-liked foods that have dairy ingredients. Dairy products add flavor, texture, and richness as well as nutrients to many foods. Dairy products also help baked goods brown.

©2011 Wisconsin Milk Marketing Board, Inc.

16-1 A glass of milk makes a healthful accompaniment to a meal or snack.

Milk

Milk, both plain and flavored, is a popular beverage, **16-1**. Milk is also an important ingredient in many foods.

Milk Processing

Milk may go through several processes between the dairy farm and the retail store. Milk and dairy products sold in the United States are pasteurized. During pasteurization, milk is heated to destroy harmful bacteria. **Pasteurization** improves the keeping quality of the milk. It does not change the nutritional value or the flavor.

Some milk is treated with **ultra-high temperature (UHT) processing**. This preservation method uses higher temperatures than regular pasteurization to increase the shelf life of foods like milk. After heating, UHT processed milk is sealed in presterilized boxes. Unopened UHT milk products can be stored without refrigeration.

Fresh whole milk is usually homogenized. **Homogenization** is a mechanical process that prevents cream from rising to the surface of milk. This process breaks globules of milkfat into tiny particles and spreads them throughout the milk. Homogenized milk has a richer body and flavor than nonhomogenized milk.

Whole milk is often fortified with vitamin D. Fat-free milk may contain added vitamins A and D. Milk fortified with calcium is available for people who are concerned about getting enough calcium in their diets.

Types of Milk

Each type of milk must meet specific standards for its composition. Whole milk must contain at least 3.25 percent milkfat and 8.25 percent milk solids. **Milkfat** is the fat portion of milk. **Milk solids** contain most of the vitamins, minerals, protein, and sugar found in milk.

All types of milk begin as whole milk. Then the milk is pasteurized. *Reduced fat milk* has some of the fat removed. *Fat-free milk* has nearly all of the fat removed. The less fat milk has, the fewer calories it provides per cup. Milk with added flavoring becomes *flavored milk*, such as chocolate milk.

Cream

Types of cream are defined according to the amount of milkfat they contain. *Heavy whipping cream* has the most fat, followed by light *whipping cream*. Both hold air when whipped, and they are often used in desserts. *Light cream*, or *coffee cream*, has less fat than light whipping cream. It can be used as a table cream and in cooking. *Half-and-half* is made from half milk and half cream. It has the least amount of fat, so it is the lowest in calories.

Yogurt and Other Cultured Dairy Products

A number of dairy products are made from milk to which helpful bacteria have been added. These bacteria are *cultured*, or specially grown for this purpose. Therefore, dairy products to which they are added are called *cultured dairy products*. The bacteria produce lactic acid, which gives these products a thick texture and tangy flavor.

Yogurt is a cultured dairy product. It may contain added nonfat milk solids and flavorings or fruits. An 8-ounce (227 g) serving of yogurt provides a bit more calcium and protein than a cup (250 mL) of milk. The amount of fat in yogurt depends on whether it was made from whole, reduced fat, or fat-free milk. Although yogurt is a nutritious food, fruit-flavored yogurt often contains about 8 teaspoons of added sugar per serving. To limit sugar intake, try stirring fresh fruit and a drizzle of honey into some plain nonfat yogurt.

Other cultured dairy products include buttermilk and sour cream. People use *cultured buttermilk* for cooking and baking as well as drinking. *Regular sour cream* is made from light cream. *Light* and *reduced fat sour cream* have fewer calories than regular sour cream because they have less fat. These sour cream products can all be used interchangeably in most recipes.

Health and Wellness

Lactose Intolerance

Many people have gas, cramps, and diarrhea after drinking milk. They have a condition called *lactose intolerance*. Their bodies cannot produce enough lactase. *Lactase* is the enzyme needed to digest *lactose*—the natural sugar in milk. People with lactose intolerance may choose to buy lactose-reduced milk. This milk has been treated with lactase to break down milk sugar. Calcium-fortified soy milk and rice milk, which are not dairy products, are also options for lactose-intolerant people.

Concentrated Milk Products

Removing water from fluid milk produces concentrated milk products. These products can be canned or dried.

Evaporated milk is sterilized, homogenized whole, reduced fat, or fat-free milk that has had some of the water removed. When diluted with an equal amount of water, it matches fresh milk in nutritional value. It can then be used in place of fluid fresh milk for drinking and in recipes. Evaporated milk costs more than fluid whole milk.

Sweetened condensed milk is whole or fat-free milk with some of the water removed and a sweetener added. It is used most often in cooking and baking. Sugar affects the flavor and texture of cooked and baked products. Therefore, sweetened condensed milk should be used only in recipes that call for it. Sweetened condensed milk cannot be used interchangeably with evaporated milk. It cannot be diluted for use in place of fluid fresh milk, either.

Removing most of the water and fat from whole milk produces *nonfat dry milk*. Nonfat dry milk can be used to add calcium and protein to many foods. It can also be reconstituted and used like fluid milk. When water is added, it costs one-half to two-thirds less than fluid milk.

Frozen Dairy Desserts

Ice cream, frozen yogurt, and sherbet are all frozen dairy desserts. The names of these products used on labels indicate fat content. *Light products* must show at least a 50 percent reduction in fat over regular products. *Fat-free products* must contain less than 0.5 grams of fat per serving.

Butter

Churning pasteurized cream produces butter. The churned product may have salt and/or artificial color added. Some cooks prefer *lightly salted butter* for use at the table and in cooking and *unsalted butter* for baking. However, the two products can usually be used interchangeably. *Whipped butter* is butter that has air whipped into it. It cannot be measured accurately for baking, so it is best used as a table spread. See **16-2**.

Nondairy Products

A few products that look and perform like dairy products contain no dairy ingredients. *Nondairy products* include *coffee whiteners*, *whipped toppings*, and *imitation sour cream*. These products do not contain real cream. They get the body and appearance of dairy products from substances such as soy protein, emulsifiers, and vegetable fats and gums.

Margarine is another nondairy product. Many people use margarine in place of butter. Compared with butter, full margarine contains the same amount of fat and calories.

16-2 The rich taste of butter enhances the flavors of many foods.

However, it contains vegetable oil, animal fat, or some of each rather than milkfat. Most margarine is lower in cholesterol and saturated fat than butter. However, most stick margarine provides *trans* fats. Tub margarines have little or no *trans* fat.

Cost of Dairy Products

National brand dairy products tend to cost more than local brands. In addition, dairy products differ in cost depending on fat content, form, size of container, and place of purchase. Whole milk usually costs more than fat-free milk. Fluid fat-free milk usually costs more than nonfat dry milk. Ounce for ounce (milliliter for milliliter), milk sold in small containers usually costs more than milk sold in large containers. Milk from a delivery service costs more than milk purchased at a store.

The cost of frozen desserts depends on the amount of fat. The kind and amount of extra ingredients, flavorings, and container size also affect cost. Rich ice cream in small containers with many added ingredients costs the most.

The cost of butter depends on form. Whipped butter may cost more than regular butter. Margarine costs less than butter, but prices vary depending on packaging and kind of oil used.

Storing Dairy Products

All dairy products are very perishable. They need careful storage to maintain their flavors and nutrients. Be sure to check the date stamped on product containers when choosing items at the store. Look for products stamped with the latest pull date.

Store dairy products in their original covered containers in the coldest part of the refrigerator or freezer. Keep containers tightly closed to prevent contamination and off flavors. Pour out just the needed amount of fresh milk and cream and return the rest to the refrigerator. If stored properly, dairy products remain wholesome and can be consumed for a few days past the pull date.

Sealed UHT milk products can be stored unrefrigerated for up to six months. Once opened, refrigerate them and use them like other milk products.

Store dried and canned milk products in a cool, dry place. Reseal opened containers of dried milk carefully. Store reconstituted dry milk like fresh milk. Cover the unused portions of canned milk products and store them in the refrigerator. Use them within a few days.

Keeping frozen dairy desserts firmly frozen will protect product texture by preventing large ice crystals from forming. For best quality, use these products within a month. See **16-3**.

Refrigerate all butter and margarine. Freezing will extend the life of both products.

Cheese

Few foods are as versatile as cheese. Its many flavors, textures, and nutrients make it suitable for any meal or snack.

©2011 Wisconsin Milk Marketing Board, Inc.

16-3 Keep ice cream and other frozen dairy desserts tightly covered and firmly frozen to protect their quality.

Cheese is a concentrated form of milk, so it is an excellent source of complete protein. A 1-pound (450 g) package of cheese contains the protein and fat of about 1 gallon (4 L) of whole milk. Cheeses are important sources of calcium and phosphorus. They are fair sources of thiamin and niacin. Whole milk cheeses are excellent sources of vitamin A.

Kinds of Cheese

All cheese is made from milk. The milk used can be from cows, goats, or other animals. In simple terms, the milk is **coagulated**, or thickened into a congealed mass, and the **curd** (solid part) is separated from the **whey** (liquid part). Cheeses made in this way are sometimes called *natural cheeses*.

Using different kinds of milk and changing the basic steps of production can produce hundreds of different cheeses. All these cheeses may be classified in two main groups: unripened and ripened.

Unripened cheeses are ready for marketing as soon as the whey has been removed. They are not allowed to ripen or age. Cottage cheese, cream cheese, farmer's cheese, and ricotta cheese are examples of unripened cheeses. They are mild in flavor.

Controlled amounts of bacteria, mold, yeast, or enzymes are used to make **ripened cheeses**. During ripening, the cheese is stored at a specific temperature to develop texture and flavor. Some cheeses become softer and more tender. Others become hard or crumbly. Over 400 varieties of ripened cheeses are produced. Each has a distinctive flavor, ranging from mild to strong.

Some ripened cheeses require further storage to develop flavor. This process is called aging. Cheese is aged anywhere from two weeks to two years, depending on the kind.

EXPLORING CAREERS

Cheese Maker

Cheese makers follow milk through a process to turn it into cheese. The process involves carefully controlled timing, temperature settings, and ingredients. These factors vary depending on the type of cheese being made.

Successful cheese makers must be able to operate and maintain equipment. They must have the ability to pay attention to details. They will use this skill as they monitor dials and gauges to be sure equipment is working correctly. They will also use this skill to measure ingredients exactly. Cheese makers must have strong sensory perception. They use this quality as they evaluate the taste, texture, and smell of samples to determine when cheese is ready for market.

In terms of formal education, cheese makers may need only high school diplomas. Learning the steps of the cheese-making process may take only a few months of training working with a skilled cheese maker. However, most cheese makers become specialists at making certain kinds of cheese. Masters at this craft may spend years honing their skills to consistently produce the highest quality cheeses.

©2011 Wisconsin Milk Marketing Board, Inc.

Feeling cheese curds with their fingers helps cheese makers determine whether cheese has reached the desired degree of firmness.

Process Cheeses

Natural cheeses can be made into other products called **process cheeses**. Several kinds of process cheese products are available in supermarkets and specialty food shops.

Pasteurized process cheese is made from a blend of unripened and ripened cheeses. The cheeses are heated and an emulsifier is added. The finished product is smooth and creamy. *Pasteurized process cheese food* is similar to pasteurized process cheese, but it contains more moisture and less fat. *Pasteurized process cheese spread* has a stabilizer added. It contains less milkfat and more moisture than cheese food.

Coldpack cheese (club cheese) is made from a mixture of unripened and aged ripened cheeses blended without heat. *Coldpack cheese food* is similar to coldpack cheese. It contains additional dairy products like cream, milk, fat-free milk, or nonfat dry milk.

Imitation cheese has a large portion of the milkfat replaced by vegetable oils. Imitation cheese may differ in texture and melting characteristics from real cheese. These differences may affect the outcome of cooked foods made with imitation cheese.

Cost of Cheese

Money can be saved by buying cheese in large pieces rather than sliced, cubed, shredded, or grated. Fully-ripened cheeses often cost more than unripened cheeses or those that ripen for only a short time. Pasteurized process cheese costs less than ripened cheese. Plain cheese costs less than cheese with added ingredients like nuts and herbs.

Online Resource

Have students visit the American Dairy Association's cheese website. Have each student find information on a different cheese and share what he or she learns about appearance, taste, texture, and recipes with the class.

Academic Connections

Combine your study of the nutritional value of choosing low-fat dairy products with the health department's study of risk factors for heart disease, stroke, and cancer. Emphasize how choosing low-fat and fat-free products easily allows dairy foods to fit into a healthful diet.

Health and Wellness

Making the Low-Fat Choice

Dairy products can add a lot of saturated fat and cholesterol to the diet. These components can raise blood cholesterol, increasing the risk of heart disease. For good health, choose low-fat and fat-free milk products most often. For every gram of fat saved, 9 calories are saved.

An example shows the calorie and fat savings from making healthier dairy choices. Using plain, nonfat yogurt in place of sour cream can save almost 3 grams of fat per tablespoon (15 mL). This difference may seem small, but it can really add up. In a recipe calling for 1 cup (250 mL) of sour cream, 48 grams of fat and 355 calories would be saved. (Larger amounts of carbohydrate and protein in yogurt take up some of the calories saved from fat.)

Low-Fat Dairy Substitutions				
Portion	Whole Milk/ Cream Product	Low-Fat/Nonfat Product	Grams of Fat Saved	Calories Saved
1 cup (250 mL)	whole milk	fat-free milk	8	63
½ cup (125 mL)	regular ice cream	light ice cream	4	20
1 tablespoon (15 mL)	sour cream	plain, nonfat yogurt	3	17
1 ounce (28 g)	Cheddar cheese	low-fat Cheddar cheese	7	65

Low-fat and nonfat dairy products can reduce fat in a health-conscious diet.

Storing Cheese

Cover or tightly wrap all cheese and refrigerate it. This will prevent the cheese from becoming dry. It will also prevent the spread of odors and flavors. Strong-flavored cheeses can flavor other foods. Mild-flavored cheeses can pick up flavors from other foods.

Cheese can become moldy if it is stored improperly or kept too long. A small amount of mold on hard cheese is not harmful. Just cut off the moldy section at least one inch (2.5 cm) into the cheese. Eat the rest of the cheese within a short time. Dispose of hard cheese with large amounts of mold and all moldy soft cheese.

Cooking with Milk and Cream

White sauce, cream soups, puddings, and frozen desserts are popular milk-based foods. Some of these foods may use cream in place of or in addition to milk.

Fresh milk, sour milk, evaporated milk, dried milk, and condensed milk are used in cooking and baking. Evaporated and dried milks may be used in place of fluid, fresh milk when they are mixed with water. Sweetened condensed milk cannot be substituted for other milk products.

Food Science Principles of Cooking with Milk

When milk is used as an ingredient, it is often heated. Heat affects proteins, and milk is a protein food. Understanding principles for cooking milk will help avoid undesirable reactions.

The same cooking principles that apply to milk also apply to cream. Because cream is richer than milk (it contains more milkfat), heat and acids affect it more quickly than milk. Therefore, extra care should be taken when cooking with cream. See **16-4**.

©2011 Wisconsin Milk Marketing Board, Inc.

16-4 Because this soup contains cream, it must be heated carefully to keep its velvety consistency.

Scum Formation

Scum is a solid layer that often forms on the surface of milk during heating. The scum is made up of milk solids and some fat. Because the scum is rubbery and tough, it should be removed. If the scum is stirred into the milk, it will float in small particles throughout the milk.

Scum formation is difficult to prevent. After scum is removed, another layer will form if heating continues. Stirring the milk during heating or covering the pan will help prevent scum formation. Beating the milk with a whisk or rotary beater to form a foam layer will also help prevent scum from forming.

Boiling Over

Scum formation is the usual cause of milk boiling over. Pressure builds up beneath the layer of scum. The scum prevents the pressure from being released as steam. The pressure continues to build until the milk finally boils over. Prevent milk from boiling over by using low heat and one of the methods suggested for preventing a scum layer.

Curdling

High temperatures, acids, tannins, enzymes, and salts can cause milk proteins to coagulate and form clumps. This is called **curdling**, and the clumps are called curds. Foods like oranges and tomatoes contain acids. Many fruits and vegetables contain tannins and enzymes. Brown sugar also contains tannins. Cured ham and other meats contain salts. These substances may cause curdling in cream of tomato soup, creamed green beans, scalloped potatoes and ham, and other milk-based foods.

Curdling can be prevented by using low temperatures and fresh milk. When acid foods are added to milk, either the milk or acid should be thickened first. For example, tomato soup made from thickened milk (or tomato juice) is less likely to curdle than tomato soup made from unthickened milk and juice.

Scorching

Scorching is burning that results in a color change. Scorched milk is brown in color and has an off taste.

Milk can scorch because it contains lactose, which is a type of sugar. Like any sugar, lactose can *caramelize*, or change to a brown, bitter substance called *caramel* when it is heated. When milk is heated, the milk proteins coagulate and settle onto the sides and bottom of the pan. If the milk is overheated, the lactose in the coagulated solids caramelizes, thus scorching the milk.

Scorching can be prevented by using low heat. Heating milk in the top of a double boiler will also help avoid scorching.

Microwaving Milk Products

Use lower settings when microwaving milk and milk products. Higher settings can cause milk to curdle. Also, watch milk carefully, as it can boil over quickly in the microwave oven. Filling containers no more than two-thirds full when microwaving milk products will help avoid this problem. Stirring during the cooking period to prevent scum formation will also help reduce the risk of boiling over.

For Example...
Heat milk to show students what scum formation, boiling over, and scorching look like. Explain how to prevent these undesirable reactions.

For Example...
Pour 1 cup of milk into a 4-cup glass measuring cup. Microwave the milk on high power for 2 minutes as students look through the microwave oven window to observe how the volume of milk increases as it comes to a boil.

Activity
Ask students what foods other than dairy products are good sources of calcium. Have them each write a menu that includes calcium-rich foods for someone who does not like to drink milk. Share and discuss the menus in class.

Food Science

Whipping Properties of Cream

The amount of milkfat affects the volume and stability of whipped cream. Cream must contain at least 25 percent milkfat to whip successfully. However, at least 30 percent milkfat is needed to produce a stable product. More milkfat (up to 40 percent) will produce a product that is still more stable.

When cream is whipped, two changes take place. The first is that air bubbles are incorporated in the cream and a foam forms. The second change is that fat particles in the cream clump together. The clumping of the fat particles produces the stiffness in whipped cream. It also is the first step in churning butter. For this reason, the amount of beating must be carefully controlled. When cream is overbeaten, too much air is incorporated into it. The emulsion around the fat particles breaks, the foam collapses, and the cream turns into butter.

Sugar decreases both the volume and stiffness of whipped cream. It also increases beating time if it is added before the cream has begun to stiffen. If cream is being sweetened, the sugar should be added after the cream has become fairly thick.

©2011 Wisconsin Milk Marketing Board, Inc.

Whipped cream has the best texture and greatest volume if served right after whipping.

Preparing Whipped Cream

For best results when whipping cream, thoroughly chill the bowl, beaters, and cream. The bowl should be large enough to hold the cream after whipping. (Cream doubles or triples in volume during whipping.)

To whip cream, pour the cream into a chilled bowl. Beat it at medium speed until thickening begins. If the cream is being sweetened, gradually start adding sugar at this point. As the sugar is added, increase the beating speed. Continue whipping the cream until it is stiff. Do not overbeat. Serve whipped cream immediately. (If the whipped cream must be held for a short time, refrigerate it promptly.)

Preparing Common Milk-Based Foods

The creamy texture and richness of milk-based foods have made them favorites for generations. Studying basic preparation techniques will allow these popular foods to be included in menu planning.

White Sauce

A **white sauce** is a starch-thickened milk product. It is used as a base for other sauces and as a component in many recipes.

The proportion of starch to milk determines the thickness of white sauce. Use *thin* sauce as the base of cream soups. Use *medium* sauce to cream vegetables and meats and *thick* sauce in soufflés. *Very thick* sauce binds the ingredients in croquettes.

Preparing White Sauce

Classic white sauce is thickened with a **roux**, which is a cooked paste of fat and flour. To prepare it, melt the fat over low heat. Then stir in flour and seasonings to form a paste. Stir milk into the roux. Stir constantly as the mixture cooks over medium heat until it thickens into a smooth sauce.

A slurry can be used as the thickening agent in a fat-free white sauce. A **slurry** is a liquid mixture of milk and flour blended together until smooth. Combine fat-free milk, flour, and seasonings in a blender container or a small, covered jar. Blend or shake until thoroughly mixed. Cook the slurry in a heavy saucepan over medium heat, stirring gently, until it reaches a boil. Cook the slurry for one minute longer until the sauce is smooth and thickened. (This cooking will also prevent a raw starch flavor.)

When preparing a white sauce, take care to prevent scorching and lumping. Using moderate heat will prevent scorching. Using cold milk and thorough blending will separate the starch granules in the flour. This, along with gentle stirring during cooking, will prevent lumping and produce a smooth-textured sauce. See **16-5**.

The principles of preparing white sauce are also used when preparing gravy. Juices from meat or poultry are used in place of some or all of the milk to give gravy flavor. Skim the fat from pan juices remaining after cooking meat or poultry. Stir a slurry into the juices. Cook and stir over medium heat until thickened. To thin or extend gravy, add milk as needed. Season to taste with salt and pepper.

Food Science

Explain to students that melting the butter and mixing it with the flour when making white sauce coats the starch granules in the flour. This separates the starch granules, making it possible for the milk to be added and stirred into a smooth sauce.

Time Management Tip

Use instant flour when making sauces and gravies to prevent lumping. This type of flour is designed to combine quickly and easily with liquids.

Community Interactions

Many teens consume too little calcium. Calcium absorption is also hindered by a high intake of phosphorus—common in a diet that includes a lot of carbonated soft drinks. Develop an ad campaign using posters and announcements on the public address system to encourage your schoolmates to drink more milk and fewer carbonated soft drinks.

Photo courtesy of National Pork Board. For more information about pork, visit TheOtherWhiteMeat.com.

16-5 A smooth white sauce gives this casserole a creamy texture.

Cream Soups

Milk-based soups, often called cream soups, are popular luncheon and supper dishes. The three basic types of cream soups are thickened cream soups, bisques, and chowders. Use a thin white sauce to make thickened cream soups. They contain vegetables, meat, poultry, or fish that is pureed or cut into small pieces. Cream of mushroom and cream of tomato soups are popular thickened cream soups.

Bisques are rich, thickened cream soups. Light cream often replaces all or part of the milk in a bisque. Bisques usually contain shellfish that is shredded or cut into small pieces. **Chowders** are made from unthickened milk. Chowders can contain vegetables, meat, poultry, or fish. (Most chowders contain potatoes, which help add thickness.) A few chowders use tomatoes and water instead of milk. Tomatoes form the base for Manhattan clam chowder, whereas milk forms the base for New England clam chowder.

Preparing Thickened Cream Soups

The first step in preparing thickened cream soups and bisques is to cook the added ingredients. Cook the vegetables, meat, poultry, or fish using only a small amount of liquid. This will help preserve as many of the water-soluble nutrients as possible. The cooking liquid may be used later as part of the liquid in the white sauce.

Many cream soup recipes require that vegetables, meat, poultry, or fish be pureed. Use a blender or sieve to make the puree as smooth as possible. Foods that do not require pureeing should be cut into small pieces.

The second step in making a cream soup is to add the prepared ingredients to a thin white sauce. Season the soup to taste. The soup may be served immediately, or refrigerated and reheated later. Be sure to use low heat when reheating a cream soup to prevent scorching.

Preparing Unthickened Cream Soups

The cooking method used to prepare chowders differs somewhat from the method used to prepare thickened cream soups. Usually, the pieces of vegetables, meat, fish, or poultry are fairly large, and they are cooked in a stock. When they are tender, add the milk to the stock and stir gently until blended. The milk should be added slowly, and the soup should be heated at a low temperature to prevent curdling.

USA Rice Federation

16-6 Cream is thickened with rice and garnished with gingered fruit to make this rich rice pudding.

Puddings

Puddings are thickened milk products usually served as desserts. Cornstarch, tapioca, rice, and bread puddings are popular You may also have tried Indian pudding. All these puddings contain milk and a thickening agent—cornstarch, tapioca, rice, bread, or cornmeal, respectively. In several types of puddings, eggs contribute additional thickening as well as protein. See **16-6**.

Of all the puddings, cornstarch pudding is the most versatile. It can be served alone or used to make fillings for other desserts.

To prepare a basic cornstarch pudding, combine the sugar, salt, and cornstarch in a heavy saucepan and mix well. Add a small amount of the cold milk and stir to make a smooth paste. (These first steps help separate the starch granules to prevent lumps.) Add the remaining milk, stirring constantly.

Cook the pudding over moderate heat, and continue stirring until the pudding boils. Cook for one minute longer to thoroughly cook the starch. Add the flavoring, and pour the pudding into dessert dishes. Chill before serving. A piece of waxed paper placed on the surface of the warm pudding will prevent the formation of a skin.

Ice Cream and Sherbet

Although many people choose to buy ice creams and sherbets, these frozen dairy desserts can be made from a few common ingredients. *Ice cream* contains milk, cream, sugar, and flavoring. Homemade ice cream can be made that is lower in fat. However, it is less creamy than regular ice cream. Simply substitute fat-free milk for the whole milk and whole milk for the cream found in ice cream recipes.

Sherbet contains fruit juices, sugar, and milk. Cooked beaten egg whites, whipped cream, or gelatin can be added to improve the texture of sherbets. The increased sugar in sherbet makes it less creamy than ice cream.

Food Science

Cooking Puddings

All puddings require the use of moderate cooking temperatures to prevent scorching and overcoagulation of the egg and milk proteins. The starch grains must be separated before cooking to prevent lumping. Rice, bread, and Indian puddings are usually placed in a dish of hot water during baking. This provides further protection against the overcoagulation of proteins.

Some old-fashioned pudding recipes call for scalded milk. Scalding means heating to just below the boiling point. In the past, this step was necessary to kill bacteria in unpasteurized milk. Because all commercially purchased milk is now pasteurized, this step can be skipped whenever it is in a recipe.

When eggs are used in pudding, first add a small amount of the hot pudding to the beaten eggs. Then the diluted egg mixture can be added to the rest of the hot pudding. (Eggs added directly to a hot mixture can coagulate into lumps.) Cook the pudding a few minutes longer after adding the eggs to completely cook the egg proteins

Food Science

Preparing Frozen Desserts

Ice cream products and sherbet must be stirred during freezing to achieve a smooth texture. This is because ice crystals form during freezing. Stirring keeps these ice crystals small. Frozen desserts that have small ice crystals taste creamy. Frozen desserts that have large ice crystals taste grainy.

Ice cream products and sherbet can be prepared in an ice cream freezer or in a refrigerator's freezer. In an ice cream freezer, stirring is continuous, so ice crystals remain small. In the refrigerator freezer, stirring is not continuous. Cooked beaten egg whites, whipped cream, whipped evaporated milk, or whipped gelatin may be added to recipes prepared in the refrigerator freezer. These ingredients inhibit the formation of ice crystals.

Cooking with Cheese

Cheeses can be eaten alone or used as ingredients in appetizers, sandwiches, casseroles, sauces, salads, and many other dishes. When used as an ingredient, cheese contributes proteins, vitamins, minerals, and flavor to other foods.

Preparing Cheese Dishes

Cheese is often combined with liquids in sauces and soups cooked on a surface unit. Cook these foods over low heat or in the top of a double boiler. The temperature must be hot enough to melt the fat so the cheese will blend smoothly. However, it must be low enough to prevent toughening of the proteins.

Cheeses that are well ripened blend more easily than less well-ripened cheeses. Well-ripened cheeses also tolerate higher temperatures.

Cheese that is grated, shredded, or cut into small pieces will blend more quickly than cheese cut into large chunks. As a result, a shorter cooking time can be used.

Process cheese blends more easily than natural cheese because of the emulsifiers it contains. A cheese sauce made with process cheese is smooth and less likely to curdle. In comparison, a cheese sauce made with natural Cheddar cheese has a grainier texture, although the cheese flavor is more pronounced.

Cheese dishes prepared in an oven or under a broiler should be cooked just until done. Place cheese-containing foods, such as sandwiches and appetizers, four to five inches (10 to 12 cm) from broiler heat. Watch food carefully while broiling. Remove food from the broiler when the cheese has melted.

Food Science

Effects of Heat on Cheese

Cheese is a concentrated form of milk. Therefore, it is a high-protein food. Like all high-protein foods, heat can adversely affect cheese. If cheese is cooked at too high a temperature or for too long a time, its proteins overcoagulate. As a result, the cheese becomes tough and rubbery and the fat in the cheese may separate.

©2011 Wisconsin Milk Marketing Board, Inc.

Baked foods containing cheese should stay in the oven just long enough to thoroughly heat the ingredients and melt the cheese.

Microwaving Cheese

Cheese requires careful timing and the use of low settings when it is being cooked in a microwave oven. Cooking for too long or at too high a power level can cause cheese to separate and become rubbery. All cheeses microwave well, but some cheeses have better melting qualities than others.

Discuss

People on weight-loss diets often say cheese is the most difficult food to give up. Ask students how cheese can be included in a low-fat diet. *(Limit*

CAREER SUCCESS

Using Staff Management Skills

Dan is a supervisor at Simons and Son Dairy Farm. He oversees a staff of four farm workers as they attend to the property and a large herd of cows. The workers handle daily chores, like milking and feeding cows. They are also responsible for seasonal and occasional jobs, like planting feed corn and mending fences. Dan needs to be sure the workers do all the critical tasks before the tanker comes for the daily milk pickup.

To be an effective worker, Dan needs skill in managing staff. In a small group, answer the following questions about Dan's need for and use of this skill:

A. Can Dan simply let the farm workers choose what tasks they want to do each day? Explain your answer.

B. How might the farm workers respond if the workdays constantly shift between periods of too little and too much work?

C. How might Simons and Son be affected if Dan lacks skill in managing staff?

D. What is another skill Dan would need in this job? Briefly explain why this skill would be important.

portion sizes. Choose reduced-fat cheeses.)

CHAPTER 16 REVIEW

Answer Key to *Review What You Have Read* **questions**

1. pasteurization
2. C
3. (List three:) yogurt, cultured buttermilk, sour cream, light sour cream, reduced fat sour cream
4. false
5. false
6. for up to six months
7. Ripened cheeses contain controlled amounts of bacteria, mold, yeast, or enzymes and are stored at specific temperatures to develop texture and flavor. Unripened cheeses are ready for marketing as soon as the whey has been removed.
8. true
9. You can prevent milk from curdling by using low temperatures and fresh milk and by thickening either the milk or the acid before combining milk with an acid food.
10. Gradually start adding sugar after the cream begins to thicken.

Summary

Dairy products include a wide range of popular foods, such as milk, cream, yogurt, ice cream, butter, and cheese. Many dairy foods are good sources of protein and calcium as well as a number of vitamins and other minerals. The cost of dairy products varies depending on fat content, container size, brand, and place of purchase. All fresh and frozen dairy products are perishable and require storage in the coldest part of the refrigerator or freezer. Canned products must be stored like fresh products once they have been opened. Dried products should be stored like fresh products after they have been reconstituted.

Cream and whole milk dairy products are high in fat. Choosing reduced fat and fat-free milk versions of dairy products can help reduce fat and calories.

Milk can form a scum layer, boil over, scorch, and curdle during cooking. Steps can be taken to help prevent these negative reactions.

Many recipes call for dairy products as ingredients. White sauces, cream soups, puddings, and frozen desserts are just a few of the foods that contain milk. When preparing these foods, remember to use moderate temperatures to prevent scorching and overcoagulating the proteins. Use moderate temperatures when cooking with cheese. This will help keep the cheese from becoming tough and rubbery and prevent the fat from separating.

Review What You Have Read

Write your answers on a separate sheet of paper, using complete sentences when appropriate.

1. The process of heating milk to destroy harmful bacteria is called _____.
2. Which of the following types of cream has the most milkfat?
   A. Coffee cream.
   B. Half-and-half.
   C. Heavy whipping cream.
   D. Light whipping cream.
3. Name three types of cultured dairy products.
4. True or false. Evaporated milk and sweetened condensed milk can be used interchangeably in recipes.
5. True or false. Margarine is a dairy product.
6. How long can sealed UHT milk products be stored without refrigeration?
7. Describe the difference between ripened and unripened cheeses.
8. True or false. A small amount of mold on hard cheese is not harmful.
9. How can you prevent milk from curdling during cooking?
10. If whipped cream is to be sweetened, when should the sugar be added?

(continued)

11. List four food products that are made with a white sauce.

12. In what type of cream soup might cream be used in place of milk?

13. How can you protect rice, bread, and Indian puddings against the overcoagulation of milk and egg proteins during baking?

14. Why is it important to stir sherbets and ice creams during freezing?

15. What are two factors that affect how easily cheese blends with other ingredients during cooking?

Link to Academic Skills

16. **Geography.** Name three animals other than cows that provide milk for some of the world's people. Identify a country in which each of these animals is used for milk. What factors contribute to the use of milk from these animals instead of or in addition to cow's milk in these countries?

17. **Social studies.** Research the prevalence of lactose intolerance in various population groups. Share your findings in class.

18. **English language arts.** Sample a variety of 10 cheeses. Be sure to choose some you have not tried before. Write a sentence describing the flavor and texture of each. Then write a paragraph describing how you would use one of the cheeses for eating and cooking.

19. **Science.** Pour 1 cup of whipping cream into a clean plastic jar. Add a clean marble to the jar and cover tightly with a lid. Working in a group, take turns shaking the jar for 30 seconds each and then passing the jar to the next group member. Note when you can no longer hear the clatter of the marble. What does this indicate? Continue shaking your jar past this point until you again hear the clatter of the marble. What does this indicate? What does this activity tell you about preparing whipped cream?

Build Critical Thinking Skills

20. **Analysis.** Set up a tasting panel. Compare the tastes and mouthfeel of whole milk, reduced fat milk, fat-free milk, cultured buttermilk, and reconstituted nonfat dry milk. Analyze the factors that contribute to the differences in flavors and textures among the products.

21. **Evaluation.** Whip heavy cream using the following methods:
    A. Chill bowl and beaters. Whip cream and sugar until stiff.
    B. Have bowl and beaters at room temperature. Whip cream until it begins to thicken. Add sugar slowly. Continue beating until stiff.
    C. Chill bowl and beaters. Whip cream until it begins to thicken. Add sugar slowly. Continue beating until stiff.
    Evaluate the beating time, appearance, volume, and stability of each sample.

11. (List four:) other sauces, cream soups, creamed vegetables, creamed meats, soufflés, croquettes

12. Cream might be used in place of milk in a bisque.

13. You can place rice, bread, and Indian puddings in a dish of hot water during baking to protect against the overcoagulation of milk and egg proteins.

14. It is important to stir sherbets and ice creams during freezing to keep the ice crystals that form small so the frozen desserts will have a smooth and creamy texture.

15. (List two:) cooking temperature, amount of ripening, size of pieces, whether cheese is process or natural

Apply Technology

22. Research how ultra-high temperature pasteurization and aseptic packaging are used to extend the shelf life of milk. Prepare a poster illustrating the pasteurization and packaging processes.

23. Choose one of four groups of dairy foods: fluid milk, cultured dairy products, frozen dairy desserts, or cheese. Using the website for the National Nutrient Database, find the calorie, protein, calcium, saturated fat, total fat, and cholesterol content for three products in your chosen group. One product should be full fat, one should be reduced fat, and one should be fat free. Also find this information for a similar nondairy item that might be used by someone following a vegan diet. Enter your findings into a chart program on a computer to make bar graphs comparing the four products for each nutrient factor. Assemble printouts of the bar graphs with a brief summary report. The report should explain what the graphs indicate about the nutritional value of including low-fat dairy products in the diet.

A Measure of Math

24. A pound of cheese yields 4 cups of shredded cheese. Calculate how many ounces of cheese you would need to buy for a recipe that calls for 1½ cups of shredded cheese.

25. Compute and compare the unit costs of the same brand and variety of block and shredded cheeses. Also compute and compare the unit costs of the same brand of ripened cheese, unripened cheese, and pasteurized process cheese.

Teamwork in Action

26. Conduct research to help you design a health pamphlet for women about the links among calcium, menopause, and osteoporosis. Make the pamphlets available at your local library or community center.

Companion Website

www.g-wlearning.com

At the website, review key terms for this chapter with crossword puzzles, matching exercises, and e-flash cards. Apply facts from the chapter to complete the activities.

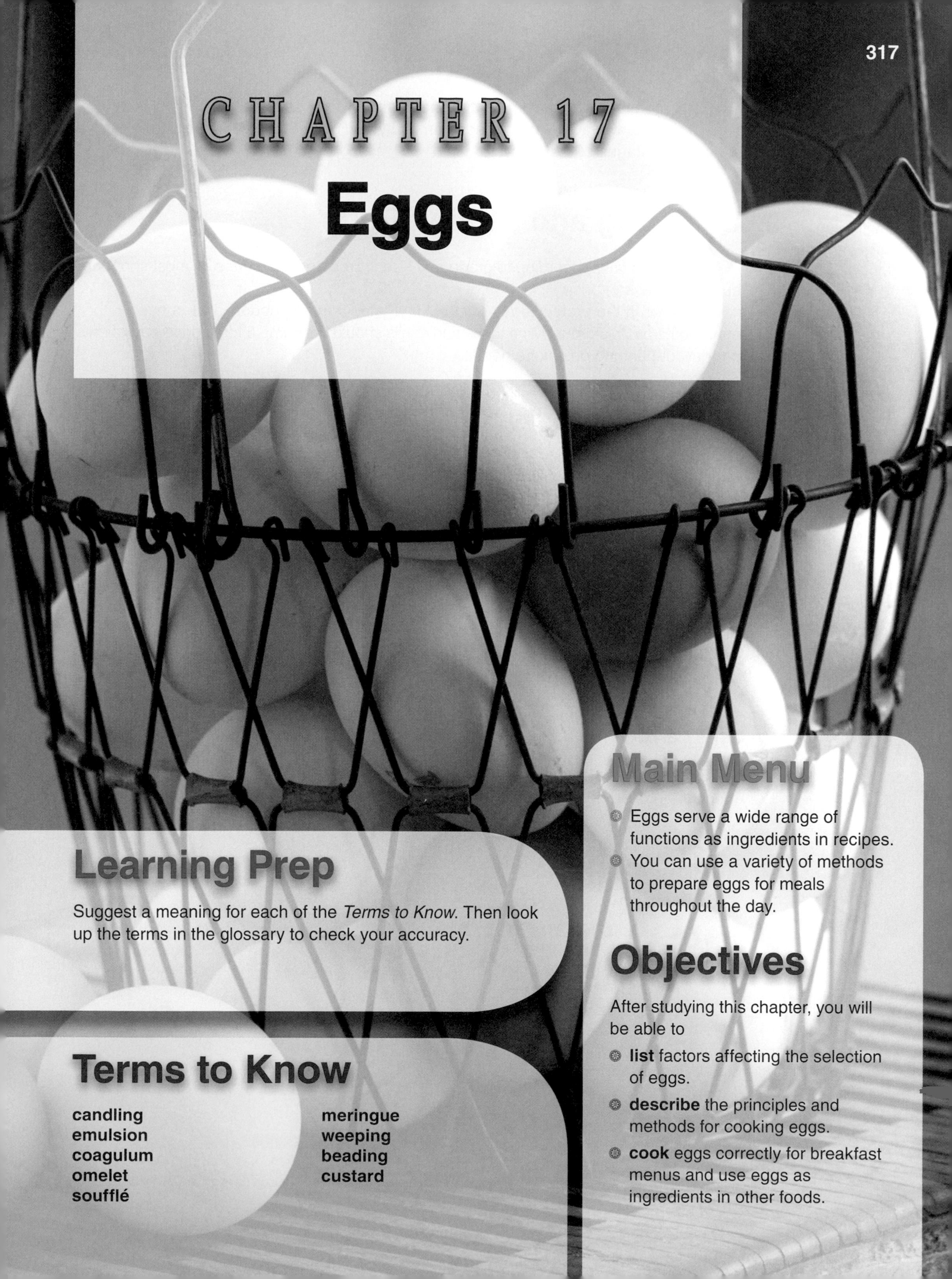

CHAPTER 17
Eggs

Learning Prep

Suggest a meaning for each of the *Terms to Know*. Then look up the terms in the glossary to check your accuracy.

Terms to Know

candling
emulsion
coagulum
omelet
soufflé

meringue
weeping
beading
custard

Main Menu

- Eggs serve a wide range of functions as ingredients in recipes.
- You can use a variety of methods to prepare eggs for meals throughout the day.

Objectives

After studying this chapter, you will be able to

- **list** factors affecting the selection of eggs.
- **describe** the principles and methods for cooking eggs.
- **cook** eggs correctly for breakfast menus and use eggs as ingredients in other foods.

Eggs are one of the most versatile and nutritious food sources. They can be prepared in many ways. Because eggs are easy to digest, they can be served to people at nearly all stages of the life cycle.

Selecting and Storing Eggs

Egg prices vary according to grade and size. Large eggs are the size most shoppers buy, regardless of price.

Eggs are in the protein foods group of MyPlate. One egg counts as 1 ounce-equivalent from this group. Most teens and adults should consume 5 to 7 ounce-equivalents per day, depending on calorie needs.

Egg Grades

Eggs for retail sale are graded for quality. **Candling** is a process by which eggs are quality-graded. The eggs move along rollers over bright lights. The lights illuminate the structure of the eggs. Skilled people can then look at the eggs carefully and remove any that do not meet standards.

Look for grade shields on egg cartons or on the tape that seals the cartons. The two grades of eggs available in most supermarkets are U.S. Grade AA and U.S. Grade A. These grades are given to high-quality eggs that have clean, unbroken shells and small air cells. The egg whites are thick and clear, and the yolks are firm and stand high above the whites.

Some eggs are rated Grade B, but these eggs are rarely seen in food stores. They are usually used in other food products.

Egg Size

Eggs are sized on the basis of an average weight per dozen. Extra large, large, and medium eggs are the most common sizes sold. Size has no relation to quality, however,

Health and Wellness

Nutrients in Eggs
Eggs are one of the best sources of complete protein. They also contain a number of vitamins and minerals. Egg yolks are high in cholesterol. Therefore, many health experts recommend using egg yolks and whole eggs with moderation. However, egg whites are cholesterol free, so they can be used freely.

Lodge Cast Iron

Eggs are rich in protein, iron, riboflavin, and vitamin A.

size does affect price. Eggs of any size can be Grade AA, A, or B. Extra large eggs cost more than large eggs, and large eggs cost more than medium eggs. Most recipes are formulated to use large eggs.

Storing Eggs

Buy eggs only from refrigerated cases. Check to be sure eggs are clean and uncracked before buying them. Cracked eggs can contain harmful bacteria, which can cause foodborne illness. Discard any eggs that become cracked or broken during transportation or storage.

Store eggs in the refrigerator as soon as they are brought home from the store. Store eggs, large end up, in their original carton. Keep them in the main compartment of the refrigerator, not on the refrigerator door, which does not stay as cold. Fresh eggs may be safely stored in the refrigerator for three to five weeks.

Some recipes call only for egg yolks or egg whites. To store leftover yolks, cover them with cold water and refrigerate in a tightly covered container. Store leftover egg whites in the refrigerator in a tightly covered container, too. Use yolks within one or two days. Use whites within four days.

Eggs as Ingredients

When eggs are used as ingredients in other food products, they contribute a number of qualities. Eggs add important nutrients to many dishes. Eggs lend flavor to foods such as custards. Eggs also give an appealing golden color to light colored foods.

In addition to these qualities, eggs serve a number of functions as ingredients. For instance, eggs add structure to baked products, such as quick breads and cakes. The heat of the oven coagulates (thickens) the egg proteins. This helps create a framework around the air cells that form in baked goods as they rise. Eggs also function as thickeners, binding agents, interfering agents, foaming agents, and emulsifiers.

Thickeners

Heat causes egg proteins to coagulate. Thus whole eggs and egg yolks can be used as thickening agents. They give foods like sauces and puddings a smooth texture.

Recipes thickened with eggs sometimes require the eggs to be added to a hot mixture. To do this, quickly but gently blend a small amount of the hot mixture into beaten eggs. Then, add the warmed eggs to the rest of the hot mixture. Warming the eggs in this way is called *tempering*. Tempering keeps the eggs from coagulating into lumps.

Binding and Interfering Agents

As the heat of cooking sets liquid eggs into a solid state, eggs act as binding agents. They hold together the ingredients in foods such as meatballs. They also bind crumb coatings to foods like breaded chicken breasts. See **17-1**.

Ice cream stays creamy because the eggs in it act as interfering agents. The eggs inhibit the formation of large ice crystals, which would ruin the texture of ice cream.

Photo courtesy of The Beef Checkoff www.BeefItsWhatsForDinner.com

17-1 Eggs act as a binding agent to hold the ingredients in meatballs together.

Foaming Agents

Eggs are used as foaming agents to add air to foods. Foams are used to make soft and hard meringues. They are also used to give structure to angel food and sponge cakes, soufflés, and puffy omelets.

Egg foams are prepared by beating air into egg whites, which causes many air cells to form. A thin film of egg white protein surrounds each cell. As beating continues, the cells become smaller and more numerous. The protein film also becomes thinner. As a result, the foam thickens.

EXPLORING CAREERS

Food Science Technician

Food science technicians work with food scientists and technologists. They might help to develop new food products. They may also get involved with food product manufacturing. This work may require testing food products and ingredients to be sure they meet standards for factors like color, texture, and nutrients. It may entail mixing and sampling products to evaluate qualities such as taste and smell. Using and cleaning lab equipment may be part of this job, too.

To be successful, food science technicians need a strong background in math and science and good analytical skills to record and assess test results and prepare reports of findings. They must be dependable, so others can count on them to complete their assigned tasks. The abilities to work well with others, deal with stress in the workplace, and accept criticism from supervisors are other qualities food science technicians should have.

A range of math classes as well as chemistry and biology can help prepare someone for this career area. Knowing how food is grown, harvested, and manufactured is also part of a good foundation for going into this field. Most food science technicians need to earn an associate's degree. However, they will gain much specific knowledge and skill on the job as they work with experienced professionals.

Food Science

Factors Affecting Egg Foams

Temperature, beating time, fat, acid, and sugar affect the formation of egg white foams. When preparing egg foams, two temperatures are needed. Eggs separate most easily when they are cold. However, egg whites reach maximum volume when they are at room temperature. Use an egg separator to separate whites from yolks when the eggs are taken from the refrigerator. Then let the egg whites stand at room temperature for 30 minutes before beating them. Store leftover yolks.

Avoid both too little and too much beating time when preparing egg foams. Too little beating time produces underbeaten egg whites, which lose volume quickly and do not hold their shape. Too much beating time produces overbeaten egg whites, which also lose volume quickly. In addition, overbeaten egg whites have little elasticity and will break down into curds.

Fat and fat-containing ingredients, such as egg yolk, interfere with the formation of egg white foams. Plastic bowls may hold traces of fat residues. Therefore, use clean glass or metal bowls and beaters when beating egg whites.

Acid makes egg white foams more stable. It also adds whiteness. This is why many recipes that use egg white foams call for a small amount of cream of tartar.

Sugar increases the stability of egg white foam. It also increases beating time. It is usually best to add sugar to the foam after it has reached most of the volume.

©Courtesy of California Tree Fruit Agreement

Cream of tartar and sugar add to the stability of the egg white foam in this meringue shell.

Recipes often direct that egg whites are beaten to one of three stages: foamy, soft peak, or stiff peak. Each stage requires increased beating time. Egg whites at the *foamy stage* have bubbles and foam on the surface. Egg whites beaten to the *soft peak stage* will form peaks that bend at the tips when the beater is lifted. Egg whites beaten to the *stiff peak stage* will form peaks that stand up straight when the beater is lifted. If egg whites are beaten past the stiff peak stage, they have been overbeaten.

When using egg foams in recipes, other ingredients are often beaten into the foams. To avoid a loss of air, this must be done quickly and gently using a process called *folding*. Wire whisks and flexible spatulas are the best tools for folding. Using either tool, cut down into the mixture, across the bottom, up the opposite side, and across the top. The whisk or spatula should remain in the mixture the entire time folding is being done.

Emulsifiers

An **emulsion** is a mixture that forms when liquids are combined that ordinarily do not mix. (Oil and water or a water-based liquid, such as lemon juice, are commonly combined to form an emulsion.) To keep the two liquids from separating, an *emulsifying agent* is needed. Egg yolk is an excellent emulsifying agent. The yolk surrounds the oil

Discuss

Ask students what would happen if they beat egg whites in a bowl that had been used to beat egg yolks. *(The egg whites would not foam well due to fat remaining in the bowl from the yolks.)*

Academic Connections

Ask a chemistry teacher to discuss the chemical structures of oils, water-based liquids, and emulsifying agents.

droplets in an emulsion. It keeps the droplets suspended in the water-based liquid so the two liquids will not separate. Mayonnaise is an example of this type of emulsion.

Methods of Cooking Eggs

Eggs can be fried, scrambled, poached, baked, soft-cooked, or hard-cooked. They can be used to prepare plain and puffy omelets, soufflés, soft and hard meringues, and stirred and baked custards, too.

In all methods of cooking eggs, low to moderate temperatures and accurate cooking times are important. Eggs coagulate when heated during cooking. (Egg white coagulates at a slightly lower temperature than egg yolk. This is why the whites will become set before the yolks during cooking.) Temperature and time affect coagulation. High temperatures and long cooking times can cause egg proteins to lose moisture, shrink, and toughen.

When frying or scrambling eggs, use a little fat or a nonstick skillet sprayed with cooking spray. Using a cool pan allows the egg white to spread too far before it sets. Therefore, heat a skillet and any cooking fat over medium heat before placing the eggs in it. The skillet is hot enough if a drop of water sizzles when it hits the surface of the pan. As soon as the eggs are in the skillet, turn the heat down to low. Cooking temperatures that are too high quickly toughen egg proteins.

Frying Eggs

To fry an egg, add the egg to a moderately hot skillet containing vegetable oil spray or a small amount of fat about 1 teaspoon (5 mL) per egg. A little water may be added to the skillet, too. Cover the skillet and cook the egg until the white is completely set and the yolk begins to thicken. The steam that forms in the covered skillet will cook the upper surface of the egg. The upper surface can also be cooked by gently turning the egg over.

Scrambling Eggs

To scramble eggs, break the eggs into a bowl. Beat the eggs with a fork or whisk until blended. Add about 1 tablespoon (15 mL) of milk or water per egg. Avoid using too much liquid, which will cause the eggs to be watery. For variety, add bits of cooked bacon or finely chopped chives to eggs before scrambling.

Pour the egg mixture into a lightly greased or nonstick heated skillet. When the egg begins to set, draw a bent-edged spatula across the bottom of the skillet. This will allow more of the liquid egg mixture to come in contact with the hot surface of the skillet. The egg will thicken into soft protein clumps, which are called **coagulum**. Gently continue drawing the spatula across the skillet until all the egg mixture has set. However, avoid constant stirring. Too much stirring will cause the coagulum to be small.

Health and Wellness

Thoroughly Cooking Eggs

Safely cooked eggs have completely set whites and thickened yolks. Yolks do not need to be hard, but they should not be runny.

Dishes made with beaten eggs are thoroughly cooked when they no longer contain any visible liquid egg. The most accurate way to test the doneness of casseroles, soufflés, and other egg dishes is with a food thermometer. These dishes should reach the safe internal temperature of 160°F (71°C).

Poaching Eggs

Eggs can be poached in water, milk, broth, or some other liquid. If using water, a small amount of salt or acid (such as vinegar) may be added. This will cause the proteins to coagulate faster and help keep the egg from spreading.

To poach an egg, break the egg into a custard cup. Slip the egg into a saucepan filled with 2 to 3 inches (5 to 7.5 cm) of simmering liquid. Cook the egg until the white is firm and the yolk is thickened. This will take about three to five minutes. Remove the egg from the cooking liquid with a slotted spoon.

Baking Eggs

Baked eggs are also called *shirred eggs*. To bake an egg, break the egg into a greased custard cup. Then put the custard cup in a shallow casserole filled with 1 inch (2.5 cm) of warm water. Bake the egg in a 350°F (175°C) oven for 12 to 18 minutes, depending on the firmness desired. Try adding variety to baked eggs by sprinkling them with finely chopped green pepper and onion or grated cheese.

Cooking Eggs in the Shell

Eggs cooked in the shell can be soft-cooked or hard-cooked, **17-2**. Time determines the degree of doneness.

To prepare soft-cooked eggs, place the eggs in a deep pan. Add enough cold water to come 1 inch (2.5 cm) above the eggs. Cover the pan and quickly bring the water to a boil. Immediately remove the pan from the heat. Let the eggs remain in the water for four to five minutes, depending on the desired degree of doneness.

To prepare hard-cooked eggs, use the same method used for soft-cooked eggs, but keep the eggs in the water longer. Large eggs will take about 15 minutes. Medium eggs will take only about 12 minutes. Extra large eggs may take about 18 minutes.

Immediately cool soft- and hard-cooked eggs under cold running water or place them in a bowl of ice water. Rapid cooling stops the eggs from cooking and prevents the formation of greenish rings around the yolks. A chemical reaction between iron in egg yolk and hydrogen sulfide in egg white causes this discoloration in overcooked eggs. The discoloration is harmless, but it looks unappetizing.

When soft-cooked eggs are cool enough to handle, they are ready to eat. A popular way to eat them is to place them in eggcups, small end down. Cut off the large end of the egg and eat the egg out of the shell.

Food Science

For

Effects of Added Ingredients on Eggs

The addition of other ingredients changes the coagulation temperature of eggs. For instance, adding milk to eggs dilutes the egg proteins. This raises the coagulation temperature. That is why eggs scrambled with added milk will take longer to set than eggs scrambled without milk. On the other hand, acid and salt both lower the coagulation temperature of eggs. Therefore, eggs poached in water containing vinegar (an acid) or added salt will set faster than eggs poached in plain water.

Example...

Hard-cooked eggs are used to make deviled, pickled, and Scotch eggs; egg, potato, and macaroni salads; and eggs goldenrod.

Rubbermaid

17-2 Hard-cooked eggs are used to make deviled eggs.

Learn About...

Egg Substitutes

Egg substitutes provide an option for people who want to limit cholesterol and saturated fat from eggs in their diets. Egg substitutes are pasteurized. Therefore, they can be used in place of raw eggs in recipes that will not be cooked.

Egg substitutes are made largely from real egg whites. They contain no egg yolks. Therefore, these products are cholesterol-free, fat-free, and lower in calories than whole eggs. They compare closely to whole eggs in most other nutrient values. However, they may cost over three times as much as fresh eggs.

Egg substitutes are nearly as versatile as whole eggs. They can be scrambled or used to prepare omelets or quiches. They can also be used in most recipes calling for eggs. Typically, ¼ cup (50 mL) of egg substitute can be used in place of each whole egg or egg yolk. Egg substitutes can even be used to make egg salad and other recipes that call for chopped hard-cooked eggs.

Reflect

Ask students if they have ever tasted food made with egg substitutes. How did they think it compared with its fresh egg counterpart?

Discuss

Ask students what kinds of ingredients might be used to fill an omelet. *(cheese, onions, green peppers, ham, tomatoes, mushrooms)*

FYI

Bake a soufflé in a straight-sided casserole or use ramekins to make individual soufflés. Prepare the baking dish by buttering the bottom and sides. Dust the buttered surfaces with grated Parmesan cheese when making a savory soufflé. Dust the surfaces with sugar for a dessert soufflé.

When hard-cooked eggs are cooled, store them in the refrigerator. They can be kept for up to one week. Do not eat hard-cooked eggs, or any other perishable food, kept at room temperature for over two hours.

Omelets

Omelets are beaten egg mixtures that are cooked without stirring and served folded in half. Omelets can be plain (also called French) or puffy. Both types of omelets can be made from eggs, a small amount of liquid (usually milk or water), and seasonings. An omelet may be served with or without a filling.

To make a plain omelet, beat together the eggs, liquid, and seasonings. Pour the mixture into a lightly greased or nonstick heated skillet or omelet pan. The edges of the egg mixture should set immediately. With a wide spatula, gently lift the cooked edges to allow the uncooked egg to run underneath. Tilting the skillet will help. The omelet is ready to fill and serve when the top has set but is still moist.

To make a puffy omelet, beat the egg whites with cream of tartar and water until stiff (but not dry) peaks form. Beat the egg yolks with salt and pepper until they are thick and lemon colored. Gently fold the beaten yolks into the beaten whites. Pour the mixture into a lightly greased ovenproof skillet that is hot enough to sizzle a drop of water. Cook the omelet slowly over medium heat until puffy, about 5 minutes. (The bottom should be lightly brown.) Place the omelet in a preheated 350°F (175°C) oven. Bake it 10 to 12 minutes, or until a knife inserted near the center comes out clean. See **17-3**.

Soufflés

Soufflés are fluffy baked preparations made with a starch-thickened sauce that is folded into stiffly beaten egg whites. Like puffy omelets, they use egg whites for structure. Soufflés can be served as a main dish or for dessert.

To prepare a soufflé, add beaten egg yolks to a basic white sauce. The white sauce may contain chocolate, fruit, cheese, or pureed vegetables or seafood. Gently fold the white sauce mixture into the beaten egg whites. Bake the soufflé in a 350°F (175°C) oven until puffy and golden, about 30 to 40 minutes. Serve the soufflé immediately.

Photograph provided courtesy of the California Strawberry Commission. ©2010 California Strawberry Commission. All rights reserved.

17-3 This puffy omelet is filled with ripe, red strawberries and dusted with powdered sugar.

Meringues

Meringues are a fluffy, white mixture of beaten egg whites and sugar. Meringues may be soft or hard. Use soft meringues in fruit whips and as toppings on pies and other baked goods like Baked Alaska. Use hard meringues to make meringue shells, which can be filled and served as desserts. Hard meringues can also be used to make confections, such as meringue cookies.

Make soft meringues from egg whites, cream of tartar, sugar, and flavoring. Beat the egg whites and cream of tartar to the foamy stage. Add the sugar gradually as the egg whites are beaten to the upper limit of the soft peak stage. When no undissolved sugar is felt when a small amount of meringue is rubbed between the thumb and forefinger, beat in the flavoring.

When using a soft meringue on a pie, spread it over hot pie filling. Carefully seal the meringue to the edge of the pastry. These important steps will help minimize weeping and beading. **Weeping** is the layer of moisture that sometimes forms between a meringue and a filling. **Beading** appears as golden droplets on the surface of a meringue. Bake the meringue-topped pie at 350°F (175°C) until lightly browned, about 12 to 15 minutes.

Hard meringues are made from the same ingredients as soft meringues. However, they contain a higher proportion of sugar, and they are beaten to the stiff peak stage. Hard meringues are usually shaped with a spoon and baked on an oiled or paper-covered baking sheet. Bake hard meringues at 225°F (105°C) for one to one and a half hours. Then turn off the oven and allow the meringues to stand in the oven with the door closed for another hour. This will produce a meringue with a crisp, dry interior.

FYI

Eggs are the only thickening agent in some food products, such as custards. In other food products, such as sauces and puddings, both eggs and starch are used as thickening agents.

Custards

Custards are a mixture of milk (or cream), eggs, sugar, and a flavoring that is cooked until thickened. Custards can be soft (sometimes called stirred) or baked. Soft custard may be served as a dessert sauce. It can also be used as the base for desserts like English trifle. Serve baked custard plain or with a topping of caramel, fruit, or toasted coconut. Bread pudding can be made by pouring custard over bread cubes before baking.

Stir soft custard constantly as it cooks. This breaks up the coagulum as it forms, giving the custard a creamy texture. Be sure to use low heat to prevent *curdling* (the formation of lumps). Soft custard will coat a metal spoon with a thin film when it is fully cooked. Place the pan of cooked custard in a bowl of ice or cold water. Stir the custard for a few minutes to cool it before covering and storing in the refrigerator.

Lack of stirring causes baked custard to become firm enough to hold its shape when removed from the baking dish. Place dishes of custard in a large baking pan. Place the pan in a preheated oven. Then pour very hot water into the pan around the custard dishes. The water should come within ½ inch (1 cm) of the top of the custard. The water helps prevent the custard from overheating, which can result in *syneresis* (the leakage of liquid from a gel). Overbaked custard will have visible bubbles and leakage. To test baked custard for doneness, insert the tip of a knife near the center. If the knife comes out clean, the custard is baked.

Health and Wellness

Using Raw Eggs

The risk of foodborne illness due to contaminated eggs is small, especially for healthy people. However, it is safest not to use raw eggs in any dish that is not thoroughly cooked. If a recipe calls for whole eggs, use a pasteurized egg product. A recipe that calls for separated eggs requires some special preparation steps.

Instead of using raw beaten egg whites in an uncooked dish, cook the whites. Using a specific technique, beat the egg whites into a fluffy frosting before adding them to a recipe. Combine the egg whites with the sugar from the recipe in a heavy saucepan or double boiler. (At least 2 tablespoons [30 mL] of sugar are needed per egg white.) Cook the mixture over low heat while beating it to the soft peak stage with an electric mixer.

Instead of adding raw egg yolks to a recipe, cook them as they would be cooked for making stirred custard. Combine the yolks with the liquid from the recipe in a heavy saucepan. (At least 2 tablespoons [30 mL] of liquid is needed per yolk.) Cook the mixture over low heat, stirring constantly until the mixture coats a metal spoon. Cool the mixture quickly and add it to the recipe when the egg yolks would be added.

Another option when preparing uncooked or lightly cooked recipes that call for raw eggs is to use pasteurized shell eggs. These are whole eggs that have been treated using the same heating process used to kill harmful bacteria in milk. This process does not affect the taste or cooking performance of the eggs.

Shutterstock

To avoid risk of foodborne illness, any recipe calling for raw eggs should be thoroughly cooked before it is eaten.

CAREER SUCCESS

Decision-Making

Deborah is an egg candler for M-G Farms. She inspects eggs as they move along rollers over bright lights. The lights allow her to see the structure of the eggs and evaluate their quality. She separates the eggs by grade. Grades AA and A are sold to supermarkets. Grade B eggs are sold to food product manufacturers.

To be a successful employee, Deborah needs skill in making decisions. Put yourself in Deborah's place and answer the following questions about your need for and use of this skill:

A. What is a decision you will make every day as an egg candler?

B. How might M-G Farms be affected if you do not have adequate skills in making decisions?

C. How might consumers be affected if you do not have adequate skills in making decisions?

D. What is a another skill you would need in this job? Briefly explain why this skill would be important.

CHAPTER 17 REVIEW

Answer Key for
Review What You Have Read **questions**

1. Candling is used in the egg industry to grade eggs for quality.

2. three to five weeks

3. Quickly but gently blend a small amount of the hot mixture into the beaten eggs. Then add the warmed eggs to the rest of the hot mixture. Warming the eggs in this way keeps the eggs from coagulating into lumps.

4. (List four:) temperature, beating time, fat, acid, sugar

5. Egg yolk acts as an emulsifying agent that surrounds the oil droplets and keeps them suspended in the water-based liquid.

6. false

7. (Describe two. Student response.)

8. Safely cooked whole eggs have completely set whites and thickened yolks. Yolks do not need to be hard, but they should not be runny. Dishes made with beaten eggs are thoroughly cooked when they no longer contain any visible liquid egg.

(continued)

Summary

Eggs are a nutritious, inexpensive, and versatile food. Grade AA and A are the grades of eggs most commonly sold at retail stores. Extra large, large, and medium are the most common sizes. Fresh eggs keep well in the refrigerator, but require careful handling to prevent cracking.

Eggs serve a number of functions in recipes. Eggs add structure to baked goods. They are used to thicken puddings and sauces and to hold ingredients together in foods like meat loaf. They interfere with the formation of ice crystals in frozen desserts. They are used as foams to add air and give structure to foods like meringues and sponge cakes. They are used as emulsifiers to keep oil suspended in water-based liquids. Several methods can be used to cook eggs. They can also be used in a variety of dishes. No matter how they are prepared, eggs require moderate cooking temperatures and carefully monitored cooking times. These factors will prevent egg proteins from shrinking and becoming tough.

Review What You Have Read

Write your answers on a separate sheet of paper, using complete sentences when appropriate.

1. How is candling used in the egg industry?

2. How long can you safely store fresh eggs in the refrigerator?

3. How should beaten eggs be added to a hot mixture? Explain why.

4. What are four factors that can affect the formation of egg white foams?

5. How does egg yolk keep the vinegar and water from separating from the oil in mayonnaise?

6. True or false. Egg yolk coagulates at a slightly lower temperature than egg white.

7. Describe two basic egg preparation methods.

8. Describe the appearance of safely cooked whole eggs and beaten egg dishes.

9. What can cause a greenish ring to form around the yolk of a soft- or hard-cooked egg and how can it be prevented?

10. Describe the appearance of a plain omelet that is ready to fill and serve.

11. How are soufflés similar to puffy omelets?

12. Golden droplets of moisture that sometimes appear on the surface of a meringue are called _____.

13. The leakage of liquid from baked custard is called _____.
    A. coagulum
    B. emulsion
    C. syneresis
    D. weeping

14. How can a recipe for an uncooked dish calling for beaten raw egg whites be prepared safely?

Link to Academic Skills

15. **Social studies.** Investigate what types of birds, other than chickens, provide eggs used as food sources by people throughout the world. In what cultures are these other types of eggs most commonly used?

16. **Science.** In a darkened room, hold an egg directly over the lens of a bright flashlight. Describe characteristics of the egg that you cannot see in normal room lighting.

17. **Science.** Pour ½ cup vegetable oil in each of two clear glass bottles. Add 1 tablespoon vinegar to one bottle and 1 tablespoon vinegar thoroughly mixed with one egg yolk to the other bottle. Put the tops on the bottles and shake them vigorously for 30 seconds. Then set the bottles on a counter and do not touch them for 10 minutes. For both bottles, record what you observe immediately after the vinegar is added, after the bottle is shaken, and 10 minutes after shaking has stopped. Use chapter information to explain your observations.

18. **English language arts.** Visit the Eggcyclopedia section of the American Egg Board's consumer website. Select a topic to research and share with the class. Conclude the activity by stating something new you learned from listening to your classmates' reports.

Build Critical Thinking Skills

19. **Analysis.** Beat four egg whites to the stiff peak stage. Before beating, add nothing to the first egg white. Add ⅛ teaspoon (0.5 mL) oil to the second egg white. Add ⅛ teaspoon (0.5 mL) cream of tartar to the third egg white. Add ¼ cup (50 mL) sugar to the fourth egg white. Analyze and compare the volume, appearance, and required beating time of the four samples. Summarize your observations in a brief written report.

20. **Evaluation.** Beat three eggs with 3 tablespoons (45 mL) milk. Divide the mixture into three equal portions. Scramble one portion over high heat. Scramble a second portion over low heat, occasionally drawing a bent-edged spatula across the bottom of the skillet. Scramble the third portion over low heat stirring constantly. Evaluate each product on the basis of appearance, tenderness and size of the coagulum, and flavor.

Apply Technology

21. Research how nutrient-enhanced eggs are produced. Summarize your findings in a brief written report.

22. Make a poster illustrating the process used to pasteurize eggs in or out of the shell. Write on the poster why you think pasteurized eggs are of value to consumers.

9. A chemical reaction between iron in egg yolk and hydrogen sulfide in egg white can cause a greenish ring to form around the yolk of a soft- or hard-cooked egg. This can be prevented by placing the egg under cold running water or in a bowl of ice water to rapidly cool the egg and stop it from cooking.

10. The top has set but is still moist.

11. They both use egg whites for structure.

12. beading

13. C

14. Combine the egg whites with the sugar from the recipe in a heavy saucepan or double boiler. Cook the mixture over low heat while beating it to the soft peak stage with an electric mixer.

A Measure of Math

23. The average hen lays about 260 eggs per year. In a recent year, 79.884 billion eggs were produced in the United States, and each person consumed about 255 eggs. Calculate how many hens would have been needed to lay all the eggs produced. Also calculate how many dozen eggs each person consumed.

24. Weigh a dozen medium eggs, a dozen large eggs, and a dozen extra large eggs. Calculate the average weight per egg for each size. Also calculate the percentage weight difference between medium and large and between large and extra large eggs.

Teamwork in Action

25. Put together a brochure about egg nutrition and safe handling, storage, and cooking of eggs. Then prepare hard-cooked eggs, color, and decorate them. Use these eggs to hold an egg hunt for children in your community, perhaps at a preschool or child care center. Be sure not to let the eggs sit out for more than two hours. At the egg hunt, distribute your brochure to parents of the children.

Companion Website
www.g-wlearning.com

At the website, review key terms for this chapter with crossword puzzles, matching exercises, and e-flash cards. Apply facts from the chapter to complete the activities.

CHAPTER 18
Meat

Learning Prep

Which of the *Terms to Know* are already familiar to you? Look up the terms in the glossary to see if your definitions match glossary definitions.

Terms to Know

meat	pork
variety meats	lamb
beef	marbling
wholesale cut	elastin
retail cut	collagen
veal	cooking losses

Main Menu

- Recognizing quality characteristics and factors that affect cost per serving can help you select meat cuts that fit your menus and your budget.
- Being familiar with principles and methods of cooking meats will allow you to prepare meats that are tender and flavorful.

Objectives

After studying this chapter, you will be able to

- **list** factors affecting the selection of meats.
- **describe** how to properly store meats to maintain their quality.
- **describe** the principles and methods of cooking meat.
- **prepare** meats by moist and dry cooking methods.

Many meal managers choose the meat course first when planning menus. Meat dishes should be tender, flavorful, and attractive.

What Is Meat?

Meat is the edible portions of mammals. It contains muscle, fat, bone, connective tissue, and water. The edible parts of the animal other than the muscles are called **variety meats**. The major meat-producing animals in the United States are cattle, swine, and sheep.

Nutritional Value of Meat

One ounce (28 g) of lean, cooked meat counts as 1 ounce-equivalent from the protein foods group of MyPlate. Most teens and adults need only 5 to 7 ounce-equivalents each day.

All meat and meat products contain proteins essential for building and repairing tissue. Meats are also good sources of B vitamins, iron, and zinc. Some processed meats contain a lot of added salt. Compare labels to choose products that are lower in sodium.

Beef

Beef comes from mature cattle. It has a distinctive flavor and firm texture. Beef is usually bright, cherry red in color with creamy white fat.

Health and Wellness

Meat in the Diet

The amount of fat meat contributes to the diet depends on the kind and quality of the meat. Ground meats are generally higher in fat than all other cuts. Fat gives meat flavor and appeal. However, experts advise limiting saturated fats and cholesterol in the diet. Diets high in these components can raise blood cholesterol, increasing the risk of heart disease.

Following a few tips can help limit fat and enjoy meat as part of a healthful diet. First, stay within suggested amounts from the meat group each day. Choose lean cuts, such as the round and loin sections of beef and the loin and leg sections of pork. Trim all visible fat before cooking. This prevents fat from melting into the meat during cooking. Use cooking methods like broiling and grilling, which allow fat to drip away during cooking. Use nonstick pans when frying and browning meat to eliminate the need for added fat during cooking. Skim the fat from the surface of chilled meat soups and stocks.

©2011 Wisconsin Milk Marketing Board, Inc.

To limit fat, choose ground meats like burgers less often than lean meat cuts.

Like all animals used for food, beef carcasses are divided into pieces, which are referred to as *cuts*. The carcasses are first cut lengthwise through the backbone into halves. The two halves are called *sides*. (Veal and lamb carcasses are much smaller than beef and do not require splitting for shipment. Pork carcasses are small enough to be shipped whole, but they are usually split.) Beef sides are cut into *quarters* and then into large pieces, called **wholesale cuts**, for easier handling. Wholesale cuts are shipped to retail grocery stores or meat markets. There, meat cutters divide the wholesale cuts into still smaller pieces, called **retail cuts**, which are sold to consumers.

Ground Beef

Some people incorrectly call ground beef hamburger. *Ground beef* contains only the fat originally attached to the meat before grinding. *Hamburger* can have extra fat added to it during grinding. For the most healthful choice, look for extra lean ground beef. The label should state that it is at least 90 percent lean.

Veal

Veal is meat that comes from young calves. Because the animals are so young, little fat has developed. Thus, most veal is lean. Veal also has quite a bit of connective tissue, but it is still considered to be tender. Veal has a light pink color and a delicate flavor.

Pork

Pork is the meat of swine. Most pork comes from animals that are 7 to 12 months old. Because the animals are so young, most pork is tender. The meat is grayish-pink to light rose in color.

Meat packing plants process many pork products. Pork can be fresh cured or smoked. *Ham* comes from the pork leg. It is cured and usually smoked. Some hams that require cooking, which may or may not include the skin and bone, can be purchased. Fully cooked canned hams can also be purchased. *Bacon* is smoked pork belly meat. It can be purchased as a slab, which can be sliced, or as precut slices. *Canadian bacon* is made from boneless pork loins.

Lamb

Lamb is the meat of sheep less than one year old. It is tender with a delicate flavor. Fresh lamb is pinkish-red in color with white fat. Older animals are marketed as *yearling lamb* (one to two years of age) and *mutton* (over two years of age). Retail outlets do not sell much mutton. It has a stronger flavor than lamb and is less tender.

Inspection and Grading of Meat

Federal inspectors must examine all meat and meat products shipped across state lines. They inspect both the live animal and the carcass. A round purple inspection stamp is placed on all wholesale cuts to indicate the meat is wholesome. This stamp also assures buyers the plant and processing conditions were sanitary. State-supported programs handle the inspection of meat processed and sold within a state.

18-1 The USDA grade shield assures consumers meat has met certain standards of quality.

Animal carcasses may be voluntarily graded for quality. *Quality grades* assure consumers meat has met set standards that predict taste appeal. The USDA oversees the grading program, **18-1**.

Quality grades for beef are based on marbling, maturity, texture, and appearance. **Marbling** refers to the flecks of fat throughout the lean muscles of meat. Cuts with more marbling are juicy, flavorful, and tender. Higher quality grades go to cuts with more marbling and fine muscle texture. Meat from younger animals that has characteristic color also qualifies for higher quality grades.

The most common grades of beef sold in retail stores are Choice and Select. *Choice meats* are high quality with good marbling. *Select meats* are leaner than Choice meats, and they usually cost less. Fine restaurants often offer *Prime meats* on their menus. Prime cuts have received the highest grade. Prime meats are also available in some grocery stores and butcher shops.

The standards used for grading veal, pork, and lamb differ somewhat from those used to grade beef. However, the highest grades are given to carcasses that are expected to provide the tastiest meat.

Selecting Meat

Meats are costly food items. Learning how to judge quality factors and identify meat cuts can help to make wise purchases.

Characteristics of the Fat

Color, firmness, and location of fat affect meat quality. Quality meats will have firm to medium-firm, creamy white fat. Fat that is yellow and coarse is a sign of poor quality.

Marbling indicates tenderness in a cut of meat. Although more marbling means more tenderness, it also means more total fat, saturated fat, cholesterol, and calories. Cooking can tenderize cuts with less marbling. Therefore, to follow the Dietary Guidelines, choose leaner cuts most often. Save cuts with more marbling for special occasions.

Location of the Meat in the Animal

The location of muscle tissue in an animal indicates the tenderness of the meat cut. Rib and loin muscles are quite tender because they lie along the backbone where they receive little exercise. Leg and shoulder muscles are less tender because the animal uses them more. See **18-2**.

The tenderness of a meat cut gives a clue about how to cook it. Tender cuts of meat can be cooked by dry heat methods, such as broiling or roasting. Sirloin and porterhouse steaks, pork and lamb loin chops, and beef and pork rib roasts are examples of tender cuts of meat. Cook less tender cuts of meat by moist heat methods, such as stewing or braising. Examples of these cuts include round steak, rump roast, and shoulder steak.

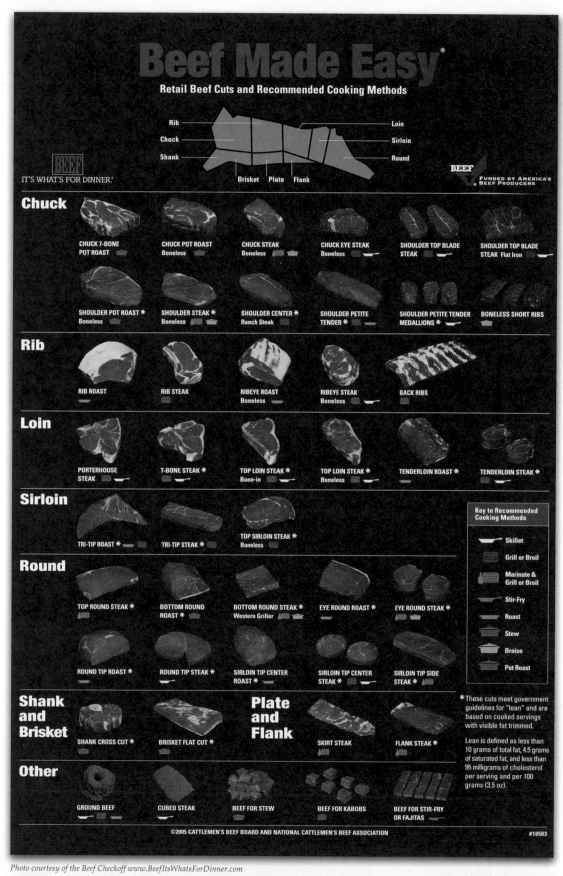

Photo courtesy of the Beef Checkoff www.BeefItsWhatsForDinner.com

18-2 The part of the animal from which meat comes indicates how tender the meat is and how to cook it.

Learn About...

Meat Labeling

To help consumers with meat selection, most retail stores follow a labeling system. Meat names on labels follow a three-part format. The kind of meat appears first. This might be *beef*. Next is the name of the wholesale cut. It tells the part of the animal from which the cut came. *Chuck* is an example of a beef wholesale cut. Third is the name of the retail cut. It tells from what part of the wholesale cut the meat comes. A *shoulder roast* is an example of a beef retail cut. Using this system, the cut described would be a *Beef Chuck Shoulder Roast*.

The label also lists the sell by date, net weight, the price per pound (kilogram), and price. This information enables easier comparison shopping.

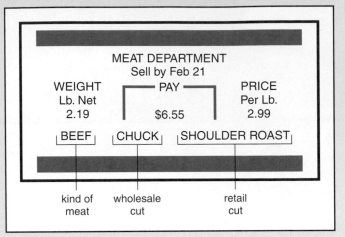

Standard three-part names on meat labels help consumers identify cuts.

FYI

As a size reference, inform students that a three-ounce (85g) serving of meat is about the size of a deck of playing cards.

How Much Meat to Buy

The amount of meat to buy depends on how many people are being served. It also depends on the cut of meat chosen and whether leftovers are wanted.

Meat is sold by the pound (kg). It is necessary to know how many people 1 pound (0.45 kg) of meat will serve. A serving size in a healthful diet is 3 ounces (85 g) of cooked, lean meat. However, the amount of raw meat required to yield this serving size varies from cut to cut. Boneless cuts will serve more people per pound (0.45 kg) than meat with bones. See **18-3**.

To determine how much to buy, multiply the amount of meat per serving by the number of people being served. Then add the amount of leftover meat planned to serve later. For instance, beef back ribs have many bones, so buy ½ to ¾ pound (225 to 340 g) per serving. If 6 people are being served and enough leftovers to serve 4 are needed, buy 10 servings. This would be between 5 and 7½ pounds (2.25 and 3.40 kg) of ribs.

Meat Purchasing Guide	
Amount of Bone	**Amount to Buy per Serving**
Boneless	¼ to ⅓ lb (115 to 150 g)
Small bone	⅓ to ½ lb (150 to 225 g)
Many bones	½ to ¾ lb (225 to 340 g)

18-3 Use this chart as a rough guide when determining how much meat to buy per serving.

Cost of Meat per Serving

The cost per serving of meat depends partly on the tenderness of the meat. Usually, tender cuts cost more than less tender cuts. That is why sirloin steak costs more than round steak.

The amount of waste in a meat cut also affects the cost per serving. Meat with bones often is priced lower per pound (0.45 kg) than boneless cuts. For example, a bone-in rump roast usually costs less per pound (0.45 kg) than a boneless rump roast.

Meat extenders like dried beans and rice can stretch meat dollars. For instance, ham will go farther when mixed with nutritious navy beans than when served alone.

Storing Meat

Store sausage and fresh, cured and smoked, and ready-to-serve meats (cold cuts) in the refrigerator for use within a few days. Also, refrigerate canned hams until ready for use unless the label says otherwise. Store meats in the meat storage compartment or the coldest part of the refrigerator. The temperature of the refrigerator should be 40°F (4°C) or lower. Refrigerate prepackaged meats in their original wrappers. After cooking meats, store them in a tightly covered container in the refrigerator.

Freeze meats for longer storage. (Canned hams should not be frozen.) The temperature in the freezer should remain at 0°F (-18°C) or colder for maximum keeping quality. Meats can be frozen in their original wrappings for up to two weeks. For extended freezer storage, rewrap meats in moistureproof and vaporproof paper. Tightly sealed heavy-duty foil and freezer bags are also good choices for freezer storage. Label each package with the date and the name and weight of the cut. Be sure to use meats within recommended storage times. See **18-4**.

Storage Times for Meat	
Refrigerated Storage	
Type of Meat	*Time*
Fresh meat cuts	3-4 days
Ground meats	1-2 days
Variety meats	1-2 days
Leftover cooked meats	3 days
Freezer Storage	
Luncheon meats, hot dogs	2 months
Ham	2 months
Ground meats	3 months
Pork cuts	6 months
Lamb	9 months
Beef	12 months

18-4 Keep fresh meat safe to eat by cooking or freezing it within a few days of purchase. Date frozen meat and use it within recommended storage times for best quality.

Food Science Principles of Cooking Meat

Cooking meat destroys harmful bacteria that can be present in raw meat. Cooking improves the flavor of meat and makes it easier to digest. Cooking also makes some meats more tender.

Remember that meat consists of muscle tissue, connective tissue, fat, and bone. Connective tissue holds together fibers in the muscle tissues. The connective tissue contains two proteins: elastin and collagen. **Elastin** is very tough and elastic, and cooking cannot soften it. **Collagen** is also tough and elastic, but cooking can soften and tenderize it.

Some meat cuts have more collagen than others. Meat cuts with little collagen are tender. Cuts with a lot of collagen are less tender.

Certain food preparation techniques can be used to break down connective tissue in meat before cooking. Elastin can be broken down mechanically or chemically. Pounding, sometimes done to round steak, and grinding, done to ground beef, are two mechanical methods of breaking down elastin. Commercial meat tenderizers can soften collagen chemically. These products contain enzymes that break down the tissue. Marinating meat can also soften collagen chemically. Marinating involves soaking meat in a solution called a *marinade*. The marinade contains an acid, such as vinegar or tomato juice, that helps tenderize the connective tissue. See **18-5**.

During cooking, heat coagulates the proteins in the muscle fibers. It also softens the collagen in the connective tissue. When cooking meats, low temperatures and careful

Photo Courtesy of The Beef Checkoff www.BeefItsWhatsForDinner.com

18-5 Marinating meat before grilling not only softens the connective tissue, it also adds flavor.

timing are needed. Cooking meats at too high a temperature or for too long a time will make them tough and dry. (Meat cuts cooked in liquid will fall apart.) This is due to overcoagulation of the proteins.

Controlling Temperature When Cooking Meat

Temperature control is a key principle to follow when cooking meat. Using too high a cooking temperature can result in excessive cooking losses. **Cooking losses** include fat, water, and other volatile (easily vaporized) substances that evaporate from the surface of the meat. Some of the cooking losses are retained in the pan drippings or cooking liquid. However, loss of these substances causes meat to shrink during cooking, decreasing in size and weight.

Cooking losses are important because they can affect the appearance and eating quality of meat. Meat cooked at too high a temperature can develop a hard crust. This can make carving and eating difficult. Excessive cooking losses can also cause meat to be tough and dry.

Learn About...

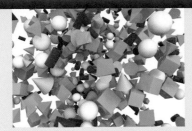

Degree of Meat Doneness

Be aware of the internal temperature of meat when cooking. The type of meat and the desired degree of doneness determine the correct internal temperature. Overcooked meat is cooked to an internal temperature that is too high. Such meat has more cooking losses than meat cooked to the correct temperature.

The only accurate way to determine the internal temperature of meat is to use a food thermometer. Insert the thermometer into the thickest part of the muscle. Make sure the probe is not touching bone, fat, or gristle. Check the temperature of uneven cuts in several places. Insert the probe sideways into thin cuts, such as chops and meat patties. Beef and pork cuts like steaks and roasts should be cooked to a minimum internal temperature of 145°F (65°C) and include a 3 minute rest time after cooking. Ground meat, such as burgers and meatloaf, should be cooked to a minimum internal temperature of 160°F (70°C).

Preventing foodborne illness is also a key reason to be aware of internal temperatures when cooking meat.

Thorough cooking kills harmful bacteria. Do not rely on the color of cooked meat as a sign that meat has reached a safe internal temperature.

Lodge Cast Iron

The reddish color of this steak indicates it has been cooked to the medium stage of doneness. However, using a food thermometer is the only sure way to know if meat has been adequately cooked.

Cooking losses can even affect the number of servings meat will provide. For instance, it can be expected that a 6-pound (2.6 kg) bone-in roast will provide about 15 servings. However, excessive cooking losses could reduce the number of servings by two or more.

Low temperatures will keep cooking losses to a minimum. Meat will be juicier, more flavorful, and easier to carve. Cleanup will be easier because less fat will have spattered on the oven walls or burned onto the pan. Although low cooking temperatures have these pluses, meat should not be cooked at temperatures below 325°F (165°C). Temperatures lower than this may allow bacteria to grow before meat has finished cooking.

Controlling Time When Cooking Meat

The total time a cut of meat is cooked affects its appearance and eating quality just as temperature does. Several factors affect cooking time.

One factor that affects cooking time is cooking temperature. Higher temperatures result in shorter cooking times. Lower temperatures result in longer cooking times. Changing the cooking temperature by just a few degrees can affect cooking time. For instance, suppose a roast is in the oven and the oven door is opened every few minutes to check it. Each time the door is opened, cool air enters the oven. This reduces the cooking temperature and will cause the roast to take longer to cook.

The size and shape of the cut of meat are factors that affect cooking time. Large cuts of meat need longer cooking times than small cuts. However, large cuts take fewer minutes *per pound* to cook than small cuts. A rolled rib roast will take longer to cook than a standing rib roast because the meat is more compact.

The desired degree of doneness is another factor that affects cooking time. The cooking time for rare beef is less than for well-done beef. The more well done the meat is to be, the longer it will take to cook.

Methods of Cooking Meat

Consider the tenderness and size and thickness of a meat cut as well as taste preferences when choosing a cooking method. Roasting, broiling, grilling, pan-broiling, and frying are *dry heat cooking methods*. Use them for tender cuts of meat, such as T-bone steaks and rib roasts. Braising and cooking in liquid are *moist heat cooking methods*. Use them for less tender cuts of meat, such as chuck roasts and corned beef brisket. Some types of meat, such as ground meat and bacon, can also be successfully prepared in a microwave oven.

Roasting Meat

Roasting is recommended for large, tender cuts of meat. For best results when roasting, place meat with the fat side up on a rack in a large, shallow pan. The fat bastes the meat during cooking, and the rack holds the meat out of the drippings. Season meat with salt and pepper, if desired. Insert a meat thermometer into the thickest part of the muscle, without having the tip touching bone or fat. Roast the meat in a slow oven (325°F to 350°F, 165°C to 180°C), uncovered, until it reaches the desired degree of doneness. (Roast smaller cuts of meat at the higher temperature and larger cuts at the lower temperature.)

Health and Wellness

Cooking Meat Safely

Meats are often identified as the source of bacteria that cause foodborne illness. Most cases of foodborne illness result from improper food handling. Using care when buying, storing, cooking, serving, and reheating foods will help avoid illness. Review the food handling precautions. In addition, be aware of the following guidelines when cooking meat:

- Store meats at or below 40°F (4°C).
- Cook or freeze refrigerated meats within recommended time frames (1 to 2 days for ground meats, 3 to 4 days for nonground products, 3 days for leftovers).
- Hands should be washed for 20 seconds with hot, soapy water before beginning to cook. Hands should be washed again after handling raw meat.
- Do not wash or rinse raw meat.
- Thoroughly wash cutting boards and utensils used for raw meat before using them to prepare raw vegetables or cooked meat.
- Marinate raw meat in the refrigerator, not at room temperature. Discard marinade after use, or boil it for 1 minute before using it on cooked meat.
- Brush sauces only on cooked surfaces of meat.
- Do not set the oven below 325°F (165°C) when cooking meats.

- Use a thermometer to make sure meat has reached a safe internal temperature. Cook ground meats to an internal temperature of 160°F (70°C) and beef and pork cuts to at least 145°F (65°C) and include a 3 minute rest time after cooking.
- Reheat leftover meats to an internal temperature of 165°F (75°C).
- Be sure to wash the probe of the meat thermometer in hot, soapy water after each use. Do not reinsert a dirty thermometer into a food or use it to check another food.

Courtesy of National Cattlemen's Beef Association and Cattlemen's Beef Board

Insert an instant-read thermometer into the side of a ground meat patty to be sure the meat has reached the safe temperature of 160°F (70°C).

Allowing a roast to stand for 10 to 15 minutes after taking it from the oven makes it easier to carve. As the roast stands, it will continue to cook. For this reason, take the roast from the oven when it is about 5°F (3°C) below the desired internal temperature.

Broiling Meat

Tender beefsteaks, lamb and pork chops, ham slices, ground beef, and ground lamb can be broiled. Steaks and chops that are too thin will dry out before they are thoroughly cooked. Therefore, these cuts should be at least ¾ inch (2.3 cm) thick for broiling. Ham slices should be at least ½ inch (1.5 cm) thick.

Broiling is done under a direct flame in gas broilers and under the direct heating element in electric broilers. The closer the meat is to the heat source, the shorter the cooking time will be. Place thick cuts of meat farther away from the heat than thin cuts. Place pork far enough away so the meat will not dry out before it is thoroughly cooked.

For best results when broiling meat, place meat on a cold broiler pan. Adjust the broiler rack to the desired distance from the heat source. Broil the top side of the meat until it is brown. (It should be about half-cooked at this point.) Turn the meat and season if desired. (Do not salt meats before broiling because salt draws juices from the meat. Cured meats should not be salted at all.) Broil the second side until brown.

Time charts can help determine the correct cooking time when broiling. They are available in basic cookbooks. Use an instant-read thermometer to check the internal temperature of the meat toward the end of the broiling time. This will help evaluate the degree of doneness. It will also assure that the meat has reached a safe internal temperature. Pork chops and ground meats should be cooked to the well-done stage.

Grilling Meat

The same cuts of meat used for broiling can be successfully grilled. Indirect grilling is recommended as the most healthful grilling method. For indirect grilling, move hot coals to the sides of the grill. To grill meat indirectly on a gas grill, turn off the central gas burners after preheating the grill. Place seasoned meat in the center of the grill and cover the grill until the meat is done. Because heat surrounds the meat in the covered grill, there is no need to turn the meat. Grill meat for the correct amount of time needed for the particular cut being cooked. A grilling time chart in a cookbook or the use and care manual for the grill will help determine cooking times.

Research suggests the high heat used in grilling and broiling can allow cancer-causing compounds to form on meat. Meat juices that drip onto hot coals and cause smoke and flare-ups increase the formation of cancer-causing agents. Several steps can be taken to keep grilled meats more healthful. First, cut any charred surfaces from meat before eating it. Meat can be marinated before grilling to help reduce the formation of harmful substances. Partially precooking meats in a microwave oven immediately before placing them on the grill will reduce grilling time. Also, try wrapping meats in foil for grilling to avoid exposing them to direct flames.

Pan-Broiling Meat

Meat cuts that can be broiled can also be pan-broiled if they are 1 inch (2.5 cm) thick or less. Pan-broiling is a good method to use when preparing small quantities of

EXPLORING CAREERS

Grill Cook

Grill cooks prepare foods in restaurants. The types of cooking and other tasks a grill cook must do depend on the kind of restaurant and the size of the kitchen staff. Tasks may involve everything from grilling meats to frying eggs to cooking soups. Larger restaurants will likely have prep cooks to do jobs like cleaning and cutting vegetables. Smaller kitchens will rely on the grill cook to handle these duties.

To be successful, grill cooks need good listening skills to hear specifics of food orders that may be called out by managers and wait staff. They need reading skills to follow written food orders and recipes. They must have hand-eye coordination when using knives and other utensils. Grill cooks use time management skills to monitor the progress of multiple food orders being prepared at once. They use sensory evaluation to judge the doneness of foods based on sight, texture, and smell. These workers need to know and follow food safety standards. Grill cooks must be able to work well with other kitchen staff, take direction from managers, and possibly train new coworkers.

Grill cooks usually need a high school diploma. Previous kitchen experience may or may not be required, depending on the restaurant. Skilled grill cooks may be able to move into chef or kitchen manager positions. However, some restaurants will require culinary training for these jobs regardless of experience as a grill cook.

Photo Courtesy of The Beef Checkoff www.BeefItsWhatsForDinner.com

18-6 Pan-broiling is a low-fat cooking method suitable for thinner cuts of meat.

FYI

Thinly slicing meats for stir-frying is easier when the meat is partially frozen.

Online Resource

Have students visit the National Cattlemen's Beef Association consumer website to find information about how to prepare meat by various cooking methods. Ask each student to choose a specific method and then search the site for a recipe that employs that method.

Vocabulary Builder

Instead of adding flour or cornstarch to thicken the juices to make gravy, students may consider reducing the juices and serving them as a sauce. *Reduce* means to decrease the volume and concentrate the flavor by boiling.

meat. It can save energy and cleanup time when cooking just one or two steaks or chops. See **18-6**.

For best results when pan-broiling, place the meat in a heavy skillet or griddle. Do not cover the pan or add fat. (If the meat is very lean, lightly brush the skillet with fat to prevent sticking.) Cook the meat slowly, turning it occasionally to ensure even cooking. Pour off any fat that accumulates. Pan-broiled meats need only about half the cooking time of broiled meats. Insert an instant-read thermometer sideways into steaks and chops to be sure they have reached the correct internal temperature.

Frying Meat

Most fried meats are prepared by pan-frying, or sautéing. A few can be deep-fried. Pan-fry meats in a small amount of fat. This fat may be added before cooking, or it may accumulate during cooking. Fairly thin pieces of tender meat, tenderized meat, ground meat patties, or cooked meat slices can be pan-fried.

For best results when pan-frying, brown meat on both sides in a small amount of fat. Season meat after browning or add the seasonings to the breading if the meat is breaded. Cook the meat uncovered at a moderate temperature, turning occasionally until done. If the temperature is too high, the fat will smoke, and the meat will burn on the outside before the inside is cooked.

A variation of pan-frying is *stir-frying*. Stir-fried meats and vegetables are often served together in Asian dishes. Cook thinly sliced meat in a small amount of oil. Use a wok or frying pan. Cook the meat over high heat and stir it constantly until done.

Braising Meat

Braising is cooking in a small amount of liquid in a tightly covered pan over low heat. Less tender meat cuts and tender cuts of pork and veal can be braised. Braising can be done in the oven or on the surface unit of a range.

For best results when braising, first brown meat slowly on all sides in a small amount of fat. (If the meat has sufficient fat, additional fat is not needed.) Browning adds flavor and color. Season browned meat if desired and add a *small* amount of liquid. Use water, broth, tomato juice, or a flavorful sauce as the braising liquid. Cover the pan tightly, and cook the meat slowly until tender. (Gently simmer braised meat. The cooking liquid should never boil.) The juices that accumulate during cooking can be thickened and made into gravy. They contain important vitamins and minerals.

Cooking Meat in Liquid

Unlike braising, when cooking meats in liquid, they are covered with the cooking liquid. Use this method for less tender cuts of meat. When used with whole cuts of meat, this method is called *simmering*. Many people simmer corned beef brisket. When small pieces of meat are cooked in liquid, this method is called *stewing*.

For best results when cooking in liquid, cover the meat entirely with water or stock. This ensures even cooking. Season cooking liquid with salt, pepper, and herbs, if desired. Cover the pot and simmer until the meat is tender. (Cooking time will vary depending on the meat being cooked. When using this method, cook most meat cuts two hours or more.) The cooking liquid should never boil. Boiling can cause meat to shrink and become dry.

If preparing a stew by this method, cut the meat into cubes of uniform size, about 1 to 2 inches (2.5 to 5 cm). Brown the cubes in a small amount of fat, if desired. Cover the meat cubes with liquid and stew until tender. Vegetables may be added to the meat later, allowing them to cook just long enough to become tender. Before serving, transfer the meat and vegetables to a warm serving platter and thicken the cooking liquid. See **18-7**.

Photo Courtesy of The Beef Checkoff www.BeefItsWhatsForDinner.com

18-7 Beef stew makes a hearty, comforting meal.

Microwaving Meat

Conventional cooking methods are often preferred for preparing cuts such as roasts, steaks, and chops. However, microwaving can be a quick, easy way to prepare meats like bacon, sausage, and ground meat patties. Remember that microwave cooking time increases as the quantity of food increases. Therefore, eight slices of bacon will take longer to cook than four slices.

Covering meats in a microwave oven holds in steam. This keeps meats such as meatballs and ham slices moist and tender and shortens cooking time even further. Cover bacon, hot dogs, and cooked sausages with paper towels to absorb grease and prevent spatters. (Remember to pierce the skin on products like sausage and hot dogs to allow steam to escape and prevent bursting.)

Arranging meats will promote even cooking in a microwave oven. Arrange uniformly shaped meat, such as meat patties and sausage links, in a circle. Overlap sliced meats, such as fully cooked ham. Rotating, turning, and rearranging meats during the cooking period will also help them microwave more evenly.

Learn About...

Variety Meats

Liver, heart, kidney, tongue, and *sweetbreads* (thymus glands) are popular variety meats. Other variety meats include beef *tripe* (stomach lining); brains; *chitterlings* (cleaned intestines); and pork jowls, tail, feet, ears, and snout. Variety meats are usually inexpensive and are rich sources of many vitamins and minerals. For instance, liver is very high in iron.

The cooking method used for preparing variety meats depends on the tenderness of each meat. Cook most variety meats by moist heat. However, brains, sweetbreads, and the liver and kidneys of veal and calf are often cooked by dry heat, usually by broiling or frying.

Brains and sweetbreads are very delicate meats. To retain their shape, precook them for about 20 minutes in salted, *acidulated* water (water that contains an acid, such as lemon juice). After precooking, they can be fried or broiled.

Meatballs, patties, and sausages will not brown in a microwave oven as they do when prepared by conventional methods. Therefore, it might be a good idea to use a sauce or topping to give them a more appealing appearance. Sauces have the added advantage of keeping meat moist in the microwave oven.

Cooking Frozen Meat

Frozen meats can be cooked from the frozen state or defrosted before cooking. Cook prepared frozen meats according to package directions.

For safety, never thaw meat on the kitchen counter. Harmful microorganisms can grow in meat thawed at room temperature, resulting in foodborne illness. Instead, leave meat in its freezer wrapping and thaw it in the refrigerator. Place it on a plate to catch any juices that may drip from the meat as it thaws. Frozen meat can also be safely defrosted in the microwave oven immediately before cooking.

Frozen meat must be cooked longer than thawed meat. A frozen roast will need to cook about 50 percent longer than a thawed roast. Cooking time for frozen steaks and chops will vary depending on size and thickness.

When broiling frozen meats, place meat farther away from the heat source. This will prevent the outside from overcooking before the inside is cooked, **18-8**. To pan-broil frozen meat, use a hot skillet to brown the meat. Then lower the heat and turn meat occasionally to ensure even cooking.

©2011 Wisconsin Milk Marketing Board, Inc.

18-8 Frozen steaks need to be placed farther from the heat source when broiling to make sure the inside of the meat cooks properly.

CAREER SUCCESS

Using Competence in Serving Customers

Kevin is a meat cutter at DeLong's Grocery Store. The store is known for its hand-trimmed, cut-to-order meats. Kevin always has a steady stream of customers, but the meat department is especially busy just before holidays.

To be an effective worker, Kevin needs competence in serving customers. Imagine you are one of Kevin's customers. Answer the following questions about his need for and use of this skill:

A. What personality characteristics would you expect Kevin to have?

B. How would you respond if you felt Kevin was not providing you with adequate service?

C. How might DeLong's Grocery Store be affected if Kevin lacked competence in serving customers?

D. What is another skill Kevin would need in this job? Briefly explain why this skill would be important.

CHAPTER 18 REVIEW

Summary

Beef, veal, pork, and lamb are the most commonly eaten types of meat in the United States. They are all high in protein as well as being good sources of several vitamins and minerals.

Meat is inspected for wholesomeness and may be graded for quality. When selecting meat, the appearance of the fat is a sign of quality. Read the label to identify the part of the animal from which the meat comes. This indicates tenderness. When deciding how much meat to buy, remember boneless cuts yield more servings per pound than bone-in cuts. Compare meats in terms of cost per serving rather than cost per pound to get the best buy.

Meats are highly perishable. Store them in the coldest part of the refrigerator and use them within a few days. Wrap them well and put them in the freezer for longer storage.

The connective tissue in meat contains two types of tough, elastic protein. One of these, collagen, can be broken down by mechanical and chemical methods and softened by cooking.

Meats cooked at lower temperatures, large cuts, and well-done meats all require longer cooking times. However, cooking times and temperatures need to be carefully monitored. Temperatures that are too high or cooking times that are too long can make meat tough and dry.

Roasting, broiling, grilling, pan-broiling, and frying are dry heat cooking methods. They generally work best for tender cuts of meat. Braising and stewing are moist heat cooking methods. They are recommended for less tender cuts. A microwave oven can be used to defrost and cook meats. Frozen meats in can be cooked from the frozen state or they can be defrosted in the refrigerator before cooking.

Review What You Have Read

Write your answers on a separate sheet of paper, using complete sentences when appropriate.

1. List three nutrients contributed to the diet by meat.

2. Give three tips for selecting and preparing meat to help limit the amount of fat supplied by meat in the diet.

3. Describe the color and fat of high-quality beef.

4. True or false. Hamburger is another name for ground beef.

5. Meat from cattle that are less than three months of age is called _____.
   A. beef
   B. lamb
   C. pork
   D. veal

6. What are the most common grades of beef sold in retail stores?

7. How does the location of the meat in the animal affect the tenderness of a cut?

8. Name two factors that affect the cost per serving of meat.

9. Within what time period should refrigerated fresh meats be used?

10. The tough and elastic meat protein that can be softened and tenderized by cooking is _____.

11. List three characteristics of overcooked meat. List three characteristics of meat cooked to the proper degree of doneness.

12. What are cooking losses and how can they affect the appearance and eating quality of meat?

13. List the dry heat cooking methods used for meats. What types of cuts are best prepared by these methods?

14. Give two tips to promote even cooking of meats in a microwave oven.

15. True or false. Frozen meats must be defrosted before cooking.

Link to Academic Skills

16. **Government/civics.** Visit the Occupational Safety and Health Administration (OSHA) website at osha.gov. Scan a variety of resources and links to get an idea of health and safety issues related to the meat packing industry. Discuss in class what types of potential hazards exist for workers in this industry. Also discuss why the federal government sets health and safety standards for this and other industries.

17. **Geography.** On a map of the United States, identify the top three states for beef, veal, pork, and lamb production. Note what geographic characteristics make these states the leading locations for meat production.

18. **English language arts.** Visit the Meat Safety website of the American Meat Institute. Find a food safety topic to use as the basis for a two-page written report.

19. **English language arts.** Look at the different cuts of meat in the meat case in a grocery store. Compare the appearance of beef, veal, pork, and lamb. Notice what variety meats are available. Compare the appearance of different grades of meat. Summarize your findings in a brief written report.

Build Critical Thinking Skills

20. **Analysis.** Prepare two identical tender cuts of beef, cooking one with high heat and the other with moderate heat. Compare appearance, flavor, and tenderness to help you analyze the effects of high cooking temperatures on meat.

21. **Evaluation.** Purchase two pieces of beef from a less tender cut. Cook one with dry heat and the other with moist heat. Compare appearance, texture, and flavor as you evaluate which preparation method you prefer for this cut.

10. collagen

11. (List three for each:) overcooked— tough, dry, large amount of shrinkage, develops a hard crust, difficult to carve and eat; properly cooked— moist and juicy, tender, flavorful, easy to carve, smaller degree of shrinkage

12. Cooking losses are fat, water, and other volatile substances that evaporate from the surface of meat. Excessive cooking losses can cause tough, dry meat with a high degree of shrinkage, resulting in a reduced number of servings.

13. Roasting, broiling, grilling, pan-broiling, and frying are dry heat cooking methods. These methods are best used for tender cuts of meat.

14. (List two:) Arrange uniformly shaped meats, such as meat patties and sausage links, in a circle. Overlap sliced meats. Rotate, turn, and rearrange meats during cooking.

15. false

Apply Technology

22. Investigate the technology used to produce textured soy protein (TSP, also known as textured vegetable protein, or TVP) as a meat alternative. Broil a ground beef patty and a patty made with TSP. Compare the two products for appearance, texture, and flavor.

23. Investigate how ultrasound technology is being used by meat producers to evaluate animal quality.

A Measure of Math

24. Use Table 18-3 to calculate how much meat you would buy in each of the following situations: ground beef for six people, pork rib chops for four people, beef short ribs for five people.

25. Buy a bone-in meat cut. Note the weight, unit cost, and total cost listed on the label. Carefully trim the meat from the bone. Also trim all visible fat from the meat. Weigh the lean meat. Then weigh the bone and fat portions. Calculate the percentage of waste in the cut you bought. Then figure the cost of the waste.

Teamwork in Action

26. Work as a class to create a pamphlet titled "Lean Is Keen," identifying the leanest cuts of meat. The pamphlet should also list tips for using moderate meat portions in a diet focused mostly on grains, vegetables, and fruits. Obtain permission to distribute pamphlets in a local library or community center.

Companion Website
www.g-wlearning.com

At the website, review key terms for this chapter with crossword puzzles, matching exercises, and e-flash cards. Apply facts from the chapter to complete the activities.

CHAPTER 19
Poultry

Main Menu

- Knowing how to select and store poultry will allow you to include it as a frequent protein source in meals.
- You can use a number of cooking methods for preparing poultry to increase variety in menu planning.

Learning Prep

Look up the definition for the term *poultry* in a dictionary. Then write a definition you would use to explain the meaning of the word *poultry* to a child.

Objectives

After studying this chapter, you will be able to

- **list** tips for buying poultry.
- **describe** how to properly store poultry to maintain its quality.
- **describe** the principles and methods for cooking poultry.
- **prepare** poultry by moist and dry cooking methods.

Terms to Know

poultry
giblets

Vocabulary Builder

Guinea hen, Rock Cornish hen, and pigeon meet the definition for *poultry* along with the more commonly consumed domesticated birds.

FYI

Removing the skin from a chicken breast before baking it results in a 29-percent reduction in calories and a 71-percent reduction in fat.

Enrich

Some farmers are now raising emus and ostriches. Have students investigate the market and preparation methods for these types of poultry.

The word **poultry** describes any domesticated bird. Chicken, turkey, goose, and duck are the types of poultry most commonly eaten in the United States. At one time, chicken and turkey were eaten only on special occasions, but today they are part of everyday meals.

Buying Poultry

Poultry is sold in a variety of forms to meet consumer needs. Poultry can be purchased as fresh, frozen, and in processed poultry products.

Inspection and Grading of Poultry

All poultry sold in interstate commerce must be federally inspected for wholesomeness. Inspection ensures that birds were healthy, processed under sanitary conditions, and labeled correctly.

Poultry can be voluntarily graded for quality. A grade shield will appear on the wing tag along with the inspection seal. Most poultry sold at the retail level is U.S. Grade A. Grade A birds are full-fleshed and meaty with well-distributed fat. Their skin has few blemishes and pinfeathers. Grade B and C birds are usually used in processed products.

All poultry that is processed and sold as canned poultry is inspected before canning. The quality depends somewhat on the brand.

Buying Fresh and Frozen Poultry

Most fresh and frozen poultry is marketed young. Young birds are tender and suitable for all cooking methods.

Chickens and turkeys have both light and dark meat. Breast meat is light and mildly flavored. The rest of the bird is dark meat, which has a stronger flavor.

Health and Wellness

Nutritional Value of Poultry

Poultry is in the protein foods group of MyPlate. Most teens and adults need only 5 to 7 ounce-equivalents from this group each day, depending on calorie needs. A small chicken breast half counts as 3 ounce-equivalents.

All poultry contains high-quality protein and is a good source of phosphorus, iron, and B vitamins. Older birds have more fat than younger birds. Dark meat is higher in fat than light meat. Poultry labeled as "self-basting" is prepared with a solution that contains added sodium.

Turkey and chicken are lower in total fat, saturated fat, and calories than many cuts of red meat. This is especially true of the light meat portions of poultry. Much of the fat in poultry is located just under the skin. Thus, the fat content can be reduced simply by removing the skin. Eating the skin or using fat when cooking poultry will provide calories that count as discretionary calories.

National Chicken Council/U.S. Poultry & Egg Association

A typical serving of poultry usually provides at least 3 ounce-equivalents from the protein foods group.

Chickens, turkeys, ducks, and geese can be purchased fresh-chilled or frozen. Chickens can be purchased whole, cut into halves, or cut into pieces. Breasts, legs, and thighs are meatier than wings and backs. When deciding what type of pieces to buy, compare prices in terms of servings.

Chicken, like all poultry, contains more bone in proportion to muscle than does red meat. Therefore, when buying chicken with bones, you need to allow about ½ pound (225 g) of meat per serving. Allow a little less per serving if buying meaty pieces like legs and breasts. Allow a little more per serving if buying bony pieces like backs and wings.

Many recipes call for boneless chicken breasts and thighs. Boneless chicken pieces cost more than pieces with bones. Some people can save money by boning chicken themselves. If buying boneless poultry, ¼ pound (115 g) of meat per serving should be adequate.

Whole turkeys are available in many sizes, making them popular for large gatherings. Turkey parts and ground turkey are also available, **19-1**. Allow ⅓ to ½ pound (150 to 225 g) of whole turkey or turkey parts per serving. Allow ¼ pound (115 g) per serving when buying ground turkey. Allow more if leftovers are desired.

Ducks and geese have all dark meat, which is tender and flavorful. Both have more fat than chickens or turkeys. Geese usually have more fat than ducks. Allow ½ pound (225 g) per serving for both duck and goose.

When buying poultry, consider the following guidelines:

- Choose birds with meaty breasts and legs, well-distributed fat, and blemish-free skin.
- Choose the type and amount of poultry that will suit the intended use.
- Look for frozen birds that are solidly frozen.
- Beware of dirty and torn wrappers and freezer burn (pale, dry, frosty areas).

Some fresh poultry carries bacteria that can cause foodborne illness. When buying poultry, put it in a plastic bag as it is removed from the poultry case. This will keep poultry drippings from getting on other items in the grocery cart.

Wheat Foods Council

19-1 Ground turkey is a tasty alternative to ground beef for making burgers, meatballs, and many other dishes.

Buying Processed Poultry Products

Turkey and chicken are available canned. Canned poultry may be whole, cut into pieces, boned, or used in items like chicken chow mein. Generally, canned poultry items are more expensive than fresh-chilled or frozen poultry.

When buying processed poultry products or food items containing poultry, read labels carefully. The ingredient list may include a poultry part, such as *turkey breast* or *chicken leg*. This indicates the fatty skin, as well as the meat, has been used in the product. However, a listing of *breast meat* or *leg meat* indicates the product contains only meat—not skin.

Storing Poultry

All poultry, except canned, is very perishable. Poultry parts are more perishable than whole birds. Poultry needs proper storage to retard spoilage. Proper storage is also important to inhibit the growth of salmonellae, an illness-causing bacteria often found in poultry.

For refrigerator storage, remove store wrapping. Rewrap the bird loosely in waxed paper. Wrap and store giblets separately. Place poultry in the coldest part of the refrigerator and use within two to three days.

For longer storage, wrap the bird in moistureproof and vaporproof wrapping and store it in the freezer. Place poultry that is purchased frozen in the freezer immediately after purchase. Poultry can be stored in the freezer for six to eight months. Once poultry is thawed, however, it should not be refrozen.

Store all canned poultry products in a cool, dry place. Store all unused portions and cooked poultry in tightly covered containers in the refrigerator. Remove stuffing from cooked poultry and store it separately. Use leftovers within two or three days.

Food Science Principles of Cooking Poultry

Like meat, poultry is a protein food. Cooking principles for poultry are similar to those used for other high-protein foods. Low temperatures and careful timing are important.

Learn About...

Testing Poultry for Doneness

A food thermometer is the only accurate way to test poultry for doneness. When testing a whole bird, insert the probe of the thermometer into the thickest part of the thigh. When testing poultry pieces, insert the probe into the thickest area. The probe should not touch bone. Whole birds and pieces should reach an internal temperature of 165°F (74°C). Due to the uneven shape of whole poultry and poultry pieces, the temperature should be checked in several places.

USDA

Using a food thermometer to check the internal temperature is the only sure way to be certain poultry is thoroughly cooked.

Cooking poultry for too long or at too high a temperature can make it tough, dry, and flavorless.

Poultry must be cooked to the well-done stage, but it should not be overcooked. Pink flesh does not always mean poultry is undercooked. A chemical reaction causes a pink color in cooked poultry. Gases in the oven combine with substances in the poultry and turn the flesh pink. The pink color is not harmful.

Poultry bones will sometimes turn a dark color during cooking. Blood cells in the bone that have broken down during freezing cause this discoloration. When heated, they turn a dark brown. The color has no effect on flavor, and the meat is safe to eat.

Methods of Cooking Poultry

Poultry can be roasted, broiled, grilled, fried, braised, or stewed. The method chosen will depend mainly on taste preferences.

Do not wash poultry before cooking it. However, be sure to thoroughly wash cutting boards, knives, and other utensils after preparing raw poultry. This helps avoid the possibility of transferring harmful bacteria that may be in the poultry to other foods. These steps will help prevent cross-contamination.

Roasting Poultry

Roasting is a popular choice for cooking whole birds. When preparing poultry, be sure to remove the neck and the packet of giblets found inside the cavity of the bird. **Giblets** are the edible internal organs of poultry, such as the heart and liver. People often use them in appetizers and to flavor soups and gravies.

Large birds should be trussed before roasting. A *trussed* bird has its wing tips turned back onto the shoulder and the drumsticks tied to the tail. Trussing prevents the wing and leg tips from overbrowning. It also makes the bird easier to handle and more attractive to serve.

Place the trussed bird breast side up in a shallow pan. Season the cavity with salt and pepper unless the bird will be stuffed. Do not add stuffing until it is time to put the bird in the oven. This will prevent the growth of harmful bacteria, which can cause food-borne illness. Pack the stuffing loosely into the cavity. Any extra stuffing can be baked in a greased casserole.

Roast the bird in a 325°F (160°C) oven. Cook the bird until a meat thermometer reads 165°F (74°C). The temperature of the stuffing should also reach at least 165°F

Learn About...

Frozen Poultry

Thaw frozen poultry before cooking it. (If the bird is commercially stuffed, cook it without thawing.) To thaw, leave the bird in its original wrapping and let it thaw in the refrigerator. Place a plate under the bird to catch any drips that may form as the bird thaws.

For quicker thawing, wrap frozen poultry in a tightly closed plastic bag. Place it in a sink full of cold water. Change the water about every 30 minutes to keep it cold until the bird defrosts.

(74°C). (For faster roasting, wrap poultry in aluminum foil and cook it in a 450°F [230°C] oven.) If poultry is allowed to stand 10 to 15 minutes after being taken from the oven, it will be easier to carve.

Sometimes the breast of a large bird will brown too quickly during roasting. To prevent overbrowning, make a tent out of aluminum foil. Cover the breast with the foil when the bird is about half-cooked.

Some people prefer to roast poultry in oven cooking bags. Cooking bags shorten cooking time because they use steam to help cook the bird. Because steam is a form of moist heat, this method is not true roasting.

Broiling Poultry

Turkeys and chickens can be broiled. To broil poultry, split the bird into halves or quarters. Place pieces on a broiler pan and brush lightly with melted margarine, if desired. Broil 4 to 5 inches (10 to 12 cm) from the heat source until done. Cooking time depends on the size of the bird. Chicken usually will take about 40 minutes. Turkey will take about 80 to 90 minutes. Thinner pieces will cook faster than thicker pieces. Remove pieces from the broiler when they are cooked and keep them warm until ready to serve.

Grilling Poultry

Grilling is a popular way to cook whole birds and poultry pieces, especially during the summer. Grill poultry with bones using indirect heat. Grill boneless poultry pieces over direct heat. Grilling times depend on the size of pieces. Shorten grilling times by partially cooking poultry in a microwave oven immediately before placing it on the grill. Partial cooking also ensures grilled poultry is thoroughly cooked. Use an instant-read thermometer to test the internal temperature of grilled poultry for doneness.

Frying Poultry

Chickens and turkeys can be cut into pieces and fried. To fry poultry, first roll the pieces in flour, egg, and bread crumbs or dip them in a batter. Then brown the pieces in about ½ inch (1.5 cm) of hot fat. (The fat should not be so hot that it smokes.) Turn poultry pieces with tongs as they brown. After browning, the bird can finish cooking in the skillet over low heat. Cooking can also be completed in a moderate oven.

Oven-Frying Poultry

Oven-frying is sometimes called baking. You can oven-fry chicken pieces by coating them with seasoned flour. Place them on a baking sheet. Cook in a moderate oven until done. Brushing chicken lightly with melted margarine will produce a crisp golden crust.

Braising Poultry

To braise turkey or chicken, brown individual pieces in a small amount of fat. Add a small amount of water to the skillet and cover tightly. Cook the poultry over low heat until tender, about 45 minutes to 1 hour. Poultry can be braised on top of the range or in the oven. For a crisp crust, uncover the pan for the last 10 minutes of cooking.

EXPLORING CAREERS

Fast-Food Counter Attendant

A fast-food counter attendant plays an important role in creating a positive image of a restaurant. The counter attendant takes customer orders and enters them into a computerized cash register system. He or she takes payment and gives change. The attendant gathers prepared food items into bags or onto trays. He or she also pours beverages and may fill orders for simple food items, such as ice cream cones and premade salads. Then the attendant checks to be sure food orders are correct before handing them to customers. The counter attendant may also have to do cleaning tasks, such as wiping tables and mopping floors.

Above all, counter attendants must be friendly, polite, and helpful when serving customers. They need good listening skills to correctly hear all the details of customer orders. They must cooperate with coworkers and take direction from managers. Fast-food counter attendants will use math skills to count money. They must function well in a busy work environment. Attendants must know and follow food safety standards, too.

Fast-food counter attendant is an entry-level position. Many of these jobs require neither previous work experience nor a high school diploma. In addition, many attendants work only part-time. These qualities make counter attendant a good first job for many teen workers.

Photo provided by Culver Franchising System, Inc.

Fast-food counter attendants generally learn how to perform work tasks, such as preparing simple food items, by shadowing an experienced coworker.

Stewing Poultry

To stew poultry, put the bird in a big pot and cover it completely with water. Carrots, celery, and seasonings can be added for flavor. Cover the pot tightly and simmer over low heat until the bird is tender. (Never allow the liquid to boil.) If desired, you can remove cooled stewed meat from the bone for use in soups and casseroles.

Microwaving Poultry

A microwave oven can be used to defrost or partially cook poultry that is being immediately prepared by another method. Chicken or turkey can also be fully cooked in a microwave oven for poultry that comes out tender and juicy. Poultry generally microwaves in much less time than poultry cooks in a conventional oven. However, when roasting large birds, little or no time may be saved by using a microwave oven. In addition, most microwave ovens are not big enough to hold very large birds.

To ensure even cooking in a microwave oven, arrange poultry pieces with the bony portions to the center. Arrange drumsticks like the spokes of a wheel. Place the meaty ends toward the outside of the dish. On whole birds, the breast area and wing and leg tips may cook faster than the rest of the bird.

For Example...

Cooled stewed poultry removed from the bone can be used to make dishes like chicken salad, chicken and rice casserole, and chicken noodle soup.

Discuss

Ask students why partial cooking of poultry in a microwave oven should not be done hours before the poultry will finish cooking by another method. *(Partial cooking warms the poultry to a temperature that fosters bacterial growth. Cooking should be completed immediately to kill harmful bacteria.)*

CAREER SUCCESS

Interpreting and Communicating Information

Calvin is a sales representative for the Better Bird Feed Company. He sells feed products to poultry farmers all over the Midwest. Each time the company introduces a feed product, someone from the research department gives a presentation to the sales group. The researcher describes the new product's features. Then Calvin receives stacks of detailed handouts about the product. The handouts show lists of ingredients, charts of research results, and graphs comparing Better Bird's feed with other brands.

To be an effective worker, Calvin needs skill in interpreting and communicating information. In a small group, answer the following questions about Calvin's need for and use of these skills:

A. Why wouldn't Calvin simply let his customers read copies of the research handouts to learn about new products?

B. How might Calvin's customers be affected if he does not adequately interpret and communicate information about new products?

C. How might Calvin's company be affected if he does not adequately interpret and communicate information about new products?

D. What is another skill Calvin would need in this job? Briefly explain why this skill would be important.

CHAPTER 19 REVIEW

Summary

Poultry is a good source of protein and B vitamins. Most poultry is marketed young. When buying poultry, look for meaty birds with well-distributed fat and blemish-free skin.

All poultry is perishable. Store it in the coldest part of the refrigerator and use it within two to three days. Carefully wrap poultry and place it in the freezer for longer storage.

Always be sure poultry is thoroughly cooked before serving it. However, use moderate cooking temperatures and careful timing to avoid overcooking. Overcooking can result in meat that is tough and dry.

Because most poultry is tender, it is suitable for any cooking method. Poultry can be roasted, broiled, grilled, fried, braised, stewed, or microwaved.

Review What You Have Read

Write your answers on a separate sheet of paper, using complete sentences when appropriate.

1. Name the four kinds of poultry most commonly eaten in the United States.
2. True or false. Most poultry is tender and can be cooked by dry heat methods.
3. Why do you need to allow more weight per serving when buying poultry than when buying red meat?
4. Within what time period should refrigerated poultry be used?
5. True or false. Stuffing should be left inside a poultry carcass for refrigerator storage.
6. What is the recommended internal temperature for cooked poultry?
7. Why is it important to thoroughly wash cutting boards and utensils after preparing raw poultry?
8. Why should a large bird be trussed before roasting?
9. What are two advantages of partially cooking poultry in a microwave oven immediately before placing it on a grill?
10. How should poultry pieces be arranged in a microwave oven to ensure even cooking?

Answer Key to *Review What You Have Read* **questions**

1. Chicken, turkey, goose, and duck are the four kinds of poultry most commonly eaten in the United States.
2. true
3. Poultry contains more bone in proportion to muscle than red meat.
4. Refrigerated poultry should be used within two to three days.
5. false
6. Whole birds and pieces should reach an internal temperature of 165°F.
7. Poultry may contain harmful bacteria that can get on the cutting board and utensils. Thoroughly washing the cutting board and utensils can help avoid the possibility of transferring these harmful bacteria to other foods.
8. Trussing prevents the wing and leg tips from overbrowning. It also makes the bird easier to handle and more attractive to serve.

(continued)

Link to Academic Skills

9. Partial cooking shortens grilling time and ensures that grilled poultry is thoroughly cooked.

10. Place bony portions to the center and arrange drumsticks like the spokes of a wheel.

11. **Social studies.** Investigate poultry consumption trends in the United States in the last 100 years. Make a graph to illustrate your findings. Write a one-page summary explaining the reasons for any changes in consumption patterns.

12. **English language arts.** Write three questions about poultry selection, storage, and preparation. Then contact the U.S. Department of Agriculture's Meat and Poultry Hotline for answers to your questions.

13. **History.** Investigate the types of poultry dishes that were typically served throughout the year and at holidays in colonial America. Bring in a copy of a historical poultry recipe to share with the class.

14. **English language arts.** Visit the consumer section of the National Turkey Federation website. Select an item from the list of holiday cooking tips and summarize the information in a poster presentation to the class.

Build Critical Thinking Skills

15. **Analysis.** Roast chicken, turkey, duck, and goose. Taste and analyze the various meats to compare them in terms of appearance, flavor, and texture.

16. **Synthesis.** Find at least three recipes for stuffing. Note what ingredients the recipes have in common and which ingredients are unique to each recipe. Also note the ingredient proportions. Combine components of these recipes with your creativity to synthesize your own recipe for stuffing. Prepare and sample the recipe. Explain why you would or would not choose to serve it with poultry.

Apply Technology

17. Investigate new techniques being studied to reduce salmonella contamination in poultry. Share your findings in a brief oral report.

18. Research the production procedures used to manufacture poultry-based luncheon meats. Prepare a poster presentation illustrating the procedures.

A Measure of Math

19. Compare the price per pound of boneless, skinless chicken breasts with the price per pound of bone-in, skin-on chicken breasts. Calculate the price per ounce of each chicken product. Remove the bone and skin from the bone-in, skin-on breasts. Weigh the bone and skin on a scale. Determine the percentage of waste in the bone-in, skin-on product. Then calculate the cost per ounce of the meat portion of this product. How does this cost compare with the cost of the product sold without bone and skin?

Teamwork in Action

20. Prepare a brochure about the importance of using a thermometer to check the doneness of poultry at holiday meals. The brochure should also discuss how to properly store and reheat leftovers. Place stacks of the brochures in your local library or community center before an upcoming holiday.

Companion Website

www.g-wlearning.com

At the website, review key terms for this chapter with crossword puzzles, matching exercises, and e-flash cards. Apply facts from the chapter to complete the activities.

CHAPTER 20
Fish and Shellfish

Main Menu

⚬ Knowing how to choose fish and shellfish will help consumers get their money's worth when buying seafood.

⚬ Using careful timing and correct cooking temperatures will result in moist, tender fish and shellfish.

Learning Prep

After reading the definitions for the *Terms to Know* in the glossary, give a specific example of each term that consumers might find in the marketplace.

Objectives

After studying this chapter, you will be able to

⚬ **list** factors affecting the selection of fish and shellfish.

⚬ **describe** how to properly store fish to maintain its quality.

⚬ **describe** the principles and methods for cooking fish and shellfish.

⚬ **prepare** fish by moist and dry cooking methods.

Terms to Know

finfish
shellfish
lean fish
fat fish
drawn fish

dressed fish
fish steak
fish fillet
crustacean
mollusk

Commercial fishers in the United States catch several billion fish each year for food, **20-1**. However, the U.S. is a small consumer of fish and fish products compared with other countries.

Choosing Fish and Shellfish

Two kinds of water animals are eaten as food: finfish (often called *fish*) and shellfish. **Finfish** have fins and backbones. **Shellfish** have shells instead of backbones.

Nutritional Value of Fish and Shellfish

Both fish and shellfish are excellent sources of complete protein. One ounce of fish and shellfish counts as 1 ounce-equivalent from the protein foods group of MyPlate. Most teens need 5 to 7 ounce-equivalents from this group each day, depending on calorie needs. It is recommended that at least 8 ounce-equivalents per week come from a variety of seafood.

Most fish have fewer calories and less saturated fat and cholesterol than moderately fat red meat. Eating fish regularly can help increase the intake of mono- and poly-unsaturated fats. These types of fats should make up the bulk of fats in the diet.

Overall, fish is slightly higher in minerals than red meat. Shellfish have even more minerals than finfish. Fish

Shutterstock
20-1 Commercial fishing is an important industry in coastal regions.

EXPLORING CAREERS

Fish Hatchery Manager

Fish hatchery managers work in facilities that breed and raise fish and shellfish for food, sport fishing, and research. They train, oversee, and help employees in the use of techniques and equipment to fertilize eggs and produce large numbers of young fish. They must monitor the feeding and growth of the fish. Managers check for diseases among the fish and specify treatments, if needed. They determine when fish need to be transferred to different tanks or ponds. They also identify when the fish are ready to be harvested for food or released into the wild.

To be successful, fish hatchery managers need to be good leaders and communicators. They will have to train, schedule, direct, evaluate, and correct workers. They need to make the best use of resources such as equipment, supplies, and money. They will use analytical skills as they examine the progress of the fish. Hatchery managers must be problem solvers when concerns arise with the health of the fish or the condition of the facilities. They will use math skills as they calculate numbers of fish produced. They will also use computer skills to keep records of breeding, shipping, and harvest or release dates.

This career involves some time spent inside doing office work. However, managers must be willing to work outdoors in all types of weather, too. Fish hatchery managers usually need several years of experience and a bachelor's degree in a field such as fishery science.

provide fair amounts of iron. Canned salmon and sardines prepared with their bones are especially good sources of calcium. Saltwater fish are one of the most important sources of iodine.

Fish and shellfish contribute the same vitamins as red meat. Fattier fish provide higher amounts of vitamins A and D.

Forms of Finfish

Finfish can be lean or fatty. **Lean fish** have very little fat in their flesh. Because their flesh is white, they are often called *white fish*. Swordfish, haddock, and cod are lean fish. **Fat fish** have flesh that is fattier than that of lean fish. Their flesh is usually pink, yellow, or gray. Mackerel, trout, and salmon are fat fish. Lean fish have fewer calories than fat fish. However, fat fish are better sources of omega-3 fatty acids, which some studies show may reduce the risk of heart disease.

Both lean and fat fish fresh can be purchased as whole, drawn, or dressed fish or as steaks or fillets. A *whole (round) fish* is marketed as it comes from the water. It must be cleaned before cooking. A **drawn fish** has the *entrails* (insides) removed. A **dressed fish** has the entrails, head, fins, and scales removed. It is ready for cooking. **Fish steaks** are cross-sectional slices taken from a dressed fish. **Fish fillets** are the sides of the fish cut lengthwise away from the backbone. Fillets have few, if any, bones. See **20-2**.

Buying Fresh Finfish

The cost of seafood depends on the form and the region of the country. Fish fillets generally cost more than whole fish because they require more handling. Money can be saved by buying dressed fish and filleting it at home. Fresh fish purchased where it is taken from the water will be less expensive than fish that must be shipped inland.

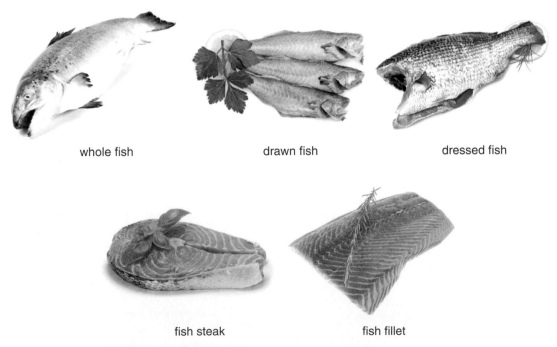

whole fish   drawn fish   dressed fish

fish steak   fish fillet

Shutterstock
20-2 Fresh fish can be purchased in several forms.

When buying fresh fish, look for a stiff body, tight scales, and firm flesh. The gills should be red, and the eyes bright and bulging. A finger pushed into the flesh should leave no indentation. The outside should have little or no slime, and the fish should smell fresh.

The amount of fish to buy depends on the kind and form. Fish, as a rule, have a large amount of waste. Dressed fish have less waste than whole and drawn fish. Fillets and steaks have even less waste.

Buying Fresh Shellfish

Shellfish can be divided into two groups: crustaceans and mollusks. **Crustaceans** are covered by firm shells and have segmented (divided into sections) bodies. Shrimp, lobsters, and crabs are crustaceans. **Mollusks** have soft bodies that are partially or fully covered by hard shells. Oysters, clams, and scallops are mollusks.

Most shellfish, except for small oysters, are expensive regardless of location. However, knowing what to look for can help consumers get the most for the money.

Crustaceans

Shrimp are the most important shellfish in the United States in terms of the amount eaten. Several varieties of shrimp can be purchased. They differ in color and size when they are raw. Shrimp are marketed by sizes such as jumbo, large, medium, and small. Sizes are based on the number needed to weigh 1 pound (0.45 kg).

Most shrimp are sold without the head and thorax (middle division of the body). Shrimp labeled as *deveined* have had the intestinal tract removed. (The intestinal tract appears as a dark streak that runs along one side of the shrimp.) When buying fresh shrimp, look for those that are odorless with firmly attached shells.

Lobster shells are dark blue green when removed from the water. They become red when cooked. When buying live lobsters, look for those with tails that snap back quickly after being flattened.

The blue crab and Dungeness crab are the two most common species sold in the United States. They can be bought live in the shell. Fresh king crab legs and claws are popular, too.

Mollusks

Several kinds of oysters and clams are eaten in the United States. Oysters are packed according to size. Fresh oysters and clams can be purchased live in the shell or *shucked* (removed from shell). Both should have tightly closed shells or the shells should close when touched. Shucked oysters and clams should be plump, creamy in color, and odorless.

Tiny bay scallops and larger deep-sea scallops are available on the market. A fresh bay scallop is creamy white or pink. A fresh deep-sea scallop is white. The whole bodies of these mollusks are edible. However, the large muscle used to close the shell is the only part commonly eaten in the United States. Unlike oysters and clams, fresh scallops are not available in the shell. See **20-3**.

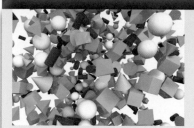

shrimp   lobster   crab

clams   oyster   scallop

Shutterstock

20-3 Both crustaceans and mollusks are available in most markets that sell shellfish.

Health and Wellness

Food Safety at the Fish Market

Fresh seafood can be a source of bacteria that cause foodborne illness. To ensure the safety of the fish and shellfish, deal only with reputable sellers. Look for the signs of quality described earlier. Be sure the market is clean and the fish is properly stored on beds of ice, preferably under a cover. The employees should be practicing safe food handling procedures, including wearing disposable gloves when handling seafood.

Frozen Fish and Shellfish

Drawn and dressed fish, as well as fish steaks and fillets, can be purchased frozen. Frozen fish should be solidly frozen in moisture-proof and vaporproof wrapping. There should be no discoloration and little or no odor.

Shrimp, lobster, crab, oysters, clams, and scallops are all available frozen. Uncooked shrimp can be purchased either peeled or unpeeled. Shrimp is also available cooked and peeled or peeled, cleaned, and breaded. Lobsters and crabs can be purchased cooked whole and as frozen cooked meat. Lobster tails are also available cooked. Frozen oysters, clams, and scallops are sold shucked.

Canned Fish and Shellfish

Tuna, salmon, sardines, shrimp, crab, lobster, and clams are among the fish and shellfish available in cans and foil pouches. Read labels to be sure of what is being purchased. To reduce fat in the diet, choose tuna packed in water instead of oil. If making shrimp cocktail, choose large, fancy shrimp rather than small shrimp.

Storing Fish and Shellfish

Fish is very perishable, so it must be stored with care. Wrap fresh fish tightly in waxed paper or foil. Place it in a tightly covered container in the coldest part of the refrigerator. Use stored fish within a day or two. For freezer storage, wrap fish in moistureproof and vaporproof material. Store it in the coldest part of the freezer.

Keep frozen fish in its original package. Place it in the freezer as soon as possible after purchase.

Store canned fish in a cool, dry place. Refrigerate any unused portions in a tightly covered container. Use it within a day or two.

Cooking Finfish

Preparing seafood with care can help to avoid foodborne illness. Practice the same precautions when handling seafood that are used when handling meat and poultry. Be sure hands are washed thoroughly before and after handling fish and shellfish. Do not thaw frozen products at room temperature. Keep cooked food from touching anything, such as utensils or marinades, that came in contact with raw seafood. Use an instant-read thermometer to be sure the internal temperature of cooked seafood has reached 145°F (63°C). Refrigerate leftover portions promptly.

Principles of Cooking Finfish

When a finfish is cooked to the proper degree of doneness, the flesh will be firm, and it will *flake* easily with a fork. (When the tines of a fork are gently inserted into the flesh and lifted slightly, the flesh will separate into distinct layers.) The flesh of a properly cooked fish will have lost its translucent appearance and will look opaque.

Methods of Cooking Finfish

All finfish are naturally tender, so both dry and moist heat cooking methods can be used. The fat content of the fish usually determines the cooking method. Generally, fat fish should be cooked by dry heat and lean fish by moist heat. See **20-4**.

Fat fish, such as mackerel, salmon, and trout, are delicious when broiled, grilled, or baked. Their fat keeps them from drying out during cooking.

Lean fish, like swordfish, halibut, flounder, haddock, and red snapper, are usually fried, poached, or steamed. Lean fish can be cooked by dry heat if they are brushed with fat or cooked in a sauce. Likewise, fat fish can be poached or steamed if they are handled gently. (Fat fish can fall apart more easily when cooked in liquid.)

Cooking methods used for fish include broiling, grilling, baking, frying, poaching, and steaming. A general guide can be used to time fish cooked by all these methods, except deep-frying. Measure fish, including stuffed and rolled fish, at its thickest point. It should be cooked about 10 minutes for every inch (2.5 cm) of thickness. Turn thick pieces of fish once during cooking. Fish that is less than ½ inch (1.25 cm) thick does not need to be turned. If fish is wrapped in foil or covered with a sauce, add 5 extra

Pyrex®

20-4 Fat fish, such as salmon, stay moist when prepared by baking and other dry heat cooking methods.

Food Science

Cooking Seafood

Finfish contain tender muscle fibers and little connective tissue. For this reason, tenderizing is not a goal when cooking fish as it is when cooking some meats. Finfish needs to cook for only a short time. They must be watched carefully to keep them from becoming dry and overcooked.

Fish should neither be undercooked nor overcooked. Undercooked fish can have an unpleasant flavor and may contain harmful bacteria. Overcooked fish is tough and dry. Some varieties become rubbery; others fall apart.

Like finfish, all kinds of shellfish are naturally tender. As a result, they should only be cooked for a short time at moderate temperatures. Overcooking will cause the proteins to overcoagulate and make the shellfish tough.

minutes to the cooking time. Fish cooked from the frozen state will require twice as much time to cook. Test fish for doneness by flaking with a fork.

Broiling Finfish

For broiling, select fish that are at least 1 inch (2.5 cm) thick. Steaks, fillets, and dressed fish can be broiled. Place the fish on a cold broiler pan and brush the fish with oil if it is lean. Broil until the fish flakes easily with a fork. Thinner fish can be cooked closer to the heat source than thicker fish. Thick pieces will need to be turned once during broiling.

Grilling Finfish

The grilling method used for fish depends on the form of fish being prepared. Grill steaks and fillets by placing them directly over hot coals. Turn over thick pieces halfway through the grilling time. Use indirect heat to grill dressed fish. Test steaks and fillets with a fork for doneness. Use an instant-read thermometer to check the internal temperature of dressed fish.

Baking Finfish

For baking, select steaks, fillets, and dressed fish. To prevent fish from drying out, brush the pieces with oil or with a sauce. Dressed fish and fillets should be stuffed just before baking. Bake fish at 400°F to 450°F (200°C to 230°C).

Frying Finfish

Finfish can be pan-fried, oven-fried, or deep-fried. Fillets, steaks, and small dressed fish can be pan-fried. Coat fish to be pan-fried with crumbs or with a batter. Then fry them in a small amount of fat until browned. See **20-5**.

Cut fish to be oven-fried into serving-sized pieces and coat them with milk and crumbs. Then drizzle them lightly with oil and place them on a greased baking sheet. To get a crispy texture that resembles deep-frying, bake fish in a 500°F (260°C) oven. At this high temperature, use caution around the oven and watch fish closely as it will cook very quickly. The breading keeps the fish from becoming dry.

USA Rice Federation

20-5 Pan-fried fish fillets have a delicate texture.

Discuss

Ask students if they have seen special fish poachers. These are long, deep, narrow containers usually used for poaching dressed fish.

Discuss

Ask students how they would distinguish a seafood fork to be used with an appetizer from one to be used with an entree. Bring samples to class for display. Ask students why they think an appetizer fork has only two prongs.

Activity

Have students contact a seafood restaurant to find out what seafood specialties they offer on their menu.

Cut fish for deep-frying into serving-sized pieces. Bread them or dip them in batter. Then fry them in 375°F (190°C) fat. If the fat is too hot, the outside of the fish will burn before the inside is cooked. If the fat is too cool, the fish will be soggy and greasy.

Poaching Finfish

Poaching is cooking in simmering liquid. To poach fish, use any tightly covered cookware that is large and deep enough to hold the fish. Add enough liquid to barely cover the fish. Use lightly salted water, milk, or water seasoned with spices or herbs as the poaching liquid. (If a dressed fish is wrapped in cheesecloth or parchment paper or placed on a rack before cooking, it will better retain its shape.) Cover the pan and poach the fish over low heat until it flakes easily with a fork. After the fish is cooked, reduce the volume of the poaching liquid by simmering it in the uncovered pan. Then the sauce can be thickened and served as a sauce.

Steaming Finfish

Steaming differs from poaching only in the amount of liquid used. Less liquid can be used because the steam that forms inside the covered cooking utensil will cook the fish. To steam fish, place dressed fish, steaks, or fillets on a rack over simmering liquid. Cover the pan tightly and steam until the fish flakes easily. (Never allow the water to boil.) Fish can also be steamed in the oven in a covered pan or wrapped in aluminum foil. The cover or foil holds in the steam that forms so the steam can cook the fish.

Cooking Frozen Finfish

Frozen fish can be cooked either frozen or thawed. If fish is thawed, it can be cooked like fresh fish. If fish is not thawed, it must cook at a lower temperature and for a longer time than fresh fish.

Cooking Shellfish

Shellfish can be simmered, baked, broiled, grilled, pan-fried (sautéed), or deep-fried. The cooking method used depends on the kind of shellfish and whether it is purchased live, frozen, or canned.

People who live in an area where fresh shellfish is available may purchase their shellfish live. Shellfish purchased live in the shell must be alive when cooked. (Fresh, uncooked shellfish deteriorates very rapidly.)

Parboil live lobster, shrimp, and crab by plunging the shellfish into boiling, salted water until it is partially cooked. (Plunge lobster into the water headfirst.) Shellfish then should be simmered, not boiled. After parboiling, shrimp can be broiled, grilled, baked, pan-fried, or deep-fried. Lobster and crab may be baked or broiled. All three may be combined with other ingredients to make such seafood specialties as Lobster Thermidor, Shrimp Scampi, and Crab Newburg.

The shells of live oysters and clams should be tightly closed. Discard oysters and clams if their shells are open. When live oysters or clams are dropped into simmering water, the shells will open. The edible part of the shellfish can then be removed from the shell. After removal, simmer, deep-fry, or sauté oysters and clams. Because fresh scallops are not sold in the shell, they are ready when purchased to be prepared by the desired cooking method, **20-6**.

©2011 Wisconsin Milk Marketing Board, Inc.

20-6 These pan-seared sea scallops are moist and tender.

In inland areas, most of the available shellfish is frozen or canned. Cook uncooked frozen shrimp in salted simmering water until pink. Frozen lobster tails are partially cooked. They may be thawed and broiled, or they may be cooked in simmering liquid like uncooked frozen shrimp. Cooked frozen shrimp, crab, or scallops may be baked, broiled or fried.

Canned shellfish can be served without further cooking. They may also be combined with other foods in salads and main dishes.

CAREER SUCCESS

Selecting Equipment and Tools

Midori is a raw shellfish preparer at The Barrier Reef, an elegant seafood restaurant. She is responsible for shucking fresh clams, oysters, and scallops; deveining shrimp; cracking crab legs; and splitting lobster tails. The owner of the restaurant prides himself in the presentation of the food. He will not allow the staff to serve anything that looks imperfect. However, he becomes quite angry when food is wasted.

To be an effective worker, Midori needs skills in selecting equipment and tools. In a small group, answer the following questions about Midori's need for and use of these skills:

A. How might the food be affected if Midori does not select the proper tools and equipment for each type of shellfish?

B. How might Midori's customers react if she does not properly prepare each type of shellfish?

C. How might Midori's employer react if she does not properly prepare each type of shellfish?

D. What is another skill Midori would need in this job? Briefly explain why this skill would be important.

CHAPTER 20 REVIEW

Summary

Consider choosing fish and shellfish often as a healthful source of protein in the diet. Finfish are available whole, drawn, dressed, or as steaks or fillets. The cost of finfish depends on the form and where it is purchased. Knowing signs of quality for both crustaceans and mollusks can help to get good value when buying shellfish. Finfish and shellfish are available frozen and canned as well as fresh. All seafood is quite perishable. It should be stored carefully and used soon after purchase.

Both finfish and shellfish require short cooking periods and moderate temperatures. Properly cooked finfish have an opaque appearance and flake easily with a fork. A number of cooking methods can be used to prepare fish. Appropriate methods include broiling, grilling, baking, frying, poaching, and steaming. However, fat fish are usually best prepared by dry heat and lean fish are usually best prepared by moist heat. The kind of shellfish, and whether purchased live, frozen, or canned, will help determine how to cook it.

Review What You Have Read

Write your answers on a separate sheet of paper, using complete sentences when appropriate.

1. Canned salmon and sardines (with bones) are especially good sources of what mineral?
2. A fish that has the entrails removed is called a _____.
   A. drawn fish
   B. dressed fish
   C. fish fillet
   D. fish steak
3. List four signs of quality for purchasing fresh fish.
4. Shrimp, lobsters, and crabs are examples of _____.
5. What are deveined shrimp?
6. Describe how to prepare fish for refrigerator storage.
7. What are two characteristics that indicate a finfish has been cooked to the proper degree of doneness?
8. What type of finfish is usually cooked by dry heat?
9. What can you do to prevent baked fish from drying out?
10. How can you help poached fish retain its shape?
11. True or false. Frozen fish is cooked for the same amount of time and at the same temperature as fresh fish.
12. True or false. Shellfish purchased live in the shell must be alive when cooked.

(continued)

Link to Academic Skills

13. **English language arts.** Read an article about the dangers of commercial fishing. Then write a paragraph describing why you would or would not be interested in this career.

14. **Government/Civics.** Find out about wild seafood populations that are in danger of being overfished. What kinds of government regulations have been enacted to protect these species? What can consumers do to help protect the earth's oceans?

15. **Social studies.** Research how fish protein concentrate (FPC) is made. Investigate how this product might be used to address protein deficiencies in some population groups.

16. **Geography.** Investigate what varieties of fish and shellfish are available from sources within 300 miles of your home. Discuss the advantages of choosing fish from local sources.

10. To help poached fish retain its shape, wrap the fish in cheesecloth or parchment paper or place it on a rack before poaching.

11. false

12. true

Build Critical Thinking Skills

17. **Analysis.** With your foods lab group, examine an unknown type of fish fillet given to you by your teacher. Predict whether the fish would be best prepared by moist or dry heat. Cut the fillet in half. Prepare one half by a moist heat method and the other half by a dry heat method. Analyze and compare the flavor and appearance of the two cooked pieces. Write a brief report stating your reasons for your original prediction and an analysis of whether your prediction was accurate.

18. **Evaluation.** Pan-fry, oven-fry, and deep-fry small, dressed fish or fish fillets using both batter and crumb coatings. Prepare a table to evaluate the color, crispness, tenderness, and flavor of the fish prepared by the various methods.

Apply Technology

19. Investigate how commercial fishers use sonar technology to detect fish in the water.

20. Explore the development of aquaculture technology and its impact on the supply of fish in consumer retail outlets. Share your findings in an oral report.

A Measure of Math

21. Compare the cholesterol and fat content of several varieties of fish and shellfish with those of several cuts of meat. Use the USDA National Nutrient Database to help you.

Teamwork in Action

22. As a class, organize a community fish fry or clambake. Visit the Simply Seafood website to read articles and review recipes in preparation for this event.

Companion Website

www.g-wlearning.com

At the website, review key terms for this chapter with crossword puzzles, matching exercises, and e-flash cards. Apply facts from the chapter to complete the activities.

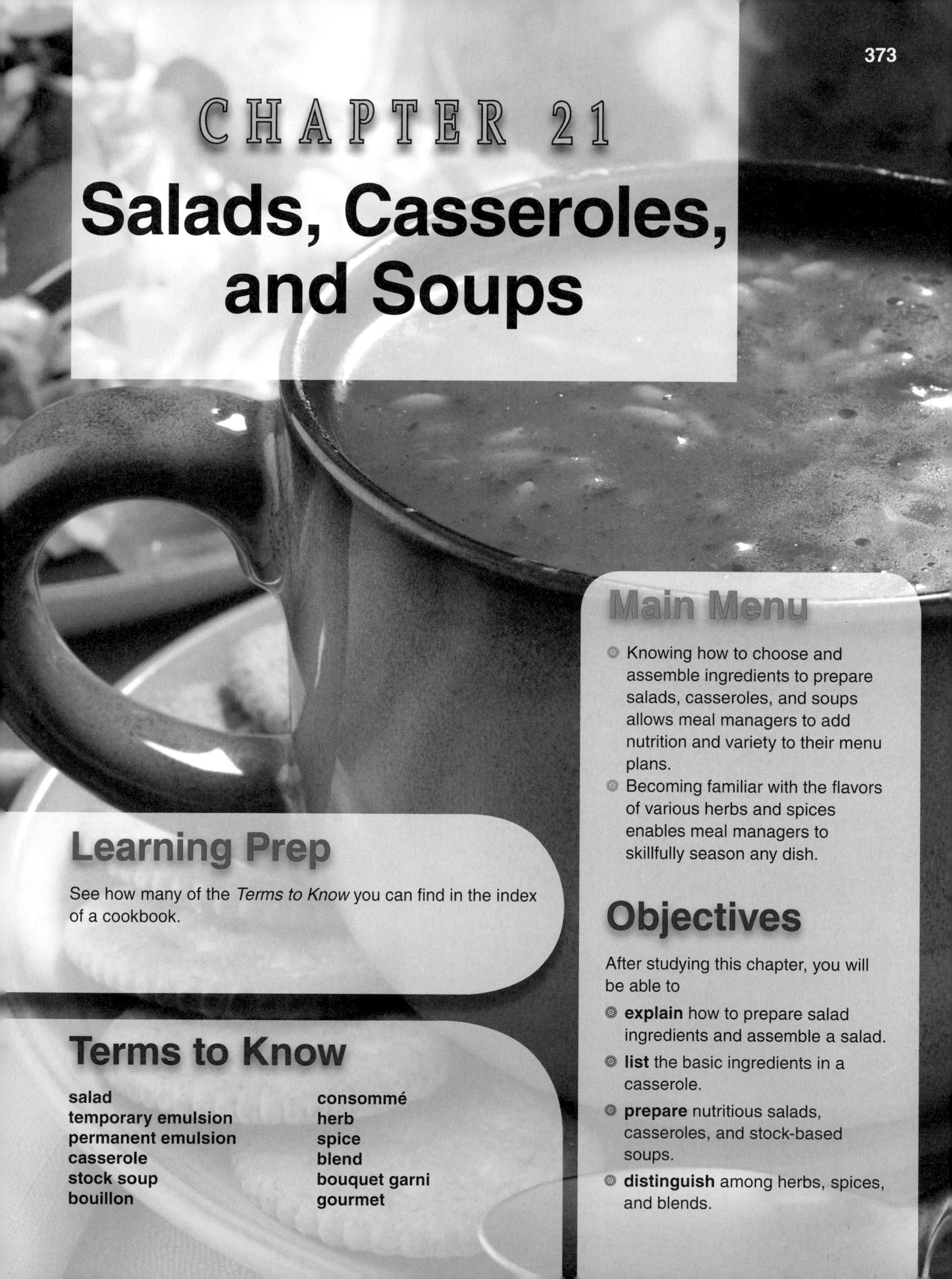

CHAPTER 21
Salads, Casseroles, and Soups

Main Menu

- Knowing how to choose and assemble ingredients to prepare salads, casseroles, and soups allows meal managers to add nutrition and variety to their menu plans.
- Becoming familiar with the flavors of various herbs and spices enables meal managers to skillfully season any dish.

Learning Prep

See how many of the *Terms to Know* you can find in the index of a cookbook.

Objectives

After studying this chapter, you will be able to

- **explain** how to prepare salad ingredients and assemble a salad.
- **list** the basic ingredients in a casserole.
- **prepare** nutritious salads, casseroles, and stock-based soups.
- **distinguish** among herbs, spices, and blends.

Terms to Know

salad
temporary emulsion
permanent emulsion
casserole
stock soup
bouillon

consommé
herb
spice
blend
bouquet garni
gourmet

Salads, casseroles, and soups add versatility to menus. They may be served as the main course or as an accompaniment to a meal. These combination dishes are nutritious as well as economical. They include a variety of ingredients, and preparing them can be a way to use leftovers.

Salads

What is a salad? A **salad** is a combination of raw and/or cooked ingredients, usually served cold with a dressing. The vegetables, fruits, and protein foods salads contain contribute important nutrients to the diet. Depending on the ingredients, salads can be served as any part of a meal—appetizer, main dish, accompaniment, or dessert.

Kinds of Salads

Most salads fit into one of five groups. *Protein salads* may have small pieces of protein food combined with a dressing. Chicken, ham, crab, and egg salads are examples of this type. Other protein salads have strips or slices of protein food arranged on a plate with cold vegetables or fruits. A chef salad is an example of this type.

Pasta, vegetable, fruit, and gelatin are the other four groups of salads. A *pasta salad* is a combination of cooked pasta, vegetables, possibly a protein food, and a dressing. *Vegetable salads* can be made from salad greens; raw vegetables; or cold, cooked vegetables. Tossed salad, coleslaw, and three-bean salad are examples of vegetable salads, **21-1**. Canned, frozen, or fresh fruits served on a bed of greens or in a hollowed fruit shell make a refreshing *fruit salad*. Commercial fruit-flavored gelatin can be used or mix fruit and vegetable juices with unflavored gelatin to make a *gelatin salad*. Almost any fruits, vegetables, and/or protein foods can be added to the gelatin for nutrition and variety.

Hamilton Beach Brands, Inc.
21-1 Tossed salad is a classic vegetable salad that goes well with many menu plans.

Preparing Salad Ingredients

Most fruits and vegetables used in salads are very perishable. Preserving their freshness is important to keep colors bright, textures crisp, and flavors full. Treating fruits, vegetables, and salad greens carefully will also help protect nutrients.

Discard outer leaves of salad greens. Wash all fresh fruits and vegetables under clean running water to remove soil and microorganisms. Trim any bruised or inedible spots. Avoid soaking fresh ingredients to prevent loss of water-soluble nutrients. Dry produce gently to remove surface moisture.

The size of pieces of food in a salad should be easy to manage. Tear salad greens into bite-sized pieces. Do not cut greens with a knife, as this will cause bruising. Avoid mincing other salad ingredients to keep them from forming a paste when mixed with the dressing.

Treat fresh cut apples, peaches, bananas, and pears with lemon juice. This will prevent enzymatic browning, making the salad look fresher and more attractive.

Canned peaches and pears can be served in large pieces because they are easy to cut with a fork. Be sure to drain liquid from canned fruits and vegetables. Extra liquid will make salads look and taste watery.

Varying the shapes of pieces will add interest to the appearance of a salad. Citrus fruits will usually need to be sectioned. Tomatoes and hard-cooked eggs might be cut into wedges. Carrots are often sliced or shredded. Meats and poultry are often diced. Fish can be flaked with a fork. Cheese might be crumbled or cut into strips.

Food Science

Ingredients That Affect Gelatin

Fresh and frozen pineapple contain an enzyme that will keep gelatin from setting. Fresh and frozen kiwi, gingerroot, papaya, figs, and guava will keep gelatin from setting, too. However, feel free to use cooked and canned forms of these foods. The heat used in cooking and canning deactivates the enzymes that affect gelatin.

Preparing Salad Dressings

There are three basic types of salad dressings: French, mayonnaise, and cooked. All three types are examples of *emulsions*, which are combinations of two liquids that ordinarily will not stay mixed. In the case of salad dressings, these liquids are usually oil and vinegar, lemon juice, or some other water-based liquid.

Make a true *French dressing* by combining oil, vinegar, and seasonings. When the dressing is agitated (shaken), an emulsion forms. When the agitation is stopped and the dressing is allowed to stand, the oil and water-based liquid separate, and the emulsion breaks. Therefore, French dressing is considered a **temporary emulsion**. French dressing must be shaken or stirred to mix it each time it is used.

Health and Wellness

Keeping Salads Healthful

To prevent nutrient losses, it is best not to clean fresh salad ingredients too far in advance. Wrap cleaned greens loosely in plastic film or a damp cloth or store them in a vegetable keeper. Washed greens can be stored for a few hours in the refrigerator. They will be crisp when ready to serve and will still retain important vitamins and minerals.

Dressing can add a lot of fat and calories to a salad. To avoid this, try using lowfat or fat-free dressing. Lowfat yogurt can be substituted for dressing on many salads. Flavor plain yogurt with herbs and use it on vegetable salads. Vanilla and fruit-flavored yogurts make creamy toppings for fruit salads.

Mayonnaise is made from vinegar (or lemon juice), oil, seasonings, and egg yolk. Mayonnaise is an example of a **permanent emulsion**. This type of emulsion will not separate on standing. This is because the egg yolk acts as an *emulsifying agent*. This is an ingredient that surrounds the droplets of oil and keeps them suspended in the liquid (vinegar or lemon juice).

A *cooked salad dressing* looks like mayonnaise. However, it is thickened with a food starch, such as cornstarch or flour. It also contains milk or water, an acid ingredient such as lemon juice, and a small amount of oil. Egg and butter are optional ingredients. Cooked salad dressings are permanent emulsions.

Other ingredients can be added to mayonnaise or basic cooked dressing. For a fruit salad, crushed pineapple might be added. For Thousand Island dressing, add catsup and pickle relish.

Assembling a Salad

Most salads have three parts: a base, body, and dressing. The *base* is the foundation on which the main salad ingredients are placed, **21-2**. It provides a color contrast with the body of the salad. It also keeps the serving dish from looking bare. The base should not extend over the edge of the plate or serving dish.

Salad greens are often used to make the salad base. A combination of three or four types of greens can add flavor, color, and texture variety to salads. Dark leafy greens also provide more nutrients than pale iceberg lettuce. Boston lettuce, watercress, spinach, escarole, endive, and leaf lettuce are some of the many salad greens available.

For convenience, bagged salad greens might be chosen. Special packaging allows them to stay fresh for an extended time. For best quality, be sure to use bagged greens by the date on the package or within two days after opening.

Courtesy of the Idaho Potato Commission
21-2 Shredded cabbage serves as a base for this Thai Idaho potato salad.

Attractively arrange the *salad body*, or main part of the salad, on top of the base. For molded gelatin, spraying the mold with nonstick cooking spray before filling will make unmolding easier. When the gelatin is firmly set, dip the mold into warm water for about 10 seconds. (Do not keep the mold in the water too long, or the gelatin will lose its shape.) Invert the loosened salad onto a serving plate.

The *dressing* is a sauce that adds flavor to a salad. The dressing is usually poured over the salad just before serving. Use just enough dressing to complement, not mask, the flavors of the other salad ingredients. Dressings may also be served separately to allow diners to dress their own salads. For some salads, the dressing is added several hours before serving to give the flavors a chance to blend.

Some salads have a fourth part—the *garnish*. A garnish can add nutrients as well as sensory appeal. It should complement the other salad ingredients. Try grape tomatoes for color, toasted nuts for crunch, or orange slices for a burst of flavor.

Some salads, such as German potato salad, are served hot. Most other salads are served well chilled. Allow a frozen fruit salad to soften slightly before serving to give flavors a chance to mellow.

Casseroles

A **casserole** is a combination of foods prepared in a single dish. Casseroles are quick and easy to prepare. They can help stretch food dollars by using starchy foods and vegetables to extend more costly protein ingredients. Casseroles can help make use of leftovers. A simple salad and dessert are all that is needed to accompany most casseroles. They also freeze well, so they can be prepared ahead of time for emergency meals.

Casseroles are a great way to emphasize plant foods in the diet. Casseroles often include a variety of vegetables and grains and only small amounts of meat. Many hearty casseroles can be made without any meat at all. Tasty combinations of rice and legumes or vegetables and pasta can become nutritious entrees.

Casserole Ingredients

Most casseroles are a combination of a protein food, vegetable, starch, and sauce. Many have a topping made of crumbs, cheese, or chopped nuts.

One or several foods high in protein can form the basis of a casserole. Turkey, chicken, ground beef, ham, luncheon meat, cheese, hard-cooked eggs, and seafood make good casserole bases.

Any canned, frozen, or cooked fresh vegetable can be used in a casserole. Try peas, green beans, carrots, spinach, or a combination of vegetables.

Starchy ingredients help make casseroles filling. Use whole-grain ingredients often. Brown rice, barley, and whole-wheat pasta combine easily with most protein foods and vegetables.

A casserole sauce can be as simple as a can of tomato sauce or as fancy as a homemade cheese sauce. Experiment with cream of tomato, shrimp, mushroom, or asparagus soups. As an alternative, try adding grated cheese and a sprinkle of seasonings to a basic white sauce. See **21-3**.

Extras can add crunch, color, and flavor to a casserole. Bean sprouts, Chinese noodles, celery, almonds, and French-fried onion rings add crunch. Tomato wedges,

Enrich

Invite a caterer to your class to demonstrate for students how to make a variety of salad garnishes, such as carrot curls and radish roses.

Vocabulary Builder

Casseroles get their name from the type of dish in which they are often prepared. Another definition of *casserole* is a deep, round baking dish.

Strengthening Family Ties

Ask each student to develop a unique family casserole recipe. Students should ask each of their family members to choose the specific food that will be used for each of the five key ingredients in the casserole. Students should combine the suggestions from their family members into a casserole, serve it for a family meal, and evaluate family members' responses.

©2011 Wisconsin Milk Marketing Board, Inc.

21-3 Creamy cheese sauce is the signature ingredient in popular macaroni and cheese casseroles.

Health and Wellness

Healthful Casseroles

As casseroles are prepared, be aware of the fat and sodium content of sauces and other ingredients. Many casserole recipes can be adapted to make them more healthful. For instance, reduced-fat mayonnaise or low-sodium condensed soup can easily be used in place of traditional ingredients. Such changes will make casseroles more nutritious without having much effect on flavor.

green pepper rings, chopped parsley, and pimiento add color. Horseradish, chili sauce, and chopped onions add flavor.

A topping helps keep a casserole from getting dry. It also adds color, flavor, and texture. Buttered bread crumbs, dumplings, and corn-bread squares are common toppings. For a nutritious change of pace, try a sprinkling of chopped nuts. Crushed unsweetened whole-grain cereals also make healthful casserole toppings.

Assembling a Casserole

The key to putting a casserole together is combining ingredients that complement each other. Consider personal likes and dislikes. Experience will also help.

Until experience in making casseroles is acquired, it is probably best to choose just one item out of each group. Use seasonings sparingly at first. Also avoid using too many highly seasoned foods at one time.

Cleanup of baked casseroles will be easier if the casserole is put in a greased dish. Most casseroles are baked in a moderate oven until they are brown and bubbly. Cooking time will depend on the size of the dish and the starting temperature of the casserole. The topping may begin to brown before the casserole heats through. A piece of aluminum foil placed loosely over the top will keep it from getting too dark.

Some casseroles can be prepared on top of the range. They are just as quick and easy as oven casseroles. However, they may require some stirring and a bit more attention during the cooking period.

Unlike soufflés and rare roast beef, most casseroles can wait for latecomers. Some casseroles even improve when they are held for a while. This is because their flavors have a chance to blend. When a casserole will not be served right away, cover it tightly and keep it warm in a low oven.

Stock Soups

People throughout the world serve soup in many forms. It can be hot or cold, hearty or light. It can be an appetizer or a main dish. It can be eaten alone or served with other foods. Soup is most popular in the United States as an appetizer or luncheon dish.

Soup can be made in two ways. **Stock soups** can be made with rich-flavored broth in which meat, poultry, or fish; vegetables; and seasonings have been cooked, **21-4**. *Cream soups* are made with milk or cream instead of broth.

Make stocks from less tender meat cuts, poultry, and fish. Vegetables, such as celery and carrots, can be added for flavor.

Preparing Stocks

Stocks obtain their flavor from the flavors of their ingredients. Meats, poultry, fish, and vegetables release their flavors slowly. To make stocks rich and flavorful, cook them over low heat for a long time.

To make a stock more flavorful, increase the amount of surface area exposed to the cooking liquid. To do this, cut the meat, poultry, fish, and vegetables for a stock into small pieces. Also, crack any large bones that are put into a stockpot.

If a *brown stock* is being prepared, begin by browning the meat. If making a *light stock*, use poultry, fish, or unbrowned meat.

To prepare a stock, place all the ingredients in a large pan with a tightly fitted lid. Cover them with cold water, and cook them slowly for several hours at a simmering temperature. The liquid should never boil.

During the first stage of cooking, foam will rise to the surface. Skim it from the stock. Use a wooden spoon or paddle for skimming.

During the final stages of cooking, fat will rise to the surface of the stock if fatty meats have been used. Remove the fat with a baster while the stock is hot. Fat can also be removed after it congeals on chilled stock.

After cooking, strain the stock. Straining separates the broth from the solid materials. The meat, poultry, or fish can be served separately or added back to the stock to make soup. Vegetables, rice, noodles or other pasta, and seasonings can be added if desired.

Photo courtesy of National Pork Board. For more information about pork, visit TheOtherWhiteMeat.com.

21-4 Chicken stock serves as the base for this flavorful Italian-inspired soup.

EXPLORING CAREERS

Prep Cook

Prep cooks are key members of restaurant kitchen crews. Their work helps ease the tasks of other workers so kitchens run smoothly. Prep cooks prepare foods that will be cooked by chefs. They often wash and chop vegetables and trim meats. They may measure and package ingredients for single servings. This allows chefs to quickly grab just the right amounts to cook for customer orders. Prep cooks may prepare foods like salads and soups. They portion and plate food items such as desserts, making them ready for servers to take to customers. Once foods are prepared, prep cooks store them to maintain safety and quality until they are ready to be used. They may also clean and organize utensils and prep areas.

To be successful, prep cooks need good listening skills and a willingness to follow directions to prepare the correct types and amounts of foods. They need attention to detail to accurately measure ingredients and follow recipes. They must assess what tasks need to be done and take responsibility to complete them. Prep cooks have to cooperate with coworkers. They must also be able to spend long hours on their feet and do some lifting and carrying.

Prep cook is an entry-level position. Some prep cook jobs are open to teens while they are still in high school. Previous foodservice experience is helpful but not required in many restaurants. Most training will take place on the job. Skilled prep cooks may be able to move into other roles on a restaurant kitchen crew.

Shutterstock

Prep cooks prepare ingredients and simple food items and organize kitchen work areas.

Preparing Bouillon and Consommé

Clear broth made from stock is called **bouillon**. Bouillon is most often made from beef stock. Clear, rich-flavored soup made from stock is called **consommé**. Both bouillon and consommé are low in calories. They make excellent appetizers and snacks for all age groups.

For both bouillon and consommé, the stock must first be clarified. Strained stock can be clarified by adding a slightly beaten egg white and a few pieces of eggshell to the boiling broth. As the egg protein coagulates, it traps any solid materials. Strain the clarified stock to remove and discard the egg, solid materials, and eggshell.

To prepare bouillon, reduce the strained and clarified stock in volume by further cooking. This additional cooking concentrates the stock, making it richer and more flavorful.

Prepare consommé by simmering the strained and clarified stock still longer. It has a richer flavor than bouillon.

Herbs and Spices

Herbs, spices, and blends can greatly enhance the flavors of salads, casseroles, soups, and all other foods. **Herbs** are food seasonings made from the leaves of plants usually grown in temperate climates. Basil, bay leaf, and mint are examples of herbs. Many herbs can be purchased fresh, but most are sold dried.

Spices are food seasonings made from the dried roots, stems, and seeds of plants grown mainly in the tropics. Cinnamon, allspice, pepper, and ginger are examples of spices. Sometimes people use the word spice to mean "hot" or pungent. Not all spices are hot, however. Most just give flavor. Spices are sold in whole or ground forms.

Blends are food seasonings made from combinations of herbs and spices. Poultry seasoning and pumpkin pie spice are examples of blends.

Using Herbs and Spices

Herbs can be used fresh or dried. Fresh herbs such as dill sprigs and basil leaves make attractive garnishes. Fresh herbs are not as concentrated as dried herbs. Use about three times more to get the same flavor. Unless the recipe says otherwise, use dried herbs when cooking.

Ground spices release their flavor immediately when added to food. Add them toward the end of cooking. Whole spices release their flavor more slowly, so they can be added at the beginning of cooking.

Sometimes whole spices and herbs are placed in a cheesecloth bag before adding them to food. This is called a **bouquet garni**. After the herbs and spices have released their flavors, they can be easily removed from the food.

Gourmet Cooking

Gourmets are people who value and enjoy fine food. Some people think gourmet cooking requires hours of work and expensive ingredients that are hard to find. However, this is not necessarily the case. Gourmet food is simply food that is expertly seasoned and prepared. Creative use of herbs and spices can make gourmet dishes out of some of the simplest foods.

Becoming familiar with a range of herbs and spices can help give foods a gourmet touch. As cooks work with seasonings, they learn that some herbs and spices go especially well with certain foods. For instance, many recipes for custard call for nutmeg. Rosemary and mint complement the flavor of lamb. People often add cinnamon to apple dishes. See **21-5**.

Reflect

Ask students what herbs, spices, and blends are used to flavor some of their favorite foods.

Reflect

Ask students what herbs they have seen sold fresh in grocery stores.

Activity

Have students try the test described in the text to evaluate the strength of three herbs, spices, or blends in the foods lab.

Learn About...

Storing Herbs and Spices

Heat can cause herbs and spices to deteriorate. Therefore, avoid storing seasonings near or over a range. Instead, store herbs and spices in a cool, dry place away from light. Keep the containers tightly closed.

Buy herbs and spices in small amounts for ordinary cooking. Most spices and herbs will keep their flavor and aroma for about a year when properly stored. However, they lose their strength as they age, so date all containers. Whole spices will last longer than ground spices. To determine if a spice or herb has lost its strength, simply rub a little of it between your hands and smell it. If it has little or no odor, it has been stored too long.

Seasoning Success	
Food Item	**Herbs and Spices**
Beef	Basil, bay leaves, cayenne, cloves, garlic, ginger, oregano, pepper, sage, tarragon, thyme
Fish	Allspice, cayenne, dill weed, garlic, ginger, mint, paprika, rosemary, sage, thyme
Lamb	Mint, rosemary
Pork	Cloves, cumin, garlic, ginger, sage
Poultry	Rosemary, sage, tarragon, thyme
Eggs	Basil, cayenne, chives, oregano, paprika, tarragon
Vegetables	Allspice, basil, bay leaves, cayenne, cloves, dill weed, garlic, ginger, nutmeg, oregano, paprika, rosemary, tarragon, thyme
Fruits	Allspice, cinnamon, cloves, ginger, nutmeg
Breads and stuffings	Cayenne, cinnamon, dill weed, rosemary, sage, thyme
Desserts	Allspice, cinnamon, cloves, ginger, mint, nutmeg

21-5 Learning which seasonings complement various food items gives cooks the confidence to be creative when combining ingredients and cooking new dishes.

Using herbs and spices well requires practice and skill. When learning to use seasonings, start with small amounts. Ideally, herbs and spices should enhance food, not overpower it.

CAREER SUCCESS

Using Reading Skills

Sandy is the soup cook at The Country Hearth restaurant. The restaurant is known throughout the area for its delicious homemade soups and European-style, hearth-baked breads. Sandy's employer expects her to prepare three soup recipes each day of the week.

To be a successful employee, Sandy needs basic reading skills. Put yourself in Sandy's place and answer the following questions about your need for and use of these skills:

A. How will you use your reading skills as a soup cook?

B. How might customers of the restaurant be affected if you do not have adequate reading skills?

C. How might other people who work at the restaurant be affected if you do not have adequate reading skills?

D. What is another skill you would need in this job? Briefly explain why this skill would be important.

CHAPTER 21 REVIEW

Summary

A salad can be served as almost any part of a meal, from appetizer to dessert. There are five main types of salads—protein, pasta, vegetable, fruit, and gelatin. To prepare most salads, begin with a base of washed and trimmed salad greens. Cut ingredients for the body of the salad into bite-sized pieces. Salad dressings may be temporary or permanent emulsions. When assembling a salad, keep flavor, texture, and color in mind.

Casseroles are both easy and economical to prepare. They generally contain a protein food, vegetable, starch, sauce, and topping. Although some casseroles are cooked on the rangetop, most casseroles are baked in a conventional oven.

Stocks are made by covering meat, poultry, or fish with water and simmering it for a long time. Vegetables may be added for extra flavor. After cooking, stock can be strained and ingredients can be added to make a hearty soup. Stock can also be clarified stock and then reduced through further cooking to prepare bouillon or consommé.

Herbs, spices, and seasoning blends are important ingredients in many foods. With practice, they can be used to enhance the flavor of almost any dish.

Review What You Have Read

Write your answers on a separate sheet of paper, using complete sentences when appropriate.

1. Give an example of each of the five main types of salads.
2. Give two tips for preventing nutrient losses when preparing salad ingredients.
3. What are the three basic types of salad dressings?
4. What are the three main parts of a salad?
5. List five components of a casserole and give an example of each.
6. Give three guidelines to follow when preparing casseroles.
7. What liquid serves as the base of a stock soup?
8. How does bouillon differ from consommé?
9. List three common herbs and three common spices.
10. When should ground spices be added to food? When should whole spices be added?

Answer Key to *Review What You Have Read* **questions**

1. (Give one example of each. Student response.)
2. (List two:) treat ingredients with care, avoid soaking ingredients, do not clean fresh ingredients too far in advance
3. The three basic types of salad dressings are French dressing, mayonnaise, and cooked salad dressing.
4. The three main parts of a salad are the base, the body, and the dressing.
5. The five components of a casserole are a protein food, vegetable, starch, sauce, and topping. (Examples are student response.)
6. (List three. Student response.)
7. The base of a stock soup is a rich-flavored broth in which meat, poultry, or fish; vegetables; and seasonings have been cooked.

(continued)

Link to Academic Skills

8. Bouillon is clear broth made from stock. Consommé is clear, rich-flavored soup made from stock. Consommé is simmered longer than bouillon.

9. (List three of each. Student response.)

10. Ground spices should be added to food toward the end of cooking. Whole spices should be added to food at the beginning of cooking.

11. **Science**. Wash and dry 10 leaves from a head of iceberg lettuce. Using your hands, gently tear 5 leaves into bite-sized pieces. Seal the torn lettuce in a labeled, dated zip-top bag. Cut the remaining 5 leaves into bite-sized pieces using a knife. Seal the cut lettuce in a second labeled, dated zip-top bag. Place both bags in a refrigerator. Compare the appearance and texture of the lettuce in the two bags every day for five days, making notes of your daily observations. Use chapter information to explain your observations. Write a paragraph with your recommendations about preparing and storing salad greens.

12. **Science**. In a small group, take turns adding the following ingredients for French dressing to a bottle. Add liquid ingredients by pouring slowly. Add solid ingredients by sprinkling. All group members should record their observations after each ingredient is added.
    - ½ cup chilled red wine vinegar
    - ⅓ cup olive oil
    - ¾ teaspoon salt
    - ½ teaspoon paprika
    - ⅛ teaspoon ground black pepper
    - ¼ teaspoon dried thyme
    - ⅛ teaspoon dried tarragon
    - 1 clove garlic, crushed
    - 1 teaspoon lemon juice

    When all the ingredients have been added, discuss the reasons for your various observations. Cover and shake the bottle vigorously. Observe how long it takes for the liquids to separate. Then add ¾ teaspoon ground dry mustard. Cover and shake the bottle again. Note whether there is a difference in how long it takes the liquids to separate. What does this indicate? Sample the dressing on salad greens.

13. **English language arts**. Write two dinner menus featuring meat, fish, or poultry entrees. Write a short story describing how a fictional meal manager takes time to carefully plan, shop for, and prepare these meals. Be sure to include sensory details about how the food items look, smell, and taste as the meal manager performs these tasks. Continue your story by describing another time during the week when the meal manager has little time to prepare meals. Then write two more menus featuring casseroles the meal manager could make with the leftovers from the first two menus.

14. **History**. Research the role spices played in the establishment of early trade routes and the exploration of new lands. Share your findings in a class discussion.

Build Critical Thinking Skills

15. **Synthesis**. Use input from all lab groups to plan and prepare a class salad buffet. Each lab group should prepare a different type of salad greens, tossed salad topping, and dressing. Each lab group should also choose a different type of salad to prepare. Coordinate recipe choices with other lab groups to plan for a variety of flavors, textures, colors, sizes, shapes, and temperatures.

16. **Evaluation.** Smell samples of three herbs and three spices. Use the aromas to propose a food item whose flavor would be enhanced by each herb or spice. Sample your proposed flavor combinations and prepare a written evaluation.

Apply Technology

17. Find out how Modified Atmosphere Packaging (MAP) is used to keep bagged salads fresh. Summarize your findings in a written report.

18. Investigate how and why spices are irradiated. Share what you learn in a class discussion.

A Measure of Math

19. Calculate and compare the cost per serving for instant, canned, and homemade bouillon. Taste samples of each and discuss when you might choose to use each product in cooking.

Teamwork in Action

20. Organize a canned and packaged food drive for needy people in your community. Place cans of protein foods, vegetables, and cream soups in bags with packages of rice or pasta. Then write recipe suggestions for combining the food items in each bag into a casserole. Distribute the foods through a local relief agency.

Companion Website

www.g-wlearning.com

At the website, review key terms for this chapter with crossword puzzles, matching exercises, and e-flash cards. Apply facts from the chapter to complete the activities.

CHAPTER 22
Breads

Learning Prep

Suggest definitions for each of the *Terms to Know*. Then look up the terms in the glossary to check your accuracy.

Terms to Know

batter
dough
leavening agent
gluten
fermentation

Main Menu

❋ Knowing how to select, store, and prepare baked products can help meal managers include them in any meal plan.

❋ Varying ingredient proportions and mixing methods creates distinctions among quick bread and yeast bread products.

Objectives

After studying this chapter, you will be able to

❋ **describe** how to select and store baked goods.

❋ **identify** the functions of ingredients in baked products.

❋ **prepare** quick breads and yeast breads.

Quick breads can be prepared in a short amount of time. Quick breads include biscuits, muffins, popovers, cream puffs, pancakes, and waffles. They also include coffee cakes and breads leavened with baking powder. See **22-1**.

Yeast breads require more time to prepare than quick breads. Yeast breads include breads, rolls, English muffins, raised doughnuts, and many other yeast-raised products.

Selecting and Storing Baked Products

Quick breads and yeast breads are *baked products.* Cakes, cookies, and pies are baked products, too. Some of the following information applies to *all* baked products. However, preparation of cakes, cookies, and pies differs from preparation of breads. Therefore, cakes, cookies, and pies will be discussed further in another chapter.

Baked products can be purchased as freshly baked, partially baked, refrigerated, and frozen. *Freshly baked items* are sold in bakeries, in bakery sections of supermarkets, and on supermarket shelves. They are ready to serve. *Brown-and-serve baked goods* are partially baked. They need a final browning in the oven before serving. Refrigerated doughs are ready to bake. They are handy for quickly preparing items like biscuits, turnovers, cookies, and rolls. *Frozen doughs* and *baked goods* require thawing and/or baking. Yeast doughs and cookie doughs are available frozen. Frozen pies, cakes, coffee cakes, and doughnuts, can be purchased, too.

©2011 Wisconsin Milk Marketing Board, Inc.

22-1 Although simple to prepare, pancakes—a popular quick bread product—are a special breakfast treat.

Cost of Baked Products

The cost of rolls, cakes, and other bakery products depends a lot on the amount of convenience. Ready-to-serve items usually cost more than items that require some preparation. Bakery yeast rolls, for instance, usually cost more than frozen yeast rolls.

Bread costs depend on size of loaf, extra ingredients, and brand. Large loaves usually cost less per serving than small loaves. Breads with fruit and nuts cost more than plain white or wheat bread. Store brands generally cost less than national brands.

Storing Baked Products

Store freshly baked items at room temperature or in the freezer, tightly wrapped. Freezing bread in hot, humid weather prevents mold growth. Slices of bread can be taken from the freezer as needed to thaw and eat. Refrigerate any baked products with cream, custard, or other perishable fillings or frosting.

Refrigerated doughs should be kept refrigerated until they are baked. Likewise, frozen doughs and baked products should be stored in the freezer until they will be used.

Academic Connections

Plan your study of this chapter in conjunction with the social studies department. In your classes, students will learn about quick bread and yeast bread preparation. In social studies classes, students can study the economic, political, environmental, and technological factors that affect the supplies of staple grains in different countries. They can also investigate the types of breads people make from these grains.

Reflect

Ask students when they would choose to use each of the following types of baked products: freshly baked, brown-and-serve, refrigerated dough, and frozen dough and baked goods.

Health and Wellness

Daily Bread

Breads, which are part of the grains group of MyPlate, are an excellent source of complex carbohydrates. They also supply B vitamins and iron. Most teens need 6 to 10 ounce-equivalents from the grains group each day, depending on calorie needs. One slice of bread and one small biscuit or muffin each count as one ounce-equivalent. Half a sandwich bun or one-fourth of a large bagel also counts as one ounce-equivalent. When buying breads, choose whole grain items most often. They are higher in fiber than refined bread products.

Quick Breads

Quick breads may be made from batters or doughs. Both batters and doughs are mixtures of flour and liquid. **Batters** range in consistency from thin liquids to stiff liquids. Thin batters are called *pour batters*. They have a large amount of liquid and a small amount of flour. A pour batter is used to prepare pancakes and popovers. Stiff batters are called *drop batters*. They have a high proportion of flour, and they can be dropped from a spoon. A drop batter is used to prepare drop biscuits and some muffin recipes. **Doughs** have an even higher proportion of flour. They are stiff enough to shape by hand. Soft dough is used to prepare shortcake and rolled biscuits. Stiff dough is used to make rolled cookies and pastry.

Quick Bread Ingredients

Flour is a basic ingredient in all quick breads. However, the kinds of ingredients added to the flour distinguish one product from another. Leavening agents, liquid, fat, eggs, sugar, and salt are among the other ingredients that may be part of quick breads. Each ingredient serves a specific purpose.

Flour

Flour gives structure to baked products. White wheat flours are most often used for baking. Most quick breads are made with *all-purpose flour*. Some recipes call for *self-rising flour*. This is all-purpose flour with added leavening agents and salt.

Leavening Agents

Leavening agents are ingredients that produce gases in batters and doughs. These gases make baked products rise and become light and porous. Two leavening agents used in quick breads are baking soda and baking powder. Chemical reactions during baking cause these ingredients to release carbon dioxide gas.

Two gases other than carbon dioxide that make baked products rise are steam and air. *Steam* is produced when liquid ingredients reach high temperatures during baking. Popovers and cream puffs are leavened almost entirely by steam. *Air* is incorporated into baked products by beating eggs, creaming fat and sugar together, folding doughs, and beating batters. Almost all baked products contain some air.

Food Science

Chemical Leaveners

One chemical leavening agent added to many baked products is *baking soda*. Baking soda is sodium bicarbonate, which is an alkali. It is used in quick bread recipes that contain food acid ingredients. When combined with a food acid, baking soda releases carbon dioxide. Acid ingredients also help neutralize the alkaline batter. This prevents a bitter flavor and disagreeable color from forming in the bread. Food acid ingredients include buttermilk, molasses, brown sugar, vinegar, honey, applesauce or other fruit, and citrus juices.

A second chemical leavener often used in baked goods is baking powder. *Baking powders* contain a dry acid or acid salt, baking soda, and starch or flour. Be sure to follow guidelines for using the recommended amount of baking powder. Too much baking powder will produce too much carbon dioxide, and the baked product will collapse. Too little baking powder will not produce enough carbon dioxide, and the product will be small and compact.

Most baking powders are *double-acting baking powders*. They release some of their carbon dioxide when they are moistened. However, they release most of their carbon dioxide when they are heated.

©2011 Wisconsin Milk Marketing Board, Inc.

These waffles contain buttermilk and baking soda: a combination that produces carbon dioxide to make the waffles rise.

Liquids

Water, milk, and fruit juices are liquids commonly used in baked products. Eggs and fats are also considered to be liquid ingredients.

Liquids serve several functions. They *hydrate* (cause to absorb water) the protein and starch in flour. Proteins must absorb water to later form gluten. Starches must absorb water to gelatinize during baking. Another function of liquids is to moisten or dissolve ingredients such as baking powder, salt, and sugar. Liquids also serve as leavening agents when they are converted to steam during baking.

Fat

Fat serves primarily as a tenderizing agent in baked products. The fat coats the flour particles and causes the dough structure to separate into layers. Fat also aids leavening. When fat is beaten, air bubbles form. The fat traps these air bubbles and holds them.

FYI

Small clumps of baking powder and baking soda can give baked goods a bitter taste. Measuring these ingredients through a small strainer will help break up clumps for better distribution.

Enrich

Have students design a bulletin board illustrating the functions of the basic ingredients in baked goods.

Discuss

Ask students why they think many recipes call for more than the minimum amounts of ingredients discussed in the "Health and Wellness" box.

Eggs

When beaten, eggs help incorporate air into baked products. They also add color and flavor and contribute to structure. During baking, the egg proteins coagulate. The coagulated proteins give the batter or dough elasticity and structure.

Sugar

Sugar gives sweetness to baked products. It also has a tenderizing effect and helps crusts brown. In yeast breads, sugar serves as food for the yeast. Brown sugar gives a distinctive flavor to baked products. It also produces baked products that are moister than products made with granulated sugar.

Health and Wellness

Adjusting Bread Ingredients

A few simple guidelines can be followed to adjust quick bread and yeast bread recipes to make them more healthful. For instance, fat-free milk can be substituted for whole milk in bread recipes. This change will reduce fat in each serving of bread products. Also, some recipes call for more baking powder, fat, eggs, sugar, and salt than are really needed. Cutting down on these ingredients will result in breads that are lower in calories, fat, and sodium. Such changes are in line with the Dietary Guidelines for Americans.

Adjusting bread recipes can help increase the intake of fruits, vegetables, and whole grains. Try adding blueberries or sliced bananas to pancakes to add fruit to the diet. Stir some shredded zucchini or carrots into muffin batter to help meet needs from the vegetable group. To increase whole grains in the diet, replace half the all-purpose flour in recipes with whole wheat flour or ground oatmeal. Count these ingredients as flour when figuring proportions of ingredients. However, these flours are heavier and may require a little extra baking powder for proper leavening.

Minimum Ingredient Proportions per 1 Cup (250 mL) of Flour					
Product	**Fat**	**Eggs**	**Sugar**	**Salt**	**Baking Powder**
Biscuits	2 tablespoons (30 mL)	—	—	¼ teaspoon (1 mL)	1¼ teaspoons (6 mL)
Muffins	2 tablespoons (30 mL)	½	1 tablespoon (15 mL)	¼ teaspoon (1 mL)	1¼ teaspoons (6 mL)
Popovers	1 tablespoon (15 mL)	2	—	¼ teaspoon (1 mL)	—
Cream puffs	½ cup (125 mL)	4	—	¼ teaspoon (1 mL)	—
Traditional yeast breads	1 tablespoon* (15 mL)	½*	1 teaspoon* (5 mL)	¼ teaspoon (1 mL)	—
Bread machine yeast breads	2 teaspoons (10 mL)	*	1 tablespoon (15 mL)	½ teaspoon (2 mL)	—

*Many traditional yeast breads can be made without any fat or eggs. When recipes for richer breads call for these ingredients, the minimums shown here will produce a suitably rich dough. Sugar is not an essential ingredient in traditional unsweetened yeast breads. However, most recipes call for a small amount to serve as food for the yeast. Fat and sugar are not optional ingredients in yeast breads prepared in bread machines. Adding an egg and decreasing other liquids by ¼ cup (50 mL) will improve structure and volume of whole grain bread machine recipes.

Following these proportions will reduce the sugar, fat, and sodium in many quick bread and yeast bread recipes.

Salt

Salt adds flavor to many baked products. In yeast breads, salt also regulates the action of the yeast and inhibits the action of certain enzymes. If yeast dough contains no salt, the yeast will produce carbon dioxide too quickly. The bread dough will be difficult to handle, and the baked product will have a poor appearance.

Food Science Principles of Preparing Quick Breads

Food science principles can be observed at work in quick breads in the development of gluten. **Gluten** is a protein that gives strength and elasticity to batters and doughs and structure to baked products. It also holds the leavening gases, which are what make quick breads rise. Gluten is created by the proteins *gliadin* and *glutenin*, which are found in wheat flour. When wheat flour is combined with liquid and stirred or kneaded, the mixture, the glutenin and gliadin, form gluten.

To understand gluten, think of a piece of bubble gum. When gum is first put into the mouth, it is soft and easy to chew. As it is chewed, the gum becomes more elastic, and bubbles can be blown. The gum becomes more elastic as it is chewed.

Gluten behaves in a similar way. If a batter or dough is handled too much, the gluten will overdevelop. This can cause a quick bread to be compact and tough. To keep quick breads light and tender, mix them for only a short time and handle them carefully.

Each kind of white wheat flour contains different amounts of gliaden and glutenin. Thus, the strength of the gluten produced by each of the flours differs. Do not replace more than half the all-purpose flour with whole grain flour when adjusting recipes. Otherwise, the product being prepared may not have the right amount of gluten, **22-2**. Yeast breads need a strong gluten structure. Cakes should have a delicate structure. Most quick breads fall somewhere in between.

Preparing Biscuits

The method used to mix baked products is another factor that distinguishes one baked product from another. When preparing biscuits, combine the ingredients using the *biscuit method*. This method involves sifting dry ingredients together into a mixing bowl. Use a pastry blender or two knives to cut the fat into the dry mixture. Continue cutting in until the particles are the size of coarse cornmeal. Then add the liquid all at once and stir until the dough forms a ball. This is the same mixing method that is used when making pastry.

Discuss

Ask students how the properties of gluten affect the preparation of bread products. *(Gluten's strength gives structure to bread products. Gluten's elasticity causes dough to rise as trapped leavening gases expand, allowing bread to become light.)*

©*Courtesy of California Tree Fruit Agreement*

22-2 These muffins contain bran cereal. An equal amount of all-purpose flour ensures sufficient gluten development.

Time Management Tip

Make your own baking mix to save money as well as time. You can find recipes on the Internet to prepare a homemade baking mix in large batches from flour, buttermilk powder, salt, sugar, baking powder, baking soda, and shortening. This mix will keep for at least a month in a sealed container, and it can be stored longer in the freezer. It will save you measuring time when you use it as a basic ingredient in a number of muffin, pancake, waffle, and quick bread recipes.

Enrich

Ask each student to find three variations to a basic muffin recipe calling for different added ingredients.

Discuss

Ask students the following:

What basic ingredients found in most baked products are not found in popovers? *(leavening agent and sugar)*

How could insufficient baking occur if popovers are cooked for the specified amount of time? How could this problem be avoided? *(Insufficient baking could occur if the oven temperature is too low. Using an oven thermometer will allow you to verify the accuracy of oven temperatures.)*

The dry ingredients in biscuits are flour, baking powder, and salt. Self-rising flour, which is a mixture of these three ingredients, can also be used. The liquid in biscuits is milk or buttermilk. Drop biscuits contain a higher proportion of liquid than rolled biscuits. When making *drop biscuits,* drop the dough from a spoon onto a greased baking sheet. When making *rolled biscuits,* gently knead the dough 8 to 10 times and roll or pat it into a circle. Then cut the dough with a biscuit cutter and place the biscuits on an ungreased baking sheet. Bake both types of biscuits in a hot oven until they are golden brown.

Characteristics of Biscuits

A high-quality rolled biscuit has an even shape with a smooth, level top and straight sides. The crust is an even brown. When a biscuit is broken open, the *crumb,* or soft interior, is white to creamy white. It is moist and fluffy and peels off in layers.

Biscuits require gentle handling. An undermixed biscuit has a low volume and a rounded top with a slightly rough crust. The crumb is tender. An overmixed biscuit also has a low volume and a rounded top, but the top is smooth. The crumb is tough and compact.

Preparing Muffins

When preparing muffins, combine ingredients using the *muffin method.* For this method, measure the dry ingredients into a mixing bowl. Make a well in the center of the dry ingredients. In a separate bowl, combine beaten eggs with milk and oil or melted fat. Pour all the liquid mixture into the well in the dry ingredients. For muffins, stir the batter just until the dry ingredients are moistened. This mixing method will also be used when preparing waffles, pancakes, popovers, and some coffee cakes. Batter for some of these baked products may require more stirring than the batter for muffins.

The dry ingredients in muffins are flour, baking powder, salt, and sugar. Fruits, nuts, cheese, and other ingredients may be added to muffin batter for variety. After combining ingredients, drop muffin batter into a greased muffin pan and bake.

Characteristics of Muffins

A high-quality muffin has a thin, evenly browned crust. The top is symmetrical, but it looks rough. When broken apart, the texture is uniform, and the crumb is tender and light.

An undermixed muffin has a low volume and a flat top. The crumb is coarse. An overmixed muffin has a peaked top and a pale, slick crust. When broken apart, narrow, open areas called *tunnels* are visible.

Preparing Popovers

Popovers look like golden brown balloons, **22-3**. They are often eaten with jam or their hollow centers are filled with mixtures of meat, poultry, seafood, and/or vegetables. A variety of sweet fillings, such as ice cream, pudding, fruit, and custard, are also popular in popovers.

Popovers contain flour, salt, eggs, milk, and a small amount of fat. Use the muffin method to combine these ingredients. Then place popovers in a hot oven for the first part of the baking period. This allows steam to expand the walls of the popovers.

©2011 Wisconsin Milk Marketing Board, Inc.

22-3 High-quality popovers look like golden brown balloons on the outside with moist strands of dough on the inside.

Following this expansion, lower the temperature to prevent overbrowning before the interior has set. Do not open the oven door to check popovers during baking. If the oven door is opened, and they have not set, the steam can condense and cause the popovers to collapse.

Characteristics of Popovers

A high-quality popover has good volume. The shell is golden brown and crisp, and the interior contains slightly moist (but not raw) strands of dough.

Insufficient baking is one of the biggest causes of popover failures. If a popover has not baked long enough, it will collapse when it is taken from the oven. The exterior will be soft instead of crisp, and the interior will be doughy.

Preparing Cream Puffs

A cream puff is a golden brown, hollow shell with crisp walls. Cream puffs can be filled with pudding, custard, ice cream, fruit, or whipped cream and served as a dessert. They can be filled with creamed meat, poultry, or fish and served as a main dish. Small

Strengthening Family Ties

Have students make popovers or cream puffs for their families as a special treat. Students should allow their family members to choose the fillings for the quick breads— savory fillings for entrees or sweet fillings for desserts. Invite students to share their family members' reactions in class. If recipes are a hit with family members, make copies of the recipes to share with class members.

Reflect

Ask how many students have eaten homemade yeast bread. Invite those who have to describe the taste and smell of homemade bread and compare it to commercially prepared sandwich bread.

Discuss

Ask students why they should not use bread flour when making cakes or cake flour when making breads. (Breads made with cake flour would not have strong enough gluten to support the structure of the bread. Cakes made from bread flour would be tough and elastic because the gluten would be too strong.)

cream puffs can be filled with cream cheese, shrimp salad, or another light filling and served as appetizers. Elongated cream puffs filled with custard are called *eclairs*.

Cream puffs are made from water, fat, flour, and eggs. They require a special mixing method. Begin by bringing the water and fat to a boil. Then add the flour and stir vigorously over low heat until the mixture forms a ball. After removing the mixture from the heat, stir in the eggs until the mixture is smooth. The resulting dough is called *puff paste*.

Drop the puff paste onto an ungreased baking sheet. Begin baking the cream puffs in a hot oven so the steam will cause them to puff (rise). Then reduce the temperature. This will prevent the exteriors of the cream puffs from overbrowning before the interiors have set. Do not open the oven door to check the cream puffs during baking. If the oven door is opened, and the cream puffs have not set, the steam can condense and cause them to collapse.

Characteristics of Cream Puffs

A properly prepared cream puff has a good volume and a brown, tender crust. When broken apart, the interior of the cream puff is hollow. A few strands of moist, tender dough may be visible.

Cream puff failures usually are the result of underbaking. When an underbaked cream puff is taken from the oven, it will collapse. The interior is moist and filled with strands of dough. Occasionally, cream puffs will ooze fat during baking. The evaporation of too much liquid can cause this. Evaporation may take place when the water and fat are heated together or when the puff paste is cooked.

22-4 The flavor, texture, and aroma of homemade yeast bread create a feast for the senses.

Yeast Breads

Homemade yeast bread is decidedly different from commercially prepared sandwich breads. It has a distinctively appealing sweet smell and delicious taste that cannot be matched, **22-4**.

Yeast Bread Ingredients

All yeast breads must contain flour, liquid, salt, and yeast. Most recipes call for a small amount of sugar, and some include fat and eggs.

Flour

All-purpose flour can be used for making traditional yeast breads. When mixed with liquid and kneaded, the flour develops gluten to support the carbon dioxide produced by the yeast.

Bread flour contains larger amounts of gliadin and glutenin than all-purpose flour. It produces the strongest and most elastic gluten of all the white wheat flours. Whole wheat and nonwheat flours, such as rye, soy, corn, and oat, have a lower protein content than all-purpose flour.

They will produce a denser loaf than all-purpose or bread flour. Many recipes calling for whole grain flours also call for an equal amount of all-purpose flour. The all-purpose flour produces more gluten and will help give the bread a better texture.

Liquid

Plain water, potato water, or milk can be used as the liquid in yeast breads. Milk produces a softer crust and helps breads stay fresh longer than water. Other options for liquid ingredients in yeast breads include buttermilk, fruit juices, yogurt, applesauce, and cottage cheese. These options add nutrients and distinctive flavors.

Salt

Salt regulates the action of the yeast and inhibits the action of certain enzymes in the flour. Without salt, a traditional yeast dough is sticky and hard to handle. When baked, the bread may look moth-eaten.

Yeast

Yeast is a microscopic, single-celled plant used as a leavening agent in yeast breads. It is available in three forms. *Compressed yeast* is made from fresh, moist yeast cells that are pressed into cakes. Compressed yeast must be refrigerated because it is very perishable. *Active dry yeast* is made from an active yeast strain that has been dried and made into granules. *Fast-rising yeast* products are highly active yeast strains. The granules of these products are smaller than those of active dry yeast, which allows them to act more quickly. Active dry and fast-rising yeast are both available in small foil packets and glass jars. Store these yeast products in a cool, dry place and refrigerate jars after opening. For fastest action, buy yeast in small quantities and use it promptly.

For best results, use the amount of yeast specified in the recipe. A general guideline is ¾ teaspoon (3 mL) active dry yeast or ½ teaspoon (2 mL) fast-rising yeast per cup of flour. Using too much yeast will cause the dough to rise too quickly. Excess yeast will also give the bread an undesirable flavor, texture, and appearance. Using too little yeast will lengthen the rising time.

Sugar

Sugar, brown sugar, honey, and molasses can all be used in yeast bread recipes. These ingredients influence browning, flavor, and texture. They also provide extra food for the yeast so the dough will rise faster. If too much sugar is used, however, the yeast will work more slowly.

Fat

Fat is optional in some yeast bread recipes. When used, its function is to increase tenderness of the bread. Most recipes call for solid fat, but some call for oil.

Food Science

Temperature of Liquids in Yeast Breads

The temperature of the liquids affects yeast cells. Liquids used in traditional yeast breads need to be warm. The recipe will specify the temperature to which liquids should be heated. Temperatures that are too high kill the yeast cells. Temperatures that are too low can slow or stop yeast activity.

FYI

Some older recipes call for scalding milk used in yeast breads. This step was intended to kill enzymes in milk that can cause doughs to soften during fermentation. Scalding is now unnecessary because pasteurization destroys these enzymes.

A ¼-ounce (7 g) package of yeast contains about 2¼ teaspoons (11 mL). One package active dry yeast is enough for 3 cups (750 mL) flour. One package fast-rising yeast is enough for 4½ cups (1125 mL) flour.

Artificial sweeteners cannot be successfully substituted for sugar in yeast bread recipes. These sweeteners are proteins and cannot be fermented by yeast.

Vocabulary Builder

The term *yeast* comes from an Old High German word that means to ferment. Ask students why this etymology seems logical.

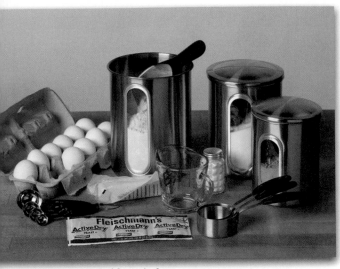

Courtesy ACH Food Companies, Inc.

22-5 In addition to yeast, basic yeast bread ingredients include flour, liquid, salt, sugar, fat, and eggs.

Eggs

Eggs are considered part of the liquid in yeast bread recipes. Eggs add flavor and richness to breads. They also add color and improve the structure. See **22-5**.

Other Ingredients

Other ingredients, such as raisins, nuts, cheese, herbs, and spices, may be added to bread dough. They add flavor and variety. However, these ingredients tend to lengthen the rising time.

Mixing Methods for Yeast Breads

The traditional, one-rise, mixer, or batter method will be used when mixing yeast dough. The recipe will specify which method to use.

Traditional Method

For the *traditional method*, dissolve the yeast in a small amount of warm water. The water should be 105°F to 115°F (41°C to 46°C). Then add remaining liquid, sugar, fat, salt, and some of the flour. Like the water used to dissolve the yeast, remaining liquid should be 105°F to 115°F (41°C to 46°C). Cold liquid will slow the rising action when added to activated yeast. If the recipe calls for eggs, stir them in before adding the remaining flour to form a soft dough.

Doughs prepared by the traditional method are allowed to rise twice. The first rising takes place after the ingredients are mixed. Then the dough is shaped and allowed to rise a second time. See **22-6**.

One-Rise Method

The *one-rise method* requires the use of fast-rising yeast. Mix the yeast with some of the flour and all the other dry ingredients. Heat the liquid and fat together to a temperature of 120°F to 130°F (49°C to 54°C). Add the warmed liquids to the dry ingredients. If eggs are required, add them before adding the remaining flour to form a soft dough.

After combining the ingredients, the dough may be kneaded. Then cover it and allow it to rest for 10 minutes. This resting period replaces the first rising required in the traditional method. After resting, shape the dough and allow it to rise before baking.

Mixer Method

The *mixer method* works well with active dry or fast-rising yeast. Like the one-rise method, begin by mixing the yeast with some of the flour and all the other dry ingredients. Heat the liquid and fat together to a temperature of 120°F to 130°F (49°C to 54°C). Using an electric mixer, add the warmed liquids to the dry ingredients. Add eggs if required. Then stir in the remaining flour with a spoon to form a soft dough. This method allows ingredients to blend easily. Using the mixer helps develop gluten and, therefore, shortens the kneading time.

A— Combine ingredients and beat until smooth. Stir in enough additional flour to make a moderately stiff dough.

B— On a lightly floured pastry board or cloth, knead dough until smooth and elastic.

C— Place dough in a lightly greased bowl; turn once to grease top.

D— Let dough rise in a warm place until double in bulk. Test dough for lightness with two fingers.

E— When dough is light, punch down.

F— Shape dough into loaves or rolls. Allow the dough to rise a second time, then bake as directed.

Courtesy ACH Food Companies, Inc.

22-6 To prepare yeast bread by the traditional method, follow these easy steps.

Activity

Have each student use text information to prepare a table comparing the traditional, one-rise, mixer, and batter methods of mixing yeast doughs. Column headings in the table might include *Type of Yeast*, *Temperature of Liquid*, *Mixing Steps*, and *Number of Risings*.

Career Path

Discuss with students what this description of a family and consumer sciences teacher tells them that they had never known before now.

Batter Method

Some recipes use the *batter* or *no-knead method*. These recipes use less flour, so the yeast mixture is thinner than dough. Vigorous stirring, rather than kneading, helps develop the gluten. Batter recipes that require two risings rise first in the mixing bowl. Then the batter is spread in a pan for the second rising before baking.

EXPLORING CAREERS

Family and Consumer Sciences Teacher

Family and consumer sciences (FCS) teachers help students learn to make informed choices about their health, relationships, and resources. Their goal is to give students the skills they will need to attain a high quality of personal and family life. They also teach principles that will prepare students for careers. FCS teachers use a variety of methods, such as lecture, demonstration, and lab activities, to help students learn. They make and evaluate assignments and keep records of student progress. They promote safety and maintain discipline in the classroom, too.

Above all else, the most successful FCS teachers care about students and have a true desire to help them do well. They need to be excellent leaders, time managers, and communicators. FCS teachers need speaking and listening skills to explain concepts, address questions, and clarify misunderstandings. They will use reading skills to study curriculum guides, textbooks, and other resources. They will use writing skills to write lesson plans, assignments, and test questions. FCS teachers need keen observation skills to evaluate students and see when further instruction is required. They must be able to use computers, educational tools, and lab equipment. They also need to be creative, flexible, and persistent.

FCS teachers need a four-year bachelor's degree. This program of study typically includes a number of weeks of student teaching. During this time, future teachers work under the guidance of experienced teachers. This gives them practice working with students in a classroom setting. After graduating, FCS teachers must obtain a teaching certificate to show they have met the requirements for teaching in a given state. Many FCS teachers continue to take classes and go on to get master's degrees.

Food Science Principles of Preparing Yeast Breads

Like preparing quick breads, preparing yeast breads requires the development of gluten and the formation of carbon dioxide. During mixing and kneading, the gluten develops. The gluten will form the framework of the bread. It will trap the carbon dioxide produced by the yeast as the dough rises. As the amount of carbon dioxide increases, the dough will rise, giving volume to the bread. The preparation of successful yeast bread depends on careful measuring, sufficient kneading, and controlled fermentation temperatures. Correct pan size and baking temperature are also important.

Kneading

After forming yeast dough by the traditional, one-rise, or mixer method, it must be kneaded. Although some of the gluten develops during initial beating, kneading develops most of the gluten. To knead, press the dough with the heels of the hands, fold it, and turn it. This motion must be rhythmically repeated until the dough is smooth and elastic. See **22-7**.

Avoid adding too much extra flour when kneading the dough. Too much flour will make the dough stiff. It is also important not to be too rough with the dough. Too much pressure at the beginning of kneading can keep the dough sticky and hard to handle. Too much pressure toward the end of kneading can tear or mat the gluten strands that have already developed.

A— If dough is sticky, sprinkle the surface with a small amount of flour.

B— Fold dough in half toward your body.

C— Push against the dough with the heels of your hands.

D— Turn dough one-quarter turn.

Courtesy ACH Food Companies, Inc.

22-7 To knead dough, repeat these steps for 4 to 10 minutes until dough becomes smooth and elastic.

Fermentation

After kneading yeast dough, allow it to rest in a warm place. During this resting time, the yeast acts on the sugars in the bread dough to form alcohol and carbon dioxide. This process is called **fermentation**. The alcohol evaporates during baking. The carbon dioxide causes the bread to rise.

The dough should at least double in volume during fermentation. To see if dough has doubled in size, gently push two fingers into the dough. If an indentation remains, the dough has risen enough.

Fermentation time varies depending on the kind and amount of yeast, the temperature of the room, and the kind of flour. Breads made with fast-rising yeast rise up to 50 percent faster than products made with regular yeast. The dough should be kept in a warm place for optimal fermentation. The temperature range of 80°F to 85°F (27°C to 29°C) is ideal for the production of carbon dioxide by the yeast. Create such a warm environment by placing the bowl of dough over a pan of steaming water. Avoid temperatures that are too warm, which will cause the yeast to work too quickly, causing the dough to rise too fast.

Punching the Dough

When the dough is light (has completed the first rising), it must be punched down to release some of the carbon dioxide. Punch dough down by firmly pushing a fist into the dough. Then fold the edges of the dough toward the center, and turn the dough over so the smooth side is on top. At this point, some doughs require a second rising time. (Doughs made with bread flour need a second rising.)

Shaping

After punching the dough down, use a sharp knife to divide it into portions as the recipe directs. Allow the divided dough to rest about 10 minutes. After resting, the dough will be easier to handle and shape as desired.

To shape yeast dough, first flatten the dough into a rectangle. The width of the dough should be about the length of the bread pan. Using a rolling pin will help to work out any large air bubbles. Fold the ends of the rectangle to the center, overlapping them a little. This should give a smaller rectangle. Use the rolling pin to flatten the rectangle into a square. Roll the dough into a cylinder. Pinch the edge of the dough into the roll to seal it. Seal each end of the roll by pressing down on it with the side of the hand. Fold the ends under. Place the shaped dough, seam side down, in a greased loaf pan. Brush the top with melted butter, if desired. Cover the loaf with a clean towel, and shape the remaining dough. Let the loaves rise in a warm, draft-free place until they have doubled in bulk.

Baking

Baking times and temperatures vary somewhat depending on the kind of dough and size of the loaf. Place most yeast breads in a moderately hot oven. During baking, the gas cells formed during fermentation expand. The walls of dough around these cells set and become rigid. During the first few minutes of baking, the dough will rise dramatically. This rapid rising is called *oven spring*.

After baking, immediately remove bread from the pans and place it on cooling racks. Cool the bread thoroughly before slicing or storing.

For Example...

Besides traditional loaves baked in loaf pans, yeast dough can be shaped into round loaves, elongated loaves, braids, rings, and bread sticks.

FYI

To prevent overbrowning of yeast bread crusts, cover loaves with foil tents during the last 10 to 15 minutes of baking time.

Enrich

Ask each student to interview someone who owns a bread machine. Students should find out how long the person has owned the machine and how often he or she uses it. Students should also ask what types of bread products the owner makes with the bread machine. Have students share their findings in class.

Meeting Special Needs

Provide a bread slice holder for students with limited manual dexterity. This device will hold a slice of bread in place on a countertop, allowing students to more easily cut or spread it.

Hamilton Beach Brands, Inc.

22-8 Uniform texture of the air cells is a sign of quality in homemade yeast bread.

Characteristics of Yeast Bread

A high-quality loaf of yeast bread has a large volume and a smooth, rounded top. The surface is golden brown. When sliced, the texture is fine and uniform. The crumb is tender and elastic, and it springs back when touched. See **22-8**.

If yeast dough has been under- or overworked, the finished product will have a low volume. This is because carbon dioxide has leaked out of the dough.

If bread is allowed to rise for too long a time before baking, it may have large, overexpanded cells. The top of the loaf may be sunken with overhanging sides, much like a mushroom. The texture will be coarse, and it may be crumbly.

If bread has not been allowed to rise long enough before baking, it may have large cracks on the sides of the loaf. Its texture will be compact.

Timesaving Yeast Bread Techniques

Bread making no longer has to be the all-day task it once was. Fast-rising yeast can cut rising time in half. Using the one-rise mixing method saves rising time. The mixer method speeds the blending of ingredients and shortens kneading time. The batter method eliminates kneading entirely.

Besides timesaving ingredients and mixing methods, some recipes allow bread making to fit conveniently into most schedules. These include recipes for cool-rise, refrigerator, and freezer doughs. Of course, a bread machine is the ultimate time-saver.

Cool-Rise Doughs

Cool-rise doughs are prepared from recipes that are specially designed to rise slowly in the refrigerator. Mix ingredients and knead the dough. Then after a brief rest, shape the dough and place it in a pan. Cover the dough and place it in the refrigerator. The dough will rise and be ready to bake at any convenient time from 2 to 24 hours later.

Refrigerator Doughs

Like cool-rise doughs, *refrigerator doughs* are prepared from recipes that are specially designed to rise slowly in the refrigerator. The batter method is often used to prepare these doughs. Therefore, they are not kneaded like cool-rise doughs. Refrigerator doughs are also shaped after, rather than before refrigeration. Refrigerator doughs can usually remain in the refrigerator for 2 to 24 hours. Then shape the dough, let it rise, and bake it.

Freezer Doughs

Another type of specially formulated yeast bread recipe is for *freezer doughs*. These recipes allow the dough to be mixed and kneaded. Then the dough is frozen before or after shaping. The dough can be stored in the freezer for up to one month. When it is needed, simply thaw, shape if necessary, let it rise, and bake.

Learn About...

Bread Machines

Many meal managers rely on the ease of bread machines to make homemade bread an option in their menu plans. All a meal manager has to do is measure the ingredients, and the bread machine does the rest.

Proportions of ingredients vary a bit between traditional yeast breads and those prepared in bread machines. Unlike traditional recipes, fat is not optional in bread machine recipes. Bread machine recipes require more salt and sugar, too.

Bread flour is recommended in bread machine recipes. This is because the actions of a bread machine require stronger gluten. When using whole grain flour, it is essential to combine it with bread flour. The combination of flours will produce more gluten and help bread rise. Adding an egg to a recipe calling for whole grain flour will also help improve the structure and volume of the finished product.

Guidelines for ingredients and operation vary from model to model. The best way to ensure success when using a bread machine is to follow the manufacturer's directions.

Yeast Bread Variations

Add variety to yeast bread by combining white flour with whole wheat flour, rye flour, or cornmeal. Try adding dried fruits, nuts, herbs, or cheese to the basic dough. Brush the tops of the loaves with butter and sprinkle them with poppy, sesame, or caraway seeds.

Basic bread dough can be shaped into rolls. After punching the dough down, allow it to rest for a short time. Then divide it into portions and shape it into rolls. Crescent rolls, cloverleaf rolls, Parker House rolls, fan tans, and bows are popular roll shapes. Directions for shaping rolls can be found in many cookbooks. See **22-9**.

Courtesy ACH Food Companies, Inc.

22-9 Shaping yeast dough into crescent rolls is an easy way to make ordinary bread seem extra special.

CAREER SUCCESS

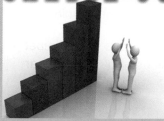

Time Management

Darnell is a baker at The Village Bakeshop, a popular spot among commuters who ride the morning train. Darnell arrives at work at 3 o'clock every morning to begin making a variety of breads and pastries. Using cool-rise dough prepared the day before, Darnell shapes, bakes, fills, and frosts loaves, rolls, and coffee cakes. When the bakeshop opens at 6:00 a.m., Darnell must have a variety of baked goods ready to sell.

To be a successful employee, Darnell needs time management skills. Put yourself in Darnell's place and answer the following questions about your need for and use of these skills:

A. How will having time management skills help you as a baker?

B. How might commuters respond if you lack time management skills?

C. How might The Village Bakeshop be affected if you lack time management skills?

D. What is another skill you would need in this job? Briefly explain why this skill would be important.

CHAPTER 22 REVIEW

Summary

Quick breads and yeast breads are baked products. All baked products are available in various forms. Convenience tends to affect the cost of these products. Unless they contain perishable fillings or frostings, most baked products can be kept at room temperature. Use the freezer for longer storage.

Biscuits, muffins, popovers, and cream puffs are four popular types of quick breads. Flour, leavening agents, liquids, fat, eggs, sugar, and salt each serve specific functions in these baked products. Varying ingredient proportions and mixing methods results in the distinctive differences among these baked products.

The mixing methods used to prepare yeast breads are different from those used to prepare quick breads. Most yeast breads require kneading to develop the gluten needed to form the structure of the bread. Yeast breads also need time for fermentation to occur. This is the time during which yeast acts on sugars, causing the dough to rise. The dough must be punched down and shaped before baking. Adding different ingredients to the dough and changing the shaping can produce a variety of yeast breads.

Review What You Have Read

Write your answers on a separate sheet of paper, using complete sentences when appropriate.

1. Explain the difference between quick breads and yeast breads. Give three examples of each.

2. What is the advantage of freezing bread in hot, humid weather?

3. What is the difference between a batter and a dough?

4. What are the three gases that make baked products rise?

5. What is the minimum amount of fat, sugar, and salt needed per cup of flour when preparing muffins?

6. Why should no more than half the all-purpose flour be replaced with whole grain flour when adjusting a recipe?

7. Match the following quick breads with their descriptions:

   _____ May be rolled or dropped.

   _____ Has a peaked top and tunnels when overmixed.

   _____ Leavened almost entirely by steam; baked in muffin pans or custard cups.

   _____ Made with a dough called puff paste.
   A. biscuit
   B. cream puff
   C. muffin
   D. pancake
   E. popover

8. What type of flour produces the strongest and most elastic gluten of all the white wheat flours?

9. How does fast-rising yeast differ from active dry yeast?

10. Which mixing method for yeast breads eliminates the need for kneading?
    A. The traditional method.
    B. The one-rise method.
    C. The mixer method.
    D. The batter method.

11. What is the function of kneading yeast dough?

12. List three factors that affect the length of fermentation for yeast doughs.

13. What are three types of recipes that are specially formulated to help bread making conveniently fit into a meal manager's schedule?

14. True or false. Fat is an optional ingredient in both traditional and bread machine yeast bread recipes.

Link to Academic Skills

15. **Social studies**. Nearly every culture on earth eats some type of bread product as a dietary staple. Investigate the type or types of bread featured in the cuisine of a culture other than your own. Find a bread recipe from this culture to prepare and share with the class.

16. **Science**. Working in your lab group, have one student place ½ cup of an assigned type of flour in a bowl. One student should stir the flour while another student gradually adds water until the mixture forms a sticky dough. This sticky dough is gluten. Have lab group members take turns stirring the dough, noting changes in the consistency. As a class, discuss the differences in gluten development among the different types of flour used by the various lab groups.

17. **Science**. Use a microscope to watch yeast grow. Explain how yeast differs from other leavening agents.

18. **English language arts**. Visit a website that features consumer reviews of various products and search for bread machines. Each student in your class should read a different review. Then compile your findings of models, product ratings, price ranges, and pros and cons. As a class, vote on which machine you would choose based on the reviews you read.

Build Critical Thinking Skills

19. **Analysis**. Prepare a plain muffin batter. Drop half of the batter from a large spoon into the depressions of a muffin pan. Place the pan in an oven and bake the muffins as the recipe directs. Continue beating the remaining batter for two more minutes. Drop it into the depressions of another muffin pan and bake as the recipe directs. Analyze the differences in appearance, flavor, and texture of the two products.

5. When preparing muffins, the minimum ingredient amounts per cup of flour are as follows: fat— 2 tablespoons (30 mL); sugar— 1 tablespoon (15 mL); and salt— ¼ teaspoon (1 mL).

6. If more than half the all-purpose flour is replaced, you may not have the right amount of gluten for the product being prepared.

7. A, C, E, B

8. Bread flour produces the strongest and most elastic gluten of all the white wheat flours.

9. Fast-rising yeast products are highly active yeast strains. The granules of these products are smaller than those of active dry yeast, which allows them to act more quickly.

10. D

11. Kneading yeast dough develops most of the gluten.

12. (List three:) kind of yeast, amount of yeast, temperature of the room, kind of flour

(continued)

13. Recipes for cool-rise, refrigerator, and freezer doughs are specially formulated to help bread making

conveniently fit into a meal manager's schedule.

14. false

20. **Evaluation.** Bake a traditional loaf of white bread and a loaf in a bread machine. Evaluate the two loaves along with a loaf of purchased white bread. Rate each product in terms of appearance, texture, flavor, and cost.

Apply Technology

21. Research the mass production processes used to manufacture bread.
22. Use spreadsheet software to compare the nutrient profiles of three bread products.

A Measure of Math

23. Visit the bread aisle in a local grocery store. List 25 bread products in order according to cost, beginning with the least expensive. Share your findings in a class discussion on factors that affect bread costs.

Teamwork in Action

24. Research celiac disease and other medical reasons for following a gluten-free diet. Summarize your findings in a brief brochure. Include several gluten-free bread recipes in the brochure. Prepare and distribute samples of the recipes along with the brochures at a local health fair.

Companion Website
www.g-wlearning.com

At the website, review key terms for this chapter with crossword puzzles, matching exercises, and e-flash cards. Apply facts from the chapter to complete the activities.

CHAPTER 23

Cakes, Cookies, Pies, and Candies

Main Menu

⊛ Proper ingredient proportions are needed to produce desired quality characteristics in cakes, cookies, and pastry.

⊛ Careful attention to recipe details, such as mixing methods and cooking temperatures, will ensure success when preparing cakes, cookies, pies, and candies.

Learning Prep

Look in the index of a cookbook to see which of the *Terms to Know* you can find listed.

Objectives

After studying this chapter, you will be able to

⊛ **describe** the functions of basic ingredients used in cakes.

⊛ **identify** six types of cookies.

⊛ **explain** principles of pastry preparation.

⊛ **compare** characteristics of crystalline and noncrystalline candies.

⊛ **prepare** cakes, cookies, pies, and candies.

Terms to Know

shortened cake
unshortened cake
chiffon cake
pastry
crystalline candy
noncrystalline candy
sugar syrup

Academic Connections

Team up with the business department to help students plan an entrepreneurship experience. Have students choose a cake, cookie, pie, or candy recipe they think will sell well to other students in your school. You can help students use ingredient prices to determine the unit cost of their product. The business teachers can help students identify other business expenses, determine an appropriate profit margin to price the product, and prepare a marketing strategy.

For many people, a meal is not complete without something sweet. Restaurants are famous for the richness of their cheesecakes. Bakeries pride themselves on their pastries. Candy stores guard their recipes for fudge, peanut brittle, and English toffee.

Cakes, cookies, and pies are three of the most popular desserts, **23-1**. Candies are not really desserts, but because they are sweet, many people serve them at the end of a meal.

Most desserts are high in calories because they contain large amounts of sugar and fat. Desserts should never replace grain foods, fruits, vegetables, milk products, or protein foods in the diet.

Cakes

Cakes are a favorite dessert of many people. They add festivity to many special occasions. They also add variety to lunch boxes and make a plain meal something special.

Kinds of Cakes

Cakes are classified into two groups: shortened and unshortened. **Shortened cakes** contain fat. This is why some people call shortened cakes *butter cakes*. Most shortened cakes contain leavening agents. Shortened cakes are tender, moist, and velvety.

Courtesy ACH Food Companies, Inc.

23-1 Who can resist a dessert of warm apple pie with a side of rich vanilla ice cream?

Unshortened cakes, sometimes called *foam cakes*, contain no fat. They are leavened by air and steam rather than chemical leavening agents. Angel food and sponge cakes are unshortened cakes. The main difference between these two cakes is the egg content. Angel food cakes contain just egg whites. Sponge cakes contain whole eggs. Unshortened cakes are light and fluffy.

Chiffon cakes are a cross between shortened and unshortened cakes. They contain fat like shortened cakes and beaten egg whites like unshortened cakes. They have large volumes, but they are not as light as unshortened cakes.

Cake Ingredients

Cakes contain flour, sugar, eggs, liquid, and salt. All shortened cakes also contain fat, and most cakes contain a leavening agent. Unshortened cakes contain cream of tartar, too.

Flour gives structure to a cake. The gluten that develops when flour is moistened and mixed holds the leavening gases that form as cakes bake. Cakes can be made with cake flour or all-purpose flour. Cakes made with cake flour are more delicate and tender. This is because cake flour has lower protein content, so it yields less gluten. It is also more finely ground than all-purpose flour.

Sugar gives sweetness to cakes. It also tenderizes the gluten and improves the texture of cakes. Recipes may call for either granulated or brown sugar. Both should be free of lumps.

Eggs improve both the flavor and color of cakes. The coagulated egg proteins also add structure to cakes. In angel food and sponge cakes, eggs are important for leavening. Eggs hold the air that is beaten into them, and the evaporation of liquid from the egg whites creates steam.

Liquid provides moisture and helps blend ingredients. Most cake recipes call for fluid fresh milk. However, some call for buttermilk, sour milk, fruit juices, or water instead. In angel food cakes, egg whites are the only source of liquid needed, **23-2**.

Salt provides flavoring. Cakes require a smaller amount of salt than quick breads and yeast breads.

Fat tenderizes the gluten. Shortened cakes may contain butter, margarine, or hydrogenated vegetable shortening. (For best results in cooking and baking, margarines must contain at least 80 percent oil.) Chiffon cakes contain oil instead of solid fat.

Leavening agents are added to most shortened cakes to make the cakes rise and become porous and light. Most recipes call for baking powder or baking soda and sour milk.

Angel food and sponge cake recipes call for *cream of tartar*. Cream of tartar is an acid that makes egg whites whiter and makes the cake grain finer. Cream of tartar also stabilizes the egg white proteins, which increases the volume of the baked cake.

Flavorings are not essential ingredients in cakes, but they help make cakes special. Spices, *extracts* (concentrated flavors), fruits, nuts, poppy seeds, and coconut can be added to cake batters for variety.

©2011 Wisconsin Milk Marketing Board, Inc.

23-2 Egg whites serve as the liquid that provides moisture and helps blend ingredients in angel food cake.

Health and Wellness

Dessert Ingredient Proportions

Like bread recipes, many dessert recipes call for more of some ingredients than are needed to perform their specific functions. Try adjusting cake, cookie, and pastry recipes to use minimum amounts of fat, eggs, sugar, salt, and baking powder. The resulting products will be lower in fat, sugar, and sodium.

Minimum Dessert Recipe Proportions per 1 Cup (250 mL) of Flour					
Product	Fat	Eggs	Sugar	Salt	Baking Powder
Shortened cakes and dropped cookies	2 tablespoons (30 mL)	½	½ cup (125 mL)	⅛ teaspoon (0.5 mL)	1 teaspoon (5 mL)
Pastry	¼ cup (50 mL)	—	—	½ teaspoon (2 mL)	—

Using these proportions can help you cut the calories, fat, and sodium from some dessert recipes.

Food Science Principles of Preparing Cakes

Successfully preparing a cake depends on measuring, mixing, and baking. Ingredients must be measured accurately and mixed correctly. The cake batter must be baked in the correct pans at the correct temperature. Baking time must be watched carefully.

Measuring Ingredients

Flour, fat, sugar, liquid, and eggs affect the development of gluten. The correct proportions of each ingredient will produce a cake that is light and tender. Too much or too little of one or more ingredients may affect the finished product.

The optimum amount of flour provides the correct amount of gluten needed for structure. A cake made with too much flour is compact and dry. A cake made with too little flour is coarse, and it may fall.

Optimum amounts of fat and sugar tenderize gluten. Too much fat or sugar overtenderizes the gluten and weakens it. A cake made with too much of either ingredient will be heavy and coarse, and it may fall. A cake made with too little of either ingredient will be tough.

The optimum amount of liquid provides the moisture needed for gluten to develop. Too much liquid will make a cake soggy and heavy. Too little liquid will make a cake dry and heavy.

The optimum number of eggs contributes proteins that strengthen the gluten framework. Too many eggs will make a cake rubbery and tough.

Mixing Cakes

The correct proportions of ingredients must be mixed according to the method specified in the recipe. Cake batters should be neither overmixed nor undermixed. Overmixing will cause the gluten to overdevelop. As a result, the cake will be tough. Overmixing angel food and sponge cakes will cause air to be lost from the beaten egg whites. As a result, the volume of the cake will be smaller. See **23-3**.

Baking Cakes

Bake cake batter in pans that are neither too large nor too small. If the pans are too small, the batter will overflow. If the pans are too large, the cake will be too flat and may be dry. The correct pan size will produce a cake with a gently rounded top.

For most shortened cakes, grease the pans and flour them lightly. Grease and flour both the bottoms and sides of the pans or just the bottoms. Do not grease the pans for unshortened cakes. This is because angel food and sponge cake batters must cling to the sides of the pan during baking.

Place cakes in a preheated oven set at the correct temperature and bake them just until they test done. Cakes baked at too high a temperature may burn. Cakes baked too long may be dry.

Preparing a Shortened Cake

Shortened cakes can be mixed by the conventional method or the quick mix method. For the conventional method, cream the fat and sugar together until light and fluffy. Beat the eggs into the creamed fat and sugar. Then add the dry ingredients alternately with the liquid.

The *quick mix method*, also called the *one-bowl method*, takes less time than the conventional method. Measure the dry ingredients into the mixing bowl. Beat the fat and part of the liquid with the dry ingredients. Add the remaining liquid and unbeaten eggs last.

Pour cake batter into prepared pans. Then arrange the pans in the oven so the heat circulates freely around the cake. The pans should not touch each other or any part of the oven. If they do, hot spots may form, and the cake may bake unevenly.

To test a cake for doneness, lightly touch the center with your fingertip. If the cake springs back, it is baked. A toothpick can be inserted into the center of the cake. If the toothpick comes out clean, the cake is baked.

Most recipes say to let cakes cool in the pans for about 10 minutes after removing the pans from the oven. This cooling period makes it easier to remove the cakes from the pans. To remove a cake from the pan, run the tip of a metal spatula around the sides of the cake to loosen it. Invert a cooling rack over the top of the pan and gently flip the cooling rack and the pan. The cake should slide out of the pan. Carefully remove the pan and place a second cooling rack on top of the cake. Flip the cake and the cooling racks so the cake is right side up. Let cake layers cool thoroughly before frosting them.

Characteristics of a Shortened Cake

A high-quality shortened cake is velvety and light. The interior has small, fine cells with thin walls. The crusts are thin and evenly browned. The top crust is smooth or slightly pebbly and gently rounded. The flavor is mild and pleasing.

Pyrex®

23-3 Measuring ingredients accurately and using the correct mixing method will help cakes turn out light and delicious.

Discuss

Ask students what will happen if they fail to grease and flour the pans when baking a shortened cake. *(Removing the cake from the pans will be difficult.)*

FYI

When greasing and flouring pans for chocolate cakes and brownies, shake a little cocoa into the flour. This will prevent white flour deposits from forming on your finished product.

Vocabulary Builder

Pound cakes get their name from their ingredients. Original recipes called for a pound of butter, a pound of sugar, and a pound of flour.

Learn About...

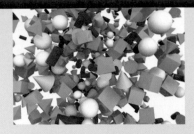

Pound Cakes

Pound cakes are shortened cakes that contain no chemical leavening agents. Pound cakes rely on air and steam for leavening. The fat and sugar must be thoroughly creamed when making pound cake. Beat the eggs into the creamed mixture until fluffy to incorporate enough air. Add the dry ingredients and the liquid to the creamed mixture. Pound cakes are more compact than other shortened cakes, and they have a closer grain.

©2011 Wisconsin Milk Marketing Board, Inc.

Fresh fruit sauce is a perfect accompaniment to moist, tender pound cake.

Preparing an Unshortened Cake

Angel food cake is the most frequently prepared unshortened cake. When preparing an angel food cake, the ingredients should be at room temperature. Egg whites that are cold will not achieve maximum volume when beaten.

Angel food cakes are mixed by a different method from those used for shortened cakes. For an angel food cake, beat the egg whites with some of the sugar until stiff. Carefully fold the flour and remaining sugar into the beaten egg whites.

Carefully pour the batter for an unshortened cake into an ungreased tube pan. Run a spatula through the batter to release large air bubbles and seal the batter against the sides of the pan. Bake the cake in a preheated oven for the recommended time. Test the cake for doneness by gently touching the cracks. They should feel dry and no imprint should remain.

When an unshortened cake is removed from the oven, immediately suspend the pan upside down over the neck of a bottle. Hanging the cake upside down prevents a loss of volume during cooling. Cool the cake completely before removing it from the pan.

Characteristics of an Unshortened Cake

A high-quality angel food cake has a large volume. The interior is spongy and porous and has thin cell walls. The cake is tender and moist, but it is not gummy.

Learn About...

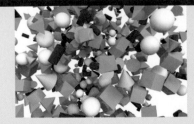

Sponge Cakes

Sponge cakes contain whole eggs rather than just egg whites. To make a sponge cake, a variation of the mixing method used for angel food cakes is used. Beat the egg yolks until they are thick and lemon colored. Add the liquid, sugar, and salt to the yolks. Continue beating until the mixture is thick. Gently fold the flour into the yolk mixture. Then fold the stiffly beaten egg whites into the flour-yolk mixture.

Preparing a Chiffon Cake

Mix a chiffon cake by combining the egg yolks, oil, liquid, and flavoring with the dry ingredients. Beat the mixture until smooth. Beat the egg whites with the sugar and cream of tartar. Then fold the egg white mixture into the other mixture.

Characteristics of a Chiffon Cake

A high-quality chiffon cake has a large volume, although not quite as large as that of an angel food cake. The interior is moist and has cells with thin walls. The cake is tender and has a pleasing flavor.

Filling and Frosting Cakes

Fillings and frostings can make a simple cake into a really special dessert. Fillings and frostings come in as wide a variety as the cakes they enhance.

Fluffy whipped cream, creamy puddings, and sweet fruits are among the popular fillings for cakes. Fillings can be spread between layers of cake or roll into the center of a jelly roll. Fillings can also be spooned into a cavity dug into the middle of a cake.

Canned frostings and frosting mixes are available, but frostings can easily be made from scratch. Frostings may be cooked or uncooked. Cooked frostings use the principles of candy making. They include ingredients that interfere with the formation of crystals in a heated sugar syrup. Then they are beaten until fluffy.

Uncooked frostings are popular for their creamy texture. They are easily made by beating the ingredients together until they reach a smooth, spreadable consistency. Cream cheese frosting and butter cream are well-liked uncooked frostings.

Frostings not only enhance the flavor of cakes, they also enhance the appearance. Cake layers can be cut into pieces and reassembled to form the shapes of animals and objects. Frosting is used as the "glue" to hold the pieces together.

Vocabulary Builder

Have students compare the terms *shortened cake*, *unshortened cake*, and *chiffon cake*.

Enrich

Invite a professional baker to your class to demonstrate various techniques for filling and frosting cakes.

Strengthening Family Ties

Have each student prepare and decorate a cake for a family celebration. Invite students to share family members' comments about the taste and appearance of the cakes.

Learn About...

Cake Decorating Tools

Use decorators' frosting to personalize cakes and trim them with pretty flowers and fancy borders. A few simple tools are all that is needed. A *decorators' tube* is a cloth, plastic, or paper bag that is filled with frosting. A *coupler* holds various plastic or metal *decorating tips* onto the tube. Squeeze the frosting through these tips to create various designs.

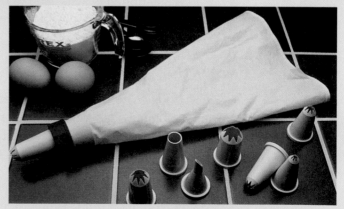

Progressive International Corp.

These accessories can be used to give any cake a festive trim.

Reflect

Ask students what their favorite kinds of cookies are and when their families bake cookies.

Activity

Have students find another example of each type of cookie in a cookbook.

Meeting Special Needs

Provide tube squeezers to help students squeeze icing from tubes when decorating cakes and sugar cookies.

Reflect

Ask students if they would prefer to eat cookies baked on a bright, shiny cookie sheet or on a dark cookie sheet.

Cookies

Children and adults find it hard to resist a cookie jar filled with fresh homemade cookies. People enjoy chocolate chip, peanut butter, oatmeal, and sugar cookies year-round. At holiday times, many families make special cookies like Swedish pepparkakor, Norwegian krumkakke, and Scottish shortbread.

Kinds of Cookies

All cookies belong to one of six basic groups: rolled, drop, bar, refrigerator, pressed, or molded. The ingredients used to make different kinds of cookies are similar. However, the doughs differ in consistency, and they are shaped differently.

A stiff dough is used to make *rolled cookies.* Roll the dough on a pastry cloth or board to a thickness of ⅛ to ¼ inch (3 to 6 mm). Cut the cookies from the dough with a cookie cutter and transfer them to a cookie sheet. Cookie cutters are available in many shapes and sizes. Sugar cookies are popular rolled cookies.

A soft dough is used to make *drop cookies.* Drop or push the dough from a spoon onto cookie sheets. Leave about 2 inches (5 cm) of space between cookies. Drop cookies will spread more than rolled cookies. Chocolate chip cookies are popular drop cookies.

A soft dough is also used to make *bar cookies.* Spread the dough evenly in a jelly roll pan or square cake pan and bake it. Depending on the thickness of the dough, bar cookies may be chewy or cakelike. Bar cookies can be cut into different shapes after baking. Brownies are popular bar cookies.

Refrigerator cookies contain a high proportion of fat. Form the stiff dough into a long roll, about two inches (5 cm) in diameter. Wrap the roll in foil or plastic wrap and refrigerate it until firm. When the dough has hardened, cut it into thin slices. Place the cookies on lightly greased cookie sheets and bake them. Pinwheel cookies are popular refrigerator cookies.

A very rich, stiff dough is used to make *pressed cookies.* Pack the dough into a *cookie press.* This utensil has perforated disks through which the dough is pushed onto cookie sheets. The cookies vary in shape and size, depending on the disk used. Swedish spritz cookies are pressed cookies.

A stiff dough is also used to make *molded cookies.* Small pieces of dough are broken off and shaped with the fingers. Crescents and small balls are popular shapes.

Cookie Ingredients

Cookies contain the same basic ingredients used to make cakes. They contain flour, sugar, liquid, fat, salt, egg, and leavening agents. Most cookies contain more fat and sugar and less liquid than cakes. Rolled cookies often contain no liquid. The proportion of ingredients, as well as the way the cookies are shaped, determines if cookies are soft or crisp.

Many cookie recipes call for ingredients such as spices, nuts, coconut, chocolate chips, and dried fruits. Some recipes say to add these ingredients to the dough during mixing. Other recipes say to sprinkle cookies or roll them in colored sugars, coconut, or nuts after baking. See **23-4**.

Mixing Methods for Cookies

Many cookies are made using the conventional mixing method used for shortened cakes. Blend the sugar and fat until smooth. Add the eggs, liquid, and flavorings, followed by the dry ingredients. Most cookies are crisp or chewy rather than light and delicate. Therefore, the fat and sugar do not need to be creamed as thoroughly as they are for a cake. Also, in most cases, the flour can be added all at once rather than in parts.

Macaroons, meringues, and kisses contain beaten egg whites. They are mixed like angel food and sponge cakes. A few cookies, like Scottish shortbread, are mixed using the biscuit method. The recipe will specify which method to use.

©2011 Wisconsin Milk Marketing Board, Inc.

23-4 Aside from basic ingredients, these cookies call for cocoa and spices in the batter, a caramel filling, and a sprinkling of ground almonds.

Pans for Baking Cookies

Bake drop, rolled, refrigerator, pressed, and molded cookies on flat baking pans or cookie sheets. Cookie sheets should not have high sides, or cookies will bake unevenly. Bake bar cookies in pans with sides.

Baking pans made of bright, shiny aluminum reflect heat. Cookies baked on bright, shiny cookie sheets will have a light, delicate brown color. Dark pans absorb heat. Cookies baked on dark cookie sheets will have dark bottoms.

Cookie sheets should be cool when cookies are placed on them for baking. Warm sheets will cause cookies to spread and lose their shape.

If two sheets of cookies are baked at one time, the pans may need to be rotated during baking. This will help the cookies brown evenly. Baking pans should never touch each other or the sides of the oven.

Storing Cookies

Store crisp cookies in a container with a loose-fitting cover. To retain their crispness, crisp cookies need to remain dry. Store soft cookies in a container with a tight-fitting cover. Exposure to the air will dry out soft cookies. (Never store crisp and soft cookies together. The soft cookies will soften the crisp cookies.) Bar cookies can be stored in their baking pan if they are covered and they will be eaten in a short time.

For longer storage, freeze cookies. Many cookies freeze well both in dough form and after baking.

To freeze refrigerator cookie dough, wrap the shaped rolls tightly in plastic wrap and then in aluminum foil. Label the package and freeze. Molded, rolled, and drop cookie doughs can be shaped into large balls. Then they can be wrapped and labeled for freezer storage. The dough will need to be thawed before molding, rolling, or dropping it. Bar cookie dough can be frozen in the baking pan. Press dough for pressed cookies or drop dough for drop cookies onto cookie sheets and quickly freeze it. The frozen dough can then be removed from the cookie sheet with a spatula. The unbaked cookies can be placed in airtight containers or plastic bags. Before baking, thaw the cookies at room temperature on a cookie sheet. To freeze baked cookies, pack them in a sturdy container with a tight-fitting cover. Separate layers of cookies with waxed paper or plastic wrap. Cover the container tightly and label.

Discuss

Ask students what the advantage of freezing unbaked cookie dough would be. *(You can prepare cookies quickly because the measuring and mixing have already been done.)*

Enrich

Ask students what healthful alternatives to cakes, cookies, and pies they might choose for desserts. Have them survey the school to find out if students prefer cakes, cookies, and pies to some of the other more healthful alternatives.

Learn About...

Freshening Stale Cookies

Cookies that have lost their characteristic texture can be freshened. If crisp cookies have become soft or begun to stale, they can be made crisp again. Place cookies on a cookie sheet in a 300°F (150°C) oven for a few minutes. If soft cookies have become hard, they can be made soft again. Place a piece of bread, an apple slice, or an orange section in the cookie container. Replace bread or fruit every other day.

Enrich

Have students investigate the difference between all-purpose flour and the pastry flour used by commercial bakeries.

Courtesy ACH Food Companies, Inc.

23-5 Tender, flaky pastry can be used to make hearty main dishes, such as chicken potpie.

Pies

Apple pie is a favorite dessert in the United States. Who can resist the flavor, aroma, and eye appeal of golden flaky pastry filled with warm, spicy apples? Apple pie begins with pastry. **Pastry** is the dough used to make piecrusts. Pastry making is not difficult. However, it does require practice and patience.

Uses for Pastry

Pastry can be used in many ways. It is mainly used when making dessert pies. However, pastry can be used when making main dish pies, such as meat pies and quiche. Small pastry shells can be filled with foods such as creamed tuna or chicken a la king to make potpies. Small pastry shells can be used to make tarts filled with pudding or ice cream. Pastry squares can be folded in half over fruit filling to make turnovers. Pastry can also be used to make appetizers such as cheese sticks. See **23-5**.

Kinds of Pies

The four basic kinds of pies are fruit, cream, custard, and chiffon. *Fruit pies* usually are two-crust pies. They may have a solid top crust, or they may have a lattice or other decorative top. Commercially prepared pie filling or filling made from canned, frozen, dried, or fresh fruit may be used.

Cream pies usually are one-crust pies. Use a cornstarch-thickened pudding mixture to make a cream filling. Cream pies often have a meringue topping.

Custard pies are one-crust pies filled with custard made from milk, eggs, and sugar. The custard may or may not contain other ingredients. Pumpkin pie is a popular custard pie.

Chiffon pies are light and airy. They are one-crust pies filled with a mixture containing gelatin and cooked beaten egg whites. Some chiffon pie fillings also contain whipped cream. Chill all chiffon pies until the filling sets.

Ingredients for Pastry

Four basic ingredients are used to make pastry—flour, fat, water, and salt. When combined correctly, the four ingredients will produce pastry that is tender and flaky.

Flour gives structure to pastry. Most home bakers use all-purpose flour to make pastry.

Fat makes pastry tender by inhibiting the development of gluten. It contributes to flakiness by separating the layers of gluten. Most bakers use lard or hydrogenated vegetable shortening. These fats produce tender and flaky pastry. Some pastry recipes call for oil. Oil-based pastry will be tender, but it will be mealy rather than flaky.

Water provides the moisture needed for the development of the gluten and the production of steam. Only a small amount of water is needed. For each 1 cup (250 mL) of flour, 2 tablespoons (30 mL) of water is ample.

Salt contributes flavor to pastry. If salt is eliminated, it will not affect the pastry in any other way.

Food Science Principles of Preparing Pastry

To make pastry that is both tender and flaky, the correct ingredients must be used. They must be measured accurately. The dough must be handled gently and as little as possible.

Measuring the Ingredients

Flour, fat, and liquid all affect the tenderness and flakiness of pastry. If these ingredients are not measured accurately, a poor-quality pastry will result.

Gluten develops when flour is moistened and stirred. The gluten creates a framework that traps air and holds steam formed during baking. This trapped air and steam is what causes pastry to be tender and flaky. Too much flour will make pastry tough.

The fat forms a waterproof coating around the flour particles. This prevents too much water from coming in contact with the proteins of the flour. It also prevents the subsequent development of too much gluten. Layers of fat physically separate the layers of gluten that form. As a result, the pastry is both tender and flaky. Too little fat will make pastry tough; too much fat will make pastry crumbly.

Water hydrates the flour so the gluten will develop. It also produces the steam needed for flakiness. The right amount of liquid will moisten the flour just enough to

For Example...

Apple, cherry, peach, strawberry, blueberry, and raspberry are among the popular fillings used for fruit pies.

Enrich

Have students prepare one piecrust using hydrogenated vegetable shortening and another using oil. After students compare the texture, flavor, and appearance of the two crusts, ask them to explain why they prefer one to the other.

Food Science

Handling Pastry Dough

Too much flour, too much liquid, and too little fat can make pastry tough. Too much handling can also make pastry tough. Handling causes gluten to develop. The more the gluten develops, the tougher the pastry will be.

Pastry should be handled gently at all times. It should also be handled as little as possible to prevent overdeveloping the gluten. It is especially important not to
- overmix the dough when adding the liquid
- use the rolling pin too vigorously when rolling the pastry
- stretch the pastry when fitting it into the pie plate

©Courtesy of California Tree Fruit Agreement

Handling pastry dough gently when fitting it into a pie plate can help prevent a tough pie crust.

develop the optimum amount of gluten. Too much liquid will make the pastry tough. Too little liquid will make it crumbly and difficult to roll.

Preparing Pastry

Several methods can be used to mix pastry, but the biscuit method (sometimes called the *pastry method*) is most popular. This method produces pastry that is both tender and flaky.

When making a one-crust pie that will be filled after baking, flute the edges. Prick the bottom and sides of the piecrust with a fork to prevent blistering during baking. Do not prick the bottom or sides of a crust that will be filled before baking.

Characteristics of Pastry

High-quality pastry is both tender and flaky. The amount and distribution of gluten determines tenderness. Flakiness is due to layers of gluten (with embedded starch grains) separated by layers of fat and expanded (puffed up) by steam.

If pastry is tender, it will cut easily with a fork and "melt in the mouth" when eaten. If pastry is flaky, thin layers of dough separated by empty spaces will be visible when the pastry is cut with a fork.

Aside from having pastry that is tender, flaky, and crisp, a pie should be lightly and evenly browned. The filling should have a pleasing flavor and be neither too runny nor too firm.

Candy

People enjoy eating candy throughout the year. At holiday times, however, many people take the time to make candy . Homemade fudge, divinity, peanut brittle, toffee, and caramels are fun to make and give as gifts.

EXPLORING CAREERS

Candy Maker

Candy making involves a number of steps. A large candy plant hires many machine operators and factory line workers. Each of these workers focuses on a single step, such as shaping, cutting, or wrapping candy. In a small candy business, all candy making tasks may be done by a master candy maker and a few assistants. The candy industry also has a lot of specialization. For instance, some candy makers produce fudge, others make caramels, and others pride themselves in taffy.

Candy factory workers need a basic skill set to be successful in their jobs. They may need only a high school education. They will likely receive on-the-job training in how to run their particular machines. They need good listening and observation skills to follow directions and pay attention to the details of their work. They also need to be able to cooperate with coworkers.

Master candy makers, on the other hand, need a broad range of skills. They may be required to have culinary training, with a focus on confectionery skills. They may also receive training as apprentices under the guidance of skilled candy makers. Master candy makers use reading skills to follow recipes and math skills to figure weights and measurements. They need to understand principles of food science to formulate new recipes. They must be able to evaluate their products for qualities such as taste, texture, and color. Master candy makers also need leadership skills to direct the work of their assistants.

To make good candy, directions must be followed exactly. Candies must be mixed correctly and cooked to the exact temperature specified in the recipe. Otherwise, they are likely to fail.

Kinds of Candy

Many kinds of candy can be made. A few kinds of candies do not need to be cooked, but these require special recipes. Most candies are cooked. Cooked candies are either crystalline or noncrystalline candies.

Crystalline candies contain fine sugar crystals. They are smooth and creamy. Fudge, fondant, and divinity are crystalline candies, **23-6**.

Noncrystalline candies do not contain sugar crystals. They can be chewy or brittle. Caramels, peanut brittle, and toffee are noncrystalline candies.

Food Science Principles of Candy Making

All cooked candies begin with **sugar syrup**. This is a mixture of sugar and liquid that is cooked to a thick consistency. Successful candy making depends on how this sugar syrup is treated.

When making crystalline candies, the sugar syrup should form crystals. However, these crystals need to be very small and fine. To produce small sugar crystals, the sugar syrup must be heated to a specific temperature. It must then be cooled to a specific temperature and beaten vigorously.

Fudge is one of the most popular crystalline candies. High-quality fudge tastes smooth and creamy because it contains small sugar crystals. It has a deep brown color and a satiny sheen. Poor-quality fudge tastes grainy because it contains large sugar crystals.

When making noncrystalline candies, the sugar syrup should not form crystals. Crystal formation can be prevented by heating the syrup to a very high temperature. Substances like corn syrup, milk, cream, or butter can be added, which interfere with crystallization. A combination of high temperatures and interfering substances can also be used to prevent crystals from forming.

Peanut brittle is a popular noncrystalline candy. High-quality peanut brittle has a golden color and looks foamy. Cooking the candy to a very high temperature and using interfering substances prevent crystal formation.

Whether making crystalline or noncrystalline candies, temperature is very important. A candy thermometer is the most accurate method of testing the temperature of sugar syrups. Each type of candy requires a specific temperature. The candy thermometer will accurately indicate when sugar syrup reaches the correct temperature.

A heavy saucepan or an iron skillet should be used to cook candy. Mixtures that contain large amounts of sugar burn easily. A heavy saucepan will help prevent scorching.

©2011 Wisconsin Milk Marketing Board, Inc.

23-6 Nothing can compare with the taste of smooth, creamy homemade fudge.

FYI
Each cacao tree yields
enough beans to
make just one to three
pounds of chocolate
per year.

Chocolate

In the minds of some sweet lovers, no candy can match chocolate. The most exquisite chocolates may be best left to professional candy makers. However, even novices can melt chocolate to make simple candies. Melted chocolate can be poured into molds. It can be used to make clusters of raisins, nuts, or coconut. Fondant or caramels can also be dipped in a coating of melted chocolate.

To melt chocolate, chop bars into small pieces or use chocolate chips. Place chocolate in the top of a double boiler over hot water and stir constantly. Remove chocolate from heat as soon as it is melted to prevent scorching. Chocolate can also be melted in a microwave oven. Place the chocolate in a glass bowl. Microwave on high power for 30 seconds at a time until chocolate is melted. Be sure to stir the chocolate after each microwaving period.

Learn About...

Types of Chocolate

Chocolate is made from the beans of the cacao tree. The beans are first roasted. Then they are shelled, pressed, and heated until they form a liquid, which is called *chocolate liquor*. At this point, some of the fat, or *cocoa butter*, may be removed. However, a high cocoa butter content is a sign of quality in chocolate.

Baking and eating chocolate is made from chocolate liquor. It comes in various degrees of sweetness. *Unsweetened chocolate* contains no sugar. *Bittersweet,* *semisweet,* and *milk chocolate* each contain progressively more sugar. Sweetened chocolates also contain vanilla, and milk chocolate contains milk solids.

Other products related to chocolate include cocoa, white chocolate, and imitation chocolate. Cocoa is made from dried chocolate liquor that has been ground to a fine powder. *White chocolate* is made from cocoa butter, sugar, milk solids, and flavorings. Because it contains no chocolate liquor, it is not truly chocolate. *Imitation chocolate* or chocolate-flavored products are made with vegetable oil instead of cocoa butter. Imitation chocolate is less expensive than real chocolate. However, it lacks the creamy smoothness and delicious flavor characteristic of true chocolate.

CAREER SUCCESS

Leadership

Judi is the pastry chef on the Caribbean Empress, which is a cruise ship noted for its world-class meals. Judi supervises three dessert cooks. Each day they prepare pastries, confections, and ice cream to coordinate with the executive chef's elaborate menus. Once a week, they also put together an expansive dessert buffet, which becomes a highlight of every cruise. Judi makes sure the cooks correctly prepare and attractively plate each of 1,800 servings of dessert daily.

To be an effective worker, Judi needs leadership skills. In a small group, answer the following questions about Judi's need for and use of these skills:

A. How might Judi's leadership skills help the dessert cooks do their work?
B. How might the ship's guests be affected if Judi lacks leadership skills?
C. How might the Caribbean Empress be affected if Judi lacks leadership skills?
D. What is another skill Judi would need in this job? Briefly explain why this skill would be important.

CHAPTER 23 REVIEW

Summary

The two basic types of cakes are shortened, which contain fat, and unshortened, which do not contain fat. Chiffon cakes are a cross between shortened and unshortened cakes. All cakes contain the same essential set of ingredients, each of which performs a specific function. When making cakes, ingredients must be measured carefully and then mixed using the method described in the recipe. Correct pan sizes, oven temperatures, and baking times must be used to make sure cakes bake properly. After baking, cakes can be filled and/or frosted to enhance flavor and appearance.

Rolled, drop, bar, refrigerator, pressed, and molded cookies all contain ingredients similar to cakes. Most cookies are mixed by the conventional mixing method. Crisp cookies should be stored in containers with loose-fitting lids and soft cookies should be stored in containers with tight-fitting lids.

Pastry is the primary component of fruit, cream, custard, and chiffon pies. Flour, fat, water, and salt are the basic ingredients in pastry. Carefully measuring these ingredients and gently handling the dough will help produce tender, flaky pastry.

Both crystalline and noncrystalline candies can be made. Both types begin with sugar syrup. For crystalline candies, sugar syrups are heated, cooled, and then beaten to produce fine sugar crystals. For noncrystalline candies, sugar syrups are heated to high temperatures and/or interfering substances are added to keep crystals from forming.

Review What You Have Read

Write your answers on a separate sheet of paper, using complete sentences when appropriate.

1. True or false. Both shortened and unshortened cakes contain chemical leavening agents.

2. List the seven basic ingredients of a shortened cake (other than pound cake) and briefly describe a major function of each.

3. What are two functions of cream of tartar in angel food cake?

4. What would happen if a cake were made with too much fat?

5. Why do baking pans need to be the correct size when baking a cake?

6. What are the two most common mixing methods for making shortened cakes?

7. True or false. An angel food cake should be removed from the pan as soon as it comes out of the oven.

8. How do proportions of cookie ingredients differ from proportions of cake ingredients?

9. Describe the appearance of cookies baked on a shiny aluminum cookie sheet and cookies baked on a dark cookie sheet.

Answer Key to *Review What You Have Read* questions

1. false

2. Flour provides structure. Sugar provides sweetness. Eggs improve color. Liquid helps blend ingredients. Salt provides flavor. Fat tenderizes the gluten. Leavening agents make the cake rise. (Students may justify other functions.)

3. (List two:) makes egg whites whiter; makes the cake grain finer; stabilizes the egg white proteins, which increases the volume of the baked cake

4. Too much fat would overtenderize the gluten and weaken it. A cake made with too much fat would be heavy and coarse, and it might fall.

5. If the pans are too small, the batter will overflow. If the pans are too large, the cake will be too flat and it may become dry. A cake baked in pans that are the right size will have a gently rounded top.

(continued)

6. The two most common mixing methods for making shortened cakes and the conventional method and the quick mix method.

7. false

8. Most cookies contain more fat and sugar and less liquid than cakes.

9. Cookies baked on a shiny cookie sheet have light, delicately browned crusts. Those baked on dark cookie sheets have dark bottoms.

10. Omitting salt from pastry will affect only the flavor.

11. (List three:) too much flour, too much liquid, too little fat, dough overmixed, rolling pin used too vigorously, pastry stretched when fitting it into a pie plate

12. Two characteristics used to describe high-quality pastry are tender and flaky.

13. Crystalline candy is smooth and creamy. Noncrystalline candy may be chewy or brittle.

14. A candy thermometer is the most accurate method of testing the temperature of sugar syrups used in candy making.

10. How will pastry be affected if salt is omitted from the recipe?

11. List three reasons pastry might be tough.

12. What two characteristics are used to describe high-quality pastry?

13. How does a crystalline candy differ in texture from a noncrystalline candy?

14. What is the most accurate method of testing the temperature of sugar syrups used in candy making?

Link to Academic Skills

15. **English language arts**. Visit the Sugar Association website. Research a type of sugar or a basic functional role of sugar in baked products. Share your findings in a brief oral report.

16. **Science**. Observe the different densities of common liquid ingredients. Working in lab groups, pour ¼ cup each of corn syrup, colored water, and vegetable oil into a liquid measuring cup. Gently drop a chocolate chip, an ice cube, and a miniature marshmallow into the measuring cup, noting the respective densities of these foods in relation to the liquids.

17. **Science**. Prepare two angel food cakes. In one cake, add cream of tartar to egg whites during beating. Do not add cream of tartar to the egg whites used in the other cake. Discuss the appearance, texture, and volume of the two cakes.

18. **English language arts**. Prepare enough pastry for a two-crust pie. Divide the dough in half. Roll half the dough and cut it into 1-inch (2.5-cm) strips. Place the strips on a cookie sheet. Knead the other half of the dough for several minutes. Roll and cut the dough into 1-inch (2.5-cm) strips and place them on a second cookie sheet. Bake the pastry strips. After comparing the appearance and texture of the two samples, write a paragraph explaining why overhandling pastry should be avoided.

Build Critical Thinking Skills

19. **Analysis**. Prepare two batches of a shortened cake recipe—one with granulated sugar and the other with brown sugar. Store the cakes in covered containers for several days. Analyze the impact changing the type of sugar used makes by comparing the flavor and texture of the two cakes.

20. **Evaluation**. Prepare two batches of fudge. Follow directions exactly for the first batch. For the second batch, stir fudge occasionally during cooling. After the fudge has set, evaluate the texture, flavor, and appearance of both samples.

Apply Technology

21. Use spreadsheet software with an automatic sum function. Create a program that will calculate the minimum amounts of fat, eggs, sugar, salt, and baking powder to use in shortened cakes. The formula for each ingredient should immediately show the correct amount when you enter the amount of flour required in a cake recipe.

22. Choose a type of artificial sweetener and investigate how it is made. Prepare two batches of a cake or cookie recipe using the artificial sweetener in place of the sugar in one batch. Compare and evaluate the two products.

A Measure of Math

23. Choose a favorite cookie recipe. Write down the amount of each ingredient you would need to prepare a double batch. Also note the yield for the double batch.

Teamwork in Action

24. Working as a class, calculate the area of common bakeware pieces, such as 8-inch round, 9-inch round, 8-inch square, 9-inch square, 13-by-9-inch oblong, 11-by-7-inch oblong, 9-by-5-inch loaf, and 8-by-4-inch loaf. Arrange your calculations into a chart along with some tips about substituting pans when baking. Laminate the charts and attach magnets to the back so they can be placed on refrigerators. Invite local bakeware retailers to distribute the charts to customers.

Companion Website

www.g-wlearning.com

At the website, review key terms for this chapter with crossword puzzles, matching exercises, and e-flash cards. Apply facts from the chapter to complete the activities.

CHAPTER 24
Food and Entertaining

Learning Prep

Suggest a definition for each of the *Terms to Know*. Then look up the terms in the glossary to check your accuracy.

Terms to Know

RSVP
appetizer
American (family style) service
Russian (continental) service
English service
compromise service
blue plate service
buffet service

manners
etiquette
reservation
entree
table d'hôte
a la carte
Dutch treat
gratuity
tip

Main Menu

* Planning can help a host reduce stress and keep food safe and guests comfortable at a social gathering.
* Using proper behavior when dining out shows self-respect and concern for restaurant staff and other diners.

Objectives

After studying this chapter, you will be able to

* **plan** a social gathering.
* **wait** on a table correctly.
* **prepare** appetizers.
* **describe** guidelines for safely preparing, transporting, and serving food for outdoor entertaining.
* **use** appropriate behavior when dining out.

Eating food is more enjoyable when others eat it with you. Entertaining and dining out give people chances to renew longstanding relationships and meet new friends.

Planning for Entertaining

Most people enjoy getting together with coworkers, friends, and family members. You might host a formal dinner party, a special birthday celebration, a business gathering, or an impromptu get-together. No matter what the event is, a little planning will help it go more smoothly. See **24-1**.

Social gatherings should allow both guests and hosts to enjoy themselves. Guests may find it hard to relax if their host is running around tending to last minute details. Hosts may find it hard to have a good time if they have not completed preparations before their guests arrive. Careful planning helps prevent these problems and set a festive mood for a party.

Planning a gathering involves money, time, and energy. The kind of gathering you have and the number of guests you invite depend on these and other important factors.

The Theme

Social gatherings often have themes. Almost any idea can be turned into a party theme. Sports events and holidays are popular themes. You could plan a gathering with an international theme using information from the last part of this text.

The theme helps determine what people should wear and what foods might be served. The theme can give ideas for decorations and activities, too. For instance, guests could wear traditional Mexican clothes to go with a Mexican fiesta theme. Tacos and enchiladas could be served. Cacti, colorful streamers, and a piñata could be used for decorations. Activities could include breaking the piñata and dancing to Latin music.

Shutterstock

24-1 Any type of gathering or celebration will be more enjoyable when there is a little planning behind it.

EXPLORING CAREERS

Meeting Planner

Meeting planners are in charge of all aspects of setting up meetings for businesses and organizations. They work with their clients to determine goals and a budget for an event. Then they put together an event schedule. They find a meeting location, arrange for food, hire entertainment, and order AV equipment, as needed. They may contact speakers and arrange for their transportation and lodging. Meeting planners send out details promoting the event. They also have agendas and other materials printed for attendees.

To be successful, meeting planners need outstanding organizational skills. They need good communication skills as they listen to clients and relay information to others. They need to pay attention to details, manage time, and oversee people. They will use math skills to handle budgeting issues. Meeting planners must be able to handle stress and adapt to change. They must be creative problem solvers. They must also be willing to do some traveling and work rather long and irregular hours.

Most meeting planners have four-year degrees. A degree may not be required, but classes in business and communications will help people who want to enter this career. Meeting planners typically start out as part of a staff. At this level, they carry out assignments and follow up to be sure tasks have been done as required. With experience, meeting planners may move into decision-making positions. They may also apply to become Certified Meeting Professionals (CMPs). This certification shows employers meeting planners have knowledge and background in the field.

Career Path

Ask students what aspects of a meeting planner's work they would find most challenging. What aspects would they find most rewarding?

Discuss

Ask students what factors they should consider when planning a guest list for a party. *(personalities, interests, and backgrounds of guests)*

Ask students why a host needs to know how many people will be attending his or her party. *(to decide how much food and space will be needed)*

The Guest List

When putting together a guest list, keep people's interests and personalities in mind. Common interests will help guests get to know one another. Compatible personalities will help create a setting in which everyone gets along and has a good time.

The number of people invited to a party should fit comfortably in the amount of space available. The guest list should also fit the host's cooking skills and available equipment. Unless extra help or a large freezer are available, very large parties might not be practical.

The Invitations

Most parties have no rules for invitations. Friends might be invited for a spur-of-the-moment party or casual gathering in person or over the phone. For large parties, e-mail invitations sent through an online service are convenient. A formal event always requires a printed invitation.

All invitations should include the date, time, and place of the party. Including a map can be helpful for people who might not be familiar with the location. Invitations should specify if a party is to honor a special event, such as a birthday. They should also indicate any need for special clothing, such as swimsuits for a pool party.

You may wish to include the letters **RSVP** on your invitations. This is the abbreviation for a French phrase that means "please respond." Also include your phone number and/or e-mail address so your guests can let you know if they are coming.

Keep a list of all replies as you receive them. You will need this list for later planning.

The Menu

Almost any foods can be party foods. Sometimes the kind of gathering helps to plan the menu. Cookies and hot chocolate might be served at a sledding party. Heartier foods, such as sandwiches and pizza, might be served for an after-the-game get-together. See **24-2**.

Of course, a key consideration when planning a menu is the guests' food preferences. Choose foods you think your guests will like. If any of your guests has special dietary needs, try to serve some foods and drinks that meet those needs. For instance, offer meatless items for guests who are vegetarians. Also, avoid serving foods to which you know a guest is allergic.

Other factors to consider when planning a party menu include the budget, cooking skills, time schedule, and equipment. Party food can be costly. Preparing food yourself is likely to be less expensive than buying ready-made snacks. You may wish to give a party with friends who can help split the costs. For a casual gathering, you might ask each guest to bring a dish to share.

When you are having guests, choose familiar recipes you know you can prepare successfully. Save new recipes for a trial run later with your family or close friends. Limit the number of dishes that will require your last minute attention. Choose one or more dishes you can prepare in advance. This gives you more time to enjoy your guests.

Do not finalize the menu until you check your equipment. See if you have all the cookware and serving utensils you will need. For instance, if you do not have a deep, straight-sided dish, do not plan to make a soufflé. Also check to see when you will need to use certain appliances. You may not have enough room to microwave two dishes at the same time. (You may be able to borrow or rent equipment, but check first.)

Appetizers

Appetizers are light foods or beverages served to stimulate the appetite. They are often served at the beginning of a meal. Appetizers are also popular as party foods.

Hamilton Beach Brands, Inc.

24-2 Chips, veggies, and appetizer meatballs would be popular foods at many types of get-togethers.

Learn About...

Serving Party Foods

Always try to make food look appetizing when you serve it. This is especially important when serving foods to guests. Arrange food attractively on platters and trays and in serving bowls. Use garnishes to add color and give guests a hint of what is in foods. For example, use jalapeño peppers to garnish a spicy hot Mexican cheese dip. Fresh raspberries can be used to garnish a chocolate raspberry torte.

Be sure an appropriate serving utensil accompanies each dish. Use serving spoons for soft foods and serving forks for meats. Tongs work well for serving individual items, such as shrimp and fresh vegetables. When guests will be approaching a buffet table from both sides, place two serving utensils with each dish.

©2011 Wisconsin Milk Marketing Board, Inc.

The garnish of grated cheese on these chicken strips helps party guests know there is cheese in the coating on the strips.

For Example...

Cocktail wieners, barbecued meatballs, vegetables and dip, and cheese balls are party appetizers that can be made at least a day ahead.

Enrich

Invite a caterer or chef to speak to your class about presentation of food. Ask the speaker to demonstrate how to prepare some eye-catching garnishes and arrange foods attractively for serving.

Many appetizers can be prepared in advance, so they require little last minute attention. You can conveniently serve appetizers to a large group because guests can eat them while standing. You are also likely to spend less money for party food when serving appetizers than when serving a full meal.

Instead of serving chips and pretzels at your next party, be creative and try making appetizers. Choose appetizers that guests will find easy to nibble while they mingle. Remember to select both hot and cold appetizers, using ingredients with a variety of flavors, colors, and textures.

A microwave oven might be used to save time when preparing hot appetizers. Mini pizzas, toasted nuts, cocktail sausages, chicken wings, and hot dips are just a few of the tasty appetizers that can be microwaved. Many of these foods can be prepared ahead of time and then microwaved at the last minute.

The Meal Service

If serving a meal at a gathering, decide how to serve it. Perhaps appetizers may be served in the living room before the meal. This will help eliminate clutter at the table. Likewise, a dessert can be served in the living room after the meal. This will give you a chance to clear the table and start to clean up the kitchen. Trays or a serving cart can help you serve both of these courses away from the table more easily.

Meals can be served in several ways. The style of service selected will depend on the formality of the meal, the menu, and the availability of help.

The six major styles of meal service are American or family, Russian or continental, English, compromise, blue plate, and buffet. They differ in the way the guests are served and in the number of courses.

American (family style) service is the style most often used in homes in the United States. In this style of service, the host fills serving dishes in the kitchen and takes them to the table. Diners serve themselves as they pass the serving dishes around the table. After clearing the table, the host may serve dessert at the table or from the kitchen.

Russian (continental) service is the most formal style of meal service. In Russian service, serving dishes are never placed on the table. Instead, waiters serve guests filled plates of food, one course at a time. Plate replaces plate as one course is removed and another is served. This type of service is often used in fine restaurants and at state dinners.

In **English service**, one of the hosts fills plates at the table and passes them from guest to guest until everyone is served. Because English service requires a lot of passing, it is best for use with small groups.

Compromise service is a compromise between Russian service and English service. The salad or dessert course is often served from the kitchen. For the other courses, one of the hosts fills the plates and passes them around the table. One person acts as waiter to clear one course and bring in the next.

Blue plate service is used in homes when serving small groups of people. It is also used at banquets where waiters are able to serve a crowd quickly. In blue plate service, the host fills plates in the kitchen and carries them to the dining room. The host may offer second helpings at the table or refill plates in the kitchen. One person clears the main course and then brings in the dessert course.

Buffet service is often used for serving large numbers of people. A dining table, a buffet, or another surface may hold the serving dishes and utensils, dinnerware, flatware, and napkins. The guests serve themselves from the buffet.

Depending on the amount of space available, guests may eat at one large table, at several smaller tables, or from lap trays. If space is limited, they may eat from plates held in their hands while sitting or standing. If guests will be seated at a table, the host may place napkins, flatware, and beverageware on the table ahead of time.

Buffet service requires careful menu planning. Equipment may be needed to keep hot foods hot and cold foods cold. Precutting foods into individual servings and pouring beverages ahead of time will make serving easier. See **24-3**.

The Host's Responsibilities

As the host, you have certain responsibilities to your guests. Before your guests arrive, be sure the house is clean and tidy. Put fresh soap and clean towels in the bathroom. Be sure to have a specific place for your guests' coats.

Enrich
Have students role-play situations in which the various styles of meal service would be used.

VISIT FLORIDA
24-3 Having poured beverages on a buffet table will make it easier for guests to serve themselves.

Learn About...

Making Introductions

As your guests begin to arrive, make introductions. Introduce a younger person to an older person by giving the older person's name first. Try to say something interesting about each person for a conversation starter. You might say, "Mary Lewis, I would like you to meet LaVarre Johnson. LaVarre worked as a camp counselor last summer."

A planned activity helps people get to know one another. Games, music, and dancing are good ways to break the ice.

Try to participate in your party as much as possible. Circulate from guest to guest instead of spending the evening with just one or two close friends. It is up to you to make all your guests feel welcome.

Waiting on the Table

If your gathering includes a meal, one of your responsibilities as host will be to wait on the table. Rules for waiting on the table are as flexible as rules for setting the table. The style of service and the menu help determine the way in which you clear the table and serve new courses.

Clear the table in a counterclockwise direction, beginning with the person seated to your right. Serve a new course in the same manner. You will use both hands when serving and clearing, but usually at different times. When serving or clearing plates, you should stand at the guest's left and place or remove the plate with your left hand. This avoids a possible collision with the water glass on the right.

Remove beverageware and unused knives and spoons from the guest's right side with your right hand. Place dessert flatware in the same manner, and pour water from the right with the right hand.

When clearing or serving, a cart or large tray can save time and steps. The order for removing and serving a course is listed in **24-4**.

Waiting on the Table	
Removing a Course	
1.	Remove all serving dishes and utensils from the table and take them to the kitchen.
2.	Beginning with the appropriate person, remove the dinner plate from each guest's left with your left hand. Transfer the first plate to your right hand. Place the second plate on top of the first plate. Then remove the third plate with your left hand. Take cleared plates to a serving cart or the kitchen. Continue this process around the table in a counterclockwise direction until you have cleared all covers.
3.	Use a small tray to remove flatware and other items not needed for the next course.
4.	If necessary, refill water glasses from each guest's right, using your right hand. Use a clean napkin to catch drips.
Serving a Course	
1.	Place needed flatware, such as cake forks or dessertspoons, at each cover.
2.	Place cream, sugar, and other needed items on the table.
3.	Place needed dinnerware at each cover.
4.	Place food and/or beverages.

24-4 Following a standard order for clearing and serving courses makes meal service more efficient.

The Guest's Responsibilities

A good guest also has responsibilities. These begin with the invitation. Always answer an invitation as soon as possible. You may be able to give an immediate response to a telephoned invitation. If not, you should answer within a day or two. Formal events require a written response. When responding to an invitation, repeat the time and the date to avoid any misunderstandings.

Arrive at a party at the designated time. Guests who arrive too early can disrupt last minute preparations. Guests who arrive late can be the cause of a ruined meal.

Greet any members of your host's family who happen to be present. Follow house rules and always be courteous.

Table Manners

When dining in a friend's home, use your best table manners. **Manners** refer to social behavior. Society sets rules of **etiquette**, which guide manners. Knowing proper etiquette will help you relax in unfamiliar settings because you will know how to behave. Those around you will also feel more at ease because your behavior will not be offensive to them. The table manners below will help you feel more comfortable and show your consideration for others when eating.

- Shortly after sitting down, open your napkin to a comfortable size and place it in your lap.
- When passing dishes at the table, always pass them in one direction.
- Wait for the host to begin eating.
- Try to eat at least a small portion of each food served. If you cannot eat something, leave it without comment.
- Use eating utensils in the order in which they have been placed on the table—from the outside toward the plate.
- Never set a used eating utensil on the table. Place dirty utensils on the plates with which you used them. For instance, leave the salad fork on the salad plate.
- If you drop an eating utensil, do not use it anymore. Your host should give you another one.
- Do not place your elbows on the table while eating.
- Keep one hand in your lap while eating.
- Do not reach in front of another diner for food. Ask someone to pass the food to you. Take helpings of average size.
- Do not take a bite from a whole slice of bread. Tear bread into quarters; tear biscuits and rolls in half. Put butter on your bread and butter plate with the knife that accompanies the butter. Then use your table knife to spread butter on one piece of bread, biscuit, or roll at a time.
- Remove seeds, pits, or fish bones from your mouth with your fingers as inconspicuously as possible. Place them on the side of your plate.
- Corn on the cob, pizza, and hot dogs are generally considered to be finger foods. At informal events, you can also pick up fried chicken, French fries, and whole fresh fruits with your fingers. However, you should use utensils when eating these foods at formal gatherings. Even at formal events, you may use your fingers when eating many appetizers.
- Do not put foods into a bowl of dip after you have had them in your mouth. Use a serving spoon to put a small amount of dip on your plate for dipping chips and vegetables. See **24-5**.

Enrich

Have students role-play various party scenarios in which a guest fails to practice proper etiquette. Discuss how the guest should have behaved in each situation.

Academic Connections

Work with a psychology teacher in presenting chapter material on party and restaurant etiquette. As you focus on table manners, ordering from a menu, and tipping, the psychology teacher can address small group behavior and factors that affect social interactions.

- If you cough or sneeze at the table, use your handkerchief and quietly excuse yourself. If you have a coughing or sneezing spell, quietly excuse yourself and leave the table.
- When you have finished eating, place your knife on the rim of the plate with the sharp edge pointing toward the center. Place the fork parallel to the knife. Lay your napkin casually to the left of the plate. Wait for your host to invite you to leave the table.
- Offer to assist with last minute details or cleanup tasks if you see the host needs help. Most hosts will appreciate your help filling serving dishes or picking up used glasses and plates. If the host refuses help, do not insist.

©2011 Wisconsin Milk Marketing Board, Inc.

24-5 Fresh vegetables are considered to be finger foods at informal events. Remember to put the dip on your plate rather than dipping into the serving bowl.

Outdoor Entertaining

Outdoor meals are an important part of warm weather entertaining. An outdoor meal can be as simple as fresh fruit, cheese, and a loaf of bread shared on a park bench. A neighborhood clambake on the beach is a more elaborate type of outdoor entertaining.

You can prepare picnic foods at home or cook them at the picnic site. Besides traditional hot dogs and hamburgers, consider expanding your picnic menus to include casseroles, soups, and ethnic dishes.

The food you serve for a picnic and how you carry it depend somewhat on transportation and available facilities. If you plan to bicycle or hike to your picnic site, you will need foods that are compact and easy to carry. Finger foods, such as sandwiches, vegetable relishes, fresh fruits, and bar cookies, would be good choices.

Picnics on the water usually have some space limitations, though not as many as bicycle picnics. On small boats, serve foods prepared in advance. On larger boats with cooking facilities, you can finish last minute preparations on the boat. Drinking water is often limited on board boats. For this reason, you might want to carry some high-moisture foods and avoid salty foods when picnicking on the water.

Grilling

Picnics that include grilled foods are called cookouts or barbecues. You can cook food over an open fire or on a grill.

Following safety precautions when grilling can help you and others avoid accidents. Always place the grill in the open, away from foliage, furniture, and buildings. Wear tight-fitting clothes and a heavy-duty apron. If you have long hair, tie it back away from your face. Do not use gasoline or kerosene to start the fire. Never pour lighter fluid over the coals once the fire has started. Keep all flammable materials away from the fire.

Light the charcoal in a grill about 30 minutes before you want to begin cooking. The time will vary somewhat depending on the wind, the location of the grill, and the kind of charcoal. Coals covered with a gray ash are ready for good heat distribution.

Learn About...

Grilling Tools

The grill is the major barbecuing tool. Except for gas and electric grills, all grills use charcoal briquettes for fuel. Place charcoal in the grill's *fire box*. An electric starter or lighter fluid and matches or a lighter will be needed to ignite the charcoal. Put the *grate*, which will hold the food, in place over the charcoal.

In addition to a grill, tongs, a long-handled fork, and a broad turner are useful. A basting brush, fireproof mitts, and heavy-duty foil also come in handy when grilling. A food thermometer is needed so the temperature of the food that is being grilled can be checked.

USDA

A food thermometer can help make sure grilled foods have reached a safe internal temperature.

Many foods can be cooked outdoors. Meats, fish, and poultry are probably the most commonly grilled foods. You can put fruits and vegetables on skewers and cook them as kabobs. You might also try wrapping them in heavy-duty foil and cooking them over the coals. You can wrap breads and biscuits in foil and warm them on a grill, too.

Transporting and Serving Food Outdoors

Hot foods must be kept hot and cold foods must be kept cold when transporting and serving foods for outdoor meals. The general guideline is to leave food at room temperature for no more than two hours. However, if temperatures are 90°F (32°C) or higher, food should not be left out for more than one hour. Vacuum containers and insulated picnic coolers can keep foods at proper temperatures during transport. Keep foods for grilling in the cooler until the coals are ready.

Remove food from coolers in small amounts. Second helpings can always be served. Return all perishable foods to the insulated cooler as soon as possible.

Bring along plenty of aluminum foil. Use it to line grills, shape serving trays, and wrap leftovers. Use plastic containers when possible. They are unbreakable, and they are lighter to carry than glass or metal containers.

Keep a supply list inside the picnic basket. Frequently forgotten items include can openers, paring knives, salt and pepper, paper towels, eating utensils, and matches.

Cleaning Up

Litter is unsightly and often illegal. It attracts insects and animals, and it can cause fires. Most parks, forest preserves, and camping grounds have refuse containers available. Be sure to use them to properly dispose of all refuse.

Discuss

Ask students to describe the function of each of the grilling utensils mentioned on this page. *(Tongs, forks, and turners are used to lift and turn foods. Basting brushes are used to apply sauces.)*

Reflect

Ask students what they do and do not enjoy about eating outdoors.

Enrich

Have each student survey three teens about how often they eat out and where they eat out. Compile findings of all students. Have one student write an article for the school newspaper.

Strengthening Family Ties

Have each student survey his or her family members to find out which local restaurant each person would choose for a casual family meal. Students should ask why family members selected specific restaurants over others. In a class discussion, ask students what factors seemed to be most important to family members when choosing a restaurant.

Enrich

Have students role-play calling a restaurant to make a reservation.

Also, pack a couple of large plastic bags with the picnic supplies. They will come in handy when picnicking in an area that does not have refuse containers. Use one of the bags to hold trash until a suitable container can be found. Use the other bag to collect cans and bottles to take to a recycling facility.

Be sure to extinguish all fires, whether in a grill or on the ground. Use plenty of water and stir the coals. Be sure all the embers have stopped smoldering before leaving. Place your hand above the ashes. If they still feel warm, add more water.

Dining Out

When you want to socialize without going to a lot of trouble, dining out is an option for entertaining. However, eating in restaurants is not just for social occasions. Many meal managers use eating out as an alternative to food preparation time.

The cost of eating out varies according to where you go and what you order. However, eating out almost always costs more than eating at home, even when you consider the cost of labor. The cost difference may be small when you look at the price of a single meal. The difference increases when you figure the price of feeding several people.

Eating out requires time as well as money. You save shopping, preparation, and cleanup time. However, you tend to spend more time at the table when dining out. You must allow time to be seated, place your order, receive your food, eat, and pay your check.

Restaurant Basics

Regardless of the time and cost factors, dining out is an enjoyable experience. Following some basic guidelines will help you feel comfortable in any restaurant setting, **24-6**.

Being Seated

A **reservation** is a request for a restaurant to hold a table for a guest. Some small or formal restaurants require reservations. In busy restaurants, reservations can ensure you will get a table when you arrive. To make a reservation, call the restaurant and request a table for the number of people in your group. Give your name and state the day and time you would like the table.

In some casual restaurants, diners seat themselves. Most restaurants, however, have a host. The host will greet you at the door and ask how many people are in your group. If you have made a reservation, give the host your name. The host will then show you to a table when one is available.

Ordering from a Menu

As you are seated, you will receive a printed menu listing the food items that are available. Items will generally be grouped under headings, such as *Appetizers*, *Salads*, *Entrees*, and *Desserts*. (**Entrees** are main courses.) Being familiar with terms used on menus will help you know how foods are prepared. This will allow you to choose items that suit your tastes. See **24-7**.

GE Lighting

24-6 Using good table manners will help make eating in a restaurant a more pleasant experience for everyone.

Menu Terms

a la. In the style of. For instance, *a la Suisse* means *Swiss style*.

a la Kiev. Containing butter, garlic, and chives.

a la king. Served with a cream sauce that contains mushrooms, green peppers, and pimientos.

a la mode. Served with ice cream.

almondine. Made or garnished with almonds.

au gratin. Served with cheese.

au jus. Served with natural juices.

du jour. Of the day. For instance, *soup du jour* means *soup of the day*.

en brochette. Broiled and served on a skewer.

en coquille. Served in a shell.

en croquette. Breaded and deep-fried.

en papillote. Cooked in parchment paper to seal in juices.

Florentine. Prepared with spinach.

lyonnaise. Sliced and sauteed with onion.

marengo. Sauteed with mushrooms, tomatoes, and olives.

picata. Prepared with lemon.

piquant. Highly seasoned.

Provencale. Prepared with garlic and olive oil.

24-7 Becoming familiar with these terms will help you when ordering from restaurant menus.

Think Outside the Box

Point out to students that if a colleague in an office where they work invites them to lunch, they would be expected to pay for their own meal. If a supervisor asks them to lunch to discuss a specific work-related topic, then this person will probably offer to pay for their lunch. Ask students how they might thank a business associate who took them to lunch. Is sending an e-mail message an appropriate way to say thanks in such a case?

Activity

Have students look through cookbooks to find names of dishes that include some of the terms listed in Figure 24-7. Ask students to share what they found about the kinds of food items that are often used in these styles of preparation.

Vocabulary Builders

• *Table d'hôte* is French for host's table. In some restaurants, table d'hôte menus are called *prix fixe*, which is French for fixed price.

• *A la carte* is French for the *bill of fare*, and bill of fare is another term for *menu*.

Pricing of menu items may be table d'hôte or a la carte. **Table d hôte** pricing means there is one price for an entire meal. Usually, this price includes salad, bread, a main course, and side dishes. It may also include an appetizer, soup, dessert, and beverage. **A la carte** pricing means there is a separate price for each menu item.

You will have a few minutes to decide what you want to eat. Then your waiter will come to your table and ask what you wish to order. If you would like an appetizer, order it first. Then tell the waiter what entree you would like. State your preferences for optional items, such as side dishes and salad dressings. On some menus, items are numbered. You can simply order the number of the meal or food item you want.

Restaurants generally serve food in courses. Your waiter will usually bring out beverages right after you place your order. If you have ordered appetizers, your waiter will serve them first. He or she will then serve soups and salads followed by entrees and side dishes. The waiter will serve dessert last. You may order dessert with the rest of the meal or after you have finished eating the entree.

Dining in Public

When dining in public, you are a guest of the restaurants to which you go. Your behavior should be that of a well-mannered visitor. Dress appropriately for the setting of the restaurant. Even in casual restaurants, it is important to look neat and clean and use good table manners. Follow the same guidelines you would use when eating in a friend's home.

Occasionally, you may have a problem with the food or service in a restaurant. Perhaps your food seems unwholesome or is not prepared as you ordered it. Maybe the service is slow or the waiter forgot part of your order. Whatever the problem is, quietly call it to your waiter's attention. Avoid making a scene and disturbing other diners. If the waiter is unwilling or unable to correct the problem, ask to speak to the manager.

Your satisfaction can affect the success of a restaurant. In most cases, restaurant staff members will do their best to make your dining experience a pleasant one.

Paying the Bill

At the end of the meal, the waiter will bring a bill showing how much money you owe. When dining with others, you should know in advance who is going to pay the bill. When someone invites a person to go out for a meal, the person extending the invitation generally pays. When a group of friends goes out to eat, they often go **Dutch treat**. This means each person pays for his or her meal.

Sometimes it may be easiest to simply split the bill equally among everyone in the group. Other times, each person will pay just for the foods he or she ordered. If you intend to pay this way, ask the waiter when ordering if you can have separate checks. This will make it easy for each person to know how much he or she owes.

Sometimes the bill will be in a folder or on a plate or small tray. Place either cash or a credit card in the folder or on the plate or tray. The waiter will take the payment and bring you your change. (If you are paying with a credit card, your waiter will bring you a receipt to sign.) In casual restaurants, you may pay a cashier on the way out the door, **24-8**. Whether you pay the waiter or a cashier, it is customary to leave a **gratuity**, or **tip**, for service received.

Learn About...

Restaurant Tipping

Some restaurants automatically include a gratuity on the bill, especially for larger groups. If no gratuity is indicated, leave whatever you feel is proper. For average service, about 15 percent of the total bill is usually appropriate. If a waiter has given you special service, you may want to leave a larger tip.

If the waiter collects payment, you can leave the tip in the folder or on the plate or tray. If you pay the cashier, leave the tip inconspicuously on the table. If you pay with a credit card, you can write the amount of your tip on the receipt. Then add the cost of the meal and the tip. Write the total on the receipt before signing your name.

Types of Restaurants

The variety of restaurants is almost limitless. Restaurants offer all cuisines and a range of prices and formality.

Fast-Food Restaurants

Fast-food restaurants specialize in speedy service. They cater to people who are looking for quick, inexpensive meals.

Most fast-food restaurants have rather limited menus. The menu is usually posted above the counter near the restaurant entrance. All the foods on the menu can be prepared quickly. Many items are fried because frying allows foods to cook rapidly.

Food at fast-food restaurants is relatively inexpensive. The high sales volume and limited service help keep prices down. Because customers do not receive service from waiters, they do not have to leave tips in fast-food restaurants. This also saves customers money.

Cafeterias and Buffets

Cafeterias have a variety of prepared foods placed along a serving line. Customers carry a tray along the line and select the foods they want. Foods are served in individual portions and each item is priced separately. Customers pay for the items on their tray when they reach the end of the line.

Buffets are similar to cafeterias as far as the way the food is served. However, at buffets, customers generally pay a fixed price for the meal. They can serve themselves as much of each food on the buffet line as they like. They can also return to the serving line for more food as many times as they wish.

Neither cafeterias nor buffets have waiters to take customers' food orders at the table. However, servers may take beverage orders, refill coffee, and clear dirty dishes. For these services, leaving a tip of about 10 percent of the food bill is appropriate.

Photo provided by Culver Franchising System, Inc.

24-8 At fast-food restaurants, you pay at the counter when you place your order.

Discuss

Ask students to discuss the advantages and disadvantages of eating at a buffet. *(People who have hearty appetites may find buffets to be a good value. However, unlimited quantities of food encourage some people to overeat.)*

VISIT FLORIDA

24-9 Family restaurants offer foods and an atmosphere that appeal to people of all ages.

Family Restaurants

Family restaurants offer casual, comfortable dining. These restaurants appeal to people dining out with children. Prices are reasonable, so meals can fit into a family food budget. Family restaurants offer a variety of popular menu items. This allows each person to order a different favorite food. See **24-9**.

Formal Restaurants

Formal restaurants offer an elegant dining atmosphere. Customers dine on fine foods and receive excellent service. In keeping with the atmosphere, guests in formal restaurants should dress formally.

Skilled chefs usually prepare the foods served at formal restaurants. They use only the freshest ingredients. Menus may list daily specials created by the chef.

The high-quality food and service at formal restaurants often cause them to be rather expensive. Some people also tend to tip a bit more in these restaurants than they would elsewhere. Be prepared for these expenses before you go to a formal restaurant.

Specialty Restaurants

Specialty restaurants focus on a specific type of food. Pizza parlors, steak houses, and ethnic restaurants are all specialty restaurants.

Specialty restaurants come in all price ranges. Some fast-food, family, and formal restaurants are also specialty restaurants.

Discuss

Ask students what would be appropriate dress in a family restaurant and a formal restaurant. *(family restaurant— anything as long as it is neat, clean, and unrevealing, formal—men wear jackets and ties; women wear dresses)*

CAREER SUCCESS

Using Listening Skills

Rashid is a formal waiter at Emerald Palms Restaurant. This elegant restaurant is known for its wonderful Caribbean cuisine and impeccable service. Each day, the chef plans a unique menu of exotically named dishes prepared with the freshest ingredients available. Like other waiters at Emerald Palms, Rashid is not permitted to write down patrons' food orders. If he gets an order wrong, however, he may be suspended from his job.

To be a successful employee, Rashid needs basic listening skills. Put yourself in Rashid's place and answer the following questions about your need for and use of these skills:

A. How will you use your listening skills as a formal waiter?

B. How might customers of the restaurant be affected if you do not have adequate listening skills?

C. How might other people who work at the restaurant be affected if you do not have adequate listening skills?

D. What is another skill you would need in this job? Briefly explain why this skill would be important.

CHAPTER 24 REVIEW

Summary

Planning a gathering begins with choosing a theme. Then you need to make up a guest list and extend invitations. You need to choose a menu and determine how you will serve it. As a host, you have the responsibility of making your guests feel comfortable. In return, your guests have the responsibility of showing respect and using their best manners.

Almost everyone enjoys picnics and barbecues when the weather is nice. No matter what type of outdoor entertaining you do, you need to transport and serve food carefully to keep it safe. You also need to be sure the outdoor area is clean when your party leaves.

Dining out can be an everyday experience or a special treat. Knowing how to make reservations, order, and tip in a restaurant will help you feel more comfortable when dining out. Your choice of restaurants includes fast-food, cafeteria, buffet, family, formal, and specialty establishments. You should be able to find a menu and a price range to suit any taste.

Review What You Have Read

Write your answers on a separate sheet of paper, using complete sentences when appropriate.

1. What information should be included on all invitations?
2. List four factors that should be considered when planning a party menu.
3. What are two functions garnishes serve when added to foods?
4. What type of meal service is used most often in homes in the United States?
5. Give three responsibilities of a host.
6. List five examples of table manners.
7. List four important safety precautions you should follow when cooking outdoors.
8. True or false. Picnic foods should sit out so picnickers can enjoy them all afternoon.
9. On what type of restaurant menu are food items priced individually?
10. What would be an appropriate tip for average service on a restaurant bill totaling $13.35?
11. What terms might be used on a menu to describe foods prepared in the following ways?
    A. Garnished with almonds.
    B. Sautéed with mushrooms, tomatoes, and olives.
    C. Served with ice cream.
    D. Prepared with spinach.

(continued)

Answer Key for *Review What You Have Read* **questions**

1. The date, time, and place of the party should be included on all invitations.
2. (List four:) guests' food preferences, guests' special dietary needs, budget, cooking skills, time schedule, equipment
3. Garnishes can add color and give guests a hint of what is in foods.
4. American or family style meal service is used most often in homes in the United States.
5. (Give three. Student response.)
6. (List five. Student response.)
7. (List four:) place grill in the open, wear tight-fitting clothes, tie hair back away from the face, never use gasoline or kerosene to start the fire, never pour more lighter fluid on coals after they have been lighted, keep all flammable materials away from the fire, keep water handy for flare-ups
8. false

9. Food items are priced individually on an a la carte restaurant menu.

10. An appropriate tip for average service on a restaurant bill totaling $13.35 would be $2.00.

11.
A. almondine
B. marengo
C. a la mode
D. Florentine

12. B

12. What type of restaurant offers a variety of individually priced food items along a serving line?
A. Buffet.
B. Cafeteria.
C. Family restaurant.
D. Specialty restaurant.

Link to Academic Skills

13. **Social studies.** Choose a culture other than your own. Explore the types of events for which people in this culture entertain coworkers, friends, and family members. Do they have theme parties? What types of foods do they serve? Share your findings in class.

14. **English language arts.** Create a public service announcement (PSA) to raise awareness about using good table manners. You can focus on a single guideline or on the use of manners in general. Write a slogan and design a poster to summarize your message. Present your poster to the class.

15. **English language arts.** Investigate foodborne illnesses that can result from improperly handling food. Write a two-page report about how to safely transport and serve picnic and barbecue food in order to avoid illness.

16. **History.** Research the evolution of fast-food restaurants. Find out when and where fast-food restaurants started operating. Also note who has been given credit for developments in the fast-food industry.

Build Critical Thinking Skills

17. **Synthesis.** Working in a small group, brainstorm to plan a social gathering. Begin by choosing a theme. Then create an invitation and write a menu.

18. **Analysis.** Analyze menus from several restaurants ranging from casual to formal. Identify each menu as table d'hôte or a la carte. Find terms from Table 24-7 used in the menus.

Apply Technology

19. Use a computer and card-making software to create party invitations. Use the computer's printer to print addresses on the envelopes or make address labels in an attractive font before sending the invitations.

20. Use a video camera and editing software to make a training video for foodservice workers. The video should demonstrate how to serve meals using one of the styles of meal service discussed in the chapter.

A Measure of Math

21. Vegetable trays are popular party foods. Compare the cost of purchasing a vegetable tray from the deli department of a supermarket with the cost of assembling a vegetable tray at home.

22. Calculate a 15 percent tip for restaurant bills of $15.45 and $22.46. Calculate a 20 percent tip for restaurant bills of $26.76 and $32.04.

Teamwork in Action

23. Research shows that parents tend to make lower-calorie food choices for their children when they have calorie information for menu items. Investigate calorie information for children's menu items at local fast-food restaurants. Compile this information into an organized food guide. Copy and laminate the food guide and distribute it to parents. Encourage parents to keep copies of the guide in their cars and refer to them when making trips through fast-food drive-thrus.

Companion Website
www.g-wlearning.com

At the website, review key terms for this chapter with crossword puzzles, matching exercises, and e-flash cards. Apply facts from the chapter to complete the activities.

CHAPTER 25
Preserving Foods

Main Menu

- Home canning, freezing, and drying use controlled temperature and moisture conditions to preserve foods.
- Food manufacturers process foods using hi-tech methods that follow the same principles used to preserve foods at home.

Learning Prep

Suggest a definition for each of the *Terms to Know*. Then look up the terms in the glossary to check your accuracy

Objectives

After studying this chapter, you will be able to

- **generalize** about factors that cause food spoilage.
- **describe** techniques for home canning and making jellied products.
- **explain** procedures for freezing and drying foods.
- **identify** methods of commercial food preservation..

Terms to Know

mold
yeast
enzyme
canning
raw pack
hot pack
headspace
processing time
botulism
pectin

quick-freezing
freezer burn
ascorbic acid
sulfuring
freeze-drying
aseptic packaging
retort packaging
irradiation
shelf life

Even primitive people realized food was perishable (subject to spoilage). They understood they needed some form of preservation to keep food from decaying. They learned to preserve food when it was bountiful for times of scarcity.

Today's consumers can buy foods in all seasons, but many people still like to preserve food. This is especially true of people who have fruit and vegetable gardens. Three popular methods of food preservation are canning, freezing, and drying.

FYI
Microorganisms multiply rapidly on damaged or diseased areas of food.

Food Spoilage

Bacteria, mold, and yeast are all microorganisms related to food preservation. Bacteria can cause foodborne illnesses. Bacteria can also cause chemical reactions in food, some of which lead to spoilage. **Mold** is a growth produced on damp or decaying organic matter or on living organisms. **Yeast** is a microscopic fungus that can cause fermentation in preserved foods, resulting in spoilage.

These microorganisms, along with enzymes, have both good and bad effects on food. (**Enzymes** are complex proteins produced by living cells that cause specific chemical reactions.) Some bacteria are used to make buttermilk and sauerkraut. Certain molds are used in curing some cheeses such as Roquefort and Camembert. Yeast makes breads rise. Enzymes ripen foods and tenderize meats. See **25-1**.

The bad effect of microorganisms is food spoilage. Enzymes can cause foods to deteriorate. They can soften the texture, change the color, and impair the flavor of foods. To preserve food, the bacteria, mold, yeast, and enzymes must be inactivated or destroyed.

Cherry Marketing Institute
25-1 Yogurt gets its thick, creamy texture from the desirable effects of a certain type of bacteria.

Canning Foods

Canning is a food preservation process that involves sealing food in airtight containers. The food is heated and held at a high temperature for a period long enough to kill harmful microorganisms.

People can foods at home for many reasons. Many home canners enjoy preserving their own special recipes of items like barbecue or spaghetti sauces. Some people can to avoid wasting an overabundance of seasonal fruits and vegetables. Others want to avoid the preservatives added to commercially canned foods.

Still another reason for home canning is the low cost. Home canning can reduce food costs if it is done frequently. The equipment is expensive, so it should be purchased only if it will be used for several years. People who can foods may find they can save more money if they grow the food themselves.

Food Science

Controlling Microorganisms
Microorganisms need food, moisture, and favorable temperatures to grow. By removing one of these conditions, the spoiling action of microorganisms can be stopped and the goods can be preserved. Freezing temperatures prevent microorganisms from growing and retard the action of enzymes. High temperatures, such as those used in canning, destroy both microorganisms and enzymes. Drying preserves food by removing moisture needed for the growth of microorganisms. To control enzyme activity, fruits and vegetables are treated before drying.

Canning procedures must be followed carefully to ensure proper preservation of food. Step-by-step directions on home canning can be obtained from manufacturers of canning products and county extension agents.

Canning Jars and Closures

Most foods that are canned at home are put into *glass* jars. Use only jars especially made for home canning. Do not use jars from commercially canned foods, such as peanut butter or mayonnaise. These will not seal tightly.

The most popular canning jar closures are two-piece vacuum caps. The pieces are a metal screw band and a flat metal lid that has a sealing compound on one side. When using this type of closure, wipe the rim of the filled jar. Put the flat lid on the jar with the sealing compound next to the glass. Then screw the band down tightly over the lid.

A flat metal lid with sealing compound should be used only once. However, canning jars and screw bands can be reused as long as they are in good condition. Be sure all jars are perfect. Discard jars that have cracks or chips, as these defects prevent airtight seals. Discard metal bands that are dented or rusty.

Preparing Jars and Closures

Wash all canning jars in hot, soapy water and rinse them well before using them. Then heat the jars to help keep them from breaking. When canning foods that are processed less than 10 minutes, such as jellies, the jars need to be sterilized. Leave the jars in the hot environment until they needed. Then remove and fill them one at a time.

Like the jars, the lids and screw bands need to be washed before using them. After washing in hot, soapy water, dry the screw bands and set them aside. Allow the flat metal lids to heat in very hot, but not boiling, water for at least 10 minutes. Remove them one at a time, as needed.

Filling Canning Jars

Jars can be filled by either the raw pack or hot pack method. For **raw pack**, pack raw fruits or vegetables into containers. Cover with boiling water, juice, or syrup. For **hot pack**, heat food in water, steam, syrup, or juices. Pack loosely in jars and cover with cooking liquid or boiling water.

When filling the jars, leave some headspace. **Headspace** is space between the food and the closure of a food storage container. Follow the canning recipe to determine the correct amount of headspace. Leaving too much or too little headspace may prevent jars from sealing properly. See **25-2**.

Liquid in the canning jars should fill all spaces between food and cover all the food. Food that is not covered tends to darken. Remove air bubbles trapped in the food with a nonmetal spatula to prevent food from darkening.

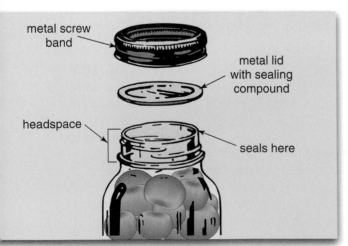

25-2 The amount of headspace left between food and the two-piece vacuum cap sealing a canning jar depends on the food being canned.

Pressure Canning

The high temperatures used in canning destroy microorganisms and enzymes. The temperatures obtained vary with the canning method. Since some microorganisms are more heat-resistant than others, the canning method used depends on the type of food being canned.

Use *pressure canning* for green beans and other low-acid vegetables. Use it for meats, poultry, and fish, too. These foods need a higher temperature than that of boiling water to destroy food-spoiling microorganisms and enzymes.

This type of canning is done in a *pressure canner*. This type of canner can reach 240°F to 250°F (115°C to 120°C) by building up steam under pressure. Pack low-acid foods into sterilized canning jars. Cover the food with liquid, and cap the jars. Put water in the bottom of the canner, and place the filled jars in the canner on a rack. Lock down the lid of the pressure canner to make the canner steam-tight. After sealing the canner, place it on the range.

A vent in the lid, called a *petcock*, allows air to be exhausted and steam to be released as needed. When the petcock is closed, the temperature and pressure inside the canner rise. A *pressure gauge* measures steam pressure inside the canner. A *safety valve* in the lid prevents explosions. It works only if pressure or temperature inside the canner becomes dangerously high.

Processing Time

When the proper pressure has been reached inside the canner, processing time begins. **Processing time** is the amount of time canned goods remain under heat (or under heat and pressure) in a canner. Processing time varies according to the food being processed.

When processing time is complete, remove the canner from the heat and allow pressure to return to zero. Lift the cover of the canner away from the body to prevent steam burns. Then remove the jars from the canner and allow them to cool.

Boiling Water Canning

Use boiling water canning for high-acid foods, such as acidified tomatoes, fruits, and pickled vegetables. This method of canning is done in a *boiling water canner*. The temperature of boiling water is enough to destroy the microorganisms and enzymes that cause food spoilage in these foods.

For this method of canning, pack food into clean canning jars, cover it with liquid, and cap the jars. For raw-pack jars, heat water in the canner until it is hot. For hot-pack jars, heat the water to boiling. Set the filled jars on the rack in the canner so water surrounds each one. Add boiling water to bring the water level above the tops of the jars. Cover the canner and allow the water to come to a rolling boil.

When the water comes to a rolling boil, the processing time begins. As with pressure canning, processing time varies with the type of food being canned. The water boils steadily throughout the processing time. When processing time is up, quickly remove the jars from the canner and allow them to cool.

After Canning

When jars are completely cool, carefully remove screw bands. Wash bands and store them in a dry place for future use.

Wipe jars clean with a soapy cloth, rinse them well, and dry them thoroughly. Label each jar, listing the type of food and the date. If more than one lot was canned on the same day, list the lot number, too.

For Example...

Low-acid vegetables other than green beans that should be processed in a pressure canner include okra, carrots, beets, turnips, spinach, asparagus, lima beans, peas, and corn.

Discuss

Ask students why fruits do not need to be processed in a pressure canner like most vegetables. *(Fruits have a higher acid content than vegetables. This high acid level does not support the growth of bacteria, which require the high temperatures of pressure canning to be destroyed.)*

Discuss

Ask students why it is important to label canning jars with the date and lot number. *(A date can identify foods that have been stored too long. A lot number can identify other jars of affected food in a batch found to be contaminated.)*

Online Resource

Have students visit the Ball website. Ask each student to find a detail about home canning that is not mentioned in the text. Ask students to share their findings in class as you discuss the importance of reviewing current recommendations before preserving foods at home.

Learn About...

Testing Canning Seals

Test the seals the day after canning. To do this, press the center of each lid. Make sure it is concave and does not flex up and down. Then remove the screw band and make sure the lid cannot be lifted off with the fingertips. If the jars pass this inspection, they have formed a good vacuum seal.

Photo courtesy of National Presto Industries, Inc.

Check the lids on canning jars to be sure they have formed a good seal before storing food for future use.

Properly canned foods stored in a cool, dry, dark place will last as long as a year. A cool temperature helps foods maintain appearance, flavor, and nutrients. Do not allow canned foods to freeze, as this will cause a loss of texture and appeal. Dampness may corrode metal lids and cause leakage. This makes the foods spoil. Heat and light may cause food to lose some of its eating quality after only a few weeks.

Checking for Spoilage

Before eating home-canned foods, take certain safety precautions. When the jars are opened, look for bulging lids, leaks, spurting liquid, off odors, mold, gas bubbles, and unusually soft food. These are signs of broken seals and spoilage. If any of these signs are present, do not taste the food. Dispose of it so neither humans nor animals will eat it. Use a food waste disposer, or burn it.

Botulism is a foodborne illness caused by eating foods containing the spore-forming bacteria *Clostridium botulinum*. These bacteria can occur in home-canned foods that were improperly processed. Botulism is the most dangerous type of foodborne illness. Even a taste of food containing the toxin produced by these bacteria can be fatal. This is why following only the latest, researched recommendations for canning methods and processing times is so important. Using proper canning methods is especially important for low-acid foods.

The texture of foods spoiled by botulism may be very soft and mushy. The foods may smell like rancid cheese. However, some spoiled foods look and smell normal. If there is any question about the safety of a home-canned food, do not take any chances. Throw it out. If the food looks spoiled, foams, or has an off odor during heating, *destroy it!*

Making Jellied Products

Canning principles are used in making jellied products. Jellied products include jelly, jam, marmalade, preserves, and conserves. *Jelly* is a firm, clear product made from fruit juice. *Jam* is a less firm product made from crushed fruit that is cooked to a fairly even consistency. *Marmalade* is a tender jelly containing small pieces of fruit and fruit rind. It is often made from citrus fruit and it may contain a mixture of fruits. *Preserves* are slightly jellied products that contain whole fruits or large pieces of fruit in thick syrup. *Conserves* are jams made from a mixture of fruits, usually including citrus fruits and sometimes raisins and nuts. *Fruit butters* are not jellied products. They are spreads made from cooked, pureed fruit.

Ingredients

Four basic ingredients are needed to make jellied products. The first of these is fruit. Fruit gives jellied products their flavors and colors. Almost any flavorful fruit can be used. Fruit also contributes some or all of two other basic ingredients—pectin and acid.

Pectin is a carbohydrate found in all fruits. It makes fruit juices jell. Some fruits have more pectin than others. If the fruit being used is low in pectin, pectin can be purchased in powdered or liquid form. Either kind can be used with any fruit. However, they are not interchangeable. Follow the recipe. Use the form and amount of pectin it suggests.

Acid is the third basic ingredient in jellied products. It works with pectin to make the products jell. It also adds flavor. All fruits contain varying amounts of acids. Lemon juice or citric acid can be added to fruits that are low in acid.

Sugar is the fourth basic ingredient. It helps jellied products become firm. It also adds flavor and helps preserve the products. Leaving some of the sugar out of a recipe will cause the jellied product to be runny. However, recipes are available for making jellied products with artificial sweeteners for people who want to avoid sugar.

Processing Jellied Products

Jellied products must be processed by the boiling water method. After combining and boiling the ingredients, pour the mixtures into hot, sterilized canning jars. Then seal and process the jars. After cooling, label the products and store them in a dark, dry, cool place.

Uncooked jam is a jellied product that is easy to make and does not require boiling water processing. It can be prepared by adding sugar and commercial pectin to crushed, fully-ripe fruit. Uncooked jams keep up to three weeks in the refrigerator or up to a year in the freezer. However, they spoil quickly at room temperature. See **25-3**.

Freezing Foods

One of the best ways to preserve the fresh flavor of food is to freeze it. Frozen foods are popular because they offer consumers many advantages. Frozen foods have the appearance, taste, and nutritive value of fresh foods. They are available at any time of year, and they are easy to prepare. Frozen foods can also help save money. They can be purchased when prices are low and stored for later use.

Many frozen foods that are bought at the grocery store are preserved by **quick-freezing**. Quick-frozen foods are subjected to temperatures between -25°F and -40°F (-32°C and -40°C) for a short time. These extremely low temperatures produce very small ice crystals in foods. When foods are frozen more slowly, larger ice crystals may form. These large crystals damage the cell structure of foods and change their textures. After quick-freezing, foods are maintained at a normal freezing temperature of 0°F (-18°C).

Driscoll's

25-3 Homemade strawberry jam is a special treat spread on bread or used as an ice cream topping.

Foods frozen at home have the same advantages as commercially frozen foods. Using the right equipment and following recommended procedures will ensure the highest quality in home-frozen foods.

Equipment

A properly operating freezer and suitable containers are needed to freeze foods at home. Containers used in freezing must be moisture- and vapor-resistant. This protects foods from exposure to air and loss of moisture during frozen storage. Foods that have not been wrapped securely may develop off flavors and lose nutrients, texture, and color. Some foods may develop **freezer burn**, or dry, tough areas. Freezer burn occurs where dry air from the freezer has come in contact with food surfaces, causing dehydration.

Properly sealed aluminum, glass, plastic-coated paper, and plastic containers are all suitable for freezer storage. Freezer bags, aluminum foil, and plastic-coated or transparent freezer wraps can also be used. These flat packaging materials work especially well when freezing bulky items, such as roasts and cakes.

Freezing Fruits and Vegetables

When selecting fresh produce for freezing, choose ripe, top-quality fruits and young, tender vegetables. Work with small batches. Carefully sort and wash each piece but do not allow them to soak. Pit, trim, and slice fruits and vegetables as desired.

Preparing Fruits and Vegetables for Freezing

Some fruits need treatment with ascorbic acid to prevent darkening. **Ascorbic acid** is a food additive that prevents color and flavor loss. It also adds nutritive value. (Ascorbic acid is another name for vitamin C.) Ascorbic acid is available in crystalline form or in a mixture with sugar and perhaps citric acid. Follow manufacturer's instructions for use.

Most vegetables must be blanched in boiling water or steam before freezing. This inactivates the enzymes. When blanching is complete, cool vegetables quickly and drain well. Quick cooling prevents vitamin loss and spoilage.

Packing Fruits and Vegetables for Freezing

Pack most vegetables and some fruits using the *dry pack* method. Carefully pour prepared produce into freezer containers. Gently tap containers to pack food closely without crushing. Do not add liquid.

Frozen sweetened fruits, usually have a better texture than unsweetened fruits. Therefore, many people use the sugar pack or syrup pack method when freezing fruits. For the *sugar pack* method, place prepared fruit in a shallow pan. Add sugar. Turn pieces of fruit gently until the sugar dissolves and forms a syrup. Carefully pack fruit into freezer containers. Gently tap each container to exclude air. For the *syrup pack* method, prepare syrup and chill. Place prepared fruit directly into container. Pour chilled syrup over fruit.

For all packing methods, leave 1 inch (2.5 cm) of headspace to allow for expansion. Wipe the top of each container with a clean, damp cloth. Seal tightly and label with the name of the food and the date.

Freeze all foods at 0°F (-18°C) or lower immediately after packing. When food freezes too slowly, a loss in quality or food spoilage may occur. Freeze food in batches, giving each batch a chance to freeze before adding the next batch. This will keep freezer temperature constant. Leave a little space between items in the freezer to allow room for cold air to circulate. Follow the freezer manufacturer's instructions concerning quantity and placement of foods. See **25-4**.

Freezing Meat, Poultry, and Fish

Meats and poultry require no special preparation before freezing. Often, however, large meat cuts are trimmed and packaged in serving-sized pieces. Choose only top quality meat cuts for freezing. Poultry may be frozen whole or in pieces.

Meat and poultry can be frozen in their original wrappers for up to two weeks. For extended freezer storage, rewrap these foods in moistureproof and vaporproof paper. Exclude as much air as possible.

Rubbermaid

25-4 Be sure to allow room for air to circulate around food items in a freezer.

Purchased fish require washing and drying before freezing. Game fish must be scaled and eviscerated (remove entrails) before freezing. Their heads and fins should also be removed.

Fish can be wrapped in moistureproof and vaporproof paper for short-term freezing. For better keeping quality and longer storage, an ice glaze is recommended. Place cleaned fish in the freezer and freeze until firm. Then dip fish in very cold water and return to the freezer so a layer of ice forms on the fish. Repeat the dipping and freezing process until the fish has a coating of ice that is about ¼ inch thick. Place glazed fish in freezer bags or wrap it in moistureproof and vaporproof paper.

Freeze meat, poultry, and fish as soon as possible after purchasing them. Be sure to label with product name, weight, and date. Turn the freezer control to its lowest possible setting for the first 24 to 48 hours. Then maintain the temperature at 0°F (-18°C) as for fruits and vegetables.

Freezing Prepared Foods

Baked pastry, cookies, breads, and cakes all freeze well. Wrap these items carefully in moistureproof and vaporproof wrapping.

Casseroles and stews can be frozen in their baking dishes. To save space, line the baking dish with foil. Fill the dish with food, wrap well, and freeze. When frozen, remove the food from the dish. Wrap it well, label it, and return it to the freezer. The casserole dish can then be used for other foods.

Be sure to label all prepared foods with the name of the product and the date. Freeze promptly and use within the recommended time.

Some foods do not freeze well. These include salad greens, custards, gelatin products, meringues, sour cream, and hard-cooked egg whites. Sandwiches containing salad dressing or mayonnaise do not freeze well, either.

Some foods can be stored longer than others. Beef, cheese, whole turkeys, and vegetables, for example, can be stored for a year. Cookies and soups can be stored for six months and unbaked pies for three months.

Discuss

Ask students how freezing temperatures affect bacteria. *(Freezing temperatures prevent bacteria from growing.)*

FYI

Food should be able to freeze within 24 hours after being placed in a freezer. A good guideline is to store no more than three pounds of food per cubic foot of freezer capacity at one time.

FYI

Salad greens lose their crispness when frozen. Custards become watery and lumpy, meringues and egg whites become tough, and mayonnaise separates.

FYI

During a power failure, you can use dry ice to keep food frozen for two to four days, depending on how full the freezer is. Do not place dry ice directly on frozen food packages, and do not touch it with bare hands.

Learn About...

Thawing Frozen Foods

Organisms that cause foodborne illnesses multiply quickly at room temperature. Therefore never thaw foods, especially meat, poultry, and fish, at room temperature. Allow them to thaw overnight in a refrigerator. Use the defrost setting on a microwave oven to thaw foods quickly right before cooking. Foods can also be allowed to thaw during the cooking process.

Some frozen foods, such as vegetables, should be cooked without thawing. Thaw prepared and baked products in their original wrappers to prevent dehydration. Thaw fruits in their original covered containers to prevent *enzymatic browning* (discoloration caused by exposure to air). Fruits have the best flavor if served with a few ice crystals remaining.

Meats, poultry, and fish can be cooked either frozen or thawed. Cooking frozen food, however, takes longer than cooking fresh or thawed foods. Consider the extra cooking time when planning meals.

If meat is partially thawed but still firm, it can be refrozen. The meat will have a loss in quality, but it will still be safe to eat. Refreeze it and use it as soon as possible. If the meat is fully thawed but still very cold, refrigerate it and use it immediately. Do not refreeze it.

Cherry Marketing Institute

Serving frozen fruit before it is completely thawed keeps it from having a mushy texture.

Drying Foods

Food drying is one of the oldest and simplest methods of food preservation. Microorganisms that cause food spoilage need moisture to grow. Drying removes moisture, thus stopping the growth of microorganisms. When drying foods, speed is important. Using a temperature that will dry food without cooking it is important, too.

The many advantages of dried foods make them especially popular with campers, cyclists, and backpackers. Dried foods are lightweight. They take up less space than fresh foods, and they taste good.

Campers are not the only ones who use dried foods. Many people add dried vegetables to soups. A variety of dried mixes are popular convenience products. People enjoy jerky and dried meat sticks as snacks. Dried fruits can be added to salads, desserts, and a variety of other foods.

Fruit leathers are pliable sheets of dried fruit puree. They can be made from almost any fruit. Fruit leathers are nutritious and lightweight for packing in school lunches or taking on camping trips.

Preparing Fruits and Vegetables for Drying

Vegetables must be dried completely to prevent spoilage. Fruits, because of their high sugar content, may retain more moisture than vegetables after drying.

Choose fruits at optimum maturity. Wash, sort, and discard bruised, overripe fruit. Peel and core fruits, if necessary. Berries and other smaller fruits can be dried whole.

Larger fruits will dry more evenly and quickly if cut into halves, quarters, or ¼-inch (6 mm) slices.

A salt solution can be used to keep fruit from darkening. **Sulfuring** can also be used as an antidarkening treatment for some fruits. Prepare a sulfuring solution using sodium metabisulfite purchased from a drugstore. Soak fruits for 15 minutes. Drain. Spread fruit to dry.

Select young, tender vegetables in prime condition. Wash vegetables thoroughly and drain. Trim and cut them into small pieces. Smaller pieces dry more quickly and evenly. Blanch prepared vegetables using steam or boiling water. Drain well and dry with a towel.

Procedure for Drying

Two popular methods of drying fruits and vegetables at home are sun drying and oven drying. Sun drying is less costly, but it relies on the weather.

Drying in the oven does not depend on the weather, so it can be done at any time. Oven drying can be done in a food dehydrator following manufacturer's instructions. Oven drying can also be done in a conventional oven.

To dry food in a conventional oven, spread food evenly in a single layer on trays. Make trays of wire screening tacked to a wooden frame. Preheat oven to 150°F (64°C) or as low as the oven thermostat will allow. Place lower oven rack about 3 inches (7.5 cm) from oven bottom. Stack trays evenly.

Rotate trays periodically because food on trays near the bottom of the oven will dry more quickly. Occasional stirring ensures even drying.

Drying time depends on the food being dried. When dry, vegetables will feel hard and brittle. Fruits will feel leathery but pliable. Cool thoroughly.

Online Resource

Have pairs of students visit the National Center for Home Food Preservation website. Have each pair give a poster presentation to the class on one of the food drying topics found on the website.

Reflect

Ask students what types of dried foods they have eaten either dried or rehydrated.

Learn About...

Storing and Using Dried Foods

Package dried foods in insectproof and moistureproof containers. Plastic containers, glass jars, and waxed cartons are all suitable. Seal, label, and store them in a cool, dark place.

Dried fruits may be eaten in their dry state, or they can be rehydrated. Most dried vegetables are rehydrated. To rehydrate, soak foods for an hour or two. Simmer in the same liquid used for soaking until foods are tender. Do not overcook.

Cherry Marketing Institute
Dried fruits add a burst of flavor and a chewy texture variation to baked goods.

Commercial Food Preservation

Of course, canning, freezing, and drying are not just home preservation methods. They are common commercial food preservation methods as well. Technical advances in food processing have improved the quality of preserved foods in recent years. Commercially preserved foods keep more nutrients than foods preserved at home. Commercial processing is done quickly and very soon after foods are harvested. This allows preserved foods to have nutritional values that are close to fresh foods.

The principles used in commercial food preservation are the same as those used at home. Moisture and temperature conditions are controlled to stop the spoiling action of microorganisms and enzymes.

Freeze-Drying

Food manufacturers preserve foods in a number of ways besides canning, freezing, and drying. One of these ways is freeze-drying. **Freeze-drying** involves the removal of water vapor from frozen foods. This process produces high-quality food products. It also saves transportation and refrigeration costs. Freeze-drying is used to preserve a variety of foods, including instant coffee.

Aseptic Packaging

With **aseptic packaging**, a food and its packaging material are sterilized separately. Then the food is packed in the container in a sterile chamber. Aseptic packaging allows some perishable foods to be stored without refrigeration. Foil-lined paper boxes used for milk products and juices are examples of aseptic packaging.

Retort Packaging

Retort packaging is similar to aseptic packaging. In **retort packaging**, food is sealed in a foil pouch. Then it is sterilized in a steam-pressure vessel known as a retort. This type of packaging is often used for shelf-stable entrees.

The advantages of aseptic and retort packaging include improved flavor and nutrition. The packages use minimal storage space and require no refrigeration. The foods inside these packages can be easily prepared in minutes.

Irradiation

Irradiation exposes food to controlled doses of gamma rays, electron beams, or X rays. Irradiation can limit sprouting in potatoes. It can slow the ripening of fruits and vegetables and control insects and microorganisms in seasonings and wheat. It can also control disease-causing trichinae in pork and salmonella in chicken. The FDA has approved all of these uses of irradiation. Even so, irradiation has not caught on as a trend in the food industry. Currently, irradiation in the United States is mainly being used to preserve spices. Use of irradiation may increase in the future if it becomes more economical for food processors. It must also gain a wider degree of acceptance among consumers.

Irradiated food products are labeled with the statement "treated with radiation" or "treated by irradiation." A special logo also appears on the label of irradiated foods.

Preservation techniques increase a food's **shelf life**. This is the amount of time a food can be stored and remain wholesome. However, preserved foods cannot be kept forever. Table **25-5** shows how long various foods can be stored in a refrigerator, freezer, or pantry.

Shelf Life of Foods	
Foods Stored in a Refrigerator	
beef, pork, lamb	2 to 4 days
poultry, fish	1 to 2 days
bacon, ham	5 to 7 days
milk	1 week
butter	2 weeks
natural, process cheeses	4 to 8 weeks
fruits and vegetables	varies according to type
Foods Stored in a Freezer	
Beef	6 to 12 months
Pork	3 to 6 months
lamb	6 to 9 months
ground beef, pork, lamb	3 months
ham, hot dogs	2 months
poultry	6 to 8 months
fish	3 to 4 months
fruits and vegetables	9 to 12 months
bread	2 to 3 months
ice cream	2 months
Foods Stored at Room Temperature	
dried fruits and vegetables	1 year
staple items (cereal, flour, sugar)	1 year
home-canned foods	1 year
onions and potatoes	4 weeks
commercially packaged foods in unopened cans and jars	1 year
aseptically packaged products (milk products, juices, soups)	6 months
freeze-dried foods	1 year
shelf-stable entrees	6 months

25-5 Even preserved foods have a limited storage life.

EXPLORING CAREERS

Quality Control Microbiologist

Quality control (QC) microbiologists work for food manufacturers. Their job is to help assure products meet company standards. They look for microorganisms that can affect the safety and quality of food. These scientists check samples of water and other ingredients that come into a food plant before they are used in food products. They also check samples of finished products before the products are released to the market. If microbiologists detect contamination, they run tests to find its source. They keep detailed records of when and how samples are collected and all test results. They may have to maintain an inventory of lab supplies. They may also train and supervise lab technicians to assist them.

QC microbiologists must be able to use math skills as they analyze data. They need to be able to handle stress, adapt to change, and quickly deal with problems. These scientists must pay careful attention to details when gathering and testing samples to be sure test results are correct. They will use writing skills to prepare reports of their findings. QC microbiologists must know how to do routine lab procedures and use technical equipment. They must know and follow safety and sanitation standards. Although they need to be able to work independently, they also need to cooperate with other lab workers.

QC microbiologists need at least a four-year bachelor's degree. Many of these scientists have advanced degrees. Employers often look for workers who have two or more years of experience working in a lab. Knowledge of food manufacturing processes is also helpful.

Agricultural Research Service, USDA

This food microbiologist is studying how to prevent microorganisms from contaminating fish.

CAREER SUCCESS

Using Self-Management Skills

Henry is a dehydrator tender for the Purist's Produce company. Purist's Produce packages a variety of dried fruits. Henry spends his entire shift spreading fresh fruit onto trays for drying and emptying dried fruit into totes for packaging. The drying tunnel requires only one person to tend it, so Henry does his routine work alone.

To be a successful employee, Henry needs skills in self-management. In a small group, answer the following questions about Henry's need for and use of these skills:

A. What characteristics of Henry's job make having good self-management skills so important?

B. How will having self-management skills help Henry as a dehydrator tender?

C. How might the quantity and quality of Purist's Produce dried fruit products be affected if Henry lacks self-management skills?

D. What is another skill Henry would need in this job? Briefly explain why this skill would be important.

CHAPTER 25 REVIEW

Summary

Enzymes and microorganisms cause food spoilage. Food, moisture, and favorable temperatures need to be present for spoilage to occur. Removing any one of these items will help preserve food.

Canning uses high temperatures to preserve foods. Home-canned foods are stored in jars with two-piece vacuum caps used as closures. Low-acid foods need to be processed in a pressure canner. High-acid foods can be processed in a boiling water bath. After canning, the lids on canning jars need to be checked to be sure they have formed good seals. Label canned foods clearly and store them in a cool, dry, dark place. Always check for signs of spoilage before using home-canned foods.

Jellied products are popular home-canned foods. The four basic ingredients in jellied products are fruit, pectin, acid, and sugar. Besides jelly, marmalade, jams, preserves, conserves, and fruit butters can be made.

Freezing uses low temperatures to preserve foods. A freezer and food storage containers are all that is needed to keep foods on hand for months. Some fruits need an antidarkening treatment before freezing. Most vegetables need blanching before freezing. Some frozen foods must be thawed before preparing them. Others can be cooked in their frozen state.

Drying removes moisture to preserve foods. Vegetables need to be blanched and some fruits need to be sulfured before drying. Foods can be dried in the sun or in a conventional oven. Store dried foods in tightly sealed containers to prevent moisture from affecting them.

Commercial food preservation follows the same principles as home preservation. Freeze-drying, aseptic packaging, retort packaging, and irradiation are all commercial preservation techniques.

Review What You Have Read

Write your answers on a separate sheet of paper, using complete sentences when appropriate.

1. True or false. Bacteria, mold, and yeast can have good effects on food.
2. What are three reasons people can foods at home?
3. Space between the food and the closure of a food-storage container is called _____.
4. What are two foods that must be processed by pressure canning? Explain why.
5. List three factors that can cause home-canned foods to lose eating quality during storage.
6. What are five signs of spoilage in home-canned foods?
7. A tender jelly containing small pieces of fruit and fruit rind is _____.

Answer Key for *Review What You Have Read* questions

1. true
2. (List three:) enjoy eating home-canned foods, can special recipes, avoid wasting an overabundance of seasonal fruits and vegetables, avoid preservatives, save money
3. headspace
4. (List two:) green beans, other low-acid vegetables, meats, poultry, fish These foods need a higher temperature than that of boiling water to destroy food-spoiling microorganisms and enzymes.
5. (List three:) freezing temperatures, dampness, heat, light
6. (List five:) bulging lids; leaking jars; spurting liquid; off odor; mold; gas bubbles; unusually soft food; looks spoiled, foams, or has an off odor during heating
7. marmalade
8. Fruit juice gives jelly flavor and color. Pectin makes fruit juices jell. Acid works with pectin to make fruit juices jell and adds flavor to jelly. Sugar helps jelly become firm, adds flavor, and helps preserve jelly.

(continued)

9. false
10. Quick-freezing produces very small ice crystals. Slow-freezing causes large ice crystals to form that damage the cell structure of food and change the texture.
11. The three packing methods that may be used when freezing fruits are dry pack, sugar pack, and syrup pack.
12. (List five:) lettuce, salad greens, custards, gelatin products, meringues, sour cream, hard-cooked egg white, sandwiches containing salad dressing or mayonnaise
13. Two methods for drying fruits and vegetables at home are sun drying and oven drying.
14. A

8. What is the function of each of the four basic ingredients needed to make jellied products?
9. True or false. Because acid and sugar act as natural preservatives, jellied products do not require further preservation methods.
10. Describe the advantage quick-frozen foods have over foods frozen more slowly.
11. What are the three packing methods that may be used when freezing fruits?
12. List five foods that do not freeze well.
13. What are two methods for drying fruits and vegetables at home?
14. What type of commercial food preservation involves separate sterilization of a food and its packaging material?
    A. Aseptic packaging.
    B. Commercial canning.
    C. Freeze-drying.
    D. Retort packaging.

Link to Academic Skills

15. **Science.** Puree three fruits and three vegetables. Use litmus paper to test the acidity of each puree. Find recommended canning procedures for each of these fruits and vegetables. How does your litmus testing compare with recommendations in terms of whether each of these fruits and vegetables should be treated as high-acid or low-acid foods?
16. **Science.** Research the symptoms and treatment of botulism. Summarize your findings in a written report.
17. **History.** Conduct research to find out what foods were dried by Native Americans and early settlers in the United States. You should also investigate drying procedures that were used by these people. Create a poster illustrating your findings.
18. **English language arts.** Prepare an oral report explaining how the food industry prevents food spoilage by microorganisms and enzymes.

Build Critical Thinking Skills

19. **Analysis.** Make two batches of a jellied product. Add commercial pectin to one batch. Do not add pectin to the other batch. Analyze the effects of added pectin on the flavor, consistency, cooking time, yield, and appearance of the jellied product.
20. **Evaluation.** Make a batch of cookies. Sample and evaluate the cookies, making notes about their quality characteristics. Package and freeze half of the remaining cookies in a loosely rolled paper bag. Package and freeze the other half of the cookies in a tightly sealed plastic container. After one month, thaw, sample, and evaluate the cookies. Which type of container best preserved the flavor, texture, and appearance of fresh cookies?

Apply Technology

21. Choose a product sold in aseptic or retort packaging. Write a paper identifying advantages and disadvantages of this product as compared to a similar canned product.

22. Prepare a poster illustrating the procedure used to irradiate foods.

A Measure of Math

23. Calculate the value of wasted food due to spoilage based on national averages.

24. Figure the costs of growing and canning tomatoes, including equipment. Compare these costs with buying commercially canned tomatoes. Calculate how many years you would need to can tomatoes at home to save money over buying commercially canned tomatoes.

Teamwork in Action

25. Design a brochure about the safe use of home-canned foods. The brochure should describe how to check for spoilage. Also list types of spoilage of which people should be aware. Explain what to do with spoiled food. Finally, discuss how to prepare canned foods that appear to be wholesome. Place the brochures in a public library.

Companion Website

www.g-wlearning.com

At the website, review key terms for this chapter with crossword puzzles, matching exercises, and e-flash cards. Apply facts from the chapter to complete the activities.

Part 4
Food and Careers

Study Starters

1. The word *career* comes from a Medieval Latin word meaning "road for vehicles." Review the definition for *career* given in this text. Discuss in class how the current use of this term relates to its Medieval Latin roots.

2. Make a list of adjectives or phrases you believe describes someone who has achieved success in his or her career. Share your list in class and give an example of someone you feel meets your description. Be prepared to explain why you chose to write each item on your list as well as why you chose your particular career success example.

26 Investigating Careers

27 Career and Job Success

FCCLA: Taking the Lead

Use this section of the text to plan and carry out a project for the *Career Connection* national program. Chapter 26 provides information to help you understand work for the *Plug In* unit. This chapter will also help you link interests, skills, and goals to career clusters for a project in the *Sign On* unit. Chapter 27 discusses habits and behaviors workers need to be productive and promotable. This information could help you develop a project for the *Access Skills* unit. Chapter 27 focuses on managing the interconnected roles in families, careers, and communities for the *Integrate* unit, too. Both chapters include topics that relate to the *Program* unit.

CHAPTER 26
Investigating Careers

Main Menu

- Learning about career clusters and pathways can acquaint you with the many career options available.
- Developing career goals and making a career plan prepares you for future career and entrepreneurship opportunities.

Learning Prep

Read the summary at the end of the chapter before you begin to read the chapter. On a sheet of paper, note the main points outlined in the summary. As you read the chapter, take additional detailed notes for each main point.

Objectives

After studying this chapter, you will be able to

- **summarize** how career clusters and pathways can help you choose a career.
- **explain** how to make a career plan.
- **evaluate** important factors involved in considering careers.
- **demonstrate** how to use sources of career information.
- **investigate** entrepreneurship opportunities.

Terms to Know

career
occupation
career clusters
lifelong learning
transferable skills

aptitude
abilities
networking
entrepreneur

The actions you take now will lay the groundwork for the career you will have in the future. Preparing for your career may seem overwhelming at first, but doing a step at a time will make the process easier. If you have not started to think about your future, now is a good time to begin. What would you like to do for a living? Whether your future will be in a food field or some other, this chapter presents guidelines that are useful for planning your career.

Career Planning

Do not be fooled into thinking the right job will simply "come along." In today's highly competitive workplace, that is most unlikely. People who make no career plans usually find themselves left with jobs no one else wants.

Having a career means you will hold several occupations related by a common skill, purpose, or interest over your lifetime. A **career** is a series of related occupations that show progression in a field of work. The term *job* is commonly used to mean *occupation*. Strictly speaking, a *job* is a task, while an **occupation** is paid employment that involves handling one or more jobs.

Career Clusters and Pathways

Career clusters are 16 groups of occupations or career specialties that are similar or related to one another. See **26-1**. The occupations within a cluster require a set of common knowledge and skills for career success. These are called *essential knowledge and skills*.

Activity
Have each student identify a career and list at least three occupations through which someone might progress in that field of work. Then have students name a job a worker might handle in each occupation listed.

Sixteen Career Clusters

Agriculture, Food & Natural Resources

Architecture & Construction

Arts, A/V Technology & Communications

Business Management & Administration

Education & Training

Finance

Government & Public Administration

Health Science

Hospitality & Tourism

Human Services

Information Technology

Law, Public Safety, Corrections & Security

Manufacturing

Marketing

Science, Technology, Engineering & Mathematics

Transportation, Distribution & Logistics

The Career Clusters icons are being used with permission of the States' Career Clusters Initiative
www.careerclusters.org

26-1 The career clusters can help you determine your career area of interest.

Enrich

Invite a member of FCCLA to speak to your class about the value of his or her involvement in this organization.

Online Resource

Have each student visit the Study Abroad website and search for a program of interest. Ask students to share their findings in class.

If one or two job titles in a career cluster appeal to you, it is likely that others will, too. This is because the jobs grouped together share certain similarities. To help you narrow down your options, each career cluster is further divided into *career pathways*. These subgroups often require more specialized knowledge and skills.

Knowing the relationship between careers in a given pathway is helpful when researching facts about careers. The skills required for related jobs in a career field are similar. Preparing for more than one career in a related field allows more flexibility when you are searching for employment. If you cannot find the exact position you desire, your skills will be needed by other occupations in the same pathway.

Programs of Study

Since occupations in a career pathway require similar knowledge and skills, they also require similar programs of study. A *program of study* is the sequence of instruction used to prepare students for occupations in a given career pathway. The program includes classroom instruction and co-curricular activities such as student organizations. The program also involves other learning experiences including work-site learning.

Customizing a program of study for an individual learner results in a *personal plan of study*. A plan of study will help prepare you for the career direction you choose. You start by taking the appropriate classes and participating in related student organizations. One organization you may want to think about joining is Family, Career and Community Leaders of America (FCCLA). FCCLA prepares young men and women for future roles at home and in the workplace. FCCLA chapters are often organized through family and consumer sciences classes.

Once you have laid this foundation, seek out programs that address your career interest. You may even find that some high school classes can count toward college credit. Your plan of study does not expire with high school. Students should update their plans at least yearly, but more often if plans change.

Global Perspective

Study Abroad

Expand your horizons by exploring opportunities to study abroad. Studying abroad is an excellent way to gain international experience and cultural awareness. Being immersed in another culture gives students a new view of global affairs—from politics to economics to social issues. Because international exposure is important to future careers, students are venturing all over the world to take advantage of study abroad opportunities. Today's companies especially value employees with an international knowledge base.

Many colleges and universities offer study abroad programs that allow students to earn credit toward graduation while experiencing their major area of study from a new perspective. If studying abroad interests you, talk with the school's guidance counselor. You will want to be sure the program is accredited. Other things to consider when choosing to study abroad include costs associated with your program and your living arrangements. Will you live on your own, with a host family, or in a group situation? Summer programs can be a good alternative to spending a year or semester away. These programs are usually less expensive.

Setting Goals

Preparing for a career involves setting goals. A *goal* is an aim you try to reach. Goals are the endpoints of your efforts. When you decide what career you would like to have, you are setting a career goal. Because this goal will take a number of years to achieve, it is a *long-term goal*. You can set short-term goals that will help you reach your long-term goal. *Short-term goals* can be achieved in a matter of weeks or months. Successfully completing a high school class and getting a part-time job related to your career are short-term goals.

The classes you take in high school can help you prepare for a career. If you think you would like a career in a particular field, take courses related to that field. For instance, some family and consumer sciences classes would help you prepare for a career in the food industry.

Understand Your Values

Your family, friends, and life experiences shape your *values*, or beliefs that are important to you. What you value will determine the career you choose and shape the way you live your life. People who value independence, for example, desire flexibility in their work hours. People who value education want a job that pays for job-related degrees they earn while employed. A person who values family life avoids employment options that require constant travel. Carefully considering your values will point you to the job that best suits you.

Lifelong Learning

No matter what career you enter, you will be expected to keep pace with the changes in your field. Continually updating your knowledge and skills is known as **lifelong learning**. The term implies that your need for learning will never end. You cannot assume that the skills you have will be all you ever need in life. Technology and other advances mean you must continue to learn so you can keep up with changes in the field. Employers usually provide some training. However, employees are often expected to use time outside the job to stay up-to-date in their field of expertise. People who enjoy their work will view lifelong learning as an exciting challenge.

Possessing **transferable skills** helps you succeed in whatever job you choose. The transferable skills useful in all jobs include accurate reading, writing, speaking, and math skills. Also included are common computer skills.

Transferable skills are basic skills, while the essential knowledge and skills for a given career cluster are more advanced. An example of such a skill is "to identify the uses of new technologies and their impact on agricultural systems." Careers within the Agriculture, Food and Natural Resources cluster need this skill.

Many people may change career directions at some point and pursue other interests. In that case, they may need additional training or education to succeed in a new career area.

Reflect

Ask students what their long-term and short-term career goals are.

For Example...

The skill of instructing, teaching others how to do something, would obviously be needed by a classroom teacher to educate students. A teacher who wanted to pursue an interest in athletic training could transfer this skill to educate athletes.

Career Path

Have students review the *Exploring Careers* boxes that appear in each chapter to get a brief idea about the wide variety of food-related careers they might consider as they begin making career decisions.

Reflect

Ask students how much they think they would like to earn to support their desired lifestyles.

Considering Career Options

Before you can set career goals, you need to consider your values and explore the real you. You also need to identify your interests, aptitudes, and abilities.

Once you decide which careers interest you, begin to evaluate other important factors. Among these are the kind of wages you might earn and the education or training you would need. Knowing the job duties and responsibilities will also impact your decision.

Career Interests, Aptitudes, and Abilities

Few teens know exactly what career they want. Sometimes adults who have prepared for one career decide they want to pursue another. As you grow older, you may notice that your interests change. This is perfectly normal. Active people are constantly developing new interests. By reviewing your likes and dislikes, you will get a better picture of the tasks you would enjoy in a career.

Career planning cannot take place until you know what you can do well. What are your aptitudes? An **aptitude**, or natural talent, is an ability to learn something quickly and easily. Are some of your subjects in school much easier than others? You may not be aware of all of your aptitudes if you have never been challenged to use them. A school counselor can give you an aptitude test to help reveal your strengths. See **26-2**.

Abilities are skills you develop with practice. As you prepare to handle a new responsibility, you will learn that it requires certain skills. Can you develop those skills with practice? For example, can a person who is afraid of heights become a good roofer? Can someone lacking finger dexterity learn to manipulate precision tools? It is impossible to excel at every skill, so find out what you can do well.

Shutterstock

26-2 Working with a career counselor can help you to identify your aptitudes and develop a program of study for your future career.

Earning Levels

You will want to check average earnings before choosing a career. What is the average beginning pay? What does it take to achieve higher earnings? Are additional degrees or training generally required? When checking pay levels for various careers, you can expect professional positions to get higher pay.

When investigating earning levels, research those of other careers in the same career pathway. You may discover another occupation in the pathway that suits you, yet earns higher pay.

Education and Training Requirements

Some employment opportunities in food-related careers require completion of a postsecondary program. Some require occupational training and others require college and advanced degrees. When planning your career, you will need to decide how much education you need and want. There are a number of ways to acquire the education and training you need.

Work-Based Learning Programs

Work-based learning programs offer students an opportunity for job placement while still taking classes. A program coordinator works with students and the work sites to make these work experiences successful. Participating in such work-based learning programs can help ease the transition from school to career. Here are some program options to explore.

- *Cooperative programs (co-ops).* High school work-based learning programs are often called *cooperative programs*. The program coordinators place students in part-time positions. Students generally attend school for at least half the day and then work the remainder of the day. The program coordinators and workplace supervisors evaluate student performance on the job. This gives students a realistic view of job realities and responsibilities.
- *Internships.* Work-based learning opportunities at the postsecondary or college level are called *internships*. Such internships offer paid or unpaid practical work experience that is supervised. Students enroll in internship programs much like they enroll in courses. They may work several days per week with a reduced class load or during the summer. Students generally receive college credit for internships while gaining valuable work skills. See **26-3**.

Enrich

Ask students to investigate the cooperative programs in foodservice that are available through your high school.

Shutterstock

26-3 Students working in an internship program gain valuable work experience.

For Example...
Occupations that
offer apprenticeships
include carpenter, chef,
child care development
specialist, dental
assistant, electrician,
fire medic, law
enforcement agent,
over-the-road truck
driver, and pipefitter.

Discuss
Ask students
what colleges and
universities are located

Occupational Training

Occupational training is available through apprenticeship programs, technical schools, and trade schools.

Apprenticeship programs offer students the opportunity to learn a trade or skill on-the-job under the direction of a skilled worker. Apprenticeships may last several months or many years. Requirements for entering these programs vary from state to state and one trade to another.

Technical schools offer job training at both secondary and postsecondary levels. Students who attend classes at technical schools during high school often receive a certificate for a specific job skill with their high school diplomas. Postsecondary programs at technical schools may offer a two-year degree or a certificate.

Trade schools provide job-specific training at the postsecondary level. Programs at trade schools may take one to three years to complete. Successful completion of these programs may result in a certificate or possibly an associate's degree.

Colleges and Universities

Careers that require a high skill level and have great potential for advancement are highly competitive. A college degree is generally needed for such positions. You can obtain degrees from community or junior colleges, four-year colleges, and universities.

Attending a community or junior (two-year) college leads to earning an *associate's degree*. Completing a program at a four-year college or university results in a *bachelor's degree*. For careers that require a higher level of education, students can earn a *master's degree*. It usually takes another one to two years of study to obtain a master's. Other professional occupations, such as research scientists, require a *doctorate*, or *Ph.D.* Doctoral degrees often require three to six years of study beyond a master's degree. See **26-4**.

Talk with your school guidance counselor to find out about schools that offer the education and training you desire. You may also want to explore schools of interest on the Internet.

Shutterstock

26-4 A college degree can open doors to careers that require a high skill level and a potential for advancement.

Certification and Licensing

People who work in jobs that deal with people's lives, health, or safety often have certification or a license. Doctors, dentists, and teachers are examples of such professions. Many people in health-related food fields have these requirements, too.

Meeting certification and licensing requirements means a person has a clear grasp of the science involved. It also means the person has proven ability to apply

in your area. For what
fields of study are
these schools noted?
scientific principles correctly with each client or patient. These extra requirements keep unqualified people from holding important jobs. The requirements also help prevent physical harm that may result from bad advice.

Certification is a special standing within a profession as a result of meeting specific requirements. A *license* is a work requirement set by a government agency. Licensing requirements are similar or identical to the certification requirements. The one main difference is license requirements carry the force of law. The government controls the performance standards of licensed professionals.

Certification and licensing usually require the following:

- completion of an approved program of study
- acceptable level of education or degree(s)
- completion of an internship and/or on-the-job experience
- acceptable grade or score on a national exam
- continuing education

Those who meet the requirements receive a certificate or license. Many professionals display these documents at their workplaces. This allows clients to know they are dealing with qualified professionals.

Certificates and licenses usually have expiration dates. If the person takes the suggested courses and/or attends a required number of approved meetings, renewal is granted. Having regular renewal requirements helps ensure professionals keep their knowledge and skills up-to-date.

The use of certain initials after a person's name often indicates certification. A certified dietitian is called a *registered dietitian*. He or she uses the initials *RD*. A certified fitness director uses the initials *ACSM*. This indicates the American College of Sports Medicine. A certified family and consumer sciences professional uses the initials *CFCS*. Examples include a teacher or a youth services counselor,

EXPLORING CAREERS

Caterer

Caterers play an essential role in celebrating special occasions and successful corporate events. They work closely with private customers and event planners to design menus for a variety of functions. Some caterers may specialize in a certain kind of cuisine or type of event. Others work with a wide range of foods in a wide variety of events. Some caterers are one-person entrepreneurs, while others work for large companies.

Caterers must be skilled in food preparation and service, cleanup, and sales and marketing. They must be able to prepare large quantities of food and serve it creatively. They must have good customer service and communication skills. Good business skills are essential to calculate budgets and pricing when planning menus. Caterers also need to know how and where to order high-quality ingredients at affordable prices.

Artistry and efficiency are both important in the catering business. Sometimes knowledge of specialty foods and decor is required. For instance, a client may request a one-of-a-kind birthday cake for a circus-themed child's birthday party. Industrial caterers must provide appetizing menus and prompt service.

The work can be physically tiring. It involves transporting and setting up equipment, carrying heavy food trays, and standing for many hours. Caterers can expect to work nights, weekends, and holidays. They need the ability to work well under pressure.

Training to become a caterer varies. There are several ways to learn the business. Some people learn on the job, beginning as kitchen helpers, advancing to the position of cook or chef, and then starting their own catering service. Others learn cooking in technical or trade schools or by joining a family business. Many two-year colleges offer training in food service. Another way to prepare for a catering career is by earning a family and consumer sciences degree or a restaurant management degree from a four-year college or university. Many states require caterers to be licensed. State and local inspectors visit caterers periodically to check on cleanliness and safe food handling procedures.

When a license is a job requirement, the government controls the use of related titles and initials. For example, a person who uses the initials *LD* or the title *Licensed Dietitian* must have the qualifications to do so. If not, fines or penalties may result.

Many states have licensing requirements for dietitians. Some have them for anyone using the term *nutritionist*. The licensing process for nutrition and fitness professionals in general is expanding due to increasing consumer complaints. Consumers are concerned about deceitful people who give harmful nutrition or exercise advice. Such frauds lack proper training and are primarily interested in selling a product or service.

Professional associations are also expanding their certification efforts to cover more job categories. Jobs that direct, counsel, or treat people are their main focus. Their goal is to keep unqualified people from spreading wrong information.

Job Responsibilities and Rewards

It is important to find out exactly what a job entails. Remember, you will be fulfilling these duties every day for many years. If they do not sound appealing now, it is unlikely that you will enjoy them in a few years' time.

When exploring different occupations, look carefully at what each involves and what is expected of the jobholder. Also study the qualifications for entering that field.

People have different ideas about what constitutes a "reward." For example, does the occupation involve frequent travel? Adventurous people would consider this job factor a reward. However, people who like to stay at home would be annoyed, perhaps irritated and angry, at so much traveling. Each job situation presents certain conditions that involve personal preferences.

Personality Traits

Some people have personality traits that are in conflict with the requirements of certain occupations. Choosing one of these occupations would not lead to career satisfaction or success. For instance, if you prefer a quiet working environment, you may not enjoy working in a noisy setting. If you prefer a routine, you may resent a job that involves constant change. Think carefully about your personality while you are exploring career choices and keep your preferences in mind.

Desired Lifestyle

The career you choose affects your lifestyle in many ways. It affects your income, which determines how much you can spend on housing, clothing, food, and luxury items. Your career choice may also affect where you live. You will want to locate where the work is plentiful. If you prefer not to live in a large city, you should be sure to choose work that is available in other areas.

Your friendships are affected by your career choice, too. You are likely to become friends with some of your work associates. You may meet other friends through the people you know from work. Your leisure time is affected by the hours and vacation policies of your job. If you prefer to work weekdays from 9 to 5, you should avoid jobs that require overtime, late shifts, or working weekends.

Employment Outlook

In 10 years, will the need for a certain career increase, stay the same, or decrease compared to average employment trends? Are too many people flocking to a field that is not growing? If the employment outlook for a career is poor, you will have fewer employment choices. It is best to focus on career areas that are growing. They will offer you greater employment options when you are ready to begin your career. You can research job trends when investigating other career information.

Sources of Career Information

You can obtain career information from many sources. Talk to your school counselor, teachers, and parents. Find people in your community involved in various careers and ask them questions. Research careers on the Internet. If you know the career of your choice requires further education, research colleges that have the curriculum you will need. Many high school libraries have college catalogs and career manuals.

When you are ready to find employment, you can get job leads through a variety of sources. Start your search at the placement office of your school. Usually school counselors and teachers can direct you to helpful job information. You can check newspaper want ads and job fairs. Good information is also available in libraries. The professional journals in your career field and the leading professional organizations often announce job openings. See **26-5**. Family members and neighbors can provide help, too.

Reflect

Ask students which source of career information they would be most likely to use first when starting a job search. Ask why this would be the first source they use.

Activity

Have each student visit the website of one of the professional organizations listed in Figure 26-5. Ask students to find out what types of resources are available for professionals and consumers at each site.

Organizations for Professionals in the Food Industry		
Organization	**Website**	**Functions**
American Association of Family and Consumer Sciences (AAFCS)	aafcs.org	Serves family and consumer sciences professionals. Works to provide leadership and support for professionals whose work assists individuals, families, and communities in making informed decisions about their well-being, relationships, and resources to achieve optimal quality of life.
American Dietetic Association (ADA)	eatright.org	Serves dietetic professionals, registered dietitians, and dietetic technicians. It is committed to improving the nation's health and advancing the profession of dietetics through research, education, and advocacy.
Food Marketing Institute (FMI)	fmi.org	Serves grocery retailers and wholesalers. It provides leadership to retailers and wholesalers of food and consumer products, as well as to their supplier partners, by fostering their growth and promoting their role in feeding families and enriching the lives of their customers.
Institute of Food Technologists (IFT)	ift.org	Serves technical personnel in food industries, production, product development, research, and product quality. Its function is to advance the science of food and to promote the application of science and engineering to the evaluation, production, processing, packaging, distribution, preparation, and utilization of foods.
National Restaurant Association (NRA)	restaurant.org	Serves personnel in all areas of the foodservice industry. It supports foodservice education and research.

26-5 You can investigate professional organizations using these websites.

Internet Sites

Today, one of the best ways to find jobs is using the Internet. You can search for open positions, and many sites also offer tips for job hunting. You can start at the U.S. Department of Labor's website to search the following helpful sources:

- The *Occupational Outlook Handbook* describes the major U.S. jobs and their working conditions, requirements, average salaries, and future outlook. This publication is available in most libraries, too.
- The *O*NET* (the *Occupational Information Network*) website replaces the *Dictionary of Occupational Titles* and is the most complete online resource available. It provides tools for exploring careers, examining job trends, and assessing personal abilities and interests. It also includes options for finding jobs within a career cluster or searching for jobs related to specific skills.
- The *CareerOneStop* website has components for exploring careers, salaries, benefits, education, training, and other resources.

    One part of CareerOneStop is *America's Career InfoNet*. You can use this site for exploring careers, including occupational trends, wage information, and state resources.

    America's Service Locator is another component of CareerOneStop. This site helps users find jobs and job-related resources in their local area. One-Stop Career Centers offer assistance in job-seeking skills, such as résumé writing. They also offer help with various types of job training.

Networking

Many people find employment through networking. **Networking** is the exchange of information or services among individuals or groups. As a newcomer to the career field, the goal of your networking is to learn about possible job leads.

Learn About...

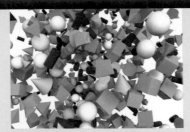

Managing Your Online Image

If future employers searched the Internet for information about you, what would they find? Many employers also use the Internet to check job applicants as well as employees.

A first step in managing your online image is to identify what is currently posted about you. Plug your name into one or more search engines and examine what comes up. Delete anything you wouldn't want a prospective employer to see. However, since you cannot control the flow of information online, be prepared to answer questions employers may ask. Here are some additional pointers.

- Do not say or do anything that is unethical or illegal.
- Do not take photos or videos that show you in a bad light. Images that depict drinking, drugs, gang signs, firearms, and lewd behavior have created problems for those pictured.
- Do not say anything negative about current or former employers, jobs, or coworkers. Negative comments and anything profane, sexist, or racist can result in the rejection of a job application or being named in a lawsuit.

Remember that cybercriminals are searching the Internet for victims. They collect and piece together data that they use to commit crimes. Avoid posting personal information, especially your address, date of birth, and phone number. Revealing your future whereabouts is also risky.

Social networking sites have become popular places to find information on companies and their available positions. Many companies network on these sites because it is an additional source of advertising for them. Users find that these sites expand their job search possibilities. In addition, these sites allow a personal exchange between users and company representatives.

Considering Entrepreneurship

Some people do not want to work for an employer. They prefer to find opportunities, make decisions, and set schedules on their own. In other words, they prefer to be self-employed. These people are often called **entrepreneurs**. Entrepreneurs are people who start and run their own business.

Many people in food-related businesses are entrepreneurs. Farmers are frequently self-employed. Grocers, butchers, and bakers often own their stores. Many restaurateurs and caterers operate their own businesses. Dietitians may go into business as freelance consultants. Food stylists may work alone to set up contracts with clients.

Entrepreneurship holds great appeal for some people. Being their own bosses makes them feel independent. They achieve a sense of satisfaction from setting and reaching business goals.

Entrepreneurship involves risks as well as rewards. Starting a business takes money. The amount depends on the type of business. However, every business has some operating costs and requires the purchase of some equipment and supplies.

Starting a business requires responsibility and organization. If a customer is unhappy, an entrepreneur must fix the problem. Entrepreneurs must keep orderly records of the money they take in and pay out. They must also keep track of meetings, customer orders, employee files, and taxes.

If entrepreneurship interests you, you should first consider several factors. Think about what kind of business you would like to start. Find out how much need there is for a business of this nature. Be sure it is something you can manage.

Advantages and Disadvantages

Many people become entrepreneurs so they can be their own boss. They enjoy being able to make all the decisions and work whatever hours they choose. See **26-6**.

Some people start a business for the satisfaction of working with subjects they understand or enjoy. Starting a business may also provide a sense of accomplishment. It is likely that an entrepreneur will value profit. The profit motive is a big incentive for starting a business. The success of a business is based on its ability to make a profit and grow.

Enrich

Have students debate whether they think it is appropriate for employers to use information and images from social networking sites when screening job applicants.

Reflect

Ask students if they would be interested in becoming entrepreneurs. Have them think about why or why not.

Shutterstock

26-6 An entrepreneur can face many challenges and rewards.

Chief among the disadvantages to becoming an entrepreneur is the hard work. At first, you may work nonstop just to get the business started. During this period, very little money—if any—is coming in. You may have to put most of your savings into the business since affordable loans for an unproven business are rare. If the business fails, you could lose everything. About 30 percent of new businesses do not last two years. Fifty percent close within five years. All these factors add to a heightened sense of stress. Too much stress could even affect your health.

Common Characteristics of Entrepreneurs

First, entrepreneurs must be optimistic. They have to believe their business will succeed. Entrepreneurs must be self-starters who can recognize when they need to initiate action. They should be hard workers who are willing to put extreme effort into the business. They must have interesting new ideas about doing or providing something that is not available anywhere else. Usually, a business succeeds by fulfilling a consumer need. A smart entrepreneur will be able to recognize a need that could become a money-making opportunity.

An entrepreneur needs to be committed to the business. This involves using his or her personal money, time, and other resources to make the business succeed. Entrepreneurs must be energetic and in good health to handle long work days. An entrepreneur must also be willing to take risks. It is a huge risk to give up a steady paycheck for a business that may not succeed.

Importance of Entrepreneurship

Over 95 percent of businesses in the U.S. are considered small businesses. These businesses each have less than 500 employees. About half the people employed in the United States work for small businesses. Of the people who do not work in government jobs, more than half are employed by small businesses.

Small businesses help create jobs. More jobs help keep the economy strong. A strong economy creates more demand for goods and services, which raises the standard of living. This, in turn, spurs the growth of small businesses that offer the goods and services desired.

Because small businesses usually produce highly specialized products, they may fulfill a focused need. However, to fill this need, they may require employees who are highly trained or experienced in one specialty. Many small businesses employ workers who are just starting their careers. This helps workers gain employment experience.

Getting Started

Consider working for someone else before starting a business of your own. This will give you work experience and show you what is involved in operating a business.

Once you have thought through your business idea, you need to write a detailed business plan. This will include a complete description of any product or service you will sell. The plan should explain everything you must do to get the business started and keep it going.

It is unlikely that you are an expert in all areas of entrepreneurship. Where can you go for support?

First, consult the Small Business Administration. Its website has helpful answers to many common questions. It also links to the state Departments of Commerce. Many of the regulations that affect small businesses are set by the states. You would be wise to investigate these regulations before starting a business. Your local chamber of commerce may also be able to check for local regulations. These sources may be free or require a small fee.

From time to time, you will also need support in specialized business areas. A lawyer will make sure you fulfill all legal requirements. An accountant can handle or check your bookkeeping and tax-related records. An insurance agent will determine the amount and types of insurance you need. These professionals can be expensive, but they limit your business risk and provide peace of mind.

With your business plan in hand, the sky is your limit. Teen entrepreneurs have started such food-related ventures as party planning, pizza delivering, and cookie baking. If you are ambitious, you too can be successful in starting a business.

Online Resource

Have students visit the Small Business Administration website at sba.gov. Ask each student to read about a different topic related to starting a business and share information in a brief oral report.

Learn About...

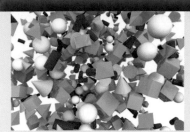

Questions for Entrepreneurs

According to the Small Business Administration, entrepreneurs should ask themselves the following questions:

- Why am I starting a business? What kind of business do I want? Am I prepared to spend the time, money, and resources needed to get my business started? How will I market my business?
- What products/services will my business provide? What is my target market? Who is my competition? What is unique about my business idea and the products/services I will provide? How long will it take before my products/services are available?
- How much money do I need to get my business set up? Will I need to get a loan? How long must I finance the company until I start making a profit? How will I price my product compared to my competition?
- How will I set up the legal structure of my business? What do I need to ensure I am paying my taxes correctly? How will I manage my business?
- Where will I house my business? How many employees will I need? What types of supplies will I need? What kind of insurance do I need?

CAREER SUCCESS

Computer Skills

Sherry is a career placement services counselor at West Barton Community College. Each year she interviews over 100 students who are looking for jobs. She gives them interest surveys and aptitude tests. She also reviews the students' school and employment records. Then Sherry analyzes all this information to help students identify career opportunities for which they would be well suited.

To be an effective worker, Sherry needs skill in using computers to process information. Put yourself in Sherry's place and answer the following questions about your need for and use of this skill:

A. How would having skill in using computers make it easier for you to help each student?

B. How might your lack of skill in using computers to process information affect the students who come to see you?

C. How might West Barton Community College be affected if you cannot adequately use computers to process information?

D. What is another skill you would need in this job? Briefly explain why this skill would be important.

CHAPTER 26 REVIEW

Answer Key for
Review What You Have Read **questions**

1. A career is a series of related occupations that show progression in a field of work. An occupation is paid employment that involves handling one or more jobs.

2. true

3. The skills required for related jobs in a career field are similar. Preparing for more than one career in a related field allows flexibility in searching for employment.

4. A program of study is the sequence of instruction used to prepare students for occupations in a given career pathway. The program includes classroom instruction, co-curricular activities, such as student organizations, and other learning experiences including work-site learning.

5. lifelong learning

6. Possessing transferable skills can help you succeed in whatever job you choose. They can help smooth career transitions.

(continued)

Summary

Studying the career clusters can make choosing a career less overwhelming. Within each career cluster are career pathways that are grouped by similar knowledge and skills. Programs of study can help you plan now how to get the education and training you need for the job you want. Belonging to organizations can also help you learn more about a career.

Careers exist at all job levels. No matter what type or level of job a person holds, staying skilled and knowledgeable is important for career success and advancement.

Knowing the real you—your interests, abilities, and aptitudes—is the first step in choosing a career. Other factors to consider include wages and earning levels; education and training; and job duties and responsibilities. Your personal traits and your lifestyle may impact your decision. You should also research the career outlook, related rewards, employer, and workplace before making a choice. Sources such as O*NET and CareerOneStop can help you thoroughly research career details.

You may want to become an entrepreneur by starting and running a business yourself. There are certain advantages and disadvantages to becoming an entrepreneur. Being committed to your business and having a well-prepared business plan will help you succeed.

Review What You Have Read

Write your answers on a separate sheet of paper, using complete sentences when appropriate.

1. What is the difference between a career and an occupation?
2. True or false. Career clusters are 16 groups of occupations or career specialties that are similar or related to one another.
3. How can knowing the relationship between careers in a given pathway be helpful when researching information about careers?
4. Describe a program of study.
5. Continually updating your knowledge and skills is known as _____ _____.
6. Why are transferable skills important?
7. What is the difference between an aptitude and ability?
8. Give two examples of work-based learning programs.
9. What is the difference between a certification and a license?
10. Name three sources of career information.
11. _____ are people who start and run their own businesses.
12. Explain why you should consider working for someone else before starting a business of your own.

Link to Academic Skills

13. **English language arts.** Obtain a copy of a career-search book (such as the latest edition of *What Color Is Your Parachute?*). Read the book. Then write a book report identifying the important guidelines the author suggests for finding meaningful employment. Select two topics you found most valuable to share with the class. Give evidence to support your reasoning.

14. **Government/Civics.** Prepare a poster listing and describing government-sponsored sources of career information. With permission, display the poster at a school career day.

15. **English language arts.** Select two careers to research on O*NET (www.onetcenter.org). Read the summary reports for these careers, especially the knowledge, skills, abilities, and interests required to do the work. Analyze whether your personal interests, skills, and abilities are a logical fit with one or both careers. Write a summary explaining why you think you are well suited for either career.

16. **Social studies.** Conduct research about various occupations in your area. Based on your survey, what is the predominate occupation in your community? How does this occupation affect the standard of living among members of the community?

17. **History.** Interview older adults about how they searched for their first jobs. Compare that to how young people search for jobs today. What are the similarities and differences?

Build Critical Thinking Skills

18. **Synthesis.** After reviewing this chapter and one or more career websites, draw conclusions about which careers appear to have excellent job outlooks. Why? Report your conclusions and your reasoning to the class.

19. **Evaluation.** Suppose a classmate posted untrue, negative remarks about you on a social networking site. You are in the process of submitting college applications and waiting for acceptance. You know that your first-choice college examines social networking sites looking for information about their applicants. Predict the potential consequences of these remarks on your pending college acceptance. How could these remarks impact future employment opportunities? What are some ways you can safely deal with cyber-bullying?

20. **Analysis.** What type of job environment do you think best suits your abilities and interests? Do you think you would be more successful as a member of a team in an established company or as an entrepreneur? Compare and contrast the benefits and challenges each choice offers.

7. An aptitude, or natural talent, is an ability to learn something quickly and easily. An ability is a skill you develop with practice.

8. cooperative programs (co-ops), internships

9. A certification is a special standing within a profession as a result of meeting specific requirements. A license is a work requirement set by a government agency.

10. (Name three:) the placement office of your school, school counselors, teachers, newspaper want ads, job fairs, libraries, professional journals, professional organizations, family members, neighbors, Internet sites, networking

11. Entrepreneurs

12. This will give you work experience and show you what is involved in operating a business.

Apply Technology

21. Use such online self-assessments as the *Skills Profiler*, *Interest Profiler*, or *Work Importance Locator* on the CareerOneStop (www.careerinfonet.org) and O*NET (www.onetcenter.org) websites. Take the assessments. Then evaluate how these assessments can help you locate a career that matches your skills and interests.

22. Search the Internet for three sources of information about the job requirements for a position you might pursue. Use one or more references from the U. S. Department of Labor. Investigate the salary potential and job outlook for the profession. Is demand for the career increasing or declining? Summarize your findings and cite your sources.

A Measure of Math

23. Ask your school counselor to administer an aptitude assessment and explain your results. Ask your counselor to explain how the results are tabulated and how the counselor uses these numbers to interpret the results. Based on your assessment results, determine which types of careers present the best opportunities for you to succeed.

Teamwork in Action

24. Team up with other classmates to role-play networking situations. Use the role-play to demonstrate how networking can help in finding career leads.

Companion Website
www.g-wlearning.com

At the website, review key terms for this chapter with crossword puzzles, matching exercises, and e-flash cards. Apply facts from the chapter to complete the activities.

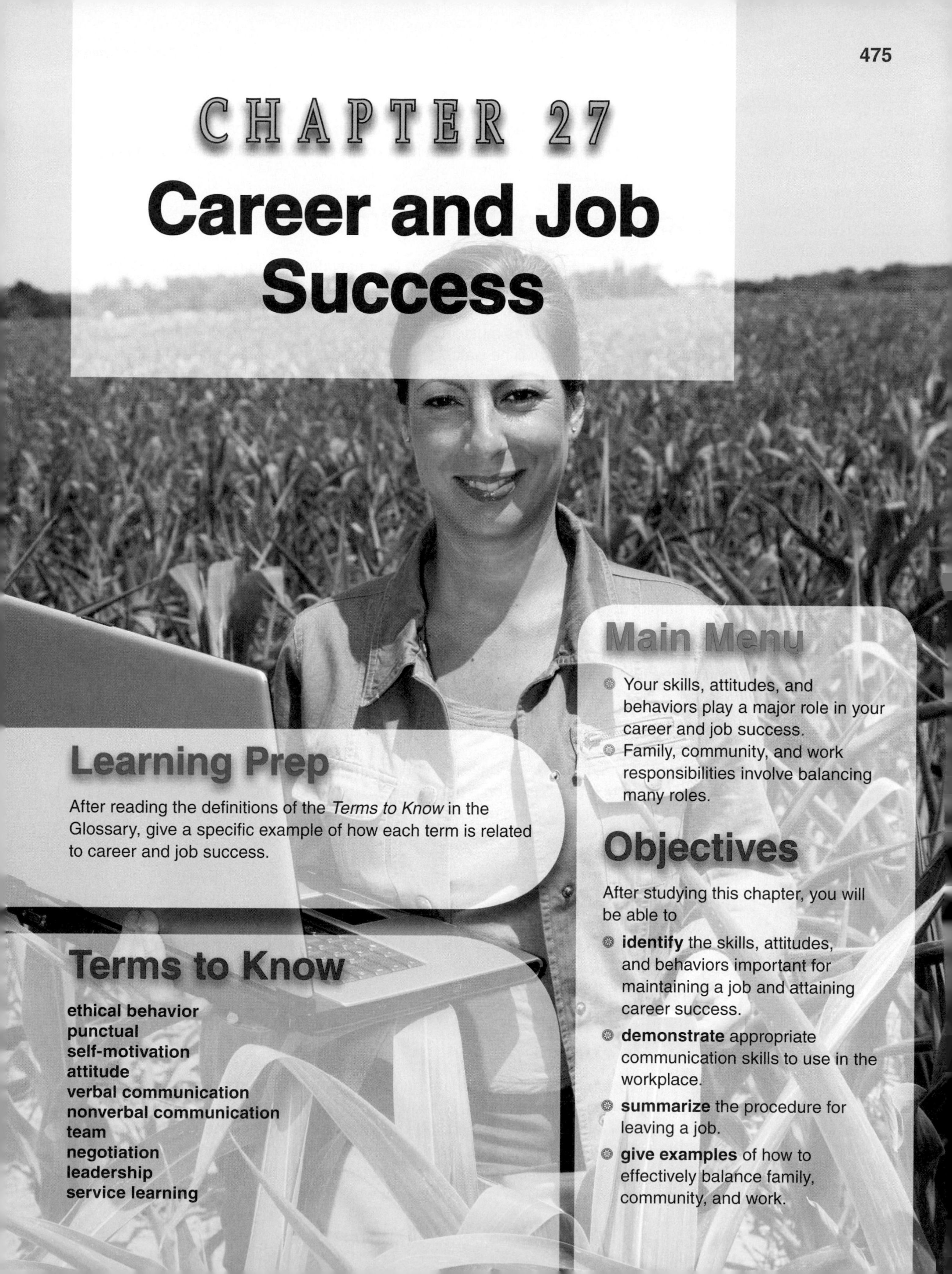

CHAPTER 27
Career and Job Success

Learning Prep

After reading the definitions of the *Terms to Know* in the Glossary, give a specific example of how each term is related to career and job success.

Terms to Know

ethical behavior
punctual
self-motivation
attitude
verbal communication
nonverbal communication
team
negotiation
leadership
service learning

Main Menu

- Your skills, attitudes, and behaviors play a major role in your career and job success.
- Family, community, and work responsibilities involve balancing many roles.

Objectives

After studying this chapter, you will be able to

- **identify** the skills, attitudes, and behaviors important for maintaining a job and attaining career success.

- **demonstrate** appropriate communication skills to use in the workplace.

- **summarize** the procedure for leaving a job.

- **give examples** of how to effectively balance family, community, and work.

Career and job success depend on many factors. Your skills, attitudes, and behaviors are critical in keeping a job and succeeding in a career. Effectively balancing your family, community, and work responsibilities can help you to achieve the lifestyle you desire.

Succeeding in the Workplace

After securing employment, adjusting to your new duties and responsibilities will occupy your first few weeks. Your supervisor and coworkers will help you learn the routine. An introduction to company policies and procedures as well as the special safety rules that all employees must know is common for new employees.

While your coworkers will be watching what you do, they will also pay attention to "how you work." How to behave in the workplace is an important lesson all employees should learn. Making an effort to do your best will help you succeed.

Professional Behavior

You will be expected to behave professionally on the job. This includes showing respect for your boss and coworkers. Limit personal conversations and phone calls to break times or lunch. Act courteously; remember that others are focusing on their work. Interruptions can cause them to lose concentration.

Part of behaving professionally is responding appropriately to *constructive criticism*. Every employee, no matter how knowledgeable or experienced, can improve his or her performance. If you receive criticism from a supervisor or coworker, do not be offended. Instead, use the feedback to improve yourself. The more you improve, the more successful you will be in your work.

Ethical Workplace Behavior

Ethical behavior on the job means conforming to accepted standards of fairness and good conduct. It is based on a person's sense of what is right to do. Individuals and society as a whole regard ethical behavior as highly important. Integrity, confidentiality, and honesty are crucial aspects of ethical workplace behavior. *Integrity* is firmly following your moral values.

Unfortunately, employee theft is a major problem at some companies. The theft can range from carrying office supplies home to stealing money or expensive equipment. Company policies are in place to address these concerns. In cases of criminal or serious behavior, people may lose their jobs. If proven, the charge of criminal behavior stays on the employee's record. Such an employee will have a difficult time finding another job.

Work Habits

Employers want employees who are punctual, dependable, and responsible. They want their employees to be capable of taking initiative and working independently. Other desirable employee qualities include organization, accuracy, and efficiency.

A **punctual** employee is always prompt and on time. This means not only when the workday starts, but also when returning from breaks and lunches. Being dependable means that people can rely on you to fulfill your word and meet your deadlines. If you are not well, be sure to call in and let the employer know right away. If there are reasons you cannot be at work, discuss this with your employer and work out an alternate arrangement. Many people have lost jobs by not checking with their supervisor about time off.

Taking *initiative* means that you start activities on your own without being told. When you finish one task, you do not wait to hear what to do next. Individuals who take initiative need much less supervision. They have **self-motivation**, or an inner desire to perform well. Generally, this motivation will drive you to set goals and accomplish them. All these qualities together show that you are capable of working *independently*. See **27-1**.

You are expected to be as accurate and error-free as possible in all that you do. This is why you were hired. Complete your work with precision and double-check it to assure accuracy. Your coworkers depend on the careful completion of your tasks.

Time Management

A good employee knows how to manage time wisely. This includes ability to prioritize assignments and complete them in a timely fashion. It also involves not wasting time. Time-wasting behaviors include visiting with coworkers,

Shutterstock

27-1 Employers value employees who work independently and stay focused on their work.

EXPLORING CAREERS

Grocery Store Manager

Grocery store managers oversee the work of employees, such as produce managers, cashiers, customer service representatives, and stock clerks. They are responsible for interviewing, hiring, and training employees. They also may prepare work schedules and assign workers to specific duties. Grocery store managers ensure that customers receive satisfactory service and quality goods. They also answer customers' inquiries, deal with complaints, and sometimes handle purchasing, budgeting, and accounting responsibilities. They organize shelves, displays, and inventories. Grocery store managers inspect merchandise to ensure that products are not outdated. They develop merchandising techniques and coordinate sales promotions. In addition, they may greet and assist customers and promote sales and good public relations. The work hours of grocery store managers are long and irregular, particularly during sales, holidays, busy shopping seasons, and inventory checks.

Grocery store managers must possess good communication skills and get along with everyone.

They need initiative, self-discipline, good judgment, and decisiveness. Patience is necessary when dealing with demanding customers. They also must be able to motivate, organize, and direct the work of their employees. They need good math and business skills as well as strong customer service and public relations skills.

Grocery store managers usually gain knowledge of management principles and practices through work experience. Many supervisors begin their careers as salespersons, cashiers, or customer service representatives. There is no standard educational requirement for grocery store managers. For some jobs, a college degree is required. Grocery store managers who have college degrees often hold associate or bachelor's degrees in liberal arts, social sciences, business, or management. College graduates usually can enter directly into management training programs sponsored by their company, without much experience. Regardless of education level or major area of study, several high school or college courses are recommended. These include those related to business, such as accounting, marketing, management, and sales, as well as those related to social science, such as psychology, sociology, and communication. To gain experience, many college students participate in internship programs that usually are developed jointly by schools and businesses.

making personal phone calls, texting, sending e-mails, or doing other nonwork activities during work hours.

While it is important to complete all your work thoroughly, you must also be able to gauge which assignments are most important. Avoid putting excessive efforts into minor assignments when crucial matters require your attention. Even though you are still accomplishing work, this is another way of wasting of time.

Attitude on the Job

Your attitude can often determine the success you have on your job. Your **attitude** is your outlook on life. It is reflected by how you react to the events and people around you. A smile and courteous behavior can make customers and fellow employees feel good about themselves and you. Clients and customers prefer to do business in friendly environments. Being friendly may take some effort on your part, but it does pay off.

Enthusiasm spreads easily from one person to another. Usually, enthusiasm means a person enjoys what he or she is doing. In a sales environment, enthusiasm increases sales. In an office, enthusiasm builds a team spirit for working together.

People who do a good job feel pride in their work. They feel a sense of accomplishment and a desire to achieve more. This attitude can inspire others as well.

Health and Hygiene

As an employee, you are a representative of your company. Therefore, your employer expects you to be neat and clean on the job. Taking care of yourself gives the impression that you want people to view you as a professional. See **27-2**.

Employers expect workers to dress appropriately. Many places of work have a dress code. If your workplace does not, use common sense and avoid extremes. Refrain from wearing garments that are revealing or have inappropriate pictures or sayings. Some employers have rules requiring that tattoos or piercings beyond pierced ears

Shutterstock

27-2 Having a neat, clean appearance shows you care about your work. This is especially important when serving food.

remain covered. Good appearance is especially important for employees who have frequent face-to-face contact with customers.

Staying Safety Conscious

Safety on the job is everyone's responsibility. Many workplace accidents occur because of careless behavior. Often poor attitudes can cause unsafe behavior, too. Common causes of accidents include the following:

- taking chances
- forgetting safety details

- disobeying company rules
- daydreaming
- losing your temper
- falling asleep

Practicing good safety habits is essential for preventing accidents and injuries on the job. A healthy worker is more alert and less likely to make accident-prone mistakes. Knowing how to use machines and tools properly is the responsibility of both the employer and employees. Wearing protective clothing and using safety equipment correctly helps keep workers safe. Your employer will emphasize the safety practices that employees must follow in your workplace.

The government agency that promotes safety in the workplace is the Occupational Safety and Health Administration (OSHA). You will be required to follow the specific OSHA regulations that apply to your workplace.

Reflect

Ask students which of the common causes of accidents listed they think would pose the greatest risk to each of them in the workplace.

Discuss

Ask students to name pieces of safety equipment workers in various careers would need to wear.

Learn About...

OSHA for Teen Workers

Work-related injuries claim the lives of 60-70 teen workers each year, while about 200,000 teen workers seek emergency medical treatment. All employees, including teens, have a right to a safe, healthy workplace. They also have a responsibility to be safe.

As a teen worker, you have the following responsibilities:

- Trust your instincts about dangerous situations.
- Follow all safety rules.
- Wear proper safety equipment.
- Ask questions about potentially dangerous situations or equipment.
- Tell your supervisor or parent if you suspect unsafe conditions.

- Be aware of your work environment.
- Work safely.
- Stay sober and drug-free.
- Know your workplace rights.

Employers have the following responsibilities:

- Provide a workplace that protects workers from injuries, illnesses, and fatalities.
- Know the law about working limits for teens, including the number of hours they can work and the kinds of jobs they can perform.
- Emphasize the importance of safety.
- Make sure that young workers are trained properly.
- Teach workers to recognize hazards and use safe work practices.

There are practical steps teens and their employers can take to help make sure that responsibilities are being met. Visit the OSHA Teen Workers website at www.osha.gov/teens.

Decision Making and Problem Solving

Employers value workers who have the ability to make sound decisions. This process applies in the workplace as well as other aspects of life. The process will help you identify the issue, identify possible solutions, make a decision, implement the decision, and evaluate the results.

Having ability to solve problems on the job shows an employer that you are able to handle more responsibility. Solving problems as a group can help employees feel more pride in their work.

Online Resource

Have students visit the OSHA Teen Workers website. Ask each student to choose a different topic to read. Have students make posters summarizing key points from their reading.

Activity

Ask students to suggest an everyday activity or a learning task at school that helps them develop and/or practice critical thinking skills. Examples might include thinking creatively in art class, making decisions when shopping, and solving word problems in math class.

Activity

Write the following words on a card: *you make your own appetizers*. Pass the card around the room and ask students to take turns reading it, emphasizing different words and using attitude and tone of voice to make statements, exclamations, and questions. Discuss how nonverbal communication can change or confuse the meaning of a message.

The ability to make decisions and solve problems requires *critical-thinking skills*. These are higher-level skills that enable you to think beyond the obvious. You learn to interpret information and make judgments. Supervisors appreciate employees who can analyze problems and think of practical solutions. See **27-3**.

Communication Skills

Communicating effectively with others is important for job success. Being a good communicator means that you can share information well with others. It also means you are a good listener.

Good communication is central to a smooth operation of any business. Communication is the process of exchanging ideas, thoughts, or information. Poor communication is costly to an employer, as when time is lost because an order was entered incorrectly. Poor communication can result in lost customers, too.

Types of Communication

The primary forms of communications are verbal and nonverbal. **Verbal communication** involves speaking, listening, and writing. **Nonverbal communication** is the sending and receiving of messages without the use of words. It involves *body language*, which includes the expression on your face and your body posture.

Listening is an important part of communication. If you do not understand, be sure to ask questions. Also give feedback to let others know you understand them and are interested in what they have to say. Leaning forward while a person is talking indicates interest and keen listening. See **27-4**. Slouching back in a chair and yawning give the opposite signal—that you are bored and uninterested.

Shutterstock

27-3 When several people pool their ideas, the result is often better than any one person could accomplish.

Shutterstock

27-4 Being a good listener is a key communication skill to have when working with clients.

The message you convey in telephone communication involves your promptness, tone of voice, and attitude. Answering the phone quickly with a pleasant voice conveys a positive image for the company. Learning to obtain accurate information from the caller without interrupting that person's message is important.

Communication tools have advanced with the development of new technologies. To be an effective employee, you need to know how to communicate well with the common tools of your workplace. For example, when sending e-mail communications, remember to think through each message as you would before sending a postal letter. Often messages are sent quickly without thought of how the recipient may interpret them. The same is true of voicemail.

The development of good communication skills is an ongoing process. Attending communication workshops and practicing often can keep your skills sharp. You should periodically give yourself a communications checkup by asking your supervisor to suggest areas that need improvement.

Customer Relations Skills

Working with customers takes special communication skills. The most important aspect of customer relations is always remaining courteous. This may also require patience in some situations. When customers visit your business, you want them to have the best possible service and to leave happy. Remember that your behavior and skills at handling customers can determine if the customer will return to your business. The customer may spread the word about his or her experience to other potential customers. Make sure your customers know you appreciate their business.

Customer relations may also involve problem solving. If a customer needs help, you must provide answers as quickly and accurately as possible while remaining pleasant and polite. When a situation becomes stressful, you must be able to control your own level of stress without letting it affect your performance. At the same time, you must be able to lessen the customer's stress and attempt to eliminate its source.

Global Perspective

International Business

Increasingly, more business is transacted internationally. Even within the United States, dealing with people from different cultures is common. Make a point of learning about the culture of your business associates. This will allow you to be sensitive to their cultural differences. Your consideration will enhance communication as well as have a positive impact on your success in the workplace.

Interpersonal Skills

Interpersonal skills involve interacting with others. Some workplace activities that involve these skills include teaching others, leading, negotiating, and working as a member of a team. Getting along well with others can require great effort on your part, but it is essential for accomplishing your employer's goals.

Teamwork

Employers seek employees who can effectively serve as good team members. Due to the nature of most work today, teamwork is necessary. A **team** is a small group of people working together for a common purpose. Often cooperation requires flexibility and willingness to try new ways to get things done. If someone is uncooperative, it takes longer to accomplish the tasks. When people do not get along, strained relationships develop and get in the way of finishing the tasks.

A big advantage of a team is its ability to develop plans and complete work faster than individuals working alone. Team members need some time before they become comfortable with one another and function as a unit. Team development goes through various stages. In the beginning, people are excited about being on a team. Later, disagreements may replace harmony. The good result of this is people express themselves and learn to trust the other team members. Eventually leaders emerge and the team develops a unique way to interact and achieve goals. Finally, the team becomes very productive and performs at its highest level. It takes time and a genuine desire to work together to build a strong team. See **27-5**.

Discuss

Ask students to name organizations and activities at school in which students must use teamwork skills to help groups achieve their goals.

Discuss

Ask students to identify specific leadership opportunities for students in your school.

Shutterstock

27-5 Effective leaders get along well with their coworkers and inspire them to perform better as a team.

Creative ideas often develop from building on another person's idea. Honesty and openness are essential. Also, trying to understand the ideas of others before trying to get others to understand your ideas is an effective skill to develop.

Negotiation

Often there are times when employees and employers must negotiate on a task or work-related issue. **Negotiation** is the process of agreeing to an issue that requires all parties to give and take. The goal is a "win-win" solution in which both parties get some or all of what they are seeking.

Negotiation begins with trying to understand the other party's interests. Possible solutions that meet their mutual concerns can be developed. Often the best solution becomes clear when both parties have ample time to explain what they are trying to accomplish.

Leadership

All careers require leadership skills. **Leadership** is the ability to guide and motivate others to complete tasks or achieve goals. It involves communicating well with others, accepting responsibility, and making decisions with confidence. Those employees with leadership skills are most likely to be promoted to higher levels.

Leaders often seem to carry the most responsibility of a group. Other group members look to them for answers and direction. The most important role of leaders is to keep the team advancing toward its goal. Leaders do this by inspiring their groups and providing the motivation to keep everyone working together.

Good leaders encourage teamwork, because a team that is working together well is more likely to reach goals. They listen to the opinions of others and make sure all team members are included in projects. Leaders also want to set a good example by doing a fair share of the work. In these ways, leaders cultivate a sense of harmony in the group.

Belonging to Organizations

Leading others may not be easy for some people, but everyone can improve their leadership skills with practice. Becoming involved in a school club or organization can help. Taking a role as an officer or a committee chair will give you even more practice.

Belonging to an organization can also help you develop your teamwork skills. You will learn how to work well in a group as you plan events, create projects, and accomplish goals together.

Leaving a Job

More money, more responsibility, and better benefits are some of the reasons for leaving a job. There are others, too, but all job departures need to be handled in a way that is considerate of the employer. You should try not to leave your job with noticeable anger and hostility. Employers know that employees will not stay forever. However, they dislike a too-short notice, especially during a busy season.

When you make the decision to leave your job, let the employer know in writing by giving at least a two-week notice. It would be helpful to give a longer notice if you can. A letter of resignation should state your reason for leaving and the date you expect to

Reflect

Ask students to think of a time when they used negotiation to solve a problem with another person. How did this approach benefit each person?

leave. The letter allows the employer to begin looking for your replacement. Perhaps there will be enough time to hire someone who can work with you during your final days. Many people have found that a past employer became their greatest ally when they needed a good reference for a future position.

Balancing Family, Community, and Work

Your success in a career will affect your satisfaction with your personal and family life. Likewise, your roles and responsibilities related to home and community life will affect your career. Balancing career and home and community life is important in any lifestyle.

Belonging to a family involves roles and responsibilities. As a son or daughter, your responsibilities at home may involve watching younger siblings, helping with family meals, and keeping your clothes and room clean. Usually these tasks do not interfere with your responsibilities to attend school and perform well. Adding a part-time job can complicate matters, however, and force you to manage your time more carefully.

The roles of spouse, parent, homemaker, and employee are much more demanding and may conflict at times. People with *multiple roles* must balance their responsibilities to fully meet them all. Sometimes family responsibilities will dictate the career decisions you make. See **27-6**.

Parents may adjust work responsibilities so they can spend more time with the family. These adjustments might include telecommuting, working less overtime, taking a part-time job, or starting a home-based business. If both parents work away from the home, they must provide *substitute care* for young children.

Belonging to a community also involves roles and responsibilities. As a citizen of a community, you may choose to volunteer to help others. You may choose to volunteer because you want to be a good citizen or because you care about a cause. Volunteers are not paid for their services. However, volunteering can be rewarding and may provide valuable experiences that may help you in a future career.

Shutterstock
27-6 Balancing work and family life can be both rewarding and challenging.

Examples of ways to volunteer in your community may include the following suggestions:

- work with a recycling program
- help at an animal shelter
- take part in organizations such as Special Olympics, Habitat for Humanity, or Toys for Tots
- assist campaigns against drunk driving or drug abuse
- work at a food bank
- raise money for a homeless shelter or veterans' group
- work as an aide at a hospital or retirement home
- help the park department in planting flowers or trees or in cleanup efforts

Learn About...

Protecting the Planet

Regardless of what type of career you choose, be a good citizen by taking steps to care for the earth's environment.

Small efforts made by you and your coworkers can make a big difference. Consider the following ideas:

- Carpool to your job.
- Use a reusable lunch bag to carry your lunch to work.
- Keep a ceramic mug in your workplace so you will not have to use disposable cups.
- Recycle office paper and cardboard cartons.
- Reuse manila envelopes.

Many communities benefit from service learning projects. Using what you learn in the classroom to meet a need in the community is called **service learning**. If your school does not have a service learning program, consider starting one. Involvement in service learning projects will help make your community a better place to live.

CAREER SUCCESS

Problem-Solving Skills

Alberto is a production line coordinator at a produce freezing plant. He coordinates the arrival of harvested crops, their processing, and shipments to warehouses. He schedules workers for the production line and makes sure equipment is maintained. Throughout the year, and especially during harvesting season, he must keep the production line staffed and the equipment maintained.

To be an effective worker, Alberto needs skills in problem-solving. Put yourself in Alberto's place and answer the following questions about your need for and use of these skills:

A. How would maintaining processing equipment and freezers help you to keep the production line running smoothly?

B. How would keeping the production line fully staffed during harvest season help productivity and minimize profit losses?

C. How might your failure to solve equipment failures or staffing issues affect company profits?

D. What is another skill you would need in this job? Briefly explain why this skill would be important.

CHAPTER 27 REVIEW

Summary

Successfully keeping a job involves being clean and neat on the job, having good work habits, and using effective time management. A positive attitude and professional behavior on the job are also essential. Developing your decision-making, communication, and interpersonal skills can help you succeed. Having ethics and integrity will help you maintain good conduct. Staying safety conscious will help you prevent workplace accidents.

Terminating the job has procedures to follow, too, including notifying the employer in writing. Leaving a job properly can help guarantee that your employer will give you good references in the future.

Having a family and a career involves balancing multiple roles and responsibilities. Being a good citizen of a community also involves responsibilities and gives you opportunities of volunteering and service learning.

Review What You Have Read

Write your answers on a separate sheet of paper, using complete sentences when appropriate.

1. What does being professional on the job involve?

2. True or false. Having initiative means that you must be constantly supervised to accomplish tasks.

3. Why does an employer expect you to be neat and clean on the job?

4. Practicing good _____ habits is essential for preventing accidents and injuries on the job.

5. True or false. Having the ability to solve problems on the job shows an employer that you are able to handle more responsibility.

6. What is the difference between verbal and nonverbal communication?

7. What is the goal of negotiation?

8. What is leadership?

9. How can belonging to an organization help you develop your teamwork skills?

10. What is the proper procedure for leaving a job?

11. Give an example of how you would balance family, community, and a career.

12. Using what you learn in the classroom to meet a need in the community is called _____ _____.

Link to Academic Skills

13. **English language arts.** Talk with the manager of a local supermarket or food-related firm about company procedures for reporting accidents. If possible, obtain samples of forms used for reporting such incidents. Then, with a classmate, role-play a scenario for the class in which an employee is talking with the manager about an accident. Demonstrate the procedure to follow when reporting such incidents.

14. **Social studies.** Select a local employer that offers jobs you might want to pursue as part of your career plan. Make arrangements with the employer and your school to "shadow" one of the employees. During your job-shadowing experience, be sure to discuss issues the employee feels are essential for career success. Observe the "culture" of the workplace. Write a summary of your experience.

15. **English language arts.** Imagine you have part-time job at a local pizza restaurant. You have just found out that your family is relocating to another state. Write a letter of resignation for your part-time job.

16. **Government/Civics.** Interview someone elected to a local office. Ask the person how he or she became interested in holding a leadership position. Ask about local volunteer or service learning opportunities. Report your findings to the class.

8. Leadership is the ability to guide and motivate others to complete tasks or achieve goals.

9. You will learn how to work well in a group as you plan events, create projects, and accomplish goals together.

10. Let the employer know in writing by giving at least a two-week notice. A letter of resignation should state your reason for leaving and the date you expect to leave.

Build Critical Thinking Skills

17. **Synthesis.** Have you ever had an informal communication experience in which you felt totally misunderstood? How could such experiences impact workplace communication? Draw conclusions about ways to prevent such misunderstandings.

18. **Analysis.** In teams, brainstorm a list of ethical behaviors you have observed in real life. What characteristics help you and your team members recognize these behaviors as ethical? How do ethical behaviors in nonwork situations transfer to workplace behaviors?

11. (Student response.)

12. service learning

Apply Technology

19. Contact a local employer to find out what their policies are on the use of personal use of communication technology in the workplace. Ask the employer why the policies are in place.

20. Interview a family that has one or more members who telecommutes. Find out the advantages and disadvantages of this arrangement. How does telecommuting affect family life? Prepare a report and share it with the class.

A Measure of Math

21. Conduct a cookie sale. Calculate how much it would cost to produce the cookies. Then decide how much profit you want to make to determine a price. Sell the cookies and donate the profits to a local charity.

22. Imagine your life 10 years from now. Prepare a schedule for one day that balances family, community, and career responsibilities.

Teamwork in Action

23. As a service learning project, recruit a group of students to volunteer to work at a local food pantry or soup kitchen. Write a brief report describing the role teamwork played in accomplishing the tasks you were assigned.

Companion Website

www.g-wlearning.com

At the website, review key terms for this chapter with crossword puzzles, matching exercises, and e-flash cards. Apply facts from the chapter to complete the activities.

Shutterstock
Voluteering to work with a recycling program is one way to contribute to your community.

Part 5 Foods of the World

Study Starters

1. Obtain menus from one type of ethnic restaurant. In a small group, identify menu terms and food items with which you are not familiar. Then help your group prepare a brief presentation on the cuisine featured in your menus.
2. Use words and pictures from magazines and travel brochures to make a collage about international cuisine.

FCCLA: Taking the Lead

Use this section of the text to help you as you create a Hospitality, Tourism, and Recreation STAR Event project. Text information would be especially helpful for a project in the culinary focus area. Descriptions of dishes, regional influences, and cooking techniques provide useful details for developing a menu for a restaurant with an international cuisine. Information in Chapter 28 would also be useful for preparing dining and attraction material for a project in the lodging or tourism focus area.

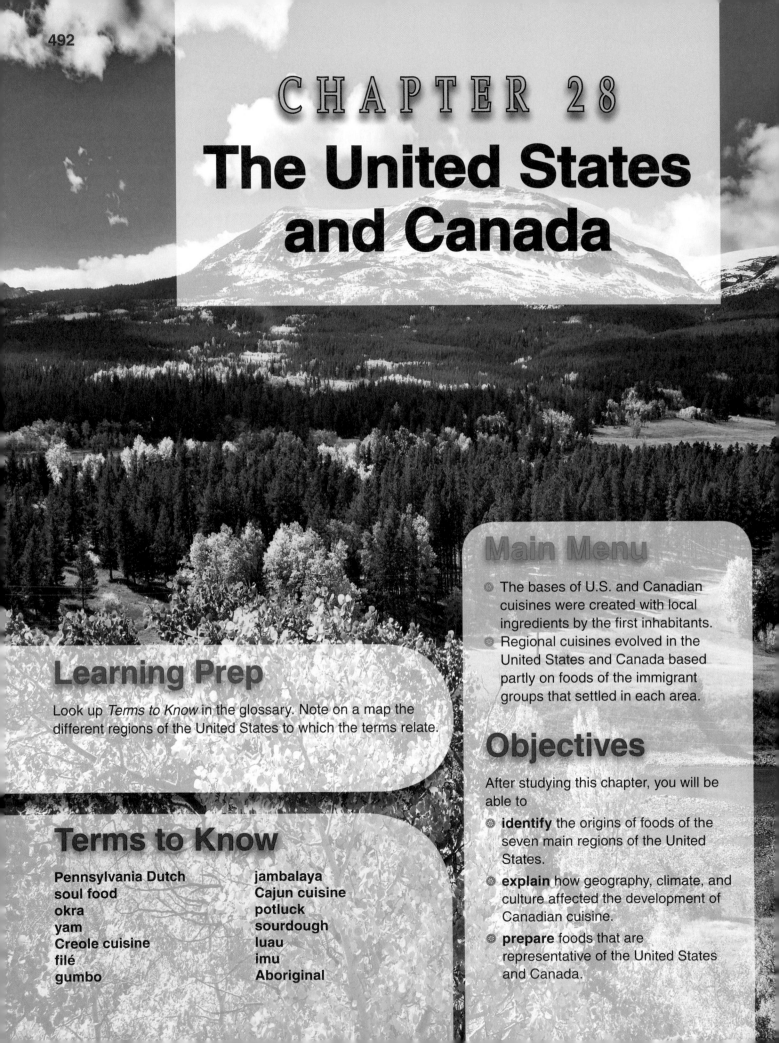

CHAPTER 28
The United States and Canada

Main Menu

- The bases of U.S. and Canadian cuisines were created with local ingredients by the first inhabitants.
- Regional cuisines evolved in the United States and Canada based partly on foods of the immigrant groups that settled in each area.

Learning Prep

Look up *Terms to Know* in the glossary. Note on a map the different regions of the United States to which the terms relate.

Objectives

After studying this chapter, you will be able to

- **identify** the origins of foods of the seven main regions of the United States.
- **explain** how geography, climate, and culture affected the development of Canadian cuisine.
- **prepare** foods that are representative of the United States and Canada.

Terms to Know

Pennsylvania Dutch
soul food
okra
yam
Creole cuisine
filé
gumbo

jambalaya
Cajun cuisine
potluck
sourdough
luau
imu
Aboriginal

Photo courtesy of National Pork Board. For more information about pork, visit TheOtherWhiteMeat.com.

28-1 This Asian stir-fry is just one example of the international heritage that flavors the cuisines of the United States and Canada.

The food customs of the United States and Canada are as diverse as the inhabitants of these nations. People who live in these two countries have roots that stretch around the world. See **28-1**.

A Historical Overview of the United States

Since shortly after Columbus' arrival in North America in 1492, people began leaving their homelands to move to the New World. They had many reasons for making this major life change. Some moved to escape debtor's prison. Others sought religious freedom. Many fled famine and disease. Some came as forced laborers, whereas others came in search of fame and fortune.

The Early Settlers

The British and Spanish were the first permanent colonists in the United States. They established the early settlements of Jamestown and Plymouth (British) and St. Augustine (Spanish). The French who settled in the United States established provinces in Louisiana. A little later, the Dutch arrived and established the New Netherland Colony, which later became New York.

Each group of settlers had to adjust to the climate and geography of the area in which they settled. However, they were able to adapt many of their food customs to take advantage of New World ingredients.

As the colonists' knowledge grew, they added many new dishes to their diets. They used local lobster, crab, and other fish in seafood chowders. They salted pork and preserved beef for use in a variety of meat dishes throughout the winter. They used pumpkin and wild berries to make pies, puddings, and cakes.

Culture and Social Studies

Native American Influence

Food customs of the United States began with the Native Americans. The Native Americans were excellent farmers. Although they cultivated many fruits and vegetables, beans, corn, and squash supplied the basis of their diets. They hunted wild game, gathered nuts and berries, and fished to supplement these staple foods. The high nutritional quality of their diets made the Native Americans healthier than the Europeans of that time.

The life of the first colonists was a struggle for survival. The Native Americans contributed to the success of the first colonial settlements in the New World. They taught colonists how to hunt, fish, and plant crops. Within a few years, the colonists had cleared land, built small groups of homes, and planted simple gardens. The colonists grew new varieties of vegetables and fruits. They learned to eat animals and fish that had been unfamiliar to them.

Discuss

Ask students why they think immigrant groups tended to settle together. *(Being near people who shared their culture and language helped ease their transition in the new land.)*

Strengthening Family Ties

Have students survey their parents to find out how many parents moved to your area from another state or country at some point in their lives. Have students ask when and why the moves took place. Students should also ask if parents remember any food products available where they last lived that are not available in your area. Invite students to share their findings in class.

The Immigrants

As more and more people came to the New World, communities sprang up along the east coast. People also began to settle on more fertile lands farther inland. Many immigrants stayed together in groups and settled in particular regions. Many British, Dutch, German, and French people settled in the Northeast. British, French, and Spanish immigrants settled in the Deep South. Other Spanish settlers chose to live in the Southwest. As the South was settled, the slave trade became established. Africans were brought to the United States to work on Southern plantations.

During the 1800s, many people came to the United States in search of economic opportunities, land, and freedom. Most of these immigrants tended to settle in areas with climates similar to those of their homelands. Chicago, New York, and other large industrial cities attracted large groups of Poles, Irish, French, and Italians. Many of these immigrants worked as unskilled laborers. Scandinavians and Germans traveled to Wisconsin and Minnesota to farm. Chinese, Japanese, and other South Asians settled along the Pacific Coast where they mined and worked on the railroads.

The new immigrants brought their native food customs with them to North America. They adapted their recipes to the foods that were readily available. Italian immigrants made rich pasta sauces from tomatoes, basil, and onions sold by street vendors in New York. The Chinese used chicken, bamboo shoots, and water chestnuts to make their chow mein. The Poles stuffed cabbage leaves with ground beef and tomato sauce to make their traditional cabbage rolls. These citizens of the New World helped create the cuisine eaten in the United States today.

Holidays in the United States

Immigrants brought their holiday traditions to the United States along with their food customs. Many holidays are ethnic celebrations. Therefore, some holidays are celebrated only in regions of the country where certain ethnic groups are found.

One regional holiday in the United States is *Mardi Gras*. It is celebrated in some parts of the South, where French settlers introduced it. Mardi Gras is French for fat Tuesday. It falls on the day before Ash Wednesday, which marks the beginning of Lent in the Christian church. Lent is a 40-day period of prayer and fasting. Mardi Gras began as a last celebration before entering into this solemn time. Festivities often begin the week before the actual holiday. They include colorful parades with floats and marching bands. People wear ornate costumes and masks and attend gala balls and parties.

Cajun favorites featuring locally caught seafood are served at many Mardi Gras parties. A typical menu might include shrimp mold appetizer, crab bisque, and crawfish stew. The classic Mardi Gras dessert is king cake. This is a ring of cinnamon-filled dough decorated with purple, green, and gold sugar. A tiny plastic baby doll is baked inside the cake. Whoever gets the piece of cake containing the doll is supposed to throw the next Mardi Gras party.

Some holidays are observed mainly by people of certain cultures. *Cinco de Mayo* is a cultural holiday observed by Mexican Americans. The name is Spanish for Fifth of May, which is the day of celebration. It marks the victory of severely outnumbered Mexican troops over French troops at the Battle of Puebla in 1862. Parades, music, dancing, and carnivals are all part of the celebration. The day may conclude with Mexican foods, including sweet breads and coffee or hot chocolate flavored with cinnamon. See **28-2**.

Another cultural holiday is *Kwanzaa*. This is a family-centered observance of cultural unity among people of African heritage. The name comes from a Swahili word for first fruits. This weeklong celebration occurs between Christmas and New Year's Day. People use this time to think about their ancestry, family, and community. On the next to the last night of Kwanzaa, families hold the *karamu*, which is a ritual feast. Kwanzaa was developed in the United States. However, this celebration is becoming popular among people of African descent all over the world.

CincinnatiUSA.com

28-2 Dancing and traditional costumes are part of some Cinco de Mayo celebrations.

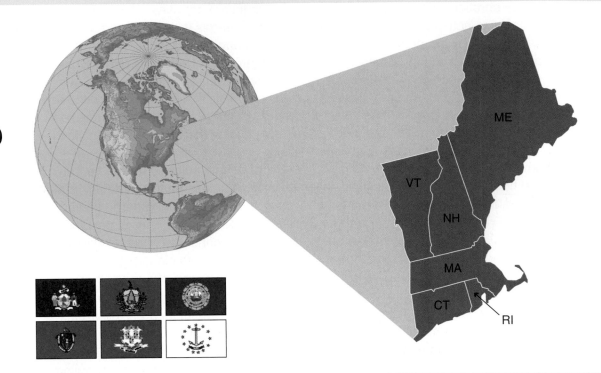

New England

Online Resource

Have students visit the Maine Office of Tourism website. Ask students to find information about a tourist attraction that interests them and write one-paragraph descriptions. Compile all the descriptions into a booklet.

Activity

Ask students to find recipes for Indian bread, Sally Lunn, and johnnycakes. Have them note the types of ingredients used in typical New England recipes.

The British were the first people to settle in the area now called New England. Much of the land was rocky, mountainous, or forested, and winters were long and severe. The early colonists had to work hard to survive.

The character of the people and the land they inhabited shaped the character of New England cooking. Most of the farms that sprang up were isolated and self-sufficient. Seafood and wild game supplemented the foods New Englanders could grow at home. The waters provided lobsters, crabs, clams, and other shellfish, which later became New England specialties. The forests provided wild turkeys, geese, ducks, and pheasants.

Each home had a large fireplace the family used for cooking. New Englanders prepared most foods in iron pots that hung over the fire. They made baked goods in covered Dutch ovens over the coals of the fireplace or in beehive ovens. These baked goods included Indian bread, Sally Lunn, and johnnycakes.

New England cooks used foods that were readily available to create hearty, substantial meals. For instance, they used corn to make corn sticks, Indian pudding, and corn-meal mush. They also used it for succotash (a combination of corn and lima beans).

To survive the long, cold winters, the early New Englanders learned to dry and salt foods to preserve them. They commonly dried beans, corn, and apples. Later, they soaked these foods in water and cooked them until tender. Early New Englanders made baked beans in this way. The Native Americans taught the early settlers how to soak the dried beans overnight. Then cooks would flavor the beans with molasses and salt pork and cook them slowly in big pots.

One-dish meals were popular in New England because they gave the cooks more time to do other tasks. One of the most common one-dish meals of that time, the *New England boiled dinner*, is still popular today. It is a combination of meat (usually corned beef), potatoes, onions, carrots, beets, cabbage, and other available vegetables. The ingredients cook together slowly until they are tender.

The colonists used a variety of meats, seafood, and vegetables to make stews and chowders. Clam chowder was one of the most popular. Many people continue to associate New England cooking with this creamy soup made with potatoes and clams.

From the sap of New England's sugar maple trees came maple syrup, **28-3**. Native Americans taught the New Englanders how to tap the maple trees. After the colonists boiled down the sap, they used the syrup to make cakes, candies, sauces, and puddings. They also used it to flavor baked beans, squash, and other vegetables.

Blueberries, cranberries, blackberries, and other fruits were another important food source. New England cooks gathered the berries and used them to make a variety of nourishing desserts. Two examples are *blueberry mush* (a steamed pudding) and *blueberry grunt* (berries simmered in a thickened sauce and topped with fluffy dumplings).

New Englanders used leftovers in creative ways. For instance, they would grind the leftovers from a boiled dinner and fry them in a large iron skillet. Beets give this dish a red color, which reminded the New Englanders of red flannel underwear worn during the cold winters. Thus, the dish earned the name *red-flannel hash*.

Enrich

Have students investigate the differences between New England clam chowder and Manhattan clam chowder. Have lab groups prepare both types of chowder to taste and compare.

FYI

It takes 35 to 45 gallons of maple sap to make 1 gallon of maple syrup.

State of Vermont—Stephen Goodhue

28-3 Pure maple syrup is a valued food product of the New England states.

New England Menu

New England Clam Chowder

Boiled Dinner

Boston Baked Beans

Brown Bread

Blueberry Muffins

Pumpkin Pie

Tea

New England Clam Chowder

Serves 6

3	slices bacon
2	cans minced clams, 8 ounces each
1	large potato, peeled and cubed
1	medium stalk celery, chopped
½	cup finely chopped onion
¼	teaspoon pepper
⅛	teaspoon thyme
2	cups fat-free milk
1½	cups evaporated fat-free milk

1. In large, heavy saucepan, cook bacon until crisp.
2. Remove bacon to a piece of absorbent paper to drain. Pour excess fat from pan.
3. Drain clams, reserving liquid. Set clams aside.
4. In saucepan used to cook bacon, add potato, celery, onion, pepper, and thyme to liquid from clams. Bring to a boil; simmer covered until vegetables are tender (about 10 minutes).
5. Add milk, evaporated milk, and clams and heat almost to the boiling point. Taste to see if additional seasonings are needed. Serve immediately.

Per serving: 268 cal. (13% from fat), 28 g protein, 30 g carbohydrate, 4 g fat, 54 mg cholesterol, 1 g fiber, 261 mg sodium.

Boiled Dinner

Serves 8

2	pounds corned beef
8	medium-sized beets*
2	pounds green cabbage, cored and quartered
4	medium-sized red potatoes, scrubbed, peeled, and cut in half
8	small carrots, scraped
16	small white onions, peeled and trimmed parsley, chopped

1. Place corned beef in a large kettle of cold water (water should rise at least 2 inches above meat). Bring to a boil and skim off any scum that rises to surface.
2. Cover kettle and reduce heat to slow simmer; cook corned beef 3 to 4 hours or until tender. (Check water level during cooking.)
3. Scrub beets, cut off tops leaving 1 inch and cover with water. Simmer until tender. Cool slightly and slip off skins.
4. Cook cabbage, potatoes, carrots, and onions in salted, simmering water until tender.
5. To serve the dinner, slice the meat and arrange on serving platter. Surround meat with vegetables and top with chopped parsley. Serve with horseradish sauce or mustard.

*One medium can whole beets can be substituted for fresh.

Note: Vegetables (with the exception of the beets) can be added to the corned beef about 30 to 40 minutes before serving as is done in New England. However, some people object to the salty flavor the corned beef gives the vegetables.

Per serving: 417 cal. (39% from fat), 23 g protein, 45 g carbohydrate, 18 g fat, 61 mg cholesterol, 8 g fiber, 229 mg sodium.

Boston Baked Beans

Serves 8

2	cups dried great northern or navy beans*
8	cups water
½	cup molasses
½	cup brown sugar
⅓	cup onions, coarsely chopped
2	teaspoons dry mustard
½	teaspoon pepper
2	slices Canadian bacon

1. Place beans in large saucepan and cover with cold water (water should be at least 2 inches higher than the beans). Bring beans to a boil and let boil 2 minutes.
2. Remove pan from heat and let beans soak about 1 hour.
3. Return pan to heat, bring water to a boil. Reduce heat and slowly simmer beans until almost tender (about 1 to 1½ hours); drain and reserve liquid.
4. Preheat oven to 300°F.
5. Place beans in 2-quart bean pot or heavy casserole.
6. Add enough water to bean liquid to make 2 cups.
7. Combine bean liquid, molasses, brown sugar, onions, dry mustard, and pepper; pour over beans.

8. Cut Canadian bacon into bite-sized pieces and add to beans.
9. Cover pot tightly; bake beans 1½ to 2 hours, stirring occasionally and adding water if needed.
10. Remove cover and bake beans an additional 30 minutes without stirring.

*Three 16-ounce cans of beans can be substituted for dried. Begin recipe preparation with step 4.

Per serving: 266 cal. (4% from fat), 12 g protein, 54 g carbohydrate, 1 g fat, 3 mg cholesterol, 5 g fiber, 142 mg sodium.

Brown Bread

Makes 3 small loaves

1	cup whole wheat flour
1	cup rye flour
1	cup cornmeal
1½	teaspoons baking soda
½	teaspoon salt
¾	cup raisins
2	cups buttermilk
¾	cup dark molasses
2	tablespoons melted shortening

1. Preheat oven to 350°F.
2. Grease three 1-pound coffee cans.
3. In large mixing bowl, combine flours, cornmeal, soda, salt, and raisins; mix well.
4. Combine buttermilk, molasses, and melted shortening; add to dry ingredients mixing well.
5. Pour batter into greased cans filling ⅔ full; cover with foil.
6. Place cans on rack in shallow pan. Place pan in oven. Pour boiling water around cans to depth of 2½ inches.
7. Steam breads 3 hours until toothpick inserted in center comes out clean.
8. Cool 15 minutes and remove from cans. Serve warm.

Per slice: 85 cal. (13% from fat), 2 g protein, 17 g carbohydrate, 1 g fat, 1 mg cholesterol, 2 g fiber, 103 mg sodium.

Blueberry Muffins

Makes 12 muffins

2	cups all-purpose flour
2½	teaspoons baking powder
3	tablespoons sugar
½	teaspoon salt
3	tablespoons shortening
1	egg, well beaten
1	cup fat-free milk
1	cup blueberries

1. Preheat oven to 400°F.
2. Stir flour, baking powder, sugar, and salt together in mixing bowl.
3. Melt shortening; cool.
4. Combine egg and milk; add cooled shortening.
5. Add liquid ingredients to dry ingredients all at once. Stir only until blended. (Batter will be lumpy.)
6. Gently fold in blueberries.
7. Fill greased muffin pans ⅔ full of batter.
8. Bake muffins 20 to 25 minutes or until brown.

Per muffin: 173 cal. (26% from fat), 3 g protein, 22 g carbohydrate, 4 g fat, 23 mg cholesterol, 1 g fiber, 167 mg sodium.

Pumpkin Pie

Makes one 9-inch pie

2	eggs
¾	cup light brown sugar, packed
2	cups canned pumpkin
1½	cups evaporated fat-free milk
1	teaspoon cinnamon
½	teaspoon ground cloves
½	teaspoon ginger
½	teaspoon nutmeg
1	unbaked pastry shell, 9-inch

1. Preheat oven to 450°F.
2. In large mixing bowl, beat eggs slightly; add pumpkin, milk, and spices and mix well.
3. Pour mixture into pastry shell.
4. Bake 10 minutes.
5. Reduce temperature to 300°F and continue baking until knife inserted in center comes out clean, about 40 to 50 minutes.
6. Cool. Serve with whipped cream.

⅙ of pie: 394 cal. (28% from fat), 10 g protein, 63 g carbohydrate, 13 g fat, 94 mg cholesterol, 2 g fiber, 284 mg sodium.

Mid-Atlantic

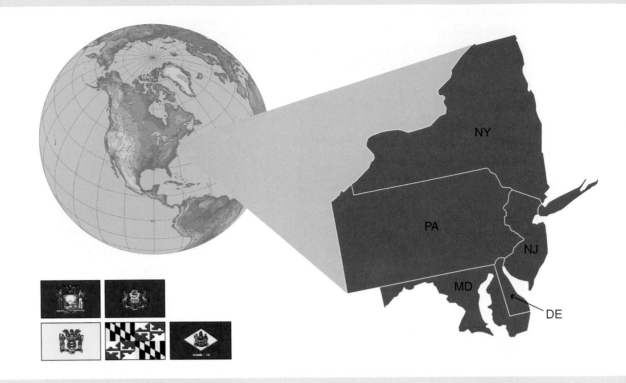

South of New England, the climate is milder. The land in the mid-Atlantic region is rich and fertile, and farming is profitable. New Jersey is a major center of fresh fruit and vegetable production. New Jersey ships apples, peaches, beans, cranberries, tomatoes, onions, asparagus, cucumbers, peas, and melons to many parts of the country.

The mid-Atlantic region was settled by Dutch, German, Swedish, and British immigrants. The Dutch were excellent farmers. They had large vegetable gardens and kept their root cellars well stocked. Many had their own orchards, too.

The Dutch were also excellent bakers. Cookies (koekjes), doughnuts (olykoeks), molasses cake, and gingerbread figures all have Dutch origins, **28-4**. The Dutch also introduced waffles, coleslaw, cottage cheese, and griddle cakes.

2011 Wisconsin Milk Marketing Board

28-4 Gingerbread figures were brought to the United States by Dutch settlers.

The Pennsylvania Dutch

One group of mid-Atlantic settlers, the Pennsylvania Dutch, deserves special mention. The **Pennsylvania Dutch** were a group of German immigrants who settled in the southeast section of Pennsylvania. (The word *Dutch* comes from the word *Deutsch*, which means *German*.) These immigrants came from the Rhine Valley, where they were farmers. When they came to the United States, they were successful in adapting their farming techniques to the soil in Pennsylvania.

The food customs of the Pennsylvania Dutch were very different from those of their neighbors. They developed a style of cooking that was rural, hearty, and inventive. They based it on cooking techniques practiced in the Old World. The thrifty *hausfrau* (housewife) canned, pickled, and dried the produce, meat, and poultry raised on the farm. The Pennsylvania Dutch did not waste anything. They used their thriftiness and ingenuity to create many new dishes. Examples are pickled pigs' feet, blood pudding, *scrapple* (pork combined with cornmeal), smoked beef tongue, stuffed heart, sausages, and bologna.

Soup was one of the most popular dishes. The Pennsylvania Dutch made it from whatever foods were available. Since they were especially skillful in the production of vegetables and poultry, they served vegetable and chicken soups often. *Chicken corn soup* remains a traditional favorite.

Hearty German foods, such as sauerbraten, sauerkraut, liverwurst, and pork, were mainstays of the Pennsylvania Dutch diet. Noodles, dumplings, potato pancakes, and other filling foods were served as accompaniments.

Each meal included seven sweets and seven sours. These usually were in the form of pickled vegetables and fruits, relishes, jams, preserves, salads, and apple butter. Homemakers made all these foods during the summer and stored them in cellars for the winter.

The Pennsylvania Dutch were excellent bakers. Coffee cakes, sticky buns, funnel cakes, crumb cakes, and *shoofly pie* (pastry with a filling made of molasses and brown sugar) are some of their specialties.

Several religious groups, including the Amish and the Mennonites, shared a German heritage with the Pennsylvania Dutch. However, they chose to live in isolated groups. Their isolation, however, helped preserve their hearty homestyle cooking and native crafts. Some small colonies of Amish and Mennonites still exist throughout the country.

Enrich

Have students research average high and low summer and winter temperatures in Maine and compare them with average temperatures in New Jersey. Discuss how the climate of New England compares with the climate of the mid-Atlantic states.

Discuss

Ask students why they think such hearty, filling foods were so common in the diets of the Pennsylvania Dutch. *(These foods gave the Pennsylvania Dutch the energy they needed to do the physical tasks farm life entails.)*

Vocabulary Builder

Shoofly pie allegedly gets its name from bakers having to shoo away the flies when preparing this sweet dessert.

Mid-Atlantic Menu

Stewed Chicken and Dumplings
Buttered Green Beans
Coleslaw
Rye Bread
Shoofly Pie
Coffee

Stewed Chicken and Dumplings

Serves 8

4   skinless chicken breast halves
4   skinless chicken legs and thighs
1   onion, quartered
3   stalks celery, cut in ½-inch slices
3   carrots, diced
½   teaspoon sage
    salt and pepper
    cold water
¼   cup all-purpose flour
1   cup cold fat-free milk

Dumplings:
1¼   cups all-purpose flour
¼   teaspoon salt
2½   teaspoons baking powder
¼   cup shortening
½   cup fat-free milk

1. Wash chicken and place in a large kettle with onion, celery, carrots, sage, and salt and pepper to taste. Add enough cold water to barely cover chicken and vegetables.
2. Cover kettle and bring to a boil over high heat.
3. Reduce heat and simmer 1 hour, until chicken is tender.
4. About 45 minutes after the chicken begins to simmer, start to mix the dumplings. Begin by stirring the flour, salt, and baking powder together into a medium mixing bowl.
5. Cut in shortening with pastry blender or two knives until particles are the size of coarse cornmeal.
6. Add milk, stir with a fork to make a sticky dough.
7. Divide the dough into eighths and drop by spoonfuls onto the chicken (not into the liquid). Allow space between dumplings for them to double in size.
8. Cover pan and continue to simmer chicken for 15 more minutes without lifting the lid.
9. Lift out the dumplings onto a plate.
10. Place chicken on a serving platter.
11. Shake ¼ cup flour with 1 cup cold milk in a small covered container until thoroughly blended.
12. Stir flour mixture into the chicken stock.
13. Heat and stir until stock thickens.
14. Pour thickened stock and vegetables over chicken. Arrange dumplings on top.

Per serving: 331 cal. (24% from fat), 31 g protein, 26 g carbohydrate, 9 g fat, 74 mg cholesterol, 2 g fiber, 298 mg sodium.

Buttered Green Beans

Serves 6

2   pounds fresh green beans*
¾   cup water
    salt
    margarine
    pepper

1. Wash beans under cool running water. Snap off ends; then snap beans in half.
2. Place water and salt in medium saucepan; bring to a boil.
3. Add beans. Return to a boil, then reduce heat and simmer beans gently just until crisp-tender, about 10 to 15 minutes.
4. Drain beans, top with margarine, and season with salt and pepper to taste. Serve immediately.

* Two 10-ounce packages of frozen green beans may be substituted for fresh. Follow package directions for cooking.

Per serving: 47 cal. (36% from fat), 1 g protein, 7 g carbohydrate, 2 g fat, 0 mg cholesterol, 3 g fiber, 202 mg sodium.

Coleslaw

Serves 6 to 8

1	large white cabbage, shredded
2	large carrots, shredded
1	medium green pepper, diced
½	cup evaporated fat-free milk
¾	cup plain nonfat yogurt
1	teaspoon prepared mustard
3	tablespoons lemon juice
1	tablespoon sugar
1	teaspoon celery seed
	salt and pepper

1. Combine vegetables in large mixing bowl.
2. In small bowl, beat together the evaporated milk, yogurt, mustard, lemon juice, sugar, celery seed, and salt and pepper.
3. Pour over vegetables, tossing well.
4. Refrigerate 1 hour before serving.

Per serving: 68 cal. (6% from fat), 4 g protein, 13 g carbohydrate, 1 g fat, 1 mg cholesterol, 2 g fiber, 76 mg sodium.

Rye Bread

Makes 2 loaves

2	cups all-purpose flour
3	tablespoons brown sugar, firmly packed
1½	teaspoons salt
1	teaspoon caraway seeds
½	teaspoon baking soda
2	packages active dry yeast
1	cup buttermilk
¼	cup dark molasses
¼	cup shortening
1	cup water
4 to 4¼	cups rye flour

1. In large mixing bowl, combine all-purpose flour, brown sugar, salt, caraway seeds, baking soda, and dry yeast. Mix well.
2. In small saucepan, heat buttermilk, molasses, shortening, and water until very warm (120°F to 130°F).
3. Add milk mixture to dry ingredients blending at lowest speed of electric mixer until moistened.
4. Beat at medium speed 3 minutes.
5. By hand, stir in enough rye flour to make a stiff dough.

6. Turn out onto lightly floured board or pastry cloth. Knead until smooth and elastic, about 5 minutes.
7. Place in greased bowl, turning once to grease top. Cover with a clean towel; and let rise in warm place until doubled in bulk, 1 to 1½ hours.
8. Punch down.
9. Shape into two round loaves.
10. Place on lightly greased baking sheet. Cover with a clean towel and let rise in a warm place until doubled in bulk, about 1 hour.
11. Bake in a preheated 350°F oven for 45 to 50 minutes or until loaves test done. Cool.

Per slice: 114 cal. (16% from fat), 4 g protein, 21 g carbohydrate, 2 g fat, 0 mg cholesterol, 3 g fiber, 125 mg sodium.

Shoofly Pie

Makes one 9-inch pie

1½	cups all-purpose flour
½	cup margarine
1	cup light brown sugar, packed
1	teaspoon baking soda
1	cup boiling water
½	cup molasses
½	cup honey
1	unbaked pastry shell, 9-inch

1. Preheat oven to 375°F.
2. In large mixing bowl, cut margarine into flour with pastry blender or two knives until mixture resembles small peas.
3. Stir in brown sugar and set aside.
4. Dissolve soda in boiling water. Then add molasses and honey.
5. Pour molasses mixture into pastry-lined pie plate with fluted edge.
6. Sprinkle the flour mixture over the top.
7. Bake pie at 375°F for 10 minutes.
8. Reduce heat to 350°F and continue baking another 25 to 30 minutes or until the filling has set.
9. Cool completely before serving.

⅛ of pie: 507 cal. (33% from fat), 4 g protein, 83 g carbohydrate, 19 g fat, 0 mg cholesterol, 1 g fiber, 407 mg sodium.

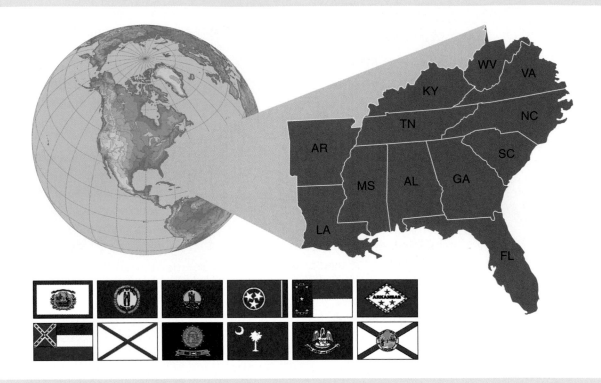

South

Immigrants from France, England, Ireland, Scotland, and Spain settled in the South. Once they were established, they brought African slaves to the United States. The slaves worked on the large plantations and served in the huge mansions.

The mild climate of the South made year-round production of many crops possible. Sugarcane, rice, and peanuts were the most economically important food crops. Southern farmers also grew fruits and vegetables, but on a smaller scale.

The waters and forests of the South were important sources of food. Southerners found catfish, bass, trout, and terrapin (turtle) in rivers and streams. They found crabs, crayfish, oysters, and shrimp in the Gulf waters. Wild game was abundant. Squirrel, goose, and turkey were especially well liked. From these foods evolved the popular *Brunswick stew* (vegetables and game, poultry, or beef cooked together slowly until tender).

Corn is a staple food in the South. Southerners serve it in many ways. At breakfast, they serve corn as hominy or hominy grits. They use cornmeal to make delicious hot breads, such as corn bread and spoon bread. *Spoon bread* is baked in a casserole like a pudding until it is crispy on the outside but still soft in the center.

Two other hot breads, buttermilk biscuits and shortnin' bread, are also Southern specialties. Today, Southern cooks still pride themselves on the tenderness and light-ness of their biscuits.

Pigs and chickens were the most common types of livestock in the South. As a result, pork and chicken played an important part in the region's cuisine. Spareribs, cured ham, fat back, chitterlings, and pigs' feet often appeared on Southern tables. Fried chicken became a Southern specialty, **28-5**.

Rice grew abundantly in the Carolinas. Southern cooks used it in many of their dishes. They often combined rice with beans, meat, or seafood to make economical and nutritious dishes.

Aside from corn, popular vegetables included beans, sweet potatoes, and a variety of greens. Southern cooks often prepared turnip and dandelion greens with pork fat for flavor. Black-eyed peas, grits, and nuts were other staple foods used in Southern cooking. *Hoppin' John* (a combination of black-eyed peas and rice) and pecan pie are two popular dishes made from these staple foods.

Soul Food

Soul food is a distinct cuisine that developed in the South. **Soul food** combines the food customs of African slaves with the food customs of Native Americans and European sharecroppers. It developed around those few foods that were readily available to all three groups of people.

Some plantation owners allowed their slaves to have small gardens. Some slave families were also able to keep a few chickens, but no other domestic animals were allowed. Fishing, however, was allowed, and the slaves could eat all the catfish they were able to catch. Those slaves who worked in the fields received a small amount of meat at harvest time. They also received the less desirable parts of the hogs and cattle. Poor sharecroppers and Native Americans had small gardens and they hunted game animals, such as squirrel, deer, and opossum.

Slaves used the few foods available to them in many creative ways. They mixed leftovers from the plantation house with rice or beans for nutritious and tasty main dishes. The cooks used the cornmeal portions allotted to each family member to make a variety of hot breads and puddings. Batter bread, hush puppies, corn bread, hoecake, and cracklin' corn bread were a few of the most popular ones.

The slaves used all the parts of hogs and cattle discarded by the plantation owners. They cleaned *chitterlings* (the intestines of the hog) and boiled them with spices or dipped them in batter for deep-frying. They even used the hogs' feet, tails, snouts, and ears. Slaves often pickled these parts or boiled them to add to stews, soups, beans, or rice.

Vegetables used in soul food dishes included corn, squash, black-eyed peas, okra, and greens. Corn and squash had been grown in the South by Native Americans for many years. **Okra** is a green, pod-shaped vegetable that was brought to the United States from Africa. Slaves breaded and fried it or added it to soups and stews. Greens, such as spinach, mustard, sorrel, beet tops, collards, turnip, kale, dock, and dandelion, grew wild and in gardens. When cooked with salt pork, bacon, pork shank, pork jowl, or ham bone, they were nutritious and flavorful.

Yams are dark orange tubers that have moist flesh. (They are often confused with sweet potatoes.) Slaves added them to stews, fried them as fritters, and made them into a pudding called *pone*. They also used yams to make the popular *sweet potato pie*.

Creole Cuisine

New Orleans is the home of Creole cuisine. However, people throughout the South enjoy Creole dishes.

Creole cuisine combines the cooking techniques of the French with ingredients of the Africans, Caribbeans, Spanish, and Native Americans. The contributions of each group have come together to give Creole foods a character all their own. For instance,

National Chicken Council/U.S. Poultry & Egg Association

28-5 Although it is served throughout the United States, many would claim the best fried chicken is prepared from Southern recipes.

Enrich

Have students visit a local butcher or supermarket meat department to learn more about the parts of the hog used in the preparation of soul food. Then have them find some interesting recipes using these parts.

Enrich

Have students look up *yam* and *sweet potato*. Ask them to explain why the term *yam* is a misnomer for most vegetables grown in the United States.

For Example...

Thickening gumbo with roux reflects French influence, with filé reflects Choctaw influence, and with okra reflects African influence.

Vocabulary Builder

Have students
compare the terms
Cajun cuisine and
Creole cuisine.

the French contributed *bouillabaisse* (a highly seasoned fish stew), court bouillon, and pastries. The Africans contributed okra, which is used as both a vegetable and a thickening agent in soups and stews. The Spanish contributed tomatoes, red and green peppers, and mixtures of rice, seafood, poultry, and meat. The Choctaw Indians were the first to use filé. (**Filé** is a flavoring and thickening agent made from sassafras leaves, which are dried and ground into a powder.) The addition of red beans, rice, and a variety of fish and seafood native to Louisiana resulted in many unusual and delicious dishes.

Photo courtesy of National Pork Board. For more information about pork, visit
TheOtherWhiteMeat.com.

28-6 Red beans and rice is a classic Creole dish.

Gumbo is a soup that reflects the various cultures of Southern Louisiana. Although recipes vary, meats, poultry, seafood, okra, and other vegetables are common ingredients. Cooks may thicken gumbo with roux, okra, or filé. Families often hand their gumbo recipes down from generation to generation.

Jambalaya is a traditional Creole rice dish. It contains rice; seasonings; and shellfish, poultry, and/or sausage. Some cooks also add tomatoes. Creole cooks use a hot pepper sauce to season both gumbo and jambalaya.

Gumbo, jambalaya, and red beans and rice (a main dish made from red beans simmered with a small amount of meat) are economical. Creole cooks often made these dishes from leftovers. See **28-6**.

Other Creole specialties include beignets, café au lait, café brulot, and pralines. *Beignets* are deep-fried squares of bread dough. Small cafés scattered throughout New Orleans serve them hot with a dusting of powdered sugar. Strong coffee flavored with chicory usually is served with them. *Café au lait* is a beverage made from equal portions of this chicory-flavored coffee and hot milk. *Café brulot* is strong coffee flavored with spices, sugar, citrus peel, and brandy. It often is flamed. Pralines are a sweet, rich candy made with sugar, pecans, and sometimes milk or buttermilk. They are sold in candy shops all over the South.

Culture and Social Studies

Cajun Cuisine

Cajun cuisine is the hearty fare of rural Southern Louisiana. It reflects the foods and cooking methods of the Acadians, French, Native Americans, Africans, and Spanish. (Acadians are French-speaking immigrants from a part of Nova Scotia called Acadia.) Like Creole cuisine, jambalayas and gumbos characterize Cajun cuisine. These dishes are seasoned heavily with hot peppers and other spicy seasonings. Cajun dishes are generally prepared from foods that are commonly available in Southern

Louisiana. Crawfish, okra, rice, pecans, beans, and *andouille* (smoked pork sausage) frequently appear in Cajun recipes. Many dishes center on locally available game and seafood. They are creative combinations of whatever happens to be on hand and are often prepared from leftovers.

Traditional Cajun dishes include chaudin, rice dressing, and tartes douces. *Chaudin* is braised pig stomach stuffed with ground pork, onions, bell peppers, garlic, and diced yams. *Rice dressing* is rice cooked with bits of chicken liver, chicken gizzard, and/or ground pork and seasoned with parsley and onion tops. *Tartes douces* are pies made with a soft, sweet crust and fillings like custard, blackberry, coconut, or sweet potato.

Southern Menu

Southern Fried Chicken
Squash Pudding
Greens with Vinegar and Oil Dressing
Buttermilk Biscuits
Pecan Pie
Chicory Coffee

Southern Fried Chicken

Serves 5

1	3-pound fryer, cut into pieces
½	cup all-purpose flour
1	teaspoon salt
¼	teaspoon pepper
½	cup evaporated fat-free milk
1	egg
	shortening or oil for frying

1. Wash chicken pieces and pat dry with a paper towel.
2. Combine flour, salt, and pepper in a shallow pan.
3. Beat milk and egg together in a pie plate.
4. Dip chicken pieces in seasoned flour, then in milk mixture, then in flour. Set aside until all pieces are coated.
5. In large, heavy skillet, heat shortening or oil until hot but not smoking.
6. Add chicken pieces, a few at a time. Brown all sides, turning occasionally.
7. When all pieces have been browned, return them to the skillet. Reduce heat, cover tightly, and cook chicken until tender, about 30 minutes. Remove cover the last 10 minutes to crisp chicken.

Per serving: 349 cal. (59% from fat), 29 g protein, 6 g carbohydrate, 23 g fat, 135 mg cholesterol, 0 g fiber, 330 mg sodium.

Squash Pudding

Serves 6 to 8

2	cups hot butternut squash, mashed
1½	tablespoons margarine
½	cup sugar
⅓	cup fat -free milk
½	teaspoon salt
1	teaspoon cinnamon
1	teaspoon nutmeg
3	eggs

1. Preheat oven to 325°F.
2. Add margarine to squash; stir until melted.
3. Add sugar, milk, salt, cinnamon, and nutmeg.
4. Beat with an electric or rotary beater until blended.
5. Beat eggs; blend in squash mixture.
6. Pour into a greased 1½-quart casserole.
7. Bake until internal temperature reads 160°F on a thermometer, about 30 minutes.

Per serving: 163 cal. (33% from fat), 4 g protein, 24 g carbohydrate, 6 g fat, 137 mg cholesterol, 2 g fiber, 253 mg sodium.

Greens with Vinegar and Oil Dressing

Serves 8

1	bunch beet tops
1	bunch kale
1	bunch spinach
1	bunch collards
¼	cup water
6	slices bacon, cooked and cut into pieces
1	clove garlic, chopped

1. Clean greens. Trim tough ends and bruised spots. Tear into pieces.
2. Place greens in large saucepan with water, bacon, and garlic.
3. Cover and simmer slowly until tender, about 15 minutes.
4. Drain and serve with vinegar and oil.

Per serving: 77 cal. (65% from fat), 3 g protein, 4 g carbohydrate, 6 g fat, 4 mg cholesterol, 0 g fiber, 143 mg sodium.

Buttermilk Biscuits

Makes about 15 biscuits

2	cups all-purpose flour
1	tablespoon baking powder
½	teaspoon salt
¼	cup shortening
⅔ to ¾	cup buttermilk

1. Preheat oven to 425°F.
2. In large mixing bowl, combine flour, baking powder, and salt.
3. Using a pastry blender or two knives, cut in shortening until mixture resembles small peas.
4. Add buttermilk, stirring gently with fork until soft dough forms.
5. Turn dough out onto lightly floured board. Knead 8 to 10 times.
6. Roll to ½-inch thickness. Cut into rounds with 2-inch biscuit cutter.
7. Place biscuits close together on an ungreased baking sheet.
8. Bake 10 to 12 minutes or until golden brown. Serve hot.

Per biscuit: 97 cal. (34% from fat), 2 g protein, 14 g carbohydrate, 4 g fat, 0 mg cholesterol, 1 g fiber, 147 mg sodium.

Pecan Pie

Makes one 9-inch pie

4	eggs
⅓	cup light brown sugar, packed
¼	cup melted margarine
1¼	cups dark corn syrup
½	teaspoon salt
1½	teaspoons vanilla
1¼	cups chopped pecans
1	unbaked pastry shell, 9-inch

1. Preheat oven to 350°F.
2. In large mixing bowl, beat eggs and brown sugar together until blended.
3. Add melted margarine, corn syrup, salt, vanilla, and chopped pecans and mix thoroughly; pour into unbaked pie shell.
4. Bake until filling is puffed and golden brown, about 35 to 40 minutes.
5. Serve pie slightly warm or cool and top with whipped cream.

⅛ of pie: 426 cal. (56% from fat), 6 g protein, 42 g carbohydrate, 28 g fat, 137 mg cholesterol, 2 g fiber, 388 mg sodium.

Shutterstock

Homemade biscuits are a common food in the Southern region.

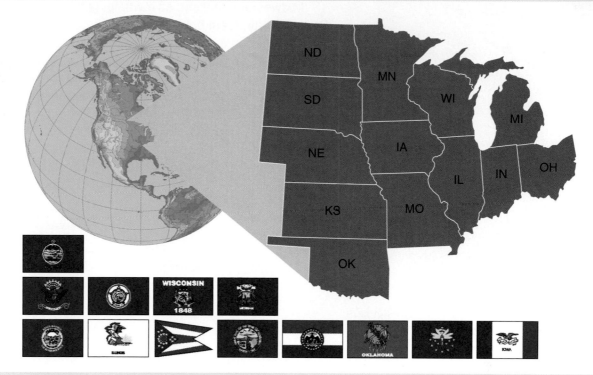

People often call the Midwest the "breadbasket" of the nation. Rich soil, good climate, and advanced farming techniques have made the Midwest one of the world's most agriculturally productive regions. Corn, wheat, and soybeans grow in large enough quantities to be exported to many parts of the world.

Beef, pork, lamb, and poultry are produced in large quantities in the Midwest. Lakes and streams in this region provide a variety of fish. People throughout the United States recognize Wisconsin and Minnesota for their dairy products. Small farms throughout the Midwest grow many kinds of fruits and vegetables.

Fairs, festivals, and picnics are popular in the Midwest. Food plays an important part at these gatherings. Homemade breads, cakes, pies, cookies, jams, and jellies are judged at county and state fairs. Cities and towns in many parts of the Midwest hold festivals centered on apples, pumpkins, strawberries, and other fruits and vegetables.

Buffet dinners and potlucks are traditional gatherings in the Midwest. For a buffet dinner, cooks fill a large table with meat dishes, potatoes, other vegetables, fruits, and baked goods.

A **potluck** is a shared meal to which each person or family brings food for the whole group to eat. These meals get their name from a tradition of hospitality in which a prepared meal would be shared with an unexpected guest. Since the cook did not know the guest was coming, the guest would have to take "the luck of the pot." Potlucks are popular social gatherings with churches, clubs, and family groups.

FYI

Kansas is the leading producer of wheat in the United States. Iowa is the top producer of soybeans and corn.

Reflect

Ask students if they have ever attended a buffet dinner or a potluck. Ask what they do and do not like about these types of meal events.

Photo courtesy of National Pork Board. For more information about pork, visit TheOtherWhiteMeat.com.

28-7 Bratwurst, which reflects the German heritage of many Midwesterners, is popular for summer grilling and Oktoberfest celebrations in the fall.

Midwestern cooking, as a whole, is hearty and uncomplicated. Broiled steak, roast beef, baked and hash brown potatoes, and corn on the cob are staples of the Midwestern diet. Coleslaw, fresh tomatoes from the garden, apple pie, and brownies also belong to the Midwest. Fruit, pancakes, bacon, eggs, and coffee might be served at a filling Midwestern breakfast.

Ethnic foods from immigrants who settled in large Midwestern cities have been added to locally grown foods. Swedish meatballs, Greek moussaka, German bratwurst, Polish sausage, and Italian lasagna have become almost as common as steak and potatoes. See **28-7**.

Midwestern Menu

Broiled Steak

Baked Potatoes

Sautéed Zucchini

Sliced Tomatoes

Warm Whole Wheat Bread

Deep Dish Apple Pie

Milk Coffee

Broiled Steak

Serves 8

2   sirloin steaks, each about 1-inch thick and
       weighing 1 pound, 10 ounces
       salt
       pepper
       garlic powder

1. Preheat broiler.
2. Trim fat from edges of steaks with a sharp knife.
3. Wipe steaks with damp paper towels; place on broiler pan.
4. Broil steaks 2 to 3 inches from the heat until brown.

5. Season with salt, pepper, and garlic powder and turn; finish broiling. Test doneness with a meat thermometer. Medium rare steaks should reach an internal temperature of 145°F in about 18 to 22 minutes. Medium steaks should reach an internal temperature of 160°F in about 20 to 25 minutes.

Per serving: 196 cal. (38% from fat), 29 g protein, 0 g carbohydrate, 8 g fat, 83 mg cholesterol, 0 g fiber, 240 mg sodium.

Baked Potatoes

Serves 6

6   medium baking potatoes
       margarine
       salt
       pepper

1. Preheat oven to 350°F.
2. Scrub potatoes under cold running water.
3. Pierce skins in several places with the tines of a fork.
4. Place potatoes in oven and bake until fork pierces potato easily, about 45 minutes to 1 hour.
5. Remove from oven.
6. Using pot holders, roll potatoes gently between hands for a minute or two.
7. Make a slit in the top of each potato and push gently.

8. Top with margarine, salt, and pepper. If desired, serve potatoes with shredded reduced fat cheese or plain nonfat yogurt and chives.

Per potato: 180 cal. (19% from fat), 3 g protein, 34 g carbohydrate, 4 g fat, 0 mg cholesterol, 3 g fiber, 410 mg sodium.

Sautéed Zucchini

Serves 6

6	small zucchini
2	tablespoons margarine
¾	teaspoon dried dill weed

1. Wash zucchini. Trim and discard ends. Cut into ¼-inch slices.
2. Melt margarine in a skillet. Add zucchini and sauté until crisp-tender (about 5 to 8 minutes), stirring occasionally.
3. Sprinkle with dill weed. Serve immediately.

Per serving: 61 cal. (59% from fat), 2 g protein, 6 g carbohydrate, 4 g fat, 0 mg cholesterol, 2 g fiber, 51 mg sodium.

Whole Wheat Bread

Makes 2 loaves

5½ to 6 cups all-purpose flour
2	cups whole wheat flour
3	tablespoons sugar
2	teaspoons salt
2	packages active dry yeast
2	cups fat-free milk
¾	cup water
¼	cup softened margarine

1. On a large sheet of waxed paper, combine all-purpose and whole wheat flours.
2. In large mixing bowl, combine 2½ cups flour mixture, sugar, salt, and dry yeast.
3. In small saucepan, combine milk, water, and margarine. Heat over low until very warm (120°F to 130°F). Margarine does not need to completely melt.
4. Gradually add warm liquids to dry ingredients; beat at medium speed of electric mixer two minutes.
5. Add 1 cup flour mixture and beat on high speed another 2 minutes, scraping bowl occasionally.
6. Stir in enough additional flour mixture to make a stiff dough.

7. Turn dough out onto lightly floured board or pastry cloth. Knead until smooth and elastic, about 8 to 10 minutes.
8. Cover with plastic wrap and then a towel. Let rest 20 minutes.
9. Divide dough in half. Roll each half into a rectangle.
10. Shape into loaves and place in two greased 9-by-5-inch loaf pans.
11. Brush tops with oil.
12. Cover with plastic wrap and refrigerate 2 to 24 hours.
13. When ready to bake, remove dough from refrigerator; let stand 10 minutes.
14. Using a greased toothpick, prick any bubbles that may have formed.
15. Bake bread at 400°F about 40 minutes or until loaves are golden and sound hollow when tapped with knuckles.
16. Remove bread from pans and cool thoroughly before storing.

Per slice: 134 cal. (12% from fat), 4 g protein, 25 g carbohydrate, 2 g fat, 0 mg cholesterol, 2 g fiber, 159 mg sodium.

Deep Dish Apple Pie

Serves 9

1	cup sugar
½	cup light brown sugar, packed
½	cup all-purpose flour
1	teaspoon cinnamon
¾	teaspoon nutmeg
2	tablespoons lemon juice
12	cups sliced, pared tart apples
2	tablespoons margarine, cut into chunks

pastry for a single-crust, 9-inch pie

1. Preheat oven to 425°F.
2. In large mixing bowl, combine sugars, flour, cinnamon, and nutmeg; mix well.
3. Sprinkle lemon juice over apples. Toss to coat.
4. Stir sugar mixture into apples.
5. Pour fruit into ungreased 9-inch square baking dish.
6. Dot with margarine.
7. Roll pastry into a 10-inch square and place over top of filling.
8. Fold edges of pastry under to fit just inside baking dish. Make steam vents.
9. Bake until juice is bubbly and apples are tender, about 1 hour.

Per serving: 366 cal. (22% from fat), 2 g protein, 72 g carbohydrate, 9 g fat, 0 mg cholesterol, 4 g fiber, 165 mg sodium.

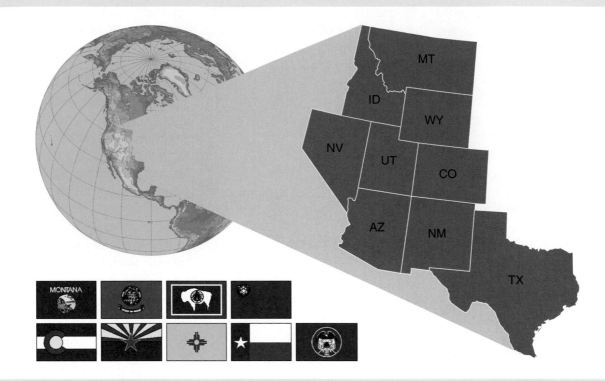

West and Southwest

Enrich

Have students investigate the population density of the states of the West and Southwest.

Vocabulary Builder

The term *barbecue* comes from the American Spanish word *barbacoa*, which is the name of a structure that was used to hold meat over a fire.

Discuss

Ask students how movies and television have influenced the way people in other parts of the United States view the West and Southwest.

The western part of the United States is a land of contrasts. Abandoned mining towns, desolate deserts, sprawling ranches, mountains, plateaus, and oil fields make up much of the landscape.

The climate of the Southwest is hot and sunny, so many fruits and vegetables grow year-round. Texas produces large quantities of grapefruit, oranges, and strawberries. Farmers in the Rio Grande valley grow early season melons, lettuce, and other fruits and vegetables. Refrigerated trucks transport this fresh produce to all parts of the United States.

Westerners tend to eat simply. Their diets are based on locally produced meat, game, and farm products. These staples are flavored with ingredients introduced by various groups to create the characteristic cuisine of this region.

Beef plays an important part in Western cooking. Western cooks grill, spit barbecue, and pit barbecue. Depending on the occasion, they might even roast a whole steer at one time. People in this region often baste their meat with a spicy tomato-based sauce during grilling.

Lamb is also quite popular in some parts of the West. It usually is roasted or stewed. In remote areas, wild game accounts for quite a bit of the meat in the diet. Antelope, rabbit, deer, and pheasant are among the game animals used for meat.

Native Americans, Spaniards, and Mexicans shaped the development of Southwestern cuisine. The foods of Native Americans in this region included corn, squash, and beans. To these, the Spanish added cattle, sheep, saffron, olive oil, and anise. The Aztecs of Mexico introduced red and green peppers.

Many foods from across the Rio Grande made their way into Southwestern cuisine. Foods like tortillas, tostadas, tacos, tamales, and sopapillas all have Mexican origins. *Tamales* are a mixture of cornmeal and peppered ground meat that is wrapped in corn husks and steamed. *Sopapillas* are sweet fried pastries.

Culture and Social Studies

Cowboy Influence on Southwestern Cuisine

The cattle introduced by the Spanish eventually developed into the longhorn breed. They roamed the plains from Texas to California and north into the Dakotas. Long cattle drives ended at the railroad yards where the cattle were shipped east. Here, stories of the cowboy and the chuck wagon originated.

Beef has always been an important staple food in the Southwest. Trail cooks used the tongue, liver, sweetbreads, and heart of a freshly slaughtered steer to make *son-of-a-gun stew*, a favorite of the cowboys. They often served beans and homemade biscuits with the spicy stew. They used chunks of beef in chili, chuck wagon beans, and many other filling dishes.

Although some people think of chili as a Mexican dish, Texans claim to have originated it. They made the first chili with cubes of beef, peppers, and seasonings. It did not include beans.

Courtesy of the Beef Checkoff Program

Traditional Texas chili is made with chunks of beef in a rich, pepper-seasoned tomato base.

Southwestern Menu

Nachos
Barbecued Beef Short Ribs
Three Bean Salad
Tossed Greens with Ranch Dressing
Mexican Corn Bread
Sopapillas
Coffee

Nachos

Makes 24 appetizers

   cooking spray
6   corn tortillas
¼   pound sharp Cheddar cheese, grated
3   jalapeno peppers, sliced
½   cup light sour cream

1. Coat a baking sheet with cooking spray.
2. Cut tortillas into quarters and spread on prepared baking sheet.
3. Bake at 350°F for 10 minutes, or until golden and crispy.

4. Remove baking sheet from oven. Sprinkle tortilla wedges with grated cheese and top each with a jalapeno slice.
5. Place pan under broiler and broil just until cheese melts.
6. Top each nacho with a teaspoon of sour cream. Serve immediately.

Per nacho: 36 cal. (50% from fat), 2 g protein, 3 g carbohydrate, 2 g fat, 6 mg cholesterol, 0 g fiber, 33 mg sodium.

Barbecued Beef Short Ribs

Serves 6

3   pounds beef short ribs, cut into serving-sized pieces
1½ cups tomato sauce
1   teaspoon beef bouillon granules
⅓   cup red wine vinegar
¼   cup brown sugar, firmly packed
2   tablespoons Worcestershire sauce
1½ teaspoons garlic salt
1½ teaspoons prepared mustard
2   lemons, sliced thinly
1   medium onion, sliced thinly

1. Preheat oven to 350°F.
2. Place short ribs in a deep roasting pan.
3. In a small bowl, combine tomato sauce, bouillon granules, red wine vinegar, brown sugar, Worcestershire sauce, garlic salt, and prepared mustard.

4. Pour sauce over ribs; place lemon and onion slices over sauce.
5. Bake ribs, covered, until tender, 1½ to 2 hours.
6. Serve ribs with sauce.

Per serving: 304 cal. (41% from fat), 27 g protein, 19 g carbohydrate, 14 g fat, 75 mg cholesterol, 2 g fiber, 456 mg sodium.

Three Bean Salad

Serves 6 to 8

1½   cups canned red kidney beans, drained
1   cup canned green beans, drained
1   cup canned chickpeas, drained
½   cup finely chopped onion
¼   teaspoon garlic powder
1½   tablespoons chopped parsley
2   small green peppers, seeded and chopped
½   teaspoon salt
     dash pepper
⅓   cup red wine vinegar
1   teaspoon sugar
⅓   cup vegetable oil

1. Using a strainer or colander, rinse drained beans and chickpeas under cold running water; drain and rinse beans again. Pat beans dry with paper towels.
2. In a large bowl, combine beans, chickpeas, onion, garlic powder, parsley, green pepper, salt, and pepper; mix well.
3. In small bowl, combine vinegar, sugar, and oil.
4. Pour dressing over beans and toss.
5. Let salad stand in refrigerator for an hour before serving.

Per serving: 171 cal. (50% from fat), 5 g protein, 17 g carbohydrate, 10 g fat, 0 mg cholesterol, 5 g fiber, 318 mg sodium.

Tossed Greens with Ranch Dressing

Serves 6

¾   cup plain nonfat yogurt
1½   teaspoons prepared mustard
1½   teaspoons lemon juice
1   tablespoon chopped green onion (tops and bottoms)
1   tablespoon chives
5 to 6 cups assorted salad greens

1. In small bowl, combine yogurt, mustard, lemon juice, onion, and chives.
2. Cover and refrigerate dressing until well chilled.
3. Clean salad greens and tear into bite-sized pieces.
4. When ready to serve, place greens in large salad bowl. Toss with dressing and serve immediately.

Per serving: 33 cal. (17% from fat), 3 g protein, 5 g carbohydrate, 1 g fat, 2 mg cholesterol, 1 g fiber, 60 mg sodium.

Mexican Corn Bread

Serves 8

1   cup cornmeal
1   cup all-purpose flour
1   cup buttermilk
¾   teaspoon baking soda
¼   teaspoon salt
½   cup onion, chopped
2   eggs, beaten
2   tablespoons cooking oil
1   can cream-style corn, low sodium
½   cup green pepper, chopped
¼   pound Cheddar cheese, grated

1. Preheat oven to 350°F.
2. In medium bowl, combine all ingredients except cheese.
3. Pour half the batter in a 2½-quart casserole.
4. Cover with half the grated Cheddar cheese.
5. Add the other half of the batter and cover with the remaining cheese.
6. Bake until corn bread is golden brown and tests done, about 40 minutes.

Per serving: 219 cal. (41% from fat), 9 g protein, 26 g carbohydrate, 10 g fat, 69 mg cholesterol, 4 g fiber, 334 mg sodium.

Sopapillas

Makes about four dozen pastries

2   cups all-purpose flour
2½   teaspoons baking powder
½   teaspoon salt
1   tablespoon shortening
½   cup lukewarm water
     shortening or oil for frying

1. In large mixing bowl, stir together flour, baking powder, and salt.
2. Cut in shortening until mixture resembles coarse cornmeal.
3. Add water gradually, stirring with a fork until dough clings together.
4. Turn dough out onto lightly floured board or pastry cloth. Knead until smooth.
5. Divide dough in half. Let rest for 10 minutes.
6. Roll each half into a 10-by-12-inch rectangle about ⅛-inch thick.
7. Cut into 2-inch squares.
8. In deep fryer or large saucepan, heat shortening or oil until it reaches 375°F.
9. Add sopapillas, a few at a time. Fry about ½ minute on each side.
10. Serve warm with butter and honey or sprinkle with confectioner's sugar.

Per sopapilla: 31 cal. (41% from fat), 1 g protein, 4 g carbohydrate, 1 g fat, 0 mg cholesterol, 0 g fiber, 39 mg sodium.

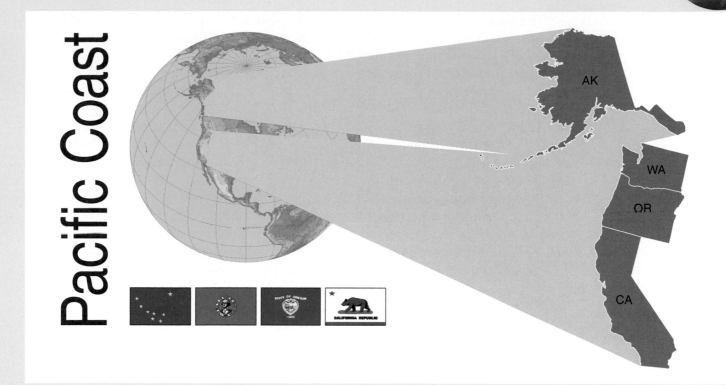

Pacific Coast

The Pacific Coast includes the states of California, Oregon, Washington, and Alaska. These diverse states vary widely in geography, climate, culture, and food customs.

Most parts of California have rich, fertile soil; a warm, sunny climate; and adequate rainfall. Fruits and vegetables of all kinds grow in abundance. Avocados, papayas, pomegranates, dates, Chinese cabbage, kale, and okra are common, as are oranges, grapefruit, lettuce, and tomatoes.

The ocean and inland lakes provide a bounty of fish and shellfish. Shad, tuna, salmon, abalone, lobsters, crabs, shrimp, and oysters are especially popular.

Few rules or traditions hamper California-style cuisine. They might simply broil salmon steaks and top them with a fresh dill sauce. However, more unusual combinations, such as crab and artichoke hearts or chicken and anchovies, are also popular.

Many of the foods that are part of California's cuisine are also available in Oregon and Washington. Many fruits, including peaches, apples, apricots, strawberries, raspberries, blackberries, blueberries, and boysenberries, grow in Washington and Oregon. Other fruits and vegetables are shipped there from California.

Steaks, chops, and other standard fare of the United States make up much of the diet of the Pacific Northwest. These foods are supplemented by wild game, fish, and seafood. Dungeness crabs, butter clams, Columbia River salmon, and Olympia oysters are especially popular.

Cooking techniques of all the Pacific states are, for the most part, simple. They take advantage of the natural flavors and colors of the foods. Cooks usually bake or broil fresh fish and shellfish. They serve vegetables raw in large salads or cooked just until crisp-tender. They often serve fresh fruits for dessert. See **28-8**.

Enrich

Have each student write a report about the annual yield, growing conditions, and uses of one type of fruit or vegetable grown in California. Have them include recipes for preparing their chosen items.

Courtesy of the Idaho Potato Commission

28-8 Fresh salmon, garnished with crisp-tender vegetables and thin potato wafers, typifies the use of natural flavors and colors found in Pacific Coast cooking.

The people who settled the Pacific Coast influenced California's cuisine (and to a lesser extent that of Oregon and Washington). From the Far East came Chinese, Japanese, and Koreans, and from the South Pacific came Polynesians. Many of these immigrants worked as cooks, thus contributing native foods and dishes. Chop suey, for example, was supposedly invented in California by a Chinese cook. He named the dish *chop suey*, which means everything chopped up.

The Mexicans who settled in Southern California brought native dishes with them. Tacos, tamales, enchiladas, guacamole, chili, and refried beans are all popular in this area of the state. The Spanish brought a type of stew called *cocido* (a mixture of vegetables, beef, lamb, ham, fowl, and a sausage called chorizo).

The prospectors who flocked to the Pacific states in search of gold brought sourdough with them. **Sourdough** is a dough containing active microscopic yeast plants. It is used as a leavening agent. The prospectors made sourdough by mixing together flour, water, and salt. They exposed the mixture to the air to absorb yeast cells. Then they added the dough to flour, water, and other available ingredients to make a variety of baked products. They always kept a small amount of the dough after each baking to serve as a starter for the next batch. They replenished the starter by adding more flour and water.

Only that part of Alaska that lies within the Arctic region has the long, frigid winters many people associate with the state. Farther south, the climate is more mild, and vegetable, grain, and dairy farms dot the countryside.

Caribou sausage and reindeer steak are Alaskan specialties. Alaskans also enjoy rabbit and bear hunted in the wilderness. The icy, clear waters of the Pacific Ocean provide Alaskan king crab. Glacier-fed lakes and streams provide delicious salmon and trout.

Alaskan cooks use the blueberries, huckleberries, and cranberries that grow wild to make pies and sauces. Other Alaskan specialties include fiddlehead ferns (young leaves of certain ferns eaten as greens), raw rose hips (the ripened false fruit of the rosebush), and cranberry catsup.

Pacific Coast Menu

Salmon Steaks with Dill Sauce
New Potatoes and Peas
Avocado Salad
Sourdough Bread
Blackberry Buckle
Iced Tea

Salmon Steaks with Dill Sauce

Serves 6

1	teaspoon dehydrated minced onion
1	teaspoon chicken bouillon granules
½	tablespoon lemon juice
1	teaspoon dill weed
2	cups water
3	salmon steaks (about ½ pound each)
2	tablespoons all-purpose flour
¾	cup evaporated fat-free milk
¼	cup plain nonfat yogurt
2	teaspoons dill

1. In large skillet, combine onion, bouillon granules, lemon juice, dill weed, and water. Bring to a boil.
2. Add salmon steaks. Reduce heat and cover pan tightly. Simmer steaks over low heat about 8 to 10 minutes or until fish flakes easily with a fork.
3. Remove salmon to a heated platter and keep warm. Reserve ¼ cup poaching liquid.
4. Shake flour and evaporated milk in a small covered container until thoroughly blended.
5. Pour flour mixture into the skillet; add reserved poaching liquid.
6. Cook sauce over low heat, stirring constantly, until smooth and bubbly.
7. Remove from heat and quickly stir in yogurt and dill.
8. Pour sauce over salmon steaks and serve immediately.

Per serving: 306 cal. (44% from fat), 33 g protein, 7 g carbohydrate, 15 g fat, 98 mg cholesterol, 0 g fiber, 299 mg sodium.

New Potatoes and Peas

Serves 5 to 6

1½ pounds new potatoes (or small red skinned potatoes)
1¾ cups fresh or frozen peas
    margarine
    salt and pepper

1. Carefully scrub potatoes.
2. With vegetable peeler or paring knife, remove one thin strip of peel from around the center of each potato.
3. Place potatoes in large saucepan.
4. Cover with cold, lightly salted water. Bring to a boil.
5. Reduce heat and simmer potatoes until tender, about 20 to 25 minutes.
6. About 15 to 20 minutes before you are ready to serve (a little less if frozen peas will be used), shell and wash peas.
7. Bring a small amount of salted water to a boil.
8. Add peas and return water to a boil.
9. Reduce heat and simmer peas, covered, 15 to 20 minutes or until tender. (Check package directions for cooking time for frozen peas.)
10. Drain both potatoes and peas.
11. Toss together with margarine and sprinkle with salt and pepper. Serve immediately.

Per serving: 179 cal. (12% from fat), 5 g protein, 35 g carbohydrate, 2 g fat, 0 mg cholesterol, 5 g fiber, 82 mg sodium.

Avocado Salad

Serves 8

1   large pink grapefruit (or 1 cup canned grapefruit sections)
2   large navel oranges
1   cup green grapes
½   cup pomegranate seeds (optional)
4   cups mixed salad greens
2   avocados
⅓   cup walnuts, chopped
¾   cup low-fat French dressing

1. Section grapefruit and oranges; set aside.
2. Wash grapes and drain well.
3. Remove seeds from pomegranate; set aside.
4. In large salad bowl or on individual salad plates, arrange salad greens. Top with orange and grapefruit sections.
5. Peel and slice avocados. Arrange avocado slices over citrus fruits.
6. Sprinkle with grapes, pomegranate seeds, and walnuts.
7. Serve with French dressing.

Per serving: 167 cal. (54% from fat), 5 g protein, 16 g carbohydrate, 11 g fat, 1 mg cholesterol, 3 g fiber, 27 mg sodium.

Sourdough Bread

Makes 3 loaves

Sourdough starter:
3½ cups bread flour
1   tablespoon sugar
1   package active dry yeast
2   cups warm water

Sourdough bread:
5 to 6 cups all-purpose flour
1   package active dry yeast
3   tablespoons sugar
1¼ teaspoons salt
¾   cup fat-free milk
¼   cup water
2   tablespoons margarine
1½ cups sourdough starter

1. In large bowl or crock, prepare starter by combining flour, sugar, and yeast.
2. Gradually add warm water, beating until smooth.
3. Cover starter tightly and let stand in a warm place for 2 days.
4. When ready to prepare bread, combine 2½ cups flour, yeast, sugar, and salt in a large mixing bowl.
5. Heat milk, water, and margarine until very warm (120°F to 130°F). Margarine does not need to completely melt.
6. Gradually add milk mixture and sourdough starter to dry ingredients. Beat 2 minutes at medium speed, scraping bowl occasionally. Then beat 2 more minutes at high speed.
7. Add enough additional flour to form a stiff dough.
8. Turn out onto a lightly floured board or pastry cloth and knead dough until smooth and elastic, about 8 to 10 minutes.
9. Cover dough with a clean towel and let rise in a warm place until doubled in bulk, about 1 hour.

10. Punch down and divide dough into three equal parts.
11. Shape each into a round loaf.
12. Place loaves on lightly greased baking sheet and slash tops with sharp knife.
13. Cover with a clean towel and let rise in a warm place until doubled in bulk, about 1 hour.
14. Bake at 400°F for about 25 minutes or until loaves sound hollow when lightly tapped with the knuckles.
15. Remove loaves from pans and place on cooling racks.

Per slice: 100 cal. (8% from fat), 3 g protein, 20 g carbohydrate, 1 g fat, 0 mg cholesterol, 1 g fiber, 85 mg sodium.

Blackberry Buckle

Serves 9

¼	cup margarine
½	cup sugar
1	egg, well beaten
1	cup all-purpose flour
1½	teaspoons baking powder
⅛	teaspoon salt
⅓	cup fat-free milk
1	teaspoon vanilla
2	cups blackberries

Topping:

¼	cup sugar
2	tablespoons margarine
2	tablespoons all-purpose flour
¼	teaspoon cinnamon

1. Preheat oven to 375°F.
2. In medium mixing bowl, cream margarine and sugar until light and fluffy.
3. Add egg and beat well.
4. Sift together flour, baking powder, and salt. Add vanilla to milk.
5. Add liquid and dry ingredients alternately to creamed mixture, beginning and ending with dry ingredients.
6. Pour batter into a greased and floured 9-by-9-inch pan. Cover with blackberries.
7. In small bowl, combine sugar, margarine, flour, and cinnamon.
8. Sprinkle topping over blackberries.
9. Bake buckle for 40 minutes or until cake tests done.
10. Serve warm with whipped cream or ice cream.

Per serving: 221 cal. (36% from fat), 3 g protein, 33 g carbohydrate, 9 g fat, 32 mg cholesterol, 2 g fiber, 183 mg sodium.

FCVB
Blueberries are just one type of wild berry that grows in Alaska.

Hawaiian Islands

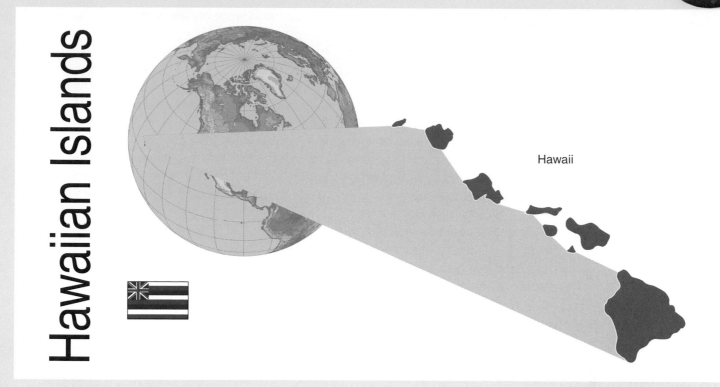

Hawaii

The Hawaiian Islands are much more than a tourist's paradise. They have a rich history and colorful culture. They also have beautiful scenery and delicious food.

Historians believe Hawaii's first settlers were Polynesians from other Pacific islands. After their arrival, Hawaii was isolated from the rest of the world for many years. Although no written records exist, the Hawaiians have a rich heritage of songs and stories.

One of the outstanding figures in Hawaiian history is Kamehameha. Kamehameha eventually captured all of the islands and became king. He was able to establish order and peace throughout the islands.

Christian missionaries and European traders came to Hawaii in the 1800s. Some enterprising foreigners began large sugar plantations. The increasing numbers of Europeans slowly weakened the traditional monarchy. It finally ended with the death of Kamehameha V. Then, in 1898, the United States annexed Hawaii. Hawaii became a state in 1959.

During the last century, Hawaii has grown rapidly. Today, pineapple, sugarcane, and tourism are Hawaii's three largest industries. See **28-9**.

The traditional Hawaiian diet was not highly varied. It consisted mainly of *poi*, a smooth paste made from the starchy root of the taro plant. The Hawaiians also ate *limu*, or seaweed, as a relish. Their main sources of protein were the numerous varieties of fish they harvested from the waters surrounding the Islands.

The early Hawaiians had some interesting food customs. Unlike many cultures, in the Hawaiian culture men typically prepared the food. Men and women were

Shutterstock

28-9 Hawaiian pineapple fields produce the sweet, delicious fruit that is so popular in this tropical island state.

not permitted to eat at the same table. Their foods were not allowed to be prepared in the same oven, either.

Today, most Hawaiians eat three meals a day and have adopted food customs of the mainland. Breakfast may consist of fruit, cereal, eggs, and coffee. However, lunch and dinner may incorporate more traditional Hawaiian foods. Poi, fish, and seaweed may be a typical noon meal. These foods may also be served for dinner, along with a vegetable and a dessert, such as baked bananas.

Throughout history, various groups of people who came to Hawaii each contributed different foods. The first Polynesians are thought to have brought coconuts and *breadfruit* (a round, starchy fruit). European traders are believed to have introduced chicken and pork. The missionaries brought the stews, chowders, and corn dishes of their native New England. Curries reflect Indian influence.

Sugar plantation owners imported large groups of Chinese workers to labor in the fields. The Chinese brought rice, bean sprouts, Chinese cabbage, soybeans, snow peas, and bamboo shoots. They also introduced the stir-fry technique for cooking foods quickly over high heat.

A number of Japanese immigrated to the Hawaiian Islands. They brought with them a variety of rice and fish dishes and pickled foods.

Contributions from all these groups led to the amazing variety visitors find in Hawaiian markets today. Water chestnuts, watercress, squash, and lotus root are just a few of the many vegetables sold. Papayas, mangoes, and pineapples are among the many locally grown fruits. Lobsters, crabs, opihi (a clamlike mollusk), oysters, shrimp, tuna, snapper, and salmon come from the bounty of the surrounding waters. Other popular items are fresh *tofu* (bean curd), soybean cakes, Japanese fish cake, Korean kim chee, and persimmon tea.

The native Hawaiians held lavish feasts on special occasions. **Luaus** are elaborate outdoor feasts that are still popular in the islands today. At these feasts, kalua puaa is often served as a main course. This is a whole, young pig that is dressed, stuffed, and cooked in a pit called an **imu**. The imu is lined with hot rocks covered with banana leaves. The dressed pig is stuffed with hot rocks and placed on a wire rack. More leaves are placed over the top of the imu followed by more hot rocks and earth. Bananas, sweet potatoes, and meat or seafood dishes wrapped in leaves may be roasted with the pig. After several hours, the pig and other foods are dug from the pit and are ready to serve.

No traditional Hawaiian meal would be complete without poi. Other Hawaiian foods that may be served at a luau include *kamano lomi*. This is salted salmon that is mashed with tomatoes and green onions. *Haupia* is a pudding made of milk, sugar, cornstarch, and grated fresh coconut. A variety of fresh fruits, macadamia nuts, and kukui nuts may be served along with the haupia for dessert.

Musical entertainment, singing, and dancing usually accompany a luau. Guests often join in the festivities. See **28-10**.

Shutterstock
28-10 Hula dancing, one of Hawaii's rich cultural traditions, is often part of the entertainment at a luau.

Hawaiian Menu

Shrimp Curry

Rice

Spinach with Evaporated Milk

Banana Biscuits

Tropical Fruit Medley

Coffee

Per serving: 369 cal. (32% from fat), 24 g protein, 39 g carbohydrate, 13 g fat, 167 mg cholesterol, 3 g fiber, 383 mg sodium.

Shrimp Curry

Serves 8

1½	pounds fresh shrimp*
1	tablespoon margarine
2	finely chopped green onions
1	teaspoon grated fresh ginger root*
3	tablespoons flour
1	cup cold fat-free milk
1½	cups coconut milk*
½	teaspoon salt
2 to 3	teaspoons curry powder
6	cups cooked brown rice

1. Clean, peel, and devein the shrimp. Set aside.
2. Melt margarine in a skillet over medium-high heat.
3. Add onion and ginger root. Sauté 2 to 3 minutes until onion is tender.
4. Shake flour and milk in a small, tightly covered container until thoroughly blended.
5. Reduce heat to low. Add flour mixture to skillet. Cook sauce, stirring constantly, until smooth and bubbly.
6. When sauce begins to thicken, stir in coconut milk, salt, and curry powder.
7. Cover and allow mixture to simmer over low heat for 10 minutes.
8. Add shrimp. Continue simmering just until shrimp are cooked through, about 5 minutes.
9. Serve over rice. Pass small dishes of several of the following accompaniments: shredded coconut, finely chopped green pepper, finely chopped green onion, pineapple chutney, and/or orange marmalade.

*You can substitute 1½ pounds cooked boneless, skinless chicken breast cut into bite-sized pieces for the shrimp. You can use 1½ teaspoons ground ginger in place of the fresh ginger root. If fresh or canned coconut milk is not available, combine 1½ cups shredded packaged coconut with 1½ cups fat-free milk in a small saucepan. Allow coconut to soak for 20 minutes. Then simmer over low heat for 10 minutes. Allow mixture to cool. Then strain through two thicknesses of cheesecloth, squeezing out as much milk as possible.

Spinach with Evaporated Milk

Serves 8

2	pounds fresh spinach
½	teaspoon salt
1	tablespoon margarine
¼	cup water
¼	cup fat-free evaporated milk

1. Wash spinach thoroughly and remove stems.
2. Place spinach, salt, margarine, water, and evaporated milk in a large nonstick saucepan. Cover and cook over medium heat until the spinach begins to wilt.
3. Uncover and cook until spinach is tender, stirring frequently. Serve immediately.

Per serving: 43 cal. (42% from fat), 4 g protein, 5 g carbohydrate, 2 g fat, 0 mg cholesterol, 3 g fiber, 255 mg sodium.

Banana Biscuits

Makes about 15 biscuits

1½	cups all-purpose flour
2	teaspoons baking powder
2	teaspoons sugar
½	teaspoon salt
1	cup mashed bananas
3	tablespoons shortening
¼	cup fat-free milk
1	egg, beaten

1. Preheat oven to 425°F.
2. In a large mixing bowl, combine flour, baking powder, sugar, and salt.
3. In a smaller bowl, thoroughly combine mashed bananas with shortening.
4. Add banana mixture to flour mixture. Using a pastry blender or two knives, cut in bananas until mixture resembles small peas.
5. Combine milk with beaten egg. Gently stir liquids into flour mixture with a fork until a soft dough forms.
6. Turn dough out onto lightly floured board. Knead 8 to 10 times.
7. Roll to ½-inch thickness. Cut into rounds with a 2-inch biscuit cutter.
8. Place biscuits close together on an ungreased baking sheet.
9. Bake 12 to 15 minutes or until golden brown. Serve hot.

Per biscuit: 86 cal (31% from fat), 2 g protein, 13 g carbohydrate, 3 g fat, 14 mg cholesterol, 1 g fiber, 114 mg sodium.

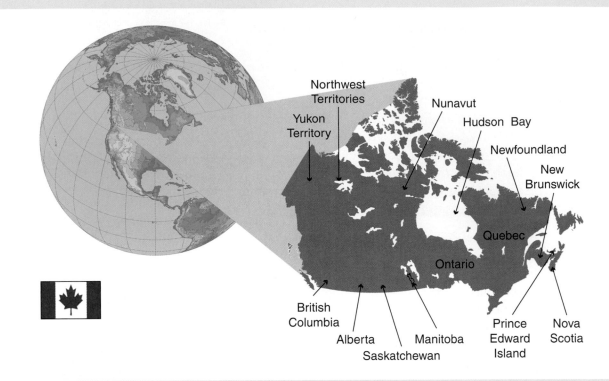

Canada

Reflect

Ask how many students have visited Canada. Ask how these students would compare the lifestyle they observed there to the lifestyle in the United States.

Enrich

Assign teams of students to investigate different Canadian regions and provinces. Have teams prepare media presentations to summarize their findings for the class.

In terms of land mass, Canada is the second largest country in the world. However, it has a population smaller than the state of California. The majority of Canadians live within a few hundred miles of the country's southern border. Over half the people live in the area around the Great Lakes and the St. Lawrence River.

Like the United States, Canada is a land that was settled by immigrants from many nations. These settlers combined their cultures with those of native peoples. Their food customs were major influences on Canadian cuisine.

Geography and Climate of Canada

Canada is divided into 10 provinces and 3 territories. Diverse geography partly accounts for the country's varied climate. Canada boasts the world's longest coastline. On the Atlantic side, air currents from over the ocean bring high annual levels of rain and snow. Along the Pacific coast, ocean airstreams give British Columbia the warmest average temperatures throughout the year. Just off the mainland, Vancouver Island's tremendous annual rainfall combines with the warm air to create a rain forest climate. The Arctic Ocean to the north surrounds many islands. It borders a region with long, dark winters. Temperatures here stay below freezing all but a few weeks a year.

Several mountain ranges break up the landscape and shape the climate of Canada's interior regions. Rain and snow are common in the mountain areas. The valleys, by contrast, are often described as desertlike.

The key geographical feature of central and eastern Canada is a rocky, U-shaped region called the *Canadian Shield*. This area, which encircles Hudson Bay, is made up mostly of low hills and lakes. The soil in this region is not very suitable for farming.

Between the Rocky Mountains and the Canadian Shield lie the vast Interior Plains. The southern part of this region is home to some of the most productive grain fields in the world. This region reports some of the lowest levels of annual rainfall in Canada. However, much of the rain that falls comes in the spring, preparing the fields for planting. The summers in this area are hot, but the winters bring some of the lowest temperatures south of the Arctic.

FYI

Some of the houses that still sit along the U.S.-Canadian border were constructed before the international boundary line was established. In some of these homes, people bathe in Canada and sleep in the United States!

Canadian Culture

By European standards, Canada is a young country. Despite its youth, Canada has developed into one of the world's leading nations. It is strengthened by a rich history and a diversity of cultures.

Influences on Canadian Culture

The **Aboriginals**, or first inhabitants of the land, influenced Canadian culture and food customs. Canadian Aboriginals form two groups—*First Nations* and *Inuit*. First Nations lived throughout Canada. Some were farmers; others were fishers or nomadic hunters. Inuit (once known as Eskimo) lived in the far northern regions where the land was not suitable for cultivation. Therefore, Inuit hunted inland game animals or marine mammals. See **28-11**.

In the early 1600s, British and French fur trappers and traders began establishing settlements in Canada. The British settled primarily along the Atlantic coast and in the Hudson Bay area. The French explorers claimed a vast territory along the St. Lawrence River and the Great Lakes. This territory became known as New France. The Inuit had little contact with these early settlers. However, the First Nations helped the settlers learn how to hunt, fish, and plant crops.

A series of wars between the French and English colonists in Canada took place between 1689 and 1763. As a result, most of New France came under British rule and was renamed Quebec. Through the Quebec Act in 1774, Britain granted the French-speaking citizens in this area political, religious, and linguistic rights.

The following year, the Revolutionary War broke out in the American colonies. Thousands of colonists who chose to remain loyal to the British crown moved north

Dave Thompson—Tourism Squamish

28-11 Stone figures called inukshuk were built by the Inuit people to mark the land for such purposes as travel routes, food supplies, and ancestral memorials.

FYI

Canada is a constitutional monarchy. The monarch of England is also the monarch of Canada. The monarch is represented in Canada by the Governor General.

Activity

Have students use an encyclopedia or the Internet to link specific natural resources and agricultural products with specific regions of Canada.

Discuss

Ask students what national holiday in the United States parallels Canada Day. *(Independence Day, July 4)*

into Canada. This led Britain to split Quebec into two colonies. They were later reunited as the Province of Canada. In 1867, this colony was joined with Nova Scotia and New Brunswick to form a new country—the Dominion of Canada. Each of the former colonies became a province in the new country.

Exploration and settlement of western Canada had been increasing since the first half of the early 1800s. Within four years of the formation of the Dominion of Canada, two more provinces were added. By 1949, a total of 10 provinces had joined the Dominion.

Modern Canadian Culture

Today, Canada is a federal state with a democratic parliament. The Parliament is modeled after the British government system. It is made up of a Senate and a House of Commons.

Canada has a multicultural society. Most of Canada's people have a British or French background. However, many Canadians claim ties to other European countries. Others have an Asian heritage. In addition, three to four percent of Canada's people are of native descent.

Canada has two national languages. English is the primary language of the majority of Canadians. However, French is the main language of a sizable percentage of the people. The largest segment of the French-speaking population lives in the province of Quebec.

Canadian Agriculture

Food products play a large role in the Canadian economy. Much of Canada's land is well suited for agriculture. Wheat, barley, apples, berries, and potatoes are among the economically important crops grown by Canadian farmers. Dairy products and livestock are significant, too. Fishing is an important industry in coastal regions. Cod, flounder, lobster, and salmon are among the most valuable catches brought in by Canadian fishers.

Learn About...

Canadian Holidays

As in all countries, holidays are an important part of the lifestyle in Canada. Many of these events involve the sharing of traditional foods.

Spring and summer holidays include Easter and Canada Day. Spring vegetables, such as asparagus and fiddlehead ferns, are often served with ham for Easter dinner. Canada Day, which is observed on July 1, honors Canada's freedom from British rule. Strawberry festivals are often held at the time of this holiday. Picnics, fireworks, parades, and concerts are also part of the festivities.

The fall and winter months bring a number of holidays in Canada. Thanksgiving is observed on the second Monday in October. A turkey dinner ended with hot pumpkin pie is the typical feast. A traditional Christmas dinner reflects the British heritage of many Canadians. This meal is likely to include roast goose with plum pudding. Shortbread and fruitcake are also common holiday treats.

Canadian Cuisine

The typical Canadian diet is nutritious. It includes a variety of foods. It features a bounty of fruits, vegetables, and grain products. Meat and dairy products also play key roles in Canadian cuisine.

Health experts in Canada encourage people to read labels to make wise choices from the array of available foods. They want people to limit calories, fat, sugar, and salt in the foods they eat. They promote the use of whole grains, lean meats, and lower fat dairy products. Canadian health experts also encourage people to be active to maintain healthy body weight and help reduce disease risk. See **28-12**.

Canada's diverse climate and geography have caused available foods to vary from one part of the country to another. Different native and immigrant influences also affected each area. Like the United States, therefore, Canada has a regional cuisine.

Traditional Canadian foods were based largely on native ingredients. Canadian cooks could not obtain these ingredients all year long. Therefore, classic Canadian cuisine was seasonal in nature. The distinctive qualities of what was once standard Canadian fare have become less striking in recent years. Food products are made by large manufacturers instead of small-scale entrepreneurs. Busy lifestyles have led to widespread use of processed foods. Modern transportation has brought cooks a broad range of foods that are not produced in Canada. It has also allowed year-round availability of foods that were once seasonal. These factors have worked together to remove some of the unique character from everyday menus in Canada. However, traditional dishes still appear at holidays and other special occasions.

In the past, food was central to many Canadian social events, such as teas, church suppers, and quilting bees. It was the main focus of parties celebrating the harvest of

Ontario Tourism

28-12 Canada's health department encourages Canadian citizens to get daily physical activity.

Discuss

Ask students what regions of the United States have large Amish and Mennonite communities. *(Pennsylvania, Virginia, Ohio, Indiana, Illinois, Iowa, Kansas, Nebraska, Oregon)*

Discuss

Ask students why early Canadian cookbooks might have included more recipes for baked goods than for main dishes, side dishes, and salads. *(Ingredient proportions are not as critical to the success of main dishes, side dishes, and salads as they are to baked goods. Therefore, cooks did not rely as much on recipes when preparing these products.)*

such foods as strawberries, smelts, apples, and maple sugar. Food also played a key role at weddings, funerals, picnics, and other family gatherings. At these functions, cooks proudly displayed their pickles, preserves, and baked goods for all to enjoy.

Immigrant Influence on Canadian Cuisine

British, Scottish, Irish, French, and German settlers all had an effect on the development of Canadian cuisine. British influence can be seen in the popularity of such dishes as steak and kidney pie. *Yorkshire pudding* is a British food that appears in some Canadian cookbooks. It is a quick bread flavored with drippings from beef roast. Tea (both the drink and the light afternoon meal) are also signs of British influence on Canadian cuisine. Scones, custards, and baked and steamed puddings are other British favorites that have become part of Canadian fare.

Two traditional entrees served in Canada for Christmas and New Year's dinners are Irish in origin. Spiced beef and stuffed pork tenderloins are often the center of winter holiday meals.

Provincial French influence is most prominent in the cuisine of Quebec. It also plays a role in the foods of the East Coast provinces. Hollandaise sauce and oil and vinegar salad dressings flavored with garlic are examples of French influence.

German influence is seen in foods brought to Canada by groups of Mennonite and Amish settlers. One example is dandelion salad with bacon and sour cream dressing. German influence is also seen in the quality baked goods that are popular in areas with large Amish and Mennonite populations.

Even the United States influenced the cuisine of Canada. Many people from New England moved north and settled along the east coast of Canada. Their effect is seen in such dishes as seafood chowders, baked beans, and steamed brown bread. People from the mid-Atlantic states settled in Ontario. Pancakes, gingersnap cookies, and hearty soups may be among the Canadian foods that reflect their influence. Another example of U.S. influence is in the traditional foods served for Thanksgiving in Canada—turkey, cranberries, and pumpkin pie.

Canadian Main Dishes

Main dishes in Canada generally include meat, poultry, or fish. Not surprisingly, menus in the coastal provinces often feature seafood. The East Coast is known for cod, flounder, lobster, crab, and oysters. In this part of Canada, seafood chowders, boiled lobster, oyster dressing, and fish salads are popular dishes. Salmon is the primary catch in the West Coast province of British Columbia. Canadians enjoy salmon poached, smoked, broiled, and grilled. Inland lakes and streams, especially in the northern provinces, provide freshwater fish including trout, pickerel, and whitefish. Commercial ice fishing makes these fish widely available during the winter months. Pan-frying and baking with stuffing are two popular preparation methods. See **28-13**.

Canadian people eat more beef than any other meat. Throughout Canada, people enjoy grilled steaks, roast prime rib, and beef sandwiches. Spiced beef, which is preserved with a mixture of salt, cloves, nutmeg, and allspice, is a Canadian Christmas specialty.

Pork was once the most commonly eaten meat in some parts of Canada, and it is still quite popular. In Canada's early days, hogs were raised on almost every farm. Butchering and sausage making were annual fall events. Most pork cuts were salted to

Ontario Tourism

28-13 Fishing is important to the economy in Canada's coastal areas, and fish is important to the cuisine in these areas, too.

preserve them for use throughout the winter. Better cuts, such as the hams, were cured in brine and smoked. This extra processing inspired many people to save hams for special occasions, such as Easter dinner.

Poultry is also common as a Canadian main dish. Chicken is most popular, and it is served in a variety of ways. Roasted chicken, grilled chicken, and chicken salads are favorite entrees. Canadians enjoy other types of poultry, too, especially at holiday times. Turkey is the traditional entree for Thanksgiving in Canada. Goose is often the bird of choice for Christmas dinner.

Game meats are not unusual on the menus of people living in rural northern regions. Bear, caribou, and moose are abundant in these wilderness areas. In other parts of Canada, rabbit is a more likely game entree. Stewing and roasting are two favorite cooking methods.

Canadian Fruits and Vegetables

The soil and climate in Southern Canada are suitable for growing a wide variety of fruits and vegetables. Apples are probably the most popular fruit in Canada. Different species are available from midsummer to late fall. Canadians use apples to make cider, apple butter, and a number of desserts and condiments.

Gooseberries, strawberries, and rhubarb are available in Canada in the spring. Blueberries, raspberries, and blackberries are part of the harvest of summer fruits. Plums, peaches, and cherries are among the tree fruits grown in this region. With this range of fruits, few would wonder why fruit pies are such popular desserts in Canada. Canadians also have a long tradition of putting up their bounty of native fruits in jams, jellies, and other preserves.

Reflect

Ask students what game meats they have tried. Ask how they felt these meats compared with domestic beef and pork.

Discuss

Ask students how the nutritional value of fresh fruit compares with the nutritional value of fruit jams and jellies. *(Fresh fruits are generally high in vitamins, minerals, and fiber. Jams and jellies are much lower in these nutrients and they are high in sugars.)*

Academic Connections

Ask an economics teacher to talk to your class about factors that affect international monetary exchange rates. Have the teacher mention how often rates fluctuate, how students can find out current exchange rates, and where they can get the best rates of exchange. Then have students investigate the current exchange rate between Canadian and U.S. dollars.

Integrating Math Concepts

Have students compare the costs of wild rice and long grain white rice. Ask students why the wild rice costs more. *(Wild rice costs more because it is harvested by hand.)*

Canadian vegetables are just as varied as the fruits. Asparagus and watercress are often the first vegetables ready for picking in the spring. Peas, leaf lettuce, radishes, tomatoes, cucumbers, and corn follow in the summer. Canadians enjoy vegetables in soups, salads, and side dishes.

Canadian Grain Products

Canada has an abundant wheat crop, and bread products are part of most meals. Breakfasts may include buckwheat pancakes or muffins, which are sometimes called *gems*. Lunches and teas are likely to feature sandwiches on hearty yeast breads. Yeast rolls or quick breads flavored with fruits are popular accompaniments to dinner entrees.

Baked goods such as cakes, cookies, and pies are also Canadian standards. Early Canadian cookbooks included a wealth of recipes for these treats, which were the pride of many cooks. Many of these traditional recipes were sweetened with maple sugar or maple syrup, which was made locally every spring.

Classic Canadian menus seldom include pasta products. However, wild rice may appear as a side dish or in a stuffing. Wild rice grows in shallow Canadian lakes and streams. It must be harvested by hand from canoes and then dried. The labor-intensive harvesting process causes wild rice to be fairly costly. See **28-14**.

Canadian Dairy Products

Large herds of dairy cows make dairy products popular in Canada. A variety of flavorful cheeses are produced throughout the country. Cheddar may be the most commonly produced cheese, but Oka, Ermite blue, and St. Benoit are uniquely Canadian.

The use of dairy products is prominent throughout traditional Canadian recipes. Oysters may be poached in milk. Cream is added to various soups, which are a filling first course in many winter menus. In the summer, home-made ice cream is a classic dessert.

Shutterstock
28-14 Wild rice, with its long, dark grains, adds a firm texture and nutty flavor to some Canadian side dishes.

Canadian Menu

Cheddar Cheese Soup

Harvest Pork Roast

Spicy Lemon Squash

Wild Rice Medley

Watercress and Mushroom Salad

Nova Scotia Oatcakes with Maple Butter

Cranberry-Orange Sorbet

Apple Cider

Cheddar Cheese Soup

Serves 6

⅓	cup minced onion
1	tablespoon butter
2½	cups low-sodium chicken broth
½	cup fat-free milk
2	tablespoons flour
1½	cups evaporated fat-free milk
1½	cups shredded Cheddar cheese
½	teaspoon dry mustard
⅛	teaspoon cayenne pepper

1. In a large nonstick saucepan, sauté onion in butter over medium heat until tender.
2. Stir in chicken broth, reduce heat to low, and simmer for 15 minutes.
3. Combine milk and flour in a small, tightly covered container. Shake vigorously to mix thoroughly.
4. Slowly pour flour mixture into broth, stirring constantly. Continue stirring gently until soup begins to thicken.
5. Add evaporated milk, cheese, dry mustard, and cayenne pepper.
6. Continue stirring gently until cheese is melted and soup is heated through. Do not allow soup to boil.

Per serving: 211 cal. (51% from fat), 14 g protein, 12 g carbohydrate, 12 g fat, 37 mg cholesterol, 0 g fiber, 347 mg sodium.

Harvest Pork Roast

Serves 6

1	2-pound boneless pork loin roast
1	tablespoon oil
½	cup apple cider
½	teaspoon dried thyme
¼	teaspoon dried marjoram
1	tablespoon dried parsley

1. Trim exterior fat from pork loin.
2. Combine oil and apple cider in blender. Blend for 15 seconds.
3. Generously brush cider mixture over the pork loin. Sprinkle moist surface with thyme, marjoram, and parsley.
4. Place pork loin on a rack in a shallow roasting pan.
5. Place roasting pan in 350°F oven and roast for 45 minutes to an hour, until internal temperature measures 145°F on a meat thermometer.
6. Remove pork loin from oven. Let it stand for 10 minutes before slicing.

Per serving: 176 cal. (41% from fat), 24 g protein, 2 g carbohydrate, 8 g fat, 67 mg cholesterol, 0 g fiber, 58 mg sodium.

Spicy Lemon Squash

Serves 6

1	teaspoon grated lemon peel
¼	cup brown sugar
½	teaspoon ground ginger
½	teaspoon ground cinnamon
¼	teaspoon ground nutmeg
3	tablespoons butter, melted
1	teaspoon rum extract
3	acorn squash

1. In a small bowl, combine lemon peel, brown sugar, ginger, cinnamon, and nutmeg.
2. Stir in butter and rum extract.
3. Wash squash. Cut in half and remove seeds.
4. Sprinkle the insides of the squash with the spice mixture.
5. Place squash halves, cut sides up, in a shallow baking dish. Add ¼ inch of water to the dish.
6. Cover the dish with aluminum foil and bake at 400°F for 30 minutes, or until tender.

Per serving: 128 cal. (42% from fat), 1 g protein, 18 g carbohydrate, 6 g fat, 16 mg cholesterol, 3 g fiber, 63 mg sodium.

Wild Rice Medley

Serves 6

¼   cup chopped onion
¼   cup minced celery
1   tablespoon butter
½   cup wild rice
2¾ cups low-sodium chicken broth
¼   teaspoon salt
½   cup brown rice
1   tablespoon chopped fresh parsley

1. In medium saucepan, sauté onion and celery.
2. Add wild rice, chicken broth, and salt. Increase heat to high and bring to a boil.
3. Cover, reduce heat to low, and simmer for 15 minutes.
4. Add brown rice, cover, and simmer an additional 30 minutes.
5. Remove from heat. Drain any unabsorbed liquid. Sprinkle with parsley.

Per serving: 133 cal. (20% from fat), 5 g protein, 23 g carbohydrate, 3 g fat, 5 mg cholesterol, 2 g fiber, 197 mg sodium.

Nova Scotia Oatcakes

Makes 36

1   cup flour
⅓   cup brown sugar
¾   teaspoon salt
½   teaspoon baking soda
3   cups oatmeal, quick or old fashioned, uncooked
½   cup shortening
⅓ to ½ cup cold water

1. Preheat oven to 425°F.
2. In a medium mixing bowl, combine flour, sugar, salt, baking soda, and oats.
3. Cut in the shortening with a pastry blender or two knives until the mixture resembles coarse crumbs.
4. With a fork, add water a tablespoon at a time until dough will hold together but is not sticky.
5. Press dough into a greased 10-by-15-inch jelly roll pan.
6. Cut dough into 36 squares (divide 10-inch side into fourths and 15-inch side into ninths); do not separate.
7. Bake in preheated oven for 15 minutes, or until browned.

8. Separate squares into a napkin-lined basket. Serve warm with maple butter.

Per oatcake: 71 cal. (38% from fat), 1 g protein, 9 g carbohydrate, 3 g fat, 0 mg cholesterol, 1 g fiber, 67 mg sodium.

Maple Butter

Makes 3/4 cup

⅓   cup butter, softened
3   tablespoons brown sugar
¼   cup maple syrup
⅛   teaspoon cinnamon

1. In a small mixer bowl, beat butter until light and fluffy.
2. Beat in brown sugar, maple syrup, and cinnamon.

Per teaspoon: 25 cal. (72% from fat), 1 g protein, 3 g carbohydrate, 2 g fat, 5 mg cholesterol, 0 g fiber, 18 mg sodium.

Watercress and Mushroom Salad

Serves 6

¼   pound mushrooms, sliced
1   tablespoon chopped fresh parsley
1   tablespoon chopped fresh chives
¼   cup vegetable oil
1   tablespoon lemon juice
½   teaspoon dry mustard
¼   teaspoon pepper
¼   teaspoon salt
2   bunches watercress

1. Place mushrooms, parsley, and chives in a large bowl.
2. Combine the oil, lemon juice, dry mustard, pepper, and salt and pour over mushroom mixture. Stir gently, cover, and refrigerate for 15 minutes.
3. Meanwhile, wash the watercress and pat dry with paper towels.
4. Add the watercress to the mushrooms. Toss well to blend. Serve immediately.

Per serving: 75 cal. (84% from fat), 1 g protein, 2 g carbohydrate, 7 g fat, 0 mg cholesterol, 1 g fiber, 108 mg sodium.

Cranberry-Orange Sorbet

Serves 6

2 cups fresh or frozen cranberries
¾ cup water
¾ cup sugar
1 cup water
½ cup orange juice concentrate

1. In a small saucepan, combine the cranberries and ¾ cup water. Cook over medium heat until cranberries are tender, about 10 minutes.
2. Remove from heat and set aside to cool.
3. In a separate saucepan, bring sugar and 1 cup water to a boil, stirring to dissolve sugar.
4. Boil for 5 minutes. Set aside to cool slightly.
5. Press cooled cranberry mixture through a large strainer into a mixing bowl.
6. Stir in orange juice concentrate and cooled sugar syrup.
7. Cover mixture and chill.
8. Pour the mixture into the canister of a 1-quart ice cream freezer and freeze according to the manufacturer's directions.

Per serving: 150 cal. (0% from fat), 1 g protein, 38 g carbohydrate, 0 g fat, 0 mg cholesterol, 2 g fiber, 4 mg sodium.

CAREER SUCCESS

Graphic Interpretation Skills

Zaleeka is a tourist-information assistant at a state information center in the South. She provides travel information to tourists, helping them map routes to places of interest around the state.

To be an effective worker, Zaleeka needs graphic interpretation skills. She needs to be able to organize and process symbols, pictures, charts, and other information. In a small group, answer the following questions about Zaleeka's need for and use of these skills:

A. What types of symbols, pictures, and charts might Zaleeka be required to interpret in her job?
B. How would the clients Zaleeka serves be affected if she lacked skill in organizing and processing symbols, pictures, charts, and other information?
C. How might the tourism industry in Zaleeka's state be affected if she lacked skill in organizing and processing symbols, pictures, charts, and other information?
D. What is another skill Zaleeka would need in this job? Briefly explain why this skill would be important.

CHAPTER 28 REVIEW

Summary

The Aboriginals and the first explorers laid the foundations of cuisine in the United States and Canada. As immigrants came from many parts of the globe, they added foods and cooking techniques from their homelands. This blend of cultures and traditions has evolved into the cuisines found in the United States and Canada today.

Immigrants from certain countries tended to settle together. Therefore, the cuisine of the United States has some regional characteristics. For instance, hearty one-dish meals and foods made with locally produced maple syrup are popular in New England. German foods of the Pennsylvania Dutch can be found in the mid-Atlantic region. The South is known for fried chicken and buttermilk biscuits. Soul food and Creole cuisine also originated in the South. In the Midwest, where much of the nation's grain is grown, meat and potatoes are standard fare.

Native Americans, Mexicans, and Spaniards influenced the foods of the West and Southwest. Chili and barbecued meats are favorites in this region. Sourdough bread, Alaskan seafood, and fresh fruits and vegetables are typical of the Pacific Coast. Tropical fruits and vegetables, often prepared with an Asian flair, are common in Hawaii.

Classic Canadian dishes were created with ingredients that were locally produced. Canada's climate and geography caused available foods to vary from area to area. Seasonal and regional distinctions are less apparent in Canadian cuisine today. In coastal regions, main dishes often feature seafood. Beef and pork are more standard in inland areas. Apples and potatoes are common. However, Canadian meals feature a broad range of fruits and vegetables. Baked goods made from wheat grown in the prairie provinces are staples of the Canadian diet. Dairy products, including cheeses, cream soups, and frozen desserts, are also well liked.

Review What You Have Read

Write your answers on a separate sheet of paper, using complete sentences when appropriate.

1. Name three reasons immigrants came to the New World.

2. How did New Englanders preserve foods for winter?

3. Name three culinary contributions of the Pennsylvania Dutch.

4. Name two distinct forms of cooking that developed in the South.

5. Name six agricultural products of the Midwest.

6. What four groups of people had the most influence on cooking in the Southwest?

7. How did the prospectors make and use sourdough?

8. Identify three groups that influenced Hawaiian cuisine and give an example of a food contributed by each group.

(continued)

9. Match the following foods to the regions of the United States with which they are associated:

_____ poi
_____ baked beans
_____ salmon
_____ tamales
_____ gumbo
_____ shoofly pie

A. New England
B. mid-Atlantic
C. South
D. Midwest
E. West and Southwest
F. Pacific Coast
G. Hawaii

10. Identify foods that are typically associated with two Canadian holidays.

11. How did people in the United States influence the cuisine of Canada?

12. True or false. Pasta is a common side dish on Canadian menus.

Link to Academic Skills

13. **Social studies.** Use a map of the United States and Canada to identify the regions that were colonized by various groups of Europeans. Discuss ways the influence of these European groups can still be found in these regions today.

14. **English language arts.** Research the first Thanksgiving in the United States or Canada. Write a report about the foods that were served. Note how many of these foods are still served today.

15. **Social studies.** Make a bulletin board with large cutouts of the Pacific states. Use pictures from magazines and catalogs to show where various plant and animal foods are produced.

16. **History.** Prepare a time line illustrating important dates in Canada's history.

17. **English language arts.** Debate the statement "Mass production, convenience foods, and modern transportation have improved the Canadian diet."

Build Critical Thinking Skills

18. **Analysis.** Choose one of the immigrant groups that helped settle a particular region of the United States. Find two regional recipes that reflect the influence of your chosen group. Then find two recipes for similar foods that are from your group's homeland. Compare the pairs of recipes, analyzing them for similarities and differences. Share with the class your conclusions about how and why the original recipes were adapted when they were brought to the United States.

19. **Synthesis.** As a class, plan a Hawaiian luau fund-raiser. Divide into groups for food, decorations, music, games, program, and promotion. Each group should conduct research to come up with ideas for their part of the event. Combine input from all the groups to finalize the details, assign tasks, and create a preparation schedule.

7. The prospectors mixed together flour, water, and salt and then exposed the mixture to air to absorb yeast cells. They used the dough as a leavening agent to make a variety of baked products. They kept a small amount of the dough after each baking to serve as a starter for the next batch.

8. (List three and give an example for each. Student response.)

9. G, A, F, E, C, B

10. (Student response.)

11. Some New Englanders settled along the east coast of Canada, contributing such dishes as seafood chowders, baked beans, and steamed brown bread. People from the mid-Atlantic states settled in Ontario, bringing with them pancakes, gingersnap cookies, and hearty soups. U.S. influence is also seen in the turkey, cranberries, and pumpkin pie served for Thanksgiving in Canada.

12. false

Apply Technology

20. Use a computer and word processing software to prepare a template for a travel journal. If you have access to a laptop computer, take the computer with you on a trip and use your template files to create documents for each day's journal entries.

21. Use map-making software or visit a mapmaking website on the Internet. Use these resources to plan a travel route from your school to the U.S. or Canadian destination of your choice. You should also investigate tourist attractions along your route and identify restaurants, gas stations, and lodging facilities at which you would stop.

A Measure of Math

22. Find the total area of the United States in square miles. Add the area of each state in a region to figure the total area of each region discussed in this chapter. Then calculate the percentage of the total U.S. area occupied by each region.

Teamwork in Action

23. As a class, vote on a dish you think best represents your region of the country. Research the cultural origins of this dish. Design a brochure describing how it evolved, classic ingredients, and why it has become popular in your region. Then organize a cook-off, inviting residents of your community to prepare their favorite recipes for the regional dish. Invite faculty members to serve as judges. Distribute your brochures to the contestants and others attending the event.

Companion Website
www.g-wlearning.com

At the website, review key terms for this chapter with crossword puzzles, matching exercises, and e-flash cards. Apply facts from the chapter to complete the activities.

CHAPTER 29
Latin America

Learning Prep

Use graph paper and the *Terms to Know* to make up a crossword puzzle, using the definitions as clues. Give your puzzle to a partner to work. Check your partner's answers after the puzzle has been completed.

Terms to Know

Latin America
tortilla
frijoles refritos
chilies
guacamole
mole
plantain
comida
siesta

manioc
cassava
arepa
ceviche
ají
gaucho
empanada
dendé oil
feijoada completa

Main Menu

◎ Geography and climate have helped shape the distinctive foods of Latin America.
◎ Latin American food customs reflect the culture of Mexico and South America.

Objectives

After studying this chapter, you will be able to

◎ **identify** geographic and climatic factors that have influenced the characteristic foods of Mexico and the South American countries.

◎ **describe** cultural factors that have affected the food customs of Mexico and South America.

◎ **prepare** foods native to Latin America.

Academic Connections

Partner with the foreign language department in teaching this chapter. You will teach the impact of climate, geography, and culture on the development of Latin American cuisine. The Spanish teacher will teach recipe translation and ordering from a menu in a Latin American restaurant.

The landmass that stretches southward from the Rio Grande to the tip of South America is known as **Latin America**. It is called Latin America because the official language of most of the countries is either Spanish or Portuguese, both of which are based on Latin.

Latin America was first explored and settled by the Spanish. Later, other Europeans established settlements. A large number of Portuguese settled along the eastern shores of South America in what today is Brazil.

Extremes are the rule rather than the exception in Latin America. Dense, tropical rain forests are as common as snow-capped mountains. Large, modern cities may not be far away from wild jungles.

The food customs of Latin America are rich and varied. They reflect the culture, climate, and geography of each country. The ancient Aztecs and the Spanish conquistadores influenced Mexico. The foods of Peru reflect the ancient Inca civilization. The foods of Argentina are an unusual mixture of European influences and native foods grown in the rich soil. The foods of Brazil reflect strong African and Portuguese heritage.

For the most part, the cuisines of Latin America are healthful. They include large amounts of fruits and vegetables and daily portions of grains and beans, **29-1**. In many regions, meat and poultry are costly, so people use them in limited amounts. Experts believe this plant-based diet is partly the reason for the low cancer rates in many Latin American countries. One aspect of Latin American cuisine that is a health concern is the frequent use of animal fats in cooking. The popularity of pickled, smoked, and salted foods in some regions is a nutritional concern, too. These factors have been linked with increased cancer risk.

Shutterstock

29-1 Fruits, vegetables, rice, and beans are common ingredients in Latin American cuisine.

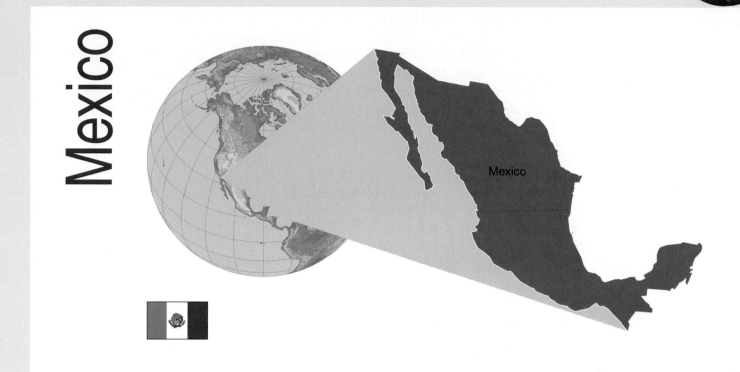

Mexico

Mexico

Of all the Latin American countries, Mexico is most familiar to the majority of people in the United States. The close proximity of Mexico has made possible a rich cultural exchange.

Thousands of United States tourists visit Mexico each year. Mexican foods, such as tacos, enchiladas, and refried beans, are popular in the Southwest and throughout the United States.

Discuss

Ask students what most of the popular tourist spots in Mexico have in common. *(warm, sunny climate and beach areas)*

Geography and Climate of Mexico

Mexico is a land of deserts, mountains, grasslands, woodlands, and tropical rain forests. The Rio Grande separates Mexico from Texas. The Pacific Ocean, Gulf of California, Caribbean Sea, and Gulf of Mexico form its coastline. Much of Mexico is mountainous, with valleys separating the different ranges. Although the climate in a few regions is wet and humid, nearly half of Mexico is arid or semiarid.

Both geography and climate have affected food customs in Mexico. In those sections of the country bordered by water, fish is an important part of the cuisine. The areas that border the United States have land that is too dry for large scale crop production. However, it is suitable for raising cattle. As a result, beef is a staple food in these areas. A variety of tropical fruits and vegetables grow along the southern Gulf Coast where rainfall is adequate. In the central plateau, the level land, adequate moisture, and cool temperatures make the production of crops like corn and beans profitable.

Mexican Culture

Living quarters in all but the wealthiest Mexican homes are simple. Beds, tables, and chairs are often hand-carved. Dishes and cooking utensils may be handmade.

Traditionally, Mexican families are close-knit. Children learn to help their parents at an early age. The children of rural families work in the fields, help with housework, and take care of their younger brothers and sisters. Many city children must work to supplement the family income.

Courtesy ACH Food Companies, Inc.

29-2 Pan de Muerto is a symbolic Mexican bread shaped to resemble bones and teardrops for the Days of the Dead.

Mexican Holidays

Most Mexicans are Roman Catholic. Many holidays throughout the year focus on religious celebrations.

Food plays a role in some Mexican holidays. The Feast of Epiphany on January 6 falls at the end of a 22-day Christmas celebration. This day celebrates the coming of three kings to see the infant Jesus. People get together and share a special supper, which includes a ring-shaped cake with a tiny plastic baby baked inside. The person who gets the piece of cake with the baby hosts a tamales party for all who are present. This party is held on February 2, which is Candlemas Day. Mexicans celebrate this as the day Jesus' parents took him to the temple in Jerusalem.

The observance of the Days of the Dead also involves a food tradition. Mexicans believe dead souls return to visit the living between October 31 and November 2. During this time, many families set up altars in the corners of their homes. They set these altars with candles, photos, and favorite foods and drinks of dead loved ones. See **29-2**.

Global Perspective

Mexican Agriculture

A little more than half of Mexico's people are farmers. Because good, rich soil is scarce, farming is difficult. Many farmers cannot afford modern machinery or fertilizers. As a result, crop yields are poor. In recent years, government irrigation projects and credit to farmers have helped farmers improve yields.

Corn is Mexico's major crop. Bean production is second. Other important crops include sugarcane, coffee, tomatoes, green peppers, peas, melons, citrus fruits, strawberries, and cacao beans. Wheat is grown in the North as are smaller amounts of barley, rice, and oats. Cattle graze on northern pastures.

Coastal waters provide a variety of seafood. Large quantities of shrimp are caught and exported. Sardines, tuna, turtles, and mackerel are also important.

Mexican Cuisine

The *Aztecs* were the original inhabitants of Mexico. In 1520, Hernando Cortes and the *conquistadores* (conquerors) explored Mexico and took control of the land for Spain. Both the Aztecs and the Spaniards made many contributions to Mexican cuisine.

The Aztecs contributed chocolate, vanilla, corn, peppers, peanuts, tomatoes, avocados, squash, beans, sweet potatoes, pineapples, and papayas. The Aztecs boiled, broiled, or steamed their food or ate it raw. Their more elaborate dishes were similar to modern stews.

The Spanish added oil, wine, cinnamon, cloves, rice, wheat, peaches, apricots, beef, and chicken. With the introduction of oil, many of the early Aztec foods could be fried. Today, frying is an important part of Mexican cooking. Mexican cooks fry foods in deep fat or on lightly greased griddles.

Another contribution to Mexican cuisine was made in the mid 1860s by Emperor Maximilian. Maximilian was from Austria. He introduced dishes from his homeland as well as sophisticated French and Italian dishes to Mexico.

Characteristic Foods of Mexico

Corn, beans, and peppers are staple ingredients in Mexican cuisine. Mexican cooks use a variety of other locally grown vegetables and fruits, too. Flavorful sauces and stews, as well as some distinctive desserts and beverages, are also typical foods of Mexico.

Corn

Corn has formed the basis of Mexican cuisine since the days of the Aztec civilization. Mexican cooks use corn in many ways, but its most important use is in the production of tortillas. A **tortilla** is a flat, unleavened bread made from cornmeal or wheat flour and water. The dough is shaped into a thin pancake in a tortilla press. Then it is cooked on a lightly greased griddle called a *comal*.

Mexican cooks make many popular dishes from tortillas. They fill tortillas with a mixture of shredded meat or sliced chicken, onions, garlic, and chilies to make *enchiladas*. Then they bake and serve the enchiladas with cheese and a red or green tomato sauce. Mexicans fry tortillas until crisp and garnish them with chopped onion, chilies, beans, shredded lettuce, meat, and cheese to make *tostadas*. *Quesadillas* are toasted turnovers made of tortillas filled with meat, sauce, cheese, beans, or vegetables. Tortillas wrapped around a meat or bean filling are called *burritos*. Crisp, fried tortillas filled with meat, beans, shredded lettuce, and cheese and seasoned with chili are called *tacos*.

Mexican cooks never waste corn. They do not even discard the husks. They use the husks to make *tamales*. The cooks stuff small amounts of corn dough with meat and beans and tuck it into the corn husks. They fold the husks into small parcels and steam them or roast them over an open fire.

Beans

Like corn, beans are a staple food in Mexico. Local farmers grow many varieties of beans. Sometimes people boil the beans and eat them from the pot as was done during Aztec times. Often they cook the beans until they are soft, then they mash the beans and fry them slowly. The Mexicans call this dish **frijoles refritos** (refried beans) and frequently serve the beans with grated cheese.

Discuss

Ask students what holiday in the United States falls at the same time of year as the Days of the Dead. Ask students to describe how the U.S. holiday is celebrated. *(Halloween; children wear costumes and go from house to house asking for candy.)*

Discuss

Ask students why the Mexican government would be interested in helping farmers. *(Farmers who become self-sufficient will not have to rely on government-funded social support programs.)*

Activity

Ask students to find three recipes for Mexican foods. Have them identify the Aztec and Spanish contributions in each recipe.

FYI

One small (6-inch diameter) corn or flour tortilla counts as 1 ounce-equivalent from the grains group of MyPlate. One large (12-inch diameter) tortilla equals 4 ounce-equivalents.

Peppers

People throughout Latin America use peppers, but they are especially important in Mexico. Strings of peppers hang outside many Mexican homes to dry.

Mexican cooks use over 30 varieties of peppers. The peppers range in size and color. They can be sweet, pungent, or burning hot. Generally, the mild peppers are called *sweet peppers*, and the hot ones are called **chilies**.

The peppers used most often in cooking can be divided into two groups according to color—red and green. Mexican cooks use red peppers dried, except for ripe red bell peppers and pimientos. They use green peppers fresh. See **29-3**.

Mexican Vegetables and Fruits

Mexican farmers grow a variety of vegetables. Mexicans usually do not eat vegetables plain. Instead, they add them to casseroles and use them as garnishes for other dishes.

Mexican vegetables that are common in the United States include zucchini, artichokes, white potatoes, spinach, chard, lettuce, beets, cauliflower, and carrots. Less common are *huazontle* (wild broccoli), *jicama* (a large, gray root), *nopole* (tender cactus leaves), and *chayotes* (a tropical squash).

Many fruits grow in Mexico. Avocados have a bland flavor and are often added to other foods. **Guacamole**, for example, is a spread made from mashed avocado, tomato, and onion. It may be served with tortillas or crisp corn chips. Bananas, pineapples, guavas, papayas, and prickly pears are other tropical fruits that are popular in Mexico. The fruits are often served alone or in syrup as a light, refreshing dessert.

Shutterstock

29-3 Mexican cooking is flavored with a variety of chilies.

Sauces and Stews

Mexican cooks often use thick sauces. They pour some sauces over other foods. Other sauces contain pieces of meat, vegetables, tortillas, or beans and are served as main dishes.

Very simple sauces are made from chilies and/or sweet peppers mixed with finely chopped onions and tomatoes. More complex sauces are called **moles**. The word *mole* is derived from the Aztec word *molli*, which means a chili-flavored sauce. Cooks make one type of mole from a variety of chilies, almonds, raisins, garlic, sesame seeds, onions, tomatoes, cinnamon, cloves, coriander seeds, and anise seeds. They finely chop these ingredients and add them to chicken stock. They add the final ingredient, unsweetened chocolate, just before serving. This type of mole is part of turkey mole, which is a traditional dish.

Mexican stews are as unique as moles. Stews begin with a sauce. Cooks grind dried peppers and mix them with ground spices and vegetables. They add some meat or poultry stock to the ground mixture to make a thick paste. Then they fry the paste, thin it, and add it to cooked meat or poultry.

Long, slow cooking gives Mexican stews their characteristic flavors. Because of the high altitude, the boiling point in many parts of Mexico is lower. As a result, stews can be simmered for many hours to develop flavor without becoming overcooked.

Mexican Desserts

Other than fresh fruits and sweet tamales, the Aztecs had few desserts. Catholic convents begun by the Spaniards developed many of the desserts and sweets eaten in Mexico today. Early Spanish and Portuguese cooks influenced those desserts that use large amounts of egg and sugar, such as *flan* (a caramel custard).

Enrich

Invite a cook from a Mexican restaurant to speak to your class about Mexican ingredients and dishes.

Reflect

Ask students what Mexican foods they have eaten.

Learn About...

Mexican Beverages

Chocolate drinks and coffee are popular Mexican beverages. The cacao bean, known since the days of the Aztecs, is toasted and ground into cocoa or made into chocolate. Mexican chocolate is similar to the hot chocolate drink served in the United States. However, it has a different texture and is lighter than the chocolate served in other Latin American and European countries. A tool called a *molinillo* is used to beat the chocolate into a foam before serving. Coffee often is served with milk and called *café con leche*. It also can be boiled to a thick syrup and served black or with sugar.

©2011 Wisconsin Milk Marketing Board, Inc.

Atole de Canela is a warm Mexican holiday drink made with sweetened, cinnamon-spiced milk and masa harina.

Activity

Have students sample wheat and corn tortillas, both plain and as the basis for an entree. Discuss which students prefer and why.

Enrich

Challenge students to create a new dish made with tortillas.

Discuss

Ask students how Mexican meal patterns differ from those of the United States.

Mexican Regional Cuisine

Although many foods are common throughout Mexico, regional differences exist. These occur mainly as a result of geographic and climatic conditions.

In the climate of northern Mexico, farmers can grow wheat and raise cattle. Therefore, tortillas in this area are made from wheat rather than corn. People commonly eat beef, which they may dry or cook with onions, peppers, and tomatoes and serve with beans. Cheese is also popular in several northern states. In Chihuahua, for example, people fry beans in lard and then carefully heat them with cheese. In Senora, cooks cover a potato soup with a thick layer of melted cheese.

Finfish and shellfish are important protein sources for people living in coastal areas. People in these regions use seafood in appetizers, soups, and main dishes. Cooks near the Gulf coast make a popular dish from plantains. **Plantains** are green, starchy fruits that have a bland flavor and look much like large bananas. The cooks fry the plantains with onions and tomatoes and serve the mixture with shrimp (or other seafood) and chili sauce. *Paella*, derived from the Spanish dish with the same name, contains seafood, chicken, and peas cooked in chicken broth and served with rice.

Wild duck is popular in eastern Mexico. Turkey is one of the most important foods of the Yucatan (peninsula that forms Mexico's southern tip).

Squash blossoms and sea chestnuts (a type of crustacean) are popular in southern Mexico. Because banana trees are abundant, tamales in this region are wrapped in fresh banana leaves rather than corn husks.

Mexican Meals

Mexican meal patterns differ somewhat from those of the United States. Families with ample incomes often eat four meals a day.

The first meal of the day, *desayuno*, is a substantial breakfast. Fruit, tortillas, bread or sweet rolls, eggs or meat, and coffee or chocolate are served. *Huevos rancheros* (eggs prepared with chilies and served on tortillas) are a popular breakfast dish.

The main meal of the day, **comida**, is served in the middle of the day between one and three o'clock. Six courses are not unusual. These may consist of an appetizer, a soup, a small dish of stew, a main course, beans, dessert, and coffee. Tortillas are traditionally served, but bread sometimes is substituted. A **siesta** (rest period) usually follows comida.

A light snack, *merienda*, is served around five or six o'clock. It includes chocolate or coffee, fruit, and *pan dulce* (sweet breads).

Mexicans may eat *cena*, supper, between eight and ten o'clock. Cena is similar to comida, but smaller and lighter. (Many Mexican families combine merienda and cena and eat one meal in the early evening.) See **29-4**.

Photo courtesy of National Pork Board. For more information about pork, visit TheOtherWhiteMeat.com.

29-4 A dish of stew, like this pork with mole, might be served for comida or cena in Mexico.

Mexican Menu

Enchiladas Verdes
(Chicken-Filled Tortillas with Green Sauce)

Tacos

Ensalada de Valenciano
(Pepper Salad)

Frijoles Refritos
(Refried Beans)

Piña
(Pineapple Slices)

Polverones
(Mexican Wedding Cookies)

Zumo Granada
(Pomegranate Juice)

Tortillas
(Flat Cornbread)

Makes 12

2¼   cups instant masa harina (corn flour)
1   teaspoon salt
1⅓   cups cold water

1. In medium mixing bowl, combine corn flour and salt.
2. Gradually add all but 3 tablespoons of the water.
3. Knead mixture with hands, adding more water (1 tablespoon at a time) until dough no longer sticks to the fingers.
4. Divide the dough in half. With a rolling pin, roll dough between sheets of waxed paper to a thickness of ¹⁄₁₆ inch.
5. Using a 6-inch plate as a pattern, cut around the plate with a sharp knife or pastry wheel.
6. Place rounds of dough between pieces of waxed paper.
7. Preheat oven to 250°F.
8. Heat a heavy 7- to 8-inch skillet over moderate heat.
9. Cook tortillas one at a time.
10. When lightly browned (about 2 minutes on each side), transfer to foil and keep warm in the oven. Fill as desired.

*Note: Tortillas may be made ahead and refrigerated lightly covered. To rewarm tortillas, brush both sides with water and heat a few minutes in a skillet, one at a time.

Per tortilla: 94 cal. (4% from fat), 2 g protein, 20 g carbohydrate, 0 g fat, 0 mg cholesterol, 2 g fiber, 178 mg sodium.

Enchiladas Verdes
(Chicken-Filled Tortillas with Green Sauce)

Makes 6

1   whole boneless, skinless chicken breast
½   cup chicken stock
3   ounces Neufchâtel cheese
1   cup evaporated fat-free milk
⅓   cup finely chopped onions
3   fresh green peppers
⅓   cup canned Mexican green tomatoes, drained
1   hot chili (canned) drained, rinsed, and chopped finely
2½   teaspoons chopped, fresh cilantro
1   egg
      dash pepper
1½   tablespoons shortening
6   tortillas
3   tablespoons grated Parmesan cheese

1. Place chicken breast in small skillet.
2. Pour stock over chicken breast and cover; simmer until chicken is tender, about 20 minutes.
3. Remove chicken to plate and reserve stock.
4. When chicken is cool enough to handle, shred meat and set it aside.
5. In small mixing bowl, beat Neufchâtel cheese until smooth.
6. Add ½ cup evaporated milk, a little at a time.
7. Add onions and chicken, stirring with wooden spoon or rubber spatula. Set aside.
8. Skin peppers. (To skin peppers, place them on a baking sheet in a 350°F oven for 20 to 30 minutes. Turn the peppers every 5 to 8 minutes. When the skins appear to have pulled away from the peppers, remove them from the oven. Place them immediately into a plastic bag for 5 minutes. Slip off skins with a sharp knife.)
9. Remove stem and seeds; coarsely chop peppers and place in blender container.
10. Add tomatoes, hot chili, cilantro, and ¼ cup reserved stock. Blend on high speed until sauce is smooth.
11. Add rest of evaporated milk, egg, and pepper. Blend 10 more seconds; pour into bowl.
12. Preheat oven to 350°F.

13. Grease a small baking dish or 8-inch square cake pan.
14. Melt shortening in small skillet.
15. Fry tortillas one at a time; filling each before frying the next.
16. To fill, place ¼ cup filling in center of tortilla. Fold one side to center; roll tortilla up completely to form a cylinder.
17. Place filled tortillas side by side in baking dish.
18. When all the tortillas have been filled, pour remaining sauce over them and sprinkle with cheese.
19. Bake about 15 minutes or until cheese has melted. Serve immediately.

Per enchilada: 253 cal. (36% from fat), 19 g protein, 24 g carbohydrate, 10 g fat, 81 mg cholesterol, 2 g fiber, 280 mg sodium.

Tacos
Makes 6

¾ pound lean ground beef
1 envelope commercial taco or chili seasoning mix
¾ cup tomato juice
6 tortillas
softened margarine
shredded lettuce
shredded Monterey Jack cheese
coarsely chopped tomatoes
salsa

1. In large skillet, brown ground beef, pouring off fat as it accumulates.
2. When meat is browned, add seasoning mix and tomato juice. Stir well.
3. Simmer, covered, about 10 minutes; stir occasionally.
4. Arrange tortillas on greased baking sheet; brush with margarine.
5. Bake at 400°F 10 to 15 minutes. (Tortillas should begin to set, but they should still be flexible.)
6. Remove from pan and fold in half to form shells.
7. To serve tacos, set out individual bowls of meat mixture, lettuce, cheese, and tomatoes. Each person can prepare his or her own taco and top with salsa, if desired.

Per taco: 282 cal. (50% from fat), 17 g protein, 19 g carbohydrate, 16 g fat, 52 mg cholesterol, 1 g fiber, 440 mg sodium.

Ensalada de Valenciano (Pepper Salad)
Serves 6

1 head iceberg lettuce
5 green peppers
4 medium tomatoes
2 small onions, chopped
¾ cup low-calorie French dressing
1 tablespoon chopped parsley

1. Core, rinse, and thoroughly drain lettuce; chill in plastic bag or refrigerator crisper.
2. Roast peppers in a 350°F oven, turning them every 5 minutes. When the skins appear to have pulled away from the peppers, remove them from the oven and place them in a plastic bag for 5 minutes. Peel peppers with a sharp knife; remove seeds and cut in thin strips.
3. Peel and seed tomatoes; dice. Chill peppers and tomatoes.
4. Line 6 salad plates with outer lettuce leaves; shred remaining lettuce and toss with peppers, tomatoes, onion, and dressing.
5. Arrange salad on lettuce-lined plates; sprinkle with parsley.

Per serving: 113 cal. (34% from fat), 3 g protein, 17 g carbohydrate, 5 g fat, 0 mg cholesterol, 5 g fiber, 630 mg sodium.

Frijoles Refritos (Refried Beans)
Serves 5 to 6

2 cups dried pinto, black, red, or kidney beans (soaked in cold water overnight and drained)
2 tablespoons vegetable shortening
1 onion, finely chopped
3 medium tomatoes, seeded and finely chopped
2 small, fried, hot chilies, crumbled
⅔ cup Monterey Jack or Cheddar cheese, crumbled
salt
pepper

1. Place beans in large saucepan and add enough cold water to completely cover beans.
2. Over moderate heat, bring water to a boil. Reduce heat to low, cover pan, and simmer beans until tender, about 1½ hours. Drain.
3. Puree beans in a blender (or push them through a fine sieve).
4. In a large, heavy skillet, melt shortening.
5. Add onions and cook until lightly browned.

6. Add tomatoes and chilies; cook, stirring frequently, for 5 minutes.
7. Add pureed beans, cheese, and salt and pepper to taste.
8. Cook, stirring occasionally, until cheese melts and beans are hot, about 10 minutes. Serve immediately.

Per serving: 220 cal. (28% from fat), 11 g protein, 29 g carbohydrate, 7 g fat, 10 mg cholesterol, 7 g fiber, 65 mg sodium.

Polverones
(Mexican Wedding Cookies)

Makes 4 dozen cookies

½   cup margarine
½   cup shortening
1   teaspoon vanilla
½   cup confectioner's sugar
2   cups all-purpose flour
¾   cup finely chopped nuts
     confectioner's sugar

1. Preheat oven to 425°F.
2. In medium mixing bowl, cream margarine, shortening, and vanilla until fluffy.
3. Mix the ½ cup confectioner's sugar, flour, and nuts together; add to creamed mixture, stirring to form a soft dough.
4. Shape dough into small balls and place on ungreased baking sheet.
5. Bake cookies about 10 minutes or until lightly brown.
6. Roll warm cookies in confectioner's sugar.

Per cookie. 71 cal. (65% from fat), 1 g protein, 5 g carbohydrate, 5 g fat, 0 mg cholesterol, 0 g fiber, 22 mg sodium.

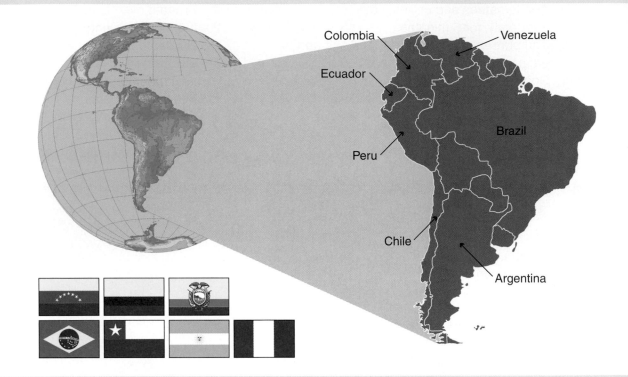

South America

Colombia

Venezuela

Ecuador

Brazil

Peru

Chile

Argentina

Think Outside the Box

Ask students how they could find out about business practices in another country before visiting associates in the country.

Activity

Have students look at a map illustrating the climate and/or annual precipitation in South America.

The Atlantic and Pacific Oceans and the Caribbean Sea form the boundaries of South America. South America is nearly twice the size of the United States. It is a land of contrasts—dense rain forests and snowcapped mountains; deserts and lush farmland; large, modern cities and untamed jungles.

Geography and Climate of South America

The geography in South America is varied. Mountains, grasslands, jungles, forests, plateaus, and deserts divide the continent. The Andes Mountains form the longest and second highest mountain chain in the world. These mountains and dense jungles have made travel impossible in many parts of the continent. As a result, each country has developed independently and has preserved a unique culture.

You can find nearly every kind of climate in South America. In parts of Chile, meteorologists have never recorded any rainfall. The area is an arid wasteland. However, rain falls daily in the tropical rain forests of Brazil. Snow and high winds bring bitter cold to the peaks of the Andes, yet the jungles below are hot and humid.

South American Culture

A number of peoples influenced the development of South American culture. These include ancient native tribes like the *Inca*. Spanish and Portuguese explorers left their marks on this land. African slaves brought to work on Brazilian sugar plantations made contributions as well. The influences of all these groups can still be seen in the lifestyle of South America today, **29-5**.

Shutterstock

29-5 Machu Picchu is an ancient Incan city built in the Andes Mountains of Peru.

Global Perspective

South American Economy

Today, South America is in a process of evolution. Most South American countries are experiencing rapid population growth.

Great economic and technological progress can be seen in skyscrapers, modern highways, and industrial plants. Brasilia, Rio de Janeiro, Caracas, and Buenos Aires are modern cities. Their architecture and transportation systems resemble those of cities in Europe and the United States. However, intermingled with modern buildings are churches that date back to the Spanish conquistadores and the Inca.

South America has both great wealth and great poverty. Some landowners control vast amounts of the most productive farmland. However, many farmers barely survive on small plots with poor soil. The members of the upper classes enjoy the best foods, entertainment, and housing. At the same time, the lower classes are hindered by illiteracy, lack of transportation, antiquated farming methods, and poor wages.

South American Holidays

Many festivals in South America are blends of Christian celebrations and other beliefs. In Brazil, many holidays combine traditions of African religions with days honoring saints in the Catholic Church. In Peru, ancient Incan beliefs are mixed with church holy days.

Many South American festivals last for several days. They are public celebrations with processions through village streets. Music, dancing, parades, and colorful costumes are part of many of these celebrations. Vendors often sell food to the crowds of people who gather to celebrate.

The most elaborate of the South American festivals is Carnival. This is the Brazilian festival that parallels the Mardi Gras festival celebrated in the southern United States. Carnival is held the six days before Ash Wednesday, which is the beginning of Lent in the Christian church. All year, people plan the floats, costumes, and exotic masks that will be part of this celebration.

South American Cuisine

South American cuisine combines influences of native tribes with those of the Spanish, Portuguese, and Africans. Many staple foods, such as corn, potatoes, and manioc, are found throughout the continent. (**Manioc**, known as **cassava** in some regions, is a starchy root plant eaten as a side dish and used in flour form in cooking and baking.) However, most food customs have developed on a regional basis because of geographic isolation. Each region reflects cultural influences as well as geographic and climatic ones. The following discussion will give you an overview of some of the unique dishes typical of some South American countries.

Venezuela

The Spanish who explored Venezuela found rich, fertile soil and a temperate climate in the valleys formed by the Andes. The cuisine of this country reflects these two factors. It also reflects the tropical climate found in the jungle lowlands just south of the valleys and the food customs of the Spanish explorers.

Much of Venezuela is inhabited by families who do small-scale farming. **Arepa**, a corn pancake similar to a tortilla, is a traditional Venezuelan bread. It forms the basis of the farmer's diet. Cooks make arepa by mixing corn flour with water and salt. They shape the stiff dough into balls or patties and toast it on a lightly greased griddle, **29-6**.

©2011 Wisconsin Milk Marketing Board, Inc.

29-6 Venezuelan corn pancakes called arepas are served here with eggs and salsa.

Although people often eat arepa plain, they also use it to make more elaborate dishes. *Bollos pelones*, for example, are balls of arepa dough stuffed with a meat mixture. These dumplings are then deep-fried or simmered in soup or sauce.

Those people living in the tropical lowlands make good use of the banana, plantain, and coconut. Bananas and plantains are boiled, fried, baked, and added to stews and soups. Plantains, thinly sliced and fried until crisp, are a popular Venezuelan snack. Banana leaves are used to wrap *hallacas*, Venezuela's national dish, which is cornmeal dough filled with other foods. Candies, puddings, and cakes are made from coconuts. Coconut and coconut milk are also added to stewed meats. A sponge-type cake moistened with *muscatel* (a type of wine) and covered with coconut cream is a famous Venezuelan dessert.

Colombia

Potatoes, which are grown high in the mountains, are especially important in the diets of northern Colombians. Farther south, cassavas are used instead of potatoes.

Colombians who are poor eat little meat. However, stews and thick soups are popular in Colombia. Cooks make one soup, *ajiaco*, with potatoes, chicken, corn, and cassava.

Colombia is an important coffee-producing country. The coffee trees thrive on the cool slopes of the Andes Mountains. The coffee served in Colombia is much stronger than that served in the United States. However, Colombians do not drink as much coffee as people in the United States.

Ecuador

Because Ecuador is a large producer of bananas, local dishes often feature bananas. Ecuadorian people make bananas into flour, which they use to make breads and pastries. They cut firm green bananas and plantains into chips and deep-fry them. The simplest and most common banana dessert is made by slowly frying ripe bananas in butter. As the slices begin to brown, sugar is added little by little until the bananas are brown on both sides. Before serving, the sautéed banana slices are splashed with brandy and dusted with powdered sugar.

Peru

The descendants of the Inca still live in Peru. They have retained many of the customs of their ancestors. Their cuisine reflects both Incan and Spanish traditions.

Peruvians often make *cuy* (guinea pig) into a stew. They also brush cuy with olive oil and garlic and roast it. Vendors on Peruvian streets sell another popular meat dish called *anticuchos*. They marinate small strips of beef heart overnight and thread them on skewers. They baste the meat with a sauce and grill it over hot coals.

Peruvians who live along the coast eat a variety of seafood. Shrimp is especially popular in both appetizers and main dishes. *Chupe*, a thick soup made from milk, vegetables, and shellfish, is served as a main dish.

Peruvians invented **ceviche**, a marinated raw fish dish. However, people throughout South America enjoy it. Cooks usually make ceviche from *corvinas* (a type of whitefish found off the Peruvian coast), but they can use other types of whitefish. They cut the fish into small cubes. Then they cover it with a marinade made of lime juice, lemon juice, salt, pepper, garlic, onion, and ají. **Ají** is the Peruvian and Chilean term for chilies.

Enrich

Show students how to prepare fresh coconut by piercing the eyes and draining the juice. Then tap the grooved shell with a hammer to crack it and pry out the meat with a sturdy knife. Allow students to sample the meat and the juice.

Online Resource

Assign each of four teams one of the following Ecuadorian regions: coast, highlands, Amazon, or Galapagos. Have each team visit the Exploring Ecuador website to find information to include in a report on their assigned region. Each team member should present a different aspect of the report.

Reflect

Ask students if they would be willing to eat guinea pig and explain how this would differ from eating beef or pork.

Discuss

Ask students how the freeze-drying process used by the

After the fish has marinated for several hours, its texture becomes similar to that of cooked fish. The ceviche is then ready to eat. Peruvians often serve ceviche with corn and sweet potatoes. People in other South American countries often serve it as an appetizer.

Peruvian tamales contain a variety of foods including meat, chicken, sausage, eggs, peanuts, raisins, and olives. Unlike Mexican tamales, they often are somewhat sweet.

Learn About...

Peruvian Potatoes

Since the days of the Inca, the *papa* (potato) has been the staple food of the Peruvian people. The Inca developed over 100 potato varieties. To preserve their potatoes, they freeze-dried them. The cold night air of the Andes quickly froze the potatoes. When the sun came out, the potatoes thawed. At night, they froze once again. The moisture that formed evaporated. Soon the potatoes became hard as stone but very lightweight. The Inca could then store the potatoes indefinitely.

The poorest people of Peru eat boiled potatoes alone or with a few local herbs or ají. Those who are not quite so poor prepare potatoes in many unusual and delicious ways. One popular potato dish is made by pouring a thick sauce made of cheese, milk, ají, and various local spices over boiled potatoes. Another flavorful potato dish of Incan origin is *causa a la limena.* A mixture of stiff mashed potatoes, olive oil, lemon juice, salt, pepper, chopped onions, and ají is pressed into small molds. The unmolded dish is garnished with hard-cooked eggs, cheese, sweet potatoes, *prawns* (a shrimplike crustacean), and olives.

Shutterstock

Potatoes have long been a staple of the Peruvian diet, and they are served in a variety of ways.

Inca compares with commercial freeze-drying done today.

Chile

Chile is a long, thin country. The upper third of Chile is arid desert, and the lower third is mountainous. The central region has fertile valleys, irrigated fields, and forests.

Because the land is not suitable for raising cattle or sheep, Chileans eat little meat. Instead, seafood, beans, and small amounts of meat are combined with vegetables in many delicious stews. *Porotos granados*, for example, contains cranberry beans, corn, squash, garlic, and onion.

Another popular dish in Chile is *pastel de choclo*. It is a meat pie made with a sugar-coated topping of ground fresh corn. Beef, or a combination of beef and chicken, usually is used in the filling. Raisins and olives may be added. Some cooks also add pepper or ají. However, most Chilean dishes are not peppery.

Of all the South Americans, Chileans probably eat the most seafood. Seafood is both plentiful and inexpensive, and shellfish are particularly popular. Crabs, lobsters, clams, scallops, and sea urchins are used in many dishes. *Chupe de marisco* (scallop stew) is baked in a deep dish. A creamy cheese sauce flavored with paprika, nutmeg, pepper, and onion complements the flavors of scallops and rice.

Argentina

The Pampas are the richest lands in South America. They cover the southeastern part of the continent and reach into the countries of Argentina and Uruguay. Here, large herds of cattle and sheep graze until they are ready for market.

Because it is so readily available, the people of Argentina eat large amounts of meat. Much of the meat is roasted in the style of the gauchos. The **gauchos** were nomadic herders of the Pampas during the eighteenth and nineteenth centuries. They put meat from freshly slaughtered cattle on large stakes placed at an angle around a fire. (This prevented the juices from dripping into the coals.) A peppery herb and parsley sauce called *chimichurri* accompanied the freshly roasted meat.

Argentine cooks also prepare meat in other ways. They make one popular dish, *metambre*, by layering spinach, hard-cooked eggs, carrots, and onions on top of a marinated flank steak. Then they roll the metambre, tie it, and either poach it or roast it until tender.

Argentine appetizers are called **empanadas**. They are small turnovers filled with chopped meat, olives, raisins, and onions.

Although most of the foods of Argentina have a strong flavor, mild-flavored squashes and pumpkins have been popular for centuries. Cooks use squash to make fritters, soups, and puddings. They sometimes thicken and decorate stews with squash. *Carbonada criolla*, a colorful stew, contains pieces of beef, squash, tomatoes, corn on the cob, and fresh peaches. It sometimes is served in a squash or pumpkin shell.

Humitas are similar to Mexican tamales. Unripe kernels of corn are mixed with onions, tomatoes, salt, pepper, sugar, and cinnamon. Sometimes cheese is also added. Humitas may be cooked with milk until tender and served plain. They may also be rolled into corn husks, tied, and boiled or steamed.

Brazil

Brazilian culture is a mixture of Native South American, Portuguese, and African cultures. The native inhabitants of Brazil were more primitive than the Inca of the Andes. They did not practice agriculture on a wide scale. However, they did produce manioc, which is still a staple food in Brazil.

Explorers from Portugal landed in the area that is now Brazil. The Portuguese stayed in the area and built large plantations where they grew sugarcane. Today, Portuguese is the official language of Brazil.

The Portuguese brought Africans to Brazil to work in the sugar fields. African women were skilled cooks and worked in the kitchens of the Portuguese. The Africans made a great impact on Brazilian cuisine. They raised crops of foods from their homeland, including bananas, yams, and coconuts. These ingredients are now used in many Brazilian dishes. African cooks also introduced the use of red pepper and **dendé oil** (palm oil that gives Brazilian dishes a bright yellow-orange color).

Discuss

Ask students how geography has affected the cuisine of Chile. *(Chile's large mountain and desert regions are not suitable for raising livestock. However, Chile's long coastline makes seafood readily available. Therefore, Chile's cuisine uses little meat but much seafood.)*

Enrich

Have students write research reports comparing the gauchos of Argentina with the cowboys of the western United States.

FYI

The cuisines of Argentina and Uruguay are exceptions to the plant-based cuisine typical of most of Latin America. People in these countries eat over twice as much beef each year as people in the United States.

Enrich

Have students research Portugal's role in triangular trade and share their findings in poster reports.

The African women made use of the readily available shrimp and fish. *Vatapa*, for example, is a delicious stew made of pieces of shrimp and fish cooked with coconut milk, palm oil, and pieces of bread. Vatapa is usually served over rice.

The Brazilians serve rice, a second staple food, in a variety of ways. One popular dish is a casserole made of layers of rice, shrimp, ham, chicken, cheese, and tomato. A popular Afro-Brazilian coconut pudding also contains rice.

Beans, a third staple food, are as important to Brazilian cooking as they are to Mexican cooking. Brazilians prefer shiny black beans they can cook to a paste. They use these beans to make **feijoada completa**, Brazil's national dish, **29-7**. Feijoada completa is made with meat and beans. It can be simple or elaborate depending on the ingredients used. Traditional feijoada completa includes dried beef and smoked tongue. Other meats, such as fresh beef, pork, bacon, sausage, and pigs' feet, can also be added. The meats are cooked until tender and then arranged on a large platter. The black beans, cooked to a pulp, are served in a separate pot. Bowls of hot sauces, cooked rice, manioc meal, shredded kale or collard greens, and orange slices accompany the beans and meat.

A Brazilian version of the tamale, called *abara*, is African in origin. Abara is a mixture of cowpeas, shrimp, pepper, and dendé oil rolled into banana leaves and cooked over an open fire.

Cuscuz, a steamed grain dish, is either Arabian or North African in origin. The Brazilians adopted it and developed two different forms of it.

One kind of cuscuz is sweet and is served as a dessert. Cooks mix tapioca, freshly grated coconut, coconut milk, sugar, and water together with boiling water. They pour the mixture into a mold and refrigerate it. Later, they slice and serve the chilled cuscuz. The other type of cuscuz, often called *cuscuz paulista*, is served as a main dish. Cuscuz paulista is made with specially prepared cornmeal mixed with shredded vegetables and meat and a small amount of fat. The mixture is steamed and garnished decoratively.

Shutterstock

29-7 Brazilian cooks combine black beans, meat, and a variety of fresh ingredients to make their national dish, feijoada completa.

South American Menu

Empanadas
(Turnovers)

Carbonada Criolla
(Beef Stew)

Couve à Mineira
(Shredded Kale)

Tortillas de Maiz
(Corn Pancakes)

Plàtanos Tumulto
(Broiled Bananas)

Brasileiras
(Brazilian Coconut Cookies)

Café
(Coffee)

1. Sift flour, salt, and baking powder into a large mixing bowl.
2. With pastry blender or two knives, cut shortening into dry ingredients until particles are the size of coarse cornmeal.
3. Add ice water, stirring gently with a fork until dough forms a ball.
4. On lightly floured board or pastry cloth, roll out dough.
5. Using a 2-inch biscuit cutter, cut dough into circles.
6. Place about 1 tablespoon filling in the center of each circle. Fold dough over filling and seal edges well with a little cold water.
7. Bake in a 450°F oven until lightly browned, about 10 to 15 minutes. (For a more authentic dish, empanadas can be fried, a few at a time, in 375°F oil until golden brown.)

Per serving: 126 cal. (50% from fat), 5 g protein, 11 g carbohydrate, 7 g fat, 11 mg cholesterol, 1 g fiber, 95 mg sodium.

Empanadas
(Turnovers)

Makes about 24

Filling:

1	pound lean ground beef
1	onion, finely chopped
½	clove garlic, chopped
2	medium tomatoes
8	large green olives, chopped
½	cup raisins
	salt
	pepper

1. In large, heavy skillet, brown ground beef.
2. Add onions and garlic.
3. When browned, add tomatoes, olives, raisins, and salt and pepper to taste.
4. Simmer mixture uncovered until cooked, about 20 minutes.
5. Remove from heat and refrigerate until you are ready to fill empanadas.

Pastry:

2	cups all-purpose flour
½	teaspoon salt
1	teaspoon baking powder
½	cup shortening
⅓	cup ice water

Carbonada Criolla
(Beef Stew)

Serves 10

2	tablespoons vegetable oil
2½	pounds beef chuck, cut into 1-inch cubes
¾	cup coarsely chopped onions
½	cup coarsely chopped green pepper
½	teaspoon finely chopped garlic
4½	cups beef stock
3	medium tomatoes, seeded and chopped
½	teaspoon oregano
1	bay leaf
1¼	teaspoons salt
½	teaspoon pepper
4½	cups sweet potatoes, cut into ½-inch cubes (about 1½ pounds)
4½	cups white potatoes, cut into ½-inch cubes (about 1½ pounds)
¾	pound zucchini, cubed
4	small ears sweet corn, shucked and cut into rounds, 1 inch wide
6	canned peach halves, rinsed in cold water

1. Heat oil in a large Dutch oven.
2. Add meat and brown.
3. Transfer browned meat to a platter and cook onions, green peppers, and garlic until lightly browned.
4. Add beef stock and bring to a boil.

5. Return meat to stock and add tomatoes, oregano, bay leaf, salt, and pepper.
6. Cover Dutch oven and reduce heat to low. Simmer stew for 15 minutes.
7. Remove cover and add sweet potatoes and white potatoes. Simmer for 15 minutes more.
8. Remove cover and add zucchini. Cover and cook 10 minutes more.
9. Remove cover and add corn and peach halves, cover and cook 5 minutes more.

Per serving: 312 cal. (32% from fat), 20 g protein, 34 g carbohydrate, 11 g fat, 53 mg cholesterol, 4 g fiber, 403 mg sodium.

Couve à Mineira (Shredded Kale)

Serves 6

1½   pounds kale*
2   tablespoons bacon drippings
½   teaspoon salt
      dash pepper

1. Under running water, carefully wash kale. With a sharp knife, remove any bruised spots and cut tender leaves from tough stems. Discard stems. Shred kale into strips about ½ inch wide.
2. In large saucepan, bring 2 quarts water to a boil.
3. Add kale and cook uncovered 3 minutes.
4. Drain kale in a colander, removing as much water as possible.
5. In a large, heavy skillet, melt bacon drippings.
6. When hot, add kale. Cook, stirring frequently, until kale is tender, about 30 minutes. (Kale should still be slightly crisp.)
7. Add salt and pepper and serve immediately.

*Collard greens may be substituted for kale.

Per serving: 58 cal. (62% from fat), 1 g protein, 4 g carbohydrate, 4 g fat, 8 mg cholesterol, 3 g fiber, 193 mg sodium.

Tortillas de Maiz (Corn Pancakes)

Makes 8 pancakes

1   cup frozen corn kernels, thawed
1   egg
2   tablespoons all-purpose flour
¼   teaspoon salt
3 to 4 tablespoons margarine
½   cup plain nonfat yogurt
1½   tablespoons chopped fresh parsley

1. Using paper towels, pat corn completely dry.
2. Heat a large, heavy skillet, sprayed with nonstick cooking spray.
3. Add corn and cook until lightly browned.
4. Remove corn to plate lined with paper towels.
5. In large mixing bowl, beat egg until foamy; add flour, salt, and corn.
6. In small skillet or crepe pan, heat 1 tablespoon margarine until it foams.
7. Pour in ⅛ cup batter. As tortilla cooks, gently lift edges to allow uncooked batter to flow underneath.
8. When tortilla is brown on the bottom, flip with spatula and cook other side 1 minute.
9. Slide tortilla onto a heated platter and keep warm in a 225°F oven.
10. Continue making tortillas, adding a teaspoon of margarine before frying each.
11. Serve tortillas topped with 1 tablespoon of yogurt and chopped parsley.

Per tortilla: 79 cal. (55% from fat), 2 g protein, 7 g carbohydrate, 5 g fat, 35 mg cholesterol, 1 g fiber, 137 mg sodium.

Plàtanos Tumulto (Broiled Bananas)

Serves 6

6   firm, medium bananas
      lemon juice
3   tablespoons light brown sugar, packed
¾   teaspoon cinnamon
3   tablespoons margarine

1. Preheat broiler.
2. Peel bananas and slice in half lengthwise.
3. Place banana halves cut side up on broiler pan; sprinkle with lemon juice.
4. Combine brown sugar and cinnamon in small bowl; cut in margarine until mixture resembles large peas. Sprinkle over banana halves.
5. Place bananas 2 inches from heat and broil until sugar has melted. (Watch carefully.) Serve immediately.

Per serving: 198 cal. (29% from fat), 1 g protein, 34 g carbohydrate, 7 g fat, 0 mg cholesterol, 2 g fiber, 71 mg sodium.

Brasileiras
(Brazilian Coconut Cookies)

Makes about 3 dozen

1	cup granulated sugar
½	cup water
4	egg yolks, slightly beaten
¼	cup all-purpose flour
2¼	cups freshly grated or packaged coconut
½	teaspoon vanilla

1. In heavy saucepan, combine sugar and water. Cook over moderate heat, stirring until sugar dissolves.
2. Cook syrup undisturbed until candy thermometer reads 230°F. (A small amount of syrup dropped into ice water should immediately form a hard thread.)
3. In small mixer bowl, combine egg yolks and flour until well blended.
4. Add 2 tablespoons of the hot syrup, stirring constantly.
5. Slowly add this mixture to the syrup remaining in the pan, stirring constantly.
6. Add coconut and simmer over low heat, stirring constantly, until mixture becomes thick. (Do not let it boil.)
7. Remove from heat and quickly stir in vanilla. Let mixture cool to room temperature.
8. Preheat oven to 375°F.
9. Shape cookie dough into small balls.
10. Arrange balls 1 inch apart on lightly greased baking sheets.
11. Bake 15 minutes or until cookies are a delicate golden brown.
12. Remove to wire racks to cool.

Per serving: 50 cal. (41% from fat), 1 g protein, 7 g carbohydrate, 2 g fat, 30 mg cholesterol, 1 g fiber, 2 mg sodium.

CAREER SUCCESS

Sociability

Armando is a Spanish interpreter for a travel agency that serves mainly Latin American clients traveling in the United States. His job is to translate his clients' questions and comments to tour guides and hotel and restaurant staff who do not speak Spanish.

To be an effective worker, Armando needs to display sociability toward his clients. He must demonstrate understanding, friendliness, and empathy to people who are in unfamiliar surroundings and are unable to communicate. Put yourself in Armando's place and answer the following questions about your need for and use of this quality:

A. How might your clients be affected if you lack sociability?
B. How might tour guides and hotel and restaurant staff interacting with your clients be affected if you lack sociability?
C. How might your travel agency be affected if you lack sociability?
D. What is another skill you would need in this job? Briefly explain why this skill would be important.

CHAPTER 29 REVIEW

Summary

The Aztecs and the Spanish conquistadores played a role in Mexico's history. They also contributed to Mexico's cuisine. Many Mexicans are farmers. The corn and beans they grow are important to the economy. These foods are important ingredients in Mexican cuisine, too. Mexican cooks also make much use of peppers, fruits, and vegetables in their cooking. They prepare a variety of flavorful sauces and stews and unique desserts and beverages. Many of these dishes have evolved on a regional basis due to Mexico's varied climate and geography.

Spanish, Portuguese, and African influences are blended with foods of native tribes to form South American cuisine. Throughout the continent, corn, potatoes, and manioc are used as staple foods. However, geographic isolation is the reason the way these foods are used vary from region to region.

Review What You Have Read

Write your answers on a separate sheet of paper, using complete sentences when appropriate.

1. How have climate and geography affected Mexican food customs?

2. The Aztecs and the Spaniards made many contributions to Mexican cuisine. Name four contributions of each.

3. What is a tortilla and how is it made? Describe three Mexican foods made from the tortilla.

4. What are the colors of peppers used in Mexican cooking and how are they used?

5. True or false. Guacamole is a popular spread made from mashed bananas.

6. Describe one type of mole.

7. What is Mexico's main meal of the day called? What foods are usually served at this meal?

8. A corn pancake similar to a tortilla that is a traditional Venezuelan bread is _____.

9. What has been the staple food of the Peruvian people since the days of the Inca? How did the Inca preserve this food?

10. With which South American country are the following words associated: Pampas, gaucho, chimichurri, and carbonada criolla?
    A. Argentina
    B. Brazil
    C. Chile
    D. Venezuela

11. Brazilian culture is a mixture of three cultures. Name them.

12. True or false. Feijoada completa is a Peruvian national dish made with meat and beans.

(continued)

Answer Key for
Review What You Have Read **questions**

1. (Student response.)

2. (Name four contributions of each:) Aztecs—chocolate, vanilla, corn, peppers, peanuts, tomatoes, avocados, squash, beans, sweet potatoes, pineapples, papayas. Spaniards—oil, wine, cinnamon, cloves, rice, wheat, peaches, apricots, beef, chicken.

3. A tortilla is flat, unleavened bread made from cornmeal or wheat flour. The dough is shaped into a thin pancake in a tortilla press. Then it is cooked on a lightly greased griddle called a comal. (Descriptions of three foods made from the tortilla are student response.)

4. The peppers used in Mexican cooking are red and green. Red peppers are used dried except for ripe bell peppers and pimientos. Green peppers are used fresh.

5. false

Link to Academic Skills

13. **History/English language arts.** Write a research report comparing the lifestyle and conquest of the Mexican Aztec civilization with that of the South American Incan Empire.

14. **Geography.** On a map of Mexico, identify areas in which fish would play a main part in the diet and areas in which beef would be more prevalent.

15. **Social studies.** Investigate how the celebration of Mardi Gras in the United States compares with the celebration of Carnival in Brazil. Share your findings in a class discussion.

16. **Geography.** Borrow several travel videos from your local library to learn more about the geography of South America. Then participate in a class discussion about how the geography of South America differs from one country to another.

Build Critical Thinking Skills

17. **Synthesis.** Visit the Mexico Online website. Navigate the site and related links to find information about the Mexican tourist destination of your choice. Investigate lodging, tours, restaurants, and activities in your chosen city to plan a four-day, three-night vacation. Compile your findings into the form of a travel itinerary.

18. **Evaluation.** Some South American baked goods are made with cassava flour instead of wheat flour. Research the nutritional value of cassava flour compared with the nutritional value of white wheat all-purpose flour. Evaluate the nutritional impact on a typical U.S. diet that would result if cassava flour were used in place of wheat flour. Share your findings in class.

Apply Technology

19. Use the Internet to find out which airlines fly to Mexico and South America. Identify the nearest point of departure as well as three Mexican and three South American destinations. Share your findings in class.

20. Work in a small group to choose a specific aspect of a Latin American country on which you want to focus a presentation. Your group should scan or download images and then use presentation software to create a slide show to present to the class.

6. The mole used to prepare the traditional turkey mole is made from a variety of chilies, almonds, raisins, garlic, sesame seeds, onions, tomatoes, cinnamon, cloves, coriander seeds, and anise seeds that are finely chopped and added to chicken stock. Unsweetened chocolate is added just before serving.

7. Mexico's main meal of the day is called comida. Foods usually served at this meal include an appetizer, a soup, a small dish of stew, a main course, tortillas or bread, beans, dessert, and coffee.

8. arepa

9. The papa (potato) has been the staple food of the Peruvian people since the days of the Inca. The Inca preserved potatoes by freeze-drying.

10. A

(continued)

A Measure of Math

11. Brazilian culture is a mixture of Native South American, Portuguese, and African cultures.

12. false

21. Identify a list of 10 popular ingredients you might opt to include in a Mexican entree such as tacos or burritos. Be sure to specify the quantity of each ingredient you would use. Use the Internet or nutrition software to find information to create a bar graph for each ingredient. Illustrate the calorie, total fat, sodium, and fiber content of each ingredient. Use the bar graphs to create nutritional profiles of three combinations of ingredients. Note how adding or eliminating certain ingredients affects the nutritional value of Mexican entrees.

Teamwork in Action

22. Plan a Mexican or South American holiday celebration to share with other students in your school. Prepare and display informative posters about the culture and cuisine you are celebrating.

Companion Website

www.g-wlearning.com

At the website, review key terms for this chapter with crossword puzzles, matching exercises, and e-flash cards. Apply facts from the chapter to complete the activities.

CHAPTER 30
Europe

Learning Prep

Write each of the *Terms to Know* on a slip of paper. Place all the slips in a container and mix them up. Pass the container around the room so each student can draw a slip from the container. Suggest a meaning and an associated country for each term you draw.

Terms to Know

cockles	escargot
fish and chips	quiche
pudding basin	braten
tea	kartoffelpuffer
haggis	sauerkraut
colcannon	spätzle
haute cuisine	strudel
provincial cuisine	crayfish
nouvelle cuisine	smørrebrød
fines herbes	lutefisk
hors d'oeuvres	smörgåsbord
croissant	husmankost
crêpe	lingonberry
truffles	sauna

Main Menu

- Regional dishes as well as national specialties are common in Europe.
- Culture and traditions have shaped diverse meal patterns in the European countries.

Objectives

After studying this chapter, you will be able to

- **identify** food customs of the British Isles, France, Germany, and the Scandinavian countries.
- **explain** how and why these customs have evolved.
- **prepare** foods native to each of these countries.

Enrich

Have students write papers comparing the nutritive values of Northern European and Southern European cuisines.

Reflect

Ask students which of the countries of the British Isles they would most like to visit and explain their choices.

Europe is the second smallest continent in terms of land area. Despite its small size, it is one of the most heavily populated continents. Nearly one-fifth of the world's people live in Europe.

Europe has been a cultural, political, and economic leader for centuries. Its history is rich and varied.

Because so many countries are part of Europe, this chapter will focus on the British Isles, France, Germany, and Scandinavia. Spain, Italy, and Greece are discussed in another chapter.

Each European country has a unique cuisine, but some common diet patterns emerge. The diets of Northern European countries include a variety of fruits, vegetables, and breads. However, meals in these countries tend to center around meat, fish, poultry, or game. Dairy products also play an important role in many Northern European cuisines. Rich desserts are popular in these cuisines, too. Together, these characteristics describe a diet that tends to be fairly high in fat.

To include Northern European foods in a healthful diet, choose generous portions of vegetable and grain dishes. Limit portion sizes of meat and dairy foods. Select fruits for dessert often. Enjoy rich desserts only occasionally.

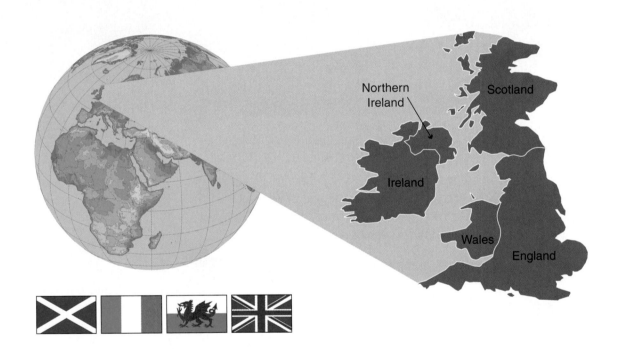

The British Isles are a group of two large islands and several small islands. They are located northwest of mainland Europe. The largest island, Great Britain, includes England, Scotland, and Wales. The second largest island, Ireland, is politically divided between two countries. Northern Ireland is joined with England, Scotland, and Wales to form the United Kingdom of Great Britain and Northern Ireland. The United Kingdom has four political divisions united under a single government. The southern part of the island of Ireland is the country of Ireland, which is an independent nation with its own government.

The people of the British Isles share a common ancestry and culture. Due to geographic isolation, however, each region of the British Isles has separate customs and traditions.

Geography and Climate of the British Isles

The Atlantic Ocean, North Sea, Irish Sea, and English Channel are the bodies of water that surround the British Isles. Much of England is composed of fertile farmlands, **30-1**. The Pennine Chain is a mountain range that runs northward through the center of England to the Scottish border. Southern Scotland is made up of rolling hills. The central lowland region is the location of most of Scotland's population, industry, and farmland. Northern Scotland is a rugged, mountainous area known as the Highlands. Wales can be divided into two parts. North Wales is mountainous country. South Wales is marked by valleys and coastal plains. Much of Ireland is covered with rolling hills and windswept plains. The landscape of Northern Ireland rises into low mountains along the northeast coast.

The weather changes in Britain from hour to hour and from village to village. Fog along the coasts is common, and the air is often raw and bone-chilling.

Culture of the British Isles

The British Isles have a long and colorful history. For centuries, this was the center of one of the world's greatest empires. It was a wellspring of contributions in the areas of art, architecture, and literature. The United Kingdom is still one of the most influential nations on earth.

British History

A number of groups of people shaped the culture of the British Isles. These included the Celts, Romans, Germanic tribes, and Normans. The Celts lived on the British Isles from about 500 BC until the Romans invaded some 600 years later.

FYI

The total area of the British Isles is roughly equal to that of the state of Arizona.

Enrich

Have students write research reports about one of the early groups of people who invaded Britain and the contributions they made to British culture.

Online Resource

Have each student navigate the British Tourist Authority website to take a virtual tour of a British destination. Ask students to share something they learned on their virtual tours. Also, ask students to state why they would or would not want to visit the British destinations in person someday.

Shutterstock

30-1 The English countryside is dotted with farms that produce grain and livestock.

The Jutes, Angles, and Saxons were Germanic tribes that invaded England from mainland Europe in the AD 400s. Eventually, the Angles and Saxons set up kingdoms throughout England. (The name *England* comes from "land of the Angles.") In 1066, William the Conqueror led a Norman army into England. (The Normans were a group of Scandinavian Vikings who had settled in northern France.) Through a military victory, William became the new king of England. Under William's reign, Norman influence spread throughout the British Isles.

The English language developed from the Germanic and Norman languages. It is the official language used throughout the United Kingdom. Welsh is a second official language in Wales. Many people in Scotland and Northern Ireland speak a form of an ancient Celtic language called *Gaelic*. Gaelic and English are both official languages in Ireland.

British Government

Wales was united with England in 1536 under King Henry VIII. In 1707, Scotland was united with England and Wales to form the Kingdom of Great Britain. Ireland became joined with Great Britain in 1801 to form the United Kingdom of Great Britain and Ireland.

London is the capital of the United Kingdom. It is the home of the Houses of Parliament, where British laws are made. The House of Lords and the House of Commons are the two bodies that make up Parliament. The monarchy has no real power. Instead, the head of government is the Prime Minister. The Prime Minister is usually the political party leader with the most members in the House of Commons.

Global Perspective

Ireland

Most of the people on the island of Ireland had been Roman Catholic for centuries. During the early 1600s, land on the northern part of the island was given to Protestants. Ongoing conflict existed between the Protestants in the north and the Catholics in the south. In 1921, the British Parliament agreed to the formation of the Irish Free State in southern Ireland. In 1937, this state adopted a new constitution and changed its name to Ireland, or Eire in Gaelic. In 1949, Ireland severed all connections with the United Kingdom and became an independent nation. Northern Ireland remains part of the United Kingdom.

British Agriculture

Much of the land on the British Isles is suitable for growing crops and raising livestock. Wheat, oats, and barley are the key grains grown in the British Isles. Potatoes are also an important crop throughout this area. Ireland has always been known for its excellent cattle, and Irish pedigree bulls are traded all over the world. Chickens, hogs, and dairy cattle are important sources of food. Sheep are raised for their wool as well as their meat.

Because water surrounds the British Isles, fishing is an important industry. Cod, haddock, and mackerel are among the most important catches. Along the Welsh coast, a type of mussel called **cockles** has flourished for hundreds of years. People still go to the shore and dig cockles out of the sand to sell in nearby markets.

Recreation in the British Isles

The people of the British Isles enjoy outdoor activities and sporting events throughout the year. Golf, hiking, mountain climbing, horseback riding, cycling, fishing, and tennis are well-liked activities when the weather is warm. In colder weather, skiing and curling are favorite pastimes. Popular sporting events in the British Isles include soccer, rugby, cricket, and hurling.

In Scotland, the Highland games are an annual recreational event. They are held in different areas throughout the spring, summer, and fall. The games include a variety of events, similar to a track meet.

Throughout the British Isles, a favorite social activity is relaxing with friends in a local public house, or *pub*. People gather to enjoy a glass of beer, play darts, and talk. See **30-2**.

Discuss

Ask students what the most popular sporting events in the United States are. *(baseball, basketball, football, ice hockey)*

Enrich

Have students write research reports on the origin and celebration of one of the British holidays discussed in the text.

British Holidays

Festivals and holiday traditions are reflections of culture among the people of the British Isles. In Scotland, New Year's Eve is called *Hogmanay*. It is celebrated with bonfires and feasts. A Scottish tradition centers on the first person to enter a family's home after midnight. This person is called the *first-footer*. The Scots look for the first-footer to carry bread, coal, and money. They believe this means the family will not be hungry, cold, or poor in the coming year. The Scots drink a New Year's toast of sweet or spiced ale from a *wassail bowl*. This name comes from "Waes hael," which is Gaelic for "Be well."

An annual Welsh festival is *St. David's Day*, which honors the patron saint of Wales. This celebration takes place on March 1. Welsh people pin daffodils (a spring flower) or leeks (a winter vegetable) to their clothes. This symbolizes the passing of winter into spring. St. David's Day feasts feature traditional Welsh foods, such as leek soup, lamb, and Welsh wines and cheeses.

St. Patrick's Day is a national celebration held in honor of Ireland's patron saint. People often dress in green and display shamrocks to observe St. Patrick's Day. Green represents the color of Ireland's countryside. Shamrocks are Ireland's national emblem. This day is celebrated by Irish people throughout the world with food, folk music, and parades. In Ireland, however, St. Patrick's Day is an important religious holiday spent quietly with family and friends.

November 5 is a distinctly English holiday—*Guy Fawkes Night*. This celebration is named for a man who tried to blow up the Houses of Parliament in 1605. The British gather for fireworks and bonfires. The bonfires are topped with figures made of paper or straw stuffed into old clothes to represent Guy Fawkes.

Courtesy of the Idaho Potato Commission

30-2 Bangers and mash, or sausages and mashed potatoes, is a classic British dish that might be offered as pub fare.

Cuisine of the British Isles

The cuisine of the British Isles is hearty and filling. Cooks use many locally grown foods. They prepare them in a variety of ways to create dishes that are substantial yet simple and economical.

Culture and Social Studies

Development of British Cuisine

The early Anglo-Saxons hunted, fished, and gathered nuts and berries for food. They eventually made small gardens and grew grain along the edges of the forests.

Using techniques they had brought from their homelands, the Anglo-Saxons brewed ale from barley. They ground grain for use in baking bread. They made the milk of sheep and cattle into butter and cheese. The Anglo-Saxons also grew apple trees for cider and kept bees for honey. They either roasted the meat from freshly caught game or cooked it in large iron pots. By the eleventh century, the Anglo-Saxons had added puddings and pies to their cuisine.

Several other contributions to British cuisine were made during the reign of William the Conqueror. The Normans prepared delicious breads and pastries. They made some unusual dishes, such as *tripe* (stomach tissue of cattle and oxen). They also used spices and herbs in large quantities.

Norman meals had several courses. Normans served their meat course on *trenchers* (wooden or metal platters or large slices of bread). This was an example of the more refined manners the Normans used.

British Cuisine

The bread, meat, cheese, pies, and puddings of the Anglo-Saxons are still staples of the British diet today. For centuries, England has specialized in a variety of dishes based on these staple foods. Steamed puddings and pickled meats are among the many foods for which British cooks are famous. Savory and sweet pies, crumpets, and a slightly sweet yeast bread called Sally Lunn are also popular British foods.

British Main Dishes

The British enjoy beef, pork, lamb, mutton, and wild game. The British perfected the art of roasting centuries ago, and roasting is still popular.

Rivaling the British love of meat is the love of fish. The British eat fresh mackerel, whiting, cod, haddock, Dover sole, halibut, salmon, and many other varieties. They often prepare these fish by baking or poaching. *Kippers* (split and salted herring) are popular smoked fish.

Shops selling fish and chips are scattered throughout England. **Fish and chips** are battered, deep-fried fish fillets served with the British version of French fries. The type of fish vendors use often depends on the particular day's catch. Cod, haddock, and sole are the most popular.

Creative British cooks turn leftovers into a number of popular dishes. *Bubble and squeak* is the name for a dish made from leftover beef and potatoes. Cold cooked beef and potatoes are mixed with either raw cabbage or Brussels sprouts and cooked until crisp. *Shepherd's pie* is a mixture of finely chopped meat and leftover vegetables

Courtesy of the Idaho Potato Commission

30-3 Hearty shepherd's pie is a filling British main dish that can be made from leftovers.

FYI

Bubble and squeak reportedly gets its name from the sounds the ingredients make while the dish is cooking.

Reflect

Ask students if main-dish pies and puddings appeal to them. Have them consider why or why not.

topped with mashed potatoes and baked, **30-3**. *Toad in the hole* is made by pouring a thick batter over pieces of leftover meat and baking the mixture.

British Fruits and Vegetables

Apples have grown in England for centuries, and British cooks use apples in many simple but creative ways. Baked apples, apple charlotte, apple crumble, apple pudding, and apple sponge are popular desserts. British people enjoy other fruits, too. They serve fresh strawberries with rich, thick cream. They use a variety of berries as well as apples, plums, and other fruits to make jams, jellies, and preserves.

Carrots, spinach, parsnips, peas, beans, cabbage, cauliflower, onions, and potatoes grow well in British gardens. Sauces appear occasionally, but the British usually serve vegetables right from the garden cooked with just butter and simple seasonings.

British Pies and Puddings

A discussion of British foods would not be complete without mentioning pies and puddings. Both can be either desserts or main dishes.

Steak and kidney pie is one of the best known British pies. Cooks combine diced kidney with cubes of beef and a savory gravy and cover it with a pastry crust. A plum pie dusted with sugar is a popular dessert pie.

The British serve hundreds of sweet puddings. Each pudding begins with the same basic ingredients—milk, sugar, eggs, flour, and butter. Extra ingredients, such as dried fruit, spices, and lemon juice, make each pudding unique.

Most puddings are steamed in a **pudding basin**. The traditional basin is a deep, thick-rimmed bowl. A cook pours the pudding mixture into the basin and covers it with a clean cloth. Then the basin goes into a large kettle that is partially filled with water to steam the pudding. Cooks make boiled puddings by wrapping the dough in a piece of floured cloth. Then they tie the cloth at the top and immerse the pudding in a kettle of boiling water.

A *summer pudding* is neither boiled nor steamed. A basin is lined with slices of bread. The lined mold is then filled to the top with sweetened, fresh berries, covered with more bread, weighted, and chilled. During chilling, the bread soaks up the fruit juices. The unmolded pudding often is served with heavy cream.

The *trifle* is another popular British dessert. You might call it a pudding-cake. A mold or serving dish is lined with slices of pound cake spread with a fruit jam. The cake is soaked with sherry. The mold is then filled with layers of custard, fresh fruit, whipped cream, and slivered almonds. See **30-4**.

British Meals

Traditional British breakfasts are hearty, including eggs, bacon, baked beans, fried bread served with marmalade, and tea. People in many parts of England also eat fruits, main dish pies, ham, smoked fish, and porridge as breakfast foods.

During the week, lunch often is little more than a hearty meat or cheese sandwich and tea. On Sunday, however, lunch is the main meal of the day.

People in all the countries of the British Isles serve tea throughout the day as a beverage. The term **tea** also refers to a light meal. In rural areas, for example, the evening meal is called tea. In the cities, where people usually serve dinner in the evening, tea is a snack in the afternoon.

The British serve many foods for tea. A simple tea may consist of tea and a few cookies or a piece of cake. More elaborate teas may include a variety of sandwiches, sausages, cheeses, breads, cakes, and cookies. In England, people often serve crumpets with butter and homemade jam. *Crumpets* are a bread product similar to the English muffin served in the United States.

©2011 Wisconsin Milk Marketing Board, Inc.

30-4 Layers of pound cake, custard, fresh fruit, and whipped cream come together to make trifle, a colorful and delicious British dessert.

Scottish Cuisine

Oats and barley grow well in Scotland. Both grains have long been staple foods. Cooks often use them to make breads and porridges. Cooks also use oats to prepare the traditional Scottish holiday dish called haggis. **Haggis** is a pudding made from oatmeal, seasonings, and a sheep's organs boiled in a sheep's stomach. Barley is basic to the production of ales and liquors, many of which are exported. Fine Scotch whiskey, for example, is known throughout the world.

Scottish cooks are known for the good, simple, wholesome foods they prepare. Many Scottish dishes contain locally produced beef, lamb, or mutton. Others contain fish caught in coastal waters. Fresh fruits and vegetables, cereal products made of oats and barley, and dairy products may be added. For example, a hearty broth made from meat bones and vegetables often forms the basis for soup. Scotch broth and cock-a-leekie are two traditional Scottish soups. *Scotch broth* is made with lamb and barley; *cock-a-leekie* is made from chicken broth and leeks.

Fishing is an important industry in Scotland. As a result, the Scots eat fish often. Kippers and *finnan haddie* (split and smoked haddock) are especially popular in Scotland.

The Scots eat even heartier breakfasts than the British. They eat large amounts of porridge with *baps* (soft breakfast rolls), kippers, and many steaming cups of tea. Dundee is the birthplace of marmalade, which is eaten throughout the British Isles. Aberdeen is the birthplace of the breakfast sausage.

Learn About...

Scottish Baked Goods

Scottish cooks consider baking to be one of their greatest skills. Their baking skills are most apparent at high tea, which they serve at around six o'clock. Scottish specialties served at high tea include scones, shortbread, Dundee cake, and black bun. *Scones* are rich, triangle-shaped biscuits. They are usually split in half and spread with butter and marmalade. *Shortbread* is a rich, buttery cookie made from flour, sugar, and butter. *Dundee cake* is a rich fruitcake sprinkled with almonds. *Black bun* is a fruitcake covered with pastry. Gingerbread cakes, oatcakes, and brown and white rolls are other favorites.

Welsh Cuisine

Welsh food is similar to the foods of England and Scotland in its simplicity. The Welsh use homegrown foods to prepare dishes that are substantial yet plain and economical.

The rugged hills found in much of Wales are suitable for sheep production. The finest spring lambs in the British Isles graze on the grasses in the Brecon Beacons of Wales. Understandably, lamb and mutton are prominent in the Welsh diet. *Cawl* is a hearty soup made from mutton and leeks and other vegetables.

Besides lamb, the Welsh eat beef, pork, veal, and seafood. The Welsh often serve ham boiled. They eat cockles with a dash of vinegar. See **30-5**.

The Welsh grow potatoes, carrots, and other vegetables in local gardens and add them to soups and stews. *Tatws slaw* (potatoes mashed with buttermilk) frequently accompanies ham.

The Welsh serve tea in late afternoon or early evening. Various baked goods accompany cups of steaming tea. *Crempog* (buttermilk cakes) and *bara ceirch* (oatcakes spread with butter and eaten with buttermilk) are especially popular. Sponge cake and *bara brith* (a bread filled with currants) are enjoyed as well.

Familiar to many people in the United States is Welsh rabbit (or rarebit). *Welsh rabbit* is toast covered with a rich cheese sauce. One story says this dish got its name

Shutterstock

30-5 Cockles gathered along the coast of Wales are a popular seafood item in Welsh cuisine.

Activity

Have students make a table comparing the similarities and differences among British, Scottish, and Welsh cuisines.

FYI

Some reports state that cabbage and leeks were once the only vegetables that could be legally grown in Wales. These two vegetables are still featured in many Welsh recipes today.

Enrich

Have students use Internet and/or library resources to investigate the Irish potato famine. Ask them to present their findings in oral reports in class.

Enrich

The five-line verses known as limericks get their name from Limerick, Ireland. Challenge students to write a limerick about Irish cuisine.

Activity

Have students prepare recipes for soda bread, oatcakes, and scones. Serve these items as part of an Irish tea in your classroom.

because Welsh peasants were too poor to buy meat, even rabbit meat. The closest dish they could afford was this cheese dish, which they nicknamed "Welsh rabbit."

Irish Cuisine

Though the island of Ireland is divided politically, the people share a culinary heritage. Local dishes are still prepared with recipes that have been handed down from generation to generation.

Irish Vegetables

Potatoes have been the mainstay of the Irish diet for centuries. Their importance can best be seen in the results of the 1847 potato crop failure. Thousands of Irish people died, and over a million fled to the United States to escape the "black famine."

In many Irish homes, potatoes are still part of the daily diet. The Irish cook potatoes in a small amount of salted water and serve them with butter. They also use potatoes in soups, stews, breads, rolls, and cakes. Crisp, fried cakes made from grated raw potatoes, flour, salt, and milk are called *boxty*. Potatoes mashed with finely chopped scallions and milk and served with melted butter are called *champ*. Mashed potatoes mixed with chopped scallions, shredded cooked cabbage, and melted butter are called **colcannon**.

A variety of other vegetables are also grown in small gardens across Ireland. Cabbage, onions, carrots, cauliflower, parsnips, turnips, and peas are plentiful. The Irish may serve these vegetables creamed, baked, or cooked in water. Mushrooms gathered from the fields are sauteed in butter or added to soups and stews. Garlic and parsley add both color and flavor to meats, poultry, soups, and stews.

Irish Main Dishes

The excellent beef cattle produced in Ireland account for the popularity of *corned beef and cabbage*. This Irish dish is economical because it is made with the beef brisket. The Irish also use beef for roasting, braising, and adding to stews. The Irish steak and kidney stew is similar to the steak and kidney pie served in England.

Sheep thrive in the mountainous areas of Ireland where the land is too poor for farming. The Irish serve the first lamb of the year on Easter Sunday to mark the beginning of spring. They usually roast the leg of lamb. However, they use less tender parts of the animal to make Irish stew. *Irish stew* is pieces of lamb and potatoes in hearty gravy.

The Irish eat pork both fresh and cured, but Ireland is best known for its boiled hams. Traditionally, the Irish covered a whole boiled ham with sugar and bread crumbs and studded it with cloves.

The Irish who live close to the sea carry home buckets of seafood from fishing boats on the wharf. Most kinds of seafood are inexpensive because they are readily available. Favorites include crabs, mussels, prawns, and scallops.

Irish Baked Goods

Many people consider Irish breads to be some of the best in the world. Some Irish farm families still bake *soda bread* and *brown bread* every day. See **30-6**.

Baking is most important at tea. The Irish sometimes serve eggs, cold meats, and salads at tea. However, they always serve a variety of breads and cakes. They spread soda bread, brown bread, oatcakes, and scones thickly with butter. *Barmbrack*, a light fruitcake served with butter, is one of the most popular Irish cakes. On All Hallows' Eve (October 31), the family baker adds a wedding ring wrapped in paper to the batter before baking. Legend says the person who receives the slice of barmbrack with the ring will marry before the year ends. Two other favorite desserts served for tea are sponge cake and Irish whiskey cake.

Irish Meals

In Ireland, as in other parts of the British Isles, the day begins with a hearty breakfast. Breakfast commonly includes porridge, eggs, bread, butter, and tea. The Irish serve dinner in the middle of the day. It is the main meal for many people, especially those who live in rural areas. The Irish serve tea at about six o'clock in the evening.

Courtesy ACH Food Companies, Inc.

30-6 Irish soda bread is a traditional bread served often in many Irish homes.

British Menu

Welsh Rabbit

Corned Beef and Cabbage

Parsley-Buttered Potatoes and Carrots

Scones and Marmalade

English Trifle

Tea

Welsh Rabbit

Serves 6

2   tablespoons all-purpose flour
¾   cup fat-free milk
⅛   teaspoon pepper
¼   teaspoon dry mustard
½   teaspoon Worcestershire sauce
1   cup shredded Cheddar cheese
6   slices toast, cut diagonally into quarters

1. Combine flour and milk in a small, tightly covered container. Shake until thoroughly blended.
2. Pour flour mixture into a small saucepan. Blend in pepper, mustard, and Worcestershire sauce, stirring until mixture is smooth.
3. Cook over medium heat, stirring constantly, until sauce comes to a boil. Cook and stir for one additional minute until sauce is thick and smooth.
4. Remove sauce from heat and add cheese, stirring constantly until the cheese is melted.
5. Serve over toast pieces. Garnish with hard-cooked egg wedges, parsley, or paprika.

Per serving: 164 cal. (38% from fat), 9 g protein, 16 g carbohydrate, 7 g fat, 20 mg cholesterol, 0 g fiber, 274 mg sodium.

Corned Beef and Cabbage

Serves 8

2   pounds corned beef
1   sprig thyme
1   onion studded with 6 cloves
¼   teaspoon pepper
1   bay leaf
1   carrot, cut into 8 sticks
    cold water
1   small head cabbage, cut into wedges

1. Place beef, thyme, studded onion, pepper, bay leaf, and carrot in a large pot. Cover with cold water. Do not cover the pot.
2. Slowly bring to a boil. Simmer for 3 hours, skimming when necessary.
3. Remove thyme sprig and bay leaf and add cabbage. Simmer for another 10 to 15 minutes or until the cabbage is crisp-tender.
4. Remove corned beef to heated serving platter. Surround with cabbage wedges, carrot sticks, and onion.

Per serving: 261 cal. (59% from fat), 18 g protein, 8 g carbohydrate, 17 g fat, 61 mg cholesterol, 3 g fiber, 162 mg sodium.

Parsley Buttered Potatoes

Serves 6 to 8

2½   pounds small new potatoes*
2   tablespoons margarine
      fresh parsley, coarsely chopped

1. Carefully scrub potatoes. Remove one strip of peel around the center of each potato.
2. Place potatoes in a large pan filled with cold water. Bring to a boil. Gently simmer 35 to 40 minutes or until potatoes are tender.
3. Drain potatoes well. Add margarine and parsley; stir gently until potatoes are coated. Serve immediately.

*Red potatoes may be substituted for the new potatoes.

Per serving: 124 cal. (25% from fat), 3 g protein, 23 g carbohydrate, 4 g fat, 0 mg cholesterol, 1 g fiber, 49 mg sodium.

Carrots

Serves 6 to 8

2   pounds carrots
1½   tablespoons margarine
      salt and pepper

1. Wash and peel carrots. Leave carrots whole if small, otherwise slice or dice.
2. Bring a small amount of salted water to a boil in a saucepan; add carrots.
3. Bring water again to a boil. Then reduce heat and let carrots gently simmer until crisp-tender, about 10 to 15 minutes.
4. Drain carrots well and toss with margarine. Season with salt and pepper to taste. Serve immediately.

Per serving: 75 cal. (33% from fat), 2 g protein, 12 g carbohydrate, 3 g fat, 0 mg cholesterol, 4 g fiber, 75 mg sodium.

Scones

Makes 8 scones

2½   cups all-purpose flour
2½   teaspoons baking powder
½   teaspoon salt
1   tablespoon sugar
3   tablespoons margarine
1   egg
1   cup fat-free milk

1. Preheat oven to 400°F.
2. Grease a baking sheet and set aside.
3. In a large bowl, combine flour, baking powder, salt, and sugar.
4. Cut in margarine until mixture resembles coarse cornmeal.

5. Beat the egg until frothy, reserving 1 tablespoon.
6. Add the milk to the beaten egg and pour into the flour mixture.
7. Stir dough lightly with a fork until it forms a soft ball.
8. On a floured board, roll the dough into a square ½ inch thick. With a sharp knife, cut the square into quarters. Then cut each quarter diagonally into a triangle.
9. Place the triangles about 1 inch apart on the baking sheet; brush the tops with reserved beaten egg.
10. Bake scones for 15 minutes or until light brown. Serve at once.

Per scone: 207 cal. (23% from fat), 6 g protein, 33 g carbohydrate, 6 g fat, 35 mg cholesterol, 1 g fiber, 306 mg sodium.

English Trifle

Serves 12

1   pound cake (homemade or packaged)
4   tablespoons raspberry jam
1   cup blanched almonds, halved
2   cups fresh raspberries or 2 packages frozen raspberries, 10 ounces each
2   cups soft custard (homemade or prepared vanilla pudding)
2   cups heavy cream
2   tablespoons confectioner's sugar

1. Cut the pound cake into slices, ½ inch thick.
2. Coat about half of the slices with jam and place them, jam side up, along the bottom and sides of a glass bowl.
3. Cut the remaining slices into cubes and scatter the cubes over the jam-covered slices.
4. Sprinkle ½ cup of the almonds over the cake.
5. Reserve 12 of the best raspberries. (Drain juice from frozen berries.) Sprinkle the remaining berries over the cake.
6. Using a flexible spatula, gently spread the custard over the fruit.
7. In a small, chilled bowl, whip cream until slightly thick.
8. Add sugar gradually, beating until cream forms soft peaks.
9. Spread half the whipped cream over the custard.
10. Using a pastry bag, pipe the remaining cream decoratively around the edge of the trifle. Garnish with reserved berries and almonds.

Per serving: 436 cal. (59% from fat), 8 g protein, 38 g carbohydrate, 30 g fat, 147 mg cholesterol, 3 g fiber, 179 mg sodium.

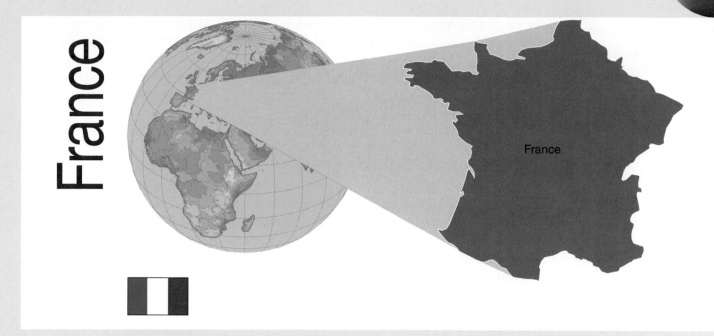

France is the largest country in Western Europe. France also is the oldest unified nation in Europe. It has been an important world power for centuries. The French have had an impact on the development of the entire Western civilization. They have made many contributions in art, science, government, and philosophy.

Geography and Climate of France

The Atlantic Ocean, the Mediterranean Sea, and the English Channel border France. Belgium, Luxembourg, Germany, Switzerland, Italy, and Spain also border France. All these nations have influenced the development of French culture.

The eastern and southwestern areas of France are mountainous. The northern and western parts of the country are rolling plains. Both highlands and lowlands are found in the central provinces.

The climate of France is moderate. In the higher elevations, snow falls during the winter. However, most of the country has cool, rainy weather instead of snow. Throughout much of France, spring is humid, summer is moderate, and autumn is long and sunny. These climatic conditions are especially favorable for the production of the grapes used to make famous French wines, **30-7**.

French Culture

The French are a mixture of many different peoples who originally came to France from areas throughout Europe. Each group settled in a different part of the country.

Shutterstock

30-7 Wines made from French grapes are regarded as some of the finest in the world.

Enrich

Invite someone who has visited France to speak to your class and show travel slides and videos.

Enrich

France has been a leader in the arts for centuries. Have students write a two-page biography of a French artist, composer, architect, or writer.

Reflect

Ask students if they think they could play a key role in defending their country the way Joan of Arc did. Have them think about the reasons behind their answers.

Reflect

In many parts of France, cooks buy food fresh each day, shopping in small specialty shops rather than large supermarkets. Ask students how this type of shopping compares with the way their families buy food.

Vocabulary Builder

Have students compare the terms *haute cuisine*, *provincial cuisine*, and *nouvelle cuisine*.

In the Middle Ages, France was divided into areas called *domains*. A member of the nobility ruled each domain and peasants worked the land. During the Renaissance, France became a unified country. However, many of the people of France did not think of themselves as French citizens. Instead, they considered themselves citizens of the regions in which they lived, such as Brittany and Burgundy. Today, regional ties continue to be strong in many parts of France, especially in rural areas.

France is a republic headed by a president. Paris, France's largest city and marketing and distribution center, is the seat of government. The official language is French. The greatest percentage of the population is Roman Catholic.

Fishing and agricultural industries are important to France. Fishers catch large amounts of cod, crab, herring, lobster, mackerel, oysters, sardines, shrimp, and tuna along the French coastlines. Grapes grow throughout much of the southern part of the country. They are used in wine production. Cattle provide meat and dairy products. Wheat, corn, oats, and barley are important grain crops. Sugar beets, fruits, vegetables, flax, flowers, and other livestock are also important agricultural commodities.

French Holidays

Joan of Arc Day is a national holiday in France, which is observed on the second Sunday in May. This day is named for a 17-year-old girl who became a French national heroine and a Catholic saint. French people celebrate the holiday held in her honor by decorating the streets with statues and pictures of Joan.

France's national independence day, Bastille Day, is July 14. On this date in 1789, a crowd of French citizens captured a Paris prison called the Bastille. This volatile event signaled the start of the French Revolution. The French celebrate this holiday with parades, parties, dancing, and fireworks.

Many other celebrations throughout the year in France are church holidays. On January 6, the eve of Epiphany, children lay fruit and cake on the church altar for the Christ child. *Mardi Gras* heralds the beginning of Lent with parades of flower-covered floats. *Pâques*, the French name for Easter, comes from the name of the Jewish Passover. On this day, children receive colored candy eggs and chocolate chickens. Corpus Christi is a festival in early June honoring the bread and wine used for Holy Communion. These sacred elements are taken from church altars in gold and silver bowls and carried through the streets. Small altars covered with boughs and flowers are set up at village crossroads. *Noël*, or Christmas, is a time for family reunions, carol singing, and gifts for the children.

French Cuisine

In France, good food and wine are an important part of daily life. In many parts of France, cooks buy food fresh each day, and they take great care in selecting it. The French usually shop in small specialty shops rather than in large supermarkets.

French cooking can be divided into three main classes: haute cuisine, provincial cuisine, and nouvelle cuisine. **Haute cuisine** is characterized by elaborate preparations, fancy garnishes, and rich sauces. Chefs make lavish use of eggs, cream, and butter in this style of French cooking. Haute cuisine is seen most often in leading restaurants and hotels.

Provincial cuisine is the style of cooking practiced by most French families. Provincial cooks make fewer fancy sauces and lavish creations. Instead, the flavors of locally grown foods are enhanced by simple cooking methods. Many provincial dishes were once regional specialties. See **30-8**.

Nouvelle cuisine emphasizes lightness and natural taste in foods. Flavor, color, texture, and presentation are as important in nouvelle cuisine as they are in haute cuisine. However, nouvelle cooks believe the richness and heaviness of haute cuisine spoil the natural flavors of food. The idea behind nouvelle cuisine is to preserve the nutrients and natural taste of foods. Nouvelle cuisine appeals to people who love French food but are concerned about fat and calories.

Nouvelle cooks serve less butter, cream, and other high-calorie foods. They use fewer starches and sauces. When they do serve a sauce, they do not thicken it with flour. Instead, nouvelle cooks use vegetable purees to thicken sauces. Nouvelle cuisine includes more fresh fruits and vegetables. (The vegetables are served nearly raw.) Meat, fish, and poultry are often broiled or poached.

Foundations of French Cooking

Two basic points form the secret of good French cooking. First, the ingredients used must be of top quality. Bread, for example, is baked twice a day in French bakeries to ensure its freshness. Second, successful cooks are very patient. Patience can make the difference

Courtesy of the Idaho Potato Commission

30-8 Salade nicoise is an example of provincial cuisine. This salad, which comes from the region of Provence, features the fresh flavors of locally grown vegetables.

Learn About...

French Sauces

The French use a variety of sauces. A sauce can be used as the basis for a dish or as a finishing touch.

A *roux* is a mixture of butter (or other fat) and flour. It forms the base of all white sauces. When milk is added to a roux, the mixture becomes a *béchamel* sauce. If chicken, veal, or fish stock is added to a roux, the mixture becomes a *velouté* sauce. Many variations of these sauces can be made by adding extra ingredients like mustard or cheese.

The classic French brown sauce is called a *demi-glace* sauce. Cooks make it from a slightly thickened stock-based sauce they have simmered for a long time.

They add additional stock and flavorings to this basic sauce. They may or may not use a thickening agent, such as a roux.

Hollandaise sauce contains egg yolks, lemon juice, and butter. The cook must warm and gently thicken the beaten egg yolks to prevent curdling. Then the butter must be added slowly to keep the sauce from separating. Hollandaise sauce often accompanies green vegetables such as asparagus.

Vinaigrettes are made by combining wine vinegar, oil, and seasonings. Many variations are possible. Vinaigrettes are commonly used as dressings on green salads and as marinades for vegetables.

Butter sauces include *cold flavored butters*, *white butter sauce*, and *brown butter* sauce. Cooks use them when baking and broiling seafood, when preparing vegetables and poultry, and when making other sauces.

between a dish that is good and one that is excellent. Cooks may simmer some sauces for hours to develop the flavors of all their ingredients.

French Seasonings

Herbs are just as important to French cooking as sauces. **Fines herbes** is a mixture of fresh chives, parsley, tarragon, and chervil. Many French chefs use this combination of herbs to flavor soups and stews. Marjoram, rosemary, basil, saffron, oregano, fennel, bay leaves, thyme, and savory are also common in French cooking.

Cooks add herbs directly to some dishes. For other dishes, such as stews, they tie herbs in a cheesecloth bag and add it to the liquid. (They remove the bag before serving.)

French Appetizers and Soups

A French meal would not be complete without hors d'oeuvres. **Hors d'oeuvres** are small dishes designed to stimulate the appetite. They may be hot or cold, but chefs always plan for them to complement the other menu items.

Soup often follows hors d'oeuvres. French soups fall into four basic categories: consommés, puree soups, cream soups, and velouté soups. *Consommés* have a meat stock base. They are rich and clear and may be served hot or cold. Puree soups are made from meat, poultry, fish, or vegetables that have been cooked in liquid and pureed. Cream soups generally use a béchamel sauce as a base. Pureed meat, fish, poultry, or vegetables are added to the béchamel sauce along with cream. *Velouté soups* are similar to cream soups. Meat, fish, poultry, or vegetables are added to a velouté sauce. Egg yolks, butter, and cream thicken the soup.

French Main Dishes

Seafood and poultry form the basis of many French main dishes. As a rule, the French eat red meat less often than people in the United States.

Many types of freshwater and saltwater fish are popular in France. Frog legs, crabs, scallops, and mussels are especially popular. Poaching is the preparation technique used most often for fish fillets and whole fish.

The French eat all types of poultry. They often truss and roast chicken, duck, and goose whole with or without a stuffing. They also add chicken to stews, such as *chicken fricassee*. This dish is made by cutting chicken into pieces that are stewed and served with a white sauce. French cooks finely chop and season the meat of game birds, such as pigeons, to make a spread called *pâté*.

The French usually broil beef steaks and serve them with a sauce. They often braise other beef and veal cuts and use some of them in stews. Lamb is particularly popular in the spring. The French consider organ meats of all kinds to be delicacies. See **30-9**.

The American Lamb Board

30-9 The French roast lamb with herbs to give it a delicately-seasoned flavor.

French Vegetables and Salads

Vegetables are an important part of a French meal. The French often serve two or more fresh vegetables with a main dish. They cook vegetables just to the crisp-tender stage and then serve them immediately to preserve their textures.

The French often serve vegetables with just butter and seasonings. Vegetables can also be creamed, braised, glazed, or served with a cheese or hollandaise sauce. Some vegetables, such as spinach, adapt particularly well to soufflés.

The French usually serve a green salad after the main course but before dessert. They often dress it with a vinaigrette sauce. Other salads, such as potato salads and meat salads, are popular additions to lighter and more casual meals. One of the best-known salads of this type is *salade nicoise*. This popular salad is a colorful combination of potatoes, green beans, and tomatoes, served with a vinaigrette sauce.

France is famous for its cheeses, and cheese is an important part of meals. The French serve cheese and fresh fruit after the green salad and before the sweet dessert in a large meal. Many simpler meals include only cheese, sausage, bread, fresh fruit, and wine.

French Baked Goods

The French serve bread at every meal. *Baguette* is the most popular. It contains only yeast, flour, salt, and water. People buy the long, crusty loaves daily from local bakers. Other breads are popular, too. *Brioche* is a rich yeast roll that contains egg. **Croissants** are flaky, buttery yeast rolls shaped into crescents.

The dessert course may be simple or elaborate. Some of the most elegant desserts in the world originated in France. *Napoleons* are layers of puff pastry separated by creamy fillings. *Éclairs* are slender pastry shells filled with custard or a cream filling and iced. *Baba au rhum* is a yeast cake soaked in a rum syrup. Chocolate, vanilla, liqueur, or fruit-based soufflés are popular. Fruit tarts filled with fruit, custard, or other sweet filling are also favorite desserts.

Regional Nature of French Cuisine

French cuisine is regional in nature. A visitor can travel throughout the country and never eat the same dish prepared in the same way twice. A traveler can even identify certain regions by their local dishes.

Normandy is located in the northwestern corner of France. Cattle graze in the fertile green pastures, and apple orchards dot the countryside. Normandy is known for tender veal, rich cream and butter, and apples. *Calvados*, a liquor made from apple cider, is produced locally for export around the world.

Brittany, Normandy's neighbor to the southwest, is relatively poor. Much of the land is rocky and wooded. Because agriculture is difficult, much of the local food comes from the sea. In early spring, vegetables are harvested from small gardens throughout Brittany. The asparagus, artichokes, and cauliflower are reported to be the best in France. Brittany is also known for its **crêpes** (thin, delicate pancakes usually rolled around a filling).

To the southwest, in the *Aquitaine* region, the finest pâté is produced. It is made from expensive goose liver and truffles. **Truffles** are a rare type of fungi that grow underground near oak trees. This region is also known for its poultry, veal, and pork.

Cassoulet is a traditional stew of the *Languedoc-Roussillon* region located in southern France. It is made with white beans, goose or chicken, pork, bacon, and herbs.

Provence is a rich agricultural region in southeastern France. Fresh vegetables are used in many colorful dishes. One of the most popular vegetable dishes is *ratatouille*. It is a vegetable casserole containing tomatoes, eggplant, green pepper, zucchini,

Discuss

Ask students how serving salad after the main course compares with the order in which courses are typically served in the United States. *(In the United States, salad is usually served before the main course.)*

Academic Connections

Teach this section of the chapter in conjunction with the foreign language department. Students can learn the meaning and pronunciation of French menu and cooking terms, and practice writing menus and making dinner conversation in French.

Activity

Have students find the various regions of France on a map.

Vocabulary Builders

One of the meanings of the word *burgundy* is a *reddish purple color*. Ask students how burgundy got this meaning. *(from the color of Burgundy wine)*

Ask students which of the French terms found throughout this section have been familiar to them. Ask why they think these terms are familiar.

Photo courtesy of The Beef Checkoff www.BeefItsWhatsForDinner.com

30-10 Boeuf à la Bourguignonne is a French regional dish made with cubes of beef and fresh vegetables simmered in broth flavored with Burgundy wine.

onions, and seasonings. The olive trees that grow on the sunny slopes along the Mediterranean Sea provide the oil needed to make aioli. (*Aioli* is a regional sauce made from olive oil and garlic.) *Bouillabaisse* (a seafood stew), leg of lamb, grilled fish, and chicken are equally popular. Many of the dishes of Provence are flavored with locally grown herbs.

Burgundy, located in central France, is famous for its vineyards and the wines they produce. Many Burgundy dishes are flavored with the local wines. *Boeuf à la Bourguignonne* (beef Burgundy) is one of the most famous of these dishes, **30-10**. **Escargots** (snails eaten as food) are another Burgundy specialty. They often are served in their shells with garlic butter.

For centuries, the people of the *Rhône-Alpes* region have based their diets on local foods. Potatoes grow in the hilly land. The cows that graze on mountain grasses provide milk and cheese. Many Alpine dishes combine these three staple foods.

The Germans have influenced the foods of the *Alsace* and *Lorraine* regions. Sausages and smoked hams are popular throughout these regions, as are fruit pies and tarts. Fine white wines are produced in Alsace. **Quiche**, a custard tart served in many variations as an appetizer and a main dish, originated in Lorraine. The most famous type of quiche is called *Quiche Lorraine*. It contains grated Swiss cheese, crumbled bacon, and diced onions along with eggs and cream.

Learn About...

French Meals

Most French people eat three meals a day. *Le petit dejeuner* (breakfast) usually is light. The French often have *café au lait* (hot milk and coffee) and brioche or crusty bread with butter and jam.

Traditionally, *le dejeuner* (the midday meal) was the main meal of the day. People ate it leisurely. In many parts of France this is still the case. People in the major cities, however, often eat the heavier meal in the evening. A traditional midday meal might include hot or cold hors d'oeuvres, soup, and a main dish. A vegetable, a green salad, bread and butter, dessert, and wine would also be served. If the main dish contains vegetables, a separate vegetable usually would be eliminated.

In France, bread usually remains on the table through the end of the meal. The salad usually is served after the main course, and coffee usually accompanies dessert.

The traditional evening meal is light. Soup, an omelet, bread and butter, fruit, and a beverage are typical supper dishes. City dwellers, however, may eat a more substantial evening meal. Business hours are later in France than they are in the United States. Therefore, the evening meal usually is not served before eight o'clock.

French Menu

Soupe à l'Oignon
(Onion Soup)

Poulet au Citron
(Chicken with Lemon)

Ratatouille
(Vegetable Casserole)

Salade Verte
(Green Salad)

Pain
(French Bread)

Mousse au Chocolat
(Chocolate Mousse)

Café
(Coffee)

Soupe à l'Oignon
(Onion Soup)

Serves 6

5	medium onions
2	tablespoons margarine
	dash pepper
6	cups low-sodium beef broth
6	thick slices French bread
3	tablespoons grated Parmesan cheese
¾	cup shredded Swiss cheese

1. Clean onions, cut into thin slices.
2. In a large, heavy skillet, melt margarine.
3. Add onions and pepper and sauté until onions are golden brown and transparent (about 10 minutes).
4. Slowly stir in beef broth. Bring soup to a boil, reduce heat and simmer for 30 minutes.
5. Toast bread slices in the oven.
6. Place one piece of toasted bread in each of six ovenproof soup bowls or use one large tureen; sprinkle with Parmesan cheese.
7. Preheat broiler.
8. Pour soup over bread. Sprinkle Swiss cheese on top.
9. Place soup bowls under broiler and broil until cheese is light brown. Serve soup immediately.

Per serving: 192 cal. (42% from fat), 9 g protein, 18 g carbohydrate, 9 g fat, 11 mg cholesterol, 2 g fiber, 407 mg sodium.

Pullet au Citron
(Chicken with Lemon)

Serves 8

1	tablespoon margarine
1	tablespoon vegetable oil
2	broilers, 2 pounds each, cut-up, skin removed
¾	teaspoon salt
	pepper to taste
2	tablespoons finely chopped parsley
1	tablespoon minced chives
1	teaspoon marjoram
2	teaspoons paprika
	grated rind and juice of one lemon
1	cup low-sodium chicken broth
2	tablespoons cornstarch
3	tablespoons cold water

1. Preheat oven to 350°F.
2. Heat margarine and oil together in a large nonstick skillet.
3. Brown chicken pieces.
4. Place chicken in a large casserole or baking pan. Season with salt and pepper, parsley, chives, marjoram, and paprika. Sprinkle with lemon juice and rind.
5. Cover pan tightly, and bake chicken until tender, about 45 minutes. Use a meat thermometer to check the internal temperature of chicken pieces. Breast pieces should reach an internal temperature of 170°F. Wings and thighs should reach an internal temperature of 180°F.
6. Remove chicken to a heated platter.
7. Pour juices into a small saucepan. Add chicken broth and bring to a boil.
8. Quickly whisk in cornstarch dissolved in cold water.
9. Simmer sauce until thickened, about 2 minutes. Serve with chicken.

Per serving: 162 cal. (44% from fat), 19 g protein, 3 g carbohydrate, 8 g fat, 57 mg cholesterol, 0 g fiber, 310 mg sodium.

Ratatouille
(Vegetable Casserole)

Serves 6 to 8

1	medium eggplant
1	teaspoon salt
2	tablespoons vegetable oil
1½	large onions, cut into rings
2	cloves garlic, crushed
2	green peppers, cut into strips
3	medium zucchini, cut into bite-sized pieces
2	medium tomatoes, cut into wedges
1	bay leaf
½	teaspoon thyme
¼	teaspoon salt
	pepper to taste

1. Cut eggplant first into thick slices and then into bite-sized pieces. Sprinkle with salt and let eggplant stand 30 minutes. Rinse and pat dry with paper towels.
2. In a large skillet, heat oil. Sauté onions and garlic until golden.
3. Add green pepper strips and cook for 2 minutes.
4. Add eggplant and cook for 3 minutes, stirring constantly.
5. Add zucchini and continue stirring and cooking another 3 minutes.
6. Add tomatoes and seasonings. Simmer uncovered for 40 minutes or until vegetables are tender.
7. Remove bay leaf. Ratatouille can be served immediately or refrigerated and reheated later.

Per serving: 98 cal. (46% from fat), 2 g protein, 12 g carbohydrate, 5 g fat, 0 mg cholesterol, 3 g fiber, 273 mg sodium.

Salade Verte
(Green Salad)

Serves 6

6	cups assorted salad greens
1	tablespoon lemon juice
1	tablespoon white wine vinegar
	salt
	pepper
⅓	cup olive oil

1. Wash salad greens and tear into bite-sized pieces.
2. In small bowl, whisk together lemon juice, wine vinegar, and salt and pepper to taste.
3. Add oil, a few drops at a time while beating with whisk. Continue to beat dressing until all of the oil has been added.
4. Toss greens together in a salad bowl with dressing. (If dressing has separated, shake well before using.)

Per serving: 119 cal. (91% from fat), 1 g protein, 2 g carbohydrate, 12 g fat, 0 mg cholesterol, 1 g fiber, 105 mg sodium.

Pain
(French Bread)

Makes 2 loaves

2¼	cups water
6½	cups all-purpose flour
2	packages active dry yeast
2	teaspoons salt
	cornmeal
	vegetable oil
	cold water

1. In small saucepan, heat water to 120°F.
2. In large mixer bowl, combine 3 cups flour, yeast, and salt.
3. Add warm water and mix by hand or on medium speed of electric mixer for 3 minutes. Gradually add enough remaining flour to form a stiff dough.
4. Turn dough out onto lightly floured board or pastry cloth; knead until smooth and satiny, about 8 to 10 minutes.
5. Place dough in a greased bowl, turning once to grease top. Cover and let rise in a warm place 30 minutes.
6. Punch down and divide into 2 equal parts.
7. Roll each half of dough into a 15-by-8-inch rectangle on a lightly floured board.
8. Beginning with long side, roll dough up tightly, sealing edges and ends well.
9. Place loaves seam side down, diagonally, on a lightly greased baking sheet that has been sprinkled with cornmeal. Brush loaves with oil, cover. Refrigerate 2 to 24 hours.
10. When ready to bake, preheat oven to 400°F.
11. Remove bread from refrigerator, uncover and let stand 10 minutes.
12. Brush bread with water. Slash tops of loaves diagonally at 2-inch intervals just before baking.
13. Bake at 400°F, 35 to 40 minutes.

Per slice: 98 cal. (6% from fat), 3 g protein, 20 g carbohydrate, 1 g fat, 0 mg cholesterol, 1 g fiber, 134 mg sodium.

Mousse au Chocolat
(Chocolate Mousse)

Serves 6

¼	pound semisweet chocolate, broken into chunks
4	eggs, separated
4	tablespoons margarine, softened
4	teaspoons water
½	cup sugar
6	strips orange peel

1. Melt chocolate in the top of a double boiler over barely simmering water.
2. In small bowl, using an electric mixer, beat egg yolks until thick and lemon-colored (about 10 minutes).
3. Add margarine a tablespoon at a time to chocolate, beating until mixture is smooth.
4. Add the beaten egg yolks and cook, beating constantly, until the mixture has thickened and is smooth, about 5 minutes. (Do not let mixture come to a boil.)
5. Remove pan from the heat. Set top portion of double boiler aside, and cool chocolate mixture to room temperature, about 30 minutes.
6. In a heavy saucepan or double boiler, stir together egg whites, water, and sugar.
7. Cook egg whites over low heat, beating with a portable mixer until the whites stand in soft peaks.
8. Gently fold chocolate mixture into egg whites, folding until no streaks of white are visible.
9. Pour mousse into a pretty bowl or individual serving dishes and refrigerate until set, at least four hours.
10. Garnish mousse with strips of orange peel.

Per serving: 272 cal. (56% from fat), 5 g protein, 29 g carbohydrate, 17 g fat, 145 mg cholesterol, 0 g fiber, 133 mg sodium.

Shutterstock

Chateaubriand (beef tenderloin with bernaise sauce) is one example of French haute cuisine.

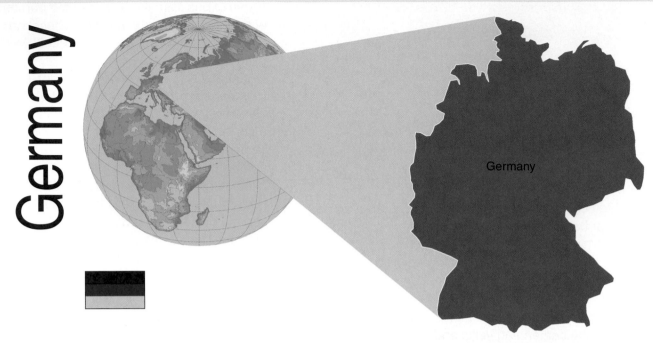

Germany

Germany

Reflect
Ask students how many German foods they can name.

Germany is in the heart of Western Europe. Germany's boundaries have changed several times over the years. Many of these changes were the result of wars.

German culture and cuisine developed with more unity than German politics. Common heritage and ingredients have led to the origin of dishes that are liked throughout Germany. However, Germany also has many regional dishes.

Geography and Climate of Germany

To the north of Germany are the Baltic and North Seas. The Rhine and the Elbe are the most important rivers in Germany.

Lowlands (flat, sandy plains) make up much of the northern part of the country. Highlands are in the central and southern regions. Two other important geographical regions, the Bavarian Alps and the Black Forest, are in southern Germany. See **30-11**.

Germany's climate is generally moderate. However, the Baltic region has extremes of temperature. Also, the higher elevations in the southern mountains receive large amounts of snow.

Shutterstock

30-11 The Black Forest region of Germany gets its name from the dense growth of pine trees, which block out daylight in the forest.

Global Perspective

German History

Until the last half of the nineteenth century, Germany was a loose mixture of states, kingdoms, duchies, and principalities. Following the unification of these territories, Germany became involved in the two World Wars. Both wars left much of the country devastated. World War II resulted in the split of the country. West Germany had a democratic government. East Germany had a communistic government.

For years, the people of both German nations longed to live under a common flag. In 1989, they tore down the Berlin Wall—a symbol of the political division between the countries. In the following year, the two nations were reunited under a single democratic government.

German Culture

After the collapse of the Roman Empire, a series of empires rose and fell. Each one brought new peoples to Germany. Many of these peoples came from what are now Poland, Denmark, Switzerland, Austria, and France.

German Agriculture

The northern lowlands and southern highlands of Germany are primarily agricultural. Potatoes and sugar beets are the main crops of the northern lowlands. In addition, farmers grow some rye, oats, wheat, and barley and raise some cattle. The southern highlands are known for their cattle, wheat, and dairy products. Grapes and other fruits grow in the west and southwest regions. Hops grow in Bavaria, the center of the German brewing industry.

German Holidays

The Germans celebrate many church holidays with traditional foods. One of these holidays is St. Martin's Day, which is a harvest festival held on November 11. Roast goose and breads baked in symbolic shapes are among the foods typically served on St. Martin's Day. At dusk, children sing and parade with paper lanterns.

During Advent, the four-week period leading to Christmas, German bakers prepare holiday cakes, cookies, and breads. On December 6, children receive candy and fruit from St. Nicholas. Children also go door to door receiving candy and money from friends and neighbors. Advent ends on Christmas Eve, which is a bigger celebration than Christmas Day. German parents decorate Christmas trees as a surprise for their children. Family members exchange gifts and enjoy a festive meal. The traditional Christmas meal was carp because the church forbade the eating of meat. Today, however, roast turkey, goose, or duck is more common. The Germans observe 12 Days of Christmas, which last until January 6. On this date, German boys dress up in celebration of the kings who visited the infant Jesus.

Enrich

Have students write five-page research reports about some aspect of Germany's involvement in one of the World Wars.

Academic Connections

As you cover information in this section of the chapter, ask music teachers to discuss famous German composers with students in their classes. Then bring recordings of these composers to class to play during lab time. Ask students if they are familiar with the music they hear.

FYI

Potatoes are the only German food crop grown in sufficient quantities to meet the needs of the German population. Germany has to import about a third of its food.

Reflect

Ask students what kinds of special foods are prepared in their homes for holidays.

FYI

Westphalia is a northwestern region of Germany that borders the Netherlands where hog production is still a major part of the economy.

Discuss

Ask students what the national dish in the United States is. (hot dogs)

German Cuisine

German cuisine is characterized by roasted meats, filling side dishes, and delicious baked goods. World-famous beers and fine white wines are also typical German fare.

German Main Dishes

Meat has been the foundation of German cuisine for centuries. The **braten** (roast) is Germany's national dish. A variety of traditional German dishes contain pork, beef, veal, and game.

Pork, both fresh and cured, is the most popular of all meats. Hams are roasted, marinated in wine, or cut in slices and then fried and served with a sauce. One of the most popular pork dishes is called *kasseler rippenspeer*. It is a whole smoked pork loin that is roasted. It is served with sauerkraut, apples or chestnuts, peas, white beans, mushrooms, and browned potatoes. See **30-12**.

Shutterstock

30-12 Eisbein is a popular German dish made of a pickled, boiled ham hock.

Boiled beef served with a horseradish sauce is one of the most popular beef dishes. *Sauerbraten*, a sweet-sour marinated beef roast, is popular, too. The ingredients used in the marinade vary from one region to another. One method uses red wine, wine vinegar, onion, peppercorns, juniper berries, and bay leaves. Sauerbraten gravy may be thickened and flavored with crushed gingersnaps and raisins.

Hasenpfeffer is rabbit that is first marinated in wine, vinegar, onions, and spices. Then the meat is stewed in the marinade. Sour cream is often added to the stew for thickening and flavor.

Many German meat dishes have regional origins. One such dish is schnitzel. *Schnitzel* is a breaded, sauteed veal cutlet. Schnitzel originated in Holstein where it is served with a fried egg. Richly flavored, smoked uncooked *Westphalian ham* originated in Westphalia, but it is served throughout Germany.

Learn About...

German Sausages

A discussion of German meat dishes would not be complete without mentioning sausage. The Germans produce hundreds of types of sausages. Some are ready-to-eat. Others must be grilled, boiled, or fried. Some sausages are smoked, and a few are pickled.

Some sausages bear the names of the cities where they were first produced. Braunschweiger, for example, is a type of liver sausage. It was first produced in Braunschweig. The *frankfurter* (hot dog) originated in the German city of Frankfurt. Other well-known German sausages include *blutwurst*, which is blood sausage. *Bratwurst* is sausage made of fresh-ground, seasoned pork that is usually cooked by grilling. *Knockwurst* is smoked, precooked sausage made of beef and pork. *Schinkenwurst* is a ready-to-eat pork sausage that contains pieces of ham.

The German people use leftovers to make hearty soups and one-dish meals. Filling lentil soups and *eintopf*, a popular stew, are both made with leftover meats.

German Seafood

Open-air fish markets scattered throughout northern Germany sell a variety of seafood obtained from the North and Baltic Seas. Smoked eel, enjoyed by many northern Germans, is inexpensive. Herring is prepared in a variety of ways. Salty, sharp, pickled Bismarck herring bears the name of a chancellor who helped unify the German territories.

German Side Dishes

Germans usually serve fruit accompaniments with pork and game dishes. Apples, prunes, raisins, and apricots accompany pork. Tart fruits like currants and *preiselbeeren* (small, cranberry-like fruits) accompany game.

At least one meal a day in Germany includes potatoes. Potatoes cooked in salted water, drained, and steamed until dry are known as *salzkartoffeln*. Salzkartoffeln are served most often as a side dish with melted butter, parsley, and bits of bacon. *Kartoffelsalat* is hot or cold potato salad made with a vinegar dressing and bits of cooked bacon. **Kartoffelpuffer** are the famous potato pancakes enjoyed throughout Germany. They are served with mixed stewed fruit or applesauce. *Kartoffelklösse* are potato dumplings.

Sauerkraut, another German specialty, is fermented or pickled cabbage. German cooks usually flavor sauerkraut with caraway, apple, onion, or juniper berries and serve it hot. The Germans often eat sauerkraut with pig's knuckles, spareribs, pork chops, and pork roasts.

The Germans may serve vegetables as side dishes or add them to stews. Cabbage and root vegetables are especially popular during winter months. Asparagus and mushrooms are spring delicacies. Cooks use fresh greens to make delicious salads, which they often serve with a vinegar dressing flavored with bacon.

Spätzle (small dumplings made from wheat flour) are another popular side dish. Cheese spätzle and liver spätzle are just two of the many kinds of spätzle eaten in Germany.

German Baked Goods

The German people serve bread at nearly every meal. Many breads and rolls are produced all over the country, while others are strictly regional. Some breads are baked in round or oblong rolls. Others are made into fanciful shapes and called *gebildbrote* (picture breads).

Rye, pumpernickel, and other dark breads are favorites. Bakers make *pumpernickel* bread from unsifted rye flour. They let it rise and bake for long periods. This allows the natural sugars in the rye to sweeten the bread evenly.

Sweet baked goods are also popular in Germany. Sweet rolls, breads, and coffee cakes are served at coffee time. Snail-shaped *schnecken*, streusel-topped coffee cakes, and *apfelkuchen* (apple cake) are served throughout Germany, **30-13**. *Stollen* is a rich yeast bread filled with almonds, raisins, and candied fruit. It usually is served at Christmastime.

Reflect

Ask students when they have eaten bratwurst or any other variety of German sausage.

Vocabulary Builder

Have students note the similarities among the names of the various German potato dishes mentioned. They should be able to identify that *kartoffel* means *potato*.

Activity

Have students make gebildbrote by shaping yeast bread dough into various shapes before baking it.

Courtesy ACH Food Companies, Inc.

30-13 Apfelkuchen is a delicious, apple-filled yeast cake topped with a sweet butter sauce.

German bakers have traditionally made cakes with honey or honey and spices. *Lebkuchen*, one of Germany's best known honey-spice cakes, has a long history. For centuries, the Germans have used decorated lebkuchen to celebrate weddings, birthdays, and anniversaries. Sometimes young men and women have given lebkuchen to their sweethearts as gifts.

Glamorous *torten* (tortes) are made of layers of cake separated by sweet fillings. The most famous German torten is the *Schwarzwälder Kirschtorte* (Black Forest cherry cake). Bakers make this rich dessert with three layers of chocolate sponge cake. They moisten the cake with *Kirschwasser*, which is brandy made from a special variety of cherry. They spread kirsch-flavored whipped cream and cherries between the cake layers. They then decorate the torten with tart cherries, chocolate curls, and more whipped cream.

Another popular German dessert with a regional origin is strudel. **Strudel** is paper-thin layers of pastry filled with plums, apples, cherries, or poppy seeds. It usually is sprinkled with confectioners' sugar and served warm. (People in some parts of Germany also make strudel with a protein-based filling and serve it as a main dish.)

German Beverages

Beer drinking is one of Germany's oldest customs. Germans drink beer by itself and with meals. Beer halls are familiar sights in all German cities and towns.

Many wine experts agree the finest table wines are produced in France and Germany. They also agree the best German wines are white wines. Most of the grapes used to make Germany's white wines grow in the valleys bordering the Rhine and Moselle Rivers.

The Germans serve table wines with meals and snacks. Both wine and beer festivals are common in many parts of the country.

German Meals

Traditionally, Germans who could afford to do so ate five meals a day. Some Germans still follow this custom.

Frühstück (breakfast) is hearty. The Germans serve eggs with dark bread and freshly baked crisp rolls. They eat butter and jams with the breads, and serve their coffee with milk. People in northern Germany often serve ham, sausage, and cheese with the eggs.

The Germans eat *zweites frühstück* (second breakfast) during midmorning. Office workers may eat thick sandwiches made of sausage and cheese. Other Germans leave their morning's work for a snack of beer and sausage at a beer hall. Still others prefer fresh pastries at the *bäckerei* (bakery) or cheese sandwiches at the *mölkerei* (dairy).

Mittagessen is the main meal of the day for those Germans who are able to go home at noon. A typical mittagessen might include soup, eintopf, dumplings, and a simple dessert like rote grutze. *Rote grutze* is a pudding made of raspberry, cherry, or red currant juice thickened with cornstarch.

The Germans eat *kaffee* (a sociable snack) in late afternoon. They serve coffee and a variety of small sandwiches, cakes, and rich pastries. Kaffee is important to the Germans, for it is a time to talk with friends.

The Germans usually serve *abendroft* (light supper) in the early evening. Traditionally, abendroft is nothing more than buttered breads served with a variety of cold meats, sausages, and cheeses, **30-14**. For those who cannot eat a hearty meal at noon, however, abendroft is the main meal of the day. An appetizer, soup, main dish, vegetable, bread, and dessert are typical.

Courtesy ACH Food Companies, Inc.

30-14 A simple assortment of breads and cheeses might be served for a traditional German abendroft.

German Menu

Sauerbraten
(Marinated Beef in Sweet-Sour Sauce)

Kartoffelpuffer mit Apfelmus
(Potato Pancakes with Applesauce)

Rotkohl
(Red Cabbage)

Grün Salat mit Heisser Specksosse
(Green Salad with Hot Bacon Dressing)

Pumpernickel
(Rye Bread from Westphalia)

Pflaumenkuchen
(Plum Cake)

Kaffee
(Coffee)

Sauerbraten
(Marinated Beef in Sweet-Sour Sauce)

Serves 8

1	cup water
1	cup vinegar
¼	cup brown sugar, firmly packed
1	teaspoon salt
1	teaspoon peppercorns
½	teaspoon pepper
3	bay leaves
1	medium onion, sliced
2	pounds boneless beef rump roast
1	tablespoon shortening
¼	cup brown sugar, firmly packed
¼	cup seedless raisins
6	gingersnaps, broken
1	cup plain nonfat yogurt

1. In a 2- or 3-quart saucepan, combine water, vinegar, ¼ cup brown sugar, salt, peppercorns, pepper, bay leaves, and onion and bring to a boil.
2. Remove marinade from heat and let cool to room temperature.
3. Place roast in a deep crock or a deep stainless steel (or enameled) pot large enough to hold the meat and marinade.
4. Pour the cooled marinade over the meat. Cover the pan tightly and refrigerate for 24 to 48 hours, turning meat occasionally.
5. Remove meat and pat dry with paper towels.
6. Melt shortening in a large Dutch oven.
7. Add meat and brown on all sides.
8. Add marinade. Cover and simmer meat until tender, about 2 hours.
9. Take meat from Dutch oven and slice; keep warm.
10. Meanwhile strain liquid. Add ¼ cup brown sugar to Dutch oven. Add strained marinade gradually and stir until sugar dissolves.
11. Add raisins and gingersnaps. Cook sauce until smooth and thick, about 5 minutes, stirring constantly.
12. Blend in yogurt. Do no let sauce boil. Serve sauce over sliced meat.

Per serving: 260 cal. (28% from fat), 21 g protein, 27 g carbohydrate, 8 g fat, 58 mg cholesterol, 1 g fiber, 384 mg sodium.

Kartoffelpuffer mit Apfelmus (Potato Pancakes with Applesauce)

Makes 18 pancakes

2	tablespoons all-purpose flour
1	teaspoon salt
½	teaspoon sugar
¼	teaspoon baking powder
⅛	teaspoon pepper
3	cups grated potatoes (6 medium potatoes)
2	eggs, well beaten
1	tablespoon grated onion
1	tablespoon minced parsley
	no-stick cooking spray
	applesauce

1. Sift flour, salt, sugar, baking powder, and pepper together in large mixing bowl; set aside.
2. Drain grated potatoes thoroughly. Press potatoes against the sides and bottom of a sieve with spoon to remove excess moisture.
3. Combine eggs, onion, and parsley; add to sifted ingredients.
4. Stir in grated potatoes. Mix thoroughly.
5. Spray heavy nonstick skillet with no-stick cooking spray.
6. For each pancake, drop about 2 tablespoons batter into skillet and spread with the back of the spoon to make a 3-inch round.
7. Fry pancakes until crisp and golden brown. Turn carefully and brown other side.
8. Drain on paper toweling. Serve with applesauce.

Per pancake: 65 cal. (20% from fat), 2 g protein, 12 g carbohydrate, 1 g fat, 30 mg cholesterol, 1 g fiber, 127 mg sodium.

Rotkohl (Red Cabbage)

Serves 6 to 8

1	head red cabbage (about 2 pounds)
3¼	cups water
¼	cup light brown sugar
3	tablespoons vinegar
3	tablespoons bacon drippings
¾	teaspoon salt
1½	teaspoons all-purpose flour
⅛	teaspoon allspice
4	whole cloves
	dash pepper

1. Coarsely shred cabbage.
2. Put water into 2- to 3-quart saucepan and bring to a boil.
3. Add cabbage, cover, and bring water again to a boil.
4. Reduce heat and gently simmer cabbage until tender, about 10 minutes.
5. Drain cabbage well.
6. Combine brown sugar, vinegar, bacon drippings, salt, flour, allspice, cloves, and pepper.
7. Pour sauce over cabbage; toss well and serve.

Per serving: 110 cal. (52% from fat), 1 g protein, 13 g carbohydrate, 7 g fat, 6 mg cholesterol, 2 g fiber, 252 mg sodium.

Pumpernickel (Rye Bread from Westphalia)

Makes 2 loaves

6	cups all-purpose flour
2	cups rye flour
2	teaspoons salt
⅔	cup whole bran cereal
½	cup yellow cornmeal
1	package plus 1 teaspoon active dry yeast
2¼	cups plus 1 tablespoon water
3	tablespoons dark molasses
1	square (1ounce) unsweetened chocolate
2½	teaspoons softened margarine
1⅓	cups mashed potatoes (at room temperature)
1½	teaspoons caraway seeds

1. Combine all-purpose and rye flours.
2. In a large mixing bowl, combine 1½ cups of flour mixture, salt, bran cereal, cornmeal, and dry yeast; mix well.
3. In a large saucepan, combine water, molasses, chocolate, and margarine. Heat over low heat until liquid is very warm (120°F to 130°F). (The margarine and chocolate do not have to be completely melted.)
4. Gradually add liquid ingredients to dry ingredients and beat 2 minutes with an electric mixer, at medium speed, scraping bowl occasionally.
5. Add potatoes and 1 cup flour mixture. Beat at high speed 2 minutes, scraping bowl occasionally.
6. Stir in caraway seeds and enough additional flour mixture to make a soft dough.

7. Turn dough out onto lightly floured board or pastry cloth. Knead until smooth and elastic, about 15 minutes.
8. Place dough in greased bowl, turning once to grease top. Cover with a clean towel and let rise in a warm place until doubled in bulk, about 1 hour.
9. Punch dough down and let rise again for 30 minutes.
10. Punch down, and turn out onto lightly floured board or cloth. Divide dough in half and shape each half into a round ball.
11. Place shaped dough in two 8- to 9-inch greased round cake pans. Cover with a clean towel and let rise in a warm place until doubled in bulk, about 45 minutes.
12. Bake breads at 350°F about 50 minutes or until loaves sound hollow when tapped with the knuckles.
13. Remove bread from pans and cool on racks.

Per serving: 140 cal. (8% from fat), 4 g protein, 29 g carbohydrate, 1 g fat, 0 mg cholesterol, 3 g fiber, 186 mg sodium.

Grün Salat mit Heisser Specksosse
(Green Salad with Hot Bacon Dressing)

Serves 8

2	cups fresh spinach
2	cups iceberg lettuce
2	cups red leaf lettuce
2	cups escarole
1	medium sweet onion cut into rings
½	pound bacon finely diced (about 1½ cups)
½	cup finely chopped onions
¼	cup cider vinegar
¼	cup water
½	teaspoon salt
¼	teaspoon pepper

1. Place greens in a large salad bowl and add onion slices.
2. In a heavy skillet, cook bacon over moderate heat until crisp. Remove bacon from skillet and place on paper towels.
3. Add chopped onions to bacon fat remaining in skillet. Cook onions until soft and transparent, stirring constantly, about 5 minutes.
4. Add vinegar, water, salt, and pepper; cook, stirring constantly for a minute or so.

5. Add bacon and pour over salad greens. Serve immediately. Dressing also may be served alongside the greens, if desired.

Per serving: 85 cal. (43% from fat), 5 g protein, 7 g carbohydrate, 4 g fat, 7 mg cholesterol, 4 g fiber, 289 mg sodium.

Pflaumenkuchen
(Plum Cake)

Serves 8

Topping:

1½	tablespoons all-purpose flour
¾	cup sugar
½	teaspoon cinnamon
2	tablespoons margarine

Cake:

1¼	cups all-purpose flour
1	teaspoon sugar
1	teaspoon baking powder
½	teaspoon salt
¼	cup margarine
1	tablespoon fat-free milk
1	egg
3	cups purple plum halves

1. Prepare topping by combining flour, sugar, and cinnamon in small mixing bowl.
2. With pastry blender or two knives, cut in margarine until mixture resembles coarse crumbs. Set aside.
3. Preheat oven to 350°F.
4. Sift flour, sugar, baking powder, and salt onto a large piece of waxed paper; set aside.
5. In large mixer bowl, cream margarine until fluffy.
6. Add dry ingredients and mix well.
7. Gently beat milk and egg together until combined; add to flour mixture.
8. Press dough into a greased 8-inch square pan.
9. Overlap plum halves in neat rows on top of dough; sprinkle with topping.
10. Bake for about 45 to 50 minutes or until cake tests done.
11. Serve warm or at room temperature with ice cream or whipped cream.

Per serving: 287 cal. (28% from fat), 3 g protein, 49 g carbohydrate, 9 g fat, 34 mg cholesterol, 3 g fiber, 280 mg sodium.

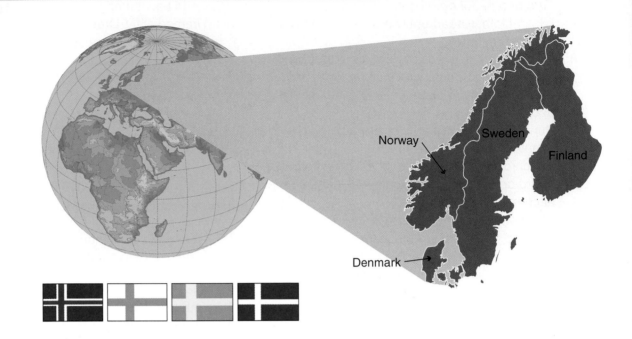

Scandinavia

Reflect

Ask students why they would or would not like to live in a land where the sun shines around the clock.

Integrating Math Concepts

Social welfare programs in Scandinavia include old age pensions and health care, hospitalization, disability, and survivor's insurance. Have students investigate the tax rates in Scandinavian countries that allow them to afford these social programs. Have students compare Scandinavian tax rates with those in the United States.

Scandinavia is a land of rugged wilderness and breathtaking beauty. Lakes made centuries ago by glaciers are crystal clear. Dense forests, snowcapped mountains, and lush valleys dot the landscape once ruled by Vikings.

Geography and Climate of Scandinavia

Scandinavia includes the countries of Denmark, Norway, Sweden, and Finland. Norway, Sweden, and Finland are part of a large peninsula that extends above the Arctic Circle. In the northern sections of these three countries, winters are long and severe. Summers are short and cool, thus making the growing season short. Above the Arctic Circle, however, the sun does not set for about two months during the summer. For this reason, the Scandinavian regions above the Arctic Circle are often called the "Land of the Midnight Sun." See **30-15**.

Norway is a long, narrow country. Its rocky, mountainous coast makes up much of its land area. Norway is known for its *fjords*, which are slender, deep bays that cut deeply into the land. Norway's greatest wealth is in timber and seafood.

Mountains separate Sweden from Norway, and forests cover much of the northern part of Sweden. The most fertile areas are located in the southern tip of the peninsula.

Glaciers have left much of Finland stony, rough, and dotted with over 60,000 lakes. The glaciers also formed large marshy areas. These areas give the country its Finnish name, Swomi, which means swamp. Forests cover much of the rest of the land.

Of the four Scandinavian nations, Denmark has the most moderate climate and the least rugged geography. Forests fringe the eastern shore, and irregular hills cut through the central part of the country. The climate is mild with plenty of rainfall. The average winter temperature is 32°F (0°C), which is considerably warmer than the rest of Scandinavia.

Photo: www.imagebank.sweden.se/Tomas Utsi/Thomas Utsi

30-15 In Northern Sweden, as in some other Scandinavian regions, the midnight sun appears for about two months each year.

Discuss

Ask students what role the Vikings played in North America. *(Erik the Red and Leif Eriksson were Viking explorers who sailed to North America in the late ninth and early tenth centuries.)*

For Example...

In addition to fish harvested from the seas, Norway produces substantial amounts of fish through aquaculture. Norway exports about 90 percent of their fish harvest.

Scandinavian Culture

As the Viking Age was ending, the people of Norway, Sweden, Denmark, and Finland began a series of governments. Some of these were joint governments; others were single. These governments lasted into the nineteenth century.

Today, governments in Sweden, Norway, and Denmark differ in form but are similar in effect. Denmark and Norway have constitutional monarchies, and Sweden has a limited monarchy. Finland has a representative government headed by a President. All four nations are peace-loving, and all are known for their advanced forms of social welfare.

Scandinavians, for the most part, have the height, light hair, and blue eyes of their Viking forebears. They are industrious, hard-working people with deep family ties. Scandinavians enjoy singing, dancing, and a variety of sports. They like to ski and ice skate in the winter. They enjoy swimming, sailing, and hiking in the summer.

Scandinavian Agriculture

Many Scandinavians make their living in the large fishing industries found in all four countries. They catch herring, cod, haddock, salmon, and a variety of other fish and shellfish. They sell some locally, but they export much of their catch.

All the Scandinavian countries obtain as many agricultural products as possible from the land. Denmark's climate and geography help make it the most agriculturally prosperous. In Denmark, the climate is mild and about 75 percent of the land can be farmed. (Only 8 percent of the land in Finland and 10 percent of the land in Sweden can be farmed.) Denmark's main wealth is in pigs, cows, and chickens. These animals provide bacon, dairy products, and eggs, which the Danes export. Danish farmers grow grain and other crops for home use and to feed livestock.

Culture and Social Studies

The Vikings

The *Vikings* are the ancestors of the Scandinavian peoples. (The Finns' origins are found in the Central Asian steppes, but Viking influence is present.) The Vikings were both industrious and warlike. They sailed to all parts of the known world during the eighth, ninth, and tenth centuries.

Niclas Jessen

The Scandinavian people are proud of their Viking heritage.

Grain and livestock (including dairy cattle) are the main agricultural products of the other Scandinavian countries. Norway also produces large quantities of potatoes.

Scandinavian Holidays

Throughout the year, festivals and holidays are times for merrymaking in Scandinavia. One annual event in Denmark is not Danish at all. It is the July 4 celebration of Independence Day in the United States. Like U.S. citizens, Danes enjoy this day by singing, dancing, eating, listening to speeches, and watching fireworks. This event promotes international unity. It also honors values Denmark shares with the United States.

In Norway, as in other Scandinavian countries, Midsummer's Eve is a time to celebrate. This festival, which is held on June 23, really falls at the beginning of summer in Scandinavia. In the part of Norway that lies above the Arctic Circle, the sun never sets at this time of year. Norwegians welcome the sunshine and warm weather by dancing around a maypole. New potatoes with dill are a traditional food at Midsummer celebrations. Fresh strawberries are a classic Midsummer dessert.

A traditional Swedish festival is Lucia Day, which is December 13. Before dawn, young girls dress in long white robes with red sashes. Wearing crowns of candles on their heads, they awaken their families with a traditional song. They serve hot coffee, saffron buns called *lussekatter*, and gingerbread biscuits called *pepparkakor*.

In Finland, July 21 marks the beginning of an annual tradition—the crayfish party. **Crayfish** are crustaceans related to the lobster. The Finns drop the crayfish one-by-one into a pot of boiling water flavored with fresh dill. As they cook, the crayfish turn bright red. The Finns serve them with toast, butter, schnapps, and beer. The atmosphere at these parties is casual and fun as guests feast on this summer treat.

Scandinavian Cuisine

The basic diets of the Danes, Norwegians, Swedes, and Finns are all rather plain and hearty. However, preparation and serving methods differ.

Learn About...

Factors Affecting Scandinavian Cuisine

Three major factors have affected Scandinavian cuisine. The first of these is geography. The geography of Scandinavia has made it hard to produce food. (Denmark is an exception.) Scandinavians have had to work to gain enough food from the water, forests, and tillable land.

Human isolation is the second factor affecting Scandinavian cuisine. Mountains and seas have separated the Scandinavian countries from most of Europe. As a result, other European countries have had little impact on Scandinavian cuisine. Geography has also kept the Scandinavian people apart from one another. Therefore, many local and regional dishes can be found.

The third factor affecting Scandinavian cuisine is climate. The Scandinavian climate includes long winters. The growing seasons are short. Therefore, much effort has to be put into preserving food. Pickled, dried, and salted foods are common.

Mads Armgaard

Drying is a common way to preserve foods for use throughout the long Scandinavian winters.

Danish Foods

Of all Scandinavian foods, Danish foods are the richest. The Danes use butter, cream, cheese, eggs, pork, and chicken in large quantities. Fish is not nearly as popular in Denmark as it is in the other Scandinavian countries.

The Danes are famous for their smørrebrød, which is literally translated as *buttered bread*. **Smørrebrød** are open-faced sandwiches usually made with thin, sour rye bread spread thickly with butter. (Soft white bread is used for smørrebrød with shellfish toppings.) Toppings can be nearly any type of meat, fish, cheese, or vegetable. Danish blue cheese with raw egg yolk is a typical topping. Sliced roast pork garnished with dried fruit and smoked salmon and scrambled eggs garnished with chives are also popular toppings.

The Danes frequently accompany their smørrebrød with glasses of chilled aquavit. *Aquavit* is a clean, potent spirit distilled from grain and potatoes and flavored with caraway seeds. It is served throughout Denmark, Sweden, and Norway.

FYI

To reduce fat and calories when preparing rich Danish dishes, substitute fat-free evaporated milk for heavy cream.

For Example...

Other examples
of toppings for
smørrebrød include
eggs with caviar,
havarti with radishes,
chicken salad with
mushrooms, and liver
paté with fried bacon.

Reflect

Ask students how
the Danish breakfast
described on this page
compares with what
they typically eat for
breakfast.

Discuss

Ask students why cattle
would be less common
in Norway than goats
and sheep. *(Cattle
are not as adept at
climbing steep hills as
goats and sheep.)*

Danish cheeses are exported and used in Danish homes to make smørrebrød. Tybo, Danbo, Danish brie, havarti, Danish blue, and Danish Camembert are particularly well known.

Danes eat a great deal of pork. They often stuff pork roasts with dried fruits. They mix ground pork with ground veal to make *frikadeller* (meat patties). The Danes use pork liver to make liver paste, which is an important part of the Danish cold table. This cold table, which is a buffet similar to the Swedish smörgåsbord, is called *koldebord*.

Most Danes love desserts. Fruit pudding, apple cake, rum pudding, and pancakes wrapped around ice cream are favorites.

The Danes often begin their day with a substantial breakfast. This meal consists of several dairy products, such as yogurt, sour milk served with cereal, and ymer. *Ymer* is a high-protein milk product. This may be followed with cheese, bread, a boiled egg, juice, milk, strong coffee, and weinerbrød. *Weinerbrød* are layers of buttery pastry filled with fruit or custard and sprinkled with sugar or nuts. The famous smørrebrød are eaten for lunch. Dinner may include a roast, vegetables, bread, and a rich fruit and cream dessert.

Norwegian Food

Norwegians begin the day with a big breakfast. They may eat herring, eggs, bacon, potatoes, cereals, breads, pastries, fruit, juice, buttermilk, and coffee.

The Norwegians work from early in the morning to midafternoon. Norwegians enjoy foods that are quick to prepare, yet filling and nourishing. Such foods include hearty soups like Bergen fish soup and rich desserts like sour cream waffles. *Lefse*, a thin potato pancake, is also a traditional Norwegian food.

Because of their nearness to the sea, Norwegians have relied on seafood as a staple in their diets. Herring (smoked, pickled, and fresh), halibut, cod, and salmon are all popular. The Norwegians often poach fish or add it to nourishing stews and soups. **Lutefisk** (dried cod that have been soaked in a lye solution before cooking) is a traditional Norwegian fish dish.

The Norwegians raise goats and sheep on their mountainous land. They use goats' milk to make cheese, **30-16**. They use lamb and mutton in a variety of dishes. The Norwegians make a stew called *får i kål* from mutton and cabbage. One of the most popular smoked meat dishes is *fenalår*, which the Norwegians make from smoked mutton.

Gaby Bohle/Innovation Norway

30-16 Norwegians make cheese from the milk of goats that graze on their rugged terrain.

Danish cooks use sweet and whipped cream, but Norwegian cooks traditionally use sour cream. Soups, sauces, salads, and meat dishes are all likely to contain sour cream. Sour cream spread on bread or crackers is a popular snack.

Norwegians take great pride in their baked goods. They serve many traditional cookies and cakes at Christmastime. *Krumkaker* are thin, delicate cookies baked on a special iron and rolled around a wooden spoon while still warm. The cooled cookies are eaten plain or filled with whipped cream and fruit. *Rosettes* are light and airy cookies cooked on the ends of special irons in hot fat. *Fattigman*, diamond-shaped cookies, are also fried in fat. *Kringla* are rich with sour cream or buttermilk and tied in figure eights or knots.

Swedish Food

The famous smörgåsbord originated in Sweden where it is served in private homes as well as in restaurants. A **smörgåsbord** is a buffet that includes a wide variety of hot and cold dishes. The word *smörgåsbord* means "bread and butter table." However, smörgåsbords can be elegant and may include 30 or more dishes, depending on the occasion. Typical smörgåsbord dishes include herring dishes; cold fish, meats, and salads; hot meats, eggs, or fish; breads; cheeses; and desserts. Diners return to the smörgåsbord several times to partake of the different courses.

Generally, people save the smörgåsbord for large gatherings and special occasions. The traditional, everyday style of cooking, called **husmankost**, is very simple. Visitors in Swedish homes are likely to see rich yellow pea soup and salt pork served for supper. Traditionally, these foods are followed by Swedish pancakes and **lingonberries** (tart, red berries) for dessert.

Baked brown beans, herring and sour cream, fried pork sausages, pickled beets, and fruit soups are other traditional Swedish foods. *Nyponsoppa* is a fruit soup made with rose hips (the orange seed capsules of the rose). It is served with whipped cream and almonds and is a Swedish specialty.

Reindeer is not exclusively Swedish, for reindeer herds roam the northern sections of Norway and Finland as well as Sweden. Reindeer flesh has a mild, wild flavor. Shaving reindeer meat into hot fat and frizzling it is one popular preparation method.

Some Swedes consider dessert to be the best part of a meal. Ostkaka and spettekaka are two of their favorites. They make *ostkaka*, a rich puddinglike cake, from milk, heavy cream, eggs, sugar, rennet, and flour. Strawberries, lingonberries, or raspberries are common accompaniments. *Spettekaka* is a delicate cake made of eggs, sugar, and flour. Swedish bakers slowly pour the batter onto a cone-shaped spit placed in front of a fire. As they rotate the cone, the batter dries in layers and forms a pattern.

Finnish Food

In Finland, forests are everywhere. The Finns gather raspberries, strawberries, lingonberries, arctic cloudberries, Finnish cranberries, and mesimarja from the forests. (Finnish cranberries are smaller than those grown in the United States. *Mesimarja* are small, delicate fruits similar to raspberries.) The Finns use berries to make liqueurs, puddings, tarts, and snows (light puddings containing beaten egg whites). One popular fruit pudding is called *vatkattu marjapuuro*. Finnish cooks make it by whipping fruit juice, sugar, and a cereal product similar to farina until light and fluffy.

FYI

The elaborate smörgåsbord described here is typical of restaurants. However, visitors in private homes are more likely to be offered just a few specialties.

Discuss

Each of the Scandinavian countries is about the size of one of the states in the U.S. Ask students how the differences in cuisines among four states compare with the differences in cuisines among these countries. *(The differences among four adjacent states would probably be less distinct because they share a national heritage.)*

For Example...

Another food common in Finland is fish, which the Finns may eat bones and all as a source of calcium. Pike, perch, eel, herring, whitefish, cod, and salmon all live in local waters.

Finnish foods are hearty, often in a primitive way. *Vorshmack*, which is ground mutton, salt herring, and beef combined with onions and garlic, is a traditional Finnish dish. Pork gravy, black sour rye bread, and rutabagas and other root vegetables help warm the Finns during the bitter winters. The Finns add mushrooms to soups, sauces, salads, gravies, and stews. They make porridges and gruels from whole grains, just as their ancestors did centuries ago. *Mämmi* is a pudding made of molasses, bitter orange peel, rye flour, and rye malt. The Finns serve it at Easter with sweet cream.

At one time, the Finns lived under Russian rule. As a result, some Russian foods have become part of Finnish cuisine. Two of the most popular Finnish dishes with Russian origins are pasha and piirakka. *Pasha* is a type of cheesecake and *piirakka* are pastries or pies. The Finns fill piirakka with meat, fish, vegetables, and fruits. They serve the piirakka as appetizers, side dishes, or desserts.

A Finnish tradition is the sauna. The **sauna** is a steam bath in which water is poured on hot stones to create steam, **30-17**. Finns follow the heat of the sauna with a quick dip in a chilly lake or swimming pool. They serve snacks during the sauna. They often serve salty fish to help replace the salt lost through sweat during the sauna. After the sauna, the Finns eat a light meal. Grilled sausages, piirakka, poached salmon, salads, and Finnish rye bread are popular after-sauna supper dishes. The Finns may serve chilled vodka or beer with the meal.

Shutterstock

30-17 After sitting in a steam-filled sauna, Finns jump in a frigid lake or pool before enjoying a light meal.

Scandinavian Menu

Sill med Kremsaus
(Herring in Cream Sauce)

Kesäkeitto
(Summer Soup)

Frikadeller
(Danish Meat Patties)

Brunede Kartofler
(Caramelized Potatoes)

Syltede Rødbeder
(Pickled Beets)

Limpa
(Swedish Rye Bread)

Kringla
(Double-Ring Twist Biscuits)

Fattigman
(Poor Man's Cookies)

Kaffe
(Coffee)

Sill med Kremsaus
(Herring in Cream Sauce)

Serves 6

1½	cups coarsely chopped herring (salt, pickled, or Bismark herring)
2	tablespoons finely chopped onion
2	tablespoons fresh dill, divided
	dash pepper
3	tablespoons white wine vinegar, divided
2	chilled hard-cooked egg yolks
1	teaspoon prepared mustard
1	tablespoon vegetable oil
3½	tablespoons evaporated fat-free milk

1. In a small mixing bowl, combine herring, onion, 1 tablespoon dill, pepper, and 1½ tablespoons white wine vinegar; set aside.
2. In another bowl, mash egg yolks with a wooden spoon.
3. Add mustard, remaining 1½ tablespoons vinegar, and oil, beating until smooth.
4. Gradually add evaporated fat-free milk, beating constantly, until sauce is the thickness of heavy cream.
5. Pour sauce over herring mixture and refrigerate, covered, at least two hours.
6. Garnish with remaining fresh dill just before serving.

Per serving: 168 cal. (73% from fat), 16 g protein, 2 g carbohydrate, 11 g fat, 114 mg cholesterol, 0 g fiber, 108 mg sodium.

Kesäkeitto
(Summer Soup)

Serves 6 to 8

1	cup fresh green peas*
1	small head cauliflower, separated into small florets
5	small carrots, diced
2	small potatoes, diced
½	pound fresh string beans, cut into narrow strips*
4	cups cold water
¼	pound fresh spinach, finely chopped
2	tablespoons all-purpose flour
1	cup fat-free milk
¼	cup evaporated fat-free milk
1	egg yolk
	salt and white pepper to taste
	chopped parsley

1. With the exception of the spinach, place vegetables in a large saucepan, cover with cold water, and simmer until just tender, about 5 minutes.
2. Add spinach and cook another 5 minutes.
3. Remove from heat and strain liquid into a bowl; set aside.
4. Place vegetables in a second bowl.
5. Combine flour and milk in a covered jar or blender container. Shake or blend until smooth.
6. Pour flour mixture into the saucepan used for the vegetables. Cook over medium heat, stirring constantly until sauce comes to a boil. Cook and stir for one additional minute until sauce is thick and smooth.
7. Add hot vegetable stock slowly, stirring constantly.
8. In a small bowl combine the evaporated fat-free milk and egg yolk.
9. Add a few tablespoons of hot soup to the egg mixture, beating constantly. Then add the warmed egg mixture to the hot soup.
10. Add vegetables and bring soup to a simmer. Simmer uncovered over low heat for 3 to 5 minutes.
11. Taste and add salt and pepper as needed.
12. Pour into a tureen and garnish with chopped parsley.

*If fresh peas, string beans, or spinach are not available, substitute frozen June peas, French-style green beans, and chopped spinach. Adjust cooking time accordingly.

Per serving: 148 cal. (6% from fat), 7 g protein, 28 g carbohydrate, 1 g fat, 46 mg cholesterol, 7 g fiber, 362 mg sodium.

Frikadeller
(Danish Meat Patties)

Makes about 15 meat patties

½   pound ground pork shoulder or fresh ham
½   pound ground shoulder of veal
½   cup flour
2   eggs
1   large onion, chopped
       salt and pepper to taste
⅔   cup fat-free milk
       margarine for frying

1. In a large bowl, mix the meats with the flour, eggs, onion, salt, and pepper.
2. Add milk gradually and mix thoroughly. Let the mixture stand 15 minutes to allow the flour to absorb the milk.
3. Shape the mixture into small meat patties.
4. Melt margarine in an electric skillet or frying pan over medium heat.
5. Fry patties about 5 minutes on each side. Use a meat thermometer to be sure the internal temperature has reached 160°F.
6. Drain on paper towels.

Per meat patty: 98 cal. (50% from fat), 7 g protein, 5 g carbohydrate, 5 g fat, 58 mg cholesterol, 0 g fiber, 40 mg sodium.

Brunede Kartofler
(Caramelized Potatoes)

Serves 6

2   pounds small red potatoes
¼   cup sugar
2   tablespoons melted margarine

1. Scrub potatoes carefully. Do not remove skins.
2. Fill a heavy 2- to 3-quart saucepan with water and bring it to a boil.
3. Add potatoes and simmer 15 to 20 minutes or until potatoes are tender.
4. Cool potatoes slightly; slip off skins.
5. In a large, heavy skillet, melt sugar. Use a low heat and stir sugar constantly until it turns into light brown syrup. (Heat must be low or sugar will scorch.)
6. Add melted margarine.
7. Add potatoes, a few at a time, shaking pan to coat all sides with syrup. Serve immediately.

Per serving: 216 cal. (17% from fat), 3 g protein, 43 g carbohydrate, 4 g fat, 0 mg cholesterol, 3 g fiber, 54 mg sodium.

Syltede Rødbeder
(Pickled Beets)

Makes 2 1/2 cups

¼   cup cider vinegar
¼   cup white vinegar
½   cup sugar
½   teaspoon salt
       dash pepper
2½   cups thinly sliced canned beets

1. In a 1½- to 2-quart stainless steel saucepan, combine all ingredients but beets. Boil briskly for 2 minutes.
2. While marinade boils, place beets in a deep stainless steel or glass bowl.
3. Pour hot marinade over beets; let cool for 20 minutes, uncovered.
4. Cover bowl and refrigerate at least 12 hours, stirring occasionally.

Per ½-cup serving: 105 cal. (0% from fat), 1 g protein, 28 g carbohydrate, 0 g fat, 0 mg cholesterol, 2 g fiber, 466 mg sodium.

Limpa
(Swedish Rye Bread)

Makes 2 loaves

1   package active dry yeast
1¾   cups warm water (105°F to 115°F)
½   cup light brown sugar, packed
½   cup light molasses
1½   teaspoons salt
2   tablespoons shortening
1   tablespoon grated orange peel
½   cup dark seedless raisins
2½   cups rye flour
3½ to 4 cups all-purpose flour

1. In a large bowl, dissolve yeast in warm water.
2. Add brown sugar, molasses, salt, shortening, orange peel, raisins, and rye flour; beat well.
3. Add enough all-purpose flour to make a soft dough.
4. Turn dough out onto a lightly floured board or pastry cloth. Cover; let rest 10 minutes.
5. Knead dough until smooth and elastic, about 10 minutes.
6. Place dough in a lightly greased bowl, turning once to grease surface. Cover with a towel. Let dough rise in a warm place until doubled in bulk (about 1½ to 2 hours).

7. Punch dough down. Turn dough out on lightly floured board or cloth and divide into 2 portions.
8. Shape each portion into a ball; cover, let rest 10 minutes.
9. Pat balls of dough into 2 round loaves and place on a greased baking sheet. Cover loaves and let rise in a warm place until double (about 1½ to 2 hours).
10. Bake loaves at 375°F for 25 to 30 minutes.
11. Remove bread from pans to cooling racks. For a soft crust, butter tops of loaves while hot.

Per slice: 119 cal. (8% from fat), 3 g protein, 25 g carbohydrate, 1 g fat, 0 mg cholesterol, 2 g fiber, 107 mg sodium.

Kringla
(Double-Ring Twist Biscuits)

Makes about 24 cookies

1	cup sugar
1	cup plain nonfat yogurt
1	cup fat-free sour milk
1	egg
1	teaspoon baking soda
	pinch salt
½	teaspoon cinnamon
1½ to 2	cups all-purpose flour

1. Preheat oven to 375°F.
2. Combine sugar, yogurt, sour milk, egg, baking soda, salt, and cinnamon in a large bowl.
3. Add enough flour to make a fairly stiff dough.
4. Roll dough between palms to form pencil-sized rolls; shape rolls into figure eights.
5. Place cookies on lightly greased baking sheet and bake until lightly browned, about 10 to 12 minutes.

Per cookie: 92 cal. (4% from fat), 2 g protein, 20 g carbohydrate, 0 g fat, 12 mg cholesterol, 0 g fiber, 51 mg sodium.

Fattigman
(Poor Man's Cookies)

Makes about 3 dozen cookies

4	eggs
½	cup sugar
	dash salt
4	tablespoons evaporated fat-free milk
1½	cups all-purpose flour
	shortening or oil for frying
	sugar

1. Beat eggs, sugar, and salt until thick and light.
2. Add evaporated milk and enough flour to make a soft dough.
3. Cut dough into diamond shapes and fry in hot shortening (375°F).
4. While warm, sprinkle cookies with sugar.

Per cookie: 53 cal. (13% from fat), 2 g protein, 10 g carbohydrate, 1 g fat, 31 mg cholesterol, 0 g fiber, 10 mg sodium.

CAREER SUCCESS

Honesty and Integrity

Ian owns a small travel agency called European Excursions. In addition to managing the business, Ian serves as the main tour guide. He arranges transportation and meal and lodging accommodations for groups of tourists traveling throughout Europe. He also accompanies the tour groups on their trips. He makes sure the groups follow their schedules and reach planned stopping points along the way.

To be an effective worker, Ian needs to display honesty and integrity. He knows he could make a bigger profit by booking groups into lower-class hotels or second-rate restaurants. However, Ian wants his business to have a reputation for giving tour groups the best value for their travel dollar. Imagine you are a client in one of Ian's tour groups. Answer the following questions about Ian's need for and use of the qualities of honesty and integrity:

A. Suppose you didn't know anything about Ian's character and business philosophy. How would you assume you would be treated by the owner of a travel agency who was arranging your vacation?
B. How would Ian's obvious honesty and integrity make you feel once you were on your trip?
C. What impact would Ian's behavior have if you were planning a second European trip or talking to a friend who was planning a European trip?
D. What is another skill Ian would need in this job? Briefly explain why this skill would be important.

CHAPTER 30 REVIEW

Summary

The British Isles include the countries of England, Scotland, Wales, Northern Ireland, and Ireland. These countries have a common climate and culture. However, each has unique aspects to its cuisine. Roasted meats, baked apples, main dish pies, and steamed puddings are among the popular foods in England. Simple, wholesome foods of the Scots often include such basic ingredients as oats, barley, lamb, and fish. The hearty fare of Wales is similar to that of its neighbors. Potatoes are the staple of the Irish diet. Tea is a popular beverage throughout the British Isles. It is also the name of a light meal served in the late afternoon or early evening.

France has long been known for its fine cuisine. French cooks use three main cooking styles: haute cuisine, provincial cuisine, and nouvelle cuisine. A variety of sauces and delicate seasonings characterize French cooking. Local dishes are popular throughout the various regions of France.

German cuisine is filling and flavorful. Roasted meats and a variety of sausages are common main dishes in Germany. Potatoes, sauerkraut, and dumplings are popular as hearty side dishes. Delicious breads as well as sweet rolls and cakes are the pride of German bakers. Of course, people throughout the world know Germany for its beers and wines.

Denmark, Norway, Sweden, and Finland are all part of Scandinavia. Much of Scandinavia is characterized by rugged terrain. This has made farming difficult in many areas and has isolated one region from another. Scandinavia is also typified by a cold climate. These factors have all affected the development of Scandinavian cuisine. Danish foods tend to be rich, often containing butter, cream, cheese, eggs, and pork. The Norwegians eat much fish and use sour cream in many of their recipes. Special occasions in Sweden often feature a smörgåsbord, but the everyday style of cooking is much simpler. Some Finnish dishes have Russian origins, and many include berries, mushrooms, and potatoes gathered from local forests.

Review What You Have Read

Write your answers on a separate sheet of paper, using complete sentences when appropriate.

1. What annual festival is celebrated in Wales on March 1, and what foods are traditionally served on this day?
2. What are four staples of the British diet that were introduced by the Anglo-Saxons?
3. What foods might be served for a traditional breakfast in England?
4. True or false. Haggis is an Irish porridge made with potatoes and cabbage.
5. Define haute cuisine, provincial cuisine, and nouvelle cuisine.
6. Name and describe three types of French sauces.
7. True or false. The French serve the salad as a first course.
8. Name three foods that are eaten in the Provence region of France.

9. Describe three popular German potato dishes.

10. True or false. German bakers have traditionally made their cakes with molasses.

11. How do German meal patterns differ from those in the United States?

12. What are two specific toppings commonly eaten on Danish smørrebrød?

13. Describe three kinds of Norwegian cookies.

14. What dishes are typically included at a smörgåsbord?

15. What do Finns often snack on during a sauna and why?

Link to Academic Skills

16. **English language arts.** Investigate how widely used the English language is in the world today. Create a bulletin board on which each student posts the name of a country in which English is a primary language.

17. **Government/civics.** Explore how the monarchy in Great Britain differs from the presidency in the United States. Share your findings in a class discussion.

18. **English language arts.** Research the celebration of a French holiday. Share your findings about traditional customs, decorations, and foods in a brief oral report.

19. **History.** Work in pairs to research milestones in German history. String a piece of yarn or twine across the classroom to create a time line. Working in chronological order, pairs of students should give brief oral reports on their historical events. As each pair reports, they should hang a sign on the time line with the date(s) and an illustration of the event on which they are reporting.

20. **Social studies.** Divide the class into four groups. Each group should visit the Scandinavia Tourist Board's website to find information about one of the Scandinavian countries discussed in this chapter. Each group should give a report on their assigned country. Reports should include information about the country's geography, history, government, economy, and lifestyle. Each group member should be responsible for presenting a different aspect of the report.

Build Critical Thinking Skills

21. **Evaluation.** Create a dish using leftovers from another meal. Give your dish an interesting name, like those coined by British cooks. Prepare a form to help your classmates evaluate your dish for appearance, texture, and flavor. Your evaluation form should also invite your classmates to offer suggestions for improving the dish.

22. **Synthesis.** Work with a small group to organize the thorough research of one of the regions of France. Each member of the group should be responsible for a different part of the research. Research topics should include the geography, agriculture, culture, and cuisine of the region. Work as a team to coordinate your research findings and prepare a multimedia presentation to share with the class.

11. Traditionally, Germans who could afford to do so ate five meals. The two "extra" meals were a second breakfast and an afternoon coffee.

12. (List two:) Danish blue cheese with raw egg yolk, sliced roast pork garnished with dried fruit, smoked salmon and scrambled eggs garnished with chives

13. (Describe three. Student response.)

14. Herring dishes; cold fish, meats, and salads; hot meats, eggs, or fish; breads; cheeses; and desserts are foods typically included at a smörgåsbord.

15. Finns often snack on salty fish during a sauna to help replace the salt lost through sweat.

Apply Technology

23. Use a computer and the table function in word processing software to create a two-column survey form. The first column should be headed *Rank*, and the second column should be headed *Attractions*. Leave the first column blank and list 10 popular European attractions in the second column. Use the sort function to alphabetize the list in the second column.

24. Give printouts of the European attractions survey form created in the preceding activity to five friends. Ask your friends to rank the listed attractions from 1 to 10, with 1 being their favorite attraction. Have them write their rankings in the first column. Then use a computer to tally the results of the survey and sort the attractions according to ascending numbers. Discuss the results in class.

A Measure of Math

25. Europeans use the metric system of measurement. List the metric equivalents for each ingredient in the British, French, German, or Scandinavian recipes found in this chapter.

Teamwork in Action

26. Parliamentary procedure is a set of rules for conducting meetings. It began in the British Parliament in the 16th century. Divide your class into teams to find out how to use parliamentary procedure to run a meeting, handle debates, and vote on issues. Use your information to put together a simple pamphlet. Hand out the pamphlet to adult and student leaders of all the clubs and organizations in your school. Encourage them to use it to help make their meetings more effective.

Companion Website
www.g-wlearning.com

At the website, review key terms for this chapter with crossword puzzles, matching exercises, and e-flash cards. Apply facts from the chapter to complete the activities.

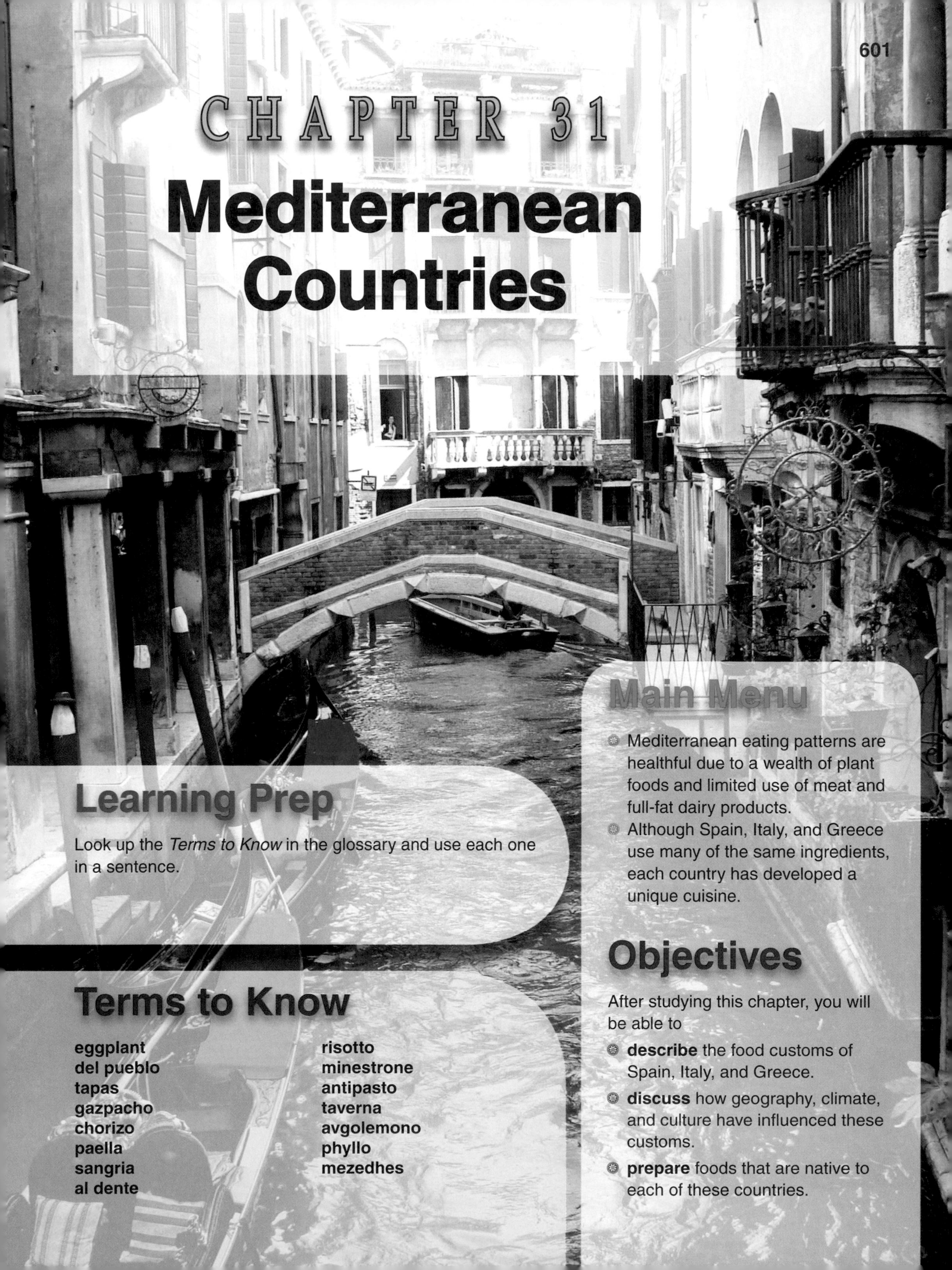

CHAPTER 31
Mediterranean Countries

Learning Prep

Look up the *Terms to Know* in the glossary and use each one in a sentence.

Terms to Know

eggplant
del pueblo
tapas
gazpacho
chorizo
paella
sangria
al dente

risotto
minestrone
antipasto
taverna
avgolemono
phyllo
mezedhes

Main Menu

- Mediterranean eating patterns are healthful due to a wealth of plant foods and limited use of meat and full-fat dairy products.
- Although Spain, Italy, and Greece use many of the same ingredients, each country has developed a unique cuisine.

Objectives

After studying this chapter, you will be able to

- **describe** the food customs of Spain, Italy, and Greece.
- **discuss** how geography, climate, and culture have influenced these customs.
- **prepare** foods that are native to each of these countries.

The Mediterranean Sea is a warm, salty body of water that lies south of Europe. The Mediterranean region supports crops like citrus fruit, olives, grapes, wheat, barley, peaches, and apricots. The sea itself harbors a variety of fish as well as sponges and coral. For ages, people in the Mediterranean region have harvested these products and the sea salt to earn a living.

The climate in this region is balmy with plenty of sunshine throughout the year. The winters are mild with average rainfall. The summers are hot and dry. This weather makes the Mediterranean a popular vacation area.

Three European countries that lie along the Mediterranean Sea are Spain, Italy, and Greece. Because of their similar climates and resources, the cuisines of these countries resemble one another. Vegetables like tomatoes, eggplant, and green peppers are used in many dishes in each of these countries. (**Eggplant** is a fleshy, oval-shaped vegetable with a deep purple skin.) Seafood is also common in each of these cuisines.

As you read about Spain, Italy, and Greece, you will recognize how their food customs are similar. You will also note unique aspects of each cuisine.

Health and Wellness

Mediterranean Eating Patterns

In recent years, nutrition experts have focused much attention on the health benefits of traditional Mediterranean-style eating patterns. Such eating patterns are linked to lower rates of cancer and heart disease.

A number of features add to the healthfulness of Mediterranean eating patterns. The most notable characteristic is the broad use of plant foods. Tomatoes, eggplant, peppers, legumes, onions, and garlic form the basis of many dishes. Pasta, rice, and/or bread are staples at most meals. Many of the grain foods served are whole grains. Nuts are also commonly included in Mediterranean eating patterns. Fruits such as grapes, oranges, figs, and melons grow well in the warm Mediterranean climate. They, rather than rich desserts, are often served at the end of Mediterranean meals. Olive oil, which has no cholesterol and is high in monounsaturated fats, is the main cooking fat in the Mediterranean. People in this region tend to eat much seafood but only limited portions of meat. Use of full-fat dairy products is limited as well. These characteristics define eating patterns that are fairly low in fat. Mediterranean eating patterns provide good sources of vitamins, minerals, fiber, and other helpful plant substances, too.

Shutterstock

Olive oil adds flavor and a source of healthful monounsaturated fats to the Mediterranean diet.

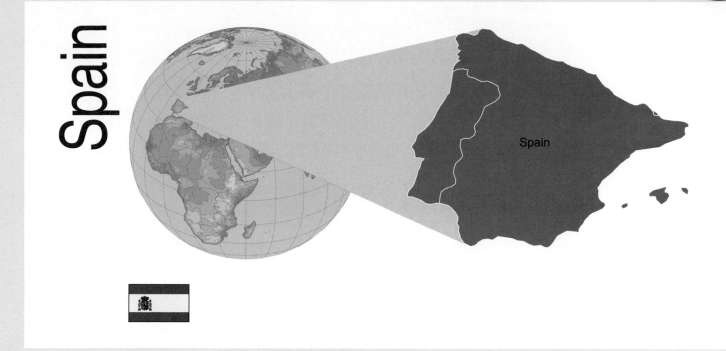

The Iberian Peninsula lies between the Mediterranean Sea and the Atlantic Ocean. This land mass forms the southwestern corner of Europe. Spain and Portugal share the peninsula. Spain occupies the largest part.

Geography and Climate of Spain

The two main geographic features of Iberia are water and mountains. Water nearly surrounds the peninsula, and several mountain ranges crisscross the land.

Most Spaniards live along the coast of the Bay of Biscay and the Mediterranean Sea. There the land is fertile and agriculture is prosperous.

In the North, the Pyrenees separate Spain from France and the rest of Europe. Four other mountain ranges divide the rest of the land into isolated units. Within the circle formed by the mountain ranges is the Meseta. The *Meseta* is a large plateau. It occupies more than half of the total area of Spain.

Spain has a surprising range of climates for a country that is relatively small. Much of Spain has a Mediterranean climate with hot, dry summers, mild winters, and light rainfall, **31-1**. Northern Spain has cool summers with mild, damp winters. The Meseta of central Spain has the most severe climate with extremes of both heat and cold. The southernmost tip of Spain is semidesert with virtually no winter.

Vocabulary Builder

The word *peninsula* comes from two Latin words meaning *almost island*.

FYI

Poor soil that is unsuitable for farming covers most of the Meseta. Madrid, Spain's capital and largest city, is located in the center of the Meseta.

FYI

Many Spaniards became Muslim under Moorish rule.

Discuss

Ask students how Spain's agricultural products are used in Spanish cuisine.

Reflect

Ask students how they feel about bullfighting as a spectacle.

Shutterstock

31-1 The warm weather along the Mediterranean Sea offers a climate suitable for growing a variety of crops.

Spanish Culture

Spain has a rich cultural heritage. This heritage has influenced life in the country today.

Spanish Agriculture

Many Spaniards make their living fishing or farming. There are some large landowners in Spain. However, most people live on their own small farms. Wheat, olives, barley, oats, rye, potatoes, rice, beans, grapes, and honey are Spain's primary crops. Valencian oranges grown in Spain are among the best oranges in the world. Farmers raise sheep on the Meseta and in mountainous areas. They raise some cattle in grassy areas.

The land along the southeastern Mediterranean coast is the "gardenland" of Spain. Extensive irrigation systems built in this once arid land have allowed a variety of crops to thrive. Today, almonds, oranges, lemons, figs, dates, melons, pomegranates, and sugarcane grow in this region. Spain's two most popular wines are also produced there.

Spanish Celebrations

Annual Spanish celebrations include some unique traditions. One interesting custom is part of the New Year's Eve celebration. People pop a grape into their mouths each time the clock strikes at midnight. Twelve grapes represent twelve months of good luck.

Bullfights are part of the festivities during the annual feast day observed for the patron saint of each town. Besides bullfighting, feast days are celebrated with parades, bonfires, and beauty contests.

A well-known Spanish festival is the *Fiesta of San Fermin*, which is held in Pamplona each July. As part of this celebration, a herd of bulls is set loose to run through the streets of the town. Young men run ahead of the bulls to a bullring where they take part in amateur bullfights.

Spanish Cuisine

Spanish cuisine can best be described as **del pueblo**, or food of the people. It is simple for the most part. Its goodness relies on fresh ingredients and basic preparation methods.

Culture and Social Studies

History of Spanish Cuisine

Spanish cuisine began centuries ago with the Romans, who ruled Spain for a period of six centuries beginning in the 200s B.C. The Romans contributed olive oil and garlic. Spanish cooks still use these two ingredients in many dishes.

In A.D. 711, the Moors, a Muslim people from northern Africa, crossed into Spain and started taking control. The Moors brought citrus fruits, peaches, and figs. They introduced the cultivation of rice. They also grew a number of spices, including saffron, pepper, nutmeg, and anise. The Romans knew of the almond. However, it was the Moors who planted large almond groves and often used almonds in cooking.

In the fifteenth century, during the reign of Ferdinand and Isabella, Spanish explorers journeyed to the New World. The explorers claimed land for Spain. Spain's colonies in the New World provided tomatoes, chocolate, potatoes, and sweet and hot peppers.

Invasion by various enemy groups and Spain's rugged terrain further affected the development of food customs. These two factors helped divide the country into distinct culinary regions.

Characteristics of Spanish Cuisine

Today, each of Spain's regions still clings to its style of cooking. However, cooks throughout the country use similar ingredients and cooking methods.

Spaniards made many contributions to Mexican cuisine. However, Spanish cooking differs from the spicy cooking of Mexico. Throughout Spain, tomatoes, onions, and garlic form the base of many sauces. Garlic, pepper, and paprika flavor many main dishes, soups, and salads. Olive oil replaces butter in most recipes. Parsley serves as more than a garnish. In *salsa verde*, for example, large amounts of parsley add flavor as well as color. Spaniards eat raw almonds as appetizers. They use toasted almonds in sauces, cookies, cakes, pastries, and appetizers. See **31-2**.

A traditional Spanish cooking method is to slowly simmer foods in earthenware pots. Cooks gently move the pots back and forth across the flame as they slowly stir the food inside. They often use the natural juices when cooking meat, fish, or poultry as the base for a sauce. They add other ingredients only to heighten the natural flavors of these juices.

Spanish cooks like to mix two or more food flavors in a single dish. They prepare mixtures of meat and fish; fish and vegetables; and meat, fish, and rice. One of the best

Courtesy of the Almond Board of California

31-2 Almonds are popular as appetizers in Spain.

examples of this method of mixing flavors is the *cocido*. Vegetables, beef, lamb, ham, poultry, and a spicy sausage cook together in a large pot. Spaniards first eat the thick soup in large bowls. Then they follow with the tender meats, poultry, and vegetables as a separate course.

Spanish Appetizers

Spanish meals often begin with **tapas** (appetizers). Friends at a sidewalk cafe may also enjoy sharing tapas. Tapas may be as simple as a few olives or toasted almonds. However, some are fancier and require hours to prepare. Scallops, prawns, pickled herring, ham, marinated mushrooms, and anchovies are popular tapas that are simple to prepare. Fancier tapas include *buñuelitos*, which are small fritters. They are prepared by deep-frying small pieces of vegetables, meat, poultry, or fish that have been coated with a batter. *Empanadillas* are small pastries filled with chopped meat, fish, or poultry. They can be eaten hot or cold. *Banderillas* are colorful tapas served on long toothpicks. *Pinchos* are grilled foods.

Spanish Salads and Soups

A salad often follows the tapas. Sometimes it is little more than lettuce and tomato with a simple oil and vinegar dressing. Other times, it may be an attractive arrangement of raw vegetables on a plate.

Soups are popular throughout Spain. One of the heartiest soups is a fish soup called *sopa al cuarto de hora*, or 15-minute soup. It is made with mussels, prawns, whitefish, rice, peas, hard-cooked eggs, saffron, salt, pepper, and meat broth. All the ingredients cook together for 15 minutes—just long enough to blend the flavors.

People throughout Spain enjoy garlic soup. Cooks prepare one of the simplest versions by slowly sautéing two cloves of garlic in olive oil. Once the garlic browns, a few slices of bread, salt, pepper, and water are added. Then the soup cooks for just a few minutes. Other versions include a small amount of minced ham and tomatoes.

Another popular Spanish soup is **gazpacho**. This soup is often made with coarsely pureed tomatoes, onions, garlic, cucumbers, and green peppers; olive oil; and vinegar. It can be thick or thin, served icy cold or at room temperature.

Spanish Main Dishes

Most culinary experts agree that few cooks can prepare seafood as well as the Spaniards. Mussels, shrimp, and crab are popular shellfish in Spain. Tuna, hake, sole, squid, and cod are also caught off Spain's coasts. Cooks bake, fry, and poach fish and shellfish. In some parts of Spain, they serve seafood with *all-i-oli* (garlic mayonnaise).

Although methods for cooking meat are not as refined as those for seafood, Spain produces some excellent meat dishes. Veal, lamb, and pork are the most popular meats. The lean, dark Spanish pig is used in many ways. Raw ham, which is air cured high in the mountains, is a specialty. Filet of cured pork is sliced thinly and served as

Enrich

Hold a debate to compare the value of enjoying tapas and beverages with friends at a café with the value of watching television as an evening pastime.

Reflect

Ask students if they would enjoy soup served cold or at room temperature and explain why or why not.

an appetizer. However, the best known pork product is **chorizo**, a dark sausage with a spicy, smoky flavor.

People throughout Spain eat poultry. Although Spaniards eat pigeon, pheasant, and partridge, chicken is by far the most popular type of poultry. Cooks stew and roast chicken. They also use it in the famous Spanish dish called paella. **Paella** is a Spanish rice dish that has many variations. All versions of paella, however, are colorful and delicious. The version most often seen in the United States contains chicken, shrimp, mussels, whitefish, peas, and rice. It is flavored with saffron, salt, pepper, and pimiento.

Spanish Accompaniments

The Spanish serve bread with soups, salads, and main dishes. A variety of breads are popular. *Pan de Santa Teresa* (fried cinnamon bread) is a sweet bread similar to French toast. *Picatostes* (fried sugar breads) are more like a pastry. They are served as an afternoon snack with coffee.

Tortillas (Spanish omelets) may be served as a separate course or as an accompaniment. Spanish cooks use a variety of fillings for tortillas. Potato, onion, white bean, and eggplant are the most popular. Sometimes cooks pile several tortillas with different fillings on top of one another. They serve them the way people serve pancakes in the United States. See **31-3**.

Spaniards generally serve vegetables as a separate course. However, potatoes or grilled tomatoes may accompany a main dish. Vegetables served alone are often cooked in a tomato sauce or coated with a batter and deep-fried. Two or more vegetables are often combined and cooked in liquid. Many Spanish vegetable dishes contain artichokes, cauliflower, and eggplant. Spaniards also enjoy dried beans, lentils, and chickpeas, which they call *pulses*. Dried beans often appear in one-dish meals with meat, poultry, and fish.

Spanish Desserts

Simple desserts like fresh fruit, dried figs, cheese, or almonds often follow a meal. Spaniards usually save fancy cakes, cookies, pastries, and other rich desserts for guests. They may also serve these desserts as afternoon snacks. Rice pudding, sponge cake, and *flan* (caramel custard) are especially popular.

Spanish cakes and pastries contain very little baking powder or butter. However, they do contain many eggs and powdered almonds. They are flavored with cinnamon, anise, and orange and lemon peel. Spaniards fry rather than bake many cakes and pastries. This is because most Spanish homes did not have ovens until recent years.

Courtesy of the Idaho Potato Commission

31-3 Potatoes make a hearty filling for Spanish tortillas.

Activity

Have students find two paella recipes. Ask them to compare the similarities and differences between the two recipes.

Vocabulary Builder

Ask students where else they have seen the word *tortilla*. Ask how the meaning of the term in Mexican cuisine differs from the meaning in Spanish cuisine.

Spanish Meals

Spanish meals are similar to Mexican meals with the same names. The people of Spain begin each day with *desayuno* (breakfast). They may just have coffee or a chocolate drink. Sometimes they have bread and jam or a sweet roll. *Churro*, a thin pastry fried in deep fat, is especially popular at breakfast.

People who have slept late or workers who find themselves hungry around 11 o'clock eat a second morning meal, *almuerzo*. It is more substantial than desayuno. This meal varies depending on locale and personal taste. It may include an omelet, grilled sausage, fried squid, open-faced sandwiches, fish, or lamb chops.

The *comida* is the main meal of the day. Spaniards eat this meal in the middle of the afternoon, around two or three o'clock. Most businesses close to escape the hottest part of the day, and workers come home to eat. A main course of fish, poultry, or meat usually follows salad or soup. Fruit or another light dessert ends the meal.

Spaniards serve *merienda* around six o'clock. It usually is a light snack of cakes and cookies or bread and jam. If a family has visitors, however, the meal may be more substantial.

Dusk is a pleasant time of day in Spain. The sidewalk cafés fill with people, and the odors of the tapas drift out to the streets. Around nine o'clock, the streets empty, and everyone goes home for *cena* (supper). Cena is a light meal similar to almuerzo.

Wine is Spain's national drink, and both the rich and poor serve it with every meal. Two popular Spanish wines are Malaga and sherry. *Malaga* has a brown color and a sweet taste. *Sherry* has a characteristic nutlike flavor. Restaurants and taverns throughout Spain serve **sangria**, a wine-based punch. There are many versions of the punch, but they all include red wine, fruit juice, and sparkling water. See **31-4**.

Shutterstock
31-4 Mock sangria, a fruity punch, can be made without alcohol.

Spanish Menu

Empanadillas
(Turnovers)

Gazpacho
(Cold Vegetable Soup)

Paella
(Saffron Rice with Seafood and Chicken)

Ensalada Catalan
(Catalan Salad)

Flan
(Caramel Custard)

Sangria Falsa
(Mock Red Wine Punch)

Empanadillas
(Turnovers)

Makes 40

Pastry:

3	cups all-purpose flour
1	teaspoon salt
½	cup olive oil
½	cup cold water

Filling:

2	tablespoons olive oil
2	small onions, chopped
2	small tomatoes, peeled and chopped
1	clove garlic, minced
2	hard-cooked eggs
¾	cup diced, cooked chicken
1	egg, beaten (optional)

1. Mix flour and salt together in a large mixing bowl.
2. Add ½ cup oil and water.
3. With fingers, mix dough until it forms a ball. Let dough rest while preparing the filling.
4. Heat 2 tablespoons oil in large skillet until very hot (but not smoking).
5. Add onions and sauté until golden.
6. Add tomatoes and garlic and continue cooking vegetables until the liquid has evaporated.
7. In small bowl, mash hard-cooked eggs.
8. Add mashed eggs and chicken to skillet. Cook mixture 2 to 3 minutes, stirring occasionally; remove from heat. Taste filling and add salt and pepper, if needed.
9. Preheat oven to 425°F.
10. On a lightly floured board, roll pastry to a thickness of ⅛ inch. Cut circles from pastry with a 3-inch biscuit cutter.
11. Place a rounded tablespoon of filling on one-half of each circle. Fold the other half of the dough over the filling and press edges together with a fork to seal.
12. Place turnovers on lightly greased baking sheet and brush surface with beaten egg, if desired.
13. Bake turnovers until brown and crisp, about 25 minutes.

Per turnover: 77 cal. (47% from fat), 2 g protein, 8 g carbohydrate, 4 g fat, 16 mg cholesterol, 0 g fiber, 60 mg sodium.

Gazpacho
(Cold Vegetable Soup)

Serves 8

1	quart low-sodium chicken broth
4	medium tomatoes, chopped
2	cucumbers, peeled and chopped
1	large onion, sliced
½	green pepper, chopped
2	cups bread cubes
2	tablespoons wine vinegar
1	clove garlic, minced
1	teaspoon sugar
	dash cayenne

Garnish:

1¼	cups bread cubes (¼ inch)
⅓	cup chopped onion
½	cup chopped green peppers
½	cup peeled and chopped tomato

1. In a large bowl, combine chicken broth, tomatoes, cucumbers, onion, green pepper, bread cubes, vinegar, garlic, sugar, and cayenne.
2. Puree mixture in a blender, 2 cups at a time.
3. Chill thoroughly.
4. Just before serving, stir soup lightly. Pour into a tureen or individual soup bowls. Pass garnishes separately.

Per serving: 85 cal. (11% from fat), 4 g protein, 16 g carbohydrate, 1 g fat, 0 mg cholesterol, 3 g fiber, 169 mg sodium.

Paella
(Saffron Rice with Seafood and Chicken)

Serves 10

12	medium-sized canned shrimp
7	small hard-shelled clams
½	pound garlic-seasoned smoked pork sausage
1	2-pound chicken, cut into serving-sized pieces, skin removed
¾	teaspoon garlic salt
	dash pepper
½	cup olive oil
¼	pound lean boneless pork, cut into ½-inch cubes
½	cup chopped onions
1	large green pepper, cleaned and cut
1	large tomato, peeled and finely chopped
2	cloves garlic, crushed
3	cups uncooked long grain rice
¼	teaspoon ground saffron
6	cups water
¾	cup frozen peas, thoroughly defrosted

1. Drain and rinse shrimp; place in small bowl and set aside.
2. Scrub clams with stiff brush under cold running water. Place clams on plate and set aside.
3. Prick sausage in several places with a fork. Place in a large, heavy skillet and cover with cold water.
4. Bring water to a boil, then reduce heat to low. Simmer sausage uncovered for 5 minutes.
5. Drain sausage well and slice into rounds about ¼ inch thick; set aside.
6. Rinse chicken and pat dry with paper towels. Season with garlic salt and pepper.
7. Heat ¼ cup olive oil in large skillet until very hot but not smoking.
8. Add chicken pieces, a few at a time, and fry until golden brown.
9. Remove browned pieces to a plate lined with paper towels and continue cooking the rest of the chicken.
10. Add sausage slices to skillet and quickly brown; transfer to a plate lined with paper towels and drain.
11. Remove oil from skillet and wipe skillet with paper towels.
12. Add ¼ cup fresh olive oil and heat until hot but not smoking.

13. Add pork cubes and brown quickly.
14. Add onions, green peppers, tomatoes, and garlic. Cook vegetables and meat, stirring constantly, until most of the liquid has evaporated. (This is called a sofrito.) Set aside.
15. Preheat oven to 400°F.
16. In an ovenproof skillet or casserole, which is at least 14 inches wide and 2 inches deep, add the sofrito, rice, and saffron.
17. Bring the 6 cups of water to a boil and pour into skillet.
18. Bring mixture to a boil, stirring constantly.
19. Remove from heat immediately and taste for seasonings.
20. Arrange shrimp, clams, sausage, and chicken over the top of the rice. Sprinkle peas over meats and seafood.
21. Place pan or skillet on bottom rack in oven and bake for 25 to 30 minutes or until the liquid has been absorbed. (Do not stir the paella.)
22. When paella is cooked, remove it from oven and place a clean kitchen towel over the top. Let the paella rest about 5 minutes. Serve immediately.

Note: All of the ingredients can be prepared a short time ahead. The oven should be preheated one-half hour before paella is to be served.

Per serving: 418 cal. (22% from fat), 30 g protein, 49 g carbohydrate, 10 g fat, 94 mg cholesterol, 3 g fiber, 539 mg sodium.

Ensalada Catalana
(Catalan Salad)

Serves 6

½	head romaine lettuce
3	medium tomatoes
1	large sweet onion
1	green pepper
1	red pepper
¼	cup green olives
¼	cup pitted black olives
	olive oil
	wine vinegar

1. Clean romaine under cool running water. Separate and dry leaves. Break into bite-sized pieces.
2. Wash tomatoes, slice into wedges.
3. Peel onion; cut into rings.

4. Wash and clean green and red peppers; cut into thin rings.
5. Set six chilled salad plates on a tray. Make a bed of romaine on each plate.
6. Attractively arrange the rest of the ingredients on the top of the lettuce.
7. Serve salads with olive oil and wine vinegar.

Per serving: 107 cal. (71% from fat), 2 g protein, 7 g carbohydrate, 9 g fat, 0 mg cholesterol, 3 g fiber, 145 mg sodium.

Sangria Falsa
(Mock Red Wine Punch)

Serves 8

1	lemon, cut into slices
1	orange, cut into slices
1	lime, cut into slices
2	bottles red grape juice, well chilled
1	bottle club soda, well chilled
	ice cubes

1. In large pitcher, combine fruits and grape juice. Refrigerate until ready to serve.
2. Just before serving, add club soda. Serve sangria immediately over ice.

Per serving: 136 cal. (1% from fat), 0 g protein, 35 g carbohydrate, 0 g fat, 0 mg cholesterol, 1 g fiber, 31 mg sodium.

Flan
(Caramel Custard)

Serves 8

½	cup sugar
2	tablespoons water
2	cups fat-free milk
2	cups evaporated fat-free milk
6	eggs
	pinch salt
¾	cup sugar
1½	teaspoons vanilla

1. To caramelize mold: In small, heavy saucepan combine ½ cup sugar and water. Cook over moderate heat, stirring constantly, until the sugar melts and turns a golden brown.
2. Quickly pour syrup into a 6-cup mold (or 8 custard cups), which has been warmed by placing it in hot water. Turn mold or custard cups in all directions so syrup coats both bottom and sides. Set aside.
3. In a large saucepan, combine milk and evaporated milk and heat to just below boiling.
4. Remove from heat and cool slightly.
5. Preheat oven to 350°F.
6. In a mixer bowl, beat eggs and salt slightly.
7. Add ¾ cup sugar gradually as you continue beating.
8. Add combined milks slowly, beating constantly, then add vanilla.
9. Pour custard into the mold. Place mold in a larger pan; fill the pan with very hot water to about ½ inch from the top of the mold.
10. Bake about 1 hour (25 to 30 minutes for custard cups), until a knife inserted near the center comes out clean.
11. Cool custard 10 minutes, then refrigerate until well chilled.
12. To unmold, run a knife between the custard and mold. Place a serving dish on top of mold and invert. Custard should slide out.

Per serving: 254 cal. (14% from fat), 12 g protein, 42 g carbohydrate, 4 g fat, 164 mg cholesterol, 0 g fiber, 193 mg sodium.

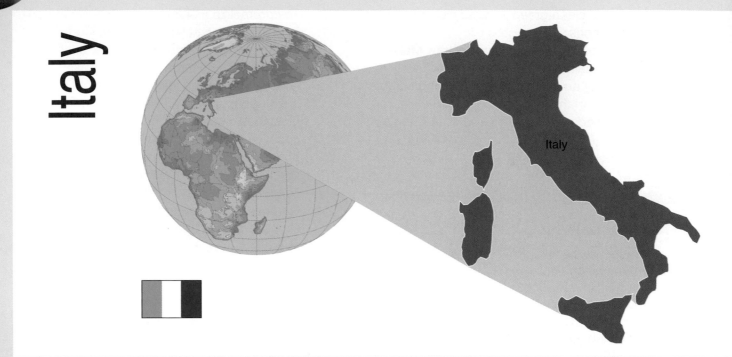

Italy

31-5 Calamari (fried squid) is one of the many Italian dishes enjoyed from the harvest of Mediterranean seafood.

Reflect

Ask students what Italian foods are most familiar to them.

Italy's warm, sunny climate and awesome scenery make it a popular vacation spot. Italy's remarkable art, architecture, and history appeal to culture lovers. Of course, everyone enjoys Italy's delicious food.

Geography and Climate of Italy

Italy is a rather small country. Many islands and a boot-shaped peninsula that juts into the Mediterranean Sea make up Italy. Italy's expansive coastline makes seafood important in Italian cuisine. See **31-5.**

Much of Italy is mountainous. The rugged Italian Alps form a semicircular barrier in the North, shutting out neighboring countries.

The Apennines run in a bow shape, dividing the peninsula in half. Between the Alps and the Apennines lies the Po Valley, which is a rich agricultural area. Narrow coastal plains that border both sides of the peninsula are also suitable for agriculture. Farming takes place in small valleys formed by the mountains, too.

Italy has three distinct geographic regions. Northern Italy has great beauty and rich land. The fertile Po River basin makes the Po Valley the most productive farming area in the country. Central Italy is mountainous and hilly. Grain, grapes, and olives grow on the terraced hillsides. Southern Italy is poor in terms of natural resources. However, olives, tomatoes, and mozzarella cheese are important agricultural products of this region.

Italy's climate is as variable as its geography. Much of Italy has a Mediterranean climate. Summers are sunny and dry with most of the rainfall occurring in the winter. In the North, however, temperatures are cooler, and rain can come during any season. As a result, Italy has a range of vegetation. Pine trees grow in the North. Citrus fruits grow in the South.

Italian Culture

Italy has been the site of many major historical and cultural events. The city of Rome was once the head of a mighty empire. Rome's rule and cultural influence reached through Europe, northern Africa, and western Asia. With the fall of the Roman Empire, which began in A.D. 330, the Roman Catholic Church slowly gained power. The Church met the people's need for leadership and became a center of learning. The structure of the Church became more governmental.

Academic Connections

Plan a unit with the cooperation of a teacher of ancient history. The history teacher can focus on the influence of the Roman Empire and the cultural advancements of ancient Greece.

Activity

Have students use an art history book to find examples of paintings

Culture and Social Studies

The Renaissance

The Roman Catholic Church continued to be a shaping force in Italian culture. Centuries after Rome fell, the Church and some wealthy Italian families encouraged the development of the arts in Italy. This led to the start of the *Renaissance*, a time of a great rebirth in art and learning. The movement spread all through Europe. The Renaissance spanned the fourteenth to the seventeenth centuries. During this time, literature and science flourished along with the arts.

Italian Agriculture

Agriculture is vital to Italy's economy. About half of the nation's land is used for farming. In many areas, farmers cannot use machines to do farm work. Therefore, they must do it by hand.

The richest and most productive farmland is located in Northern Italy in the Po River Valley. Leading crops are wheat, corn, rice, sugar beets, and flax. The many dairy herds make this region the largest cheese-producing region in the country. Olive trees thrive in Southern Italy. Farmers grow vegetables and fruits for local use and for export to other European countries.

Vineyards are scattered throughout the country. They supply grapes for Italy's large wine industry. Italian wine makers produce a variety of red, white, and sparkling wines for domestic use and export.

and sculptures done by Italian artists of the Renaissance period.

For Example…

Oranges, peaches, apples, tomatoes, potatoes, and artichokes are among Italy's important fruit and vegetable crops.

Italian Holidays

Almost all Italians are Roman Catholics. Many Italian holidays celebrate events in the church. *Pasqua*, or Easter, is one important holiday. A number of foods are used to celebrate this holy day that ushers in spring. Cakes and breads made with fruits and

Courtesy ACH Food Companies, Inc.

31-6 Bread shaped like a dove is one of the traditional foods that are part of the Easter celebration in Italy.

nuts are baked in shapes such as doves, **31-6**. People serve lamb as a symbol of spring. Eggs symbolize life, and wheat symbolizes the resurrection of Christ.

Italians hold harvest festivals in the late summer and early fall. These events celebrate the gathering of important foods. At an olive festival, farmers and workers who have brought in the olive crop sit at a long outdoor table. They feast on a meal of pasta, olives, and wine. At fishing festivals held in coastal towns, people enjoy eating seafood barbecued along the shore.

On November 2, Italians celebrate *Festa Dei Morti*, or All Souls' Day. On this day, they pay respect to dead relatives by visiting cemeteries to place flowers and candles on the graves. People may also leave buns, fruit-shaped candies, and lentils in their kitchens at night. They believe the souls of their relatives will enter the home through an open window and enjoy the food.

Christmas is a special time of celebration in Italy. Some people travel to Rome to hear the Pope deliver a Christmas sermon. Many families decorate trees and display nativity scenes depicting the birth of Christ. Children receive gifts from *Babbo Natale*, or Father Christmas. Italians refrain from eating meat on Christmas Eve, but they enjoy a meal of roast meat on Christmas Day.

Italian Cuisine

During the Renaissance, Italian cooking became the "mother cuisine." It is the source of many Western cuisines.

History of Italian Cuisine

The beginning of Italian cuisine belongs to the Greeks, who colonized Southern Italy and the island of Sicily around 1000 B.C. During the time of the Roman Empire, Rome was known for its elaborate feasts. Romans paid high prices for Greek chefs because good food was a status symbol.

Cooking declined somewhat after the fall of the Roman Empire. Cooking and food experienced a rebirth during the Renaissance. Many people say the French have the greatest Western cuisine. However, even the French grudgingly give Italy credit for laying the foundation for haute cuisine. Catherine de Medici, an Italian, brought her cooks to France when she married the future French king, Henri II. These cooks taught new cooking skills to the French. They also introduced new foods like peas, haricot beans, artichokes, and ice cream.

Characteristics of Italian Cuisine

Italian food, as a whole, is lively, interesting, colorful, and varied, yet it is basically simple. The Italians believe in keeping the natural flavors of food, and they insist on fresh, high-quality ingredients. Many Italian cooks shop daily so foods will be as fresh

Academic Connections

As your class studies information on the culture and cuisine of Italy, ask teachers from the art department to discuss the work of Italian painters and sculptors with their classes.

Reflect

Ask students how shopping for food on a daily basis and eliminating convenience foods from their diets would affect their lifestyles.

as possible. They do not indulge in convenience foods. If a particular food is too costly or out of season, an Italian cook substitutes whatever is available.

Italian cooks use many kinds of herbs, spices, and other seasonings. They stock their kitchens with parsley, marjoram, sweet basil, thyme, sage, rosemary, tarragon, bay leaves, oregano, and mint. Other commonly used flavorings include cloves, saffron, coriander, celery, onions, shallots, garlic, vinegar, olives, and lemon juice.

Fresh fruits and vegetables are as important to the Italian kitchen as herbs and spices. Those who live in the country grow many of the fruits and vegetables they use. City dwellers make trips to the local market each day. There, they select the ripest and freshest tomatoes, artichokes, peas, beans, and other produce.

Italian cooks prepare many dishes on top of the range, either by simmering or frying. Because fuel is relatively expensive, they use the oven as little as possible.

Italian Staple Foods

People throughout Italy eat pasta. Pasta refers to any paste made from wheat flour that is dried in various shapes. Pasta may be made from just flour and water. However, pasta may have added ingredients like eggs. It may be made at home, or it may be made commercially.

Italians serve pasta in many ways, but they always serve it cooked **al dente** (slightly resistant to the bite). They may serve it with butter, a sprinkling of cheese, or a variety of sauces. They may add it to soups or stews or stuff it with meat, poultry, vegetables, or cheese.

After pasta, Italy's most important staple food is seafood. Every locale with a coast-line has developed unique methods of preparing and serving fish. Sole, sea bass, anchovies, sardines, mackerel, tuna, eel, squid, and octopus are some of the varieties of seafood caught. Equally popular are the shellfish, including oysters, clams, mussels, spiny lobsters, shrimp, and crayfish. See **31-7.**

Rice is both an important agricultural product and a staple food. Italians cook the rice so the grains remain separate with a slight firmness.

Pork, lamb, veal, and beef are produced and eaten in Italy. Sausage, wild game, and poultry are equally popular. Meat is relatively expensive, so many Italian dishes rely on meat extenders. The sauces for many pasta dishes contain little meat. If large cuts of meat are served, they usually are roasted.

Italian Dairy Products

Among the best-known Italian cheeses sold in the United States are Parmesan, mozzarella, Romano, ricotta, provolone, and Gorgonzola. Some varieties of cheese, such as Parmesan, are named after their place of origin.

The Italians introduced ice cream to the rest of Europe. There are two basic varieties. *Granita* is a light sherbet made with powdery ice and coffee or fruit-flavored syrup. *Gelati* is made with milk. It resembles the vanilla and chocolate ice creams familiar to people in the United States.

For Example...

Bring in samples of a variety of Italian pasta shapes to show students. Ask students to find a sauce, casserole, or soup recipe that would be appropriate for use with each pasta shape.

Vocabulary Builder

Have students use the etymology references in a dictionary to identify the place of origin for *Parmesan*, *Romano*, and *Gorgonzola* cheeses.

©2011 Wisconsin Milk Marketing Board, Inc.

31-7 Shrimp, olives, pasta, and Parmesan cheese—this dish includes a flavorful array of Italian staple ingredients.

Italian Beverages

Caffe espresso is a rich, dark, flavorful coffee served throughout Italy. It is made in a special type of coffeemaker called a *caffettiera*. Darkly roasted, finely ground coffee beans must be used. (This type of coffee is often called *French roast* in stores in the United States.)

Even more important to the Italians than caffe espresso is *vino* (wine). Even children drink it. Mild burgundy or Chianti usually replaces water at Italian meals.

Regional Italian Specialties

Thanks to modern transportation, people throughout Italy can now buy foods that were once strictly regional. Pizza, for example, originated in Naples. Today it is eaten all over Italy and much of the rest of the world as well. Despite this, Italian cooking is regional cooking. Most culinary experts agree the best regional foods are still found within their home regions.

Culture and Social Studies

An Italian Culinary Division

Geography and climate create a culinary division between the North and South in Italy. Northern Italy has more resources than Southern Italy. Meat is easier to obtain and less expensive. Dairy products are more common. Foods are not as heavily spiced as they are in the South. Cooks use delicate sauces instead of heavier tomato sauces.

Most of the farming and grazing land in Southern Italy is of poor quality. This region is rather sparsely populated and many of the people have lower incomes. Meat is expensive and eaten in small amounts. Dairy products, except for cheese, are rare. Most foods are hearty, filling, and economical. Southern Italian cooking is the cooking with which most people in the United States are familiar. This is because most Italian restaurants in the United States are Neapolitan, and Naples is the heart of Southern Italian cooking.

Cooking fats and pasta varieties also differ between the North and the South. Northern Italy is too cold to raise olive trees but has excellent grazing land for dairy cattle. Southern Italy is warm enough for olive trees but has poor grazing land. Therefore, butter is the favored cooking fat in the North. In the South, cooks prefer olive oil.

Northern Italy is the home of the fat, ribbon-shaped groups of pastas called *pasta bolognese*. These pastas usually are made at home and contain egg. Southern Italy is the home of the tubular-shaped groups of pastas called *pasta napoletania*. These pastas are usually produced commercially. They do not contain egg, and they have a longer shelf life.

Specialties of Northern Italy

The specialties of Northern Italy include the simple *minestras* (soups) of the Friuli-Venezia region. The elegant stuffed pastas and rich meat sauces of the city of Bologna are also part of this fare.

The North is known for its sausages and other pork products. Bologna's *mortadella* is one of the best-known Italian sausages in the United States. It is made with beef and pork and seasoned with pepper and garlic. Delicately-flavored *Parma ham* is a popular appetizer.

In the North, people often serve risottos, gnocchi, and polenta instead of pasta. **Risottos** are rice dishes made with butter, chopped onion, stock or wine, and Parmesan cheese. They may have meats or seafood and vegetables added. Because many of the northern regions lie along the sea, risottos in this area often contain seafood. *Gnocchi* are dumplings. They may be made of potatoes or wheat flour, **31-8**. *Polenta* is a porridge made of cornmeal. It sometimes is combined with butter and cheese and served as a filling side dish.

In several of the northeastern regions, Austrian influences are evident. Foods such as *apfelstrudel* (apple strudel) and *crauti* (sauerkraut) have retained their original names.

Other Northern Italian specialties popular in the United States are chicken cacciatore, minestrone soup, and osso buco. *Pollo alla cacciatore* (chicken hunter-style) is prepared by simmering pieces of chicken with tomatoes and mushrooms. **Minestrone** is a satisfying soup made with onions, carrots, zucchini, celery, cabbage, rice or pasta, and seasonings. It is served with Parmesan cheese. *Osso buco* is the portion of a calf's leg between the knee and hock. It is served with the marrow that fills the center of the bone. The flavorful marrow is eaten with rice.

Famous Northern Italian sweets include zabaglione and panettone. *Zabaglione* is fluffy egg custard flavored with Marsala wine. *Panettone* is a sweet cake filled with fruit and nuts. It is often served for breakfast.

Courtesy of the Idaho Potato Commission

31-8 Potato gnocchi provides a delicious and filling alternative to pasta in Northern Italy.

Specialties of Central Italy

Several of Central Italy's specialties have Roman origins. Roman cooks serve spaghetti in at least 25 ways. Of these, people in the United States may be most familiar with the spaghetti dish called *spaghetti alla carbonara*. The sauce for this dish contains eggs, pork, pepper, and cheese.

Of all meats, Romans enjoy lamb the most. Cooks rub young lambs with garlic, rosemary, pepper, and salt. Then they cover the lambs with rosemary and roast them until tender.

The Romans must be given credit for inventing cheesecake. The early Romans made their *crostata di ricotta* (cheese pie) without any sweetening. It contained flour, cheese, and eggs. Today's cooks sweeten crostata di ricotta with sugar and flavor it with candied fruits, almonds, and vanilla.

In the rich countryside of Tuscany, home-grown vegetables, beans, and charcoal-grilled meats are specialties. Tuscan cooks add beans to minestras. They also cook beans with garlic and tomatoes or flavor them with sage and cheese. They prepare beans *nel fiasco* by cooking them with garlic, water, and olive oil in an empty wine flask. Tuscan cooks grill large beefsteaks on gridirons. The steaks are sprinkled with coarse salt and pepper to make *bistecca alla fiorentina*.

Cenci and panforte are sweets with Central Italian origins. *Cenci* are deep-fried pastry strips shaped like bows. *Panforte* is a honey cake flavored with cinnamon and cloves.

Specialties of Southern Italy

Southern Italian cooks serve pasta with rich tomato sauces. They may flavor the sauces with meat, seafood, or vegetables. Spaghetti and lasagne are the southern pastas with which people in the United States are most familiar. However, Southern Italian cooks do not limit themselves to just these varieties. *Fusilli* (pulled out spirals),

Reflect

Ask students which of these Northern Italian specialties they have eaten.

Online Resource

Have each student navigate the Italian Government Tourist Board website to learn about a chosen region, including food specialties. Have students share their findings.

Activity

Have students make a chart identifying some of the main differences between the cuisines of Northern Italy and Southern Italy.

Community Interactions

Have the class organize a spaghetti dinner for the community. Students should choose Italian music and decorations to coordinate with the theme of the menu.

orecchietta (little ears), and *ricci di donna* (ladies' curls) are equally popular. Large tubular pastas like cannelloni and rigatoni are used as well.

With pasta, the Southern Italians love rich tomato sauces. The traditional Neapolitan tomato sauce is simple. Cooks combine fresh tomatoes with fried onions, larded filet of beef, and a sprig of basil. The mixture simmers in an earthenware pot for several hours to bring out all the flavors.

One popular Neapolitan dish is *stuffed lasagne*. Long, wide noodles are layered with cheeses and meats. Cheeses include ricotta, mozzarella, and grated Parmesan. The filling may contain pieces of sausage, minced pork, strips of ham, and hard-cooked egg slices. A thick tomato sauce is poured over the mixture and the lasagne is baked until bubbly. See **31-9**.

Tomatoes and mozzarella cheese are two of Southern Italy's major agricultural products. They are also key ingredients in the popular Neapolitan dish called *pizza*. The Italians make many kinds of pizza. Most pizzas contain tomato sauce, cheese, and a crust made from yeast dough. Sausage, anchovies, mushrooms, green peppers, olives, and other ingredients are optional.

Other Southern Italian specialties feature vegetables. *Soffritti* is lightly fried onions and other vegetables mixed with a small amount of meat. *Eggplant Napoli* is eggplant layered with tomato sauce and cheese. *Zucchini Parmesan* is sliced zucchini and cubed tomatoes tossed with Parmesan cheese.

Italian Meals

Like many Europeans, Italians typically eat a light breakfast and a hearty noon meal. The noon meal is the largest meal of the day and people usually eat it at home.

The well-known **antipasto** is an appetizer course that often begins the meal. Foods in an antipasto may include salami, Parma ham, anchovies, and hard-cooked eggs. Celery, radishes, pickled beets, black olives, marinated red peppers, and stuffed tomatoes are popular antipasto foods, too. Regardless of the selection of foods, the tray must have both color and taste appeal.

Minestra may follow or replace the antipasto at the start of a meal. Each region has its favorite soups. One common soup is *pasta in brodo*, which is a simple broth with pasta.

A main course of a meat, poultry, or fish dish usually follows the soup. Italians often roast their meat, and lamb is particularly popular when roasted. Poultry often is served in a sauce, whereas fish is baked or broiled. (If meat is too costly, a large serving of pasta may replace the main dish. Pasta is usually served with a sauce containing small pieces of meat or fish.) A vegetable or salad usually accompanies the main dish. Salads always contain tomatoes and other vegetables.

Fruit and cheese end a typical meal. Italians reserve fancier desserts for special occasions.

The evening meal usually is light. Soup, omelets, and risottos are popular supper dishes. Bread, wine, and a simple fruit dessert complete the meal.

Corelle®

31-9 Stuffed lasagne is one of the most popular dishes at many Italian restaurants in the United States.

Italian Menu

Antipasto
(Appetizers)

Minestrone
(Vegetable Soup)

Pollo alla Cacciatore
(Chicken Hunter-Style)

Fettuccine Verde
(Green Noodles)

Panne
(Italian Bread)

Spumoni with Cenci
(Three-Flavored Ice Cream with Deep-Fried
Sweet Pastry)

Caffe Espresso
(Rich Coffee)

Antipasto
(Appetizers)

Many different foods can appear in an antipasto. Regardless of the number of types of foods chosen, however, all antipasto ingredients should be attractively arranged on the serving platter. The following foods frequently are part of an antipasto.

Anchovy fillets
Artichoke hearts
Black olives
Celery hearts
Finocchio (Italian celery)
Peperoncini (small green peppers pickled in
 vinegar)
Prosciutto (smoky-flavored Italian ham)
Provolone cheese
Radishes
Salami
Sautéed cold mushrooms marinated in vinegar
 and oil
Sliced hard-cooked eggs
Sliced tomatoes
Sweet red peppers

Minestrone
(Vegetable Soup)

Serves 8

2   quarts low-sodium chicken bouillon
1¾   cups canned Italian peeled tomatoes
1   medium onion, chopped
2   ribs celery, cut into 1-inch pieces
¼   cup chopped parsley
½   teaspoon oregano
⅛   teaspoon pepper
1   clove garlic, minced
1¾   cups canned chickpeas, rinsed and drained
1   cup cubed zucchini
1   cup fresh or thoroughly defrosted frozen peas
1   cup diced carrots
1   cup chopped cabbage
½   cup uncooked white rice or orzo pasta
½   cup grated Parmesan cheese
     chopped fresh parsley

1. In kettle, combine bouillon, tomatoes, onion, celery, ¼ cup parsley, oregano, pepper, and garlic. Simmer, stirring occasionally, 20 to 30 minutes.
2. Add chickpeas, zucchini, peas, carrots, cabbage, and rice or pasta; simmer an additional 20 to 25 minutes or until vegetables and rice or pasta are tender.
3. Before serving, taste soup and adjust seasonings if needed.
4. Pour soup into large tureen or individual soup bowls. Pass bowls of grated Parmesan cheese and chopped parsley separately.

Per serving: 123 cal. (22% from fat), 9 g protein, 19 g carbohydrate, 3 g fat, 4 mg cholesterol, 3 g fiber, 359 mg sodium.

Pollo alla Cacciatore
(Chicken Hunter-Style)

Serves 6

1	4-pound broiler
½	cup all-purpose flour
½	teaspoon salt
¼	teaspoon pepper
2	tablespoons olive oil
2	medium onions, chopped
1	clove garlic, finely minced
1	cup canned whole tomatoes, low sodium
1	cup sliced green pepper
1½	cups sliced mushrooms

1. Rinse chicken; pat dry with paper towels. Cut into serving-sized pieces and remove skin.
2. Combine flour, salt, and pepper.
3. Coat chicken pieces with seasoned flour.
4. In large skillet, heat oil until hot but not smoking.
5. Add chicken pieces, a few at a time, and fry until golden brown.
6. Combine onions, garlic, tomatoes, and green peppers in a mixing bowl; add to chicken.
7. Cover skillet and simmer chicken slowly until tender, about 40 minutes.
8. Add mushrooms and simmer an additional 10 to 15 minutes.
9. Use a meat thermometer to check the internal temperature of chicken pieces. Breast pieces should reach an internal temperature of 170°F. Wings and thighs should reach an internal temperature of 180°F.
10. Taste; add additional seasonings if needed. Serve immediately.

Per serving: 267 cal. (37% from fat), 27 g protein, 14 g carbohydrate, 11 g fat, 76 mg cholesterol, 2 g fiber, 274 mg sodium.

Fettuccine Verde
(Green Noodles)

Serves 8

2	packages frozen chopped spinach, 10 ounces each
2	cups all-purpose flour
½	teaspoon salt
2	eggs
6 to 8	quarts water
2	tablespoons margarine, softened

1. In medium saucepan, cook spinach in a small amount of simmering salted water until tender. Drain well and squeeze dry.
2. Using fine blade of food processor, grind spinach 2 or 3 times.
3. Transfer chopped spinach to mixing bowl. Add flour, salt, and eggs.
4. Using hands, mix to form a soft dough.
5. Turn dough out onto a floured board and knead until smooth and no longer sticky, adding additional flour if needed.
6. Roll dough very thin into a rectangle. Cover with damp towels and let stand 1 hour.
7. Starting at the narrow end closest to you, fold dough over and over until it is about 3 inches wide.
8. Using a sharp knife, cut folded dough into very thin strips, about ¼ inch wide.
9. Unroll strips on flat surface and let dry 2 to 3 hours or overnight.
10. When ready to cook, bring water to boil in large kettle. Add noodles and simmer until tender.
11. When noodles are tender, drain well. Toss with margarine and serve immediately.

Per serving: 174 cal. (26% from fat), 7 g protein, 27 g carbohydrate, 5 g fat, 53 mg cholesterol, 3 g fiber, 242 mg sodium.

Panne
(Italian Bread)

Makes 2 loaves

4½ to 5½	cups all-purpose flour
1	tablespoon sugar
1½	teaspoons salt
2	envelopes active dry yeast
1	tablespoon softened margarine
1¾	cups very warm water (120°F to 130°F)
	cornmeal
	olive oil
1	egg white
1	tablespoon cold water

1. In large mixing bowl, combine 1½ cups flour, sugar, salt, and dry yeast.
2. Work in margarine.
3. Gradually add warm water and beat 2 minutes on medium speed of electric mixer, scraping bowl occasionally.
4. Add ¾ cup flour and beat 2 more minutes on high speed.

5. Stir in enough additional flour to make a stiff dough.
6. Turn dough out onto lightly floured board or pastry cloth. Knead until smooth and elastic, about 8 to 10 minutes.
7. Place dough in greased bowl and turn once to grease top. Cover with plastic wrap and a clean towel and let rest 20 minutes.
8. Divide dough in half and shape into two long loaves. (Shape by rolling each piece into an oblong. Beginning at wide end, roll tightly like a jelly roll and seal edges well.)
9. Place loaves on lightly greased baking sheets that have been sprinkled with cornmeal. Brush loaves lightly with olive oil and cover with plastic wrap. Refrigerate dough 2 to 24 hours.
10. When ready to bake, remove dough from refrigerator. Uncover dough carefully and let stand at room temperature 10 minutes.
11. Meanwhile, preheat oven to 425°F.
12. Slash loaves diagonally 4 to 5 times with a sharp knife.
13. Bake for 20 minutes.
14. Remove from oven and brush with beaten egg white mixed with water.
15. Return to oven and bake an additional 5 to 10 minutes or until loaves are golden brown and sound hollow when tapped with the knuckles.
16. Remove to cooling racks.

Per slice: 73 cal. (8% from fat), 2 g protein, 14 g carbohydrate, 1 g fat, 0 mg cholesterol, 1 g fiber, 106 mg sodium.

Cenci
(Deep-Fried Sweet Pastry)
Makes about 4 dozen pastries

2	cups all-purpose flour
2	whole eggs
2	egg yolks
1	teaspoon rum extract
1	tablespoon sugar
	vegetable shortening for frying
	confectioner's sugar

1. Place flour in a large mixing bowl. Make a well in the center and add the eggs, egg yolks, rum extract, and 1 tablespoon sugar.
2. Using a fork or fingers, mix until soft dough forms.
3. Turn dough out onto a lightly floured board or pastry cloth. Knead until dough is smooth, adding more flour if needed.
4. Refrigerate for one hour.
5. Heat 4 inches of shortening to 350°F.
6. Roll the dough until paper thin.
7. Cut into strips 6 inches long and ½ inch wide. Tie the strips into loose knots and fry until golden brown.
8. Drain on absorbent paper and sprinkle with confectioner's sugar. Serve immediately.

Per pastry: 40 cal. (37% from fat), 1 g protein, 5 g carbohydrate, 2 g fat, 23 mg cholesterol, 0 g fiber, 14 mg sodium.

Hamilton Beach Brands, Inc.

Espresso and biscotti are often served as a snack or after dinner.

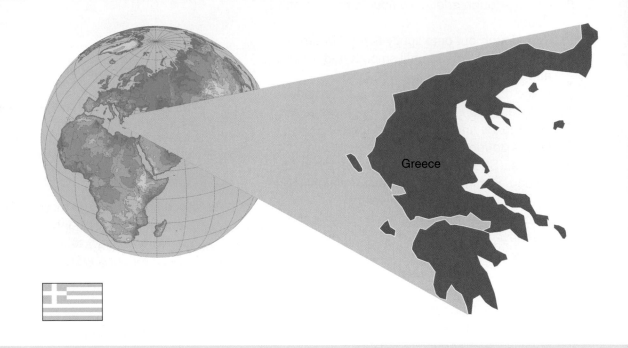

Greece

Greece is a land of terraced gardens, busy seaports, and ancient temples. In this sunny land, the art, literature, science, and philosophy that form the basis of Western civilization began. Parts of Greek culture, such as some Greek foods, have their roots in the older civilization of the Middle East. The foods moussaka and baklava are examples.

Geography and Climate of Greece

Greece forms the southern tip of Europe's Balkan Peninsula. The country is made up of one large landmass and many islands.

The geography of Greece is varied. Mountain ridges form the jagged coastline. To the east lie Mount Olympus and another strip of mountains separated by fertile valleys. The mountainous land with its stony, dry soil makes farming difficult. However, olive trees and grapevines, with their deep roots, can be cultivated in this terrain. Sheep thrive on the short grasses of the more mountainous areas. See **31-10**.

Greece has mild winters and warm, sunny summers. Rainfall rarely exceeds 20 inches (50 cm) per year, and most of the rain falls in the winter. Because Greece has little or no frost, subtropical fruits and flowers can be grown.

The American Lamb Board

31-10 Greece's terrain is suitable for raising sheep, making lamb the country's favorite meat.

Greek Culture

Just under half of the Greek population lives in urban areas. The people of Greece share a common language, Greek, and a common religion. The majority of Greeks belong to the Greek Orthodox Church.

Greece is a relatively poor country. Many Greeks are farmers, despite the lack of fertile farmland. They produce wheat and corn on small acreages. They raise vegetables in terraced gardens. Grapes, olives, and citrus fruits grow in more fertile areas. Goats and sheep, which graze in the mountains, provide milk, cheese, and meat. Farming is difficult, and many families are able to provide only enough food for themselves. With new agricultural methods, however, food production in Greece's fertile areas has increased tremendously in recent years.

The Greek people are skilled mariners, and Greek ships carry cargo to ports all over the world. Fishing is an important industry on the islands and in coastal areas. Much of the seafood that is caught is eaten in Greece. However, some is exported along with olive oil and raisins.

In small communities, the **tavernas** are cafés that serve as public meeting places. Guests who gather in the tavernas often order glasses of retsina or ouzo. (*Retsina* is a resin-flavored wine. *Ouzo* is a strong spirit with the flavor of anise.) Often, someone will play a mandolin-like instrument called a *bouzoukia* while the other guests talk, play games, or dance.

Discuss

Ask students to name four foods they would expect to be common in the Greek diet considering the geography of Greece. (*seafood, olives, grapes/wine, lamb*)

FYI

In ancient Athens, teachers operated separate schools for music where they taught students to sing and play an instrument.

FYI

The city-states Athens and Sparta opposed each other in the Peloponnesian War, which lasted 27 years before Sparta finally

Culture and Social Studies

Ancient Greece

Greek history spans centuries. Ancient Greece is sometimes called *Classical Greece.* Achievements in art, literature, science, and philosophy mark this period in Greek history. The philosophers Socrates, Aristotle, and Plato and the jurist Solon were products of Ancient Greece. The playwrights Sophocles, Aristophanes, and Euripides and the scientist Hippocrates were from this culture, too. This is also the era that produced examples of classical architecture, such as the Parthenon in Athens.

Ancient Greece was divided into city-states. These were self-governing political units consisting of a city and surrounding territory. Although Ancient Greece never became unified, two of the city-states, Athens and Sparta, became seats of power. Athens was democratic, and the Athenians originated the basic concepts of Western law. Sparta, on the other hand, was not democratic. Spartans lived a strict, military life with stern laws. The Spartan ideal was individual sacrifice for community welfare.

The city-states fell to the Roman Empire. After the seat of Roman government moved to Constantinople, Greece became less of a world power.

won. Athens had a stronger navy; Sparta had a stronger army.

Reflect

Ask students what traditions they follow to affect the outcome of the new year.

Greek Holidays

Religious holidays hold great importance in Greece. People devote much time and energy to their celebration. Many of these celebrations involve special food traditions.

The year of Greek celebrations begins with Saint Basil's Day, which is also New Year's Day. On this day (rather than on Christmas) Greek people exchange gifts.

Discuss

Ask students what
the staple foods of
the diet in the United
States would be.
*(meat, especially beef;
potatoes; bread)*

Children receive a Saint Basil's cake, which is covered with almonds and walnuts and has a coin baked inside. Eating something sweet on New Year's Day is believed to bring a sweet year.

Easter is the most important religious holiday in Greece. A seven-week fast characterizes the Lenten season that precedes Easter. The fast is broken on Holy Saturday (the day before Easter) with a dish called *mayeritsa*. This is the internal organs of a lamb cooked in a seasoned broth. After midnight on Holy Saturday, people watch displays of fireworks. Then early the next morning, the rest of the lamb is roasted whole and served for Easter dinner.

Each village and town in Greece has a patron saint. The feast day for the local patron saint is a holiday. On the feast day and the evening before, people go to a church service. Then the feast day is celebrated with food, wine, singing, and dancing. Some people wear traditional Greek clothes for the celebration.

Many Greek towns also hold annual harvest festivals. For example, the town of Megara has a fish festival in the spring.

Greek Cuisine

For thousands of years, the Greeks have been developing their cuisine. Early records show that the Greeks cooked foods while the rest of the world ate raw foods. Early Greek foods included roast lamb with capers, wild rice with saffron, and honey cakes. As Greek civilization spread throughout the Mediterranean, so did Greek cuisine. The Greeks taught the Romans how to cook, and a Greek named Hesiod wrote one of the first cookbooks.

Greek cooking has a rich, varied past. A pre-Greek people living in the Stone Age brought foods like lamb and beans to Greece. Other foods, like olives, grapes, and seafood, are native to the area. Invading groups of peoples added their food customs to these native foods. The many Greek pasta dishes, for example, are Italian in origin. Layers of pasta, ground lamb, and cheese covered with a rich custard and baked is called *pastitsio*. Kebabs, yogurt, Greek coffee, and rich sweet pastries are Turkish in origin. (*Kebabs* are pieces of meat, poultry, fish, vegetables, or fruits threaded onto skewers and broiled.) See **31-11**.

Greek Staple Foods

A number of foods are basic to Greek cooking. Greek cooks make liberal use of lemon juice, tomatoes, and green peppers. **Avgolemono**, one of the most popular Greek sauces, is a mixture of egg yolks and lemon juice. The Greeks use it to flavor soups and stews. They serve it with vegetables and fish, too. Greek cooks stuff tomatoes and green peppers with meat and other vegetables. They

The American Lamb Board
31-11 Famous Greek kebabs actually have a Turkish background.

also thread them on skewers and broil them and add them to soups and stews. Tomato sauces are used with both meat and fish dishes.

Greek cooks use many herbs and spices to bring out the natural flavors of lamb, fish, and vegetables. The most widely used herbs and spices include cinnamon, basil, dill, bay leaves, garlic, and oregano.

The Greeks serve eggplant as a side dish or add it to main dishes. Cooks prepare *moussaka* by layering slices of eggplant, ground lamb, and cheese. (They often cook the lamb with tomato paste, wine, cinnamon, and onion.) They pour a rich cream sauce over the meat, vegetable, and cheese mixture before baking.

Lamb

Sheep have been raised in Greece since prehistoric times. Greek cooks roast lamb whole or thread it onto skewers and broil it. They also grind and layer it with other ingredients in casseroles. They use lamb as a filling for vegetables and add it to soups and stews, too.

Seafood

Because of Greece's location, seafood is an important part of the Greek diet. Fishers catch red mullet, crawfish, cuttlefish, sea bass, red snapper, swordfish, squid, and shrimp in the Mediterranean Sea.

Greek cooks prepare freshly caught seafood simply, usually by baking or broiling. They often bake fresh vegetables, such as tomatoes and zucchini, with the fish. Squid is particularly popular. Fresh squid stuffed with rice, onions, nuts, and seasonings is poached and served as a favorite main dish. Raw squid served with raw green beans or artichokes is eaten as an appetizer. Another popular appetizer or snack is *taramasalata*, a pâté made from fish roe (eggs).

Discuss

Ask students what the information about the history of Greek cuisine indicates about the advancement of early Greek civilization. *(The use of fire to cook food indicates the Greeks had a more highly evolved society than those who ate their food raw.)*

FYI

In the United States, the average consumption of lamb equals less than 1 pound per person per year.

Reflect

Ask students how they would respond if someone invited them to eat raw squid.

Learn About...

Greek Olives

Olives grow in abundance in Greece. Their many sizes, shapes, and colors often amaze people from the United States. The flavor of olive oil dominates Greek cuisine. People throughout Greece eat olives as appetizers and snacks or add them to other dishes. The popular *salata horiatiki* (rural salad) contains olives, a variety of greens, tomatoes, and feta cheese. (*Feta cheese* is a slightly salty, crumbly, white cheese made from goat's milk.)

Honey

Greek honey is world famous. In Ancient Greece, people used honey to make *melamacarons* (honey cakes), which they offered as gifts to the gods. Today, Greek bakers prepare the same honey cakes to celebrate the New Year. Honey is the basic sweetener used in the preparation of many Greek desserts, pastries, and cakes.

Although the Greeks enjoy sweets, they usually serve sweets only on special occasions. The Greeks make many of their desserts with **phyllo**, a paper-thin pastry made with flour and water. Some Greek cooks still make phyllo; others prefer to buy sheets of phyllo ready-made. *Baklava* is thin layers of phyllo filled with nuts and soaked with a honey syrup. *Galatoboureko* is phyllo layered with rich custard and honey. *Kopenhai* is a nut cake with phyllo.

Other popular sweets contain flour, eggs, and oil rather than phyllo. They are deep-fried and are similar to fritters. *Diples*, for example, are small thin sheets of dough that are rolled with two forks as they are fried. They may be coated with a honey and nut syrup flavored with cinnamon.

Greek Meals

The Greeks appreciate simple pleasures. Their meals reflect this simplicity. Breakfast is often no more than a slice of dry bread and a cup of warm milk. Sometimes, eggs or cheese accompanies the bread.

Both lunch and dinner are hot meals. The Greeks eat lunch at noon and dinner late in the evening.

Early evening is generally the most pleasant and enjoyable time of day. Many Greek families go for an evening walk. Some choose to sit at small outdoor cafes and enjoy a variety of appetizers called **mezedhes**. Olives, feta cheese, pistachio nuts, garlic-flavored sausage, shrimp, and hard-cooked eggs are popular mezedhes. Ouzo and conversation accompany this early snack. See **31-12**.

Later, families gather at home for the evening meal. This meal might include either baked or broiled fish, a vegetable, and bread. Fresh fruit would complete the meal.

Western Pistachio Association and TheGreenNut.org

31-12 Pistachios might be enjoyed as an evening snack by patrons of a local cafe in a Greek village.

Greek Menu

Soupa Avgolemono
(Egg-Lemon Soup)

Moussaka
(Baked Eggplant and Lamb with Cream
Sauce)

Salata Horiatiki
(Rural Salad)

Psomi
(Greek Bread)

Kourambiedes
(Walnut Cookies)

Kafés
(Greek Coffee)

Soupa Avgolemono
(Egg-Lemon Soup)

Serves 6 to 8

8	cups low-sodium chicken bouillon
½	cup uncooked white rice
3	eggs
2 to 3	tablespoons lemon juice
	salt
	pepper
	finely chopped parsley

1. In a large saucepan, bring chicken bouillon to a boil.
2. Add rice and simmer until tender.
3. Pour contents of saucepan through a strainer, catching excess bouillon in a large liquid measure. Set rice and bouillon aside.
4. Put eggs and lemon juice into blender container. Cover and process at high speed until frothy.
5. Remove cover and slowly pour the hot bouillon into the egg mixture while processing at low speed.
6. Pour soup into saucepan; add rice. Cook over low heat until thoroughly heated. Do not let soup boil.
7. Season soup with salt and pepper. Serve immediately garnished with parsley.

Per serving: 114 cal. (28% from fat), 5 g protein, 16 g carbohydrate, 4 g fat, 137 mg cholesterol, 0 g fiber, 43 mg sodium.

Salata Horiatiki
(Rural Salad)

Serves 6

6	cups assorted salad greens
3	medium tomatoes, washed and cut into wedges
½	cup chopped green onion
1	medium cucumber, washed and sliced thinly
⅓	cup olive oil
2	tablespoons lemon juice
2	teaspoons sugar
½	teaspoon salt
	few dashes pepper
1½	ounces feta cheese
6	canned anchovy filets, drained
6	whole pitted ripe olives
	crumbled dry oregano

1. Wash greens and pat dry.
2. In a large salad bowl, combine greens with tomatoes, onions, and cucumber.
3. In a small bowl, mix olive oil, lemon juice, sugar, salt, and pepper to taste. Toss with greens mixture.
4. Crumble cheese coarsely and sprinkle over salad in a ring.
5. Wrap each anchovy around an olive and place inside ring of cheese.
6. Sprinkle oregano over all.

Per serving: 178 cal. (76% from fat), 4 g protein, 9 g carbohydrate, 15 g fat, 10 mg cholesterol, 3 g fiber, 474 mg sodium.

Moussaka
(Baked Eggplant and Lamb with Cream Sauce)

Serves 12

3	medium eggplants
	salt
2	pounds ground lamb
3	onions, chopped
2	tablespoons tomato paste
½	cup tomato sauce
¼	cup parsley, chopped
	salt and pepper to taste
½	cup water
	dash cinnamon
½	cup grated Parmesan cheese
½	cup bread crumbs
3	tablespoons all-purpose flour
3	cups fat-free milk
	dash nutmeg

4 egg yolks, lightly beaten
2 tablespoons olive oil
¼ cup grated Parmesan cheese

1. Remove ½-inch wide strips of peel lengthwise from eggplants, leaving ½ inch peel between the strips.
2. Cut eggplant into thick slices. Sprinkle slices with salt and let stand between two heavy plates while browning meat and making sauce.
3. In large skillet, sauté ground lamb and onions until meat is browned.
4. Add tomato paste, tomato sauce, parsley, salt, pepper, and water. Simmer until liquid is absorbed; cool.
5. Add cinnamon, ½ cup cheese, and half of the bread crumbs to meat mixture. Set aside.
6. Combine flour and milk in a covered jar or blender container. Shake or blend until smooth.
7. Pour milk mixture into a heavy saucepan. Cook over medium heat, stirring constantly until sauce comes to a boil. Cook and stir for one additional minute until sauce is thick and smooth; add nutmeg.
8. Stir a little of the hot sauce into beaten egg yolks, then stir egg mixture into sauce and cook over very low heat for 2 minutes, stirring constantly. Set aside.
9. Preheat oven to 350°F.
10. In large skillet, heat oil.
11. Brown eggplant slices on both sides.
12. Grease a 13-by-9-inch baking dish and sprinkle bottom with remaining bread crumbs. Cover with layer of eggplant slices, then a layer of meat. Repeat layering until all eggplant and meat have been used, finishing with a layer of eggplant.
13. Cover eggplant and meat with sauce, sprinkle with ¼ cup grated cheese and bake 1 hour or until hot and bubbly.

Per serving: 300 cal. (48% from fat), 21 g protein, 18 g carbohydrate, 16 g fat, 126 mg cholesterol, 4 g fiber, 273 mg sodium.

Psomi
(Greek Bread)

Makes 2 loaves

3¾ to 4¼ cups all-purpose flour
1 package active dry yeast
1⅓ cups fat-free milk
2 tablespoons sugar
1 tablespoon plus 1 teaspoon shortening
1½ teaspoons salt
    melted margarine
    sesame seeds

1. In large mixing bowl, combine 1½ cups flour and yeast.
2. Combine milk, sugar, shortening, and salt in saucepan and heat until very warm (120°F to 130°F). (Shortening does not need to be completely melted.)
3. Add warm milk mixture to yeast and flour. Beat on low speed of electric mixer (or with wooden spoon) ½ minute (75 strokes) scraping the sides of the bowl often.
4. Beat an additional 3 minutes at high speed (900 strokes). Add enough additional flour to make a soft dough.
5. Turn dough out onto lightly floured board or pastry cloth and knead until smooth and elastic (about 8 to 10 minutes).
6. Place dough in lightly greased bowl, turning once to grease top. Cover with a clean towel and let rise in a warm place until doubled in bulk (about 1½ hours).
7. Punch dough down and divide in half. Shape each half into a round loaf.
8. Place loaves on a lightly greased baking sheet. Brush tops with melted margarine and sprinkle with sesame seeds. Cover with a clean towel and let rise in a warm place until almost doubled in bulk (about 1 hour).
9. Bake loaves at 375°F until they are golden brown and sound hollow when gently tapped with the knuckles.
10. Remove breads to cooling racks and cool thoroughly before storing.

Per slice: 65 cal. (10% from fat), 2 g protein, 13 g carbohydrate, 1 g fat, 0 mg cholesterol, 0 g fiber, 106 mg sodium.

Kourambiedes
(Walnut Cookies)

Makes 3 dozen cookies

¾ pound margarine
3 tablespoons confectioner's sugar
½ teaspoon vanilla
1½ teaspoons baking powder
3½ cups all-purpose flour, minus 1 tablespoon
½ cup finely chopped walnuts
½ cup confectioner's sugar

1. Melt margarine in small saucepan and cool to lukewarm.
2. Preheat oven to 350°F.
3. In large mixing bowl, combine melted margarine, 3 tablespoons sugar, vanilla, and baking powder; stir with a wooden spoon until mixed.
4. Add flour, ¼ cup at a time, beating well after each addition.
5. Add walnuts, stirring until mixed.
6. On a lightly floured board, roll about 2 tablespoons of dough into an S-shaped rope, 6 inches long and ¼ inch thick. Repeat with remaining dough.
7. Place cookies 1 inch apart on baking sheet. Bake until light brown, about 15 minutes.
8. Sprinkle with remaining confectioner's sugar.

Per cookie: 130 cal. (60% from fat), 2 g protein, 12 g carbohydrate, 9 g fat, 0 mg cholesterol, 0 g fiber, 102 mg sodium.

CAREER SUCCESS

Resource Organization and Distribution

Antonio is an Italian chef at a trendy new restaurant called Pasta Roma. He supervises a number of cooks and assistants as they prepare a variety of popular Italian dishes. He also orders ingredients and sees they are stored properly. He sets up workstations for the cooks and makes sure each station includes the necessary equipment.

To be an effective worker, Antonio needs skill in organizing and distributing resources of materials and facilities. In a small group, answer the following questions about Antonio's need for and use of this skill:

A. What are some specific material and facility resources Antonio would need to organize? How would he need to distribute these resources?
B. How might the cooks and assistants Antonio supervises be affected if Antonio lacked skill in organizing and distributing resources?
C. How might the patrons of Pasta Roma be affected if Antonio lacked skill in organizing and distributing resources?
D. What is another skill Antonio would need in this job? Briefly explain why this skill would be important.

CHAPTER 31 REVIEW

Summary

The mild climate of the Mediterranean region is favorable for the growth of a bounty of fruits and vegetables. These foods, along with fish from the sea, appear in a variety of dishes throughout Spain, Italy, and Greece. Despite common ingredients, however, each of these countries has a distinct cuisine.

Spanish cuisine is simple and colorful, focusing on the natural flavors of fresh ingredients. Spaniards enjoy an assortment of tapas at the beginnings of meals or while socializing with friends. Attractive salads and flavorful soups are popular throughout Spain. Main dishes such as cocido and paella include a variety of ingredients cooked together to produce a blend of flavors. Breads, tortillas, vegetables, and desserts round out Spanish meals.

Italy was the center of the Roman Empire, the birthplace of the Renaissance, and the home of the Roman Catholic Church. The foods of Italy are as notable as its cultural heritage. Italian cuisine focuses on fresh fruits and vegetables, a variety of seasonings, and rangetop cooking methods. Pasta, rice, and seafood are staples of the Italian diet.

The cuisine in each of Italy's three main geographic regions has distinct features. In Northern Italy, foods are cooked in butter, and homemade, ribbon-shaped pastas are popular. This region is also known for its soups, sausages, and risottos. The Central region is known for roasted lamb and cheesecake from Rome and grilled meats and bean dishes from Tuscany. In the South, cooks use olive oil and tubular pastas. This region is the home of rich tomato sauces, stuffed lasagne, and pizza.

Greek cuisine has been evolving for centuries. Staple foods of the Greek diet include lamb, seafood, olives, and honey. Lemon juice, tomatoes, green peppers, garlic, and eggplant also appear in many Greek dishes. Greek cooks flavor their foods with a number of herbs and spices.

Review What You Have Read

Write your answers on a separate sheet of paper, using complete sentences when appropriate.

1. Name three culinary advances the Moors made to Spanish cuisine.
2. Spanish meals often begin with appetizers called _____.
3. What is the difference between tortillas in Spain and tortillas in Mexico?
4. Why is Italian cuisine known as the "mother cuisine"?
5. Describe three ways Italians may serve pasta.
6. True or false. Northern Italian cooks favor olive oil for cooking, but Southern Italian cooks prefer butter.
7. List the courses that would make up a typical noon meal in Italy. Give an example of a food that might be served for each course.
8. Name three dishes invading groups of people contributed to Greek cuisine and two foods that are native to Greece.

9. Which of the following foods would most likely be served as a main dish in Greece?
   A. Avgolemono.
   B. Diples.
   C. Moussaka.
   D. Taramasalata.

10. What is the basic sweetener used in the preparation of many Greek desserts, pastries, and cakes?

Link to Academic Skills

11. **English language arts.** Research the similarities and differences between Spanish and Mexican cuisine. Summarize your findings in a two-page written report.

12. **History.** Prepare a time line illustrating major events in Italian history from the Roman Empire to today. Explain to the class the significance of one of the events shown on your time line.

13. **Geography.** Make a map of Italy showing the three main culinary regions. Use icons to illustrate the chief agricultural products of each region. Be sure to include a key identifying the meaning of each icon. Attach a recipe for an Italian regional specialty dish to your map. Highlight the use of locally produced ingredients in the recipe.

14. **English language arts.** Give an oral biographical report on one of the notable figures of Ancient Greece.

Build Critical Thinking Skills

15. **Analysis.** Working in lab groups, research and prepare a regional version of paella. Each group should choose a different version. Serve all the paellas buffet-style. Analyze the major differences that are apparent among the dishes.

16. **Synthesis.** Divide the class into four groups. Then synthesize information and efforts to turn your classroom into a Greek taverna. One group should find appropriate music and learn a traditional Greek dance to teach the rest of the class. One group should be responsible for decorations. One group should learn a few Greek games to teach the rest of the class. The fourth group should choose a menu of Greek appetizers and find recipes to distribute. Each group should prepare one of the appetizer recipes.

7. A typical noon meal in Italy might include antipasto, minestra (soup), a main course served with a vegetable or salad, fruit, and cheese. (Pasta replaces the main course if meat is too costly.) (Examples are student response.)

8. (Name three dishes contributed by invading groups:) pasta dishes, kebabs, yogurt, rich pastries, Greek coffee, lamb, beans (Name two native Greek foods:) olives, grapes, seafood

9. C

10. The basic sweetener used in the preparation of many Greek desserts, pastries, and cakes is honey.

Apply Technology

17. Go to a weather information website to find average high and low temperatures for each month for a specific Mediterranean location. Use graphing software to create a line chart of your data. Share your chart in class.

18. Use a computer and language translation software to translate the phrase "Celebrate the tastes of the Mediterranean" into Greek, Italian, and Spanish. Then use the computer's printer to print banners of the English phrase and the three translations. Use the banners as classroom decorations on days when your class is sampling Mediterranean foods.

A Measure of Math

19. Suppose a school organization wants to hold a spaghetti dinner as a fund-raiser. Find a spaghetti sauce recipe and calculate the amounts of ingredients that would be needed to serve 250 people.

20. Visit a grocery store to calculate the cost per serving of the ingredients for the sauce mentioned in the previous activity. Assume the sauce equals one-fourth of the total costs of the food items for the dinner. Calculate the cost per person to hold the dinner. Assume the organization wants to earn 100 percent profit. Calculate how much they would need to charge for tickets to the fund-raiser.

Teamwork in Action

21. Divide the class into six groups. Each group of students should focus on research of a different food group: vegetables; fruits and juices; grains; dairy products; protein foods; and oils, solid fats, and added sugars. Research typical daily intakes of your assigned food group for a Mediterranean-style eating pattern and a typical U.S. eating pattern. Investigate the health benefits for your food group of the Mediterranean levels of intake over the U.S. levels. Summarize your group's findings into a poster presentation. Give your presentation, along with the presentations of the other groups, at a school or community health fair. Also prepare an illustrated fact sheet based on your presentation to pass out at the fair.

Companion Website
www.g-wlearning.com

At the website, review key terms for this chapter with crossword puzzles, matching exercises, and e-flash cards. Apply facts from the chapter to complete the activities.

CHAPTER 32
Middle East and Africa

Learning Prep

Use the *Terms to Know* to make a crossword puzzle. Use the definitions as clues.

Terms to Know

Haram	milchig
Halal	fleishig
bulgur	pareve
mazza	felafel
chelo kebab	cacao
kibbutzim	pita bread
matzo	injera
kashrut	teff
kosher	wat
shohet	

Main Menu

- Religious laws affect food customs throughout much of the Middle East and Africa.
- The cuisines of this region use some common ingredients, but each country has developed unique dishes.

Objectives

After studying this chapter, you will be able to

- **describe** the food customs of the Middle East and Africa.
- **discuss** how geography, climate, and culture have influenced these customs.
- **prepare** foods that are native to each of these countries or regions.

The Middle East and Africa cover a large area. These regions are home to people of several races and many nationalities. They speak a number of major languages and hundreds of dialects.

Geographical features in the Middle East and Africa vary widely. In Egypt, the hot, dry, sandy desert stretches for miles. In Eastern Africa, rugged, snowcapped mountains rise above the arid plains. Along the equator, tropical rain forests boast lush vegetation.

The climate limits the types of foods that are available in each of the countries in this area. Strict religious doctrines also restrict the foods that many Middle Eastern and African people can eat. These factors have caused a number of distinct cuisines to emerge in these regions.

Cooking styles vary. However, there are some similarities in foods from this part of the world. For instance, many foods eaten in Israel originated in other Middle Eastern countries and parts of Africa. See **32-1**.

The cuisines of these regions are nutritious. Cooks in the Middle East and Africa use only limited amounts of meat. A starchy food, such as cassava, rice, plantains, or some type of bread, accompanies every meal. Meals also include a wide variety of vegetables and fruits. These mealtime staples are rich in complex carbohydrates, vitamins, minerals, and fiber. Because frying is a favored cooking method, some dishes can be high in fat. However, many foods are prepared by low-fat cooking methods, such as broiling and stewing. By practicing balance when planning menus, all Middle Eastern and African foods can fit into a healthful diet.

As you read about these regions, you will become more familiar with their cultures, climates, and customs. You will begin to identify differences and similarities in their cuisines.

The American Lamb Board

32-1 Skewered lamb cubes and couscous are foods that would be found in several parts of the Middle East as well as Northern Africa.

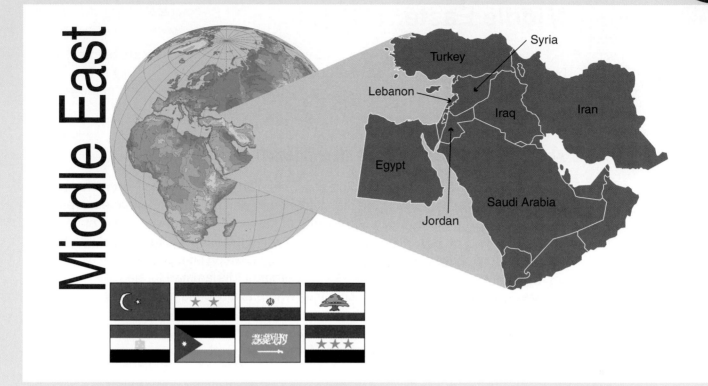

The Middle East forms a large horseshoe from the eastern edge of the Mediterranean Sea to North Africa. This land is the cradle of civilization. Christianity, Judaism, and Islam began in this region. This is where the Byzantine, Persian, Arab, and Ottoman Empires flourished.

The exact boundaries of the Middle East are sometimes disputed. However, the countries of Iran, Iraq, Syria, Lebanon, Jordan, Egypt, and Saudi Arabia form its center. (Israel is also part of the Middle East, but because its cuisine has unique qualities, Israel will be discussed separately.) Turkey, which lies just to the north and east, shares some characteristics with its Middle Eastern neighbors.

Geography and Climate of the Middle East

Mountains, high plateaus, and deserts are important geographical features of the Middle East. Much of the land is arid and barren. However, fertile oases are scattered throughout the region.

Seven major bodies of water border the nations that form the core of the Middle East. Three of the world's most famous rivers, the Nile, Tigris, and Euphrates, are in this region. The lands along the banks are among the world's richest. Coastal lands and inland mountain valleys are also excellent farming areas.

Rainfall varies in the Middle East. Areas in southern Egypt may not have rain for 10 to 20 years. However, some coastal regions may have 20 to 30 inches (50 to 70 cm) of rain during one season. As a whole, much of the Middle East is hot and dry. Therefore, irrigation is essential. When rain does fall, it is often so heavy that flooding occurs.

The climate along the Mediterranean coasts is subtropical with warm, dry summers and mild, rainy winters. Mountain valleys have hot, dry summers and cool winters. Desert areas have daytime temperatures above 100°F (38°C) and little, if any, rain.

FYI

Because the climate in the Middle East is so warm, outdoor pools are often chilled rather than heated to keep them at a comfortable temperature for swimming.

Activity

On a map, have students locate the seven bodies of water that border the core nations of the Middle East.

Middle Eastern Culture

Egypt has one of the world's oldest civilizations. Thousands of years before the birth of Christ, the Egyptians had reached a high level of civilization. They had an orderly government and a written language. They traded with other parts of the world and built great structures of stone.

Ancient Empires of the Middle East

Much of the history of the Middle East centers around large empires that rose to power, weakened, and fell. The first of the four greatest Middle Eastern empires was the Persian Empire. Today, the country of Iran is all that remains of this once mighty empire. The Byzantine Empire formed when the Roman Empire split into East and West. Its headquarters were in Constantinople, which later became the capital of the Ottoman Empire. The followers of the prophet Muhammad formed the Arab Empire. People in Middle Eastern countries where Islam is the primary faith still speak the Arabic language. Eventually, the Ottoman Turks combined parts of the Persian, Byzantine, and Arab Empires to form the Ottoman Empire. As a result, Turkish foods and customs are evident in many parts of the Middle East.

Middle Eastern Agriculture

Today, many Middle Easterners make their living as farmers or herders. Sheep, goats, and camels graze on the short, stubby grasses of the arid regions. They supply meat, milk (used to make yogurt and cheese), and hides. Camels also serve as pack animals.

A variety of crops grow in areas where there are irrigation systems or where there is enough rain. Wheat and barley are the major grain crops. Corn grows in some areas. Citrus fruits, Persian melons, olives, bananas, figs, grapes, and other fruits grow in the subtropical climate of the coastal regions. Other important food crops include sugar beets and rice. Families grow vegetables for home use on small plots of land.

Middle Eastern Holidays

With the large Muslim population, it is not surprising that many Middle Eastern celebrations are Muslim holidays. Each country may have different names for and ways of celebrating these holidays.

The first month of the Muslim year is called *Muharram*. This is also the name given to the 10-day Muslim New Year Festival. The last day of this festival is another Muslim holiday called *Ashura*. This day commemorates the death of the martyr Husain, who was the grandson of the prophet Muhammad. It also celebrates the safe landing of Noah's ark. On Ashura, Muslim people eat a pudding of the same name. This pudding is made with dates, raisins, figs, and nuts as was a legendary pudding made by Noah's wife.

Another Muslim observance is the *Fast of Ramadan*. Ramadan is the ninth month of the Muslim calendar, and the fast lasts the entire month. Muslims are to abstain from food and drink throughout the day. Each night they may break the fast. In some regions the fast is broken with a light meal, in other areas, people feast during the night. *Id-al-Fitr* is a three-day celebration that marks the end of the Fast of Ramadan.

Culture and Social Studies

Religion in the Middle East

More than 90 percent of the people living in the Middle East practice the same religion. This religion is Islam, and those people who follow it are called *Muslims*. Islam is based on the teachings of the prophet Muhammad. Islam greatly affects the lifestyle and food choices of the Muslims.

The *Koran* is a book of sacred writings in the Islamic religion. It specifies foods Muslims should and should not eat. It forbids the eating of animals that have died from disease, strangulation, or beating. Only animals that have been slaughtered by a proper ritual are considered edible. The Koran also forbids Muslims to eat pork and drink wine and other alcoholic beverages.

Shutterstock

The Islamic religion influences many aspects of lifestyle, including food customs, in the Middle East.

Another Muslim holiday is *Maulid an-Nabi*. This is a nine-day celebration of Muhammad's birthday. Fairs, parades, and community feasting may be part of the observance.

Middle Eastern Cuisine

Middle Eastern cuisine, which is sometimes called Eastern Mediterranean cuisine, has been developing for centuries. As traders crossed the deserts and one group of people conquered another, recipes were exchanged and modified. As a result, it is often difficult to determine the exact origin of a particular dish.

Foods Found Throughout the Middle East

Basic to all Middle Eastern cooking are five ingredients: garlic, lemon, green pepper, eggplant, and tomato. These ingredients appear again and again in dishes served throughout the area. Both olives and olive oil are common in Middle Eastern cuisine. Olives come in a variety of shapes, sizes, and colors. People eat them as appetizers and snacks. They use olive oil in place of butter or lard for cooking. Fresh olive oil gives a special flavor to Middle Eastern foods.

Spice caravans were once a common sight in the Middle East. Therefore, it seems only natural to expect cooks to use spices liberally. Middle Eastern foods are not spicy hot. Instead, spices and herbs add delicate flavor to foods.

Activities

Have students make three-column charts, listing the five basic ingredients of Middle Eastern cooking in the first column. In the second column, have them list foods containing each ingredient. In the third column, students should identify the country with which each food is associated.

CERTIFIED
HALAL
حلال
ISLAMIC FOOD AND NUTRITION
COUNCIL OF AMERICA

32-2 This symbol on a food product label assures Muslims the food is Halal, or in keeping with Islamic dietary laws.

Throughout the Middle East, there is a taboo against eating pork. Both Judaism and Islam forbid their followers to eat the meat of swine. Pork and other foods that are forbidden according to the Islamic religion are called **Haram**. Foods considered lawful are called **Halal**. See **32-2**.

In the Middle East, lamb is the staple meat. It is often roasted whole. Chunks of lamb sometimes are threaded on skewers and served as *shish kebabs* or added to hearty stews. Ground lamb is used to make dolmas. *Dolmas* are a mixture of ground meat and seasonings wrapped in grape leaves or stuffed into vegetables.

Middle Eastern yogurt is curdled milk with a tangy flavor. It is not at all like the yogurt eaten in the United States. People throughout the Middle East eat it as a side dish, snack, and dessert. They also use it to make cakes and hot and cold soups. In some areas, people serve diluted yogurt as a beverage.

Middle Eastern Grains and Legumes

Wheat, beans, rice, lentils, and chickpeas are the staple grains and legumes of the Middle East. Middle Easterners use wheat flour to make bread. Middle Eastern people serve bread at every meal and often buy it from the village baker twice a day.

Middle Eastern people also serve wheat as bulgur. **Bulgur** is a grain product made from whole wheat that has been cooked, dried, partly debranned, and cracked. Middle Easterners add bulgur to soups, stews, stuffings, and salads. They also serve it as a side dish with ground lamb. *Felafel* is a deep-fried mixture of bulgur, ground chickpeas, and spices. Street vendors sell felafel and people eat it much as people in the United States eat hot dogs. See **32-3**.

Rice is as popular as bulgur, and in Iran, it is even more popular. People in the Middle East often serve rice plain. However, they may cook it with tomato juice or saffron and make it into a seasoned rice dish called *pilav*.

Middle Eastern Dessert and Coffee

Middle Eastern people, as a group, enjoy sweets and rich desserts. However, they usually eat these foods as snacks or serve them on special holidays. They eat fruit at the end of most meals. Quince, pomegranates, figs, and melons are particularly popular.

People throughout most of the Middle East drink coffee. (Iran is an exception. There, tea is the main beverage.) All Middle Eastern coffee is strong, but it can be prepared in several ways. People who make *khave* (Turkish-style coffee) use a long-handled pot with a wide bottom and thin neck. They combine and heat water, coffee, and sugar just until the mixture begins to foam. They quickly remove the pot from the heat. Then they return the pot to the heat once or twice to again build up the foam. Finally, they pour the foaming liquid into small cups and top it with the remaining coffee, grounds and all.

Shutterstock

32-3 Felafel—fried balls of mashed chickpeas with seasonings—is a popular Middle Eastern food.

More sugar can be added if desired. *Arab-style coffee* rarely contains sugar. People who make this type of coffee bring it to a boil only once. They pour it into a second pot to get rid of the grounds and sediment. They may add cloves and cardamom seeds before serving.

Turkish Foods

Many people do not regard Turkey as part of the Middle East. However, it lies next to three Middle Eastern countries. Therefore, the influence of Turkish cuisine is found throughout this region. Any discussion of Middle Eastern cuisine would be lacking if it did not include information about Turkish foods.

The waters that border Turkey on three sides provide a variety of fish and shell-fish. Seafood vendors in Istanbul sell lobster, salty red caviar, jumbo shrimp, mussels, haddock, bass, and mackerel.

Lamb is the most readily available and most popular meat. Lamb cubes marinated in a mixture of olive oil, lemon juice, and onions are threaded onto skewers and charcoal broiled. Rice, sliced tomatoes, and bread often accompany this dish, which is called *shish kebab*. Another type of kebab, the *döner kebab*, is a large cone made of thin pieces of lamb. As the cone rotates over a bed of charcoal, the outside slices of meat become crisp and flavorful. Turkish cooks slice these crisp pieces from the cone with large knives. They serve the meat with a salad, onion rings, cucumbers, and tomato slices. By the time they serve one helping, the next layer of meat has become crisp.

Stuffed vegetables, cacik, and pilav are other common Turkish foods. (*Cacik* is slices of cucumber in a yogurt sauce flavored with mint.) Turkish cooks may serve pilav plain or mix it with currants, nuts, and tomato sauce.

Snacking is popular in Turkey. Nuts, pumpkin seeds, and toasted chickpeas are favorite snack foods. Vendors in the streets of Istanbul sell crisp bracelets of bread from long poles. Other vendors look like walking refreshment stands. Each carries a container of sweet, fruit-flavored syrup, a jug of water, and a rack of glasses. The vendor mixes a little of the syrup with some of the water and sells the beverage by the glass.

Sweets are popular in Turkey. *Halva* is a candylike sweet made from farina or semo-lina and sugar. *Baklava* is a sweet pastry made from phyllo, nuts, and honey. *Kurabiye* is a rich butter cookie. *Rahat lokum* (Turkish delight) is a candylike sweet made from grape jelly coated with powdered sugar.

Other sweets have even more exotic names. The "vizier's finger" is a sweet roll fried in olive oil until crisp. A "lady's navel" is a deep-fried fritter with a depression in the center. "Sweetheart's lips" are rounds of dough filled with nuts and folded in a way that resembles human lips.

Foods of the Arab States

The countries of Lebanon, Iraq, Jordan, Syria, Saudi Arabia, and Egypt are often called the Arab States. The Arab States include the area once called the *Fertile Crescent*. This is where people first learned to grow crops.

People can buy a variety of spices at bazaars throughout the Arab world. Vendors scoop cinnamon, cumin, ginger, coriander, allspice, and hot peppers onto pieces of paper, which they roll into cones. Arab cooks add spices to many dishes. They use rose water and orange-flower water to flavor their sweets.

No Arab meal is complete without **mazza** (appetizers). Arak, an anise-flavored

Discuss

Ask students how Middle Eastern coffee preparation methods differ from the way coffee is usually prepared in the United States.

Ask students why charcoal broiling might be a popular cooking method in Turkey. (*The hot climate makes outdoor cooking appealing.*)

Reflect

Ask students how the Turkish snacks mentioned compare to the types of foods they choose for snacking.

Activity

Ask students to make up exotic names for chocolate chip cookies, brownies, and other sweets they enjoy. Have them be prepared to explain why they chose each name.

Reflect

Ask students how often they eat appetizers with their meals.

USA Rice Federation

32-4 Although tabbouleh is often made with bulgur, this version is made with brown rice instead.

Vocabulary Builder

Bedouin comes from an Arabic word meaning *desert dweller*.

liqueur, is usually served with the mazza. One kind of mazza, called *tabbouleh*, is actually a salad. It is made of chopped tomatoes, radishes, green and white onions, parsley, mint, and bulgur. People break off pieces of *shrak* (a flat bread) and use them to scoop up the tabbouleh. See **32-4**.

Islam law forbids the eating of pork, but the Arabs enjoy both camel and lamb. Camel, boiled in sour milk until it is tender, is popular among the nomadic Bedouin people. Most other Arabs prefer lamb.

Kibbi (called *kibbi* in Syria, *kobba* in Jordan, and *kubba* in Iraq) is a popular Arab lamb dish. Arab cooks pound raw lamb and bulgur into a paste and shape it into flat patties or hollow balls. They fry the patties. They stuff the hollow balls with ground lamb, pine nuts, rice, or vegetables and either bake or broil them.

Arab cooks love both color and pattern, and they use both lavishly. For example, they often garnish hummus with red pepper, green parsley, and brown cumin. *Hummus* is a mixture of chickpeas and sesame paste. They serve torshi the way people serve pickle relish in the United States. *Torshi* is a mixture of pickled turnips, onions, peppers, eggplant, cucumbers, and occasionally beets. They use saffron to give a bright gold color to a variety of dishes.

Along the eastern Mediterranean coastline, fishers catch a variety of fish daily. Cooks quickly clean mullet, sea bass, turbot, swordfish, cod, sardines, and other fish. Then they bake or poach the fish or cook them over charcoal. Restaurants that line the riverbanks of the Tigris serve smoked shabait (a kind of trout).

Culture and Social Studies

Dining with Bedouins

Bedouins are a nomadic group of Arabs. In the tent of a Bedouin *sheikh*, or chief, it is customary to dine on the rug-covered floor. The sheikh's family members serve trays covered with Arab bread, rice, pine nuts, almonds, and lamb. According to Arab custom, diners must eat the food with the right hand only. At the end of the meal, coffee and tea are served in small cups.

Iranian Foods

The Persians (predecessors of the present day Iranians) laid the foundation for Middle Eastern cooking. Scholars believe that wine, cheese, sherbet, and ice cream were first made in Persia. The Persians were also the first to extract the essence of roses and combine exotic herbs and spices with foods.

For centuries, rice has been the staple food of the Iranians. They serve many kinds of rice dishes. All these dishes belong to one of two groups: chelo or polo. *Chelo* is plain boiled, buttered rice served with *khoresh* (a topping made of varied sauces, vegetables, fruits, and meats). *Polo* is similar to pilaf in that all the accompaniments cook with the rice.

Iran's national dish is called **chelo kebab**. The kebab consists of thin slices of marinated, charcoal-broiled lamb. Diners combine three accompaniments with the chelo: a pat of butter, a raw egg, and a bowl of sumac. (*Sumac* is a tart-flavored spice.)

Iran's proximity to the Caspian Sea with its many sturgeon makes caviar a bargain. (*Caviar* is the processed eggs of a large fish, often the sturgeon.) Over 95 percent of the world's caviar comes from the Caspian Sea.

Iranians use yogurt to make a variety of hot and cold soups. One popular version contains grated cucumber and is served with a topping of raisins and fresh mint leaves. When combined with plain or carbonated water, yogurt becomes a refreshing drink.

Iranians are not quite as fond of rich pastries as other Middle Easterners. They eat fresh fruits instead. Iran produces some of the finest Persian melons, watermelons, peaches, pomegranates, apricots, quinces, dates, pears, and grapes, **32-5**. Iranians often eat these fruits plain. However, sometimes they slice and sweeten the fruits and serve them with crushed ice or make them into sherbets.

Shutterstock

32-5 Pomegranates are one of the many fruits Iranians may serve at the end of a meal.

Middle Eastern Menu

Shish Kebabs
(Chunks of Meat Threaded on Skewers)

Pilav
(Seasoned Rice)

Mast va Khiar
(Cucumber and Yogurt Salad)

Pita Bread
(Pocket Bread)

Baklava
(Layered Pastry with Walnuts and Honey Syrup)

Khave
(Turkish Coffee)

Shish Kebabs
(Chunks of Meat Threaded on Skewers)

Serves 8

1	large onion
4	tablespoons olive oil
½	cup lemon juice
1	teaspoon salt
½	teaspoon pepper
½	teaspoon garlic powder
2	pounds lean, boneless lamb cut into 2-inch cubes
4	large tomatoes, quartered
4	large green peppers, cut into chunks
¼	cup evaporated fat-free milk

1. Remove papery covering from onion and slice into rings.
2. Put onion rings into deep pan. Add oil, lemon juice, salt, pepper, and garlic powder.
3. Add lamb cubes to marinade and stir well. Cover and place in refrigerator for at least 4 hours, turning lamb occasionally.
4. Preheat broiler.
5. Thread lamb cubes on eight long skewers.
6. Thread tomato quarters and green pepper chunks on two more skewers.
7. Place skewers of meat side by side along the length of a deep roasting pan. Brush meat with evaporated milk.
8. Broil 4 inches from the heat, turning occasionally, until meat reaches the desired degree of doneness, about 10 minutes for pink lamb and 15 minutes for well-done lamb.
9. Add vegetables to roasting pan about a third of the way through the cooking period. Watch carefully and remove when tender. Serve lamb with broiled vegetables and pilav.

Per serving: 157 cal. (42% from fat), 16 g protein, 7 g carbohydrate, 7 g fat, 50 mg cholesterol, 2 g fiber, 133 mg sodium.

Pilav
(Seasoned Rice)

Serves 6 to 8

2   tablespoons margarine
1½   cups uncooked white rice
3   cups low-sodium chicken stock
       salt
       pepper
1   tablespoon melted margarine

1. In heavy saucepan, melt 2 tablespoons margarine.
2. Add rice and stir for several minutes to evenly coat rice with fat. (Do not let rice brown.)
3. Add chicken stock and salt and pepper to taste.
4. Bring mixture to a boil, stirring constantly.
5. Cover pan, reduce heat, and simmer rice slowly for 20 minutes or until all the liquid has been absorbed.
6. Add melted margarine, stir with a fork.
7. Let rice stand, covered with a clean towel, for 20 minutes before serving.

Per serving: 224 cal. (24% from fat), 3 g protein, 38 g carbohydrate, 6 g fat, 0 mg cholesterol, 1 g fiber, 160 mg sodium.

Mast va Khiar
(Cucumber and Yogurt Salad)

Serves 8

2   medium cucumbers
4   tablespoons finely chopped green pepper
3   tablespoons finely chopped green onion
2   tablespoons dried tarragon or dill
1   teaspoon lime juice
½   teaspoon salt
2   cups plain nonfat yogurt

1. Wash cucumbers and peel.
2. Slice each cucumber in half lengthwise. Scoop out seeds and chop cucumber coarsely.
3. Put cucumber in a deep bowl and add green pepper, green onion, tarragon or dill, lime juice, and salt. Mix well.
4. Add yogurt and stir to coat vegetables.
5. Chill at least one hour before serving.

Per serving: 40 cal. (4% from fat), 4 g protein, 6 g carbohydrate, 0 g fat, 1 mg cholesterol, 0 g fiber, 178 mg sodium.

Pita Bread
(Pocket Bread)

Makes 18

5 to 6 cups all-purpose flour
1   package active dry yeast
2   cups water
2   tablespoons sugar
1½   teaspoons salt

1. In large mixing bowl, stir together 2 cups flour and yeast.
2. Heat water, sugar, and salt over low heat until warm (105°F to 115°F), stirring to blend.
3. Add liquid ingredients to flour mixture and beat until smooth, about 2 minutes on medium speed of electric mixer.
4. Add 1 cup flour and beat 1 minute more.
5. Stir in enough additional flour to make a moderately stiff dough.
6. Turn dough out onto lightly floured board or pastry cloth and knead until smooth and satiny, about 18 to 20 minutes.
7. Divide dough into 18 portions. Roll each into a 3-inch circle.
8. Place circles on lightly greased baking sheet. Cover with a clean towel and let rise in warm place until doubled, about 45 minutes.
9. Bake on middle shelf of preheated 450°F oven, 10 to 12 minutes or until lightly browned. Cool.

Per pita: 133 cal. (2% from fat), 4 g protein, 28 g carbohydrate, 0 g fat, 0 mg cholesterol, 1 g fiber, 179 mg sodium.

Baklava
(Layered Pastry with Walnuts and Honey Syrup)

Makes about 3 dozen pieces

4   cups walnuts, finely chopped
5   tablespoons sugar
1   teaspoon ground cinnamon
       dash ground cloves
¾   cup margarine
1   pound phyllo (about 20 to 30 sheets Greek pastry dough)
1   cup sugar
1   cup water
1   tablespoon lemon juice
½   cup honey
4   thin slices lemon
1   3-inch cinnamon stick, broken
2   teaspoons vanilla

1. Butter a 13-by-9-by-2-inch pan.
2. In a mixing bowl, combine walnuts, 5 tablespoons sugar, ground cinnamon, and cloves; set aside.
3. Melt margarine and keep it warm over very low heat.
4. Unfold room temperature stack of phyllo sheets on a slightly damp dish towel. Cover the phyllo with another slightly damp dish towel. Keep the stack covered as you work.
5. Place 2 sheets of phyllo pastry in the prepared pan, folding edges to fit pan. Brush evenly with melted margarine. Place another sheet of phyllo in the pan and brush it with margarine. Continue layering phyllo sheets and brushing them with margarine until 5 sheets have been used.
6. Sprinkle 1 cup nut mixture over the buttered top sheet. Place 5 more sheets of phyllo over the nut layer, brushing each sheet with margarine. Repeat this step three more times, using all the nut mixture and ending with 5 sheets of phyllo brushed with margarine on top.
7. Preheat oven to 350°F.
8. With a very sharp knife, cut the baklava diagonally into diamond-shaped pieces.
9. Sprinkle any remaining margarine over the top.
10. Bake baklava for 30 minutes.
11. Reduce heat to 300°F and continue to bake for 45 minutes more.
12. While baklava is baking, prepare syrup. In medium saucepan, combine 1 cup sugar, water, lemon juice, honey, lemon slices, and cinnamon stick. Bring to a boil, stirring until sugar is dissolved.
13. Simmer syrup uncovered for 10 minutes.
14. Remove lemon slices and cinnamon stick. Add vanilla. Set syrup aside to cool.
15. As soon as baklava comes out of the oven, pour the syrup over the hot pastry. Allow the pastry to set for several hours before serving.

Per serving: 196 cal. (55% from fat), 3 g protein, 20 g carbohydrate, 12 g fat, 0 mg cholesterol, 1 g fiber, 107 mg sodium.

Courtesy of the Almond Board of California

This mixture of nuts, spices, and olive oil are used as a dip with pita bread for an Egyptian appetizer.

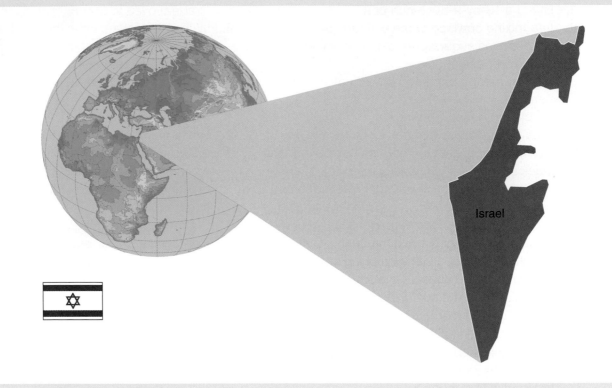

Israel

Israel

The state of Israel was established in 1948. Since that time, Israel has grown at a rapid rate. This country is known for its agricultural production. Heavy industry flourishes in Haifa, the nation's largest seaport, **32-6**. As the home of many talented writers, artists, and musicians, Israel is rich in cultural assets, too.

Shutterstock

32-6 Cargo ships are a common sight at the Port of Haifa in Israel.

Israel is also a religious center. The capital city of Jerusalem has been an important place to people of many races and religions for centuries. Jerusalem is called the "Holy City" by Christians, Jews, and Muslims alike.

Geography and Climate of Israel

The Mediterranean Sea forms Israel's western border. The northern part of the country borders Syria and Lebanon. There, the land rises from a fertile coastal plain to the hills of Galilee. Galilee's scattered green valleys are suitable for agriculture. To the east is the Jordan River, which separates Israel from Jordan. To the south lies the triangular Negev Desert bordered by Egypt and the Red Sea.

Israel has four climatic regions. Along the Mediterranean Sea, summers are warm, and winters are mild with occasional rain. In the central highlands, summers are again warm and dry, but the winters are cold and wet. The Negev Desert is hot and dry in the summer and cool and dry in the winter. The Jordan Valley has hot, dry summers and mild winters. Almost no rain falls in Israel from May to October. This makes irrigation necessary for the production of most crops.

Israeli Culture

Some of Israel's citizens live in collective communities called **kibbutzim**. Members of a kibbutz own their property collectively and live together in a cluster of dwellings. They receive no wages for their work, but all their needs are met. Food, clothing, medical care, and entertainment are supplied. Children who live in a kibbutz are educated communally according to age. A kibbutz may have from 30 to 2,000 members and may or may not have a few small industries.

Many kibbutzim operate farms. Almost all the fruits and vegetables eaten in Israel are grown there. Guavas, citrus fruits, mangoes, dates, bananas, avocados, and melons are some of the most popular fruits. Cattle, sheep, poultry, and fish are also available from local sources. Cattle breeds that are suitable for the semiarid land are raised. Fresh fish and ducks are scientifically raised on farm ponds.

Enrich

Ask students to locate on a map and investigate the significance to Israel of the following areas: Palestine, West Bank, Gaza Strip, Golan Heights, and Sinai Peninsula.

Discuss

Ask students how farms in the United States compare with those operated by kibbutzim. *(U.S. farms are generally individually owned and operated family farms or corporate farms where farmers may be contracted employees of corporations that own the farms.)*

Vocabulary Builder

The movement of the Jews back to Palestine was called *Zionism*. This term comes from the word *Zion*, which is the name Jews give to their homeland.

Global Perspective

A Land of Jewish Heritage

Israel was founded on the land that had been called Palestine for centuries. This land was the birthplace of the Jews. However, the Jewish population dwindled as a result of revolts, invasions, and periods of foreign rule. Some Jews were killed or sold into slavery. Some fled to nearby Middle Eastern countries and to other countries around the world.

The Jews were physically separated from their homeland and from one another. Even so, they were able to keep their identity and religion. Jews around the world waited for the time when they could return.

The movement of Jews back into Palestine began in the second half of the nineteenth century. However, the present state of Israel was not declared until May 14, 1948. This date marked the first time in more than 2,000 years that Jews were able to govern themselves.

Israeli Holidays

Holidays are an important part of the culture in Israel. Over 80 percent of Israel's citizens are Jewish, so most of the holidays revolve around the Jewish faith. These celebrations always begin and end at sunset. Many of them involve special food traditions. For instance, *Rosh Hashanah* begins a period called the Ten Days of Repentance. This holiday celebrates the Jewish New Year. On this day, Jews in Israel eat sweet foods, such as sliced apples, honey cookies, and sweet potato pudding. They hope eating these foods will bring a new year that is sweet and happy. The last of the Ten Days of Repentance is called *Yom Kippur*. This is the holiest day of the year. Jewish people spend the day at the synagogue fasting, praying, and reading.

Chanukah is an eight-day festival in December. It commemorates the regaining of Jewish control of the Temple in Jerusalem. Chanukah is sometimes called the Festival of Lights. During this holiday, families light candles in a nine-branched candlestick called a *menorah*. Traditional Chanukah foods include *latkes* (potato pancakes) and *sufganiyah* (doughnuts), **32-7**.

Pesakh, or Passover, is celebrated for eight days in the spring. It commemorates the Jews' freedom from slavery in Egypt thousands of years ago. On the first evening of Passover, families share the *Seder*. This is a traditional meal of specific foods, each with a symbolic meaning. Bitter herbs, such as horseradish, are eaten as a symbol of the bitterness of slavery. Parsley represents the coming of spring. **Matzo** is an unleavened bread. It reminds the Jews their ancestors had no time to let bread rise when they were fleeing Egypt. A roasted egg and a shank of lamb symbolize beasts given to God as sacrifices. A dish of salt water stands for the tears of the Hebrew slaves. *Charoset*, a mixture of nuts, apples, and wine, represents the cement the slaves used to build cities for the Egyptians.

Courtesy of the Idaho Potato Commission

32-7 Potato latkes are a classic dish at many Chanukah celebrations.

Israeli Cuisine

When the Jews fled from Palestine, they settled in many parts of the world. Thus, Jewish cuisine is multinational. This is most noticeable in Israel. For there, people of 80 nationalities have added their foods to the area's native Middle Eastern cuisine. Borscht, sauerbraten, and shish kebab might be listed in an Israeli cookbook along with kreplach, challah, and blintzes.

Besides this mixture of native and ethnic Jewish foods, Israeli cooks have developed totally new dishes. These dishes are based on foods readily available in Israel. Many of them contain fish, poultry, and fresh fruit.

Jewish Dietary Laws

People in most Israeli homes and restaurants observe the Jewish **kashrut** (dietary laws). Foods prepared according to the dietary laws are considered **kosher**.

The first of these laws concerns foods that are suitable for eating. Only animals that have cloven (split) hoofs and chew their cud are considered fit to eat. Therefore, Jews cannot eat pigs because pigs do not chew their cud. Fish must have both scales and fins. Therefore, people cannot eat shellfish. They can eat domesticated fowl, but not wild fowl. Cooks must carefully check vegetables and cereals to be sure they are free of insects. They must break eggs into a separate dish and inspect them for blood spots before using them. Manufactured products must not contain any nonkosher ingredients.

Other dietary laws describe the proper methods of slaughter. According to these laws, a **shohet** (licensed slaughterer) must slaughter all animals and fowl.

In a kosher kitchen, there are distinctions between what is considered milchig and what is considered fleishig. **Milchig** describes foods made with milk, and utensils used to prepare, serve, and eat them. **Fleishig** describes foods made with meat or poultry as well as utensils and dishes used with these foods. People cannot cook or eat milchig and fleishig foods together. For this reason, kosher kitchens contain two complete sets of eating, serving, and food preparation utensils. Cooks use one set for milchig foods. They use the other set for fleishig foods. The two sets of utensils must be washed and stored separately. People may eat fleishig foods after milchig foods—but only if they thoroughly cleanse their mouths first. They must wait a period of time after eating fleishig foods before eating milchig foods.

Foods and utensils that are neither milchig nor fleishig are described as pareve. **Pareve** foods include eggs, fruits, vegetables, cereals, fish, and baked goods made with vegetable shortening, **32-8**. Except for fish, pareve foods can be prepared and eaten with either milk or meat dishes.

Traditional Jewish Dishes

For centuries, soups have played an important part in Jewish cooking. They are hot, filling, and relatively inexpensive. Soups may be clear or thick. Chicken soup is perhaps the best-known clear soup. Lentil soup is perhaps the best-known thick soup. Other popular soups include borscht, barley and bean, and fruit soup.

Jewish cooks serve many Jewish soups with *knaidlach* or *mandlen*. Both are similar to dumplings and are frequently made with *matzo meal* (meal made from matzos).

Gefilte fish is another popular Jewish dish. A variety of freshwater fish may be used to make gefilte fish. However, pike, carp, and whitefish are most common. The cook forms a minced fish mixture into balls the size of small dumplings. Then he or she either bakes the gefilte fish or simmers it in fish stock with a few vegetables.

Chicken is both versatile and economical. Cooks boil and roast chicken and use it to make soup. Other popular Jewish chicken dishes include gizzards simmered in seasoned gravy. Chopped chicken liver and neck skin stuffed with seasoned bread crumbs are well-liked chicken dishes, too.

Homemade noodles and dumplings are frequent additions to soups, main dishes, and puddings. They are also used to make the popular kreplach. *Kreplach* are squares of noodle dough stuffed with a filling made of meat,

Courtesy ACH Food Companies, Inc.

32-8 Baked goods, like this challah, are considered pareve foods if they are made with vegetable margarine instead of butter.

cheese, potato, chicken, or chicken liver. Kreplach may also be stuffed with *kasha*, which is cooked, coarsely ground, hulled buckwheat.

Kugels, which resemble puddings, may contain vegetables, fruits, noodles, rice, or fish. A kugel may be a separate course or a side dish. Sweet kugels are often served for dessert.

Tzimmes are combinations of meats, vegetables, and fruits. Although the cook's imagination determines the choice of ingredients, long, slow cooking improves the flavor of all tzimmes.

Blintzes, knishes, latkes, and challah have been Jewish specialties for centuries. Blintzes are thin pancakes similar to French crêpes. *Blintzes* are browned on one side only. Then they are filled with a cheese or fruit filling and folded like a napkin with the browned side up. Knishes are dumplings. They may be filled with potato, cheese, meat, or chicken. See **32-9**. *Latkes* (pancakes) can be made from matzo meal, buckwheat, or wheat flour. However, potato latkes, which are similar to German potato pancakes, are particularly popular. *Challah* is a braided, rich egg bread. Jewish people often serve it at holiday meals.

Courtesy of the Idaho Potato Commission

32-9 These tasty knishes are filled with potatoes and cheese.

Middle Eastern Foods

Many of the foods found in Israel originated in other Middle Eastern countries. One of these foods, felafel, has become one of Israel's national dishes. **Felafel** is a mixture of ground chickpeas, bulgur, and spices that is formed into balls and deep-fried. The warm balls of felafel are tucked inside a piece of pita bread and served with a salad.

A variety of salads and colorful, spicy hot hashes have North African origins. *Couscous*, for example, is a thick, steamed semolina porridge flavored with chicken and spices.

Leben is an Israeli delicacy. It is a type of cheese made from sour milk. Jewish people often serve it with crackers as an appetizer.

Israeli Additions

The citrus fruits, figs, dates, almonds, grapes, and melons that grow abundantly in Israel have inspired many new dishes. Turkey pieces coated with flour, browned, and stewed in orange juice with peas and mushrooms is uniquely Israeli. Avocado halves stuffed with a mixture of walnuts, pistachios, sour cherries, and marinated herring is a new native dish, too.

Some desserts are also uniquely Israeli. For instance, sabra liqueur has the flavor of the Jaffa orange. Jewish cooks use it to make a rich dessert. They dip chocolate cookies into hot, strong coffee. Then they arrange the cookies in layers with whipped cream flavored with the liqueur. After chilling, the dessert is cut into pieces and served like a cake.

Israeli Menu

Lentil Soup

Gefilte Fish with Horseradish

Roasted Chicken

*Noodle Kugel
(Noodle Pudding)*

*Gezer Hai
(Carrot and Orange Salad)*

*Challah
(Braided Egg Bread)*

Honey Cake

Coffee

Lentil Soup

Serves 6 to 8

1¼	cups uncooked lentils
1	cup sliced onions
1	tablespoon vegetable oil
2½	cups canned low-sodium whole tomatoes, mashed slightly
1	cup diced celery
¾	cup diced carrots
¾	cup diced parsnips
¾	cup chopped green pepper
6	cups cold water
¾	teaspoon salt
½	teaspoon pepper

1. Wash and sort lentils. Set aside.
2. In Dutch oven or large saucepan, sauté onions in oil until browned.
3. Add lentils, tomatoes, celery, carrots, parsnips, green pepper, water, and seasonings. Bring to a boil.
4. Reduce heat and cover pan. Simmer soup about 40 minutes, or until lentils are very tender.

Per serving: 205 cal. (13% from fat), 11 g protein, 35 g carbohydrate, 3 g fat, 0 mg cholesterol, 16 g fiber, 339 mg sodium.

Gefilte Fish

Makes 6 to 8 appetizer servings

1	pound skinless whitefish fillets
1	medium onion
1	egg
½	teaspoon salt
¼	teaspoon pepper
2 to 3	tablespoons matzo meal
4	cups vegetable stock
1	medium onion, chopped
1	carrot, diced
1	stalk celery, diced
2	teaspoons parsley

1. Grind fish with one of the onions in a food processor.
2. Add egg, salt, pepper, and enough matzo meal to make fish mixture easy to handle.
3. In a large saucepan, combine vegetable stock, onion, carrot, celery, and parsley. Bring to a boil, then reduce heat to a simmer.
4. With wet hands, shape fish mixture into balls, using about ¼ cup mixture for each.
5. Gently lower the fish balls into the simmering stock.
6. Cover and simmer for 1 hour and 10 minutes without stirring.
7. Remove fish balls carefully to a bowl. Strain stock and pour it over the fish balls.
8. Chill. Serve with horseradish.

Per serving: 177 cal. (36% from fat), 20 g protein, 8 g carbohydrate, 7 g fat, 93 mg cholesterol, 1 g fiber, 267 mg sodium.

Roasted Chicken

Serves 8

2   roasting chickens, 2 pounds each
     margarine, softened
     salt and pepper

1. Preheat oven to 350°F.
2. Remove heart, liver, and giblets from chickens.
3. Rinse chickens under cool running water. Pat dry with paper towels.
4. Place chickens breast side up on rack in roasting pan.
5. Rub skin with margarine. Sprinkle with salt and pepper.
6. Roast, uncovered, about 1½ hours or until meat thermometer inserted into the thickest part of the thigh reads 180°F.
7. Carve chickens and remove skin before serving.

Per serving: 165 cal. (44% from fat), 21 g protein, 0 g carbohydrate, 8 g fat, 65 mg cholesterol, 0 g fiber, 96 mg sodium.

Noodle Kugel
(Noodle Pudding)

Serves 8

3   eggs
4   tablespoons light brown sugar
¼   teaspoon nutmeg
½   teaspoon cinnamon
4   cups cooked wide egg noodles
⅔   cup seedless raisins
½   cup sliced blanched almonds
1   tablespoon lemon juice
2   tablespoons melted margarine
3   tablespoons bread crumbs

1. Preheat oven to 350°F.
2. In large bowl, beat eggs until foamy.
3. Add brown sugar, nutmeg, and cinnamon and continue beating until well mixed.
4. Fold in noodles, raisins, almonds, lemon juice, and melted margarine.
5. Pour into a 1½-quart greased casserole or ring mold.
6. Sprinkle with bread crumbs.
7. Bake for 50 minutes or until browned.

Per serving: 277 cal. (34% from fat), 8 g protein, 39 g carbohydrate, 11 g fat, 128 mg cholesterol, 3 g fiber, 83 mg sodium.

Gezer Hai
(Carrot and Orange Salad)

Serves 8

1   cup fresh orange juice
¼   teaspoon ground ginger
¼   teaspoon salt
2   tablespoons lemon juice
1   tablespoon honey
4   cups coarsely grated carrots
2   navel oranges
     salad greens

1. In small bowl, mix together orange juice, ginger, salt, lemon juice, and honey.
2. Pour over carrots, cover, and refrigerate for at least an hour.
3. When ready to serve, peel and section oranges.
4. Line 8 small salad plates with salad greens.
5. Top greens with grated carrots.
6. Garnish with orange sections. Serve at once.

Per serving: 72 cal. (0% from fat), 2 g protein, 17 g carbohydrate, 0 g fat, 0 mg cholesterol, 4 g fiber, 98 mg sodium.

Challah
(Braided Egg Bread)

Makes 2 loaves

4½ to 5½ cups all-purpose flour
2   tablespoons sugar
1½   teaspoons salt
1   package active dry yeast
⅓   cup softened margarine
     pinch powdered saffron (optional)
1   cup very warm water (120°F to 130°F)
3   eggs (at room temperature)
1   teaspoon cold water
1   teaspoon poppy seeds

1. In large mixing bowl, combine 1¼ cups flour, sugar, salt, and dry yeast.
2. Work in softened margarine with pastry blender or two knives.
3. Dissolve saffron in the very warm water. Gradually add water to dry ingredients, beating on medium speed of electric mixer for 2 minutes, scraping bowl occasionally.

4. Divide one of the eggs and set aside the yolk. Add the egg white and the other two eggs to the dough mixture along with ½ cup flour. Beat at high speed for 2 minutes.

5. Stir in enough additional flour to form a stiff dough.

6. Turn dough out onto a lightly floured board or pastry cloth. Knead until smooth and elastic, about 8 to 10 minutes.

7. Place dough in greased bowl, turning once to grease top.

8. Cover with a clean towel and let rise in a warm place until doubled in bulk, about 1 hour.

9. Punch dough down and divide it in half. Divide each half into three strips. Place strips side by side on a lightly greased baking sheet and braid, pinching ends to seal.

10. Braid the second loaf.

11. Beat together reserved egg yolk with 1 teaspoon cold water.

12. Brush loaves with egg wash and sprinkle with poppy seeds.

13. Let rise in a warm place until doubled in bulk, about 1 hour.

14. Bake at 400°F for 20 to 25 minutes or until loaves sound hollow when tapped with knuckles.

15. Remove loaves from baking sheets and place on cooling racks.

Per slice: 92 cal. (25% from fat), 2 g protein, 14 g carbohydrate, 3 g fat, 26 mg cholesterol, 1 g fiber, 129 mg sodium.

Honey Cake

Serves 12

2	tablespoons vegetable oil
1	cup sugar
3	eggs
⅔	cup cold strong coffee
1	cup honey
3	cups cake flour
2	teaspoons baking powder
1	teaspoon baking soda
1	teaspoon cinnamon
½	teaspoon ginger
½	teaspoon nutmeg
½	cup blanched almonds, chopped (reserve a few for the top)
½	cup seedless raisins

1. Preheat oven to 350°F.

2. In large mixer bowl, combine oil, sugar, and eggs. Beat until light and fluffy.

3. In small bowl, combine coffee and honey.

4. Sift together flour, baking powder, baking soda, cinnamon, ginger, and nutmeg.

5. Add dry ingredients alternately with liquid ingredients to egg mixture.

6. Fold in almonds and raisins.

7. Pour batter into a greased and floured 9-inch tube pan.

8. Sprinkle batter with the reserved almonds.

9. Bake for 45 minutes to 1 hour, or until toothpick inserted in center comes out clean.

Per piece: 332 cal. (18% from fat), 5 g protein, 66 g carbohydrate, 7 g fat, 69 mg cholesterol, 2 g fiber, 143 mg sodium.

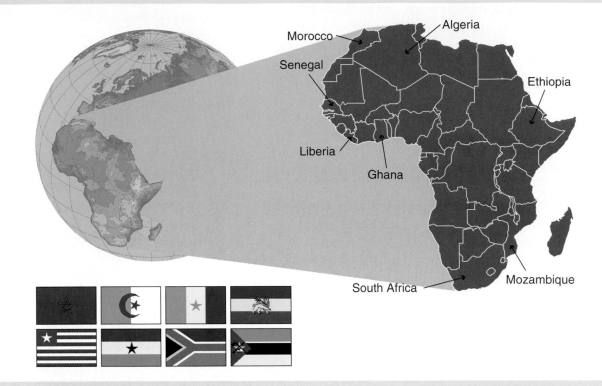

Africa

Activities

Africa is made up of over 50 countries. Ask students to see how many they can name.

Africa is the second largest continent; only Asia is larger. Africa shares the title of warmest continent with South America. The geographic extremes of Africa range from sandy deserts to tropical forests.

The countries of Africa are as varied as its geography. Therefore, Africa does not have a typical cuisine. Each African nation has unique foods.

Climate and Geography of Africa

Since the equator runs through the middle of Africa, both the extreme northern and southern countries have subtropical climates. Summers are dry, with the highest monthly average temperature above 72°F (22°C). Monthly winter temperatures average above 50°F (10°C). In these areas, grains such as millet, teff, and sorghum grow well.

Along the equator in central and western Africa, temperatures range between 64°F (18°C) and 80°F (27°C) year round. This area has rainfall throughout the year. In these tropical, humid sections, root crops and vegetables are grown. Other products include palm oil, groundnuts (peanuts), bananas, dates, figs, plantains, citrus fruits, sugarcane, coffee, and cacao. (**Cacao** is a plant that produces beans that are ground into cocoa or made into chocolate.) See **32-10**.

The majority of the people in Africa live on the savannas, or grasslands. These are the broad areas above and below the equatorial belt. They receive less precipitation and have greater temperature ranges. Raising crops is difficult and unprofitable on the savannas because the soil is poor. The soil has little *humus*, a substance formed by decayed matter. Humus holds water near the ground surface, within reach of plant roots.

North and south of the savannas are the deserts. Average summer temperatures may reach 98°F (37°C) and winter temperatures never drop below 59°F (15°C). Rain, when it falls, is brief. In the deserts, there are places called *oases* where water is available. Groups of people known as *nomads* move from one oasis to another. They herd sheep, goats, and camels as was done in primitive times.

African Culture

Native Africans make up over 70 percent of Africa's population. Over five million people of European descent also live in Africa.

More than 800 languages are spoken in Africa. Most Africans speak a local language in their home village. They also speak an interchange language to communicate with people outside their village.

Much of Africa is in a state of political, economic, and cultural development. Many of the people in Africa have not had an opportunity to attend school. Therefore, a number of Africans are unable to read or write. This has made it hard for African governments to communicate modern ideas to their people. To help solve this problem, some African governments choose students to send to schools in Europe and the United States. In payment, the governments expect students to return to their native lands and help educate others.

African Holidays

Many of the holidays in African countries are religious festivals. Therefore, holidays vary from region to region, depending on the main form of religion. Muslims in Africa observe such events as the Fast of Ramadan. Christmas and Easter are celebrated by African Christians. Besides these holy days, New Year festivals are popular in Africa. Many areas hold harvest festivals in the autumn. Independence day celebrations are also common in Africa. The people celebrate the days their nations gained freedom from the European countries that colonized them. These festivals often involve parades, speeches, parties, and fireworks. Music, dancing, and the wearing of masks are part of many African festivals, too.

African Cuisine

Each African country has unique dishes. However, similarities exist among the foods of a region. For instance, *akla* is a popular snack food in Ghana, a country in western Africa. It is made of cowpeas, which are cooked, mashed, formed into balls, and fried. This dish, known by many other names, is also found in other west African countries.

Most African people do not have refrigerators. Cooks who live in cities are likely to take daily trips to the market to buy fresh ingredients. Those who live in rural areas often grow the fruits and vegetables they need.

A wide variety of fruits and vegetables grow in Africa. A *papaya* is a small melonlike fruit. A *guava* is a small fruit with many seeds. A *plantain* is like a banana, but it is much larger and has a bland flavor. *Cassava* is a root vegetable much like a sweet potato. *Okra*, which also grows in the United States, is a native African vegetable. See **32-11.**

Shutterstock

32-10 Cacao beans from Africa are valued all over the world for the wonderful chocolates made from them.

Online Resource

Have each student visit the Africa Guide website to research a different item of interest about the continent or one of the African countries. Ask each student to share what he or she learned.

Activity

Haggling over prices is a common practice in African markets. Give students play money and allow them to haggle over prices for samples of African food items prepared by each lab group.

Shutterstock

32-11 Okra is a green, pod-shaped vegetable that was brought to the United States from Africa.

Some of the breads and pastries prepared in Africa are kesra, brik, and pita. *Kesra* is a round oven bread made in mountain villages. A *brik* is a pastry that is filled and then deep-fried. **Pita bread** is found throughout Africa as well as the Middle East. It is a flat, round, hollow bread. When cut in half, each half opens like a pocket and can be filled with meat or vegetables.

The French influenced the foods of the North African countries of Morocco, Senegal, and Algeria. In the nineteenth century, the French invaded these countries and brought their European customs to the region. A common meat in Algeria is lamb. It is usually grilled or stewed. *Mechoui* is lamb that has smoldered and cooked over a fire for many hours. The smoked head of a sheep is a delicacy.

Ghana is located on the midwestern coast of the African continent. This has made seafood an important ingredient in many of the spicy soups and stews served in this country. These main dishes are usually served with a starchy side dish, such as boiled yams, cassava, or plantains. These starchy vegetables may also be boiled and pounded into a dish called *fufu*, which is similar to dumplings.

Another country along the western coast is Liberia. Freed slaves from the United States founded Liberia in the late 1800s after the Civil War. The food of Liberia is similar to soul food in the United States. It is a combination of American and African cooking.

One of the oldest countries in Africa is Ethiopia, which is located in the East. Christianity is the predominant religion in Ethiopia. Therefore, Ethiopian cuisine is not bound by the many religious dietary restrictions found in neighboring Muslim countries. Ethiopia's main dish is **injera**, which is a large sourdoughlike pancake made from teff. **Teff** is a milletlike grain grown only in Africa and the Middle East. Injera is served with **wat**, a spicy sauce or stew. Diners tear the injera into pieces, roll it around in the wat, and eat it with their fingers.

South Africa is an African country with many contrasts. Dutch, French, German, and British colonists brought foods to South Africa from their home nations. These European foods have been blended with native foods over the years.

Portuguese influence can be seen in the foods of Mozambique, a country in southeastern Africa. Chicken is cooked the Portuguese way with tomatoes and wine. Hot curries are another food typical of Mozambique.

African Meals

In urban areas of Africa, some people follow a daily meal pattern that includes breakfast, lunch, and dinner. However, people in rural areas are more likely to follow the traditional pattern of eating just two meals a day. Both meals, the first at midday and the second in the evening, are quite similar. They typically consist of a main dish soup or stew and a starchy accompaniment, such as rice or bread, **32-12**.

Snacking is popular in Africa. In city streets, vendors sell such foods as fried plantains and broiled meat to satisfy hunger between meals.

Reflect

Ask students if they would be comfortable dining at low tables while sitting on pillows, folded carpets, or the floor.

Activity

Have students practice the African hand-washing ritual described here before eating foods prepared in an African foods lab.

Culture and Social Studies

African Meal Traditions

Africans often serve meals on low tables with pillows, folded carpets, or the floor used as seats. Food is often served in the brass or earthenware vessels in which it was cooked. The food is usually arranged on one large tray and placed in the center of the table. Then each household member takes his or her individual share. Although diners do not use knives and forks, they may use spoons. However, they use the fingers of their right hands to eat most foods. They use flat breads to sop up the stews and sauces.

In most of Africa, a hand-washing ritual takes place before meals. A servant or member of the household brings in a long-necked pitcher of water and a bowl or basin. This person pours water over the hands of each household member and catches it in the basin. He or she then offers a small towel to dry the hands. Since diners eat most of the food with their fingers, this ritual is usually repeated after the meal.

Photo Courtesy of The Beef Checkoff www.BeefItsWhatsForDinner.com

32-12 This flavorful stew served over starchy couscous would be a typical meal in many parts of Africa.

African Menu

Meat on a Stick
(East Africa)

Spinach Stew
(West Africa)

Rice

Salatat Fijl wa Latsheen
(Radish and Orange Salad - North Africa)

Melktert
(Milk Pie - South Africa)

Coffee

Meat on a Stick

Serves 8

¾	teaspoon cayenne pepper
1	teaspoon garlic salt
1	pound round steak
1	medium onion

1. Place 8 12-inch bamboo skewers in a 13-by-9-inch oblong pan. Cover with water and allow to soak for 30 minutes.
2. Cut round steak into 1-inch cubes.
3. Cut onion into 1-inch chunks.
4. Combine cayenne pepper and garlic salt in a resealable plastic bag.
5. Toss steak cubes, a few at a time, into the bag with the seasonings. Seal and shake to coat. Remove coated cubes from the bag and set aside while repeating coating process with remaining cubes.
6. Alternately thread steak cubes and onion chunks onto skewers.
7. Place skewers under broiler. Broil 4 to 5 minutes. Turn; broil another 4 to 5 minutes until meat is cooked and onions are browned.

Per serving: 72 cal. (38% from fat), 11 g protein, 1 g carbohydrate, 3 g fat, 28 mg cholesterol, 0 g fiber, 168 mg sodium.

Spinach Stew

Serves 6

1	medium onion, chopped
2	tablespoons peanut oil
1	medium tomato, cubed
6	tablespoons tomato paste, unsalted
1	10-ounce package frozen chopped spinach, thawed
1	12-ounce can corned beef hash
1	teaspoon cayenne pepper
4½	cups hot, cooked rice

1. In a large, nonstick skillet, sauté onion in peanut oil over medium heat until tender.
2. Add tomatoes and tomato paste. Cook, stirring gently, until tomatoes are tender, about 5 minutes.
3. Add spinach, corned beef hash, and cayenne pepper. Reduce heat to low, cover, and cook for 30 minutes.
4. Serve over rice.

Per serving: 416 cal. (30% from fat), 21 g protein, 51 g carbohydrate, 14 g fat, 48 mg cholesterol, 2 g fiber, 615 mg sodium.

Salatat Fijl wa Latsheen
(Radish and Orange Salad)

Serves 6

6	seedless oranges
⅓	cup lemon juice
3	tablespoons sugar
¼	teaspoon salt
1	bunch radishes
¼	teaspoon cinnamon

1. Peel and section oranges into a large bowl.
2. In a separate bowl, combine lemon juice, sugar, and salt. Stir until sugar and salt are dissolved.
3. Wash and coarsely grate radishes.
4. Toss radishes and lemon juice mixture with the orange sections.
5. Sprinkle with cinnamon and serve immediately.

Per serving: 89 cal. (0% from fat), 1 g protein, 23 g carbohydrate, 0 g fat, 0 mg cholesterol, 3 g fiber, 101 mg sodium.

Melktert
(Milk Pie)

Serves 6

1¾   cups fat-free milk
1   tablespoon butter
1   cinnamon stick
1   small orange, peeled and cut into pieces
¼   cup sugar
⅓   cup flour
¼   cup fat-free milk
2   eggs, beaten
      pastry for one single-crust, 9-inch pie
1½   teaspoons sugar
¼   teaspoon cinnamon

1. In a 2-quart heavy saucepan, combine 1¾ cups milk, butter, cinnamon stick, and orange pieces. Bring to a boil.
2. Remove from heat. Remove cinnamon stick and orange pieces with a slotted spoon.
3. Combine ¼ cup sugar with the flour. Add ¼ cup milk and stir until smooth.
4. Stir flour mixture into the milk in the sauce pan. Place over low heat and cook, stirring constantly, until thickened.
5. Remove from the heat. Stir a small amount of the hot liquid into the beaten eggs. Then add the eggs to the hot mixture, mixing well.
6. Pour the pudding into a pastry-lined pie plate.
7. Bake at 450°F for 20 minutes.
8. Reduce heat to 350°F and bake for another 10 minutes.
9. Combine 1½ teaspoons sugar with the cinnamon and sprinkle over the top of the pie. Serve warm.

Per serving: 303 cal. (39% from fat), 8 g protein, 40 g carbohydrate, 13 g fat, 78 mg cholesterol, 1 g fiber, 283 mg sodium.

CAREER SUCCESS

Responsibility

Abira is a foreign correspondent in the Middle East for NWN, a cable news network. She must gather information about newsworthy events and analyze it for accuracy. Sometimes this involves a lot of effort and perseverance as she tracks down sources of information and confirms facts. Then she uses credible information to write news stories for broadcast on her network.

To be an effective worker, Abira needs to display responsibility. In a small group, answer the following questions about Abira's need for and use of this quality:

A. In what kinds of situations would the quality of responsibility be especially important to Abira?
B. How might Abira's information sources respond if she failed to display responsibility?
C. How might the viewers of Abira's broadcasts be affected if she failed to display responsibility?
D. What is another skill Abira would need in this job? Briefly explain why this skill would be important.

CHAPTER 32 REVIEW

Summary

The climate throughout much of the Middle East and Africa is hot and dry. Irrigation is essential for growing crops in many Middle Eastern and African countries. Religion is an important part of the culture in this part of the world. Religious laws as well as the climate have an impact on the foods of this region.

A number of ingredients and foods are common throughout the Middle East. However, unique dishes are found in each Middle Eastern country. Lamb is the staple meat of this region and bulgur and rice are often served as side dishes. Fish is popular in coastal countries. Middle Eastern cooks use a variety of spices to season foods. Fruits and rich pastries are common desserts. Coffee is a favorite beverage, although Iranians prefer tea.

Israel has a rather eclectic cuisine. Jewish people from many parts of the world have made contributions to the foods of Israel. The neighboring Middle Eastern and African countries have had an influence, too. Of course, Jewish dietary laws also affect many foods.

The Islamic religion influences food habits throughout much of Africa. European countries that colonized various parts of Africa also left their mark on the cuisine. Although each African country has unique dishes, some foods are common all over the continent. Such foods include a variety of fruits and vegetables and several breads and pastries.

Review What You Have Read

Write your answers on a separate sheet of paper, using complete sentences when appropriate.

1. How do Muslims observe the Fast of Ramadan?

2. List the five ingredients basic to all Middle Eastern cooking.

3. True or false. Both Islam and Judaism forbid their followers to eat poultry.

4. Describe three Turkish sweets.

5. Which of the following is an Arabian mazza?
   A. Hummus.
   B. Kibbi.
   C. Tabbouleh.
   D. Torshi.

6. Name and describe the two types of rice dishes served in Iran.

7. Explain the symbolism of five foods eaten as part of the Seder shared by Jewish families during Passover.

8. Match the following terms and definitions associated with Jewish dietary laws:

_____ Someone who, in accordance with Jewish dietary laws, is licensed to slaughter all animals and fowl used as food.

_____ Foods that are prepared according to Jewish dietary laws.

_____ Foods made with milk, and utensils and dishes used to prepare, serve, and eat them.

_____ Foods made with meat or poultry, and utensils and dishes used to prepare, serve, and eat them.

_____ Fruits, vegetables, cereal, fish, and baked goods made with vegetable shortening.

A. fleishig
B. Halal
C. kosher
D. milchig
E. pareve
F. shohet

> 12. Africans often sit on pillows, folded carpets, or the floor during meals.

9. Name four foods used to stuff kreplach.

10. Most of the world's chocolate is made from a plant grown in Africa called _____.

11. What is injera? How is it served and eaten?

12. On what do Africans often sit during meals?

Link to Academic Skills

13. **Geography.** On a world or regional map, identify populated areas of the Middle East and Africa in which water resources are most limited. Find out the lengths to which some people in these areas must go to get water each day. Share your findings in class.

14. **Government/Civics.** Work as part of an investigative team. Research the political system and any sources of political unrest in a Middle Eastern or African country. Use media resources to compile your findings into a brief documentary presentation.

15. **Social studies.** Explore the history and meaning of Egyptian hieroglyphics. Write a message in Egyptian hieroglyphics and translate it for the class. As an alternative, work in a small team to develop your own set of symbols for a system of hieroglyphic writing.

16. **History.** Use library resources to read about the establishment of the state of Israel. Summarize your findings in a brief written report.

Build Critical Thinking Skills

17. **Analysis.** Investigate the average annual rainfall in various regions of the Middle East. Analyze how rainfall affects agricultural production in these regions.

18. **Synthesis.** Work in a small group to trace the origins of some specific food customs of one African country. Use visual aids to put together a presentation about the ingredients, cooking methods, eating habits, and meal patterns in your chosen country. Each member of your team should be responsible for a different part of the presentation. Following the group presentations, each group should prepare a dish typical of their country to contribute as part of an African banquet

Apply Technology

19. Find a report about a recent incident in the Middle East at each of two news websites. Copy the two reports into a word processing document file. Search for the same three key terms in both reports, highlighting each term in a different color. Make color printouts of the two highlighted reports. Use the highlighting to compare the angle and emphasis of the two reports. Share your findings in class.

20. Use a computer and the table function in word processing software to make a table comparing Islam, Judaism, and Christianity.

A Measure of Math

21. Choose an African country. Research the following statistics for your chosen country and for the United States:
    • male and female literacy rates
    • male and female life expectancies
    • under age five mortality rate
    • per capita gross domestic product
    • percentage of urban and rural population using improved drinking water sources
    • percentage of urban and rural population using adequate sanitation facilities

    Create a poster display using charts to compare these numerical statistics for the two countries. Present your poster in class.

Teamwork in Action

22. Arrange for your class to accompany a class of young children on a trip to a zoo in your area. Before the trip, prepare a short presentation about African culture for the children. You might also prepare African snacks and research African games to play with the children. While on the trip, help the children identify all the animals that are native to Africa.

Companion Website
www.g-wlearning.com

At the website, review key terms for this chapter with crossword puzzles, matching exercises, and e-flash cards. Apply facts from the chapter to complete the activities.

CHAPTER 33
Asia

Learning Prep

Use the *Terms to Know* to make a matching activity. List terms in one column and definitions, in random order, in a second column. Have a partner complete your activity; then check your partner's accuracy.

Terms to Know

kasha	korma
zakuska	vindaloo
caviar	chasnidarth
schi	wok
borscht	congee
beef stroganov	chopsticks
paskha	gohan
kulich	soybean
caste system	tofu
curry	sukiyaki
masala	tsukemono
ghee	kaiseka
chapatis	nihon-cha
tandoori	

Main Menu

* Russia, India, China, and Japan all have very different sets of influences on their cuisines.
* The countries of Asia each developed distinct foods, meal patterns, and eating customs.

Objectives

After studying this chapter, you will be able to

* **describe** how geography, climate, and culture have influenced the food customs of Russia, India, China, and Japan.
* **name** foods that are native to each of these countries.
* **use** recipes to prepare foods that are native to each of these countries.

Asia is the largest continent in the world. It covers nearly a third of the earth's total land surface. Asia is also the home of over three-fifths of the world's people. Deserts, jungles, swamps, and mountains cover much of Asia. Therefore, most of its people are crowded into small areas that can better support crops.

When people in the rest of the world were making crude tools, people in Asia were becoming highly advanced. Asian art, architecture, and technology laid the groundwork for the later development of Western civilization.

Russia, India, China, and Japan dominate Asia in area and population. (The largest portion of Russia lies in Asia. The smaller portion lies in Europe.) Interest in these nations, however, goes far beyond size and population statistics. Each of these nations has a unique culture. The culture of Russia is a mixture of Eastern and Western influences. The cultures of India, Japan, and China are far different from those of any Western nation. Despite growing Western influence, many of the customs and traditions of these countries have been preserved.

Russia

Inside Russia's borders are vast natural resources. Forests provide timber. Thousands of rivers provide power, food, water, and transportation. A large population representing a range of cultures has added to the diversity of Russian cuisine.

Geography and Climate of Russia

Russia is the largest country in the world. It is almost twice the size of the United States. Most of Russia is a vast lowland, but mountains are important, too. The Ural Mountains divide Europe from Asia. The other important mountain ranges form a large arc along the southern and southwestern borders. The rivers of Russia are important transportation arteries. Because many of the rivers run north and south, canals have been built to improve east-west transportation. See **33-1**.

The climate in a large portion of Russia is marked by short, cool summers; long, severe winters; and light precipitation. Much of the European part of Russia (including Moscow) has short, mild summers. The winters are long and cold, and precipitation is moderate. In the northern Arctic regions, summers are short and chilly, and winters are long and bitterly cold. Temperatures of -94°F (-70°C) have been recorded in northeastern Siberia. The Pacific Ocean brings monsoons to the far southeastern portion of the country.

Russian Culture

Russian history and cultural influences date back for centuries. However, Russia has been an independent country for only a short time. Russia had been ruled by an imperial government for hundreds of years. Then in the early twentieth century, Russia became part of the Union of Soviet Socialist Republics (U.S.S.R., or Soviet Union). The U.S.S.R. was ruled by a Communist dictatorship. In 1991, the Communist Party was dissolved. The Soviet Union was broken up into 15 independent countries, one of which is Russia.

Russian Holidays

The Communist government had a great impact on the celebration of holidays in Russia. Many traditional holidays are linked to the Russian Orthodox Church. During the years of Communist rule, the government closed churches and discouraged the celebration of religious holidays. With the fall of Communism, churches reopened. Religious holidays, such as Christmas and Easter, regained importance in the lives of the Russian people.

Two of Russia's winter festivals involve some special food traditions. Most Russian people consider New Year to be the best holiday. Children receive candy and gifts from Grandfather Frost and the Snow Maiden, who arrive in a horse-drawn sled. Families get together to enjoy a meal that includes borscht, beef stroganov, pickled tomatoes, and salads. Festival of Winter is a period of several weeks during which parks are decorated with lights and Christmas trees. People stroll through the parks and enjoy blinis and tea purchased from vendors. *Blinis* are pancakes made from buckwheat flour. Russians fry them in butter and serve them with butter and sour cream, caviar, smoked fish, or jam. Their round shape symbolizes the sun and the coming of spring.

Shutterstock

33-1 Canals are an important part of the transportation system in Russia.

Discuss

Ask students how the Russian Festival of Winter compares to the weeks leading up to Christmas in the United States.

Academic Connections

As you cover material on Russian cuisine, ask the music teacher to introduce students to the music of famous Russian composers and Russian folk music.

Discuss

Ask students what types of foods the forests, mountains, and waters would probably have provided to diets of the first Slavs. *(game animals, such as deer and rabbit; wild berries; fish)*

Russian Agriculture

Wheat is Russia's major grain crop, followed by rye, barley, oats, and corn. Other important crops include sugar beets, sunflower seeds, and flax. Fruit and vegetable crops are not as varied as they are in the United States. However, hardy fruits and vegetables, such as cabbage, potatoes, and apples, grow where climate and soil are suitable.

Russian Cuisine

Russian cuisine is, for the most part, hearty and filling. The Russian diet is also nutritious, with bread and other grain products forming the foundation. Vegetables frequently appear in healthful soups and side dishes. Russians make more liberal use of meat and dairy products than many of their Asian neighbors. Although these foods add a balance of nutrients, they also increase the amount of fat in the diet. Serving moderate portions is important to help keep fat under control. Smoked and pickled foods, which are linked with certain types of cancer, should be enjoyed in limited amounts, too.

Culture and Social Studies

Contributions to Russian Cuisine

Russian cuisine has Slavic origins. Thousands of years ago, the Slavs were a group of people who lived in the land that is now Russia. The first Slavs depended on the forests, mountains, and waters for most of their food. Cream sauces and the queen cake are examples of Scandinavian foods contributed by these early people. (*Queen cake* is apples and cherries baked between layers of sweet pastry and topped with meringue.)

The next major contribution to Russian cuisine came from the Mongols, who invaded Russia in the thirteenth century. The Mongols taught the Slavs how to broil meat and how to make sauerkraut, yogurt, kumys, and curd cheese. (*Kumys* is a mild alcoholic beverage.) The Mongols also introduced tea drinking and the *samovar* (a special piece of equipment used to make Russian tea).

In 1547, Ivan the Terrible became the first in a line of Russian czars. (The word *czar* means ruler.) The czars influenced Russian cuisine by staging elaborate banquets and introducing European foods. For instance, Peter the Great brought French soups and Dutch cheeses to the Russian court. He also introduced the custom of serving fruit preserves with meat.

Enrich

Have students analyze the nutritional quality of the Russian peasant diet.

Staple Foods of Russian Peasants

During the time of the czars, most people living in Russia were peasants. They ate foods they could grow themselves or obtain from the forests and rivers. Some peasant families had enough money to have small vegetable gardens and some livestock. The gardens supplied potatoes, cabbage, cucumbers, beets, carrots, and turnips. Cows provided milk and milk products. Chickens gave eggs, and hogs and cattle provided meat.

Bread, kasha, and soup formed the basis of the diet for Russian peasants. These foods are still important in Russian cuisine today.

Peasant bread was dark, nourishing, and filling. Peasants usually made it from rye flour because they could grow rye in the short, cool growing season. See **33-2**.

Kasha was another staple food. The peasants usually made **kasha** from buckwheat, but they also used other grains. They first fried the raw grain. Then they simmered it until tender. The peasants could eat the kasha alone. However, those who could afford to do so added vegetables, meat, eggs, or fish.

The third staple food of the peasants was soup. Cabbage, beet, and fish soups were the most common.

Modern Russian Cuisine

The Russian cuisine of today combines native Russian foods with foods of neighboring European and Asian countries.

Russian Appetizers and Soups

Zakuska (appetizers), such as smoked salmon, pickled herring, fish in aspic, and sliced cold meats, begin many Russian meals. Pâtés, salads, cheese, pickles, and breads are also among the many foods that appear on a zakuska table. However, the star of the table is always caviar.

Caviar is the processed, salted roe (eggs) of large fish. The roe of the sturgeon are used most often. Russians serve their fine black caviar on small pieces of white bread.

Soup usually follows the zakuska. **Schi** (cabbage soup) is one of the most popular Russian soups. Cooks obtain different flavors by varying the vegetables and broth. **Borscht** (beet soup) can be thin and clear or thick with chunks of beets and other vegetables. Russians often top borscht with a dollop of sour cream. Other popular soups include *ouba*, which is a clear fish broth. *Rasolnik* is made with a mixture of vegetables garnished with chopped veal or lamb kidneys. *Solianka* contains meat or fish and salted cucumber.

Russian Main Dishes

Many Russian meat dishes have regional origins. *Shashlik* (cubes of marinated lamb grilled on skewers), for example, developed in Georgia (a country that borders Turkey).

One of the best-known Russian meat dishes was created for a Russian count of the late nineteenth century. **Beef stroganov** is made with tender strips of beef, mushrooms, and a seasoned sour cream sauce.

Other Russian main dishes are made with chicken. *Chakhokhbili* is stewed chicken with tomato sauce, onions, vinegar, wine, peppers, and olives. *Kurnik* is a chicken and rice pie and *kotmis satsivi* is roasted chicken with walnut sauce. *Kotlety po-kyivskomu*

Courtesy ACH Food Companies, Inc.

33-2 Today, as in the times of the peasants, Russian farmers grow a lot of rye, making hearty rye breads a staple of the Russian diet.

Discuss

Ask students what other countries have a dish similar to shashlik. Ask what this dish is called. *(Some Middle Eastern countries grill cubes of lamb on skewers and call them kabobs.)*

(chicken Kiev) is pounded chicken breasts wrapped around pieces of sweet butter. The rolls of chicken are then breaded and deep-fried until golden brown. When a fork pierces the golden coating, the butter spurts out and serves as a sauce.

More than 100 types of fish live in the waters that border Russia. Sturgeon, pike, carp, bream, salmon, and trout were favorites of the Russian czars. A branch of Russian cuisine developed around these and other varieties of fish. In one region, sturgeon and swordfish are prepared on skewers. White-fleshed fish are served in aspic, and crisp fish cakes are eaten with a mustard sauce.

Russian Side Dishes

Russian vegetable dishes have always changed with the seasons. During the cold winters, rutabagas and other root vegetables, potatoes, pickles, dried mushrooms, and sauerkraut are eaten. During the summers, asparagus, peas, and fresh cabbage are more common.

Cereals are available year-round. Because they are both filling and inexpensive, they serve as staples in the Russian diet. Russian cooks use cereals to make dark breads, white breads, and sweet breads. They use cereals to make kasha, which is still popular in Russia. Russians may serve kasha plain or add it to soups. They may combine it with other foods and serve it as a side dish or a puddinglike dessert. Russian cooks use flour doughs to make noodles, dumplings, and pirozhki. *Pirozhki* are pastries filled with protein-based or sweet fillings.

Milk and milk products are an important part of Russian cooking. Russian cooks use *smetana* (sour cream) on top of borscht and in cakes, pastries, salads, sauces, and main dishes, **33-3**. They also use *prostokvasa* (sour milk), *kefir* (a type of yogurt), and *koumys* (sour mare's milk).

©2011 Wisconsin Milk Marketing Board, Inc.

33-3 Rich sour cream is a common ingredient in Russian cooking.

Russian Desserts

Russian desserts have varied origins. Some Russian desserts, like *charlotte russe* (ladyfinger mold with cream filling) and fruit tarts, were favorites of the czars. Other desserts, like *kisel* (pureed fruit), were eaten by the peasants. Many desserts are strictly regional in origin. These include *samsa* (sweet walnut fritters) and *medivnyk* (honey cake).

Two of the most popular Russian desserts are part of the Easter celebrations of the Russian Orthodox Church. **Paskha** is a rich cheesecake. It is molded into a pyramid and decorated with the letters *XB*. These are the initials of the Greek phrase *Christos voskres*, meaning Christ has risen. **Kulich** is a tall, cylindrical yeast cake filled with fruits and nuts. Russians always serve kulich by first removing the top half of the cake and placing it on a serving plate. Then they slice the rest of the cake and arrange the slices around the mushroom-shaped top.

Russian Meals

The average Russian family eats three meals a day. Breakfast generally is simple. Kasha with milk, bread, butter, jam, hot tea, and an occasional egg are typical.

Lunches may be eaten wherever workers find themselves in the middle of the day, such as factory cafeterias or farm fields. Lunch may consist of a hearty soup, thick slices of bread with a little cheese or sausage, and tea. In wealthier families, a fish or meat course and vegetables may follow the soup.

Dinner is the main meal of the day. Russians serve a small assortment of zakuska with glasses of vodka or *kvas* (similar to European beers). They often follow zakuska with soup. Then they serve the main course of meat, poultry, or fish. Potatoes, vegetables, and bread usually accompany the main course. A simple dessert, such as kisel and hot tea, follows.

Russian Menu

Borscht
(Beet Soup)

Chernyi Hleb
(Black Bread)

Tvorog
(Cottage Cheese)

Cranberry Kisel

Tchai
(Tea)

Borscht
(Beet Soup)

Serves 6

2	pounds beef brisket
8	medium beets, coarsely grated
4	medium onions, sliced
2	medium tomatoes, coarsely chopped
2	tablespoons sugar
2	tablespoons lemon juice
1½	teaspoons salt
⅛	teaspoon pepper
½	pound white cabbage, shredded
	sour cream

1. Fill a large Dutch oven with water. Add brisket, beets, onions, and tomatoes; simmer until meat is tender, about 1½ hours.
2. Remove meat. Add sugar, lemon juice, salt, and pepper to stock. Stir until sugar has dissolved.
3. Add cabbage and simmer an additional 25 minutes.
4. Skim fat.
5. Shred meat and add to soup.
6. Pour soup into large tureen and serve immediately with dollops of sour cream. (Soup may also be served cold, if desired.)

Per serving: 310 cal. (26% from fat), 36 g protein, 22 g carbohydrate, 9 g fat, 104 mg cholesterol, 4 g fiber, 723 mg sodium.

Chernyi Hleb
(Black Bread)

Makes 2 loaves

4	cups rye flour
3	cups all-purpose flour
1	teaspoon sugar
2	teaspoons salt
2	cups whole-bran cereal
1½	tablespoons caraway seeds, crushed
2	teaspoons instant coffee
1	teaspoon onion powder
½	teaspoon fennel seed, crushed
2	packages active dry yeast
2½	cups water
¼	cup vinegar
¼	cup molasses
1	square unsweetened chocolate, 1 ounce
¼	cup margarine
1	egg white
1	teaspoon cold water

1. On a sheet of waxed paper, combine rye flour and all-purpose flour.

2. In a large mixer bowl, combine 2⅓ cups mixed flour, sugar, salt, bran cereal, caraway seeds, instant coffee, onion powder, fennel seed, and dry yeast.

3. In medium saucepan, combine 2½ cups water, vinegar, molasses, chocolate, and margarine. Heat over low heat until very warm (120°F to 130°F). (Margarine and chocolate do not need to melt.)

4. Gradually add warm liquids to dry ingredients in mixer bowl and beat on medium speed of electric mixer 2 minutes, scraping bowl occasionally.

5. Add ½ cup of mixed flour and beat on high speed 2 minutes.

6. Add enough remaining mixed flour to form a soft dough.

7. Turn dough out onto a lightly floured board or pastry cloth. Cover with a clean towel and let rest 15 minutes.

8. Knead dough until smooth and elastic, about 10 to 15 minutes. (Dough will still be a little sticky.)

9. Place dough in greased bowl, turning to grease top. Cover with a clean towel and let rise in a warm place until doubled in bulk, about 1 hour.

10. Punch dough down; turn out onto lightly floured board. Divide in half and shape each half into a ball about 5 inches in diameter.

11. Place each ball in a greased 8-inch round cake pan. Cover with a clean towel and let rise in a warm place until doubled in bulk, about 1 hour.

12. Bake at 350°F for 45 to 50 minutes or until loaves sound hollow when gently tapped with knuckles.

13. Remove to cooling rack and brush tops with egg white that has been mixed with 1 teaspoon water.

Per slice: 130 cal. (16% from fat), 4 g protein, 26 g carbohydrate, 3 g fat, 0 mg cholesterol, 5 g fiber, 206 mg sodium.

Cranberry Kisel

Serves 4

2	cups fresh cranberries
1½	cups cold water, divided
⅔	cup sugar
3	tablespoons corn starch

1. Wash cranberries and put them in a medium saucepan with 1¼ cups of cold water.

2. Place cranberries over medium heat and bring to a boil. Reduce heat and simmer for 5 to 10 minutes, until cranberries pop.

3. Remove cranberries from heat and allow to cool for 10 minutes. Then puree the cranberries in a blender or food processor until smooth.

4. Return the puree to the saucepan. Stir in sugar.

5. Combine corn starch with ¼ cup cold water; stir until smooth.

6. Add corn starch mixture to cranberry puree. Place over medium heat. Bring mixture to a boil; reduce heat and simmer for 1 minute, stirring constantly. Remove from heat.

7. Pour kisel into a bowl or serving dishes and chill. Serve with whipped cream, if desired.

Per serving: 175 cal. (0% from fat), 0 g protein, 45 g carbohydrate, 0 g fat, 0 mg cholesterol, 2 g fiber, 1 mg sodium.

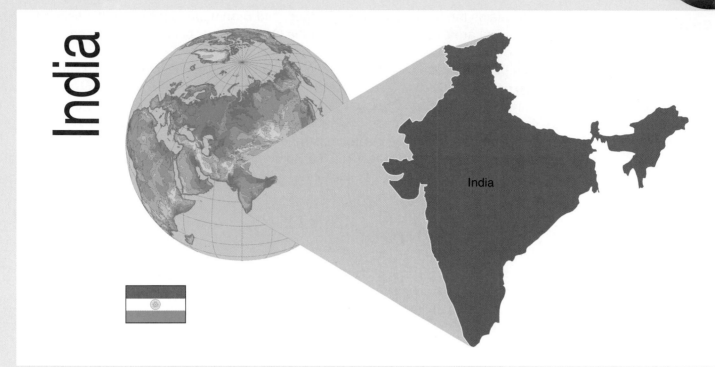

India

The local people call it Bharat. The English call it India. Both names belong to the seventh largest country in the world. It is a beautiful country with mountains, jungles, rich valleys, and miles of coastline.

Geography and Climate of India

India is located on a peninsula of southern Asia. The Himalayan Mountains form one of three distinct geographical areas in India. The mountains form a natural barrier from the rest of Asia. The hilly regions beneath the mountains are forests or grazing lands. See **33-4**.

Activity

Have students locate the Indus, Ganges, and Brahmaputra rivers on a map of India.

Enrich

Invite someone who has lived in or visited India to speak to your class about the country and its people. Have students prepare questions in advance.

Shutterstock
33-4 The hilly lands beneath India's Himalayan Mountains are suitable for grazing.

Discuss

Hindus are born into a caste and can never become a member of another caste. Ask students how this philosophy compares with the social climate in the United States.

FYI

In addition to food, cotton is an important agricultural product in India. The spinning and weaving of cotton is one of India's most important industries. A large percentage of the textile industry in India is a cottage industry. Millions of Indians work at home, weaving fine fabrics by hand. These fabrics are exported around the world.

Discuss

Ask students what nutrients might be lacking in the vegetarian diet of a Hindu. *(Vitamin B$_{12}$, calcium, riboflavin, and protein may be lacking, depending on food choices and degree of vegetarianism.)*

The plains formed by the Indus, Ganges, and Brahmaputra rivers are the second geographical area. The rich, deep soil of the Ganges River basin allows farmers to plant two crops each year.

The third geographical area lies to the south of the fertile river plains. It is a large plateau called the *Deccan*, which covers most of the peninsula. Agriculture is possible in level areas of the Deccan where rainfall or irrigation systems provide enough moisture.

India has a tropical climate. Cool weather lasts only from about December to March. The monsoon season lasts from June until the end of September. (*Monsoons* are storms with high winds and heavy rains.) The monsoon rains provide needed moisture for the dry earth. In just a short time, however, they can force rivers to flood their banks.

Indian Culture

The people of India belong to a number of races. Indians speak over 700 languages and dialects. This variety is the result of foreign invasions that lasted many centuries.

Religion plays an important role in the culture of India's people. Most Indians are Hindus. Muslims are the next largest group. Small groups of Christians, Sikhs, Jains, Buddhists, and Parsees also live in India.

One influence of religion on Indian culture is the observance of the **caste system**. This ancient social system, which evolved from Hinduism, divided people into groups, or castes. The four major castes were the *Brahmins* (priests), *Kshatriyas* (warriors), *Vaisyas* (farmers), and *Sudras* (laborers). Below the Sudras were the outcasts, or "untouchables." The untouchables were forced to live away from the rest of the people. They were even forbidden to use public roads or bridges.

Today, many of the old caste restrictions have been relaxed. It is now illegal to view anyone as untouchable. Caste divisions are observed mainly for choosing marriage partners.

Holidays in India

Another way religion influences Indian culture is in the celebration of holidays. Three popular festivals honor Hindu gods. The *Pongal Harvest Festival* is a time of thanksgiving for the winter harvest of rice, an important crop in India. It honors Surya, the sun god, for helping to ripen the rice. Hindu families offer a special rice pudding to Surya before eating it themselves. *Janmashtami* celebrates the birthday of one of the most popular Hindu gods, Krishna. The traditions of this holiday include going to the temple and bathing a statue of Krishna. The statue is bathed with clarified butter mixed with milk, sugar, and honey. The people in the temple then eat the sweet mixture with which they washed the statue. The *Ganesha Festival* is named for an elephant-headed god. Hindu people ask Ganesha to bring them success when they start new projects. During the festival, people place statues of Ganesha in their homes and present offerings of candy and fruit to it.

Indian Agriculture

Over 70 percent of India's people are farmers. Rice is India's major crop. Wheat, barley, millet, corn, and sorghum are grown in areas lacking the moisture needed for rice. Other important crops are chickpeas, beans, peas, and other legumes; sugarcane; and tea. Smaller quantities of coffee, coconuts, and spices are also grown.

Indians raise more cattle than any other type of livestock. Cows provide some milk, but Indians primarily use cattle as work animals. They also raise smaller numbers of goats, hogs, sheep, and water buffalo and export the hides and skins.

Indian Cuisine

Indian cuisine gets a high rating on the nutrition scale. Many Indian dishes are vegetarian. Even those dishes that include meat generally do so in small amounts. This plant-based diet, which centers on grains, vegetables, and legumes, is high in fiber, **33-5**. It includes a variety of seasonings, which researchers believe may offer health benefits. The Indian diet is also rich in vitamins, minerals, and many other nutrients. However, the fat content of some dishes can be high due to the liberal use of fat in cooking.

Geography and climate have influenced India's cuisine. Geographically, the major division occurs between the North and the South. Invading groups of people, especially the Mongols in the thirteenth century, influenced Northern India. The Mongols brought the meat-based cuisine of their central Asian home. This cuisine developed in the royal kitchens and became characterized by foods that are rich and heavily seasoned. Foreigners had less influence on Southern India. Its foods are hotter and not as subtle or refined as those of the North.

Climate has played a large part in the development of the two styles of Indian cooking. The heavy rainfall of the South allows large crops of rice, fruits, and vegetables to grow. In the drier North where wheat grows, bread sometimes replaces rice.

Shutterstock

33-5 Grains and legumes make many Indian dishes rich in fiber and other nutrients.

Culture and Social Studies

Influence of Religion on Indian Cuisine

Religion has been a third major influence on the development of Indian cuisine. Most Indian people are either Hindu or Muslim. Therefore, the dietary restrictions of these two religions have had the greatest impact.

Many Hindu taboos concern food. Hindus cannot eat beef because they consider the cow to be sacred.

Most Hindus are vegetarians. However, some Hindus, usually members of lower castes, eat mutton, poultry, goat, and fish. A member of the diner's caste must prepare these foods with cooking utensils belonging to that caste. In addition, food cannot be organically altered. (Artificial color and chemical processes used as preservatives are allowed.)

Although Muslims cannot eat pork, they do eat beef, mutton, lamb, fish, and poultry. These animal foods are more common in Northern India where most Indian Muslims live.

Indian Vegetable Dishes

Vegetable dishes are common in Indian cooking. This is especially true in the South where many people are vegetarians. There, *pulses* (legumes) are an important source of protein.

One way Indian cooks prepare pulses is to combine them with other vegetables in filling stews. Another way they serve pulses is by mashing or pureeing them with spices to make *dal*. Dal may be thinned and eaten as soup. It may also be poured over rice or served as a dipping sauce for bread.

Indian cooks prepare many vegetable dishes by frying the vegetables with spices. They shape mashed vegetables into balls, deep-fry them, and serve them with a sauce. They skin eggplant; flavor it with oil, pepper, and lemon; and grill it. *Raita*, a salad made of yogurt, vegetables, and seasonings, is a cool accompaniment to spicy dishes. *Rayata*, a potato salad flavored with yogurt, cucumber, tomatoes, cumin, and paprika, is served as a main dish.

Indian Main Dishes

Rice is a staple food throughout much of India. Rice often is served as a side dish. However, it sometimes is used in a variety of main dishes and desserts. Rice also is served as part of a group of dishes called curries.

Literally, **curry** is a variation of a word meaning sauce. It describes a type of stew. Curry can be prepared in many ways depending on the region. However, all curries are made with a mixture of spices called **masala**. One common curry is prepared by adding the masala to pickled fruit. This mixture is cooked with sugar and vinegar. The curry may be combined with vegetables, meat, poultry, or fish and accompanied by a variety of condiments, **33-6**.

India's many miles of coastline provide a variety of fish. Fish are dried, marinated, and smoked. One specialty is a marinated fish prepared by layering fillets of fish with spices, salt, and tamarind pulp. *Bombil*, a small, nearly transparent fish, is caught in large quantities. When dried, it can be stored for long periods. *Pomfret* often is stuffed with a mixture of spices. It is then wrapped in a banana leaf and steamed, baked, or fried.

Shellfish are also widely available in India. Shrimp and prawns are baked, grilled, or used in curries. Cooks often coat these crustaceans with a spicy batter and deep-fry them. Crabs and lobsters are shredded; mixed with coconut milk, eggs, and spices; and fried in butter.

Most Indian meat dishes are made with goat or mutton. Few Indians eat pork, and beef is both scarce and expensive. Indians prepare meat in many ways. Meat braised in yogurt, cream, or a mixture of the two is called *korma*. *Bhona* is meat that is first sautéed and then baked. Kebabs are made from mutton that has been spiced, minced, and grilled. *Koftas* are spicy meatballs.

The American Lamb Board
33-6 Many types of curry are found throughout India.

Discuss
Ask students what group of MyPlate pulses would be in. *(protein foods group)*

Discuss
Ask students what foods in the United States are prepared in different ways depending on the region. *(Chili is one example—beans may or may not be a standard ingredient.)*

Chicken dishes are also popular in parts of India. People in the North marinate chicken in a mixture of yogurt and spices and roast it on a spit. People in the South add chicken to a spicy, coconut-flavored curry.

Indians cook many dishes in oil or fat. **Ghee** (Indian clarified butter) is the preferred cooking fat. Ghee is prepared by simmering butter and then straining it to remove solids that could cause rancidity during storage.

Discuss

Ask students why the keeping quality of butter might be a concern to Indian cooks. *(Most Indian*

Learn About...

Indian Seasonings

The essence of Indian cooking lies in mastering the art of using spices. A key example is in preparing the masala used to make curry. The combination of spices in masala can vary. However, each ingredient must retain its identity without overpowering the other flavors.

The spicy dishes of the coastal South use *wet masalas*. These are prepared by mixing the spices with vinegar, coconut milk, or water. They must be used immediately. Northern Indians use dry masalas. *Dry masalas* contain no liquid and cooks can prepare them ahead and store them for a short time.

Saffron, fenugreek, cumin seed, coriander seed, turmeric, and fennel seed are basic to Indian cooking. Other seasonings essential to Indian cooking are garlic, onions, and hot chili peppers. Spices add color as well as flavor to Indian dishes. Saffron and turmeric give rice and potato dishes a bright yellow color. Red and green chilies add vivid color to curries.

Fresh herbs add flavor to Indian foods. They are also used to make sauces and *chutneys* (condiments containing fruits, onions, spices, and herbs). Coriander leaves, mint, and sweet basil are the most popular fresh herbs.

Shutterstock

Indian cooks use spices liberally to enhance the flavors of foods.

Indian Breads

Indians eat several kinds of *roti*, or bread. Most Indian breads are made from wheat, and they are unleavened and round. The most common is **chapatis**, a flat bread. Indian bakers make *naan* with yeast or baking powder and bake it in an Indian oven called a *tandoor*. When bakers make *paratha*, they roll and fold it several times so layers form when the bread bakes. Indians often stuff paratha with a meat or vegetable mixture.

Indian Sweets

Indians make many of their sweets from milk. Cooks simmer the milk into a thickened mass called *mawa*. They cook the mawa with sugar and add flavorings, such as almonds and coconut.

homes do not have refrigerators.)

Activity

Have students read the ingredient label on a container of curry powder. Ask them how they think this seasoning got its name.

Another group of confections is made from semolina, chickpea flour, wheat flour, or corn flour. *Halva*, one type of flour-based sweet, is made from semolina.

Indian Cooking Techniques

A number of cooking techniques characterize Indian cuisine. **Tandoori**, the simplest cooking technique, is used most often in Northern India. It requires a clay oven called a *tandoor*. Tandoori chicken, lamb on skewers, and naan are three traditional foods prepared by this method.

Korma is the second major cooking technique. Foods prepared in this fashion are braised, usually in yogurt. Lamb traditionally is prepared in this way.

Vindaloo is the third major technique. Foods prepared in this way have a hot, slightly sour flavor created by combining vinegar with spices.

Chasnidarth is the fourth major technique. This simply is an Indian version of the Chinese sweet and sour.

Indian Meals

During Indian meals, all dishes are served at one time. The serving dishes usually are placed on a thalis. A *thalis* is a large, round tray, which is often made of brass, stainless steel, or silver. (In some parts of India, a banana leaf replaces the thalis.)

Rice generally is placed in the center of the thalis. Chutneys, pickles, yogurt, and other condiments surround it. The main dishes are placed around the edges of the tray. Diners help themselves to the food by using their fingers.

In middle-class Indian homes, the main meal of the day usually includes a meat or fish dish. (Vegetarian families would omit this dish.) Several vegetable dishes, rice, or lentils and bread are also included. Occasionally, appetizers may be served. One popular appetizer is *samosas*, which are small pastries stuffed with vegetables, fish, or meat. If sweets are served, Indians eat them with the meal rather than afterward. See **33-7**.

Family etiquette requires that diners wash their hands and rinse their mouths following a meal. They frequently follow this ritual with paan. *Paan* is a betel leaf spread with lime paste and wrapped around chopped betel nuts. As people chew it, it acts as a mouth freshener and digestive aid.

Courtesy of the Idaho Potato Commission

33-7 Hariyali tikki is an Indian appetizer made with green vegetables that are held together with potatoes.

Indian Menu

Samosas
(Savory Stuffed Pastries)

Chatni
(Mixed Fruit Chutney)

Raita
(Yogurt with Vegetables)

Dal
(Lentil Puree)

Chapatis
(Unleavened Bread)

Pongal Rice
(Rice Pudding)

Tea

Ghee
(Clarified Butter)

Makes about 3/4 cup

½   pound sweet butter

1. In a heavy saucepan, melt butter over very low heat.
2. When butter has melted, increase heat just enough to bring it to a boil.
3. Stir once and reduce the heat to very low. Simmer the butter, uncovered, for 50 minutes.
4. Line a strainer with 3 or 4 thicknesses of cheesecloth.
5. Carefully strain the clear liquid ghee through the cheesecloth. Make sure none of the solids in the bottom of the pan go through the cheesecloth.
6. Pour the ghee into a jar, cover, and store in a cool place.

Per tablespoon: 100 cal. (100% from fat), 0 g protein, 0 g carbohydrate, 11 g fat, 31 mg cholesterol, 0 g fiber, 2 mg sodium.

Garam Masala
(Indian Spice Mixture)

24   large cardamom seeds
2   ounces coriander seeds
2   ounces black peppercorns
1½   ounces caraway seeds
½   ounce whole cloves
½   ounce ground cinnamon

1. Remove skin from the cardamom seeds.
2. Grind cardamom seeds, coriander seeds, peppercorns, caraway seeds, and cloves until fine.
3. Add cinnamon and mix thoroughly.
4. Seal in airtight container.

Samosas
(Savory Stuffed Pastries)

Makes about 30

Pastry:
1½   cups all-purpose flour
1   tablespoon vegetable oil
¾   teaspoon salt
½   cup warm water

1. In medium mixer bowl, blend flour, oil, salt, and water until soft dough forms.
2. Turn dough out onto lightly floured board. Knead until dough is smooth and elastic, about 10 minutes.
3. Cover and set aside while preparing filling.

Filling:
1   tablespoon ghee
1   clove garlic, chopped
1   teaspoon chopped ginger root
1   medium onion, chopped
1½   cups mashed potatoes
½   cup cooked peas
1   teaspoon garam masala
1   tablespoon fresh coriander or mint
    vegetable oil for frying

1. In a large skillet, heat ghee over medium heat. Add garlic, ginger root, and onion. Sauté until vegetables are tender.
2. Remove from heat. Stir in mashed potatoes and peas. Season with garam masala and coriander or mint.
3. Using fingers, shape tablespoons of pastry dough into small balls. Roll each ball into a flat circle about 6 inches in diameter.
4. Cut each circle in half. Place 1 teaspoon of filling on one side of each half circle.
5. Moisten the edge of the pastry with water.

Fold dough over to form a triangle and press edges together to seal.

6. In a deep saucepan, heat vegetable oil to 375°F.

7. Fry samosas a few at a time until golden brown.

8. Drain on absorbent paper. Serve immediately.

Per samosa: 50 cal. (36% from fat), 1 g protein, 7 g carbohydrate, 2 g fat, 1 mg cholesterol, 1 g fiber, 90 mg sodium.

Chatni
(Mixed Fruit Chutney)

Serves 8

½	pound cooking plums
½	pound cooking apples
½	pound pears or apricots
1	clove garlic
¼	ounce fresh ginger root
2	teaspoons garam masala
1	teaspoon caraway seeds
1	teaspoon salt
2	tablespoons raisins
1½	teaspoons chili powder
½	cup brown sugar
1	cup vinegar

1. Peel fruit, core or pit, and cut into small pieces.

2. Mince garlic and ginger root.

3. Put fruit, garlic, and ginger in large saucepan.

4. Add garam masala, caraway seeds, salt, raisins, and chili powder. Bring mixture to a boil and simmer over moderate heat for 35 minutes, stirring frequently.

5. Remove from heat, stir in sugar and vinegar, and cool. Serve cold as an accompaniment.

Per serving: 106 cal. (4% from fat), 1 g protein, 29 g carbohydrate, 1 g fat, 0 mg cholesterol, 2 g fiber, 278 mg sodium.

Raita
(Yogurt with Vegetables)

Serves 6 to 8

3	medium cucumbers
3	tablespoons chopped onions
1	teaspoon salt
3	medium firm ripe tomatoes
3	tablespoons chopped coriander
3	cups plain nonfat yogurt
1	tablespoon cumin

1. With a small sharp knife, peel cucumbers. Slice them lengthwise into halves. Scoop out the seeds. Make lengthwise slices about ⅛ inch thick. Then cut slices crosswise into ½-inch pieces.

2. In medium mixer bowl, combine cucumbers, onions, and salt and mix thoroughly. Let rest at room temperature for five minutes.

3. Squeeze cucumbers and onions gently to remove the excess liquid and transfer to a clean bowl.

4. Add the tomato and coriander and toss together thoroughly.

5. Combine the yogurt and cumin. Pour over the vegetables.

6. Refrigerate until ready to serve.

Per serving: 93 cal. (10% from fat), 7 g protein, 14 g carbohydrate, 1 g fat, 2 mg cholesterol, 1 g fiber, 386 mg sodium.

Dal
(Lentil Puree)

Serves 6

1½	cups dried lentils
3	cups water
2	tablespoons ghee or butter
3	cloves garlic, crushed
½	teaspoon ground ginger
1	teaspoon coriander seeds
¾	teaspoon salt
½	teaspoon cayenne pepper

1. Wash and sort lentils.

2. Place lentils and water in a large saucepan. Bring to a boil over medium-high heat.

3. Reduce heat, cover, and simmer until lentils are very tender, about 20 minutes.

4. In large skillet, heat ghee or melt butter.

5. Add the garlic, ginger, and coriander seeds. Stir over medium heat for about 3 minutes.

6. Add lentils and any remaining cooking water to skillet. Mash lentils until smooth as you stir them into the seasonings. Add water as needed to reach desired consistency for dipping.

7. Add salt and cayenne pepper.

8. Serve hot with chapatis for dipping.

Per serving: 152 cal. (24% from fat), 9 g protein, 21 g carbohydrate, 4 g fat, 10 mg cholesterol, 8 g fiber, 294 mg sodium.

Chapatis
(Unleavened Bread)

Makes 8

2   cups whole-wheat flour
½   teaspoon salt
4   tablespoons margarine
¾   cup water
1   tablespoon ghee

1. Mix flour and salt together in mixing bowl.
2. With pastry blender, two knives, or fingers, cut margarine into dry ingredients until particles are the size of small peas.
3. Add ¼ cup water all at once. Mix with fingers, gradually adding enough additional water to form a soft dough.
4. Turn dough out onto a lightly floured board or pastry cloth. Knead dough until smooth and elastic, about 10 minutes.
5. Place dough in bowl, cover and let stand at room temperature 30 minutes.
6. Turn dough out onto floured surface. Divide into 8 pieces. Roll each piece into a thin circle about 5 inches in diameter.
7. Meanwhile, heat a heavy skillet over moderate heat.
8. Put chapatis, one at a time, in skillet. When small blisters appear on surface, turn and cook other side until golden.
9. Remove from skillet. Brush with ghee and keep warm in 200°F oven until all chapatis are cooked. Serve warm.

Per piece: 163 cal. (40% from fat), 4 g protein, 21 g carbohydrate, 8 g fat, 4 mg cholesterol, 6 g fiber, 201 mg sodium.

Pongal Rice
(Rice Pudding)

Serves 6 to 8

½   cup uncooked rice
1   cup water
6   cups fat-free milk
¾   cup sugar
¼   teaspoon cardamom
¼   teaspoon cinnamon
¼   cup raisins
¼   cup slivered, blanched almonds

1. Place rice and water in a medium saucepan. Bring to a boil over high heat.
2. Reduce heat, cover, and simmer for 5 minutes. Drain.
3. In a large, heavy saucepan, heat milk over medium heat until steaming, but not boiling.
4. Add rice. Reduce heat to low and simmer, stirring frequently, for 45 minutes.
5. Stir in sugar and continue simmering for 15 more minutes, until pudding is thick.
6. Remove pudding from heat. Stir in cardamom, cinnamon, raisins, and almonds.
7. Pour pudding into serving dishes. Chill well before serving.

Per serving: 291 cal. (12% from fat), 12 g protein, 52 g carbohydrate, 4 g fat, 5 mg cholesterol, 1 g fiber, 147 mg sodium.

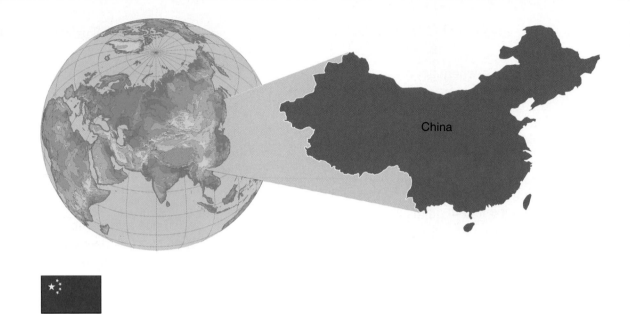

China

China

FYI

Although the geographical region that defines western China equals about 50 percent of China's total area, only about 10 percent of China's population lives there.

Online Resource

Have students navigate the China National Tourist Office website to find tourism statistics showing how many tourists from the United States have visited China in recent years. What features make China most attractive as a tourist destination?

The People's Republic of China (commonly called China) is the home of one of the oldest civilizations. In modern history, China has gone through many changes. Some of these changes have affected the nation's diet. However, the roots of Chinese cuisine date back centuries.

Geography and Climate of China

China is the third largest country in the world. It occupies nearly one-fourth of Asia. Geographical features have kept China isolated for much of its history.

The Pacific Ocean and the South China Sea form China's coastlines. Western China is mountainous. The Himalayan and Tien Shan Mountains are most familiar to the Western world. Much of western and southwestern China is barren. The mountains are too high and rugged, and the valleys are too cold and dry for food production.

Eastern China is more suitable for human life. The mountains and hills are lower, and the rolling plains are fairly level. The wide valleys formed by China's great rivers have rich soil. Historically, most of China's people have crowded within this geographic area.

Because China's borders extend so far north and south, there are extremes in climate. In China's northernmost regions, the ground stays frozen two-thirds of the year. Subarctic conditions keep temperatures below zero for months at a time, **33-8**. Rainfall is scarce. In the southernmost provinces, however, the climate is subtropical with ample rainfall.

The monsoons that come off the Pacific Ocean bring dust storms to the North. They also bring undependable rainfall to much of the eastern third of the country. Both drought and flooding are common.

Chinese Culture

China has a population larger than any other nation. Many notable achievements have taken place in China throughout the ages. The Chinese are credited with numerous inventions, including paper, gunpowder, and the magnetic compass. They built the Great Wall, which stretches about 4,000 miles through northern China. The Chinese also created beautiful works of art and made important contributions in literature.

The People's Republic of China was established in 1949 under Communist rule. In pre-Communist days, most Chinese were Buddhists, Taoists, or Confucianists. Smaller groups of Chinese Christians and Muslims lived in scattered groups. Today, most people do not openly practice religion in China.

Shutterstock

33-8 Frigid temperatures dominate the climate for much of the year in China's northern regions.

Chinese Holidays

The most widely celebrated festival in China is the *Spring Festival*, which recognizes the new year. The Chinese zodiac follows a 12-year cycle, with each year being named for a different animal. Each new year is welcomed with a special dinner of festive foods, including candied fruits and dumplings.

The *Dragon Boat Festival* falls in midsummer. People used to throw rice cakes into the river to appease a mythical dragon. Now they recognize this occasion by holding boat races and eating rice cakes that have been wrapped in bamboo leaves.

The *Moon Festival* comes in midautumn. The Chinese celebrate this festival by eating moon cakes, which are pastries filled with bean paste or lotus seeds. Adults sit outside and enjoy the full moon while children parade through the streets with lanterns.

FYI
More than a third of all the hogs in the world live in China. Hogs provide China's main source of meat. They also provide organic fertilizer, which Chinese farmers use extensively.

Chinese Agriculture

Today, many of China's people are farmers, just as they were thousands of years ago. Some small family farms still exist. There, the farming methods are primitive. Farmers do nearly all the work by hand or with the help of a single water buffalo or donkey. The government controls other farms and operates them as communes.

China's chief agricultural product is rice. Other important products include wheat, corn, millet, sorghum, oats, rye, barley, soybeans, tea, and sugarcane. Chinese celery, turnips, radishes, and eggplant are the most important vegetable crops. The Chinese also grow pears, grapes, oranges, apricots, kumquats, lychee nuts, and figs where weather permits.

The Chinese raise few beef or dairy cattle. Instead, they raise pigs, chickens, ducks, geese, and other small animals that can eat scraps. A few sheep and goats graze in mountainous and grassy areas. China's waters provide an abundance of fish.

Enrich
Have students visit a supermarket to see how many of the Chinese ingredients described in the text they can find. Ask students to identify whether items are available fresh, canned, frozen, or dried.

Chinese Cuisine

The Chinese enjoy a nutritious cuisine. Their meals include large amounts of rice and vegetables but only small amounts of meat. They stir-fry, steam, or simmer many of their dishes. This combination of healthful ingredients and light cooking methods makes Chinese cuisine fairly low in fat. However, it is high in vitamins, minerals, and fiber. One nutritional drawback of the Chinese diet is the high sodium level that results from liberal use of soy sauce.

Besides nourishing the body, Chinese cuisine delights the senses. An old Chinese proverb describes a well-prepared dish as one that smells appealing as it is brought to the table. The dish must stimulate the appetite by its harmonious color combinations. The food must taste delicious and sound pleasing as it is being chewed. Today, the best Chinese dishes still live up to these high standards.

Learn About...

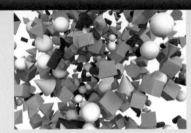

Chinese Ingredients

In the past, many Chinese ingredients were difficult to obtain in the United States. Today, many large cities have specialty shops that stock Chinese foods. Chinese items can also be found in international sections of most supermarkets.

The ingredients described below often appear in Chinese recipes. Besides these ingredients, Chinese cooks use many seasonings. Important seasonings include ginger root, scallions, garlic, sugar, bean paste, and fermented black bean. Monosodium glutamate (MSG), hot pepper, sesame seed oil, star anise, Chinese peppercorns, and five spice powder are also common.

Basic Ingredients Used in Chinese Cooking

bamboo shoots. Cream-colored vegetable that adds a crisp, chewy texture to foods.

bean curd. Gelatinous, cream-colored cake made from soybeans that is a major source of protein in the Chinese diet.

bean sprouts. Sprouts of mung beans.

bean threads (cellophane noodles). Thin, smooth, and translucent noodles.

black mushrooms. Very dark mushrooms that are sold dried.

Chinese cabbage (bok choy). Type of cabbage with a white celerylike stalk topped with green leaves that is used for cooking and stewing.

Chinese pea pods. Tender, crisp, green, pod-shaped vegetable.

golden needles. Parts of the tiger lily plant that look like brown shriveled stems.

hoisin sauce. Dark, thick sauce made from beans, salt, spices, and sugar that is used in cooking and at the table.

oyster sauce. Dark brown sauce that is made from oysters and seasonings and is used with dark-colored dishes and as a dipping sauce.

soy sauce. Brown sauce made from soybeans, wheat, flour, salt, and water.

water chestnuts. Round, cream-colored vegetables that can be purchased canned or fresh.

winter melon. Large melon with pale green skin and white flesh that is cooked with vegetables and meat or added to soup.

wood ears. Type of brown fungus that grows on trees.

Some of these Chinese ingredients are available in most supermarkets. Others can be found at Asian specialty stores.

Chinese Cooking Utensils

Of all Chinese cooking utensils, the wok is the most versatile. A **wok** looks like a metal bowl with sloping sides. Some woks have covers. A metal ring makes it possible to use a wok on a gas or electric range.

Woks are ideal for stir-frying because they conduct heat evenly and rapidly. (A heavy, smooth skillet can also be used for this type of cooking.) There are few foods that cannot be cooked in a wok. Other cooking methods, such as deep-frying, can be done in a wok, too.

A second piece of Chinese cooking equipment is the *steamer*. A steamer looks like a round, shallow basket with openings. Steamers often are sold in sets of five so several foods can steam at the same time. Most Chinese steamers are made from bamboo. In the United States, aluminum steamers are more common.

A third cooking tool is the *cleaver*. Because the Chinese eat with chopsticks, cooks must cut all the ingredients into pieces that diners can handle easily. Small pieces of food also cook more evenly and rapidly. Chinese cooks use cleavers to perform all cutting tasks as well as crushing and pounding tasks. They use the wide, flat sides of cleaver blades to scoop and transfer food.

A number of other tools will come in handy when preparing Chinese foods. A *curved spatula* that fits the shape of the pan is ideal for stirring and turning foods in the wok. *Long chopsticks* are useful for loosening and mixing food. A *wire-mesh strainer* helps lift deep-fried foods out of hot oil. A *ladle* can be used to serve foods and spoon liquids over ingredients in a wok. A *bamboo brush* is helpful for cleaning the wok. See **33-9**.

Chinese Cooking Methods

Because most Chinese dishes cook so quickly, cooks must assemble all the ingredients in advance. In fact, the Chinese spend more time preparing food to be cooked than they spend cooking.

Much of the preparation time involves slicing, chopping, shredding, dicing, and mincing vegetables and meats. Many ingredients can be prepared hours or even days in advance and refrigerated until needed.

Once the ingredients are prepared, the Chinese may use one of four main cooking methods: stir-frying, steaming, deep-frying, or simmering. Less often, they might choose roasting as the cooking method.

Stir-Frying

Stir-frying is the most common Chinese cooking method. Meat, poultry, fish, and vegetables can be stir-fried. All ingredients must be cut into uniform pieces so they will cook evenly.

Enrich

Invite a cook from a Chinese restaurant to demonstrate how to prepare ingredients for Chinese dishes using Chinese cooking utensils.

Enrich

Have students visit the culinary department of a department store to see which of the Chinese cooking utensils described in the text are available.

curved spatula

ladle

wire-mesh strainer

long chopsticks

bamboo brush

33-9 These Chinese utensils are especially helpful when preparing foods in a wok.

To stir-fry foods, heat a small amount of oil in a wok. When the oil becomes hot, add the ingredients that need the longest cooking time. Then add the ingredients that cook more quickly. Stir continuously throughout the cooking period. When the vegetables are crisp-tender, the dish is ready to serve. (Sometimes, a little stock or water and seasonings might be added to form a sauce.)

Stir-fried foods cook rapidly, so they must be watched carefully. Stir-fried foods retain their color, texture, flavor, and nutrients. They must be served immediately, however, or they will lose their texture and flavor. Never overfill a wok. If more than a few people are being served, several batches of the same dish will need to be prepared.

Steaming

Steaming is the second most common cooking method in China. Because most Chinese do not have ovens, steaming replaces baking. Meats, poultry, dumplings, bread, and rice can be steamed. The kettle used for steaming must be large enough to allow the steam to circulate freely around the food. (The water never should touch the food.) Like stir-frying, steaming is economical. Because several dishes can be steamed at the same time, energy is saved.

Deep-Frying

Deep-frying seals in juices and gives foods a crisp coating. Meat, poultry, egg rolls, and wontons are often deep-fried.

Foods to be deep-fried are first cut into cubes. The cubes can be coated with cornstarch or dipped in a flour and egg batter. (Sometimes the cubes might be marinated before being coated.) Plunge the coated food into hot fat a few pieces at a time. Drain all deep-fried foods on absorbent paper.

Simmering

Chinese soups and large pieces of meat may be prepared by *simmering*. In this method of cooking, the ingredients are cooked in simmering liquid over low heat. If a clear liquid, such as chicken broth, is used this method is called *clear-simmering*.

Roasting

The Chinese occasionally use several other cooking methods. Of these methods, *roasting* is most popular. The Chinese sometimes roast pork and poultry. They first rub the meat or bird with oil and/or marinate it. A quick searing over an open flame makes the skin crisp. Then they place the meat or bird on a rack or hang it on a hook to roast slowly. Of all roasted dishes, *Peking duck* is the best known. The Chinese roll slices of the crisp duck skin and tender flesh inside thin pancakes with scallions and hoisin sauce. (*Hoisin sauce* is a soy-based barbecue-type sauce.)

Traditional Chinese Foods

From basic ingredients and cooking methods, the Chinese prepare a variety of traditional foods.

Chinese Grain Products

For centuries, rice has been the backbone of the southern Chinese diet. This is mainly because rice is both inexpensive and filling, **33-10**.

The Chinese use glutinous, short-grain rice to make rice flour and translucent rice noodles. They use rice flour to make pastries and dumplings. They serve long-grain rice as a side dish and use it to make the main dish called *fried rice*. For this dish, Chinese cooks mix rice with meat, poultry, or fish; eggs; vegetables; and seasonings.

The Chinese prepare most rice by steaming. When ready to serve, the rice should be fluffy with firm, distinct grains.

In some parts of China, noodles or flat pancakes made from wheat flour are used in place of rice. One type of noodle is called *lo mein*. It is made from flour and eggs and resembles spaghetti.

The Chinese also use wheat flour to make the skins or wrappers for *wontons* (dumplings) and *egg rolls*. The dough for both contains wheat flour and eggs. The Chinese usually fill egg rolls and wontons with a mixture of minced vegetables and meat, poultry, or shellfish. They prepare wontons by steaming, deep-frying, or boiling them in soups. Egg rolls usually are deep-fried.

Hamilton Beach Brands, Inc.

33-10 Some people in China eat rice every day.

Chinese Vegetables

Vegetables are used to a greater extent than meat in the Chinese diet. The Chinese grow many varieties of vegetables. These include Chinese cabbage, broccoli, spinach, pea pods, radishes, mushrooms, and cauliflower. The Chinese eat vegetables alone, in salads, and in soups. They also use vegetables to stretch small amounts of meat, fish, and poultry. Vegetables help make Chinese cooking economical and nutritious.

Chinese Main Dishes

Although the Chinese eat chicken and duck, they eat little beef. This is partly because beef is scarce and not very good. Also, some religions forbid the eating of beef. Religions may forbid the eating of pork as well. *Sweet and sour pork* is a popular dish among those allowed to eat pork. Sweet and sour pork is a mixture of deep-fried pork cubes, pineapple, and vegetables in a sweet-sour sauce.

Fish are more important to the Chinese diet than meat. Many kinds of fresh- and saltwater fish and shellfish are available. The Chinese preserve some fish by drying. This allows them to transport the fish inland or store it for times of need.

The Chinese also like eggs, which they consider a sign of good luck. The Chinese eat both chicken eggs and duck eggs, but they prefer chicken eggs. They use eggs in soups, such as egg drop soup. (*Egg drop soup* is seasoned chicken broth containing beaten eggs.) They also use eggs in main dishes, such as fried rice and egg foo yung. (*Egg foo yung* is the Chinese version of an omelet.) The Chinese scramble, steam, and smoke eggs, too.

Discuss

Ask students what nutrients rice contributes to the diet. *(complex carbohydrates, iron, thiamin, and niacin)*

For Example…

Other vegetables grown widely in China include sweet potatoes, corn, potatoes, carrots, and tomatoes.

FYI

Fish farming is an important Chinese industry. Pond-raised fish serve as a source of fertilizer as well as a source of food.

Chinese Soups

Soups are popular throughout China. Some soups, such as *Chinese noodle soup*, are very light. Others, such as velvet-corn soup, are heavier. The Chinese use exotic ingredients to make *shark fin soup* and *bird nest soup*.

Most Chinese soups are accompaniments rather than filling main dishes. Soup is the only dish the Chinese eat without chopsticks. They use spoons instead.

Chinese Desserts

Chinese cooks use few dairy products. Chinese recipes rarely call for milk, cheese, butter, or cream. However, some Chinese people now eat ice cream, and they sometimes serve Peking dust at banquets. *Peking dust* is a dessert made of whipped cream covered with chestnut puree and garnished with nuts.

Sweet desserts are much less common in China than in other Asian countries. The Chinese reserve sweet desserts for banquets. Then they serve the desserts in the middle of the meal rather than at the end. Fresh or preserved fruits, almond cookies, almond float, and eight treasure rice pudding are popular desserts. (*Almond float* is cubes of almond-flavored gelatin garnished with fruit. *Eight treasure rice pudding* is a molded rice pudding made with candied or dried fruits.)

Culture and Social Studies

Chinese Tea

Tea is China's national drink. The Chinese serve black teas, oolong teas, and green teas. (In China, black tea is called *red tea* because black is considered to be an unlucky color.) Some teas are scented with fragrant blossoms. The Chinese never add cream, lemon, or sugar to their tea. They usually serve tea at the end of meals. They also offer tea to arriving and departing guests as a sign of hospitality.

Hamilton Beach Brands, Inc

The Chinese enjoy a variety of teas.

Chinese Meals

The Chinese eat three meals a day. Breakfast may be just a bowl of **congee** (a thick porridge made from rice or barley), rice, or boiled noodles. More well-to-do families often serve the congee with several salty side dishes. They may also serve hot sesame muffins, Chinese doughnuts, or pastries bought from a nearby street vendor.

Lunch and dinner are similar. At both meals, all the dishes are served at once. The soup is placed in the center of the table. Four other dishes of pork, chicken, or fish, with or without vegetables, and one vegetable dish surround the soup. Rice always accompanies the main dishes.

Although the Chinese eat few sweets, they do enjoy snacks. *Dim sum* (steamed dumplings) are delicate pastries filled with meat, fish, vegetables, or occasionally a sweet fruit. Most are steamed, but a few are deep-fried.

At a Chinese table, each person's cover is set with a rice bowl, soup spoon, and shallow soup bowl. A shallow sauce dish, a larger dish for entrees, and a tea cup are also placed at each cover. The Chinese use **chopsticks** as their eating utensils for all dishes except soup and finger foods.

Reflect

Ask students whether they would find salty foods appealing at breakfast. Have them explain why or why not.

Chinese Menu

Ch'un-Chuan
(Egg Rolls)

Tan-Hau-T'ang
(Egg Drop Soup)

T'ien-Suan-Ku-Lao-Jou
(Sweet and Sour Pork)

Chao-Hsueh-Tou
(Stir-Fried Snow Peas with Chinese Mushrooms and Bamboo Shoots)

Pai-Fan
(Steamed Rice)

Preserved Kumquats

Hsing-Jen-Ping
(Almond Cookies)

Ch'a
(Tea)

Ch'un-Chuan
(Egg Rolls)

Makes 16 to 18 egg rolls

½   pound ground pork
1½   teaspoons cornstarch
    dash pepper
1   tablespoon light brown sugar
1   tablespoon low-sodium soy sauce
3   tablespoons vegetable oil
2   cups shredded cabbage
1   cup finely chopped celery
3   cups raw bean sprouts, washed and drained
¼   cup sliced mushrooms
1   tablespoon cornstarch
2   tablespoons cold water
1   1-pound package commercial egg roll wrappers
3   cups oil for frying

1. In medium mixing bowl, combine pork, cornstarch, pepper, brown sugar, and soy sauce. Let stand while heating oil.
2. Heat 1 tablespoon oil in wok or large skillet over high heat for 30 seconds.
3. Swirl oil over bottom and sides of wok and heat another 30 seconds. (If oil begins to smoke, reduce heat to moderate.)
4. Add pork and fry 2 minutes stirring constantly. (Meat should lose its reddish color.) Put meat in bowl and set aside.
5. Add the remaining 2 tablespoons of oil to the wok.
6. Add cabbage, celery, and bean sprouts, stir-fry 3 minutes.
7. Add mushrooms, stir-fry another 2 minutes.
8. Return pork to wok. Continue cooking and stirring over moderate heat until liquid comes to a boil.
9. Remove meat and vegetables. Remove all but 3 tablespoons of the cooking liquid from the wok.

10. Mix cornstarch with cold water. Add to cooking liquid and stir until slightly thickened.

11. Return meat and vegetables to wok to glaze with sauce and then transfer entire contents of wok to shallow pan. Cover and refrigerate until cool enough to handle, about 20 minutes.

12. Place one egg roll wrapper diagonally on the surface in front of you.

13. Use fingers to shape about ¼ cup of cooled filling into a cylinder about 4 inches long. Place the cylinder parallel to the edge of your work surface in the center of the wrapper.

14. Fold the corner of the wrapper closest to you over the filling. Fold the two side corners toward the center like an envelope. Brush a little water on the top corner. Then roll the egg roll toward the top corner and seal well.

15. Place filled egg rolls on a baking sheet and cover with a slightly damp towel.

16. Place 3 cups of oil in a wok or deep saucepan. Heat oil to 375°F.

17. Fry egg rolls, 5 at a time, until crisp and golden brown, about 3 or 4 minutes.

18. Place cooked egg rolls on a plate lined with paper towels to drain while you finish frying. Serve immediately or keep warm for a short time in a 225°F oven.

Per egg roll: 124 cal. (31% from fat), 6 g protein, 16 g carbohydrate, 4 g fat, 27 mg cholesterol, 1 g fiber, 132 mg sodium.

Tan-Hau-T'ang
(Egg Drop Soup)

Serves 5 to 6

5	cups low-fat chicken broth
¾	cup minced, cooked chicken
1	tablespoon cornstarch
3	tablespoons cold water
2	eggs, lightly beaten
2	scallions, finely chopped

1. In a large saucepan, bring chicken broth to a boil.

2. Reduce heat to moderate and add chicken. Simmer 5 minutes.

3. Mix cornstarch with cold water. Add to soup, stirring until soup thickens and becomes clear.

4. Slowly pour in eggs and stir once, gently. Turn off the heat.

5. Transfer soup to a heated tureen and garnish with chopped scallions.

Per serving: 60 cal. (45% from fat), 6 g protein, 3 g carbohydrate, 3 g fat, 87 mg cholesterol, 0 g fiber, 188 mg sodium.

T'ien-Suan-Ku-Lao-Jou
(Sweet and Sour Pork)

Serves 5 to 6

2	eggs, lightly beaten
1	teaspoon low-sodium soy sauce
½	cup cornstarch
½	cup flour
½	cup low-fat chicken broth
1	pound lean pork, trimmed and cut into 1-inch cubes
3	cups vegetable oil for frying

Sauce:

2	tablespoons vegetable oil
3	green onions, finely chopped
3	medium green peppers, cleaned, seeded, and cut into strips
2	cups canned pineapple chunks, drained (reserve juice)
3	tablespoons brown sugar
½	teaspoon ground ginger
¾	cup reserved pineapple juice
4½	tablespoons cider vinegar
1½	tablespoons red wine vinegar
3	tablespoons reduced-sodium soy sauce
1½	tablespoons cornstarch dissolved in
2	tablespoons cold water

1. In large bowl, prepare coating batter by combining eggs, 1 teaspoon soy sauce, ½ cup cornstarch, flour, and chicken broth. Set aside.

2. Prepare and assemble all other ingredients.

3. Just before cooking, add pork cubes to coating batter. With fork or chopsticks, stir to coat cubes evenly.

4. Preheat oven to 250°F.

5. Put 3 cups oil into wok or very large skillet. Over high heat, heat oil to 375°F.

6. Add pork cubes, a few at a time, fry until crisp and golden.

7. Remove pork to paper towel-lined baking pan to drain. Then, put pork in baking dish and keep warm in oven.

8. Pour remaining oil from wok or skillet. Add 2 tablespoons fresh oil and heat over high heat for 30 seconds.

9. Add green onions and green peppers to wok or skillet. Stir-fry about 2 to 3 minutes.

10. Add pineapple and stir-fry an additional minute.

11. Add brown sugar, ginger, pineapple juice, cider vinegar, red wine vinegar, and soy sauce. Cook until bubbly.

12. Add dissolved cornstarch to sauce. Cook, stirring constantly, until sauce thickens and becomes clear.
13. Pour sauce over fried pork cubes and serve immediately.

Per serving: 494 cal. (42% from fat), 18 g protein, 60 g carbohydrate, 23 g fat, 121 mg cholesterol, 2 g fiber, 477 mg sodium.

Chao-Hsueh-Tou
(Stir-Fried Snow Peas with Chinese Mushrooms and Bamboo Shoots)

Serves 6

⅔ cup dried Chinese mushrooms
1½ pounds fresh snow peas (or thoroughly defrosted frozen snow peas)
2 tablespoons vegetable oil
1 cup canned bamboo shoots, rinsed and sliced thinly
2 teaspoons sugar
1½ tablespoons low-sodium soy sauce

1. In a small bowl, combine mushrooms with ½ cup boiling water. Let soak 15 minutes.
2. Drain, squeezing excess water from mushrooms with fingers. (Reserve soaking liquid.)
3. Cut off stems and cut mushrooms into quarters.
4. Remove tips from fresh snow peas and string from pods.
5. In wok or heavy skillet, heat the oil over high heat.
6. Add mushrooms and bamboo shoots and stir-fry for 2 minutes.
7. Add snow peas, sugar, 2 tablespoons of the reserved soaking liquid, and soy sauce. Cook over high heat, stirring constantly, until water evaporates, about 2 to 3 minutes.
8. Transfer contents of wok to a serving dish and serve immediately.

Per serving: 92 cal. (49% from fat), 3 g protein, 8 g carbohydrate, 5 g fat, 0 mg cholesterol, 2 g fiber, 262 mg sodium.

Pai-Fan
(Steamed Rice)

Serves 6

1 cup uncooked long grain rice
2 cups cold water

1. Put rice and cold water in heavy saucepan and bring to a boil. Stir once or twice.
2. Cover pan, reduce heat to low and simmer 15 minutes.
3. Remove from heat and let rest 5 minutes. (Do not uncover pan.)
4. Remove cover and fluff rice with chopsticks or a fork. Serve immediately.

Per serving: 112 cal. (1% from fat), 2 g protein, 25 g carbohydrate, 0 g fat, 0 mg cholesterol, 1 g fiber, 2 mg sodium.

Hsing-Jen-Ping
(Almond Cookies)

Makes 5 dozen cookies

4 cups all-purpose flour
1½ cups sugar
½ teaspoon baking powder
1 teaspoon salt
1 cup shortening
1 egg, beaten
1 tablespoon water
1 teaspoon almond extract
5 dozen white blanched whole almonds
1 egg yolk
2 tablespoons fat-free milk

1. Preheat oven to 375°F.
2. In large mixing bowl, combine flour, sugar, baking powder, and salt.
3. With pastry blender or two knives, cut in shortening until particles are the size of small peas.
4. In small bowl, combine egg, water, and almond extract.
5. Add egg mixture to flour mixture all at once. Mix well.
6. Knead dough in the bowl for 1 minute.
7. Roll dough into small balls. Place 2 inches apart on ungreased baking sheets.
8. Flatten dough balls to about ⅜-inch thickness. Top each cookie with a blanched almond and brush with egg glaze made by combining the egg yolk with milk.
9. Bake cookies until lightly browned, about 12 minutes.

Per cookie: 93 cal. (46% from fat), 1 g protein, 11 g carbohydrate, 5 g fat, 9 mg cholesterol, 1 g fiber, 40 mg sodium.

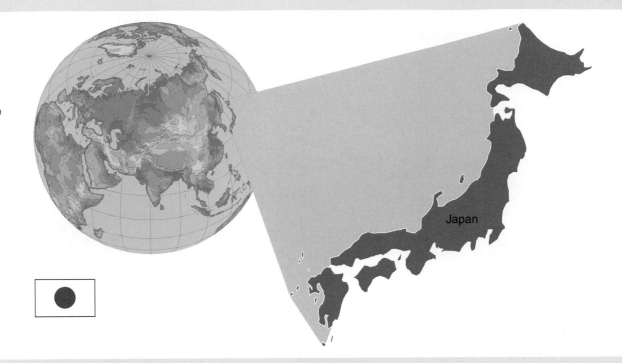

Japan

Japan has successfully adapted to Western ways without losing its sense of identity. Japan's traditional values are still alive today. These values include respect for family, love of nature, and belief in hard work. The Japanese word *sappari* means "clean, light, and sparkling with honesty." Sappari still describes the Japanese people, their country, and their cuisine.

Geography and Climate of Japan

Japan is a nation of islands. Three-fourths of Japan's total land area is mountainous or hilly. The mountains have made farming difficult and have caused crowded living conditions in the few lowlands.

Swift-flowing rivers and crystal clear lakes dot Japan's landscape. Many of the rivers end in picturesque waterfalls. Others bring the water used to irrigate rice fields. A few provide hydroelectric power.

Because the islands cover such a large latitude, Japan has a variety of climates. The southern part of the country is subtropical. Summers are hot and humid, and winters are mild. The bulk of the population lives in this area. Their housing, clothing, and farming methods are suited to a warm climate.

Hokkaido, Japan's northernmost island, has cold winters. Temperatures fall below freezing for at least four months during the winter, and snowfall is heavy.

Japan receives more than adequate moisture. Seasonal winds, called *monsoons*, bring rain in summer and snow in winter. During September, severe storms, called *typhoons*, bring heavy rains and damaging winds, **33-11**.

Shutterstock

33-11 Seasonal typhoons can lead to flooding in some parts of Japan.

Japanese Culture

In the decades that followed World War II, Japan experienced rapid industrial growth. Today, Japan plays a major role in world affairs.

Japanese Festivals

Festivals are an important part of Japanese culture, and foods are an important part of many festivals. The biggest celebration in Japan is the New Year festival. The Japanese eat long noodles on New Year's Eve as a symbol for living a long life. They also make offerings of rice cakes to the New Year god.

Soybeans play a symbolic role in a second Japanese New Year celebration called *Setsubun*. This holiday takes place in early February—the time of the new year according to Japan's archaic lunar calendar. Japanese people still celebrate this event by eating one soybean for each year they have lived. They also throw handfuls of roasted soybeans in and around their homes to chase away demons. Celebrities stand near shrines and throw soybeans into crowds of people. People who catch the beans are believed to be blessed with good fortune throughout the following year.

A third annual tradition in Japan is the welcoming of spring with Cherry Blossom celebrations. The cherry blossom is Japan's national flower. Families enjoy picnicking under the blooming trees. People also recognize this time of year by eating cherry blossom cakes. These cakes are made of cooked, sweetened azuki beans wrapped in a pounded rice mixture to look like cherry blossoms.

Japanese Agriculture

Rice is Japan's most important crop. Over half the tillable land is used for rice production. In the far south, Japanese farmers can grow two crops each year. Other important crops include sweet potatoes, wheat, and sugar beets.

The Japanese raise tea bushes on terraced hillsides. They grow mandarin oranges and strawberries in the South. They grow peaches, pears, persimmons, cherries, apples, and other hearty fruits in the North. The Japanese also grow beans, large radishes, cucumbers, lettuce, onions, cabbage, turnips, carrots, and spinach. They grow many varieties of peas, squash, and pumpkins, too.

The teachings of Buddhism, which is practiced by a large number of Japanese people, forbid the eating of meat. In addition, land has always been scarce in Japan. Therefore, the Japanese have traditionally raised little livestock. In recent years, however, livestock production has increased. This is partly due to the abandonment of Buddhist dietary laws. Also, a taste for eggs, milk, meat, and poultry has been developing among the Japanese people.

Seafood provides most of the protein in the Japanese diet. Japan's fishing industry is one of the world's largest. Sardines, salmon, herring, cuttlefish, yellowtail, and other kinds of fish, as well as seaweed, live in coastal waters. The Japanese freeze or can some of the seafood catch for export.

Japanese Cuisine

Japan's staple foods can be easily obtained from the sea and the country's limited land resources. Rice, which forms the basis of the Japanese diet, is rich in complex carbohydrates. Soybeans and fish are the main sources of protein. These foods keep the cuisine lower in fat, saturated fat, and cholesterol than a cuisine based on meat. Vegetables, fruits, and seaweed supply vitamins, minerals, and fiber. Light cooking methods help retain the nutritional value of Japanese staple foods. However, the Japanese diet is rather high in sodium due to the popularity of soy sauce as a flavoring agent.

An important element of Japanese cuisine is subtlety of taste. Cooks achieve this subtlety through the careful selection of ingredients and cooking methods.

Another important element is aesthetic appearance. Japanese cooks place great emphasis on the color, shape, and arrangement of food on a serving dish, **33-12**. Many times an arrangement may suggest a particular season or mood. For instance, a cook might arrange ingredients to represent the mountains, rivers, trees, and flowers of a Japanese spring. Such a dish might be served at the spring fish festival.

Basic Japanese Ingredients

Ingredients commonly used in Japanese cooking include sesame oil, mild rice vinegar, mushrooms, daikon, mirin, and sake. Kanpyo, gobo, and shirataki are common ingredients, too. *Kanpyo* is strips of dried gourd. *Gobo* is burdock root, and *shirataki* is a mixture made from a

Shutterstock

33-12 The color, shape, and arrangement of foods is an important aspect of Japanese cuisine.

yamlike tuber. The Japanese also use salt, pepper, sugar, chives, onions, mustard, scallions, and other familiar seasonings. However, four ingredients are basic to Japanese cookery: rice, soybeans, seaweed, and fish.

Rice

Rice is so important to the Japanese diet that the Japanese word for meal is **gohan**, which means rice. Japanese rice is a short-grain variety. Cooks usually steam it and serve it plain. Sometimes they cook rice with other ingredients or serve it with a sauce. Two other products, *sake* (Japanese rice wine) and *mirin* (sweet wine), are obtained from rice.

Soybeans

The Chinese introduced the soybean to the Japanese. The **soybean** is a legume with seeds that are rich in protein and oil. The Japanese use soybeans in many forms.

Miso is a fermented soybean paste. The Japanese use miso in a soup they serve for breakfast. It may also be an ingredient in a marinade used to prepare fish and vegetables.

Tofu is a custardlike cake made from soybeans. It has a very mild flavor. The Japanese may roll tofu in cornstarch and deep-fry it. They may scramble it with eggs. They may also sauté, boil, or broil it. Sometimes, they add tofu to soups. *Sumashi* (clear broth with tofu and shrimp) is an example.

Shoyu, Japanese soy sauce, contains wheat or barley, salt, water, and malt along with soybeans. Shoyu is an all-purpose seasoning in the Japanese kitchen. (Chinese soy sauce is heavier and does not make a suitable substitute.)

Reflect

Rice is served at almost every meal in Japan. Ask students if they would mind eating one food item that often. Have them think about why or why not.

Reflect

Ask students if they would feel comfortable eating fugu if they knew a licensed fugu chef had properly cleaned it. Have them think about the reasons behind their responses.

Learn About...

Fish in Japanese Cuisine

Tuna, bass, flounder, cod, mackerel, *ayu* (sweet fish), carp, and squid are popular in Japan. The Japanese also eat many varieties of shellfish and more unusual subtropical species. *Katsuo* (dried bonito) is an essential ingredient of *dashi*, a Japanese fish stock. *Fugu* (blowfish) is a Japanese delicacy. Fugu contains a lethal toxin that can kill a diner unless the fish has been properly cleaned. Licensed fugu chefs perform this task.

Japanese cooks demand that all fish and shellfish must be fresh. Therefore, they do not kill shellfish until minutes before cooking. They keep freshwater varieties that will be eaten raw alive until serving time.

Two of the most popular fish dishes are sashimi and sushi. *Sashimi* are raw fillets of fish eaten alone or with a sauce. *Sushi* are balls of cooked rice flavored with vinegar. They are served with strips of raw or cooked fish, eggs, vegetables, or seaweed. Sashimi and sushi restaurants and snack bars are found throughout Japan.

Shutterstock

Raw fish fillets, called sashimi, are a popular Japanese dish.

Seaweed

The Japanese use seaweed from the surrounding oceans in both fresh and dried forms. They roll *nori*, a dried variety of seaweed, around fish or rice. They also use it as a garnish. The Japanese use *konbu* (dried kelp) in dashi. They use other varieties of seaweed as flavorings, garnishes, and vegetables in soups.

Japanese Vegetables and Fruits

Japanese farmers grow many vegetables. Traditional Japanese vegetables include *daikon*, which is a giant white radish. *Negi* is a thin Japanese leek. *Wasabi* is Japanese horseradish, and *bakusai* is Chinese cabbage. Lotus roots and shoots, edible chrysanthemum leaves, burdock, spinach, ginger root, and bamboo shoots are also popular. Many types of peas, beans, ferns, and mushrooms are common, too.

Japanese cooks often mix vegetables together in salads. Japan has two kinds of salads: *aemono* (mixed foods) and *sunomono* (vinegared foods). Aemono salads contain several raw or cooked vegetables in a thick dressing. Sunomono salads contain crisp, raw vegetables and cold, cooked fish or shellfish. They are served with a thin dressing made of rice vinegar, sugar, and soy sauce. *Namusu* (vegetables in a vinegar dressing) is an example of a sunomono salad.

Japanese fruits are plentiful. Persimmons and many types of oranges grow in Japan. One of the best-known oranges is the *mikan*, or mandarin orange. Apples, pears, cherries, strawberries, plums, and melons also grow well.

Japanese Main Dishes

Meat traditionally was not part of the Japanese diet. Today, however, meat appears on many Japanese tables. Because it is costly, the Japanese usually serve meat in small amounts with other foods.

Although the Japanese eat both pork and beef, their beef is famous. The tenderness of the meat results in part from the treatment the cattle receive. Japanese farmers feed the animals bran, beans, rice, and beer. They massage each steer daily with *shochu* (Japanese gin).

Poultry production in Japan has grown in recent years. Chickens are less costly to raise, so they appear more often in Japanese recipes than meat. Eggs are becoming more popular, too. *Tamago dashimaki* is the Japanese version of an omelet.

Japanese Cooking Methods

In Japan, cooks always cut food into small pieces before cooking. This makes the food easy to pick up with chopsticks. (The Japanese use knives only for food preparation. They do not place knives on the table.)

Japanese cooks boil a variety of foods, including meat, poultry, seafood, and vegetables. The cooking liquid may be a strongly flavored stock or a mild broth. Foods cooked in boiling liquid are called *nimono*. Examples of nimono are *kimini* (sake-seasoned shrimp with egg yolk glaze) and *kiriboshi daikon* (chicken simmered with white radish threads).

Steaming is the simplest of all cooking methods. *Mushimono* (steamed foods) retain their fresh flavors, colors, and nutrients. Japanese cooks use two steaming methods. *Mushi* foods are foods cooked on a plate suspended over boiling water. *Chawan mushi* foods are foods steamed in an egg custard. Mushi foods are mild in flavor, so the Japanese usually serve them with a dipping sauce. Chawan mushi foods are richer in flavor and usually are served without a sauce.

The Japanese use frying to prepare *tempura*. Japanese cooks prepare tempura by coating vegetables, meat, poultry, and seafood in a light batter. Then they quickly fry the coated pieces in oil. Other Japanese *agemono* (fried foods) are deep-fried in oil. All Japanese agemono are light and delicate. They are never greasy or heavy.

The Japanese usually use broiling for meat, poultry, and fish. One popular *yakimono* (broiled food) is beefsteak. It is dipped in a mixture of soy sauce and mirin and grilled over charcoal. Beef teriyaki and yakitori are two types of yakimono popular in the United States. *Beef teriyaki* is slices of beef glazed with a special sauce. *Yakitori* is chicken, scallions, and chicken livers broiled on a skewer, **33-13**.

Japanese cooks prepare many dishes at the table. They use one or a combination of the above cooking methods. **Sukiyaki** is a popular Japanese dish that combines two cooking methods—nimono and *nabemono* (dishes cooked at the table). It is made of thinly sliced meat, bean curd, and vegetables cooked in a sauce. Cooks prepare all the raw ingredients in the kitchen. Then they cook the beef and vegetables with their accompanying sauce in a skillet at the table. Another method of preparing food at the table uses the hibachi. A *hibachi* is a small grill that can be freestanding or built into the center of the table.

Shutterstock

33-13 Broiled foods, like this yakitori, are referred to as yakimono in Japanese cuisine.

Culture and Social Studies

Japanese Eating Customs

The Japanese do not use napkins. Instead, small, soft towels called *oshibori* are brought to the table at the beginnings and ends of meals. The oshibori are warm, damp, and fragrant. The Japanese use them to wipe their faces and hands.

Bowls used for hot foods are served covered. Diners usually remove the cover of the individual rice bowl first. This indicates that rice is Japan's most honored food. The Japanese do not eat rice all at once. Instead, they eat it with the other foods in much the same way people in the United States eat bread. The Japanese must use both hands to place a rice bowl on a tray for refilling. To use one hand is a breach of courtesy.

The Japanese drink soup from a cup rather than spooning it from a bowl. They remove the cup from the table and hold it in the left hand. Then they hold their chopsticks in the right hand to secure the food. The oldest guest always picks up his or her chopsticks first as a token of respect. After use, diners return their chopsticks to the chopstick rest.

To show appreciation for the cook's skill, it is quite proper to smack the lips or make sucking sounds. Guests often exchange sake cups with their host as a sign of respect.

Japanese Meals

Japanese meals are made up of many light dishes. The quantities served are much smaller than those served in the West.

In the morning, some Japanese people eat eggs and other breakfast foods popular in the United States. In many parts of Japan, however, people eat more traditional breakfast foods. Such foods include umeboshi and miroshiru. *Umeboshi* is a tiny, red, pickled plum. *Miroshiru* is a hearty soup made of dashi, miso, and rice. Japanese breakfast foods also include rice, which is often sprinkled with nori.

Japanese families may serve a carefully prepared lunch if family members come home at noon or they are expecting guests. Otherwise, Japanese cooks usually prepare simple lunches. The morning rice is reheated and served with leftover vegetables and meat or a simple sauce.

The evening meal is much more elaborate. Because businesses stay open later in Japan than in the United States, the meal usually is served later. The young children eat their meal first. The Japanese prepare children's versions of many popular foods. An example is *kushizashi* (meats, fowl, and vegetables grilled on a skewer). Cooks make kushizashi with hot peppers for adults. However, they use milder scallions when preparing the dish for children.

The Japanese usually serve all the dishes in the main meal together. They usually serve broiled or fried meat, poultry, or fish as a main course. Although the main course can vary, rice, soup, and tsukemono must be served. **Tsukemono** (soaked foods) are lightly pickled pieces of daikon, cucumber, melon, eggplant, and other vegetables. The Japanese eat them with rice near the end of the meal.

The Japanese rarely eat sweet desserts. They reserve sweets for special occasions. Instead, most meals end with fresh fruit.

Another meal enjoyed by the Japanese is **kaiseka**. This is a delicate meal that may be served after the tea ceremony. Tea is Japan's national drink. The Japanese serve green teas, which they call **nihon-cha**. The Japanese perform the tea ceremony just as their ancestors did hundreds of years ago. Each step of the ceremony is done according to established rules. Each movement the host makes is designed to bring pleasure to the guest. Harmony must exist among all the elements of the ceremony and among all the people present. Simple tea ceremonies may last just 40 minutes. Those that include kaiseka may last as long as four hours. See **33-14**.

Shutterstock

33-14 The tea ceremony is a ritual that has been performed in Japan for hundreds of years.

Japanese Menu

Sumashi Wan
(Clear Broth with Tofu and Shrimp)

Sukiyaki
(Beef and Vegetables Cooked
in Seasoned Liquid)

Namasu
(Vegetables in a Vinegar Dressing)

Gohan
(Steamed Rice)

Snow Peas

Mikan
(Mandarin Oranges)

Nihon-Cha
(Green Tea)

Sumashi Wan
(Clear Broth with Tofu and Shrimp)

Serves 6

2	cups water
1	cake tofu, 6 ounces, cut into 6 equal squares
1	cup water
	salt
7	spinach leaves (or ½ package frozen leaf spinach thoroughly defrosted and separated into leaves)
4	cups clam broth
2	cups low-fat chicken broth
6	small canned shrimp

1. In small saucepan, bring 2 cups of water to a boil.
2. Add tofu and let water return to a simmer.
3. Remove from heat immediately and cover. Set aside until ready to serve soup.
4. In a second saucepan, bring 1 cup lightly salted water to a boil.
5. Add spinach and cook just until tender.
6. Drain immediately and rinse under cold running water. Remove excess moisture with paper towels and set aside.
7. Wash saucepan. Combine clam broth and chicken broth and bring to a boil.
8. Meanwhile, set six soup bowls on a tray. Place a spinach leaf, a shrimp, and a cube of tofu in the bottom of each.

9. Pour broth into bowls, filling each about ¾ full and being careful not to disturb garnish. (Pour broth down the sides of the bowls.) Serve immediately.

Per serving: 50 cal. (41% from fat), 5 g protein, 2 g carbohydrate, 2 g fat, 7 mg cholesterol, 0 g fiber, 169 mg sodium.

Sukiyaki
(Beef and Vegetables Cooked in Seasoned Liquid)

Serves 4 to 6

1	pound beef tenderloin or sirloin steak
1	cup water
8	ounces shirataki (long noodlelike threads) or cooked vermicelli
2	medium onions, sliced crosswise
5	leeks, split lengthwise and cut in 1½-inch lengths
¾	pound fresh mushrooms, washed and sliced
5	stalks celery, cut diagonally into ¼-inch slices
1	pound fresh spinach, cleaned (or 1 package frozen leaf spinach, thoroughly defrosted)
½	pound tofu, cut into cubes
½	cup low-sodium soy sauce
2	tablespoons sugar
1½	cups low-sodium beef broth
¼	cup margarine

1. Slice beef cross-grained into paper-thin slices, 1 by 2 inches. (Slightly frozen meat is easier to slice.) Trim fat. Arrange slices attractively on a plate, cover with plastic wrap, and refrigerate.
2. Bring one cup of water to a boil.
3. Add shirataki and return water to a boil.
4. Drain and slice shirataki into thirds.
5. Arrange shirataki, vegetables, and tofu attractively on a serving platter, cover with plastic wrap, and refrigerate.
6. Combine soy sauce, sugar, and beef broth in a small bowl. Cover and refrigerate.
7. To cook sukiyaki, heat two tablespoons margarine in a wok over moderately high heat or an electric skillet preheated to 425°F.
8. Add half of the beef slices and cook until meat loses its pink color. Push meat to the side.
9. Add half of the onions and leeks and cook until transparent and lightly browned. (Turn meat as needed.) Push vegetables to the side.
10. Add half of the mushrooms and half of the celery in two groups. Stir-fry 2 to 3 minutes.
11. Add half the sauce and simmer about 5 minutes. Turn all foods occasionally.

12. Add half of the spinach and cook 1 minute.
13. Add half of the noodles or vermicelli and tofu. (These will absorb the broth.) Serve immediately or keep warm in a 225°F oven while you cook the remaining half of the ingredients.

Per serving: 474 cal. (23% from fat), 28 g protein, 66 g carbohydrate, 12 g fat, 26 mg cholesterol, 7 g fiber, 992 mg sodium.

Namasu
(Vegetables in a Vinegar Dressing)

Serves 6

½   pound daikon or white turnip, peeled and shredded
1   medium carrot, scraped and shredded
1   teaspoon salt
1   cup cold water
¼   cup preflaked, dried bonito
1   tablespoon white vinegar
2   teaspoons sugar
     monosodium glutamate (MSG), optional

1. In small bowl, combine daikon, carrot, salt, and water. Stir to mix and let stand 30 minutes.
2. Put dried bonito in a small pan and heat over low heat for 3 to 4 minutes to dry further.
3. Transfer bonito to a blender container and grind to a fine powder.
4. Drain carrot and daikon. Squeeze dry and put in mixing bowl.
5. Add vinegar, sugar, and two pinches of monosodium glutamate. Mix well and add powdered bonito. Serve at room temperature.

Per serving: 38 cal. (5% from fat), 5 g protein, 4 g carbohydrate, 0 g fat, 8 mg cholesterol, 1 g fiber, 451 mg sodium.

Gohan
(Steamed Rice)

Makes 3 cups

1   cup uncooked short-grain rice
2   cups cold water

1. Place rice and water in a large, heavy saucepan.
2. Bring water to a boil, reduce heat to low and cook rice covered for about 15 minutes, or until rice has absorbed all the liquid.
3. Remove from heat. Let the rice rest, undisturbed, 5 minutes.
4. Remove cover, fluff with fork, and serve.

Per serving: 112 cal. (1% from fat), 2 g protein, 25 g carbohydrate, 0 g fat, 0 mg cholesterol, 1 g fiber, 2 mg sodium.

Snow Peas

Serves 6

1½   pounds snow peas (or two 10 ounce packages frozen snow peas)
     water
     salt

1. Snap ends from fresh snow peas and remove center rib. Rinse in cool water.
2. In a medium saucepan, bring small amount of salted water to a boil.
3. Add snow peas and return water to a boil. Simmer peas until crisp-tender.
4. Drain and serve immediately.

Per serving: 46 cal. (4% from fat), 3 g protein, 8 g carbohydrate, 0 g fat, 0 mg cholesterol, 1 g fiber, 86 mg sodium.

CAREER SUCCESS

Teamwork

Chen is a Chinese-style food cook at Szechwan East, a small Chinese carryout owned by his uncle. Chen's uncle takes telephone orders and collects payment from customers when they come in to pick up the orders. Chen works in the small kitchen with his aunt and two cousins to prepare food items. Chen and his family members must avoid getting in one another's way as they work together to quickly fill orders.

To be an effective worker, Chen needs skill in working as a member of a team. Put yourself in Chen's place and answer the following questions about his need for and use of this skill:

A. What are some tasks of a Chinese-style food cook that might especially require teamwork skills when working in a small kitchen?
B. How might your aunt and cousins be affected if you lack skill in working as a member of a team?
C. How might customers of Szechwan East be affected if you lack skill in working as a member of a team?
D. What is another skill you would need in this job? Briefly explain why this skill would be important.

CHAPTER 33 REVIEW

Summary

Russia, India, China, and Japan have cuisines that differ greatly from the cuisine of the United States. The cuisines of these countries also differ greatly from one another.

Russian cuisine was influenced by the Slavs and Mongols. The czars also made a number of contributions. However, the staple foods of Russian peasants—bread, kasha, and soup—remain basic components of the Russian diet. Today, Russian meals often begin with appetizers, called zakuska. A hearty soup, such as schi or borscht, and a meat, fish, or poultry main dish would follow. Rye bread, potatoes, and a seasonal vegetable would accompany the main dish. A simple dessert of pureed fruit might round out the meal.

Religious dietary restrictions play a major role in the cuisine of India. Different climates and influences have created some specific distinctions between the cuisines of Northern and Southern India. Four basic cooking techniques are used to prepare Indian cuisine: tandoori, korma, vindaloo, and chasnidarth. Curry is a dish found throughout India. However, cooks in different regions prepare and season it in different ways.

Chinese foods contain some unique ingredients. A few special utensils, including a wok, are helpful for preparing Chinese foods. Most Chinese foods are prepared by stir-frying, steaming, deep-frying, or simmering. Rice is a staple of the Chinese diet. Vegetables also play an important role. Vegetables and meat or poultry are cut into small pieces to make them easier to eat with chopsticks.

Four ingredients are basic to Japanese cuisine: rice, fish, seaweed, and soybeans. Many Japanese foods feature vegetables with smaller amounts of meat, poultry, or fish. The Japanese often boil, steam, fry, or broil their foods. The aesthetic appearance of foods is an important aspect of Japanese cuisine. The Japanese also follow some specific eating customs. Many of these are observed in the traditional tea ceremony.

Review What You Have Read

Write your answers on a separate sheet of paper, using complete sentences when appropriate.

1. What are four contributions the Mongols made to Russian cuisine?
2. Name and describe two Russian soups.
3. Name and describe two Russian desserts.
4. In general, how does the cuisine of Northern India differ from the cuisine of Southern India?
5. Many Indian dishes are cooked in a clarified butter called _____.
6. Which of the following Indian cooking techniques involves braising foods in yogurt?
   A. Chasnidarth.
   B. Korma.
   C. Tandoori.
   D. Vindaloo.

(continued)

Answer Key for *Review What You Have Read* **questions**

1. (List four:) broiled meats, sauerkraut, yogurt, kumys, curd cheese, tea drinking
2. (Name and describe two:) schi—cabbage soup; borscht—beet soup; ouba—clear fish broth; rasolnik—made with a mixture of vegetables garnished with chopped veal or lamb kidneys; solianka—contains meat or fish and salted cucumber
3. (Name and describe two:) charlotte russe—ladyfinger mold with cream filling; fruit tart—sweetened fruit filling in a pastry shell; kisel—pureed fruit; samsa—sweet walnut fritters; medivnyk—honey cake; paskha—rich cheese cake; kulich—tall, cylindrical yeast cake filled with fruits and nuts
4. In Northern India, foods are rich and heavily seasoned. In Southern India, foods are hotter and not as subtle or refined.

5. ghee

6. B

7. China's chief agricultural product is rice.

8. (List and define four. Student response.)

7. What is China's chief agricultural product?

8. Choose four important ingredients in Chinese cooking and briefly define each.

9. What is the most versatile of all Chinese cooking utensils?

10. Why have the Japanese traditionally raised little livestock?

11. Name and describe three food products made from soybeans in Japan.

12. Describe two Japanese eating customs.

Link to Academic Skills

9. The most versatile of all Chinese cooking utensils is the wok.

10. Land is scarce and the teachings of Buddhism forbid the eating of meat.

11. miso—fermented soybean paste; tofu—custardlike cake with a mild flavor; shoyu—Japanese soy sauce that is used as a seasoning

12. (Describe two. Student response.)

13. **Social studies.** Divide the class into four teams. Each team will research trade between the United States and one of the countries discussed in this chapter. Identify top products exported to and imported from the country. Find out dollar values of imports and exports for the five most recent years for which data is available. Note the trade deficit or surplus each year. Prepare a poster or multimedia presentation to share your team's findings with the class.

14. **History.** Use library resources to research one of the Russian czars. Write a two-page biographical report about the czar and one of the notable events that occurred during his reign.

15. **History.** According to archaeologists, the region that is now India was a highly developed society as early as 3000 B.C. Examples of this society include sewers; brick houses; irrigation ditches; and systems of counting, measuring, weighing, and writing. Research one of these advances, then find or create an illustration of it to share with the class.

16. **Geography.** Investigate one of the provinces of China. Point out your chosen province on a map of China and share an interesting fact about the province with your classmates.

17. **English language arts.** Haiku is a form of unrhymed Japanese poetry. In simplified terms, haiku is made up of three lines. The first line has five syllables, the second line has seven, and the third line has five. Write a haiku about a Japanese food. Then write a haiku about a popular food in the United States. Display your haikus on a class bulletin board titled "A Taste of Poetry."

Build Critical Thinking Skills

18. **Analysis.** Prepare ghee. Fry potatoes in lard, vegetable shortening, margarine, and ghee. Analyze differences in browning and flavor.

19. **Evaluate.** Design an evaluation form for a tea tasting. Then complete the form as you taste and compare several varieties of tea popular in China.

20. **Synthesis.** Work as part of a team to research the traditional Japanese tea ceremony. Pool your ideas to prepare a demonstration for the class. Each member of the team should plan to be responsible for demonstrating a different aspect of the ceremony.

Apply Technology

21. Search online for a photo of a Russian landmark. Save a copy of the image in a picture file on your computer. Then insert the photo into a word processing document. Write a creative caption about the photo. Type the caption under the image and then make a printout of the photo with the caption to display on a class bulletin board.

22. Use Internet resources to find out more about the culture in one of the Asian countries covered in the chapter. Use clipart and photos to prepare a PowerPoint presentation to share your findings with the class.

A Measure of Math

23. Identify the basic units and subunits of currency used in Russia, India, China, and Japan. Look up current exchange rates and calculate the equivalent of $100 U.S. dollars in each currency.

Teamwork in Action

24. As a class, choose one of the countries from this chapter. Then work as part of a small team to write lesson plans for two activities focusing on the country for specific learning centers in a preschool. Be sure to clearly define your objectives for each activity. List needed supplies and write detailed steps for conducting the activities. Also state how the preschoolers' learning will be assessed after completing the activities. Submit your team's lesson plans along with the lesson plans from the other teams to a local preschool teacher to incorporate into his or her curriculum. Ask the teacher to share feedback with your class.

Companion Website

www.g-wlearning.com

At the website, review key terms for this chapter with crossword puzzles, matching exercises, and e-flash cards. Apply facts from the chapter to complete the activities.

APPENDIX A

Nutritional Goals for Age-Gender Groups

Based on Dietary Reference Intakes and 2010 Dietary Guidelines Recommendations

Nutrient (units)	Source of goal[a]	Child 1–3	Female 4–8	Male 4–8	Female 9–13	Male 9–13	Female 14–18	Male 14–18	Female 19–30	Male 19–30	Female 31–50	Male 31–50	Female 51+	Male 51+
Macronutrients														
Protein (g)	RDA[b]	13	19	19	34	34	46	52	46	56	46	56	46	56
(% of calories)	AMDR[c]	5–20	10–30	10–30	10–30	10–30	10–30	10–30	10–35	10–35	10–35	10–35	10–35	10–35
Carbohydrate (g)	RDA	130	130	130	130	130	130	130	130	130	130	130	130	130
(% of calories)	AMDR	45–65	45–65	45–65	45–65	45–65	45–65	45–65	45–65	45–65	45–65	45–65	45–65	45–65
Total fiber (g)	IOM[d]	14	17	20	22	25	25	31	28	34	25	31	22	28
Total fat (% of calories)	AMDR	30–40	25–35	25–35	25–35	25–35	25–35	25–35	20–35	20–35	20–35	20–35	20–35	20–35
Saturated fat (% of calories)	DG[e]	<10%	<10%	<10%	<10%	<10%	<10%	<10%	<10%	<10%	<10%	<10%	<10%	<10%
Linoleic acid (g)	AI[f]	7	10	10	10	12	11	16	12	17	12	17	11	14
(% of calories)	AMDR	5–10	5–10	5–10	5–10	5–10	5–10	5–10	5–10	5–10	5–10	5–10	5–10	5–10
alpha-Linolenic acid (g)	AI	0.7	0.9	0.9	1.0	1.2	1.1	1.6	1.1	1.6	1.1	1.6	1.1	1.6
(% of calories)	AMDR	0.6–1.2	0.6–1.2	0.6–1.2	0.6–1.2	0.6–1.2	0.6–1.2	0.6–1.2	0.6–1.2	0.6–1.2	0.6–1.2	0.6–1.2	0.6–1.2	0.6–1.2
Cholesterol (mg)	DG	<300	<300	<300	<300	<300	<300	<300	<300	<300	<300	<300	<300	<300
Minerals														
Calcium (mg)	RDA	700	1,000	1,000	1,300	1,300	1,300	1,300	1,000	1,000	1,000	1,000	1,200	1,200
Iron (mg)	RDA	7	10	10	8	8	15	11	18	8	18	8	8	8
Magnesium (mg)	RDA	80	130	130	240	240	360	410	310	400	320	420	320	420
Phosphorus (mg)	RDA	460	500	500	1,250	1,250	1,250	1,250	700	700	700	700	700	700
Potassium (mg)	AI	3,000	3,800	3,800	4,500	4,500	4,700	4,700	4,700	4,700	4,700	4,700	4,700	4,700
Sodium (mg)	UL[g]	<1,500	<1,900	<1,900	<2,200	<2,200	<2,300	<2,300	<2,300	<2,300	<2,300	<2,300	<2,300	<2,300
Zinc (mg)	RDA	3	5	5	8	8	9	11	8	11	8	11	8	11
Copper (mcg)	RDA	340	440	440	700	700	890	890	900	900	900	900	900	900
Selenium (mcg)	RDA	20	30	30	40	40	55	55	55	55	55	55	55	55

(Continued)

(Continued)

Nutrient (units)	Source of goal[a]	Child 1–3	Female 4–8	Male 4–8	Female 9–13	Male 9–13	Female 14–18	Male 14–18	Female 19–30	Male 19–30	Female 31–50	Male 31–50	Female 51+	Male 51+
Vitamins														
Vitamin A (mcg RAE)	RDA	300	400	400	600	600	700	900	700	900	700	900	700	900
Vitamin D[h] (mcg)	RDA	15	15	15	15	15	15	15	15	15	15	15	15	15
Vitamin E (mg AT)	RDA	6	7	7	11	11	15	15	15	15	15	15	15	15
Vitamin C (mg)	RDA	15	25	25	45	45	65	75	75	90	75	90	75	90
Thiamin (mg)	RDA	0.5	0.6	0.6	0.9	0.9	1.0	1.2	1.1	1.2	1.1	1.2	1.1	1.2
Riboflavin (mg)	RDA	0.5	0.6	0.6	0.9	0.9	1.0	1.3	1.1	1.3	1.1	1.3	1.1	1.3
Niacin (mg)	RDA	6	8	8	12	12	14	16	14	16	14	16	14	16
Folate (mcg)	RDA	150	200	200	300	300	400	400	400	400	400	400	400	400
Vitamin B_6 (mg)	RDA	0.5	0.6	0.6	1.0	1.0	1.2	1.3	1.3	1.3	1.3	1.3	1.5	1.7
Vitamin B_{12} (mcg)	RDA	0.9	1.2	1.2	1.8	1.8	2.4	2.4	2.4	2.4	2.4	2.4	2.4	2.4
Choline (mg)	AI	200	250	250	375	375	400	550	425	550	425	550	425	550
Vitamin K (mcg)	AI	30	55	55	60	60	75	75	90	120	90	120	90	120

Notes

[a] Dietary Guidelines recommendations are used when no quantitative Dietary Reference Intake value is available; apply to ages 2 years and older.
[b] Recommended Dietary Allowance, IOM.
[c] Acceptable Macronutrient Distribution Range, IOM.
[d] 14 grams per 1,000 calories, IOM.
[e] Dietary Guidelines recommendation.
[f] Adequate Intake, IOM.
[g] Upper Limit, IOM.
[h] 1 mcg of vitamin D is equivalent to 40 IU.
AT = alpha-tocopherol; DFE = dietary folate equivalents; RAE = retinol activity equivalents.

APPENDIX B

Eating Well with Canada's Food Guide

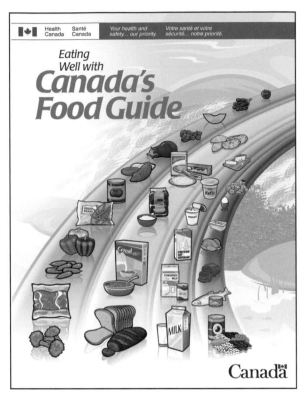

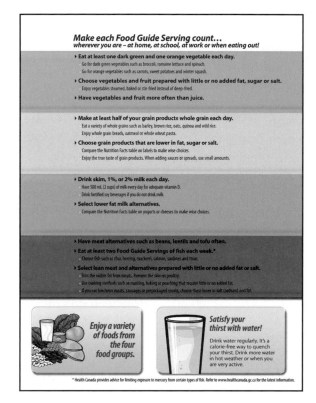

Make each Food Guide Serving count...
wherever you are – at home, at school, at work or when eating out!

▸ **Eat at least one dark green and one orange vegetable each day.**
   Go for dark green vegetables such as broccoli, romaine lettuce and spinach.
   Go for orange vegetables such as carrots, sweet potatoes and winter squash.

▸ **Choose vegetables and fruit prepared with little or no added fat, sugar or salt.**
   Enjoy vegetables steamed, baked or stir-fried instead of deep-fried.

▸ **Have vegetables and fruit more often than juice.**

▸ **Make at least half of your grain products whole grain each day.**
   Eat a variety of whole grains such as barley, brown rice, oats, quinoa and wild rice.
   Enjoy whole grain breads, oatmeal or whole wheat pasta.

▸ **Choose grain products that are lower in fat, sugar or salt.**
   Compare the Nutrition Facts table on labels to make wise choices.
   Enjoy the true taste of grain products. When adding sauces or spreads, use small amounts.

▸ **Drink skim, 1%, or 2% milk each day.**
   Have 500 mL (2 cups) of milk every day for adequate vitamin D.
   Drink fortified soy beverages if you do not drink milk.

▸ **Select lower fat milk alternatives.**
   Compare the Nutrition Facts table on yogurts or cheeses to make wise choices.

▸ **Have meat alternatives such as beans, lentils and tofu often.**

▸ **Eat at least two Food Guide Servings of fish each week.***
   Choose fish such as char, herring, mackerel, salmon, sardines and trout.

▸ **Select lean meat and alternatives prepared with little or no added fat or salt.**
   Trim the visible fat from meats. Remove the skin on poultry.
   Use cooking methods such as roasting, baking or poaching that require little or no added fat.
   If you eat luncheon meats, sausages or prepackaged meats, choose those lower in salt (sodium) and fat.

Enjoy a variety of foods from the four food groups.

Satisfy your thirst with water!
Drink water regularly. It's a calorie-free way to quench your thirst. Drink more water in hot weather or when you are very active.

* Health Canada provides advice for limiting exposure to mercury from certain types of fish. Refer to www.healthcanada.gc.ca for the latest information.

Advice for different ages and stages...

Children
Following *Canada's Food Guide* helps children grow and thrive.

Young children have small appetites and need calories for growth and development.

- Serve small nutritious meals and snacks each day.
- Do not restrict nutritious foods because of their fat content. Offer a variety of foods from the four food groups.
- Most of all... be a good role model.

Women of childbearing age
All women who could become pregnant and those who are pregnant or breastfeeding need a multivitamin containing **folic acid** every day. Pregnant women need to ensure that their multivitamin also contains **iron**. A health care professional can help you find the multivitamin that's right for you.

Pregnant and breastfeeding women need more calories. Include an extra 2 to 3 Food Guide Servings each day.

Here are two examples:
- Have fruit and yogurt for a snack, or
- Have an extra slice of toast at breakfast and an extra glass of milk at supper.

Men and women over 50
The need for **vitamin D** increases after the age of 50.

In addition to following *Canada's Food Guide*, everyone over the age of 50 should take a daily vitamin D supplement of 10 µg (400 IU).

How do I count Food Guide Servings in a meal?

Here is an example:

Vegetable and beef stir-fry with rice, a glass of milk and an apple for dessert	
250 mL (1 cup) mixed broccoli, carrot and sweet red pepper	= **2 Vegetables and Fruit** Food Guide Servings
75 g (2 ½ oz.) lean beef	= **1 Meat and Alternatives** Food Guide Serving
250 mL (1 cup) brown rice	= **2 Grain Products** Food Guide Servings
5 mL (1 tsp) canola oil	= part of your **Oils and Fats** intake for the day
250 mL (1 cup) 1% milk	= **1 Milk and Alternatives** Food Guide Serving
1 apple	= **1 Vegetables and Fruit** Food Guide Serving

Eat well and be active today and every day!

The benefits of eating well and being active include:
- Better overall health.
- Lower risk of disease.
- A healthy body weight.
- Feeling and looking better.
- More energy.
- Stronger muscles and bones.

Be active
To be active every day is a step towards better health and a healthy body weight.

Canada's Physical Activity Guide recommends building 30 to 60 minutes of moderate physical activity into daily life for adults and at least 90 minutes a day for children and youth. You don't have to do it all at once. Add it up in periods of at least 10 minutes at a time for adults and five minutes at a time for children and youth.

Start slowly and build up.

Eat well
Another important step towards better health and a healthy body weight is to follow *Canada's Food Guide* by:
- Eating the recommended amount and type of food each day.
- Limiting foods and beverages high in calories, fat, sugar or salt (sodium) such as cakes and pastries, chocolate and candies, cookies and granola bars, doughnuts and muffins, ice cream and frozen desserts, french fries, potato chips, nachos and other salty snacks, alcohol, fruit flavoured drinks, soft drinks, sports and energy drinks, and sweetened hot or cold drinks.

Read the label
- Compare the Nutrition Facts table on food labels to choose products that contain less fat, saturated fat, trans fat, sugar and sodium.
- Keep in mind that the calories and nutrients listed are for the amount of food found at the top of the Nutrition Facts table.

Limit trans fat
When a Nutrition Facts table is not available, ask for nutrition information to choose foods lower in trans and saturated fats.

Nutrition Facts
Per 0 mL (0 g)

Amount	% Daily Value
Calories 0	
Fat 0 g	0 %
Saturates 0 g	0 %
+ Trans 0 g	
Cholesterol 0 mg	
Sodium 0 mg	0 %
Carbohydrate 0 g	0 %
Fibre 0 g	0 %
Sugars 0 g	
Protein 0 g	
Vitamin A 0 %	Vitamin C 0 %
Calcium 0 %	Iron 0 %

Take a step today...
✓ Have breakfast every day. It may help control your hunger later in the day.
✓ Walk wherever you can – get off the bus early, use the stairs.
✓ Benefit from eating vegetables and fruit at all meals and as snacks.
✓ Spend less time being inactive such as watching TV or playing computer games.
✓ Request nutrition information about menu items when eating out to help you make healthier choices.
✓ Enjoy eating with family and friends!
✓ Take time to eat and savour every bite!

For more information, interactive tools, or additional copies visit Canada's Food Guide on-line at:
www.healthcanada.gc.ca/foodguide

or contact:
Publications
Health Canada
Ottawa, Ontario K1A 0K9
E-Mail: publications@hc-sc.gc.ca
Tel.: 1-866-225-0709
Fax: (613) 941-5366
TTY: 1-800-267-1245

Également disponible en français sous le titre :
Bien manger avec le Guide alimentaire canadien

This publication can be made available on request on diskette, large print, audio-cassette and braille.

© Her Majesty the Queen in Right of Canada, represented by the Minister of Health Canada, 2007. This publication may be reproduced without permission.
No changes permitted. HC Pub.: 4651 Cat.: H164-38/1-2007E ISBN: 0-662-44467-1

APPENDIX C

Applying and Interviewing for a Job

Apply for a Position

When you hear of a job that interests you, contact the employer to express your interest. Depending on the job and the employer's requirements for application, you may make this contact by e-mail, letter, telephone, or in person.

If the job is still available, the next step is to fill out an application. Many employers now require potential job candidates to complete their applications online. When filling out online applications, it is extremely important to use the key words from the employer's job listing to describe your abilities as they relate to the job. Online applications are screened for such key words and help employers sort through the applications. If you are filling out a form in person, be sure to bring a pen. Be prepared to provide all information an application is likely to request.

You will need to write your name, address, phone number, and possibly an e-mail address. The form may also ask you to state the position for which you are applying, your expected wages, and when you can start working. You will need to list the names and locations of schools attended and provide information about any current or previous jobs held. Be ready to give the names of *references*, the people employers can call to ask about your capabilities as a worker.

Employers may not request your Social Security number until they are interested in hiring you. All workers need a Social Security number for tax and identification purposes.

Interview for the Position

A neat, well-written application can lead to an interview. An *interview* is a chance for an employer and a job applicant to discuss the job and the applicant's qualifications.

To make a good impression at an interview, you should be well groomed and neatly dressed. Speak in a clear voice and have a positive attitude. Be prepared to answer a variety of questions about your skills, interests, and work experiences. In addition, do your homework—know some background information about the employer. This will help you ask more specific questions about the company and the job.

Common Interview Questions

In what position are you interested?

Would you be interested in any other position(s)?

What other jobs have you had?

How many hours a week can you work?

Are you involved in other activities that could cause time conflicts with your work schedule?

What kinds of classes do you take in school?

What class do you like best?

Would you have transportation to and from work?

How much do you expect to earn?

How well do you work with others?

Why should we hire you?

If the interview goes well, the employer may decide to offer you the job. However, the employer is likely interviewing other applicants for the same job. At the interview, ask the employer when you can expect to hear his or her decision.

Handling an Offer or a Rejection

When you receive an offer, let the employer know as soon as possible if you will accept the job. Ask when you should report to work. Find out any necessary information regarding items such as uniforms and training sessions.

If the employer does not offer you the job, ask yourself the following questions:

- Was my application accurate and neat?
- Did I arrive for the interview on time and appropriately dressed?
- Did I show interest in the job and willingness to work?
- Did I appear friendly and cooperative?
- Did I answer all questions accurately?

Answering *no* to a question may give you a clue about why you did not receive a job offer. This will help you improve for your next interview.

GLOSSARY

Note: See also the Glossary of Food Preparation Terms on pages 236-238 in Chapter 12, "Recipes and Work Plans." Numbers in parentheses refer to the chapter in which each term is defined.

A

abdominal thrust. A procedure used to save choking victims. (6)

abilities. Skills developed with practice. (26)

Aboriginal. One of the first, or native, inhabitants of a land. (28)

absorption. The process of taking nutrients into the body and making them part of the body. (2)

aerobic activity. A physical activity that speeds heart rate and breathing, promoting endurance. (5)

agriculture. The use of knowledge and skill to tend soil, grow crops, and raise livestock. (1)

ají. The Peruvian and Chilean term for chilies. (29)

a la carte. Type of menu in which each menu item is individually priced. (24)

al dente. Italian term describing the way pasta is cooked so its texture is slightly resistant to the bite. (31)

alternative. An option a person might choose when making a decision. (1)

American (family style) service. Style of meal service in which diners pass serving dishes from hand to hand around the table and serve themselves. (24)

amino acid. A chemical compound that serves as a building block of proteins. (2)

anemia. A condition resulting from deficiencies of various nutrients, which is characterized by a reduced number of red blood cells in the bloodstream. (2)

anorexia nervosa. An eating disorder characterized by self-starvation. (5)

anthocyanin. A reddish pigment found in vegetables. (14)

antioxidant. A substance that prevents or slows down damage caused by chemical reactions involving oxygen. (2)

antipasto. An Italian appetizer course. (31)

appetite. A psychological desire to eat. (1)

appetizer. Light food or beverage that begins a meal and is designed to stimulate the appetite. (24)

aptitude. A natural talent; an ability to learn something quickly and easily (26)

arcing. Sparking that occurs in a microwave oven when metal comes in contact with the oven walls. (12)

arepa. A corn pancake similar to a tortilla that is a traditional Venezuelan bread. (29)

artificial light. Light that most often comes from electrical fixtures. (7)

artificial sweetener. A product that sweetens food without providing the calories of sugar. (11)

ascorbic acid. A food additive that prevents color and flavor loss and adds nutritive value; another name for vitamin C. (25)

aseptic packaging. A commercial method of packaging food in which a food and its packaging material are sterilized separately and then the food is packed in the container in a sterile chamber. (25)

attitude. Your outlook on life. It is reflected by how you react to the events and people around you. (27)

avgolemono. A popular Greek sauce made from a mixture of egg yolks and lemon juice. (31)

B

bacteria. Single-celled or noncellular microorganisms that live almost everywhere. (6)

basal metabolism. The amount of energy the human body needs to stay alive and carry on vital processes. (5)

batter. Flour-liquid mixture with a consistency ranging from thin to thick, depending on the proportion of dry to liquid ingredients. (22)

beading. Golden droplets of moisture that sometimes appear on the surface of a meringue. (17)

beef. Meat that comes from mature cattle. (18)

beef stroganov. A popular Russian meat dish made with tender strips of beef, mushrooms, and a seasoned sour cream sauce. (33)

beriberi. A disease of the nervous system resulting from a thiamin deficiency, which is characterized by numbness in the ankles and legs followed by severe cramping and paralysis and potentially fatal heart disturbances. (2)

berries. Classification of fruits, including strawberries, raspberries, and grapes, that are small and juicy and have thin skins. (15)

beverageware. Drinking glasses, often called glassware, of many shapes and sizes used for a variety of purposes. (7)

binge eating disorder. An eating disorder characterized by repeated episodes of uncontrolled eating of large amounts of food. (5)

bisque. A rich, thickened cream soup. (16)

blend. Several varieties of coffee beans mixed to produce a particular flavor and aroma (12); a food seasoning made from a combination of spices and herbs. (21)

blue plate service. Type of meal service in which the plates are filled in the kitchen, carried to the dining area, and served. (24)

body composition. Proportions of bone, muscle, fat, and other tissues that make up body weight. (5)

body mass index (BMI). A calculation involving a person's weight and height measurements used by health professionals to assess a person's weight. (5)

borscht. Russian beet soup. (33)

botulism. Foodborne illness caused by eating foods containing the spore-forming bacteria *Clostridium botulinum*. (25)

bouillon. Clear broth made from strained, clarified stock, most often made from beef stock. (21)

bouquet garni. Whole spices and herbs tied together in a cheesecloth bag and added to a food during cooking for flavor. Parsley, thyme, and bay leaf usually are used. (21)

bran. The outer protective covering of a kernel of grain. (13)

brand name. The name a manufacturer puts on products so people will know that company makes the products. (11)

braten. German term for roast, which is Germany's national dish. (30)

budget. A plan for managing income and expenses. (10)

buffet service. Style of meal service in which a large table or buffet holds the utensils, dinnerware, flatware, napkins, and serving dishes from which guests serve themselves. (24)

bulgur. Grain product made from whole wheat that has been cooked, dried, partly debranned, and cracked. (32)

bulimia nervosa. An eating disorder characterized by repeated eating binges followed by inappropriate behaviors to prevent weight gain. (5)

C

cacao. A plant that produces beans that are ground into cocoa or made into chocolate. (32)

caffeine. A compound found in coffee and some other plant products that acts as a stimulant. (12)

Cajun cuisine. Hearty fare of rural Southern Louisiana that reflects the foods and cooking methods of the Acadians, French, Native Americans, Africans, and Spanish. (28)

calorie. The unit used to measure the energy value of foods. (3)

calorie balance. When calories consumed equal calories burned. (3)

candling. Process by which eggs are quality-graded. (17)

canning. A food preservation process that involves sealing food in airtight containers. (25)

carbohydrate. One of the six basic types of nutrients that is the body's chief source of energy. (2)

cardiovascular health. A strong heart and blood vessels. (4)

career. A series of related occupations that show progression in a field of work. (26)

career clusters. Sixteen groups of occupations or career specialties that are similar or related to one another. (26)

carotene. Chemical substance found in orange fruits and vegetables that can be converted into vitamin A by the body; chemical substance that gives orange vegetables and fruits their color. (14)

cassava. A starchy root plant (also known as manioc) eaten as a side dish and used in flour form in cooking and baking in South America. (29)

casserole. A baking dish with high sides (9); combination of foods prepared in a single dish. (21)

caste system. A social system in India that evolved from Hinduism and divided people into groups, or castes. (33)

caviar. The processed, salted roe (eggs) of large fish, most often sturgeon. (33)

cereal. Starchy grain that is suitable to use as food. (13)

ceviche. A marinated raw fish dish served throughout South America. (29)

chapatis. A flat bread that is common in India. (33)

chasnidarth. A major cooking technique in Indian cuisine that resembles Chinese sweet and sour. (33)

chef's knife. Also known as a *French knife*, it is a versatile kitchen knife that has a long, smooth blade for chopping, dicing, and mincing fresh fruits, vegetables, and herbs. (9)

chelo kebab. Iran's national dish, which consists of thin slices of marinated, charcoal-broiled lamb served with plain rice accompanied by a pat of butter, a raw egg, and a bowl of ground sumac. (32)

chiffon cake. Cake that is a combination of a shortened and unshortened cake; cake that contains fat and beaten egg whites. (23)

chilies. Term used in Mexico for hot peppers. (29)

chlorophyll. Green pigment found in green plants (including vegetables). (14)

cholesterol. A fatlike substance that occurs naturally in the body and is found in every cell. It occurs only in foods of animal origin. (2)

chopsticks. Chinese eating utensils. (33)

chorizo. A dark sausage with a spicy, smoky flavor. (31)

chowder. Cream soup that contains pieces of seafood, vegetables, poultry, or meat and is made from unthickened milk. (16)

citrus fruits. Classification of fruits, including oranges, lemons, and grapefruit, that have a thick outer rind and thin membranes separating the flesh into segments. (15)

coagulate. To thicken or form a congealed mass. (Proteins are coagulated by heat and can cause a mixture to thicken.) (16)

coagulum. Clumps of a protein food. (17)

cockles. A type of mussel common along the coast of Wales. (30)

colander. A perforated bowl used to drain fruits, vegetables, and pasta. (9)

colcannon. An Irish dish made with mashed potatoes mixed with chopped scallions, shredded cooked cabbage, and melted butter. (30)

collagen. Protein constituent of connective tissue in meat. Collagen is tough and elastic but can be softened and tenderized by cooking. (18)

combination oven. An oven that can do two types of cooking, such as conventional and convection. (8)

comida. The main meal of the day in Mexico and Spain. (29)

comparison shopping. Evaluating different brands, sizes, and forms of a product before making a purchase decision. (11)

compromise service. Style of meal service that is a compromise between Russian service and English service in which part of the food is served from the kitchen and part is served at the table. (24)

congee. A thick porridge made from rice or barley often served for breakfast in China. (33)

conservation. The planned use of a resource to avoid waste. (10)

consommé. Clear, rich-flavored soup made from strained, clarified stock. (21)

contaminant. A substance that may be harmful that has accidentally gotten into food. (6)

convection cooking. Method of cooking in which foods are baked or roasted in a stream of heated air. (8)

convenience food. Food product that has had some amount of service added to it. (10)

cooking losses. Fat, water, and other volatile substances that evaporate or are retained in pan drippings or cooking liquid when meats are cooked. (18)

cooking time. The total amount of time food in a microwave oven is exposed to microwave energy. (12)

course. A part of a meal made up of all the foods served at one time. (10)

cover. The amount of space needed by each person at a dining table; area on a table that contains the linen, dinnerware, flatware, and glassware needed by one person. (7)

crayfish. A crustacean related to the lobster. (30)

Creole cuisine. Style of food popular in the Southern United States that combines cooking techniques of the French with ingredients of the Africans, Caribbeans, Spanish, and Native Americans. (28)

crêpe. A thin, delicate pancake that is usually rolled around a filling. (30)

crisp-tender. Term used to describe vegetables that have been cooked to the proper degree of doneness. (14)

croissant. A flaky, buttery French yeast roll shaped into a crescent. (30)

cross-contamination. The transfer of harmful bacteria from one food to another food. (6)

crustacean. Shellfish with a segmented body that is covered by a crustlike shell. (20)

crystalline candy. Type of candy with fine sugar crystals, which give it a smooth and creamy texture. (23)

culture. The traditions and beliefs of a racial, religious, or social group. (1)

curd. Solid part of coagulated milk. (16)

curdling. Formation of clumps or curds (coagulated proteins) that can happen when milk is overheated or exposed to acids, tannins, enzymes, or salts. (16)

curry. A type of Indian stew. (33)

custard. Mixture of milk (or cream), eggs, sugar, and a flavoring that is cooked until thickened. (17)

custom. A typical way of behaving. (1)

D

Daily Values. Recommended nutrient intake levels that are used on food labels. (11)

decaffeinated. Term describing a product, such as coffee or tea, made by removing most of the caffeine. (12)

decision-making process. A method for thinking about possible options and outcomes before making a choice. (1)

deficiency disease. An illness caused by the lack of a sufficient amount of a nutrient. (2)

dehydration. An abnormal loss of body fluids. (5); the process of drying; the removal of water from foods or other items. (12)

del pueblo. Term meaning of the people, which is used to describe Spanish cuisine. (31)

dendé oil. Palm oil that gives Brazilian dishes a bright yellow-orange color. (29)

diabetes mellitus. A body's lack of or inability to use the hormone insulin to maintain normal blood glucose levels. (4)

diet. All the food and drink a person regularly consumes. (4)

Dietary Guidelines for Americans. The federal government's nutritional advice. They are intended to promote health and reduce the risk of chronic (long-term) diseases. They are also aimed at reducing the rate of overweight and obesity in the United States. They urge people to use improved nutrition and physical activity to reach these goals. (3)

Dietary Reference Intakes (DRIs). Estimated nutrient intake levels used for planning and evaluating the diets of healthy people. (3)

dietary supplement. A purified nutrient or nonnutrient substance that is manufactured or extracted from natural sources. (2)

digestion. The bodily process of breaking food down into simpler compounds the body can use. (2)

dinnerware. Plates, cups, saucers, and bowls. (7)

discretionary calories. The calories left in a person's daily allowance after making nutrient-dense choices for all food group servings. (3)

double boiler. Small pan that fits into a larger pan. Food is put in the smaller pan, and water is placed in the larger pan. The food cooks by steam heat. (9)

dough. Flour-liquid mixture that is stiff enough to be shaped by hand. (22)

dovetail. To overlap tasks to use time more efficiently. (12)

drawn fish. Fish that has the entrails (insides) removed. (20)

dressed fish. Fish that has the entrails (insides), head, fins, and scales removed. (20)

drupes. Classification of fruits, such as cherries, peaches, and plums, that have an outer skin covering a soft flesh that surrounds a single, hard seed, which is called a stone or pit. (15)

Dutch treat. A way of paying for a meal in a restaurant in which each person in a group pays for his or her own meal. (24)

E

eating disorder. Abnormal eating behavior that risks physical and mental health. (5)

eggplant. A fleshy, oval-shaped vegetable with a deep purple skin frequently used in Mediterranean dishes. (31)

elastin. Protein constituent of connective tissue in meat that is tough and elastic and cannot be softened by cooking. (18)

empanada. An Argentine appetizer. (29)

emulsion. Mixture that forms when liquids that ordinarily do not mix, such as oil and water, are combined. (17)

endosperm. The largest part of a kernel of grain containing most of the starch and the protein of the kernel, but few minerals and little fiber. (13)

EnergyGuide label. A yellow tag that shows an estimated yearly energy usage for the major appliance on which it appears. (8)

ENERGY STAR® mark. A label manufacturers voluntarily place on appliances that are energy efficient and meet guidelines set by the U.S. Environmental Protection Agency (EPA). (8)

English service. Style of meal service in which the plates are served by one of the hosts and passed around the table until each guest has been served. (24)

enriched. Having added nutrients to replace those lost through processing. (13)

entree. Main course. (24)

entrepreneur. A person who starts and runs his or her own business. (26)

environment. Interrelated factors, including air, water, soil, mineral resources, plants, and animals, that ultimately affect the survival of life on earth. (1)

enzymatic browning. Darkening process some fruits undergo when exposed to the air. (15)

enzyme. Complex protein produced by living cells that causes specific chemical reactions. (25)

escargot. A snail eaten as food. (30)

ethical behavior. Conforming to accepted standards of fairness and good conduct. It is based on a person's sense of what is right to do. (27)

etiquette. Rules set by society to guide manners. (24)

F

fad. A practice that is very popular for a short time. (1)

fallacy. A mistaken belief. (1)

fasting. Denying oneself food. (1)

fat. One of the six basic types of nutrients that is an important energy source belonging to a larger group of compounds called lipids. (2)

fat fish. Fish having flesh that is fattier than the flesh of lean fish. (20)

fat-soluble vitamin. A vitamin that dissolves in fats and can be stored in the fatty tissues of the body. (2)

fatty acid. A chemical chain containing carbon, hydrogen, and oxygen that is the basic component of all lipids. (2)

feijoada completa. Brazil's national dish, which is made with meat and black beans. (29)

felafel. A mixture of ground chickpeas, bulgur, and spices that is formed into balls and deep-fried. (32)

fermentation. Process that takes place when yeast cells act on sugars to form alcohol and carbon dioxide. (22)

fiber. A form of complex carbohydrate from plants that humans cannot digest. (2)

filé. Flavoring and thickening agent made from the leaves of the sassafras tree, which have been dried and ground into a powder. (28)

fines herbes. A mixture of fresh chives, parsley, tarragon, and chervil used to flavor many French soups and stews. (30)

finfish. Fish that have fins and backbones. (20)

finished food. Convenience food that is ready for eating either immediately or after heating or thawing. (10)

fish and chips. Battered, deep-fried fish fillets served in England with a British version of French fries. (30)

fish fillet. The side of a fish cut lengthwise away from the backbone. (20)

fish steak. Cross-sectional slice taken from a dressed fish. (20)

fitness. The body's ability to meet physical demands. (4)

fixed expense. A regularly recurring cost in a set amount, such as rent, mortgage, or installment loan payments. (10)

flatware. Forks, knives, spoons, serving utensils, and specialty utensils used to serve and eat food. (7)

flavones. Pigments that make white vegetables, such as cauliflower, white. (14)

fleishig foods. Food made with meat or poultry as well as the utensils and dishes used with these foods as described by Jewish dietary laws. (32)

flexible expense. A regularly recurring cost that varies in amount, such as food, clothing, or utility bills. (10)

food additive. A substance that is added to food for a specific purpose, such as adding nutrients, preserving quality, aiding processing or preparation, or enhancing flavors or colors. (11)

food allergy. A response of the body's immune system to a food protein. (4)

Food and Drug Administration (FDA). The federal agency that ensures the safety and wholesomeness of all foods sold across state lines, except meat, poultry, and eggs. (1)

foodborne illness. A disease transmitted by food. (6)

food-drug interaction. An effect a drug has on the way the body absorbs or uses a nutrient or an effect a food has on the way the body absorbs or uses a drug. (4)

food intolerance. A negative reaction to a food substance that does not involve the body's immune system. (4)

fortified food. A food to which nutrients are added in amounts greater than what would naturally occur in the food. (2)

freeze-drying. A method of commercial food preservation in which water vapor is removed from frozen food items. (25)

freezer burn. Dry, tough areas that occur on food surfaces that have become dehydrated due to exposure to dry air in a freezer. (25)

frijoles refritos. Refried beans, a popular Mexican dish. (29)

fritters. Fruits, vegetables, or meats that are dipped into a batter and fried in hot fat. (15)

functional food. A food that provides health benefits beyond the nutrients it contains. (1)

G

gaucho. Nomadic herders of the Pampas in South America during the eighteenth and nineteenth centuries. (29)

gazpacho. A Spanish soup made with coarsely pureed tomatoes, cucumbers, onions, garlic, green peppers, olive oil, and vinegar. (31)

gelatinization. Swelling and subsequent thickening of starch granules when heated in water. (13)

germ. The reproductive part of a kernel of grain, which is rich in vitamins, minerals, protein, and fat. (13)

ghee. Indian clarified butter. (33)

giblets. The edible internal organs of poultry. (19)

glucose. The form of sugar carried in the bloodstream for energy use throughout the body. (2)

gluten. A protein that gives strength and elasticity to batters and doughs and structure to baked products. (22)

goal. An aim a person tries to reach. (1)

gohan. The Japanese word for meal, which means rice. (33)

goiter. A visible enlargement of the thyroid gland resulting from an iodine deficiency. (2)

gourmet. A person who values and enjoys fine food. (21)

grade. An indication of food quality. (11)

GRAS list. List of food additives that are "Generally Recognized as Safe" by the Food and Drug Administration (FDA). (11)

gratuity. Sum of money given to a waiter in a restaurant for service rendered. (24)

ground. To connect an appliance electrically with the earth. (7)

growth spurt. A period of rapid growth. (4)

guacamole. A spread made from mashed avocado, tomato, and onion that is popular in Mexico. (29)

gumbo. A Creole specialty that is a thick, souplike mixture containing a variety of seafood, poultry, meats, vegetables, and rice. (28)

H

haggis. A Scottish dish made from a pudding made from oatmeal, seasonings, and the sheep's organs boiled in the sheep's stomach. (30)

Halal. Foods considered lawful for consumption according to the Islamic religion. (32)

Haram. Foods that are forbidden to be eaten according to the Islamic religion. (32)

haute cuisine. A style of French cooking characterized by elaborate preparations, fancy garnishes, and rich sauces. (30)

headspace. Space between the food and the closure of a food storage container. (25)

healthy weight. A body mass index of 18.5 to 24.9 in an adult. (5)

herb. A leaf of a plant usually grown in a temperate climate and used to season food. (21)

holloware. Tableware, such as bowls, tureens, and pitchers, used to serve food and liquids. (7)

homogenization. Mechanical process by which milkfat globules are broken into tiny particles and spread throughout milk or cream to keep the cream from rising to the surface of the milk. (16)

hors d'oeuvres. Small dishes designed to stimulate the appetite. (30)

hot pack. Process of packing vegetables or fruits that have been preheated in water, steam, syrup, or juices into canning jars and covering them with cooking liquid or boiling water. (25)

hunger. The physical need for food. (1)

husmankost. The traditional, everyday style of cooking enjoyed in Swedish homes. (30)

hydrogenation. A process by which hydrogen atoms are chemically added to unsaturated fatty acids in liquid oils to turn the oils into more highly saturated solid fats. (2)

hypertension. High blood pressure. (2)

I

immature fruit. Fruit that is small and has such characteristics as poor color, flavor, and texture, which will not improve with time. (15)

impulse buying. Making an unplanned purchase without much thought. (11)

imu. A pit lined with hot rocks used to roast a whole, young pig at a Hawaiian luau. (28)

income. Money received. (10)

injera. Ethiopia's main dish, which is a large, sourdoughlike pancake made from a grain called teff. (32)

irradiation. A commercial food preservation method that exposes food to low-level doses of gamma rays, electron beams, or X rays. (25)

J

jambalaya. A Creole specialty that is a mixture of rice; seasonings; and shellfish, poultry, and/or sausage. (28)

K

kaiseka. A delicate meal served after the Japanese tea ceremony. (33)

kartoffelpuffer. German potato pancakes. (30)

kasha. A Russian staple food made of buckwheat or other grains that is fried and then simmered until tender. (33)

kashrut. Jewish dietary laws. (32)

kernel. A whole seed of a cereal. (13)

kibbutzim. Cooperative communities in Israel. (32)

korma. A major Indian cooking technique in which foods are braised, usually in yogurt. (33)

kosher. Foods prepared according to Jewish dietary laws. (32)

kulich. A tall, cylindrical Russian yeast bread filled with fruits and nuts. (33)

L

lamb. The meat of sheep less than one year old. (18)

Latin America. The landmass that stretches southward from the Rio Grande to the tip of South America. (29)

leadership. The ability to guide and motivate others to complete tasks or achieve goals. (27)

lean fish. Fish that have very little fat in their flesh. (20)

leavening agent. An ingredient that produces gases in batters and doughs, causing baked products to rise and become light and porous. (22)

legumes. Peas, beans, and lentils. (14)

lifelong learning. Continually updating your knowledge and skills. (26)

lifestyle. The way a person usually lives. (1)

lingonberry. A tart, red berry used in Swedish desserts. (30)

luau. Elaborate outdoor feast popular in the Hawaiian Islands. (28)

lutefisk. A traditional Norwegian fish dish made from dried cod that have been soaked in a lye solution before cooking. (30)

M

macromineral. A mineral needed in the diet in amounts of 100 or more milligrams each day. (2)

malnutrition. A lack of the right proportions of nutrients over an extended period, which can be caused by an inadequate diet or the body's inability to use the nutrients from foods. (2)

manioc. A starchy root plant (also known as cassava) eaten as a side dish and used in flour form in cooking and baking in South America. (29)

manners. Social behavior. (24)

marbling. Flecks of fat found throughout the lean muscles of meat. (18)

masala. A mixture of spices used to make Indian curry. (33)

matzo. Unleavened bread that is part of Jewish cuisine. (32)

mazza. Arabian appetizers. (32)

meal manager. Someone who uses resources to reach goals related to preparing and serving food. (10)

meat. The edible portion of mammals. (18)

medical nutrition therapy (MNT). A health care strategy that helps people learn to use their eating habits as part of their treatment. (4)

melons. Classification of fruits, including cantaloupe, casaba, honeydew, Crenshaw, Persian, and watermelon, that are large, juicy fruits produced by plants in the gourd family and usually have thick rinds and many seeds. (15)

menu. A list of the foods to be served at a meal. (10)

meringue. Fluffy white mixture of beaten egg whites and sugar, which may be soft or hard. (17)

metabolism. The chemical processes that take place in the cells after the body absorbs nutrients. (2)

mezedhes. Greek appetizers. (31)

microorganism. A living substance so small it can be seen only under a microscope. (6)

microwave. High-frequency energy wave used in microwave ovens to cook foods quickly. (8)

milchig foods. Dairy foods and the utensils used to prepare, serve, and eat them as described by Jewish dietary laws. (32)

milkfat. Fat portion of milk. (16)

milk solids. Nonfat portion of milk, which contains most of the vitamins, minerals, protein, and sugar found in milk. (16)

mineral. One of the six basic types of nutrients that is an inorganic substance and becomes part of the bones, soft tissues, and body fluids. (2)

minestrone. A popular Italian vegetable soup made with onions, carrots, zucchini, celery, cabbage, rice or pasta, and seasonings. (31)

mold. Growth produced on damp or decaying organic matter or on living organisms. (25)

mole. A complex sauce used in Mexican cuisine. (29)

mollusk. Shellfish that has a soft body fully or partially covered by a hard shell. (20)

MyPlate. A food guidance system with a set of interactive tools to help people make healthful eating choices consistent with the Dietary Guidelines. The MyPlate icon helps people visualize how the food groups fit together to build a healthy plate at mealtime. (3)

N

national brand. A brand that is advertised and sold throughout the country. (11)

natural light. Light that comes from the sun. (7)

negotiation. The process of agreeing to an issue that requires all parties to give and take. (27)

networking. The exchange of information or services among individuals or groups. (26)

new potatoes. Potatoes that are harvested and sent directly to market. (14)

night blindness. A condition resulting from a vitamin A deficiency, which is characterized by a reduced ability to see in dim light. (2)

nihon-cha. Japanese term for green teas. (33)

noncrystalline candy. Type of candy that does not contain sugar crystals, which makes it chewy or brittle. (23)

nonstick finish. Coating with nonstick properties used on some cookware and bakeware. (9)

nonverbal communication. Communication that involves the sending and receiving of messages without the use of words. It involves body language. (27)

nouvelle cuisine. A style of French cooking that emphasizes lightness and natural taste in foods. (30)

nutrient. A chemical substance from food the body needs to live. (2)

nutrient dense. Foods and beverages that provide vitamins, minerals, and other healthful substances with relatively few calories. (3)

nutrition. The study of how the body uses the nutrients in foods that are eaten. (2)

nutrition labeling. A breakdown of how a food product fits in an average diet that appears on the product packaging. (11)

O

obesity. A condition characterized by excessive deposits of body fat. In an adult, obesity is defined as a body mass index of 30 or more. (5)

occupation. Paid employment that involves handling one or more jobs. (26)

okra. A green, pod-shaped vegetable brought to the United States from Africa that is popular in the Deep South. (28)

omelet. A beaten egg mixture that is cooked without stirring and served folded in half. (17)

open dating. A system of putting calendar dates on perishable and semiperishable foods to help retailers to know how long to display products and to help consumers to choose products that will maintain quality the longest and to help consumers know which product to use first. (11)

open stock. A way of purchasing tableware in which each piece is purchased individually. (7)

organic food. A food produced without the use of synthetic fertilizers, pesticides, or growth stimulants. (11)

osteoporosis. A condition resulting from a calcium deficiency, which is characterized by porous, brittle bones. (2)

overweight. A condition characterized in an adult by a body mass index of 25 to 29.9. (5)

P

paella. A Spanish rice dish often containing chicken, shrimp, mussels, whitefish, peas, and rice and flavored with saffron, salt, pepper, and pimiento. (31)

pareve foods. Foods (and utensils used with them) that contain neither meat nor milk or as described by Jewish dietary laws. (32)

paskha. A rich cheesecake that is a popular Russian dessert. (33)

pasta. A dough made from wheat flour that may or may not be dried that comes in various shapes, such as macaroni and spaghetti. (13)

pasteurization. Process by which milk and milk products are heated to destroy harmful bacteria. (16)

pastry. The dough used to make piecrusts. (23)

pectin. Carbohydrate found naturally in fruits that makes fruit juices jell. (25)

peer pressure. Influence that comes from people in a person's social group. (1)

pellagra. A disease resulting from a niacin deficiency that is characterized by skin lesions and digestive problems. Mental disorders and death may follow if left untreated. (2)

Pennsylvania Dutch. Group of German immigrants who settled in the southeast section of Pennsylvania. (28)

peristalsis. Waves of muscle contractions that push food through the digestive tract. (2)

permanent emulsion. Type of emulsion that will not separate on standing; type of emulsion that is formed when an emulsifying agent is added to a mixture of oil and a water-based liquid. (21)

pesticide. An agent used to kill insects, weeds, and fungi that attack crops. (11)

phyllo. A paper-thin pastry made with flour and water used to make many Greek foods. (31)

pita bread. Flat, round, hollow bread common to the cuisines of Africa and the Middle East. (32)

pitting. Tiny indentations that mark the surface of some aluminum cookware due to a reaction with some foods and minerals. (9)

place setting. A set of all the dinnerware or flatware pieces used by one person. (7)

plantain. A green, starchy fruit that has a bland flavor and looks much like a large banana. (29)

pomes. Classification of fruits, including apples and pears, that have a central, seed-containing core surrounded by a thick layer of flesh. (15)

porcelain enamel. Glasslike material fused at very high temperatures to a base metal, such as the outer surfaces of cookware and bakeware. (9)

pork. The meat of swine. (18)

pot. A two-handled cooking utensil. (9)

potluck. A shared meal to which each person or family brings food for the whole group to eat. (28)

poultry. Any domesticated bird. (19)

precycling. Thinking about how packaging materials can be reused or recycled before buying a product. (11)

prepreparation. Any step done in advance to save time when getting a meal ready. (10)

pressure saucepan. Saucepan that cooks foods more quickly than a conventional pan because as pressure is increased, temperature also increases. (9)

process cheese. One of several types of products, including pasteurized process cheese, pasteurized process cheese food, pasteurized process cheese spread, coldpack cheese, and coldpack cheese food, made from various cheeses. (16)

processed food. A food that has undergone some preparation procedure, such as canning, freezing, drying, cooking, or fortification. (3)

processing time. The amount of time canned goods remain under heat (or under heat and pressure) in a canner. (25)

produce. Fresh fruits and vegetables. (11)

protein. One of the six basic types of nutrients, made up of amino acids, that is required for growth, repair, and maintenance of every body cell. (2)

protein-energy malnutrition (PEM). A condition that may result from a diet that does not contain enough protein and calories. (2)

provincial cuisine. The style of French cooking practiced by most French families using locally grown foods and simple cooking methods. (30)

pudding basin. A deep, thick-rimmed bowl used to steam British puddings. (30)

punctual. Prompt and on time. (27)

Q

quiche. A French custard tart served in many variations as an appetizer and a main dish. (30)

quick-freezing. Process of subjecting foods to extremely low temperatures for a short time and then maintaining them at a normal freezing temperature. (25)

R

raw pack. Process of packing raw vegetables in canning jars and covering them with boiling water or syrup. (25)

recipe. A set of instructions for preparing a specific food. (12)

refined. Term used to refer to cereal products made from grain that has had the bran and germ, along with the nutrients they provide, removed during processing and contains only the endosperm. (13)

reservation. An arrangement made with a restaurant to hold a table for a guest on a given date at a given time. (24)

retail cut. A smaller cut of meat taken from a larger wholesale cut and sold to consumers in retail stores. (18)

retort packaging. A commercial method of packaging food in which food is sealed in a foil pouch and then sterilized in a steam-pressure vessel known as a retort. (25)

rickets. A disease resulting from a vitamin D deficiency, which is characterized by crooked legs and misshapen breast bones in children, and bone abnormalities in adults. (2)

ripened cheese. Cheese in which controlled amounts of bacteria, mold, yeast, or enzymes were added and that was stored for a certain period at a specific temperature to develop texture and flavor. (16)

risotto. An Italian rice dish made with butter, chopped onion, stock or wine, and Parmesan cheese. Meats or seafood and vegetables may also be added. (31)

roux. Cooked paste of fat and flour used as the thickening agent in many sauces and gravies. (16)

RSVP. Letters often included on an invitation that stand for a French phrase meaning please respond. (24)

Russian (continental) service. Style of meal service in which waiters serve guests filled plates of food, one course at a time. (24)

S

salad. Combination of raw and/or cooked ingredients, usually served cold with a dressing. (21)

saliva. A mucus- and enzyme-containing liquid secreted by the mouth that makes food easier to swallow and begins to break down starches. (2)

sangria. A Spanish punch made with red wine, fruit juice, and sparkling water. (31)

sanitation. Maintaining clean conditions to prevent disease and promote good health. (6)

saucepan. A one-handled cooking utensil. (9)

sauerkraut. Fermented or pickled cabbage. (30)

sauna. A steam bath in which water is poured on hot stones to create steam. (30)

schi. Russian cabbage soup. (33)

scorching. Burning that results in a color change. (16)

scum. Solid layer made up of milk solids and some fat that often forms on the surface of milk during heating. (16)

scurvy. A disease resulting from a vitamin C deficiency, which is characterized by bleeding gums, loss of teeth, and internal bleeding. (2)

self-motivation. An inner desire to perform well. (27)

semiprepared food. Convenience food that still needs to have some service performed. (10)

serrated blade. A sawtooth edge on a knife. (9)

service contract. A contract that is like an insurance policy for a major appliance that can be purchased from an appliance dealer to cover the cost of needed repairs for a period after the warranty has expired. (8)

service learning. Using what you learn in the classroom to meet a need in the community. (27)

shelf life. The amount of time a food can be stored and remain wholesome. (25)

shellfish. Fish that have shells instead of backbones. (20)

shohet. A licensed slaughterer who butchers animals and fowl following methods described in Jewish dietary laws. (32)

shortened cake. Cake made with fat. (23)

siesta. A rest period that usually follows the midday meal in Mexico. (29)

slurry. A liquid mixture of milk and flour blended until smooth, which is used as a thickening agent in sauces and gravies. (16)

smörgåsbord. A Swedish buffet that includes a wide variety of hot and cold dishes. (30)

smørrebrød. Danish open-faced sandwiches usually made with thin, sour rye bread spread thickly with butter. (30)

soufflé. Fluffy baked preparation made with a starch-thickened sauce into which stiffly beaten egg whites are folded. (17)

soul food. A cuisine developed in the Southern United States that combines food customs of African slaves with food customs of Native Americans and European sharecroppers. (28)

sourdough. A dough containing active microscopic yeast plants that is used as a leavening agent. (28)

soybean. A legume with seeds that are rich in protein and oil, which is used in many different forms in Japanese and Chinese cooking. (33)

spätzle. Small dumplings made from wheat flour, which are a popular German side dish. (30)

spice. A dried root, stem, or seed of a plant grown mainly in the tropics and used to season food. (21)

springform pan. A round pan with a removable bottom that is held together by means of a spring or latch on the side of the pan. (9)

standing time. The time during which foods finish cooking by internal heat after being removed from a microwave oven. (12)

starch. Complex carbohydrates stored in plants. (13)

stemware. Glassware with three distinct parts: a bowl, a stem, and a base. (7)

stockinette. A cloth cover for a rolling pin used to keep dough from sticking to the rolling pin. (9)

stock soup. Soup made with a rich-flavored liquid in which meat, poultry, or fish; vegetables; and seasonings have been cooked. (21)

store brand. A brand sold only by a store or chain of stores. (11)

stress. Mental tension caused by change. (1)

strudel. A German dessert made with paper-thin layers of pastry filled with fruit. (30)

sugar syrup. A mixture of sugar and liquid that is cooked to a thick consistency. (23)

sukiyaki. A popular Japanese dish made of thinly sliced meat, bean curd, and vegetables cooked in a sauce. (33)

sulfuring. Antidarkening treatment used on some fruits before they are dried. (25)

sustainability. Practices that are productive and profitable while still caring for the environment. (1)

syneresis. Leakage of liquid from a gel. (13)

T

table appointments. All the items needed at the table to serve and eat a meal. (7)

table d'hôte. Type of menu in which one price is given for an entire meal. (24)

table linens. Table coverings and napkins. (7)

tandoori. A simple Indian cooking technique, which requires a clay oven called a *tandoor*. (33)

tang. Prong that attaches a knife blade to the handle. (9)

tapas. Spanish appetizers. (31)

taste buds. Flavor sensors covering the surface of the tongue. (10)

taverna. A Greek café that serves as a public meeting place in small communities. (31)

tea. Leaves of a tropical evergreen or bush used to make a beverage, which is also called tea (12); the evening meal in rural areas or an afternoon snack in cities throughout the British Isles. (30)

team. A small group of people working together for a common purpose. (27)

technology. The use of knowledge to develop improved methods for doing tasks. (1)

teff. A milletlike grain grown only in Africa and the Middle East. (32)

temporary emulsion. Type of emulsion that forms when oil and a water-based liquid are agitated but breaks when the agitation stops and it is allowed to stand. (21)

therapeutic diet. An eating plan prescribed by a physician. (4)

time-work schedule. A written plan listing actual times for doing specific tasks to prepare a meal or food product. (12)

tip. Sum of money given to a waiter in a restaurant for service rendered. (24)

tofu. A mild-flavored, custardlike cake made from soybeans. (33)

tortilla. Flat, unleavened bread made from cornmeal or wheat flour and water used to make many Mexican dishes. (29)

toxicity. Poisoning. (2)

toxin. Poison. (6)

trace element. A mineral needed in the diet in amounts less than 100 milligrams per day. (2)

trans **fatty acid.** A fatty acid with an odd molecular shape that is created in hydrogenated oils and found naturally in dairy products, beef, and lamb. (2)

transferable skills. Skills useful in all jobs, such as reading, writing, speaking, basic math, and basic computer skills. (26)

tropical fruits. Classification of fruits, including avocados, bananas, and pineapples, that are grown in warm climates and are considered to be somewhat exotic. (15)

truffles. A rare type of fungi that grow underground near oak trees and are used in many French recipes. (30)

tsukemono. Soaked foods, or lightly pickled pieces of daikon, cucumber, melon, eggplant, and other vegetables, which are a standard part of the main course at Japanese meals. (33)

tumbler. A piece of glassware without a stem. (7)

U

ultra-high temperature (UHT) processing. A preservation method that uses higher temperatures than regular pasteurization to increase the shelf life of foods like milk. (16)

underripe fruit. Fruit that has reached full size but has not yet reached peak eating quality. (15)

underweight. A condition characterized by a body mass index of less than 18.5. (5)

United States Department of Agriculture (USDA). The federal agency that enforces standards for the quality and wholesomeness of meat, poultry, and eggs. (1)

unit pricing. A listing of a product's cost per standard unit, weight, or measure. (11)

universal design. Features of rooms, furnishings, and equipment that are usable by as many people as possible. (7)

universal product code (UPC). A series of lines, bars, and numbers that appears on the package of a food or nonfood item. This code is used by a computer scanner to identify a product, its manufacturer, and its size and form. (11)

unripened cheese. Cheese that is prepared for marketing as soon as the whey has been removed without being allowed to ripen or age. (16)

unshortened cake. Cake made without fat. (23)

V

value. An item or idea that a person or group considers important. (1)

variety meats. Edible parts of animals other than muscle, such as liver, heart, and tongue. (18)

veal. Meat that comes from young calves. (18)

vegetarian diet. A diet that is built partly or entirely on plant foods. (4)

verbal communication. Communication that involves speaking, listening, and writing. (27)

vindaloo. A major Indian cooking technique in which foods have a hot, slightly sour flavor created by combining vinegar with spices. (33)

vitamin. One of the six basic types of nutrients that is a complex organic substance needed by the body in small amounts for normal growth, maintenance, and reproduction. (2)

W

waist circumference. The distance around the natural waistline. The measurement used to assess whether a high BMI is due to excess fat. (5)

warranty. A seller's promise that a product will be free of defects and will perform as specified. (8)

wat. A spicy sauce or stew that is part of Ethiopian cuisine. (32)

water-soluble vitamin. A vitamin that dissolves in water and is not stored in the body to any great extent. (2)

watt. A unit of power; the cooking power of microwave ovens is measured and expressed in watts. (12)

weeping. Layer of moisture that sometimes forms between a meringue and a filling. (17)

weight management. Using resources like food choices and physical activity to reach and/or maintain a healthy weight. (5)

wellness. A state of being in overall good physical, mental, and social health. (1)

whey. Liquid part of coagulated milk. (16)

whisk. A mixing tool made of loops of wire attached to a handle used to incorporate air into foods and to keep sauces from lumping. (9)

white sauce. A starch-thickened milk product used as a base for other sauces and as a component in many recipes. (16)

whole grain. Term used to refer to cereal products made from grain that contains all three parts of the kernel—bran, germ, and endosperm. (13)

wholesale cut. Large cut of meat shipped to a retail grocery store or meat market. (18)

wok. A versatile Chinese cooking utensil, which looks like a metal bowl with sloping sides. (33)

work center. Section in a kitchen that has been designed around a specific activity or activities. (7)

work simplification. Act of performing tasks in the simplest way possible in order to conserve time and energy. (10)

work triangle. Imaginary triangle formed by the focal points of the three major work centers found in a kitchen. (7)

Y

yam. Dark orange tuber with moist flesh often confused with a sweet potato. (28)

yeast. Microscopic fungus that can cause fermentation in preserved foods resulting in spoilage. (25)

yield. The average amount or number of servings a recipe makes. (12)

Z

zakuska. Russian appetizers. (33)

INDEX

C

N

O

V

values, 11, 461
variety meats, 332, 343
veal, 333
vegetable group, 64–65
vegetables, 271–284
    British, 565
    Canada, 527–528
    canned, 276
    China, 683
    classifications, 272–273
    cooking methods, 280–282
    dried, 277
    drying, 448–449
    food science principles of cooking, 279
    France, 574–575
    freezing, 446–447
    fresh, 272–276
    frozen, 276–277
    India, 672
    Irish, 568
    Japan, 692
    Mexico, 540
    MyPlate and, 272
    Peruvian potatoes, 550
    preparing, 278–283
    serving, 283–284
    storing fresh, 276
    washing, 278
vegetarian diets, 96
Venezuela, 548–549
vent, 238
ventilation, 156
verbal communication, 480
Vikings, 590
vindaloo, 674
vitamins, 34–42
    biotin, 41
    definition, 34
    folate, 40–41
    niacin, 39–40
    pantothenic acid, 41
    riboflavin, 39
    thiamin, 38–39
    vitamin A, 35
    vitamin B_{12}, 41
    vitamin B_6, 40
    vitamin C, 37–38
    vitamin D, 35–36
    vitamin E, 36–37
    vitamin K, 37
    water-soluble vitamins, 35, 42
volunteering, 484–485

W

waist circumference, 114
wall coverings, 155
warranty, 165
wat, 654
water, 48–50
    bottled, 49
    functions, 48
    intake and excretion, 49
    requirements, 49–50
water-soluble vitamins, 35, 42
watts, 239
weeping, 325
weight loss, 115–120
    aids, 118
    controlling energy intake, 116–117
    deciding to lose weight, 115–116
    identifying eating habits, 116
    increasing physical activity, 117–118
    tips for success, 118–120
weight management, 104–124
    body mass index, 113–114
    definition, 112
    determining healthy weight, 112–113
    hazards of obesity, 114
    maintaining healthy weight, 120
    overeating, 114–115
    social events, 119
    underweight, 120–122
    weight loss, 115–120
weight, measuring, 242
wellness, 8
Welsh cuisine, 567–568
whey, 304
whip, 238
whipped cream, 308
whipped toppings, 302
whisk, 183
white sauce, 308–309
whole grain, 72, 249, 262
wholesale clubs, 217
wholesale cuts, 333
WIC, 98–99
wok, 681
Women, Infants, and Children, 98–99
work. *See* careers
work center, 151–152
work-based learning programs, 463
work plans, 243–247. *See also* time-work schedule
work simplification, 211
work triangle, 152

Y

yams, 505
yeast, 441
yeast breads, 394–401
    characteristics, 400
    food science, 295, 398–400
    ingredients, 394–396
    mixing methods, 396–397
    timesaving techniques, 400
    variations, 401
yield, 234
yogurt, 301

Z

zakuska, 665
zinc, 47

RECIPE INDEX

W

T

Y

V